PRENTICE HALL

Algebra 1

Stanley A. Smith

Randall I. Charles

John A. Dossey

Marvin L. Bittinger

PEARSON

Prentice
Hall

Needham, Massachusetts
Upper Saddle River, New Jersey

REVIEWERS

Donald R. Price
Alvarado Intermediate School
Rowland Heights, California

Joyce F. Henderson
Millikan High School
Long Beach, California

CONTENT CONSULTANTS

Elizabeth Cunningham
Mathematics
Prentice Hall National Consultant
Mansfield, Texas

Shawyn Jackson
Mathematics
Prentice Hall National Consultant
Bayshore, New York

Bridget Hadley
Mathematics
Director, Prentice Hall National Consultants
Hopkinton, Massachusetts

Sandra Mosteller
Mathematics
Prentice Hall National Consultant
Anderson, South Carolina

Loretta Rector
Mathematics
Prentice Hall National Consultant
Foresthill, California

ISBN 0-13-133770-X
7 8 9 10 V063 10

AUTHORS

Stanley A. Smith

Formerly, Coordinator,
Office of Mathematics
Baltimore County Public Schools
Baltimore, Maryland

Randall I. Charles

Professor Emeritus
Department of Mathematics
and Computer Science
San Jose State University
San Jose, California

John A. Dossey

Distinguished University Professor
of Mathematics Emeritus
Department of Mathematics
Illinois State University
Normal, Illinois

Marvin L. Bittinger

Professor of Mathematics Education
Indiana University - Purdue University
Indianapolis, Indiana

Table of Contents

CHAPTER 1 ▷ Introduction to Algebra

ASSESSMENT

Try This exercises after every Example

Contents   **v**

2 ▷ Integers and Rational Numbers

REVIEW

ASSESSMENT

CHAPTER

3 ▷ Equations

CHAPTER

4 ▷ Inequalities

REVIEW

ASSESSMENT

CHAPTER 5

Exponents and Polynomials

REVIEW

ASSESSMENT

CHAPTER 6

Polynomials and Factoring

CHAPTER 8

Systems of Equations

Inequalities and Absolute Values

CHAPTER 11

Radical Expressions and Equations

CHAPTER

12 ▷ Relations and Functions

REVIEW

Mixed Review in every Lesson

ASSESSMENT

Try This exercises after every Example

CHAPTER

13 ▷ Quadratic Equations

ASSESSMENT

Try This exercises after
every Example

CHAPTER 1

Skills & Concepts You Need for Chapter 1

Add or subtract. Simplify answers if possible.

1. $\frac{3}{7} + \frac{2}{7}$ **2.** $\frac{3}{8} + \frac{1}{6}$ **3.** $6\frac{3}{4} + 9\frac{5}{8}$ **4.** $3\frac{1}{2} + 4\frac{2}{3} + 7\frac{1}{4}$

5. $\frac{5}{9} - \frac{2}{9}$ **6.** $\frac{5}{6} - \frac{2}{5}$ **7.** $1\frac{7}{8} - \frac{3}{4}$ **8.** $7 - \frac{5}{8}$

Multiply. Simplify answers if possible.

9. $\frac{3}{4} \times \frac{3}{4}$ **10.** $\frac{5}{8} \times 18$ **11.** $4\frac{1}{5} \times 3\frac{5}{7}$ **12.** $2\frac{3}{10} \times 3\frac{1}{3}$

Divide. Simplify answers if possible.

13. $\frac{7}{12} \div \frac{7}{12}$ **14.** $\frac{3}{4} \div 2$ **15.** $3\frac{1}{3} \div 1\frac{1}{4}$ **16.** $3 \div \frac{1}{3}$

Add.

17. $0.5 + 0.35 + 1.5$ **18.** $14 + 3.75 + 8.6$ **19.** $1 + 0.02 + 0.2$

Subtract.

20. $7 - 4.38$ **21.** $11.2 - 6.09$ **22.** $8.9 - 0.76$

Multiply.

23. $\begin{array}{r} 8.75 \\ \times\ \ \ \ 6 \\ \hline \end{array}$ **24.** $\begin{array}{r} 0.75 \\ \times 0.003 \\ \hline \end{array}$ **25.** $\begin{array}{r} 7.82 \\ \times\ \ 7.9 \\ \hline \end{array}$ **26.** $\begin{array}{r} 0.0004 \\ \times\ \ \ \ \ 57 \\ \hline \end{array}$

Divide. Round answers to the nearest hundredth, if necessary.

27. $7\overline{)8.1}$ **28.** $0.08\overline{)396.7}$ **29.** $1.1\overline{)0.44}$

30. $\frac{5.82}{0.6}$ **31.** $0.065\overline{)333}$ **32.** $8\overline{)0.91}$

Introduction to Algebra

The memory of a personal computer is measured in bytes. In Lesson 1-3, you will learn how to use exponential notation to express the number of different characters each byte can represent.

Symbols and Expressions

Math in Action

The time for a high-speed train to travel 396 km from Paris, France to Lyon, France is determined by the velocity of the train.

Velocity (km/h)	Time (hours)
180	$396 \div 180$, or 2.2
200	$396 \div 200$, or 1.98
220	$396 \div 220$, or 1.8
v	$396 \div v$

The average velocity of a high-speed train for the 396-km trip from Paris to Lyon is 198 km/h. What is the average time for the trip?

PART 1 **Algebraic Expressions**

Objective: Evaluate algebraic expressions.

In algebra we use symbols to stand for various numbers. One type of symbol used is a **variable.** A variable is a letter, such as v or x or m, that represents one or more numbers. In the last line of the table above, we let the letter v stand for the velocity of the train.

An expression may be a number, or two or more numbers involving operation signs. An expression, such as $396 \div v$, that contains at least one variable is called an **algebraic expression.** We can replace a variable with a number. This is called **substituting** for the variable. To **evaluate** an algebraic expression, substitute a number for each variable and calculate.

EXAMPLE 1   Evaluate $n - 7$ for $n = 15$.

$$n - 7 = 15 - 7 \quad \text{Substituting 15 for the variable } n$$
$$= 8$$

Try This   Evaluate.

a. $y + 8$ for $y = 9$ **b.** $2 + x$ for $x = 6$ **c.** $t + 3 + t$ for $t = 4$

Algebraic expressions involving multiplication can be written in several ways. For example, "3 times a" can be written as $3 \times a$, $3 \cdot a$, $3(a)$, or simply $3a$. Algebraic expressions involving division can also be written in several ways. For example, "m divided by 4" can be written as $m \div 4$ or simply as $\frac{m}{4}$. The fraction bar is a division symbol.

Writing Math

The multiplication symbol $\times$ looks similar to the variable x. To avoid confusion, use $\cdot$ or ( ) for multiplication.

EXAMPLE 2   Evaluate $5y$ for $y = 6$.

$5y = 5(6)$ Substituting 6 for the variable y
  $= 30$

Try This   Evaluate.

d. $\frac{x}{12}$ for $x = 36$ **e.** $6m$ for $m = 3$ **f.** $\frac{18}{g}$ for $g = 2$

EXAMPLE 3   Evaluate $\frac{x}{y}$ for $x = 10$ and $y = 5$.

$\frac{x}{y} = \frac{10}{5}$ Substituting 10 for x and 5 for y and dividing

  $= 2$

Try This   Evaluate.

g. $a + b$ for $a = 3$ and $b = 7$ **h.** mn for $m = 2$ and $n = 6$

We also use several different sets of numbers in algebra. Here are two you already know.

- ■ **Natural numbers** are the numbers used for counting: 1, 2, 3, and so on.
- ■ **Whole numbers** are the natural numbers and zero: 0, 1, 2, 3, and so on.

We will also work with numbers of the form $\frac{a}{b}$, where $b \neq 0$. Some examples are $\frac{2}{3}$, $\frac{6}{3}$, and $\frac{4}{1}$. These numbers, which include natural and whole numbers, are contained in a set of numbers called **rational numbers.** Rational numbers are explored further in Chapter 2.

PART 2 Order of Operations

Objective: Evaluate expressions using grouping symbols and the order of operations.

Parentheses are called **grouping symbols.** When an expression contains parentheses, any operation inside the parentheses should be done first. The fraction bar is also a grouping symbol. In expressions containing a fraction bar, do all computations above and below the bar before dividing.

$$\frac{4 + 6}{2 \cdot 1} = \frac{10}{2} = 5$$

EXAMPLE 4 Evaluate $a(3 + b)$ for $a = 5$ and $b = 2$.

$$
\begin{aligned}
a(3 + b) &= 5(3 + 2) && \text{Substituting 5 for } a \text{ and 2 for } b \\
&= 5(5) && \text{Working inside parentheses} \\
&= 25
\end{aligned}
$$

Try This   Evaluate.

i. $14 - (b + 5)$ for $b = 3$

j. $\frac{x + 5}{2 \cdot 3}$ for $x = 7$

k. $3 + (6x)$ for $x = 2$

l. $s(t - 4)$ for $s = 4$ and $t = 8$

We need a rule for the order in which the operations should be done.

Order of Operations

1. Compute within grouping symbols.
2. Multiply and divide in order from left to right.
3. Add and subtract in order from left to right.

EXAMPLE 5   Simplify.

$$
\begin{aligned}
8 \cdot 4 + \frac{16}{2} &= 32 + 8 && \text{Multiplying and dividing first} \\
&= 40 && \text{Adding}
\end{aligned}
$$

Try This   Simplify.

m. $36 \div (4 + 5)$ **n.** $24 - (12 + 3) \div 5$ **o.** $4 \times 3 + 6 \div 2$

EXAMPLE 6   Evaluate $\frac{2m}{n}$ for $m = 6$ and $n = 3$.

$$
\begin{aligned}
\frac{2m}{n} &= \frac{2 \cdot 6}{3} && \text{Substituting 6 for } m \text{ and 3 for } n \\
&= \frac{12}{3} \\
&= 4
\end{aligned}
$$

Try This   Evaluate.

p. $3x + y$ for $x = 2$ and $y = 5$

q. $\frac{2a + b}{5}$ for $a = 4$ and $b = 2$

Order of Operations

You should determine whether or not your calculator follows the Order of Operations. Calculate 3 + 4(2).

3 **+** 4 **×** 2 **=** → ?

If your calculator displays 11, the correct answer, your calculator is programmed to follow the Order of Operations.

If your calculator displays 14, you must always enter the operations in the correct order to get the correct answer.

4 **×** 2 **+** 3 **=** → 11

1-1 Exercises

Extra Help On the Web

Look for worked-out examples at the Prentice Hall Web site.
www.phschool.com

A

Mental Math   Evaluate.

1. $x + 6$ for $x = 7$

2. $3 + y$ for $y = 9$

3. $m - 2$ for $m = 12$

4. $9 - h$ for $h = 3$

5. $t + 24$ for $t = 11$

6. $18 + x$ for $x = 30$

7. $12 - x$ for $x = 5$

8. $k - 6$ for $k = 15$

9. $4 - x - x$ for $x = 1$

10. $k + 8 - k$ for $k = 10$

11. $4h$ for $h = 12$

12. $8m$ for $m = 3$

13. $3t$ for $t = 9$

14. $6y$ for $y = 12$

15. $\frac{12}{y}$ for $y = 2$

16. $\frac{p}{5}$ for $p = 30$

17. $\frac{h}{7}$ for $h = 63$

18. $\frac{x}{y}$ for $x = 16$ and $y = 4$

19. $a - b$ for $a = 12$ and $b = 3$

20. mn for $m = 3$ and $n = 7$

21. $p + q$ for $p = 7$ and $q = 9$

22. $\frac{m}{n}$ for $m = 36$ and $n = 9$

Simplify.

23. $13 + 54 \div 9$

24. $64 \div 16 + 8$

25. $12 + 3 - 7 \cdot 2 + 8$

26. $12 \div 2 \times 3 \div 9$

27. $4 + 12 \times 2 - 8 \div 4$

28. $15 \div 5 \times 5 \times 0$

29. $32 \div 8 + 4 \times 3$

30. $18 \times 2 \div 9 - 3$

Evaluate.

31. $2x + y$ for $x = 5$ and $y = 4$

32. $x + 4y$ for $x = 2$ and $y = 3$

33. $3m + 4n$ for $m = 2$ and $n = 6$

34. $\frac{x + y}{4}$ for $x = 4$ and $y = 8$

35. $\frac{a + 3b}{5}$ for $a = 4$ and $b = 2$

36. $\frac{4p}{3q}$ for $p = 6$ and $q = 8$

B

Evaluate.

37. $\frac{n}{3m}$ for $n = 12$ and $m = 4$

38. $\frac{ab}{8}$ for $a = 5$ and $b = 8$

39. $\frac{3x}{2y + 1}$ for $x = 7$ and $y = 3$

40. $\frac{a + b}{2a}$ for $a = 5$ and $b = 15$

41. $2x + 3x - 4x$ for $x = 5$

42. $\frac{24}{2x} + \frac{36}{3x} + \frac{6}{x}$ for $x = 6$

43. $\frac{x + y}{4} + \frac{x - y}{4}$ for $x = 12$ and $y = 8$

44. $\frac{4y}{4y} + (2x + y) - 3z$ for $x = 3$, $y = 2$, and $z = 1$

45. $\frac{y + x}{2} + \frac{3y}{x}$ for $x = 2$ and $y = 4$

46. *Critical Thinking*   Use each of the numbers 2, 4, 6, 8, and 10 exactly once, with any operation signs and grouping symbols, to write an expression equal to 0.

47. *Error Analysis*   When Rob simplified the expression $72 \div 6 + 3$, his answer was 8. What was Rob's error?

48.   **TEST PREP**   For what value of x will $\frac{4x + 2}{2} - x$ equal 7?

A. 4 **B.** 5 **C.** 6 **D.** 7

Challenge

49. The sum of two numbers, $a + b$, is 17, and the product of these numbers, ab, is 60. What numbers do a and b represent?

50. Write as many of the whole numbers from 0 to 10 as you can, using only the digit 4 with operation signs and grouping symbols as many or as few times as you need to. For example, $\frac{(4 + 4)}{4} = 2$.

Mixed Review

Calculate.   **51.** $251 - 179$ **52.** $307 + 94$ **53.** $1824 \div 32$

54. $2.66 - 0.93$ **55.** $5.74 + 8.36$ **56.** $(4.9)(3.04)$ **57.** $\frac{3}{4} + \frac{2}{7}$

58. $\frac{5}{8} - \frac{1}{3}$ **59.** $2\frac{5}{6} - \frac{2}{3}$ **60.** $4 \div \frac{1}{2}$ **61.** $1\frac{1}{4} \div 2\frac{1}{3}$ *Pre-Course*

The Commutative and Identity Properties

In this lesson you will begin to study number properties as they apply to algebraic expressions. You already know that the order in which you add two numbers does not affect the sum.

$$3 + 4 = 7 \quad \text{and} \quad 4 + 3 = 7$$

You also know that the order in which you multiply two numbers does not affect the product.

$$8 \cdot 2 = 16 \quad \text{and} \quad 2 \cdot 8 = 16$$

You will now see how these relationships apply to algebraic expressions.

PART 1 Commutative Properties

Objective: Use the commutative properties for addition and multiplication of whole numbers.

The expressions $x + 2$ and $2 + x$ have the same value for every replacement for the variable x. Similarly, the expressions $3y$ and $y(3)$ have the same value for every replacement for the variable y. The **commutative properties** state that these relationships will always be true.

Commutative Properties

Addition

For any numbers a and b, $a + b = b + a$. (We can change the order when adding without affecting the sum.)

Multiplication

For any numbers a and b, $ab = ba$. (We can change the order when multiplying without affecting the product.)

Expressions such as $2 + x$ and $x + 2$, which always result in the same number when we substitute any value for their variables, are called **equivalent expressions.**

EXAMPLE 1 Write an expression equivalent to $y + 5$ using a commutative property.

$y + 5 = 5 + y$ using the commutative property of addition.

What You'll Learn

1 To use the commutative properties for addition and multiplication

2 To use the identity properties for addition and multiplication

3 To simplify expressions

. . . And Why

To write equivalent expressions

EXAMPLES Write an expression equivalent to each using a commutative property.

2 xy An equivalent expression is yx by the commutative property of multiplication.

3 $5 + ab$ An equivalent expression is $ab + 5$ by the commutative property of addition.

Another is $5 + ba$ by the commutative property of multiplication.

Another is $ba + 5$ by both commutative properties.

Try This   Use a commutative property to write an equivalent expression.

a. $x + 9$ **b.** pq **c.** $xy + t$

PART 2 Identity Properties

Objective: Use the identity properties for addition and multiplication of whole numbers.

When 0 is added to any number, the sum is the number. We call 0 the **additive identity.** When any number is multiplied by 1, the product is that number. We call 1 the **multiplicative identity.**

Identity Properties

Addition

For any number a, $a + 0 = a$ and $0 + a = a$. (Adding 0 to any number gives that number.)

Multiplication

For any number a, $1 \cdot a = a$ and $a \cdot 1 = a$. (Multiplying a number by 1 gives that number.)

Recall that the bar in expressions written as $\frac{a}{b}$ means to divide.

Using this idea, we see that the expressions $\frac{5}{5}$, $\frac{3}{3}$, and $\frac{26}{26}$ all name the number 1.

Dividing a Number by Itself

For any number a, $a \neq 0$, $\frac{a}{a} = 1$.

Here are some algebraic expressions that have the value 1 for all replacements, except those that would make the denominator zero. (In Chapter 2 we will discuss why division by zero is not allowed.)

$$\frac{n}{n} \qquad \frac{m+3}{m+3} \qquad \frac{5y+4}{5y+4}$$

We can use the identity property for multiplication to write equivalent expressions. If we multiply a fraction by 1, written in the form $\frac{a}{a}(a \neq 0)$, we get a fraction equivalent to the original one.

EXAMPLE 4   Write an equivalent expression for $\frac{2}{3}$ by multiplying by 1. Use $\frac{5}{5}$ for 1.

$\frac{2}{3} = \frac{2}{3} \cdot 1$ Multiplying by the identity

$\quad = \frac{2}{3} \cdot \frac{5}{5}$ Substituting $\frac{5}{5}$ for 1

$\quad = \frac{10}{15}$ Multiplying numerators and denominators

Quick Review

If a number has two different names, such as 1 and $\frac{5}{5}$, then either can be substituted in place of the other.

Try This

d. Write an equivalent expression for $\frac{7}{5}$ by multiplying by 1. Use $\frac{4}{4}$ for 1.

e. Write an equivalent expression for $\frac{3}{8}$ by multiplying by 1. Use $\frac{5}{5}$ for 1.

We can also use the identity property for multiplication to write equivalent algebraic expressions. In this lesson we will assume that all variables in the denominator are nonzero.

EXAMPLE 5   Write an expression equivalent to $\frac{x}{2}$ by multiplying by 1. Use $\frac{y}{y}$ for 1.

$\frac{x}{2} = \frac{x}{2} \cdot \frac{y}{y}$ Multiplying by 1

$\quad = \frac{xy}{2y}$

The expressions $\frac{x}{2}$ and $\frac{xy}{2y}$ have the same value for all replacements for x and y, $y \neq 0$. The expressions $\frac{x}{2}$ and $\frac{xy}{2y}$ are equivalent.

Try This

f. Write an expression equivalent to $\frac{y}{2x}$ by multiplying by 1. Use $\frac{z}{z}$ for 1.

g. Write an expression equivalent to $\frac{2m}{n}$ by multiplying by 1. Use $\frac{p}{p}$ for 1.

Objective: Simplify expressions.

When two or more numbers are multiplied to form a product, each number is called a **factor** of the product. For example, $3 \times 5 = 15$, so 3 and 5 are factors of 15. When the only common factor of the numerator and the denominator of a fraction is 1, the fraction is in **simplest form.** The process of finding the simplest form is called **simplifying.**

EXAMPLES Simplify.

6 $\frac{10}{15} = \frac{2 \cdot 5}{3 \cdot 5}$ Factoring the numerator and denominator

$\phantom{\frac{10}{15}} = \frac{2}{3} \cdot 1$ Substituting 1 for $\frac{5}{5}$

$\phantom{\frac{10}{15}} = \frac{2}{3}$ Using the identity property of multiplication

7 $\frac{36}{24} = \frac{6 \cdot 6}{4 \cdot 6}$ Factoring the numerator and denominator

$\phantom{\frac{36}{24}} = \frac{3 \cdot 2 \cdot 6}{2 \cdot 2 \cdot 6}$ Further factoring

$\phantom{\frac{36}{24}} = \frac{3}{2} \cdot 1$ Substituting 1 for $\frac{2 \cdot 6}{2 \cdot 6}$

$\phantom{\frac{36}{24}} = \frac{3}{2}$

Try This   Simplify.

h. $\frac{18}{27}$ **i.** $\frac{48}{18}$ **j.** $\frac{56}{49}$

The number of factors of the numerator and denominator may not always "match." If they do not, you can always use the factor 1.

EXAMPLES Simplify.

8 $\frac{18}{72} = \frac{2 \cdot 9}{4 \cdot 2 \cdot 9}$

$\phantom{\frac{18}{72}} = \frac{1 \cdot 2 \cdot 9}{4 \cdot 2 \cdot 9}$ Using the identity property (inserting a factor of 1)

$\phantom{\frac{18}{72}} = \frac{1}{4} \cdot \frac{2 \cdot 9}{2 \cdot 9}$ Factoring the fraction

$\phantom{\frac{18}{72}} = \frac{1}{4}$

9 $\quad \dfrac{72}{9} = \dfrac{8 \cdot 9}{1 \cdot 9}$ Factoring and inserting a factor of 1 in the denominator

$\qquad\quad = \dfrac{8}{1} \cdot \dfrac{9}{9}$

$\qquad\quad = \dfrac{8}{1}$

$\qquad\quad = 8$

Try This   Simplify.

k. $\dfrac{27}{54}$ **l.** $\dfrac{48}{12}$

We can simplify algebraic expressions using the identity property for multiplication and procedures like those used above with numbers. Note that whenever two algebraic expressions are equivalent, we can **substitute** one for the other. In Example 11, substituting $1 \cdot x$ for x helps us simplify the fractions.

EXAMPLES   Simplify.

10 $\quad \dfrac{xy}{3y} = \dfrac{x \cdot y}{3 \cdot y}$ Factoring numerator and denominator

$\qquad\quad = \dfrac{x}{3} \cdot \dfrac{y}{y}$ Factoring the fraction

$\qquad\quad = \dfrac{x}{3}$ Using the identity property (removing a factor of 1)

11 $\quad \dfrac{x}{5xy} = \dfrac{1 \cdot x}{5 \cdot x \cdot y}$ Substituting $1 \cdot x$ for x.

$\qquad\quad = \dfrac{1}{5y} \cdot \dfrac{x}{x}$ Using the commutative property and factoring the fractional expression

$\qquad\quad = \dfrac{1}{5y}$

12 $\quad \dfrac{4cd}{2c} = \dfrac{4 \cdot c \cdot d}{2 \cdot c \cdot 1}$

$\qquad\quad = \dfrac{4 \cdot d}{2 \cdot 1} \cdot \dfrac{c}{c}$

$\qquad\quad = \dfrac{2d}{1}$

$\qquad\quad = 2d$

Try This   Simplify.

m. $\dfrac{5xy}{3x}$ **n.** $\dfrac{m}{8mn}$ **o.** $\dfrac{14ab}{7b}$

Journal

Illustrate the commutative, associative, and identity properties of addition and multiplication as follows: for each property, write an algebraic expression, then use the property to write an equivalent algebraic expression.

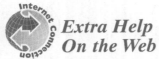
1-2 Exercises

A

Write an equivalent expression using a commutative property.

1. $y + 8$ **2.** $x + 3$ **3.** mn **4.** ab

5. $9 + xy$ **6.** $11 + ab$ **7.** $ab + c$ **8.** $rs + t$

Write an equivalent expression. Use the indicated expression for 1.

9. $\frac{5}{6}$ Use $\frac{8}{8}$ for 1.   **10.** $\frac{9}{10}$ Use $\frac{11}{11}$ for 1.   **11.** $\frac{6}{7}$ Use $\frac{100}{100}$ for 1.

12. $\frac{y}{10}$ Use $\frac{z}{z}$ for 1.   **13.** $\frac{s}{20}$ Use $\frac{t}{t}$ for 1.   **14.** $\frac{m}{3n}$ Use $\frac{p}{p}$ for 1.

Simplify.

15. $\frac{13}{104}$ **16.** $\frac{56}{7}$ **17.** $\frac{132}{11}$ **18.** $\frac{5y}{5}$ **19.** $\frac{ab}{9b}$

20. $\frac{x}{9xy}$ **21.** $\frac{q}{8pq}$ **22.** $\frac{8a}{3ab}$ **23.** $\frac{9p}{17pq}$ **24.** $\frac{3pq}{6q}$

25. $\frac{51d}{17sd}$ **26.** $\frac{9nz}{19tn}$ **27.** $\frac{13rv}{3vh}$ **28.** $\frac{9abc}{3ab}$ **29.** $\frac{32prq}{4qrp}$

B

Tell whether each pair of expressions is equivalent.

30. $3t + 5$ and $3 \cdot 5 + t$ **31.** $4x$ and $x + 4$

32. $bxy + bx$ and $yxb + bx$ **33.** $ab + bc$ and $ac + db$

34. $a + c + e + g$ and $ea + cg$ **35.** $abc \cdot de$ and $a \cdot b \cdot c \cdot ed$

Simplify.

36. $\frac{33sba}{2 \cdot (11a)}$ **37.** $\frac{36 \cdot 2rh}{3 \cdot (9hg)}$ **38.** $\frac{3 \cdot (4xy) \cdot (5)}{2 \cdot (3x) \cdot (4y)}$

39. *Critical Thinking*   Find two expressions that simplify to $\frac{4ab}{c}$.

Challenge

40. *Mathematical Reasoning*   Is there a commutative property for division of whole numbers? If not, give a counterexample. A **counterexample** is one case where a rule is false.

Mixed Review

Simplify.   **41.** $12 + 8 \div 2$ **42.** $16 \div 8 \cdot 2 \div 4$ **43.** $(3 + 4)6$ *1-1*

Calculate.   **44.** $\frac{2}{5} + \frac{3}{8}$ **45.** $\frac{5}{8} \div \frac{2}{3}$ **46.** $(3.1)(0.02)$ **47.** $\frac{4.8}{10}$ *Pre-Course*

Exponential Notation

Math in Action

In a computer, information is read in units called "bits" and "bytes." A bit is like an on-off switch and is read by the computer as 1 (on) or 0 (off). A byte is a group of 8 bits, put together to represent one unit of data such as a letter, digit, or special character. Each byte, therefore, can represent $2 \times 2 \times 2 \times 2 \times 2 \times 2 \times 2 \times 2$ or 256 different characters.

This book was edited on a personal computer with 2^7 megabytes of built–in memory. If the prefix *mega-* means one million, how many bytes of built-in memory does this computer have?

What You'll Learn

1 To express numbers with exponents

2 To evaluate expressions with exponents

... And Why

To use exponential notation to simplify expressions with repeated factors

 PART 1 Using Exponents

Objective: Express numbers using exponential notation.

A product in which the factors are the same is called a **power.** We can write $2 \times 2 \times 2 \times 2 \times 2 \times 2 \times 2 \times 2$ as 2^8. The number 8 is called the **exponent,** and 2 is called the **base.** The exponent tells how many times the base is used as a factor. Similarly, we can write $a \cdot a \cdot a = a^3$. Here the exponent is 3 and the base is a. When an expression is written with exponents, we say the expression is written using **exponential notation.**

$$\text{Exponent} \longrightarrow$$
$$\text{Base} \longrightarrow b^n$$

We read b^n as the "nth power of b," or simply "b to the nth," or "b to the n." We may also read b^2 as "b squared" and b^3 as "b cubed."

EXAMPLES What is the meaning of each expression?

1 2^2 2^2 means $2 \cdot 2$ **2** 3^5 3^5 means $3 \cdot 3 \cdot 3 \cdot 3 \cdot 3$

3 n^4 n^4 means $n \cdot n \cdot n \cdot n$ **4** $2y^3$ $2y^3$ means $2 \cdot y \cdot y \cdot y$

Try This   What is the meaning of each expression?

a. 5^4 **b.** b^3 **c.** $2x^3$ **d.** $12y^4$

EXAMPLES   Write using exponential notation.

5 $7 \cdot 7 \cdot 7 \cdot 7$ can be written as 7^4

6 $n \cdot n \cdot n \cdot n \cdot n \cdot n$ can be written as n^6

7 $3 \cdot x \cdot x$ can be written as $3x^2$

8 $2 \cdot y \cdot y \cdot y \cdot y$ can be written as $2y^4$

Try This   Write using exponential notation.

e. $9 \cdot 9 \cdot 9$ **f.** $y \cdot y \cdot y \cdot y \cdot y$ **g.** $4 \cdot n \cdot n \cdot n \cdot n$

h. $15 \cdot x \cdot x \cdot x \cdot x$ **i.** $10 \cdot b \cdot b \cdot b$

Here are some definitions for exponents.

Definitions

b^1 means b for any number b.

If n is a whole number greater than 1, b^n means $\overbrace{b \cdot b \cdot b \cdot b \cdot \ldots \cdot b}^{n \text{ factors}}$.

PART 2   Evaluating Expressions

Objective: Evaluate expressions containing exponents.

EXAMPLES   Evaluate each expression.

9 x^4 for $x = 2$
$x^4 = 2^4$ Substituting
$\quad = 2 \cdot 2 \cdot 2 \cdot 2$
$\quad = 16$

10 y^2 for $y = 5$
$y^2 = 5^2$ Substituting
$\quad = 5 \cdot 5$
$\quad = 25$

Try This   Evaluate each expression.

j. a^2 for $a = 10$ **k.** y^5 for $y = 2$ **l.** x^4 for $x = 0$

We now extend the rules for the order of operations to include exponents.

Order of Operations—Extended

1. Compute within grouping symbols first.
2. Compute powers.
3. Multiply and divide in order from left to right.
4. Add and subtract in order from left to right.

EXAMPLES Evaluate each expression.

11 $y^4 + 3$ for $y = 2$
$y^4 + 3 = 2^4 + 3$
$= 2 \cdot 2 \cdot 2 \cdot 2 + 3$
$= 16 + 3$
$= 19$

12 $m^3 + 5$ for $m = 4$
$m^3 + 5 = 4^3 + 5$
$= 4 \cdot 4 \cdot 4 + 5$
$= 64 + 5$
$= 69$

Try This Evaluate each expression.

m. $x^3 + 2$ for $x = 3$ **n.** $n^5 + 8$ for $n = 2$

When an expression inside parentheses is raised to a power, everything inside the parentheses is the base. Compare $3a^3$ and $(3a)^3$.

$3a^3$ means $3 \cdot a \cdot a \cdot a$ *a* is the base
$(3a)^3$ means $(3a)(3a)(3a)$ *3a* is the base

EXAMPLES Evaluate.

13 $(3a)^3$ for $a = 2$
$(3a)^3 = (3a)(3a)(3a)$
$= (3 \cdot 2)(3 \cdot 2)(3 \cdot 2)$
$= 6 \cdot 6 \cdot 6$
$= 216$

14 $3a^3$ for $a = 2$
$3a^3 = 3 \cdot a \cdot a \cdot a$
$= 3 \cdot 2 \cdot 2 \cdot 2$
$= 24$

Try This Evaluate.

o. $(2x)^2$ for $x = 4$ **p.** $(5y)^3$ for $y = 2$ **q.** $3x^2$ for $x = 3$

Evaluating Expressions Involving Exponents

You can evaluate expressions like $y^3 + 3$ for $y = 2$ on a calculator with an exponent key. Calculate $2^3 + 3$.

2   y^x 3   =   +   3   =   →   11

1-3 Exercises

Extra Help On the Web
Look for worked-out examples at the Prentice Hall Web site.
www.phschool.com

A
What is the meaning of each expression?

1. 2^4 **2.** 5^3 **3.** 3^1 **4.** 1^3 **5.** a^3 **6.** $5y^4$

Write using exponential notation.

7. $10 \cdot 10 \cdot 10 \cdot 10 \cdot 10 \cdot 10$ **8.** $6 \cdot 6 \cdot 6 \cdot 6$ **9.** $x \cdot x \cdot x \cdot x \cdot x$
10. $4 \cdot y \cdot y \cdot y$ **11.** $5 \cdot m \cdot m \cdot m \cdot m$ **12.** $2 \cdot n \cdot n \cdot n \cdot n \cdot n \cdot n$

Evaluate each expression.

13. m^3 for $m = 3$ **14.** x^6 for $x = 2$ **15.** p^1 for $p = 19$

16. x^{19} for $x = 0$ **17.** $x^4 - 8$ for $x = 4$ **18.** $y^{15} + 4$ for $y = 1$

19. $x^3 + 2$ for $x = 4$ **20.** $y^2 - 3$ for $y = 5$ **21.** $3m^3$ for $m = 1$

22. $4x^2$ for $x = 3$ **23.** $2n^4$ for $n = 2$ **24.** $(4x)^3$ for $x = 2$

25. $(2a)^4$ for $a = 3$ **26.** $(5n)^2$ for $n = 6$ **27.** $(6y)^4$ for $y = 2$

B

28. Evaluate $(2ab)^3$ for $a = 2$ and $b = 4$.

29. Evaluate $(3mn)^3$ for $m = 2$ and $n = 0$.

Write with a single exponent.

For example, $\dfrac{3^5}{3^3} = \dfrac{3 \cdot 3 \cdot 3 \cdot 3 \cdot 3}{3 \cdot 3 \cdot 3} = 3 \cdot 3 = 3^2$

30. $\dfrac{10^5}{10^3}$ **31.** $\dfrac{10^7}{10^2}$ **32.** $\dfrac{5^4}{5^2}$ **33.** $\dfrac{8^6}{8^2}$

34. Evaluate $x^3 y^2 + zx$ for $x = 2$, $y = 1$, $z = 3$.

35. *Critical Thinking*   Does $x^y = y^x$ for all whole numbers x and y? If yes, justify your answer. If no, provide a counterexample.

36. *Mathematical Reasoning*   Square any number, then double the result. Is your answer *always, sometimes,* or *never* greater than the result of doubling the number, then squaring it? Justify your answer.

37. *Error Analysis*   Elaine wrote in her math journal "The square of any number is always greater than the number." Find a counterexample to show that Elaine's statement is incorrect.

Challenge

38. Find yx^{149} for $x = 13$ and $y = 0$.

39. Find $x^{410} y^2$ for $x = 1$ and $y = 3$.

40. 10^{127} is 1 followed by how many zeros?

41. Find $(x^2)^2$ if $x = 3$.

Mixed Review

Calculate. **42.** $8\frac{1}{3} + 2\frac{2}{3}$ **43.** $1\frac{5}{8} - \frac{3}{4}$ **44.** $\frac{3}{8} \div 3$ **45.** $5 \times 2\frac{1}{2}$ *Pre-Course*

Evaluate. **46.** $2(m + n)$ for $m = 7$, $n = 1$ **47.** $(3 + n)n$ for $n = 2$ *1-1*

Simplify. **48.** $\frac{7}{56}$ **49.** $\frac{96}{12}$ **50.** $\frac{r}{8rs}$ **51.** $\frac{18x}{2xy}$ **52.** $\frac{3ab}{12b}$ *1-2*

The Associative Properties

PART 1 Parentheses

Objective: Evaluate expressions involving parentheses.

You have learned to calculate within parentheses first. You also know that you simplify powers before doing other operations.

EXAMPLES Calculate.

1 $(3 \cdot 4)^2 = 12^2$ Working within parentheses first
       $= 144$

2 $3 \cdot 4^2 = 3 \times 16$ There are no parentheses, so we find 4^2 first.
       $= 48$

Try This Calculate.

a. $(3 \cdot 5)^2$ **b.** $3 \cdot 5^2$ **c.** $4 \cdot 2^3$ **d.** $(4 \cdot 2)^3$
e. $4 + 2^2$ **f.** $(4 + 2)^2$ **g.** $(5 - 1)^2$ **h.** $5 - 1^2$

EXAMPLES Evaluate each expression.

3 $(3x)^3 - 2$ for $x = 2$
       $(3x)^3 - 2 = (3 \cdot 2)^3 - 2$ Substituting
       $= 6^3 - 2$ Multiplying within parentheses first
       $= 216 - 2$
       $= 214$

4 $(2 + x)(y - 1)$ for $x = 3$ and $y = 5$
       $(2 + x)(y - 1) = (2 + 3)(5 - 1)$
       $= 5 \cdot 4$ Working within parentheses first
       $= 20$

Try This Evaluate each expression.

i. $(4y)^2 - 5$ for $y = 3$ **j.** $6(x + 12)$ for $x = 8$

k. $t + \dfrac{6}{5t^2}$ for $t = 2$ **l.** $(x - 4)^3$ for $x = 6$

m. $(4 + y) \cdot (x - 3)$ for $y = 3$ and $x = 12$

What You'll Learn

1 To evaluate expressions involving parentheses

2 To use the associative properties of addition and multiplication

3 To write equivalent expressions using properties

...And Why

To use the associative properties to make calculations easier

Evaluating Expressions

You can use a calculator to evaluate algebraic expressions.

Evaluate $\frac{x + 2y}{3}$ for $x = 9$ and $y = 3$.

Key sequence for scientific calculators, which follow the Order of Operations:

| (| 9 | + | 2 | × | 3 |) | ÷ | 3 | = | → 5 |

Key sequence for arithmetic calculators, which do not follow the Order of Operations:

| 2 | × | 3 | + | 9 | = | ÷ | 3 | = | → 5 |

PART 2 Using the Associative Properties

Objective: Write equivalent expressions using the associative properties.

Reading Math

You read the expression 3 + (7 + 5) as "3 plus the quantity 7 plus 5."

When addition is the only operation in an expression, the parentheses can be moved without affecting the value of the expression. For example, the expressions $3 + (7 + 5)$ and $(3 + 7) + 5$ are equivalent.

$$
\begin{array}{cc}
3 + (7 + 5) & (3 + 7) + 5 \\
3 + 12 & 10 + 5 \\
15 & 15
\end{array}
$$

When multiplication is the only operation in an expression, parentheses can be moved without affecting the value of the expression. For example, the expressions $3 \cdot (4 \cdot 2)$ and $(3 \cdot 4) \cdot 2$ are equivalent.

$$
\begin{array}{cc}
3 \cdot (4 \cdot 2) & (3 \cdot 4) \cdot 2 \\
3 \cdot 8 & 12 \cdot 2 \\
24 & 24
\end{array}
$$

The **associative properties** state that this will always be true.

Associative Property of Addition

For any numbers a, b, and c,

$$a + (b + c) = (a + b) + c$$

(Numbers can be grouped in any order for addition.)

Associative Property of Multiplication

For any numbers a, b, and c,

$$a \cdot (b \cdot c) = (a \cdot b) \cdot c$$

(Numbers can be grouped in any order for multiplication.)

EXAMPLES   Use an associative property to write an equivalent expression.

5 $y + (z + 3) = (y + z) + 3$ Using the associative property of addition

6 $5 \cdot (x \cdot y) = (5 \cdot x) \cdot y$ Using the associative property of multiplication

Try This   Use an associative property to write an equivalent expression.

n. $a + (b + 2)$ **o.** $3 \cdot (v \cdot w)$

PART 3 Using the Properties Together

Objective: Write equivalent expressions using the commutative and associative properties.

If addition or multiplication is the only operation in an expression, then the associative and commutative properties allow us to group and change order as we please. For example, in a calculation like $(5 + 2) + (3 + 5) + 8$, addition is the only operation. Therefore, we can change the grouping and order to make our calculations easier.

$$(5 + 5) + (2 + 8) + 3 = 10 + 10 + 3 = 23$$

In algebra we often need to change the order or grouping of an expression. The associative and commutative properties allow us to do this.

EXAMPLE 7   Use the commutative and associative properties to write three expressions equivalent to $(x + 5) + y$.

$(x + 5) + y = x + (5 + y)$ Using the associative property first
$\qquad\qquad\quad = x + (y + 5)$ and then the commutative property

$(x + 5) + y = y + (x + 5)$ Using the commutative property and
$\qquad\qquad\quad = y + (5 + x)$ then the commutative property again

$(x + 5) + y = 5 + (x + y)$ Using the commutative property first
$\qquad\qquad\qquad\qquad$ and then the associative property

EXAMPLE 8   Use the commutative and associative properties to write three expressions equivalent to $(3 \cdot x) \cdot y$.

$(3 \cdot x) \cdot y = 3 \cdot (x \cdot y)$ Using the associative property first
$ = 3 \cdot (y \cdot x)$ and then the commutative property

$(3 \cdot x) \cdot y = y \cdot (x \cdot 3)$ Using the commutative property twice

$(3 \cdot x) \cdot y = x \cdot (y \cdot 3)$ Using the commutative property, then the associative property, and then the commutative property again

Try This   Use the commutative and associative properties to write three equivalent expressions.

p. $4 \cdot (t \cdot u)$ **q.** $r + (2 + 5)$

Extra Help On the Web

Look for worked-out examples at the Prentice Hall Web site.
www.phschool.com

1-4 Exercises

A

Mental Math   Calculate.

1. $(5 \cdot 4)^2$ **2.** $(6 \cdot 3)^2$ **3.** $5 \cdot 4^2$ **4.** $6 \cdot 3^2$

5. $7 + 2^2$ **6.** $5 + 3^2$ **7.** $(7 + 2)^2$ **8.** $(5 + 3)^2$

9. $(5 - 2)^2$ **10.** $(3 - 2)^2$ **11.** $10 - 3^2$ **12.** $16 - 4^2$

13. $12 - 2^3$ **14.** $30 - 3^3$ **15.** $(2 + 3)^3$ **16.** $3 \cdot 2^3$

Evaluate each expression.

17. $5x^2 - 4$ for $x = 4$ **18.** $3a^3 + 2$ for $a = 1$

19. $(5y)^3 - 75$ for $y = 2$ **20.** $(7x)^2 + 59$ for $x = 3$

21. $3(a + 10)$ for $a = 12$ **22.** $b(7 + b)$ for $b = 5$

23. $(t + 3)^3$ for $t = 4$ **24.** $(12 - w)^3$ for $w = 7$

25. $(x + 5)(12 - x)$ for $x = 7$ **26.** $(y - 4)(y + 6)$ for $y = 10$

27. $\dfrac{y + 3}{2y}$ for $y = 5$ **28.** $\dfrac{(4x) + 2}{2x}$ for $x = 5$

29. $\dfrac{w^2 + 4}{5w}$ for $w = 4$ **30.** $\dfrac{b^2 + b}{2b}$ for $b = 5$

Use the associative properties to write an equivalent expression.

31. $(a + b) + 3$ **32.** $(5 + x) + y$ **33.** $3 \cdot (a \cdot b)$ **34.** $(6 \cdot x) \cdot y$

Use the commutative and associative properties to write three equivalent expressions.

35. $(a + b) + 2$ **36.** $(3 + x) + y$ **37.** $5 + (v + w)$

38. $6 + (x + y)$ **39.** $(x \cdot y) \cdot 3$ **40.** $(a \cdot b) \cdot 5$

41. $7 \cdot (a \cdot b)$ **42.** $5 \cdot (x \cdot y)$ **43.** $2 \cdot c \cdot d$

B

Use the commutative and associative properties to write two expressions equivalent to each expression.

44. $(4a + 2) + b$ **45.** $(7 \cdot m) \cdot n + 3$ **46.** $(5x^3 + 2) + 6$

47. $(6m)(np)$ **48.** $2(x + 3)y$ **49.** $5 + (3 + 7y) + 4$

Find a replacement for the variable for which the two expressions are *not* equivalent.

50. $3x^2; (3x)^2$ **51.** $(a + 2)^3; a^3 + 2^3$

52. $\frac{x + 2}{2}; x$ **53.** $\frac{y^6}{y^3}; y^2$

54. *Critical Thinking* If it is true that $A + B = 25$ and $(A + C) + B = 85$, what is the value of $A + (C + B)$? of C?

Challenge

55. *Mathematical Reasoning* Evaluate $a - (b - c)$ and $(a - b) - c$ for $a = 12, b = 7, c = 4$. Is there an associative property for subtraction?

56. *Mathematical Reasoning* Evaluate $a \div (b \div c)$ and $(a \div b) \div c$ for $a = 32, b = 8$, and $c = 4$. Is there an associative property for division?

57. *Mathematical Reasoning* Suppose we define a new operation @ on the set of whole numbers as follows: $a @ b = 2a + b$. For example, $4 @ 5 = 2(4) + 5 = 13$.
  a. Determine whether @ is commutative for whole numbers. That is, does $a @ b = b @ a$ for all whole numbers a and b?
  b. Determine whether @ is associative for whole numbers. That is, does $(a @ b) @ c = a @ (b @ c)$ for all whole numbers a, b, and c?

Self-Test On the Web
Check your progress. Look for a self-test at the Prentice Hall Web site. www.phschool.com

Mixed Review

Calculate. **58.** $12\frac{1}{4} + 7\frac{3}{8}$ **59.** $3\frac{3}{5} + 5\frac{1}{2}$ **60.** $8\frac{1}{3} + 3\frac{3}{5}$

61. $3\frac{3}{4} - 2\frac{1}{3}$ **62.** $\frac{7}{8} \times \frac{2}{3}$ **63.** $1\frac{1}{5} \times 1\frac{1}{3}$ **64.** 3.75×0.3 *Pre-Course*

Simplify. **65.** $\frac{6x}{7xy}$ **66.** $\frac{12t}{24t}$ **67.** $\frac{6mn}{11mt}$ **68.** $\frac{14n}{28ny}$ *1-2*

Evaluate. **69.** $(3a^3)$ for $a = 5$ **70.** $4y^2$ for $y = 7$

71. $2w^3 - 9$ for $w = 2$ **72.** $4r + \frac{3t}{6}$ for $r = 4$ and $t = 8$

73. $3(m + 2n)$ for $m = 4$ and $n = 3$ **74.** $2a + 5b$ for $a = 2$ and $b = 6$

75. $\frac{3s + 7}{t}$ for $s = 1$ and $t = 5$ **76.** $\frac{x + x}{7}$ for $x = 7$

77. $\frac{w + 2z}{z}$ for $w = 6$ and $z = 3$ **78.** $\frac{6 + 3x}{6y}$ for $x = 4$ and $y = 1$ *1-3*

What You'll Learn

1 To use the distributive property to write equivalent expressions

2 To use the distributive property to factor expressions

3 To use the distributive property to collect like terms

...And Why

To simplify expressions by collecting like terms

Introducing the Concept: The Distributive Property

Formulas for the perimeter of a rectangle are used often by surveyors in designing land plots. One surveyor used Formula A; another used Formula B. Do both formulas give the same number for the perimeter?

Formula A: P = 2l + 2w
$$P = (2 \cdot 8) + (2 \cdot 5)$$

Formula B: P = 2(l + w)
$$P = 2 \cdot (8 + 5)$$

PART 1   Using the Distributive Property

Objective: Use the distributive property to write equivalent expressions.

The activity above shows that expressions like $2 \cdot (8 + 5)$ and $(2 \cdot 8) + (2 \cdot 5)$ are equivalent. The **distributive property of multiplication over addition** states that this will always be true.

The Distributive Property of Multiplication Over Addition

For any numbers a, b, and $c, a(b + c) = ab + ac$.
For any numbers a, b, and $c, (b + c)a = ba + ca$.

We can omit the parentheses in expressions like $(4 \cdot 5) + (3 \cdot 7)$ and just write $4 \cdot 5 + 3 \cdot 7$, since this will not change the order of the operations. If we omit the parentheses in expressions like $2(3 + 5)$, however, we will no longer have equivalent expressions.

$$2(3 + 5) = 2(8) = 16 \qquad\qquad 2 \cdot 3 + 5 = 6 + 5 = 11$$

The distributive property must be used to remove the parentheses.

$$2(3 + 5) = 2 \cdot 3 + 2 \cdot 5 = 6 + 10 = 16$$

The following diagram illustrates the distributive property.

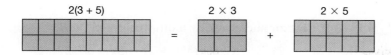

2(3 + 5)　　　2 × 3　　　2 × 5

EXAMPLES   Use the distributive property to write an equivalent expression.

1 $3(x + 2) = 3x + 3 \cdot 2 = 3x + 6$

2 $(s + t + w)6 = s(6) + t(6) + w(6)$
                    $= 6s + 6t + 6w$ Using the commutative property

3 $4(2s + 5) = 4(2s) + 4(5)$
              $= 8s + 20$

Try This   Use the distributive property to write an equivalent expression.

a. $4(x + y + z)$ **b.** $(y + 3)5$

c. $(8a + 3)2$ **d.** $6(x + 2y + 5)$

PART 2   **Factoring**

Objective: Factor expressions.

If the statement of the distributive property is reversed, we have the basis of a process called factoring: $ab + ac = a(b + c)$. To factor an expression, write an equivalent expression as a product of the factors.

EXAMPLES   Factor.

4 $3x + 3y = 3(x + y)$ Look for a common factor. Then use the distributive property.

5 $5x + 5y + 5z = 5(x + y + z)$ The common factor is 5.

6 $7y + 14 + 21z = 7 \cdot y + 7 \cdot 2 + 7 \cdot 3z$ The common factor is 7.
               $= 7(y + 2 + 3z)$

7 $9x + 27y + 9 = 9 \cdot x + 9 \cdot 3y + 9 \cdot 1$ The common factor is 9.
               $= 9(x + 3y + 1)$

Try This   Factor.

e. $5x + 10$ **f.** $12 + 3x$

g. $6x + 12 + 9y$ **h.** $5x + 10y + 5$

Factoring can be checked by multiplying. We multiply the factors to see if we get the original expression.

EXAMPLE 8   Factor and check by multiplying.

$$5x + 10 = 5(x + 2) \qquad \text{Check: } 5(x + 2) = 5x + 5 \cdot 2$$
$$= 5x + 10$$

Try This   Factor and check by multiplying.

i. $9x + 3y$ **j.** $5 + 10x + 15y$

PART 3   Collecting Like Terms

Objective: Collect like terms.

In an expression like $6s + 6t + 6w$, $6s$, $6t$, and $6w$ are called **terms.**

Terms such as $5x$ and $4x$, whose variable factors are exactly the same, are called **like terms.** Similarly, $3y^2$ and $9y^2$ are like terms. Terms such as $4y$ and $5y^2$ are not like terms. We often simplify expressions using the distributive property to collect like terms.

EXAMPLES   Collect like terms.

9 $3x + 4x = (3 + 4)x$ Using the distributive property
$$= 7x$$

10 $x + x = 1 \cdot x + 1 \cdot x$ Using the identity property
$$= (1 + 1)x \qquad \text{Using the distributive property}$$
$$= 2x$$

11 $2x + 3y + 5x + 2y = 2x + 5x + 3y + 2y$ Using the commutative property
$$= (2 + 5)x + (3 + 2)y \qquad \text{Using the distributive property}$$
$$= 7x + 5y$$

12 $5x^2 + x^2 = 5x^2 + 1 \cdot x^2$ Using the identity property
$$= (5 + 1)x^2 \qquad \text{Using the distributive property}$$
$$= 6x^2$$

Try This   Collect like terms.

k. $6y + 2y$ **l.** $7x + 3y + 5y + 4x$
m. $10p + 8q + 4p + 5q$ **n.** $7x^2 + x^2$

1-5 Exercises

Extra Help On the Web

Look for worked-out examples at the Prentice Hall Web site.
www.phschool.com

A

Use the distributive property to write an equivalent expression.

1. $2(b + 5)$

2. $4(x + 3)$

3. $(1 + t)7$

4. $6(v + 4)$

5. $3(x + 1)$

6. $(x + 8)7$

7. $4(1 + y)$

8. $9(s + 1)$

9. $6(5x + 2)$

10. $9(6m + 7)$

11. $7(x + 4 + 6y)$

12. $(5x + 8 + 3p)4$

Factor.

13. $2x + 4$

14. $5y + 20$

15. $30 + 5y$

16. $7x + 28$

17. $14x + 21y$

18. $18a + 24b$

19. $5x + 10 + 15y$

20. $9a + 27b + 81$

21. $14c + 63d + 7$

22. $4y + 10 + 8x$

23. $9r + 27s + 18$

24. $24x + 72y + 8$

Factor and check by multiplying.

25. $9x + 27$

26. $6x + 24$

27. $9x + 3y$

28. $15x + 5y$

29. $8a + 16b + 64$

30. $5 + 20x + 35y$

31. $11x + 44y + 121$

32. $7 + 14b + 56w$

33. $5x + 10y + 45z$

34. $9p + 3q + 27r$

Collect like terms.

35. $9a + 10a$

36. $12x + 2x$

37. $10a + a$

38. $16x + x$

39. $2x + 9z + 6x$

40. $3a + 5b + 7a$

41. $7x + 6y^2 + 9y^2$

42. $12m^2 + 6q + 9m^2$

43. $41a + 90 + 60a + 2$

44. $42x + 6 + 4x + 2$

45. $8a + 8b + 3a + 3b$

46. $100y + 200z + 190y + 400z$

47. $8u^2 + 3t + 10t + 6u^2 + 2$

48. $5 + 6h + t + 8 + 9h$

49. $23 + 5t + 7y + t + y + 27$

50. $45 + 90d + 87 + 9d + 3 + 7d$

51. $\frac{1}{2}b + \frac{1}{2}b$

52. $\frac{2}{3}x + \frac{1}{3}x$

53. $2y + \frac{1}{4}y + y$

54. $\frac{1}{2}a + a + 5a$

Simplify each expression. Collect like terms as needed.

55. $4x + 5y + 6x$

56. $6z + 3k + 9z$

57. $4p^2 + 2p + 4p + 8p^2$

58. $2m + 3mn + 2m + mn$

59. $7xy + 3y + 6x + 2xy$

60. $6tp + 3t^2 + 9t^2 + 2tp$

B

Simplify each expression.

61. $4(x + 3) + 5(x + 3)$ **62.** $7(m^2 + 2) + 7(m^2 + 2)$

63. $8(a + b) + 4(a + 2b)$ **64.** $4(5x + 6y + 3) + 2(x + 2y)$

65. a. The money you deposit in a bank is called the principal. When you deposit money in a bank and earn interest, the new principal is given by the expression $P + Prt$, where P is the principal, r is the rate of interest, and t is the time. Factor the expression $P + Prt$.
   b. If \$400 is invested at 3% interest, find the new principal at the end of one year by substituting $P = 400$, $r = 0.03$, and $t = 1$ in the expression in part (a).

66. a. Factor $17x + 34$. Then evaluate both expressions when $x = 10$.
   b. Do you get the same answer for both expressions? Why?

67. *Critical Thinking*   Does $(x + y)^2 = x^2 + y^2$ for all whole numbers? When are the expressions equal? Explain.

68. *Critical Thinking*   You know that $a(b + c) = ab + ac$ for any numbers $a, b,$ and c. Use this fact and the properties introduced earlier to write a paragraph explaining why $(b + c)a = ba + ca$ is also true for any numbers $a, b,$ and c.

69. *Mathematical Reasoning*   A student factored $ax + ay + bx + by$ as $a(x + y) + b(x + y)$. Another student factored the same expression as $x(a + b) + y(a + b)$. Are both answers correct, or is one of them incorrect? Justify your answer.

Challenge

70. Find a simpler expression equivalent to $\frac{3a + 6}{2a + 4}$.

71. Find a simpler expression equivalent to $\frac{4x + 12y}{3x + 9y}$.

Collect like terms, if possible, and factor the result.

72. $x + 2x^2 + 3x^3 + 4x^2 + 5x$

73. $q + qr + qrs + qrst$

74. $21x + 44xy + 15y - 16x - 8y - 38xy + 2x + xy$

75. Simplify $a\{1 + b[1 + c(1 + d)]\}$. (Hint: Begin with $c(1 + d)$ and work outwards.)

Mixed Review

Calculate.   **76.** $(4 \cdot 3)^2$ **77.** $6 \cdot 2^3$ **78.** $(3 - 2)^3$ **79.** $8 - 2^3$ *1-4*

Simplify.   **80.** $\frac{8xy}{2x}$ **81.** $\frac{6b}{18ab}$ **82.** $\frac{15c}{30c}$ **83.** $\frac{24xy}{3y}$ *1-2*

Evaluate.   **84.** $6(t + 4)$ for $t = 2$ **85.** $w(5 + w)$ for $w = 3$

86. k^1 for $k = 5$ **87.** $(x + 3) \cdot (5 - x)$ for $x = 2$ *1-1*

Writing Expressions

Objective: Write algebraic expressions involving one operation.

Many problems can be solved by translating data given with words into algebraic expressions. To do this, you must know which phrases suggest each of the operations (addition, subtraction, multiplication, and division).

What You'll Learn

1 To write algebraic expressions involving one operation

. . . And Why

To prepare for solving word problems

EXAMPLES Write as an algebraic expression.

1 5 more than a number

$n + 5$ Think of a specific number, say 3. "5 more than 3" would be 3 + 5, so "5 more than a number" would be $n + 5$.

2 3 less than a number

$n - 3$ Think of a specific number, say 5. "3 less than 5" would be 5 − 3, so "3 less than a number" would be $n - 3$.

3 3 times a number

$3n$ Think of a specific number, say 6. "3 times 6" would be 3 · 6, so "3 times a number" would be $3n$.

4 a number divided by 5

$\frac{n}{5}$ Think of a specific number, say 20. "20 divided by 5" would be $\frac{20}{5}$, so "a number divided by 5" would be $\frac{n}{5}$.

Try This   Write as an algebraic expression.

a. the sum of a number and 7
b. the product of a number and 4
c. 4 less than y
d. 6 fewer than x
e. the difference of m and n
f. twice y
g. a less than b
h. 7 times a number

EXAMPLES

5 Let L be the amount of money Lila earned. Glenn earned twice as much as Lila. Write an expression for the amount Glenn earned.

$2L$ "Twice as much" suggests multiplying by 2.

6 Let h be the number of hits John had in a baseball game. John had 2 more walks than hits. Write an expression for the number of walks.

$h + 2$ "2 more walks than hits" suggests adding 2 to the number of hits.

Try This

i. Let a be the amount of money Barbara has. Barbara divides her money among 7 people. Write an expression for the amount each person receives.

j. Let c be the number of coins. Ilene has 24 fewer stamps than coins. Write an expression for the number of stamps she has.

Extra Help On the Web

Look for worked-out examples at the Prentice Hall Web site.
www.phschool.com

1-6 Exercises

A

Write as an algebraic expression.

1. 6 more than b	**2.** 8 more than t
3. 9 less than c	**4.** 4 less than d
5. 6 greater than q	**6.** 11 greater than z
7. b more than a	**8.** c more than d
9. x less than y	**10.** c less than h
11. x added to w	**12.** s added to t
13. m subtracted from n	**14.** p subtracted from q
15. the sum of r and s	**16.** the sum of d and f
17. twice x	**18.** three times p
19. 5 multiplied by t	**20.** 9 multiplied by d
21. the product of 3 and b	**22.** x divided among 5
23. double h	**24.** half of x
25. y fewer than x	**26.** n more than 6
27. 5 less than m	**28.** q less than p

29. Let a be Connie's age. Robin is 5 years older than Connie. Write an expression for Robin's age.

30. Let p be the number of points the Tigers scored. The Lions scored double the number of points the Tigers scored. Write an expression for the number of points the Lions scored.

31. Let m be the amount of money Bob had before he went shopping. Bob spent \$4.50 while shopping. Write an expression for the amount Bob had left after shopping.

32. Let t be the total amount Rosalie spent for blouses. Each of the 5 blouses cost the same. Write an expression for the cost of each blouse.

33. Let a be the amount Greg earned last week. Greg earned \$45 more this week than last week. Write an expression for the amount he earned this week.

34. Let n be the number of magazines Scotty sold. Sherry sold half as many magazines as Scotty. Write an expression for the number of magazines that Sherry sold.

35. Let w be Tom's weight last week. Tom lost 2 pounds this week. Write an expression for Tom's weight this week.

36. Let a be the amount Gil has left after buying a record. The record cost $8. Write an expression for the amount he had before buying the record.

37. Let K be the amount Kelly earns. Geri earns three times as much as Kelly. Write an expression for the amount Geri earns.

38. Let w be the width of a racing-eight crew shell. A racing-eight shell is 32 times as long as it is wide. Write an expression for the length of a racing-eight crew shell.

39. Let t be the total amount of money collected. The total amount was divided evenly among 4 charities. Write an expression for the amount received by each charity.

40. Let d be the distance Paul ran. Steve ran a third as far as Paul. Write an expression for the distance Steve ran.

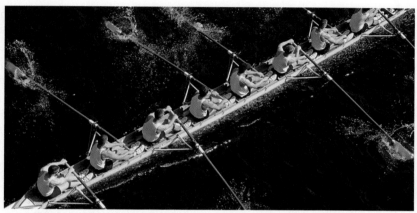

A racing-eight shell is 32 times as long as it is wide. How long is a 22 in.-wide shell? (See Exercise 38.)

41. Let R be Randy's age 3 years from now. Write an expression for Randy's age now.

B

Write as an algebraic expression.

42. a number x increased by three times y

43. a number y increased by twice x

44. a number a increased by 2 more than b

45. a number that is 3 less than twice x

46. a number x increased by itself

47. the area of a rectangle with length l and width w

48. the perimeter of a square with side s

Evaluate.

49. $\dfrac{256y}{32x}$ for $y = 1$ and $x = 4$

50. $\dfrac{y + x}{2} + \dfrac{3 \cdot y}{x}$ for $x = 2$ and $y = 4$

51. $\dfrac{a + b}{4} + \dfrac{a \cdot b}{2}$ for $a = 3$ and $b = 4$

Evaluate $\frac{x + y}{4}$ when

52. $y = 2$ and x is 14. **53.** $x = 9$ and y is three times x.

54. $y = 8$ and x is twice y. **55.** $x = 64$ and y is half of x.

56. *Critical Thinking* Describe a real-world situation that could be translated to the expression $25a + 10b$.

57. *Multi-Step Problem* Let x be the number of students in the art club.

  a. All but 6 students in the club went on a field trip. Write an expression for the number of students on the field trip.

  b. When the students got to the museum, they were divided into three groups of equal size. Write an expression for the number of students in each group.

  c. Four students from another school joined the group that Ed was in. Write an expression for the number of students in Ed's group.

  d. Before lunch, some students (not including Ed) left Ed's group to go to a special exhibit. The number of students that left was equal to one-ninth of the number of students in the art club. Write an expression for the number of students that remained in Ed's group.

  e. There are 27 students in the art club. How many students were in Ed's group at lunchtime?

58. *Critical Thinking* Let n be a whole number. Tell whether each expression always represents an odd number. Justify your answers.

  a. $2(n + 1)$ **b.** $2n + 1$ **c.** $10n - 1$ **d.** $11n$

Challenge

59. Let $w + 3$ represent a whole number. Give an expression for the next whole number after it.

60. Let $d + 2$ represent an odd whole number. Give an expression for the preceding odd number.

61. The difference between two numbers is 3. One number is t. What are two possible values for the other number?

62. Two numbers are $v + 2$ and $v - 2$. What is their sum?

63. Two numbers are $2 + w$ and $2 - w$. What is their sum?

Mixed Review

Evaluate.   **64.** $4c^2$ for $c = 6$ **65.** $3t^4$ for $t = 2$ **66.** $(4x)^2$ for $x = 3$ *1-3*

Factor.   **67.** $3x + 6$ **68.** $20a + 30b$ **69.** $8 + 16x + 40y$ *1-5*

Collect like terms.   **70.** $14c + 8c$ **71.** $4a + 7b + 8a$ **72.** $\frac{1}{3}c + \frac{2}{3}c$

73. $3y + 7y + y$ **74.** $\frac{1}{4}d + \frac{3}{4}d$ **75.** $5 + 7c + 4$ *1-5*

Solving Equations: An Introduction

Introducing the Concept: Equations

A block and two marbles balance six marbles on a scale. The marbles each weigh one ounce. How much does the block weigh?

Which of the following scales balance?

Much of your work in algebra will involve solving equations. In this lesson we introduce solving simple equations. An **equation** is a mathematical sentence that uses an equal sign to state that two expressions represent the same number or are equivalent. Here are some examples.

$$3 + 2 = 5 \qquad 7 - 2 = 4 \qquad x + 15 = 12$$

PART 1 True, False, and Open Equations

Objective: Determine whether an equation is true, false, or open.

An equation that contains only numbers may be either true or false. For example, $3 + 2 = 5$ is true, but $7 - 2 = 4$ is false. An equation containing a variable may be neither true nor false. For example, $x + 5 = 12$ is neither true nor false because you do not know the value of the variable. An equation that contains at least one variable is called an **open sentence.**

EXAMPLES State whether each sentence is true, false, or open.

1 $18 + 32 = 50$ True

2 $42 - 15 = 25$ False

3 $12 = 4 + x$ Open

Try This State whether each sentence is true, false, or open.

a. $3 \cdot 5 + 2 = 13$ **b.** $4 \cdot 2 - 3 = 5$ **c.** $y + 5 = 6$

Objective: Find solution sets of an equation.

The set of numbers from which you can select replacements for the variable is called the **replacement set.** A replacement for a variable that makes an equation true is called a **solution.** To **solve** an equation means to find all of its solutions. The collection of all the solutions is called the **solution set.**

When the replacement set contains a small number of elements, one way to solve the equation is to substitute each element in the set to see if it makes a true sentence.

EXAMPLE 4

Solve $2x = x + 3$ for the replacement set $\{0, 1, 2, 3\}$.

$$2x = x + 3$$

Replace the variable with each number in the replacement set.

$2(0) = 0 + 3$
$\quad 0 = 3$ False

$2(1) = 1 + 3$
$\quad 2 = 4$ False

$2(2) = 2 + 3$
$\quad 4 = 5$ False

$2(3) = 3 + 3$
$\quad 6 = 6$ True

The solution to the equation is 3. The solution set is $\{3\}$.

Try This

d. Solve $x^2 + 3 = 12$ for $\{0, 3, 9\}$.

e. Solve $\frac{12}{x} = 3x$ for $\{2, 4, 12\}$.

If the replacement set is large, trying numbers is not a good method for solving an equation. If an equation contains small numbers and one operation, the equation can often be solved mentally.

EXAMPLES Solve mentally. The replacement set is all whole numbers.

5 $x + 6 = 13$

  $x = 7$ Think: What number added to 6 gives 13?

6 $4y = 32$

  $y = 8$ Think: What number multiplied by 4 gives 32?

Try This   Solve mentally. The replacement set is all whole numbers.

f. $x + 4 = 10$ **g.** $\frac{y}{6} = 4$

h. $14 = y + 9$ **i.** $x - 5 = 12$

PART 3 Equivalent Equations

Objective: Recognize equivalent equations.

Two equations with the same solution set are **equivalent.**

Equivalent Equations		*Nonequivalent Equations*	
	Solution Set		Solution Set
$x + 4 = 10$	{6}	$x + 8 = 10$	{2}
$x + 6 = 12$	{6}	$x + 8 = 14$	{6}

An equation is like a balanced scale. If you add the same weight to both sides of the scale, it will remain balanced. Likewise, if you add the same quantity to both sides of an equation, the equations will be equivalent.

$x + 4 = 10$
$x + 4 + 2 = 10 + 2$ Adding 2 to both sides
$x + 6 = 12$

The equation $x + 4 = 10$ is equivalent to the equation $x + 6 = 12$.

You can
   add the same number to both sides of an equation,
   subtract the same number from both sides of an equation,
   multiply both sides of an equation by the same nonzero number, or
   divide both sides of an equation by the same nonzero number
and still have an equivalent equation.

EXAMPLE 7 Each pair of equations is equivalent. What was done to the first equation to get the second one?

  $x + 2 = 5$
  $x + 5 = 8$ $x + 2 + 3 = 5 + 3$

Three was added to both sides of the first equation to get the second equation.

Each pair of equations is equivalent. What was done to the first equation to get the second one?

8 $4x = 20$
$x = 5$ $\qquad \frac{4x}{4} = \frac{20}{4}$

Both sides of the first equation were divided by 4 to get the second equation.

9 $\frac{1}{3}x = 8$
$\frac{2}{3}x = 16$ $\qquad 2 \cdot \frac{1}{3}x = 2 \cdot 8$

Both sides of the first equation were multiplied by 2 to get the second equation.

Try This Each pair of equations is equivalent. What was done to the first equation to get the second one?

j. $x + 8 = 20$
$\quad x + 12 = 24$

k. $2x - 4 = 56$
$\quad 2x - 9 = 51$

l. $6x = 42$
$\quad 3x = 21$

Extra Help On the Web

Look for worked-out examples at the Prentice Hall Web site.
www.phschool.com

1-7 Exercises

A

State whether each sentence is true, false, or open.

1. $2 + 3 \cdot 5 = 25$ **2.** $3a - 4 = 5$ **3.** $2^3 + 8 = 16$

Solve for the given replacement set.

4. $3n + 2 = 23 \{5, 7, 9\}$ **5.** $6u - 2 = 46 \{5, 6, 8\}$

6. $2m^2 - 1 = 7 \left\{1, \frac{3}{2}, 2\right\}$ **7.** $x^2 + x = 0 \{0, 100, 1000\}$

8. $8 - n = 2n \{1, 2, 4\}$ **9.** $t - 8 = 4t - 44 \{8, 12, 18\}$

Mental Math Solve mentally. The replacement set is all whole numbers.

10. $x + 10 = 20$ **11.** $m + 7 = 30$ **12.** $x - 7 = 12$

13. $y - 8 = 19$ **14.** $6a = 54$ **15.** $8y = 72$

16. $\frac{x}{6} = 5$ **17.** $\frac{c}{8} = 6$ **18.** $d + 98 = 100$

Each pair of equations is equivalent. Tell what was done to the first equation to get the second equation.

19. $3x - 5 = 12$
$\quad 3x = 17$

20. $4r + 3 = 12$
$\quad 4r = 9$

21. $x + 5 = 12$
$\quad x - 5 = 2$

22. $12x = 36$
 $4x = 12$

23. $\frac{r}{4} = 6$
 $r = 24$

24. $\frac{3y}{5} = 3$
 $3y = 15$

25. $\frac{x}{8} = 4$
 $x = 32$

26. $5 = \frac{n}{3}$
 $15 = n$

27. $7 = \frac{2y}{4}$
 $28 = 2y$

B

Mental Math Simplify; then solve mentally. The replacement set is all whole numbers.

28. $5x + 3x = 24$

29. $9y + 4y = 26$

30. $6t + 3t = 0$

31. $\frac{y}{2} + \frac{y}{2} = 31$

32. $\frac{2}{3}y + \frac{1}{3}y = 2$

33. $20x - 6x = 7$

34. $\frac{10d}{5} = 10$

35. $\frac{20k}{4} = 10$

36. $4t^2 = 0$

What can be done to each side of the equation to get the variable alone on one side of the equal sign?

37. $x - 12 = 34$

38. $g + 34 = 60$

39. $3x = 23$

40. $5v = 35$

41. $\frac{t}{8} = 12$

42. $\frac{m}{5} = 14$

Error Analysis A student made the claim that each pair of equations below is equivalent. Explain why the student is incorrect.

43. $n - 5 = 21$
 $n - 5 + 5 = 21 - 5$

44. $\frac{x}{6} = 12$
 $12 \cdot \frac{x}{6} = 6 \cdot 12$

45. **TEST PREP** For which replacement set does the equation $25 = \frac{n}{5}$ have a solution?

 A. $\{5, 25\}$ **B.** $\{25, 75\}$ **C.** $\{\frac{1}{5}, 5\}$ **D.** $\{10, 125\}$

46. *Critical Thinking* Write an equation with no solution if the replacement set is the set of all odd whole numbers.

Challenge

47. Write an equation that has *no* whole number solution.

48. Write an equation for which *every* whole number is a solution.

49. Write an equation of the type $ax = b$ where $x = 0$ is a solution.

Mixed Review

Write using exponential notation. **50.** $m \cdot m \cdot m$ **51.** $n \cdot n \cdot 5 \cdot n \cdot n \cdot n$ *1-3*

Calculate. **52.** $(3 \cdot 2)^2$ **53.** $(4 + 4)^2$ **54.** $9 + 3^2$ **55.** $(9 - 6)^3$ *1-4*

Factor. **56.** $4x + 12$ **57.** $13t + 52$ **58.** $10t + 25m$

59. $16 + 8y$ **60.** $8a + 16b$ **61.** $9x + 3$ **62.** $8 + 24c$ *1-5*

1-8 ▷ Reasoning Strategies

What You'll Learn

1 To solve nonroutine problems using the strategy *Draw A Diagram*

...And Why

To increase efficiency in solving problems by applying reasoning skills

PART 1 Draw a Diagram

Objective: Solve nonroutine problems using the strategy *Draw a Diagram*.

You can use the Problem-Solving Guidelines below to help you solve problems.

PROBLEM-SOLVING GUIDELINES

■ **Phase 1: UNDERSTAND the problem**

What am I trying to find?
What data am I given?
Have I ever solved a similar problem?

■ **Phase 2: Develop and carry out a PLAN**

What strategies might I use to solve the problem?
How can I correctly carry out the strategies I selected?

■ **Phase 3: Find the ANSWER and CHECK**

Does the proposed solution check?
What is the answer to the problem?
Does the answer seem reasonable?
Have I stated the answer clearly?

The planning phase involves selecting and carrying out one or more *strategies* for solving problems. One of the most useful strategies is to *draw a diagram* of the situation.

EXAMPLE

A mining company estimates that it needs to tunnel about 2000 ft into a mountain to reach the mineral deposits. Each day the company is able to tunnel about 500 ft into the mountain. Each night, when equipment is removed for maintenance, about 200 ft of the tunnel refills with rocks. At this rate, estimate how many days it will take the company to reach the mineral deposits.

■ **UNDERSTAND the problem**

Question: How many days will the company need to tunnel?
Data: Each day it gains 500 ft; each night it loses 200 ft.

■ Develop and carry out a PLAN

We can *draw a diagram* to show the action in the problem.

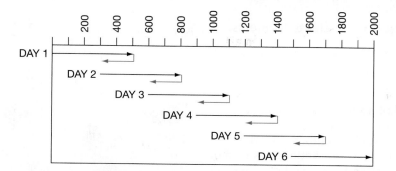

■ Find the ANSWER and CHECK

The diagram shows that the company will reach the deposit in 6 days. This answer seems reasonable, since each day the progress is 300 ft.

1-8 Problems

Extra Help On the Web

Look for worked-out examples at the Prentice Hall Web site.
www.phschool.com

Solve by drawing a diagram.

1. The tip of a large underwater mountain in the Pacific Ocean is about 8700 ft from the surface. The distance from the bottom of the mountain to the water's surface is about 14,250 ft. What is the approximate height of this underwater mountain?

2. The manager of a shopping mall was asked to rope off a rectangular section of the parking lot for an automobile show. The area roped off was 250 ft by 300 ft. Posts were to be placed every 25 ft around the lot. How many posts were needed?

3. A rocket is divided into three sections: the cargo and navigation section at the top, the fuel tank in the middle, and the booster rocket at the bottom. The cargo and navigation section is one sixth as long as the booster rocket. The booster rocket is one half the total length of the rocket. The total length is 180 ft. How long is each section?

4. *Write a Convincing Argument*   Solve the problem below. Then write an argument to convince a classmate that your solution is correct.

A teacher has to select 1 of her 20 students to attend a leadership conference. To be fair she places them in a circle and gives each student a number, in order, from 1 through 20. Then, starting with 1, she points to every other student, sending them back to their seats. She sends student number 2 back, student number 4 back, student number 6 back, and so on, until she goes completely around the circle. She continues skipping every other student until only 1 person is left. In which position should a student stand in order to be selected to attend the conference?

1-9 ▷ Using Formulas

Objective: Evaluate formulas.

What You'll Learn

▼ **1** To evaluate formulas

...And Why

To use formulas to solve geometric problems and rate problems

Math in Action

The speed of a supersonic airplane, which travels near or above the speed of sound, is given as a "Mach" number. The Mach number (M) is the quotient of the speed of the airplane (a) and the speed of sound (s). We can express this as a formula.

A **formula** is an equation that shows a relationship between two or more variables. The formula for the Mach number is $M = \frac{a}{s}$. An equivalent formula is $a = Ms$. We can evaluate this formula just as we evaluate any algebraic expression.

In 1947, Chuck Yeager broke the sound barrier flying at Mach 1.015. Supersonic passenger jets now cruise at twice this speed. What is the Mach number of this cruising speed?

EXAMPLE 1

What is the speed of a supersonic airplane traveling at Mach 1.5 at an altitude where the speed of sound is 720 mi/h?

We will use the formula $a = Ms$ to find the answer, where $M = 1.5$ and $s = 720$ mi/h.

$$a = Ms$$
$$a = 1.5(720) \text{ mi/h}$$
$$a = 1080 \text{ mi/h}$$

Since the speed of sound is in miles per hour, the speed of the airplane is also in miles per hour.

Try This

a. Find the speed of a supersonic airplane traveling at Mach 1.5 at an altitude where the speed of sound is 1130 km/h.

b. Find the speed of a supersonic airplane traveling at Mach 2 at an altitude where the speed of sound is 685 mi/h.

The units of the quantities must always be compatible. Consider, for example, the formula $d = rt$, where d is the distance a moving object travels, r is the rate of travel, and t is the time the object travels. If the rate is given in miles per *hour*, the time must be in *hours*.

EXAMPLE 2

Find the distance (d) traveled by a moped moving at the rate (r) of 27 mi/h for the time (t) of 8 h using the formula $d = rt$.

$$d = rt$$

$$d = 27\,\frac{mi}{h} \cdot 8\,h \qquad \text{The units of measurement are compatible.}$$

$$d = 216\,mi \qquad \frac{mi}{h} \cdot h = mi$$

EXAMPLE 3

Find the perimeter (P) of a rectangle with length (l) of 9 ft and width (w) of 48 in. using the formula $P = 2l + 2w$.

The length and width must be expressed in the same units. Change 48 inches to feet by dividing by 12, the number of inches in one foot. Carrying the dimensions through a computation is called **dimensional analysis.**

$$l = 9\,ft \quad w = \frac{48\,in.}{12\,in./ft} = 4\,ft \qquad \frac{in.}{\frac{in.}{ft}} = in. \cdot \frac{ft}{in.} = ft$$

$$P = 2(9\,ft) + 2(4\,ft)$$
$$P = 18\,ft + 8\,ft$$
$$P = 26\,ft$$

EXAMPLE 4

Find the amount of sales tax (T) paid on an item selling for a price (p) of \$14 using the formula $T = 0.05p$ (5% tax rate).

$$T = 0.05(\$14) \qquad \text{Substituting 14 for } p$$
$$T = \$0.70$$

Try This

c. Find the perimeter (P) of an equilateral triangle with sides (s) of 13 cm using the formula $P = 3s$.

d. Find the area (A) of a square with sides of 7 in. using the formula $A = s^2$.

e. Find the rate (r) at which an object is traveling if it goes a distance (d) of 63 feet in 7 seconds (t) using the velocity formula $r = \frac{d}{t}$.

f. Find the volume (V) of a toy box with length (l) of 4 ft, width (w) of 24 in., and height (h) of 30 in. using the formula $V = lwh$.

1-9 Exercises

A

1. Find the distance (d) traveled by a truck moving at a rate (r) of 55 mi/h for the time (t) of 8 h using the formula $d = rt$.

2. Find the approximate area (A) of a circle with a radius (r) of 4 m using the formula $A = 3.14\,r^2$.

3. Find the amount of sales tax (T) paid on an item selling for a price (p) of $170 using the formula $T = 0.04p$ (4% tax rate).

4. Find the number of kilometers (km) in 2500 meters (m) using the formula $\text{km} = \frac{\text{m}}{1000}$.

5. Find the speed of a supersonic airplane (a) traveling at Mach (M) 1.4 at an altitude where the speed of sound (s) is 1025 ft/s using the formula $a = Ms$.

6. Find the speed of a supersonic airplane (a) traveling at Mach (M) 2.3 at an altitude where the speed of sound (s) is 714 mi/h using the formula $a = Ms$.

7. Find the area (A) of a basketball court with length (l) of 26 m and width (w) of 1400 cm using the formula $A = lw$.

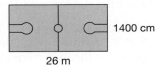

1400 cm

26 m

8. Find the area (A) of a triangle with a base (b) of 1 ft and a height (h) of 9 in. using the formula $A = \frac{1}{2}bh$.

9 in.

1 ft

9. Find the perimeter (P) of an ice skating rink with length (l) of 66 yd and width (w) of 99 ft using the formula $P = 2(l + w)$.

10. Find the temperature in degrees Celsius (C) given a temperature 75° Fahrenheit (F) using the formula $C = \frac{5}{9}(F - 32)$.

11. Find the amount of simple interest (I) paid on a principal (p) amount of $2000 at a rate ($r$) of 0.15 (15% interest rate) for a term (t) of 3 years using the formula $I = prt$.

12. Find the unit price of (U) of a 40 oz (n) box of rice selling for a price (P) of $2.50 using the formula $U = \frac{P}{n}$.

The formula below gives a rule for the amount of medicine a child should have if you know the age of the child (a) and the amount, or dosage, (D) of the medicine an adult would take. Find the child's dosage (d) for the given values of a and D. Round answers to the nearest tenth.

$$d = \frac{a}{a + 12} \cdot D$$

13. $a = 5$ yr, $D = 2.5$ mL

14. $a = 10$ yr, $D = 8$ mL

15. $a = 2$ yr, $D = 4$ mL

16. $a = 1$ yr, $D = 1.5$ mL

B

The formula below gives the approximate stopping distance (d) in feet for an automobile driving at x miles per hour (mi/h). Find the approximate stopping distance for each speed given.

$$d = x + \frac{x^2}{20}$$

17. $x = 25$ mi/h   **18.** $x = 10$ mi/h   **19.** 55 mi/h   **20.** 50 mi/h

The formula below gives the area of a trapezoid. As shown in the picture, h is the height, b is the length of one base, and c is the length of the other base. Use this formula to find the area for the different values given below.

$$A = \tfrac{1}{2}h\,(b + c)$$

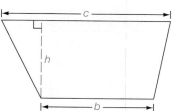

21. $h = 2$ ft, $b = 5$ ft, $c = 12$ ft

22. $h = 10$ in., $b = 8$ in., $c = 14$ in.

23. $h = 4$ m, $b = \tfrac{1}{2}$ m, $c = \tfrac{3}{4}$ m

24. *Critical Thinking*   The length and width of a rectangle are each whole numbers. Find possible areas for this rectangle if its perimeter is 14 cm. Use the formulas $A = lw$ and $P = 2l + 2w$.

25. *Error Analysis*   A rectangular field is 150 m wide and 0.5 km long. To find the area, Andrew and Marie each used the formula $A = lw$. Andrew found the area of the field to be 75 m². Marie found the area of the field to be 75 km². Both of these answers are incorrect.
  a. Identify each student's error.
  b. Find the actual area of the field.

Challenge

26. Find the length of a rectangle (l) with area (A) 64 cm² and width (w) 16 cm. Use the formula $A = lw$.

Write a formula for the area of each figure.

27.

28.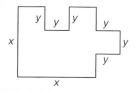

Mixed Review

Write as an algebraic expression.   **29.** 5 more than t

30. the sum of x and y **31.** 3 times k **32.** 3 less than m *1-6*

Collect like terms.   **33.** $15c + c$ **34.** $3x + 4 + 5x$ *1-5*

Solve mentally.   **35.** $x + 6 = 15$ **36.** $6m = 42$ *1-7*

1-10 ▷ Reasoning Strategies

What You'll Learn

1 To solve problems using the strategy *Try, Test, Revise*

. . . And Why

To increase efficiency in solving problems by applying reasoning skills

---

PART 1 Try, Test, Revise

Objective: Solve problems using the strategy *Try, Test, Revise* and other strategies.

PROBLEM-SOLVING GUIDELINES
■ UNDERSTAND the problem
■ Develop and carry out a PLAN
■ Find the ANSWER and CHECK

Some problems can be solved by choosing a possible solution, testing it, and, if necessary, using information gained from the test to revise the possible solution.

This strategy for solving problems is called *Try, Test, Revise.*

EXAMPLE 1 Use the *Try, Test, Revise* strategy to find the missing number.

$$\frac{3 \cdot \square + 7}{2} = 11$$

■ Try 8 for □. Test. $\frac{3 \cdot 8 + 7}{2} = \frac{24 + 7}{2}$

$$= \frac{31}{2} = 15\frac{1}{2}$$

Since $15\frac{1}{2}$ is greater than 11, 8 was too large. Try 4.

■ Try 4 for □. Test. $\frac{3 \cdot 4 + 7}{2} = \frac{12 + 7}{2}$

$$= \frac{19}{2} = 9\frac{1}{2}$$

Since $9\frac{1}{2}$ is less than 11, 4 is too small. Try 5.

■ Try 5 for □. Test. $\frac{3 \cdot 5 + 7}{2} = \frac{15 + 7}{2}$

$$= \frac{22}{2} = 11 \text{ Correct.}$$

The missing number is 5.

The missing number in the example was found using the *Try, Test, Revise* strategy. The missing number also could have been found using equation-solving techniques that you will learn in later chapters. *Many problems in mathematics can be solved correctly in more than one way.*

Use the *Try, Test, Revise* strategy to solve the following problem.

EXAMPLE 2   One number is 12 more than another number. The sum of the two numbers is 48. What are the two numbers?

■ Try 5 for the first number. $5 + 12 = 17$, the second number

   $17 + 5 = 22$ Too low, try a higher first number.

■ Try 20 for the first number. $20 + 12 = 32$, the second number

   $20 + 32 = 52$ Too high but close. Try a lower number.

■ Try 18 for the first number. $18 + 12 = 30$

   $18 + 30 = 48$ Correct.

The two numbers are 18 and 30.

Reasoning Strategies

Draw a Diagram	Try, Test, Revise	Write an Equation
Make an Organized List	Use Logical Reasoning	Make a Table
Look for a Pattern	Simplify the Problem	Work Backward

1-10 Problems

Extra Help On the Web

Look for worked-out examples at the Prentice Hall Web site.
www.phschool.com

Solve using the *Try, Test, Revise* strategy.

1. $\dfrac{4 \cdot \square - 12}{2} = 8$ **2.** $\dfrac{2 \cdot \square + 18}{4} = 6$

3. $\dfrac{\square \cdot 3 + 19}{2} = 20$ **4.** $\dfrac{5 \cdot 8 + \square}{4} = 12$

5. $\dfrac{30}{2 + \square} = 3$ **6.** $\dfrac{12}{2 + \square} = 2$

7. $7(14 - \square) = 35$ **8.** $5(3 + \square) = 40$

9. $2 \cdot \square - 1 = 4 + \square$ **10.** $6 \cdot \square + 3 = 2 \cdot \square + 11$

11. One number is 4 times larger than another number. Their sum is 60. What are the two numbers?

12. Consecutive numbers are numbers that follow each other when counting. For example, 5, 6, and 7 are consecutive numbers. Find three consecutive numbers whose sum is 72.

13. The length of a rectangle is twice as long as the width. The perimeter of the rectangle is 72 in. What are the length and width of this rectangle?

14. The length of a rectangle is 8 more than the width. The area is 308 square units. What are the dimensions of the rectangle?

15. The sum of the interior angles of a triangle is 180°. Two angles are the same. The other angle is two times as large as one of the smaller angles. What are the angles of the triangle?

16. One angle of a triangle is twice as large as the smallest. Another is three times as large as the smallest. What are the three angles?

17. The sum of two numbers is 33. Their product is 242. What are the numbers?

18. The product of two numbers is 800. Their difference is 7. What are the two numbers?

19. The sum of the digits of a two-digit number is 14. If the digits are reversed, the new number is 36 greater than the original number. What is the original two-digit number?

20. The sum of three numbers is 47. The second number is 5 more than the smallest number. The third number is 5 times larger than the smallest number. What are the three numbers? Copy and complete a table like the one below to record your tests.

	1st Number	2nd Number	3rd Number	Sum
1st test				
2nd test				
3rd test				

Solve using one or more of the strategies.

21. Eunpyo worked a total of 33 hours in 1 week. She worked half as many overtime hours as she worked regular hours. How many overtime hours did she work?

22. A photography expedition planned an 8-day crossing of an animal preserve. Each person can carry at most a 5-day supply of water. What is the smallest number of people that must start the trip in order for one member of the group to cross the preserve and the others to return safely to the starting point?

23. Peter earned $45.75 in the second week of his new job. This amount was 3 times what he earned the first week. How much did Peter earn the first week?

24. *Write a Convincing Argument*   Solve the problem below. Then write an argument that would convince a classmate that your solution is correct.

    Juanita installs wheels on lawnmowers. She works on 4-wheel and 5-wheel lawnmowers. One day she installed 98 wheels. She earns $6 for each lawnmower. How much money could she have earned that day?

1 ▷ Chapter Wrap Up

1-1

To evaluate an **algebraic expression, substitute** a number for each variable and calculate the results. When an expression contains grouping symbols, any operation inside the grouping symbols must be done first. When an expression contains a fraction bar, all computations above and below the bar must be done before dividing. When no grouping symbols are used, follow the **Order of Operations.**

Evaluate.

1. $y + 7$ for $y = 4$

2. $n - 6$ for $n = 15$

3. $\frac{30}{x}$ for $x = 6$

4. $4t$ for $t = 8$

5. ab for $a = 8$ and $b = 9$

6. $x - y$ for $x = 19$ and $y = 11$

7. $\frac{a}{3b}$ for $a = 18$ and $b = 3$

8. $p(6 + q)$ for $p = 3$ and $q = 5$

Simplify.

9. $15 \div 3 + 6 \cdot 8$

10. $2 \cdot 10 \div 5 + 6$

Evaluate.

11. $\frac{4a}{2b + 3}$ for $a = 7$ and $b = 2$

12. $6x + \frac{3y}{2}$ for $x = 8$ and $y = 4$

1-2

The **commutative properties,** $a + b = b + a$ and $ab = ba$, and **identity properties,** $1 \cdot a = a$ and $0 + a = a$, are used to write **equivalent expressions** and to **simplify** expressions.

Write an equivalent expression using a commutative property.

13. $x + 8$

14. $11 + ab$

Write an equivalent expression. Use the indicated expression for 1.

15. $\frac{4}{5}$ Use $\frac{9}{9}$ for 1.

16. $\frac{2x}{y}$ Use $\frac{z}{z}$ for 1.

Simplify.

17. $\frac{6}{18}$

18. $\frac{56}{16}$

19. $\frac{35ab}{105bc}$

20. $\frac{96z}{24xyz}$

21. $\frac{mn}{6m}$

22. $\frac{9pq}{72p}$

Key Terms

additive identity (p. 10)
algebraic expression (p. 4)
associative properties (p. 20)
base (p. 15)
commutative properties (p. 9)
counterexample (p. 14)
dimensional analysis (p. 41)
distributive property (p. 24)
equation (p. 33)
equivalent (p. 35)
equivalent expressions (p. 9)
evaluate (p. 4)
exponent (p. 15)
exponential notation (p. 15)
factor (p. 12)
formula (p. 40)
grouping symbols (p. 5)
identity properties (p. 10)
like terms (p. 26)
multiplicative identity (p. 10)
natural numbers (p. 5)
open sentence (p. 33)
power (p. 15)
rational numbers (p. 5)
replacement set (p. 34)
simplest form (p. 12)
simplifying (p. 12)
solution (p. 34)
solution set (p. 34)
solve (p. 34)
substitute (p. 13)
substituting (p. 4)
terms (p. 26)
variable (p. 4)
whole numbers (p. 5)

1-3

We write $10 \times 10 \times 10 \times 10$ using **exponential notation as** 10^4. The **exponent,** 4, tells how many times the **base,** 10, is used as a factor. When an expression inside parentheses is raised to a power, everything inside the parentheses is the base.

Write using exponential notation.

23. $6 \cdot 6 \cdot 6 \cdot 6 \cdot 6$ **24.** $3 \cdot y \cdot y \cdot y \cdot y$

Evaluate each expression.

25. y^3 for $y = 4$ **26.** $2x^2$ for $x = 6$

27. $a^2 - 2$ for $a = 8$ **28.** $b^4 + 3$ for $b = 2$

29. $(2a)^3$ for $a = 3$ **30.** $(5t)^5$ for $t = 2$

1-4

The **associative properties,** $(a + b) + c = a + (b + c)$ and $(ab)c = a(bc)$, are used to write equivalent expressions. When evaluating an expression, you must use the order of operations correctly.

Calculate.

31. $(4 \cdot 5)^2$ **32.** $6 + 7^2$

Evaluate.

33. $6 + (4y)^2$ for $y = 2$ **34.** $(6 + a) \cdot (b - 4)$ for $a = 8$ and $b = 6$

Use an associative property to write an equivalent expression.

35. $(a + b) + 6$ **36.** $(7 \cdot y) \cdot x$

Use the commutative and associative properties to write three equivalent expressions.

37. $(1 + m) + n$ **38.** $4 \cdot (x \cdot y)$

1-5

The **distributive property of multiplication over addition,** $a(b + c) = ab + ac$, is used to write equivalent expressions and to collect like terms. We can multiply: $3(4x + 3) = 12x + 9$; factor expressions: $3xy + 9 = 3(xy + 3)$; and collect like terms: $4y + 7y = 11y$.

Use the distributive property to write an equivalent expression.

39. $7(y + 5)$ **40.** $(6m + 4n + 5)3$

Factor.

41. $18x + 6y$ **42.** $4 + 12b + 36a$

Collect like terms.

43. $3a + 2b + 5a + 7b$ **44.** $15m^2 + 12m + 4m^2$

1-6

It is often necessary to translate data given in words into algebraic expressions. We use a variable to represent each unknown number.

Write as an algebraic expression.

45. fives times a number

46. seven less than a number

47. four more than a number

48. twice a number

49. Suppose x is the amount of money Jenny earned on Monday, and she earned twice that amount on Tuesday. Write an expression for the amount Jenny earned on those two days.

50. Suppose a was Robert's age 12 years ago. Write an expression for Robert's age now.

1-7

An equation that contains only numbers may be either true or false. An equation that contains at least one variable is called an **open sentence.** A replacement for a variable that makes an equation true is called a **solution.** The collection of all the solutions is called the **solution set.** Two equations with the same solution set are **equivalent.**

Solve for the given replacement set.

51. $3n + 7 = 16$ $\{1, 3, 5\}$

52. $x^2 - x = 0$ $\{0, 1, 10\}$

Solve mentally. The replacement set is all whole numbers.

53. $5a = 35$

54. $\frac{c}{4} = 6$

Each pair of equations is equivalent. What was done to the first equation to get the second one?

55. $2x - 8 = 20$
$2x - 13 = 15$

56. $\frac{r}{5} = 10$
$2r = 100$

1-9

To evaluate a **formula,** substitute the given numerical values for the variables and calculate the results.

57. Find the area (A) of a figure with base (b) of 12.5 cm and height (h) of 7.5 cm using the formula $A = bh$.

58. Find the approximate area (A) of a circle with radius (r) of 3 ft using the formula $A = 3.14r^2$.

1-8, 1-10

There are many strategies involved in solving all kinds of problems. You will use a variety of reasoning strategies throughout your study of algebra.

1 ▷ Chapter Assessment

Evaluate.

1. $p - 11$ for $p = 25$ **2.** $\frac{40}{x}$ for $x = 8$

3. $\frac{3x}{y}$ for $x = 10$ and $y = 5$ **4.** $a - 2b$ for $a = 16$ and $b = 3$

Simplify.

5. $16 \div 8 + 8$ **6.** $3 \cdot 4 + 2 \cdot 8$

Evaluate.

7. $3(2a + b)$ for $b = 4$ and $a = 2$ **8.** $\frac{2x + y}{4}$ for $x = 3$ and $y = 6$

Write an equivalent expression using a commutative property.

9. $xy + 3$ **10.** $a + 6$

Write an equivalent expression. Use the indicated expression for 1.

11. $\frac{3}{7}$ Use $\frac{4}{4}$ for 1.   **12.** $\frac{6}{3y}$ Use $\frac{x}{x}$ for 1.

Simplify.

13. $\frac{16}{24}$ **14.** $\frac{81}{45}$

15. $\frac{xy}{12x}$ **16.** $\frac{9xy}{15yz}$

What is the meaning of each expression?

17. 2^4 **18.** $5x^3$

Write in exponential notation.

19. $7 \cdot 7 \cdot 7 \cdot 7$ **20.** $8 \cdot x \cdot x \cdot x \cdot x \cdot x$

Evaluate each expression.

21. $(5x)^2$ for $x = 4$ **22.** $(3y)^4$ for $y = 0$

23. x^3 for $x = 3$ **24.** $3y^2$ for $y = 4$

25. $b^2 - 5$ for $b = 7$ **26.** $(4t)^3$ for $t = 2$

Calculate.

27. $(3 \cdot 6)^2$ **28.** $6 + 3^3$

Evaluate.

29. $(3x)^3 + 4$ for $x = 2$ **30.** $(r + 5)(s - 4)$ for $r = 5$ and $s = 10$

Use an associative property to write an equivalent expression.

31. $(x + y) + 5$

Use the commutative and associative properties to write three equivalent expressions.

32. $3 \cdot (a \cdot b)$

Use the distributive property to write an equivalent expression.

33. $6(4y + 3)$

Factor.

34. $8a + 12b$ **35.** $18x + 6y + 12$

36. $3 + 12b + 36a$ **37.** $8a + 4 + 12c$

Collect like terms.

38. $7a + 3b + 8a + 4b$

39. $6m + 9m^2 + 3m + 7m^2$

Write as an algebraic expression.

40. 11 fewer than x **41.** half of a number

42. twice a number   **43.** six more than a number

44. Suppose w was Lisa's weight last year. Lisa lost 7 pounds this year. Write an expression for Lisa's weight this year.

45. Suppose t is the total amount of tickets sold to the dance. If each of the ninth, tenth, and eleventh grades sold the same number of tickets, write an expression for the number of tickets sold by each grade.

Solve for the given replacement set.

46. $5n - 4 = 11$ $\{2, 3, 4\}$

47. $x^2 - x = 2$ $\{0, 2, 4\}$

48. $7.2y = 36$ $\{5, 50, 500\}$

Each pair of equations is equivalent. What was done to the first equation to get the second one?

49. $\frac{2}{5}m = 3$ **50.** $2x = 10$

$\frac{4}{5}m = 6$ $2x + 4 = 14$

Evaluate.

51. Find the distance (d) traveled by a train moving at the rate (r) of 50 mi/h for the time (t) of 3 h using the formula $d = rt$.

52. Find the temperature in degrees Celsius (C) given a temperature of 77° Fahrenheit (F) using the formula $C = \frac{5}{9}(F - 32)$.

CHAPTER

What You'll Learn in Chapter 2

- How to use integers and rational numbers to model real situations

- How to add, subtract, multiply, and divide rational numbers and how to use these operations in solving problems

- How to use the distributive property to simplify algebraic expressions

- How to apply the properties of numbers, axioms and theorems, to algebraic expressions

Skills & Concepts You Need for Chapter 2

1-2 Simplify.

1. $\frac{12}{27}$ **2.** $\frac{a}{4ab}$ **3.** $\frac{13xy}{xy}$ **4.** $\frac{18cd}{15d}$

1-3 Evaluate.

5. $(4n)^2$ for $n = 2$ **6.** p^1 for $p = 24$ **7.** $3x^3$ for $x = 2$

1-5 Multiply.

8. $5(a + b + d)$ **9.** $11(w + 4)$ **10.** $7(3z + y + 2)$

1-5 Factor.

11. $45 + 9y$ **12.** $3a + 12b$ **13.** $4x + 10 + 8y$

1-5 Collect like terms.

14. $5x + 3y + 2x$ **15.** $b^2 + 3a + 4b^2$ **16.** $5t + 2 + 3t + 7$

Solve for the given replacement set.

17. $4x + 2 = 30$ $\{3, 5, 7\}$ **18.** $8a = 4$ $\{0.5, 5, 50\}$

Integers and Rational Numbers

In Death Valley National Park, the elevation ranges from 282 feet below sea level at the valley floor to 14,494 feet at the peak of Mt. Whitney. What is the difference in elevation?

2-1 ▷ Integers and the Number Line

What You'll Learn

1 To give an integer that corresponds to a real-world situation

2 To compare integers using > or <

3 To find the absolute value of a number

... And Why

To learn how integers can model real-world situations

Math in Action

Some computer spreadsheets show amounts of money less than zero using parentheses. You can also write amounts less than zero using a "negative sign." ($35,000) is the same as −$35,000.

	A	B
1		October
2	Income	$129,000
3	Expenses	($164,000)
4	Balance	($35,000)

PART 1 The Set of Integers

Objective: Give an integer that corresponds to a real-world situation.

We know that the set of whole numbers consists of 0, 1, 2, 3, 4, and so on. On a number line we can match each whole number with another number that is the same distance from 0 but on the opposite side of 0. Numbers such as 3 (read "positive three" or just "three") and −3 (read "negative three") that are the same distance from 0, but on opposite sides of 0, are called **opposites.** Zero is its own opposite. The set of **integers** consists of the whole numbers and their opposites. On the number line, the **positive integers** are to the right of 0, and the **negative integers** are to the left of 0. Zero is neither positive nor negative. The number line below shows some examples of opposites.

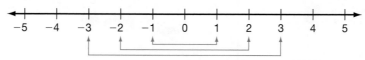

Definition

The set of **integers** consists of the positive integers, negative integers, and zero. {... −4, −3, −2, −1, 0, 1, 2, 3, 4, ...}

EXAMPLES   Name the integer that is suggested by each situation.

1   Death Valley is 282 ft below sea level.

−282   Below sea level suggests a negative integer.

2 The temperature is 3° below 0.

   −3   Below 0 suggests a negative integer.

3 Mickey's juice stand made an $18 profit on Monday.

   18   A profit suggests a positive integer.

Try This   Name the integer that is suggested by each situation.

a. Julia has a debt of $12.

b. The halfback made a gain of 8 yd.

c. The quarterback lost 5 yd.

d. Ignition occurs 3 seconds before liftoff.

This thermometer has both Fahrenheit (F) and Celsius (C) scales. The temperature is about 0°F. What is the temperature in degrees Celsius? For what temperature are the Fahrenheit and Celsius readings the same?

PART **2** **Order on the Number Line**

Objective: Compare integers using > or <.

We use the symbol < to mean *is less than*. For example, 6 < 8 means "6 is less than 8." The symbol > means *is greater than*. For example, 2 > −4 means "2 is greater than −4." The symbols > and < are called inequality symbols. A mathematical sentence that contains an inequality symbol is called an **inequality.** We can read an inequality in two ways. For example, the sentence 5 < 7 means "5 is less than 7." This sentence can also be reversed and read as "7 is greater than 5." An inequality can be true or false. The sentence 12 > 2 is true. The sentence 5 > 16 is false.

On the number line, numbers increase as we move from left to right. For any two numbers, the one farther to the right is the greater and the one to the left is the lesser. This means that all negative numbers are less than 0 and all positive numbers are greater than 0.

EXAMPLES   Write a true sentence using > or <.

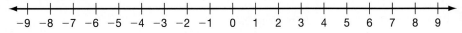

−9 −8 −7 −6 −5 −4 −3 −2 −1 0 1 2 3 4 5 6 7 8 9

4   2 < 9   Since 2 is to the left of 9, 2 is less than 9.

5   −7 < 3   Since −7 is to the left of 3, −7 is less than 3.

6   6 > −12   Since 6 is to the right of −12, 6 is greater than −12.

7 −18 < −5   Since −18 is to the left of −5, −18 is less than −5.

Try This   Write a true sentence using > or <.

e. 14 □ 7   **f.** 11 □ −2   **g.** −15 □ −5

Objective: Find the absolute value of an integer.

The integers 4 and −4 are both the same distance, 4 units, from 0 on the number line.

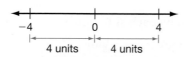

The **absolute value** of a number is its distance from 0 on the number line. We use the symbol |n| to represent "the absolute value of n." The absolute value of a number is either positive or zero. The number line above shows that |4| = 4 and |−4| = 4. The absolute value of 0 is 0.

Definition

Absolute Value

For any number n,
$|n| = n$ if n is a positive number or 0, and
$|n| = -n$ if n is a negative number.

Note that −n means the opposite of n. It does not necessarily stand for a negative number. For instance, the opposite of −8, written −(−8), is 8. And 8 is a positive number.

EXAMPLES Find the absolute value.

8 |12| = 12   12 is 12 units from 0.

Using the definition of absolute value, |12| = 12 since 12 is a positive number.

9 |−7| = 7   −7 is 7 units from 0.

Using the definition of absolute value, |−7| = the opposite of −7 = 7. Notice that the absolute value is always nonnegative.

10 |−3.04| = 3.04   −3.04 is 3.04 units from 0.

Using the definition of absolute value, |−3.04| = the opposite of −3.04 = 3.04.

Try This   Find the absolute value.

h. |17| **i.** |−8| **j.** |−14|

k. |21| **l.** |0| **m.** |−21|

2-1 Exercises

Extra Help On the Web

Look for worked-out examples at the Prentice Hall Web site.
www.phschool.com

A

Name the integer that is suggested by each situation.

1. In one game Carlos lost 12 marbles.

2. Jana won 5 marbles in her first game.

3. The temperature Wednesday was 18° above zero.

4. Ramona has a debt of $17.

5. Jane's business had a profit of $2500 in one week.

6. The Dead Sea, between Jordan and Israel, is 1299 feet below sea level.

7. On Friday, Vicki withdrew $125 from her savings account.

8. Terry's bowling team won by 34 pins.

9. In foreign trade, the U.S. had an excess of $3 million.

Write a true sentence using $<$ or $>$.

10. 5 □ 0   **11.** 9 □ 0   **12.** -9 □ 5   **13.** 8 □ -8

14. -6 □ 6   **15.** 0 □ -7 **16.** -8 □ -5 **17.** -4 □ -3

18. -5 □ -11 **19.** -3 □ -4 **20.** -6 □ -5 **21.** -10 □ -14

Find the absolute value.

22. $|-3|$ **23.** $|-7|$ **24.** $|10|$ **25.** $|11|$

26. $|0|$ **27.** $|-4|$ **28.** $|-24|$ **29.** $|325|$

30. $|-125|$ **31.** $|5.5|$ **32.** $|-4.2|$ **33.** $|-120.2|$

34. $|755|$ **35.** $|-340|$ **36.** $|-5.8|$ **37.** $|-0.3|$

38. $|12.75|$ **39.** $|-0.07|$ **40.** $|-80|$ **41.** $|-3.75|$

B

Evaluate.

42. $|-5| + |-6|$ **43.** $|17| + |-17|$ **44.** $|12| \cdot |-3|$

45. $|-5| \cdot |-6| \cdot |0|$ **46.** $|-3| \cdot |-7| + |-4|$ **47.** $|8| \cdot |-2| - |5|$

Write the following integers in order from least to greatest.

48. $13, -12, 5, -17$

49. $-23, 4, 0, -17$

50. $-24, -26, -18, -32, -5, -16$

51. $15, -24, -5, -16, 12, -13, -14$

Evaluate each expression.

52. $|x| + 24$ for $x = -7$

53. $|t| - 15$ for $t = -36$

54. $|a| + |b|$ for $a = -5$ and $b = -12$

55. $2|x| + |y|$ for $x = 8$ and $y = 15$

56. $3a - |b| + |c|$ for $a = 5, b = -4, c = -12$

57. *Critical Thinking* Find the next three numbers in each pattern by thinking about integers and the number line.

    a. 13, 9, 5, 1, ____, ____, ____

    b. 6, 5, 3, 0, ____, ____, ____

    c. $-3, -5, -8, -12,$ ____, ____, ____

    d. $-1, -3, -4, -7,$ ____, ____, ____

TEST PREP Compare the boxed quantity in column A with the boxed quantity in column B. Choose the best answer.

  A. The quantity in column A is greater.

  B. The quantity in column B is greater.

  C. The two quantities are equal.

  D. The relationship cannot be determined with the information supplied.

	column A	column B		column A	column B
58.	5.3	$\|5.3\|$	**59.**	-3.1	$\|-3.1\|$
60.	0	$\|0\|$	**61.**	2.7	$-\|2.7\|$
62.	x	$\|x\|$	**63.**	$\|x\|$	$-\|x\|$

Challenge

Use $<, >,$ or $=$ to write a true sentence.

64. $|-3| \;\square\; 5$ **65.** $2 \;\square\; |-4|$ **66.** $-2 \;\square\; |-1|$ **67.** $0 \;\square\; |0|$

68. $|-5| \;\square\; |-2|$ **69.** $|4| \;\square\; |-7|$ **70.** $|x| \;\square\; -1$ **71.** $|-8| \;\square\; |8|$

72. List in order from least to greatest. $7^1, -5, |-6|, 4, |3|, -100, 0, 1, \frac{14}{4}$

Mixed Review

Collect like terms.   **73.** $6m + 11m + 4m$ **74.** $\frac{1}{2}a + \frac{1}{2}a$

75. $8x^2 + 3x^2 + 7x$ **76.** $4c^2 + 7c + 2c^2$ *1-5*

Factor.   **77.** $4m + 24c$ **78.** $7b + 14$ **79.** $14x + 28y + 7$ *1-5*

Solve for the given replacement set.   **80.** $y + 3 = 42$ $\{14, 39, 45\}$

81. $w + 3911 = 4272$ $\{361, 7183, 8183\}$ **82.** $14t = 42$ $\{2, 3, 28\}$

83. $c + 9.7 = 12.4$ $\{2.7, 3.3, 22.1\}$ **84.** $2.6n = 7.8$ $\{3, 5.2, 10.4\}$ *1-7*

Mental Math   **85.** $x - 4 = 18$ **86.** $c - 25 = 30$

87. $y - 80 = 10$ **88.** $\frac{a}{4} = 20$ **89.** $\frac{x}{10} = 2.4$ **90.** $\frac{d}{7} = 20$ *1-7*

Rational Numbers

PART 1   Showing a Number Is Rational

Objective: Show a number is rational.

Much of your work in algebra will involve rational numbers. The word "rational" comes from the word *ratio*.

> ### Definition
>
> Any number that can be expressed as the ratio of two integers, $\frac{a}{b}$, where $b \neq 0$, is called a **rational number.**

There are three ways to write a negative rational number. You can write "negative three fourths" as follows.

$$-\frac{3}{4} \qquad \frac{-3}{4} \qquad \frac{3}{-4}$$

To show that a number is rational, we only have to find one way of naming it as a ratio of two integers.

EXAMPLES   Show that each can be written as the ratio of two integers.

1 $3 = \frac{3}{1}$

2 $-9.2 = -\frac{92}{10}$

Try This   Show that each can be written as the ratio of two integers.

a. 4.5 **b.** -10 **c.** -14.3 **d.** -0.01

PART 2   Graphing Rational Numbers

Objective: Graph rational numbers.

There is a point on the number line for every rational number. The number is called the **coordinate** of the point. The point is the **graph** of the number. When we draw a point for a number on a number line, we say that we have graphed the number.

What You'll Learn

1 To show that a number is rational

2 To graph rational numbers

3 To compare rational numbers using > or <

. . . And Why

To learn how rational numbers can model real-world situations

EXAMPLES   Graph each of these numbers.

3 $\frac{5}{2}$ The number $\frac{5}{2}$ can be named $2\frac{1}{2}$.
Its graph is halfway between 2 and 3.

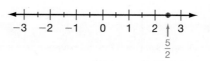

. Divide the units of the number line into halves.

4 -1.2

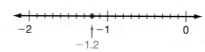

Divide the units of the number line into tenths.

5 $\frac{7}{4}$

Divide the units of the number line into fourths.

Try This   Graph each rational number.

e. $\frac{12}{5}$ **f.** -4.8 **g.** $-\frac{18}{4}$ **h.** 0.5

PART 3   **Order of the Rational Numbers**

Objective: Compare rational numbers using > or <.

The relations < (is less than) and > (is greater than) are the same for rational numbers as they are for integers. Recall that numbers on the number line increase from left to right.

EXAMPLES   Use either < or > to write a true sentence.

6 $1.38 < 1.83$ 38 hundredths is less than 83 hundredths.

7 $-3.45 < 1.32$ Negative rational numbers are always less than positive rational numbers.

8 $-4.23 > -5.2$ –4 is farther to the right on the number line than –5, so –4 > –5.

9 $\frac{3}{4} \;\square\; \frac{5}{8}$

$\frac{6}{8} \;\square\; \frac{5}{8}$ Find a common denominator. $\frac{3}{4} = \frac{6}{8}$

$\frac{6}{8} > \frac{5}{8}$ $\frac{6}{8}$ is farther to the right on the number line than $\frac{5}{8}$.

$\frac{3}{4} > \frac{5}{8}$

10 $-\frac{2}{3} \ \square \ -\frac{5}{8}$

$-\frac{16}{24} \ \square \ -\frac{15}{24}$ Find a common denominator. $-\frac{2}{3} = -\frac{16}{24}$ $-\frac{5}{8} = -\frac{15}{24}$

$-\frac{16}{24} < -\frac{15}{24}$ $-\frac{16}{24}$ is farther to the left on the number line than $-\frac{15}{24}$.

$-\frac{2}{3} < -\frac{5}{8}$

Try This   Use either < or > to write a true sentence.

i. 4.62 $\square$ 4.26   **j.** $-3.11 \ \square \ -3.22$ **k.** $\frac{5}{6} \ \square \ \frac{7}{8}$ **l.** $-\frac{2}{3} \ \square \ -\frac{4}{5}$

Rational numbers are part of a larger set of numbers called the **real numbers.** In Chapter 11, we will work with real numbers in more detail. The diagram below shows the relationships among these sets of numbers.

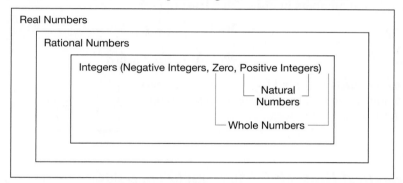

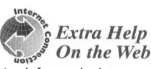

2-2 Exercises

Extra Help On the Web

Look for worked-out examples at the Prentice Hall Web site.
   www.phschool.com

A

Show that each number can be written as the ratio of two integers.

1. 14	**2.** -7	**3.** 4.2	**4.** 1.5
5. -0.5	**6.** -0.03	**7.** 3.444	**8.** -5.333
9. -0.68	**10.** -4	**11.** $7\frac{1}{2}$	**12.** $1\frac{2}{3}$

Graph each rational number.

13. $\frac{10}{3}$ **14.** $-\frac{17}{5}$ **15.** -4.3 **16.** 6.4

17. **TEST PREP**   To which sets of numbers does $\frac{-10}{2}$ belong?

I. Integers   II. Rational numbers   III. Whole numbers

a. I only   **b.** II only   **c.** I and II   **d.** II and III

Use either $<$ or $>$ to write a true sentence.

18. $2.14 \ \square \ 1.24$ **19.** $-3.3 \ \square \ -2.2$ **20.** $7.075 \ \square \ 7.750$

21. $-14.5 \ \square \ 0.011$ **22.** $17.2 \ \square \ -1.67$ **23.** $-345 \ \square \ -354$

24. $-12.88 \ \square \ -13$ **25.** $-14.34 \ \square \ -17.88$ **26.** $-0.606 \ \square \ -0.660$

27. $\frac{4}{10} \ \square \ -\frac{1}{2}$ **28.** $-\frac{5}{12} \ \square \ -\frac{3}{8}$ **29.** $-\frac{5}{3} \ \square \ -\frac{7}{5}$

30. *Mathematical Reasoning*   Show that $\frac{1}{3} > 0.33$ and that $-\frac{1}{3} < -0.33$.

B

The **density property** of rational numbers states that between any two rational numbers, there is another rational number. Find a number between the following pairs of numbers.

31. $\frac{1}{2}, \frac{1}{4}$ **32.** $\frac{1}{5}, \frac{2}{5}$ **33.** $0.45, 0.46$ **34.** $0.012, 0.013$

Write these rational numbers in order from least to greatest.

35. $\frac{3}{8}, \frac{7}{8}, \frac{1}{8}, -\frac{4}{8}, \frac{5}{8}, -\frac{8}{8}$ **36.** $\frac{6}{5}, -\frac{4}{5}, -\frac{2}{5}, \frac{4}{5}, -\frac{7}{5}, -\frac{1}{5}$

37. $\frac{4}{5}, \frac{4}{3}, \frac{4}{8}, \frac{4}{6}, \frac{4}{9}, \frac{4}{2}$ **38.** $-\frac{2}{3}, \frac{1}{2}, -\frac{3}{4}, -\frac{5}{6}, \frac{3}{8}, \frac{1}{6}$

39. *Critical Thinking*   Find five ways the numbers 2, 3, 4, 5, and 7 can be placed in the boxes to make a true statement.

$$\frac{\square}{\square} > \frac{\square}{\square}$$

Challenge

40. *Mathematical Reasoning*   Show that for any positive rational numbers, $\frac{a}{b}$ and $\frac{c}{d}$, if $\frac{a}{b} < \frac{c}{d}$, then $ad < cb$. (*Hint:* Find a common denominator.)

41. *Reasoning*   Is the following generalization always, sometimes, or never true? $\frac{a}{b} = \frac{a + c}{b + c}$, where $b \neq 0$ and $c \neq 0$. Explain.

Mixed Review

Write as an algebraic expression.   **42.** 11 less than m

43. y divided among x **44.** the sum of 9 and t **45.** 4 times w *1-6*

Find the absolute value.   **46.** $|0.06|$ **47.** $|-2.3|$ **48.** $|-41|$ *2-1*

Solve.   **49.** $y + \frac{3}{5} = \frac{4}{5}$ **50.** $a - \frac{1}{7} = \frac{6}{7}$ **51.** $x + \frac{2}{3} = \frac{5}{6}$

52. $\frac{a}{7} = 8$ **53.** $\frac{c}{6} = 12$ **54.** $\frac{y}{4} = 32$ **55.** $\frac{y}{3} = 7 + \frac{1}{3}$ *1-7*

Mental Math   Evaluate.   **56.** $D = r \cdot k$ for $r = 45$ and $k = 3$ **57.** $A = bh$ for $b = 10.2$ and $h = 5$ **58.** $P = 2w + 2l$ for $w = 17$ and $l = 2.5$ *1-1*

Addition of Rational Numbers

Math in Action

The school refreshment stand started selling popcorn during lunch and after school. They kept a record of profits and losses for the first five days of operation. What was the total profit or loss?

Monday	Tuesday	Wednesday	Thursday	Friday
$18 profit	$7 loss	$5 loss	$11 profit	$2 loss

Profit and loss statements often involve the addition of integers. This problem can be solved by finding this sum.

$$18 + (-7) + (-5) + 11 + (-2)$$

PART 1 — **Addition Using a Number Line**

Objective: Add rational numbers using a number line.

Addition of whole numbers can be shown by moves on a number line. To add 2 and 5, we start at 2, the first number. Then we move a distance of 5 units to the right. We end up at 7, the sum.

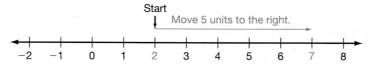

We can also add any two rational numbers using moves on the number line. When we add a negative number, however, we must move to the left. Recall that 0 plus any number is that number.

EXAMPLES   Add using the number line.

1 $3 + (-5)$

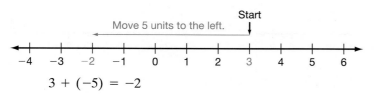

$$3 + (-5) = -2$$

What You'll Learn

1 To add rational numbers using a number line

2 To add rational numbers without using a number line

3 To give the additive inverse of a number

. . . And Why

To learn how to operate with rational numbers so that you will be able to use them to solve real-world problems

2 $-4 + (-3)$

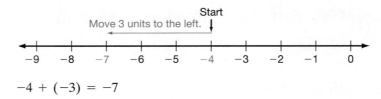

$-4 + (-3) = -7$

3 $-4 + 9$

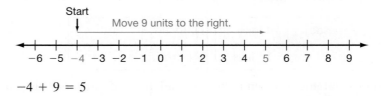

$-4 + 9 = 5$

4 $\frac{2}{3} + \left(-\frac{4}{3}\right)$

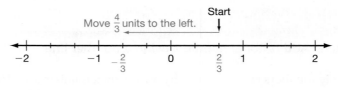

$\frac{2}{3} + \left(-\frac{4}{3}\right) = -\frac{2}{3}$

Try This   Add using the number line.

a. $4 + 3$ **b.** $-5 + 2$ **c.** $3 + (-5)$ **d.** $-4 + (-2)$ **e.** $-\frac{3}{4} + \frac{7}{4}$

PART 2 **Addition Without a Number Line**

Objective: Add rational numbers without a number line.

We can use the number line to suggest how to add rational numbers.

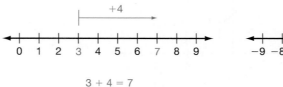

$3 + 4 = 7$ $-4 + (-2) = -6$

These illustrations suggest the following.

Adding Two Positive or Two Negative Numbers

Add the absolute values. The sum has the same sign as the addends.

In these illustrations, we add a positive number and a negative number.

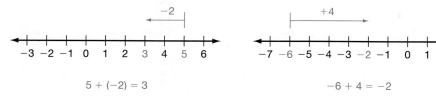

$$5 + (-2) = 3 \qquad -6 + 4 = -2$$

These illustrations suggest the following.

Adding a Positive and a Negative Number

Subtract the absolute values. The sum has the sign of the addend with the greater absolute value.

EXAMPLES Add without using the number line.

5 $-12 + (-7) = -19$ Since both addends are negative, the sum is negative.

6 $-1.4 + 8.5 = 7.1$ The difference of the absolute values is 7.1. The positive addend has the greater absolute value, so the sum is positive.

7 $21 + (-36) = -15$ The difference of the absolute values is 15. The negative addend has the greater absolute value, so the sum is negative.

8 $-\frac{2}{3} + \frac{4}{5} = -\frac{10}{15} + \frac{12}{15}$

$= \frac{2}{15}$ The difference of the absolute values is $\frac{2}{15}$. The positive addend has the greater absolute value, so the sum is positive.

Try This Add without using a number line.

f. $-17 + 17$ **g.** $-13 + (-7)$ **h.** $-15 + (-10)$

i. $-0.17 + 0.7$ **j.** $-12 + 25$ **k.** $14 + (-21)$

l. $\frac{3}{4} + \left(-\frac{5}{4}\right)$ **m.** $-\frac{5}{8} + \left(-\frac{1}{4}\right)$ **n.** $-\frac{4}{5} + \frac{5}{7}$

The commutative and associative properties hold for rational numbers, so we can group and order addends as we please. One way is to group the positive numbers together and group the negative numbers together.

EXAMPLE 9   Add.

$18 + (-7) + (-5) + 11 + (-2)$
$\quad = (18 + 11) + [(-7) + (-5) + (-2)]$ Grouping the positive and the negative numbers together

$\quad = 29 \qquad + \qquad (-14)$ Adding the results
$\quad = 15$

Try This   Add.

o. $(-15) + (-37) + 25 + 42 + (-59) + (-14)$

p. $42 + (-81) + (-28) + 24 + 18 + (-31)$

PART 3   **Additive Inverses**

Objective: Give the additive inverse.

When opposites such as 6 and -6 are added, the sum is 0. Number pairs such as 6 and -6 are also called additive inverses.

Definition

Two rational numbers whose sum is 0 are called **additive inverses** of each other.

Every rational number has an additive inverse.

Property of Additive Inverses

For each rational number a, there is one and only one rational number $-a$ such that $a + (-a) = 0$.

EXAMPLES   Find the additive inverse of each.

10   34

The additive inverse is -34. $34 + (-34) = 0$

11 -2.96

The additive inverse is 2.96. $-2.96 + 2.96 = 0$

12 $-\frac{5}{4}$

The additive inverse is $\frac{5}{4}$. $-\frac{5}{4} + \frac{5}{4} = 0$

Try This   Find the additive inverse of each.

q. -19 **r.** 54 **s.** 0 **t.** -7.4 **u.** $-\frac{8}{3}$

The symbol -8 is usually read "negative 8." It could also be read "the additive inverse of 8" or "the opposite of 8" because the additive inverse of 8 is negative. A symbol like $-x$ should be read "the additive inverse of x" or "the opposite of x" and not "negative x," however, because we do not know if $-x$ represents a negative number, a positive number, or 0 until we know the value of x.

Inverse of the Inverse

The inverse of the inverse of a rational number is the number itself.
$$-(-n) = n$$

EXAMPLES

13   Find $-x$ and $-(-x)$ when x is 16.

If $x = 16$, then $-x = -(16)$ Replacing x with 16
$= -16$
$-(-x) = -(-16)$ Replacing x with 16
$= 16$

14   Find $-x$ and $-(-x)$ when x is -3.

If $x = -3$, then $-x = -(-3)$ Replacing x with -3
$= 3$
$-(-x) = -(-(-3))$ Replacing x with -3
$= -3$

Try This   Find $-x$ and $-(-x)$ when x is each of the following.

v. 14 **w.** 1 **x.** -19

EXAMPLE 15

A submarine is cruising at a depth of 30 m. It climbs 12 m, then dives 21 m, and then climbs 13 m. At what depth is the submarine?

$-30 + 12 + (-21) + 13 = -26$ We can represent depth with a negative number. Use a positive number to represent climbing.

The submarine is at a depth of -26 m.

Try This   Solve.

y. Rico carried the ball six times in the third quarter of a football game. Here are his gains and losses: 11-yd gain, 4-yd loss, 6-yd loss, 5-yd gain, 8-yd gain, 2-yd loss. What was the total number of yards he gained (or lost)?

Extra Help On the Web

Look for worked-out examples at the Prentice Hall Web site.
www.phschool.com

2-3 Exercises

A

Add using a number line.

1. $-9 + 2$
2. $2 + (-5)$
3. $-10 + 6$
4. $8 + (-3)$
5. $-8 + 8$
6. $6 + (-6)$
7. $-3 + (-5)$
8. $-4 + (-6)$

Add without using a number line.

9. $-7 + 0$
10. $-13 + 0$
11. $0 + (-27)$
12. $0 + (-35)$
13. $17 + (-17)$
14. $-15 + 15$
15. $-17 + (-25)$
16. $-24 + (-17)$
17. $-14 + (-29)$
18. $-\frac{5}{8} + \frac{1}{4}$
19. $-\frac{5}{6} + \frac{2}{3}$
20. $-\frac{3}{7} + \left(-\frac{2}{5}\right)$
21. $-\frac{5}{8} + \left(-\frac{1}{3}\right)$
22. $-\frac{3}{5} + \left(-\frac{2}{15}\right)$
23. $-\frac{5}{9} + \left(-\frac{1}{18}\right)$
24. $-44 + \left(-\frac{3}{8}\right) + 95 + \left(-\frac{5}{8}\right)$
25. $\frac{-3}{12} + \frac{3}{18} + \frac{-7}{6} + 2$
26. $24 + 3.1 + (-44) + (-8.2) + 63$
27. $-17 + 28 + (-12) + (-20.5) + 16.5$
28. $24 + (-36) + 75 + (-75) + 82 + (-63)$
29. $98 + (-54) + 113 + (-998) + 44 + (-612) + (-18) + 334$
30. $-455 + (-123) + 1026 + (-919) + 213 + 111 + (-874)$

Estimation   Which of the two numbers is greater? Use estimation to decide.

31. $14 + (-36)$ or $14 + (-35)$
32. $-32 + (-9)$ or $-32 + (-8)$
33. $-\frac{3}{5} + \frac{2}{5}$ or $-\frac{3}{5} + \frac{3}{5}$
34. $-16 + 9$ or $-16 + (-9)$

Find the additive inverse of each.

35. 24
36. -64
37. -9
38. $\frac{7}{2}$
39. -26.9
40. 48.2

Find $-x$ when x is

41. 9
42. -26
43. $-\frac{14}{3}$
44. $\frac{1}{328}$
45. 0.101
46. 0

Find $-(-x)$ when x is

47. -65 **48.** 29 **49.** $\frac{5}{3}$ **50.** -9.1

Mathematical Reasoning Use *sometimes*, *always*, or *never* to make the statement true.

51. The sum of two negative numbers is ___?___ positive.

52. The sum of two positive numbers is ___?___ positive.

53. The sum of a positive and a negative number is ___?___ positive.

54. The additive inverse of a number is ___?___ negative.

55. The sum of two numbers is ___?___ greater than either number.

56. The sum of two numbers is ___?___ less than either number.

Solve.

57. The barometric pressure at Omaha was 1012 millibars (mb). The pressure dropped 6 mb, then it rose 3 mb. After that it dropped 14 mb and then rose 4 mb. What was the pressure then?

58. In a football game, the quarterback attempted passes with the following results. Find the total gain (or loss).

first try	13-yd gain
second try	incomplete
third try	12-yd loss (tackled behind the line)
fourth try	21-yd gain
fifth try	14-yd loss

Barometric pressure is also measured in inches of mercury (the length of a column of mercury that is supported by the atmosphere). A pressure of 1012 mb is equivalent to 29.88 in. of mercury. How many inches of mercury are equivalent to 999 mb?

59. The average attendance at a soccer game last year was 1755 people. The table below shows the attendance for each game this year compared to last year's average. By how much was the total attendance for all 6 games above or below last year's?

Game 1	Game 2	Game 3	Game 4	Game 5	Game 6
+357	−144	−250	+347	+420	−188

60. The business class kept a record of the change in a stock market for a period of 5 weeks. After 5 weeks, how many points had the market gained or lost?

Week 1	Week 2	Week 3	Week 4	Week 5
down 120 pts	down 150 pts	up 350 pts	down 100 pts	up 180 pts

61. In a board game, Alice started with $1475. After these transactions how much did Alice have?

purchased properties	1700
collected rents	1640
purchased houses	900
passed start (collected money)	1200

62. The table below shows the profits and losses of a company over a six-year period. Find the total profit or loss for this period of time.

Year	Profit or loss ($)
1994	+32,056
1995	−2,925
1996	+81,429
1997	−19,365
1998	−13,875
1999	+384

63. Francine received an allowance of $5.00, bought a pen for $0.59, gave $1.75 to Pat, made $10.50 baby sitting, and spent $6.75 at a movie. How much did she have left?

B

64. For what numbers x is $-x$ negative?

65. For what numbers x is $-x$ positive?

Mathematical Reasoning   Tell whether the sum is *positive*, *negative*, or *zero*. Explain your answers.

66. n is positive, m is negative. $n + (-m)$ is _____.

67. n is positive, m is negative. $-n + m$ is _____.

68. $n = m$, n and m are negative. $-n + (-m)$ is _____.

69. $n = m$, n and m are negative. $n + (-m)$ is _____.

70. Name the largest negative integer.

71. *Write a Convincing Argument*   Write an argument to convince a classmate that $-(-n) = n$.

Challenge

Solve.

72. $x + x = 0$

73. $x + (-5) = x$

74. $3y + (-2) = 7$

75. $x + (-5) = 16$

76. Does $x - y = x + (-y)$ for all numbers x and y?

Mixed Review

Solve.   **77.** $2.6n = 6.24$ **78.** $w - 1.07 = 3.24$ **79.** $7r = 84$ *1-7*

Use either $<$ or $>$ to write a true sentence.   **80.** $-9 \ \square \ 2$

81. $-4 \ \square \ -6$ **82.** $-1 \ \square \ 0$ **83.** $3.62 \ \square \ 3.26$ **84.** $0 \ \square \ 0.001$ *2-1*

Find the absolute value.   **85.** $|2|$ **86.** $|-4|$ **87.** $|-2.03|$ **88.** $|0|$ *2-1*

89. Each of the members of Miss Odell's class read 8 books. If the class read 104 books in all, how many members are in the class?   *1-10*

Subtraction of Rational Numbers

The floor of Death Valley, California, can be seen betweeen the two mountain ranges.

What You'll Learn

1 To subtract rational numbers using a number line

2 To subtract rational numbers without using a number line

...And Why

To learn how to operate with rational numbers so that you will be able to use them to solve real-world problems

Math in Action

The lowest point in Asia is the Dead Sea, 396 meters below sea level. The lowest point in the United States is Death Valley, 86 meters below sea level. How much higher is Death Valley than the Dead Sea?

Drawing a diagram can help you understand the problem.

Let d be the difference between the altitude of Death Valley and the Dead Sea. You can solve this problem by subtracting rational numbers.

$$d = -86 - (-396)$$

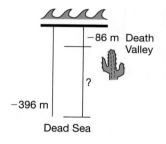

PART 1 — Subtraction on a Number Line

Objective: Subtract rational numbers using a number line.

We can subtract rational numbers by using the definition of subtraction and a number line.

Definition

For all rational numbers a and b, the **difference** $a - b$ is the number c, such that $c + b = a$.

EXAMPLE 1 Subtract.

  10 − 12

From the definition of subtraction, the number that can be added to 12 to get 10 will be the answer. On a number line we start at 12 and move to 10.

We moved 2 units in the negative direction. The answer is −2. Therefore, 10 − 12 = −2. We can check by adding, 12 + (−2) = 10.

EXAMPLE 2 Subtract.

  −1 − (−5)

We read this "negative 1 minus negative 5." From the definition of subtraction, the number that can be added to −5 to get −1 will be the answer. Start at −5 and move to −1.

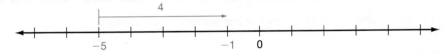

We moved 4 units in the positive direction. The answer is 4. Therefore, −1 − (−5) = 4. Check by adding, −5 + 4 = −1.

Try This Subtract using a number line.

a. −2 − 6   **b.** 4 − 10   **c.** −9 − (−4)

PART 2 **Subtraction Without a Number Line**

Objective: Subtract rational numbers without using a number line.

The examples below show that adding the opposite of a rational number gives the same result as subtracting the rational number.

$$8 - 3 = 5 \qquad\qquad 8 + (-3) = 5$$
$$4 - 7 = -3 \qquad\qquad 4 + (-7) = -3$$
$$-4.5 - 2 = -6.5 \qquad -4.5 + (-2) = -6.5$$

These examples suggest the following rule.

Subtracting Numbers

For all rational numbers a and b, $a - b = a + (-b)$.
(To subtract a rational number, add its additive inverse or opposite.)

EXAMPLES Subtract.

3 $2 - 6 = 2 + (-6)$ Writing as addition; adding the opposite of 6
$ = -4$ Adding

4 $-86 - (-400) = -86 + 400$
$ = 314$

5 $-4.2 - (-3.6) = -4.2 + 3.6$
$ = -0.6$

6 $-\frac{1}{2} - \frac{3}{4} = -\frac{1}{2} + \left(-\frac{3}{4}\right) = -\frac{5}{4}$

Try This   Subtract.

d. $4 - 9$ **e.** $6 - (-4)$ **f.** $-4 - 17$

g. $-3 - (-12)$ **h.** $\frac{3}{8} - \left(-\frac{1}{4}\right)$

When addition and subtraction occur several times, we can use the rule for subtracting rational numbers to make them all additions.

EXAMPLE 7   Simplify.

$$8 - (-4) - 2 - (-4) + 2 = 8 + 4 + (-2) + 4 + 2$$
$$= 16$$

EXAMPLE 8   Simplify.

$$-4 - (-2x) + x - (-5) = -4 + 2x + x + 5$$
$$= 3x + 1 \qquad \text{Combining like terms}$$

Try This   Simplify.

i. $-6 - (-2) - (-4) - 12 + 3$
j. $3 - (-7.1) + 6.3 - (-5.2)$
k. $-8 - (-3x) + 2x - (-13)$

EXAMPLE 9

Mr. Casper had $75.50 in his checking account. He wrote a check for $95.00. By how much has he overdrawn his checking account? Let c = the amount in his checking account.

$$c = 75.50 - 95.00$$
$$c = -19.50$$

He has overdrawn his checking account by $19.50.

Try This   Solve.

l. Juan has saved $35 toward a new stereo system. The total cost of the system is $125. How much more money does Juan need?

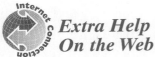

**Extra Help
On the Web**

Look for worked-out
examples at the Prentice
Hall Web site.
www.phschool.com

2-4 Exercises

A

Subtract using a number line.

1. $3 - 7$ **2.** $4 - 9$ **3.** $0 - 7$ **4.** $0 - 10$

5. $5 - (-2)$ **6.** $-6 - (-8)$ **7.** $-10 - (-10)$ **8.** $-8 - (-8)$

Subtract.

9. $7 - 7$ **10.** $0.9 - 0.9$ **11.** $7 - (-7)$

12. $4 - (-4)$ **13.** $8 - (-3)$ **14.** $-7 - 4$

15. $-6 - 8$ **16.** $6 - (-10)$ **17.** $-4 - (-9)$

18. $15 - (-6)$ **19.** $0 - 5$ **20.** $0 - 0.6$

21. $-51 - (-2)$ **22.** $-39 - (-41)$ **23.** $-79 - 114$

24. $-197 - 216$ **25.** $0 - (-500)$ **26.** $500 - (-1000)$

27. $-2.8 - 0$ **28.** $6.04 - 1.1$ **29.** $7 - 10.53$

30. $8 - (-9.3)$ **31.** $\frac{1}{6} - \frac{2}{3}$ **32.** $-\frac{3}{8} - \left(-\frac{1}{2}\right)$

33. $\frac{12}{5} - \frac{12}{5}$ **34.** $-\frac{4}{7} - \left(-\frac{10}{7}\right)$ **35.** $-\frac{7}{10} - \frac{10}{15}$

36. $-\frac{4}{18} - \left(-\frac{2}{9}\right)$ **37.** $\frac{1}{13} - \frac{1}{12}$ **38.** $-\frac{1}{7} - \left(-\frac{1}{6}\right)$

Simplify.

39. $18 - (-15) - 3 - (-5) + 2$

40. $22 - (-18) + 7 + (-42) - 27$

41. $-31 + (-28) - (-14) - 17$

42. $-43 - (-19) - (-21) + 25$

43. $-34 - 28 + (-33) - 44$

44. $39 + (-88) - 29 - (-83)$

45. $84 + (-99) + 44 - (-18) - 43$

46. $-5 - (-3x) + 3x + 4x - (-12)$

47. $14 + (-5x) + 2x - (-32)$

48. $13x - (-2x) + 45 - (-21)$

49. $8x - (-2x) - 14 - (-5x) + 53$

50. *Error Analysis*   A student claims that $-12 - (-3)$ equals -15. How would you convince the student that the answer is incorrect?

Solve.

51. Mrs. Kang has $619.46 in her checking account. She wrote a check for $950.00. By how much did she overdraw her checking account?

52. Omar had $137.40 in his checking account. He wrote a check for $225.20. By how much has he overdrawn his checking account?

53. On a winter night the temperature dropped from −5°C to −12°C. How many degrees did the temperature drop?

54. The temperature at 6 P.M. was 5°C. At 9 P.M. the temperature had dropped to −5°C. How many degrees did the temperature fall?

55. There are 47 females in the band. If there is a total of 163 band members, how many males are in the band?

56. Sarah had a balance of $45 in her checking account. She wrote two checks totaling $12. How much money does she have in her checking account now?

57. The lowest point in Africa is Lake Assal, which is 156 m below sea level. The lowest point in South America is the Valdes Peninsula, which is 40 m below sea level. How much lower is Lake Assal than the Valdes Peninsula?

58. The deepest point in the Pacific Ocean is the Marianas Trench, which is 10,415 m deep. The deepest point in the Atlantic Ocean is the Puerto Rico Trench, which is 8,648 m deep. How much deeper is the Marianas Trench than the Puerto Rico Trench?

TEST PREP   Compare the boxed quantity in column A with the boxed quantity in column B. Choose the best answer.
A. The quantity in column A is greater.
B. The quantity in column B is greater.
C. The two quantities are equal.
D. The relationship cannot be determined with the information supplied.

	column A	column B		column A	column B
59.	$10 - 1$	$10 - 5$	**60.**	$10 - (-1)$	$10 - (-5)$
61.	$-10 - 1$	$-10 - 5$	**62.**	$-10 - (-1)$	$-10 - (-5)$
63.	$x - 1$	$x - 5$	**64.**	$x - (-1)$	$x - (-5)$

B

65. Evaluate each expression using the values from the table.

a	b	x	y	z
5	−8	−2.3	4.1	0

a. $(a + x) - b$
c. $(x - y) + (a - b)$
e. $b - |x - a|$

b. $z - (b - x)$
d. $(y - x) - (b - a)$
f. $|x| - a - (|b| + y)$

66. *Critical Thinking* Study the first scale and then add items to the right side of the second scale so it will balance.

a.

b.

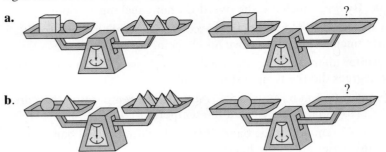

Challenge

Mathematical Reasoning If a statement is not true for all integers m and n, give a counterexample.

67. $n - 0 = 0 - n$

68. $0 - n = n$

69. If $m \neq n$, then $m - n \neq 0$.

70. If $m = -n$, then $m + n = 0$.

71. If $m + n = 0$, then m and n are additive inverses.

72. If $m - n = 0$, then $m = -n$.

73. Do the commutative and associative properties hold for subtraction of integers?

74. Simplify $-[-(-5)]$ and $-\{-[-(-5)]\}$. Give a rule for determining the sign of expressions like these, which involve any number of negative signs.

75. Is $a - 1 \leq a$ for all, some, or no rational numbers? Explain.

76. Does $|a| \cdot (b + c) = |a| \cdot b + |a| \cdot c$ for all integers a, b, and c?

Journal

Describe how you can subtract a number from 10 to get a difference that is greater than 10. Give examples.

Self-Test On the Web

Check your progress. Look for a self-test at the Prentice Hall Web site. www.phschool.com

Evaluate. **77.** $(n + 3)^2$ for $n = 4$ **78.** $(3n)^3 - 100$ for $n = 2$

79. t^4 for $t = 3$ **80.** n^5 for $n = 2$ **81.** $9y^3$ for $y = 3$

82. m^3 for $m = 0$ **83.** $3t^2 + 6$ for $t = 2$ **84.** $2|m|$ for $m = -3$ *1-3*

Mental Math Solve. **85.** $3y = 3$ **86.** $\frac{a}{2} = 4$ **87.** $4y = 1$ *1-7*

Combine like terms.

88. $3x + 5x^2 + 5x + 2x^2$ **89.** $2a + 3b + 4c + 5b$ *1-5*

Factor. **90.** $3c^2 + 5c$ **91.** $6x + 24y - 18z$ **92.** $6m + 9p$ *1-5*

Multiplication of Rational Numbers

Objective: Multiply rational numbers.

Introducing the Concept: Multiplication of Integers

We know that one interpretation of multiplication is as repeated addition. For example, $5 \cdot 3$ can be written as $3 + 3 + 3 + 3 + 3 = 15$. Therefore, $5 \cdot 3 = 15$. Use this interpretation of multiplication to copy and complete the table below. What patterns do you see?

Factor	Factor	Repeated Addition	Product
5	4	$4 + 4 + 4 + 4 + 4$	20
5	3	$3 + 3 + 3 + 3 + 3$	15
5	2		
5	1		
5	0		
5	-1		
5	-2		
5	-3		

The table above suggests the following rule.

Multiplying a Positive Number and a Negative Number

To multiply a positive number and a negative number, multiply their absolute values. The sign of the product is negative.

EXAMPLES   Multiply.

1 $8(-5) = -40$ **2** $-\frac{1}{3} \cdot \frac{5}{7} = -\frac{5}{21}$ **3** $(-7.2)5 = -36.0 \text{ or } -36$

Try This   Multiply.

a. $(-3)6$ **b.** $20(-5)$ **c.** $4.5(-20)$ **d.** $-\frac{2}{3}\left(\frac{9}{4}\right)$

How do we multiply two negative numbers? Since -3 is the opposite of 3, it seems reasonable that $-3(-5)$ would be the opposite of $3(-5)$. You saw above that $3(-5) = -15$. So, $-3(-5) = 15$ (the opposite of -15). This example suggests the following rule.

Multiplying Two Negative Numbers

To multiply two negative numbers, multiply their absolute values. The sign of the product is positive.

Multiplicative Property of Zero

For any rational number n, $n \cdot 0 = 0$.
(The product of 0 and any rational number is 0.)

We already know how to multiply two positive numbers. The only case we have not considered is multiplying by 0.

EXAMPLES Multiply.

4 $\quad -3(-4) = 12$ **5** $\quad -1.6(-2) = 3.2$ **6** $\quad -\frac{5}{6}\left(-\frac{1}{9}\right) = \frac{5}{54}$

Try This Multiply.

e. $-5(-4)$ **f.** $-8(0)$ **g.** $-4.2(-3)$ **h.** $-\frac{3}{8}\left(-\frac{1}{7}\right)$

The commutative and associative properties of multiplication hold for rational numbers. We can, therefore, choose the order and grouping.

EXAMPLES Multiply.

7 $\quad -8(2)(-3) = -16(-3) \qquad$ Multiplying the first two numbers

$\qquad\qquad\quad = 48 \qquad\qquad\qquad$ Multiplying the results

8 $\quad -8(2)(-3) = 24 \cdot 2 \qquad\quad$ Multiplying the negative numbers

$\qquad\qquad\quad = 48$

9 $\quad -\frac{1}{2}(8)\left(-\frac{2}{3}\right)(-6) = (-4)4$

$\qquad\qquad\qquad\qquad\quad = -16$

Try This Multiply.

i. $-5(-6)(-3)$

j. $-4(5)(-3)(2)$

k. $(-7)\left(-\frac{2}{3}\right)\left(-\frac{1}{7}\right)(9)$

2-5 Exercises

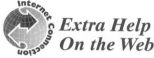

Extra Help On the Web

Look for worked-out examples at the Prentice Hall Web site.
www.phschool.com

A

Multiply.

1. $-8 \cdot 2$ **2.** $-2 \cdot 5$ **3.** $-7 \cdot 6$ **4.** $-9 \cdot 2$

5. $8(-3)$ **6.** $9(-5)$ **7.** $-9 \cdot 8$ **8.** $-10 \cdot 3$

9. $-8(-2)$ **10.** $-2(-5)$ **11.** $-7(-6)$ **12.** $-9(-2)$

13. $15(-8)$ **14.** $-12(-10)$ **15.** $-14(17)$ **16.** $-13(-15)$

17. $-25(-48)$ **18.** $39(-43)$ **19.** $-3.5(-28)$ **20.** $97(2.1)$

21. $\frac{1}{5}\left(\frac{-2}{9}\right)$ **22.** $-\frac{3}{5}\left(-\frac{2}{7}\right)$

23. $-7(-21)(13)$ **24.** $-14 \cdot 34 \cdot 12$

25. $-4(-1.8)(7)$ **26.** $-8(-1.3)(-5)$

27. $-\frac{1}{9}\left(\frac{-2}{3}\right)\left(\frac{5}{7}\right)$ **28.** $-\frac{7}{2}\left(\frac{-5}{7}\right)\left(\frac{-2}{5}\right)$

29. $4(-4)(-5)(-12)$ **30.** $-2(-3)(-4)(-5)$

31. $0.07(-7)(6)(-6)$ **32.** $80(-0.8)(-90)(-0.09)$

33. $-\frac{5}{6}\left(\frac{1}{8}\right)\left(-\frac{3}{7}\right)\left(-\frac{1}{7}\right)$ **34.** $\frac{4}{5}\left(\frac{-2}{3}\right)\left(-\frac{15}{7}\right)\left(\frac{1}{2}\right)$

35. $(-14)(-27)(0)$ **36.** $7(-6)(5)(-4)(3)(-2)(1)(0)$

37. $0.02(-4)(1.3)$ **38.** $-5.1(0.03)(-1.1)$

B

Simplify.

39. $-6[(-5) + (-7)]$ **40.** $7[(-16) + 9]$

41. $-3[(-8) + (-6)]\left(-\frac{1}{7}\right)$ **42.** $8[17 - (-3)]\left(-\frac{1}{4}\right)$

43. $-(3^5) \cdot [-(2^3)]$ **44.** $4(2^4) \cdot [-(3^3)] \cdot 6$

45. $(-2)^5$ **46.** $(-1)^{23}$

Evaluate for $x = -2$, $y = -4$, and $z = 5$.

47. $xy + z$ **48.** $-4y + 3x + z$

49. $-6(3x - 5y) + z$ **50.** $(-9z)(-5x)(-7y)$

51. $y(x^4) - z$ **52.** $3z^2 - xy$

53. *Critical Thinking*   Find a pair of integers with a product of -84 and a sum of 5.

54. **TEST PREP**   Which of these numbers is the least?

   A. $-1.08\left(-\frac{4}{3}\right)$ B. $-1.08\left(\frac{4}{3}\right)$ C. $-1.08\left(-\frac{2}{3}\right)$ D. $-1.08\left(\frac{2}{3}\right)$

Challenge

55. What must be true of m and n if $-mn$ is positive?

56. What must be true of m and n if $-mn$ is negative?

57. For any rational numbers a and b, is it *sometimes*, *always*, or *never* true that $|ab| = |-a||-b|$? Explain.

58. What must be true of x if $x(x - 2) < 0$?

59. What must be true of z if $|z| \cdot z < 0$?

Mixed Review

Add or subtract. **60.** $4 - 9$ **61.** $3 - (-1)$ **62.** $0 + (-4)$

63. $-8 + 8$ **64.** $6 - (-2)$ **65.** $-37 + 52$ **66.** $67 + (-8)$ *2-3, 2-4*

Use $<$, $>$, or $=$ to write a true sentence. **67.** $-1.01 \square -1$

68. $2.5 \square -2.4$ **69.** $\frac{7}{2} \square 4$ **70.** $|-3| \square |3|$ *2-1*

Factor. **71.** $4x + 10 + 8y$ **72.** $10a + 15b + 5$ *1-5*

Evaluate. **73.** $3x^3$ for $x = 2$. **74.** $5x^3$ for $x = 1$ *1-3*

Subsets of the Rational Numbers

We can use the diagram on page 61 and set notation to write subsets of the rational numbers. Consider these sets:

Natural numbers or positive integers

$$N = \{1, 2, 3, \ldots\}$$

Whole numbers

$$W = \{0, 1, 2, 3, \ldots\}$$

Integers

$$I = \{\ldots, -3, -2, -1, 0, 1, 2, 3, \ldots\}$$

Consider these definitions: Each number in a set is called an element or member of the set. The symbol $\in$ is read "is an element of." We write: $-3 \in I$. Set A is a subset of set B if every element of set A is an element of set B. The symbol $\subset$ is read "is a subset of." We write: $A \subset B$.

The following are true statements.

$N \subset W$ The natural numbers are a subset of the whole numbers.

$W \subset I$ The whole numbers are a subset of the integers.

$I \subset R$ (rational numbers) The integers are a subset of the rational numbers.

1. Write at least five subset statements using the sets shown in the diagram on page 61.

2. The empty set or null set, symbolized $\emptyset$, is a set with no elements. Is $\emptyset$ a subset of the rational numbers?

Division of Rational Numbers

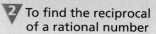

PART 1 Division

Objective: Divide rational numbers.

To divide rational numbers, we can use the definition of division.

Definition

For all rational numbers a and b, the **quotient** $\frac{a}{b}$ (or $a \div b$), where $b \neq 0$, is the number c such that $cb = a$.

EXAMPLES Divide. Check your answers.

1 $14 \div (-7) = -2$ Check: $(-2)(-7) = 14$

2 $\frac{-32}{-4} = 8$ Check: $8(-4) = -32$

3 $\frac{-10}{2} = -5$ Check: $-5(2) = -10$

These examples suggest the following rule.

Dividing Positive and Negative Numbers

To divide positive and negative numbers, divide their absolute values. Use the following rules to determine the sign of the quotient.

■ When we divide a positive number by a negative number or a negative number by a positive number, the quotient is negative.

■ When we divide two positive numbers or two negative numbers, the quotient is positive.

Try This   Divide. Check your answer.

a. $15 \div (-3)$ **b.** $-21 \div (-7)$ **c.** $\frac{-44}{-11}$ **d.** $\frac{35}{-5}$

e. $\frac{-8}{-4}$ **f.** $\frac{45}{-9}$ **g.** $-24 \div -8$ **h.** $\frac{105}{-5}$

What You'll Learn

1 To divide rational numbers

2 To find the reciprocal of a rational number

...And Why

To learn how to operate with rational numbers so that you will be able to use them to solve real-world problems

We can show why we cannot divide any nonzero number by 0. For $\frac{a}{0}$, $a \neq 0$, we look for a number which, when multiplied by 0, gives a. There is no such number because the product of 0 and any number is 0. If we divide $\frac{0}{0}$, we look for a number r such that $r \cdot 0 = 0$. But $r \cdot 0 = 0$ for any number r. Thus $\frac{0}{0}$ could be any number we choose. Since for any operation there must be only one answer, we agree that we shall not divide 0 by 0. In general, we cannot divide by 0.

PART 2 **Reciprocals**

Objective: Find the reciprocal of a rational number.

When pairs of numbers like $-\frac{1}{8}$ and -8 are multiplied, their product is 1. Number pairs such as $-\frac{1}{8}$ and -8, whose product is 1, are called multiplicative inverses or reciprocals.

Definition

Two rational numbers whose product is 1 are called **multiplicative inverses** or **reciprocals** of each other.

Any nonzero rational number has a reciprocal.

Property of Multiplicative Inverses

For each nonzero rational number a, there is one and only one rational number $\frac{1}{a}$ such that $a \cdot \frac{1}{a} = 1$.

If a nonzero rational number is named with fractional notation $\frac{a}{b}$, then its reciprocal can be named $\frac{b}{a}$. Also, the reciprocal of a positive number is positive, and the reciprocal of a negative number is negative.

Reading Math

Since we cannot divide by 0, assume that any variable in the denominator of a rational expression represents a nonzero number.

EXAMPLES Find the reciprocal.

4 $\frac{7}{8}$ The reciprocal of $\frac{7}{8}$ is $\frac{8}{7}$ because $\frac{7}{8} \cdot \frac{8}{7} = 1$.

5 -5 The reciprocal of -5 is $\frac{1}{-5}$ because $-5\left(\frac{1}{-5}\right) = 1$.

6 0.8 The reciprocal of $0.8 = \frac{8}{10}$ is $\frac{10}{8}$ because $\frac{8}{10} \cdot \frac{10}{8} = 1$.

7 $\frac{m}{n}$ The reciprocal of $\frac{m}{n}$ is $\frac{n}{m}$ because $\frac{m}{n} \cdot \frac{n}{m} = 1$.

Try This Find the reciprocal.

i. $\frac{3}{6}$ **j.** -4 **k.** -0.5 **l.** $1\frac{1}{3}$ **m.** $\frac{x}{y}$

PART 3 Division and Reciprocals

Objective: Divide by multiplying by the reciprocal.

We know we can subtract a rational number by adding its inverse. Similarly, we can divide by a rational number by multiplying by its reciprocal.

Dividing Numbers

For all rational numbers a and b ($b \neq 0$),

$$\frac{a}{b} = a \cdot \frac{1}{b}$$

EXAMPLES Rewrite each division as multiplication.

8 $-4 \div 3 = -4 \cdot \frac{1}{3}$

9 $\frac{x+2}{5} = (x+2) \cdot \frac{1}{5}$ Parentheses are necessary here.

10 $\frac{-17}{\frac{1}{b}} = -17 \cdot b$

11 $\frac{3}{5} \div \left(-\frac{9}{7}\right) = \frac{3}{5}\left(-\frac{7}{9}\right)$

Try This Rewrite each division as multiplication.

n. $-6 \div \frac{1}{5}$ **o.** $\frac{-5}{7}$ **p.** $\frac{x^2 - 2}{3}$ **q.** $\frac{x}{y}$

r. $\frac{-15}{\frac{1}{x}}$ **s.** $-\frac{4}{7} \div -\frac{3}{5}$ **t.** $\frac{13}{\frac{2}{3}}$ **u.** $\frac{a}{\frac{1}{b}}$

When doing division calculations, we sometimes multiply by a reciprocal and we sometimes divide directly. With fractional notation, it is usually easier to multiply by a reciprocal. With decimal notation, it is usually easier to divide directly.

EXAMPLES Divide.

12 $\frac{4}{3} \div \left(-\frac{9}{7}\right) = \frac{4}{3}\left(-\frac{7}{9}\right)$

$\qquad\qquad = -\frac{4 \cdot 7}{3 \cdot 9} = -\frac{28}{27}$

13 $-27.9 \div (-3) = \frac{-27.9}{-3} = 9.3$

Try This   Divide.

v. $-\frac{3}{5} \div \left(-\frac{12}{11}\right)$ **w.** $-\frac{8}{5} \div \frac{2}{3}$ **x.** $-64.8 \div 4$ **y.** $78.6 \div (-3)$

Extra Help On the Web

Look for worked-out examples at the Prentice Hall Web site.
www.phschool.com

2-6 Exercises

A

Divide. Check your answer.

1. $36 \div (-6)$ **2.** $\frac{28}{-7}$ **3.** $\frac{-16}{8}$

4. $-22 \div (-2)$ **5.** $\frac{-48}{-12}$ **6.** $-63 \div (-9)$

7. $\frac{-50}{25}$ **8.** $-100 \div (-50)$ **9.** $\frac{-200}{8}$

10. $-108 \div 9$ **11.** $\frac{-63}{-7}$ **12.** $\frac{200}{-25}$

13. $(-300) \div (0)$ **14.** $\frac{75}{5}$ **15.** $\frac{0}{-5}$

Find the reciprocal. Recall that all variables represent nonzero rational numbers.

16. $\frac{15}{7}$ **17.** $\frac{3}{8}$ **18.** $\frac{47}{13}$ **19.** $-\frac{31}{12}$

20. 13 **21.** -10 **22.** 0.3 **23.** -0.4

24. $1\frac{1}{2}$ **25.** $2\frac{2}{3}$ **26.** $\frac{p}{q}$ **27.** $\frac{s}{t}$

28. $\frac{1}{4y}$ **29.** $\frac{-1}{8a}$ **30.** $\frac{2a}{3b}$ **31.** $\frac{-4y}{3x}$

Rewrite each division as multiplication.

32. $3 \div 19$ **33.** $4 \div (-9)$ **34.** $\frac{6}{-13}$ **35.** $-\frac{12}{41}$

36. $\frac{13.9}{-1.5}$ **37.** $\frac{x}{\frac{1}{y}}$ **38.** $\frac{3x + 4}{5}$ **39.** $\frac{5a - b}{5a + b}$

Divide.

40. $\frac{3}{4} \div \left(-\frac{2}{3}\right)$ **41.** $\frac{7}{8} \div \left(-\frac{1}{2}\right)$ **42.** $-\frac{5}{4} \div \left(-\frac{3}{4}\right)$

43. $-\frac{5}{9} \div \left(-\frac{5}{6}\right)$ **44.** $-\frac{2}{7} \div \left(-\frac{4}{9}\right)$ **45.** $-\frac{3}{5} \div \left(-\frac{5}{8}\right)$

46. $-44.1 \div (-6.3)$ **47.** $-42.3 \div 0$ **48.** $0 \div -2.5$

49. $-\frac{1}{3} \div \frac{1}{3}$ **50.** $-\frac{1}{4} \div \frac{1}{2}$ **51.** $-\frac{5}{6} \div \frac{3}{4}$

TEST PREP Compare the boxed quantity in column A with the boxed quantity in column B. Choose the best answer.
A. The quantity in column A is greater.
B. The quantity in column B is greater.
C. The two quantities are equal.
D. The relationship cannot be determined with the information supplied.

	column A	column B		column A	column B
52.	$\frac{20}{10}$	$\frac{20}{5}$	**53.**	$\frac{-20}{10}$	$\frac{-20}{5}$
54.	$\frac{20}{-10}$	$\frac{20}{-5}$	**55.**	$\frac{-20}{-10}$	$\frac{-20}{-5}$
56.	$\frac{x}{10}$	$\frac{x}{5}$	**57.**	$\frac{x}{-10}$	$\frac{x}{-5}$

B
Simplify.

58. $\dfrac{(-9)(-8) + (-3)}{25}$ **59.** $\dfrac{-3(-9) + 7}{-4}$ **60.** $\dfrac{(-2)^7}{(-4)^2}$ **61.** $\dfrac{(-3)^4}{-9}$

62. $5\frac{3}{7} \div 4\frac{2}{5}$ **63.** $\frac{10}{7} \div 1\frac{3}{4}$ **64.** $2\frac{2}{3} \div \frac{40}{15}$ **65.** $\dfrac{(-4)^3}{(-8)^3}$

66. Use a calculator to find the reciprocal of -10.5.

67. Use a calculator to find the reciprocal of 4.2.

68. What should happen if you enter a number on a calculator and press the reciprocal key twice? Why?

69. *Critical Thinking* Is it possible for a number to be its own reciprocal? Explain.

Challenge

Write a Convincing Argument Write a convincing argument or give a counterexample.

70. Is division of rational numbers commutative? That is, does $a \div b = b \div a$ for all rational numbers a and b?

71. Is division of rational numbers associative? That is, does $(a \div b) \div c = a \div (b \div c)$ for all rational numbers a, b, and c?

72. Is it possible for the additive inverse of a number to be its reciprocal?

73. Are both $\frac{b}{a}$ and $\frac{1}{\left(\frac{a}{b}\right)}$ reciprocals of a nonzero rational number $\frac{a}{b}$?

Mixed Review

Simplify.   **74.** $6 + (-3) - 5 - (-9)$ **75.** $12 - 7 - (-4) + (-2)$

76. $9 + (11) + (-8) - 4$ **77.** $8 + (-15) - 4 - (-18)$ *2-3, 2-4*

Write as an algebraic expression.   **78.** 5 more than t **79.** twice m

80. 36 divided among y **81.** x less than 25   **82.** m times n *1-1*

Solve.   **83.** $12 = 24p$ **84.** $20n = 5$ **85.** $42x = 14$ **86.** $3 = 6y$ *1-7*

Terminating and Repeating Decimals

We have learned that a rational number can be expressed as the ratio of two integers. A rational number can also be expressed as either a **terminating decimal** or a **repeating decimal.** When we divide the integer a by the integer b in the rational number $\frac{a}{b}$, the resulting decimal will either terminate or repeat.

$$\frac{3}{8} = 0.375$$ The decimal ends or terminates in the thousandths place.

$$\frac{3}{11} = 0.272727\ldots = 0.\overline{27}$$ The digits 27 repeat. We use a bar to indicate which digits repeat.

A decimal that neither terminates nor repeats, such as $2.35335333533335\ldots$ names an **irrational number.**

Exercises

Write as a decimal. If the decimal repeats, use a bar for the repeating decimal part.

1. $\frac{4}{11}$ **2.** $\frac{7}{20}$ **3.** $\frac{23}{9}$ **4.** $\frac{5}{18}$ **5.** $\frac{4}{9}$ **6.** $\frac{2}{13}$

To find the decimal equivalent to $\frac{1}{7}$, you can divide 1 by 7. Several steps of the long division are shown at the right. In the first three subtractions, the remainders are 1, 3, and 2.

7. Continue the long division to find a repeating pattern of remainders. How many digits are in this pattern?

8. What repeating decimal equals $\frac{1}{7}$? How many digits repeat?

9. *Write a Convincing Argument*   What is the greatest number of digits that can repeat in the repeating decimal for $\frac{1}{17}$? Explain.

$$
\begin{array}{r}
0.14 \\
7\overline{)1.00} \\
\underline{0} \\
10 \\
\underline{7} \\
30 \\
\underline{28} \\
2
\end{array}
$$

Lever Problems

The principles that allow small forces to lift heavy bridges and provide for movement on playground teeter-totters also provide ways for small forces to move heavy loads. Consider the problem of lifting a 1500-pound bale of hay. If a farmer uses a tower boom crane to lift the bale of hay, how many pounds of force are needed to lift the bale with the crane?

The problem is like the problem of lifting a person off the ground on a seesaw. A force needs to be applied to the opposite side of the seesaw or to the opposite side of the boom on the crane.

A "square" bale of hay with dimensions 14" × 18" × 36" weighs 50 to 60 lb. This rolled bale weighs about 1500 lb. How many square bales are equivalent to the rolled bale?

You can use integers to predict what will happen when forces are applied to a seesaw or boom. Both of these situations are examples of **levers**. The diagram represents the physical situation involved.

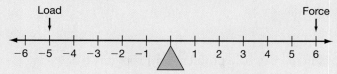

The 0 point, where the lever pivots, is called the fulcrum. The moment, or torque, for both the load and the force, is the product of the force each exerts and its distance from the fulcrum: Moment = (force)(distance). Downward forces, such as weight or force applied, are negative. Distances to the left of the fulcrum can be thought of as negative, and distances to the right can be thought of as positive, as on a number line.

The farmer uses a hydraulic jack to pull on the end of the other side of the boom to lift the bale. He notes that the force required was 750 pounds to lift and balance the bale. This force caused the moments of the two sides to be equal.

Farmer's moment: $(-750)(-20) = 15,000$
Bale's moment: $(-1500)(10) = -15,000$
Sum of the two moments: $15,000 + (-15,000) = 0$

When the sum of the moments is 0, the boom balances.

The Principle of Moments

When several parallel forces act on an object, it will be in balance if the sum of the moments is 0.

To move an object using a lever and fulcrum, the moment on one side of the fulcrum has to exceed the moment created by the load to be moved. Exact solutions of such problems must also take into account the mass of the lever.

EXAMPLE

To lift a heavy load, one end of an eight-foot pry bar is placed two feet beyond a pivot point and inserted into a chain link. How many pounds of force are needed to balance the chain link if 200 pounds of force are placed on the other end of the pry bar?

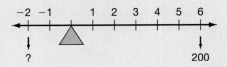

The force of 200 pounds acting downward at a distance of 6 feet from the fulcrum creates a moment of $(-200)(6)$ or -1200. The chain link end is acting through a distance of 2 feet on the negative side of the fulcrum. If f represents the force exerted here, we have a moment of $-2f$ being in balance with the moment on the other side of -1200. Hence, f must equal 600 pounds.

Problems

Solve. Use the conditions in the hay bale problem for Problems 1–3.

1. Show two other places the farmer could hook the jack to the boom and lift the hay bale. Give the force required to balance the bale for each of these points.

2. How long a boom on the farmer's side would be required to balance the bale with a force of 125 pounds?

3. Suppose the hay bale was attached at a point 8 feet from the fulcrum. How much force 20 feet from the fulcrum would be required to balance the bale?

4. One end of a 10-foot pry bar is inserted under a 420-pound rock. If the fulcrum is 3 feet from the rock, how many pounds of force have to be exerted on the other end of the bar to balance the rock?

5. A meter bar has a 10-kg weight on one end and a 15-kg weight on the other end. Where would the fulcrum have to be placed to balance the loads?

Using the Distributive Property ◁ 2-7

PART 1   **The Distributive Property Over Subtraction**

Objective: Multiply using the distributive property over subtraction.

In Chapter 1 you learned how to use the distributive property over addition with whole numbers. The distributive property over addition applies to all rational numbers.

The Distributive Property of Multiplication Over Addition

For any rational numbers a, b, and c, $a(b + c) = ab + ac$, and
$$(b + c)a = ba + ca$$

We can use the basic properties and previous definitions to show that the distributive property holds for subtraction as well.

The Distributive Property of Multiplication Over Subtraction

For any rational numbers a, b, and c, $a(b - c) = ab - ac$, and
$$(b - c)a = ba - ca$$

We refer to this property as the **distributive property over subtraction.**

EXAMPLES   Multiply.

1 $9(x - 5) = 9x - 9(5)$
$$= 9x - 45$$

2 $-3(y - 3) = -3y - (-3)(3)$
$$= -3y + 9$$

3 $\frac{4}{3}(s - t + w) = \frac{4}{3}s - \frac{4}{3}t + \frac{4}{3}w$

4 $-4(x - 2y + 3z) = -4 \cdot x - (-4)(2y) + (-4)(3z)$
$$= -4x - (-8y) + (-12z) = -4x + 8y - 12z$$

Try This   Multiply.

a. $8(y - 7)$ **b.** $\frac{5}{6}(x - y + 7z)$ **c.** $-5(x - 3y + 8z)$

What You'll Learn

1 To multiply using the distributive property of multiplication over subtraction

2 To factor expressions

3 To collect like terms in an expression

... And Why

To be able to simplify algebraic expressions

Factoring

Objective: Factor expressions.

Recall that we can use the distributive properties to **factor** an expression.

$$ab + ac = a(b + c)$$
$$ab - ac = a(b - c)$$

EXAMPLES   Factor.

5 $5x - 5y = 5(x - y)$

6 $8x - 16 = 8 \cdot x - 8 \cdot 2 = 8(x - 2)$

7 $ax - ay + az = a(x - y + z)$

8 $9x - 27y - 9 = 9(x) - 9(3y) - 9(1)$
$$= 9(x - 3y - 1)$$

9 $-3x + 6y - 9z = 3(-x + 2y - 3z)$ or $-3(x - 2y + 3z)$

10 $18z - 12x - 24 = 6(3z - 2x - 4)$

11 $\frac{1}{2}x + \frac{3}{2}y - \frac{1}{2} = \frac{1}{2}(x + 3y - 1)$

Try This   Factor.

d. $4x - 8$ **e.** $3x - 6y - 15$ **f.** $bx - by + bz$
g. $-2y + 8z - 2$ **h.** $12z - 16x - 4$

Collecting Like Terms

Objective: Collect like terms.

If there are subtractions in an expression, we can think of an equivalent expression without subtraction signs. Then the terms are separated by addition signs.

EXAMPLE 12

What are the terms of $3x - 4y + 2z$?

The terms are $3x$, $-4y$, and $2z$.   Think $3x + (-4y) + 2z$.

In the first term, $3x$, 3 and x are the factors. In the second term, $-4y$, -4 and y are the factors. In the last term, $2z$, 2, and z are the factors.

Try This   What are the terms of each expression?

i. $5a - 4b + 3$ **j.** $-5y - 3x + 5z$

We can collect like terms by using the distributive property of multiplication over addition or subtraction to factor.

EXAMPLES   Collect like terms.

13 $2k + 7k = (2 + 7)k = 9k$

14 $2x + 3y - 5x - 2y = 2x - 5x + 3y - 2y$
$$= (2 - 5)x + (3 - 2)y \quad \text{Factoring}$$
$$= {}^-3x + y$$

15 $3x - x = (3 - 1)x = 2x$

16 $x - 0.24x = 1 \cdot x - 0.24x = (1 - 0.24)x = 0.76x$

17 $x - 6x = 1 \cdot x - 6x = (1 - 6)x = {}^-5x$

Try This   Collect like terms.

k. $6x - 3x$
l. $7y - y$
m. $m - 0.44m$
n. $5x + 4y - 2x - y$
o. $3x - 7x - 11 + 8y - 4 - 13y$

2-7 Exercises

A
Multiply.

1. $7(x - 2)$ **2.** $5(x - 8)$

3. $-7(y - 2)$ **4.** $-9(y - 7)$

5. $-9(-5x - 6y + 8)$ **6.** $-7(-2x - 5y + 9)$

7. $-4(x - 3y - 2z)$ **8.** $8(2x - 5y - 8z)$

9. $3.1(-1.2x + 3.2y - 1.1)$ **10.** $-2.1(-4.2x - 4.3y - 2.2)$

11. $\frac{2}{3}(3a - 6b + 9)$ **12.** $\frac{1}{2}(4c + 5d - 6)$

13. $-\frac{4}{5}\left(-\frac{1}{2}x + \frac{2}{3}y - 1\right)$ **14.** $-\frac{7}{8}\left(\frac{2}{3}x - \frac{1}{2}y - 8\right)$

Factor.

15. $8x - 24$ **16.** $-10x - 50$ **17.** $32 - 4y$

18. $24 - 6m$ **19.** $8x + 10y - 22$ **20.** $-9a + 6b - 15$

21. $ax - 7a$ **22.** $by - 9b$ **23.** $ax - ay - az$

24. $cx + cy - cz$ **25.** $\frac{3}{4}x - \frac{1}{4}y - \frac{1}{4}$ **26.** $\frac{2}{3}x - \frac{1}{3}y + \frac{1}{3}$

What are the terms of each expression?

27. $4x + 3z$

28. $8x - 1.4y$

29. $7x + 8y - 9z$

30. $8a + 10b - 18c$

31. $12x - 13.2y + \frac{5}{8}z - 4.5$

32. $3ab - 4cd$

Collect like terms.

33. $x - 3x$

34. $9t - 17t$

35. $6n - n$

36. $y - 17y$

37. $9x + 2y - 5x$

38. $8y - 3z + 4y$

39. $11x + 2y - 4x - y$

40. $13a + 9b - 2a - 4b$

41. $2.7x + 2.3y - 1.9x - 1.8y$

42. $6.7a + 4.3b - 4.1a - 2.9b$

43. $5y - 3x - 7y$

44. $13m + 5m - 3n - 18m$

45. $-8t + p + 4p - t$

46. $q + q + q + 5p$

47. $17a - 17b - 17c + 15a$

48. $6m - 3.5n + 2.5m - 7n$

49. $5.5d - 1.2a + 3d + 4.2a$

50. $17z + 3x - 2y + y - 5z - 3x$

51. $\frac{1}{5}x + \frac{4}{5}y + \frac{2}{5}x - \frac{1}{5}y$

52. $\frac{7}{8}x + \frac{5}{8}y + \frac{1}{8}x - \frac{3}{8}y$

B

Write as an algebraic expression.

53. eight times the difference of x and y

54. nine times the difference of y and z, increased by $3z$

55. three times the sum of a and b, decreased by $7a$

56. the total cost if you buy x cassette tapes at \$2.95 on Monday and y cassettes at the same price on Wednesday

57. *Critical Thinking*   For all rational numbers a, b, and c, does $a \cdot (b - c) = a - (b \cdot c)$? Explain.

Challenge

58. If the temperature is C degrees Celsius, it is $\frac{9}{5}C + 32$ degrees Fahrenheit. What is the Fahrenheit temperature if the Celsius temperature drops $5°$?

59. Jill has 5420 shares of a stock that she bought at $41\frac{1}{8}$. The stock is now worth $37\frac{3}{4}$. Show two ways of determining how much she has lost. Solve.

Mixed Review

Find the reciprocal.   **60.** $\frac{2}{15}$ **61.** $-\frac{6}{11}$ **62.** 4   **63.** $\frac{1}{3c}$ *2-6*

Simplify.   **64.** $11 - |-3| + (-9) - 16$ **65.** $4x - (-9x) - x$ *1-5, 2-3, 2-4*

Calculate.   **66.** $\frac{4}{5}\left(\frac{2}{3}\right)$ **67.** $-\frac{3}{8}\left(\frac{1}{2}\right)$ **68.** $\frac{2}{3} \div -\frac{1}{2}$ **69.** $\frac{4}{5} \div \frac{2}{5}$ *2-5, 2-6*

Inverse of a Sum and Simplifying

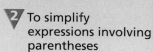

2-8

PART 1 Inverse of a Sum

Objective: Find the inverse of a sum.

What happens when we multiply a rational number by -1?

$$-1 \cdot 7 = -7 \qquad -1 \cdot (-5) = 5 \qquad -1 \cdot 0 = 0$$

The product is the additive inverse of the number.

The Property of -1

For any rational number a,
$$-1 \cdot a = -a.$$
(Negative one times a is the additive inverse of a.)

The property of -1 enables us to find an equivalent expression for the additive inverse of a sum.

EXAMPLES Rename each additive inverse without parentheses.

1
$$\begin{aligned}
-(3 + x) &= -1(3 + x) && \text{Using the property of } -1 \\
&= -1 \cdot 3 + (-1)x && \text{Using a distributive property} \\
&= -3 + (-x) && \text{Using the property of } -1 \\
&= -3 - x && \text{Using the subtraction rule}
\end{aligned}$$

2
$$\begin{aligned}
-(3x + 2y + 4) &= -1(3x + 2y + 4) \\
&= -1(3x) + (-1)(2y) + (-1)4 \\
&= -3x - 2y - 4
\end{aligned}$$

Try This Rename each additive inverse without parentheses.

a. $-(x + 2)$ **b.** $-(5x + 2y + 8)$

c. $-(a - 7)$ **d.** $-(3c - 4d + 1)$

What You'll Learn

1 To find the inverse of a sum

2 To simplify expressions involving parentheses

3 To simplify expressions containing multiple grouping symbols

...And Why

To learn how to simplify complex expressions and equations that are obtained when modeling real-life situations

Examples 1 and 2 illustrate an important property of rational numbers.

The Inverse of a Sum Property

For any rational numbers a and b,
$$-(a + b) = -a + (-b)$$
(The additive inverse of a sum is the sum of the additive inverses.)

The inverse of a sum property holds for differences as well as sums because any difference can be expressed as a sum. It also holds when there is a sum or difference of more than two terms. When we apply the inverse of a sum property we sometimes say that we "change the sign of every term."

EXAMPLES   Rename each additive inverse without parentheses.

3 $-(5 - y) = -5 + y$ Changing the sign of every term

4 $-(2a - 7b - 6) = -2a + 7b + 6$

Try This   Rename each additive inverse without parentheses.

e. $-(6 - t)$ **f.** $-(-4a + 3t - 10)$ **g.** $-(18 - m - 2n + 4t)$

PART 2 Simplifying Expressions Involving Parentheses

Objective: Simplifying expressions involving parentheses.

When an expression inside parentheses is added to another expression as in $5x + (2x + 3)$, the associative property allows us to move the parentheses and simplify the expression to $7x + 3$. When an expression inside parentheses is subtracted from another expression as in $3x - (4x + 2)$, we can subtract by adding the inverse. Then we can use the inverse of a sum property and simplify.

EXAMPLE 5   Simplify.

$$\begin{aligned}
3x - (4x + 2) &= 3x + (-(4x + 2)) && \text{Using the definition of subtraction} \\
&= 3x + (-4x + (-2)) && \text{Using the inverse of sum property} \\
&= 3x - 4x - 2 \\
&= -x - 2 && \text{Collecting like terms}
\end{aligned}$$

We can combine the first two steps of Example 5 by changing the sign of every term inside the parentheses.

Simplify.

6 $5y - (3y + 4) = 5y - 3y - 4$ Changing the sign of the terms inside
parentheses
$\qquad\qquad = 2y - 4$ Collecting like terms

7 $3y - 2 - (2y - 4) = 3y - 2 - 2y + 4$
$\qquad\qquad\qquad = y + 2$

Try This   Simplify.

h. $5x - (3x + 9)$ **i.** $5x - 2y - (2y - 3x - 4)$

Next consider subtracting an expression consisting of several terms preceded
by a number.

EXAMPLES   Simplify.

8 $x - 3(x + y) = x + (-3(x + y))$ Adding the inverse of $3(x + y)$
$\qquad\qquad = x + (-3x - 3y)$ Using the distributive property
$\qquad\qquad = x - 3x - 3y$
$\qquad\qquad = -2x - 3y$ Collecting like terms

9 $3y - 2(4y - 5) = 3y + (-2(4y - 5))$ Adding the inverse of $2(4y - 5)$
$\qquad\qquad\quad = 3y + (-8y + 10)$
$\qquad\qquad\quad = 3y - 8y + 10$
$\qquad\qquad\quad = -5y + 10$

Try This   Simplify.

j. $y - 9(x + y)$ **k.** $5a - 3(7a - 6)$

PART 3   Grouping Symbols

**Objective: Simplify expressions containing multiple grouping
symbols.**

Some expressions contain more than one grouping symbol. **Parentheses ( ),
brackets [ ],** and **braces { }** are all grouping symbols we use in algebra.
When an expression contains more than one grouping symbol, the
computations in the innermost grouping symbols should be done first.

EXAMPLES   Simplify.

10 $[3 - (7 + 3)] = [3 - 10]$ Computing $7 + 3$
$\qquad\qquad\quad = -7$

11 $\{8 - [9 - (12 + 5)]\} = \{8 - [9 - 17]\}$ Computing $12 + 5$
$\qquad\qquad\qquad\quad = \{8 - [-8]\}$ Computing $9 - 17$
$\qquad\qquad\qquad\quad = 16$

EXAMPLES Simplify.

12 $4(2 + 3) - \{7 - [4 - (8 + 5)]\}$
$= 4 \cdot 5 - \{7 - [4 - 13]\}$ Working with innermost parentheses first
$= 20 - \{7 - [-9]\}$ Computing $4 \cdot 5$ and $4 - 13$
$= 20 - 16$ Computing $7 - [-9]$
$= 4$

13 $[5(x + 2) - 3x] - [3(y + 2) - 7(y - 3)$
$= [5x + 10 - 3x] - [3y + 6 - 7y + 21]$ Working with innermost parentheses first

$= [2x + 10] - [-4y + 27]$ Collecting like terms
$= 2x + 10 + 4y - 27$
$= 2x + 4y - 17$

Try This   Simplify.

l. $[9 - (6 + 4)]$ **m.** $3(4 + 2) - \{7 - [4 - (6 + 5)]\}$

n. $[3(4 + 2) + 2x] - [4(y + 2) - 3(y - 2)]$

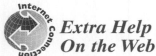

Extra Help On the Web

Look for worked-out examples at the Prentice Hall Web site.
www.phschool.com

2-8 Exercises

A

Rename each additive inverse without parentheses.

1. $-(2x + 7)$ **2.** $-(3x + 5)$

3. $-(5x - 8)$ **4.** $-(6x - 7)$

5. $-(4a - 3b + 7c)$ **6.** $-(5x - 2y - 3z)$

7. $-(6x - 8y + 5)$ **8.** $-(8x + 3y + 9)$

9. $-(3x - 5y - 6)$ **10.** $-(6a - 4b - 7)$

11. $-(-8x - 6y - 43)$ **12.** $-(-2a + 9b - 5c)$

Simplify.

13. $9x - (4x + 3)$ **14.** $7y - (2y + 9)$

15. $2a - (5a - 9)$ **16.** $11n - (3n - 7)$

17. $2x + 7x - (4x + 6)$ **18.** $3a + 2a - (4a + 7)$

19. $2x - 4y - 3(7x - 2y)$ **20.** $3a - 7b - 1(4a - 3b)$

21. $15x - y - 5(3x - 2y + 5z)$ **22.** $4a - b - 4(5a - 7b + 8c)$

23. $(3x + 2y) - (5x - 4y)$ **24.** $(-6a - b) - (4b + a)$

25. $6m - n - 4m - (5n - m)$ **26.** $7p - (q + 8p) - 5p + 3q$

27. $-(7u - 8v) - (8v - 7u)$ **28.** $7m + 8n - (4n - 5m) + n$

29. $5a - 3b - (-6b + 4a) - (-b)$

30. $-(-4x - 3y) - 6y + 3x - x - y$

Simplify.

31. $[9 - 2(5 - 4)]$

32. $[6 - 5(8 - 4)]$

33. $8[7 - 6(4 - 2)]$

34. $10[7 - 4(7 - 5)]$

35. $[4(9 - 6) + 11] - [14 - (6 + 4)]$

36. $[7(8 - 4) + 16] - [15 - (7 + 3)]$

37. $[10(x + 3) - 4)] + [2(x - 1) + 6)]$

38. $[9(x + 5) - 7] + [4(x - 12) + 9]$

39. $[7(x + 5) - 19] - [4(x - 6) + 10]$

40. $[6(x + 4) - 12] - [5(x - 8) + 11]$

B

Find an equivalent expression for each of the following by enclosing the last three terms in parentheses preceded by a minus sign.

41. $x - y - a - b$

42. $6y + 2x - 3a + c$

43. $6m + 3n - 5m + 4b$

44. $3q - 2p + 4q - 5$

Simplify.

45. $3a + 4 - \{-2 - [-3 - (a - 1)]\}$

46. $2s + 2 - \{-3 - [2 - (3 - s)]\}$

47. *Critical Thinking*   If $-(a + b)$ is $-a + (-b)$, what should be the sum of $(a + b)$ and $-a + (-b)$? Show that your answer is correct.

Challenge

Simplify.

48. $z - \{2z - [3z - (4z - 5z) - 6z] - 7z\} - 8z$

49. $\{x - [f - (f - x)] + [x - f]\} - 3x$

50. $x - \{x - 1 - [x - 2 - (x - 3 - \{x - 4 - [x - 5 - (x - 6)]\})]\}$

51. A bar, or vinculum, can be used as a grouping symbol. Simplify the following.
$$\{y - [y + (3 - y)] - \overline{y + 1}\} + 5y$$

Mixed Review

Factor.   **52.** $3x + 12y$ **53.** $2a - 6b + 12$ **54.** $an + 2a$ *2-7*

Evaluate for $x = 3$, $y = 2$, and $z = 5$.   **55.** $2x^3$ **56.** $-3z^2$

57. $6x + 2y^4$ **58.** $2x^2 + 3z$ **59.** $x + 2y - 3z$ *1-4*

Calculate.   **60.** $\frac{2}{3} + \frac{1}{4} - \left(-\frac{3}{8}\right)$ **61.** $\frac{1}{2}\left(\frac{4}{5}\right) + \left(\frac{5}{6}\right)\left(-\frac{2}{3}\right)$ *2-3, 2-4*

Collect like terms.   **62.** $8b + 7b + b$ **63.** $x^2 + x + x^2$ *1-5*

Write as an algebraic expression.   **64.** a number squared plus 3

65. five less than three times a number   *1-1*

What You'll Learn

1 To write an equation that can be used to solve a problem

... And Why

To be able to solve real-world problems using algebraic reasoning skills

PART 1 Write an Equation

Objective: Write an equation that can be used to solve a problem.

In the past you have been introduced to strategies that you can use to solve mathematical problems. A powerful strategy is *Write an Equation.* Many of the problems you will work with in your study of algebra can be solved by writing and solving an equation.

PROBLEM-SOLVING GUIDELINES
■ UNDERSTAND the problem
▢ Develop and carry out a PLAN
■ Find the ANSWER and CHECK

The Problem-Solving Guidelines were introduced in Chapter 1. The three phases can help you solve many kinds of problems.

The planning phase involves selecting and carrying out strategies for solving problems. Here are some tips you can use when your plan involves writing an equation.

PLANNING to write and solve an equation

Can I use a variable to represent an unknown number?
Can I represent other conditions in terms of the variable?
Can I find equivalent expressions?
Can I write and solve an equation?

EXAMPLE 1   Which equation(s) can be used to solve the problem?

Jose's salary this year was $23,400. This is $1700 more than he made last year. What was his salary last year?

(A) $l - 1700 = 23,400$ (B) $1700 + l = 23,400$
(C) $l = 23,400 - 1700$

■ **UNDERSTAND the problem**

Question: What was Jose's salary last year?

Data: Jose earned $23,400 this year. This is $1700 more than he made last year.

Clarifying the question and identifying the data given

▢ **Develop and carry out a PLAN**

Let l = last year's salary.

Using a variable to represent what you are trying to find

Our data tell us that 23,400 is 1700 more than l. This is the same as equation (B). We can also say that last year's salary was 1700 less than this year's salary. This is the same as equation (C).

Either (B) or (C) are correct equations.

EXAMPLE 2 Write an equation that could be used to solve the problem.

A color television set uses about 420 kilowatt hours (kWh) of electrical energy in a year. That is 3.5 times the amount of energy used by a black-and-white set. How many kWh does a black-and-white set use in a year?

■ **UNDERSTAND the problem**

Question: How many kWh does a black-and-white set use in 1 year?

Data: A color set uses 420 kWh a year. This amount is 3.5 times as much as the amount used by a black-and-white set.

Clarifying the question and identifying the data given

■ **Develop and carry out a PLAN**

Let $b =$ number of kWh used by a black-and-white set.

$3.5b =$ number of kWh used by a color set

Using a variable to represent what you are trying to find

3.5 times the number of kWh for a black-and-white TV equals the amount used by a color TV.

$$(3.5)b = 420$$

EXAMPLE 3 Write an equation that could be used to solve the problem.

In baseball, a player's batting average multiplied by the number of times at bat equals the number of hits. A player had 125 at-bats and 36 hits. What was this player's batting average?

■ **UNDERSTAND the problem**

Question: What was this player's batting average?

Data: A player had 125 at-bats and 36 hits.

Clarifying the question and identifying the data given

■ **Develop and carry out a PLAN**

Let $b =$ player's batting average.

$125b =$ player's batting average after 125 at-bats

Using a variable to represent what you are trying to find

$$(125)b = 36$$

Extra Help On the Web

Look for worked-out examples at the Prentice Hall Web site.

www.phschool.com

2-9 Problems

Which equation(s) can be used to solve each problem?

1. Nita had 25 points on the second quiz. That was 8 more points than she had on the first quiz. How many points did she have on the first quiz? Let x = number of points on her first quiz.
   - (A) $x - 25 = 8$
   - (B) $x + 8 = 25$
   - (C) $x = 25 - 8$

2. A golfer hit two shots for a total of 375 yards. Her first shot was 240 yards. How far was her second shot? Let s = length of the second shot.
   - (A) $240 + s = 375$
   - (B) $s - 240 = 375$
   - (C) $s = 375 + 240$

3. There are 775 dogs and cats in an animal shelter. There are 423 dogs in the shelter. How many cats are there? Let c = number of cats.
   - (A) $775 - 423 = c$
   - (B) $423 + c = 775$
   - (C) $c - 423 = 775$

4. The San Francisco Giants won 39 more games than the St. Louis Cardinals. The Giants won 101 games. How many games did the Cardinals win? Let c = number of games the Cardinals won.
   - (A) $c - 39 = 101$
   - (B) $c + 39 = 101$
   - (C) $101 + 39 = c$

5. A game board has 64 squares. If you win 35 squares, how many does your opponent get? Let o = number of squares your opponent gets.
   - (A) $o - 35 = 64$
   - (B) $35 + o = 64$
   - (C) $o = 64 - 35$

6. A dozen balloons cost \$3.50. How much is each balloon? Let b = the cost of each balloon.
   - (A) $3.50 \div 12 = b$
   - (B) $3.50 - b = 12$
   - (C) $12b = 3.50$

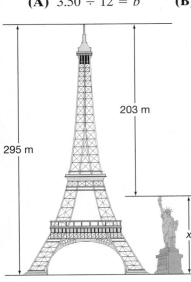

203 m

295 m

x

Write an equation that can be used to solve the problem.

7. The height of the Eiffel Tower is 295 m, which is about 203 m higher than the Statue of Liberty. What is the height of the Statue of Liberty?

8. Dennis sold a total of 318 tickets in two days. He sold 127 tickets the second day. How many did he sell the first day?

9. Alberto has \$48 less than Mariana. Mariana has \$115. How much does Alberto have?

10. A bakery charges \$3.12 for a dozen bagels. How much does it cost to buy a single bagel?

11. A movie theater took in $438.75 from 117 customers. What was the price of a ticket?

12. A consultant charges $80 an hour. How many hours did the consultant work to make $53,400?

13. The area of Lake Superior is about 4 times the area of Lake Ontario. The area of Lake Superior is 78,114 km². What is the area of Lake Ontario?

14. It takes a 60-watt bulb about 16.6 hours to use 1 kWh of electricity. That is about 2.5 times as long as it takes a 150-watt bulb to use 1 kWh. How long does it take a 150-watt bulb to use 1 kWh?

15. The area of Alaska is about 483 times the area of Rhode Island. The area of Alaska is 1,519,202 km². What is the area of Rhode Island?

16. The boiling point of ethyl alcohol is 78.3°C. That is 13.5°C higher than the boiling point of methyl alcohol. What is the boiling point of methyl alcohol?

17. The distance from Earth to the sun is about 150,000,000 km. That is about 391 times the distance from Earth to the moon. What is the distance from Earth to the moon?

18. In three-way light bulbs, the highest wattage is the sum of the two lower wattages. If the lowest is 30 watts and the highest is 150 watts, what is the middle wattage?

19. The distance traveled (D) equals the rate of travel (r) times the time traveled (t). How long would it take a boat traveling 50 miles per hour to travel 325 miles, assuming there are no stops?

20. A roll of film costs $3.14 and developing costs $10.39. What is the total cost for each of the 36 prints?

21. The dryers at Franklin Laundry cost a quarter for 7 minutes. How many quarters will you have to use to dry your clothes for 45 minutes?

22. One inch equals 2.54 centimeters. A meter is 100 centimeters. How many inches are there in a meter?

23. Sound travels at 1087 feet per second. How long does it take the sound of an airplane to reach you when it is 10,000 feet overhead?

24. In baseball, a player's batting average multiplied by the number of times at bat equals the number of hits. A player had 125 at-bats and 36 hits. What was this player's batting average?

Write a problem that can be solved using the given equations. Specify what the variable represents.

25. Let x = ?
$x - 2 = 32$

26. Let a = ?
$a + 24 = 42$

27. Let r = ?
$42 - r = 11$

28. Let m = ?
$m + 2m = 18$

2-10 ▷ Number Properties and Proofs

What You'll Learn

1 To identify applications of the number properties

2 To identify the properties of equality

3 To prove number properties

... And Why

To become familiar with the properties of numbers and be able to use them to simplify algebraic expressions

Writing Math

How would you convince a fellow student that the opposite of a number equals the number subtracted from zero?

PART 1 Number Properties and Definitions

Objective: Identify applications of the number properties.

Number properties are important in algebra because they allow us to write equivalent expressions. For example, the associative property allows us to write $(x + 3) + 5$ and $x + (3 + 5)$ and know they are equivalent.

How do we know that the properties we have used so far are true? We accept some number properties as obvious, and then, using these properties, we prove the rest. The properties that we accept without proof are called **axioms.** The properties that we prove are called **theorems.**

Following is a list of properties that we will accept as axioms.

Axioms for Rational Numbers

For any rational numbers a, b, and c

- The Closure Properties
    1. Addition: $a + b$ is a rational number.
    2. Multiplication: ab is a rational number.
- The Commutative Properties
    3. Addition: $a + b = b + a$
    4. Multiplication: $ab = ba$
- The Associative Properties
    5. Addition: $a + (b + c) = (a + b) + c$
    6. Multiplication: $a(bc) = (ab)c$
- The Identity Properties
    7. Addition: $a + 0 = a$
    8. Multiplication: $a \cdot 1 = a$
- The Inverse Properties
    9. Addition: For each a, there is an additive inverse, $-a$, such that $a + (-a) = 0$.
    10. Multiplication: For each a ($a \neq 0$), there is a multiplicative inverse, $\frac{1}{a}$, such that $a \cdot \frac{1}{a} = 1$.
- The Distributive Property of Multiplication over Addition
    11. $a(b + c) = ab + ac$

These axioms hold for rational numbers, and they also hold in some other number systems. Any number system in which these axioms hold is called a **field.** Hence the axioms are known as the **field axioms.**

EXAMPLES   Which axiom guarantees the truth of each statement?

1 $2(y + 3) = 2y + 2 \cdot 3$ Distributive property

2 $(3m)(n) = 3(mn)$ Associative property for multiplication

Try This   Which axiom guarantees the truth of each statement?

a. $4 + (5 + x) = (4 + 5) + x$ **b.** $7\left(\frac{1}{7}\right) = 1$ **c.** $-12 + 12 = 0$

The closure properties for rational numbers guarantee that the sum and product of any two rational numbers are also rational numbers. We say that the set of rational numbers is **closed** for addition and multiplication.

EXAMPLE 3   Is the set $\{0, 1\}$ closed for addition? for multiplication?

No; $1 + 1 = 2$ and 2 is not in $\{0, 1\}$.

Yes; the only possible products of 0 and 1 are 0 and 1.

Try This   **d.** Is the set $\{-1, 0, 1\}$ closed for addition? for multiplication?

Here are some important definitions.

Definitions

Subtraction
The difference $a - b$ is the number c such that $c + b = a$.

Division
The quotient $\frac{a}{b}$, or $a \div b$, where $b \neq 0$, is the number c such that $c \cdot b = a$.

Equality
A sentence $a = b$ states that a and b are expressions for the same number.

PART 2   Properties of Equality

Objective: Identify the properties of equality.

The following are some important properties related to equality.

Properties of Equality

For any rational numbers a, b, and c,

Reflexive Property	**Symmetric Property**	**Transitive Property**
$a = a$ is always true.	If $a = b$, then $b = a$.	If $a = b$ and $b = c$, then $a = c$.

EXAMPLES   Which property of equality justifies each statement?

4 $a(b + c) = ab + ac$, so
$ab + ac = a(b + c)$ Symmetric property

5 $2x^3 = 2x^3$ Reflexive property

6   If $5xy^2 = 5y^2x$ and $5y^2x = 5 \cdot y \cdot y \cdot x$
then $5xy^2 = 5 \cdot y \cdot y \cdot x$.   Transitive property

Try This   Which property of equality justifies each statement?

e. $3a + 5b = 3a + 5b$

f. $(b + c)a = a(b + c)$ and $a(b + c) = ab + ac$. Therefore,
$(b + c)a = ab + ac$.

g. If $a(b - c) = ab - ac$, then $ab - ac = a(b - c)$.

Theorems and Proofs

Objective: Prove number properties.

We now consider some number properties that can be proved. The first theorem is a restatement of the distributive property. To prove this theorem, we write a sequence of statements. Each statement must be supported by a reason, which can be an axiom or a definition.

Theorem

For any rational numbers a, b, and c, $(b + c)a = ba + ca$.

EXAMPLE 7   Prove the above theorem.

Statement	Reason
1. $(b + c)a = a(b + c)$	1. Commutative property of multiplication
2. $\quad\quad = ab + ac$	2. Distributive property
3. $\quad\quad = ba + ca$	3. Commutative property of multiplication
4. $(b + c)a = ba + ca$	4. Transitive property of equality

Here is another theorem dealing with the distributive property. It involves three addends.

Theorem

For any rational numbers a, b, c, and d, $a(b + c + d) = ab + ac + ad$.

Try This

h. Complete the following proof by supplying the missing reasons.

Statement	Reason
1. $a(b + c + d) = a[(b + c) + d]$	1. Associative property of addition
2. $\qquad = a(b + c) + ad$	2.
3. $\qquad = ab + ac + ad$	3.
4. $a(b + c + d) = ab + ac + ad$	4. Transitive property of equality

The next theorem was stated on page 78 as the multiplication property of zero.

Theorem

For any rational number a, $a \cdot 0 = 0$.

Try This

i. Complete the following proof by supplying the missing reasons.

1. $a \cdot 0 = a \cdot 0 + 0$	1. Additive identity
2. $\qquad = a \cdot 0 + a + (-a)$	2. Additive inverse
3. $\qquad = a \cdot 0 + a \cdot 1 + (-a)$	3. Multiplicative identity
4. $\qquad = a(0 + 1) + (-a)$	4.
5. $\qquad = a \cdot 1 + (-a)$	5. Additive identity
6. $\qquad = a + (-a)$	6.
7. $\qquad = 0$	7.
8. $a \cdot 0 = 0$	8. Transitive property of equality

2-10 Exercises

**Extra Help
On the Web**

Look for worked-out examples at the Prentice Hall Web site.
www.phschool.com

A

Which axiom guarantees each statement?

1. $a + b = b + a$

2. $(a + b) + c = c + (a + b)$

3. $x(y + z) = xy + xz$

4. $3(b + c) = 3b + 3c$

5. $y + [x + (-x)] = y + 0$

6. $3x(x + 2) = 3x^2 + 6x$

7. $-(x - 3) = -x + 3$

8. $6x - 3y = 3(2x - y)$

Which axiom or property guarantees the truth of each statement?

9. $(a \cdot b)c = a(b \cdot c)$

10. $(a + b) \cdot 1 = a + b$

11. $17(2b + 1) = 34b + 17$

12. $(2a + 3b) + 19 = 19 + (3b + 2a)$

13. $\frac{1}{x + y} \cdot (x + y) = 1$

14. $-(a + b) + (a + b) = 0$

Which axiom or property guarantees the truth of each statement?

15. $3x(y + z) = 3x(y + z)$ **16.** $\frac{1}{x} \cdot x = 1$. Thus $1 = \frac{1}{x} \cdot x$

17. $4ab = 4ab$ **18.** $5(a + b) = (a + b)5$

Are the sets closed for addition, subtraction, multiplication, and division (except by 0)? If not, give counterexamples.

19. whole numbers   **20.** rational numbers   **21.** integers

Complete the following proof by supplying the missing reasons.

22. Property of -1. For any number a, $-1 \cdot a = -a$.

1. $-1 \cdot a = -1 \cdot a + 0$	1.
2. $\quad\quad = -1 \cdot a + (a + (-a))$	2. Additive inverse
3. $\quad\quad = (-1 \cdot a + a) + (-a)$	3.
4. $\quad\quad = (-1 \cdot a + 1 \cdot a) + (-a)$	4. Multiplicative identity
5. $\quad\quad = (-1 + 1) \cdot a + (-a)$	5.
6. $\quad\quad = 0 \cdot a + (-a)$	6. Additive inverse
7. $\quad\quad = 0 + -a$	7.
8. $\quad\quad = -a$	8.
9. $-1 \cdot a = -a$	9. Transitive property of equality

B

Write a Convincing Argument   Write a convincing argument or give a counterexample.

23. The set of whole numbers is *closed* for addition. The set of even numbers $\{0, 2, 4, 6, 8, 10, \ldots\}$ consists of numbers of the form $2a$ where a is a whole number. Is the set of even numbers closed for addition?

24. Is the set of odd whole numbers $\{1, 3, 5, 7, 9, \ldots\}$ closed for addition?

25. The set of whole numbers is closed for multiplication. The set $\{0, 3, 6, 9, 12, \ldots\}$ consists of numbers of the form $3a$ where a is a whole number. Is this set closed for multiplication?

Challenge

26. Prove that for any rational numbers a and b, $(-a)b = -ab$.

27. Prove the inverse of a sum property: For any rational numbers a and b, $-(a + b) = -a + (-b)$. (Hint: Use the property of -1 and the distributive property).

Mixed Review

Write an equation.   **28.** A roll of film costs \$4.80 and developing costs \$8.35. What is the total cost for each of the 36 prints?   *2-9*

Factor.   **29.** $16a - 48$ **30.** $8y - 10 + 12x$ **31.** $45 - 15n$ *2-7*

Collect like terms.   **32.** $6a + 9c - 8a$ **33.** $7 + 8c - 25c + 2$ *1-5*

Chapter Wrap Up

2-1

The set of **integers** consists of the **positive integers,** the **negative integers,** and zero. Numbers that are the same distance from 0, but on opposite sides of 0 on the number line, are called **opposites.** For any two numbers on the number line, the one farther to the right is greater. The **absolute value** of a number is its distance from 0 on the number line.

Name the integer suggested by each situation.
1. Tanya's mom owes $25.
2. Keiko deposited $50 in her savings account.

Find the absolute value.
3. $|-38|$
4. $|91|$
5. $|-0.02|$

2-2

A **rational number** can be expressed as the ratio of two integers, $\frac{a}{b}$, where $b \neq 0$. There is a point on the number line for every rational number. The number is called the **coordinate** of the point, and the point is the **graph** of the number.

Graph each rational number on a number line.
6. -2.5
7. $\frac{4}{3}$
8. $-\frac{16}{5}$

Use $<$ or $>$ to write a true sentence.
9. $-2.5 \;\square\; -4.5$
10. $-\frac{2}{3} \;\square\; -\frac{1}{10}$
11. $-\frac{1}{2} \;\square\; \frac{3}{5}$

Show that each number can be written as the ratio of two integers.
12. -4.2
13. $1\frac{3}{5}$
14. -8

2-3

To add two positive numbers or two negative numbers, add the absolute values; the sum has the same sign as each addend. To add a positive number and a negative number, subtract the absolute values; the sum has the same sign as the addend with the greater absolute value. Number pairs whose sum is 0 are called **additive inverses.**

Add.
15. $-6 + (-13)$
16. $\frac{3}{4} + \left(-\frac{9}{4}\right)$
17. $-3.9 + 7.4$
18. $6 + (-9) + (-8) + 7$
19. $-3.8 + 5.1 + (-12) - (-4.3)$

Key Terms
absolute value (p. 56)
additive inverse (p. 66)
axiom (p. 102)
braces (p. 95)
brackets (p. 95)
closed (p. 103)
coordinate (p. 59)
density property (p. 62)
difference (p. 71)
distributive properties (p. 89)
field (p. 102)
field axioms (p. 102)
graph of a number (p. 59)
inequality (p. 55)
integers (p. 54)
inverse of a sum property (p. 94)
irrational number (p. 86)
multiplicative inverse (p. 82)
multiplicative property of zero (p. 78)
negative integers (p. 54)
opposites (p. 54)
parentheses (p. 95)
positive integers (p. 54)
property of −1 (p. 93)
property of additive inverses (p. 66)
property of multiplicative inverses (p. 82)
quotient (p. 81)
rational numbers (p. 59)
real numbers (p. 61)
reciprocal (p. 82)
repeating decimal (p. 86)
terminating decimal (p. 86)
theorem (p. 102)

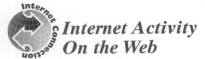
Find the additive inverse of each.

20. 27   **21.** -7.45 **22.** $-\frac{7}{3}$

23. Find $-x$ when x is -34.   **24.** Find $-(-x)$ when x is 5.

25. On a first, second, and third down a football team had these gains and losses: a 5-yd gain, a 12-yd loss, and a 15-yd gain. Find the total number of yards gained or lost.

2-4

To subtract a rational number, add its inverse. When addition and subtraction occur several times, use the rule for subtracting rational numbers to make them all additions.

Subtract.

26. $5 - 7$ **27.** $-7 - (-3)$ **28.** $-\frac{9}{10} - \frac{1}{2}$

Simplify.

29. $13 - 4 + 8 - (-2)$ **30.** $4y - 19 - (-7y) + 3$

31. An airplane is 2500 ft above the rim of the Grand Canyon at a point where the Grand Canyon is 1500 ft deep. How high is the plane above the floor of the canyon?

32. Mr. Jones had a balance of \$89.00 in his checking account. He wrote a check for \$105.95. By how much has he overdrawn his checking account?

2-5

When you multiply a positive number and a negative number, the product is negative. When you multiply two negative numbers or two positive numbers, the product is positive. The product of 0 and a rational number is 0.

Multiply.

33. $6(-4)$ **34.** $\frac{2}{3}\left(-\frac{3}{7}\right)$ **35.** $3(-7)(-2)(5)$

2-6

When you divide a positive number by a negative number or a negative number by a positive number, the quotient is negative. When you divide two negative numbers, the quotient is positive. Two numbers are **multiplicative inverses** or **reciprocals** if their product is 1. To divide by a rational number, multiply by its reciprocal.

Divide.

36. $21 \div (-7)$ **37.** $\frac{-45}{-9}$ **38.** $-\frac{7}{8} \div \frac{5}{4}$

2-7

The **distributive property of multiplication over subtraction** is used to multiply and factor algebraic expressions and to collect like terms.

Multiply.

39. $2(6x - 1)$ **40.** $-7(1 + 4x)$ **41.** $-3(2a - 3b + c)$

Factor.

42. $9a - 9$ **43.** $8x - 32y - 8$ **44.** $42z - 21x + 7$

Collect like terms.

45. $5x + 3x - x$ **46.** $5a - 3a$ **47.** $8m - 6m + 6$

2-8

The property of -1 states that $-1 \cdot a = -a$. The property of -1 and the distributive property allow us to rename the inverse of a sum as the sum of the inverses, $-(a + b) = -a + -b$.

Rename each additive inverse without parentheses.

48. $-(x + 7)$ **49.** $-(7a + 12b + c)$ **50.** $-(6 - z)$

When an expression contains more than one grouping symbol, you must do the computation in the innermost grouping symbols first.

Simplify.

51. $3a - (8a + 3)$ **52.** $7x - 5 - (10x - 4)$

53. $a - 5(a + b)$ **54.** $3p - 4(8p - 3)$

Simplify.

55. $[12 - (8 + 3)]$ **56.** $15 - [9 - (11 + 4)]$

2-9

Write an equation is a powerful strategy for many of the problems you will encounter while studying algebra. You should use the Problem-Solving Guideline, Develop and carry out a PLAN, when you need to write an equation.

Which equation(s) can be used to solve the problem?

57. A dozen roses cost $30. How much does each rose cost?

Let $r =$ the cost of one rose.

(A) $\frac{30}{12} = r$ **(B)** $30 - r = 12$ **(C)** $12r = 30$

Write an equation that could be used to solve the problem.

58. A professional baseball player made $1,289,196 for the 1999 baseball season. His team played 162 games in the season. How much did the player make per game?

Name the integer suggested by each situation.

1. Ed lost 16 points in a card game.

2. The highest points on the Grand Canyon are 9000 ft above sea level.

Find the absolute value.

3. $|6.5|$

4. $|-105.5|$

Graph each rational number on a number line.

5. $\frac{9}{2}$

6. -2.5

Use > or < to write a true sentence.

7. $-3.2 \ \square \ 1.2$

8. $-\frac{3}{4} \ \square \ -\frac{5}{8}$

Show that each number can be written as the ratio of two integers.

9. -3.5

10. $2\frac{1}{3}$

Add.

11. $3.1 + (-4.7)$

12. $-\frac{3}{5} + \left(-\frac{4}{5}\right)$

13. $-8 + 4 + (-7) + 3$

Find the additive inverse of each.

14. $\frac{2}{3}$

15. -1.4

16. Wendy had $43 in her savings account. She withdrew $25. Then she made a deposit of $30. How much money does she have in her savings account now?

Subtract.

17. $\frac{1}{3} - \frac{2}{3}$

18. $2 - (-8)$

19. $3.2 - 5.7$

Simplify.

20. $6 + 7 - 4 - (-3)$

21. $3y + 16 - (-4y) + 7$

22. On a winter night the temperature dropped from 5°C to −7°C. How many degrees did the temperature drop?

23. Your total assets are $170. You borrow $300 to go on vacation. What is your net worth now?

Multiply.

24. $4(-12)$

25. $\left(-\frac{1}{2}\right)\left(-\frac{3}{8}\right)$

26. $5(-4)(-6)(2)$

Divide.

27. $-35 \div 7$ **28.** $\frac{-54}{-9}$ **29.** $\frac{-125}{25}$

Find the reciprocal.

30. $-\frac{8}{7}$ **31.** $-\frac{24}{7}$ **32.** $3y$

Divide.

33. $\frac{4}{9} \div \left(\frac{-7}{3}\right)$ **34.** $\frac{-15}{\frac{1}{x}}$ **35.** $\frac{-3}{5} \div \left(-\frac{5}{6}\right)$

Multiply.

36. $-7(x + 3)$ **37.** $\left(\frac{5}{3}\right)(x - 2y + z)$ **38.** $-7(-3a - 2b - 8)$

Factor.

39. $4x - 12$ **40.** $4a + 12b - 16$ **41.** $\frac{2x}{3} - \frac{y}{3}$

Collect like terms.

42. $-5x - 6x + 4x$ **43.** $q + t - 2t + q$ **44.** $4m - m + 3$

Multiply.

45. $(-1)(-21)$ **46.** $-1 \cdot 17$

Rename each additive inverse without parentheses.

47. $-(y - 8)$ **48.** $-(2a + 5b - c)$

Simplify.

49. $5n - (2n + m)$ **50.** $4x - 3(y + 2x)$
51. $50 - [12 - (16 + 5)]$ **52.** $6(9 - 4) - [10 - (6 + 8)]$

Which equation(s) can be used to solve the problem?

53. Saturnina got a 92 on the Chapter 2 test. That was 9 more points than she got on the Chapter 1 test. What was her score on the Chapter 1 test?

    (A) $n - 92 = 9$ **(B)** $n = 92 + 9$ **(C)** $n + 9 = 92$

Write an equation that can be used to solve the problem.

54. A museum took in \$3456 from 576 patrons. What was the price of admission to the museum?

55. Marta rode her bike 57 miles in two days. She rode 31 miles the first day. How far did she ride the second day?

Skills & Concepts You Need for Chapter 3

2-3 Add.

1. $-3 + (-8)$ **2.** $8 + (-3) + (-11)$ **3.** $-3.1 + 6.8$

2-4 Subtract.

4. $9 - (-13)$ **5.** $-7.2 - (-10.1)$ **6.** $\frac{2}{3} - \frac{9}{10}$

2-5 Multiply.

7. $9 \cdot (-4)$ **8.** $\frac{3}{2} \cdot \frac{-4}{7}$ **9.** $-\frac{2}{3} \cdot \frac{5}{8}$

10. $-6 \cdot 8$ **11.** $-11(-3)$ **12.** $-7(-5)$

2-6 Divide.

13. $\frac{3}{4} \div -\frac{1}{8}$ **14.** $-\frac{7}{9} \div -\frac{2}{3}$ **15.** $-9.37 \div -0.1$

2-7 Factor.

16. $9y - 45$ **17.** $bw + bx - by$

18. $3y + 15 - 21x$ **19.** $6w - 12x + 10$

2-7 Multiply.

20. $3(x - 5)$ **21.** $8(4 + w)$

2-8 Simplify.

22. $5x - (6 + 3x)$ **23.** $7w - 3 - (4w - 8)$

24. $[3(5 - 2) + 18] - [12 - (3 + 4)]$

25. $[2(4x + 7) - 3] + [5(3 + x) + 2x]$

Equations

The tallest building in Los Angeles, Library Tower, rises 565 ft higher than the venerable City Hall to stand 1017 ft tall. Use the equation $h + 565 = 1017$ to find the height h of City Hall.

3-1 ▷ The Addition Property of Equality

What You'll Learn

1 To use the addition property of equality in solving equations

2 To solve problems using an equation

...And Why

To use and solve algebraic models of the forms $x + a = b$ and $x - a = b$

Introducing the Concept: The Addition Property

The scales at the right are balanced. Suppose you have as many of each object as you want.

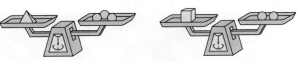

What are five different ways you can add objects to both sides of the scale below so it remains balanced?

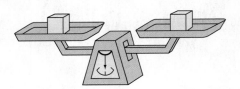

PART 1 Using the Addition Property of Equality

Objective: Use the addition property of equality to solve equations.

In Chapter 1 you learned two ways to solve equations: using mental math and the problem-solving strategy *Try, Test, Revise*. Recall that replacements that make an equation true are called solutions and that to solve an equation means to find all of its solutions.

You also learned that you can add the same number to both sides of an equation and get an equivalent equation. We call this the **addition property of equality.**

The Addition Property of Equality

For all rational numbers a, b, and c, if $a = b$, then $a + c = b + c$.

To solve an equation like $x + 5 = -7$, we need to get the variable alone on one side of the equation. In this equation, we have to add a number to 5 to "get rid of" the 5. Since -5 is the additive inverse, or the opposite of 5, $5 + (-5) = 0$. If we add -5 to both sides of the equation, we will get the variable alone. The following examples show these steps.

EXAMPLES   Solve.

1
$$x + 5 = -7$$
$$x + 5 + (-5) = -7 + (-5)$$

We must add -5, the opposite of 5.
Using the addition property to add -5 to both sides

$$x + 0 = -12$$
$$x = -12$$

Using the additive inverse property
Using the additive identity property

Check: $\dfrac{x + 5 = -7}{\begin{array}{c|c} -12 + 5 & -7 \\ -7 & -7 \checkmark \end{array}}$

Substituting -12 for x

The solution is -12.

2
$$-6 = y - 8$$
$$-6 + 8 = y - 8 + 8$$

We must add 8, the opposite of -8.
Using the addition property to add 8 to both sides of the equation

$$2 = y$$

Check: $\dfrac{-6 = y - 8}{\begin{array}{c|c} -6 & 2 - 8 \\ -6 & -6 \checkmark \end{array}}$

Substituting 2 for y

The solution is 2.

3
$$x - 5.4 = 2.3$$
$$x - 5.4 + 5.4 = 2.3 + 5.4$$

We must add 5.4, the opposite of -5.4.
Using the addition property to add 5.4 to both sides of the equation

$$x = 7.7$$

The solution is 7.7.

Substitution will show that 7.7 checks.

Try This   Solve.

a. $x + 7 = 2$ **b.** $y - 8 = -3$ **c.** $5 = -4 + a$

PART
2   **Solving Problems**

Objective: Solve problems using an equation.

PROBLEM-SOLVING GUIDELINES
■ UNDERSTAND the problem
▢ Develop and carry out a PLAN
■ Find the ANSWER and CHECK

Many problems can be solved by translating the situation into an equation (Lesson 2-9) and then solving the equation.

EXAMPLE 4

In a basketball game Paula scored 18 points. This was 4 points higher than her average. What was her average?

Let $a =$ Paula's average.

$$\underbrace{\text{Paula's average}}_{a} \;\; \overset{\text{plus}}{\underset{+}{\downarrow}} \;\; \underbrace{\text{4 points}}_{4} \;\; \overset{\text{is}}{\underset{=}{\downarrow}} \;\; \underbrace{\text{18 points.}}_{18}$$ Translating to an equation

$$a + 4 + (-4) = 18 + (-4)$$ Adding -4 to both sides
$$a + 0 = 14$$
$$a = 14$$

Paula's average was 14 points.
The answer is reasonable, since 14 is less than 18.

Try This   Translate to an equation and solve.

d. The weekly rent on an ocean-front apartment was increased by $82. The new rental cost is $675. What was the previous rent?

Extra Help On the Web

Look for worked-out examples at the Prentice Hall Web site.
www.phschool.com

3-1 Exercises

A

Solve.

1. $x + 2 = 6$ **2.** $x + 5 = 8$ **3.** $x + 15 = 26$

4. $y + 9 = 43$ **5.** $x + 6 = -8$ **6.** $t + 9 = -12$

7. $x + 16 = -2$ **8.** $y + 25 = -6$ **9.** $x - 9 = 6$

10. $x - 8 = 5$ **11.** $x - 7 = -21$ **12.** $x - 3 = -14$

13. $5 + t = 7$ **14.** $8 + y = 12$ **15.** $-7 + y = 13$

16. $-9 + z = 15$ **17.** $-3 + t = -9$ **18.** $-6 + y = -21$

19. $b - 31 = 12$ **20.** $-18 = y - 4$ **21.** $-14 = p + 6$

22. $a + 1.5 = 3$ **23.** $n - 0.6 = 4$ **24.** $x + 3.2 = 7$

25. $c + 4 = -2.5$ **26.** $x + 5.7 = 15$ **27.** $s - 10 = -3.1$

28. $r + \frac{1}{3} = \frac{8}{3}$ **29.** $t + \frac{3}{8} = \frac{5}{8}$ **30.** $m + \frac{5}{6} = -\frac{11}{12}$

31. $x + \frac{2}{3} = -\frac{5}{6}$ **32.** $x - \frac{5}{6} = \frac{7}{8}$ **33.** $y - \frac{3}{4} = \frac{5}{6}$

34. $x - \frac{3}{8} = \frac{1}{4}$ **35.** $a + \frac{4}{5} = \frac{1}{10}$ **36.** $m + \frac{2}{9} = \frac{2}{3}$

Translate to an equation and solve.

37. Six more than a number is 57. Find the number.

38. A number decreased by 18 is -53. Find the number.

39. Four less than a number is eleven. Find the number.

40. A number increased by 42 is -100. Find the number.

41. TEST PREP   If $x + 4 = -4$, then $x - 4 = ?$

  A. -12 **B.** -8 **C.** 0 **D.** 4

42. *Write a Convincing Argument*   Tell why it is not necessary to state a subtraction property of equality.

43. In Churchill, Manitoba, the average daily low temperature in January is $-35°C$. This is $55°$ less than what it is in Key West, Florida. What is the average daily low temperature in Key West in January?
Let $t =$ the average low temperature for Key West in January.

  a. Write an expression, using t, that represents the average low temperature in Churchill.

  b. What is the average low temperature in Churchill in January?

  c. What are you asked to find in this problem?

  d. Write an equation using the information you know.

  e. Solve the equation and answer the problem.

44. For many years, the tallest building in Los Angeles was City Hall. As "earthquake-proof" construction improved, however, building heights soared. In 2000, the tallest building was the 1017-ft Library Tower. It is 565 ft taller than City Hall. How tall is City Hall?
Let $h =$ the height of City Hall.

  a. Write an expression, using h, that represents the height of Library Tower.

  b. What is the height of Library Tower?

  c. What are you asked to find?

  d. Write an equation using the information you know.

  e. Simply by looking at the equation, how can you tell that the height of City Hall is less than the height of Library Tower?

  f. Solve the equation and answer the problem.

Library Tower in Los Angeles is shorter than the Sears Tower in Chicago by 437 ft. How tall is the Sears Tower?

45. In 2000 a TV magazine had a circulation of 18,870,730. That was 15,918,215 more than the circulation of a certain newspaper. What was the newspaper's circulation?
Let $c =$ circulation for the newspaper.

  a. Write an expression, using c, for the circulation of the magazine.

  b. What was the actual circulation for the TV magazine?

  c. What are you asked to find in this problem?

  d. Write an equation using the information you know.

  e. Without solving the equation, decide whether the circulation for the newspaper is more than or less than the circulation for the magazine.

  f. Solve the equation and answer the problem.

B

Solve each equation for x.

46. $8 - 25 = 8 + x - 21$ **47.** $16 + x - 22 = -16$

48. $x + 5 = x - (3 + x)$ **49.** $x + 3 = 3 + a - b$

50. $x + 7 = b + 10$ **51.** $1 - c = a + x$

Solve.

52. The end-of-month inventory indicated that there were 319 blank videocassettes in stock. This was after sales of 142 and a restocking of 75 during the month. How many videocassettes were in stock at the beginning of the month?

53. At the end of the week, Andrea found that she had $124.23 in her checking account. During the week, she had written checks for $12.24, $15.05, and $22.00, and she had deposited $55.12. How much was in her checking account at the beginning of the week?

54. *Critical Thinking*   Write an equation for which the solution $-\frac{7}{12}$ is found using addition.

Challenge

55. *Mathematical Reasoning*   If k is a solution of $x + a = b$, is $-k$ sometimes, always, or never a solution of $x + a = b$? Of $x - a = -b$? Explain.

56. Solve $x - 1 + 2x - 2 + 3x - 3 = 30 + 4x$.

57. If $x - 4720 = 1634$, find $x + 4720$.

58. Solve $x + x = x$.

59. *Mathematical Reasoning*   Solve each equation. Explain each result.

    a. $x + 3 = 3 + x$ **b.** $x - 3 = 3 + x$

60. *Error Analysis*   One student solved the equation $6 - x = 10$ by subtracting 6 from both sides and got 4. Explain what that student did wrong.

Mixed Review

Simplify.   **61.** $9y - (2y + 4)$ **62.** $7c - (8c + 2)$

63. $8w - 3(5w - 8)$ **64.** $6a + 2c - 3(2a + 3c)$

65. $3[5 + 4(3 - y)]$ **66.** $5t - (3 + 9t)$ *2-8*

Evaluate.   **67.** $(5a)^2$ for $a = 2$ **68.** $5a^2$ for $a = 2$ **69.** s^1 for $s = 32$ *1-3*

Multiply.   **70.** $3(-5)$ **71.** $\left(-\frac{1}{3}\right)\left(-\frac{3}{5}\right)$ **72.** $4(-2)(-1)(-3)$ *2-5*

Divide.   **73.** $-4 \div 2$ **74.** $\frac{2}{7} \div \left(-\frac{3}{8}\right)$ **75.** $-\frac{14}{15} \div \frac{5}{7}$ *2-6*

76. Mario spent half of his weekly allowance to buy a book. The book cost $5.75. Write an equation to find Mario's allowance.   *2-9*

The Multiplication Property of Equality

Math in Action

The California condor can be reclassified from "endangered" to "threatened" if its numbers reach about 459 (and other conditions apply). This would be 17 times as many as were alive in 1987 when all living condors were captured in an effort to save them from extinction. How many condors were there in 1987?

In this lesson you will learn how to solve equations like $17c = 459$. This equation can be used to find how many condors there were in captivity in 1987.

The number of endangered California condors grew to 161 by 1999. This is about 6.7 times the number counted in 1982. How many condors were counted in 1982?

What You'll Learn

1 To use the multiplication property of equality in solving equations

2 To solve problems using an equation

. . . And Why

To use and solve algebraic models of the forms
$ax = b$ and $\frac{a}{b}x = c$

PART 1 Using the Multiplication Property of Equality

Objective: Use the multiplication property to solve equations.

Equations such as $17c = 459$ can be solved using the **multiplication property of equality.**

The Multiplication Property of Equality

For all rational numbers a, b, and c, if $a = b$, then $ac = bc$.

When using the multiplication property of equality, we can say that "we multiply both sides of the equation by the same number."

To solve an equation like $17c = 459$, we need to get the variable alone on one side of the equal sign. Here we have to multiply $17c$ by some number to "get rid of" the 17. Since $\frac{1}{17}$ is the multiplicative inverse or reciprocal of 17, $\frac{1}{17} \cdot 17 = 1$. Therefore, if we multiply both sides of the equation by $\frac{1}{17}$, we will get the variable alone. The following example shows these steps.

EXAMPLE 1   Solve.

$$17c = 459$$ We must multiply by $\frac{1}{17}$, the reciprocal of 17.

$$\frac{1}{17} \cdot 17c = \frac{1}{17} \cdot 459$$ Using the multiplication property to multiply both sides of the equation by $\frac{1}{17}$

$$1 \cdot c = 27$$ Using the multiplicative inverse property

$$c = 27$$ Using the multiplicative identity property

Check:

$$\begin{array}{c|c} \multicolumn{2}{c}{17c = 459} \\ \hline 17 \cdot 27 & 459 \\ 459 & 459 \checkmark \end{array}$$ Substituting 27 for c

The solution is 27.

EXAMPLE 2   Solve.

$$-x = 9$$

$$-1(-x) = -1(9)$$ Using the multiplication property to multiply both sides by -1

$$-(-x) = -9$$ Using the property of -1, $-1 \cdot a = -a$

$$x = -9$$ The inverse of the inverse of a number is the number itself.

Check:

$$\begin{array}{c|c} \multicolumn{2}{c}{-x = 9} \\ \hline -(-9) & 9 \\ 9 & 9 \checkmark \end{array}$$ Substituting -9 for x

The solution is -9.

EXAMPLE 3   Solve.

$$\frac{3}{8} = -\frac{5}{4}x$$

$$-\frac{4}{5} \cdot \frac{3}{8} = -\frac{4}{5}\left(-\frac{5}{4}x\right)$$ Using the multiplication property to multiply both sides by $-\frac{4}{5}$, the reciprocal of $-\frac{5}{4}$

$$-\frac{3}{10} = x$$

Check:

$$\begin{array}{c|c} \multicolumn{2}{c}{\frac{3}{8} = -\frac{5}{4}x} \\ \hline \frac{3}{8} & -\frac{5}{4}\left(-\frac{3}{10}\right) \\ \frac{3}{8} & \frac{3}{8} \checkmark \end{array}$$ Substituting $-\frac{3}{10}$ for x

The solution is $-\frac{3}{10}$.

Try This   Solve.

a. $5x = 25$ **b.** $4a = -7$ **c.** $-3y = -42$

d. $-\frac{1}{3}y = 4$ **e.** $\frac{5}{6} = -\frac{2}{3}x$ **f.** $-x = 6$

An equation like $\frac{y}{9} = 14$ can also be solved using the multiplication property. In Chapter 2 you learned that $\frac{y}{9}$ can be written

$$\frac{y}{9} = \frac{1}{9} \cdot y$$

We know that the multiplicative inverse of $\frac{1}{9}$ is 9, since $\frac{1}{9} \cdot 9 = 1$. Example 4 shows how to use this relationship to solve the equation $\frac{y}{9} = 14$.

EXAMPLE 4 Solve.

$$\frac{y}{9} = 14$$

$$9 \cdot \frac{y}{9} = 9 \cdot 14$$

$$y = 126$$

Check:
$$\frac{y}{9} = 14$$

$\frac{126}{9}$	14
14	14 ✔

The solution is 126.

Try This Solve.

g. $\frac{x}{5} = 10$ **h.** $\frac{m}{-3} = -12$ **i.** $\frac{-t}{4} = 6$

PART 2 Solving Problems

Objective: Solve problems using an equation.

PROBLEM-SOLVING GUIDELINES
■ UNDERSTAND the problem
▢ Develop and carry out a PLAN
■ Find the ANSWER and CHECK

After translating a problem to an equation, we may need to use the multiplication property to solve the equation.

EXAMPLE 5 Solve.

In 1990, the population of Napa, California, was about 61,800. That was about one sixth the population of Sacramento, the California state capital. What was the approximate population of Sacramento?

Let s = population of Sacramento.

$\frac{1}{6}s$ = population of Napa   The population of Napa, about $\frac{1}{6}$ the size of Sacramento's, can be written as $\frac{1}{6}s$.

We can write the following equation.

$$\frac{1}{6}s = 61{,}800$$ $\frac{1}{6}s$ and 61,800 both represent the approximate population of Napa.

$$6 \cdot \frac{1}{6}s = 6 \cdot 61{,}800$$ Using the multiplication property

$$s = 370{,}800$$

There were about 370,800 people in Sacramento in 1990. If we estimate using 360,000 rather than 370,800, we get $\frac{1}{6} \cdot 360,000 = 60,000$, which is close to 61,800. Therefore, the number 370,800 seems reasonable.

Try This   Solve.

j. Penny bought a 12-bottle case of juice on sale for $6.72. What was the price for each bottle?

Extra Help On the Web
Look for worked-out examples at the Prentice Hall Web site.
www.phschool.com

3-2 Exercises

A

Solve.

1. $6x = 36$	**2.** $3x = 39$	**3.** $5x = 45$
4. $9x = 72$	**5.** $84 = 7x$	**6.** $56 = 8x$
7. $-x = 40$	**8.** $100 = -x$	**9.** $-x = -1$
10. $-68 = -r$	**11.** $7x = -49$	**12.** $9x = -36$
13. $-12x = 72$	**14.** $-15x = 105$	**15.** $-21x = -126$
16. $-13x = -104$	**17.** $\frac{t}{7} = -9$	**18.** $\frac{y}{-8} = 11$
19. $\frac{3}{4}x = 27$	**20.** $\frac{4}{5}x = 16$	**21.** $\frac{-t}{3} = 7$
22. $\frac{-x}{6} = 9$	**23.** $-\frac{m}{3} = \frac{1}{5}$	**24.** $\frac{1}{9} = -\frac{z}{7}$
25. $-\frac{3}{5}r = -\frac{9}{10}$	**26.** $-\frac{2}{5}y = -\frac{4}{15}$	**27.** $-\frac{3}{2}r = -\frac{27}{4}$
28. $\frac{5}{7}x = -\frac{10}{14}$	**29.** $6.3x = 44.1$	**30.** $2.7y = 54$
31. $-3.1y = 21.7$	**32.** $-3.3y = 6.6$	**33.** $38.7m = 309.6$

Translate to an equation and solve.

34. Eighteen times a number is -1008. Find the number.

35. Some number multiplied by negative eight is 744. Find the number.

36. *Critical Thinking*   If a, b, and c are rational numbers such that $a = b$ and $c = 0$, does $ac = bc$? Explain.

37. Katha paid the same price for each of 8 tickets to a concert. If she paid a total of $170, what was the price of each ticket?
Let p = price of each ticket.
a. Write an expression using p that represents the price of all 8 tickets.
b. What did Katha pay for all 8 tickets?
c. What are you asked to find in this problem?
d. Write an equation using the information you know.
e. Without solving the equation, decide whether the price of each ticket is more than or less than $30. How do you know?
f. Solve the equation and answer the problem.

38. Deployment of the Chandra X-ray Observatory, named in honor of the Indian-American scientist Subrahmanyan Chandrasekhar, was the main objective of the 26th mission of the shuttle *Columbia*. When main engine cut-off occurred at about 8 min after launch, the *Columbia* was traveling about 16,700 mi/h. This is about 5.8 times its speed at about 2 min when it jettisoned its huge solid rocket boosters. What was *Columbia's* speed 2 min into flight?

Let s = speed at 2 min.

The 1999 *Columbia* space-shuttle mission commanded by Eileen Collins was launched just after midnight in Florida. The *Columbia* landed in Florida after averaging about 15,100 miles each hour for 1,796,000 miles. Did it land in the daylight or the dark?

   a. Write an expression, using s, that represents the speed at 8 min.

   b. What was the speed at 8 min?

   c. What are you asked to find in this problem?

   d. Write an equation using the information you know.

   e. Without solving the equation, estimate the speed at 2 min.

   f. Solve the equation and answer the problem.

39. In 1990 the population of Las Vegas, the largest city in Nevada, was 258,295. That was about 42 times the population of Winnemucca, Nevada's tenth largest city. What was the population of Winnemucca?

Let $w =$ the population of Winnemucca, Nevada.

   a. Write an expression, using w, for the population of Las Vegas in 1990.

   b. What was the population of Las Vegas in 1990?

   c. What are you asked to find in this problem?

   d. Write an equation using the information you know.

   e. Without solving the equation, estimate the population of Winnemucca, Nevada, in 1990.

   f. Solve the equation and answer the problem.

40. A case of a dozen videocassette tapes costs $23.40. Find the cost of a single tape.

41. A wildlife expert estimates that in a certain year the number of male fawns born will be about $\frac{1}{3}$ the number of adult female deer. Suppose 1131 male fawns are born. About how many female deer are there?

42. *Write a Convincing Argument*   Tell why it is not necessary to state a division property of equality.

43. The 1996 population of San Diego, California, was estimated to be about 1,170,000. This was about $\frac{3}{7}$ of the estimate for Chicago. What was the approximate population of Chicago?

B

44. *Multi-Step Problem*   Joe Montana and John Elway were pro football quarterbacks. Montana completed 3409 passes in his career. This is about $\frac{7}{11}$ of the passes he threw. It is also about $\frac{3}{4}$ the number that Elway completed. Elway completed about $\frac{4}{7}$ of the passes he threw. Who threw more passes? About how many more?

Mathematical Reasoning   Use the first equation to find the missing value in the second equation. Justify your result.

45. $6a + 6b = 72$

$\quad a + b = ??$

46. $\frac{x}{3} + 2 = 12$

$\quad x + 6 = ??$

47. $\frac{2m}{5} - 2 = 12$

$\quad 2m - 10 = ??$

48. $\frac{2a^2}{3} + 1 = 8$

$\quad 2a^2 + 3 = ??$

Solve each equation for x.

49. $ax = 5a \ (a \neq 0)$

50. $3x = \frac{b}{a} \ (a \neq 0)$

51. $cx = a^2 + 1 \ (c \neq 0)$

52. $abx = 1 \ (ab \neq 0)$

53. *Critical Thinking*   Write two different equations that each have the solution 2 and could be solved using the multiplication property.

Challenge

54. *Mathematical Reasoning*   Solve each equation. Explain each result.

    a. $0 \cdot x = 0$ **b.** $0 \cdot x = 9$

55. Explain or give a counterexample. a and b are integers.

    a. If $a = b$, does $a^2 = b^2$?   **b.** If $a^2 = b^2$, does $a = b$?

Mixed Review

Simplify.   **56.** $8x + 4y - (4x - 5y)$ **57.** $3 - (4a + 7)$

58. $7r - (s + 2r) - 4s$ **59.** $(2a + 4b) - (2a + 4b)$ *2-8*

Multiply.   **60.** $-5 \cdot 8 \cdot 2$ **61.** $(-7) \cdot (-24) \cdot 0$ **62.** $(-2.1)(-1.2)$

63. $(-3)(-7)(-2)$ **64.** $(-4)(-2.2)(-5)$ **65.** $(-2)(-3.1)3$ *2-5*

Evaluate.   **66.** $t^4 + 1$ for $t = 2$ **67.** $8y^3$ for $y = 3$

68. $3|x|$ for $x = -8$ **69.** $y^2 + 2y$ for $y = -3$

70. $4z + |z|$ for $z = -1$ *1-3, 2-1*

Factor.   **71.** $4x + 8y - 12z$ **72.** $6a - 12b - 9c$ *2-7*

Using the Properties Together

PART
1 **Applying Both Properties**

Objective: Solve equations using the addition and multiplication properties.

To solve some equations, you may need to use both the addition property and the multiplication property.

EXAMPLE 1 Solve.

$$3x + 4 = 13$$
$$3x + 4 + (-4) = 13 + (-4)$$ Using the addition property to add -4 to both sides

$$3x = 9$$
$$\tfrac{1}{3} \cdot 3x = \tfrac{1}{3} \cdot 9$$ Using the multiplication property to multiply both sides by $\tfrac{1}{3}$

$$x = 3$$

Check:

$3x + 4 = 13$	
$3(3) + 4$	13
$9 + 4$	13
13	13 ✔

The solution is 3.

EXAMPLE 2 Solve.

$$-5x + 6 = 16$$
$$-5x + 6 + (-6) = 16 + (-6)$$ Using the addition property to add -6 to both sides

$$-5x = 10$$
$$-\tfrac{1}{5} \cdot (-5x) = -\tfrac{1}{5} \cdot 10$$ Using the multiplication property to multiply both sides by $-\tfrac{1}{5}$

$$x = -2$$

Check:

$-5x + 6 = 16$	
$-5(-2) + 6$	16
$10 + 6$	16
16	16 ✔

The solution is -2.

What You'll Learn

1 To solve equations by using the addition and multiplication properties

2 To solve equations by first collecting like terms

3 To solve equations containing parentheses

...And Why

To use and solve algebraic models in various forms

Try This Solve.

a. $9x + 6 = 51$ **b.** $-8y - 4 = 28$
c. $-18 - 3x = -57$ **d.** $4 - 8x = 12$

PART 2 Collecting Like Terms in Equations

Objective: Solve equations by first collecting like terms.

If there are like terms on one side of an equation, we collect them before using the properties.

EXAMPLE 3 Solve.

$$6x + 2x = 15$$
$$8x = 15 \qquad \text{Collecting like terms}$$
$$\tfrac{1}{8} \cdot 8x = \tfrac{1}{8} \cdot 15 \qquad \text{Multiplying both sides by } \tfrac{1}{8}$$
$$x = \tfrac{15}{8}$$

Substitution will show that $\tfrac{15}{8}$ checks.
The solution is $\tfrac{15}{8}$.

Try This Solve.

e. $4c + 3c = 21$ **f.** $9x - 4x = 20$

PART 3 Equations Containing Parentheses

Objective: Solve equations containing parentheses.

Equations containing parentheses can often be solved by first using the distributive property.

EXAMPLE 4 Solve.

$$2(2y + 3) = 14$$
$$4y + 6 = 14 \qquad \text{Using the distributive property}$$
$$4y + 6 + (-6) = 14 + (-6) \qquad \text{Using the addition property}$$
$$4y = 8$$
$$\tfrac{1}{4} \cdot 4y = \tfrac{1}{4} \cdot 8 \qquad \text{Using the multiplication property}$$
$$1 \cdot y = 2$$
$$y = 2$$

Substitution will show that 2 checks.

The solution is 2.

Solve.

$$4(3x - 2) + 12x = 40$$
$$12x - 8 + 12x = 40 \qquad \text{Using the distributive property}$$
$$24x - 8 = 40 \qquad \text{Collecting like terms}$$
$$24x - 8 + 8 = 40 + 8 \qquad \text{Using the addition property}$$
$$24x = 48$$
$$\tfrac{1}{24} \cdot 24x = \tfrac{1}{24} \cdot 48 \qquad \text{Using the multiplication property}$$
$$1 \cdot x = 2$$
$$x = 2$$

Substitution will show that 2 checks.
The solution is 2.

Try This   Solve.

g. $9 = 3(x + 6)$ **h.** $24 - 2(2m + 1) = -6$
i. $3a + 5(a - 2) = 6$

3-3 Exercises

Extra Help On the Web

Look for worked-out examples at the Prentice Hall Web site.
   www.phschool.com

A
Solve.

1. $5x + 6 = 31$

2. $3x + 6 = 30$

3. $8x + 4 = 68$

4. $7z + 9 = 72$

5. $4x - 6 = 34$

6. $6x - 3 = 15$

7. $3x - 9 = 33$

8. $5x - 7 = 48$

9. $7x + 2 = -54$

10. $5x + 4 = -41$

11. $-4x + 7 = 35$

12. $-5x - 7 = 108$

13. $-7x - 24 = -129$

14. $-6z - 18 = -132$

Solve.

15. $5x + 7x = 72$

16. $4x + 5x = 45$

17. $4x + 3x = 42$

18. $6x + 19x = 100$

19. $4y - 2y = 10$

20. $8y - 5y = 48$

21. $-6y - 3y = 27$

22. $-4y - 8y = 48$

23. $-7y - 8y = -15$

24. $-10y - 3y = -39$

25. $10.2y - 7.3y = -58$

26. $6.8y - 2.4y = -88$

27. *Critical Thinking*   Solve $4x - 8 = 32$ by using the multiplication property first. Then solve it using the addition property first. Are the results the same?

Solve.

28. $5(3x - 2) = 35$

29. $3(2y - 3) = 27$

30. $-2(4y - 3) = 6$

31. $(4 + 3x)(-3) = -9$

Solve.

32. $2(3 + 4m) - 9 = 45$

33. $3(5 + 3m) - 8 = 88$

34. $12 - 3(x - 5) = 21$

35. $5 - 2(y + 1) = 21$

36. $5r - 2(2r + 8) = 16$

37. $6b - 4(2b + 8) = 16$

38. $2(2x - 4) + 3x = -1$

39. $-5a + 4(2 + 2a) = -1$

40. $\frac{1}{3}x + 2\left(\frac{1}{3}x + 5\right) = 12$

41. $3\left(\frac{1}{8}m - \frac{1}{2}\right) + \frac{3}{4}m = \frac{3}{2}$

42. When Erica learned that her company matches employee gifts to schools, she added $15 to her gift. This made the value of her gift $90. How much did Erica originally intend to give?

B

Mathematical Reasoning   Provide a reason to justify each step.

43. $6(2x - 8) = 36$

  a. $12x - 48 = 36$ _____

  b. $12x - 48 + 48 = 36 + 48$ _____

  c. $12x = 84$ _____

  d. $\frac{1}{12} \cdot 12x = \frac{1}{12} \cdot 84$ _____

  e. $x = 7$ _____

44. $6(2x - 8) = 36$

  a. $\frac{1}{6} \cdot 6(2x - 8) = \frac{1}{6} \cdot 36$ _____

  b. $2x - 8 = 6$ _____

  c. $2x - 8 + 8 = 6 + 8$ _____

  d. $2x = 14$ _____

  e. $\frac{1}{2} \cdot 2x = \frac{1}{2} \cdot 14$ _____

  f. $x = 7$ _____

45. $7y + (8 + 3y) = 38$

  a. $7y + (3y + 8) = 38$ _____

  b. $(7y + 3y) + 8 = 38$ _____

  c. $10y + 8 = 38$ _____

  d. $10y + 8 - 8 = 38 - 8$ _____

  e. $10y = 30$ _____

  f. $\frac{1}{10} \cdot 10y = \frac{1}{10} \cdot 30$ _____

  g. $y = 3$ _____

46. $9m - 2(2m + 6) = 28$

  a. $9m - 4m - 12 = 28$ _____

  b. $5m - 12 = 28$ _____

  c. $5m - 12 + 12 = 28 + 12$ _____

  d. $5m = 40$ _____

  e. $\frac{1}{5} \cdot 5m = \frac{1}{5} \cdot 40$ _____

  f. $m = 8$ _____

Solve.

47. $(0.26 + y) + 3y = 0.98$ **48.** $0 = y - (-14) - (-3y)$

49. $12 - (-5m) + 3m + 12 = 0$ **50.** $4a + 5a - 2(2a) + 35 = 0$

51. $4(a - 2) + 3(2a + 1) = 5$ **52.** $2(3x + 5) + 3(2x + 5) = 1$

53. Rafael spent $2011 to operate his car last year. He drove 12,500 miles. He paid $972 for insurance and $114 for the registration fee. Rafael's only other expense was for gas. How much did the gas cost per mile?

Challenge

Solve the first equation for x. Substitute your result into the second equation. Then solve for y. Check your work.

54. $9x - 5 = 22$

$4x + 2y = 2$

55. $9x + 2 = -1$

$4x - y = \frac{11}{3}$

56. *Error Analysis*   The "Check" suggests an error was made. Explain.

Solve:

$$1.2x + 7.7 = 2.9$$
$$1.2x + 7.7 + (-7.7) = 2.9 + (-7.7)$$
$$1.2x = -4.8$$
$$\frac{1}{1.2} \cdot 1.2x = \frac{1}{1.2} \cdot -4.8$$
$$x = -4$$

Check:

$1.2x + 7.7 = 2.9$	
$1.2x + 7.7$	2.9
$1.2(-4) + 7.7$	2.9
$-4.8 + 7.7$	2.9
$3.9 \neq 2.9$	

Mixed Review

Use $>$ or $<$ to write a true sentence.   **57.** $-5.2 \ \square \ 4$ **58.** $-2.3 \ \square \ 2.2$

59. $\frac{2}{3} \ \square \ \frac{3}{5}$ **60.** $\frac{1}{5} \ \square \ -\frac{3}{5}$ **61.** $-6.7 \ \square \ -3.9$ *2-2*

Divide.   **62.** $\frac{5}{12} \div \frac{3}{4}$ **63.** $-\frac{2}{5} \div -\frac{5}{6}$ **64.** $\frac{2}{9} \div -\frac{1}{2}$ *2-6*

Solve.   **65.** $x + 10 = 25$ **66.** $t - 84 = 72$ **67.** $5y = 30$ *3-1, 3-2*

Factor.   **68.** $4t + 4n - 12m$ **69.** $3a - 3c - 3d$ **70.** $4c - 12d$ *2-7*

Multiply.   **71.** $4(3x - 4y)$ **72.** $3(2q - r - 4)$ *2-7*

◈ Connections: Geometry

Find the length of each side, given the perimeter.

1. a square with perimeter 64 ft

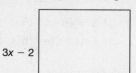
$3x - 2$

2. a rectangle with perimeter 36 in.

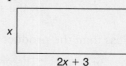
x

$2x + 3$

3-4 ▷ Expressions and Equations

What You'll Learn

1 To translate phrases to algebraic expressions

2 To solve problems by writing and solving equations

...And Why

To apply algebraic models to real-life situations

Math in Action

The distance from Exit 18 to Exit 19 on the interstate highway is 18 miles. The first 3 miles have been paved. The same number of miles will be paved each day. How many miles should be paved each day to complete this section of highway in the next 10 days?

In this lesson you will learn techniques for solving problems similar to the one above.

After paving 10 ft, this paver needed 12 loads of concrete to finish a 100-ft section. How much roadway did the paver complete for each load of concrete?

Quick *Review*

To review how to translate simple phrases to algebraic expressions, see Lesson 1-6.

Reading Math

The phrase *the quantity* suggests a grouping of the terms that follow. A pause after reading "the quantity" will help you understand the grouping.

The words *sum, difference, product,* and *quotient* also suggest a grouping of the terms that follow.

PART 1 ▽ Phrases to Algebraic Expressions

Objective: Translate phrases to algebraic expressions.

In Chapters 1 and 2 you translated simple phrases like "5 less than a number" to algebraic expressions. In this lesson you will translate more difficult phrases to algebraic expressions.

EXAMPLES Write as an algebraic expression.

1 5 times the quantity 3 less than a number

$5(n - 3)$ "The quantity 3 less than a number" translates to $(n - 3)$, and "5 times the quantity . . . " translates to $5(n - 3)$.

2 $\frac{1}{2}$ the sum of a number and 4

$\frac{1}{2}(n + 4)$ "The sum of a number and 4" translates to $(n + 4)$, and "$\frac{1}{2}$ the sum . . . " translates to $\frac{1}{2}(n + 4)$.

3 14 less than the product of 3 and a number

$3n - 14$ "The product of 3 and a number" translates to $3n$, and "14 less than . . . " translates to $3n - 14$.

Try This   Write as an algebraic expression.

a. 3 less than twice a number

b. $\frac{1}{2}$ the difference of a number and 1

c. 4 times the quantity 3 greater than a number

d. 2 fewer than the product of 10 and a number

EXAMPLE 4

Jason's weekly salary is $35 less than twice David's weekly salary. Let D = David's weekly salary in dollars. Write an expression, using D, for Jason's weekly salary.

David's weekly salary = D

Jason's weekly salary = $2D - 35$ "Twice David's weekly salary" translates to $2D$, and "$35 less than . . . " translates to $2D - 35$.

Try This

e. This year Todd sold five fewer houses than twice as many as he sold last year. Let n = the number he sold last year. Write an expression for the number of houses that Todd sold this year.

f. Ellen Ikeda scored two points more than half the number scored by the whole team. Let t = the number of points scored by the whole team. Write an expression for the number of points Ellen scored.

PART 2   Using Equations to Solve Problems

Objective: Solve problems by writing and solving equations.

You can use the Problem-Solving Guidelines below to help you solve problems when your plan involves writing and solving an equation.

PROBLEM-SOLVING GUIDELINES

■ **Phase 1: UNDERSTAND the problem**

What am I trying to find?
What data am I given?
Have I ever solved a similar problem?

■ **Phase 2: Develop and carry out a PLAN**

What strategies might I use to solve the problem?
How can I correctly carry out the strategies I select?

■ **Phase 3: Find the ANSWER and CHECK**

Does the proposed solution check?
What is the answer to the problem?
Does the answer seem reasonable?
Have I stated the answer clearly?

EXAMPLE 5

The number of girls in the band is 6 more than twice the number of boys. There are 88 girls in the band. How many boys are in the band?

■ **UNDERSTAND the problem**

Question: How many boys are in the band?

Data: The number of girls is 6 more than twice the number of boys; 88 girls are in the band.

Clarifying the question and identifying the data given in the problem

■ **Develop and carry out a PLAN**

Let b = the number of boys in the band.
$2b + 6$ = the number of girls in the band

Choosing a variable

The number of girls is given in terms of the number of boys.

$$2b + 6 = 88$$
$$2b + 6 + (-6) = 88 + (-6)$$
$$2b = 82$$
$$\tfrac{1}{2} \cdot 2b = \tfrac{1}{2} \cdot 82$$
$$1 \cdot b = 41$$
$$b = 41$$

The number of girls is also 88.
Using the addition property

Using the multiplication property

■ **Find the ANSWER and CHECK**

There are 41 boys in the band. If there were 40 boys in the band, $2 \cdot 40 + 6 = 86$, so 41 is a reasonable answer.

Estimating to check whether the answer is reasonable

EXAMPLE 6

Kara has driven 75 miles. She averages 55 mi/h. How many more hours must Kara drive to travel a total of 350 mi?

■ **UNDERSTAND the problem**

Question: How many additional hours must Kara drive?
Data: She averages 55 mi/h; she has already traveled 75 mi; she wants to travel a total of 350 mi.

■ **Develop and carry out a PLAN**

Let h = the number of additional hours she must drive.
$55h$ = the additional distance she must travel

Drawing a diagram can often help you understand a problem.

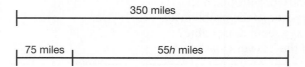

$55h + 75 =$ the total distance for the trip

Since $55h + 75$ represents the total distance for the trip, and we know that the total distance is 350 miles, we have the equation

$$55h + 75 = 350$$

We can solve this equation.

$$55h + 75 = 350$$
$$55h + 75 + (-75) = 350 + (-75)$$
$$55h = 275$$
$$\frac{1}{55} \cdot 55h = \frac{1}{55} \cdot 275$$
$$h = 5$$

■ **Find the ANSWER and CHECK**

Kara must drive for 5 more hours.
$5 \cdot 55 = 275$ miles. This plus 75 miles gives the total of 350 miles. The answer checks.

Try This   Solve.

g. When Jill sells 2 more buckets, she will have sold 3 times as many buckets as Jack sold. Jill has sold 19 buckets. How many buckets has Jack sold?

h. An 18-mile section of highway is being paved. The first 3 miles are done. The same number of miles will be paved each day. How many miles should be paved each day to complete this section in the next 10 days?

3-4 Exercises

Extra Help On the Web

Look for worked-out examples at the Prentice Hall Web site.
www.phschool.com

A

Write as an algebraic expression.

1. 3 less than the product of 5 and a number

2. 5 more than twice a number

3. 18 fewer than half a number

4. 12 more than half a number

5. 3 less than the quotient of a number and 5

6. 3 more than the quotient of a number and 2

7. 4 times the quantity 1 less than a number

8. 2 times the quantity 4 greater than a number

9. $\frac{1}{2}$ the sum of a number and 6

10. $\frac{3}{4}$ the difference of a number and 3

11. 4 less than a third of a number

12. 7 greater than half a number

13. Today Harvey ran 2 km more than twice as far as he ran yesterday. Let y = the number of kilometers he ran yesterday. Write an expression for the number of kilometers he ran today.

14. Darrell sold 3 fewer subscriptions than 4 times the number Brenda sold. Let B = the number Brenda sold. Write an expression for the number Darrell sold.

15. Lyle still has $2 more than half of his allowance. Let a = the amount of his allowance. Write an expression for the amount he has.

16. Last year Chu found 3 more customers than Ralph found. This year Chu found 2 times as many customers as he found last year. Let r = the number of customers Ralph found last year. Write an expression for the number of customers Chu found this year.

17. **Critical Thinking**   Large drinks cost 15¢ more than small drinks.
   a. Let s = the cost of a small drink. Write an expression for the cost of the large drink.
   b. Let L = the cost of a large drink. Write an expression for the cost of a small drink.

18. **Critical Thinking**   The cost of a small television set is $25 more than half the cost of a large TV.
   a. Let C = the cost of a large television set. Write an expression for the cost of the small television.
   b. Let c = the cost of a small television set. Write an expression for the cost of the large television.

19. Elena has ridden 20 mi on her bike so far. She travels at an average rate of 10 mi/h. How many more hours will she have to ride to go a total of 55 mi?

   Let h = number of additional hours of travel needed.

   $10h$ = distance traveled in h hours

   a. Draw a diagram that shows this situation.
   b. Write an expression using h that represents 55 miles.
   c. What are you asked to find in this problem?
   d. Write an equation using the information you know.
   e. Solve the equation and answer the problem.

20. One hundred twenty-two vans were supposed to be shipped by railroad, but 2 vans could not fit on the railroad cars. There were 8 railroad cars, each holding the same number of vans. How many vans were on each car?

   Let v = the number of vans on each railroad car.

   a. What does the expression $8v$ represent?
   b. Write an expression using v that represents the 122 vans.
   c. Write an equation using the information you know.
   d. Solve the equation and answer the problem.

21. **TEST PREP**   Let c = the number of cows in a herd. Then $2(c + 4)$ represents which quantity?

A. 4 more than twice the number of cows in the herd

B. twice the number of cows in a herd that has 4 more cows

C. the number of cows in a herd that has 6 more cows

D. the number of cows in a herd that has 8 more cows

B

22. The number of boys in the tennis club is 10 more than half the number of girls. There are 30 boys in the tennis club. Altogether, how many boys and girls are in the club?

23. A salesman rented a car that got 35 miles per gallon. He paid $19.50 a day for the car plus $0.26 per mile. He rented the car for 1 day and paid $39. How many miles did he travel?

24. Bowling at Sunset Lanes cost Danny and Zorina $9. This included shoe rental of $0.75 a pair. How much did each game cost if Danny bowled 3 games and Zorina bowled 2 games?

25. Popcorn costs $0.75 a box. Carl and Diane each bought 1 box of popcorn at the ball game. Carl bought 3 cans of juice and Diane bought 2 cans of juice during the game. Each can cost the same. They spent a total of $5.25. What did they pay for each can of juice?

26. *Critical Thinking*   If you add 2 to a certain number, multiply the result by 3, subtract 1 from the product, and divide the difference by 2, you get 10. Find the number.

Challenge

27. Ronald can do a job alone in 3 days. His assistant can do the same job alone in 6 days. How long would it take Ronald and his assistant to do the same job together? (Hint: Determine what part of the job each can do in one day.)

28. One cashier works at a rate of 3 minutes per customer and a second cashier works at a rate of 2 customers per minute. How many customers can they serve in 1 hour?

29. Ruth has some money in a savings account. After the bank adds 5% interest to her account, she has $126. How much was in her account before the interest was added?

Mixed Review

Solve. **30.** $3x + 2x = 15$ **31.** $-\frac{1}{2}x + 3 = 1$ **32.** $3(4y - 2) = 18$ *3-3*

Write using exponential notation.   **33.** $4 \cdot n \cdot n \cdot m \cdot 3 \cdot m \cdot n$

34. $y \cdot y \cdot y \cdot x$ **35.** $5 \cdot t \cdot 3 \cdot t \cdot 2 \cdot t$ **36.** $2 \cdot 6 \cdot r \cdot r$ *1-3*

Solve.   **37.** $\frac{w}{-5} = -4$ **38.** $\frac{1}{2} = -\frac{1}{8}c$ **39.** $\frac{5}{7} = \frac{2}{3}x$ **40.** $\frac{4}{9}y = 2$ *3-2*

3-5 ▷ More on Solving Equations

What You'll Learn

1 To solve equations by first getting all variables on the same side of the equation

2 To solve equations that contain parentheses

...And Why

To use and solve algebraic models in various forms

Objective: Solve equations by first getting all variables on the same side of the equation.

If there are variable terms on opposite sides of an equation, we can get them on the same side by using the addition property. Then we collect like terms.

EXAMPLE 1 Solve.

$$2x - 2 = -3x + 3$$
$$2x + 3x - 2 = -3x + 3x + 3$$ Using the addition property; adding $3x$ to both sides

$$5x - 2 = 3$$ Collecting like terms and simplifying

$$5x - 2 + 2 = 3 + 2$$ Using the addition property
$$5x = 5$$
$$\tfrac{1}{5} \cdot 5x = \tfrac{1}{5} \cdot 5$$ Using the multiplication property
$$x = 1$$

Substitution will show that 1 checks.
The solution is 1.

If there are like variable terms on the same side of the equation, they should be collected first.

EXAMPLE 2 Solve.

$$6m + 5 - 7m = 10 - 5m + 3$$
$$-m + 5 = 13 - 5m$$ Collecting like terms
$$-m + m + 5 = 13 - 5m + m$$ Using the addition property; adding m to both sides

$$5 = 13 - 4m$$ Collecting like terms and simplifying

$$-13 + 5 = -13 + 13 - 4m$$ Using the addition property
$$-8 = -4m$$

$$-\tfrac{1}{4}(-8) = -\tfrac{1}{4}(-4m)$$ Using the multiplication property
$$2 = m$$

Substitution will show that 2 checks.
The solution is 2.

Try This   Solve.

a. $7y + 5 = 2y + 10$

b. $5 - 2p = 3p - 5$

c. $7x - 17 + 2x = 2 - 8x + 15$

d. $3n - 15 = 5n + 3 - 4n$

PART 2 Equations Containing Parentheses

Objective: Solve equations that contain parentheses.

Some equations containing parentheses can be solved by first using the distributive property.

EXAMPLE 3   Solve.

$$
\begin{aligned}
3(n - 2) - 1 &= 2 - 5(n + 5) \\
3n - 6 - 1 &= 2 - 5n - 25 \qquad &\text{Using the distributive property} \\
3n - 7 &= -5n - 23 \qquad &\text{Simplifying} \\
3n + 5n - 7 &= -5n + 5n - 23 \qquad &\text{Using the addition property} \\
8n - 7 &= -23 \\
8n - 7 + 7 &= -23 + 7 \qquad &\text{Using the addition property} \\
8n &= -16 \\
\tfrac{1}{8} \cdot 8n &= \tfrac{1}{8} \cdot -16 \qquad &\text{Using the multiplication property} \\
n &= -2
\end{aligned}
$$

Substitution will show that -2 checks. The solution is -2.

Try This   Solve.

e. $3(7 + 2x) = 30 + 7(x - 1)$

f. $4(3 + 5y) - 4 = 3 + 2(y - 2)$

3-5 Exercises

Extra Help On the Web

Look for worked-out examples at the Prentice Hall Web site.
www.phschool.com

A

Solve.

1. $4x - 7 = 3x$

2. $9x - 6 = 3x$

3. $8x - 1 = 23 - 4x$

4. $5y - 2 = 28 - y$

5. $2x - 1 = 4 + x$

6. $5x - 2 = 6 + x$

7. $6x + 3 = 2x + 11$

8. $5y + 3 = 2y + 15$

9. $5 - 2x = 3x - 7x + 25$

10. $10 - 3x = 2x - 8x + 40$

11. $4 + 3x - 6 = 3x + 2 - x$

12. $5 + 4x - 7 = 4x + 3 - x$

13. 2 less than 3 times a number is the same as 3 more than 2 times the number. Find the number.

14. 3 less than 2 times a number is the same as 2 more than 3 times the number. Find the number.

Solve.

15. $5r - (2r + 8) = 16$

16. $6b - (3b + 8) = 16$

17. $3g - 3 = 3(7 - g)$

18. $3d - 10 = 5(d - 4)$

19. $5(d + 4) = 7(d - 2)$

20. $9(t + 2) = 3(t - 2)$

21. $8(3t - 2) = 4(7t - 1)$

22. $7(5x - 2) = 6(6x - 1)$

23. $3(r - 6) + 2 = 4(r + 2) - 21$

24. $5(t + 3) + 9 = 3(t - 2) + 6$

25. $19 - (2x + 3) = 2(x + 3) + x$

26. $13 - (2c + 2) = 2(c + 2) + 3c$

27. $\frac{1}{4}(8y + 4) - 17 = \frac{-1}{2}(4y - 8)$

28. $\frac{1}{3}(6x + 24) - 20 = \frac{-1}{4}(12x - 72)$

29. Placing planks of equal length end to end, Jules found that 3 planks were one foot short of the porch length, while 4 planks were two feet too long. How long was each plank?

B

Solve.

30. $\frac{2x + 4}{4} = 3x - 4$

31. $\frac{3x - 14}{-2} = 3x - 2$

32. $5(x - 1) = \frac{2(x + 4)}{-2}$

33. $-4(2x + 2) = \frac{-4(x + 1)}{4}$

Solve.

34. Terry has walked 3 miles. He averages 4 miles an hour. In how many more hours will he have traveled 13 miles?

35. *Critical Thinking*   An **identity** is an equation that is true for all acceptable replacements. Is each equation an identity? Explain.

a. $2x + 4 + x = 4 + 3x$

b. $2(x - 3) + 5 = 3(x - 2) + 5$

Challenge

Solve for x. Assume that all variables represent positive numbers.

36. $a - b(x + c) = d$

37. $a(bx - c) = d - (x + e)$

38. How many equations having different solutions can you find by using parentheses to group the terms below? What are the solutions?

$$4 - 2x - 3 = 2 - x + 1$$

Mixed Review

Collect like terms.   **39.** $\frac{2}{5}x + \frac{1}{7}y - \frac{3}{5}x + \frac{2}{7}y$

40. $\frac{3}{8}m - \frac{7}{8}n + \frac{1}{8}m + \frac{3}{8}n$

41. $\frac{2}{3}a - \frac{1}{3}a + \frac{4}{9} - \frac{1}{9}$ *2-7*

Write as an algebraic expression.   *3-4*

42. 3 more than twice a number

43. 5 times the difference of a number and 2

44. 4 more than the quotient of a number and 2

Clearing an Equation of Fractions or Decimals

Objective: Clear an equation of fractions or decimals.

In equations containing fractions, you can use the multiplication property to make the equation easier to solve. To clear the equation of fractions, multiply both sides of the equation by the least common denominator of all the fractions in the equation.

EXAMPLE 1 Solve.

$$\frac{2}{3}x + \frac{1}{2}x = \frac{5}{6} + 2x$$

The number 6 is the least common denominator.

$$6\left(\frac{2}{3}x + \frac{1}{2}x\right) = 6\left(\frac{5}{6} + 2x\right)$$ Multiplying both sides by 6

$$6 \cdot \frac{2}{3}x + 6 \cdot \frac{1}{2}x = 6 \cdot \frac{5}{6} + 6 \cdot 2x$$ Using the distributive property

$$4x + 3x = 5 + 12x$$
$$7x = 5 + 12x$$
$$7x - 12x = 5 + 12x - 12x$$
$$-5x = 5$$
$$x = -1$$

Substitution will show that -1 checks.

The solution is -1.

If you wish to clear the decimals in an equation, multiply on both sides by the appropriate power of 10.

EXAMPLE 2 Solve.

$$16.3 - 7.2y = -8.18$$ Multiplying by 100 will clear the decimals.

$$100(16.3 - 7.2y) = 100(-8.18)$$
$$100(16.3) - 100(7.2y) = 100(-8.18)$$ Using the distributive property
$$1630 - 720y = -818$$
$$-720y = -818 - 1630$$
$$-720y = -2448$$
$$y = \frac{-2448}{-720}$$
$$y = 3.4$$

Substitution will show that 3.4 checks.

The solution is 3.4.

What You'll Learn

1 To clear an equation of fractions or decimals

. . . And Why

To make an equation easier to solve

Quick Review

The least common denominator of two fractions is the least common *multiple* of their denominators. In Example 1, the least common multiple of 2 and 3 is 6.

Try This   Solve.

a. $\frac{7}{8}x + \frac{3}{4} = \frac{1}{2}x + \frac{3}{2}$ **b.** $\frac{5}{6}x + \frac{1}{2} = \frac{2}{3}x + 4$

c. $26.45 = 4.2x + 1.25$ **d.** $41.68 = 4.7 - 8.6y$

The following summarizes the steps for solving an equation.

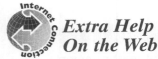

Quick Review

Step 1: This lesson

Step 2: Lesson 3-3

Step 3: Lessons 3-5, 3-1

Step 4: Lesson 3-3

Step 5: Lesson 3-2

Solving Equations
1. Multiply both sides to clear fractions or decimals, if necessary.
2. Collect like terms on each side, if necessary.
3. Use the addition property to move the variable to one side and all other terms to the other side of the equation.
4. Collect like terms again, if necessary.
5. Use the multiplication property to solve for the variable.

Extra Help On the Web

Look for worked-out examples at the Prentice Hall Web site.
    www.phschool.com

3-6 Exercises

A

Mental Math   By what number would you multiply to clear the fractions?

1. $\frac{1}{4}x + 2 = \frac{3}{4}x$ **2.** $5d - \frac{2}{3} = \frac{1}{3}d$ **3.** $\frac{3}{4}k + 1 = \frac{3}{8} - 2k$

4. $2 - \frac{4}{5}w = \frac{7}{15}w + \frac{1}{5}$ **5.** $\frac{1}{3}g + \frac{1}{2} = \frac{5}{6}g$ **6.** $\frac{3}{4} - \frac{1}{6}m = \frac{2}{3}m$

Solve. Clear the fractions first, if necessary.

7. $\frac{7}{2}x + \frac{1}{2}x = 3x + \frac{3}{2} + \frac{5}{2}x$ **8.** $\frac{1}{2} + 4m = 3m - \frac{5}{2}$

9. $\frac{5}{3} + \frac{2}{3}x = \frac{25}{12} + \frac{5}{4}x + \frac{3}{4}$ **10.** $1 - \frac{2}{3}y = \frac{9}{5} - \frac{y}{5} + \frac{3}{5}$

11. $\frac{4}{5}x - \frac{3}{4}x = \frac{3}{10}x - 1$ **12.** $\frac{8}{5}y - \frac{2}{3}y = 23 - \frac{1}{15}y$

13. $\frac{7}{8}x - \frac{1}{4} + \frac{3}{4}x = \frac{1}{16} + x$ **14.** $\frac{2}{3} + \frac{1}{4}t = \frac{1}{3}$

15. $-\frac{3}{2} + x = -\frac{5}{6} - \frac{4}{3}$ **16.** $\frac{2}{3} + 3y = 5y - \frac{2}{15}$

17. $\frac{2}{7}x + \frac{1}{2}x = \frac{3}{4}x + 1$ **18.** $\frac{5}{16}y + \frac{3}{8}y = 2 + \frac{1}{4}y$

19. $2.1x + 45.2 = 3.2 - 8.4x$ **20.** $0.96y - 0.79 = 0.21y + 0.46$

21. $1.03 - 0.62x = 0.71 - 0.22x$ **22.** $0.42 - 0.03y = 3.33 - y$

23. $1.7t + 8 - 1.62t = 0.4t - 0.32 + 8$

24. $0.7n - 15 + n = 2n - 8 - 0.4n$

B

Solve.

25. $7\frac{1}{2}x - \frac{1}{2}x = 3\frac{3}{4}x + 39$

26. $\frac{1}{5}t - 0.4 + \frac{2}{5}t = 0.6 - \frac{1}{10}t$

27. $\frac{1}{4}(8y + 4) - 17 = -\frac{1}{2}(4y - 8)$

28. $\frac{1}{3}(6x + 24) - 20 = -\frac{1}{4}(12x - 72)$

29. $30,000 + 20,000x = 55,000$

30. $25,000(4 + 3x) = 125,000$

31. *Critical Thinking*   After the death (about 290 A.D.) of Diophantus, a famous Greek mathematician, someone described his life as a puzzle.

> He was a boy for $\frac{1}{6}$ of his life.
>
> After $\frac{1}{12}$ more, he acquired a beard.
>
> After another $\frac{1}{7}$, he married.
>
> In the fifth year after his marriage his son was born.
>
> The son lived half as many years as his father.
>
> Diophantus died 4 years after his son.

How old was Diophantus when he died?

Challenge

32. Apples are collected in a basket for six people. One third, one fourth, one eighth, and one fifth of the apples are given to four people, respectively. The fifth person gets ten apples with one apple remaining for the sixth person. Find the original number of apples in the basket.

33. Carol shared a package of graph paper with 3 of her friends. She gave $\frac{1}{4}$ of the pack to Willy. Sara got $\frac{1}{3}$ of what was left. Then Marcy took $\frac{1}{6}$ of what was left in the package. Carol kept the remaining 30 sheets. How many sheets were in the package to start?

Mixed Review

Write a true sentence using $<$ or $>$.   **34.** $7.301 \;\square\; 7.310$

35. $5.4 \;\square\; |-5|$ **36.** $-0.783 \;\square\; -0.781$ **37.** $|6| \;\square\; |-7|$ *2-1, 2-2*

Write as an algebraic expression.   **38.** 7 more than half a number

39. 5 less than twice a number   **40.** twice the sum of a number and 3   *3-4*

Solve.   **41.** $-4(2t + 7) = -4$ **42.** $3a + 2(2a + 5) = 3$

43. $x + \frac{1}{3}x = 8$ **44.** $x + \frac{1}{4}x = 10$ **45.** $\frac{3}{8}y + \frac{3}{4}y = 3$ *3-2, 3-5*

Evaluate each expression for $x = -2$.   **46.** $9x^2 - 4$ **47.** $\frac{1}{2}x^3 + 32$ *1-3*

3-7 ▷ Formulas

Objective: Solve for a given variable in a formula.

What You'll Learn

▼ To solve for a given variable in a formula

...And Why

To find formulas equivalent to the given formula

Math in Action

Computers are used by air traffic controllers to quickly determine the flight times of thousands of airplanes. The computer program must include a formula that will compute the time given the rate and distance for each flight. The formula that is needed is based on the formula for distance, $d = rt$, where d is the distance, r is the rate, and t is the time.

We can solve the formula $d = rt$ for the variable t using the same rules as for solving equations.

EXAMPLES

1 Solve $d = rt$ for t.

$$d = rt$$
$$\frac{1}{r} \cdot d = \frac{1}{r} \cdot rt$$

Using the multiplication property to multiply both sides by the multiplicative inverse of r, $\frac{1}{r}$

$$\frac{d}{r} = t$$

2 A formula for the average A of three numbers, a, b, and c is

$$A = \frac{a + b + c}{3}$$

Solve for a. Justify each step.

$$A = \frac{a + b + c}{3}$$

$$3A = a + b + c \qquad \textit{Multiplication property of equality}$$

$$3A - b - c = a \qquad \textit{Addition property of equality}$$

Reading Math

Formulas and other equations that use more than one letter are often called *literal equations*.

Try This

a. Solve $C = 2\pi r$ for r.

b. Solve $P = 2l + 35$ for l. Justify each step.

c. A formula for the average A of four numbers a, b, c, and d is

$$A = \frac{a + b + c + d}{4}$$

Solve for c.

EXAMPLE 3

A formula for computing the earned-run average A of a pitcher who has given up R earned runs in I innings of pitching is

$$A = \frac{9R}{I}$$

Solve for I.

$$A = \frac{9R}{I}$$

$AI = 9R$ Multiplying both sides by I

$I = \frac{9R}{A}$ Multiplying both sides by $\frac{1}{A}$

Try This

d. A formula for a football player's rushing average r with a total of y yards rushed in n carries of the ball is $r = \frac{y}{n}$. Solve for n.

In 1999, Pedro Martinez gave up 49 earned runs for an earned-run average of 2.067. How many innings did he pitch that year?

3-7 Exercises

A
Solve.

1. $A = bh$, for b (an area formula)
2. $A = bh$, for h
3. $d = rt$, for r (a distance formula)
4. $d = rt$, for t
5. $I = Prt$, for P (an interest formula)
6. $I = Prt$, for t
7. $F = ma$, for a (a physics formula)
8. $F = ma$, for m
9. $P = 2l + 2w$, for w (a perimeter formula)
10. $P = 2l + 2w$, for l
11. $A = \pi r^2$, for r^2 (an area formula)
12. $A = \pi r^2$, for π
13. $A = \frac{1}{2}bh$, for b (an area formula)
14. $A = \frac{1}{2}bh$, for h
15. $E = mc^2$, for m (a relativity formula)
16. $E = mc^2$, for c^2
17. $A = \frac{a + b + c}{3}$, for b
18. $A = \frac{a + b + c}{3}$, for c
19. $v = \frac{3k}{t}$, for t
20. $P = \frac{ab}{c}$, for c

Extra Help On the Web

Look for worked-out examples at the Prentice Hall Web site.
www.phschool.com

Writing Math

Mathematicians may solve Exercise 17 in much the same way that you do. Then, however, they will quickly give the answer to Exercise 18, writing "by symmetry" to justify it. Can you solve Exercise 18 by using the "symmetry" of Exercises 17 and 18?

A formula for the area of a sector of a circle is $A = \frac{\pi r^2 S}{360}$ where r is the radius and S is the central angle measure of the sector.

21. Solve for S.

22. Solve for r^2.

A formula to find the horsepower H of an N-cylinder engine is

$$H = \frac{D^2 N}{2.5}$$

23. Solve for D^2.

24. Solve for N.

B

In Exercises 25–33, solve. Justify each step.

25. $A = \frac{1}{R}$, for R

26. $g = 40n + 20k$, for k

27. $r = 2h - \frac{1}{4}f$, for f

28. $\frac{s}{t} = \frac{t}{v}$, for s

29. $a^2 = b^2 + 2xc$, for x

30. $m = ax^2 + bx + c$, for b

31. $\frac{a}{b} = \frac{c}{d}$, for $\frac{a}{c}$

32. $d = \frac{1}{e + f}$, for f

33. $l = a + (n - 1)d$, for n

34. If $a^2 = b^2$, does $a = b$?

35. The formula $R = -0.00625t + 3.85$ can be used to estimate the world record in the 1500 m run t years after 1930. Solve for t.

36. *Critical Thinking* In Exercise 23, you solved for D^2. How might you solve for D?

Challenge

Solve.

37. $y = a - ab$, for a

38. $ax + b = cb$, for b

39. $x = a + b - 2ab$, for a

40. $x - a = a(y - b)$, for a

41. *Mathematical Reasoning* Solve $2p - q = 2r - s$ for $4p + 2s$.

42. **TEST PREP** If $\frac{a}{b - c} = d$, then $b = $?

A. $\frac{a + c}{d}$ **B.** $\frac{a + cd}{d}$ **C.** $\frac{a}{d - c}$ **D.** $\frac{d + c}{a}$

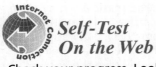
Mixed Review

Factor.   **43.** $4x + 12$ **44.** $3c + 12d - 9$ *2-7*

Collect like terms.   **45.** $2x + 3y - 4x$ **46.** $8a - 3c + 4 - 2a$ *1-5*

Solve.   **47.** $16 - 2c = 4c - 2$ **48.** $1.7m + 16.8 = 25.8 - 0.55m$

49. $\frac{1}{2}(8m + 4) + 2 = \frac{1}{3}(18m - 18)$ **50.** $\frac{2}{5} + 3y = 10y - 1$

51. $15.4 - 9.1t = 2.4t - 19.1$ **52.** $27 - 3(t + 4) = 9(t - 2) - 15$ *3-5, 3-6*

Solving Equations Involving Absolute Value

Objective: Solve equations involving absolute value.

In Chapter 2 you learned that the absolute value of a number is its distance from zero on a number line. You also learned that the absolute value of a number is always positive or zero. In this lesson you will solve equations involving absolute values.

What You'll Learn

1 To solve equations involving absolute value

. . . And Why

To learn what to do with the simple form $|x|$ when it appears in an equation

EXAMPLES Solve.

1
$$|x| = 6$$
$$x = 6 \text{ or } x = -6$$

6 and −6 are both 6 units from 0 on the number line.

Check:
$$
\begin{array}{c|c}
|x| = 6 & \\
\hline
|6| & 6 \\
6 & 6 ✔
\end{array}
\qquad
\begin{array}{c|c}
|x| = 6 & \\
\hline
|-6| & 6 \\
6 & 6 ✔
\end{array}
$$

The solutions are 6 and −6.

2
$$|x| + 2 = 12$$
$$|x| + 2 + (-2) = 12 + (-2) \qquad \text{Using the addition property}$$
$$|x| = 10$$
$$x = 10 \text{ or } x = -10$$

Check:
$$
\begin{array}{c|c}
|x| + 2 = 12 & \\
\hline
|10| + 2 & 12 \\
10 + 2 & 12 \\
12 & 12 ✔
\end{array}
\qquad
\begin{array}{c|c}
|x| + 2 = 12 & \\
\hline
|-10| + 2 & 12 \\
10 + 2 & 12 \\
12 & 12 ✔
\end{array}
$$

The solutions are 10 and −10.

3
$$3|b| - 4 = 2$$
$$3|b| - 4 + 4 = 2 + 4 \qquad \text{Using the addition property}$$
$$3|b| = 6$$
$$\tfrac{1}{3} \cdot 3|b| = \tfrac{1}{3} \cdot 6 \qquad \text{Using the multiplication property}$$
$$|b| = 2$$
$$b = 2 \text{ or } b = -2$$

Substitution will show that the numbers 2 and −2 check.

The solutions are 2 and −2.

Try This Solve.

a. $|y| = 17$ **b.** $|y| - 5 = 1$ **c.** $2|x| + 1 = 15$

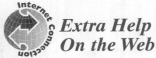

**Extra Help
On the Web**

Look for worked-out
examples at the Prentice
Hall Web site.
www.phschool.com

3-8 Exercises

A

Mental Math   Solve.

1. $|x| = 19$

2. $|y| = 9$

3. $4 = |m|$

4. $|n| = 7$

5. $|h| = 0$

6. $3 = |a|$

7. $|b| = 12$

8. $|x| = 15$

9. $|a| = |-2|$

10. $|-20| = |-x|$

11. $|y| = 12 - 5$

12. $|y| + 5 = 16$

13. $|a| - 7 = 21$

14. $4 + |m| = 9$

15. $-2 + |n| = 0$

16. $|x| + 3 + 9 = 15$

17. $5 + |x| - 9 = 2$

18. $|x| - 23 = 34$

19. $|-4| + |-6| + |m| = 10$

20. $|-8| + |x| = |-8| + |-3|$

21. $5|x| = 35$

22. $3|y| = 27$

Solve.

23. $2|x| + 6 = 12$

24. $4|r| - 2 = 18$

25. $\frac{|m|}{4} = 5$

26. $\frac{|t|}{-2} = -9$

27. $-4|x| = -5$

28. $4|x| + |-4| = |-6|$

29. $-3|a| - 5 = -17$

30. $-2|b| + 4 = 2$

31. $\frac{|x|}{5} + 7 = 42$

32. $\frac{1}{4} + \frac{1}{2}|x| = \frac{5}{8}$

33. Write a Convincing Argument $|x| = -5$ has no solutions. Why?

Mathematical Reasoning   Show that the statement is sometimes true.
Then give a counterexample to show that the statement is not always true.

34. $|x| = x$

35. $|x| = -x$

36. $|-x| = x$

37. $|-x| = -x$

38. $|x + y| = |x| + |y|$

39. $|x + y| < |x| + |y|$

B
Solve.

40. $-|x| = -4$

41. $-12 = -|y|$

42. $-2|a| + 5 = 1$

43. $2|x| + 3|x| + 4 = 24$

44. $-3|m| + 5|m| - 3 = 1$

45. $|n| - 3 + 5|n| = 15$

46. $|x| + 12 = 5|x| - 4$

47. $6 - 3|a| = 2|a| + 1$

48. $-\frac{2}{3}|m| - \frac{4}{5} = -4$

49. $-\frac{1}{3}|y| + \frac{5}{6} = \frac{1}{6}$

50. $|3m| = 6$

51. $|2a| = 8$

52. $|-m| = 5$

53. $|-x| = 7$

Critical Thinking   Complete.

54. If $x > 0, |x| = $?   **55.** If $x < 0, |x| = $?   **56.** If $x = 0, |x| = $?

Challenge

Solve.

57. $|x + 2| = 7$ **58.** $|m - 4| = 1$ **59.** $|2a + 1| = 5$

Mathematical Reasoning   Is the statement sometimes true, always true, or never true? Explain.

60. $|x| > x$ **61.** $|x| = |-x|$ **62.** $|x^2| = x^2$

63. $|x| + |y| > 0$ **64.** $|xy| = |x||y|$ **65.** $|x - y| = |x| - |y|$

66. If $|x| > |y|$, what is the most you know about x and y?

Error Analysis   The solution of each equation has an error commonly made by algebra students. Find and correct the error.

67. $4 - 3x = 5$

$3x = 9$

$x = 3$

68. Solve $ax - b = c$ for b.

$ax = b + c$

$x = \dfrac{b + c}{a}$

69. $4|c| - 3 = 1$

$4|c| - 3 = 1$ or $4|c| - 3 = -1$

$4|c| = 4$ or $4|c| = 2$

$|c| = 1$ or $|c| = \frac{1}{2}$

$c = 1$ or $c = -1$ $c = \frac{1}{2}$ or $c = -\frac{1}{2}$

70. $|x| = -3$

$x = 3$ or $x = -3$

Mixed Review

Solve.   **71.** $-12t - 4 = 32$ **72.** $3m + 2m + 15 = 35$

73. $x + 0.75x = 21$ **74.** $\frac{1}{2}n + \frac{2}{5}n = -\frac{9}{10}$ **75.** $\frac{2}{5}(m - 4) = 4$ *3-3*

Collect like terms.   **76.** $2x - \frac{1}{2}x + \frac{3}{4}x - 4x$

77. $3a - \frac{2}{5}b - \frac{1}{2}a - 6b$ **78.** $5x + \frac{2}{3}y - \frac{1}{4}x + y$ *2-7*

Translate to an equation and solve.

79. The sum of two consecutive even integers is 94. What are the integers?

80. The sum of three consecutive odd integers is 123. What are the integers?

81. One angle of a triangle is 3 times as large as another. The third angle is 60° less than the sum of the other two angles. Find the measure of each angle.

82. The length of a rectangle is twice the width. The perimeter is 24 m. Find the length and the width.   *3-4*

3-9 ▷ Proportions

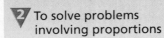

What You'll Learn

1 To solve proportions

2 To solve problems involving proportions

. . . And Why

To develop and solve proportional relationships

PART
1 **Solving Proportions**

Objective: Solve proportions.

A **ratio** of two quantities is a comparison, often expressed as a fraction. For example, the ratio of the age of a 34-year-old parent to that of a 10-year-old child is 34 to 10 or $\frac{34}{10}$. The ratio of 34 to 10 can be expressed in several ways.

$$34:10 \qquad 34 \div 10 \qquad \frac{34}{10} \qquad 3.4$$

An equation that states that two ratios are equal is called a **proportion.** These are proportions.

$$\frac{2}{3} = \frac{6}{9} \qquad \frac{5}{7} = \frac{25}{35} \qquad \frac{x}{24} = \frac{2}{3} \qquad \frac{9}{y} = \frac{32}{81}$$

Since proportions are equations, we can use equation-solving properties to solve them.

EXAMPLE 1 Solve.

$$\frac{x}{63} = \frac{2}{9}$$
$$63 \cdot \frac{x}{63} = 63 \cdot \frac{2}{9} \qquad \text{Using the multiplication property}$$
$$x = 14$$

EXAMPLE 2 Solve.

$$\frac{65}{10} = \frac{13}{x}$$
$$10x \cdot \frac{65}{10} = 10x \cdot \frac{13}{x} \qquad \text{Using the multiplication property;}$$
$$\text{multiplying by 10x to clear fractions}$$
$$65x = 130$$
$$\frac{1}{65} \cdot 65x = \frac{1}{65} \cdot 130 \qquad \text{Using the multiplication property}$$
$$x = 2$$

Try This Solve.

a. $\frac{3}{5} = \frac{12}{y}$ **b.** $\frac{1}{2} = \frac{x}{5}$ **c.** $\frac{m}{4} = \frac{7}{6}$

148 Chapter 3 *Equations*

Objective: Solve problems involving proportions.

PROBLEM-SOLVING GUIDELINES
■ UNDERSTAND the problem
▢ Develop and carry out a PLAN
■ Find the ANSWER and CHECK

Some problems can be solved by writing and solving a proportion. Use the Problem-Solving Guidelines to help you solve the following problems.

EXAMPLE 3

The property tax on a house is $8 per $1000 assessed valuation. What is the tax on a house assessed at $165,000?

$$\frac{8}{1000} = \frac{x}{165,000}$$

Think: $8 is to $1000 as x dollars is to $165,000.

$$\frac{8}{1000} \cdot 165,000 = \frac{x}{165,000} \cdot 165,000$$

$$1320 = x$$

The tax is $1320.

EXAMPLE 4

A certain car can travel 180 miles on 8 gallons of gasoline. How far can this car travel on 19 gallons of gasoline?

Solve:
$$\frac{180}{8} = \frac{x}{19}$$

Think: 180 miles is to 8 gallons as x miles is to 19 gallons.

$$\frac{180}{8} \cdot 19 = \frac{x}{19} \cdot 19$$

$$\frac{180 \cdot 19}{8} = x$$

$$427.5 = x$$

The car can travel 427.5 miles on 19 gallons.

Try This Solve.

d. The scale on a map says that 0.5 cm represents 25 km. On the map the measurement between two cities is 5 cm. What is the actual distance between these two cities?

e. According to the scale on a road map, 3 inches represent 40 miles. If two cities measure 10 inches apart on the map, how many miles apart are they?

**Extra Help
On the Web**

Look for worked-out
examples at the Prentice
Hall Web site.
www.phschool.com

3-9 Exercises

A

Solve these proportions.

1. $\frac{y}{3} = \frac{9}{27}$ **2.** $\frac{7}{8} = \frac{m}{4}$ **3.** $\frac{9}{x} = \frac{2}{3}$ **4.** $\frac{25}{75} = \frac{1}{x}$

5. $\frac{2}{y} = \frac{5}{9}$ **6.** $\frac{16}{m} = \frac{1}{4}$ **7.** $\frac{8}{5} = \frac{40}{y}$ **8.** $\frac{12}{15} = \frac{t}{5}$

9. $\frac{y}{4} = \frac{5}{8}$ **10.** $\frac{3}{8} = \frac{12}{x}$ **11.** $\frac{5}{x} = \frac{9}{11}$ **12.** $\frac{2}{7} = \frac{5}{y}$

13. $\frac{x}{40} = \frac{3}{5}$ **14.** $\frac{n}{20} = \frac{3}{4}$ **15.** $\frac{18}{c} = \frac{2}{7}$ **16.** $\frac{24}{x} = \frac{4}{3}$

17. $\frac{15}{y} = \frac{10}{8}$ **18.** $\frac{63}{144} = \frac{u}{16}$ **19.** $\frac{12}{30} = \frac{10}{k}$ **20.** $\frac{5}{3} = \frac{y}{42}$

21. $\frac{7}{b} = \frac{4}{9}$ **22.** $\frac{100}{a} = \frac{90}{45}$ **23.** $\frac{4}{5} = \frac{28}{h}$ **24.** $\frac{y}{18} = \frac{150}{126}$

Solve.

25. A car travels 150 km on 12 L of gasoline. How many liters of gasoline are needed to travel 500 km?

26. A baseball pitcher strikes out an average of 3.6 batters per 9 innings. At this rate, how many batters would the pitcher strike out in 315 innings?

27. A watch loses 2 minutes every 15 hours. How much time will it lose in 2 hours?

28. A school has a policy that 2 adults must accompany every group of 15 students on school trips. How many adults are needed to take 180 students on a trip?

29. Four shovels of sand are used for every 5 shovels of gravel in making concrete. How much gravel is needed for 64 shovels of sand?

30. The ratio of international students to U.S. students at a college is 2 to 35. How many international students are there if there are 1575 U.S. students?

31. A loading crew estimates that it can load 8 boxes in 20 minutes. At this rate, how many boxes could it load in 1 hour?

32. On a map, 1 cm represents 3.27 km. It is 24.5 cm between two cities on this map. What is the actual distance between the two cities?

33. A television station found that 145 out of the 350 people surveyed watched a special program on education on Monday night. If this survey is representative of the total viewing population (12,250 people), about how many people watched the television special?

34. A survey of 250 people in a city found that Channel 5 is the favorite station of 52 people. If this survey is representative of the city's population of 35,000, about how many people in this city favor Channel 5?

35. If two out of five people wear red to support the Ohio State football team, then how many in a full Ohio Stadium (capacity 89,841) are wearing red?

B

Solve.

36. An automobile engine crankshaft revolves 3000 times per minute. How long does it take to revolve 50 times?

37. A refrigerator goes on a defrost cycle for 1 hour out of every 14 hours. How many hours is this each week?

38. The ratio of full seats to empty seats in an auditorium is 5 to 2. If there are 120 empty seats, what is the seating capacity of this auditorium?

39. *Critical Thinking* $9m = 5n$. Find the ratio $m:n$.

Challenge

40. *Mathematical Reasoning*   The boy : girl ratio in a school is $4:5$.

   a. If there are 225 girls, how many students are in the school?

   b. If there are 225 students, how many girls are in the school?

41. *Mathematical Reasoning*   Alena wants to guess the number of marbles in an 8-gal jar in order to win a moped. She knows there are 128 oz in a gallon, and she finds that 46 marbles fill an 8-oz jar. What should be her guess?

42. *Critical Thinking*   It takes 12 minutes to cut a log into 4 pieces. How long would it take to cut a log into 8 pieces?

43. A scale model of an experimental airplane measures 2.5 m from wingtip to wingtip. The actual plane will measure 60 m from wingtip to wingtip. If the highest point on the model will just fit under a $\frac{1}{2}$ m workbench, how tall does the airplane hangar doorway have to be?

In this sample, about 67 of 200 people are wearing red. If there were 85,000 people at this Ohio State game, estimate how many wore red.

Mixed Review

Divide.   **44.** $\frac{-32}{-8}$ **45.** $-\frac{7}{8} \div \frac{1}{4}$ **46.** $\frac{1}{6} \div -\frac{2}{3}$ *2-6*

Solve.   **47.** $9a - 6 = 30 - 3a$ **48.** $17 - 5c = 2c + 3$

49. $-11w = -132$ **50.** $|x| = 15$ **51.** $|c| + 9 = 12$

52. $6|m| = 24$ **53.** $|n| = 0$ **54.** $4(3x - 12) = 12$

55. $\frac{x}{3} + 5 = \frac{3x}{5} - \frac{7}{3}$ **56.** $0.3r - 2.8 = 3.2 - 0.2r$ *3-2, 3-5, 3-6, 3-8*

Solve for the given variable.   **57.** $y = mx + b$ for m

58. $PV = nRT$ for T **59.** $I = Prt$ for r *3-7*

Simplify.   **60.** $2w - (3w - 1)$ **61.** $2[3x - 2(3x + 4)]$ *2-8*

3-10 ▷ Using Percent

What You'll Learn

1 To express decimals and fractions as percents and vice versa

2 To solve equations involving percent

3 To solve percent problems

...And Why

To become proficient with percent

Math History

The idea of percent was used as early as the Roman Empire. The Roman Emperor Augustus levied a tax at a rate of $\frac{1}{100}$ of the selling price on all goods. In the 15th century, Italian manuscripts used expressions such as "20 p 100" and "xx p cento" to indicate 20 percent. Near the end of that century, phrases such as "viii in x percento" (8 percent) were used to express percent. The percent symbol (%) probably came from the symbol " " introduced in Italy at the end of the 15th century. By 1650, the symbol "per ÷" was used for percent. Later the "per" was dropped, leaving a symbol that closely resembles the one used today.

PART 1 — Percent

Objective: Express decimals and fractions as percents and vice versa.

The ratio of a number to 100 is called **percent.** The word "percent" means *per one hundred*, and is represented by the symbol %. We can write a percent as a fraction or as a decimal.

$$78.5\% = 78.5 \times \frac{1}{100} = \frac{78.5}{100} = 0.785$$
$$4\% = 4 \times \frac{1}{100} = \frac{4}{100} = 0.04$$

To solve problems involving percent, we can first change the percent to a decimal.

EXAMPLES   Write as a decimal.

1 $35\% = 0.35$ The hundredths place is the second place to the right of the decimal point.

2 $5\% = 0.05$

3 $138\% = 1.38$

4 $0.8\% = 0.008$

Try This   Write as a decimal.

a. 48%   **b.** 3%   **c.** 145%   **d.** 0.5%

Some problems require that we change a fraction to a percent. The easiest way to do this usually is to change the fraction to a decimal first.

EXAMPLES Express as a percent. Round to the nearest tenth of a percent if necessary.

5 $\frac{2}{3} = 0.666\overline{6}$ $2 \div 3 = 0.666\overline{6}$ The bar shows that the digit 6 repeats.

≈ 0.667 Rounding to the nearest thousandth

$= \frac{66.7}{100}$ Writing in fraction form with a denominator of 100

$= 66.7\%$

6 $\frac{5}{4} = 1.25$ $5 \div 4 = 1.25$

$= \frac{125}{100}$

$= 125\%$

Try This Express as a percent. Round to the nearest tenth of a percent if necessary.

e. $\frac{3}{4}$ **f.** $\frac{3}{8}$ **g.** $\frac{24.5}{5}$

h. $\frac{12.4}{25}$ **i.** $\frac{0.02}{500}$ **j.** $\frac{3}{40}$

PART 2 Using Equations with Percent

Objective: Solve percent problems.

We can solve problems involving percent by using a proportion or by translating to an equation and solving. When fractional percents are used, translating to an equation is usually the better method.

EXAMPLE 7 Solve.

15.5% of 60 is what number?

15.5%	of	60	is	what number?	Translating to an equation
↓	↓	↓	↓	↓	
0.155	·	60	=	n	$15.5\% = \frac{15.5}{100} = 0.155$
		9.3	=	n	

15.5% of 60 is 9.3.

EXAMPLE 8 Solve.

24 is what percent of 120?

24	is	what percent	of	120?	Translating to an equation
↓	↓	↓	↓	↓	
24	=	p	·	120	Let p represent the percent expressed as a decimal.

$$\frac{24}{120} = p$$

$$0.2 = p$$

$$p = 0.2 \text{ or } 20\%$$ Express the decimal as a percent.

24 is 20% of 120.

EXAMPLE 9 Solve.

25% of what number is 15?

25%	of	what number	is	15?	Translating to an equation
↓	↓	↓	↓	↓	
0.25	·	n	=	15	Let n be the number you are trying to find. $25\% = \frac{25}{100} = 0.25$

$$n = \frac{15}{0.25}$$

$$n = 60$$

25% of 60 is 15.

Try This Solve.

k. What percent of 40 is 15? **l.** 3 is 16% of what number?

m. 7.5% of 80 is what number? **n.** What number is 12.5% of 40?

◇◇ **Connections: Estimating**

Estimating with percents is easy if you remember some key fraction-percent relationships. Here are approximate percents for the thirds.

$$\frac{1}{3} \approx 33\% \qquad \frac{2}{3} \approx 67\%$$

1. In your journal, on an index card, or on some other form of ready reference, make a chart showing fraction-percent relationships for halves, thirds, fourths, fifths, sixths, eighths, and tenths.

2. Show how you could estimate each of the following.

   a. 25% of 445 **b.** $\frac{33}{40} = ??\%$ **c.** the number that 9 is 12% of

Objective: Solve problems involving applications of percent.

PROBLEM-SOLVING GUIDELINES
■ UNDERSTAND the problem
Develop and carry out a PLAN
■ Find the ANSWER and CHECK

You can use the Problem-Solving Guidelines to help you solve problems involving percent.

EXAMPLE 10

The tax on an automobile was 6% of its price. What was the price of this car if the tax was $633?

■ **UNDERSTAND the problem**

Question: What was the price of the car?
Data: The tax was 6% of the price.

Clarifying the question and identifying the given data

■ **Develop and carry out a PLAN**

Let $p =$ the price of the car.

$$(0.6)p = 633$$

$$p = \frac{633}{0.06}$$

$$p = 10{,}550$$

Using a variable to represent the price of the car.

6% of the price is the tax, $633.

■ **Find the ANSWER and CHECK**

The price of the car was $10,550. If we find 6% of $10,550, we get $633. The answer checks.

Since 6% of 10,000 is 600, the answer is reasonable.

Try This   Solve.

o. Ms. Pelligrini received a $750 bonus with her monthly paycheck. Her regular monthly pay is $2500. What percent of her regular monthly pay was her bonus?

p. Truong's junior college expenses were $5000 last term. She spent $1500 on tuition, $2250 on room and board, and $1250 on miscellaneous expenses. What percent of her college expenses went toward tuition?

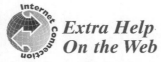
3-10 Exercises

A

Write as a decimal.

1. 41% **2.** 60% **3.** 7% **4.** 1% **5.** 125%

6. 180% **7.** 0.8% **8.** 0.6% **9.** 1.5% **10.** 2.8%

Express as a percent. Round to the nearest tenth of a percent if necessary.

11. $\frac{3}{4}$ **12.** $\frac{1}{25}$ **13.** $\frac{24}{25}$ **14.** $\frac{3}{8}$ **15.** $\frac{1}{3}$

16. $\frac{3}{25}$ **17.** $\frac{5}{8}$ **18.** $\frac{5}{6}$ **19.** $\frac{3}{16}$ **20.** $\frac{1}{20}$

Solve.

21. What percent of 68 is 17? **22.** What percent of 75 is 36?

23. What percent of 125 is 30? **24.** What percent of 300 is 57?

25. 45 is 30% of what number? **26.** 20.4 is 24% of what number?

27. 0.3 is 12% of what number? **28.** 7 is 175% of what number?

29. What percent of 80 is 100? **30.** What percent of 10 is 205?

31. What is 2% of 40? **32.** What is 40% of 2?

33. 2 is what percent of 40? **34.** 40 is 2% of what number?

35. 2 is 40% of what number? **36.** 40 is what percent of 2?

37. On a test of 88 items, a student got 76 correct. What percent were correct?

38. A softball player had 13 hits in 25 times at bat. What percent of her times at bat resulted in hits?

39. A family spent $408 one month for food. This was 26% of its income. What was its monthly income?

40. The sales-tax rate in New York City is $8\frac{1}{4}$%. How much city sales tax would be charged on a purchase of $428.86? What will be the total cost of the purchase?

41. Water volume increases 9% when it freezes. If 400 cm³ of water are frozen, how much will the volume increase? What will be the volume of the ice?

42. Sales tax in Freeberg is 5%. What would be the sales tax on a motorbike that costs $775? What would be the total cost for the motorbike, including tax?

43. A salesperson's quota was set at $7500 for one month. During this month the salesperson sold $10,000. What percent of the quota is this?

44. *Write a Convincing Argument* Which is greater,
  a. 50% of 40 or 40% of 50?
  b. 20% of 90 or 90% of 20?
  c. *a*% of *b* or *b*% of *a*?

B

45. A meal came to \$16.41 without tax. Calculate a 6% sales tax, and then calculate a 15% tip based on the sum of the meal and the tax. What is the total cost of the meal?

46. Debby's Discs charges \$12.99 for a CD. DISCount, Inc., charges \$14.95, but you have a \$2.00 DISCount coupon. A sales tax of 7% is charged on the *regular* prices. How much does the CD cost at each store?

To find the **percent of increase** (or **decrease**), divide the amount of increase (or decrease) by the original amount.

47. Wendi worked for \$6 an hour for the first month she was on the job. She was then given a raise to \$6.24 an hour. What was the percent of her wage increase?

48. A car stereo that originally cost \$175 was on sale for \$150. What was the percent of decrease for the car stereo?

49. The dimensions of a rectangular design are 7.5 cm by 12.5 cm. Each is $37\frac{1}{2}\%$ of the original design. What were the original dimensions?

50. The new price of a car is 25% higher than the old price of \$8800. The old price is less than the new price by what percent?

51. *Critical Thinking* If x is 160% of y, y is what percent of x?

Challenge

52. A store has a 30% discount on every item in stock. By how much is the 5% sales tax reduced on an item that regularly sells for \$10?

53. A bank offered two plans for a two-year investment. One was 5% the first year and 10% the second year. The other was 10% the first year and 5% the second year. Which investment plan was better?

54. *Write a Convincing Argument* Here are seven different discount plans. List them in order from best to worst. Justify your listing.

successive discounts   of 10%, 10%, 10%, 10%;   of 10%, 10%, 20%

of 20%, 10%, 10%;   of 10%, 30%;

of 30%, 10%;   of 20%, 20%;

of 40% (one discount only)

Journal

From your work with Exercise 54, list two facts that you feel are important to remember about successive discounts.

3-11 ▷ More Expressions and Equations

What You'll Learn

1 To translate compound phrases into algebraic expressions

2 To solve problems by writing and solving equations

...And Why

To use mathematical models to solve problems

Quick Review

An even integer has 2 as a factor. An odd integer does not have 2 as a factor.

Some problems contain two or more unknowns. To solve such problems, you must first decide which unknown quantity the variable will represent and then express the other unknown quantities in terms of that variable.

PART 1 Compound Phrases to Algebraic Expressions

Objective: Translate compound phrases into algebraic expressions.

EXAMPLE 1

The cost of a main-floor seat is three times as much as the cost of a balcony seat. Write an expression showing the total cost for one of each type of seat.

Let $b =$ cost of a balcony seat. $3b =$ cost of a main floor seat	The cost of a main floor seat is expressed in terms of the cost of a balcony seat. Therefore, let the variable b represent the cost of a balcony seat, and express the cost of a main floor seat in terms of b.
$b + 3b =$ total cost	To find the total cost, add the cost of each seat.

Try This

a. There are half as many boys in a certain club as there are girls. Write an expression for the total number of boys and girls in the club.

The integers 22, 23, and 24 are *consecutive integers*. These numbers follow each other when we count by ones. The integers 6, 8, and 10 are *consecutive even integers*. These numbers follow each other when we count by twos, beginning with 6. The integers 7, 9, and 11 are *consecutive odd integers* because they follow each other when we count by twos, beginning with 7.

EXAMPLE 2

Write an expression for the sum of an integer and three times the next larger integer.

Let $x =$ an integer
$(x + 1) =$ the next larger integer
$x + 3(x + 1) =$ the sum of an integer and three times the next integer

Try This

b. Write an expression for the sum of three consecutive odd integers.

Using Equations to Solve Problems

Objective: Solve problems by writing and solving equations.

You can use the Problem-Solving Guidelines on page 155 to help you solve problems when your plan involves writing and solving an equation.

EXAMPLE 3

Manuel scored 35 points fewer in his second bowling game than in his first game. His total score for two games was 395. How many points did he score in each game?

■ **UNDERSTAND the problem**

Question: How many points did Manuel score in each game?
Data: The total for the 2 games was 395. In the second game, he scored 35 points fewer than in the first.

We can show this in a diagram.

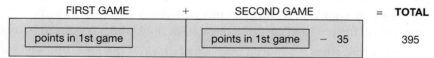

■ **Develop and carry out a PLAN**

Let f = points in the first game.
$f - 35$ = points in the second game

The points for the second game are expressed in terms of points for the first game. Therefore, let the variable represent the points in the first game.

$$f + (f - 35) = 395$$
$$2f - 35 = 395$$
$$2f - 35 + 35 = 395 + 35$$
$$2f = 430$$

$$\tfrac{1}{2} \cdot 2f = \tfrac{1}{2} \cdot 430$$

$$f = 215$$

Second game = $f - 35 = 215 - 35 = 180$

■ **Find the ANSWER and CHECK**

Manuel scored 215 points in the first game and 180 points in the second game.

If we estimate by rounding we get $200 + 200 = 400$. The answer seems reasonable.

Try This   Solve.

c. The perimeter of a rectangle is 150 cm. The length is 15 cm greater than the width. Find the dimensions.

d. The sum of an integer and twice the next consecutive integer is 29. What are the integers?

e. Mrs. Lee deposited a sum of money in a savings account that pays 4% interest per year. At the end of one year, Mrs. Lee had a total of $9620 in the account. How much did she invest originally?

3-11 Exercises

Extra Help On the Web

Look for worked-out examples at the Prentice Hall Web site.
www.phschool.com

A

1. A CD costs $3.50 more than a tape. Write an expression for the total cost of 1 CD and 1 tape.

2. The second math test was worth half as many points as the first test. Write an expression for the total number of points on the 2 tests.

3. There are 9 fewer math books than English books. Write an expression for the total number of books.

4. There are 12 more history books than science books. Write an expression for the total number of books.

5. A hardback book cost $7 more than a paperback book. Write an expression for the total cost of 1 paperback book and 3 hardback books.

6. A large drink costs 50¢ more than a small drink. Write an expression for the total cost of 3 small drinks and 2 large drinks.

Write an expression for each of the following.

7. the sum of an even integer and the next even integer

8. the sum of an odd integer and the next odd integer

9. the sum of an even integer and two times the next even integer

10. the sum of an integer and three times the next integer

11. the sum of an even integer and the next two even integers

12. the sum of $\frac{1}{4}$ of an integer, $\frac{1}{5}$ of the next integer, and $\frac{1}{2}$ of the following integer

13. the sum of an even integer, $\frac{1}{2}$ of the next even integer, and $\frac{1}{4}$ of the following even integer

14. the sum of an odd integer, $\frac{3}{4}$ of the next odd integer, and two times the following odd integer

Solve.

15. The sum of a number and $\frac{2}{5}$ of itself is 56. What is the number?

16. If you add one third of a number to the number itself, you get 48. What is the number?

17. The sum of two consecutive odd integers is 76. What are the integers?
18. The sum of two consecutive even integers is 106. What are the integers?
19. The sum of three consecutive integers is 126. What are the integers?
20. The sum of three consecutive odd integers is 189. What are the integers?
21. *Critical Thinking*   Redo Exercise 19. Let x be the second of the three consecutive integers. Then redo Exercise 20 using a similar procedure.
22. The perimeter of a rectangle is 310 m. The length is 25 m greater than the width. What are the length and the width of this rectangle?
23. One angle of a triangle is 4 times as large as another. The third angle is equal to the sum of the other two angles. What is the measure of the smallest angle? (Hint: The sum of the measures of the angles of a triangle is 180°.)
24. *Critical Thinking*   Abraham Lincoln's 1863 Gettysburg Address refers to the year 1776 as "four score and seven years ago." Write an equation and solve for a score.

25. The combined lengths of the Nile and Amazon rivers is 13,108 km. If the Amazon were 234 km longer, it would be as long as the Nile. What is the length of each river?
26. In 1999, tennis-playing sisters Venus and Serena Williams earned a total of $4,921,107. If Venus had earned $289,097 more, she would have earned the same as Serena. How much did each earn?
27. A 48-ft wire is cut into three pieces. The second piece is three times as long as the first piece. The third piece is four times as long as the second piece. How long is each piece?
28. Mrs. Gutierrez borrowed some money. At the end of the year, she repaid the loan plus 10.5% of the original amount for interest. She paid back a total of $8287.50. How much money did she borrow originally?

How many score years ago did Lincoln give his Gettysburg Address? (See Exercise 24.)

29. Mr. Horvath put some money into a savings account and deposited no more into this account for one year. At the end of the year, there was $6272 in the account, including 6% of the original amount for interest. How much did he deposit originally?
30. After a 20% discount, an item was sold for $9600. What was the original price of the item?
31. The population of the United States in 1998 was estimated to be 270 million. This was a 79% increase over the population in 1950. What was the population in 1950, to the nearest million?
32. The number of students, ages 5 to 17 years, enrolled in school in 1970 was 45.6 million. The number enrolled in 1995 was 3.3% less than in 1970.
   a. How many students were enrolled in 1995?
   b. Can you tell which year had the greater percentage of students in this age group in school? Explain.

B

33. One number is 25% of another. The larger number is 12 more than the smaller. Both numbers are positive. What are the numbers?

34. If the daily rental for a car is $38.90, and a person must drive 190 miles and stay within a $100.00 budget, what is the highest price per mile the person can afford?

35. Jane scored 78 on a test that had 4 seven-point fill-ins and 24 three-point multiple-choice questions. She had one fill-in wrong. How many multiple-choice answers did she get right?

36. The width of a rectangle is $\frac{3}{4}$ the length. The perimeter of the rectangle becomes 50 cm when the length and width are each increased by 2 cm. Find the length and width.

37. Phone charges are $13.72 per month plus 13¢ per call and 8¢ per minute. How much did it cost one month for 35 calls totaling 172 minutes?

Challenge

38. In a basketball league, the Falcons won 15 of their first 20 games. If they win only half the time from now on, how many more games will they have to play in order to win 60% of the total games?

39. *Error Analysis*   In one city, a city sales tax of 9% was added to the gasoline price registered on the pump. What, if anything, is wrong with each scenario?

    a. At one station, a driver asked for $10 worth. The attendant filled the tank until the pump read $9.10 and charged the driver $10.00.

    b. On Tuesdays, this gas station gives 9% off the total cost to the customer. On one Tuesday, the attendant simply collected the amount that registered on the pump.

40. The buyer of a piano priced at $2000 is given the choice of paying cash at the time of purchase or $2150 at the end of one year. What rate of interest is being charged if payment is made at the end of one year?

41. If you receive 7% interest on savings, but 20% tax is charged on the interest, how much do you have left from an initial $1000 deposit?

42. A storekeeper goes to the bank to get $10 worth of change. He requests twice as many quarters as half dollars, twice as many dimes as quarters, three times as many nickels as dimes, and no pennies or dollars. How many of each coin did the storekeeper get?

Mixed Review

Solve.   **43.** $7x = 10$ **44.** $7a - 9a = 6$ **45.** $-8w + 13w = 45$

46. $8c + 6 = 6c + 10$ **47.** $15 - (5m - 6) = 1$ **48.** $\frac{3}{4}b = 9$ *3-2, 3-5*

Solve.   **49.** $\frac{3}{4}a - 6 = 3 + \frac{1}{2}a$ **50.** $\frac{3}{5}y + 2 = \frac{1}{2}y$ *3-5, 3-6*

Reasoning Strategies

PART
1 **Make an Organized List**

What You'll Learn

1 To solve problems using the strategy *Make an Organized List* and other strategies

... And Why

To increase efficiency in solving problems by applying reasoning skills

Make an Organized List **and other strategies.**

PROBLEM-SOLVING GUIDELINES
■ UNDERSTAND the problem
■ Develop and carry out a PLAN
■ Find the ANSWER and CHECK

Some problems can be solved by listing information in a systematic or organized way. This strategy for solving problems is called *Make an Organized List.*

EXAMPLE Use the strategy *Make an Organized List* to solve this problem. The team that wins 3 games in a "best-3-of-5" basketball playoff wins the playoff. In how many ways can a team win 3 games?

We can solve this problem by first listing all of the ways to win if there are no losses. Next we will list the ways if there is 1 loss and then the ways with 2 losses. Listing the possibilities according to the number of losses keeps the list organized. After the list is organized, we can tell when we have listed all possibilities.

WWW   1 way to win 3 games with 0 losses

LWWW
WLWW   3 ways to win 3 games with 1 loss
WWLW

LLWWW
LWLWW
LWWLW
WLLWW   6 ways to win 3 games with 2 losses
WLWLW
WWLLW

$1 + 3 + 6 = 10$ There are 10 ways to win 3 games in the playoff.

Reasoning Strategies

Draw a Diagram	Try, Test, Revise	Write an Equation
Make an Organized List	Use Logical Reasoning	Make a Table
Look for a Pattern	Simplify the Problem	Work Backward

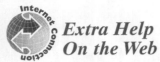

3-12 Problems

Solve using one or more problem-solving strategies.

1. There are 9 teams that play in a soccer league. During the season each team will play each other team in the league twice. How many games will be played?

2. Tennis rackets can be packaged in cartons holding 2 rackets each or in cartons holding 3 rackets each. Yesterday's packing slip showed that 38 cartons were used to pack a total of 100 rackets. How many cartons of each size were used yesterday?

3. In how many *different* ways can you arrange the shapes in each set so that at least one side of each shape is completely touching one side of another shape, and all shapes are adjacent? Sketch each arrangement. (Arrangements you can turn or flip to match each other count as one arrangement.)
   a. 3 equilateral triangles   b. 4 equilateral triangles
   c. 4 squares   d. 5 squares

4. A vending machine had to be programmed to accept any combination of nickels, dimes, and quarters that totals 40¢. How many different combinations are possible?

5. A garden plot has an area of 120 square meters. The measures of the length and width are whole numbers. The length and width of the garden were selected so that the least amount of fencing would be required to enclose the garden. What are the dimensions of this garden?

6. A sporting goods store was having a sale. One customer bought 5 different items and paid $120, not including tax. He could have chosen any of the items listed in the chart below. What combination of 5 items could he have bought?

■ soccer shoes $25	■ jogging suits $35	■ sweat shirts $15
■ basketballs $20	■ swimsuits $10	■ softball bats $15
■ leg weights $45	■ racquetball racket $40	■ tennis outfit $50

7. Charles and Eva want to have a party for their friends. Both work at night. Charles has every ninth night off from work, and Eva has every fifth night off. Today is Sunday and Charles is off work. Eva has tomorrow night off. When is the first night they would both be available to have the party?

8. *Write a Convincing Argument* Solve the problem below. Then write an argument that would convince a classmate that your solution is correct.

   A school club sold calculators to raise money for a field trip. The members sold small calculators for $5 each and large desk-top calculators for twice as much as the small calculators. At the end of the sale, they sold three times as many small calculators as large calculators for a total of $600. How many of each size calculator did they sell?

3-1

To solve an equation using the **addition property of equality,** you add the same number to both sides of the equation.

Solve.

1. $x + 12 = -8$

2. $-7 = y - 11$

3. $x - 11 = 14$

4. $w + \frac{3}{7} = -\frac{5}{7}$

Translate to an equation and solve.

5. A color TV sold for $629 in May. This was $38 more than the price in January. Find the January price.

6. In La Ciudad Fría the average daily high temperature in the winter is $-65°F$. This is 150° less than the average daily high temperature in Ciudad Caliente. What is the average daily high temperature in Ciudad Caliente in the winter?

3-2

To solve an equation using the **multiplication property of equality,** you multiply both sides of the equation by the same nonzero number.

Solve.

7. $6x = 24$

8. $-\frac{x}{4} = 48$

9. $\frac{3}{5} = \frac{-2}{5}x$

10. $-11x = 121$

Translate to an equation and solve.

11. Rosita gets a $4 commission for each small appliance that she sells. One week she got $108 in commissions. How many small appliances did she sell?

3-3

To solve an equation, you may need to use both the addition and multiplication properties of equality. Collect like terms on each side of the equation before using the properties. You may need to use the distributive property to remove parentheses before collecting like terms.

Solve and check.

12. $2x + 5 = 13$

13. $-8x + 3 = 27$

14. $50 - 4x = 14$

15. $7x + 8x = 45$

16. $4(3y + 2) = 44$

17. $6(3a - 2) + 5a = 57$

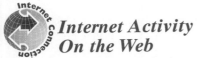

Internet Activity
On the Web

Look for extension problems
for this chapter at the
Prentice Hall Web site.
www.phschool.com

3-4

Use the Problem-Solving Guidelines to help you understand a problem, write
an equation, and check your solution.

Write as an algebraic expression.

18. 6 more than twice a number

19. 18 less than the product of 5 and a number

20. 6 less than $\frac{1}{3}$ of the number

21. $\frac{1}{2}$ of the sum of a number and 10

22. Betsy swims every day. She swam 3 fewer laps today than twice the
number of laps she swam yesterday. Write an expression for the number
of laps she swam today.

23. After 8 weeks at the exercise club, Nadia could lift 10 pounds more than
twice what she could lift before joining the club. Write an expression for
the weight Nadia could lift after 8 weeks at the club.

24. The number of girls in the swim club is 5 less than twice the number of
boys. There are 75 girls in the club. How many boys are in the club?

25. Chris has ridden her bike 10 miles. She averages 12 mi/h. How many more
minutes must she ride before she has traveled 60 miles?

26. If the Menlo High football team scored 4 more points in Friday night's
game, they would have tripled the score of Woodside High. Woodside
scored 14 points. How many points did Menlo score?

3-5

To solve an equation, you must get all variable terms on the same side of the
equation. If the equation contains parentheses, you may need to use the
distributive property first. An **identity** is an equation that is true for all
acceptable replacements of the variables.

Solve.

27. $6x - 5 = -2x + 11$

28. $3y - 6 - 7y = 12 - 2y + 6$

29. $4(x + 3) = 36$

30. $8(x - 2) = 5(x + 4)$

31. $x + 7 - 2 = 5 + x$

32. $2(x + 3) - 3x = 5 - x + 1$

3-6

To clear an equation of fractions, multiply both sides of the equation by the
least common denominator. To clear an equation of decimals, multiply both
sides of the equation by a power of 10.

Solve.

33. $\frac{3}{4}x + \frac{1}{2}x + \frac{1}{4} = 1 + 2x$

34. $12.21 - 4.3a = 24.25$

35. $\frac{4}{9}y - \frac{4}{3} = \frac{1}{6}y + \frac{11}{18}$

36. $0.83w + 0.29 = 0.5w - 0.7$

3-7

To solve a formula for a given variable, use the same rules you use to solve equations.

Solve.

37. $V = Bh$ for h

38. $b = \frac{3A}{r}$ for A

39. $P = 2x + 2w$ for x

40. $V = \frac{1}{3}Ar$ for A

3-8

To solve an equation involving absolute value, remember that the absolute value of a number is its distance from 0 on a number line. If $|a| = 3$, then $a = 3$ or -3.

Solve.

41. $|x| = 5$

42. $|x| - 4 = 6$

43. $-9 + 3|y| = 24$

3-9

An equation that states two **ratios** are equal is called a **proportion.** Some problems can be solved by writing and solving a proportion.

Solve.

44. $\frac{b}{42} = \frac{6}{7}$

45. $\frac{45}{15} = \frac{30}{x}$

Translate to a proportion and solve.

46. The winner of an election for class president won by a vote of 3 to 2, having received 324 votes. How many votes did the other candidates get?

47. A student traveled 234 km in 14 days. At this rate, how far would the student travel in 42 days?

3-10

The ratio of a number to 100 is called **percent.** When solving problems involving percent, the percent should be expressed as a fraction or a decimal. To find the **percent of increase** (or **decrease**), divide the amount of increase (or decrease) by the original amount.

Write as a decimal.

48. 48%

49. 7%

50. 150%

Express as a percent. Round to the nearest tenth if necessary.

51. $\frac{1}{3}$

52. $\frac{7}{8}$

53. 0.012

Solve.

54. 60 is what percent of 150?

55. 75% of what number is 187.5?

56. Sales tax in a certain city is 6.5% of the cost. What would the sales tax be on a motorcycle that costs $850?

57. A Shea CD player cost $80 last year and $112 this year. What was the percent of increase in its price?

3-11

To solve a problem with more than one unknown quantity, you may be able to represent all of the unknown quantities in terms of one variable. First decide which unknown quantity the variable will represent.

58. An adult's ticket to the movie theater costs twice as much as a child's ticket. Write an expression for the cost of admission for one child and one adult.

59. Write an expression for the sum of two consecutive even integers.

Translate to an equation and solve.

60. The sum of two consecutive odd integers is 116. Find the integers.

61. The perimeter of a rectangle is 56 cm. The width is 6 cm less than the length. Find the width and the length.

Chapter Assessment

Solve.

1. $x + 7 = 15$

2. $t - 9 = 17$

3. $3x = -18$

4. $-7x = -28$

5. $-\frac{x}{8} = 5$

6. $-\frac{2}{3}y = -\frac{4}{15}$

7. $8a + 11 = 35$

8. $-4y + 7 = -21$

9. $3(x + 2) = 27$

10. $45 - 3x = 30$

11. $3t + 7 = 2t - 5$

12. $-3x + 6(x + 4) = 9$

13. $0.51m + 0.03 = 0.4m - 0.74$

14. $\frac{1}{2}x - \frac{3}{5} = \frac{1}{10} + \frac{3}{10}$

15. $|x| + 3 = 8$

16. $2|y| - 4 = 8$

Write as an algebraic expression.

17. the number of days in x weeks

18. fifteen decreased by four times a number

19. the sum of two consecutive integers

20. two less than one fifth of a number

Solve the formulas for the given variable.

21. $A = 2\pi rh$ for r

22. $b = \frac{2A}{h}$ for A

23. $P = 2x + 2w$ for x

24. $V = \frac{1}{3}Ar$ for r

Solve.

25. $\frac{16}{3} = \frac{c}{12}$

26. $\frac{21}{x} = \frac{105}{5}$

Translate to a proportion and solve.

27. A sample of 184 light bulbs contained 6 defective bulbs. At this rate, how many defective bulbs would you expect to find in a sample of 1288 light bulbs?

28. In traveling 350 miles, Raul used 21 gallons of gas. How many gallons of gas would Raul use on a trip of 525 miles if his car consumed gas at the same rate?

Write as a decimal.

29. 89%

30. 3%

31. 200%

Express as a percent. Round off to the nearest tenth of a percent if necessary.

32. $\frac{2}{5}$

33. $\frac{2}{3}$

Solve.

34. 96 is what percent of 150?

35. 90% of what number is 45?

36. 87.5% of 200 is what number?

37. A family spends $660 a month for rent. This is 30% of the family's monthly income. What is their monthly income?

Translate to an equation and solve.

38. Jim scored 22 points in a basketball game. That was six points more than Frank scored. How many points did Frank score?

39. A carpenter worked on a job for 5 days and earned $440. How much did he earn per day?

40. Marisa and Lisa earned a total of $65 babysitting during the month of November. Marisa earned $5 more than $\frac{1}{2}$ of what Lisa earned. How much did they each earn?

41. The perimeter of a rectangle is 36 cm. The length is 4 cm greater than the width. Find the width and length.

42. Money is invested in a "guaranteed fund" at 12% simple interest. After one year, there is $840 in the account. How much was originally invested?

CHAPTER

Skills & Concepts You Need for Chapter 4

2-2   Graph each number on the number line.

1. $\frac{5}{3}$ **2.** $\frac{2}{5}$ **3.** $-\frac{3}{4}$

Use the proper symbol $>$ or $<$.

4. $-\frac{3}{4} \ \square \ -\frac{2}{5}$ **5.** $-1.5 \ \square \ 0.65$ **6.** $\frac{3}{4} \ \square \ -2$

3-3   Solve.

7. $3x - 2 = 7$ **8.** $-6x + 4 = 28$

9. $40 - 2x = 26$ **10.** $5x + 3x = 64$

11. $2(5y + 3) = 56$ **12.** $8(3a + 5) + a = 65$

3-4   Write as an algebraic expression.

13. the sum of three consecutive even integers

14. one half of the number plus 12

15. thirty-two less than twice the number

16. two greater than 3 times a number

3-5   Solve.

17. $2x + 20 + 33x = 80 + 15x$ **18.** $3(2x - 1) + 4 = x + 25$

19. $14p - 10 = 8 + 2p$ **20.** $4(2x + 1) = 3(x + 13)$

Solve.

21. $\frac{b}{3} - 2 = 6$ **22.** $\frac{2}{9}b + \frac{1}{3}b = \frac{4}{9} - \frac{1}{3}b$

23. $0.9x - 0.5x = 6$ **24.** $0.32y = 0.3y + 32$

Inequalities

Suppose peanuts cost $2.50/lb, almonds cost $5.60/lb, and cashews cost $7.60/lb. A 1-lb mixture has 8 oz of peanuts, 4 oz of almonds, and 4 oz of cashews. How much should the 1-lb mixture cost?

4-1 ▷ Inequalities and Their Graphs

What You'll Learn

1 To determine whether a number is a solution of an inequality

2 To graph inequalities on the number line

...And Why

To understand statements of inequality

Math in Action

The phrases italicized below are statements of inequality. An inequality tells the relationship between two numbers or expressions.

- Motorized vehicles must be able to maintain a speed *greater than or equal to* 35 miles per hour to travel on most freeways.
- Most elevators can carry a load *less than or equal to* 2000 pounds.

PART 1 Solutions of Inequalities

Objective: Determine whether a given number is a solution of an inequality.

In Chapter Two you learned the meaning of the symbols $<$ (is less than) and $>$ (is greater than). We now include the symbols $\leq$ and $\geq$.

> We read $\leq$ as "is less than or equal to."
> We read $\geq$ as "is greater than or equal to."

Mathematical sentences containing $<$, $>$, $\leq$, or $\geq$ are called **inequalities.**

A solution of an inequality is any number that makes the inequality true.

EXAMPLE 1 Determine whether each number is a solution of $x \geq 5$.

  5   Yes, 5 is a solution because $5 \geq 5$ is true.
 12   Yes, 12 is a solution because $12 \geq 5$ is true.
 −7   No, −7 is not a solution because $-7 \geq 5$ is not true.

Try This Determine whether the given number is a solution of the inequality.

a. $x < 3$ (1) 2   (2) 0   (3) −5   (4) 15   (5) 3
b. $x \geq 6$ (1) 6   (2) 0   (3) −4   (4) 25   (5) −6

PART 2 Graphing Inequalities

Objective: Graph inequalities on the number line.

A **graph** of an inequality in one variable is a picture of its solution set on a number line.

EXAMPLE 2   Graph $x < 2$ on a number line.

The solutions of $x < 2$ are all numbers less than 2. They are shown by shading all points to the left of 2 on a number line.

Note that 2 is not a solution. We indicate this by an open circle at 2. The red arrow indicates that all points to the left of 2 are solutions of the inequality.

EXAMPLE 3   Graph $x \geq -3$ on a number line.

The solutions of $x \geq -3$ are -3 and all points to the right of -3.

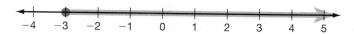

Note that -3 is a solution. We indicate this by a closed circle at -3. The red arrow indicates that all points to the right are also solutions of the inequality.

Try This   Graph on a number line.

c. $x < 8$ **d.** $y \geq -5$

4-1 Exercises

Internet Connection
Extra Help On the Web
Look for worked-out examples at the Prentice Hall Web site.
www.phschool.com

A

Mental Math   Determine whether the given number is a solution of the inequality.

1. $x > 4$	**a.** 4	**b.** 0	**c.** -4	**d.** 6
2. $y < 5$	**a.** 0	**b.** 5	**c.** -1	**d.** -5
3. $x \geq 6$	**a.** -6	**b.** 0	**c.** 6	**d.** 8
4. $x \leq 10$	**a.** 4	**b.** -10	**c.** 0	**d.** 11
5. $x < -8$	**a.** 0	**b.** -8	**c.** -9	**d.** -7
6. $x \geq 0$	**a.** 2	**b.** -3	**c.** 0	**d.** 3
7. $y \geq -5$	**a.** 0	**b.** -4	**c.** -5	**d.** -6
8. $y \leq -\frac{1}{2}$	**a.** -1	**b.** $-\frac{2}{3}$	**c.** 0	**d.** -0.5

Graph on a number line.

9. $x < 5$	**10.** $y < 0$	**11.** $t < -3$	**12.** $h < -5$
13. $y > 6$	**14.** $m > 4$	**15.** $k \geq -4$	**16.** $n \geq -2$
17. $x \leq 5$	**18.** $g \leq 8$	**19.** $b \leq -3$	**20.** $c \leq -1$

See Exercise 25.

B

Classify each statement as true or false.

21. $3 \leq 3$ **22.** $\left| -\frac{1}{4} \right| \geq 0$ **23.** $|-10| \leq 4$ **24.** $|-.08| \leq 0.4$

25. Write an inequality for the sign at the left.

Write the inequality shown by each graph.

26.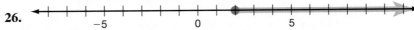

27.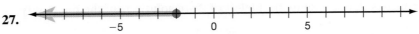

28.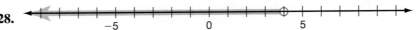

29.

30.

31.

32. *Critical Thinking*   The solutions to $|x| = 5$ are the same distance from 0. What can you say about the solutions to $|x - 2| = 5$?

Challenge

Graph on a number line.

33. all values of x such that $x < 3$ and $x > -1$

34. all values of x such that $x \geq 4$ and $x \leq 1$

35. all values of x such that $x > 2$ and $x < 5$

36. all values of x such that $|x| \geq 4$

Mixed Review

Solve.   **37.** $\frac{1}{3} + 8m = 3m - \frac{1}{2}$ **38.** $5x - (2x + 7) = 2$

39. $7.5y - 0.5y = 3.75y + 39$ **40.** $16 - 2w = 10w - 2 - 6w$

41. $|y| + 6 = 21$ **42.** $|a| = |-9|$ **43.** $|x| = -6$ *3-5, 3-6, 3-8*

Write an equation to solve.

44. The perimeter of a rectangle is 30 in. The length is 5 in. greater than the width. Find the dimensions.

45. Maury bought concert tickets at the Ticket Outlet. He paid $12 for each ticket, plus a $5 service charge for the whole set of tickets. The total cost was $77. How many tickets did he buy?   *3-11*

The Addition Property of Inequalities

Objective: Solve inequalities using the addition property.

We can use a scale to think about inequalities. We know that the inequality $3 < 7$ is true. If we add the same number to both sides of the inequality, we get another true inequality in the same direction.

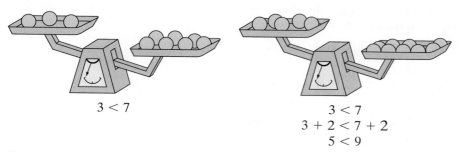

$$3 < 7$$

$$3 < 7$$
$$3 + 2 < 7 + 2$$
$$5 < 9$$

We can state this observation as a property.

The Addition Property of Inequalities

For all rational numbers a, b, and c,

if $a < b$, then $a + c < b + c$

if $a > b$, then $a + c > b + c$

Similar statements hold for $\leq$ and $\geq$.

We use the addition property of inequalities when solving inequalities just as we use the addition property of equality when solving equations.

EXAMPLE 1   Solve the inequality and graph the solution.

$$x + 3 > 4$$
$$x + 3 + (-3) > 4 + (-3) \quad \text{Using the addition property}$$
$$x > 1$$

Since there are an infinite number of solutions to an inequality, it is not possible to "check" the solution. It is possible, however, to check whether the computations used in solving the inequality were done correctly.

Write the equation $x + 3 = 4$ for the inequality $x + 3 > 4$. Then substitute 1, the boundary point of the solution, into the equation. If the computations were done correctly, the equation will check.

Check the computation.

Use $x = 1$ to check the computation.

$$x + 3 = 4$$
$$1 + 3 = 4 \qquad \text{Substituting 1 for } x$$
$$4 = 4 \checkmark$$

We can also check whether the inequality symbol in the solution is correct. Choose any number greater than 1. Substitute this number into the original inequality. An easy number to use is 3.

Check the inequality symbol.

$$x + 3 > 4$$
$$3 + 3 > 4 \qquad \text{Substituting 3 for } x$$
$$6 > 4 \checkmark$$

Any number greater than 1 is a solution.

Try This Solve each inequality and graph the solution.

a. $x + 3 > 5$

b. $x - 5 \leq 8$

c. $x - 2 \geq 7$

d. $x + 1 < 3$

EXAMPLE 2 Solve the inequality and graph the solution.

$$x + \tfrac{1}{3} \geq \tfrac{3}{4}$$
$$x + \tfrac{1}{3} + \left(-\tfrac{1}{3}\right) \geq \tfrac{3}{4} + \left(-\tfrac{1}{3}\right) \qquad \text{Using the addition property}$$
$$x \geq \tfrac{3}{4} - \tfrac{1}{3}$$
$$x \geq \tfrac{9}{12} - \tfrac{4}{12}$$
$$x \geq \tfrac{5}{12}$$

We can check the computation and the inequality symbol to ensure that the answer is correct.

Check the computation.
Use $\frac{5}{12}$, the boundary point.

$$x + \frac{1}{3} = \frac{3}{4}$$

$$\frac{5}{12} + \frac{4}{12} = \frac{3}{4}$$

$$\frac{9}{12} = \frac{3}{4}$$

$$\frac{3}{4} = \frac{3}{4} \ \checkmark$$

Check the inequality symbol.
Use any number greater than $\frac{5}{12}$, say 1.

$$x + \frac{1}{3} \geq \frac{3}{4}$$

$$1 + \frac{1}{3} \geq \frac{3}{4}$$

$$1\frac{1}{3} \geq \frac{3}{4} \ \checkmark$$

Any number greater than or equal to $\frac{5}{12}$ is a solution.

Try This   Solve each inequality and graph the solution.

e. $y + \frac{1}{8} < -\frac{3}{8}$

f. $\frac{3}{10} \leq -\frac{1}{5} + y$

As in solving equations, you should collect like terms on the same side of the inequality symbol first. Then solve the inequality.

EXAMPLE 3   Solve the inequality and graph the solution.

$$3y + 1 - 2y < -3$$
$$y + 1 < -3 \qquad \text{Collecting like terms}$$
$$y + 1 + (-1) < -3 + (-1) \qquad \text{Using the addition property}$$
$$y < -4$$

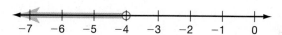

Check the computation.
Use -4, the boundary point.

$$3y + 1 - 2y = -3$$
$$3(-4) + 1 - 2(-4) = -3$$
$$-12 + 1 + 8 = -3$$
$$-3 = -3 \ \checkmark$$

Check the inequality symbol.
Choose any number less than -4,
say -6.

$$3y + 1 - 2y < -3$$
$$3(-6) + 1 - 2(-6) < -3$$
$$-18 + 1 + 12 < -3$$
$$-5 < -3 \ \checkmark$$

Any number less than -4 is a solution.

Try This   Solve each inequality and graph the solution.

g. $5y + 2 - 4y \leq -1$ **h.** $-4x + 5x + 1 < -2$

Extra Help On the Web

Look for worked-out examples at the Prentice Hall Web site.
www.phschool.com

4-2 Exercises

A

Solve each inequality and graph the solution.

1. $x + 7 > 2$ **2.** $x + 6 > 3$

3. $y + 5 > 8$ **4.** $y + 7 > 9$

5. $x + 8 \le -10$ **6.** $x + 9 \le -12$

7. $a + 12 < 6$ **8.** $a + 20 < 8$

9. $x - 7 \le 9$ **10.** $x - 3 \le 14$

11. $x - 6 > 2$ **12.** $x - 9 > 4$

13. $y - 7 > -12$ **14.** $y - 10 > -16$

15. $4m - 3m < 2$ **16.** $2x + 3 - x > 5$

Solve.

17. $3x - 2x + 9 \le 6$ **18.** $-2y + 3y + 10 \le 8$

19. $5n - 6 - 4n < -2$ **20.** $-5x + 6x - 8 < -9$

21. $3y + 4 - 2y \le -7$ **22.** $4a - 3a + 5 \ge -8$

23. $m + \frac{1}{4} \le \frac{1}{2}$ **24.** $y + \frac{1}{3} \ge \frac{5}{6}$

25. $x - \frac{1}{3} > \frac{1}{4}$ **26.** $b - \frac{1}{8} > \frac{1}{2}$

27. $c + \frac{4}{5} \le \frac{3}{10}$ **28.** $\frac{2}{3} + a \ge \frac{5}{6}$

29. **TEST PREP** Which number is *not* a solution of $t - 5 \le 1$?

    A. -5 **B.** 1 **C.** 6 **D.** 10

B

Solve.

30. $3(r + 2) - 2r < 4$ **31.** $4(r + 5) - 3r \ge 7$

32. $3a + 6 - 2a \ge -19$ **33.** $-5 \le 3m - 10 - 2m$

34. $4(x + 3) - 3x > 4$ **35.** $5(y - 2) - 4(y - 1) < 0$

36. $-6(a + 2) + 7a \le -12$ **37.** $-2(a - 3) + 3(a + 2) < 4$

Use the first inequality to find the unknown number or expression in the second inequality.

38. $y + 2 + 3y > 9$ **39.** $a^2 + 4 - b \le -2$
      $y + 3y > \text{??}$ $a^2 - b \le \text{??}$

40. $m + n - 4 \le n$ **41.** $p + q + z \ge -2$
      $m - 4 \le \text{??}$ $p + z \ge \text{??}$

42. $a + b < 2a - 4$ **43.** $x - y > 7 + y$
      $b < \text{??}$ $x > \text{??}$

44. *Error Analysis*   A student solved $t + 6 < 5$ and got the solution $t < 11$. What error did the student make?

45. *Critical Thinking*   Give two different inequalities that each have $x \le -5$ as a statement of all solutions.

Challenge

Determine whether the following statements are true or false.

46. $x + c < y + d$ when $x < y$ and $c < d$.

47. $x - c > y - d$ when $x > y$ and $c > d$.

48. If x is an integer, write a statement equivalent to $x > 5$ using $\ge$.

49. If y is an integer, write a statement equivalent to $y < 5$ using $\le$.

50. *Mathematical Reasoning*   Does the transitive property hold for $>$? Does it hold for $\le$? Explain.

51. Other inequality symbols include $\not>$, which means "is not greater than," $\not<$, "is not less than," and $\ne$, "is not equal to." Write statements equivalent to each of the following using $>$, $<$, $\ge$, $\le$, or $=$.

    a. $x \not> 5$ **b.** $x \not< -3$ **c.** $x \ne -\frac{3}{2}$

    d. $x \not< y$ **e.** $x \not> -y$ **f.** $-x \ne y$

Mixed Review

Solve each proportion.   **52.** $\frac{m}{8} = \frac{3}{4}$ **53.** $\frac{21}{m} = \frac{7}{3}$ **54.** $\frac{4}{6} = \frac{m}{9}$ *3-9*

Solve.   **55.** $-84x = 4$ **56.** $-3 = 9c$ **57.** $|t| - 4 = 21$

58. $3 - |m| = 1$ **59.** $\frac{2}{3} + \frac{1}{8}m = \frac{5}{12}m - \frac{19}{24}$ **60.** $\frac{2}{3} \cdot |y| = 8$ *3-2, 3-6, 3-8*

61. Write an algebraic expression for 3 more than twice a number. *1-6, 3-4*

62. A certain cruise ship must have 1 lifeboat for every 16 passengers. How many lifeboats are needed to accommodate 144 passengers? *3-11*

63. A certain mixed-nut snack uses 6 oz of peanuts for every 4 oz of almonds and cashews. How many ounces of peanuts are needed for a 28 oz mix of almonds and cashews? *3-11*

Suppose peanuts cost $2.50/lb, almonds cost $5.60/lb, and cashews cost $7.60/lb. A 1-lb mixture has 8 oz of peanuts, 4 oz of almonds, and 4 oz of cashews. How much should the 1-lb mixture cost?

⬦ Connections: Geometry

In the figure at the right, the measure of angle 1 is x (m∠1 = x) and the measure of angle 2 is $4x + 6$ (m∠2 = $4x + 6$). The sum of the measures of angles 1 and 2 is less than 90°. What are three possible measures for angles 1 and 2?

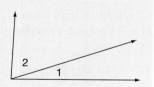

4-3 ▷ The Multiplication Property of Inequalities

What You'll Learn

1 To solve inequalities using the multiplication property

...And Why

To prepare for solving more complicated inequalities

Objective: Solve inequalities using the multiplication property.

Consider the true inequality.

$$3 < 7$$

If we multiply both numbers by 2, we get another true inequality.

$$6 < 14 \qquad \text{True}$$

If we multiply both numbers by -3, we get a false inequality.

$$-9 < -21 \qquad \text{False}$$

If we reverse the inequality symbol, however, we get a true inequality.

$$-9 > -21 \qquad \text{True}$$

We can state these observations as a property.

The Multiplication Property of Inequalities

For all rational numbers a, b, and c,

where c is positive,
if $a < b$, then $ac < bc$
if $a > b$, then $ac > bc$

where c is negative,
if $a < b$, then $ac > bc$
if $a > b$, then $ac < bc$

Similar statements hold for $\leq$ and $\geq$.

EXAMPLE 1   Solve the inequality and graph the solution.

$$4x < 28$$

$$\tfrac{1}{4}(4x) < \tfrac{1}{4} \cdot 28 \qquad \text{Multiplying both sides by } \tfrac{1}{4}$$

$$x < 7 \qquad \text{Since } \tfrac{1}{4} \text{ is positive, do not change the inequality symbol.}$$

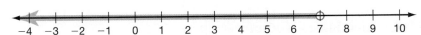

Check the computation.
Use 7 to check the computation.

$$4x = 28$$
$$4 \cdot 7 = 28$$
$$28 = 28 \ ✔$$

Check the inequality symbol.
Choose any number less than 7, say 0.

$$4x < 28$$
$$4 \cdot 0 < 28$$
$$0 < 28 \ ✔$$

Any number less than 7 is a solution.

Try This   Solve each inequality and graph the solution.

a. $8x < 64$ **b.** $5y \geq 160$ **c.** $2t < 56$ **d.** $9s > 81$

EXAMPLE 2   Solve the inequality and graph the solution.

$$-2y < 18$$

$$-\tfrac{1}{2}(-2y) > -\tfrac{1}{2} \cdot 18 \qquad \text{Multiplying both sides by } -\tfrac{1}{2} \text{ and}$$
$$\text{reversing the inequality symbol}$$

$$y > -9$$

Check the computation.   Check the inequality symbol.
Use -9 to check the computation.   Choose any number greater than -9,
say 0.

$$-2y = 18 \qquad\qquad -2y < 18$$
$$-2 \cdot -9 = 18 \qquad\qquad -2 \cdot 0 < 18$$
$$18 = 18 \ \checkmark \qquad\qquad 0 < 18 \ \checkmark$$

Any number greater than -9 is a solution.

Try This   Solve and graph the solution.

e. $-4x \geq 24$ **f.** $-5y < 13$ **g.** $-t < -5$ **h.** $-n > 2$

EXAMPLE 3   Solve the inequality and graph the solution.

$$-3x \geq \tfrac{5}{6}$$

$$-\tfrac{1}{3}(-3x) \leq -\tfrac{1}{3} \cdot \tfrac{5}{6} \qquad \text{Multiplying both sides by } -\tfrac{1}{3} \text{ and reversing the}$$
$$\text{inequality sign}$$

$$x \leq -\tfrac{5}{18}$$

Any number less than or equal to $-\tfrac{5}{18}$ is a solution.

Try This   Solve each inequality and graph the solution.

i. $-y \geq \tfrac{1}{2}$ **j.** $-3x < \tfrac{1}{6}$ **k.** $-2x \leq \tfrac{5}{8}$ **l.** $-4y \geq -\tfrac{3}{7}$

4-3 Exercises

A

Solve each inequality and graph the solution.

1. $5x < 35$
2. $8x \geq 32$
3. $9y \leq 81$

4. $10x > 240$
5. $6y > 72$
6. $9x \leq 63$

7. $7x < 13$
8. $8y < 17$
9. $4y \geq 15$

10. $3y \geq 19$
11. $6y \leq 3$
12. $14x \leq 4$

13. $7y \geq -21$
14. $6x \geq -18$
15. $12x < -36$

Solve.

16. $16y < -64$
17. $5y \geq -2$
18. $7x \geq -4$

19. $-2x \leq 12$
20. $-3y \leq 15$
21. $-4y \leq 16$

22. $-7y \leq 21$
23. $-6y > 360$
24. $-9x > 540$

25. $-12x < -24$
26. $-14y < -70$
27. $-18y \geq -36$

28. $-20x \geq -400$
29. $-2x < -17$
30. $-5y < -23$

31. $-8y \geq -31$
32. $-7x \geq -43$
33. $-3y < \frac{1}{7}$

34. *Error Analysis*   A student wrote that the solution of $-2x \geq 20$ was $x \geq -10$. What error did the student make?

B

Solve.

35. $-7x \geq -6.3$
36. $-\frac{5}{6}y \leq -\frac{3}{4}$
37. $-8x < 40.5$

38. $-\frac{3}{4}x \geq -\frac{1}{8}$
39. $5x + 6x < -33$
40. $-12 > 2y - 6y$

41. $0 > -5t + 10t$
42. $4 \leq -9n + n$
43. $4m - 9m \geq -12 - 8$

44. *Critical Thinking*   Solve $3x > 4x$.

Challenge

Mathematical Reasoning   Determine whether each statement is true or false. If it is false, give a counterexample.

45. $x^2 > y^2$ when $x > y$.
46. $\frac{x}{z} < \frac{y}{z}$ when $x < y$ and $z \neq 0$.

Mixed Review

Determine whether the given number is a solution of the inequality.

47. $-4x > 9$;   **a.** 10   **b.** 6   **c.** -8 **d.** 0   **e.** -5 *4-1*

Simplify.   **48.** $4m + 2m - m$ **49.** $7x + 5 + 4x$

50. $6(y + 4y) + 3y$ **51.** $3(2x - 4) + 2x + 12$ *1-5, 2-7*

Evaluate for $a = 2, b = 3, c = 4$.   **52.** $a(b^2 + c)$ **53.** $c(2a - 3b)$ *1-1, 2-7*

Using the Properties Together

4-4

Objective: Solve inequalities using the addition and multiplication properties.

We use the addition and multiplication properties together in solving inequalities in much the same way as for equations. We usually use the addition property first.

What You'll Learn

1 To solve inequalities using the addition and multiplication properties

. . . And Why

To solve more complicated inequalities

 **EXAMPLES** Solve.

1
$$6 + 5y > 21$$
$$-6 + 6 + 5y > -6 + 21 \qquad \text{Using the addition property of inequalities}$$
$$5y > 15$$
$$\tfrac{1}{5} \cdot (5y) > \tfrac{1}{5} \cdot 15 \qquad \text{Using the multiplication property of inequalities}$$
$$y > 3$$

Any number greater than 3 is a solution.

2
$$7x + 4 \le 4x + 16$$
$$-4x + 7x + 4 \le -4x + 4x + 16 \qquad \text{Using the addition property of inequalities}$$
$$3x + 4 \le 16$$
$$3x + 4 + (-4) \le 16 + (-4) \qquad \text{Using the addition property of inequalities}$$
$$3x \le 12$$
$$\tfrac{1}{3} \cdot 3x \le \tfrac{1}{3} \cdot 12 \qquad \text{Using the multiplication property of inequalities}$$
$$x \le 4$$

Any number less than or equal to 4 is a solution.

3
$$17 - 5y < 8y - 9$$
$$17 - 5y + (-8y) < 8y + (-8y) - 9 \qquad \text{Using the addition property}$$
$$17 - 13y < -9$$
$$-17 + 17 - 13y < -17 - 9 \qquad \text{Using the addition property}$$
$$-13y < -26$$
$$-\tfrac{1}{13} \cdot -13y > -\tfrac{1}{13}(-26) \qquad \text{Using the multiplication property, reversing the inequality symbol}$$
$$y > 2$$

Any number greater than 2 is a solution.

Try This   Solve.

a. $7 - 4x < -1$ **b.** $13a + 5 \ge 12a + 4$ **c.** $4m - 4 > 8 + 2m$

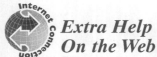

Extra Help
On the Web

Look for worked-out
examples at the Prentice
Hall Web site.
www.phschool.com

4-4 Exercises

A
Solve.

1. $4 + 3x < 28$
2. $5 + 4y < 37$
3. $3x - 5 \le 13$
4. $5y - 9 \le 21$
5. $13x - 7 < -46$
6. $8y - 4 < -52$
7. $5x + 3 \ge -7$
8. $7y + 4 \ge -10$
9. $4 - 3y > 13$
10. $6 - 8x > 22$
11. $3 - 9x < 30$
12. $5 - 7y < 40$
13. $3 - 6y > 23$
14. $8 - 2y > 14$
15. $4x + 2 - 3x \le 9$
16. $15x + 3 - 14x \le 7$
17. $8x + 7 - 7x > -3$
18. $9x + 8 - 8x > -5$
19. $6 - 4y > 4 - 3y$
20. $7 - 8y > 5 - 7y$
21. $5 - 9y \le 2 - 8y$
22. $6 - 13y \le 4 - 12y$
23. $19 - 7y - 3y < 39$
24. $18 - 6y - 9y < 63$
25. $21 - 8y < 6y + 49$
26. $33 - 12x < 4x + 97$
27. $14 - 5y - 2y \ge -19$
28. $17 - 6y - 7y \le -13$
29. $27 - 11x > 14x - 18$
30. $42 - 13y > 15y - 19$

31. **TEST PREP**   Which inequality has the same solutions as
    $3x - 1 > -7$?

    A. $-2x + 4 > 8$ **B.** $x + 3 - 2x > 5$ **C.** $4x < 6x + 4$
    D. $9 + 4x \ge 1$ **E.** None of them

B
Solve.

32. $5(12 - 3t) \ge 15(t + 4)$
33. $6(z - 5) < 5(7 - 2z)$
34. $4(0.5 - y) + y > 4y - 0.2$
35. $3 + 3(0.6 + y) > 2y + 6.6$
36. $\frac{x}{3} - 2 \le 1$
37. $\frac{2}{3} - \frac{x}{5} < \frac{4}{15}$
38. $\frac{y}{5} + 1 \le \frac{2}{5}$
39. $\frac{3x}{5} \ge -15$
40. $\frac{-x}{4} - \frac{3x}{8} + 2 > 3 - x$
41. $11 - x > 5 + \frac{2x}{5}$
42. $0.2y + 2.1 \ge 1.2y + 0.3$
43. $0.3b + 5.4 \ge -b + 0.2$
44. $0.2(30 + a) < 5$
45. $0.3(10 + 2y) \le 9$
46. $\frac{1}{5}(z + 6) \le 0.4(2 + z)$
47. $\frac{1}{2}(t + 5) \le 0.2(3 + t)$
48. $\frac{1}{2}(c + 3) - \frac{1}{3}(c - 2) > 0$
49. $\frac{3}{4}(2d + 1) + \frac{1}{3}(d - 3) < 0$
50. $0.3[4(x - 2) + x] < 0.3x$
51. $0.4[2(w + 3) - 5w] < 0.6$

Mathematical Reasoning Give a reason that justifies each step in the solution.

52. $8 + 3x - 7x \geq 32$

   a. $8 - 4x \geq 32$ _____

   b. $-8 + 8 - 4x \geq 32 - 8$ _____

   c. $-4x \geq 24$ _____

   d. $-\frac{1}{4}(-4x) \leq -\frac{1}{4} \cdot 24$ _____

   e. $x \leq -6$ _____

53. $11 - 6y < -34 + 9y$

   a. $11 - 6y + 6y < -34 + 9y + 6y$ _____

   b. $11 < -34 + 15y$ _____

   c. $34 + 11 < 34 - 34 + 15y$ _____

   d. $45 < 15y$ _____

   e. $\frac{1}{15} \cdot 45 < \frac{1}{15} \cdot 15y$ _____

   f. $3 < y$ _____

54. $3(m - 8) \geq 4(m + 4)$

   a. $3m - 24 \geq 4m + 16$ _____

   b. $3m - 24 + 24 \geq 4m + 16 + 24$ _____

   c. $3m \geq 4m + 40$ _____

   d. $-4m + 3m \geq -4m + 4m + 40$ _____

   e. $-m \geq 40$ _____

   f. $-1(-m) \leq -1 \cdot 40$ _____

   g. $m \leq -40$ _____

55. $\frac{x}{4} - \frac{1}{6} \leq \frac{2}{3}$

   a. $12\left(\frac{x}{4} - \frac{1}{6}\right) \leq 12\left(\frac{2}{3}\right)$ _____

   b. $12\left(\frac{x}{4}\right) - 12\left(\frac{1}{6}\right) \leq 12\left(\frac{2}{3}\right)$ _____

   c. $3x - 2 \leq 8$ _____

   d. $3x - 2 + 2 \leq 8 + 2$ _____

   e. $3x \leq 10$ _____

   f. $\frac{1}{3}(3x) \leq \frac{1}{3}(10)$ _____

   g. $x \leq \frac{10}{3}$ _____

Journal

Explain how solving inequalities and solving equations are similar. Explain how they are different.

Determine whether each inequality is sometimes, always, or never true for any value of the variable.

56. $w + 3 \le w - 4$ **57.** $2t < 5t$ **58.** $x^2 > x$

59. *Error Analysis*   A student solved the inequality $4x + 9 < 7x - 1$ as shown below.

$$4x + 9 < 7x - 1$$
$$8 < 3x$$
$$\tfrac{8}{3} < x$$

What error did the student make?

60. *Critical Thinking*   Solve $\frac{1}{2}(5x + 5) < \frac{1}{3}(5x - 30)$ and describe its positive solutions.

Challenge

Solve for x.

61. $-(x + 5) \ge 4a - 5$ **62.** $\frac{1}{2}(2x + 2b) > \frac{1}{3}(21 + 3b)$

63. $-6(x + 3) \le -9(y + 2)$ **64.** $y < ax + b$

65. $6x + 3 > 7x - c$ **66.** $8 - 0.5x < w + 6.7$

67. *Mathematical Reasoning*   If $x \ge y$ and $-x \ge -y$, what can we conclude about x and y?

68. If $0 < x < 1$, then which of the following is true, $x^2 < x$ or $x < x^2$?

69. If $-1 < x < 0$, then which of the following is true, $x^2 < |x|$ or $|x| < x^2$?

Mixed Review

Evaluate for $m = 6$.   **70.** $m(m + 2)$ **71.** $0.5(m)$

72. $(m + 3)(m - 4)$ **73.** $m^2 - m - 12$ *1-1*

Solve.   **74.** $9y = 3y - 45$ **75.** $3z + 45 < 36$

76. $-2.05n = -9.02$ **77.** $2x = 3x - 4$ *3-3, 3-5, 3-6*

Write each as a percent.   **78.** $\frac{6}{8}$ **79.** $\frac{27}{15}$ **80.** $\frac{60}{12}$ **81.** $\frac{45}{75}$ **82.** $\frac{18}{4}$ *3-10*

83. Let M be Michele's age. Nicole is 2 years younger than Michele. Write an expression for Nicole's age.

84. Let s be the total amount Heidi spent for scarves. Each of the 4 scarves that she bought cost the same. Write an expression for the cost of each scarf.

85. Let L be the amount Lewis earns. Harry earns three times as much as Lewis. Write an expression for the amount Harry earns.   *1-6*

Using Inequalities

4-5

1 Translating Phrases to Inequalities

Objective: Translate phrases to mathematical inequalities.

You have learned how to translate a problem to an equation and solve the equation to answer the problem. Some problems can be solved by translating to an inequality and solving the inequality to answer the problem.

EXAMPLES Translate to an inequality.

1 A number y is greater than 4.
$y > 4$

2 A number x is less than or equal to $2\frac{1}{2}$.
$x \le 2\frac{1}{2}$

3 A number m is at least 3.
$m \ge 3$ "At least 3" means the number could be 3 or greater.

4 A number p is at most $\frac{1}{3}$.

$p \le \frac{1}{3}$ "At most $\frac{1}{3}$" means the number could be $\frac{1}{3}$ or less.

5 3 is greater than or equal to some number n.
$3 \ge n$ We can also write this as $n \le 3$.

6 12 more than twice a number is less than 20.
$2x + 12 < 20$ "12 more than twice a number" translates to $2x + 12$.
                 "Is less than 20" translates to < 20.

Try This   Translate to an inequality.

a. A number x is greater than or equal to 8.
b. A number t is less than 12.

c. A number x is at most $4\frac{1}{2}$.

d. A number n is at least 0.
e. 3 less than a number is greater than 4.

What You'll Learn

1 To translate phrases to mathematical inequalities

2 To solve problems by translating and solving inequalities

...And Why

To use inequalities to solve problems

Writing Math

You can translate words for inequalities into symbols.

less than	$<$
greater than	$>$
less than or equal to	$\le$
greater than or equal to	$\ge$
at least	$\ge$
at most	$\le$

Objective: Solve problems by translating and solving inequalities.

PROBLEM-SOLVING GUIDELINES
■ UNDERSTAND the problem
▪ Develop and carry out a PLAN
■ Find the ANSWER and CHECK

You can use the Problem-Solving Guidelines at the left to help you solve problems when your plan involves writing and solving an inequality.

EXAMPLE 7

Calves weigh about 75 lb at birth and gain about 2 lb per day for a few weeks.

Ruth Anne wants to enter her newborn calf in the 4-H competition at the county fair. In order to qualify for the competition, her calf must weigh at least 200 pounds. Calves weigh approximately 75 pounds at birth and gain around 2 pounds per day for the first few weeks. How many days will it take before the calf's weight exceeds 200 pounds?

■ **UNDERSTAND the problem**

Question: How many days until the calf exceeds 200 pounds?
Data: Calf weighs 75 lb at birth; gains 2 lbs per day.

▪ **Develop and carry out a PLAN**

Let d = the number of days until the calf exceeds 200 pounds.
$2d$ = the amount of weight gained in d days

$$75 + 2d > 200$$
$$2d > 125$$
$$d > 62.5$$

$75 + 2d$ is the total weight after d days. This amount must be greater than ($>$) 200.

■ **Find the ANSWER and CHECK**

On average, a calf should reach 200 pounds in about 63 days, or about 9 weeks. At 2 lb per day plus the birth weight, this answer seems reasonable.

EXAMPLE 8

The medium-size box of dog food weighs 1 lb more than the small size. The large size weighs 2 lb more than the small size. If the total weight of the three boxes is at most 30 lb, what is the most a small box could weigh?

■ **UNDERSTAND the problem**

Question: What is the most the small box could weigh?
Data: Medium box weighs 1 lb more than the small;
large box weighs 2 lb more than the small;
total weight of the three boxes is at most 30 lb.

■ **Develop and carry out a PLAN**

Let s = the maximum weight of the small box.
$s + 1$ = the maximum weight of the medium box.
$s + 2$ = the maximum weight of the large box.

$$s + (s + 1) + (s + 2) \le 30$$ The total weight of the 3 boxes is 30 lb or less.

$$3s + 3 \le 30$$ Simplifying

$$3s \le 27$$ Adding −3 to both sides

$$s \le 9$$ Multiplying both sides by $\frac{1}{3}$

■ **Find the ANSWER and CHECK**

The small box can weigh at most 9 lb. We know that $3 \times 10 = 30$, so we can estimate that each box should weigh about 10 lb. The answer is reasonable.

Try This

f. Each student agreed to sell at least 50 seed packages for a school project. Yesterday one student sold 22 packages, and today this student sold 18. How many more packages does the student need to sell to reach the goal of 50 packages?

g. In an algebra course you must get a total of at least 360 points on four tests for a grade of A. You get 85, 89, and 92 on the first three tests. What score on the last test will give you an A?

h. The sum of two consecutive integers is less than 35. What is the greatest possible pair?

4-5 Exercises

Extra Help On the Web

Look for worked-out examples at the Prentice Hall Web site.
www.phschool.com

A
Translate to an inequality.

1. 3 is less than a number y.

2. $5\frac{1}{2}$ is greater than a number k.

3. A number h is at least $4\frac{5}{6}$.

4. A number j is at most 2.

5. A number is greater than or equal to 0.

6. 7 less than a number is less than 5.

7. 2 more than a number is greater than 9.

8. Twice a number is greater than 12.

9. Half a number is less than or equal to 6.

10. 3 more than one third of a number is less than 9.

11. 18 is greater than or equal to 4 less than twice a number.

12. 4 more than twice a number is less than the opposite of the number.

13. 2 more than the quantity 3 times a number is at most 11.

14. 5 less than a third of a number is at most 15.

Solve.

15. Your quiz grades are 73, 75, 89, and 91. What is the lowest grade you can obtain on the last quiz and still achieve an average of at least 85?

16. The sum of three consecutive odd integers is less than 100. What are the greatest possible values of these integers?

17. Find the greatest possible pair of integers such that one integer is twice the other and their sum is less than 30.

18. The sum of two integers is greater than 12. One integer is ten less than twice the other. What are the least values of the integers?

19. Find all sets of four consecutive even whole numbers whose sum is less than 35.

20. Find the length of the base of a triangle when one side is 2 cm shorter than the base and the other side is 3 cm longer than the base. The perimeter is greater than 19 cm.

21. Armando and Drew do volunteer work at an animal shelter. Drew worked 3 more hours than Armando, and together they worked more than 27 hours. What is the least number of hours each worked?

22. Mrs. Hays has promised her two teenagers that they may go to a concert if together they save more than $25.00 of their spending money. The older teenager agrees to save twice as much as the younger. How much must each save?

B

Solve.

23. The length of a rectangle is 26 cm. What width will make the perimeter greater than 80 cm?

24. The width of a rectangle is 8 cm. What length will make the area at least 150 cm^2?

25. The height of a triangle is 20 cm. What length base will make the area greater than 40 cm^2?

Translate to an inequality and solve.

26. Half of a number is at least -8.

27. 7 less than a third of a number is less than 12.

28. *Critical Thinking* A painter can be paid in two ways.

> Plan A: $500 plus $19 per hour
> Plan B: $24 per hour

Suppose the job takes n hours. For what values of n is Plan A better for the painter than Plan B?

Challenge

29. You have 5 sections of chain and each section has 3 links. The cost to have a link cut is 10¢. The cost to have a link welded is 20¢. How can you join the sections together for less than $1?

30. The Wilsons are remodeling their bathroom. A new vanity and sink will cost $151, the mirror and lights will cost $179.75, and a new tub with the vinyl behind it will cost $191. The plumber will install everything and will charge a certain percent of the total cost of the material for his labor. What is the greatest percent the Wilsons can afford to pay to keep the total for material and labor less than $1000?

Mixed Review

Evaluate for $n = \frac{2}{3}$.   **31.** $n - \frac{3}{2}$ **32.** $\left(\frac{4}{5}\right)n$ **33.** $\frac{3}{5} - n$ *1-1, 2-4, 2-5*

Solve.   **34.** $4(c + 3) = 14c - 3$ **35.** $9y + 16 = 3 - 4y$

36. $9 - 2x < -11$ **37.** $14a + 3 \leq 15a + 7$ *3-5, 4-4*

TEST PREP   Compare the boxed quantity in column A with the boxed quantity in column B. Choose the best answer.   *2-4, 3-2*
  A. The quantity in column A is greater.
  B. The quantity in column B is greater.
  C. The two quantities are equal.
  D. The relationship cannot be determined with the information supplied.

	column A	column B			column A	column B
38.	$3x - 2$	$3x + 7$	**39.**		$-2x + 1$	$7x + 1$
40.	the solution of $4x = 25$	the solution of $-3z = -18$	**41.**		the solution of $\frac{m}{3} = \frac{5}{12}$	the solution of $\frac{c}{8} = \frac{4}{15}$

Connections: Deductive Reasoning

If–Then Statements

Deductive reasoning is a process of reasoning logically from given facts to a conclusion. One of the most common statements used in deductive reasoning is a statement of the form *if A, then B*. Here are some examples:

> If an animal is a cat, then it has four legs.
> If a figure is a square, then it has four sides.
> If $x = 1$, then $x + 1 = 2$.
> If $x < 5$, then $x < 10$.

A statement of this form is called a **conditional statement.** In the statement *if A, then B*, *A* is the antecedent, or **hypothesis,** and *B* is the consequent, or **conclusion.**

The **converse** of a conditional statement can be found by interchanging the hypothesis and the conclusion. The converse of a true conditional statement may or may not be true.

EXAMPLE 1

Conditional: If the product of two numbers is 0, then at least one of the numbers must be 0.

Converse: If at least one of the numbers is 0, then the product of the two numbers is 0.

The converse is also a true statement.

EXAMPLE 2

Conditional: If a figure is a square, then it has four sides.

Converse: If it has four sides, then the figure is a square.

The converse is not necessarily true. A rectangle has four sides, but it is not a square. To show that a converse is not true, you need to give a counterexample. A rectangle is a counterexample for the statement above.

Exercises

Give the converse for each of the conditional statements below. Decide whether the converse is true. If not, give a counterexample.

1. If it's raining, then we can't play soccer.
2. If a number is divisible by 2, then it is an even number.
3. If a number is divisible by 4, then it is an even number.
4. If $5x + 4 = 24$, then $x = 4$.
5. If $x < 5$, then $x < 10$.

Connections: Inductive Reasoning

In everyday life we most commonly reach conclusions using inductive reasoning. With inductive reasoning, you make conclusions based on what you observe has happened before. A conclusion reached by inductive reasoning is sometimes called a conjecture.

EXAMPLE 1

The first five streets that cross First Avenue are Adams Street, Bedford Street, Carlisle Street, Desmond Street, and Everett Street. What is a reasonable conjecture to make about the names of the next five streets?

Since the names of the first five streets are in alphabetical order, a reasonable conjecture is that the names of the next five streets continue in alphabetical order.

A conjecture may or may not be true. One counterexample is enough to prove that a conjecture is false. In Example 1, if the tenth street is named Orange Street, then the conjecture that the street names continue in alphabetical order is false.

Try This

a. Consider this conjecture: "The square of any number is always greater than or equal to the number." Find several examples that support this conjecture. If possible, find a counterexample.

Exercises

Look at each pattern of the sums. Based on the pattern, predict the last sum shown. Verify your prediction.

1.

			2.		
1	$= 1$	$= 1^2$	1	$= 1$	$= \frac{1(2)}{2}$
$1 + 3$	$= 4$	$= 2^2$	$1 + 2$	$= 3$	$= \frac{2(3)}{2}$
$1 + 3 + 5$	$= 9$	$= 3^2$	$1 + 2 + 3$	$= 6$	$= \frac{3(4)}{2}$
$1 + 3 + 5 + 7$	$= 16$	$= 4^2$	$1 + 2 + 3 + 4$	$= 10$	$= \frac{4(5)}{2}$
sum of the first 25 positive odd integers	$= ??$		sum of the first 30 positive integers	$= ??$	

Give a counterexample to show that each conjecture is FALSE.

3. The product of two positive rational numbers is always greater than or equal to both numbers.

4. The difference of two rational numbers is always less than at least one of the numbers.

5. Explain the difference between inductive and deductive reasoning. Give an example of each.

Reasoning Strategies

What You'll Learn

1 To solve problems using the strategy *Use Logical Reasoning* and other strategies

...And Why

To increase efficiency in solving problems by applying reasoning skills

Use Logical Reasoning

Objective: Solve problems using the strategy *Use Logical Reasoning* and other strategies.

Some problems are solved by understanding the given relationships among the facts and using known facts and relationships to draw conclusions. This problem-solving strategy is called *Use Logical Reasoning*.

You can use the Problem-Solving Guidelines at the right to help you solve problems when your plan involves the strategy *Use Logical Reasoning*.

PROBLEM-SOLVING GUIDELINES
■ UNDERSTAND the problem
Develop and carry out a PLAN
■ Find the ANSWER and CHECK

EXAMPLE

A newspaper gave information about an election, but did not tell who was elected to which office. The offices were president, vice-president, secretary, and treasurer. Those elected, but not necessarily in the order of the offices above, were Mr. Berry, Ms. Wells, Mr. Murata, and Ms. Holden. Use these headlines from the paper to decide who was elected to which office.

(1) Murata and Holden Congratulate New Vice-President
(2) Wells—First Woman President
(3) Former Treasurer Holden Happy in New Office

You can solve this problem by recording the given information in a chart and making conclusions based on it. The charts below show the reasoning you might go through to solve this problem.

	B	W	M	H
P				
VP			no	no
S				
T				

Murata and Holden were not elected vice-president.

	B	W	M	H
P	no	yes	no	no
VP	yes	no	no	no
S	no	no		
T	no	no		

If Wells is president, no one else is president. Berry must be vice-president.

	B	W	M	H
P	no	yes	no	no
VP	yes	no	no	no
S	no	no	no	yes
T	no	no	yes	no

Since Holden was not treasurer, she has to be secretary. Murata must be treasurer.

Those elected were: president, Wells; vice-president, Berry; secretary, Holden; and treasurer, Murata.

Problem-Solving Strategies

Draw a Diagram	Try, Test, Revise	Write an Equation
Make an Organized List	Use Logical Reasoning	Make a Table
Look for a Pattern	Simplify the Problem	Work Backward

4-6 Problems

Solve using one or more strategies.

1. William, Carrie, Lester, and Rosa were hired as coaches at a high school. The coaching positions were for basketball, tennis, racquetball, and volleyball. William's sister was among those hired, and she was to be the tennis coach. Neither William nor Lester ever played basketball or knew how to coach it. Rosa had never learned to play tennis. Lester disliked all sports involving a racket. Who was hired to coach which sport?

2. A certain town can use the digits 0, 1, 2, 3, 7, and 9 for its telephone prefixes. How many 3-digit telephone prefixes are possible for this town if each digit can be used only once in a prefix and the first digit cannot be a 1 or a 0?

3. A student was hired by a city's maintenance department to paint house numbers on the curbs in a particular neighborhood. Each digit had to be painted separately, and the student was paid 50¢ per digit. He painted house numbers from 1 to 225. How much did he earn?

4. Two consultants were hired by a company. The total consultant fees were $18,500. If one consultant had earned $500 less, each consultant would have been paid the same. How much was each consultant paid?

5. Five tiles, each 1 foot square, were used to cover a spot on a floor. The tiles had to be placed so that the sides of any two tiles matched evenly. The perimeter of the spot that was covered was 10 feet. What are the possible shapes for the spot?

6. Five cars in a race all finished within 8 seconds of each other. Car 1 finished 1 second ahead of car 4, and car 4 was not last. Car 2 finished 6 seconds before car 5. Car 5 finished 3 seconds behind car 1. Car 1 finished 5 seconds behind car 3. In what order did the cars finish?

7. *Write a Convincing Argument* Solve the problem below. Then write an argument that would convince a classmate that your solution is correct.

   Meg, Scott, Nellie, and Jeff live in the towns Jackson, Springstown, Newton, and Mowetown. None lives in a town that has the same first letter as his or her name. Neither Jeff nor Nellie has ever been to Mowetown. Meg has spent all of her life in Springstown. Which person lives in which town?

4 ▷ Chapter Wrap Up

4-1

A sentence containing $<, >, \leq,$ or $\geq$ is an inequality. A solution of an **inequality** is any number that makes the inequality true when that number is substituted for the variable.

Determine whether the given number is a solution of the inequality.

1. $y \leq 4$ **a.** 3   **b.** 0   **c.** -2 **d.** 8
2. $x > -12$ **a.** 6   **b.** -18 **c.** 0   **d.** 18

A **graph** of an inequality is a diagram of all its solutions on a number line. A closed circle indicates that the end point is part of the solution, and an open circle indicates that the end point is not part of the solution.

Graph on a number line.

3. $x > -1$ 4. $x \leq 5$ 5. $x < -5$

4-2

The **addition property of inequalities** states that if we add the same number to both sides of an inequality, we get another inequality with the same solutions.

Solve and graph the solution.

6. $y + 5 > 3$ 7. $b - \frac{1}{4} \geq 2$ 8. $4a + 6 - 3a < 12$

Solve.

9. $4x + 6 - 3x > 2$ 10. $a + \frac{2}{3} \leq \frac{5}{6}$ 11. $-4y + 5y - 8 \leq 12$

4-3

The **multiplication property of inequalities** states that if we multiply both sides of an inequality by a positive number, we get another inequality with the same solutions. If, however, we multiply both sides of an inequality by a negative number, we must reverse the inequality symbol.

Solve and graph the solution.

12. $5x < 25$ 13. $-3b \geq 21$ 14. $-2y > 3$

4-4

The addition and multiplication properties are often used together in solving inequalities. The addition property is usually used first.

Solve.

15. $3y + 4 < 25$ 16. $4a + 9 \leq 2a - 4$ 17. $14 - 8x < 6x + 36$
18. $7 - 6y > 3y - 20$ 19. $6 - 5y > 3 - 4y$ 20. $15a + 3 - 12a \leq 14$

4-5

Some problems can be solved by translating to an inequality and solving the inequality. Use the Problem-Solving Guidelines to help you.

Internet Activity On the Web

Look for extension problems for this chapter at the Prentice Hall Web site. www.phschool.com

Solve.

21. Alicia weighs 60 lb less than her father. Their combined weights total 300 lb at most. What is the most Alicia could weigh?

22. Heather received grades of 80, 75, and 86 on three algebra tests. What must her grade be on the next test if her average for the four tests is to be at least 82?

23. The sum of three consecutive even integers is less than or equal to 42. Find the largest set of these numbers.

24. Find all sets of four consecutive odd whole numbers whose sum is less than 38.

 **Chapter Assessment**

1. Determine whether each number is a solution of $b \geq -3$.
   a. 0   **b.** -3 **c.** -5 **d.** 6

2. Determine whether each number is a solution of $x < 5$.
   a. 3   **b.** -3 **c.** -8 **d.** 0

Graph on a number line.

3. $a \geq -5$ **4.** $c < -4$ **5.** $y \leq 6$

Solve.

6. $x - 2 > 5$ **7.** $9x + 2 - 4x > 17$

8. $x + \frac{1}{3} \geq -5$ **9.** $7y > -42$

10. $-6x \leq -24$ **11.** $5x \geq 8x - \frac{3}{2}$

12. $5a - 6 \geq 3a$ **13.** $2x - 15 > 5x$

14. $-5y - 34 \geq -19$ **15.** $7 - 6x < 2x + 87$

16. $5 - 8y \geq 23$ **17.** $9a - 16 < -52$

18. Kim is 3 years older than Bridget. The sum of their ages is less than 16. What is the oldest Bridget could be?

19. The sum of two consecutive even integers is less than or equal to 90. What is the greatest possible pair?

1-1

Evaluate.

1. $\frac{y - x}{4}$ for $y = 12$ and $x = 6$ **2.** $\frac{3x}{y}$ for $x = 5$ and $y = 4$

Simplify.

3. $16 \div (4 \cdot 2) + 9 - 3$ **4.** $(48 - 8) \div 5 + 3$

1-2

Write an equivalent expression using a commutative property or an identity property. Use $\frac{4}{4}$ for 1.

5. $12 + y$ **6.** $\frac{5}{6}$

Simplify.

7. $\frac{9xy}{12yz}$ **8.** $\frac{108}{72y}$

1-3

Evaluate each expression.

9. y^4 for $y = 2$ **10.** $x^3 + 5$ for $x = 3$

11. $(2a)^4$ for $a = 5$ **12.** $3a^2$ for $a = 2$

1-4

Calculate.

13. $(3 + 7)^3$ **14.** $5 + 4^4$

Use an associative property to write an equivalent expression.

15. $(3 \cdot y) \cdot z$ **16.** $x + (y + 21)$

1-5

Use the distributive property to write an equivalent expression.

17. $5(3x + 5y + 2z)$ **18.** $8(2w + 4x + 3y)$

Factor.

19. $54y + 6$ **20.** $42x + 36y + 12$

Collect like terms.

21. $9b + 18y + 6b + 4y$ **22.** $3y + 4z + 6z + 6y$

1-6

Write as an algebraic expression.

23. four less than twice w

24. three times the sum of x and y

1-7

Solve for the given replacement set.

25. $6y = 54$ $\quad$ {7, 8, 9}

26. $x^2 - x = 3$ $\quad$ {1, 3, 9}

27. $2.5y = 15$ $\quad$ {0.6, 6, 60}

28. $m - 18 = 56$ $\quad$ {38, 64, 74}

Each pair of equations is equivalent. What was done to the first equation to get the second one?

29. $\frac{4y}{7} = 3$

$\quad$ $4y = 21$

30. $\quad$ $5x = 30$

$\quad$ $5x - 4 = 26$

1-9

Evaluate.

31. Find the perimeter (p) of a rectangle with a length (l) of 12 m and a width (w) of 8.4 m using the formula $p = 2l + 2w$.

32. Find the area (A) of a rectangle with a length (l) of 12 m and a width (w) of 8.4 m using the formula $A = l \cdot w$.

2-1

Use $>$ or $<$ to write a true sentence.

33. $-4 \ \square \ -6$

34. $-2 \ \square \ 2$

Find the absolute values.

35. $|-14|$

36. $|65|$

2-2

Use $>$ or $<$ to write a true sentence.

37. $-2.5 \ \square \ -4.25$

38. $-\frac{3}{4} \ \square \ -\frac{3}{8}$

Graph each rational number on a number line.

39. -3.5

40. $\frac{5}{4}$

2-3

Add.

41. $5 + (-9) + 7$

42. $-3.5 + 7.2$

2-4

Subtract.

43. $-7 - (-8)$

44. $-\frac{3}{4} - \frac{2}{3}$

Simplify.

45. $-2 - 4x - 6x + 5$

46. $7 - 2x - (-5x) - 8$

2-5

Multiply.

47. $5(-7)(3)(-4)$

48. $-\frac{5}{8}\left(-\frac{4}{3}\right)$

49. $(-7)(5)(-6)(-0.5)$

2-6

Divide.

50. $\frac{-10.8}{36}$

51. $\frac{-4}{5} \div \frac{25}{8}$

52. $\frac{81}{-90}$

2-7

Multiply.

53. $4(-3x - 2)$

54. $-6(2y - 4x)$

55. $-5(-x - 1)$

Factor.

56. $16y - 56$

57. $-2x - 8$

58. $5a - 15b + 25$

Collect like terms.

59. $-4d - 6a + 3a - 5d + 1$

60. $3.2x + 2.9y - 5.8x - 8.1y$

2-8

Remove parentheses and simplify.

61. $-3x - (-x + y)$

62. $-3(x - 2) - 4x$

63. $10 - 2(5 - 4x)$

2-10

Which properties of equality justify each statement?

64. $2a + 3b = 2a + 3b$

65. $60 = 45t$ and $60 = 35(t - 1)$. Therefore, $45t = 35(t - 1)$.

3-1 to 3-6

Solve.

66. $-2.6 + x = 8.3$

67. $4\frac{1}{2} + y = 8\frac{1}{3}$

68. $\frac{-3}{4}x = 36$

69. $-2.2y = -26.4$

70. $-4x + 3 = 15$

71. $-3x + 5 = -8x - 7$

72. $4y - 4 + y = 6y + 20 - 4y$ **73.** $-3(x - 2) = -15$
74. $\frac{1}{3}x - \frac{5}{6} = \frac{1}{2} + 2x$ **75.** $-3.7x + 6.2 = -7.3x - 5.8$

3-7

Solve.

76. $c = 10d + 5n$ for n **77.** $L = 2rh$ for r

3-8

Solve.

78. $|y| = 7$ **79.** $|x| + 2 = 11$ **80.** $3|a| = 27$

3-9

Solve.

81. $\frac{x}{12} = \frac{16}{18}$ **82.** $\frac{16}{6} = \frac{x}{24}$

83. A car uses 32 L of gas to travel 450 km. How many liters would be required to drive 800 km (to the nearest tenth)?

3-10

Translate to an equation and solve.

84. What percent of 60 is 18?   **85.** Two is four percent of what number?
86. What is 16.5% of 80?

3-11

87. Money is invested in a savings account at 12% simple interest. After one year there is $1680 in the account. How much was originally invested?

88. The sum of three consecutive integers is 114. Find the integers.

4-1

Determine whether each number is a solution of $a \geq -4$.

89. -6 **90.** 2   **91.** 0   **92.** -4

4-2 to 4-5

Solve and graph on a number line.

93. $x - \frac{1}{6} \geq \frac{2}{3}$ **94.** $-4x \geq 24$

95. $-3x < 30 + 2x$ **96.** $x + 3 \geq 6(x - 4) + 7$

97. Find the length and width of a rectangle when the width is 4 ft shorter than the length. The perimeter of the rectangle is greater than 72 ft.

CHAPTER 5

Skills & Concepts You Need for Chapter 5

1-3 Write using exponential notation.

1. $8 \cdot 8 \cdot 8 \cdot 8$

2. $12 \cdot b \cdot b \cdot b$

1-3 Evaluate each expression.

3. $m^4 - 5$ for $m = 2$

4. $3b^2$ for $b = 4$

1-5, 2-7 Multiply.

5. $3(s + t + w)$

6. $-7(x + 4)$

1-5 Collect like terms.

7. $2x + 8y + 7x + 5y$

8. $7b^2 + 9b + 2b^2 + 8$

2-5 Multiply.

9. $(-6)(-5)$

10. $-\frac{1}{2} \cdot \frac{5}{8}$

2-6 Divide.

11. $-\frac{16}{-2}$

12. $-\frac{24}{16}$

2-8 Rename each additive inverse without parentheses.

13. $-(4x - 7y + 2)$

14. $-(12r + 7p - 9s)$

2-8 Simplify.

15. $5y - 8 - (9y - 6)$

16. $5b - 4(6b - 2)$

What You'll Learn in Chapter 5

- How to multiply, divide, and raise a power to a power using exponents

- How to use scientific notation

- How to add and subtract polynomials

- How to multiply monomials and polynomials

Exponents and Polynomials

The thickness of
a soap bubble is
about 0.0000001 m.
You can express this
measurement with
scientific notation
as 1.0×10^{-7} m.

5-1 ▷ Exponents

What You'll Learn

1 To multiply numbers in exponential form

2 To divide numbers in exponential form

...And Why

To simplify expressions containing exponents

Recall that an exponent tells how many times we use a base as a factor. For example, $a^3 = a \cdot a \cdot a$. An expression written with exponents is written using **exponential notation.**

PART 1 Multiplying Using Exponents

Objective: Multiply numbers in exponential form.

We can use the meaning of an exponent to develop a rule for multiplying powers with like bases.

$$8^3 \cdot 8^2 \text{ means } (8 \cdot 8 \cdot 8)(8 \cdot 8) = 8^5$$
$$5^2 \cdot 5^4 \text{ means } (5 \cdot 5)(5 \cdot 5 \cdot 5 \cdot 5) = 5^6$$
$$a^5 \cdot a \text{ means } (a \cdot a \cdot a \cdot a \cdot a)(a) = a^6$$

Notice we could add the exponents to find the exponent of the product.

$$8^3 \cdot 8^2 = 8^{3+2} = 8^5$$
$$5^2 \cdot 5^4 = 5^{2+4} = 5^6$$
$$a^5 \cdot a = a^{5+1} = a^6 \qquad a = a^1$$

Multiplying Powers with Like Bases

For any rational number a, and for all whole numbers m and n,
$$a^m \cdot a^n = a^{m+n}$$

EXAMPLES   Simplify. Express using exponents.

1 $8^4 \cdot 8^3 = 8^{4+3}$ $(8 \cdot 8 \cdot 8 \cdot 8)(8 \cdot 8 \cdot 8) = 8^7$
$\qquad\qquad = 8^7$

2 $y \cdot y^2 \cdot y^5 = y^{1+2+5}$ $(y)(y \cdot y)(y \cdot y \cdot y \cdot y \cdot y) = y^8$
$\qquad\qquad\quad = y^8$

3 $(a^3 b^2)(a^3 b^5) = (a^3 a^3)(b^2 b^5)$
$\qquad\qquad\quad = a^{3+3} b^{2+5}$
$\qquad\qquad\quad = a^6 b^7$

Try This   Simplify. Express using exponents.

a. $5^2 \cdot 5^4$ **b.** $a^5 \cdot a^3$ **c.** $y^3 \cdot y^2 \cdot y^5$ **d.** $(mn^2)(m^4 n^6)$

Objective: Divide numbers in exponential form.

The following suggests a rule for simplifying expressions in the form $\frac{a^m}{a^n}$.

$$\frac{3^5}{3^2} = \frac{3 \cdot 3 \cdot 3 \cdot 3 \cdot 3}{3 \cdot 3} = 3 \cdot 3 \cdot 3 = 3^3$$

Notice that we can subtract the exponents to find the exponent of the quotient.

Dividing Powers with Like Bases

For any rational number a except 0, and for all whole numbers m and n,

$$\frac{a^m}{a^n} = a^{m-n}$$

EXAMPLES Simplify. Express using exponents.

4 $\frac{4^5}{4^2} = 4^{5-2} = 4^3$ $\qquad \frac{4 \cdot 4 \cdot 4 \cdot 4 \cdot 4}{4 \cdot 4} = 4^3$

5 $\frac{x^6}{x^2} = x^{6-2} = x^4$ $\qquad \frac{x \cdot x \cdot x \cdot x \cdot x \cdot x}{x \cdot x} = x^4$

6 $\frac{p^5 \cdot q^7}{p^2 \cdot q^5} = p^{5-2} q^{7-5}$ $\qquad$ *Think* $\frac{p^5}{p^2} \cdot \frac{q^7}{q^5}$.

$\qquad\quad = p^3 q^2$

Try This Simplify. Express using exponents.

e. $\frac{7^6}{7^2}$ $\qquad$ **f.** $\frac{a^7}{a^2}$ $\qquad$ **g.** $\frac{m^4}{m^2}$ $\qquad$ **h.** $\frac{x^4 y^3}{x^2 y^2}$

You can use the meaning of an exponent to simplify $\frac{5^2}{5^5}$.

$$\frac{5^2}{5^5} = \frac{5 \cdot 5}{5 \cdot 5 \cdot 5 \cdot 5 \cdot 5} = \frac{1}{5^3}$$

You can also use the rule above to simplify the expression $\frac{5^2}{5^5}$.

$$\frac{5^2}{5^5} = 5^{2-5} = 5^{-3}$$

This suggests that $5^{-3} = \frac{1}{5^3}$.

In general, we can state the following.

Definition

For any rational number a except 0, and for all whole numbers m,
$$a^{-m} = \frac{1}{a^m}$$

EXAMPLES Express using positive exponents.

7 $\quad 4^{-2} = \frac{1}{4^2}$

8 $\quad m^{-3} = \frac{1}{m^3}$

9 $\quad ab^{-1} = a \cdot \frac{1}{b} = \frac{a}{b}$ The exponent affects only b.

Try This   Express using positive exponents.

i. 2^{-2} **j.** y^{-4} **k.** $3c^{-2}$

You know that any nonzero number divided by itself equals 1. For example, $\frac{a^2}{a^2} = 1$. Using the rule given above, we also find that $\frac{a^2}{a^2} = a^{2-2} = a^0$. We can state the following about zero as an exponent.

Definition

$a^0 = 1$ for any rational number a except 0.

EXAMPLES Simplify.

10 $\quad 3^{-2} = \frac{1}{3^2} = \frac{1}{9}$

11 $\quad 1^{-4} = \frac{1}{1^4} = 1$

12 $\quad p^0 = 1$ Any nonzero number to the 0 power $= 1$.

Try This   Simplify.

l. 4^{-2} **m.** 1^{-10} **n.** 3^0

Internet Connection

Extra Help On the Web
Look for worked-out examples at the Prentice Hall Web site.
www.phschool.com

A

Simplify. Express using exponents.

1. $2^4 \cdot 2^3$　　　　**2.** $3^5 \cdot 3^2$　　　　**3.** $8^5 \cdot 8^9$　　　　**4.** $n^3 \cdot n^{20}$

5. $x^4 \cdot x^3$　　　　**6.** $y^7 \cdot y^9$　　　　**7.** $n^3 \cdot n$　　　　**8.** $z^7 \cdot z^7$

9. $x^3 \cdot x^1$　　　　**10.** $a^6 \cdot a^8$　　　　**11.** $m^7 \cdot m^0$　　　　**12.** $p \cdot p \cdot p$

13. $x^4 \cdot x^2 \cdot x$　　**14.** $y^2 \cdot y^4 \cdot y^3$　　**15.** $a^3 \cdot a^4 \cdot a \cdot a$　**16.** $b \cdot b^5 \cdot b^2 \cdot b^2$

17. $(a^3b^6)(a^5b)$　　　　**18.** $(x^2y)(x^5y^2)$　　　　**19.** $(p^2q^3r^2)(pqr^3)$

20. $(x^7y^4z^4)(x^2y^5z^8)$　　**21.** $(5s^2t^3)(5s^2t)$　　　　**22.** $(2xy^2)(2x^2y^2)$

23. $\dfrac{7^5}{7^2}$　　　　**24.** $\dfrac{4^7}{4^3}$　　　　**25.** $\dfrac{8^{12}}{8^6}$　　　　**26.** $\dfrac{9^{15}}{9^2}$

27. $\dfrac{6^4}{6^4}$　　　　**28.** $\dfrac{2^7}{2^7}$　　　　**29.** $\dfrac{y^9}{y^5}$　　　　**30.** $\dfrac{x^{12}}{x^{11}}$

31. $\dfrac{g^5}{g^5}$　　　　**32.** $\dfrac{h^4}{h}$　　　　**33.** $\dfrac{m^8}{m^8}$　　　　**34.** $\dfrac{x^7}{x^5}$

35. $\dfrac{a^3b^4}{ab}$　　　　**36.** $\dfrac{x^8y}{x^7y}$　　　　**37.** $\dfrac{4^3x^3}{4^2x}$　　　　**38.** $\dfrac{6^4a^5b}{6^2a^2b}$

Express using positive exponents.

39. 3^{-2}　　　　**40.** 6^{-3}　　　　**41.** x^{-4}　　　　**42.** n^{-6}

43. $3a^{-1}$　　　　**44.** $(3x)^{-1}$　　　　**45.** $(2y)^{-1}$　　　　**46.** $4x^{-3}$

47. $5c^{-4}$　　　　**48.** $8m^{-1}$　　　　**49.** $(3a)^{-1}$　　　　**50.** cd^{-2}

Mental Math　Simplify. Express without using exponents.

51. 4^{-2}　　　　**52.** 8^{-1}　　　　**53.** 5^{-3}　　　　**54.** 1^{-4}

55. 5^0　　　　**56.** 2^{-4}　　　　**57.** 10^0　　　　**58.** x^0

B

Simplify.

59. $(-2)^4(-2)^2$　　**60.** $(-5)^2(-5)$　　**61.** $\dfrac{(-3)^6}{(-3)^4}$　　**62.** $\dfrac{(-10)^7}{(-10)^6}$

63. $\dfrac{4^3}{4^5}$　　　　**64.** $\dfrac{3^4}{3^6}$　　　　**65.** $\dfrac{(-2)^2}{(-2)^5}$　　**66.** $\dfrac{(-5)^3}{(-5)^4}$

Simplify. Express using (a) negative exponents; (b) positive exponents.

67. $\dfrac{x^3}{x^7}$　　　　**68.** $\dfrac{y}{y^4}$　　　　**69.** $\dfrac{a^2}{a^6}$　　　　**70.** $\dfrac{m^5}{m^{10}}$

Evaluate each expression.

71. $x^5 \cdot x^3$ for $x = 2$　　　　**72.** $10^m \cdot 10^n$ for $m = 2$ and $n = 4$

73. $a^3 \cdot a^2 \cdot a$ for $a = -2$　　　　**74.** $2^a \cdot 2^b \cdot 2^c$ for $a = 3, b = 2, c = 2$

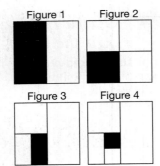

Figure 1   Figure 2

Figure 3   Figure 4

75. *Multi-Step Problem*   Use the figures at the left.

   a. What fraction of each figure is shaded?

   b. Rewrite each fraction in part (a) as a power of 2.

   c. *Mathematical Reasoning*   What pattern occurs in your answers to part (b)?

   d. If the pattern were to continue to Figure 10, what portion of the square would be shaded?

Error Analysis   Find and correct each error in Exercises 76 and 77.

76. $(3x^2)(2x^5) = 6x^{2 \cdot 5} = 6x^{10}$ **77.** $x^5 \cdot x \cdot x^2 = x^{5+2} = x^7$

78. **TEST PREP**   If $5^{x+1} = 125$, what is the value of x?

   A. 2   **B.** 3   **C.** 4   **D.** 5

Simplify.

79. $\dfrac{4^2 \cdot 4^5}{4^3}$ **80.** $\dfrac{2^5 \cdot 3^4}{2^2 \cdot 3^2}$ **81.** $\dfrac{a^2 \cdot b^3}{a^2 \cdot b^5}$ **82.** $\dfrac{m^5 \cdot n^6}{m^2 \cdot m^2}$

83. $4^{-1} \cdot 4^5$ **84.** $\dfrac{(-3)}{(-3)^{-4}}$ **85.** $\dfrac{x^6 \cdot x^{-2}}{x^2}$ **86.** $\dfrac{a^{-2} \cdot b^{-3}}{a^4 \cdot b^{-1}}$

87. *Critical Thinking*   Is $(a + b)^m = a^m + b^m$ true for all numbers? If yes, justify your answer. If no, give a counterexample.

Challenge

Write each of the following as a power of 2.

88. 16   **89.** 4^3 **90.** 8^2 **91.** $4^3 \cdot 8 \cdot 16$

92. Write $2^8 \cdot 16^3 \cdot 64$ as a power of 4.

93. Write $9 \cdot 27 \cdot 3 \cdot 81$ as a power of 3.

Simplify.

94. $\dfrac{\left(\frac{1}{c}\right)^4}{\left(\frac{1}{c}\right)^5}$ **95.** $\dfrac{\left(\frac{a}{b}\right)^3}{\left(\frac{a}{b}\right)^6}$

Mixed Review

Simplify.   **96.** $3[8 - 2(t + 3)]$ **97.** $(5m + 6n) - (6m + 9n)$

98. $6a - 9a(4a + 3)$ **99.** $7a(a + 2) + 3a^2 + 2a^2$ *2-8*

Write as an algebraic expression.   **100.** the difference of w and 4

101. 8 less than the product of a and c **102.** twice the sum of m and n *1-6*

Solve.   **103.** $m - 422 = -53$ **104.** $21t = -693$

105. $6(m + 3) = 10m - 2$ **106.** $\frac{3}{4}c + 4 = \frac{1}{4}c - 2$ *3-1, 3-2, 3-5*

107. Frank needs a new shirt and sweater and wants to spend at most \$45. If he finds a shirt for \$18, how much can he spend on a sweater? *4-5*

More with Exponents

PART 1 — Raising a Power to a Power

Objective: Find a power to a power.

We can use the meaning of an exponent to simplify an expression like $(3^2)^4$.

$$(3^2)^4 = (3^2)(3^2)(3^2)(3^2)$$
$$= 3^{2+2+2+2}$$
$$= 3^8$$

Using the rule for multiplying powers with like bases

Notice that we get the same result if we multiply the exponents.

$$(3^2)^4 = 3^{2 \cdot 4} = 3^8$$

In general, we can state the following rule for raising a power to a power.

Raising a Power to a Power

For any rational number a, and any whole numbers m and n,
$$(a^m)^n = a^{mn}$$

EXAMPLES   Simplify.

1 $(3^5)^4 = 3^{5 \cdot 4} = 3^{20}$ $(3^5)(3^5)(3^5)(3^5) = 3^{5+5+5+5} = 3^{5 \cdot 4}$

2 $((-2)^3)^2 = (-2)^{3 \cdot 2} = (-2)^6$

3 $(y^5)^3 = y^{5 \cdot 3} = y^{15}$ $(y^5)(y^5)(y^5) = y^{5+5+5} = y^{5 \cdot 3}$

4 $(m^2)^2 = m^{2 \cdot 2} = m^4$

Try This   Simplify.

a. $(5^4)^3$ **b.** $(2^2)^5$ **c.** $(a^6)^3$ **d.** $(n^4)^4$

Evaluating Expressions

We can evaluate numbers expressed in exponential notation using a calculator. For example, evaluate $(3^2)^4$.

3   y^x 2 $=$ y^x 4 $=$ → 6561

Objective: Find the power of a product or a quotient.

Recall from Chapter 1 that when an expression inside parentheses is raised to a power, everything inside the parentheses is the base. Compare $2n^3$ and $(2n)^3$.

$2n^3$ means $2 \cdot n \cdot n \cdot n$ (n is the base.)
$(2n)^3$ means $(2n)(2n)(2n)$ ($2n$ is the base.)

We can use the meaning of an exponent to write expressions like $(2n)^3$ without parentheses.

EXAMPLES   Simplify.

5 $(2n)^3$ means $(2n)(2n)(2n) = 2 \cdot 2 \cdot 2 \cdot n \cdot n \cdot n$ Using the associative and commutative properties

$$= 2^3 n^3$$
$$= 8n^3$$

6 $(4x)^2$ means $(4x)(4x) = 4 \cdot 4 \cdot x \cdot x$
$$= 4^2 x^2$$
$$= 16x^2$$

7 $(3a^2)^3$ means $(3a^2)(3a^2)(3a^2) = 3 \cdot 3 \cdot 3 \cdot a^2 \cdot a^2 \cdot a^2$
$$= 3^3 \cdot a^{2+2+2}$$
$$= 3^3 a^{2 \cdot 3}$$
$$= 27a^6$$

Try This   Simplify.

e. $(3y)^2$ **f.** $(6m)^4$ **g.** $(2a^3)^3$ **h.** $(4x^3)^2$

Note the following relationship in Example 7.

$$(3a^2)^3 = (3^1 a^2)^3$$
$$= 3^{1 \cdot 3} a^{2 \cdot 3}$$
$$= 3^3 \cdot a^6$$

Each factor inside parentheses is raised to the third power. We can use the following rule for raising a product to a power.

Raising a Product to a Power

For any rational numbers a and b, and for any whole number n,
$$(ab)^n = a^n \cdot b^n$$

EXAMPLES Simplify.

8 $(3x^2)^3 = 3^3(x^2)^3$
$= 3^3x^6$
$= 27x^6$

9 $(5x^3y^5z^2)^4 = 5^4(x^3)^4(y^5)^4(z^2)^4$
$= 625x^{12}y^{20}z^8$

10 $(-5x^4y^3)^3 = (-5)^3(x^4)^3(y^3)^3$
$= -125x^{12}y^9$

11 $[(-x)^{25}]^2 = (-x)^{50}$
$= (-1 \cdot x)^{50}$ Using the property of -1
$= (-1)^{50}x^{50}$
$= 1 \cdot x^{50}$ An even number of negative factors
$= x^{50}$ gives a positive product.

Try This Simplify.

i. $(4y^3)^4$ **j.** $(3x^4y^7z^6)^5$ **k.** $(-7x^9y^6)^2$ **l.** $[(-y)^{15}]^3$

The rule for raising a quotient to a power is similar to the rule for raising a product to a power.

Raising a Quotient to a Power

For any rational numbers a and b except $b = 0$, and for any whole number n,

$$\left(\frac{a}{b}\right)^n = \frac{a^n}{b^n}$$

Reading Math

The expression $\left(\frac{2}{3}\right)^n$ is read "Two-thirds to the nth power." The expression $\left(\frac{2^n}{3^n}\right)$ is read "Two to the nth power divided by 3 to the nth power."

EXAMPLES Simplify.

12 $\left(\frac{x^2}{4}\right)^3 = \frac{(x^2)^3}{(4)^3} = \frac{x^6}{64}$

13 $\left(\frac{a^4}{b^3}\right)^2 = \frac{a^8}{b^6}$

Try This Simplify.

m. $\left(\frac{y^3}{2}\right)^2$ **n.** $\left(\frac{a^5}{3}\right)^3$ **o.** $\left(\frac{x^2}{y^3}\right)^2$

5-2 Exercises

A

Simplify.

1. $(2^5)^2$ 2. $(3^4)^3$ 3. $(5^2)^3$ 4. $(6^8)^9$

5. $(y^5)^9$ 6. $(x^3)^5$ 7. $(m^8)^4$ 8. $(n^5)^{12}$

9. $(a^6)^5$ 10. $(y^7)^7$ 11. $(p^{10})^{10}$ 12. $(w^{12})^7$

13. $(3y)^4$ 14. $(2t)^5$ 15. $(7y)^3$ 16. $(8x)^4$

17. $(5m)^2$ 18. $(4y)^5$ 19. $(7x)^4$ 20. $(12a)^3$

21. $(2m^2)^2$ 22. $(4n^3)^2$ 23. $(5y^4)^3$ 24. $(3x^5)^4$

25. $(-6t^2)^3$ 26. $(-10b^6)^2$ 27. $(8k^4)^3$ 28. $(7x^5)^3$

29. $(2x^8y^3)^2$ 30. $(3mn^4)^3$ 31. $(-2x^2y^4)^3$ 32. $(-3m^4n^2)^2$

33. $(4x^2y^3z)^4$ 34. $(2m^5n^4p^3)^3$ 35. $\left(\frac{3}{a^2}\right)^3$ 36. $\left(\frac{7}{x^7}\right)^2$

37. $\left(\frac{x^2}{4}\right)^4$ 38. $\left(\frac{y^5}{3}\right)^2$ 39. $\left(\frac{m^4}{n^2}\right)^3$ 40. $\left(\frac{a^8}{b^4}\right)^3$

B

Simplify.

41. $\left(\frac{3 \cdot 2^2}{5}\right)^3$ 42. $\left(\frac{5 \cdot 2^4}{3}\right)^2$ 43. $\left(\frac{xy^2}{z}\right)^3$

44. $\left(\frac{ab^4}{c}\right)^3$ 45. $\left(\frac{-2x^2y^6}{5}\right)^2$ 46. $\left(\frac{3x^3y^3}{2}\right)^4$

47. $\left(\frac{-4m^2n^5}{3}\right)^3$ 48. $\left(\frac{-5p^4q^3}{2}\right)^3$ 49. $[(-x^5)]^6$

50. $[(-y)^{18}]^2$ 51. $\left(\frac{-x}{3y}\right)^3$ 52. $\left(\frac{2c}{-y}\right)^4$

53. $\left(\frac{x^2y}{z}\right)^3$ 54. $\left(\frac{m}{n^4p}\right)^3$ 55. $\left(\frac{-3a^2b^4}{4c^3}\right)^2$

56. $\left(\frac{2m^5n^5}{p^4}\right)^3$ 57. $(2n)^4\left(\frac{3}{2}n\right)^3$ 58. $(4x^3)^2 + (2x^2)^3$

59. $(7a)(4a) - (3a)^2$ 60. $(-2y^2)^3 + 4y(2y^5)$ 61. $(-3z^4)^2 - (z^2)^4$

62. $(6cd^2)^2 + 3cd(cd^3)$ 63. $3z^3(2z^4) - (-5z^3)^2$

64. $b^2(a^3b)^2 + a^2(a^2b^2)^2$ 65. $(3c^4)^2(2c)$

66. $(-2x^2y^3)^4(xy)^3$ 67. $(-3a^2b^4)^3(4a^3b)^2$

68. *Critical Thinking*   Does $(a^m)^n = (a^n)^m$ for all rational numbers a
    and all natural numbers m and n? If yes, explain why. If no, provide a
    counterexample.

69. **TEST PREP**   If $y = 2^x$, which of the following equals $4y$?

  A. 2^{2x} B. 2^{2+x} C. 2^{x^2} D. 4^x

Challenge

Simplify.

70. $x^{2a}x^4$

71. $x^{3a}x^{2b}$

72. $x^{a+4}x^3$

73. x^5x^{2a-4}

74. $(a^{n+1}b^{m+2})^3$

75. $(x^ay^{a-3})^3$

76. $(c^3d)^a(cd^7)^a$

77. $x^2(x^{a+2}y^3)$

Solve for a.

78. $x^{a+4} = x^4x^8$

79. $x^{a-3} = x^5x^3$

80. $x^{2a} = \dfrac{x^{12}}{x^9}$

81. $x^{3a} = x^4x^6$

Mixed Review

Simplify.   **82.** $6c + (-9m) - 5c + m$ **83.** $21 - 8x - 9 - (-7x)$ *2-8*

Give the reciprocal.   **84.** $\dfrac{x}{y}$ **85.** $\dfrac{5c}{8}$ **86.** $\dfrac{-5}{2a}$ **87.** $\dfrac{m}{2}$ **88.** $\dfrac{7}{t}$ *2-6*

Solve.   **89.** $m + 4 = -3m$ **90.** $4x + 2x = 9x - 6$ *3-5*

⬦ Connections: Geometry

1. Find the volume of a cube with sides of length $2x$.

2. Suppose the cube has sides of length $4x$. What would its volume be?

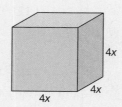

3. Suppose the cube has sides of length $8x$. What would its volume be?

4. How do the volumes of each of the cubes above change as the dimension doubles?

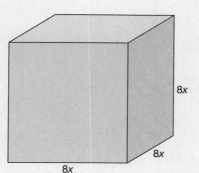

5-3 ▷ Multiplying and Dividing Monomials

What You'll Learn

1 To multiply monomials

2 To divide monomials

... And Why

To prepare for multiplication and division of polynomials

PART 1 Multiplying Monomials

Objective: Multiply monomials.

A **monomial** is an expression that is either a numeral, a variable, or a product of numerals and variables with whole number exponents. If the monomial is a numeral, we call it a **constant.**

These expressions are monomials.

$$4x^3 \qquad -7ab \qquad x \qquad \tfrac{1}{2}y^5 \qquad -8 \qquad 2x^2y$$

These expressions are not monomials.

$$\frac{1}{y} \qquad x^{\frac{1}{2}} \qquad x^2 + 4 \qquad y^2 + 2y - 4$$

We can multiply two monomials using the properties of rational numbers and the properties of exponents.

EXAMPLES Multiply.

1 $(3x)(4x) = (3 \cdot 4)(x \cdot x)$ Using the associative and commutative properties

$\qquad\qquad = 12x^2$ Multiplying

2 $(3x^2)(-x) = (3x^2)(-1x)$

$\qquad\qquad = (3 \cdot -1)(x^2 \cdot x)$

$\qquad\qquad = -3x^3$ Multiplying $(x^2 \cdot x = x^{2+1})$

3 $(-7x^2y^5)(4xy^3) = (-7 \cdot 4)(x^2 \cdot x)(y^5 \cdot y^3)$

$\qquad\qquad = -28x^3y^8$ Multiplying $(x^2 \cdot x = x^{2+1}, y^5 \cdot y^3 = y^{5+3})$

4 $(4m^2)(2m^3)(-m) = (4 \cdot 2 \cdot -1)(m^2 \cdot m^3 \cdot m)$

$\qquad\qquad = -8m^6$ Multiplying $(m^2 \cdot m^3 \cdot m = m^{2+3+1})$

5 $(-3a)(4a^2)(-a^4) = (-3 \cdot 4 \cdot -1)(a \cdot a^2 \cdot a^4)$

$\qquad\qquad = 12a^7$

Try This Multiply.

a. $(3x)(-5)$ **b.** $(-m)m$ **c.** $(-y)(-y)$

d. $(-x)^2x^3$ **e.** $(3p^5q^2)(4p^2q^3)$ **f.** $(4x^5y^5)(-2x^6y^4)$

g. $(-7y^4)(-y)(2y^3)$ **h.** $(7a^5)(3a^3)(-a^5)$

Objective: Divide monomials.

We can also divide monomials using the properties of rational numbers and the properties of exponents.

EXAMPLES Divide.

6 $\dfrac{x^5}{x^2} = x^{5-2} = x^3$

7 $\dfrac{4x^2}{5x^7} = \dfrac{4}{5} \cdot x^{2-7} = \dfrac{4}{5}x^{-5} = \dfrac{4}{5x^5}$

8 $\dfrac{8x^5y^{12}}{-2x^3y^{10}} = \dfrac{8}{-2} \cdot x^{5-3}y^{12-10} = -4x^2y^2$

Try This Divide.

i. $\dfrac{x^8}{x^5}$ j. $\dfrac{12m^5}{8m^8}$ k. $\dfrac{-5x^3y^4}{-5x^2y}$ l. $\dfrac{-32x^{15}y^7}{8x^{14}y^6}$

5-3 Exercises

Extra Help On the Web
Look for worked-out examples at the Prentice Hall Web site.
www.phschool.com

A

Multiply.

1. $(6x^2)(7)$ 2. $(5y^3)(-2)$ 3. $(-x^3)(-x)$

4. $(-y^4)(y^2)$ 5. $(-x^5)(x^3)$ 6. $(-m^6)(-m^2)$

7. $(3a^4)(2a^2)$ 8. $(5x^3)(4x^5)$ 9. $(7t^5)(4t^3)$

10. $(-3b^3)(5b^5)$ 11. $(3g^4)(-6g^3)$ 12. $(h^5)(-7h^3)$

13. $(-6x^3)(x^8)$ 14. $(-8m^7)(-4m^3)$ 15. $(-5n^4)(-5n^4)$

16. $(-x^7)(5x^{12})$ 17. $(x^3y^4)(x^4y^2)$ 18. $(2m^3n^2)(-3m^6n^5)$

19. $(4a^4b^8)(2a^4b^2)$ 20. $(-2x^3y)(-6x^9y^8)$ 21. $(y^5)(2y)(3y^2)$

22. $(3x^4)(x^4)(5x^2)$ 23. $(-4m^2)(5m^4)(-2m^3)$ 24. $(9b^2)(2b^5)(-3b^7)$

Divide.

25. $\dfrac{x^6}{x^2}$ 26. $\dfrac{a^7}{a}$ 27. $\dfrac{4x^5}{2x^2}$ 28. $\dfrac{-6a^3}{6a}$

29. $\dfrac{12m^4}{4m^4}$ 30. $\dfrac{-4x^6}{-2x^6}$ 31. $\dfrac{5a^3}{a^7}$ 32. $\dfrac{15y^8}{3}$

33. $\dfrac{-h^5}{2h^4}$ 34. $\dfrac{k^3}{3k^8}$ 35. $\dfrac{2x^{10}}{8x^5}$ 36. $\dfrac{3m^5}{6m^7}$

37. $\dfrac{16x^2}{-4x^2}$ **38.** $\dfrac{-25a^7}{-25}$ **39.** $\dfrac{45x^3}{15x^2}$ **40.** $\dfrac{6m^6}{2m^2}$

41. $\dfrac{10x^5y^4}{2x^3y}$ **42.** $\dfrac{-12m^7n^8}{4m^2n^5}$ **43.** $\dfrac{24a^6b^9}{-6a^6b^3}$ **44.** $\dfrac{48x^6y^7}{12xy^5}$

45. $\dfrac{-12p^8r^3}{4p^6r^4}$ **46.** $\dfrac{2x^{12}y^5}{3x^4y^2}$ **47.** $\dfrac{5a^{11}b^7}{-7a^5b^9}$ **48.** $\dfrac{6x^{13}y^4}{24x^5y^7}$

B

Simplify.

49. $x^3(x^4)^2$ **50.** $p(p^4)^3$ **51.** $(a^3)^2(a^4)^3$

52. $(m^2)^4(m^3)^2$ **53.** $(2x^2)(3x^3)^2$ **54.** $(3y^4)(5y^4)^2$

55. $(3x^4)^2(2x^5)^2$ **56.** $(4y)^3(-2y^2)^2$ **57.** $(2x^2y)(3x^4y^5)$

58. $(-3mn^4)(4mn^2)$ **59.** $(ab^2)^3(a^3b^4)^2$ **60.** $(m^3n)^2(mn^5)^3$

61. $\dfrac{(-2x^2)^2}{x^3}$ **62.** $\dfrac{(3a^3)^2}{18a^2}$ **63.** $\dfrac{(4y^3)^2}{(4y^2)^2}$ **64.** $\dfrac{(-5m)^4}{(-25m^2)^2}$

65. $\dfrac{a^4b^5}{3a^2b^6}$ **66.** $\dfrac{2x^6y^4}{8x^4y^7}$ **67.** $\dfrac{-2m^3}{-4m^4n^6}$ **68.** $\dfrac{-4ab^3}{-8a^2b^4}$

69. *Critical Thinking*   When a monomial is multiplied or divided by a certain monomial, you get the same result. What must be true of the certain monomial?

Challenge

Simplify.

70. $(5x^{-2})(2x^{-4})$ **71.** $(8m^{-3})(-4m^4)(m^{-4})$

72. $\dfrac{25b^{16}}{5b^{-12}}$ **73.** $\dfrac{12m^{-10}}{-4m^5}$

74. $(3a^{-2}b^4)(-4a^6b^{-7})$ **75.** $(5x^6y^7)(3x^{-6}y^{-7})$

76. $(5x^{-4}y^{-6}z^5)(-4x^5y^5z^{-3})(-4x^2yz^{-1})$ **77.** $(qrs)(-qrs^3)(-5q^{-3}r^4s^{-5})$

Each problem below involves the sum or difference of monomials. Simplify each expression by collecting like terms.

78. $3x + 2y + 4x$ **79.** $7x + 3y^2 + y^2$ **80.** $8pt + 4t + 2pt + t$ *1-5*

81. $5m - 7m$ **82.** $m - 3n - 2n$ **83.** $14a + b - 5a - 3b$ *2-7*

Write each as a decimal. **84.** 15% **85.** 0.04% **86.** 125% *3-10*

Solve.   **87.** $8x + 4 - 6x < -10$ **88.** $6x \le -36$ **89.** $3 - 6x < 9$ *4-4*

90. There were 407 books in the school library. The ninth grade returned 23 books and checked out 17; the tenth grade returned 15 books and checked out 29; the twelfth grade checked out 26 books and returned 30. How many books were left in the library?   *2-3, 2-4*

Scientific Notation

Objective: Write numbers using scientific notation.

Math in Action

The distance from Earth to the North Star is about 10,000,000,000,000,000,000 meters. The thickness of a soap bubble is about 0.0000001 meter. It is easy to make errors when working with numbers involving many zeros. If an extra zero is included, the resulting number is ten times larger or ten times smaller.

To prevent this type of error and to make it easier to work with very large and very small numbers, we can write these numbers in a form called **scientific notation.** Using scientific notation we can write a number as the product of a power of 10 and a number greater than or equal to 1, but less than 10. In scientific notation, the distance to the North Star is 1.0×10^{19} meters and the thickness of a soap bubble is about 1.0×10^{-7} meters. The numbers 10,000,000,000,000,000,000 and 0.0000001 are expressed using **standard notation.**

The thickness of a soap bubble is 0.0000001 m. How many times thicker than a soap bubble is a layer of plastic that is 0.00001 m thick?

What You'll Learn

1 To write numbers using scientific notation

... And Why

To use simple notation for very large and very small numbers

EXAMPLES

1 Write 4.58×10^4 using standard notation.

$4.58 \times 10^4 = 45{,}800$

Multiplying 4.58 by 10^4, or 10,000, moves the decimal point 4 places to the right.

2 Write 3.4×10^{-2} using standard notation.

$3.4 \times 10^{-2} = 3.4 \times \dfrac{1}{10^2}$

Multiplying by 10^{-2} is the same as dividing by 10^2, or 100, and moves the decimal point 2 places to the left.

$= \dfrac{3.4}{100}$

$= 0.034$

Try This Write using standard notation.

a. 1.25×10^3 **b.** 7×10^5 **c.** 4.8×10^{-3} **d.** 1.8×10^{-4}

EXAMPLES Write using scientific notation.

3 $12{,}450 = 1.2450 \times ?$ Moving the decimal 4 places to the left, which is the same as dividing 12,450 by 10,000 or 10^4

       $= 1.245 \times 10^4$ Multiplying by 10^4 to balance this division

4 $0.2362 = 2.362 \times ?$ Moving the decimal 1 place to the right, which is the same as multiplying 0.2362×10

       $= 2.362 \times 10^{-1}$ Multiplying by 10^{-1} to balance this multiplication

5 $0.00236 = 0\,002.36 \times ?$ Moving the decimal 3 places to the right, which is the same as multiplying 0.00236 by 1000 or 10^3

       $= 2.36 \times 10^{-3}$ Multiplying by 10^{-3} to balance this multiplication

Try This Write using scientific notation.

e. 3,200 **f.** 139,000 **g.** 0.0307 **h.** 0.2004

We can use the properties of exponents to multiply and divide numbers that are expressed in scientific notation.

EXAMPLES Multiply or divide. Express the result using scientific notation.

6 $(3.0 \times 10^5)(4.1 \times 10^{-3}) = (3.0 \times 4.1)(10^5 \times 10^{-3})$ Applying the commutative and associative properties

       $= 12.3 \times 10^2$ Adding exponents to multiply

       $= 1.23 \times 10^3$ Converting to scientific notation

7 $\dfrac{2.5 \times 10^{-7}}{5.0 \times 10^6} = \dfrac{2.5}{5.0} \times \dfrac{10^{-7}}{10^6}$ Factoring

       $= 0.5 \times 10^{-13}$ Subtracting exponents to divide

       $= 5.0 \times 10^{-14}$ Converting to scientific notation

Try This Multiply or divide. Express the result using scientific notation.

i. $(1.1 \times 10^{-8})(5 \times 10^{-7})$ **j.** $\dfrac{4.2 \times 10^5}{2.1 \times 10^2}$

Calculating with Scientific Notation

Some calculators allow you to enter numbers in scientific notation. Using a scientific calculator, follow the example below. The EXP key tells the calculator that you are entering a power of ten. If the exponent is negative, enter the negative sign after you enter the exponent.

Problem in standard notation

$$(42,000,000)(250,000,000) = 10,500,000,000,000,000$$

Problem using scientific notation

$$(4.2 \times 10^7)(2.5 \times 10^8) = (4.2)(2.5) \times (10^7)(10^8)$$
$$= 10.5 \times 10^{15} = 1.05 \times 10^{16}$$

Using a calculator

4.2 EXP 7 × 2.5 EXP 8 = 1.05 16

Notice that the calculator display shows only the 16 rather than 10^{16}.

5-4 Exercises

A

Write using standard notation.

1. 5.543×10^3
2. 3.29×10^2
3. 2.35×10^{-3}
4. 1.743×10^{-4}
5. 5.7×10^4
6. 4.89×10^5
7. 3.4×10^{-5}
8. 4×10^3
9. 6×10^{-4}
10. 1.206×10^2
11. 3.007×10^{-3}
12. 8.04×10^{-5}

Write using scientific notation.

13. 425
14. 0.478
15. 12,400
16. 32,060
17. 0.045
18. 0.00003
19. 125,000
20. 12
21. 5,200,000
22. 12,400,000
23. 0.0000056
24. 0.000000032

Multiply or divide. Express your answer in scientific notation.

25. $(7 \times 10^4)(2 \times 10^2)$
26. $(2.2 \times 10^{-3})(3.0 \times 10^5)$
27. $(4.0 \times 10^7)(8.0 \times 10^3)$
28. $(6.1 \times 10^9)(2.5 \times 10^{-4})$
29. $(2.5 \times 10^{-3})(4.0 \times 10^{-8})$
30. $(5.4 \times 10^{-6})(5.1 \times 10^{-8})$
31. $\dfrac{(6.0 \times 10^7)}{(3.0 \times 10^2)}$
32. $\dfrac{(9.0 \times 10^8)}{(3.0 \times 10^2)}$
33. $\dfrac{(8.4 \times 10^6)}{(2.0 \times 10^8)}$
34. $\dfrac{(6.9 \times 10^4)}{(3.0 \times 10^8)}$
35. $\dfrac{(1.5 \times 10^{-2})}{(3 \times 10^{-4})}$
36. $\dfrac{(2.7 \times 10^{12})}{(9.0 \times 10^{12})}$

Extra Help On the Web

Look for worked-out examples at the Prentice Hall Web site.
www.phschool.com

B

Divide. Express the result using scientific and standard notation.

37. $\dfrac{(3.4 \times 10^6)(6 \times 10^3)}{(5 \times 10^5)}$

38. $\dfrac{(4.55 \times 10^3)(2.6 \times 10^5)}{(2 \times 10^{-2})}$

39. $\dfrac{(5.2 \times 10^{-4})(4 \times 10^5)}{(2.5 \times 10^9)}$

40. $\dfrac{(5 \times 10^{-3})(3.26 \times 10^{-4})}{(4 \times 10^2)}$

41. Light traveling from the sun at about 3.0×10^5 km per second takes about 5.0×10^2 seconds to reach Earth. Approximately what is the distance, expressed in scientific notation, from the sun to Earth?

42. *Estimation*   Approximately how many seconds are there in 2000 years? Assume 365 days per year.

43. *Estimation*   About how many seconds have you been alive?

44. A certain molecule has a mass of 3.01×10^{-23} g. There are 1.3×10^{21} of these molecules in a drop. What is the approximate mass of these molecules?

45.   **TEST PREP**   Compare the quantities in Column A and Column B.

Column A   Column B

three times (3.6×10^{-3}) half of (2.16×10^{-2})

   A. The quantity in Column A is greater.

   B. The quantity in Column B is greater.

   C. The quantities are equal.

   D. The relationship cannot be determined from the information given.

46. Light travels 1.86×10^5 miles in 1 second. How far does light travel in one year (light year)?

47. Neptune is approximately 2,790,000,000 mi from the sun. About how many seconds does it take light from the sun to reach Neptune?

48. *Critical Thinking*   Use the digits 1, 2, 3, and 4 and one negative sign to write a number in scientific notation that is close to 0.001.

Challenge

Solve for y.

49. $(8 \times 10^4)y = 6.4 \times 10^7$

50. $(3.1 \times 10^5)y = 9.3 \times 10^3$

51. Simplify $\dfrac{(3.6 \times 10^6)(4 \times 10^{-3})}{(4.8 \times 10^{-2})(1.2 \times 10^6)}$

Mixed Review

Factor.   **52.** $21 - 15t$ **53.** $9a + 6$ **54.** $30 + 15k$

55. $12m - 4n$ **56.** $3a^2 + 6a + 9$ *2-7, 1-5*

Simplify.   **57.** $5x + (2x - 6)$ **58.** $(11y + 9) - 6y$

59. $4a - (3a + 15)$ **60.** $(4x - 7) - (3x - 7)$ *2-8*

Polynomials

Math in Action

Mathematicians use expressions to model real-world situations. The expression

$$-0.346y + 914.31$$

is a mathematical model of the record time (in seconds) for the mile race in any given year (y) after 1875.

The expression

$$-16t^2 + 96t$$

is a mathematical model of the height (in feet) after t seconds for a projectile with an initial vertical velocity of 96 feet per second.

Both expressions above are called polynomials. Polynomials are used in many areas of mathematics including mathematical applications.

In 1954, Roger Bannister was the first person on record to run a mile in under four minutes. Substitute 1954 for y in the expression at the left above. Is the resulting value less than four minutes? Explain.

What You'll Learn

1 To identify terms and coefficients and factors of a term

2 To simplify a polynomial by collecting like terms

3 To identify the degree of a polynomial

...And Why

To prepare for operations with polynomials

PART 1 **Identifying Terms, Factors, and Coefficients**

Objective: Identify terms and their coefficients and the factors of a term.

You have learned what a monomial is and how to simplify expressions by multiplying and dividing monomials. You will now be working with expressions like these.

$$5y + 3 \qquad 3x^2 + 2x - 5 \qquad -5a^3b^2 + \tfrac{1}{2}ab$$

Each of these expressions is a sum of monomials.

Definition
A **polynomial** is a monomial or a sum of monomials.

In a polynomial, each monomial can be called a term. Polynomials with exactly two terms are called **binomials.** Polynomials with exactly three terms are called **trinomials.**

EXAMPLES Tell whether each expression is a polynomial. If so, identify it as a monomial, binomial, or trinomial.

1 $y^2 + y$

$y^2 + y$ is a polynomial because it is the sum of the two monomials y^2 and y. It is a binomial since it has two terms.

2 $\frac{1}{x} + 2x^2 + \frac{1}{3}x^3$

$\frac{1}{x} + 2x^2 + \frac{1}{3}x^3$ is not a polynomial because $\frac{1}{x}$ is not a monomial.

3 $5x^4 - 3x^2 + 9$

$5x^4 - 3x^2 + 9$ can be rewritten as $5x^4 + (-3x^2) + 9$. Therefore, $5x^4 - 3x^2 + 9$ is a polynomial because it is the sum of the three monomials $5x^4$, $-3x^2$, and 9. It is a trinomial since it has three terms.

Try This Tell whether each expression is a polynomial. If so, identify it as a monomial, binomial, or trinomial.

a. $\frac{7}{n^2} + 4n + 3$ **b.** $8xy^2 - 4$

Be careful not to confuse *terms* and *factors*. In a polynomial, terms are added and factors are multiplied. In the polynomial $2x^3 + 5x^4y^2$, the terms are $2x^3$ and $5x^4y^2$. In the term $2x^3$, 2 and x^3 are factors. In the term $5x^4y^2$, 5, x^4, and y^2 are factors.

The numeric factor of a term is called the **coefficient.** In the term $5x^4y^2$, 5 is the coefficient.

EXAMPLES Identify the terms. Give the coefficient of each term.

4 $4x^2 + 3x - 5$

The terms are $4x^2$, $3x$, and -5.
The coefficient of $4x^2$ is 4; the coefficient of $3x$ is 3; the coefficient of -5 is -5.

5 $2a^4b^3 - 3a^2b^3 - ab + 3$

The terms are $2a^4b^3$, $-3a^2b^3$, $-ab$, and 3.
The coefficient of $2a^4b^3$ is 2; the coefficient of $-3a^2b^3$ is -3; the coefficient of $-ab$ is -1; the coefficient of 3 is 3.

Try This Identify the terms. Give the coefficient of each term.

c. $5y^3 + 6y - 3$ **d.** $m^4 - 3m - 6$ **e.** $-3m^4n^2 - m^2n + 2n$

Collecting Like Terms

Objective: Simplify a polynomial by collecting like terms.

We can often simplify polynomials by collecting like terms. Recall that terms like $3x^2y^3$ and $4x^2y^3$ whose variable factors are exactly the same are called like terms. The distributive property can be used as before to factor out the variable factors. The coefficients of the like terms can then be added to simplify the polynomial.

Quick Review

You can review collecting like terms in Lessons 1-5 and 2-7.

EXAMPLES   Collect like terms.

6 $2m^3 - 6m^3 = (2 - 6)m^3$ Using the distributive property
$$= -4m^3$$

7 $3x^5y^4 - 6y^5 - x^5y^4 + 2y^5 = (3 - 1)x^5y^4 + (-6 + 2)y^5$
$$= 2x^5y^4 + -4y^5$$
$$= 2x^5y^4 - 4y^5$$

Recall that the coefficient of a term like x^3y is 1 and the coefficient of a term like $-x^3$ is -1.

8 $7x^3y + 3x^3 - x^3 + x^3y = (7 + 1)x^3y + (3 - 1)x^3$
$$= 8x^3y + 2x^3$$

Try This   Collect like terms.

f. $2x - 4x^3 - 24 - 6x^3$ **g.** $7m^2 - m - m^2 - 7$

h. $8x^2y^2 - y^2 + y^3 - 1 - 4x^2y^2$ **i.** $4b^5 - 2ab^3 - 3b^5 + 7ab^3$

PART 3

Degrees and Coefficients

Objective: Identify the degree of a polynomial.

The **degree of a term** is the sum of the exponents of the variables. The **degree of a polynomial** is the highest degree of its terms.

EXAMPLE 9

Identify the degree of each term of $8a^4b^2 + 3ab + 7$. Give the degree of the polynomial.

The degree of $8a^4b^2$ is $4 + 2 = 6$.
The degree of $3ab$ is $1 + 1 = 2$.
The degree of 7 is 0.   Think of 7 as $7x^0$.
The degree of the polynomial $8a^4b^2 + 3ab + 7$ is 6.

The term with the highest degree is called the **leading term.** The coefficient of the leading term is called the **leading coefficient.**

Writing Math

When you simplify a polynomial by collecting like terms, you are adding or subtracting monomials.

Try This   Identify the degree of each term. Give the degree of the polynomial.

j. $-6x^4 + 8x^2 - 2x + 9$ 　　　　　　　　**k.** $9x^6y^5 - 7x^4y^3 + 3x^3y^4 + 17x$

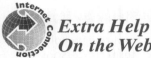

Extra Help On the Web

Look for worked-out examples at the Prentice Hall Web site.
www.phschool.com

5-5 Exercises

A

Tell whether each expression is a polynomial. If it is a polynomial, identify it as a monomial, binomial, or trinomial.

1. $\frac{1}{x}$ 　　　　　　　　　　　　　**2.** $5x^3 - 6x - 3$

3. $7 + 6x^2$ 　　　　　　　　　　　**4.** $15p^2qr^5$

5. $-4m^5 + \frac{6}{m} - 1$ 　　　　　　　**6.** $a^2 + ab + b^3$

7. $-12ab^7 - 12$ 　　　　　　　　**8.** $4 + y$

9. -43 　　　　　　　　　　　　　**10.** $y^3 - 3y^2 - 5$

11. $-h^2 - 3h + 8$ 　　　　　　　**12.** $5x^5y^3 + 5x^3y^2 + 6$

13. $\frac{r^2}{7}$ 　　　　　　　　　　　　**14.** $\frac{7}{r^2}$

Identify the terms. Give the coefficient of each term.

15. $-4m^9 + 6m - 1$ 　　　　　　**16.** $a^5 + 4a^3 - 3a^2 + a$

17. $2x^2y + 5xy^2 - 6y^4$ 　　　　**18.** $m^4n^3 - 3m^3n^2 + 6m^2n^4$

19. $8p^3 + 2pq - 4$ 　　　　　　**20.** $a^4b^6 - 2a^6b^4$

21. $-3n^6 + 3n - 3$ 　　　　　　**22.** $x^6 - 2x^5 + 3x^2 - 2x - 4$

23. $x^8y^6 - 2x^6y^6 + 8x^4y^7 - 4xy^8$

24. $12m^{12} - 8m^{11}n^{10} + 5m^5n^{11} - m^4n^{12} + n^{14}$

Collect like terms.

25. $2x - 5x$ 　　　　　　　　　　**26.** $x - 9x$

27. $2x^2 + 8x^2$ 　　　　　　　　**28.** $3x^2 - 4x^2$

29. $x^3 - 5x - 2x^3$ 　　　　　　**30.** $5x^3 + 6x^3 + 4$

31. $6x^4 - 3x^4 + 7$ 　　　　　　**32.** $6x^4 - 2x^4 + 5$

33. $5x^3 - 3 - 2x^3$ 　　　　　　**34.** $-3x^4 - 6x^4 + 5$

35. $3a^4 - 2a + 2a + a^4$ 　　　　**36.** $2x^2 - 6x + 3x + 4x^2$

37. $4xy^2 + 2x^2y - xy^2 + 3x^2y$ 　**38.** $-7m^2n^2 + 2mn - 2m^2n^2 - 4mn$

39. $2ab^2 + 3ab - 5a^2b + 4ab^2$ 　**40.** $6x^2 + 5xy^2 + 2x^2 - 3xy^2$

41. ***Error Analysis***   A student simplified $7x^3 - x^3$ and got 7 as a result. Write an explanation of the student's error using the words *coefficient* and *like terms*.

Identify the degree of each term and the degree of the polynomial.

42. $2x - 4$

43. $3x^2 - 5x + 2$

44. $-7x^3 + 6x^2 + 3x + 7$

45. $x^2 - 3x + x^6 - 9x^4$

46. $-7x^3y^3 + 6x^2y^2 + 3xy + 7$

47. $-5x^4y^5 + 6x^3y^6 - 3x^2y^2$

48. *Mathematical Reasoning*   Is the sum of the degrees of the terms of a binomial *sometimes, always,* or *never* equal to the degree of the binomial? Justify your answer.

B

Collect like terms.

49. $\frac{1}{4}x^5 - 5 + \frac{1}{2}x^5 - 2x$

50. $\frac{1}{3}x^3 + 2x - \frac{1}{6}x^3 + 4$

51. $\frac{1}{2}a^4 - 4a^2 + \frac{2}{3}a^4 - 3$

52. $\frac{2}{5}r^5 - \frac{1}{2}r^3 + \frac{7}{2}r^3$

53. Write a polynomial for the perimeter of these figures. Simplify the polynomial by collecting like terms.

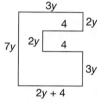
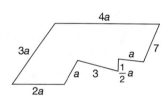

54. *Critical Thinking*   Tell why the following algebraic expressions are not polynomials.

$$\frac{1}{x} \qquad 7 + \frac{5}{y} \qquad x^2 - 5x + \sqrt{x} \qquad (y^2 + 3) \div y$$

Challenge

55. The sum of a number and 2 is multiplied by the number, and then 3 is subtracted from the result. Express the final result as a polynomial.

56. The polynomial in x has degree 3. The coefficient of x^2 is 3 less than the coefficient of x^3. The coefficient of x is 3 times the coefficient of x^2. The remaining coefficient is 2 more than the coefficient of x^3. The sum of the coefficients is -4. Find the polynomial.

Mixed Review

Simplify.   **57.** $c^2 \cdot c^5 \cdot c^3$ **58.** $(3m^2)^3$ **59.** $(x^3y^2)(x^4y^9)$

60. $(-2ab)^3$ **61.** $(3c^{-2})^2$ **62.** $(3c)^{-2}$ *5-1, 5-2*

Evaluate for $y = -\frac{1}{2}$.   **63.** $y\left(y + \frac{2}{3}\right)$ **64.** y^4 **65.** $1 - \frac{3}{4}y$ *1-1, 2-5*

Solve.   **66.** $-6x \le 12$ **67.** $2 + 9a \ge 29$ **68.** $9 - 6c = 3c + 54$ *3-5, 4-3, 4-4*

5-6 ▷ More on Polynomials

What You'll Learn

1 To write polynomials in ascending and descending order

2 To evaluate polynomials

...And Why

To write polynomials in a form that facilitates addition and subtraction

PART 1 **Ascending and Descending Order**

Objective: Write polynomials in ascending and descending order.

The polynomial $8x^4y^3 - 2x^3y^4 + 5x^2 - x + 3$ is written in **descending order** for the variable x. The term with the greatest exponent for x is first, the term with the next greatest exponent for x is second, and so on. The constant 3 can be written as $3x^0$. Thus the degree of the constant is 0.

The polynomial $5 - 3xy^3 + 4x^3y^4 - 3x^5y^3$ is written in **ascending order** for the variable x. The term with the least exponent for x is first, the term with the next larger exponent for x is second, and so on.

EXAMPLES Arrange each polynomial in descending order for the variable x.

1 $4x^4 + 4x^7 + x^2 + 2x^3 = 4x^7 + 4x^4 + 2x^3 + x^2$

2 $3y + 4x^5y^2 - 4x^2 + 5xy^4 + 3x^3 = 4x^5y^2 + 3x^3 - 4x^2 + 5xy^4 + 3y$

Try This Arrange each polynomial in descending order for the variable x.

a. $x + 3x^5 + 4x^3 + 5x^2 + 6x^7 - 2x^4$
b. $4x^2 - 3 + 7x^5 + 2x^3 - 5x^4$
c. $-14y + 7x^2y^3 - 10x^3y^2 - 14x^7$

Sometimes we may need to collect like terms before arranging a polynomial.

EXAMPLE 3 Collect like terms and arrange in descending order for the variable x.

$$2x^2y^3 - 4x^3 + 3 - x^2y^3 - 2x^3 = x^2y^3 - 6x^3 + 3 \quad \text{Simplifying}$$
$$= -6x^3 + x^2y^3 + 3 \quad \text{Writing in descending order}$$

Try This Collect like terms and arrange in descending order for the variable m.

d. $3m^2 - 2m + 3 - 5m^2 - 1 - m$
e. $-4m^2y + my - 2m^2y - my + 3m^3y$

Objective: Evaluate polynomials.

When we replace the variable in a polynomial by a number and calculate, the result is a number. This process is called **evaluating the polynomial.**

EXAMPLES   Evaluate each polynomial for the given value.

4 $3x + 5$ for $x = 6$
$$3x + 5 = 3 \cdot 6 + 5 \qquad \text{Substituting}$$
$$= 18 + 5$$
$$= 23$$

5 $2x^2 + 7x + 3$ for $x = 2$
$$2x^2 + 7x + 3 = 2 \cdot 2^2 + 7 \cdot 2 + 3$$
$$= 2 \cdot 4 + 14 + 3$$
$$= 8 + 14 + 3$$
$$= 25$$

Try This   Evaluate each polynomial for the given value.

f. $-4x - 7$ for $x = 3$
g. $-5x^2 + 7x + 10$ for $x = 3$
h. $2x^2y + 5xy - 4$ for $x = -4$ and $y = 5$

EXAMPLE 6

The height reached by a fireworks packet is given by the polynomial

$$-16t^2 + 140t$$

(height in ft, time (t) in sec).

If the fuse is set to detonate a packet of spider design fireworks five seconds after launch, at what height will the fireworks explode?

Evaluate the polynomial for $t = 5$ to find the height for the explosion of the fireworks.

$$-16t^2 + 140t = -16(5)^2 + 140(5)$$
$$= -16(25) + 700$$
$$= -400 + 700$$
$$= 300$$

The fireworks will explode at 300 feet.

In Example 6, you use the expression $-16t^2 + 140t$ to find the height of a fireworks explosion. The term $140t$ reflects the upward speed with which the fireworks packet is launched. What force do you think is represented by the term $-16t^2$?

EXAMPLE 7

For certain speeds, the cost of operating an automobile at speed s is approximated by the polynomial

$$0.005s^2 - 0.35s + 37$$

(cost in cents per mile, speed (s) in mi/h).

Evaluate the polynomial for $s = 50$ to find the cost of operating an automobile at 50 mi/h.

$$
\begin{aligned}
0.005s^2 - 0.35s + 37 &= 0.005 \cdot 50^2 - 0.35 \cdot 50 + 37 \\
&= 0.005 \cdot 2500 - 17.5 + 37 \\
&= 12.5 - 17.5 + 37 \\
&= 32
\end{aligned}
$$

The cost is approximately 32¢ per mile.

Try This

i. Evaluate the polynomial in Example 6 for $t = 7$ to find the height the fireworks will explode if set to detonate 7 seconds after launch.

j. Evaluate the polynomial in Example 7 for $s = 55$ to find the cost of operating an automobile at 55 mi/h.

k. The lung capacity in liters for a woman can be estimated by the polynomial

$$0.041h - 0.018A - 2.69$$

(height (h) in centimeters, age (A) in years).

Find the lung capacity for a 25-year-old woman who is 170 cm tall.

Evaluating Polynomials

We can evaluate polynomials using a calculator. We can use the memory key STO and the memory recall key RCL to save steps.

Evaluate $2x^3 + 4x^2 - 5$ for $x = 12$.

12 STO   Storing the variable in the memory

2   ×   RCL y^x 3   +   4   ×   RCL y^x 2

−   5   =   →   4027

5-6 Exercises

Extra Help On the Web
Look for worked-out examples at the Prentice Hall Web site.
www.phschool.com

A

Arrange each polynomial in descending order.

1. $x^5 + x + 6x^3 + 1 + 2x^2$

2. $3 + 2x^2 - 5x^6 - 2x^3 + 3x$

3. $5x^3 + 15x^9 + x - x^2 + 7x^8$

4. $9x - 5 + 6x^3 - 5x^4 + x^5$

5. $8y^3 - 7y^2 + 9y^6 - 5y^8 - y^7$

6. $p^8 - 4 + p + p^2 - 7p^4$

Collect like terms and then arrange in descending order for the variable m.

7. $3m^4 - 5m^6 - 2m^4 + 6m^6$

8. $-1 + 5m^3 - 3 - 7m^3 + m^4 + 5$

9. $-2m + 4m^3 - 7m + 9m^3 + 8$

10. $-6m^2 + m - 5m + 7m^2 + 1$

11. $3mp + 3mp + 3mp + m^2 - 4m^2$

12. $-2m - 2mp - 2m - m^3p^4 - 5m^3p^4$

13. $-m + \frac{3}{4} + 15m^4 - m - \frac{1}{2} - 3m^4$

14. $2m - \frac{5}{6} + 4m^3 + m + \frac{1}{3} - 2m$

Evaluate each polynomial for the given value.

15. $x^3 - 27$ for $x = 5$

16. $x^5 + x$ for $x = -2$

17. $x^4 - x$ for $x = 3$

18. $5x^4 - 7x + 2$ for $x = -2$

19. $2x^3 - 5x^2 + x - 3$ for $x = 3$

20. $2x - 5 + 4x^3 + x + x^2 - 2x$ for $x = -4$

21. $-4x^3 + 2x^2 + x - 3$ for $x = 5$

22. $x^5 - x^4 + x^3 - x^2 + x - 1$ for $x = -1$

Evaluate each polynomial for $x = 4$.

23. $-5x + 2$

24. $-3x + 1$

25. $2x^2 - 5x + 7$

26. $3x^2 + x - 7$

27. $x^3 - 5x^2 + x$

28. $7 - x + 3x^2$

Evaluate each polynomial for $a = -1$ and $b = 2$.

29. $3a + 5ab$

30. $6 - 2ab$

31. $a^2 - 2a + b$

32. $5a - 6 + a^2b$

33. $-3a^3 + 7a^2 - 3b - 2$

34. $-2a^3 - 5a^2 + 4a + 3b$

The daily number of automobile accidents involving drivers of age x ($x > 15$) is approximated by the polynomial $0.4x^2 - 40x + 1039$.

35. Evaluate the polynomial for $x = 18$ to find the number of daily accidents involving 18-year-old drivers.

36. Evaluate the polynomial for $x = 20$ to find the number of daily accidents involving 20-year-old drivers.

B

37. A 4-ft by 4-ft sandbox is placed on a square lawn whose side is x ft long. Express the area left over as a polynomial.

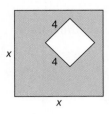

38. Express the shaded area in the figure below as a polynomial.

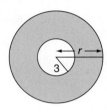

39. *Critical Thinking*   The trinomial $ax^2 + 3x + 7$ is equal to 15 when x is 1, and the trinomial is equal to 33 when x is 2. What is the value of a?

Challenge

Evaluate each expression for the given value.

40. $(-5x^3 + 3x^2 + 6)(7x - 12)$ for $x = 3$

41. $(2x^3 + 3x^2 - 4x + 8)(x^4 - x^2 + 5x)$ for $x = -2$

42. $(4x^5 - 4x^3 + 5x^2 - 4x + 6)(-3x^3 + 6x^2 - x + 8)$ for $x = -1$

43. For a polynomial of degree 2 of the form $ax^2 + bx + c$ where a, b, and c are coefficients, the extreme (highest or lowest) value of the polynomial is the value of x when $2ax = -b$. Find the age with the lowest daily accidents for the polynomial $0.4x^2 - 40x + 1039$, as given for Exercises 35 and 36.

Internet Connection

Self-Test On the Web

Check your progress. Look for a self-test at the Prentice Hall Web site. www.phschool.com

Mixed Review

Simplify.   **44.** $\dfrac{x^2y^4}{xy}$ **45.** $\left(\dfrac{x^3}{2}\right)^3$ **45.** $\dfrac{4a^9}{a^7}$ **47.** $\dfrac{21c^3}{7a^3}$ *5-2*

Write in standard notation.   **48.** 1.603×10^4 **49.** 7.662×10^{-3} *5-4*

Write an equation and solve.

50. The sum of two consecutive integers is 67. Find the integers.   *10-9*

Addition of Polynomials

PART 1 Adding Polynomials

Objective: Add polynomials.

What You'll Learn

1 To add polynomials

2 To add polynomials in column form

...And Why

To write an expression for the perimeter of a geometric figure

Some situations can be modeled by adding polynomials.

EXAMPLE 1 The areas of these figures can be expressed as polynomials.

Area: $x^2 - 16$

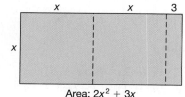

Area: $2x^2 + 3x$

The total area of the two figures can be found by adding the two polynomials.

$$(x^2 - 16) + (2x^2 + 3x)$$

This sum equals the single polynomial

$$x^2 - 16 + 2x^2 + 3x.$$

By collecting like terms as you have already done in Lessons 1-5, 2-7, and 5-6, the polynomial can be simplified to

$$3x^2 + 3x - 16.$$

Try This

a. Write a polynomial for the area of each figure. Then express the total area of the two figures as a sum of two polynomials and as a simplified polynomial.

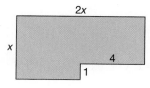

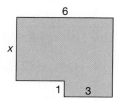

b. Express the perimeter of the triangle as the sum of three polynomials and as a simplified polynomial.

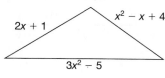

When we add polynomials, we usually arrange the terms in descending order for one of the variables.

EXAMPLES

2 $(3x^3 - 2x - 4) + (4x^3 - 3x^2 + 2)$
$= 3x^3 - 2x - 4 + 4x^3 - 3x^2 + 2$
$= 7x^3 - 3x^2 - 2x - 2$ Collecting like terms

3 $(4m^4n^2 + 3m^2n^3 - 4n) + (2n - 5m^2n^3 + 2m)$
$= 4m^4n^2 - 2m^2n^3 + 2m - 2n$

The answer in Example 3 was arranged in descending order for the variable m. The answer could be arranged in descending order for the variable n:

$$-2m^2n^3 + 4m^4n^2 - 2n + 2m$$

Try This Add.

c. $(3x^2 + 2x - 2) + (-2x^2 + 5x + 5)$
d. $(31m^4 + m^2 + 2m - 1) + (-7m^4 + 5m^3 - 2m + 2)$
e. $(4a^2b - 5a + 3) + (-2a^2b - 2a - 4)$
f. $(3n^3 - 3m^3n^2 - 5n - 3) + (5n^3 + 2m^3n^2 - 3m - 2n - 2)$

PART
2 Adding Polynomials in Columns

Objective: Add polynomials in column form.

We can also add polynomials by writing the polynomials in column form. Align the like terms so they can be easily added.

EXAMPLES Add by writing like terms in columns.

4 $(9m^5 - 2m^3 + 6m^2 + 3) + (5m^4 - 7m^2 + 6)$

$$\begin{array}{l} 9m^5 \qquad\quad - 2m^3 + 6m^2 + 3 \\ \underline{\qquad 5m^4 \qquad\quad - 7m^2 + 6} \\ 9m^5 + 5m^4 - 2m^3 - \ m^2 + 9 \end{array}$$ Aligning like terms

5 $(3x^3y + 6x^2y^3 - 4x + 3) + (2x^4y - 4x^3y + 6x - y)$

$$\begin{array}{l} \qquad\quad 3x^3y + 6x^2y^3 - 4x \qquad + 3 \\ \underline{2x^4y - 4x^3y \qquad\qquad\quad + 6x - y} \\ 2x^4y - x^3y \ + 6x^2y^3 + 2x - y + 3 \end{array}$$ Aligning like terms

232   Chapter 5   *Exponents and Polynomials*

Try This   Add using columns.

g. $(-2m^3 - 5m^2 - 2m - 4) + (m^4 - 6m^2 + 7m - 10)$

h. $(-3x^4y^3 - 5xy + 2) + (x^4y^3 + x^2 + 2xy + 5)$

5-7 Exercises

Extra Help On the Web

Look for worked-out examples at the Prentice Hall Web site.

www.phschool.com

A

Express the sum of the areas of the two figures as a simplified polynomial.

1.

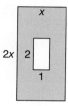
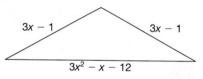

2.

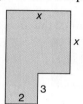

Express the perimeter of each triangle as a simplified polynomial.

3.

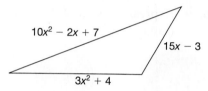

$3x - 1$ $3x - 1$

$3x^2 - x - 12$

4.

$10x^2 - 2x + 7$

$15x - 3$

$3x^2 + 4$

Add.

5. $3x + 2$ and $-4x + 3$

6. $5x^2 + 6x + 1$ and $-7x + 2$

7. $-4x^4 + 6x^2 - 3x - 5$ and $6x^3 + 5x + 9$

8. $5x^3 + 6x^2 - 3x + 1$ and $5x^4 - 6x^3 + 2x - 5$

9. $(7x^3 + 6x^2 + 4x + 1) + (-7x^3 + 6x^2 - 4x + 5)$

10. $(3x^4 - 5x^2 - 6x + 5) + (-4x^3 + 6x^2 + 7x - 1)$

11. $5x^4 - 6x^3 - 7x^2 + x - 1$ and $4x^3 - 6x + 1$

12. $8x^5 - 6x^3 + 6x + 5$ and $-4x^4 + 3x^3 - 7x$

13. $9x^8 - 7x^4 + 2x^2 + 5$ and $8x^7 + 4x^4 - 2x$

14. $4x^5 - 6x^3 - 9x + 1$ and $6x^3 + 9x^2 + 9x$

15. $(-3cd^4 + 6d^2 + 2cd - 1) + (-3d^2 + 2cd + 1)$

Add using columns.

16. $(4m^4 - 3m^3 + 6m^2 + 5m - 4) + (6m^3 - 8m^2 - 3m + 1)$

17. $(5a^4 - 2a^3 + 4a^2 + 5a) + (5a^3 - 5a^2 + 2)$

Add using columns.

18. $(5t^2 - 2t + 3) + (-3t^4 + 3t^2 + 5t - 3)$

19. $(7y^5 - 6y^4 + 3y^3 - 1) + (6y^4 - 4y^3 + 6y^2 + 5)$

20. $(-x^3y^2 + 6x^2 + 3x + 5) + (x^4 + 2x^3y^2 - 3x^2 + 2)$

21. $(-2h^3 + 3h^2k + 5hk + 3) + (-5h^2k - 2hk + 1)$

22. $(-3x^4y^3 + 6x^3y^3 - 6x^2 + 5xy^5 + 1) + (5x^5 - 3x^3y^3 - 5xy^5)$

23. $(4x^2y - 5xy + 7) + (8x^2y + 7xy^2 + 3xy - 2)$

24. $(4x^3y^4 + 7x^4y^3 - 4x^5 - 6x^4) + (-6x^3y^4 - 3x^4y^3 + 2x^4 - x^3)$

B

25. **a.** Express the sum of the areas of these rectangles as a polynomial.

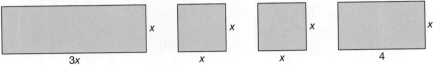

    b. Find the sum of the areas when $x = 3$.

    c. Find the sum of the areas when $x = 8$.

26. **a.** Express the sum of the areas of these circles as a polynomial (area $= \pi r^2$).

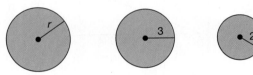

    b. Find the sum of the areas when $r = 5$.

    c. Find the sum of the areas when $r = 11.3$.

27. *Multi-Step Problem*   Use the steps below to solve the following problem. Three brothers have ages that are consecutive multiples of five. The sum of their ages two years ago was 69. Find their ages now.

    a. Let the youngest brother's age be n. Write an expression for the age of each of the other brothers.

    b. Use your answer to part (a) to write an expression for the age of each of the brothers two years ago.

    c. Use your answer to part (b) to write an expression for the sum of the brothers' ages two years ago. Simplify the expression.

    d. For what value of n will the expression in part (c) equal 69?

    e. Use the value of n you found in part (d) to find the age of each of the brothers now.

    f. Check: First check that each age you found in part (e) is a multiple of five. Then find the ages of the brothers two years ago. Check that the sum is 69.

28. a. Use the lengths of the sides of the parallelogram to explain why the value of n must be greater than 2.
  b. Express the perimeter as a simplified polynomial.
  c. Why must the perimeter be greater than 16?

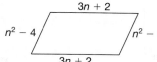

29. *Critical Thinking*   Compare and contrast the column method for adding whole numbers and the column method for adding polynomials.

Challenge

30. The sum of two polynomials is $2x^2 + x + 8$. One polynomial is $x^2 + 3$. What is the other?

31. Addition of real numbers is commutative. That is, $a + b = b + a$ where a and b are real numbers. Show that addition of binomials such as $(ax + b)$ and $(cx + d)$ is commutative.

32. Show that addition of trinomials such as $(ax^2 + bx + c)$ and $(dx^2 + ex + f)$ is commutative.

33. Show that addition of polynomials is commutative. Use
$a_nx^n + a_{n-1}x^{n-1} + \ldots + a_1x + a_0$ and
$b_nx^n + b_{n-1}x^{n-1} + \ldots + b_1x + b_0$

Writing Math

The ellipsis points "..." indicate that a pattern continues.

Mixed Review

Name the properties that guarantee that these statements are true.
34. $a(b + c) = ab + ac$ **35.** $x + (-x) = 0$ **36.** $y \cdot 1 = y$
37. $nm = mn$ **38.** $a + 0 = a$ **39.** $4 + 1 = 1 + 4$ *2-10*

Simplify. **40.** $(2t^3)^5$ **41.** $(3a^5)(6a^2)$ **42.** $x^0 \cdot x^1$ **43.** $(2m^2n)(6n)$ *5-1, 5-2, 5-3*
Factor.   **44.** $5ac + 12a$ **45.** $xyz + 5y - 9yz$ **46.** $a^2 + a + ab$ *2-7*

HISTORICAL NOTE

In 2000 B.C., the Babylonians used algebraic methods in solving problems. However, they used no mathematical symbols other than primitive numerals. This lack of symbolism in algebra continued until almost 1500 A.D.

The plus, +, and minus, −, signs first appeared in 1489 A.D. and were regularly used by 1544 A.D. The equal sign, =, was first used in 1557 by Robert Recorde in England. The raised dot, · , and juxtaposition were first used for multiplication about 1600, and the symbol × about 1620. The division symbol, ÷, appeared in 1659.

5-8 ▷ Subtraction of Polynomials

Objective: Subtract polynomials.

What You'll Learn

1 To subtract polynomials

...And Why

To perform subtraction by adding the additive inverse

We know that two numbers are additive inverses if their sum is zero. For example, 5 and -5 are additive inverses, since $5 + (-5) = 0$. The same definition holds for polynomials.

Definition

Two polynomials are **additive inverses** of each other if their sum is 0.

Consider the polynomial $8x^2 - 4x + 3$. The additive inverse of $8x^2 - 4x + 3$ is

$$-(8x^2 - 4x + 3)$$
$$= (-1)(8x^2 - 4x + 3) \qquad \text{Using the property of } -1$$
$$= (-1)(8x^2) + (-1)(-4x) + (-1)(3) \qquad \text{Using the distributive property}$$
$$= -8x^2 + 4x - 3$$

The additive inverse of a polynomial can be found by replacing each coefficient by its additive inverse.

EXAMPLE 1 Find the additive inverse of $4x^5 - 7x - 8$.

$$-4x^5 + 7x + 8 \qquad \text{Changing the sign of each coefficient gives the additive inverse of the polynomial.}$$

Try This Find the additive inverse of each polynomial.

a. $12x^4 - 3x^2 + 4x$

b. $-13x^6y^4 + 2x^4y - 3x^2 + xy - \frac{5}{13}$

Recall that we can subtract a rational number by adding its additive inverse: $a - b = a + (-b)$. This rule also applies to polynomials.

EXAMPLE 2 Subtract.

$$(a^3 - 2a^2 + 4) - (a^4 - 4a^3 - 3a^2)$$
$$= (a^3 - 2a^2 + 4) + [\,-(a^4 - 4a^3 - 3a^2)] \qquad \text{Adding the inverse}$$
$$= (a^3 - 2a^2 + 4) + (-a^4 + 4a^3 + 3a^2) \qquad \text{Using the distributive property}$$
$$= -a^4 + 5a^3 + a^2 + 4 \qquad \text{Collecting like terms}$$

EXAMPLE 3 Subtract.

$$(4x^3y + 2x^2y^2 - 3xy + 6) - (x^3y - 2x^2y^2 - 2xy - 3)$$
$$= (4x^3y + 2x^2y^2 - 3xy + 6) + [-(x^3y - 2x^2y^2 - 2xy - 3)]$$
$$= (4x^3y + 2x^2y^2 - 3xy + 6) + (-x^3y + 2x^2y^2 + 2xy + 3)$$
$$= 3x^3y + 4x^2y^2 - xy + 9$$

Try This Subtract.

c. $(5x^4 + 4) - (2x^2 - 1)$
d. $(-7m^3 + 2m + 4) - (-2m^3 - 4)$
e. $(-3a^2b^4 + 5ab - 4) - (-4a^3 + 11a^2b^4 - 2a - 6)$

We can also subtract polynomials by arranging like terms in columns.

EXAMPLES Subtract using columns.

4 $(5p^2 - 3p + 6) - (9p^2 - 5p - 3)$

(a) $\begin{array}{l} 5p^2 - 3p + 6 \\ \underline{- (9p^2 - 5p - 3)} \end{array}$ Writing like terms in columns

(b) $\begin{array}{l} 5p^2 - 3p + 6 \\ \underline{+(-9p^2 + 5p + 3)} \end{array}$ Changing subtraction to addition of the inverse

(c) $\begin{array}{l} 5p^2 - 3p + 6 \\ \underline{-9p^2 + 5p + 3} \\ -4p^2 + 2p + 9 \end{array}$ Adding

5 $(3x^3y^2 - 4xy + 1) - (-4x^3y^2 - 3x^2y^2 + 3xy - 5)$

(a) $\begin{array}{l} 3x^3y^2 \qquad\quad - 4xy + 1 \\ \underline{- (-4x^3y^2 - 3x^2y^2 + 3xy - 5)} \end{array}$ Writing like terms in columns

(b) $\begin{array}{l} 3x^3y^2 \qquad\quad - 4xy + 1 \\ \underline{+(4x^3y^2 + 3x^2y^2 - 3xy + 5)} \end{array}$ Changing signs to add

(c) $\begin{array}{l} 3x^3y^2 \qquad\quad - 4xy + 1 \\ \underline{4x^3y^2 + 3x^2y^2 - 3xy + 5} \\ 7x^3y^2 + 3x^2y^2 - 7xy + 6 \end{array}$ Adding

Try This Subtract using columns.

f. $(4x^3 + 2x^2 - 2x - 3) - (2x^3 - 3x^2 + 2)$
g. $(-3ab^2 + 4ab - 7a) - (-2ab^2 - 3a + 4)$

5-8 Exercises

A

Find the additive inverse of each polynomial.

1. $-5x$

2. $x^2 - 3x$

3. $-x^2 + 10x - 2$

4. $-4x^3 - x^2 - x$

5. $12x^4y - 3x^3 + 3$

6. $4x^3 - 6x^2y^2 - 8xy + 1$

Subtract

7. $(5x^2 + 6) - (3x^2 - 8)$

8. $(7a^3 - 2a^2 + 6) - (7a^2 + 2a - 4)$

9. $(6x^5 - 3x^4 + x + 1) - (8x^5 + 3x^4 - 1)$

10. $\left(\frac{1}{2}x^2 - \frac{3}{2}x + 2\right) - \left(\frac{3}{2}x^2 + \frac{1}{2}x - 2\right)$

11. $(6b^2 + 2b) - (-3b^2 - 7b + 8)$

12. $7x^3 - (-3x^2 - 2x + 1)$

13. $(5m^3 - 3m - 6) - (-2m^3 + 5)$

14. $(-4n^4 + n^3 + 2n^2) - (n^4 - 3n^3 - n^2 + 4)$

15. $(6y^3 - 4y - 7) - (-3y^4 - 2y^3 + y - 4)$

16. $(7t^4 + 4t) - (6t^5 - 3t^4 + 2t^2 + 3t - 1)$

17. $(8v^4u + 6v^2 - 5) - (2v^4u - 3v^2 + 2)$

18. $(-3m^3n^2 + 2m^2 - mn - 4) - (-5m^3n^2 - 4m^2 + 3mn + 2)$

19. $(8mn^5 + n^4 - 3mn^3 + 2n^2) - (-mn^5 - mn^4 - n^2 - 1)$

20. $(3x^4y + 2x^3y - x^2 - 7) - (-2x^6 - 3x^4y + 2x^3y - x^2 - 7)$

Subtract.

21. $\begin{array}{l} x^2 + 5x + 6 \\ \underline{x^2 + 2x} \end{array}$

22. $\begin{array}{l} x^3 \qquad + 1 \\ \underline{x^3 + x^2} \end{array}$

23. $\begin{array}{l} c^4 \qquad - 3c^2 + c + 1 \\ \underline{c^4 - 4c^3} \end{array}$

24. $\begin{array}{l} 3x^2 - 6x + 1 \\ \underline{6x^2 + 8x - 3} \end{array}$

Subtract using columns.

25. $(5x^4 + 6x^3 - 9x^2) - (-6x^4 - 6x^3 + 8x)$

26. $(5x^4 + 6x^2 - 3x + 6) - (6x^3 + 7x^2 - 8x - 9)$

27. $(3m^4 + 6m^2 + 8m - 1) - (4m^5 - 6m^4 - 8m - 7)$

28. $(6x^5 + 3x^2 - 7x + 2) - (10x^5 + 6x^3 - 5x^2 - 2x + 4)$

29. $(x^5y^2 - x^3y^2 + xy - 1) - (x^5y^2 - x^4y^2 - x^3y^2 - x^2y + xy - 1)$

30. $(x^5 + x^4y^2 - x^3 + x^2y - xy + 2) - (x^5 + x^4y^2 + x^3 - x^2y - xy + 2)$

B

Simplify.

31. $(y + 4) + (y - 5) - (y + 8)$

32. $(7y^2 - 5y + 6) - (3y^2 + 8y - 12) + (8y^2 - 10y + 3)$

33. $(4a^2 - 3a) + (7a^2 - 9a - 13) - (6a - 9)$

34. $(3x^2 - 4x + 6) - (-2x^2 + 4) + (-5x - 3)$

35. $(-8y^2 - 4) - (3y + 6) - (2y^2 - y)$

36. $(5x^3 - 4x^2 + 6) - (2x^3 + x^2 - x) + (x^3 - x)$

37. $(-xy^4 - 7y^3 + xy^2) + (-2xy^4 + 5y - 2) - (-6y^3 + xy^2)$

38. *Critical Thinking*   The difference of two polynomials is $2x^2 + x + 4$. One polynomial is $3x^2 + x$. What is the other polynomial?

Express the measure of the third side of each triangle as a simplified polynomial. P is the perimeter.

39. $P = 6x + 3$

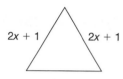

$2x + 1$ $2x + 1$

40. $P = 3x^2 - 6$

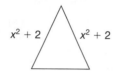

$x^2 + 2$ $x^2 + 2$

41. $P = 4x^2 - x - 16$

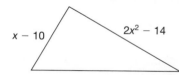

$x - 10$ $2x^2 - 14$

42. $P = 11x^2 + 10$

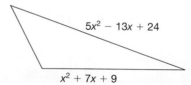

$5x^2 - 13x + 24$

$x^2 + 7x + 9$

Challenge

43. Does replacing each occurrence of x with its additive inverse in the polynomial $5x^3 - 3x^2 + 2x$ result in the additive inverse of the polynomial? Explain.

44. What is the additive identity for addition of polynomials? Show that subtraction of binomials is not commutative. Is it associative? Justify your answer.

Mixed Review

Write using scientific notation.   **45.** 1594   **46.** 0.772   **47.** 93,610   *5-4*

Identify the terms. Give the coefficient of each term.

48. $5x^3 + 3x^2 - 2x + 1$ **49.** $5n^4m + 7n^2m^2 - 2m + 3$ *5-5*

Solve.   **50.** $16 - 3a < 5a$ **51.** $21 + 4h = 11h$ *3-5, 4-4*

5-9 ▷ Multiplication of Monomials and Binomials

What You'll Learn

1 To multiply a monomial and a polynomial

2 To multiply two binomials

. . . And Why

To use the FOIL rule to find products of binomials quickly

PART 1 **Multiplying a Polynomial by a Monomial**

Objective: Multiply a monomial and a polynomial.

We can use the rule for multiplying monomials and the distributive property to multiply a polynomial by a monomial.

EXAMPLES Multiply.

1 $2x(5x + 3) = (2x)(5x) + (2x)(3)$ Using the distributive property
$$= 10x^2 + 6x$$

2 $8p(3q^4 - 2q^3p^2 + 2p) = (8p)(3q^4) + (8p)(-2q^3p^2) + (8p)(2p)$
$$= 24q^4p - 16q^3p^3 + 16p^2$$

Try This Multiply.

a. $4x(2x + 4)$ **b.** $3a^2(-5a^3 + 2a - 7)$

c. $5s(8t^4 - 4s^2 - 9t - 11)$

PART 2 **Multiplying Two Binomials**

Objective: Multiply two binomials.

We can use an area model to illustrate multiplication of two binomials.

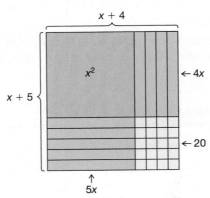

Using the model, the product $(x + 4)(x + 5)$ equals $x^2 + 4x + 5x + 20$, which simplifies to $x^2 + 9x + 20$.

We can also use the distributive property twice to multiply two binomials. For example, $(x + 5)(x + 4)$.

(1) $(x + 4)(x + 5) = x(x + 5) + 4(x + 5)$ Using the distributive property

(2) $= x \cdot x + x \cdot 5 + 4 \cdot x + 4 \cdot 5$ Using the distributive property again

(3) $= x^2 + 5x + 4x + 20$

(4) $= x^2 + 9x + 20$ Collecting like terms

We can rewrite line (2) above to show a short way to find the product of two binomials.

$$\text{First} \quad \text{Outside} \quad \text{Inside} \quad \text{Last}$$
$$(x + 4)(x + 5) = x \cdot x + 5 \cdot x + 4 \cdot x + 4 \cdot 5$$

This is called the **FOIL** method for finding the product of two binomials.

EXAMPLES   Multiply.

3 $(x + 6)(x - 6) = x^2 - 6x + 6x - 36$ Using FOIL
                  $= x^2 - 36$ Collecting like terms

4 $(x + 3)(x - 2) = x^2 - 2x + 3x - 6$
                  $= x^2 + x - 6$

5 $(x^3 + 5)(x^3 - 5) = x^6 - 5x^3 + 5x^3 - 25$
                     $= x^6 - 25$

6 $(4x^2 + 5)(3x^2 - 2) = 12x^4 - 8x^2 + 15x^2 - 10$
                         $= 12x^4 + 7x^2 - 10$

7 $(4m^2 + 5mn)(2mn - 4n) = 8m^3n - 16m^2n + 10m^2n^2 - 20mn^2$

Try This   Multiply.

d. $(x + 3)(x + 4)$ **e.** $(x + 3)(x - 5)$

f. $(2x + 1)(x + 4)$ **g.** $(2x^2 - 3)(x - 2)$

h. $(6x^2 + 5)(2x^3 + 1)$ **i.** $(y^3 + 7)(y^3 - 7)$

j. $(2x^5 + x^2)(-x^3 + x)$ **k.** $(3a + b)(-2a - 4b)$

l. $(2xy + 4x)(-2y + y^2)$ **m.** $(3rs + 2r)(r^2 + 2rs^2)$

We can also use columns to multiply. We multiply each term on the top row by each term on the bottom. Then we add.

EXAMPLE 8

Multiply $4x - 3$ and $x - 2$.

$$
\begin{array}{r}
4x - 3 \\
x - 2 \\
\hline
4x^2 - 3x \\
-8x + 6 \\
\hline
4x^2 - 11x + 6
\end{array}
$$

Multiplying the top row by x

Multiplying the top row by -2

Adding

Try This Multiply.

n. $(5x + 3)(x - 4)$

o. $(2y^2 - 3)(3y - 5)$

p. $(3a + b)(2a - b)$

q. $(6m^2 + n)(3m - n^2)$

r. $(4pq - p^2)(pq + p^2)$

s. $\left(\frac{1}{2}r^2s + s\right)\left(\frac{1}{2}r^2s - s\right)$

Extra Help On the Web

Look for worked-out examples at the Prentice Hall Web site.
www.phschool.com

5-9 Exercises

A

Multiply.

1. $3x(-x + 5)$

2. $2y(4y - 6)$

3. $4x^2(3x + 6)$

4. $5a^2(-2a + 1)$

5. $-6m^2(m^2 + x)$

6. $-4x^2(x^2 - x)$

7. $3x^3(x^3 + 5)$

8. $-5m(-3m^5 - 4m^2)$

9. $3y^2(6y^4 + 8y^3)$

10. $4y^4(y^3 - 6y^2)$

11. $2x(3x^2 + 4x - 3)$

12. $-6x(-5x^3 - x^2 + 4)$

13. $-5a^2(-3a^2 - 6a + 7)$

14. $4b^2(-6b^4 + 3b^2 - 4)$

15. $4y^6(-2y^3 - 2y^2 + y - 5)$

16. $-2x^5(x^4 + 2x^3 - x^2 - x + 3)$

17. $-7h^4(k^6 - k^4 - k^3 + k)$

18. $x^3(-y^7 + y^4 - y^3 + y^2 - y)$

19. $2a(-5a^8b + a^2 - 12ab)$

20. $10x(-y^5 - xy^3 + 12x)$

Multiply.

21. $(x + 1)(x^2 + 3)$

22. $(x^2 - 3)(x - 1)$

23. $(x^3 + 2)(x + 1)$

24. $(x^4 + 2)(x + 12)$

25. $(a + 2)(a - 3)$

26. $(x + 2)(x + 2)$

27. $(3x + 2)(3x + 3)$

28. $(4x + 1)(2x + 2)$

Multiply.

29. $(5x - 6)(x + 2)$ **30.** $(x - 8)(x + 8)$

31. $(3x - 1)(3x + 1)$ **32.** $(2x + 3)(2x + 3)$

33. $(4x - 2y)(x - y)$ **34.** $(2x - y)(3x + y)$

35. $\left(x - \frac{1}{4}\right)\left(x + \frac{1}{4}\right)$ **36.** $\left(x + \frac{3}{4}\right)\left(x + \frac{3}{4}\right)$

37. $(x - 0.1)(x + 0.1)$ **38.** $(3x^2 + 1)(x + 1)$

39. $(2x^2 + 6)(x + 1)$ **40.** $(2b^2 + 3)(2b - 1)$

41. $(-2x + 1)(x - 6)$ **42.** $(3x + 4)(2x - 4)$

43. $(x + 7y)(x + 7y)$ **44.** $(2x + 5y)(2x + 5y)$

45. $(3x^5 + 2)(2x^2 + 6)$ **46.** $(1 - 2x)(1 + 3x^2)$

47. $(8x^3 + 1)(x^3 + 8)$ **48.** $(4 - 2x)(5 - 2x^2)$

49. $(4x^2 + 3)(x - 3)$ **50.** $(7x - 2)(2x - 7)$

51. $(4x^4 + x^2)(x^2 + x)$ **52.** $(5x^6 + 3x^3)(2x^6 + 2x^3)$

53. $(ab + 3b^2)(ab - 3b^2)$ **54.** $(m^2n - 5n)(m^2n + 5n)$

B

Multiply.

55. $(a + b)^2$ **56.** $(a - b)^2$ **57.** $(2x + 3)^2$ **58.** $(5y + 6)^2$

Find an expression for the area of the shaded regions.

59.

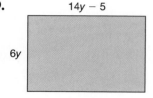

14y − 5

6y

60.

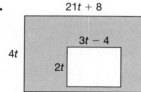

21t + 8

4t

3t − 4

2t

Find an expression for the area of the shaded portion of each square.

61.

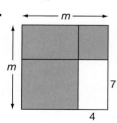

m

m

7

4

62.

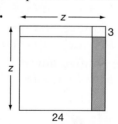

z

3

z

24

63. *Critical Thinking* The product of two binomials is $2x^2 + 5x + 2$. One of the binomials is $(x + 2)$. What is the other binomial?

Error Analysis Study each of the products below. Which are correct and which are incorrect? For those that are incorrect, give the correct answer and state what error was made.

64. $(x^2 + 3y^3)(2x^2 - y) = 2x^2 - x^2y + 6x^2y^3 - 3y^3$

65. $(4m^3)(2m^2 - 2m + 1) = 8m^5 - 8m^4 + 4m^3$

66. $(ab + 2b^2)(ab - 2b^2) = a^2b^2 + 4b$

67. $-2x^2(x^3 + 3x^2 - 3x + 2) = -2x^6 - 6x^4 + 6x^2 - 4x^2$

68. *Critical Thinking* A student claimed that the product of two binomials always results in a polynomial with at least three terms. Provide a counterexample to show that the student's claim is incorrect.

Challenge

69. A box with a square bottom is to be made from a 12-inch square piece of cardboard. Squares with side x are cut out of the corners, and the sides are folded up. Express the volume and the surface area of the outside of the box as polynomials.

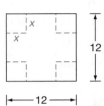

Compute.

70. a. $(x + 3)(x + 6) + (x + 3)(x + 6)$
  b. $(x + 4)(x + 5) - (x + 4)(x + 5)$

71. a. $(x - 2)(x - 7) + (x - 2)(x - 7)$
  b. $(x - 6)(x - 2) - (x - 6)(x - 2)$

72. a. $(x + 5)(x - 3) + (x + 5)(x - 3)$
  b. $(x + 9)(x - 4) - (x + 9)(x - 4)$

73. a. $(x + 7)(x - 8) + (x - 7)(x + 8)$
  b. $(x + 2)(x - 5) - (x - 2)(x + 5)$

74. If a and b are positive, how many terms are there in $(x - a)(x - b) + (x - a)(x - b)$?

75. If a and b are positive, how many terms are there in $(x + a)(x - b) + (x - a)(x + b)$?

76. If a and b are positive, how many terms are there in $(x + a)(x - b) - (x + a)(x - b)$?

Mixed Review

Write as an algebraic expression.   **77.** half of the sum of a number and 3
78. 9 more than the product of a number and 6   **79.** 3 times the difference of 7 and a number   **80.** the sum of two consecutive integers *1-6*

Solve.   **81.** $15r = 3(r + 28)$ **82.** $25 = 4(m - 3) - 3$
83. $13k = 19k + 12$ **84.** $12x = 16(x - 2) + 48$ *3-5*

Multiplying Binomials: Special Products

 PART 1 **Multiplying a Sum and a Difference**

Objective: Multiply the sum and the difference of two expressions.

You have learned the FOIL method for multiplying two binomials. Here are some products found using the FOIL method.

$$(x + 2)(x - 2) = x^2 - 2x + 2x - 4$$
$$= x^2 - 4$$
$$(3x - 5)(3x + 5) = 9x^2 + 15x - 15x - 25$$
$$= 9x^2 - 25$$
$$(3 + x)(3 - x) = 9 - 3x + 3x - x^2$$
$$= 9 - x^2$$

In these examples, the first terms of the binomials are the same and the last terms differ only in sign. These examples suggest the following rule for multiplying the sum and the difference of the same terms.

Product of $(A + B)$ and $(A - B)$

The product of the sum and the difference of two terms is the square of the first term minus the square of the second.
$$(A + B)(A - B) = A^2 - B^2$$

EXAMPLES Multiply.

1 $(x + 4)(x - 4) = x^2 - 4^2$ Squaring the first expression and subtracting the square of the second

$= x^2 - 16$ Simplifying

2 $(2w + 5)(2w - 5) = (2w)^2 - 5^2$
$= 4w^2 - 25$

3 $(-4x - 10y)(-4x + 10y) = (-4x)^2 - (10y)^2$
$= 16x^2 - 100y^2$

Try This Multiply.

a. $(x + 2)(x - 2)$

b. $(x^2 + 7)(x^2 - 7)$

c. $(3t + 5)(3t - 5)$

d. $(2x^3 + y)(2x^3 - y)$

What You'll Learn

1 To multiply the sum and difference of two expressions

2 To square a binomial

...And Why

To use rules to find special products quickly

Objective: Square a binomial.

Multiplying a binomial by itself is called *squaring the binomial*. Look for a pattern.

$$(x + 2)^2 = (x + 2)(x + 2)$$
$$= x^2 + 2x + 2x + 4$$
$$= x^2 + 4x + 4$$
$$(x - 2)^2 = (x - 2)(x - 2)$$
$$= x^2 - 2x - 2x + 4$$
$$= x^2 - 4x + 4$$
$$(3x + 5)^2 = (3x + 5)(3x + 5)$$
$$= 9x^2 + 15x + 15x + 25$$
$$= 9x^2 + 30x + 25$$
$$(3x - 5y)^2 = (3x - 5y)(3x - 5y)$$
$$= 9x^2 - 15xy - 15xy + 25y^2$$
$$= 9x^2 - 30xy + 25y^2$$

There is a quick way to square a binomial.

Squaring Binomials

The square of a binomial is the square of the first term, plus or minus twice the product of the two terms, plus the square of the last term.

$$(A + B)^2 = A^2 + 2AB + B^2$$
$$(A - B)^2 = A^2 - 2AB + B^2$$

EXAMPLES Multiply.

4 $(x + 3)^2 = x^2 + 2 \cdot x \cdot 3 + 3^2$
$$= x^2 + 6x + 9$$

5 $(t - 5)^2 = t^2 - 2 \cdot t \cdot 5 + 5^2$
$$= t^2 - 10t + 25$$

6 $(2x + 7)^2 = (2x)^2 + 2 \cdot 2x \cdot 7 + 7^2$
$$= 4x^2 + 28x + 49$$

7 $(3x - 5y)^2 = (3x)^2 - 2 \cdot 3x \cdot 5y + (5y)^2$
$$= 9x^2 - 30xy + 25y^2$$

Try This Multiply.

e. $(x + 2)(x + 2)$ **f.** $(y - 9)(y - 9)$ **g.** $(4x - 5)^2$

h. $(a - 4)^2$ **i.** $(5x^2 + 4)(5x^2 + 4)$ **j.** $(4x^2 - 3x)^2$

5-10 Exercises

Extra Help On the Web

Look for worked-out examples at the Prentice Hall Web site.
www.phschool.com

A

Multiply.

1. $(x + 4)(x - 4)$
2. $(a + 1)(a - 1)$
3. $(d - 6)(d + 6)$
4. $(y - 5)(y + 5)$
5. $(6 - m)(6 + m)$
6. $(8 + m)(8 - m)$
7. $(2x + 1)(2x - 1)$
8. $(3y - 1)(3y + 1)$
9. $(4a - 7)(4a + 7)$
10. $(5b - 2)(5b + 2)$
11. $(4x^2 - 3)(4x^2 + 3)$
12. $(2x^2 + 3)(2x^2 - 3)$
13. $(3x^4 + 2)(3x^4 - 2)$
14. $(6t^5 - 5)(6t^5 + 5)$
15. $(x^6 - x^2)(x^6 + x^2)$
16. $(3a - 4b)(3a + 4b)$
17. $(7c - 2d)(7c + 2d)$
18. $(-3m + 2n)(-3m - 2n)$
19. $(-6t + s)(-6t - s)$
20. $(x^2 + y^2)(x^2 - y^2)$

Multiply.

21. $(x + 2)^2$
22. $(a + 3)^2$
23. $(t - 3)^2$
24. $(r - 2)^2$
25. $(2x - 1)^2$
26. $(3c - 1)^2$
27. $(4a - 3b)^2$
28. $(7a - 2b)^2$
29. $(4s + 5t)^2$
30. $\left(x - \frac{1}{2}\right)^2$
31. $\left(x - \frac{1}{4}\right)^2$
32. $\left(a + \frac{2}{3}\right)^2$
33. $(2x + 7)(2x + 7)$
34. $(4x + 3)(4x + 3)$
35. $(3x - 2y)(3x + 2y)$
36. $(7x - 5y)(7x + 5y)$
37. $(5x^2 - 1)(5x^2 - 1)$
38. $(12 - 3x^2)(12 + 3x^2)$
39. $\left(2x - \frac{1}{5}\right)\left(2x - \frac{1}{5}\right)$
40. $\left(3x + \frac{3}{4}\right)\left(3x - \frac{3}{4}\right)$
41. $(2x^3 - 0.3)(2x^3 + 0.3)$
42. $(t^2 - 0.2)(t^2 + 0.2)$

B

43. **a.** Find the area of the 4 small rectangles.

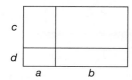

   b. What is the sum of the areas?

   c. Find the area of the blue rectangle.

   Compare your result with your answer to part b.

44. Consider the rectangle at the right. The area of the shaded region is $(a + b)(a - b)$.

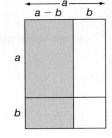

a. Find the area of the large rectangle.
b. Find the area of the two small unshaded rectangles.
c. Find the difference of the areas in part a and part b.
d. Find the area of the shaded region and compare this result with part c.

45. *Critical Thinking*   Find three consecutive integers, the sum of whose squares is 65 more than three times the square of the smallest.

46. *Mathematical Reasoning*   If $m = k^2 + 10k + 25$ and k is an integer, which of the following statements about m must always be true?

A. m is odd.
B. m is even.
C. m is divisible by 5.
D. m is not divisible by 5.
E. m is the square of an integer.

47.   **TEST PREP**   If $a^2 - 2ab + b^2 = 0$, then a must equal

A. 0   B. 1   C. -1 D. b E. $-b$

48. *Mathematical Reasoning*   Is the expression $x^2 - 6x + 9$ *sometimes*, *always*, or *never* negative? Justify your answer.

Challenge

49. a. What is the relationship between $x - y$ and $y - x$?
b. Find $(x - y)^2$ and $(y - x)^2$.
c. Explain your results.

50. Find $(10x + 5)^2$. Use your result to show how to mentally square any two-digit number ending in 5.

51. The product of the sum and difference of two expressions is $25a^2 - 49$. What are the two expressions?

52. The height of a box is one more than its length, and the length is one more than its width.
a. Find the volume of the box in terms of the width (w).
b. Find the volume in terms of the length (l).
c. Find the volume in terms of the height (h).

Mixed Review

Simplify.   **53.** $(9x - 7) + (11x - 6)$ **54.** $(4y^3 - 7y) - (2y^3 - 5y^2)$

55. $(3m^5)^3$ **56.** $(a^3b^2c)(a^2b^4c^2)$ **57.** $15(2y^2)(y^5)$ *5-2, 5-7, 5-8, 5-9*

Evaluate for $a = 3$.   **58.** $-9a^2 + 8$ **59.** $2a^2 - 9a + 15$

60. $7 - 9a + a^2$ **61.** $15a - 3a^2 - 7$ **62.** $5a^2 - 9a - 18$ *1-1*

63. 17 is 25% of what number?   **64.** What number is 8% of 750?   *3-10*

Multiplying Polynomials

5-11

Objective: Multiply any two polynomials.

To multiply two polynomials we can use the distributive property more than once.

What You'll Learn

1 To multiply any two polynomials

... And Why

To find patterns to multiply polynomials quickly

EXAMPLES Multiply.

1 $(x^2 + 4)(x^2 + 2x - 3) = \underset{①}{(x^2)(x^2 + 2x - 3)} + \underset{②}{(4)(x^2 + 2x - 3)}$

$$= (x^4 + 2x^3 - 3x^2) + (4x^2 + 8x - 12)$$
$$= x^4 + 2x^3 + x^2 + 8x - 12$$

2 $(a + 2b)(4a^2 - 2ab + 3b^2)$
$$= a(4a^2 - 2ab + 3b^2) + 2b(4a^2 - 2ab + 3b^2)$$
$$= 4a^3 - 2a^2b + 3ab^2 + 8a^2b - 4ab^2 + 6b^3$$
$$= 4a^3 + 6a^2b - ab^2 + 6b^3$$

Try This Multiply.

a. $(b^2 + 3b - 4)(b^2 + 5)$
b. $(2x - 3y + 5)(3x + 4y)$

Multiplying Polynomials

To multiply two polynomials, multiply each term of one polynomial by every term of the other. Then add the results.

We usually use columns for long multiplication. We multiply each term at the top by every term at the bottom and align like terms. Then we add.

EXAMPLE 3 Multiply $(2c^2 + 3c - 4)(2c^2 - c + 3)$.

$$
\begin{array}{r}
2c^2 + 3c - 4 \\
2c^2 - c + 3 \\
\hline
4c^4 + 6c^3 - 8c^2 \\
-2c^3 - 3c^2 + 4c \\
6c^2 + 9c - 12 \\
\hline
4c^4 + 4c^3 - 5c^2 + 13c - 12
\end{array}
$$

Multiplying by $2c^2$
Multiplying by $-c$
Multiplying by 3

Try This   Multiply.

c. $(3a^2 - 2a + 4)(a^2 + 5a + 1)$
d. $(5x^2 + 4x + 2)(-4x^2 + x - 8)$
e. $(4n^3 - 6n - 5)(2n^2 + n - 2)$
f. $(3x^4y^2 - 4x^2 - 5)(x^3 + x^2y)$

Here is a list of the rules you have learned for multiplying polynomials.

Rules for Multiplying Polynomials

A polynomial and a monomial:

(1) to find the product of a monomial and any polynomial, multiply each term of the polynomial by the monomial.

Two binomials:

(2) $(A + B)(A + B) = (A + B)^2 = A^2 + 2AB + B^2$
(3) $(A - B)(A - B) = (A - B)^2 = A^2 - 2AB + B^2$
(4) $(A + B)(A - B) = A^2 - B^2$
(5) To multiply any two binomials, find the sum of the products of the First terms, the Outside terms, the Inside terms, and the Last terms (FOIL).

Any two polynomials:

(6) To multiply any two polynomials, multiply each term of a polynomial by every term of the other polynomial.

Notice that the FOIL method will work for (2) through (4), but computation is quicker if you know these rules.

EXAMPLES   Multiply.

4 $(x + 3)(x - 3) = x^2 - 9$

Using rule 4 (the product of a sum and difference)

5 $(t + 7)(t - 5) = t^2 + 2t - 35$

Using rule 5 (the product of two binomials)

6 $(x + 7)(x + 7) = x^2 + 14x + 49$

Using rule 2 (the square of a binomial sum)

7 $2y^3(9x^2 + x - 7) = 18x^2y^3 + 2xy^3 - 14y^3$

Using rule 1 (the product of a monomial and a polynomial)

8 $(3x^2 - 7x)^2 = 9x^4 - 42x^3 + 49x^2$

Using rule 3 (the square of a binomial difference)

9 $\left(3x + \frac{1}{4}\right)^2 = 9x^2 + 2(3x)\frac{1}{4} + \frac{1}{16}$ Using rule 2 (the square of a binomial sum)

$$= 9x^2 + \frac{3}{2}x + \frac{1}{16}$$

10 $(x^2 - 3x + 2)(2x - 4)$ Using rule 6 (the product of any two polynomials)

$$= 2x^3 - 6x^2 + 4x - 4x^2 + 12x - 8$$
$$= 2x^3 - 10x^2 + 16x - 8$$

Try This   Multiply.

g. $(x + 5)(x + 6)$ **h.** $(x - 4)(x + 4)$ **i.** $4x^2(-2x^3 + 5x^2 + 10)$

j. $(9x^2 + 1)^2$ **k.** $(2x - 5)(2x + 8)$ **l.** $(x^2 - 4x - 3)(3x - 2)$

5-11 Exercises

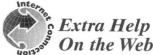

Journal

Summarize what you have learned in this chapter about operations with polynomials. Give an example of each operation.

Extra Help On the Web

Look for worked-out examples at the Prentice Hall Web site.

www.phschool.com

A

Multiply.

1. $(x^2 + x + 1)(x - 1)$ **2.** $(n^2 - n + 2)(n + 2)$

3. $(2x^2 + 6x + 1)(2x + 1)$ **4.** $(4x^2 - 2x - 1)(3x - 1)$

5. $(3y^2 - 6y + 2)(y^2 - 3)$ **6.** $(y^2 + 6y + 1)(3y^2 - 3)$

7. $(x^3 + x^2 - x)(x^3 + x^2)$ **8.** $(x^3 - x^2 + x)(x^3 - x^2)$

9. $(a - b)(a^3 + a^2b + ab^2 + b^3)$ **10.** $(c + d)(c^3 - c^2d + cd^2 - d^3)$

11. $(x^2 + x + 1)(x^2 - x - 1)$ **12.** $(x^2 - x + 1)(x^2 - x + 1)$

13. $(2x^2 + 3x - 4)(2x^2 + x - 2)$ **14.** $(2x^2 - x - 3)(2x^2 - 5x - 2)$

15. $(2t^2 - t - 4)(3t^2 + 2t - 1)$ **16.** $(3a^2 - 5a + 2)(2a^2 - 3a + 4)$

17. $(2x^2 + x - 2)(-2x^2 + 4x - 5)$

18. $(3x^2 - 8x + 1)(-2x^2 - 4x + 2)$

19. $(x^5 - x^3 + x)(x^4 + x^2 - 1)$

20. $(3x^6 + 3x^4 + 3x^2)(x^5 - x^3 + x)$

21. $(b^3 + b^2 + b + 1)(b - 1)$ **22.** $(x^3 + x^2 + x - 2)(x - 2)$

23. $(x^3 + x^2 - x - 3)(xy - 3y)$ **24.** $(x^3 - x^2 - x + 4)(xy + 4y)$

Multiply.

25. $(x - 8)(x - 8)$ **26.** $(x + 7)(x + 7)$

27. $(x - 8)(x + 8)$ **28.** $(x + 7)(x - 7)$

29. $(x - 8)(x + 5)$ **30.** $(x + 7)(x - 4)$

31. $4x(x^2 + 6x - 3)$ **32.** $8x(-x^2 - 4x + 3)$

33. $\left(2x^2 - \frac{1}{2}\right)\left(2x^2 - \frac{1}{2}\right)$ **34.** $(1 - x^2)(1 - x^2)$

Multiply.

35. $(6a^3 - 1)(6a^3 + 1)$

36. $(2b^2 - 7)(3b^2 + 9)$

37. $(2 - 3x)(2 + 3x)$

38. $(4 + 5x)(4 - 5x)$

39. $(6x^4 + 4)^2$

40. $(8 - 6x^4)^2$

41. $-6x^2(x^3 + 8x - 9)$

42. $-5x^2(x^3 - 2x + 4)$

43. $(6q^3 - 1)(2q^2 + 1)$

44. $(7p^2 + 4)(5p^2 - 8)$

45. $\left(\frac{3}{4}x + 1\right)\left(\frac{3}{4}x + 2\right)$

46. $\left(\frac{1}{5}x^2 + 9\right)\left(\frac{3}{5}x^2 - 7\right)$

47. $(x^2 + 2x + 3)(4x + 5)$

48. $(x^2 + 2x)(3x^2 + 4x + 5)$

49. $(x^3 - 4x^2)(3x^2 - 2x + 5)$

50. $(x^3 - 4x^2 + 5)(3x^2 - 2x)$

B

51. Find $(x + y)^3$.

52. Find $(x + y)^4$.

53. *Critical Thinking*   Study the pattern of your answers for Exercises 51 and 52. Without multiplying, find $(x + y)^5$.

Challenge

Multiply. Look for patterns.

54. **a.** $(x^2 + x + 1)(x - 1)$

b. $(x^2 + x + 1)(x + 1)$

c. $(x^2 - x + 1)(x - 1)$

d. $(x^2 - x + 1)(x + 1)$

e. $(-x^2 + x - 1)(x - 1)$

f. $(-x^2 + x - 1)(x + 1)$

g. $(x^3 + x^2 + x + 1)(x - 1)$

h. $(x^3 + x^2 + x + 1)(x + 1)$

i. $(x^3 - x^2 + x - 1)(x - 1)$

j. $(x^3 - x^2 + x - 1)(x + 1)$

k. $(-x^3 + x^2 - x + 1)(x - 1)$

l. $(-x^3 + x^2 - x + 1)(x + 1)$

55. What polynomial times $(x - 1)$ equals $x^5 - 1$?

56. What polynomial times $(x + 1)$ equals $x^5 + 1$?

57. What polynomial times $(x - 1)$ equals $x^6 - 1$?

58. Find $(x^2 + xy + y^2)^2$.

59. Find a trinomial $ax^2 + bx + c$ and a binomial $dx + e$ so that when they are multiplied, the coefficient of the x term is 1.

Mixed Review

Multiply.   **60.** $(x - 3)^2$ **61.** $(x + 3)^3$ **62.** $(x - 3)(x + 3)$ 5-10

Give the additive inverse.   **63.** 7a   **64.** $-21n$ **65.** $3y^2 - 9y + 1$ 2-3

Write in standard notation.   **66.** 1.1×10^{-5} **67.** 2.1×10^7 5-9

Identify the degree of each term and the degree of the polynomial.

68. $3n^2 - 4n + 11$ **69.** $3x^3y^4 + 9x^2y - 24$ **70.** $9a + 6$ 5-5

71. On a scale drawing of a certain building, 1 in. represents 2.5 ft. The length of one wall in the drawing is 3.6 in. What is the actual length of that wall?   3-9

Application

Formulas in Health Care

Doctors often use mathematics in evaluating health. For example, doctors can compare the graphs of a patient's pulse rate and blood pressure with graphs showing normal ranges for people of similar height, age, and weight.

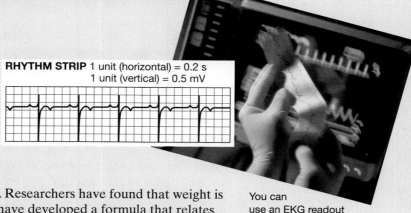

RHYTHM STRIP 1 unit (horizontal) = 0.2 s
1 unit (vertical) = 0.5 mV

Math is also used to determine body fat. Researchers have found that weight is not the best indicator of body fat. They have developed a formula that relates bone structure to actual fat in the body. The polynomial $0.49W + 0.45P - 6.36R + 8.7$, where W = waist circumference in centimeters, P = skinfold above the pectoral muscle in millimeters, and R = wrist diameter in centimeters, gives an estimate of the percent of body fat for a man.

You can use an EKG readout to find a pulse rate in beats per minute. You evaluate the expression $\frac{60}{t}$, where t is the time in seconds between peaks on the graph. Find the pulse rate for the graph shown.

EXAMPLE

Estimate the percent of body fat for a man with the measurements W = 94.2 cm, P = 6.3 mm, R = 7.5 cm.

$$0.49W + 0.45P - 6.36R + 8.7$$
$$= 0.49(94.2) + 0.45(6.3) - 6.36(7.5) + 8.7$$
$$= 9.993 \approx 10$$

The man has 10% body fat.

Problems

Solve.

1. Use the polynomial in the example to estimate the body fat of a young man with the measurements W = 86.2 cm, P = 4.8 mm, R = 6.0 cm.
2. Use the polynomial in the example to estimate the body fat of a man with the measurement W = 95.8 cm, P = 5.1 mm, R = 7.2 cm.
3. The polynomial $0.041h - 0.018A - 2.69$ gives an estimate of lung capacity in liters where h = height in cm and A = age in years. Find the lung capacity of a 29-year-old woman who is 170 cm tall.
4. Use the polynomial in Problem 3 to find the lung capacity of a person who is 18 years old and 156 cm tall.

5-12 ▷ Reasoning Strategies

What You'll Learn

1 To solve problems using the strategies *Make a Table* and *Look for a Pattern*

... And Why

To increase efficiency in problem solving by applying reasoning skills

The average starting salaries for college graduates vary according to academic majors from $22,102 to $42,758, with chemical engineering majors earning the highest average starting salary.

Objective: Solve problems using the strategies *Make a Table* and *Look for a Pattern*.

The reasoning strategies called *Make a Table* and *Look for a Pattern* are helpful when you are solving problems involving numerical relationships. Recording data from a problem in a table organizes the data. When data are organized in a table, numerical patterns are easier to recognize.

EXAMPLE

A college graduate was offered two jobs. One job had a starting salary of $30,000 a year with a guaranteed $3000-a-year raise for each of the next 10 years. The other job had a starting salary of $37,000 a year with a guaranteed $2000-a-year raise for each of the next 10 years. After 10 years, both jobs offered a 5% raise each year thereafter. Which job would pay the most in the tenth year?

To find the amount of money earned in the tenth year, you can *make a table* showing the years and the amount earned each year for each job. *Look for a pattern* to extend the table to the tenth year.

Year	1	2	3	4	5	6	7	8	9	10
Amount (in thousands)	30	33	36	39	42	45	48	51	54	57

The amount increases by $3000 each year for job A.

Year	1	2	3	4	5	6	7	8	9	10
Amount (in thousands)	37	39	41	43	45	47	49	51	53	55

The amount increases by $2000 each year for job B.

You can see in the table that job A, the one with a starting salary of $30,000, will pay the most in the tenth year.

As we have seen, problems can be solved in more than one way. This problem could also have been solved using logical reasoning.

5-12 Problems

**Extra Help
On the Web**

Look for worked-out
examples at the Prentice
Hall Web site.
www.phschool.com

Solve using one or more of the strategies.

1. In the example, in which job would this person have earned the most money altogether after 10 years?

2. A wealthy family donated money to a local university for a 10-year period. The first year they gave $1 million. The second year they gave $3 million. The third year they gave $5 million, and so on. They continued giving money in this manner. How much money did they give in all for these 10 years?

3. Members of a stamp-collecting club each bought one of the same kind of stamp at an auction. All stamps were sold at whole-dollar amounts. Each member paid the same amount, there was no tax, and no stamp at this auction was sold for less than $10. The club paid a total of $203 for the stamps. How many people from the club bought the stamp?

4. The area of a square farm field was 25 acres. The field was divided into separate square lots of 1 acre. A fence was placed around the outside of the entire field. The base price for a lot was $1200. Lots on the edge, which had fences, cost $150 more for each side that had a fence. What were the different prices for the lots in this field, and how many of each price were there?

5. A company decides to increase its sales force. In the first week, each of the 25 original salespeople hires and trains 2 new salespeople. In week two, each of the new salespeople hires and trains 2 new salespeople. Again in week three, each of the most recently hired salespeople hires and trains 2 new salespeople. If the company continues this pattern, how large is the sales force after 3 months (12 weeks)?

6. *Write a Convincing Argument* Solve the problem below. Then write an argument that would convince a classmate that your solution is correct.

   John was hired by a painter to paint doors. He was paid $10 for each door that he completed that did not need repainting by the painter. For each door that needed to be redone, he was fined $5. On a bad day, he painted 25 doors, but made a total of only $10. How many doors did he paint that did not need to be repainted?

5 ▷ **Chapter Wrap Up**

Key Terms

additive inverses (p. 236)
ascending order (p. 226)
binomial (p. 222)
coefficient (p. 222)
constant (p. 214)
degree of a polynomial (p. 223)
degree of a term (p. 223)
descending order (p. 226)
evaluating a polynomial (p. 227)
exponential notation (p. 204)
FOIL (p. 241)
leading coefficient (p. 223)
leading term (p. 223)
monomial (p. 214)
polynomial (p. 221)
scientific notation (p. 217)
standard notation (p. 217)
trinomial (p. 222)

5-1

To multiply powers with like bases, such as $x^2 \cdot x^5$, you add the exponents to get x^7. To divide powers with like bases, such as $\frac{y^6}{y^2}$, you subtract the exponents to get y^4. To divide $\frac{x^3}{x^5}$, where the larger exponent is in the denominator, you subtract the exponents to get x^{-2} or $\frac{1}{x^2}$.

Simplify.

1. $7^2 \cdot 7^4$

2. $y^3 \cdot y^5$

3. $x^7 \cdot x^3 \cdot x$

4. $(a^2b^4)(a^3b)$

5. $(x^4y^5)(x^4y^5)$

6. $(lm^7n^5)(l^2m^6n)$

Simplify.

7. $\frac{7^5}{7^3}$

8. $\frac{a^9}{a^4}$

9. $\frac{x^9y^7}{x^2y^3}$

Simplify. Express each power using positive exponents.

10. 7^{-3}

11. y^{-2}

12. a^0

5-2

To raise a power to a power, such as $(a^2)^3$, you multiply the exponents to get a^6. To find the power of a product or quotient, everything inside the parentheses is raised to the power.

Simplify.

13. $(5^3)^2$

14. $(3^4)^4$

15. $(x^6)^2$

16. $(a^3)^3$

17. $(3a)^2$

18. $(2b)^3$

19. $(2x^3)^3$

20. $(4p^2)^3$

21. $(3x^2yz^4)^2$

22. $(-2x^6y^2)^3$

23. $[(-n)^{15}]^2$

24. $\left(\frac{y^3}{3}\right)^4$

5-3

To multiply two **monomials,** multiply the numerical factors and the variable factors. Use the properties of exponents to multiply the variables: $(-3x^2y)(-5xy^5) = 15x^3y^6$. To divide two monomials, divide the numerical factors and the variable factors: $\frac{15x^3y^4}{-5xy^2} = -3x^2y^2$

Multiply.

25. $(2a)(3a)$

26. $(-2x)(3x^2)$

27. $(5b^2c^3)(-4bc^3)$

28. $(5y^3)(-2y)(-y^4)$

29. $-(3wz^4)(-5w^2z^3)$

30. $(-4x^2y)(-8xy^3)$

Divide.

31. $\frac{a^6}{a^3}$

32. $\frac{15n^5}{-15n}$

33. $\frac{-15x^3y^6}{5xy^3}$

34. $\frac{-24m^{12}n^2}{-6m^5n}$

35. $\frac{18b^{14}c^6}{-3b^7c^2}$

36. $\frac{-28x^4y^8}{-7x^2y^6}$

5-4

The numbers 3.215×10^4 and 4.17×10^{-3} are expressed using **scientific notation,** and the numbers 32,150 and 0.00417 are expressed using **standard notation.**

Internet Activity On the Web

Look for extension problems for this chapter at the Prentice Hall Web site. www.phschool.com

Write using standard notation.

37. 3.25×10^3

38. 5.7×10^{-3}

Write using scientific notation.

39. 2,426,000

40. 0.000045

5-5

In a **polynomial,** each monomial can be called a **term.** In the term $3a^2b^3$, 3 is called the **coefficient,** and factors are 3, a^2, and b^3. To collect like terms, add or subtract the coefficients of the like terms. To find the **degree of a term,** add the exponents of the variables in that term. The **degree of a polynomial** is the highest degree of its terms.

Collect like terms.

41. $5x^3 - x^3 + 4$

42. $-2x^4 + 16 + 2x^4 + 9 - 3x^5$

Identify the degree of each term and the degree of the polynomial.

43. $3x^3y^2 + 7x^2y - 5$

44. $4y^2 + 7y + 2$

5-6

To write a polynomial in **descending order** for the variable x, write the term with the greatest exponent for x first, the next greatest exponent for x second, and so on. A constant term will always be last. To evaluate a polynomial, replace the variable with the given number and calculate the result.

Arrange each polynomial in descending order for the variable x.

45. $3x^2 - 2x^4 + 5 + 7x^5 - 2x$

46. $3y - 4x^5 - 2x^3y^2 + 7x^2y^3$

47. $-x^5 + 14x^4 - 7x - 1 - 4x^4$

48. $6y + 3x^3 - 7xy^2 + 8x^4y^3$

Evaluate each polynomial for $x = 5$.

49. $7x - 10$

50. $x^2 - 3x + 6$

5-7

To add polynomials collect like terms and arrange in descending order.

Add.

51. $(5x^3 - 2x^2 + 3x) + (2x^3 + 6x^2 + x)$

52. $(3x^4 - x^3 + x - 4) + (3x^4 - 5x^3 + 3x^2 - 5)$

53. $(3x^5 - 4x^4 + x^3 - 3) + (3x^4 - 5x^3 + 3x^2)$

54. $(a^3 + 7a^2b - ab^2 - 2b^3) + (2a^3 - 3ab^2 + 2b^3)$

5-8

When you the find the **additive inverse of a polynomial,** you change the sign of each term in the polynomial. You can subtract a polynomial by adding its additive inverse.

Subtract.

55. $(7y^3 + 8) - (3y^3 - 6)$ **56.** $(5x^2 - 4x + 1) - (3x^2 + 7)$

57. $(3x^5 + 4x^4 + 2x^2 + 3) - (2x^5 - 4x^4 + 3x^3 + 4x^2 - 5)$

Use columns to subtract.

58. $(6y^2 - 5y + 3) - (8y^2 - 3y - 8)$

59. $(2x^5 - x^3 + x + 3) - (3x^5 - x^4 + 4x^3 + 2x^2 - x + 3)$

5-9

To multiply a polynomial by a monomial, multiply each term of the polynomial by the monomial. To multiply two binomials, use the **FOIL** method: multiply the **F**irst terms, the **O**utside terms, the **I**nside terms, and the **L**ast terms. Then collect like terms.

Multiply.

60. $3x(5x + 6)$ **61.** $5x^3(3x^3 - 8x^2 + 10x + 2)$

Multiply and collect like terms.

62. $(x + 4)(x - 7)$ **63.** $(a - 3)(a + 3)$

64. $(b^2 + 3)(b^2 + 2)$ **65.** $(2x^2 + 5xy)(3x^2 - 3)$

5-10

Although FOIL can be used to multiply two binomials, the rules for the following special products can be used as shortcuts.

$$(A + B)(A - B) = A^2 - B^2$$
$$(A + B)^2 \quad = A^2 + 2AB + B^2$$
$$(A - B)^2 \quad = A^2 - 2AB + B^2$$

Multiply.

66. $(x - 3)(x + 3)$ **67.** $(a - 8)(a + 8)$ **68.** $(2y + 3)(2y - 3)$

69. $(3x^2 - 4)(3x^2 + 4)$ **70.** $(-2y + 7x)(-2y - 7x)$

71. $(2 + 3y)(2 - 3y)$ **72.** $(a + 4)^2$ **73.** $(3x + 6)^2$

5-11

To multiply a trinomial by a binomial, multiply the trinomial by each term of the binomial. To multiply two polynomials, multiply each term of one polynomial by every term of the other. It may help you to use columns for long multiplications.

74. $(4x^2 - 5x + 1)(3x - 2)$ **75.** $(2a^2 + 3a - 2)(a^2 - 4)$

76. $(2b^2 + 5b - 3)(2b^2 - 2b + 1)$ **77.** $(x^4 - 2x + 3)(x^3 + x - 1)$

Simplify. Express using exponents.

1. $6^2 \cdot 6^3$

2. $x^6 \cdot x^2$

3. $a^8 \cdot a^3$

4. $(r^2 s^3)(rs^4)$

5. $\dfrac{3^5}{3^2}$

6. $\dfrac{a^4 b^5}{ab^3}$

Simplify. Express using a positive exponent.

7. 6^{-2}

8. y^{-4}

9. 3^0

Simplify.

10. $(x^3)^2$

11. $(-3y^2)^3$

12. $\left(\dfrac{a^4}{3}\right)^3$

Multiply.

13. $(-2y^2)(4y)$

14. $(6x^2)(-2x^3)(-2x^5)$

15. $(-4n^3)(-4n^3)$

Divide.

16. $\dfrac{b^3}{b}$

17. $\dfrac{7a^4}{a^4}$

18. $\dfrac{4x^5}{12x^3}$

Write using standard notation.

19. 3.265×10^5

20. 2.07×10^{-3}

Write using scientific notation.

21. 246,000

22. 0.00385

Collect like terms.

23. $4a^2 - 6 + a^2$

24. $y^2 - 3y - y + 2y^2$

Collect like terms, and then arrange them in descending order.

25. $3 - x^2 + 2x + 5x^2 - 6x$

Evaluate the polynomial for $x = -2$.

26. $x^2 - 5x - 1$

Add.

27. $(5x^4 + 7x^3 - 8) + (3x^4 - 5x^3 + 6x^2)$

Subtract.

28. $(12x^2 - 3x - 8) - (4x^2 + 5)$

Multiply.

29. $-3x^2(4x^2 - 3x - 5)$

30. $(3b + 5)(b - 3)$

31. $(6a^2 - 2)(a^2 - 1)$

32. $(3p - 2)(3p + 2)$

33. $(3x^2 + 4)(3x^2 - 4)$

34. $(x - 9)^2$

35. $(4x^7 + 3)(4x^7 - 3)$

36. $(3x^2 - 2x)^2$

37. $(2x + 1)(3x^2 - 5x - 3)$

38. $(-2a^3 + 5a^2 - 3)(3a^2 + 1)$

CHAPTER 6

Skills & Concepts You Need for Chapter 6

1-5   Factor.

1. $6x + 6y$ **2.** $24w + 24z$ **3.** $4y + 28 + 12z$

3-4   Write as an algebraic expression.

4. 10 more than twice the number

5. 2 times the sum of a number and 6

3-5   Solve.

6. $6y + 4 = 2y + 8$ **7.** $3(2a + 4) = 20$

3-11

8. The perimeter of a rectangle is 280 cm. The length is 20 cm more than the width. Find the dimensions.

5-3   Multiply.

9. $(-6x^8)(2x^5)$ **10.** $(-6x^2y^2)(4xy^4)$

5-9   Multiply.

11. $9x(4x + 7)$ **12.** $3s(6t^4 - 2s^2 - 3t - 6)$

13. $(3x + 8)(x - 7)$ **14.** $(x + 3)(5x - 7)$

15. $8x(2x^2 - 6x + 1)$ **16.** $(x + 6)(x - 4)$

17. $(y - 8)(y + 3)$ **18.** $(7w + 6)(4w - 1)$

5-10   Multiply.

19. $(x - 9)^2$ **20.** $(5x + 3)^2$

21. $(a - 7)(a + 7)$ **22.** $(2 - 5y)(2 + 5y)$

Polynomials and Factoring

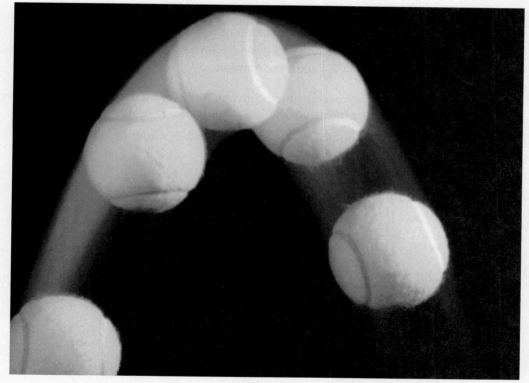

You can use the formula
$h = vt - 4.9t^2$ to find the height of a thrown tennis ball. A tennis ball bounces upward with a speed of 4.9 m per second. Evaluate the polynomial $4.9t - 4.9t^2$ for $t = 0.5$ to find its height after 0.5 seconds.

Factoring Polynomials

What You'll Learn

1 To factor monomials

2 To factor out common factors in terms of a polynomial

... And Why

To rewrite monomials as the product of two factors

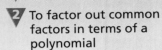

You can read $20x^2 = (2x)(10x)$ as *Twenty x squared is the product of 2x and 10x*, or *Twenty x squared equals 2x times 10x*.

Introducing the Concept: Factoring Monomials

How many pairs of monomials can you find whose product is $16x^4$? *Make an organized list* showing the pairs you find.

PART 1 Factoring Monomials

Objective: Factor monomials.

Factoring is the reverse of multiplying. To factor an expression means to write an equivalent expression that is a product of two or more expressions.

To factor a monomial, we find two monomials whose product is that monomial. Compare.

Multiplying	**Factoring**
$(4x)(5x) = 20x^2$	$20x^2 = (4x)(5x)$
$(2x)(10x) = 20x^2$	$20x^2 = (2x)(10x)$
$(-4x)(-5x) = 20x^2$	$20x^2 = (-4x)(-5x)$
$(x)(20x) = 20x^2$	$20x^2 = (x)(20x)$
$(2)(10x^2) = 20x^2$	$20x^2 = (2)(10x^2)$

There are still other ways to factor $20x^2$. Each is called a **factorization** of $20x^2$.

EXAMPLE 1 Find factorizations of $15x^3$.

Factors of $15x^3$ are $1, -1, 3, -3, 5, -5, 15, -15, x, x^2, x^3$. Some possible factorizations are

$$(15x)(1x^2) \qquad (5x)(3x^2) \qquad (3)(5x^3)$$
$$(1x)(15x^2) \qquad (3x)(5x^2) \qquad (5)(3x^3)$$

Since $(-1)(-1) = 1$, we could also have the following.

$$(-15x)(-1x^2) \qquad (-5x)(-3x^2) \qquad (-3)(-5x^3)$$
$$(-1x)(-15x^2) \qquad (-3x)(-5x^2) \qquad (-5)(-3x^3)$$

There are still other ways to factor $15x^3$.

Try This   Find three factorizations of each monomial.

a. $8x^4$ **b.** $6m^5$ **c.** $12a^2b^2$

PART 2 Factoring Terms With a Common Factor

Objective: Factor out common factors in the terms of a polynomial.

To multiply a monomial and a polynomial, we use the distributive property to multiply each term of the polynomial by the monomial. To factor, we do the reverse and *factor out* a common factor. We use the factor common to each term with the greatest possible coefficient and the variable to the greatest power.

Compare.

<table>
<tr><td>Multiply</td><td>Factor</td></tr>
<tr><td>$5(x + 3) = 5 \cdot x + 5 \cdot 3$</td><td>$5x + 15 = 5 \cdot x + 5 \cdot 3$</td></tr>
<tr><td>$= 5x + 15$</td><td>$= 5(x + 3)$</td></tr>
<tr><td>$3a(b^2 + 2) = 3a(b^2) + 3a(2)$</td><td>$3ab^2 + 6a = 3a(b^2) + 3a(2)$</td></tr>
<tr><td>$= 3ab^2 + 6a$</td><td>$= 3a(b^2 + 2)$</td></tr>
</table>

We say we have "factored out" the common factor.

EXAMPLES Factor.

2 $3x^2 + 3 = 3(x^2) + 3(1)$
$= 3(x^2 + 1)$ Factoring out the common factor, 3

3 $5y^4 - 20y^3 = 5y^3(y) = 5y^3(4)$
$= 5y^3(y - 4)$ Factoring out the common factor, $5y^3$

4 $16a^2b^2 + 20a^2 = 4a^2(4b^2) + 4a^2(5)$
$= 4a^2(4b^2 + 5)$ Factoring out the common factor, $4a^2$

5 $15x^5 - 12x^4 + 27x^3 - 3x^2$
$= 3x^2(5x^3) - 3x^2(4x^2) + 3x^2(9x) - 3x^2(1)$
$= 3x^2(5x^3 - 4x^2 + 9x - 1)$ Factoring out the common factor, $3x^2$

6 $4m^2n^3 + 2m^2n^2 + 6m^2n = 2m^2n(2n^2) + 2m^2n(n) + 2m^2n(3)$
$= 2m^2n(2n^2 + n + 3)$

Try This Factor.

d. $x^2 + 3x$

e. $a^2b + 2ab$

f. $3x^6 - 5x^3 + 2x^2$

g. $9x^4 - 15x^3 + 3x^2$

h. $2p^3q^2 + p^2q + pq$

i. $12m^4n^4 + 3m^3n^2 + 6m^2n^2$

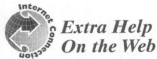

Extra Help On the Web

Look for worked-out examples at the Prentice Hall Web site.
www.phschool.com

6-1 Exercises

A

Find three factorizations for each monomial.

1. $6x^3$ **2.** $9y^4$ **3.** $-9a^5$

4. $-12x^6$ **5.** $24x^4y^2$ **6.** $15m^5n$

7. $-18p^3q^2$ **8.** $10r^2s^6$ **9.** $12a^3b^4$

Factor.

10. $x^2 - 4x$ **11.** $y^2 + 8y$ **12.** $2a^2 + 6a$

13. $3p^2 - 3p$ **14.** $3y^4 + 6y^2 + 6$ **15.** $5x^2 + 10x + 30$

16. $14m^4 - 12m$ **17.** $28y^2 + 21y^4$ **18.** $32x^5 - 17x^4$

19. $9x^3 + 25x^7$ **20.** $6a^2 - 5a^2$ **21.** $11y^4 + 7y^4$

22. $2x^2 + 2x - 8$ **23.** $6x^2 + 3x - 15$

24. $x^3y + 6x^2y$ **25.** $4a^4b^2 + a^2b$

26. $8x^4y^2 - 24x^2y$ **27.** $5m^5n + 10m^3$

28. $12m^5n^2 + 9m^4n + 6m^3n^2$ **29.** $2x^3y^2 + 6xy^3 + 8xy^2$

30. $17x^5 + 34x^3 + 51x$ **31.** $16x^6 - 32x^5 - 48x$

32. $6x^4 - 10x^3 + 3x^2$ **33.** $5x^5 + 10x^2 - 8x$

34. $x^5 + x^4 + x^3 - x^2$ **35.** $x^9 - x^7 + x^4 + x^3$

36. $2x^7 - 2x^6 - 64x^5 + 4x^3$ **37.** $10x^3 + 25x^2 + 15x - 20$

38. $4a^4b^4 - 2a^3b^2 + 6a^2$ **39.** $5p^3q^2 + 10p^2q^2 - 20pq^2$

40. $2x^3y - 4x^2y + x^2$ **41.** $6m^3n^3 + 3m^3n^2 + m^2n^2$

42. **TEST PREP**   Which polynomial has $3x$ as a factor?

     A. $15x^3 - 9x^2 + 13x$ **B.** $-21x^2 + 24y^2$

     C. $9x - x^3$ **D.** $6x^2 + 15x$

B

Two polynomials are **relatively prime** if they have no common factors other than constants. Tell which pairs are relatively prime.

43. $5x, x^2$ **44.** $3x, ax - 3$

45. $x + x^2, 3x^3$ **46.** $y - 6, y$

47. $7a, a$ **48.** $2p^2 + 2, 2p$

49. $t^2 - 4t, t^2 - 4$ **50.** $3a^2 - a, a^3 - 2a$

51. $2x + 4, 2x^2 - 4$ **52.** $m^2 + 4mn, 3mn + 2m$

53. $4x^5 + 8x^3 - 6x, 8x^3 + 12x^2 + 24x - 16$

54. $6x^2y + 4xy + 2x, 2x^3 + 8x^2y + 14x$

55. $a^3 + a^2b + ab^2 + b^3, a^2 - ab^2$

56. *Critical Thinking* Represent the area (A) of the shaded region using an expression in factored form. (Formulas for area can be found in Table 2 in appendix.)

Challenge

Find the common factor, if one exists.

57. $6t^3 + 30t^2, 9t^3 + 27t^2 + 9t$

58. $12t^4 - 15t^3 + 6t + 18, 16t^4 + 24t^3 - 48t^2 - 32t$

59. $192t^6 - 480t^4, 144t^8 + 72t^2$

60. $27x^5 - 81x^2 + 9x, 8x^4 - 16x + 4$

Mixed Review

Simplify.   **61.** $x^7 \cdot x^5 \cdot x$ **62.** $(3m^2n^3)^2$ **63.** $(9t^2)(-2t^5)$ 5-1, 5-2, 5-3

Write using scientific notation.   **64.** 0.00437 **65.** 307.5 **66.** 5613 5-4

Collect like terms and then arrange in descending order for the variable m.

67. $12 - 9m^3 + 6m^2 + 4m^3 - 8m^2$ **68.** $5m^2 + 116 - 4m^2 + 3$ 5-6

◇ Connections: Geometry

Recall that the perimeter of a polygon is the sum of the lengths of its sides. Use the idea of perimeter to complete each of the following.

1. The perimeter of the parallelogram below is $8x + 4y$. What are the lengths of the missing sides?

2. The perimeter of the trapezoid below is $16x + 3$. The base of the trapezoid is 1 more than twice the length of the opposite side. What are the lengths of the missing sides?

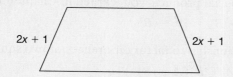

Differences of Two Squares

What You'll Learn

1 To recognize a difference of two squares

2 To factor a difference of two squares

3 To factor a difference of two squares completely

. . . And Why

To factor some binomials

Recognizing Differences of Two Squares

Objective: Recognize a difference of two squares.

For a binomial to be a **difference of two squares,** two conditions must hold.

(A) There must be two terms, both squares. Examples are $4x^2$ and $9x^4$, 16 and y^2.

(B) There must be a minus sign between the two terms.

EXAMPLES

1 Is $9x^2 - 36$ a difference of two squares?
The first term is a square. $9x^2 = (3x)^2$
The second term is a square. $36 = 6^2$
There is a minus sign between them.
Thus we have a difference of two squares.

2 Is $-4x^2 + 16$ a difference of two squares?
$-4x^2 + 16 = 16 - 4x^2$ Rewriting as a difference
$16 = 4^2$ and $4x^2 = (2x)^2$ The first and last terms are squares.
Since there is a minus sign between 16 and $4x^2$, we have a difference of two squares.

Try This   State whether each expression is a difference of two squares.

a. $x^2 - 25$ **b.** $x^2 - 24$ **c.** $-36 - x^2$

d. $4x^2 - 15$ **e.** $-49 + 16a^2$ **f.** $-1 + 9m^6$

Factoring Differences of Two Squares

Objective: Factor a difference of two squares.

Here is one of the special products you learned in Chapter 5.

$$(A + B)(A - B) = A^2 - B^2$$

We can use this relationship to factor differences of two squares.

$$A^2 - B^2 = (A + B)(A - B)$$

EXAMPLE 3 Factor.

$$x^2 - 4 = x^2 - 2^2 = (x + 2)(x - 2)$$
$$\uparrow \quad \uparrow \quad \uparrow \quad \uparrow \quad \uparrow \quad \uparrow$$
$$A^2 - B^2 = (A + B)(A - B)$$

Try This   Factor.

g. $x^2 - 9$ **h.** $y^2 - 64$

EXAMPLES Factor.

4 $4x^2 - 25 = (2x)^2 - (5)^2 = (2x + 5)(2x - 5)$
$$\uparrow \qquad \uparrow \qquad \uparrow \quad \uparrow \quad \uparrow \quad \uparrow$$
$$A^2 - \quad B^2 = \quad (A + B)(A - B)$$

5 $m^6 - 16n^2 = (m^3)^2 - (4n)^2 = (m^3 + 4n)(m^3 - 4n)$
$$\uparrow \qquad \uparrow \qquad \uparrow \quad \uparrow \quad \uparrow \quad \uparrow$$
$$A^2 \quad - \quad B^2 \ = \ (A \ + \ B) \ (A \ - \ B)$$

6 $36x^2 - 25y^6 = (6x)^2 - (5y^3)^2$ Writing as a difference of squares
$$= (6x - 5y^3)(6x + 5y^3)$$

7 $9a^8b^4 - 49 = (3a^4b^2)^2 - (7)^2 = (3a^4b^2 + 7)(3a^4b^2 - 7)$

Try This   Factor.

i. $4y^2 - 49$ **j.** $16x^2 - 25y^2$ **k.** $a^8b^4 - 4$ **l.** $25a^{10} - 36b^8$

If the terms of a binomial have a common factor, first factor out the common factor. Then continue factoring.

EXAMPLES Factor.

8 $49x^4 - 9x^6 = x^4(49 - 9x^2)$ Factoring out the
                                              common factor, x^4

$$\quad = x^4[(7)^2 - (3x)^2]$$
$$\quad = x^4(7 + 3x)(7 - 3x)$$ Factoring a difference of
                                    two squares

9 $18a^2b^2 - 50a^6 = 2a^2(9b^2 - 25a^4)$ Factoring out the
                                                   common factor, $2a^2$

$$\quad = 2a^2[(3b)^2 - (5a^2)^2]$$
$$\quad = 2a^2(3b + 5a^2)(3b - 5a^2)$$ Factoring a difference of
                                           two squares

Try This   Factor.

m. $32y^2 - 8y^6$ **n.** $5 - 20y^6$ **o.** $a^3b - 4ab^3$ **p.** $64x^4y^4 - 25x^6y^8$

PART 3

Factoring Completely

Objective: Factor a difference of two squares completely.

After you factor a difference of two squares, you can sometimes continue factoring. **Factoring completely** means to factor until factoring is no longer possible (other than for a common factor of 1).

EXAMPLE 10 Factor.

$$1 - 16x^{12} = (1)^2 - (4x^6)^2$$
$$= (1 - 4x^6)(1 + 4x^6)$$
$$= [(1)^2 - (2x^3)^2](1 + 4x^6)$$
$$= (1 + 2x^3)(1 - 2x^3)(1 + 4x^6)$$

Factoring the first binomial as a difference of squares

Try This   Factor.

q. $81x^4 - 1$ **r.** $16m^4 - n^8$

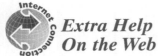

Extra Help On the Web

Look for worked-out examples at the Prentice Hall Web site.
www.phschool.com

6-2 Exercises

A

Mental Math   State whether each expression is a difference of two squares.

1. $x^2 - 4$ **2.** $x^2 - 36$ **3.** $x^2 + 36$ **4.** $x^2 + 4$

5. $x^2 - 35$ **6.** $x^2 - 50$ **7.** $-25 + 16x^2$ **8.** $-1 + 36x^2$

Factor.

9. $x^2 - 4$ **10.** $x^2 - 36$ **11.** $x^2 - 9y^2$

12. $m^2 - y^2$ **13.** $16a^2 - 9$ **14.** $25x^2 - 4$

15. $4x^2 - 25$ **16.** $9a^2 - 16$ **17.** $25m^2 - 49$

18. $100x^2 - 25$ **19.** $x^4 - 9$ **20.** $y^6 - 4$

21. $m^{16} - 25$ **22.** $-16 + a^{12}$ **23.** $-16 + 4x^4$

24. $16x^6 - 25$ **25.** $64y^4 - 81$ **26.** $4x^{10} - 25$

27. $36x^{12} - 49$ **28.** $16y^2 - 25$ **29.** $36x - 49x^3$

30. $121a^8 - 100$ **31.** $81y^6 - 25y^2$ **32.** $100y^6 - 49y^4$

33. $8x^2 - 98y^2$ **34.** $-54y^4 + 24x^2$ **35.** $-50y^2 + 32x^2$

36. $27y^2 - 48y^4$ **37.** $75m^6n^2 - 147$ **38.** $50a^{10}b^4 - 72$

39. $x^4 - 1$ **40.** $x^4 - 16$ **41.** $4x^4 - 64$ **42.** $5x^4 - 80$

43. $16 - y^4$ **44.** $25 - x^4$ **45.** $625 - m^4$ **46.** $4 - 9y^2$

B

Factor.

47. $16x - 81x^3$ **48.** $1 - y^8$ **49.** $b^8 - a^4$

50. $16x^2 - 25x^4$ **51.** $x^{16} - 9x^2$ **52.** $-16 + x^6$

53. $-81 + 49a^4$ **54.** $-64 + c^{14}$ **55.** $x^{12} - 16$

56. $x^8 - 1$ **57.** $a^{12} - 4a^2$ **58.** $16p^8 - t^4$

59. $-9 + 25a^4$ **60.** $x^8 - 81$ **61.** $-49 + 9c^8$

62. $4x^4 - 4x^2$ **63.** $3x^5 - 12x^3$ **64.** $3x^2 - \frac{1}{3}$

65. $18x^3 - \frac{8}{25}x$ **66.** $x^2 - 2.25$ **67.** $x^3 - \frac{x}{16}$

68. $3.24x^2 - 0.81$ **69.** $0.64x^2 - 1.21$ **70.** $1.28x^2 - 2$

71. $(x + 3)^2 - 9$ **72.** $(y - 5)^2 - 36$ **73.** $(3a + 4)^2 - 49$

74. $(2y - 7)^2 - 1$ **75.** $y^8 - 256$ **76.** $x^{16} - 1$

77. *Critical Thinking*   Can you find a rational nonzero value for b that allows you to factor $x^2 + b^2$? Explain.

Challenge

78. Find 2 polynomials, each with three factors, where the only common factor is $(x + 2)$.

79. Find a polynomial with 2 factors where one factor is $(x^2 - 2)$.

80. Find a third-degree polynomial where one factor is $(x + 5)$ and the other 2 factors are binomials.

81. Find a third-degree polynomial where there are three binomial factors and one factor is $(a + 2b)$.

82. Find a fourth-degree polynomial where there are three factors and one factor is $x^2 - 5$.

Mixed Review

Multiply.   **83.** $(x + 7)(x + 7)$ **84.** $(2a - 3)(2a - 3)$ *5-10*

Identify the degree of each term and the degree of the polynomial.

85. $12c + 1$ **86.** $6y^3 - 25y^2 - 8y + 15$ **87.** $9a^2c^3 + 45ac - 7$ *5-5*

Write each as a decimal.   **88.** 20%   **89.** 8%   **90.** 430%   **91.** 6.5%   *3-10*

Solve.   **92.** $26 - 3c = 10c$ **93.** $4t - 12 = t + 3$ *3-5*

94. Ana has saved \$68 to buy the bicycle at the right. How much more money does Ana need?   *3-4, 3-11*

95. Find the length of the base of a triangle if one side is 3 cm longer than the base, and the other side is 5 cm shorter than the base. The perimeter of the triangle is 52 cm.   *3-4, 3-11*

Our low price: only \$200

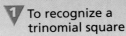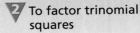

6-3 ▷ Trinomial Squares

What You'll Learn

1 To recognize a trinomial square

2 To factor trinomial squares

...And Why

To factor certain trinomials more quickly

Objective: Recognize a trinomial square.

From the study of special products in Lesson 5-10, we know that the square of a binomial is a trinomial. Such trinomials are often called **trinomial squares.**

$$(x + 3)^2 = x^2 + 6x + 9 \qquad (x - 3)^2 = x^2 - 6x + 9$$

The trinomials $x^2 + 6x + 9$ and $x^2 - 6x + 9$ are trinomial squares, as each one is the square of a binomial.

Use the following to help recognize a trinomial square.
A. Two of the terms must be squares, A^2 and B^2.
B. There must be no minus sign before A^2 or B^2.
C. If we multiply A and B and double the result, we get the third term, $2AB$, or its additive inverse, $-2AB$.

EXAMPLE 1 Is $x^2 + 6x + 9$ a trinomial square?

A. $x^2 = (x)^2$ and $9 = (3)^2$
B. There is no minus sign before x^2 or 9.
C. If we multiply x and 3 and double the result, we get the third term, $2 \cdot 3 \cdot x$, or $6x$.

Thus $x^2 + 6x + 9$ is the square of the binomial $(x + 3)$.

EXAMPLE 2 Is $x^2 + 6x + 11$ a trinomial square?

The answer is no because only one term is a square.

EXAMPLE 3 Is $16a^2 - 56ab + 49b^2$ a trinomial square?

A. $16a^2 = (4a)^2$ and $49b^2 = (7b)^2$
B. There is no minus sign before $16a^2$ or $49b^2$.
C. If we multiply $4a$ and $7b$ and double the result, we get the additive inverse of the third term, $2 \cdot 4a \cdot 7b = 56ab$.

Thus $16a^2 - 56ab + 49b^2$ is the square of $(4a - 7b)$.

Try This Which of the following are trinomial squares?

a. $x^2 + 8x + 16$ **b.** $x^2 - 10x + 25$ **c.** $x^2 - 12x + 4$
d. $4x^2 + 20x + 25$ **e.** $9x^2 - 14x + 16$ **f.** $16x^2 + 40xy + 25y^2$

Objective: Factor trinomial squares.

To factor trinomial squares, you can use the following relationships.

$$A^2 + 2AB + B^2 = (A + B)^2$$
$$A^2 - 2AB + B^2 = (A - B)^2$$

Remember to factor out a common factor first, if possible.

EXAMPLES   Factor.

4 $x^2 + 6x + 9 = x^2 + 2 \cdot x \cdot 3 + 3^2 = (x + 3)^2$ The sign of the middle term is positive.

5 $x^2 - 14x + 49 = x^2 - 2 \cdot x \cdot 7 + 7^2 = (x - 7)^2$ The sign of the middle term is negative.

6 $16a^2 - 40ab + 25b^2 = (4a - 5b)^2$

7 $27m^2 + 72mn + 48n^2 = 3(9m^2 + 24mn + 16n^2)$ Factoring out the common factor, 3.

$$= 3(3m + 4n)^2$$

Try This   Factor.

g. $x^2 + 2x + 1$ **h.** $x^2 - 2x + 1$
i. $25x^2 - 70x + 49$ **j.** $48m^2 + 120mn + 75n^2$

6-3 Exercises

Extra Help On the Web

Look for worked-out examples at the Prentice Hall Web site.
www.phschool.com

A

Mental Math   Which of the following are trinomial squares?

1. $x^2 - 14x + 49$ **2.** $x^2 - 16x + 64$ **3.** $x^2 + 16x - 64$
4. $x^2 - 14x - 49$ **5.** $x^2 - 6x + 9$ **6.** $x^2 + 2x + 4$
7. $8x^2 + 40x + 25$ **8.** $9x^2 + 18xy + 9y^2$
9. $36m^2 - 24m + 16n^2$ **10.** $16x^2 - 56xy + 49y^2$

Factor. Remember to look first for a common factor.

11. $x^2 - 14x + 49$ **12.** $x^2 - 16x + 64$ **13.** $x^2 + 16x + 64$
14. $x^2 + 14x + 49$ **15.** $x^2 - 2x + 1$ **16.** $x^2 + 2x + 1$
17. $x^2 + 4xy + 4y^2$ **18.** $x^2 - 4xy + 4y^2$ **19.** $y^2 - 6xy + 9x^2$
20. $y^2 + 6xy + 9x^2$ **21.** $2x^2 - 4x + 2$ **22.** $2x^2 - 40x + 200$
23. $x^3 - 18x^2 + 81x$ **24.** $x^3 + 24x^2 + 144x$

25. $20x^2 + 100x + 125$ **26.** $12x^2 + 36xy + 27y^2$

27. $49y^2 - 42xy + 9x^2$ **28.** $64y^2 - 112xy + 49x^2$

29. $5y^4 + 10y^2 + 5$ **30.** $a^4 + 14a^2 + 49$

31. $y^6 + 26y^3 + 169$ **32.** $y^6 + 16y^3 + 64$

33. $16x^{10} - 8x^5 + 1$ **34.** $9x^{10} + 12x^5 + 4$

35. $4x^4 + 4x^2 + 1$ **36.** $1 + 2a^4 + a^8$

37. $81x^6 + 72x^3y + 16y^2$ **38.** $9a^8 - 30a^4b + 25b^2$

B

Factor, if possible.

39. $49x^2 - 216$ **40.** $27x^3 - 13x$ **41.** $x^2 + 22x + 121$

42. $4x^2 + 9$ **43.** $x^2 - 5x + 25$ **44.** $18x^3 + 12x^2 + 2x$

45. $63x - 28$ **46.** $162x^2 - 82x$ **47.** $x^4y^4 - 9y^4$

48. $81x^2 - 64x$ **49.** $x^8 - 2^8$ **50.** $3^4 - x^4$

Factor.

51. $(y + 3)^2 + 2(y + 3) + 1$ **52.** $(a + 4)^2 - 2(a + 4) + 1$

53. $4(a + 5)^2 + 20(a + 5) + 25$ **54.** $49(x + 1)^2 - 42(x + 1) + 9$

55. $(x + 7)^2 - 4x - 24$ **56.** $(a + 4)^2 - 6a - 15$

57. *Critical Thinking*   Suppose $x^2 + a^2x + a^2$ factors into $(x + a)^2$. Find the nonzero value of a.

Challenge

Factor.

58. $9x^{18} + 48x^9 + 64$ **59.** $x^{2n} + 10x^n + 25$

Factor as the square of a binomial, then as a difference of two squares.

60. $a^2 + 2a + 1 - 9$ **61.** $y^2 + 6y + 9 - x^2 - 8x - 16$

Find c so that the polynomial will be the square of a binomial.

62. $cy^2 + 6y + 1$ **63.** $cy^2 - 24y + 9$

64. *Mathematical Reasoning*   Show that the difference of the squares of two consecutive integers is the sum of the integers. (Hint: Use x for the smaller number.)

Mixed Review

Multiply.   **65.** $(9 - x^2)(1 + 2x)$ **66.** $(y^3 + y^2)(y^3 - 4)$ *5-9*

Factor.   **67.** $6x^2 - 9x$ **68.** $24a^2 - 12a$ **69.** $9y^3 + 3y$ *6-1*

Write using standard notation.   **70.** 1.667×10^{-3} **71.** 3.594×10^5 *5-4*

Factoring $x^2 + bx + c$

PART 1 Constant Term Positive

Objective: Factor trinomials of the the type $x^2 + bx + c$ where $c > 0$.

In the polynomial $x^2 + bx + c$, recall that c is called the constant term or just the constant. If the constant of a polynomial $x^2 + bx + c$ is not a perfect square, the trinomial cannot be factored into a square of a binomial. It may, however, be possible to factor it as the product of two different binomials.

In Chapter 5, we used area models to illustrate products of two binomials. We can use these models when factoring the trinomial $x^2 + 7x + 10$. Since $1 \cdot 10 = 10$ and $2 \cdot 5 = 10$, there are two possible arrangements to try.

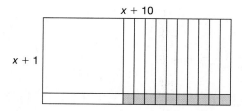 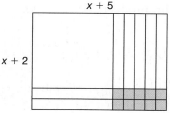

When we complete the rectangle in each model, we see that since there are 11 rectangles with area x in the model on the left and 7 rectangles with area x in the model on the right, the model on the right shows the correct factorization: $x^2 + 7x + 10 = (x + 2)(x + 5)$.

Recall the FOIL method. It is useful when factoring polynomials such as $x^2 + 7x + 10$.

$$(x + 2)(x + 5) = x^2 \underbrace{+\ 5x + 2x}_{} + 10$$
$$= x^2 \qquad + 7x \quad + 10$$

To factor $x^2 + 7x + 10$, think of FOIL in reverse. The first term, x^2, is the result of x times x. Thus the first term of each binomial factor is x.

$$(x + \_)(x + \_)$$

The coefficient of the middle term and the last term of the trinomial are two numbers whose product is 10 and whose sum is 7. Those numbers are 2 and 5. Thus the factorization is

$$(x + 2)(x + 5)$$

Quick Review

To review the FOIL method and multiplying binomials, see Lesson 5-9.

When factoring, it can be helpful to *make a table*.

EXAMPLE 1   Factor $x^2 + 5x + 6$.

The first term of each factor is x.

$$(x + \_)(x + \_)$$

Look for two numbers whose product is 6 and whose sum is 5.

Product of 6	Sum	
1, 6	7	
2, 3	5	← The numbers we need are 2 and 3.

$$x^2 + 5x + 6 = (x + 2)(x + 3)$$

Try This   Factor.

a. $x^2 + 7x + 12$
b. $x^2 + 13x + 36$

Consider this product.

$$(x - 3)(x - 4) = x^2 \overset{F}{\underset{\downarrow}{}} \underset{O \quad\quad I}{-4x - 3x} \overset{L}{+ 12}$$

$$= x^2 \quad - 7x \quad + 12$$

When the constant term of a trinomial is positive, we look for two numbers with the same sign. The sign is that of the middle term.

$$(x^2 - 7x + 12) = (x - 3)(x - 4)$$

EXAMPLE 2   Factor $x^2 - 8x + 12$.

Since the coefficient of the middle term is negative, we need two negative numbers whose product is 12 and whose sum is -8.

Product of 12	Sum	
$-1, -12$	-13	
$-2, -6$	-8	← The numbers we need are -2 and -6.
$-3, -4$	-7	

$$x^2 - 8x + 12 = (x - 2)(x - 6)$$

Try This   Factor.

c. $x^2 - 8x + 15$
d. $x^2 - 9x + 20$
e. $x^2 - 7x + 12$

EXAMPLE 3 Factor $a^2 + 7ab + 10b^2$.

Since a^2 is the product of a times a, and b^2 is the product of b times b, we are looking for binomials of the form

$$(a + \_b)(a + \_b)$$

Find the two numbers whose sum is 7 and whose product is 10.

Product of 10	Sum
1, 10	11
2, 5	7 ← The numbers we need are 2 and 5.

$$a^2 + 7ab + 10b^2 = (a + 2b)(a + 5b)$$

Try This Factor.

f. $m^2 + 8mn + 15n^2$ **g.** $a^2 + 5ab + 6b^2$ **h.** $p^2 + 6pq + 8q^2$

PART 2 Constant Term Negative

Objective: Factor trinomials of the type $x^2 + bx + c$ where $c < 0$.

Sometimes the constant term of a trinomial is negative. In this case, the middle term may be positive or negative. Consider these multiplications.

$$(x - 5)(x + 2) = x^2 \overbrace{+ 2x - 5x}^{F \quad O \quad I} - 10$$
$$= x^2 \quad - 3x \quad - 10$$

$$(x + 5)(x - 2) = x^2 \overbrace{- 2x + 5x}^{F \quad O \quad I} - 10$$
$$= x^2 \quad + 3x \quad - 10$$

Since the constant term is negative, it has a positive factor and a negative factor. Their sum is still the coefficient of the middle term.

EXAMPLE 4 Factor $x^2 - 8x - 20$.

Find two numbers whose sum is -8 and whose product is -20.

Product of −20	Sum
−1, 20	19
1, −20	−19
−2, 10	8
2, −10	−8 ← The numbers we need are 2 and −10.
4, −5	−1
−4, 5	1

$$x^2 - 8x - 20 = (x + 2)(x - 10)$$

EXAMPLE 5   Factor $a^2 + ab - 6b^2$.

We are looking for binomials of the form $(a\_b)(a\_b)$. Find two numbers whose sum is 1 and whose product is -6.

Product of -6	Sum
1, -6	-5
-1, 6	5
2, -3	-1
-2, 3	1 ← The numbers we need are -2 and 3.

$$a^2 + ab - 6b^2 = (a - 2b)(a + 3b)$$

Try This   Factor.

i. $x^2 + 4x - 12$ **j.** $x^2 - 4x - 12$
k. $a^2 + 5ab - 14b^2$ **l.** $x^2 - xy - 30y^2$

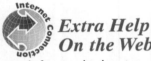

Extra Help On the Web

Look for worked-out examples at the Prentice Hall Web site.
www.phschool.com

6-4 Exercises

A
Factor.

1. $x^2 + 8x + 15$ **2.** $x^2 + 5x + 6$

3. $x^2 + 7x + 12$ **4.** $x^2 + 9x + 8$

5. $x^2 - 6x + 9$ **6.** $y^2 + 11y + 28$

7. $x^2 + 9x + 14$ **8.** $a^2 + 11a + 30$

9. $b^2 + 5b + 4$ **10.** $x^2 - 11x + 28$

11. $a^2 - 14a + 48$ **12.** $z^2 - 8z + 7$

13. $m^2 + 10m + 21$ **14.** $a^2 - 14a + 45$

15. $z^2 - 10z + 24$ **16.** $t^2 + 12tp + 36p^2$

17. $a^2 - 9ab + 20b^2$ **18.** $x^2 - 5xy + 4y^2$

19. $c^2 - 7cd + 10d^2$ **20.** $x^2 - 8xy + 15y^2$

21. $y^2 - 11yz + 10z^2$ **22.** $x^2 - 2x - 15$

23. $x^2 + x - 42$ **24.** $x^2 + 2x - 15$

25. $x^2 - 7x - 18$ **26.** $y^2 - 3y - 28$

27. $x^2 - 6x - 16$ **28.** $x^2 - x - 42$

29. $y^2 - 4y - 45$ **30.** $x^2 - 7x - 60$

31. $x^2 - 2xy - 99y^2$ **32.** $x^2 + 6xy - 72y^2$

33. $c^2 + cd - 56d^2$ **34.** $b^2 + 5bc - 24c^2$

35. $a^2 + 2ab - 35b^2$ **36.** $y^2 - xy - 2x^2$

B

Factor.

37. $x^2 + 20x + 100$

38. $x^2 + 20x + 99$

39. $x^2 - 21x - 100$

40. $x^2 - 20x + 96$

41. $x^2 - 21x - 72$

42. $4x^2 + 40x + 100$

43. $x^2 - 25x + 144$

44. $y^2 - 21y + 108$

45. $a^2 + a - 132$

46. $a^2 + 9a - 90$

47. $120y^2 - 23xy + x^2$

48. $96e^2 + 22de + d^2$

49. $108y^2 - 3xy - x^2$

50. $112z^2 + 9yz - y^2$

51. *Critical Thinking*   A hot air balloon flies at a speed of $(n + 8)$ miles per hour. At this rate, how long will it take to fly $(n^2 + 5n - 24)$ miles?

52. *Mathematical Reasoning*
Let $x^2 - 3x - 10 = (x + a)(x + b)$.
   a. What do you know about the signs of a and b?
   b. Suppose $|a| > |b|$. Which number, a or b, is a negative integer? How do you know?

53. *Mathematical Reasoning*
Let $x^2 + 3x - 10 = (x + a)(x + b)$.
   a. What do you know about the signs of a and b?
   b. Suppose $|a| > |b|$. Which number, a or b, is a negative integer? How do you know?

Hot air balloons move with wind currents. Evaluate the expressions in Exercise 51 when $n = 27$ to find the speed and length of one journey.

Challenge

54. Find all integers m for which $y^2 + my + 50$ can be factored.

55. Find all integers b for which $a^2 + ba - 50$ can be factored.

Factor completely.

56. $x^3 - x^2 - 6x$

57. $-x^3 + 22x^2 + 23x$

Self-Test On the Web

Check your progress. Look for a self-test at the Prentice Hall Web site. www.phschool.com

Mixed Review

Find three factorizations for each monomial.   **58.** $12x^3$ **59.** $8y^3$ *6-1*

Simplify.   **60.** $(3m + 14) - (m + 9)$ **61.** $\dfrac{a^6b^3}{a^2b^2}$ **62.** $\dfrac{6m^6}{3m^6}$ *2-8, 5-2*

63. $(4y^2 - 3) + (y^2 + 11)$ **64.** $\dfrac{5t^3}{11t}$ **65.** $\dfrac{4c^3}{4c^2}$ *5-3, 5-7, 5-8*

Solve.   **66.** $|x| + 3 = 7$ **67.** $3|c| - 2 = 4$ **68.** $4 - |m| = -2$ *3-8*

Factoring $ax^2 + bx + c$

Objective: Factor trinomials of the type $ax^2 + bx + c$.

Suppose the leading coefficient of a trinomial is not 1. Consider this product.

$$\underset{\downarrow}{(2x + 5)(3x + 4)} = 6x^2 \overset{\text{F \quad O \quad I \quad L}}{+ \underbrace{8x + 15x}} + 20$$

$$= 6x^2 \quad + 23x \quad + 20$$

Factoring Trinomials

To factor $ax^2 + bx + c$, we look for binomials

$$(\_x + \_)(\_x + \_)$$

where products of numbers in the blanks are as follows.
1. The numbers in the *first* blanks of each binomial have product a.
2. The numbers in the *last* blanks of each binomial have product c.
3. The *outside* product and the *inside* product have a sum of b.

EXAMPLE 1   Factor $3x^2 + 5x + 2$.

First look for a factor common to all terms. There is none. Next look for two numbers whose product is 3.

$$1, 3 \qquad -1, -3$$

Now look for numbers whose product is 2.

$$1, 2 \qquad -1, -2$$

Since the last term of the trinomial is positive, the signs of the second terms must be the same. Here are some possible factorizations.

$$(x + 1)(3x + 2) \qquad (x + 2)(3x + 1)$$
$$(x - 1)(3x - 2) \qquad (x - 2)(3x - 1)$$

When we multiply, the first term will be $3x^2$ and the last term will be 2 in each case. Only the first multiplication gives a middle term of $5x$.

$$3x^2 + 5x + 2 = (x + 1)(3x + 2)$$

Try This   Factor.

a. $6x^2 + 7x + 2$ **b.** $8x^2 + 10x - 3$ **c.** $6x^2 - 41x - 7$

EXAMPLES

2 Factor $2x^2 + 5x - 12$.

First terms: Find two numbers whose product is 2.
Last terms: Find two numbers whose product is -12 .

$(2x + 3)(x - 4)$ $(2x - 2)(x + 6)$ $(2x - 1)(x + 12)$ Possible
$(2x - 3)(x + 4)$ $(2x + 2)(x - 6)$ $(2x - 12)(x + 1)$ factorizations

The outside product plus the inside product must equal $5x$.

$$2x^2 + 5x - 12 = (2x - 3)(x + 4)$$

3 Factor $8m^2 + 8m - 6$.

$$8m^2 + 8m - 6 = 2(4m^2 + 4m - 3)$$ Factoring out the common factor, 2

First terms: Find two numbers whose product is 4.
Last terms: Find two numbers whose product is -3.

$(4m + 3)(m - 1)$ $(4m - 3)(m + 1)$ $(2m + 3)(2m - 1)$ Possible
$(4m - 1)(m + 3)$ $(4m + 1)(m - 3)$ $(2m - 3)(2m + 1)$ factorizations

The outside product plus the inside product must equal $4m$.

$$8m^2 + 8m - 6 = 2(4m^2 + 4m - 3) = 2(2m + 3)(2m - 1)$$

Try This   Factor.

d. $3x^2 - 21x + 36$ **e.** $8x^2 - 2$ **f.** $9a^2 - 15a - 6$
g. $2x^2 + 4x - 6$ **h.** $4a^2 + 2a - 6$ **i.** $6m^2 + 15mn - 9n^2$

▶ 6-5 Exercises

**Extra Help
On the Web**

Look for worked-out
examples at the Prentice
Hall Web site.
www.phschool.com

A
Factor.

1. $2x^2 - 7x - 4$ **2.** $3x^2 - x - 4$ **3.** $5x^2 + x - 18$

4. $3x^2 - 4x - 15$ **5.** $6x^2 + 23x + 7$ **6.** $6x^2 + 13x + 6$

7. $3x^2 + 4x + 1$ **8.** $7x^2 + 15x + 2$ **9.** $4x^2 + 4x - 15$

10. $9a^2 + 6a - 8$ **11.** $2x^2 - x - 1$ **12.** $15n^2 - 19n - 10$

13. $9x^2 + 18x - 16$ **14.** $2y^2 + 5y + 2$ **15.** $3x^2 - 5x - 2$

16. $18c^2 - 3c - 10$ **17.** $12x^2 + 31x + 20$ **18.** $15x^2 + 19x - 10$

19. $14x^2 + 19x - 3$ **20.** $35x^2 + 34x + 8$ **21.** $9p^2 + 18p + 8$

22. $6 - 13x + 6x^2$ **23.** $49 - 42b + 9b^2$ **24.** $15x^2 - 19x + 6$

25. $24x^2 + 47x - 2$ **26.** $16a^2 + 78a + 27$ **27.** $35x^2 - 57x - 44$

28. $9a^2 + 12a - 5$ **29.** $20 + 6x - 2x^2$ **30.** $15 + x - 2x^2$

Factor.

31. $12x^2 + 28x - 24$

32. $6c^2 - 33c + 15$

33. $30x^2 - 24x - 54$

34. $20x^2 - 25x + 5$

35. $6x^2 + 4x - 10$

36. $18y^2 - 21y - 9$

37. $3a^2 - 4a + 1$

38. $6x^2 + 13x + 6$

39. $12x^2 - 28x - 24$

40. $6x^2 + 33x + 15$

41. $2x^2 + x - 1$

42. $15s^2 + 19s + 6$

43. $9b^2 - 18b - 16$

44. $14x^2 + 35x + 14$

45. $15x^2 - 25x - 10$

46. $30b^2 - b - 20$

B

Factor, if possible.

47. $18x^2 + 3xy - 10y^2$

48. $12a^2 - 31ab + 20b^2$

49. $15m^2 - 19mn - 10n^2$

50. $14p^2 - 19pq - 3q^2$

51. $35x^2 - 34xy + 8y^2$

52. $56a^2 - 15ab + b^2$

53. $9x^4 + 18x^2 + 8$

54. $6y^2 - 13y + 6$

55. $9x^2 - 42x + 49$

56. $15x^4 - 19x^2 + 6$

57. $6a^3 + 4a^2 - 10a$

58. $18x^3 - 21x^2 - 9x$

59. $x^2 + 3x - 7$

60. $b^2 + 13b - 12$

61. $x^5 + x^3 - 6x$

62. $x^5 - 6x^3 + 5x$

63. *Critical Thinking*   What are the values of a and c in the trinomial square $ax^2 + 12x + c$ if $a \neq 1$ and $c > a$?

64. *Error Analysis*   Bobbi factored $4y^2 + 36y + 80$ as $2(y + 5)(y + 4)$. She argued that using the distributive property, $2(y + 5) = 2y + 10$ and $2(y + 4) = 2y + 8$. We know that $(2y + 10)(2y + 8) = 4y^2 + 36y + 80$. Thus $2(y + 5)(y + 4) = 4y^2 + 36y + 80$. Write a paragraph evaluating Bobbi's argument.

Challenge

Factor.

65. $20x^{2n} + 16x^n + 3$

66. $-15x^{2m} + 26x^m - 8$

67. $x^{6a} - x^{3a} - 6$

68. $x^{4n+1} + 2x^{2n+1} + x$

69. $3(a + 1)^{n+1}(a + 3)^2 - 5(a + 1)^n(a + 3)^3$

Mixed Review

Write as an algebraic expression.   **70.** 11 more than the product of m and n
71. the sum of a and b, divided by 2   **72.** the square of the difference between x and y *1-6, 3-4*
73. r divided by the sum of s and t
Solve. **74.** $3 - 4y < 7$ **75.** $6t > 9 + 9t$ **76.** $8 - 3y \leq 2$ *4-4*

Factoring by Grouping

Objective: Factor polynomials by grouping.

The distributive property can be used to factor some polynomials with four terms. Consider $x^3 + x^2 + 2x + 2$.

There is no factor common to all terms other than 1. We can, however, factor $x^3 + x^2$ and $2x + 2$ separately.

$$x^3 + x^2 = x^2(x + 1) \qquad 2x + 2 = 2(x + 1)$$

Therefore, $x^3 + x^2 + 2x + 2 = x^2(x + 1) + 2(x + 1)$. We can use the distributive property again and factor out the common factor, $x + 1$.

$$x^2(x + 1) + 2(x + 1) = (x + 1)(x^2 + 2)$$

This method is called **factoring by grouping.** Not all expressions with four terms can be factored by this method.

EXAMPLES Factor.

1 $6x^3 - 9x^2 + 4x - 6 = (6x^3 - 9x^2) + (4x - 6)$
$$= 3x^2(2x - 3) + 2(2x - 3) \qquad \text{Factoring each binomial}$$
$$= (2x - 3)(3x^2 + 2) \qquad \text{Factoring out the common factor, } 2x - 3$$

2 $x^3 + x^2 + x + 1 = (x^3 + x^2) + (x + 1)$
$$= x^2(x + 1) + 1(x + 1) \qquad \text{Factoring each binomial}$$
$$= (x + 1)(x^2 + 1) \qquad \text{Factoring out the common factor, } x + 1$$

3 $x^3 + 2x^2 - x - 2 = (x^3 + 2x^2) + (-x - 2)$
$$= x^2(x + 2) + 1(-x - 2)$$
$$= x^2(x + 2) - 1(x + 2) \qquad \text{Using } ab = (-a)(-b)$$
$$= (x + 2)(x^2 - 1)$$
$$= (x + 2)(x + 1)(x - 1) \qquad \text{Factoring completely}$$

4 $x^2y^2 + ay^2 + ab + bx^2 = y^2(x^2 + a) + b(x^2 + a)$
$$= (x^2 + a)(y^2 + b)$$

5 $x^3 + x^2 + 2x - 2 = x^2(x + 1) + 2(x - 1)$
This cannot be factored by grouping.

Try This Factor.

a. $8x^3 + 2x^2 + 12x + 3$ **b.** $4x^3 - 6x^2 - 6x + 9$
c. $x^3 + x^2 - x - 1$ **d.** $3a - 6b + 5a^2 - 10ab$

What You'll Learn

1 To factor polynomials by grouping

... And Why

To factor polynomials with more than three terms

6-6 Exercises

A

Factor.

1. $x^3 + 3x^2 + 2x + 6$

2. $6z^3 + 3z^2 + 2z + 1$

3. $2y^3 + 6y^2 + y + 3$

4. $3x^3 + 2x^2 + 3x + 2$

5. $8a^3 - 12a^2 + 6a - 9$

6. $10p^3 - 25p^2 + 4p - 10$

7. $12x^3 - 16x^2 + 3x - 4$

8. $18c^3 - 21c^2 + 30c - 35$

9. $b^3 + 8b^2 - 3b - 24$

10. $2x^3 + 12x^2 - 5x - 30$

11. $14x^3 + 18x^2 - 21x + 27$

12. $24x^3 + 27x^2 - 8x - 9$

13. $2x^3 - 8x^2 - 9x + 36$

14. $20g^3 - 4g^2 - 25g + 5$

15. $ax - bx + ay - by$

16. $bx + 2b + cx + 2c$

17. $n^2 + 2n + np + 2p$

18. $2x^2 - 4x + xz - 2z$

19. $a^2 - 3a + ay - 3y$

20. $6y^2 - 3y + 2py - p$

B

Factor.

21. $4x^5 + 6x^3 + 6x^2 + 9$

22. $4y^5 + 6y^4 + 6y^3 + 9y^2$

23. $c^6 - c^4 - c^2 + 1$

24. $x^{13} + x^7 + 2x^6 + 2$

Factor each as a difference of two squares.

25. $(x - y)^2 - z^2$

26. $4 - (2a + 3b)^2$

27. $a^2 + 2ab + b^2 - 1$

28. $c^2 - 6cd + 9d^2 - 4$

29. *Critical Thinking*   What is the relationship between the value of D in the polynomial and the values of a, b, and c in the binomials?

$$Ax^3 + Bx^2 + Cx + D = (x + a)(x + b)(x + c)$$

Challenge

30. *Mathematical Reasoning*   Factor $acx^{m+n} + adx^n + bcx^m + bd$ into two factors. Assume a, b, c, and d are constants. Verify your factorization by multiplying.

31. Find $ax^3 + bx^2 + cx + d$ so that a, b, c, and d are integers, $\frac{a}{c} = \frac{b}{d} = 4$, and $\frac{a}{b} = \frac{7}{5}$. Factor the result by grouping.

32. Subtract $(x^2 + 1)^2$ from $x^2(x + 1)^2$ and factor the result.

Mixed Review

Multiply.   **33.** $(m + n)^2$ **34.** $(m - n)^2$ **35.** $(m + n)(m - n)$ *5-10*

Factor.   **36.** $x^2 - 16$ **37.** $y^2 + 6y + 9$ **38.** $3a^2 - 6a + 3$

39. $c^2 - c - 90$ **40.** $n^2 - 15n + 54$ **41.** $20 - 4x - 5y + xy$

42. $x^2 + 3x + 2$ **43.** $9a^4 - b^2$ **44.** $25 - 40a + 16a^2$ *6-2, 6-3, 6-4, 6-5*

Factoring: A General Strategy

Objective: Factor polynomials.

Here is a good strategy for factoring.

Factoring Polynomials

A. Always look first for a common factor.
B. Then look at the number of terms.
    Two terms: Determine whether you have a difference of squares.
    Three terms: Determine whether the trinomial is a square of a binomial. If not, test the factors of the terms.
    Four terms: Try factoring by grouping.
C. Always factor completely.

...And Why

To be able to factor polynomials completely

EXAMPLES Factor.

1 $10x^3 - 40x$

A. Look first for a common factor.

$$10x^3 - 40x = 10x(x^2 - 4)$$

Factoring out the greatest common factor

B. Factor a difference of two squares.

$$10x(x + 2)(x - 2)$$

Factoring $x^2 - 4$

C. Have we factored completely? Yes, because no factor can be factored further.

2 $t^4 - 16 = (t^2 + 4)(t^2 - 4)$ Factoring a difference of two squares

$$= (t^2 + 4)(t + 2)(t - 2)$$

Factoring a difference of two squares again

3 $2a^3 + 10a^2 + a + 5 = (2a^3 + 10a^2) + (a + 5)$

$$= 2a^2(a + 5) + 1(a + 5)$$ Factoring each binomial

$$= (2a^2 + 1)(a + 5)$$ Using the distributive property

4 $x^4 - 10x^2 + 25 = (x^2)^2 - 10x^2 + 25$ Writing an equivalent expression

$$= (x^2 - 5)^2$$ Factoring a trinomial square

Try This Factor.

a. $3m^4 - 3$ **b.** $x^6 + 8x^3 + 16$ **c.** $2x^4 + 8x^3 + 6x^2$

d. $3x^3 + 12x^2 - 2x - 8$ **e.** $8x^3 - 200x$ **f.** $y^5 - 2y^4 - 35y^3$

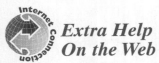
6-7 Exercises

A

Factor.

1. $2x^2 - 128$ **2.** $3t^2 - 27$ **3.** $a^2 + 25 - 10a$

4. $y^2 + 49 + 14y$ **5.** $2x^2 - 11x + 12$ **6.** $8y^2 - 18y - 5$

7. $x^3 + 24x^2 + 144x$ **8.** $x^3 - 18x^2 + 81x$ **9.** $24x^2 - 54$

10. $8x^2 - 98$ **11.** $20x^3 - 4x^2 - 72x$ **12.** $9x^3 + 12x^2 - 45x$

13. $x^2 + 4$ **14.** $t^2 + 25$ **15.** $x^5 - 14x^4 + 49x^3$

16. $2x^6 + 8x^5 + 8x^4$ **17.** $x^2 + 3x + 1$ **18.** $x^2 + 5x + 2$

19. $4x^4 - 64$ **20.** $5x^5 - 80x$ **21.** $1 - y^8$

22. $t^8 - 1$ **23.** $x^5 - 4x^4 + 3x^3$ **24.** $x^6 - 2x^5 + 7x^4$

25. $x^3 + 3x^2 - 4x - 12$ **26.** $x^3 - 5x^2 - 25x + 125$

27. $x^4 + 7x^2 - 3x^3 - 21x$ **28.** $m^4 + 8m^3 + 8m^2 + 64m$

B

Factor completely.

29. $a^4 - 2a^2 + 1$ **30.** $x^4 + 9$

31. $20 - 6x - 2x^2$ **32.** $45 - 3x - 6x^2$

33. $18 + y^3 - 9y - 2y^2$ **34.** $-(x^4 - 7x^2 - 18)$

35. $a^3 + 4a^2 + a + 4$ **36.** $x^3 + x^2 - (4x + 4)$

37. $12a^3b^2 - 6a^2b + 4a^2b^2 - 2ab$ **38.** $a^3 - 5a^2b - 14ab^2$

39. $3x^3y - 2x^2y^2 + 3x^4y - 2x^3y^2$ **40.** $m^2n^2 + 7mn^3 + 10n^4$

41. ***Critical Thinking***   The polynomials $x^4 + 3x^2 - 28$ and $x^2 + 7x + 10$ have a common binomial factor. What is it?

Challenge

42. Factor $64a^4 + 1$. (Hint: Write it as $64a^4 + 16a^2 + 1 - 16a^2$.)

43. Factor $x^{2h} - 2^{2h}$ when $h = 4$.

Mixed Review

Express using positive exponents.   **44.** m^{-2} **45.** x^{-1} **46.** $3c^{-2}$ *5-1*

Subtract.   **47.** $(8a^5 + a^3 - 1) - (2a^5 + 4a^3 - 1)$

48. $(-3a^2b + 7ab - 4a) - (-2a^2b - 4a + 3ab)$ *5-8*

Binomial Expansion

The distributive property can be used as many times as needed to expand binomials to powers. This is called a **binomial expansion.**

$$(x + 2)^3 = (x + 2)(x + 2)(x + 2) = (x + 2)(x^2 + 4x + 4)$$
$$= x^3 + 4x^2 + 4x + 2x^2 + 8x + 8$$
$$= x^3 + 6x^2 + 12x + 8$$

Consider the following expansions of $(a + b)^n$ for $n = 0, 1, 2, 3, 4,$ and 5. Look for patterns.

$$(a + b)^0 = 1$$
$$(a + b)^1 = a + b$$
$$(a + b)^2 = a^2 + 2ab + b^2$$
$$(a + b)^3 = a^3 + 3a^2b + 3ab^2 + b^3$$
$$(a + b)^4 = a^4 + 4a^3b + 6a^2b^2 + 4ab^3 + b^4$$
$$(a + b)^5 = a^5 + 5a^4b + 10a^3b^2 + 10a^2b^3 + 5ab^4 + b^5$$

Compare the above expansions with *Pascal's Triangle*.

```
              1
           1     1
        1     2     1
     1     3     3     1
  1     4     6     4     1
1     5    10    10     5     1
```

We can use Pascal's Triangle and the patterns in the above expansions to find powers of binomials.

EXAMPLE   Expand $(x + 3)^4$.

We can use the pattern shown above.

$$(a + b)^4 = a^4 + 4a^3b + 6a^2b^2 + 4ab^3 + b^4$$

We substitute x for a and 3 for b.

$$(x + 3)^4 = x^4 + 4 \cdot x^3 \cdot 3 + 6 \cdot x^2 \cdot 3^2 + 4 \cdot x \cdot 3^3 + 3^4$$
$$= x^4 + 4 \cdot x^3 \cdot 3 + 6 \cdot x^2 \cdot 9 + 4 \cdot x \cdot 27 + 81$$
$$= x^4 + 12x^3 + 54x^2 + 108x + 81$$

Exercises

Use the patterns above to expand the binomials.
1. $(m + n)^5$ **2.** $(x + 1)^3$ **3.** $(a + 4)^4$
4. Write the next row of numbers in Pascal's Triangle.
5. Use Pascal's Triangle to find $(a + b)^6$.

6-8 ▷ Solving Equations by Factoring

What You'll Learn

1 To solve equations expressed as a product of factors equal to zero

2 To factor and solve equations

...And Why

To solve polynomial equations using the principle of zero products

PART 1 **The Principle of Zero Products**

Objective: Solve equations expressed as a product of factors equal to zero.

The product of two or more numbers is 0 if any of the factors is 0. Also, if a product is 0, at least one of the factors must be 0. In general, we can state the following rule.

The Principle of Zero Products

For any rational numbers a and b, if $ab = 0$, then $a = 0$ or $b = 0$, and if $a = 0$ or $b = 0$, then $ab = 0$.

If we have an equation with 0 on one side and a factorization on the other, we can solve the equation by finding the values that make the factors 0.

EXAMPLE 1   Solve.

$$(5x + 1)(x - 7) = 0$$
$$5x + 1 = 0 \quad \text{or} \quad x - 7 = 0 \quad \text{Using the principle of zero products}$$
$$5x = -1 \quad \text{or} \quad x = 7$$
$$x = -\frac{1}{5} \quad \text{or} \quad x = 7 \quad \text{Solving the two equations separately}$$

Check to see whether $-\frac{1}{5}$ and 7 are both solutions of the equation.

Check: for $-\frac{1}{5}$

$(5x + 1)(x - 7) = 0$	
$\left(5\left(-\frac{1}{5}\right) + 1\right)\left(-\frac{1}{5} - 7\right)$	0
$(-1 + 1)\left(-7\frac{1}{5}\right)$	0
$0\left(-7\frac{1}{5}\right)$	0
0	0 ✔

Check: for 7

$(5x + 1)(x - 7) = 0$	
$(5 \cdot 7 + 1)(7 - 7)$	0
$(35 + 1)0$	0
0	0 ✔

The solutions are $-\frac{1}{5}$ and 7.

EXAMPLE 2   Solve.

$$x(2x - 9) = 0$$
$$x = 0 \quad \text{or} \quad 2x - 9 = 0 \qquad \text{Using the principle of zero products}$$
$$x = 0 \quad \text{or} \qquad 2x = 9$$
$$x = 0 \quad \text{or} \qquad x = \frac{9}{2}$$

Check: for 0   Check: for $\frac{9}{2}$

$x(2x - 9) = 0$		$x(2x - 9) = 0$	
$0(2 \cdot 0 - 9)$	0	$\frac{9}{2}\left(2 \cdot \frac{9}{2} - 9\right)$	0
$0(-9)$	0	$\frac{9}{2}(0)$	0
0	0 ✔	0	0 ✔

The solutions are 0 and $\frac{9}{2}$.

Try This   Solve using the principle of zero products.

a. $(x - 3)(x + 4) = 0$ **b.** $(x - 7)(x - 3) = 0$
c. $y(3y - 17) = 0$ **d.** $(4t + 1)(3t - 2) = 0$

PART 2   Factoring and Solving

Objective: Factor and solve equations.

You can use the following steps to solve equations using the principle of zero products.
A. Get zero on one side of the equation using the addition property.
B. Factor the expression on the other side of the equation.
C. Set each factor equal to zero.
D. Solve each equation.

EXAMPLES   Solve.

3
$$x^2 - 8x = -16$$
$$x^2 - 8x + 16 = 0 \qquad \text{Adding 16 to get 0 on one side}$$
$$(x - 4)(x - 4) = 0 \qquad \text{Factoring the square of a binomial}$$
$$x - 4 = 0 \quad \text{or} \quad x - 4 = 0$$
$$x = 4 \quad \text{or} \qquad x = 4$$

Check:

$x^2 - 8x + 16 = 0$	
$4^2 - 8 \cdot 4 + 16$	0
$16 - 32 + 16$	0
0	0 ✔

There is only one solution, 4.

4
$$x^2 + 5x + 6 = 0$$
$$(x + 2)(x + 3) = 0 \qquad \text{Factoring}$$
$$x + 2 = 0 \quad \text{or} \quad x + 3 = 0 \qquad \text{Using the principle of zero products}$$
$$x = -2 \quad \text{or} \qquad x = -3$$

Check:

$$
\begin{array}{r|l}
x^2 + 5x = -6 \\
\hline
(-2)^2 + 5(-2) & -6 \\
4 + (-10) & -6 \\
-6 & -6 \checkmark
\end{array}
\qquad
\begin{array}{r|l}
x^2 + 5x = -6 \\
\hline
(-3)^2 + 5(-3) & -6 \\
9 + (-15) & -6 \\
-6 & -6 \checkmark
\end{array}
$$

The solutions are -2 and -3.

Try This   Solve.

e. $x^2 - x - 6 = 0$ **f.** $m^2 - m = 56$ **g.** $x^2 - 3x = 28$

Example 4 shows that the value of the polynomial $x^2 + 5x + 6$ is 0 when $x = -2$ or $x = -3$. For a polynomial containing a variable, any value of the variable that makes the value of the polynomial equal 0 is called a zero or a **root** of the polynomial.

EXAMPLE 5   Find the roots of the polynomial $x^2 - 5x$.

$$
\begin{aligned}
x^2 - 5x &= 0 && \text{Setting the polynomial equal to 0} \\
x(x - 5) &= 0 && \text{Factoring}
\end{aligned}
$$

$$
\begin{array}{lll}
x = 0 & \text{or} & x - 5 = 0 \\
x = 0 & \text{or} & x = 5
\end{array}
$$

Check:
$$
\begin{array}{r|l}
x^2 - 5x = 0 \\
\hline
0^2 - 5(0) & 0 \\
0 & 0 \checkmark
\end{array}
\qquad
\begin{array}{r|l}
x^2 - 5x = 0 \\
\hline
5^2 - 5(5) & 0 \\
0 & 0 \checkmark
\end{array}
$$

The roots of $x^2 - 5x$ are 0 and 5.

EXAMPLE 6   Find the roots of $4x^2 - 25$.

$$
\begin{aligned}
4x^2 - 25 &= 0 && \text{Setting the polynomial equal to 0} \\
(2x - 5)(2x + 5) &= 0 && \text{Factoring a difference of two squares}
\end{aligned}
$$

$$
\begin{array}{lll}
2x - 5 = 0 & \text{or} & 2x + 5 = 0 \\
2x = 5 & \text{or} & 2x = -5 \\
x = \frac{5}{2} & \text{or} & x = -\frac{5}{2}
\end{array}
$$

Check:
$$
\begin{array}{r|l}
4x^2 - 25 = 0 \\
\hline
4\left(\frac{5}{2}\right)^2 - 25 & 0 \\
4\left(\frac{25}{4}\right) - 25 & 0 \\
0 & 0 \checkmark
\end{array}
\qquad
\begin{array}{r|l}
4x^2 - 25 = 0 \\
\hline
4\left(-\frac{5}{2}\right)^2 - 25 & 0 \\
4\left(\frac{25}{4}\right) - 25 & 0 \\
0 & 0 \checkmark
\end{array}
$$

The roots are $\frac{5}{2}$ and $-\frac{5}{2}$.

Try This   Find the roots of each polynomial.

h. $x^2 + 6x + 9$ **i.** $x^2 + 4x$ **j.** $25x^2 - 16$

Internet Connection

Extra Help On the Web

Look for worked-out examples at the Prentice Hall Web site.
www.phschool.com

A

Solve.

1. $(x + 8)(x + 6) = 0$

2. $(c + 3)(c + 2) = 0$

3. $(a - 3)(a + 5) = 0$

4. $(x + 9)(x - 3) = 0$

5. $(x + 12)(x - 11) = 0$

6. $(x - 13)(x + 53) = 0$

7. $x(x + 5) = 0$

8. $y(y + 7) = 0$

9. $y(y - 13) = 0$

10. $v(v - 4) = 0$

11. $0 = y(y + 10)$

12. $0 = x(x - 21)$

13. $(7x - 28)(28x - 7) = 0$

14. $(12x - 11)(8x - 5) = 0$

15. $2x(3x - 2) = 0$

16. $75x(8x - 9) = 0$

17. $\frac{1}{2}x\left(\frac{2}{3}x - 12\right) = 0$

18. $\frac{5}{7}d\left(\frac{3}{4}d - 6\right) = 0$

19. $\left(\frac{1}{3} - 3x\right)\left(\frac{1}{5} - 2x\right) = 0$

20. $\left(\frac{1}{5} + 2x\right)\left(\frac{1}{9} - 3x\right) = 0$

21. $\left(\frac{1}{3}y - \frac{2}{3}\right)\left(\frac{1}{4}y - \frac{3}{2}\right) = 0$

22. $\left(\frac{7}{4}x - \frac{1}{12}\right)\left(\frac{2}{3}x - \frac{12}{11}\right) = 0$

23. $(0.3x - 0.1)(0.05x - 1) = 0$

24. $(0.1x - 0.3)(0.4x - 20) = 0$

25. $9x(3x - 2)(2x - 1) = 0$

26. $(x - 5)(x + 55)(5x - 1) = 0$

27. $x^2 + 6x + 5 = 0$

28. $x^2 + 7x - 18 = 0$

29. $x^2 + 4x - 21 = 0$

30. $b^2 - 8b + 15 = 0$

31. $x^2 - 8x = 0$

32. $x^2 - 3x = 0$

33. $x^2 + 19x = 0$

34. $x^2 - 100 = 0$

35. $9x^2 - 4 = 0$

36. $4a^2 - 9 = 0$

37. $x^2 + 6x + 9 = 0$

38. $x^2 + 10x + 25 = 0$

39. $12y^2 - 5y = 2$

40. $2y^2 + 12y = -10$

41. $x(x - 5) = 14$

42. $t(3t + 1) = 2$

43. $64m^2 = 81$

44. $100t^2 = 49$

45. $(4x + 9)(14x - 7) = 0$

46. $(3w - 1)(w + 2) = 0$

47. $5x^2 = 6x$

48. $(5x + 1)(4x - 12) = 0$

49. $x^2 - 2x + 1 = 0$

50. $(3x - 9)(x + 3) = 0$

51. $6x^2 - 4x = 10$

52. $(2x + 5)(x + 4) = 0$

53. $(2x + 9)(x + 8) = 0$

54. $v^2 - 6v - 16 = 0$

Find the roots of each polynomial.

55. $c^2 - 16$ **56.** $d^2 + 7d + 6$ **57.** $x^2 - 9x + 14$

58. $x^2 + 12x$ **59.** $3x^2 - 7x - 20$ **60.** $7x^2 - 8x$

B
Solve.

61. $b(b + 9) = 4(5 + 2b)$ **62.** $y(y + 8) = 16(y - 1)$

63. $(t - 3)^2 = 36$ **64.** $(t - 5)^2 = 2(5 - t)$

65. $x^2 - \frac{1}{64} = 0$ **66.** $x^2 - \frac{25}{36} = 0$

67. $\frac{5}{16}x^2 = 5$ **68.** $\frac{27}{25}x^2 = \frac{1}{3}$

69. *Critical Thinking* Write all factorable second-degree trinomials whose first term is x^2 and whose last term is -16.

70. **TEST PREP** Which equation does *not* have –1 as a solution?

A. $(x + 1)(x - 2) = 0$ **B.** $(x + 3)(x - 1) = 0$

C. $x^2 - x = -2x$ **D.** $(x + 3)(x + 1) = 0$

Challenge

71. Find an equation that has the given numbers as solutions. For example, 3 and -2 are solutions to $x^2 - x - 6 = 0$.

a. $1, -3$ **b.** $3, -1$ **c.** $2, 2$ **d.** $3, 4$ **e.** $3, -4$

f. $-3, 4$ **g.** $-3, -4$ **h.** $\frac{1}{2}, \frac{1}{2}$ **i.** $5, -5$ **j.** $0, 0.1, \frac{1}{4}$

72. For each equation in the left-hand column, find an equation in the right-hand column that has the same two solutions.

a. $3x^2 - 4x + 8 = 0$ **(1)** $4x^2 + 8x + 36 = 0$

b. $(x - 6)(x + 3) = 0$ **(2)** $(2x + 8)(2x - 5) = 0$

c. $x^2 + 2x + 9 = 0$ **(3)** $9x^2 - 12x + 24 = 0$

d. $(2x - 5)(x + 4) = 0$ **(4)** $(x + 1)(5x - 5) = 0$

e. $5x^2 - 5 = 0$ **(5)** $x^2 - 3x - 18 = 0$

f. $x^2 + 10x - 2 = 0$ **(6)** $2x^2 + 20x - 4 = 0$

Mixed Review

Write as an algebraic expression. **73.** 3 times the quantity a number plus 8
74. 3 times the sum of a number and 8 **75.** half of the difference of a number and 15 **76.** the square of the sum of a and b **77.** the sum of the squares of a and b **78.** the difference of the squares of a and b *1-6, 3-4*
Factor. **79.** $4y^2 + 10y - 6$ **80.** $4x^2 - y^2$ **81.** $6y^2 - 5y - 6$ *6-2, 6-5*

Using Equations that Factor

Objective: Solve problems by writing and solving equations.

You can use the Problem-Solving Guidelines below to help you solve problems when your plan involves writing and solving an equation.

PROBLEM-SOLVING GUIDELINES

■ **Phase 1: UNDERSTAND the problem**

What am I trying to find?
What data am I given?
Have I ever solved a similar problem?

■ **Phase 2: Develop and carry out a PLAN**

What strategies might I use to solve the problem?
How can I correctly carry out the strategies I selected?

■ **Phase 3: Find the ANSWER and CHECK**

Does the proposed solution check?
What is the answer to the problem?
Does the answer seem reasonable?
Have I stated the answer clearly?

What You'll Learn

1 To solve problems by writing and solving equations

. . . And Why

To use polynomials and factoring to solve problems

EXAMPLE 1   Translate to an equation and solve.

The product of one more than a number and one less than the number is 8. Find the number.

Let $x =$ the number.

One more than a number times one less than the number is 8.

$$(x + 1) \cdot (x - 1) = 8 \qquad \text{Translating}$$

$$(x + 1)(x - 1) = 8 \qquad \text{Multiplying}$$
$$x^2 - 1 = 8$$
$$x^2 - 1 - 8 = 0$$
$$x^2 - 9 = 0$$
$$(x - 3)(x + 3) = 0 \qquad \text{Factoring}$$
$$x - 3 = 0 \quad \text{or} \quad x + 3 = 0 \qquad \text{Using the principle of zero products}$$
$$x = 3 \quad \text{or} \qquad x = -3$$

Check for 3: $3 + 1 = 4$; $3 - 1 = 2$; and the product, $4 \cdot 2$, is 8.
Check for -3: $-3 + 1 = -2$; $-3 - 1 = -4$; and the product, $-2(-4)$, is 8.

Both 3 and -3 check. They are both solutions.

EXAMPLE 2   Translate to an equation and solve.

The square of a number minus twice the number is 48. Find the number.
Let x = the number.

The square of a number   minus   twice the number   is 48.

$$x^2 \qquad\qquad - \qquad\qquad 2x \qquad\qquad = 48 \qquad \text{Translating}$$

$$x^2 - 2x = 48$$
$$x^2 - 2x - 48 = 0$$
$$(x - 8)(x + 6) = 0$$

$$x - 8 = 0 \quad \text{or} \quad x + 6 = 0 \qquad \text{Using the principle of zero products}$$
$$x = 8 \quad \text{or} \qquad\quad x = -6$$

Check for 8: $8^2 - 2(8) = 64 - 16 = 48$.
Check for -6: $(-6)^2 - 2(-6) = 36 + 12 = 48$.

Both 8 and -6 check. They are both solutions.

Try This   Translate to an equation and solve.

a. The product of seven less than a number and eight less than the number is 0.
b. A number times one less than the number is zero.
c. The product of one more than a number and one less than the number is 24.
d. The square of a number minus the number is 20.
e. One more than twice the square of a number is 73.

Sometimes it helps to reword before translating.

EXAMPLE 3   Translate to an equation and solve.

The area of the foresail on a 12-meter racing yacht is 93.75 square meters. The sail's height is 8.75 meters greater than its base. Find its base and height.

$$\text{Area} = \tfrac{1}{2} \times \text{base} \times \text{height}$$

Let h = the sail's height and $h - 8.75$ = the length of the sail's base.

The foresail of this yacht is the sail on the right. The area of the sail is 93.75 m². See Example 3.

$\frac{1}{2}$ times $\underbrace{\text{the base}}$ times $\underbrace{\text{the height}}$ is 93.75　　　Rewording

$\downarrow\ \downarrow\downarrow\downarrow\ \downarrow$

$\frac{1}{2}\ \cdot\ (h-8.75)\ \cdot\ h=93.75$　　　Translating

$\frac{1}{2}(h-8.75)h=93.75$

$(h-8.75)h=187.5$　　Multiplying both sides by 2

$h^2-8.75h=187.5$　　Using the distributive property

$h^2-8.75h-187.5=0$　　Adding -187.5 to both sides to get 0 on one side

$(h-18.75)(h+10)=0$　　Factoring

$h-18.75=0$　　or　$h+10=0$　　Using the principle of zero products

$h=18.75$　　or　　$h=-10$

The solutions of the equation are 18.75 and -10. The height of the sail cannot have a negative value, so the height must be 18.75 meters. The length of the base is then 8.75 meters shorter, or 10 meters.

EXAMPLE 4　Translate to an equation and solve.

The product of two consecutive integers is 156. Find the integers.

Let x represent the first integer. Then $x+1$ represents the second integer.

$\underbrace{\text{First integer}}$ times $\underbrace{\text{second integer}}$ is 156.　　Rewording

$\downarrow\downarrow\ \downarrow$

$x\cdot(x+1)=156$　　Translating

$x(x+1)=156$

$x^2+x=156$

$x^2+x-156=0$

$(x-12)(x+13)=0$

$x-12=0$　　or　$x+13=0$　　Using the principle of zero products

$x=12$　　or　　$x=-13$

When $x=12$, $x+1=13$, and $12(13)=156$.

When $x=-13$, $x+1=-12$, and $-12(-13)=156$.

We have two pairs of solutions, 12 and 13, and -12 and -13. Both are pairs of consecutive integers whose product is 156.

Try This　Translate to an equation and solve.

f. The width of a rectangular card is 2 cm less than the length. The area is 15 cm². Find the length and width.

g. The product of two consecutive integers is 462. Find the integers.

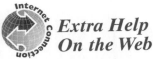

6-9 Exercises

A

Translate to an equation and solve.

1. If you subtract a number from four times its square, the result is three.

2. Fifteen more than the square of a number is eight times the number.

3. Eight more than the square of a number is six times the number.

4. If seven is added to the square of a number, the result is 32.

5. The product of two consecutive integers is 182.

6. The product of two consecutive integers is 56.

7. The product of two consecutive even integers is 168.

8. The product of two consecutive even integers is 224.

9. The product of two consecutive odd integers is 255.

10. The product of two consecutive odd integers is 143.

11. The length of a rectangle is 4 m greater than the width. The area of the rectangle is 96 m^2. Find the length and width.

12. The length of a rectangle is 5 cm greater than the width. The area of the rectangle is 84 cm^2. Find the length and width.

13. The number of square feet in the area of a square is 5 more than the number of feet in the perimeter of the square. Find the length of a side.

14. The number of inches in the perimeter of a square is 3 more than the number of square inches in its area. Find the length of a side.

15. The base of a triangle is 10 cm greater than the height. The area is 28 cm^2. Find the height and base.

16. The height of a triangle is 8 m less than the base. The area is 10 m^2. Find the height and base.

17. If the sides of a square are lengthened by 3 m, the area becomes 81 m^2. Find the length of a side of the original square.

18. If the sides of a square are lengthened by 7 in., the area becomes 121 in.^{2}. Find the length of a side of the original square.

19. The sum of the squares of two consecutive odd positive integers is 74.

20. The sum of the squares of two consecutive odd positive integers is 130.

21. **TEST PREP**   Which equation would be used to solve the following problem: The sum of the squares of two consecutive even positive integers is 52?

   A. $(x + x + 2)^2 = 52$
   C. $(x + x + 1)^2 = 52$

   B. $x^2 + (x + 1)^2 = 52$
   D. $x^2 + (x + 2)^2 = 52$

B

22. The sum of 7 times a positive number and 1 is the same as the square of 1 more than the number.

23. The sum of 6 times a positive number and 1 is the same as the square of 1 less than the number.

24. The cube of a number is the same as twice the square of the number.

25. *Error Analysis*   A student read the following exercise: *The difference of a number squared and two is 38.* The student wrote the equation $(x - 2)^2 = 38$. What error did the student make?

26. Mark launched a model rocket with an initial speed of 180 ft per second. After how many seconds will Mark's rocket reach a height of 464 ft?
    a. The formula $h = rt - 16t^2$ gives the height of an object projected upward at a rate of r feet per second after t seconds. Rewrite this equation substituting the data you are given.
    b. Solve the equation and answer the problem.
    c. After how many seconds will it be at that height again?

27. When distance is measured in meters and the speed of the object is measured in meters per second, the formula in Exercise 26 becomes $h = rt - 4.9t^2$. A tennis ball is bounced upward with speed of 9.8 m per second.
    a. After how many seconds will the ball reach a height of 4.9 m?
    b. After how many seconds will the ball hit the ground?

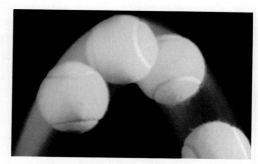

Use the formula in Exercise 27 to find the height of the ball at 0.5 seconds and 1.5 seconds.

28. *Multi-Step Problem*   A cement walk of constant width is built around a 20 ft × 40 ft rectangular pool. The total area of the pool and walk is 1500 ft². Find the width of the walk. Let w be the width of the walkway.
    a. Copy and complete the diagram below showing all of the data you are given and the unknown dimensions.

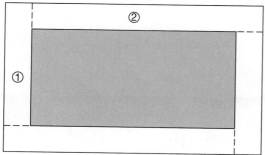

    b. What is the total area of the walkway?
    c. Write an expression for the area of section 1.
    d. Write an expression for the area of section 2.
    e. Write an expression that represents the total area of the walkway.
    f. Solve the equation and answer the problem.

29. **_Write a Convincing Argument_**   Solve the
problem below. Then write an argument that would
convince a classmate that your solution is correct.

The total surface area of a box is 350 in.^{2} The box is
9 in. high and has a square base. Find the length of
the side of the base.

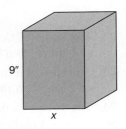

Challenge

30. Find two consecutive positive numbers such that the product of the sum
and difference of the numbers plus eight is the sum of their squares.

31. Find two consecutive positive numbers such that the sum of the squares
of the numbers is one plus the product of the numbers, plus the quantity
eight times the larger number.

32. The pages of a book are 15 cm by 20 cm. Margins of equal width surround
the printing on each page and comprise one half the area of the page.
Find the width of the margins.

33. A rectangular piece of cardboard is twice as long as it is wide. A 4-cm
square is cut out of each corner, and the sides are turned up to make a
box. The volume of the box is 616 cm^3. Find the original dimensions of
the cardboard.

34. An open rectangular gutter is made by turning up the sides of a piece of
metal 20 in. wide. The area of the cross section of the gutter is 50 in.^{2} Find
the depth of the gutter.

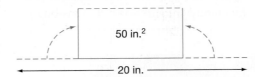

Mixed Review

Write using scientific notation.   **35.** $117{,}203$ **36.** 0.00559 _5-4_

Simplify.   **37.** $(10m^2)^4$ **38.** $(5x^5)(x^2)(16x)$ **39.** $(3a^3b^2)(-5ab^3)$ _5-2, 5-3_

Solve.   **40.** What number is 80% of 30?

41. 34 is 5% of what number?   _3-10_

Factor.   **42.** $a^2 - 8a + 16$ **43.** $6c^2 - 15c - 9$

44. $x^4 - x^2$ **45.** $2m^3 - 4m^2 - m + 2$

46. $36y^4 - 63$ **47.** $5x^2 + 70x + 245$ _6-2, 6-3, 6-5, 6-7_

Preparing for Standardized Tests

Factoring

The special products that you learned in this chapter can be very useful on college entrance exams.

$$(a - b)(a + b) = a^2 - b^2$$
$$(a + b)^2 = a^2 + 2ab + b^2$$
$$(a - b)^2 = a^2 - 2ab + b^2$$

Although the instructions may not tell you to factor, you can often solve problems more efficiently by factoring an expression first.

EXAMPLE 1

If $x^2 - 4 = (14)(18)$, then x could be
(A) 12   (B) 14   (C) 16   (D) 18   (E) 20

Here we can factor, $x^2 - 4 = (x - 2)(x + 2)$. If we write the factors under $(14)(18)$, we can see that x must be 16.

$$x^2 - 4 = (14) \cdot (18)$$
$$(x - 2)(x + 2)$$

EXAMPLE 2

$0.74^2 - 0.73^2 =$
(A) 0.00147   (B) 0.0147   (C) 0.147   (D) 14.70   (E) 147.0

If we factor, we can do the arithmetic mentally.

$$0.74^2 - 0.73^2 = (0.74 + 0.73)(0.74 - 0.73)$$
$$= (1.47)(0.01)$$
$$= 0.0147$$

Factoring in Example 2 makes the computation much simpler.

Example 3 also illustrates the value of looking for a simpler way to solve a problem rather than doing the computation in its present form.

EXAMPLE 3

$(43)^2 + 2(43)(57) + (57)^2 =$
(A) 3,467   (B) 7,842   (C) 8,900   (D) 10,000   (E) 14,959

We recognize that this problem is in the form $a^2 + 2ab + b^2$ and can be simplified to $(a + b)^2$.

$$a^2 + 2ab + b^2 = (a + b)^2$$
$$(43)^2 + 2(43)(57) + (57)^2 = (43 + 57)^2 = 100^2 = 10,000$$

EXAMPLE 4

If $x = 8.000001$, then $\dfrac{x^2 + 2x}{x}$ rounded to the nearest whole number is

(A) 4   (B) 6   (C) 8   (D) 10   (E) 12

We factor before substituting for x.

$$\frac{x^2 + 2x}{x} = \frac{x(x + 2)}{x} = \frac{8.000001(8.000001 + 2)}{8.000001} = 8.000001 + 2$$
$$\approx 10$$

Problems

1. If $x + y = 4$ and $x - y = 6$, then $x^2 - y^2 =$
   (A) 2   (B) 10   (C) 24   (D) 34   (E) 99

2. If $(r + 2)\left(\dfrac{1}{r}\right) = 0$, what is r?
   (A) 2   (B) 1   (C) -1 (D) -2 (E) any integer

3. $0.53^2 - 0.52^2 =$
   (A) 0.00105   (B) 0.0105   (C) 0.105   (D) 10.50   (E) 105.0

4. If $x + 3x$ is 7 more than $y + 3y$, then $x - y =$
   (A) 0   (B) $\dfrac{3}{7}$ (C) $\dfrac{4}{7}$ (D) $\dfrac{7}{3}$ (E) $\dfrac{7}{4}$

5. If $x^2 - 16 = (8)(16)$, then x could be
   (A) 8   (B) 10   (C) 12   (D) 14   (E) 16

6. $(23)^2 - 2(23)(13) + (13)^2 =$
   (A) 34   (B) 46   (C) 100   (D) 438   (E) 1,296

7. If $ab = 2$, $(a + b)^2 = 10$, then $a^2 + b^2 =$
   (A) 4   (B) 6   (C) 8   (D) 10   (E) 12

8. If $xy - 2y + 7x - 14 = 12$, and $x - 2 = 4$, then $y + 7 =$
   (A) 0   (B) 1   (C) 2   (D) 3   (E) 4

9. If $x + y = m$ and $x - y = \dfrac{1}{m}$, then when $m \neq 0$, $x^2 - y^2 =$
   (A) $\dfrac{1}{m}$ (B) m^2 (C) m (D) 1   (E) 2

10. If $m = 11$, then $\dfrac{m^2 + 3m}{m} =$
    (A) 9   (B) 11   (C) 14   (D) 44   (E) 124

6 ▷ Chapter Wrap Up

6-1

Factoring is the reverse of multiplying. Some of the possible **factorizations** for $12a^2b$ are $(12a)(ab)$, $(6a^2)(2b)$, $(3a)(4ab)$, and $12(a^2b)$. To factor a polynomial, factor out the greatest common factor of each term.

$$6a^2b - 12ab^2 = (6ab)a - (6ab)(2b) = 6ab(a - 2b)$$

Find three factorizations for each monomial.

1. $-10x^2$
2. $36x^5$

Factor.

3. $x^2 - 3x$
4. $6y^3 + 12y^2 + 3y$
5. $8x^6 - 32x^5 + 4x^4$
6. $6a^4b^4 - 2a^3b + 8a^2$

Key Terms

binomial expansion (p. 285)
difference of two squares
   (p. 266)
factoring by grouping (p. 281)
factoring completely (p. 268)
factoring polynomials (p. 283)
factorization (p. 262)
principle of zero products
   (p. 286)
relatively prime (p. 264)
root (p. 288)
trinomial squares (p. 270)

6-2

A binomial is a **difference of two squares** if both terms of the binomial are squares, and there is a minus sign between the two terms. The difference of two squares, $A^2 - B^2$, factors as two binomials $(A - B)(A + B)$.

Which of the following are differences of squares?

7. $4x^2 - 8y^2$
8. $-25 + 81a^2$

Factor.

9. $9x^2 - 4$
10. $4x^2 - 25$
11. $2x^2 - 50$
12. $3x^2 - 27$
13. $x^4 - 81$
14. $16x^4 - 1$

6-3

A **trinomial square** has three terms and is the square of a binomial.

$$A^2 + 2AB + B^2 = (A + B)^2$$
$$A^2 - 2AB + B^2 = (A - B)^2$$

Which of the following are trinomial squares?

15. $y^2 + 3y + 9$
16. $49a^2 - 112a + 16$
17. $c^2 + 12c + 36$
18. $4c^2 - 4c - 1$

Factor.

19. $x^2 - 6x + 9$
20. $x^2 + 14x + 49$
21. $9x^2 - 30x + 25$
22. $25x^2 - 20x + 4$
23. $18x^2 - 12x + 2$
24. $12x^2 + 60x + 75$

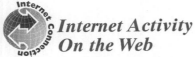
6-4

To factor a trinomial of the type $x^2 + bx + c$, think of FOIL in reverse. Look for factors of the constant term whose sum is the coefficient of the middle term.

Factor.

25. $x^2 - 8x + 15$ **26.** $x^2 + 4x - 12$ **27.** $y^2 + 9y + 20$

28. $b^2 - 3b - 18$ **29.** $m^2 + 15m + 56$ **30.** $p^2 - 7p - 8$

6-5

To factor a trinomial of the type $ax^2 + bx + c$, first check for common factors. Then test factors of the first and last terms to find the correct combination, using FOIL to test possible factorizations.

Factor.

31. $2x^2 - 7x - 4$ **32.** $6y^2 - 5y + 1$ **33.** $6a^2 - 28a - 48$

6-6

A polynomial with four terms can sometimes be **factored by grouping** and using the distributive property twice.

$$a^3 + 2a^2 + 3a + 6 = (a^3 + 2a^2) + (3a + 6)$$
$$= a^2(a + 2) + 3(a + 2)$$
$$= (a + 2)(a^2 + 3)$$

Factor by grouping.

34. $x^3 + x^2 + 3x + 3$ **35.** $x^4 + 4x^3 - 2x - 8$

36. $x^3 + 3x^2 - x - 3$ **37.** $6x^3 + 4x^2 + 3x + 2$

6-7

When you factor a polynomial, first look for a common factor. Then check the number of terms and look for special cases (difference of squares or trinomial squares). Always factor completely.

38. $7x^2 - 7$ **39.** $-75x^3 + 60x^2 - 12x$ **40.** $a^2 - 4a - 21$

41. $x^2 + 2x - 195$ **42.** $x^3 - 3x + 4x^2 - 12$ **43.** $1 - a^8$

6-8

To solve an equation using the **principle of zero products**, use the addition principle to get zero on one side of the equation and a factorization on the other side. Set each of the factors equal to 0 and solve separately. Check all solutions.

Solve.

44. $(x - 1)(x + 3) = 0$ **45.** $y(4y - 6) = 0$ **46.** $x^2 + 2x - 35 = 0$

47. $x^2 + x - 12 = 0$ **48.** $3x^2 - 2 = 5x$ **49.** $9x^2 = 16$

6-9

You can use the Problem-Solving Guidelines to help you translate a problem into an equation and solve it. After you have solved the problem, check to see if your answer is reasonable.

Translate into an equation and find all solutions.

50. The square of a number is six more than the number. Find the number.

51. The product of two consecutive even integers is 288. Find the integers.

52. The product of two consecutive odd integers is 323. Find the integers.

53. Twice the square of a number is 10 more than the number. Find the number.

54. If the sides of a square picture frame are increased by 5 cm, the area becomes 289 cm^2. Find the length of a side of the original picture frame.

 **Chapter Assessment**

Factor

1. $x^2 - 5x$

2. $6x^3 + 9x^2 - 3x$

3. $4y^4 - 8y^3 + 6y^2$

4. $4x^2 - 9$

5. $3x^2 - 75$

6. $3x^4 - 48$

7. $x^2 - 10x + 25$

8. $49x^2 - 84x + 36$

9. $45x^2 + 60x + 20$

10. $x^2 - 7x + 10$

11. $x^2 - x - 12$

12. $x^3 + 2x^2 - 3x$

13. $4x^2 - 4x - 15$

14. $5x^2 - 26x + 5$

15. $10x^2 + 28x - 48$

16. $x^3 + x^2 + 2x + 2$

17. $x^4 + 2x^3 - 3x - 6$

18. $6x^3 + 9x^2 - 15x$

19. $80 - 5x^4$

20. $y^5 - 8y^4 + 15y^3$

Solve.

21. $x^2 - x - 20 = 0$

22. $2x^2 + 7x = 15$

23. $4a^2 = 25$

24. $x(x - 3) = 28$

Translate to an equation and find all solutions.

25. Find the number whose square is 24 more than five times the number.

26. The length of a rectangle is 6 m more than the width. The area of the rectangle is 40 m^2. Find the length and the width.

27. The product of two consecutive even integers is 528. Find the integers.

CHAPTER 7

Skills & Concepts You Need for Chapter 7

1-1   Evaluate.

1. $3x + y$ for $x = 4$ and $y = 3$

2. $\frac{3m + 1}{2n}$ for $m = 5$ and $n = 2$

1-3   Evaluate each expression.

3. $y^2 + 2$ for $y = 6$ **4.** $m^2 + 7$ for $m = 7$

2-1   Make true sentences using $>$ or $<$.

5. $-3 \,\square\, 2$ **6.** $-2 \,\square\, -6$ **7.** $0 \,\square\, -8$ **8.** $5 \,\square\, -2$

3-1 to 3-3   Solve and check.

9. $\frac{5}{2} - y = \frac{1}{3}$ **10.** $w + 8 = -3$ **11.** $-4 + x = 8$

12. $6x = -12$ **13.** $\frac{7}{8}w = -\frac{2}{3}$ **14.** $\frac{2}{3}t = \frac{1}{8}$

15. $5x + 8 = 43$ **16.** $-2x + 9 = -11$ **17.** $-8x + 3x = 25$

3-5   Solve and check.

18. $5x + 6 = -2x - 8$ **19.** $6(x - 6) = 3(x - 4)$

3-7   Solve for the indicated variable.

20. $d = \frac{5k}{s}$, for k **21.** $S = \frac{Mp^2}{mv}$, for v

Graphs and Linear Equations

At the age of 8 years, a saguaro cactus is 7 ft tall. After 20 years the cactus is 10 ft tall. Predict the height of the saguaro after 200 years. (See Lesson 7-7.)

What You'll Learn

▼**1** To plot points using the coordinate system

▼**2** To identify the quadrant associated with a point

▼**3** To identify the coordinates of a point

...And Why

To establish the basic algebra-geometry relationships of the coordinate plane

Math History

In this lesson you will learn a system for graphing and naming points in a plane. This system is called the Cartesian coordinate system and is named after René Descartes (1596–1650), a French mathematician and philosopher. Before Descartes, algebra and geometry were separate areas of mathematics. Algebra dealt with numbers; geometry was the study of points, lines, and curves. Technological advances in fields such as navigation and optics made it necessary to define curves mathematically. People needed to know how much to curve lenses in microscopes and telescopes and how to plot the courses of ships traveling on Earth's curved surface. Descartes's coordinate system enabled mathematicians to represent lines and curves with algebraic equations.

PART 1 Plotting Points

Objective: Plot points using the coordinate system.

On a number line, each point is the graph of a number. On a plane, each point is the **graph** of an ordered pair of numbers. We use two perpendicular number lines called axes, which divide the plane into four regions. The horizontal axis is called the **x-axis** and the vertical axis is called the **y-axis.** The axes cross at a point called the **origin.** The arrows show the positive direction for each number line. The plane is often called a **coordinate plane,** and the axes are called **coordinate axes.**

The numbers in an ordered pair are called **coordinates.** In the ordered pair (4, 3) the first number, 4, is the **x-coordinate** (or the **abscissa**) and the second number, 3, is the **y-coordinate** (or the **ordinate**). The x-coordinate tells the distance right (positive) or left (negative) from the y-axis. The y-coordinate tells the distance up (positive) or down (negative) from the x-axis.

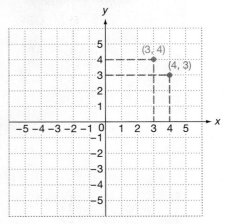

EXAMPLE 1   Plot the points $(-3, 4)$, $(2, -5)$, and $(-4, -4)$.

The coordinates of the first point $(-3, 4)$ tell us that the point is located 3 units to the left of the y-axis and 4 units up from the x-axis. The graphs of the other points are shown.

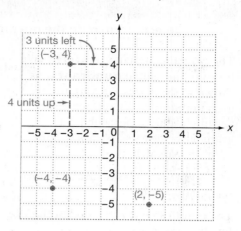

Try This   Plot these points on the coordinate plane. Write the ordered pair next to each point.

a. $(4, 6)$ **b.** $(6, 4)$ **c.** $(-2, 5)$
d. $(-3, -3)$ **e.** $(5, -3)$

When one coordinate is 0, the point is on one of the axes. The origin has coordinates $(0, 0)$.

EXAMPLE 2   Plot the points $(0, -3)$ and $(-2, 0)$.

For the point $(0, -3)$, move 0 units left or right and 3 units down. The point $(0, -3)$ is on the y-axis.

For the point $(-2, 0)$, move 2 units left and 0 units up or down. The point $(-2, 0)$ is on the x-axis.

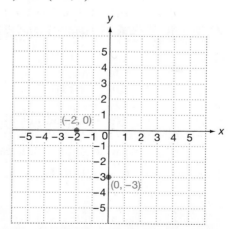

Try This   Plot the following points.

f. $(0, 7)$ **g.** $(5, 0)$ **h.** $(0, 0)$ **i.** $(0, -5)$

Objective: Identify the quadrant associated with a point.

The coordinate plane is divided into four regions called **quadrants,** as shown at the right. The quadrants are numbered counterclockwise starting at the upper right. The graph also shows some points and their coordinates.

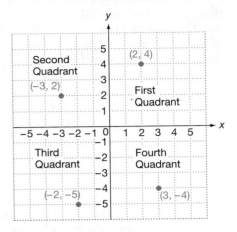

The point $(-3, 2)$ is located in the second quadrant.

The point $(3, -4)$ is located in the fourth quadrant.

The axes are not a part of any quadrant. A point on the x- or y-axis is not in a quadrant since it is on the boundary between quadrants.

The quadrants are traditionally denoted by Roman numerals.

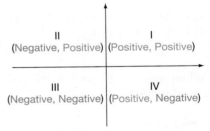

EXAMPLE 3 In which quadrant is each point located?

$(4, -5)$ Quadrant IV
$(2, 2)$ Quadrant I
$(-1, -3)$ Quadrant III
$(-6, 1)$ Quadrant II
$(-4, 0)$ Not in a quadrant

Try This   In which quadrant is each point located?

j. $(5, 3)$ **k.** $(-6, -4)$ **l.** $(10, -14)$ **m.** $(-13, 4)$

Objective: Identify the coordinates of a point.

We can count how many units a point is to the left or right of the y-axis and the units up or down from the x-axis to find the coordinates of the point.

| **EXAMPLE 4** | Find the coordinates of point B. |

Point B is 3 units to the left and
5 units up. Its coordinates are
$(-3, 5)$.

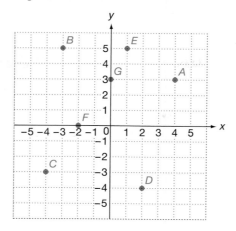

Try This

n. Find the coordinates of points A, C, D, E, F, and G in the graph above.

7-1 Exercises

**Extra Help
On the Web**

Look for worked-out
examples at the Prentice
Hall Web site.
www.phschool.com

A

Plot these points. Write the ordered pair close to each point.

1. $(2, 5)$ **2.** $(4, 6)$ **3.** $(-1, 3)$ **4.** $(-2, 4)$

5. $(3, -2)$ **6.** $(5, -3)$ **7.** $(-2, -4)$ **8.** $(-5, -7)$

9. $(0, 4)$ **10.** $(0, 6)$ **11.** $(0, -5)$ **12.** $(0, -7)$

13. $(5, 0)$ **14.** $(6, 0)$ **15.** $(-7, 0)$ **16.** $(-8, 0)$

In which quadrant is each point located?

17. $(-5, 3)$ **18.** $(-12, -1)$ **19.** $(100, -1)$ **20.** $(35.6, -2.5)$

21. $(-6, -29)$ **22.** $(-3.6, 10.9)$ **23.** $(3.8, 9.2)$ **24.** $(1895, 1492)$

25. a. In Quadrant II, ___-coordinates are positive and
___-coordinates are negative.

b. In Quadrant IV, x-coordinates are ___ and y-coordinates are ___.

26. *Critical Thinking*   There are many types of coordinate systems
that use ordered pairs. For example, the (city, state) ordered pair in
an envelope address helps locate a letter's destination.

a. Name two different (city, state) ordered pairs with the same
second coordinate. Tell why the ordered pairs are different.

b. Name two different (city, state) ordered pairs with the same
first coordinate. Tell why the ordered pairs are different.

ZIP+4 is a coordinate system used by
the United States Postal Service to
locate places as small as a post
office box. See Exercise 26.

Find the coordinates of points A, B, C, D, and E.

27.

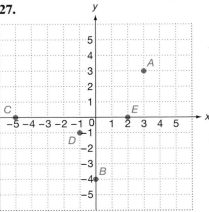

28.

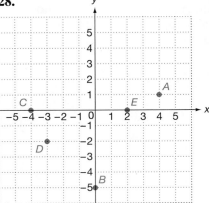

B

In Exercises 29–31, find three points that satisfy the following conditions.

29. The absolute values of the x-coordinate and the y-coordinate are equal.

30. The x-coordinate and the y-coordinate are additive inverses of each other.

31. The x-coordinate is the square of the y-coordinate.

32. Graph 12 points where the difference between the x- and y-coordinates of each point is 1.

33. *Critical Thinking*   Graph the following pairs of points: $(1, -1)$, $(-1, 1)$; $(2, 5)$, $(5, 2)$; $(-3, -4)$, $(-4, -3)$; $(3, -1)$, $(-1, 3)$; and $(1, 4)$, $(4, 1)$. Make a conclusion about the graphs of the points (q, r) and (r, q) from the pattern formed.

Challenge

34. Find three points such that the product of the two coordinates is 2.

35. Find three points such that the sum of the two coordinates is 5.

36. Find the perimeter of a rectangle whose vertices have coordinates $(5, 3)$, $(5, -2)$, $(-3, -2)$, and $(-3, 3)$.

37. Find the area of a triangle whose vertices have coordinates $(0, 9)$, $(0, -4)$, and $(5, -4)$.

Mixed Review

Factor.   **38.** $54m^2 - 24n^2$ **39.** $x^3 - 5x^2 + 2x - 10$ 6-2, 6-7

Simplify.   **40.** $(xy - 4yz) + 6yz$ **41.** $(ab - bc) + (3ab - 2bc)$

42. $(xy + 3yz) - (2xy - 5yz)$ **43.** $(mn - pq) - (2pq + 5mn)$ 2-8

Graphing Equations

 7-2

 PART 1 **Solutions of Equations in Two Variables**

Objective: Determine whether an ordered pair is a solution of an equation.

An equation such as $3x + 2 = 8$ has one number, 2, as its solution. An equation with two variables, such as $y = 2x + 1$, has many solutions, which we write as ordered pairs of numbers. We usually consider variables in alphabetical order. For an equation such as $y = 2x + 1$, we write an ordered pair in the form (x, y).

EXAMPLE 1

Determine whether $(3, 7)$ is a solution of $y = 2x + 1$.

$$y = 2x + 1$$
$$7 = 2 \cdot 3 + 1 \qquad \text{Substituting 3 for } x \text{ and 7 for } y$$
$$7 = 7$$

The equation is *true*. The ordered pair $(3, 7)$ is a solution.

EXAMPLE 2

Determine whether $(-2, 3)$ is a solution of $2y = 4x - 8$.

$$2y = 4x - 8$$
$$2 \cdot 3 = 4(-2) - 8$$
$$6 = -16$$

The equation is *false*. The ordered pair $(-2, 3)$ is *not* a solution.

Try This

a. Determine whether $(2, 3)$ is a solution of $y = 2x + 3$.
b. Determine whether $(-2, 4)$ is a solution of $4y - 3x = 22$.

We can find solutions of equations in two variables by choosing a value for one variable, substituting, and computing the value of the other variable.

EXAMPLE 3

Find three solutions of $y - 3x = -2$.

Solving for y first makes it easier to substitute for x and compute.

$$y = 3x - 2$$

 What You'll Learn

1 To determine whether an ordered pair is a solution of an equation

2 To graph equations in two variables

... And Why

To establish the relationship between the solutions and the graph of an equation

Quick Review

Replacements that make an equation true are its solutions.

We can substitute values for x and find corresponding values for y.
We choose any value for x. The easiest is 0.

$$y = 3x - 2$$
$$y = 3 \cdot 0 - 2 \qquad \text{Substituting 0 for } x$$
$$y = -2$$

The ordered pair $(0, -2)$ is a solution. We choose another number for x.

$$y = 3 \cdot 2 - 2 \qquad \text{Substituting 2 for } x$$
$$y = 4$$

A second solution is $(2, 4)$. Now try -2 for x.

$$y = 3(-2) - 2 \qquad \text{Substituting } -2 \text{ for } x$$
$$y = -8$$

A third solution is $(-2, -8)$.

We can record the ordered pairs in a table to
show the solutions at a glance.

x	y
0	−2
2	4
−2	−8

Try This

c. Find three solutions of $y - 2x = 3$.

PART 2 Graphing Equations

Objective: Graph equations in two variables.

A solution of an equation with two variables is an ordered pair of numbers,
which can be plotted on a coordinate plane. The **graph** of an equation is a
drawing that represents its solution set.

Quick Review

To "graph an equation"
means to draw the graph
of its solution set.

EXAMPLE 4 Graph the equation $y - x = 1$.

Solve for y and find several solutions by substituting values for x.

$$y - x = 1$$
$$y = 1 + x$$

If $x = 0, y = 1 + 0 = 1$
If $x = -1, y = 1 + -1 = 0$
If $x = -5, y = 1 + -5 = -4$
If $x = 1, y = 1 + 1 = 2$
If $x = 3, y = 1 + 3 = 4$

x	y
0	1
−1	0
−5	−4
1	2
3	4

Making a table to
record ordered pairs

Plot the points $(0, 1)$, $(-1, 0)$, $(-5, -4)$, $(1, 2)$ and $(3, 4)$.

The points all lie on a straight line. We can see that if we could plot all solutions, the graph would be a line. Thus we connect the points to draw the line. The arrowheads show that the line continues endlessly.

The line is the graph of the equation $y - x = 1$. Every point on the line is a solution of this equation.

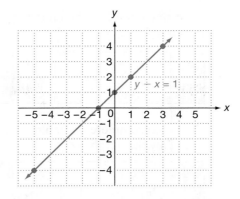

Try This   Graph each equation.

d. $y - x = 3$ **e.** $y = x$

7-2 Exercises

Extra Help On the Web

Look for worked-out examples at the Prentice Hall Web site.
www.phschool.com

A

Determine whether the given point is a solution of the equation.

1. $(2, 5)$, $y = 3x - 1$ **2.** $(1, 7)$, $y = 2x + 5$

3. $(2, -3)$, $3x - y = 3$ **4.** $(-1, 4)$, $2x + y = 2$

5. $(-2, -1)$, $2x + 3y = -7$ **6.** $(0, -4)$, $4x + 2y = 8$

Find three solutions of each equation.

7. $y = 2x + 1$ **8.** $y = 3x + 2$ **9.** $x + y = 6$

10. $x + y = 8$ **11.** $2x + y = 10$ **12.** $3x - y = 11$

13. $4x + 3y = 14$ **14.** $5x + 7y = 19$ **15.** $6x - 5y = 23$

Make a table of solutions and graph each equation.

16. $y = x$ **17.** $y = -x$ **18.** $y = -2x$

19. $y = 2x$ **20.** $y = x + 1$ **21.** $y = x - 1$

22. $y = 2x + 1$ **23.** $y = 3x - 1$ **24.** $y = -3x + 2$

25. $y = -4x + 1$ **26.** $2x + y = 3$ **27.** $5x + y = 7$

B

28. Complete the table for $y = x^2 + 1$. Plot the points on graph paper and draw the graph.

x	0	−1	1	−2	2	−3	3
y							

29. Copy and complete the table for $y = |x| + 1$. Plot the points on graph paper and draw the graph.

x	-4	-3	-2	-1	0	1	2	3	4
y									

30. Copy and complete the table for $y = \frac{1}{x}$. Plot the points on graph paper and draw the graph.

x	4	3	2	1	$\frac{1}{2}$	$\frac{1}{3}$	$\frac{1}{4}$	$\frac{1}{5}$	0	$-\frac{1}{4}$	$-\frac{1}{3}$	$-\frac{1}{2}$	-1	-2	-3	-4
y																

31. *Critical Thinking*   Looking at the graphs for Exercises 28–30, which of the equations below would you expect to graph as a straight line?

$$y = 3x - 1 \qquad x^2 + y^2 = 3 \qquad y = \frac{3}{xy} \qquad y = |x - 1|$$

Challenge

32. Joan earns $6 an hour. If she works on Saturdays, she earns $9 an hour. Joan worked x hours on Friday and y hours on Saturday.
  a. Write an expression showing Joan's total earnings for the two days.
  b. Suppose Joan earned a total of $57 on the two days. If x and y are whole numbers, find all of the possibilities for the number of hours she worked each day.

33. Machine X produces 68 rivets per hour, and machine Y produces 76 rivets per hour. Let x represent the number of hours machine X runs, and let y represent the number of hours machine Y runs. Write an equation giving the combined production of machine X and machine Y on a given day as 864. Find a solution to the equation. Explain your solution.

Mixed Review

Simplify.   **34.** 4^{-3} **35.** m^0 **36.** $(y^2)^3$ **37.** $8x^4 - (x^4 + 2x) + 3x$ *2-7, 5-1, 5-2*

Solve.   **38.** $(2y + 3)(y + 3) = 0$ **39.** $36c^2 = 0$ **40.** $9x^2 = 25$

41. $y^2 + 3y - 18 = 0$ **42.** $5x^2 = 7x$ **43.** $3x^2 + 14x + 9 = 2x$ *6-8*

Factor   **44.** $16 - 12c$ **45.** $m^2n^3 + 2mn^2$ **46.** $9a^4 - 9b^4$

47. $x^2 + 6xy + 9y^2$ **48.** $x^2 + 7x - 18$ **49.** $6x^2 - 7x + 2$ *6-1, 6-2, 6-5, 6-6*

Solve for the indicated variable.   **50.** $\frac{9}{5}C + 32 = F$ for C

51. $A = P(1 + rt)$ for r **52.** $A = \frac{1}{2}h(b_1 + b_2)$ for b_2 *3-7*

Linear Equations and Their Graphs

Introducing the Concept: Straight-line Graphs

Determine which of the following equations has a straight line as its graph.

$$xy = 4 \qquad y = 3x - 4 \qquad y - 4x = 2$$
$$2x - 3y = 0 \qquad y = 2x^2 \qquad y = \frac{3}{x}$$

PART 1 — Linear Equations

Objective: Graph linear equations in two variables.

Equations whose graphs are lines are **linear equations**. An equation is linear if the variables occur as first powers only, there are no products of variables, and no variable is in a denominator. Here are some examples.

Linear Equations $y = 2x + 1 \qquad y - 3x = -2 \qquad 5y = -4 \qquad 9x - 15y = 7$

Nonlinear Equations $y = x^2 - 4 \qquad x^2 + y^2 = 16 \qquad y = \frac{2}{x} \qquad xy = 3$

Since two points determine a line, plotting two points is sufficient for graphing linear equations. We should, however, use a third point as a check.

> **EXAMPLE 1**   Graph the equation $2y - 4 = 4x$.

Solve for y and find three solutions.

$$y = 2x + 2$$

If $x = 1, y = 2(1) + 2 = 4$
If $x = -2, y = 2(-2) + 2 = -2$
If $x = 3, y = 2(3) + 2 = 8$

x	y
1	4
−2	−2
3	8

Plot the points (1, 4), (−2, −2), and (3, 8) and draw the line containing the points.

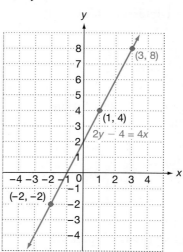

What You'll Learn

1 To graph linear equations in two variables

2 To graph linear equations using intercepts

3 To graph linear equations that graph as horizontal and vertical lines

. . . And Why

To graph linear equations using the geometric idea that two points determine a line

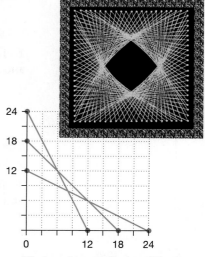

What are the coordinates of the two points that determine each of these three lines in a string design?

Try This   Graph these linear equations using three points.

a. $3y - 12 = 9x$ **b.** $4y + 8 = -16x$ **c.** $6x - 2y = -2$
d. $-10x - 2y = 8$

PART 2 Graphing Using Intercepts

Objective: Graph linear equations using intercepts.

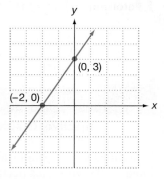

We can graph a linear equation by finding any two points that belong to the graph. Often the easiest points to find are the points where the graph crosses the axes.

The line shown at the right crosses the x-axis at $(-2, 0)$ and the y-axis at $(0, 3)$.

We say that the x-intercept is -2 and that the y-intercept is 3.

Definitions

The **x-intercept** of a line is the x-coordinate of the point where the line intercepts the x-axis.

The **y-intercept** of a line is the y-coordinate of the point where the line intercepts the y-axis.

EXAMPLE 2   Graph $4x + 3y = 12$ using intercepts.

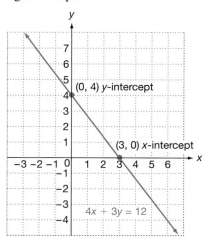

To find the x-intercept, let $y = 0$ and solve for x.

$$4x + 3 \cdot 0 = 12$$
$$4x = 12$$
$$x = 3$$

The x-intercept is 3. We plot the point $(3, 0)$.

To find the y-intercept, let $x = 0$ and solve for y.

$$4 \cdot 0 + 3y = 12$$
$$3y = 12$$
$$y = 4$$

The y-intercept is 4. We plot the point $(0, 4)$ and draw the line.

Try This   Graph using intercepts.

e. $2y = 3x - 6$ **f.** $5x + 7y = 35$ **g.** $8x + 2y = 24$

Objective: Graph linear equations that graph as horizontal and vertical lines.

The **standard form** of a linear equation in two variables is $Ax + By = C$, where A, B, and C are constants and A and B are not both 0.

EXAMPLE 3   Graph $y = 3$.

Write the equation in standard form.

$$0 \cdot x + 1 \cdot y = 3$$

You can see that for any value of x, $y = 3$. Thus any ordered pair $(x, 3)$, such as $(0, 3)$, $(4, 3)$, or $(-1, 3)$, is a solution. The line is parallel to the x-axis with y-intercept 3.

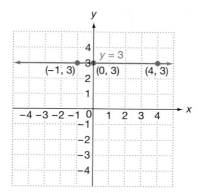

EXAMPLE 4   Graph $x = -4$.

Write this equation in standard form.

$$1 \cdot x + 0 \cdot y = -4$$

You can see that for any value of y, $x = -4$. Thus any ordered pair $(-4, y)$, such as $(-4, 3)$, $(-4, 1)$, or $(-4, -1)$, is a solution. The line is parallel to the y-axis with x-intercept -4.

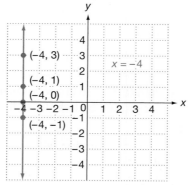

Horizontal and Vertical Lines

For constants a and b,
- the graph of $y = b$ is the x-axis or a line parallel to the x-axis with y-intercept b.
- the graph of $x = a$ is the y-axis or a line parallel to the y-axis with x-intercept a.

Try This   Graph these equations.

h. $x = 5$ **i.** $y = -2$ **j.** $x = 0$ **k.** $x = -6$

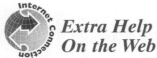
7-3 Exercises

A

Graph these linear equations using three points.

1. $x + 3y = 6$ **2.** $x + 2y = 8$ **3.** $-x + 2y = 4$

4. $-x + 3y = 9$ **5.** $3x + y = 9$ **6.** $2x + y = 6$

7. $2y - 2 = 6x$ **8.** $3y - 6 = 9x$ **9.** $2x - 5y = 10$

10. $4x + 5y = 20$ **11.** $2x + 6y = 12$ **12.** $2x + 3y = 8$

13. $3x - 4y = 12$ **14.** $y = \frac{1}{2}x + 1$ **15.** $y = \frac{1}{3}x - 1$

Graph using intercepts.

16. $x - 1 = y$ **17.** $x - 3 = y$ **18.** $2x - 1 = y$

19. $3x - 2 = y$ **20.** $4x - 3y = 12$ **21.** $6x - 2y = 18$

22. $7x + 2y = 6$ **23.** $3x + 4y = 5$ **24.** $y = -4 - 4x$

25. $y = -3 - 3x$ **26.** $-3x = 6y - 2$ **27.** $-4x = 8y - 5$

28. $3x - 6y = 12$ **29.** $-5x + y = 3$ **30.** $3x - 4y = -12$

31. $8y + 5x = 24$ **32.** $y = -6 + 2x$ **33.** $3y = 2x - 7$

Graph.

34. $x = -4$ **35.** $x = -3$ **36.** $y = -7$ **37.** $y = -8$

38. $x = 5$ **39.** $x = 7$ **40.** $y = 0$ **41.** $y = -2$

42. Write an equation whose graph is the y-axis.

43. Find the coordinates of the point of intersection of the graphs of the equations $x = -3$ and $y = 6$.

44. *Mathematical Reasoning*   Which equation, $x = -2$ or $x = 3$, has a graph that comes closer to the origin? Explain.

B

Match each equation with its corresponding graph at the right.

45. $y = \frac{1}{2}x$

46. $y = \frac{1}{2}x + 1$

47. $y = \frac{1}{2}x - 1$

48. $y = \frac{1}{2}x + 2$

49. $y = \frac{1}{2}x - 2$

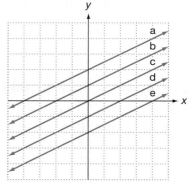

50. **TEST PREP**   Which equation is *not* a standard-form equation for a line graphed above?

A. $2y - x = 0$ **B.** $x - 2y = 0$ **C.** $x - 2y = 2$ **D.** $-x + 2y = 4$

51. *Critical Thinking*   In Exercises 45–49, what effect does changing the constant in an equation have on the graph of the equation?

Mental Math Write an equation of each line.

52. the line parallel to the *x*-axis and 5 units below it

53. the line parallel to the *y*-axis and 13 units to the right of it

54. the line parallel to the *x*-axis and intersecting the *y*-axis at $(0, 2.8)$

55. the line parallel to the *y*-axis and intersecting the *x*-axis at $(-3\frac{1}{2}, 0)$

Challenge

56. Plot the points $(10, 10)$, $(10, -10)$, $(-10, -10)$, and $(-10, 10)$. Connect the points to form a square. Then graph the following equations, but draw only the part of each line that is inside the square.

    a. $y = x - 7$ **b.** $y = x - 5$ **c.** $y = 5$ **d.** $y = 2x$

    e. $y = -x$ **f.** $y = -x + 7$ **g.** $y = -x + 5$ **h.** $2y = x$

57. The part of each line that is inside the square in Exercise 56 is called a line segment. Which of the eight line segments is the longest? Which pairs of line segments have the same length?

58. Is the following statement sometimes, always, or never true? Explain.

If $Ax + By = C$ is in standard form, then $-Ax - By = -C$ is also in standard form.

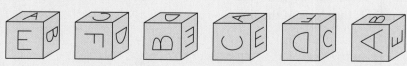

Mixed Review

Determine whether the following are squares of binomials.

59. $x^2 + 24x + 144$ **60.** $m^2 - 24m - 144$ **61.** $a^2 - 2ac + c^2$ *6-3*

Factor.   **62.** $a^2c - ac^2$ **63.** $x^2y^2 - 2xy - 8$ **64.** $a^2 - 3ab - 4b^2$ *6-2, 6-6*

Solve for the indicated variable.   **65.** $a = \frac{v^2}{r}$ for r **66.** $K = \frac{1}{2}Iw^2$ for I *3-7*

67. The office assistant types 65 words per minute. At that rate, how long will it take him to type a 2500-word document? *3-9*

◇ Connections: Reasoning

The 6 diagrams below show different views of the same cube.

Give the letter that is on the face opposite each face shown below.

    1.   **2.** B   **3.** E   **4.** C

7-4 ▷ Slope

What You'll Learn

1 To find the slope of a line given two points on the line

2 To describe slope for horizontal and vertical lines

...And Why

To represent the orientation of a line numerically

Math in Action

Attendance at men's and women's basketball games at a large university has been increasing for the past 6 years. The lines on the graph at the right approximate the growth patterns. We see that the line for women's basketball is steeper than the line for men's basketball. We can define a ratio that describes the steepness of a line. This ratio is called the slope.

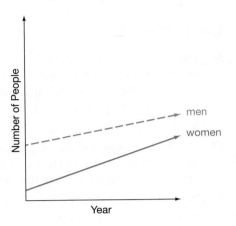

PART 1 Meaning of Slope

Objective: Find the slope of a line given two points on the line.

In the graph at the right, as we move from P to Q, the change in the x-coordinates is $6 - 2$, or 4 units. We call the change in the x-coordinates the **run.** The change in the y-coordinates is $3 - 1$, or 2 units. We call the change in the y-coordinates the **rise.** For the line at the right, the ratio of the rise to the run is 2 to 4. That is $\frac{\text{rise}}{\text{run}} = \frac{2}{4}$, or $\frac{1}{2}$. This ratio is the slope of the line.

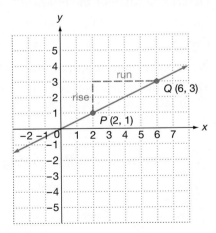

Definition

$$\textbf{Slope} = \frac{\text{rise}}{\text{run}} = \frac{\text{change in the } y\text{-coordinates}}{\text{change in the } x\text{-coordinates}}$$

$$= \frac{\text{difference of } y\text{-coordinates}}{\text{difference of } x\text{-coordinates}}$$

EXAMPLE 1

Graph the line containing points $(-4, 2)$ and $(2, -3)$ and find the slope.

We plot the points $(-4, 2)$ and $(2, -3)$ and draw the line containing these points. We can use the definition of slope to find the slope of the line.

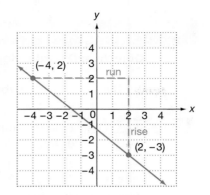

We know that the points $(-4, 2)$ and $(2, -3)$ are on the line.

$$\text{Slope} = \frac{\text{rise}}{\text{run}} = \frac{\text{change in } y}{\text{change in } x} = \frac{2 - (-3)}{-4 - 2}$$

$$= \frac{5}{-6}$$

$$= -\frac{5}{6}$$

The slope is $-\frac{5}{6}$.

Try This Graph the lines containing these points and find their slopes.

a. $(-2, 3)$ $(3, 5)$ **b.** $(0, -3)$ $(-3, 2)$

In Example 1 we found the change in y by subtracting the y-coordinates, and we found the change in x by subtracting the x-coordinates. We can also find the slope by subtracting the coordinates in reverse order.

$$\text{slope} = \frac{\text{change in } y}{\text{change in } x} = \frac{-3 - 2}{2 - (-4)} = \frac{-5}{6} = -\frac{5}{6}$$

The slope is the same. In general, the slope of a line can be found using

$$m = \frac{y_2 - y_1}{x_2 - x_1} \quad \text{The letter } m \text{ is commonly used for slope.}$$

for any two points (x_1, y_1) and (x_2, y_2) of the line, a fact that you will be able to prove when you take geometry.

Writing Math

When you write the ratio for slope thinking x and y, remember

1. y on top, x on bottom.
2. Subtract y-values in either order.
3. Subtract x-values in the same order as the y-values.

EXAMPLE 2   Find the slope of the line containing $(1, 1)$ and $(3, 5)$.

$$m = \frac{y_2 - y_1}{x_2 - x_1} = \frac{5 - 1}{3 - 1} = \frac{4}{2} = 2$$

Try This   Find the slopes of the lines containing these points.

c. $(2, 2)$ $(8, 9)$ **d.** $(-4, -6)$ $(3, -2)$
e. $(-2, 3)$ $(2, 1)$ **f.** $(5, -11)$ $(-9, 4)$

Objective: Describe slope for horizontal and vertical lines.

What about the slope of a horizontal or vertical line?

Reading Math

Because the graph of a linear equation is a line, a linear equation $ax + by = c$ is often referred to as "the line $ax + by = c$."

EXAMPLE 3 Find the slope of the line $y = 4$.

$$m = \frac{\text{change in } y}{\text{change in } x} = \frac{4 - 4}{-3 - 2} = \frac{0}{-5} = 0$$

Any two points on a horizontal line have the same y-coordinate. Thus the change in y is 0, so the slope is 0.

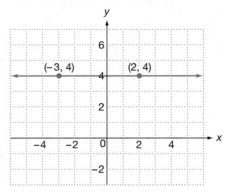

EXAMPLE 4 Find the slope of the line $x = -3$.

$$m = \frac{\text{change in } y}{\text{change in } x} = \frac{3 - (-2)}{-3 - (-3)} = \frac{5}{0}$$

Since division by 0 is not defined, this line has no slope.

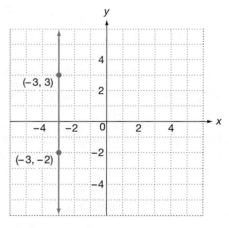

Example 3 suggests that a horizontal line has slope 0, a fact that we prove later. Example 4 shows that the slope definition does not apply to vertical lines. For them, we leave slope undefined and simply say that such lines have no slope.

Slope for Horizontal and Vertical Lines

A horizontal line has slope 0.

A vertical line has no slope.

Try This Find the slopes, if they exist, of the lines through these points.

g. $(9, 7)$ $(3, 7)$ **h.** $(4, -6)$ $(4, 0)$ **i.** $(2, 4)$ $(-1, 5)$

7-4 Exercises

Internet Connection

Extra Help On the Web

Look for worked-out examples at the Prentice Hall Web site.

www.phschool.com

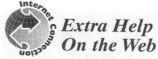

A

Find the slope of each line.

1.

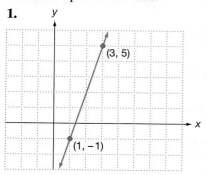

2.

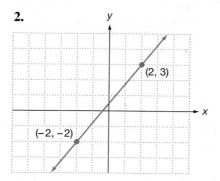

3.

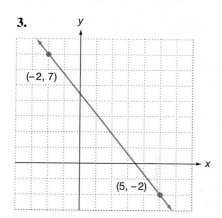

4.

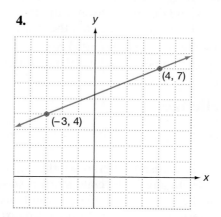

Graph the lines containing these points and find their slopes.

5. $(-4, 2)$ $(2, -3)$ **6.** $(4, 1)$ $(-2, -3)$ **7.** $(-2, 4)$ $(3, 0)$

8. $(3, 2)$ $(-1, 2)$ **9.** $(0, 5)$ $(-4, -3)$ **10.** $(1, 6)$ $(-2, -4)$

Find the slopes of the lines containing these points.

11. $(4, 0)$ $(5, 7)$

12. $(3, 0)$ $(6, 2)$

13. $(0, 8)$ $(-3, 10)$

14. $(0, 9)$ $(4, 7)$

15. $(3, -2)$ $(5, -6)$

16. $(-2, 4)$ $(6, -7)$

17. $(0, 0)$ $(-3, -9)$

18. $(0, 0)$ $(-4, -8)$

19. $\left(\frac{3}{4}, \frac{1}{2}\right)$ $\left(\frac{1}{4}, -\frac{1}{2}\right)$

20. $\left(\frac{1}{4}, \frac{1}{8}\right)$ $\left(\frac{1}{2}, \frac{3}{4}\right)$

Find the slope, if it exists, of each of these lines.

21. $x = -8$ **22.** $x = -4$ **23.** $y = 2$ **24.** $y = 17$

25. $x = 9$ **26.** $x = 6$ **27.** $y = -9$ **28.** $y = -4$

The vertical rise is 14 ft. The horizontal run is 5 ft. What is the slope of this ladder? (See Exercise 35.)

B

29. A line contains $(4, 3)$ and $(x, 7)$. It has slope 2. Find x.

30. A line contains $(9, y)$ and $(-6, 3)$. It has slope $\frac{2}{3}$. Find y.

31. A line contains $(-4, y)$ and $(2, 4y)$. It has slope 6. Find y.

32. The gradient of a road is its slope expressed as percent. What is the slope of a road with a 7% gradient?

33. Suppose an airplane climbs 11.7 ft for every 30 ft it moves horizontally. Express the slope of the climb as a percent.

34. The vertices of a triangle are $X(-1, 4)$, $Y(2, 2)$, and $Z(2, -2)$. Find the slope of each side of the triangle.

35. *Critical Thinking*   An extension ladder has a label that says, "Do not place base of ladder less than 5 ft from the vertical surface."

    a. What is the greatest slope possible if the ladder can extend to safely reach a height of 12 ft? Of 18 ft? Of 24 ft?

    b. Once, when the ladder reached to 20 ft with the base 5 ft from a wall, it slid down and away from the wall until it was flat on the ground. What slope values did the ladder have during its slide?

36. *Write a Convincing Argument*   Are the points $(-1, 3)$, $(1, 1)$, and $(10, -8)$ on one line? Explain. Hint: Use the definition of slope.

Challenge

37. A line contains points (p, q) and (q, p) where $p \neq q$. Find the slope.

38. In the chessboard drawing, the knight may move to any of the eight squares shown. If the beginning and end squares of any move determine a line, what slopes are possible?

39. *Error Analysis*   Garth found the slope of the line containing $(-2, 5)$ and $(4, -7)$ to be 2. What error did he make?

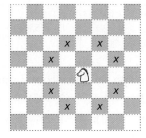

Journal

Explain how graphs of linear equations change as the coefficient of x changes.
    Illustrate using the graphs of these equations on one set of axes.

$y = x$	$y = 2x$
$y = 5x$	$y = -3x$
$y = \frac{1}{2}x$	$y = -\frac{1}{2}x$

Mixed Review

Factor.   **40.** $9m^4n^2 - 16$ **41** $a^2b^2 + ab - 2$ **42.** $3x^2 + 2xy - y^2$ *6-2, 6-7*

Determine whether the given point is a solution of the equation.

43. $(0, -2)$, $3x - y = 2$ **44.** $(2, 3)$, $3x - 2y = 2$ *7-2*

Write in standard notation   **45.** 2.575×10^{-3} **46.** 1.004×10^5 *5-4*

Solve.   **47.** $y^2 - 7y = 18$ **48.** $m^2 + 3m = 10$ **49.** $a^2 + 4a = -4$ *6-8*

Equations and Slope

Introducing the Concept: Slopes and Linear Equations

Determine the slope of each line.

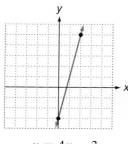

$$y = 4x - 3$$

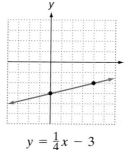

$$y = \tfrac{1}{4}x - 3$$

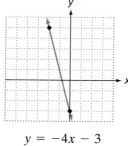

$$y = -4x - 3$$

What is the relationship between the slope and the equation of each line?

What You'll Learn

1 To find the slope of a line from an equation

2 To find the slope and *y*-intercept of a line from an equation

3 To graph lines using the slope-intercept equation

. . . And Why

To efficiently draw the graph of a linear equation

PART 1 Finding Slope from an Equation

Objective: Find the slope of a line from an equation.

It is possible to find the slope of a line from its equation. We begin by finding any two points on the line. We then use the formula for slope.

EXAMPLE 1 Find the slope of the line $y = 2x + 3$.

We choose the points $(0, 3)$ and $(1, 5)$.

$$m = \frac{\text{change in } y}{\text{change in } x} = \frac{5 - 3}{1 - 0}$$
$$= \frac{2}{1}$$
$$= 2$$

The slope is 2.

Notice that the slope, 2, is also the coefficient of the *x*-term in the equation $y = 2x + 3$. We can always find *m*, the slope of a line, if its equation is written in the form, $y = mx + b$. The coefficient of the *x*-term, *m*, is the slope, as we will prove in Lesson 7-9.

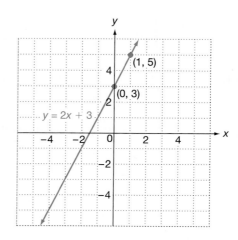

EXAMPLE 2   Find the slope of $2x + 3y = 7$.

Solve for y.

$$2x + 3y = 7$$
$$3y = -2x + 7$$
$$y = \frac{-2}{3}x + \frac{7}{3}$$

The slope is $-\frac{2}{3}$.

Try This   Find the slope of each line by solving for y.

a. $4x + 5y = 7$ **b.** $3x + 8y = 9$
c. $x + 5y = 7$ **d.** $5x - 4y = 8$

PART 2

Slope-Intercept Equation of a Line

Objective: Find the slope and *y*-intercept of a line from an equation.

In the equation $y = mx + b$, m is the slope. If $x = 0$, then $y = m(0) + b$ or $y = b$. Thus the graph crosses the y-axis at the point $(0, b)$, and b is the y-intercept. In the graph at the right, the line $y = 2x - 3$ has slope 2 and y-intercept -3.

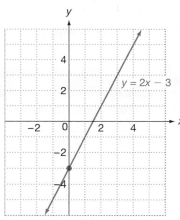

Definition

An equation $y = mx + b$ is called the **slope-intercept equation** of a line. The slope is m and the y-intercept is b.

Reading Math

To help you understand the slope-intercept form, read an equation like
$$y = 3x - 4$$
as
$$y = 3x + (-4).$$

EXAMPLE 3   Find the slope and y-intercept of $y = 3x - 4$.

$$y = 3x - 4$$

slope: 3 y-intercept: -4

The slope is 3. The y-intercept is -4.

EXAMPLE 4 Find the slope and y-intercept of $2x + 3y = 6$.

First solve for y.

$$2x + 3y = 6$$
$$y = -\frac{2}{3}x + 2$$

The slope is $-\frac{2}{3}$. The y-intercept is 2.

Try This Find the slope and y-intercept.

e. $y = 5x$ **f.** $y = -\frac{3}{2}x - 6$

g. $3x + 4y = 16$ **h.** $-7x - 5y = 25$

PART 3 Graphing Using the Slope-Intercept Equation

Objective: Graph lines using the slope-intercept equation.

We can graph lines using the slope-intercept form of an equation.

EXAMPLE 5 Graph $y = -2x + 3$ using y-intercept and slope.

From the equation $y = -2x + 3$, we know that the slope is -2 and that the y-intercept is 3.

First we plot $(0, 3)$. We can think of the slope as $\frac{-2}{1}$. Using the slope, we find another point by moving 2 units down (negative) and 1 unit right (positive). The point is $(1, 1)$. We graph the equation by drawing the line through the two points.

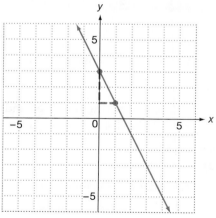

Try This Graph each equation using y-intercept and slope.

i. $y = 3x - 4$ **j.** $y = -\frac{1}{3}x + 4$

k. $y = -\frac{3}{4}x + 2$

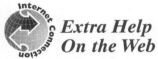

**Extra Help
On the Web**
Look for worked-out
examples at the Prentice
Hall Web site.
www.phschool.com

7-5 Exercises

A

Find the slope of each line by solving for y.

1. $3x + 2y = 6$ **2.** $4x - y = 5$ **3.** $x + 4y = 8$

4. $x + 3y = 6$ **5.** $-2x + y = 4$ **6.** $-5x + y = 5$

7. $4x - 3y = -12$ **8.** $3x - 4y = -12$ **9.** $x - 2y = 9$

10. $x - 3y = -2$ **11.** $-2x + 4y = 8$ **12.** $-5x + 7y = 2$

13. $-7x + 5y = 16$ **14.** $-3x + 2y = 9$ **15.** $-6x - 9y = 13$

16. $-8x - 5y = 18$ **17.** $8x + 9y = 10$ **18.** $7x + 4y = 13$

Find the slope and y-intercept.

19. $y = -4x - 9$ **20.** $y = -3x - 5$ **21.** $2x + 3y = 9$

22. $5x + 4y = 12$ **23.** $-8x - 7y = 21$ **24.** $-2x - 9y = 13$

25. $9x = 3y + 5$ **26.** $4x = 9y + 7$ **27.** $-6x = 4y + 2$

Graph each line using the y-intercept and slope.

28. $y = 2x + 3$ **29.** $y = -3x + 4$ **30.** $y = -x + 7$

31. $y = \frac{2}{3}x - 3$ **32.** $y = \frac{3}{4}x - 3$ **33.** $y = \frac{1}{2}x + 2$

34. $y + \frac{1}{3}x = 2$ **35.** $y - \frac{2}{3}x = 0$ **36.** $y + \frac{3}{5}x = -3$

37. $y - 5x = -4$ **38.** $y - 7 = -3x$ **39.** $y + 4 = -2x$

40. **TEST PREP**   Which line has greater slope, $-2x + 3y = 6$ or $2x - 3y = 4$?

   A. $-2x + 3y = 6$ **B.** $2x - 3y = 4$

   C. Slopes are equal.   **D.** Cannot tell.

B

Graph each line using the slope and y-intercept.

41. $2y - 6x = -8$ **42.** $4y + 2x = 12$

43. $2x - 5y = 15$ **44.** $6x + 3y = -12$

45. $8x - 3y = 15$ **46.** $-2x = -4y + 16$

47. Consider the equation $ky + 2x = 7$. For what value of k will the slope be 1?

Write an equation for each line given the slope and y-intercept. Express the equation in slope-intercept form.

48. $m = 3, b = -2$ **49.** $m = 8, b = 0$

50. $m = 0, b = -5$ **51.** $m = -7, b = 4$

52. $m = \frac{1}{2}, b = 1$ **53.** $m = -6, b = \frac{3}{4}$

54. Write an equation of a line that has the same slope as $y = \frac{2}{3}x + 5$ with a y-intercept of -8.

Find the slope and *y*-intercept. Do not graph.

55. $3(x + 4) = y - 8x + 3$ **56.** $2y + 4x = 3(y - x) + 8$

57. *Critical Thinking*   Graph $y = 3|x| + 5$. Your graph should look like an angle. Give the slope of each ray of the angle, and the coordinates of the vertex.

Challenge

58. *Mathematical Reasoning*   Copy and complete the table.

Standard Form	Slope-Intercept Form	*x*- and *y*-Intercepts
$Ax + By = C,$ $A \neq 0, B \neq 0$	?	?
?	$y = mx + b$	?
?	?	$(a, 0)$ and $(0, b)$ $a \neq 0, b \neq 0$

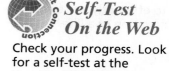

Mixed Review

In which quadrant is each point located?   **59.** $(1, -5)$ **60.** $(-1, 3)$

61. $(2, 3)$ **62.** $(-4, -1)$ **63.** $(2, -6)$ **64.** $(-3, 2)$ *7-1*

Find three solutions of each equation.   **65.** $x + 2y = 5$

66. $2x - 4y = 0$ **67.** $3x + y = 2$ **68.** $2x - 2y = 4$ *7-2*

Factor.   **69.** $25b^2 - 16a^2$ **70.** $a^4 + 4a^3b + 4a^2b^2$

71. $mn + 5m + 3n + 15$ **72.** $6x^2 + 14x + 8$ *6-2, 6-7*

Solve.   **73.** $12y^2 = 108$ **74.** $a^2 - 3a = 10$ **75.** $x^2 - 25 = 0$ *6-8*

76. The Correction Company makes erasers and packs them in boxes of 144. On Tuesday, the Correction Company produced and packed 31 boxes, with 4 erasers left over. How many erasers were produced that day?   *3-11*

◇◇ Connections: Reasoning

The graph of the equation $y = 3x - 4$ is shown at the right.

Suppose you graphed each of the following equations on the same coordinate axes. How would the graph of each equation be related to the graph at the right?

a. $y = 3x + 6$ **b.** $y = 6x - 4$
c. $2y = 6x - 8$ **d.** $4 = 3x - y$
e. $y = \frac{-x}{3} - 4$ **f.** $-y = -3x + 4$

7-6 ▷ Finding an Equation of a Line

What You'll Learn

1 To write an equation of a line using the slope-intercept equation

2 To write an equation of a line using the point-slope equation

... And Why

To efficiently write an equation of a line

PART 1 The Slope-Intercept Equation

Objective: Write an equation of a line using the slope-intercept equation.

If we can determine the slope and y-intercept of a line, we can use the slope-intercept equation, $y = mx + b$, to write an equation of the line.

EXAMPLE 1 Write an equation for the line with slope 2 that contains the point $(3, 1)$.

Use the given point $(3, 1)$ and substitute 3 for x and 1 for y in $y = mx + b$, the slope-intercept equation. Substitute 2 for m, the slope. Then solve for b.

$$y = mx + b$$
$$1 = 2(3) + b \qquad \text{Substituting}$$
$$-5 = b \qquad \text{Solving for } b, \text{ the } y\text{-intercept}$$

We can substitute 2 for m and -5 for b in $y = mx + b$.

$$y = mx + b$$
$$y = 2x - 5$$

Try This Write an equation for the line that contains the given point and has the given slope.

a. $(4, 2)$, $m = 5$ **b.** $(-2, 1)$, $m = -3$

EXAMPLE 2 Write an equation for the line containing $(1, 3)$ and $(-2, -3)$.

$$m = \frac{\text{change in } y}{\text{change in } x} = \frac{-3 - 3}{-2 - 1} = \frac{-6}{-3} = 2$$

Choose either point and substitute for x and y in $y = mx + b$. Also substitute 2 for m, the slope. Then solve for b.

$$y = mx + b$$
$$3 = 2(1) + b \qquad \text{Substituting } (1, 3) \text{ for } (x, y) \text{ and 2 for } m$$
$$1 = b \qquad \text{Solving for } b, \text{ the } y\text{-intercept}$$

Substitute 2 for m and 1 for b in $y = mx + b$.

$$y = mx + b$$
$$y = 2x + 1$$

Try This   Write an equation for the line that contains the given
two points.

c. $(8, 2)$ $(2, 6)$ **d.** $(-1, 4)$ $(-3, -5)$

PART 2 The Point-Slope Equation

Objective: Write an equation of a line using the point-slope equation.

Consider Example 2 again. We know that the line contains the point $(1, 3)$.
Let (x, y) represent any other point on this line. We can use the definition of
slope to write the following.

$$m = \frac{\text{difference of } y\text{-coordinates}}{\text{difference of } x\text{-coordinates}} = \frac{y - 3}{x - 1}$$

We know the slope is 2. Thus we can write

$$2 = \frac{y - 3}{x - 1} \quad \text{or} \quad \frac{y - 3}{x - 1} = 2$$

If we multiply both sides by $(x - 1)$, we have

$$y - 3 = 2(x - 1) \quad \text{or} \quad y = 2x + 1$$

This last equation is satisfied by every point on the line and is the equation
for the line.

Recall that we started with a line with slope 2 and containing the point $(1, 3)$.
For the point $(1, 3)$ and slope 2, we develop the equation above.

$$\underset{y\text{-coordinate}}{\underset{\downarrow}{y - 3}} \quad = \quad \underset{\text{slope}}{\underset{\downarrow}{2}} \quad \cdot \quad \underset{x\text{-coordinate}}{\underset{\downarrow}{(x - 1)}}$$

We can state this relationship in general (and you will prove it in Lesson 7-9).

The Point-Slope Equation

A nonvertical line with slope m and containing a point (x_1, y_1) has the
point–slope equation

$$y - y_1 = m(x - x_1)$$

EXAMPLE 3   Write an equation for the line with slope 3 that contains
the point $(5, 2)$. Express the equation in slope-intercept
form.

$$y - y_1 = m(x - x_1)$$
$$y - 2 = 3(x - 5) \qquad \text{Substituting 3 for } m \text{ and } (5, 2) \text{ for } (x_1, y_1)$$
$$y - 2 = 3x - 15 \qquad \text{Using the distributive property}$$
$$y = 3x - 13 \qquad \text{Simplifying}$$

Try This   Write an equation for each line with the given point and slope. Express the equation in slope-intercept form.

e. $(3, 5), m = 6$ **f.** $(1, 4), m = -\dfrac{2}{3}$

We can also use the point-slope equation to find an equation of a line if we know any two points on the line.

EXAMPLE 4   Write an equation for the line shown below. Express the equation in slope-intercept form.

We first find any two points on the line. Use $(1, 1)$ and $(2, 3)$. We next find the slope.

$$m = \frac{3 - 1}{2 - 1} = \frac{2}{1} = 2$$

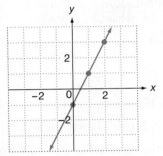

We can now use the point-slope equation to find an equation for the line. We can use either point. Using $(1, 1)$ may make the computation easier.

$$y - y_1 = m(x - x_1)$$
$$y - 1 = 2(x - 1)$$
$$y - 1 = 2x - 2$$
$$y = 2x - 1$$

Try This   Write an equation for each line in slope-intercept form.

g.

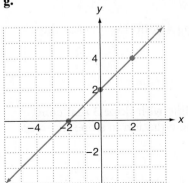

h.

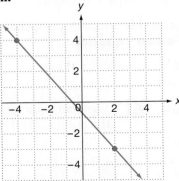

Extra Help On the Web

Look for worked-out examples at the Prentice Hall Web site.
www.phschool.com

A

Write an equation for each line with the given point and slope. Express the equation in slope-intercept form.

1. $(2, 5)$, $m = 5$ **2.** $(-3, 0)$, $m = -2$ **3.** $(2, 4)$, $m = \frac{3}{4}$

4. $\left(\frac{1}{2}, 2\right)$, $m = -1$ **5.** $(2, -6)$, $m = 1$ **6.** $(-3, 0)$, $m = -3$

7. $(0, 3)$, $m = -3$ **8.** $(4, 3)$, $m = \frac{3}{4}$ **9.** $(-2, 1)$, $m = \frac{1}{2}$

10. $(-3, -5)$, $m = -\frac{3}{5}$ **11.** $(-6, -2)$, $m = \frac{5}{2}$ **12.** $\left(-\frac{1}{2}, 0\right)$, $m = 3$

Write an equation for each line that contains the given pair of points.

13. $(-6, 1)$ $(2, 3)$ **14.** $(12, 16)$ $(1, 5)$

15. $(0, 4)$ $(4, 2)$ **16.** $(0, 0)$ $(4, 2)$

17. $(3, 2)$ $(1, 5)$ **18.** $(-4, 1)$ $(-1, 4)$

19. $(5, 0)$ $(0, -2)$ **20.** $(-2, -2)$ $(1, 3)$

21. $(-2, -4)$ $(2, -1)$ **22.** $(-3, 5)$ $(-1, -3)$

Write an equation for each line in slope-intercept form.

23.

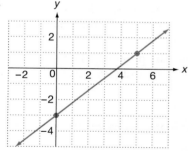

24.

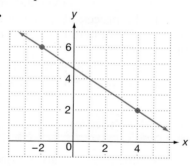

25.

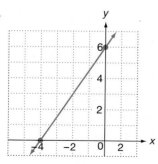

26.

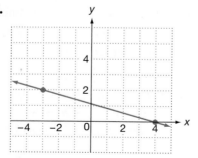

27. *Critical Thinking*   When you write an equation for a line containing one or more given points, you can check your work by checking that the coordinates of each given point satisfy the equation. Check your work in this way for the Exercises assigned from 1–26 above.

B

Write an equation in slope-intercept form of the line described.

28. has the same slope as $3x - y + 4 = 0$ and contains the point $(2, -3)$

29. has the same y-intercept as $x - 3y = 6$ and contains the point $(5, -1)$

30. has the same slope as $3x - 2y = 8$ and the same y-intercept as $2y + 3x = -4$

31. has the same slope as $2x = 3y - 1$ and contains the point $(8, -5)$

32. *Write a Convincing Argument*   A line contains the points $(12, 8)$ and $(14, 9)$. Explain why the line intercepts the y-axis at the point $(0, 2)$.

Challenge

33. If the endpoints of a line segment are (x_1, y_1) and (x_2, y_2), then the coordinates of the midpoint of the segment are

$$\left(\frac{x_1 + x_2}{2}, \frac{y_1 + y_2}{2} \right)$$

Quick Review

The sum of two numbers divided by 2 is the *average* of the two numbers.

Use this formula to find midpoints of segments with these endpoints.

a. $(-4, 3)$ and $(6, -9)$ b. $(-4, 0)$ and $(4, 0)$

c. $(-2, 1)$ and $(4, 3)$ d. $(-4, 3)$ and $(4, -3)$

34. Consider the triangle with vertices at $(1, 4), (5, 10)$, and $(9, 2)$. Form a second triangle by joining midpoints of the sides of the first triangle. Repeat this process to get a third triangle. How are the slopes of the sides of the third triangle related to the slopes of the sides of the first triangle?

35. Find the y-intercept of the line containing the point $(2, 5)$ and the midpoint of the segment with endpoints $(3, 6)$ and $(10, -2)$.

Mixed Review

Graph each line using the given information.

36. $(-6, 1)$ and $(4, 6)$ are on the line.   37. $m = 3$ and $(4, -1)$ is on the line.

38. slope $= -2$, y-intercept is 1   *7-5*

39. What number is 68% of 240?   40. 54 is 12% of what number?   *3-10*

Solve.   41. $x^2 - 49 = 0$ 42. $a^2 - a = 6$ 43. $m^2 + 5m = 36$

44. $c(c + 7) = 0$ 45. $(x - 9)(3x + 5) = 0$ 46. $81x^2 = 16$ *6-8*

Factor.   47. $4m^2 - 36m + 80$ 48. $x^5 + 4x^4 + 4x^3$

49. $9c^3 - 3c^2 - 3c + 1$ 50. $y^3 - 2y^2 - 8y$ 51. $x^2y^2 - z^2$ *6-7*

Simplify.   52. $\dfrac{4^7}{4^4}$ 53. $\dfrac{p^{18}}{p^{16}}$ 54. $(5^3)^4$ *5-1, 5-2*

55. The United States population in 1950 was 151 million. By 1990 it had increased by 65%. What was the 1990 population?   *3-10*

Fitting Equations to Data

Objective: Find an equation of a line that models given data.

The mathematical relationship between two variables is of interest in many real-world situations. The relationship between two variables can often be expressed as a linear equation, which is called a model of the situation. The model can be used to make estimates or predictions about the quantities represented by the variables.

What You'll Learn

1 To find an equation of a line that models given data

. . . And Why

To model real-life relationships algebraically and use models to make estimates and predictions

EXAMPLE 1

To produce 50 copies of a school newspaper, the cost per paper is 26¢. To produce 200 newspapers, the cost per paper is 20¢. Let n be the number of copies of a school newspaper, and let c be the cost per paper. Assume that a linear relationship fits these data with ordered pairs (n, c).
(1) Find the linear equation that fits these data.
(2) Use the linear equation to predict what it would cost per paper to produce 300 copies.

■ **UNDERSTAND the problem**

Question: How much would it cost per paper to produce 300 copies?
Data: 50 copies cost 26¢ each; 200 copies cost 20¢ each.

■ **Develop and carry out a PLAN**

(1) Use the ordered pairs $(50, 26)$ and $(200, 20)$ to find the linear equation.

$$m = \frac{26 - 20}{50 - 200} = \frac{6}{-150} = -\frac{1}{25} \qquad \text{Finding the slope}$$

$$c - 26 = -\frac{1}{25}(n - 50) \qquad \text{Using the point-slope equation}$$

$$c - 26 = -\frac{1}{25}n + 2$$

$$c = -\frac{1}{25}n + 28$$

(2) To find the cost per paper for 300 papers, substitute 300 for n and solve for c.

$$c = -\frac{1}{25}n + 28$$

$$c = -\frac{1}{25}(300) + 28$$

$$c = -12 + 28 = 16$$

■ **Find the ANSWER and CHECK**

The cost to produce 300 papers would be 16¢ per paper. The answer seems reasonable, since the cost decreases as the number produced increases.

The number of daily newspapers has been declining linearly for several years. How can you predict when there will be fewer than 1400 daily newspapers?

EXAMPLE 2

The chart shows the number of daily newspapers published in the United States during the even-numbered years from 1982 to 1996.

Daily Newspapers

Year	Number
1982	1711
1984	1688
1986	1657
1988	1642
1990	1611
1992	1570
1994	1548
1996	1520

Let a be the number of years since 1980. (For 1982, for example, $a = 2$.) Let d be the number of daily newspapers published. Graph the ordered pairs (a, d). Draw a line of best fit and find an equation of the line. Use the line to predict the number of daily newspapers in the year 2000.

Years since 1980 (a)	2	4	6	8	10	12	14	16
Number of dailies (d)	1711	1688	1657	1642	1611	1570	1548	1520

We plot each ordered pair (a, d) and see that the points suggest a linear relationship. The line that best approximates the linear relationship is the **line of best fit.**

The points $(4, 1688)$ and $(14, 1548)$ are close to the line. We use these points to approximate the line.

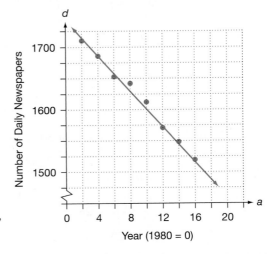

$$m = \frac{1548 - 1688}{14 - 4} = \frac{-140}{10} = -14,$$

or a loss of 14 dailies each year

$$d - 1688 = -14(a - 4)$$
$$d - 1688 = -14a + 56$$
$$d = -14a + 1744$$

For the year 2000, $a = 20$. We evaluate the equation for $a = 20$.

$$d = -14a + 1744$$
$$d = -14(20) + 1744$$
$$d = -280 + 1744$$
$$d = 1464$$

We can predict that there were about 1464 daily newspapers in the United States in 2000.

Try This

a. A college record in the 100-m dash in 1960 (t) was 10.5 seconds (r). In 1990 the new record was 10.2 seconds. Assume a linear relationship fits these data with ordered pairs (t, r).
   (1) Find a linear equation to fit the data points.
   (2) Use the linear equation to predict the record in 2000.

b. Graph the ordered pairs (d, c). Draw the line of best fit and find the equation of the line.

Distance (d) in miles	10	15	20	25	30	40	50	60
Cost (c)	10	15	20	22	24	35	42	50

7-7 Exercises

Extra Help On the Web

Look for worked-out examples at the Prentice Hall Web site.
   www.phschool.com

A

Solve. Assume a linear relationship fits each set of data.

1. A long-distance telephone company advertised the following rates: "5 minutes (m) for just 85¢ (p) and 10 minutes for just $1.10." Use the ordered pairs (m, p).

   a. Find a linear equation for these data points.

   b. Use this linear equation to find the cost of a 20-minute phone call.

2. A temperature of 0°C is the same as 32°F. A temperature of 10°C is the same as 50°F. Use the ordered pairs (C, F).

   a. Find a linear equation for these data points.

   b. Use this linear equation to find the temperature Fahrenheit when the temperature is 30°C.

3. For a ground temperature of 15°C, the air temperature (t) at an altitude of 500 m (h) is 10°C. At 2000 m, the air temperature is −5°C. Use the ordered pairs (h, t).

   a. Find a linear equation for these data points.

   b. Use this linear equation to find the air temperature at 1500 m.

4. Scores on an achievement test (a) are related linearly to scores on another test (b). Here are two students' scores $a = 500, b = 100$ and $a = 680$, $b = 127$. Use the ordered pairs (a, b).

   a. Find a linear equation for these data points.

   b. Use this linear equation to predict the score on the b test for a student with a score of 700 on the a test.

5. A school record in a certain race in 1970 (t) was 3.8 minutes (r). In 1990 the school record was 3.65 minutes. Use the ordered pairs (t, r).

   a. Find a linear equation for these data points.

   b. Use this linear equation to predict the school's record in 2000.

6. The total length (l) of a certain species of snake is related linearly to the tail length (t) of this snake. Here are the measurements for two snakes of this species. Snake 1: $l = 150$ mm and $t = 19$ mm; Snake 2: $l = 300$ mm and $t = 40$ mm. Use the ordered pairs (l, t).

   a. Find a linear equation for these data points.

   b. Use this linear equation to estimate the tail length of a snake with a total length of 200 mm.

   c. Use this linear equation to estimate the tail length of a snake with a total length of 350 mm.

7. Graph the ordered pairs (d, y). Draw the line of best fit and find an equation of the line.

Diameter of tree trunk in inches (d)	4	10	40	35	25	35	20
Age (y)	1	5	20	15	10	15	20

8. Graph the ordered pairs (m, c). Draw the line of best fit and find an equation of the line.

Miles (m)	2	3	5	10	20
Cost of a taxi (c)	$4.00	$5.25	$8.50	$16.25	$31.00

9. A motel owners' association compared the prices of motel rooms in and near a small city. Each ordered pair represents the distance (d) in miles a motel is from the center of the city and the cost (c) of a motel room for one person. Graph the ordered pairs (d, c). Draw the line of best fit and find an equation of the line.

Distance (d) in miles	1	2	2	3	3	4	5	5	6
Cost (c)	$80	$75	$55	$60	$45	$55	$40	$50	$35

10. Below are some world records for the fastest speed attained on land, in miles per hour. The speed (*s*) is linearly related to the year. Graph the ordered pairs (*y*, *s*). Draw the line of best fit and find an equation of the line. Use the equation to predict the record for the year 2000.

Speed	39	105	132	204	301	394	537
Year	1898	1904	1910	1927	1935	1947	1964

B

11. Solve, assuming a linear equation fits the situation. The value of a computer is $3500. After 2 years, the value of this computer is $2200. Find the value of the computer after 5 years.

12. Solve, assuming a linear equation fits the situation. The value of a new car is $14,000. Two years later, its value is $9000. What will be the value of this car after 5 years?

13. *Write a Convincing Argument* At the age of 8 years, a saguaro cactus is 7 ft tall. After 20 years, the cactus is 10 ft tall. Predict the height of the saguaro after 200 years. Assume a linear equation fits the situation to justify your prediction.

Challenge

14. An elevator has a capacity of 500 kg. Suppose an average child weighs 34 kg and an average adult weighs 75 kg. Find the combinations of adults and children that would exceed the weight limit of this elevator by no more than 50 kg.

15. The formula below gives an approximate value for the stopping distance (*d*), in feet, of a car traveling at speed (*s*), in miles per hour.

$$d = s + \frac{s^2}{20}$$

Find 6 ordered pairs that satisfy this relationship. Graph these ordered pairs. Is the relationship linear?

Use your work from Exercise 13 to estimate the age of a saguaro cactus that is 30 ft tall.

Mixed Review

Find the slope of each line.   **16.** $2y - 6x = 5$ **17.** $4x + y = 7$ *7-5*

Multiply.   **18.** $(x^3 - 2)(x^2 + 2)$ **19.** $3y^3(y^2 - 2y)$ **20.** $(a^2 - 2a)^2$ *5-9*

Factor.   **21.** $50y^4 - 72y^2$ **22.** $16 - 9m^2$ **23.** $ab + 3a - 6b - 18$ *6-2, 6-7*

Write an equation and solve.

24. One less than the square of a number is 143.

25. The product of two consecutive integers is 110.

26. Three times the difference of the square of a number and 1 is 72.   *6-9*

What You'll Learn

1 To determine whether the graphs of two equations are parallel

2 To determine whether the graphs of two equations are perpendicular

... And Why

To work with geometric relationships algebraically

Introducing the Concept: Slope and Line Relationships

Graph the following equations on the same set of axes.

$$y = 2x \qquad y = 2x + 3 \qquad y = 2x - 1$$

$$y = -\frac{1}{2}x \qquad y = -\frac{1}{2}x + 3 \qquad y = -\frac{1}{2}x - 1$$

What patterns do you see?

PART 1 Parallel Lines

Objective: Determine whether the graphs of two equations are parallel.

Parallel lines are lines in the same plane that never intersect. All vertical lines are parallel. Nonvertical lines that are parallel are precisely those that have the same slope and different y-intercepts (a theorem you will prove when you study geometry).

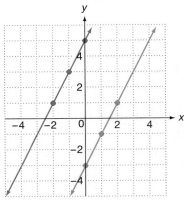

The graphs at the right are for the linear equations $y = 2x + 5$ and $y = 2x - 3$. The slope of each line is 2. The y-intercepts are 5 and -3. The lines are parallel.

EXAMPLE 1 Determine whether the graphs of $y = -3x + 4$ and $6x + 2y = -10$ are parallel lines.

We first solve each equation for y.

$$y = -3x + 4 \qquad 6x + 2y = -10$$

$$2y = -6x - 10$$

$$y = -3x - 5$$

The graphs of these lines have the same slope and different y-intercepts. Thus the lines are parallel.

Try This   Determine whether the graphs are parallel lines.

a. $3x - y = -5$ and $5y - 15x = 10$
b. $4y = -12x + 16$ and $y = 3x + 4$

Objective: Determine whether the graphs of two equations are perpendicular.

Perpendicular lines are lines that intersect to form a 90° angle (a right angle). A vertical line and a horizontal line are perpendicular. Other lines that are perpendicular are precisely those for which the product of their slopes is −1 (another theorem you will prove in geometry).

Another way to say this is that for perpendicular lines, the slope of one is the negative reciprocal of the slope of the other. For the graphs of the linear equations at the right, the slopes are 2 and $-\frac{1}{2}$. One slope is the negative reciprocal of the other. Their product is −1. The lines are perpendicular.

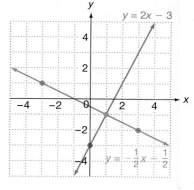

EXAMPLE 2 Tell whether the graphs of $3y = 9x + 3$ and $6y + 2x = 6$ are perpendicular lines.

We first solve for y in each equation to find the slopes.

$$3y = 9x + 3 \qquad\qquad 6y + 2x = 6$$
$$y = 3x + 1 \qquad\qquad 6y = -2x + 6$$
$$y = -\tfrac{1}{3}x + 1$$

The slopes are 3 and $-\frac{1}{3}$.

The product of the slopes of these lines is $3\left(-\frac{1}{3}\right) = -1$. Thus the lines are perpendicular.

Try This Tell whether the graphs of the equations are perpendicular.

c. $2y - x = 2$ and $y = -2x + 4$
d. $4y = 3x + 12$ and $-3x + 4y - 2 = 0$

EXAMPLE 3 Write an equation for the line containing $(1, 2)$ and perpendicular to the line $y = 3x - 1$.

The slope of the line $y = 3x - 1$ is 3. The negative reciprocal of 3 is $-\frac{1}{3}$.

$$y - y_1 = m(x - x_1) \qquad \text{Using the point-slope equation}$$
$$y - 2 = -\tfrac{1}{3}(x - 1) \qquad \text{Substituting } -\tfrac{1}{3} \text{ for } m \text{ and } (1, 2) \text{ for } (x_1, y_1)$$
$$y - 2 = -\tfrac{1}{3}x + \tfrac{1}{3}$$
$$y = -\tfrac{1}{3}x + \tfrac{7}{3}$$

Try This Write an equation for the line containing the given point and perpendicular to the given line.

e. $(0, 0)$; $y = 2x + 4$ **f.** $(-1, -3)$; $x + 2y = 8$

7-8 Exercises

A

Determine whether the graphs of the equations are parallel lines.

1. $x + 4 = y$
$y - x = -3$

2. $3x - 4 = y$
$y - 3x = 8$

3. $y + 3 = 6x$
$-6x - y = 2$

4. $y = -4x + 2$
$-5 = -2y + 8x$

5. $y = 2x + 7$
$5y + 10x = 20$

6. $y = -7x - 5$
$2y = -7x - 10$

7. $3x - y = -9$
$2y - 6x = -2$

8. $y - 6 = -6x$
$-2x + y = 5$

9. $-3x + y = 4$
$3x - y = -6$

10. $-4 = y + 2x$
$6x + 3y = 4$

11. $8x - 4y = 16$
$5y - 10x = 3$

12. $-4x = 3y + 5$
$8x + 6y = -1$

Determine whether the graphs of the equations are perpendicular lines.

13. $y = -4x + 3$
$4y + x = -1$

14. $y = -\frac{2}{3}x + 4$
$3x + 2y = 1$

15. $x + y = 6$
$4y - 4x = 12$

16. $2x - 5y = -3$
$5x + 2y = 6$

17. $y = -x + 8$
$x - y = -1$

18. $2x + 6y = -3$
$12y = 4x + 20$

19. $6x + y = -4$
$6x - y = 4$

20. $4y = x + 5$
$9y + 3x = 2$

21. $6y - x = -12$
$\frac{1}{6}x + y = 3$

22. $\frac{2}{3}x + y = 6$
$8y - 12x - 12 = 0$

23. $\frac{2}{5}x - \frac{1}{10}y = 20$
$5x + 10y = -5$

24. $\frac{1}{2}x + \frac{3}{4}y = 6$
$-\frac{3}{2}x + y = 4$

25. $\frac{3}{8}x - \frac{y}{2} = 1$
$\frac{4}{3}x - y + 1 = 0$

26. **TEST PREP** Are the graphs of $3x + 4y = 4$ and $4y = 3x + 4$ parallel, perpendicular, or neither?

     A. parallel   **B.** perpendicular   **C.** neither   **D.** Cannot tell.

B

Write an equation for the line containing the given point and perpendicular to the given line.

27. $(0, 6)$; $y - 3x = 4$

28. $(-2, 4)$; $y = 2x - 3$

29. $(0, 2)$; $3y - x = 0$

30. $(1, 0)$; $2x + y = -4$

31.–34. Write an equation for the line containing the given point and parallel to the given line in each of Exercises 27–30.

35. a. Write an equation for the line containing $(4, -1)$ and perpendicular to the line $x - 2y = 6$.

    b. *Write a Convincing Argument*   Can you write an equation for a line containing $(4, -1)$ and parallel to the line $x - 2y = 6$? Explain.

36. *Critical Thinking*   Write an equation of a line parallel to $ax + by = c$ and an equation of a line perpendicular to $ax + by = c$.

Challenge

37. Graph the line $y = 4x + 2$. Give the equations of three other lines that together with the line $y = 4x + 2$ would form a rectangle. Graph your rectangle.

38. Find the value of k so that the graphs of $4y = kx - 6$ and $5x + 20y = 12$ are parallel.

39. Using the same equations as in Exercise 38, find the value of k so that the graphs are perpendicular.

Assume the two lines are perpendicular. Find an equation for each line.

40.

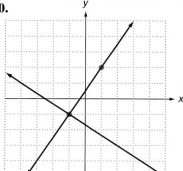

41.

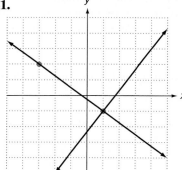

Mixed Review

Find the slope and y-intercept of each line.   **42.** $y = 3x + 5$

43. $2x + 4y = 5$ **44.** $6x = 2y + 3$ **45.** $6x = 3y - 2$

46. $5y - 3x = 15$ **47.** $2x = 3y + 4$ **48.** $3x + 4y = 8$ *7-5*

Write an equation in slope-intercept form for each line with the given slope and point.   **49.** $(1, 3), m = -2$ **50.** $(-1, 4), m = 9$ *7-6*

Factor.   **51.** $9a^2 - 49b^2$ **52.** $5x^2 + 70x + 245$

53. $2m^3 + 3m^2 - 18m - 27$ **54.** $3x^2 - 3x - 90$ *6-2, 6-5, 6-7*

Simplify.   **55.** $(3t^3)^2$ **56.** $(4ab^2c)(3abc^3)$ **57.** $(2x^2yz)(3x^3yz^2)$

58. $(y + 11)(y - 11) + 121$ **59.** $(2x + y)(3x + 3y)$ *5-2, 5-9*

7-9 ▷ Proofs

Objective: Prove theorems related to slope.

What You'll Learn

1 To prove theorems related to slope

... And Why

To give structure to convincing arguments

A proof is a convincing argument that a statement is true. Before writing a proof, we must organize our ideas and see exactly what we want to prove.

We have stated (Lesson 7-5) that in the equation $y = mx + b$, m is the slope. Before writing a proof of this statement, we must think about what it means to prove that m is the slope.

We know the definition, slope $= \dfrac{\text{change in } y}{\text{change in } x}$.

We must show that the m-value in $y = mx + b$ is also $\dfrac{\text{change in } y}{\text{change in } x}$.

Prove: The m-value in $y = mx + b$ is also $\dfrac{\text{change in } y}{\text{change in } x}$.

Consider any linear equation $y = mx + b$. Suppose that (x_1, y_1) and (x_2, y_2) are any two points on the line. Then, since each of these points must satisfy the equation, we have the two equations

$$y_2 = mx_2 + b \quad \text{and} \quad y_1 = mx_1 + b$$

(Our strategy will be to work with these two equations and to try to show $m = \dfrac{y_2 - y_1}{x_2 - x_1}$.)

From the second equation we know that y_1 and $mx_1 + b$ are the same number. Thus $-y_1$ and $-(mx_1 + b)$ are also the same number. We add this number to both sides of the first equation.

$$y_2 - y_1 = (mx_2 + b) - (mx_1 + b)$$
$$y_2 - y_1 = mx_2 - mx_1 \qquad \text{Simplifying}$$
$$y_2 - y_1 = m(x_2 - x_1) \qquad \text{Factoring out } m$$

$$\dfrac{y_2 - y_1}{x_2 - x_1} = m \qquad \text{Solving for } m$$

Since $\dfrac{y_2 - y_1}{x_2 - x_1}$ is the $\dfrac{\text{change in } y}{\text{change in } x}$ for the given two points, then the m-value in

$y = mx + b$ is also $\dfrac{\text{change in } y}{\text{change in } x}$.

Try This

a. Write a proof to show that in the equation $y = mx + b$, b is the y-intercept. (Hint: Think about what is true of a y-intercept.)

In Lesson 7-4, we stated that a horizontal line has slope 0. Before we begin to write the proof, we think about horizontal lines. On any horizontal line, all points have the same y-coordinate. This is the key to the proof. We want to show that for a horizontal line, slope = 0.

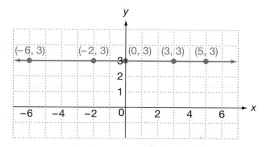

Prove: For a horizontal line, slope = 0

Consider any horizontal line. Suppose that (x_1, y_1) and (x_2, y_2) are any two points on the line. Then,

$$\text{slope} = \frac{y_2 - y_1}{x_2 - x_1}$$

Since the y-coordinates are the same,

$$\text{slope} = \frac{y_2 - y_1}{x_2 - x_1} = \frac{0}{x_2 - x_1} = 0$$

Try This

b. Prove that a vertical line has no slope. (Hint: Think about the coordinates of the points on a vertical line and division by 0.)

7-9 Exercises

Extra Help On the Web

Look for worked-out examples at the Prentice Hall Web site.
www.phschool.com

A

1. Prove the point-slope equation property of Lesson 7-6. (Hint: Show that any point (x_2, y_2) on the line described must satisfy the equation, and that any point satisfying the equation must be on the line described.)

2. Prove that if a line has slope m and y-intercept b, then an equation of the line is $y = mx + b$. (Hint: Use the point-slope equation theorem.)

Mixed Review

Identify the degree of each term and the degree of the polynomial.

3. $c^2 - 25$ 4. $3a^4b^2 + 21b^4 - 11a$ 5. $a^3b^2c - 4c^3$ *5-5*
Give the additive inverse.   6. $ax^2 + bx + c$ 7. $35 - 8c$ 8. $y - 9$ *2-3, 5-8*
Find three factorizations for each monomial.   9. $3a^3$ 10. $15a^2b$ *6-1*
Find three solutions of the equation.   11. $4y - x = 1$ *7-2*
Factor.   12. $4a^2b + 2a$ 13. $4y^2 - 9$ 14. $10c^2 + 28c - 6$ *6-1, 6-2, 6-5*

7-10 ▷ Reasoning Strategies

What You'll Learn

1 To solve problems using the strategy *Simplify the Problem* and other strategies

... And Why

To increase efficiency in solving problems by applying reasoning skills

PART 1 Simplify the Problem

Objective: Solve problems using the strategy *Simplify the Problem* and other strategies.

A problem that may seem difficult because of the large numbers involved can be solved more easily using a strategy called Simplify the Problem. A problem can be *simplified* by substituting smaller numbers. You may need to solve a series of simpler problems, each one with progressively larger numbers. Organizing the information in a *table* can help you find a pattern and the solution to the original problem.

EXAMPLE

How many phone lines are needed to connect the 10 buildings at the right? A separate line must be used to connect each pair of buildings.

Simplify the problem by determining how many lines are needed to connect 2 buildings, then 3 buildings, and so on. *Drawing a diagram, making a table,* and *looking for a pattern* are other strategies used.

2 bldgs.
1 line

3 bldgs.
3 lines

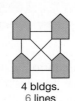
4 bldgs.
6 lines

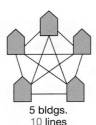
5 bldgs.
10 lines

Quick *Review*

Making a conclusion based on what you observe is inductive reasoning. See page 193.

Number of buildings	Number of lines
2	1
3	3 = 1 + 2
4	6 = 1 + 2 + 3
5	10 = 1 + 2 + 3 + 4

Organizing the data in the table helps you see a *pattern*. For n buildings, there will be a total of $1 + 2 + 3 + \ldots + (n - 1)$ lines. Thus for 10 buildings there will be a total of $1 + 2 + 3 + \ldots + 9 = 45$ lines.

344 Chapter 7 *Graphs and Linear Equations*

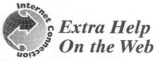

Extra Help
On the Web

Look for worked-out
examples at the Prentice
Hall Web site.
www.phschool.com

Reasoning Strategies

Draw a Diagram	Try, Test, Revise	Write an Equation
Make an Organized List	Use Logical Reasoning	Make a Table
Look for a Pattern	Simplify the Problem	Work Backward

7-10 Problems

Solve using one or more of the strategies.

1. The figure at the right was made with 4 triangles.
An architect made a long figure like this using 70
triangles. Each side of each triangle is 1 meter
long. What is the perimeter of the figure made with 70 triangles?

2. There were 12 teams in a soccer tournament. When a team lost, it was
eliminated from the tournament and it played no more games. How many
games were needed to determine a champion?

3. Three men and three women signed up for mixed-doubles tennis. In mixed
doubles, a team consists of 1 man and 1 woman. How many different
matches could be made with different mixed-doubles teams?

4. A bank has checkbook covers that are either pocket or desk size. The
covers can be orange, black, red, or tan. The customer's name will be
stamped on the cover in gold or silver. How many different choices are
available for checkbook covers?

5. Half of all baseball fans in a survey are also soccer fans. Half of all football
fans in this survey are also baseball fans. No football fan is a soccer fan. All
soccer fans are also baseball fans. There are 20 soccer fans and 30 football
fans. How many baseball fans are neither soccer fans nor football fans?

6. The Windsville Park District used a pneumatic pump to pump water into a
reservoir from a nearby river. Each day the pump raised the water level
2 m, but at night the water leaked back into the river and the level of the
reservoir dropped 50 cm. At this rate, how many days did it take the pump
to fill the reservoir to a height of 15 m?

7. *Write a Convincing Argument* How many
different squares are there in a 7-by-7 grid? Justify
your answer.

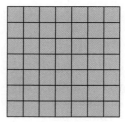

8. *Error Analysis* To evaluate $\frac{\pi}{1.344 - 4.265}$ on
her calculator, Julie couldn't remember whether the
denominator needed parentheses. She entered the
simpler form 3/1 − 4 and got −1. She concluded that
she didn't need parentheses. What was Julie's error?

Compound Interest

Interest is a charge for the use of money. When you borrow money, either by taking out a loan or by making purchases on a credit card or installment plan, you pay interest to the lender. When you put money in a savings account, the bank pays you interest for the use of your money. The amount invested or loaned is called the *principal*. The *interest rate* is given as a percent. Simple interest is interest computed on the principal alone. Today, we deal mostly with *compound interest,* or interest figured on both the principal and previously accumulated interest. Compound interest is found by the formula

$$A = P\left(1 + \frac{r}{n}\right)^{nt}$$

where principal P is invested at interest rate r compounded n times per year. In t years P will grow to amount A. The product nt is the total number of payment periods.

Suppose you invest $1000 at 8% interest. How much will be in the account at the end of 3 years if the interest is compounded

a. annually? **b.** quarterly? **c.** daily?

a. $A = P\left(1 + \frac{r}{n}\right)^{nt} = \$1000\left(1 + \frac{0.08}{1}\right)^3$

$= \$1000(1.08)^3 \approx \$1259.71$

b. $A = P\left(1 + \frac{r}{n}\right)^{nt} = \$1000\left(1 + \frac{0.08}{4}\right)^{4\times3}$

$= \$1000(1 + 0.02)^{12}$

$= \$1000(1.02)^{12} \approx \$1268.24$

c. $A = P\left(1 + \frac{r}{n}\right)^{nt} = \$1000\left(1 + \frac{0.08}{365}\right)^{365\times3}$

$\approx \$1000(1 + 0.000219)^{1095}$

$= \$1000(1.000219)^{1095} \approx \$1270.97$

Problem

Suppose you invest $10,000 for 2 years at an interest rate of 11%. How much will be in the account if interest is compounded:

a. annually? **b.** semiannually? **c.** quarterly?
d. monthly? **e.** daily? **f.** hourly?

▷ **Chapter Wrap Up**

7-1

On a plane, each point is the graph of an ordered pair. The numbers in the ordered pair are called **coordinates.** The first number in the pair, the **x-coordinate,** tells the distance right or left from the y-axis. The second number, the **y-coordinate,** tells the distance up or down from the x-axis.

Plot these points on graph paper.

1. $(2, 5)$ 2. $(0, -3)$
3. $(-4, -2)$ 4. $(5, 0)$
5. $(4, -3)$ 6. $(-4, 3)$

In which **quadrant** is each point located?

7. $(3, -8)$ 8. $(-20, -14)$
9. $(4.9, 1.3)$ 10. $(-1, 12)$

Find the coordinates of each point.

11. A 12. B 13. C

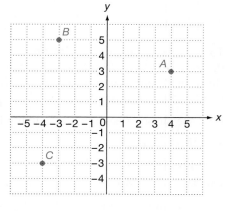

7-2

An ordered pair of numbers is a solution of an equation if the numbers make the equation true when the numbers are substituted for the variables.

Determine whether the given point is a solution of $3x + y = 4$.

14. $(0, 4)$ 15. $(1, -1)$

Make a table of solutions and draw a **graph** of each equation.

16. $2x - y = 1$ 17. $y - 5 = 2x$

7-3

An equation whose graph is a straight line is called a **linear equation.** Its **standard form** is $Ax + By = C$ (A and B not both 0). To graph a linear equation, plot two points (ordered pairs) and draw the line that contains the two points. Use a third point to check. The **x-intercept** of a line is the x-coordinate of the point where the line crosses the x-axis. To find the x-intercept, let $y = 0$ and solve for x. The **y-intercept** of a line is the y-coordinate of the point where the line crosses the y-axis. To find the y-intercept, let $x = 0$ and solve for y.

Graph using intercepts.

18. $2x - 7y = 14$ 19. $3x - 2y = -6$

Graph.

20. $y = -4$ 21. $x = 7$

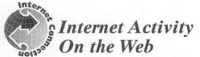

7-4

The **slope** of a line is a ratio that describes which way the line slants and how steep it is.

$$m = \text{slope} = \frac{\textbf{rise}}{\textbf{run}} = \frac{y_2 - y_1}{x_2 - x_1}$$

A horizontal line has a slope of 0 and a vertical line has no slope.

Find the slopes, if they exist, of the lines containing these points.

22. $(6, 8)\ (-2, -4)$ **23.** $(5, 1)\ (-1, 1)$

24. $(-3, 0)\ (-3, 5)$ **25.** $(3, 4)\ (5, -8)$

7-5

To find the slope and the y-intercept of a line from its equation, solve the equation for y to get the form $y = mx + b$. This is called the **slope-intercept equation.** The coefficient of the x-term, m, is the slope, and b is the y-intercept.

Find the slope of each line by solving for y.

26. $3x - 2y = -6$ **27.** $5x + 3y = 4$

Find the slope and y-intercept of each line.

28. $3x - 5y = 4$ **29.** $2x = 6y + 12$

Graph each line using the y-intercept and slope.

30. $y = -x + 5$ **31.** $y = \frac{3}{5}x - 2$ **32.** $y - \frac{3}{4}x = 0$

7-6

If you know the slope, m, and the y-intercept, b, of a line, you can use the slope-intercept equation for the line, $y = mx + b$, to find the equation of the line. If you know the slope, m, and a point on the line, (x_1, y_1), you can use the **point-slope equation,** $y - y_1 = m(x - x_1)$, to find an equation of the line. If you know two points on the line, first find the slope and then use the point-slope equation.

Write an equation for the line with each given slope and y-intercept.

33. $m = 3$, y-intercept $= -4$ **34.** $m = 5$, y-intercept $= 0$

Write an equation for the line with each given point and slope.

35. $(1, 2), m = 3$ **36.** $(0, 4), m = -2$ **37.** $(-2, 4), m = -\frac{1}{2}$

Write an equation for the line that contains each given pair of points.

38. $(5, 7)\ (-1, 1)$ **39.** $(2, 0)\ (-4, -3)$

Write an equation for each line in slope-intercept form.

40.

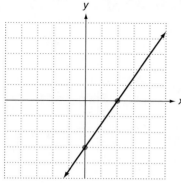

41.

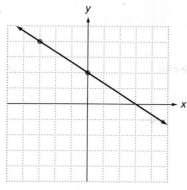

7-7

In real-world situations, the relationship between two variables can sometimes be expressed as a particular linear equation whose graph is the **line of best fit.** You can then use the linear equation to solve problems involving a prediction between two variables.

Solve.

A temperature of 59°F equals 15°C. A temperature of 68°F equals 20°C.

42. Find the linear equation with ordered pairs (F, C) for these data points.

43. Use this linear equation to find the Celsius temperature when it is 77°F.

7-8

Two nonvertical lines are **parallel** if they have the same slope and different y-intercepts. Two lines are **perpendicular** if the product of their slopes is -1.

Determine whether the graphs of the equations are parallel.

44. $y - 5 = -2x$
$y + 2x = -3$

45. $y = 3x - 4$
$y + 3x = 2$

Determine whether the graphs of the equations are perpendicular.

46. $y = \frac{2}{3}x$
$2y = -3x + 8$

47. $6y = -x + 18$
$y = -6x - 4$

Determine whether the graphs of the equations are parallel, perpendicular, or neither.

48. $4x + y = 6$
$4x + y = 8$

49. $2x + y = 10$
$y = \frac{1}{2}x - 4$

50. $x + 4y = 8$
$x = -4y - 10$

51. $3x - y = 6$
$3x + y = 8$

Use graph paper to plot these points.

1. $(-5, 3)$ **2.** $(0, -4)$

In which quadrant is each point located?

3. $(-1, -4)$ **4.** $(-1, 8)$

Find the coordinates of each point.

5. A **6.** B **7.** C **8.** D

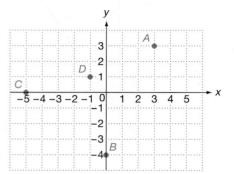

Determine whether the given point is a solution of $2x + 3y = 12$.

9. $(2, 3)$ **10.** $(3, 2)$

11. Make a table of solutions and graph $3x + y = 10$.

12. Use intercepts to graph $2x - 3y = -6$.

Graph.

13. $x = 8$ **14.** $y = -2$

Find the slopes, if they exist, of the lines containing these points.

15. $(9, 2)$ $(-3, -5)$ **16.** $(4, 7)$ $(4, -1)$

Use the equation $-4x + 3y = -6$.

17. Find the slope and y-intercept.   **18.** Graph the equation.

Write an equation for the line containing the given point and having the given slope.

19. $(3, 5)$ $m = 1$ **20.** $(-2, 0)$ $m = -3$

Write an equation for the line containing the two given points.

21. $(1, 1)$ $(2, -2)$ **22.** $(4, -1)$ $(-4, -3)$

When an electronics company produces 1000 chips, it makes a profit of $10 per unit. When it produces 5000 chips, the company makes a profit of $30 per unit. Assume that a linear relationship fits these data.

23. Find the linear equation that fits these data.

24. Use the linear equation to predict the profit per unit if the company produced 10,000 chips.

Determine whether the lines are parallel, perpendicular, or neither.

25. $2x + y = 8$ **26.** $2x + 5y = 2$ **27.** $x + 2y = 8$

      $2x + y = 4$ $y = 2x + 4$ $-2x + y = 8$

1-7 ▷ Cumulative Review

1-1   Evaluate.

1. $y + 6 + y$ for $y = 8$

2. $\frac{x}{18}$ for $x = 24$

1-2

3. Use a commutative property to write three equivalent expressions for $4x + 3y$.

Simplify

4. $\frac{16}{48}$

5. $\frac{q}{12pq}$

6. $\frac{51s}{3st}$

1-3, 1-4   Evaluate.

7. $x^2 - 5$ for $x = 3$

8. $(4y)^3$ for $y = 3$

9. $(y - 1)^2$ for $y = 6$

1-5   Use the distributive property to write an equivalent expression.

10. $3(2x + y)$

11. $4(3x + 4y + z)$

Collect like terms.

12. $7a + 7b + a + 7c$

13. $6x^2 + 2y + 2z + 3x^2$

1-6   Write as an algebraic expression.

14. 7 less than twice y

15. the difference of x and three times y

16. Let s be Shawn's age 5 years ago. Write an expression for Shawn's age now.

1-7   State whether each sentence is true, false, or open.

17. a. $15x + 325 = 90$ **b.** $9 \cdot 8 - 5 = 27$ **c.** $12x - 5x = 7$

Solve for the given replacement set.

18. $x + 2.7 = 8.5$ $\{5.4, 5.8, 6.2\}$ **19.** $112t = 4256$ $\{35, 37\}$

1-9   Evaluate.

20. $D = rt$ for $r = 55$ mi/h and $t = 270$ min

21. $F = \frac{9}{5}C + 32$ for $C = 15°$

2-1   Use $>$, $<$, or $=$ to write a true sentence.

22. $-10 \ \square \ -14$ **23.** $-3.1 \ \square \ -3.15$ **24.** $0.01 \ \square \ 0.1$

25. $-\frac{2}{3} \ \square \ -\frac{3}{4}$ **26.** $\frac{7}{8} \ \square \ \frac{8}{9}$ **27.** $\frac{-4}{10} \ \square \ \frac{5}{7}$

Find the absolute value.

28. $|-18|$ **29.** $|25|$

2-3, 2-4   Add or subtract.

30. $-\frac{1}{2} + \frac{3}{8} + (-6) + \frac{3}{4}$ **31.** $-2.6 + (-7.5) + 2.6 + (-7.5)$

32. $-6.1 - (-3.1) + 7.9 - 3.1 + 1.8$ **33.** $-\frac{5}{9} - \frac{2}{18}$

2-5   Multiply.

34. $\left(-\frac{2}{3}\right)\left(\frac{18}{15}\right)$ **35.** $\frac{3}{5}\left(-\frac{3}{5}\right)\left(-\frac{25}{9}\right)$ **36.** $-2(-7)(-3)$

2-6   Divide.

37. $-\frac{4}{3} \div \frac{-2}{9}$ **38.** $-6.262 \div 1.01$ **39.** $-\frac{72}{108} \div -\frac{2}{3}$

2-7   Factor.

40. $121x - 55$ **41.** $-6 - 2x - 12y$

2-8   Simplify.

42. $-8x - (9 - 4x)$ **43.** $-2(y + 3) - 3y$

2-10   Name the following properties.

44. $a + (-a) = 0$ **45.** $a(b + c) = ab + ac$

3-1 to 3-3   Solve.

46. $x - \frac{3}{8} = \frac{1}{2}$ **47.** $-3.2 = y - 5.8$ **48.** $-\frac{2}{3} = x - \frac{8}{12}$

49. $-4x = -18$ **50.** $-\frac{x}{3} = -16$ **51.** $-\frac{5}{6} = x - \frac{1}{3}$

52. $6y + 3 = -15$ **53.** $3(x - 2) = 24$ **54.** $-2(x - 4) = 10$

3-4, 3-11   Write an equation and solve.

55. Twelve computer disks cost \$9. How much does one disk cost?

56. The number of girls in the band is one more than twice the number of boys. There are 19 students in the band. How many are boys?

3-5, 3-6 Solve.

57. $9(t + 2) = 5(t - 3)$

58. $4 + 3x - 2 = 5x + 8 - x$

59. $\frac{5}{3} + \frac{2}{3}x = \frac{13}{12} + \frac{5}{4}x + \frac{3}{4}$

60. $\frac{1}{3}x - \frac{2}{9} = \frac{2}{3} + \frac{4}{9}x$

3-7 Solve.

61. $C = 2\pi r$ for r

3-8 Solve.

62. $4|x| = 28$

63. $|x| - 16 = 45$

3-9 Solve these proportions.

64. $\frac{24}{x} = \frac{8}{3}$

65. $\frac{12}{15} = \frac{t}{35}$

3-10 Translate to an equation and solve.

66. What is the interest on $300 at 6% for one year?

67. A football quarterback completes 21 passes out of a total of 35. What percent are completed?

4-1 Determine whether the given number is a solution of the inequality $x \geq -5$.

68. a. -2 **b.** 0 **c.** -8

4-2 to 4-5 Solve and graph the solution.

69. $4y + 4 - 2y \leq 12$

70. $4x + 3 - 3x > 2$

71. $-2y > 3$

72. $6 - 5y > 8 - 4y$

73. The sum of three consecutive odd integers is less than 100. Find the set of the largest of three such numbers.

5-1, 5-2 Simplify.

74. $x^8 \cdot x^2$

75. $\frac{z^4}{z^7}$

76. $(4y^3)^2$

77. $(3x^2y)^3$

5-3 Multiply.

78. $(-2x)(4x^3)$

79. $(3b^2c^3)(-4bc^4)(-2b^2)$

Divide.

80. $\dfrac{-25n^6}{-5n^3}$ **81.** $\dfrac{-48m^6n^8}{8m^4n^8}$ **82.** $\dfrac{36a^4b^7}{-3a^6b^2}$ **83.** $\dfrac{4p^2r^4}{12p^5r^9}$

5-4 Write in scientific notation.

84. 248,000 **85.** 0.0000375

5-5, 5-6 Collect like terms and arrange in descending order for x.

86. $-3x^2 + 4x - 5x^3 - 6x^2 + 2 - 3x$

87. $2x^3 - 7 + 3x^2 - 6x^3 - 4x^2 + 5$

Evaluate.

88. $x^2 - 6x + 8$ for $x = 4$

5-7 Add.

89. $(3x^4 + 2x^3 - 6x^2) + (-2x^4 - 3x^2 - 7)$

90. $(a^4b^2 - 3a^2b + 4b^3) + (5a^4b^2 + 6a^2b - 9b^3)$

5-8 Subtract.

91. $(-8y^2 - y + 2) - (-y^3 - 6y^2 + y - 5)$

92. $(14v^3u + 4u^2 - 3v^2) - (8v^3u - 6u^2 + 5v^2)$

5-9 to 5-11 Multiply.

93. $4x^3(2x^2 - x + 7)$ **94.** $(2x - 5)(3x + 4)$

95. $(xy - 7y^2)(xy + 7y^2)$ **96.** $3m(-m^7 + 4m^2n + 3n^3)$

97. $(2a - 5b)^2$ **98.** $(4x - 5y)(x + 6y)$

99. $(1 - 3x^2)(2 - 4x^2)$ **100.** $(2x^5 + 3)(3x^2 - 6)$

101. $(2x^3 + 1)(2x^3 - 1)$ **102.** $(8x + 3)^2$

103. $(6x - 5)^2$ **104.** $(4x^3 - x + 1)(x - 1)$

6-1 to 6-7 Factor.

105. $x^2 - 4x$ **106.** $6x^5 - 36x^3 + 9x^2$

107. $12x - 4x^2 - 48x^4$ **108.** $9x^2 - 1$

109. $2x^2 - 8$ **110.** $16x^4 - 81$

111. $x^2 - 14x + 49$ **112.** $16x^2 + 40x + 25$

113. $x^2 - 8xy + 16y^2$ **114.** $c^2 - 7cd + 6d^2$

115. $18x^2 - 48x + 32$ **116.** $x^2 - 10x + 24$

117. $x^2 - 2x - 35$ **118.** $x^3 - 4x^2 - 21x$

119. $8x^2 + 10x + 3$ **120.** $3x^2 + 10x - 8$

Factor.

121. $6x^2 - 28x + 16$

122. $x^3 + x^2 + 2x + 2$

123. $x^4 + 2x^3 - 3x - 6$

124. $3 - 12x^6$

125. $x^2 + 5x + xy + 5y$

126. $am + an - bm - bn$

6-8   Solve for x.

127. $x^2 + 4x - 12 = 0$

128. $2x^2 + 7x - 4 = 0$

6-9   Solve.

129. The product of two consecutive even integers is 224. Find the integers.

7-1   In which quadrant is each point located?

130. $(4, 3)$

131. $(-2, 7)$

132. $(4, -9)$

7-2   Graph the equations. Make a table of solutions.

133. $3x - y = 2$

134. $y - 4 = 3x$

7-3   Graph the equations. Use intercepts.

135. $3y = x + 6$

136. $2x = 3y + 9$

7-4   Find the slopes of the lines containing these points.

137. $(0, -3)$ and $(4, 0)$

138. $(2, 2)$ and $(-1, 8)$

7-5   Find the slope and y-intercept of each line.

139. $2y = -4x + 8$

140. $4x = 9y - 7$

7-6   Write an equation for each line.

141. $m = -1$, y-intercept $= 3$

142. $m = 5$, passes through $(5, 2)$

143. $m = \frac{2}{3}$, passes through $(2, 5)$

144. contains points $(6, 4)$ and $(-2, 0)$

7-8   Determine whether the graphs of the equations are parallel or perpendicular lines.

145. $y = -\frac{1}{2}x - \frac{1}{2}$, $-2y = x + 6$

146. $6x + y = -4$, $6y = x + 8$

CHAPTER **8**

Skills & Concepts You Need for Chapter 8

3-1 to 3-3 Solve.

1. $y + 3 = -2$ **2.** $9y = 2$

3. $-3x + 2 = -10$ **4.** $3x + 4 = 19$

5. $6x + 2x = 45$ **6.** $-7y - 8y = -30$

3-4 Write as an algebraic expression.

7. 8 more than twice a number

8. the value of x dimes plus the value of y nickels

3-5 Solve.

9. $6x + 5 = 2x + 13$ **10.** $9(t + 2) = 6(t - 2)$

5-6 Evaluate each polynomial for $w = -2$.

11. $3 + 4w$ **12.** $-7w - 8$ **13.** $w^2 - 2w + 3$

7-2

14. Determine whether $(3, -2)$ is a solution of $y = 4x - 14$.

15. Determine whether $(-1, 5)$ is a solution of $y = -3x - 2$.

Find three solutions of each equation.

16. $y = 3x - 1$ **17.** $2w + 4x = -7$ **18.** $-4y - 2z = 10$

7-3, 7-5 Graph the following equations.

19. $2x - 4y = 1$ **20.** $-x + 3y = 5$

21. $y = -2$ **22.** $x = 5$

Systems of Equations

To make his nonstop transatlantic flight in this plane, Charles Lindbergh had to make careful calculations about the distance, average speed, time, and amount of fuel needed. In Lesson 8-5 you will learn how to solve problems involving distance, rate, and time.

8-1 ▷ Solving Systems of Equations by Graphing

What You'll Learn

1 To determine whether an ordered pair is a solution of a system of equations

2 To find the solution of a system of equations by graphing

... And Why

To be able to solve real-world problems using algebraic reasoning skills

Introducing the Concept: Intersections of Graphs

Graph each set of equations on separate coordinate axes. For each set, how many solutions do the two equations have in common?

Set 1: $2x + 3y = 12$
$x - 4y = -5$

Set 2: $x = 2y + 1$
$3x - 6y = 9$

Set 3: $2x = 4 - y$
$6x + 3y = 12$

PART 1 Identifying Solutions

Objective: Determine whether an ordered pair is a solution of a system of equations.

A set of equations for which a common solution is sought is called a **system of equations.** A **solution** of a system of two equations in two variables is an ordered pair that makes both equations true. Since the solution of a system satisfies both equations simultaneously, we say that we have a system of simultaneous equations. When we find all the solutions of a system, we say that we have solved the system.

EXAMPLES

1 Determine whether $(1, 2)$ is a solution of the system.

$$y = x + 1$$
$$2x + y = 4$$

$y = x + 1$		$2x + y = 4$	
2	$1 + 1$	$2(1) + 2$	4
2	2 ✔	$2 + 2$	4
		4	4 ✔

$(1, 2)$ is a solution of the system.

Reading Math

In the ordered pair (–3, 2), –3 is the replacement for *a* and 2 is the replacement for *b*. The numbers in an ordered pair are in the alphabetical order of the variables.

2 Determine whether $(-3, 2)$ is a solution of the system.

$$a + b = -1$$
$$b + 3a = 4$$

$a + b = -1$		$b + 3a = 4$	
$-3 + 2$	-1	$2 + 3(-3)$	4
-1	-1 ✔	$2 - 9$	4
		-7	4

Since $(-3, 2)$ is not a solution of $b + 3a = 4$, it is not a solution of the system.

Try This Determine whether the given ordered pair is a solution of the system.

a. $(2, -3); x = 2y + 8$
$ 2x + y = 1$

b. $(20, 40); a = \frac{1}{4}b + 10$
$ b - a = -20$

Objective: Find the solution of a system of equations by graphing.

One way to solve a system of equations is to graph the equations and find the coordinates of the point(s) of intersection. Since the point, or points, of intersection are on both graphs, these ordered pairs are the solutions of the system.

EXAMPLE 3 Solve by graphing.

$$x + 2y = 7$$
$$x = y + 4$$

We graph the equations using any of the methods learned in Chapter 7. Point P appears to have coordinates $(5, 1)$.

Check $x = 5$ and $y = 1$ in *both* equations.

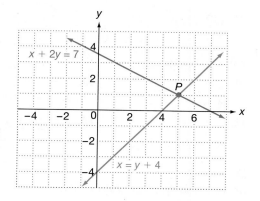

$$
\begin{array}{c|c}
x + 2y = 7 & \\
\hline
5 + 2(1) & 7 \\
7 & 7 \checkmark
\end{array}
\qquad
\begin{array}{c|c}
x = y + 4 & \\
\hline
5 & 1 + 4 \\
5 & 5 \checkmark
\end{array}
$$

$(5, 1)$ is the solution of the system.

When we graph a system of two linear equations, one of three things may happen.

1. The lines have one point of intersection. The point of intersection is the *only solution* of the system.

2. The lines are parallel. If this is so, there is no point that satisfies both equations. The system has *no solution.*

3. The lines coincide. Thus the equations have the same graph, and every solution of one equation is a solution of the other. There is an *infinite number of solutions.*

Try This Solve by graphing.

c. $x + 4y = -6$
$2x - 3y = -1$

d. $y + 2x = 5$
$2y - 5x = 10$

e. $y - 2x = 7$
$y = 2x + 8$

f. $3y - 2x = 6$
$4x - 6y = -12$

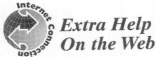

8-1 Exercises

A
Determine whether the given ordered pair is a solution of the system of equations.

1. $(3, 2); 2x + 3y = 12$
$x - 4y = -5$

2. $(1, 5); 5x - 2y = -5$
$3x - 7y = -32$

3. $(3, 2); 3t - 2s = 0$
$t + 2s = 15$

4. $(2, -2); b + 2a = 2$
$b - a = -4$

5. $(-1, 1); x = -1$
$x - y = -2$

6. $(-3, 4); 2x = -y - 2$
$y = -4$

7. $(12, 3); y = \frac{1}{4}x$
$3x - y = 33$

8. $(-3, 1); y = -\frac{1}{3}x$
$3y = -5x - 12$

Solve by graphing.

9. $x + y = 3$
$x - y = 1$

10. $x - y = 2$
$x + y = 6$

11. $x + 2y = 10$
$3x + 4y = 8$

12. $-3x = 5 - y$
$2y = 6x + 10$

13. $a = \frac{1}{2}b + 1$
$a - 2b = -2$

14. $x = \frac{1}{3}y + 2$
$-2x - y = 1$

B
Solve these systems graphically.

15. $y = 3$
$x = 5$

16. $x = 4$
$3y - 2x = 1$

17. $y = 3x$
$y = -3x + 2$

18. $x + y = 9$
$3x + 3y = 27$

19. $x + y = 4$
$x + y = -4$

20. $y = 2x - 1$
$y - 2x = 3$

21. A system of equations that has one or more solutions is called **consistent.** Which systems of equations in Exercises 9–20 are consistent?

22. A system of equations that has infinitely many solutions is called consistent and **dependent.** Which systems of equations in Exercises 9–20 are dependent?

23. A system of equations that has no solution is called **inconsistent.** Which systems of equations in Exercises 9–20 are inconsistent?

24. **TEST PREP**   Here are graphs of three systems of equations. Which of the systems are consistent?

I. 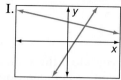   II. 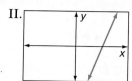   III.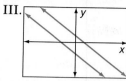

A. I only   **B.** I and II   **C.** I and III   **D.** II and III

25. Estimate the solutions to the system of equations below by studying the graph at the right. Check your solutions using substitution in both equations.

$$y = -2x^2 + 4x + 1$$
$$y = x^2 - 2x + 1$$

26. *Critical Thinking*   The solution of the following system is $(2, -3)$. Find A and B.

$$Ax - 3y = 13$$
$$x - By = 8$$

Challenge

27. Solve this system by graphing. What happens when you check your possible solution?

$$3x + 7y = 5$$
$$6x - 7y = 1$$

28. Find a system of equations with $(2, -4)$ as the solution.

29. Find an equation to go with $5x + 2y = 11$ so that the solution to the system of equations is $(3, -2)$.

Mixed Review

Find the slope and y-intercept.   **30.** $x - y = 3$ **31.** $2x = y + 1$ *7-5*

Write an equation in slope-intercept form   **32.** for the line with $m = -3$, y-intercept $= 2$ **33.** for the line that contains $(2, 4)$ and $(0, -2)$ *7-6*

Factor. **34.** $4a^2 - 14a - 18$ **35.** $y^3 + 2y^2 + 5y$ **36.** $16m^4 - 1$ *6-2, 6-5, 6-7*

Solve.   **37.** $m^2 + 5m - 14 = 0$ **38.** $2x^2 - 9x - 5 = 0$ *6-8*

39. The difference of the squares of two consecutive odd positive integers is 40. Find the integers.   *6-9*

8-2 ▷ The Substitution Method

What You'll Learn

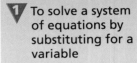 To solve a system of equations by substituting for a variable

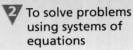 To solve problems using systems of equations

. . . And Why

To be able to solve real-world problems using algebraic reasoning skills

Solving systems of equations by graphing is often not accurate if the solutions are not integers. There are several methods for solving systems of equations without graphing. One of these is called the **substitution method.**

PART 1 | Substituting for a Variable

Objective: Solve a system of equations by substituting for a variable.

If a variable in one equation of a system of equations is alone on one side of the equation, you can substitute for that variable in the other equation.

EXAMPLE 1   Solve using the substitution method.

$$x + y = 6$$
$$x = y + 2$$

The second equation states that x and $y + 2$ are equivalent expressions. Thus in the first equation, we can substitute $y + 2$ for x.

$$x + y = 6$$
$$y + 2 + y = 6 \qquad \text{Substituting } y + 2 \text{ for } x \text{ in the first equation}$$

Since this equation now has only one variable, we can solve for y.

$$2y + 2 = 6 \qquad \text{Collecting like terms}$$
$$2y = 4$$
$$y = 2$$

Next substitute 2 for y in either of the original equations.

$$x + y = 6$$
$$x + 2 = 6 \qquad \text{Substituting 2 for } y$$
$$x = 4$$

We check $x = 4$ and $y = 2$ in *both* equations.

$$\begin{array}{c|c} x + y = 6 \\ \hline 4 + 2 & 6 \\ & 6 \mid 6 \checkmark \end{array} \qquad \begin{array}{c|c} x = y + 2 \\ \hline 4 & 2 + 2 \\ 4 \mid 4 \checkmark \end{array}$$

The solution of the system is $(4, 2)$.

Try This   Solve using the substitution method.

a. $x + y = 5$ **b.** $a - b = 4$ **c.** $y = x + 2$
      $x = y + 1$ $b = 2 - 5a$ $y = 2x - 1$

Sometimes neither equation has a variable alone on one side. We can solve one equation for one of the variables and proceed as before.

EXAMPLE 2 Solve using the substitution method.

$$x - 2y = 6$$
$$3x + 2y = 4$$

Solve the first equation for x.

$$x = 6 + 2y$$

Substitute $6 + 2y$ for x in the second equation.

$$3(6 + 2y) + 2y = 4$$
$$18 + 6y + 2y = 4$$
$$18 + 8y = 4$$
$$8y = -14$$
$$y = -\frac{7}{4}$$

We go back to either of the original equations and substitute $-\frac{7}{4}$ for y. It will be easier to use in the first equation.

$$x - 2\left(-\frac{7}{4}\right) = 6$$
$$x + \frac{7}{2} = 6$$
$$x = \frac{5}{2}$$

We check $\left(\frac{5}{2}, -\frac{7}{4}\right)$ in both equations.

$x - 2y = 6$	
$\frac{5}{2} - 2\left(-\frac{7}{4}\right)$	6
$\frac{5}{2} + \frac{7}{2}$	6
6	6 ✔

$3x + 2y = 4$	
$3 \cdot \frac{5}{2} + 2\left(-\frac{7}{4}\right)$	4
$\frac{15}{2} - \frac{7}{2}$	4
4	4 ✔

The solution of the system is $\left(\frac{5}{2}, -\frac{7}{4}\right)$.

Try This Solve using the substitution method.

d. $x - 2y = 8$
     $2x + y = 8$

e. $4x - y = 5$
     $2x + y = 10$

f. $y = x + 5$
     $2x + y = 8$

g. $3x + 4y = 2$
     $2x - y = 5$

In some books this system of equations would be written as

$$\begin{cases} x - 2y = 6 \\ 3x + 2y = 4 \end{cases}$$

The brace emphasizes that the two equations are a system of equations.

Objective: Solve problems using systems of equations.

PROBLEM-SOLVING GUIDELINES
■ UNDERSTAND the problem
■ Develop and carry out a PLAN
■ Find the ANSWER and CHECK

We can solve many problems by translating to a system of equations and using the Problem-Solving Guidelines.

EXAMPLE 3   Translate to a system of equations and solve.

The sum of two numbers is 82. One number is twelve more than the other. Find the larger number.

Let $x =$ one number and $y =$ the other number. There are two statements in this problem.

$$\underbrace{\text{The sum of two numbers}}\ \underset{\downarrow\ \downarrow}{\text{is 82.}}$$
$$x + y \qquad\ = 82$$

$$\underbrace{\text{One number}}\ \underset{\downarrow\quad\downarrow}{\text{is twelve}}\ \underbrace{\text{more than}}\ \underbrace{\text{the other number.}}$$
$$x \qquad = \quad 12 \qquad + \qquad\qquad y$$

Now we have a system of equations.

$$x + y = 82$$
$$x = 12 + y$$

We solve, substituting $12 + y$ for x in the first equation.

$$12 + y + y = 82 \qquad \text{Substituting } 12 + y \text{ for } x$$
$$12 + 2y = 82$$
$$2y = 70$$
$$y = 35$$

Next we solve for x by substituting 35 for y in the second equation.

$$x = 12 + 35$$
$$x = 47$$

The two numbers are 47 and 35. We check in the original problem. The sum of 35 and 47 is 82, and 47 is 12 more than 35. The larger number is 47.

Try This   Translate to a system of equations and solve.

h. The sum of two numbers is 84. One number is three times the other. Find the numbers.

8-2 Exercises

Extra Help On the Web

Look for worked-out examples at the Prentice Hall Web site.
www.phschool.com

A

Solve using the substitution method.

1. $x + y = 4$
$y = 2x + 1$

2. $x + y = 10$
$y = x + 8$

3. $x = y - 1$
$y = 4 - 2x$

4. $x = y + 6$
$y = -2 - x$

5. $y = 2x - 5$
$3y - x = 5$

6. $y = 2x + 1$
$x + y = -2$

7. $x = -2y$
$x = 2 - 4y$

8. $r = -3s$
$r = 10 - 4s$

9. $x = 3y - 4$
$2x - y = 7$

10. $s + t = -4$
$s - t = 2$

11. $x - y = 6$
$x + y = -2$

12. $y - 2x = -6$
$2y - x = 5$

13. $x - y = 5$
$x + 2y = 7$

14. $2x + 3y = -2$
$2x - y = 9$

15. $x + 2y = 10$
$3x + 4y = 8$

16. $x - y = -3$
$2x + 3y = -6$

17. $3b + 2a = 2$
$-2b + a = 8$

18. $r - 2s = 0$
$4r - 3s = 15$

19. $y - 2x = 0$
$3x + 7y = 17$

20. $x - 3y = 7$
$-3x + 16y = 28$

21. $8x + 4y = 6$
$4x = 3 - y$

Translate to a system of equations and solve.

22. The sum of two numbers is 27. One number is 3 more than the other. Find the numbers.

23. The sum of two numbers is 36. One number is 2 more than the other. Find the numbers.

24. Find two numbers whose sum is 58 and whose difference is 16.

25. Find two numbers whose sum is 66 and whose difference is 8.

26. The difference between two numbers is 16. Three times the larger number is seven times the smaller. What are the numbers?

27. The difference between two numbers is 18. The sum of twice the smaller number and three times the larger is 74. What are the numbers?

Journal

Describe a system of equations that you would prefer to solve using substitution. Describe a system of equations that you would prefer to solve using graphing. Give examples.

B

Solve each system of equations by using the substitution method and by graphing. Explain your results.

28. $3y + 3x = 14$
$y = -x + 4$

29. $y = x + 5$
$-3x + 3y = 15$

30. Determine whether $(2, -3)$ is a solution of this system of equations.
$$x + 3y = -7 \qquad -x + y = -5 \qquad 2x - y = 1$$

31. *Critical Thinking* Here are two equivalent systems of equations. Find the values of A and B.

$$x + 2y = 2$$
$$5x - 3y = -29$$

$$Ax + 5y = -9$$
$$x + By = 8$$

32. *Mathematical Reasoning* Justify each step in the solution of the system of equations.

$$x + y = 19$$
$$x = 5 + y$$

Solution:
$$5 + y + y = 19 \qquad \underline{\hspace{4cm}}$$
$$5 + 2y = 19 \qquad \underline{\hspace{4cm}}$$
$$2y = 14 \qquad \underline{\hspace{4cm}}$$
$$y = 7 \qquad \underline{\hspace{4cm}}$$
$$x = 5 + 7 = 12 \qquad \underline{\hspace{4cm}}$$

Challenge

Here are systems of three equations in three variables. Use the substitution method to solve.

33.
$$x + y + z = 4$$
$$x - 2y - z = 1$$
$$y = -1$$

34.
$$x + y + z = 180$$
$$x = z - 70$$
$$2y - z = 0$$

35. Why is there no solution to the system at the right? (Hint: Use substitution more than once.)

$$x + y = 10$$
$$y + z = 10$$
$$x + z = 10$$
$$x + y + z = 10$$

Mixed Review

Determine whether the graphs of the equations are parallel. *7-8*

36. $y = 2x - 9$
$y - 2x = 11$

37. $6y - 21x = 3$
$8y - 5 = 28x$

38. $4y + 9 = x$
$5 - 2y = 8x$

Factor. **39.** $9a^2 - 6ab + b^2$ **40.** $36y^4 - 25y^2$

41. $x^2 - 4xyz^2 + 4y^2z^4$ **42.** $9x^2 + 12xz^3 + 4z^6$ *6-2, 6-7*

Solve. **43.** $n^2 + 10n + 25 = 0$ **44.** $n^2 - 10n + 25 = 0$

45. $n^2 - 25 = 0$ **46.** $4n^2 - 49 = 0$ *6-8*

47. The perimeter of a rectangle is 350 cm. The width is 15 cm shorter than the length. What are the length and the width of this rectangle? *6-9*

48. If the sides of a square are lengthened by 8 in., the area becomes 169 in.^{2}. Find the length of a side of the original square. *6-9*

The Addition Method

PART 1 — Using the Addition Method

Objective: Solve a system of equations using the addition method.

Another method for solving systems of equations is called the **addition method.** It is especially useful when both equations are written in standard form, $Ax + By = C$.

EXAMPLE 1 Solve using the addition method.

$$x + y = 5$$
$$x - y = 1$$

According to the second equation, $x - y$ and 1 are equivalent expressions. The addition property of equality says that we can add the same number or expression to both sides of an equation and still have a true equation. Since $x - y$ and 1 are equal, we can add $x - y$ to the left side and 1 to the right side of the first equation.

$$
\begin{aligned}
x + y &= 5 \\
x - y &= 1 \\
\hline
2x + 0y &= 6 \quad \text{Using the addition property}\\
2x &= 6 \\
x &= 3 \quad \text{Solving for } x
\end{aligned}
$$

Next substitute 3 for x in either of the original equations.

$$
\begin{aligned}
x + y &= 5 \\
3 + y &= 5 \quad \text{Substituting 3 for } x \text{ in the first equation}\\
y &= 2 \quad \text{Solving for } y
\end{aligned}
$$

Check $x = 3$ and $y = 2$ in both equations.

Check:
$$
\begin{array}{c|c}
x + y = 5 & x - y = 1 \\
\hline
3 + 2 \mid 5 & 3 - 2 \mid 1 \\
5 \mid 5 \; \checkmark & 1 \mid 1 \; \checkmark
\end{array}
$$

The solution of the system is $(3, 2)$.

Try This Solve using the addition method.

a. $x + y = 5$
   $2x - y = 4$

b. $3x - 3y = 6$
   $3x + 3y = 0$

What You'll Learn

1. To solve a system of equations using the addition method

2. To solve a system of equations using the multiplication and addition properties

3. To solve problems using systems of equations

. . . And Why

To be able to solve real-world problems using algebraic reasoning skills

Quick *Review*

The addition property of equality is found on page 114.

Objective: Solve a system of equations by using the multiplication and addition properties.

The multiplication property for equations states that we can multiply each side of an equation by the same number and still have a true equation. Sometimes we may need to multiply both sides of an equation by a number before using the addition method.

EXAMPLE 2   Solve using the addition method.

$$2x + 3y = 8$$
$$x + 3y = 7$$

If we add the equations, no variables will be eliminated. If the $3y$ in the second equation were $-3y$, the y-terms would be additive inverses and would be eliminated when added. We use the multiplication property to multiply both sides of the second equation by -1 and add the two equations. This new equation is called a **linear combination** of the original equations.

$$2x + 3y = 8 \qquad \longrightarrow \qquad 2x + 3y = 8$$
$$-1(x + 3y) = -1(7) \quad \longrightarrow \quad \dfrac{-x - 3y = -7}{x \qquad = 1} \qquad \text{Adding}$$

Substitute 1 for x in either of the original equations.

$$x + 3y = 7$$
$$1 + 3y = 7 \qquad \text{Substituting 1 for } x \text{ in the second equation}$$
$$3y = 6$$
$$y = 2 \qquad \text{Solving for } y$$

Substitution will show that $(1, 2)$ checks in both equations. The solution of the system is $(1, 2)$.

Try This   Solve using the addition method.

c. $5x + 3y = 17$ **d.** $8x + 11y = 37$
    $5x - 2y = -3$ $-2x + 11y = 7$

In Example 2, we used the multiplication property for equations, multiplying by -1. We often need to multiply by some number other than -1.

EXAMPLE 3   Solve.

$$3x + 6y = -6$$
$$5x - 2y = 14$$

If the y-term of the second equation were $-6y$, the y-terms would be additive inverses and could be eliminated by using the addition property.

We can multiply the second equation by 3 to get $-6y$.

$$3x + 6y = -6 \quad \longrightarrow \quad 3x + 6y = -6$$
$$3(5x - 2y) = 3(14) \quad \longrightarrow \quad \underline{15x - 6y = 42}$$
$$18x \qquad = 36 \qquad \text{Adding}$$
$$x = 2$$

Substitute 2 for x in either of the original equations.

$$3(2) + 6y = -6 \qquad \text{Substituting 2 for } x \text{ in the first equation}$$
$$6 + 6y = -6$$
$$6y = -12$$
$$y = -2 \qquad \text{Solving for } y$$

Substitution will show that $(2, -2)$ checks in both equations. The solution of the system is $(2, -2)$.

Try This   Solve.

e. $4a + 7b = 11$ **f.** $7x - 5y = 76$ **g.** $5b + 10c = 15$
    $4a + 6b = 10$ $4x + y = 55$ $3b - 2c = -7$

When we use the addition method for solving systems of equations, we sometimes need to use the multiplication property more than once.

EXAMPLE 4   Solve.

$$3x + 5y = 30$$
$$5x + 8y = 49$$

We can multiply the first equation by 5 and the second by -3 to make the x-terms additive inverses.

$$5(3x + 5y) = 5(30) \quad \longrightarrow \quad 15x + 25y = 150$$
$$-3(5x + 8y) = -3(49) \quad \longrightarrow \quad \underline{-15x - 24y = -147}$$
$$y = 3 \qquad \text{Adding}$$

Substitute 3 for y in one of the original equations.

$$3x + 5y = 30 \qquad \text{Choosing the first equation}$$
$$3x + 5(3) = 30 \qquad \text{Substituting 3 for } y$$
$$3x = 15$$
$$x = 5$$

Substitution will show that $(5, 3)$ checks in both equations. The solution of the system is $(5, 3)$.

Try This   Solve.

h. $5x + 3y = 2$ **i.** $6x + 2y = 4$
    $3x + 5y = -2$ $10x + 7y = -8$

Objective: Solve problems using the addition method.

PROBLEM-SOLVING GUIDELINES
■ UNDERSTAND the problem
Develop and carry out a PLAN
■ Find the ANSWER and CHECK

Once we have translated a problem to a system of equations, we can use the addition method to solve.

EXAMPLE 5 Translate to a system of equations and solve.

The sum of two numbers is 56. The sum of one third of the first number and one fourth of the second number is 16. Find the numbers.

Let $x = $ the first number and $y = $ the second number. We translate to a system of equations.

$$x + y = 56$$
$$\tfrac{1}{3}x + \tfrac{1}{4}y = 16$$

First we clear the second equation of fractions.

$$x + y = 56 \longrightarrow x + y = 56$$
$$12\left(\tfrac{1}{3}x + \tfrac{1}{4}y\right) = 12(16) \longrightarrow 4x + 3y = 192$$

Next we multiply both sides of the first equation by -4.

$$-4(x + y) = -4(56) \longrightarrow -4x - 4y = -224$$
$$4x + 3y = 192 \longrightarrow \underline{4x + 3y = 192}$$
$$-y = -32$$
$$y = 32$$

Substitute for y in either of the first equations.

$$x + 32 = 56 \qquad \text{Substituting 32 for } y \text{ in the first equation}$$
$$x = 24$$

The two numbers are 24 and 32.

Their sum, $24 + 32$, is 56. One third of 24 is 8. One fourth of 32 is 8, and the sum, $8 + 8$, is 16. The answer checks.

Try This Translate to a system of equations and solve.

j. The difference of two numbers is 36. The difference of one sixth of the larger number and one ninth of the smaller number is 11. Find the numbers.

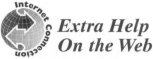

Extra Help
On the Web

Look for worked-out examples at the Prentice Hall Web site.
www.phschool.com

A

Solve using the addition method.

1. $x + y = 10$
$x - y = 8$

2. $x - y = 7$
$x + y = 3$

3. $x + y = 8$
$-x + 2y = 7$

4. $x + y = 6$
$-x + 3y = -2$

5. $3x - y = 9$
$2x + y = 6$

6. $4x - y = 1$
$3x + y = 13$

7. $4a + 3b = 7$
$-4a + b = 5$

8. $7c + 5d = 18$
$c - 5d = -2$

9. $8x - 5y = -9$
$3x + 5y = -2$

10. $3a - 3b = -15$
$-3a - 3b = -3$

11. $4x - 5y = 7$
$-4x + 5y = 7$

12. $2x + 3y = 4$
$-2x - 3y = -4$

Solve.

13. $-x - y = 8$
$2x - y = -1$

14. $x + y = -7$
$3x + y = -9$

15. $x + 3y = 19$
$x - y = -1$

16. $3x - y = 8$
$x + 2y = 5$

17. $x + y = 5$
$5x - 3y = 17$

18. $x - y = 7$
$4x - 5y = 25$

19. $2w + 3z = 17$
$3w + 4z = 24$

20. $7p + 5q = 2$
$8p - 9q = 17$

21. $2a + 3b = -1$
$3a + 5b = -2$

22. $3x - 4y = 16$
$5x + 6y = 14$

23. $x - 3y = 0$
$5x - y = -14$

24. $5a - 2b = 0$
$2a - 3b = -11$

25. $3x - 2y = 10$
$5x + 3y = 4$

26. $2p + 5q = 9$
$3p - 2q = 4$

27. $3x - 8y = 11$
$x + 6y - 8 = 0$

28. $m - n = 32$
$3m - 8n - 6 = 0$

29. $a + b = 12$
$\frac{1}{2}a + \frac{1}{4}b = 4$

30. $2p - q = 8$
$\frac{1}{3}p + \frac{1}{4}q = 3$

Translate to a system of equations and solve.

31. The sum of two numbers is 115. The difference is 21. Find the numbers.

32. The sum of two numbers is 26.4. One is five times the other. Find the numbers.

33. The sum of the length and width of a rectangle is 19 in. The length is one less than twice the width. Find the length and width of the rectangle.

34. The perimeter of a rectangle is 48 m. The width of the rectangle is 2 more than half the length. Find the length and the width.

35. Two angles are complementary. Their difference is 34°. Find the angles. (Complementary angles are angles whose sum is 90°.)

36. Two angles are complementary. One angle is 42° more than one half the other. Find the angles.

37. **TEST PREP**   Which of the following ordered $2x - y = 10$
pairs are solutions of the system of equations? $6x - 3y = 30$

I. $(0, -10)$ II. $(2, 6)$ III. $(5, 0)$ IV. $(-10, -30)$

A. I only   **B.** I and III only
C. I, III, and IV   **D.** I, II, III, and IV

B

Solve each system.

38. $3(x - y) = 9$
$x + y = 7$

39. $5(a - b) = 10$
$a + b = 2$

40. $2(x - y) = 3 + x$
$x = 3y + 4$

41. $2(5a - 5b) = 10$
$-5(6a + 2b) = 10$

42. $1.5x + 0.85y = 1637.5$
$0.01(x + y) = 15.25$

43. *Critical Thinking*   Suppose we can get a system into the form

$$ax + by = c$$
$$dx + ey = f$$

where $a, b, c, d, e,$ and f are any positive or negative rational numbers. Solve the system for x and y.

Challenge

Solve each system.

44. $y = ax + b$
$y = x + c$

45. $ax + by + c = 0$
$ax + cy + b = 0$

46. $3(7 - a) - 2(1 + 2b) + 5 = 0$
$3a + 2b - 18 = 0$

47. $\frac{2}{x} - \frac{3}{y} = -\frac{1}{2}$, and $\frac{1}{x} + \frac{2}{y} = \frac{11}{12}$

48. Use the pattern of your solution in Exercise 43 to solve the following system.

$$14x - 10y = 2600$$
$$24x + 20y = 520$$

Mixed Review

Determine whether the graphs of the equations are perpendicular.   *7-8*

49. $8y - 3x = 10$
$-6y - 3x = 4$

50. $3x + 2y = 1$
$2x - 3y = 4$

51. $8x + y = 10$
$x - 8y = 0$

Solve by graphing.   **52.** $x + 2y = 9$
$3y - x = 1$

53. $3x + 5y = -2$
$2y - 7x = 32$ *8-1*

Factor.   **54.** $2m^3 - 4m^2 - m + 2$ **55.** $3y^2 - 12$ **56.** $x^2z - xz^2$ *6-7*

Simplify.   **57.** $(a^2b + 2ab^2) - (3a^2b + ab^2)$

58. $(3y^2 - xy + 2x) + (5xy - 2y^2 + x)$ *5-7, 5-8*

Using Systems of Equations

Objective: Solve problems using systems of equations.

Systems of two equations with two variables are often used to solve problems. When you use two variables, you must remember to write two equations in order to have one solution.

After a problem is translated to a system of equations, you must decide whether to use the substitution or addition method.

PROBLEM-SOLVING GUIDELINES
■ UNDERSTAND the problem
▨ Develop and carry out a PLAN
■ Find the ANSWER and CHECK

We can use the Problem-Solving Guidelines to solve problems involving systems of equations.

What You'll Learn

1 To solve problems using systems of equations

. . . And Why

To be able to solve real-world problems using algebraic reasoning skills

---

EXAMPLE 1

A baseball team played 162 games. They won 44 more games than they lost. How many games did they lose?

■ **UNDERSTAND the problem**

Question: How many games did the team lose?
Data: Total games played = 162; 44 more games were won than lost.

▨ **Develop and carry out a PLAN**

Let $x =$ the number of games won and $y =$ the number of games lost. There are two statements in this problem.

$$\underbrace{\text{The number of games won}}_{x} \; \underbrace{\text{plus}}_{+} \; \underbrace{\text{the number of games lost}}_{y} \; \underbrace{\text{is 162}}_{= 162}$$

$$\underbrace{\text{The number of games won}}_{x} \; \underbrace{\text{minus}}_{-} \; \underbrace{\text{the number of games lost}}_{y} \; \underbrace{\text{is 44}}_{= 44}$$

We solve the system of equations by the addition method.

$$
\begin{array}{rl}
x + y = 162 & \\
\underline{x - y = 44} & \\
2x = 206 & \text{Adding} \\
x = 103 & \text{Number of games won} \\
x + y = 162 & \text{Choosing the first equation} \\
103 + y = 162 & \text{Substituting 103 for } x \\
y = 59 & \text{Number of games lost}
\end{array}
$$

■ **Find the ANSWER and CHECK**

The team lost 59 games. They won 103 games, which is 44 more than they lost, and played a total of 162 games. The answer checks.

Try This Translate to a system of equations and solve.

a. An automobile dealer sold 180 vans and trucks at a sale. He sold 40 more vans than trucks. How many of each did he sell?

EXAMPLE 2

Ramon sells cars and trucks. He has room on his lot for 510 vehicles. From experience he knows that his profits will be greatest if he has 190 more cars than trucks. How many of each vehicle should he have?

Let $x = $ the number of cars and $y = $ the number of trucks.

Number of cars plus number of trucks is 510	Rewording
$\downarrow$ $\downarrow$ $\downarrow$	
x + y $= 510$	Translating
Number of cars is 190 plus number of trucks	Rewording
$\downarrow$ $\downarrow$ $\downarrow$	
x $= 190 +$ y	Translating

We now have a system of equations.

$$x + y = 510$$
$$x = 190 + y$$

We use the substitution method to solve this system.

$$
\begin{aligned}
(190 + y) + y &= 510 && \text{Substituting } 190 + y \text{ for } x \\
190 + 2y &= 510 \\
2y &= 320 \\
y &= 160 && \text{Number of trucks}
\end{aligned}
$$

Substituting 160 for y in the second equation, we have

$$
\begin{aligned}
x &= 190 + 160 \\
x &= 350
\end{aligned}
$$

The solution of this system is (350, 160).
Ramon should have 350 cars and 160 trucks in his lot.

The number of cars, 350, plus 160 trucks is 510 vehicles. Also, 350 is 190 more than 160. The answer checks.

Try This Translate to a system of equations and solve.

b. A family went camping at a place 45 km from town. They drove 13 km more than they walked to get to the campsite. How far did they walk?

EXAMPLE 3

Shirley is 21 years older than Laura. In six years, Shirley will be twice as old as Laura. How old are they now? Let $x =$ Shirley's age and $y =$ Laura's age.

	Age now	**Age in 6 years**
Shirley	x	$x + 6$
Laura	y	$y + 6$

Recording the data in a *table* helps you write equations.

Shirley's age now is 21 more than Laura's age now.

$$x = 21 + y$$

Shirley's age in 6 years will be twice Laura's age in 6 years.

$$x + 6 = 2 \quad (y + 6)$$

We have a system of equations.

$$x = 21 + y$$
$$x + 6 = 2(y + 6)$$

Simplifying the second equation gives $x = 2y + 6$.

$$x = 21 + y$$
$$x = 2y + 6$$

Next we use the substitution method.

$$2y + 6 = 21 + y \qquad \text{Substituting } 2y + 6 \text{ for } x \text{ in the first equation}$$
$$y = 15 \qquad \text{Laura's age now}$$

We substitute 15 for y in $x = 21 + y$.

$$x = 21 + 15$$
$$x = 36 \qquad \text{Shirley's age now}$$

Shirley is 36 and Laura is 15.

Shirley's age, 36, is 21 more than Laura's age, 15. In six years, Shirley will be 42 and Laura will be 21 and 42 is twice 21. The answers check.

Try This Translate to a system of equations and solve.

c. Wilma is 13 years older than Bev. In nine years, Wilma will be twice as old as Bev. How old is Bev?

d. Stan is two thirds as old as Adam. In 7 years, Stan will be three fourths as old as Adam. How old are they now?

e. Four pencils and two pens cost $0.74. Six pencils and five pens cost $1.53. Find the cost of a pencil and a pen.

EXAMPLE 4

Badger Rent-A-Truck rents small trucks at a daily rate of $33.95 plus 30¢ per mile. Cactus Rent-A-Truck rents the same size truck at a daily rate of $32.95 plus 32¢ per mile. For what mileage is the cost the same?

Let m represent the mileage.

Let c represent the cost.

	Charge per mile ($)	Charge for m miles ($)	Daily Rate ($)
Badger	0.30	$0.30m$	33.95
Cactus	0.32	$0.32m$	32.95

To make this move with a small truck, the family had to drive about 80 miles. Was it cheaper for them to rent from Badger or from Cactus? Use the solution to Example 4 and explain your reasoning.

We write the cost for Badger. $33.95 + 0.30m$

We write the cost for Cactus. $32.95 + 0.32m$

We want the cost for both to be the same, so both can equal c.

We have a system of equations.

$$33.95 + 0.30m = c$$
$$32.95 + 0.32m = c$$

Clear the system of decimals and multiply the second equation by -1. Then we use the addition method to solve the system.

$$
\begin{array}{r}
3395 + 30m = 100c \\
-3295 - 32m = -100c \\
\hline
100 - 2m = 0 \\
100 = 2m \\
50 = m \qquad \text{mileage}
\end{array}
$$

If the trucks are driven 50 miles, the cost will be the same.

We can substitute for m in both equations to see if the cost is the same.

$$c = 33.95 + 0.30(50) = \$48.95$$
$$c = 32.95 + 0.32(50) = \$48.95$$

The cost is the same. The answer checks.

Try This Translate to a system of equations and solve.

f. Acme rents a pickup truck at a daily rate of $31.95 plus 33¢ per mile. Speedo Rentzit rents a pickup for $34.95 plus 29¢ per mile. For what mileage is the cost the same?

8-4 Exercises

Extra Help
On the Web

Look for worked-out
examples at the Prentice
Hall Web site.
www.phschool.com

A

Translate to a system of equations and solve.

1. ***Multi-Step Problem***   Marco has 150 coins, all nickels and dimes. He has 12 more dimes than nickels. How many nickels and how many dimes does he have?

   a. Let n be the number of nickels and d be the number of dimes. Write an equation that shows that the sum of the number of nickels and the number of dimes is 150.

   b. Which equation shows that there are 12 more dimes than nickels: $n + 12 = d$ or $d + 12 = n$?

   c. Show the system of equations that can be used to solve this problem.

   d. Solve the system of equations and answer the problem.

2. ***Multi-Step Problem***   Use the sales receipts at the right to find the cost of a taco and a glass of milk.

   a. Let t be the cost of a taco and m be the cost of a glass of milk. Write an expression that shows that the sum is $2.10.

1 taco

1 milk

Total $2.10

2 tacos

3 milks

Total $5.15

   b. Write an expression for the cost of two tacos.

   c. Write an expression for the cost of three glasses of milk.

   d. Write an equation that shows that the total cost for two tacos and three glasses of milk is $5.15.

   e. Show the system of equations you can use to solve this problem.

   f. Solve the system of equations and answer the problem.

3. Four oranges and five apples cost $3.56. Three oranges and four apples cost $2.76. Find the cost of an orange and the cost of an apple.

4. Zelma is eighteen years older than her son. She was three times as old as he was one year ago. How old are they now?

5. Tyrone is twice as old as his daughter. In six years Tyrone's age will be three times what his daughter's age was six years ago. How old are they at present?

6. Frederique is two years older than her brother. Twelve years ago she was twice as old as he was. How old are they now?

7. The perimeter of a rectangle is 160 ft. One fourth the length is the same as twice the width. Find the dimensions of the rectangle.

8. On a fishing trip, Mariko caught twenty-four fish. She caught some rockfish averaging 2.5 lb. and some bluefish averaging 8 lb. The total weight of the fish was 137 lb. How many of each kind of fish did she catch?

9. Safety Rent-A-Truck rents a truck at a daily rate of $41.95 plus 29¢ per mile. City Rentals rents the same size truck for $38.95 plus 31¢ per mile. For what mileage is the cost the same?

10. Sunshine Truck Rentals rents a truck at a daily rate of $57.99 plus 48¢ per mile. City Rentals rents the same size truck at $58.95 plus 46¢ per mile. For what mileage is the cost the same?

11. Six apples and three oranges cost $3.36. Two apples and five oranges cost $3.04. Find the cost of an apple and the cost of an orange.

12. Susan wants to have business cards printed. One style will cost $25 plus 2 cents per card. Another style will cost $10 plus 5 cents per card. For how many cards will the cost be the same for both styles?

13. The Booster Club voted on where they would go for their annual trip. A majority of the club voted to go to a baseball game. They bought 29 tickets. Some of the tickets cost $21 each and some cost $27 each. The total cost of all the tickets was $675. How many tickets of each price did they buy?

TICKET INFORMATION	
Lower Box.	$30.00
Upper Box.	$27.00
Lower Reserved.	$24.00
Upper Reserved.	$21.00
General Admission.	$15.50
General Admission.	$10.50
(Children under 14 and senior citizens)	

14. Jermaine was in charge of buying milk for a class picnic for 32 students. Milk is sold in half-gallon cartons and gallon cartons at a neighborhood grocery store. The half-gallon carton costs $1.46 and the gallon carton costs $2.39. When he got to the store, there was not much milk left. Jermaine bought all 21 cartons they had and paid a total of $41.82. How many cartons of each size did he buy?

15. Lorena bought 10 packs of styrofoam cups for the graduation dance. A pack of fifty 12-oz cups costs $1.80 and a pack of fifty 16-oz cups costs $2.40. Lorena paid a total of $21.60 excluding tax. How many packs of each size cup did she buy?

16. The Taylor family reunion had a record turnout of 38 people last year. For a change of pace, they decided to go ice skating instead of having a picnic. Admission for the group cost $179.50 (including skates). How many adults and how many children were at the reunion?

ICELAND SKATING RINK	
Admission:	
ADULTS	$3.75
CHILDREN	$2.50
Admission and skate rental:	
ADULTS	$5.25
CHILDREN	$4.00

B

17. In Lewis Carroll's *Through the Looking Glass,* Tweedledum says to Tweedledee, "The sum of your weight and twice mine is 361 pounds." Then Tweedledee says to Tweedledum, "Contrariwise, the sum of your weight and twice mine is 362 pounds." Find the weight of Tweedledum and Tweedledee.

18. During a publicity campaign, a cycle shop gave away 5000 miniature cycles and bumper stickers. The cycles cost 63¢ each and the bumper stickers cost 52¢ each. The cycle shop spent $2798 on the gifts. How many of each gift did they buy?

19. Fenton Rent-A-Truck charges $32.85 plus 49¢ per mile for a certain truck. Handy Truck Rents charges $31.95 plus 48¢ per mile for the same truck. For what mileage is the cost the same?

20. *Write a Convincing Argument*   Solve the problem below. Then write an argument that would convince a classmate that your solution is correct.

Several ancient Chinese books include problems that can be solved by translating to systems of equations. *Arithmetical Rules in Nine Sections* was compiled by Chang Tsang, a Chinese mathematician who died in 152 B.C. One of the problems is: Suppose there are a number of rabbits and pheasants confined in a cage. In all there are 35 heads and 94 feet. How many rabbits and how many pheasants are there?

Challenge

21. Daniel earned $288 on his investments. He invested $1100 at one yearly rate and $1800 at a rate that was 1.5% higher. Find the two rates of interest.

22. Together, a bat, a ball, and a glove cost $99.00. The bat costs $9.95 more than the ball, and the glove costs $65.45 more than the bat. How much does each cost?

Mixed Review

Graph the lines containing these points and find their slope.

23. $(2, 5), (-3, 10)$ **24.** $(-1, -1), (2, 5)$ **25.** $(4, -7), (2, 3)$ *7-1, 7-4*

26. Write an equation for the line that contains $(-2, 2)$ and $(3, 7)$.   *7-5*

27. Write an equation for the line with $m = 6$, y-intercept $= 7$.   *7-5*

Simplify. **28.** $\dfrac{x^6}{x^2}$ **29.** $\dfrac{t^9}{t^8}$ **30.** $\dfrac{n^4}{n^4}$ **31.** $\dfrac{x^3y^5}{x^3y^4}$ *5-1*

Factor. **32.** $7m^4n^2 - 7m^2n^4$ **33.** $81x^2 - 126xy + 49y^2$ *6-7*

Self-Test On the Web

Check your progress. Look for a self-test at the Prentice Hall Web site.
www.phschool.com

8-5 ▷ Motion Problems

Objective: Solve problems involving uniform motion.

What You'll Learn

1 To solve problems involving uniform motion

...And Why

To be able to solve real-world problems using algebraic reasoning skills

PROBLEM-SOLVING GUIDELINES
■ UNDERSTAND the problem
▢ Develop and carry out a PLAN
■ Find the ANSWER and CHECK

The three strategies *Write an Equation, Draw a Diagram,* and *Make a Table* will be particularly helpful for the problems in this section.

The formula $d = r \cdot t$ shows the relationship between distance (d), rate (r), and time (t). We use this formula in the following examples.

EXAMPLE 1

A train leaves Slaton traveling east at 80 kilometers per hour. An hour later, another train leaves Slaton on a parallel track at 120 km/h. How far from Slaton will the trains meet?

■ **UNDERSTAND the problem**

Question: At what distance from Slaton will the trains meet?
Data: The rate of the slow train is 80 km/h. The rate of the fast train is 120 km/h. The fast train leaves 1 hour after the slow train.

The distances will be equal.

slow train
80 km/h $\qquad d$

fast train
120 km/h $\qquad d$

▢ **Develop and carry out a PLAN**

Let d = distance traveled when the trains meet.
Let t = time for the faster train.

$t + 1$ = time for the slower train

	Distance	Rate	Time
Slow Train	d	80	$t + 1$
Fast Train	d	120	t

Recording the data in a *table* helps you write equations.

For each row in the chart we can *write an equation* in the form $d = r \cdot t$.

$$d = 80(t + 1) \text{ and } d = 120t$$

Thus we have a system of equations. We solve the system by the substitution method.

$120t = 80(t + 1)$ Substituting $120t$ for d in the first equation
$120t = 80t + 80$
$40t = 80$
$t = 2$ Time (hours)

Solve for d using either equation.

$d = 120t$
$d = 120(2)$ Substituting 2 for t
$d = 240$ Distance (kilometers)

■ **Find the ANSWER and CHECK**

The problem asks us to find how far from Slaton the trains meet. The trains meet 240 km from Slaton.

The time for the fast train is 2 h; $2 \times 120 = 240$ km. The time for the slow train is $2 + 1$ or 3 h; $3 \times 80 = 240$ km. The answer checks.

Try This Solve.

a. A car leaves Hartford traveling north at 56 km/h. Another car leaves Hartford one hour later traveling north on the same road at 84 km/h. How far from Hartford will the second car overtake the first? (Hint: The cars travel the same distance.)

EXAMPLE 2

A motorboat took 3 hours to make a downstream trip with a current of 6 km/h. The return trip against the same current took 5 hours. Find the speed of the boat in still water.

Let r represent the speed of the boat in still water. Then, when traveling downstream, the speed of the boat is $r + 6$ (the current helps the boat along). When traveling upstream the speed of the boat is $r - 6$ (the current holds the boat back). We can organize the information in a table.

	Distance	Rate	Time
Downstream	d	$r + 6$	3
Upstream	d	$r - 6$	5

From each row of the table, we write an equation of the form distance = rate × time.

$d = (r + 6)3$
$d = (r - 6)5$

Thus we have a system of equations.

We solve the system by the substitution method.

$$(r + 6)3 = (r - 6)5 \qquad \text{Substituting } (r + 6)3 \text{ for } d \text{ in the second equation}$$
$$3r + 18 = 5r - 30$$
$$-2r = -48$$
$$r = 24 \qquad \text{Rate, or speed}$$

The speed in still water is 24 km/h.

We check in the original problem. When $r = 24$, $r + 6 = 30$ and the distance is $30 \cdot 3$, or 90. When $r = 24$, $r - 6 = 18$ and the distance is $18 \cdot 5$, or 90. In both cases we get a distance of 90 km.

Try This   Solve.

b. An airplane flew for 5 hours with a tail wind of 25 km/h. The return flight against the same wind took 6 hours. Find the speed of the airplane in still air. (Hint: The distance is the same both ways.)

EXAMPLE 3

Two cars leave town at the same time going in opposite directions. One of them travels 60 mi/h and the other 30 mi/h. In how many hours will they be 150 miles apart?

We first make a diagram.

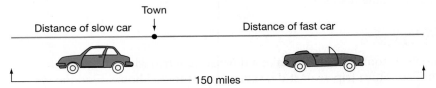

From the diagram and the wording of the problem, we see that the distances are *not* the same. We also see that the distance of the slow car plus the distance of the fast car is 150 mi. Both cars travel for the same amount of time, so we use t for both times. We organize the information in a chart. Using the chart, we translate this information.

	Distance	**Rate**	**Time**
Slow Car	distance of slow car	30	t
Fast Car	distance of fast car	60	t

$$\underbrace{\text{Distance of slow car}} \text{ plus } \underbrace{\text{distance of fast car}} \text{ is 150.}$$
$$\downarrow \qquad\qquad\qquad \downarrow \qquad\qquad\quad \downarrow\ \downarrow$$
$$30t \qquad + \qquad 60t \qquad = 150$$

We solve this equation for t.

$$30t + 60t = 150$$
$$90t = 150$$
$$t = \tfrac{5}{3}, \text{ or } 1\tfrac{2}{3} \text{ hours}$$

In $1\tfrac{2}{3}$ hours the cars will be 150 miles apart.

Try This Solve.

c. Two cars leave town at the same time in opposite directions. One travels 35 km/h and the other 40 km/h. In how many hours will they be 200 km apart?

d. Two cars leave town at the same time in the same direction. One travels 35 mi/h and the other 40 mi/h. In how many hours will they be 15 miles apart?

8-5 Exercises

Extra Help On the Web

Look for worked-out examples at the Prentice Hall Web site.
www.phschool.com

A

Solve.

1. *Multi-Step Problem* Two cars leave town at the same time going in opposite directions. One travels 55 mi/h and the other travels 48 mi/h. In how many hours will they be 206 miles apart?

  a. Draw a diagram that represents the situation. Label your diagram using data from the problem.

  b. Copy and complete the missing information in the table below.

	Distance	Rate	Time
Slow Car	distance of slow car		
Fast Car	distance of fast car		

  c. Use the data in your table to write an equation.

  d. Solve the equation and answer the question.

2. *Multi-Step Problem* Two cars leave town at the same time going in the same direction on the same road. One travels 30 mi/h and the other travels 46 mi/h. In how many hours will they be 72 miles apart?

  a. Draw a diagram that represents the situation. Label your diagram using data from the problem.

b. Copy and complete the missing information in the table below.

	Distance	Rate	Time
Slow Car	d		
Fast Car		46	

c. Use the data in your table to write a system of equations.

d. Solve the system of equations and answer the question.

3. *Multi-Step Problem*   A train leaves a station and travels east at 72 km/h. Three hours later a second train leaves on a parallel track and travels east at 120 km/h. When will it overtake the first train?

a. Draw a diagram that represents the situation. Label your diagram using data from the problem.

b. Copy and complete the missing information in the table below.

	Distance	Rate	Time
1ˢᵗ train		72	
2ⁿᵈ train	d		t

c. Use the data in your table to write a system of equations.

d. Solve the system of equations and answer the question.

4. Two cars leave town at the same time going in opposite directions. One travels 44 mi/h and the other travels 55 mi/h. In how many hours will they be 297 miles apart?

5. Two cars leave town at the same time going in the same direction on the same road. One travels 32 mi/h and the other travels 47 mi/h. In how many hours will they be 69 miles apart?

6. A private airplane leaves an airport and flies due south at 192 km/h. Two hours later a jet leaves the same airport and flies due south at 960 km/h. When will the jet overtake the plane?

7. A canoeist paddled for 4 hours with a 6-km/h current to reach a campsite. The return trip against the same current took 10 hours. Find the speed of the canoe in still water.

8. An airplane flew for 4 hours with a 20-km/h tail wind. The return flight against the same wind took 5 hours. Find the speed of the plane in still air.

9. It takes a passenger train 2 hours less time than it takes a freight train to make the trip from Central City to Clear Creek. The passenger train averages 96 km/h while the freight train averages 64 km/h. How far is it from Central City to Clear Creek?

10. It takes a small jet plane 4 hours less time than it takes a propeller-driven plane to travel from Glen Rock to Oakville. The jet plane averages 637 km/h while the propeller plane averages 273 km/h. How far is it from Glen Rock to Oakville?

11. An airplane took 2 hours to fly 600 km against a head wind. The return trip with the wind took $1\frac{2}{3}$ hours. Find the speed of the plane in still air.

12. It took 3 hours to row a boat 18 km against the current. The return trip with the current took $1\frac{1}{2}$ hours. Find the speed of the rowboat in still water.

13. A motorcycle breaks down and the rider has to walk the rest of the way to work. The motorcycle was traveling at 45 mi/h, and the rider walks at a speed of 6 mi/h. The distance from home to work is 25 miles, and the total time for the trip was 2 hours. How far did the motorcycle go before it broke down?

14. A student walks and jogs to college each day. The student averages 5 km/h walking and 9 km/h jogging. The distance from home to college is 8 km, and the student makes the trip in 1 hour. How far does the student jog?

B

15. An airplane flew for 4.23 hours with a 25.5-km/h tail wind. The return flight against the same wind took 4.97 hours. Find the speed of the plane in still air.

16. An airplane took 2.5 hours to fly 625 miles with the wind. It took 4 hours and 10 minutes to make the return trip against the same wind. Find the wind speed and the speed of the plane in still air.

17. To deliver a package, a messenger must travel at a speed of 60 mi/h on land and then use a motorboat whose speed is 20 mi/h in still water. The messenger goes by land to a dock and then travels on a river against a current of 4 mi/h. He reaches the destination in 4.5 hours and then returns to the starting point in 3.5 hours. How far did the messenger travel by land and how far by water?

18. Against a head wind, Jeff computes his flight time for a trip of 2900 miles at 5 hours. The flight would take 4 hours and 50 minutes if the head wind were half as much. Find the head wind and the plane's air speed.

19. *Write a Convincing Argument* Solve the problem below. Then write an argument that would convince a classmate that your solution is correct.

A truck and a car leave a service station at the same time and travel on the same road in the same direction. The truck travels at 55 mi/h and the car at 40 mi/h. They can maintain CB radio contact within a range of 10 miles. When will they lose contact?

Challenge

20. In 1927 Charles Lindbergh flew the *Spirit of St. Louis* from New York to Paris at an average speed of 107.4 mi/h. Eleven years later, Howard Hughes flew the same route, averaged 217.1 mi/h, and took 16 hours, 57 minutes less time. Find the length of their route.

Today commercial airlines fly from New York to Paris in about 7 hours. Use the answer to Exercise 20 to find their average speed.

21. During normal traffic it takes Ingrid 24 minutes to travel the 18 miles from her house to the train station. However, during rush hour (5:30–8:30 A.M.) Ingrid can only travel 12 miles in the same length of time. It then takes at least 5 minutes to get onto a train, 30 minutes to get to her destination, and 5 minutes to get to her office. If trains leave every 15 minutes starting at 6:00 A.M., when does Ingrid have to leave her house in order to get to her office by 8:00 A.M.?

Mixed Review

Mental Math   Is the given ordered pair a solution of the system of equations? **22.** $(6, 1)$; $4y - x = -2$ **23.** $(2, 5)$; $y - 4x = -3$

$\qquad\qquad\qquad\qquad\qquad\qquad x - 7y = 2 \qquad\qquad\qquad\qquad\qquad 2x - y = -1$ *8-1*

Solve.   **24.** $x^2 - 3x = 4$ **25.** $y^2 - 7y - 18 = 0$ *8-8*

Simplify.   **26.** $\dfrac{x^4 y^7}{xy^3}$ **27.** $\dfrac{a^9 b^8}{a^4 b^2}$ **28.** $\left(\dfrac{q^3 s^5}{qs^2}\right)^3$ **29.** $\dfrac{x^{12} y^3 z^5}{x^3 yz^3}$ *5-1, 5-2*

Error Analysis

Each exercise has an error commonly made by algebra students. Can you find and correct the error?

1.
$$3x - y = 4$$
$$2x + y = 16$$
$$\overline{5x = 20}$$
$$x = 4$$

$$3x - y = 4$$
$$3(4) - y = 4$$
$$y = 4 - 12$$
$$y = -8$$
The solution is $(4, -8)$.

2.
$$4x - y = 17$$
$$-x - y = 7$$
$$\overline{3x = 24}$$
$$x = 8$$

$$4(8) - y = 17$$
$$32 - y = 17$$
$$-y = -15$$
$$y = 15$$
The solution is $(8, 15)$.

Digit and Coin Problems

Objective: Use systems of equations to solve digit and coin problems.

Any two-digit number can be expressed as $10x + y$ where x is the digit in the tens place and y is the digit in the ones place. The number 23 can be written $10 \cdot 2 + 3$.

If we reverse the digits in the original number, the new number can be expressed as $10y + x$. The reverse of 23, 32, can be written $10 \cdot 3 + 2$. We use this relationship in the next example.

What You'll Learn

1 To use systems of equations to solve digit and coin problems

. . . And Why

To be able to solve real-world problems using algebraic reasoning skills

EXAMPLE 1

The sum of the digits of a two-digit number is 14. If the digits are reversed, the number is 36 greater than the original number. Find the original number.

Let $x =$ the tens digit and $y =$ the ones digit.

There are two statements in this problem.

The sum of the digits is 14.

$$x + y = 14 \qquad \text{Translating}$$

The new number is 36 greater than the original number.

$$10y + x = 36 + 10x + y \qquad \text{Translating}$$

Simplifying the second equation gives

$$9x - 9y = -36$$

We have a system of equations.

$$x + y = 14$$
$$9x - 9y = -36$$

We can solve the system using the addition method. Multiply the first equation by 9 to make the y-terms additive inverses.

$$
\begin{aligned}
9(x + 7) = 9(14) &\longrightarrow & 9x + 9y &= 126 \\
9x - 9y = -36 &\longrightarrow & 9x - 9y &= -36 \\
\cline{3-4}
& & 18x &= 90 \\
& & x &= 5 \qquad \text{Tens digit}
\end{aligned}
$$

$5 + y = 14$ Substituting 5 for x in the first equation
$ y = 9$ Solving for y

The solution is $(5, 9)$. The original number is $5(10) + 9$ or 59.

Try This Translate to a system of equations and solve.

a. The sum of the digits of a two-digit number is 5. If the digits are reversed, the new number is 27 more than the original number. Find the original number.

b. The sum of the digits of a two-digit number is 7. If the digits are reversed, the new number is 9 less than the original number. Find the original number.

EXAMPLE 2

Kami has some nickels and some dimes. The value of the coins is $1.65. There are 12 more nickels than dimes. How many of each kind of coin does Kami have?

Let $d =$ the number of dimes and $n =$ the number of nickels. We write an equation for the number of coins.

$$d + 12 = n$$

The value of the nickels, in cents, is $5n$ since each nickel is worth 5¢. The value of the dimes is $10d$. Since we have the values of the coins in cents, we must use 165 cents for the total value. We write an equation for the value of the coins.

$$10d + 5n = 165$$

We can solve the system using the substitution method.

$$d + 12 = n$$
$$10d + 5n = 165$$
$$10d + 5(d + 12) = 165 \qquad \text{Substituting } d + 12 \text{ for } n \text{ in the second equation}$$
$$10d + 5d + 60 = 165$$
$$15d = 105$$
$$d = 7$$

$$d + 12 = n \qquad \text{Choosing the first equation}$$
$$7 + 12 = n \qquad \text{Substituting 7 for } d$$
$$19 = n$$

The solution of this system is (7, 19). Kami has 7 dimes and 19 nickels.

Try This Translate to a system of equations and solve.

c. On a table there are 20 coins, some quarters and some dimes. Their value is $3.05. How many of each are there?

d. Calvin paid his $1.35 skate rental with dimes and nickels only. There were 19 coins in all. How many of each coin were there?

EXAMPLE 3

There were 411 people at a play. Admission was $5 for adults and $3.75 for children. The receipts were $1978.75. How many adults and how many children attended?

Let a = the number of adults and c = the number of children.

	Number	Admission Price ($)	Receipts ($)
Adult	a	5.00	$5.00a$
Child	c	3.75	$3.75c$
Total	411		1978.75

Since the total number of people is 411, we have this equation.

$$a + c = 411$$

The receipts from adults and from children equal the total receipts.

$$5.00a + 3.75c = 1978.75$$

We have a system of equations. Clear the second equation of decimals and solve the system.

$$a + c = 411$$
$$500a + 375c = 197875$$

We multiply on both sides of the first equation by -500 and then add.

$$-500a - 500c = -205500$$
$$\underline{500a + 375c = 197875}$$
$$-125c = -7625$$
$$c = \frac{-7625}{-125}$$
$$c = 61$$
$$a + c = 411 \qquad \text{Choosing the first equation}$$
$$a + 61 = 411 \qquad \text{Substituting 61 for } c$$
$$a = 350$$

The solution of the system is (350, 61). There were 350 adults and 61 children at the play.

Try This Translate to a system of equations and solve.

e. There were 166 paid admissions to a game. The price was $2 for adults and $0.75 for children. The amount taken in was $293.25. How many adults and how many children attended?

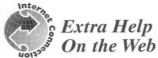
8-6 Exercises

A

1. The sum of the digits of a two-digit number is 9. If the digits are reversed, the new number if 63 greater than the original number. Find the original number.

2. The sum of the digits of a two-digit number is 10. When the digits are reversed, the new number is 36 more than the original number. Find the original number.

3. The sum of the digits of a two-digit number is 12. If the digits are reversed, the new number is 18 less than the original number. Find the original number.

4. The sum of the digits of a two-digit number if 16. If the digits are reversed, the new number is 18 less than the original number. Find the original number.

5. A jar of dimes and quarters contains $15.25. There are 103 coins in all. How many of each are there?

6. A jar of quarters and nickels contains $1.25. There are 13 coins in all. How many of each are there?

7. A vending machine takes only nickels and dimes. There are 5 times as many dimes as nickels in the machine. The face value of the coins is $4.40. How many of each coin are in the machine?

8. A vending machine takes only nickels and dimes. At the end of the day there were three times as many nickels as dimes and a total of $25. How many of each coin were in the machine?

9. There were 429 people at a play. Admission was $1 for adults and 75¢ for children. The receipts were $372.50. How many adults and how many children attended the play?

10. The attendance at a school concert was 578. Admission cost $2.00 for adults and $1.50 for children. The receipts were $985.00. How many adults and how many children attended the concert?

11. There were 200 tickets sold for a college basketball game. Tickets were $4.50 for students and $9 for adults. The total amount collected was $1485. How many of each type of ticket were sold?

12. There were 203 tickets sold for a school wrestling match. For those who held activity cards, the price was $2.50. For those who did not hold activity cards, the price was $4.00. The total amount collected was $620. How many of each type of ticket were sold?

13. A jar contains 5-gram bolts and 10-gram bolts. The contents of the jar weigh 2.35 kg (1000 g = 1 kg). If there are 300 bolts altogether, how many are there of each kind?

14. A jar contains 5-gram bolts and 10-gram bolts. The contents of the jar weigh 3.8 kg. If there are 460 bolts, how many are there of each kind?

Franklin Delano Roosevelt was paralyzed in both legs after he contracted polio in 1921. He was elected to four terms as President of the United States, serving from 1933 to his death in 1945. He has been honored on U.S. dimes since 1946.

B

15. The sum of the digits of a two-digit number is 14. If the number represented by reversing the digits is subtracted from the original number, the result is 18. What is the original number?

16. If 27 is added to a two-digit number, the result is a number with the same digits, but in reverse order. The sum of the digits is 11. What is the original number?

17. A two-digit number is 6 times the sum of its digits. The tens digit is 1 more than the units digit. Find the number.

18. *Write a Convincing Argument* Solve the problem below. Then write an argument to convince a classmate that your solution is correct.

The sum of three digits is 5. The first and last digits are the same. If the middle digit is exchanged with the first digit, the new number is 90 less than the original number. Find the original number.

Challenge

19. A three-digit number is 28 times the sum of its digits. The units digit is twice the tens digit and 3 more than the hundreds digit. Find the number.

20. Find all possible combinations of quarters and dimes that will total $2.20. What is the smallest number of coins?

21. Laurel went to the bank to get $20 worth of dimes and quarters. The teller made a mistake, interchanging the number of dimes and quarters Laurel asked for. How many dimes and how many quarters had she asked for if the teller gave her $9 too much?

22. Glenda wrote a check to pay for a radio. She accidentally transposed the numbers. The store sent her a refund for $36. She knew that the check was less than $100 and was a whole dollar amount. What are the possible amounts that the radio could have cost?

Mixed Review

Factor.   **23.** $16a^8 - 36$ **24.** $8x^3 + 10x^2 - 6x$ **25.** $c^2 - 5c$

26. $y^2 - 10y + 25$ **27.** $45m^2 - 106m + 45$ **28.** $2t^3 - 2t^2 - 4t$ *6-2, 6-5*

Solve.   **29.** $c^2 + 4c = 0$ **30.** $a^2 - 7a = -12$ **31.** $x^2 + 3x = 10$

Simplify.   **32.** $\dfrac{x^4 y^7}{x^2 y^5}$ **33.** $\dfrac{x^9 y^5 z^4}{x^6 y^2 z}$ **34.** $\left(\dfrac{a^3 b^7 c}{a^3 b}\right)^3$ *5-1, 5-2*

Multiply.   **35.** $(x + 1)^2$ **36.** $(x - 3)^2$ **37.** $(a + 7)^2$

38. $(r + 3)(r - 3)$ **39.** $(2a + 4)(a - 5)$ **40.** $(m - 4)^2$ *5-10*

Solve each system.   **41.** $3x + y = 5$ **42.** $2x + 3y = -2$
              $x + 2y = 0$ $3x + 2y = 7$ *8-1, 8-2, 8-3*

Preparing for Standardized Tests

Systems of Equations

Some items on standardized tests can be solved using the techniques you learned in this chapter for solving systems of equations. Some test items, however, can be solved more quickly using a variation of these methods.

EXAMPLE 1

If $2x + 3y = 27$ and $x + 2y = 7$, then $\dfrac{3x + 5y}{2} =$

(**A**) 10   (**B**) 12   (**C**) 17   (**D**) 20   (**E**) 34

While the addition method could be used to solve for x and y, this problem can be solved more easily using the addition principle and the multiplication principle to solve directly.

If we add the two equations and divide by 2, we find the answer immediately.

$$\begin{array}{l} 2x + 3y = 27 \\ \underline{x + 2y = 7} \\ 3x + 5y = 34 \end{array} \qquad \frac{3x + 5y}{2} = 17$$

The answer is (**C**).

EXAMPLE 2

If $5x + 4y = 12$ and $2x + y = 8$, then $3x + 3y =$

(**A**) 5   (**B**) 4   (**C**) 3   (**D**) 2   (**E**) 1

Subtracting equations results in the answer directly.

$$\begin{array}{l} 5x + 4y = 12 \\ \underline{2x + y = 8} \\ 3x + 3y = 4 \end{array}$$

The answer is (**B**).

EXAMPLE 3

If $5x - 3y = 12$ and $x = \dfrac{7y}{5}$, then $y =$

(**A**) $\dfrac{3}{5}$ (**B**) $\dfrac{5}{7}$ (**C**) 3   (**D**) $\dfrac{3}{4}$ (**E**) $\dfrac{21}{5}$

Since x is expressed in terms of y, we use the substitution method.

$$5\left(\frac{7y}{5}\right) - 3y = 12$$
$$y = 3$$

The answer is (C).

Before solving a system, decide whether it would be easier to use the addition method, the substitution method, or a variation of these methods as shown in Examples 1 and 2.

Problems

Determine the best method and solve.

1. If $x + 2y = 6$ and $3x + y = 4$, then $4x + 3y =$

(A) 8   (B) 9   (C) 10   (D) 11   (E) 12

2. If $5x - 3y = 8$ and $x = \frac{4y}{5}$, then $y =$

(A) $\frac{4}{5}$ (B) $\frac{8}{5}$ (C) 6   (D) $\frac{8}{3}$ (E) 8

3. If $x + 4y = 9$ and $4x + 3y = 7$, then $5x + 7y =$

(A) 8   (B) 9   (C) 16   (D) 18   (E) 20

4. If $3x + 3y = 17$ and $x + 4y = 3$, then $\frac{4x + 7y}{4} =$

(A) 5   (B) 7   (C) 8   (D) 10   (E) 12

5. If $4x - 3y = 12$ and $x = \frac{7y}{4}$, then $y =$

(A) 2   (B) 3   (C) 4   (D) 5   (E) 6

6. If $x + y = 3$ and $x - y = 2$, then $4x =$

(A) 16   (B) 14   (C) 12   (D) 10   (E) 8

7. If $5x + 2y = 6$ and $2x + y = 4$, then $3x + y =$

(A) 5   (B) 4   (C) 3   (D) 2   (E) 1

8. If $x + 2y = 4$ and $2x + y = 2$, then $6x + 6y =$

(A) 8   (B) 9   (C) 10   (D) 11   (E) 12

9. If $3x - 2y = 13$ and $5x + 4y = 11$, then $\frac{8x + 2y}{6} =$

(A) 24   (B) 6   (C) 4   (D) 3   (E) 2

10. If $5x + 2y = 12$ and $3x - 2y = 4$, then $\frac{2x + 4y}{4} =$

(A) 16   (B) 8   (C) 6   (D) 4   (E) 2

11. If $3x + 2y = 10$ and $5x - 2y = 6$, then $2x =$

(A) 1   (B) 2   (C) 3   (D) 4   (E) 8

Sales Taxes

Color Television Sets—This Week Only $290.00
How much would you really pay for a television set priced at $290.00? In most states, you would have to add sales tax, and would end up paying over $300.00. Sales tax is a percent of the price, and it varies by locality.

EXAMPLE 1

Gerry has $2.00 to buy a tube of toothpaste, which is priced at $1.88. The sales tax is 7%. Does he have enough money?
$$\text{total} = \$1.88 + 0.07(1.88) = \$2.01$$
He does not have enough money.

EXAMPLE 2

As the manager of a cafeteria, you would like to sell pears at exactly one dollar including tax. If sales tax is $6\frac{1}{2}\%$, what price would bring the total cost to an even dollar?

$$x + 0.065x = \$1.00$$
$$1.065x = \$1.00$$
$$x = \$0.94 \quad \text{Rounding to the hundredths place}$$

Problems

Assume the tax rate is 6%. State whether the spending money given is enough to pay for the item.

1. Soap, $1.68; spending money, $1.75

2. Clock radio, $29.98; spending money, $31.75

3. Baseball glove, $33.00; spending money, $35.00

4. Bicycle, $249.50; spending money, $270.00

You manage a cafeteria, and want to set prices that come to the total shown when sales tax of 5.5% is added. Give the price you would set for each.

5. Soup; total, $1.50

6. Chili; total, $2.00

7. Chicken sandwich; total, $3.00

8. Fruit salad; total, $2.50

9. Soft drink; total, $0.75

10. Ice cream; total, $1.00

8-1

A **solution** of a **system of equations** in two variables is an ordered pair that makes both equations true.

Determine whether the given ordered pair is a solution of the system.

1. $(6, -1)$; $x - y = 3$
$\quad\quad\quad\quad 2x + 5y = 6$

2. $(2, -3)$; $2x + y = 1$
$\quad\quad\quad\quad\quad x - y = 5$

3. $(-2, 1)$; $x + 3y = 1$
$\quad\quad\quad\quad\quad 2x - y = -5$

4. $(-4, -1)$; $x - y = 3$
$\quad\quad\quad\quad\quad\quad x + y = -5$

Solve by graphing.

5. $x + y = 4$
$\quad x - y = 8$

6. $x + 3y = 12$
$\quad 2x - 4y = 4$

7. $2x + y = 1$
$\quad x = 2y + 8$

8. $3x - 2y = -4$
$\quad 2y - 3x = -2$

8-2

To solve a system of equations without graphing, you can use the **substitution method.** First solve one of the equations for a variable. Then substitute for that variable in the other equation.

Solve using the substitution method.

9. $y = 5 - x$
$\quad 3x - 4y = -20$

10. $x + 2y = 6$
$\quad\quad 2x + 3y = 8$

11. $3x + y = 1$
$\quad\quad x = 2y + 5$

12. $x + y = 6$
$\quad\quad y = 3 - 2x$

13. $s + t = 5$
$\quad\quad s = 13 - 3t$

14. $x - y = 4$
$\quad\quad y = 2 - x$

Translate to a system of equations and solve.

15. The sum of two numbers is 30. Their difference is 40. Find the numbers.

8-3

The **addition method** can be used to solve a system of equations that are both in standard form $Ax + By = C$. Multiply one or both equations to make a pair of terms additive inverses. Then add the two equations and solve for the variable. Substitute for that variable in either of the original equations and solve for the second variable.

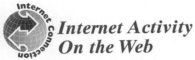

**Internet Activity
On the Web**

Look for extension problems
for this chapter at the
Prentice Hall Web site.
www.phschool.com

Solve using the addition method.

16. $x + y = 4$
$2x - y = 5$

17. $x + 2y = 9$
$3x - 2y = -5$

18. $x - y = 8$
$2x + y = 7$

19. $2x + 3y = -5$
$3x - y = -13$

20. $2x + 3y = 8$
$5x + 2y = -2$

21. $5x - 2y = 2$
$3x - 7y = 36$

22. $-x - y = -5$
$2x - y = 4$

23. $6x + 2y = 4$
$10x + 7y = -8$

Translate to a system of equations and solve.

24. The sum of two numbers is 27. One half of the first number plus one third of the second number is 11. Find the numbers.

8-4

Sometimes it is easier to use two variables when translating a word problem. Then you must find a system of two equations to solve in order to find the solution to the problem.

Translate to a system of equations and solve.

25. Roberta is 25 years older than her daughter, Cindy. In four years, Roberta will be twice as old as Cindy. How old are they now?

26. The perimeter of a rectangle is 76 cm. The length is 17 cm more than the width. Find the length and the width.

8-5

Use the formula, $d = r \cdot t$, to solve motion problems. *Drawing a diagram* and *making a table* may help you *write the equation.*

Translate to a system of equations and solve.

27. An airplane flew for 4 hours with a 15 mi/h tail wind. The return flight against the same wind took 5 hours. Find the speed of the airplane in still air.

8-6

A two-digit number can be written in the form $10x + y$. If the digits are reversed, the new number is $10y + x$. To solve coin problems, you can write one equation for the **number** of coins, and a second equation for the **value** of the coins.

28. The sum of the digits of a two-digit number is 6. When the digits are reversed, the new number is 36 more than the original number. Find the original number.

29. A collection of dimes and quarters is worth $25. There are 40 more dimes than quarters. How many of each are there?

Determine whether the given ordered pair is a solution of the system of equations.

1. $(4, 2)$; $x - y = 2$
  $x + y = 6$

2. $(-8, -7)$; $x - 2y = 6$
  $2x - 3y = 5$

Solve by graphing.

3. $x - y = 3$
  $x + y = 5$

4. $x + 2y = 6$
  $2x - 3y = 26$

5. $x = 2y + 4$
  $y = 2x - 8$

6. $x = y - 1$
  $3y = -2x - 2$

Solve using the substitution method.

7. $y = 6 - x$
  $2x - 3y = 22$

8. $x + 2y = 5$
  $x + y = 2$

9. $x + y = 31$
  $x - y = 17$

10. $7x + y = 10$
  $2y + 5x = 11$

Solve using the addition method.

11. $x - y = 6$
  $3x + y = -2$

12. $3x - 4y = 7$
  $x + 4y = 5$

13. $4x + 5y = 5$
  $6x + 7y = 7$

14. $2x + 3y = 13$
  $3x - 5y = 10$

15. $x + y = 4$
  $2x + 3y = 7$

16. $8x - 10y = 2$
  $7x - 5y = 13$

Translate to a system of equations and solve.

17. A motorboat traveled for 2 hours with an 8 km/h current. The return trip against the same current took 3 hours. Find the speed of the motorboat in still water.

18. The sum of two numbers is 8. Their difference is 12. Find the numbers.

19. A collection of dimes and quarters totals $3.55. There are 25 coins in all. How many quarters are there?

20. Tickets to a junior high school play cost $1.10 for each adult and $0.40 for each child. If 360 tickets were sold for a total of $282.60, how many tickets of each kind were sold?

21. One train leaves a station heading due west. Two hours later a second train leaves the same station heading due east. The second train is traveling 15 mi/h faster than the first. Six hours after the second train leaves, the two trains are 580 miles apart. Find the rate at which each train is traveling.

CHAPTER 9

Skills & Concepts You Need for Chapter 9

2-2 Use $>$ or $<$ to write a true sentence.

1. $-6 \;\square\; -4$ **2.** $4.5 \;\square\; -4.5$

4-1 Determine whether the given number is a solution of the inequality.

3. $x \le 6$

   (a) -12 **(b)** 0 **(c)** 6

Graph on a number line.

4. $x > -3$ **5.** $x \le 1$

4-2 to 4-4 Solve and graph the solution.

6. $2 - 3x > 20$ **7.** $28x + 18 > 26x - 8$

8. $8x - 10 > 7x - 4$ **9.** $8x - 13 \le -13$

7-2 **10.** Determine whether the given point is a solution of $2x - y = 6$.

   (a) $(1, 4)$ **(b)** $(1, -4)$ **(c)** $(2, -2)$

8-1 Determine whether the given ordered pair is a solution of the system of equations.

11. $(-4, -1);\ 2y - x = 2$
                 $x = 4y$

12. $(0, 2);\ y + 2 = x$
                   $y - 2 = -x - 4$

Solve by graphing.

13. $x + 2y = 7$
          $x = 3$

14. $3y - 2x = 4$
          $x + y = -2$

Inequalities and Absolute Value

A foundry worker pours molten gold. In Lesson 9-2, you will write a compound inequality to describe the temperature of liquid gold.

9-1 ▷ Sets, Intersections, and Unions

What You'll Learn

1 To name sets using set-builder notation

2 To find intersections of sets

3 To find unions of sets

... And Why

To understand the relationships between sets

We think of many objects in the real world in terms of sets. We refer to sets of keys, a set of dishes, and a set of luggage. A **set** is a well-defined collection of objects called **members** or **elements.** We will use capital letters to represent sets. The letter Z is commonly used to represent the set of integers.

PART 1 Set-Builder Notation

Objective: Name sets using set-builder notation.

We can write sets using two different notations, **roster notation,** which lists the members of the set, and **set-builder notation,** which gives a description of how the set is built.

Roster notation for the set of whole numbers greater than 20 is written

$$\{21, 22, 23, 24, \dots \}$$

The three dots indicate that the numbers continue, following the pattern set by the first four numbers.

Set-builder notation for the set of whole numbers greater than 20 is written

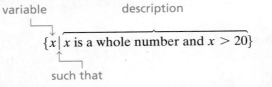

$$\{x \mid x \text{ is a whole number and } x > 20\}$$

We read this as "the set of all x such that x is a whole number and x is greater than 20."

EXAMPLES Write using (a) roster notation and (b) set-builder notation.

1 the set B of whole numbers less than 7
(a) $B = \{0, 1, 2, 3, 4, 5, 6\}$
(b) $B = \{x \mid x \text{ is a whole number and } x < 7\}$

2 the set E of positive integers
(a) $E = \{1, 2, 3, 4, \dots \}$ (b) $E = \{x \mid x \text{ is an integer and } x > 0\}$

Try This   Writing using (a) roster notation and (b) set-builder notation.

a. the set G of whole numbers greater than 5
b. the set T of multiples of 5 less than 24
c. the set P of prime numbers less than 20

Objective: Find intersections of sets.

The **intersection** of two sets A and B, written $A \cap B$, is the set of all members that are *common to both sets.* $A \cap B$ is read "A intersection B." In the diagram below, the circles represent sets A and B. The shaded region represents $A \cap B$.

$A \cap B$

EXAMPLE 3   Let $A = \{1, 2, 3, 4, 5, 6\}$ and $B = \{-2, 1, 0, 1, 2, 3\}$.

Find $A \cap B$. The numbers 1, 2, and 3 are common to both A and B.

$A \cap B = \{1, 2, 3\}$

Try This   Let $P = \{-3, -2, 0, 1, 5\}, T = \{0, 1, 6, 9\}$, and
$S = \{-3, 1, 6\}$.

d. Find $P \cap T$.   **e.** Find $T \cap S$.   **f.** Find $P \cap S$.

We can find intersections of infinite sets.

EXAMPLE 4   Let W be the set of whole numbers and Z be the set of integers. Find $W \cap Z$.

Every whole number is common to W and Z. Thus $W \cap Z = W$.

Consider the intersection of the set of even numbers and the set of odd numbers. There are no members common to both sets. Thus the intersection is empty. We say the intersection is the **empty set,** which is symbolized by $\{\ \}$ or $\emptyset$.

EXAMPLE 5   Let $G = \{0, 3, 6, 9\}$ and $H = \{2, 4, 8\}$. Find $G \cap H$.

There are no members common to G and H. $G \cap H = \emptyset$

Try This   Let E be the set of even numbers, W be the set of whole numbers, $T = \{0, 2\}$, and $S = \{1, 5\}$.

g. Find $S \cap T$.   **h.** Find $E \cap W$.   **i.** Find $T \cap E$.
j. Find $E \cap S$.   **k.** Find $W \cap S$.   **l.** Find $W \cap T$.

Objective: Find unions of sets.

The **union** of two sets A and B, written $A \cup B$, is the set of all members that are in A or in B (or in both). In other words, we form the union of two sets by putting them together. In the diagram below, the circles represent the sets. The shaded region represents the union of the sets.

Reading Math

Read $A \cup B$ as A *union* B.

$A \cup B$

$C \cup D$

EXAMPLE 6   Let $A = \{2, 3, 4\}$ and $B = \{3, 5, 7\}$. Find $A \cup B$.

The members 2, 3, 4, 5, and 7 are either in A or in B (or in both).

$A \cup B = \{2, 3, 4, 5, 7\}$

Try This   Let $W = \{-3, -2, 0, 4\}$, $X = \{-4, -2, 5, 6\}$, and $Y = \{1, 3, 5\}$.

m. Find $W \cup X$.   **n.** Find $W \cup Y$.

We can find unions involving infinite sets or the empty set.

EXAMPLE 7   Let $P = \{-2, -1, 4\}$. Find $P \cup \emptyset$.

The members -2, -1, and 4 are in P or in $\emptyset$.

$P \cup \emptyset = \{-2, -1, 4\} = P$

EXAMPLE 8   Let $S = \{4, 6, 8, 10\}$ and E be the set of even numbers.

Find $S \cup E$.

All even numbers are in S or in E.

$S \cup E = E$

Try This   Let $M = \{1, 3, 5\}$, E be the set of even whole numbers, and D be the set of odd whole numbers.

o. Find $M \cup D$.   **p.** Find $E \cup D$.   **q.** Find $M \cup \emptyset$.

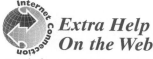

Extra Help On the Web
Look for worked-out examples at the Prentice Hall Web site.
www.phschool.com

9-1 Exercises

A

Write using (a) roster notation and (b) set-builder notation.

1. the set A of whole numbers less than 4

2. the set F of integers greater than or equal to 12

3. the set N of negative integers greater than -5

4. the set P of prime numbers less than 30

5. the set H of positive multiples of 3 less than or equal to 21

6. the set R of positive multiples of 4

7. the set E of positive even integers

8. the set T of positive factors of 12

9. the set M of even prime numbers

10. the set S of integers that are perfect squares less than 20

Let $A = \{-4, -3, -2, -1, 0\}$, $B = \{0, 1, 2\}$, $C = \{1, 2, 3, 4, 5\}$, and $D = \{4, 5, 6, 7, 8, 9, 10\}$. Find each of the following.

11. $B \cap C$	**12.** $A \cap B$	**13.** $C \cap D$	**14.** $C \cap B$
15. $A \cap C$	**16.** $B \cap D$	**17.** $A \cap \emptyset$	**18.** $D \cap \emptyset$

19. Let W be the set of whole numbers and E the set of even numbers. Find $W \cap E$.

20. Let Z be the set of integers and D the set of odd positive integers. Find $D \cap Z$.

Let $P = \{-5, -4, -3, -2, -1, 0\}$, $Q = \{-2, -1, 0\}$, $R = \{-1, 0, 1, 2, 3, 4\}$, and $S = \{5, 6, 7, 8\}$. Find each of the following.

21. $P \cup Q$	**22.** $Q \cup R$	**23.** $S \cup P$	**24.** $Q \cup S$
25. $R \cup S$	**26.** $R \cup P$	**27.** $P \cup \emptyset$	**28.** $S \cup \emptyset$

29. Let W be the set of whole numbers and E the set of even positive numbers. Find $W \cup E$.

30. Let Z be the set of integers and D the set of odd positive integers. Find $D \cup Z$.

B

Let E be the set of even numbers, J the set of integers less than -9, and P the set of odd numbers between 7 and 29. To say that -9 is an element of Z, we write $-9 \in Z$. To say that $\frac{5}{8}$ is not a member of Z, we write $\frac{5}{8} \notin Z$.

Tell whether each of the following is true or false.

31. $2 \in E$	**32.** $-7 \in J$	**33.** $19 \in P$	**34.** $0 \in J$
35. $-10 \in E$	**36.** $23 \in P$	**37.** $5 \notin P$	**38.** $16 \notin E$
39. $-8 \in P$	**40.** $10 \notin P$	**41.** $-5 \notin J$	**42.** $0 \notin E$

Mathematical Reasoning   Let A be any set. Find the following.

43. $A \cap A$ **44.** $A \cup \emptyset$ **45.** $A \cup A$ **46.** $A \cap \emptyset$

47. Find the intersection of the set of positive integers and the set of even integers.

48. Find the union of the set of integers and the set of whole numbers.

49. *Critical Thinking*   Find two sets whose intersection is {1} and whose union is {5, 1, 0, 9}.

Challenge

50. *Mathematical Reasoning*   Let $n(A)$ represent the number of members in set A. Show that $n(A \cup B) = n(A) + n(B) - n(A \cap B)$.

51. Use diagrams to show that $(A \cap B) \cap C = A \cap (B \cap C)$.

52. Use diagrams to show that $(A \cup B) \cup C = A \cup (B \cup C)$.

53. Let $A = \{3, 7, 10, 15\}$. Find a set B such that $A \cap B = A \cup B$.

Mixed Review

Factor. **54.** $18a^2 - 21a - 9$ **55.** $49 - 4c^2$ **56.** $5m^2 - 125$ *6-2, 6-5, 6-7*

57. $4a^2 - 12a + 9$ **58.** $4y^2 + 28y + 49$ **59.** $8x^2 + 18xy - 18y^2$

Solve.   **60.** $y = x - 5$ **61.** $x = y + 2$ **62.** $2x - y = -1$
$\qquad\qquad\quad y = 11 - 7x$ $x + y = 8$ $2y - x = -4$ *8-1, 8-2, 8-3*

Write an equation for the line that contains each pair of points.

63. $(0, 0), (1, 3)$ **64.** $(3, -1), (1, 1)$ **65.** $(3, -3), (-3, -5)$ *7-6*

66. The sum of two numbers is 31, the difference is 5. Find the numbers.   *8-6*

67. The sum of two numbers is 13, the product is 36. Find the numbers.   *8-6*

68. A bookstore sells paperback books for \$5.95 each and hardcover books for \$19.75 each. Last Tuesday, 86 books were sold for a total of \$939.50. How many each of paperback and hardcover books were sold?   *8-6*

◈ Connections: Reasoning

There are 220 students in the sophomore class. Suppose
115 are taking Journalism,
60 are taking Ceramics,
95 are taking Spanish,
20 are taking Journalism and Ceramics,
30 are taking Journalism and Spanish,
25 are taking Ceramics and Spanish,
15 are taking all three subjects.

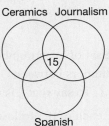

How many students are taking only one of these three subjects?
Hint: Complete a diagram like the one above.

Compound Sentences

PART 1

Conjunctions and Intersections

Objective: Solve and graph a conjunction of two inequalities in one variable.

A sentence like $x > 5$ and $x \le 12$ is called a **conjunction.** A conjunction of two statements is formed by connecting them with the word "and." A conjunction is true when *both* statements are true. A conjunction of two statements is similar to the intersection of two sets. The solution set of a conjunction is the intersection of the solution sets of the individual statements.

EXAMPLE 1 Graph the conjunction $x > 5$ and $x \le 12$.

$x > 5$

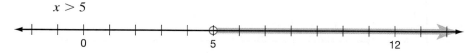

$x \le 12$

The graph of the conjunction is the intersection of the graphs of $x > 5$ and $x \le 12$.

$x > 5$ and $x \le 12$

The graph contains all numbers that are between 5 and 12, including 12. This can also be written as $5 < x \le 12$.

EXAMPLE 2 Graph the conjunction $x \ge -2$ and $x < 1$.

$x \ge -2$ and $x < 1$

This graph contains all numbers that are between -2 and 1, including -2. This can also be written as $-2 \le x < 1$.

What You'll Learn

1 To solve and graph a conjunction of two inequalities in one variable

2 To solve and graph a disjunction of two inequalities in one variable

...And Why

To solve compound inequalities

Reading Math

A compound sentence in English has two or more independent clauses. Similarly, a mathematical compound sentence has two or more inequalities or other mathematical sentences. Two types of compound sentences are *conjunctions* and *disjunctions*.

Try This   Graph each conjunction.

a. $-3 < x$ and $x < 4$ **b.** $-2 \le x$ and $x < 7$

EXAMPLE 3   Graph $-3 < x < 6$.

The inequality is the abbreviated form for the conjunction

$$-3 < x \text{ and } x < 6$$

The graph of the conjunction is the intersection of the individual graphs.

$-3 < x$

$x < 6$

$-3 < x < 6$

Try This   Graph.

c. $-2 < x \le 4$ **d.** $-7 < x < -3$

EXAMPLE 4   Solve and graph.

$$-6 \le 2x + 4 < 10$$
$$-6 \le 2x + 4 \text{ and } 2x + 4 < 10 \qquad \text{\small Writing the conjunction using \textit{and}}$$

Solve each inequality separately.

$$
\begin{array}{rcl}
-6 \le 2x + 4 & \text{and} & 2x + 4 < 10 \\
-6 + (-4) \le 2x + 4 + (-4) & \text{and} & 2x + 4 + (-4) < 10 + (-4) \\
-10 \le 2x & \text{and} & 2x < 6 \\
-5 \le x & \text{and} & x < 3
\end{array}
$$

We write the answer in abbreviated form and graph the solution.

$$-5 \le x < 3$$

The solution set is $\{x \mid x \ge -5 \text{ and } x < 3\}$ or $\{x \mid -5 \le x < 3\}$.

Try This   Solve and graph.

e. $-18 < 3x - 6 \le -3$
f. $5 < -2x + 1 \le 3$

Quick Review

To review solving inequalities, see Lesson 4-4.

PART 2   **Disjunctions and Unions**

Objective: Solve and graph a disjunction of two inequalities in one variable.

A sentence like $x < -3$ or $x > 6$ is called a **disjunction.** A disjunction of two statements is formed by connecting them with the word "or." A disjunction is true when *one or both* statements are true. A disjunction of two statements is like the union of two sets. The solution set of a disjunction is the union of the solution sets of the individual statements.

EXAMPLE 5   Graph the disjunction $x < -3$ or $x > 6$.

Try This   Graph the disjunction.

g. $x \le -1$ or $x > 4$

EXAMPLE 6   Solve and graph.

$$-3x - 4 > 8 \text{ or } x - 6 > 1$$

Solve each inequality separately.

$-3x - 4 > 8$	or	$x - 6 > 1$
$-3x - 4 + (4) > 8 + (4)$	or	$x - 6 + (6) > 1 + (6)$
$-3x > 12$		
$x < -4$	or	$x > 7$

We draw the graph of the solution set.

$$x < -4 \text{ or } x > 7$$

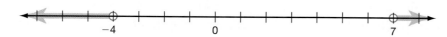

The solution set is $\{x \mid x < -4 \text{ or } x > 7\}$.

Try This   Solve and graph.

h. $-2x - 6 > 4$ or $x + 5 > 8$
i. $-5x + 2 > 27$ or $x - 3 > 2$

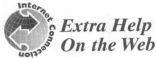

Extra Help On the Web

Look for worked-out examples at the Prentice Hall Web site.
www.phschool.com

9-2 Exercises

A

Mental Math   Graph these conjunctions.

1. $4 < x$ and $x < 9$

2. $-3 < x$ and $x < -1$

3. $0 < x$ and $x \le 5$

4. $-3 \le x$ and $x < 2$

5. $-7 \le x$ and $x \le 0$

6. $-4 \le x < 5$

Solve and graph.

7. $3 < x + 2 < 5$

8. $-4 \le x - 3 < 1$

9. $12 < 2x < 20$

10. $-18 < 3x < 3$

11. $-20 \le 5x \le 15$

12. $7 < 2x + 5 < 17$

13. $19 \le 5x + 4 \le 24$

14. $-5 < 7x - 5 \le 16$

15. $-11 \le -2x + 1 \le -3$

16. $-19 \le 5x + 6 < -4$

Mental Math   Graph these disjunctions.

17. $x < -1$ or $x > 2$

18. $x < -2$ or $x > 0$

19. $x \le -4$ or $x \ge 4$

20. $x < 0$ or $x > 5$

21. $x \le -6$ or $x > 2$

22. $x < 1$ or $x > -3$

Solve and graph.

23. $x + 8 < 10$ or $x - 5 > 2$

24. $x - 2 < 3$ or $x + 3 > 9$

25. $x + 1 \le 0$ or $x - 6 > 3$

26. $5x < -20$ or $3x > 12$

27. $4x < 16$ or $3x > 15$

28. $-2x > -14$ or $3x > 21$

29. $2x + 7 \le -3$ or $5x - 9 > 6$

30. $4x - 9 \le -17$ or $2x + 6 > 8$

31. **TEST PREP**   The solution of which inequality is $x < -10$ or $x > 4$?

A. $5x > 20$ or $2x < -20$

B. $-15 < x + 5 < 9$

C. $x + 3 > 7$ and $x + 10 < 0$

D. $-3x < -30$ or $x - 7 > -3$

B

Solve.

32. $x + 2 < 7$ or $x - 1 > -4$

33. $x - 5 < -3$ or $x + 8 > 7$

34. $3x + 12 \le 6$ and $2x - 4 > 2$

35. $-2x + 1 > 5$ and $-2x + 10 > 2$

36. $-6 > -3x - 6$ and $-3x - 6 \ge 6$

37. $3x - 8 < 13$ or $-3x + 10 > 5$

Write the inequality shown by each graph.

38.

39.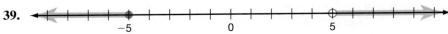

408   Chapter 9   *Inequalities and Absolute Value*

40.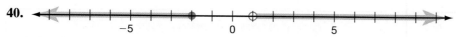

41.

42.

43.

Write a compound sentence for each situation.

44. The length of an adult triceratops dinosaur was between 20 feet and 25 feet. (Let l be the length in feet.)

45. The Mesozoic era was 145 million years ago plus or minus 85 million years.

46. Gold must be at least 1063° C and not more than 2808° C to be in liquid form.

47. Mercury is not a liquid if its temperature is below −39° C or above 357° C.

48. *Critical Thinking* If $a > b$ and $c > d$, is $ac > bd$ for all rational values of $a, b, c,$ and d? Explain.

Challenge

Write a conjunction or disjunction to describe each graph.

49.

50.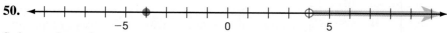

Solve and graph.

51. $(x - 3)(x + 5) \geq 0$ **52.** $(x + 8)(x - 4) < 0$

53. $x^2 + x - 2 > 0$ **54.** $x^2 - x - 6 \leq 0$

Gold is liquid between 1063°C and 2808°C. Write an inequality for temperatures where gold is not liquid.

Mixed Review

Identify the degree of each term and the degree of the polynomial.

55. $9a^2 - 25$ **56.** $7x^3y^2 + 21x^2y - 14x + 5$ **57.** $2a^2b^3c^4 - b^6$ *5-5*

Write an equation in slope-intercept form for the line that contains the given pair of points.   **58.** $(-3, 1), (4, 2)$ **59.** $(0, 5), (-2, 1)$ *7-6*

Solve. **60.** $x + y = -1$ **61.** $4x - 2y = 18$ **62.** $4x + 5y = -1$
$ x - y = 3$ $ x + 3y = -20$ $ 2x - 3y = 5$ *8-1, 8-2, 8-3*

63. A collection of nickels and dimes is worth $3.40. There are 41 coins in all. How many are nickels and how many are dimes?   *8-6*

64. The difference of two numbers is 8; the product is 65. Find the numbers.   *8-6*

Truth Tables

Recall that a statement is a sentence that is either true or false. A conjunction of two statements is only true if both statements are true. A disjunction of two statements is true if either statement is true. We can represent this with **truth tables** using T to indicate a true statement and F to indicate a false statement.

A	*B*	*A* and *B*
T	T	T
T	F	F
F	T	F
F	F	F

Truth Table for Conjunction

A	*B*	*A* and *B*
T	T	T
T	F	T
F	T	T
F	F	F

Truth Table for Disjunction

According to the table for conjunction, *A* and *B* is a true statement only if both *A* and *B* are true.

EXAMPLES

1 "Two is an even number and four is an even number" is true, since both individual statements are true.

2 "Five is an odd number and six is a prime number" is false, since one of the statements is false.

According to the table for disjunction, *A* and *B* is true in all cases except the one in which both *A* and *B* are false.

EXAMPLES

3 "Five is a prime number or eight is a prime number" is true, since one of the statements is true.

4 "Ten is a factor of twelve or eight is a prime number" is false, since both statements are false.

Exercises

True or false?

1. Five is a factor of 25 and six is a factor of 8.

2. Four is a prime number or two is a prime number.

3. Six is an even number or three is a prime number.

4. Ten is a factor of 11 or eight is an odd number.

5. An author of this book is Randall Charles and an author of this book is Stanley Smith.

Equations and Absolute Value

Objective: Solve equations involving absolute value.

Recall that the absolute value of a number is its distance from zero on the number line. $|x| = 3$ has two solutions, 3 and -3, since both have a distance of 3 units from 0 on the number line.

In general, we can state the following.

Solving Equations with Absolute Values

To solve an equation of the form $|A| = b$, where b is a positive number, solve the disjunction $A = b$ or $A = -b$.

What You'll Learn

1 To solve equations involving absolute value

...And Why

To increase the number of types of equations that can be solved

EXAMPLE 1   Solve $|x + 3| = 5$.
There are two numbers whose distance from 0 is 5, namely 5 and -5. This gives us the disjunction $x + 3 = 5$ or $x + 3 = -5$.

$$x + 3 = 5 \quad \text{or } x + 3 = -5$$
$$x = 2 \quad \text{or} \quad x = -8$$

Check:

$|x + 3| = 5$		$|x + 3| = 5$	
$|2 + 3|$	5	$|-8 + 3|$	5
$|5|$	5	$|-5|$	5
5	5 ✔	5	5 ✔

The solution set is $\{2, -8\}$.

EXAMPLE 2   Solve $|2x - 4| = 10$.
There are two numbers whose distance from 0 is 10, namely 10 and -10.

$$2x - 4 = 10 \quad \text{or} \quad 2x - 4 = -10$$
$$2x = 14 \quad \text{or} \quad 2x = -6$$
$$x = 7 \quad \text{or} \quad x = -3$$

Substitution will show that both numbers check. The solution set is $\{7, -3\}$.

EXAMPLE 3   Solve $|5x - 3| = -17$.
Since by definition the absolute value of a number is positive or it is zero, there is no solution to this equation. The solution set is $\emptyset$.

Try This   Solve.

a. $|x + 8| = 6$ **b.** $|x - 6| = 10$ **c.** $|4x - 9| = -7$

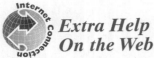
9-3 Exercises

A

Solve.

1. $|x + 9| = 18$ **2.** $|x - 4| = 9$ **3.** $|x + 11| = 6$

4. $|m - 7| = 23$ **5.** $|x - 10| = -8$ **6.** $|x + 17| = 2$

7. $|2x - 4| = 6$ **8.** $|4b - 11| = 5$ **9.** $|7x - 2| = 5$

10. $|8x + 3| = -27$ **11.** $|5x - 9| = 1$ **12.** $|4x + 3| = 67$

13. $|2y - 6| = -9$ **14.** $|4x + 3| = -5$ **15.** $|3x + 1| = 0.5$

16. $|5y + 8| = \frac{1}{2}$ **17.** $|2r - 1| = \frac{1}{4}$ **18.** $\left|\frac{1}{3}x - 9\right| = 10$

19. $|0.2x + 1| = 0.8$ **20.** $|4.2x - 1.4| = 7$ **21.** $|5x + 0.2| = 1.2$

B

Solve.

22. $|2x + 5| - 9 = 12$ **23.** $|3y - 2| + 4 = 21$

24. $|2 - a| - 3 = 1$ **25.** $8 - |1 - y| = 7$

26. $3|y + 6| = 6$ **27.** $4|t + 3| = 16$

28. $8 + |2c - 1| = 4$ **29.** $3|b - 2| + 7 = 10$

30. $4|3 - z| - 8 = 8$ **31.** $10 + |5x + 2| = 7$

32. $6 - |3y - 2| = 10$ **33.** $-|x + 1| = -2$

34. *Critical Thinking* Make one change in the equation $|x + 3| = 5$ so that the solution set of the new equation is $\{0, -6\}$.

Challenge

Solve.

35. $|x - 4| = x - 4$ **36.** $|3x| = |4x - 1|$ **37.** $|2y| = |3y + 2| + 1$

Self-Test On the Web

Check your progress. Look for a self-test at the Prentice Hall Web site.
www.phschool.com

Quick Review

To review solving equations, see Lessons 3-3 and 3-5.

Mixed Review

Find the slope and y-intercept of each line.

38. $x - 2y = 1$ **39.** $-4x - y = 7$ **40.** $3x = y - 4$

41. $5y + 4 = 2x - 1$ **42.** $3x - 5 = -4y + 7$ *7-5*

Factor. **43.** $2x^3 - 4x^2 - 6x$ **44.** $2y^2 - 9y + 4$ **45.** $9a^2 - 4$ *6-2, 6-5, 6-7*

Solve. **46.** $3y + 4x = -5$ **47.** $2x + y = -2$ **48.** $3x - y = 2$
$\qquad\qquad\quad x = y + 4 \qquad\qquad y - x = -5 \qquad\qquad 2x + y = 3$ *8-1, 8-2, 8-3*

Solve. **49.** $(m + 2)(m - 1) = 0$ **50.** $a(2a + 6)(a - 5) = 0$ *6-8*

51. Ray is 42 years old. Eight years ago, Ray was twice as old as Roy. How old is Roy today? *3-11*

Inequalities and Absolute Value

Introducing the Concept: Inequalities with Absolute Value

We know that $|x| = 3$ has two solutions, $x = 3$ and $x = -3$. Both 3 and -3 are 3 units from 0. Copy the number line below. Test points on the number line to find four other points that satisfy the condition $|x| < 3$.

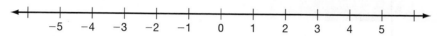

PART 1 Conjunctions and Inequalities

Objective: Solve and graph inequalities involving absolute value of the form $|A| < b$.

For the absolute value of a number to be less than 3, its distance from 0 must be less than 3. Therefore, the inequality $|x| < 3$ is true for any number between 3 and -3.

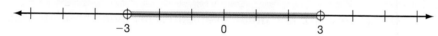

We write the solution as the conjunction $x < 3$ and $x > -3$, or $-3 < x < 3$. The solution set is $\{x| -3 < x < 3\}$.

Solving Inequalities with Absolute Values $|A| < b$

To solve an inequality of the form $|A| < b$ where b is a positive number, we solve the conjunction $-b < A < b$.
A similar rule holds for $|A| \le b$.

EXAMPLE 1   Solve and graph $|3x| < 15$.

We solve the conjunction as $-15 < 3x < 15$, first rewriting it using *and*.

$$-15 < 3x \quad \text{and} \quad 3x < 15$$
$$-5 < x \quad \text{and} \quad x < 5 \qquad \text{Solving each inequality}$$

We can abbreviate this conjunction as $-5 < x < 5$ and graph the solution.

The solution set is $\{x|-5 < x < 5\}$.

EXAMPLE 2

A lathe operator is making gears. The specifications require that the diameter (d) of the gear satisfies the inequality $|d - 2| \leq 0.01$ cm. What are the acceptable diameters for the gear?

We solve the conjunction

$-0.01 \leq d - 2 \leq 0.01$, first

rewriting it using *and*.

$$-0.01 \leq d - 2 \quad \text{and} \quad d - 2 \leq 0.01.$$
$$1.99 \leq d \quad \text{and} \quad d \leq 2.01.$$

The diameter of these gears must be within 0.01 cm of 2 cm to fit in a set of gears.

We can write this conjunction as $1.99 \leq d \leq 2.01$. The gear's diameter must be equal to a number in the interval described by the inequality.

The solution set is $\{d \mid 1.99 \leq d \leq 2.01\}$.

Try This Solve and graph.

a. $|x| < 7$ **b.** $|3x| < 18$ **c.** $|x + 5| \leq 9$ **d.** $|3x - 4| \leq 2$

PART 2 — Disjunctions and Inequalities

Objective: Solve and graph inequalities involving absolute value of the form $|A| > b$.

The inequality $|x| > 2$ is true for any value whose distance from 0 on the number line is greater than 2.

EXAMPLE 3   Graph $|x| > 2$ on a number line. Find the solution set.

For the absolute value of a number to be greater than 2, its distance from 0 must be greater than 2. Thus x must be greater than 2 or less than -2.

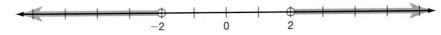

The solution is the disjunction $x < -2$ or $x > 2$.

Thus the solution set is $\{x \mid x < -2 \text{ or } x > 2\}$.

Try This Graph on a number line. Find the solution set.

e. $|x| > 1$ **f.** $|x| \geq 3$ **g.** $|x| > 5$

Solving Inequalities with Absolute Values $|A| > b$

To solve an inequality of the form $|A| > b$ where b is a positive number, we solve the disjunction $A < -b$ or $A > b$.
A similar rule holds for $|A| \geq b$.

EXAMPLE 4   Solve and graph $|3x - 8| \geq 5$.

Solve the disjunction $3x - 8 \leq -5$ or $3x - 8 \geq 5$.

$$3x - 8 \leq -5 \quad \text{or} \quad 3x - 8 \geq 5$$
$$3x \leq 3 \qquad\qquad 3x \geq 13$$
$$x \leq 1 \qquad\qquad x \geq \frac{13}{3}$$

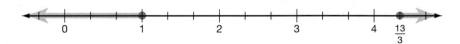

The solution set is $\left\{ x \mid x \leq 1 \text{ or } x \geq \frac{13}{3} \right\}$.

Try This   Solve and graph.

h. $|2x| > 10$ **i.** $|x - 4| \geq 5$ **j.** $|2x + 4| \geq 16$

9-4 Exercises

Extra Help On the Web

Look for worked-out examples at the Prentice Hall Web site.
   www.phschool.com

A

Solve and graph.

1. $|x| < 1$ **2.** $|t| \leq 4.5$ **3.** $|5x| \leq 20$ **4.** $|6x| \leq 24$

5. $|2x| < 11$ **6.** $|5y| \leq 5$ **7.** $|4t| < 28$ **8.** $|6x| \leq 36$

9. $|7x| \leq 35$ **10.** $|x - 3| < 12$ **11.** $|x + 2| \leq 5$ **12.** $|x - 5| \leq 7$

13. $|x + 6| < 2$ **14.** $|2y - 4| < 7$ **15.** $|4y - 2| < 7$

16. $|3x + 4| \leq 10$ **17.** $|2x + 1| \leq 5$ **18.** $|4z + 3| \leq 15$

In Example 2, suppose the diameter of the gear satisfies the following equation. What are the acceptable diameters for the gear?

19. $|d - 1| < 0.011$ **20.** $|2d - 2| \leq 1.1$ **21.** $|2d - 4| \leq 0.002$

Graph on a number line.

22. $|y| > 3$ **23.** $|t| > 4$ **24.** $|y| \geq 7$ **25.** $|x| \geq 9$

26. **TEST PREP**   Which inequality has the solution $-6 < t < 4$?

     A. $|t + 1| < 5$ **B.** $|t + 1| > 5$

     C. $|t - 1| < 5$ **D.** $|t - 1| > 5$

Solve and graph.

27. $|5x| > 20$ **28.** $|3x| \geq 18$ **29.** $|9t| \geq 27$

30. $|0.5x| > 1$ **31.** $|x - 1| \geq 6$ **32.** $|x + 5| > 9$

33. $|x - 9| \geq 11$ **34.** $\left| t - \frac{1}{2} \right| \geq 3$ **35.** $|3y + 1| > 4$

36. $|4x - 3| \geq 13$ **37.** $|6x + 1| \geq 11$ **38.** $\left| \frac{1}{5}x - \frac{1}{4} \right| > 1$

39. *Error Analysis* A student solved $|x - 3| > 5$ as shown.

$$|x - 3| > 5$$
$$x - 3 > 5 \text{ and } -5 < x - 3$$
$$x > 8 \text{ and } -2 < x$$

Therefore, x must be greater than 8.
What error did the student make?

B
Solve.

40. $|4x - 1| = 7$ **41.** $|2x + 3| \leq 9$ **42.** $|7x - 4| > 8$

43. $\left| \frac{2y + 1}{3} \right| \geq 5$ **44.** $\left| \frac{3x + 2}{4} \right| \leq 5$ **45.** $\left| \frac{13}{4} + 2t \right| = \frac{1}{4}$

46. $|3x + 2| + 2 = 3$ **47.** $|2b - 4| < -5$ **48.** $|3x + 5| > 0$

49. *Critical Thinking* Write an absolute value inequality to describe each of the graphs below.

a.
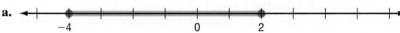

b.
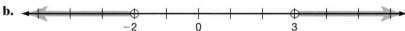

Challenge

50. Solve and graph $|5x| \geq 20$ or $|2x| \leq 4$.

Mixed Review

Write using roster notation.
51. the set A of prime numbers between 10 and 30
52. the set B of positive multiples of 4 less than 25   *9-1*
Find each of the following. Let $R = \{-6, -4, -2, 0, 2\}$,
$S = \{-2, -1, 0, 1, 2\}$, and $T = \{0, 2, 4, 6\}$.
53. $R \cap T$ **54.** $R \cup T$ **55.** $S \cup T$
56. $S \cap T$ **57.** $R \cup S$ **58.** $R \cap S$ *9-1*

Inequalities in Two Variables

What You'll Learn

1 To determine whether a given ordered pair is a solution of an inequality

2 To graph inequalities in two variables

PART 1 **Solutions of Inequalities in Two Variables**

Objective: Determine whether a given ordered pair is a solution of an inequality.

The solutions of an inequality in two variables are the ordered pairs of numbers that make the inequality true.

EXAMPLE 1

Determine whether $(5, -3)$ is a solution of the inequality $2x - y > 5$.
Replace x by 5 and y by -3.

$$2x - y > 5$$
$$2(5) - (-3) > 5$$
$$10 + 3 > 5$$
$$13 > 5 \quad \text{True}$$

Since $13 > 5$ is true, $(5, -3)$ is a solution.

Try This

a. Determine whether $(2, 1)$ is a solution of $x + y < 4$.
b. Determine whether $(4, 8)$ is a solution of $y > 2x + 1$.

PART 2 **Graphing Inequalities in Two Variables**

Objective: Graph inequalities in two variables.

The graph of the linear equation $x + y = 3$ separates the coordinate plane into three sets:

the set of points on the line,
the set of points above the line,
and the set of points below the line.

We call the regions above the line and below the line **half-planes.** We call the line a **boundary line.**

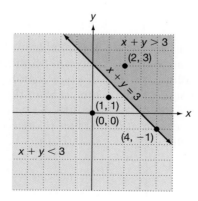

The solutions of an inequality in two variables are all the points in a half-plane and may include the points on the boundary line.

... **And Why**

To solve and graph inequalities in two variables

EXAMPLE 2 Graph $x + y < 4$ on a coordinate plane.

(a) We graph the boundary line $x + y = 4$ using any method learned in Chapter 7. We use a dashed line to show that the points on the line are not solutions of $x + y < 4$.

(b) The solutions of $x + y < 4$ must lie on one side of the boundary line. We test a point that is not on the line, such as $(0, 0)$.

$$x + y < 4$$
$$0 + 0 < 4$$
$$0 < 4 \quad \text{True}$$

Since $0 < 4$ is true, the half-plane containing $(0, 0)$ is the graph of the solution. We shade it to show that every point in that half-plane is a solution.

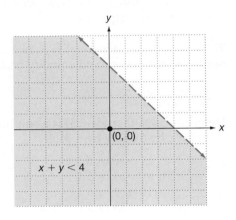

EXAMPLE 3 Graph $y - 2x \geq 0$ on a coordinate plane.

(a) We graph the boundary line $y - 2x = 0$. We use a solid line to show that the points on the line are solutions of $y - 2x \geq 0$.

(b) We determine which half-plane contains the solutions to $y - 2x \geq 0$ by testing a point that is not on the line, say $(1, 1)$.

$$y - 2x \geq 0$$
$$1 - 2(1) \geq 0$$
$$1 - 2 \geq 0$$
$$-1 \geq 0 \quad \text{False}$$

Since $-1 \geq 0$ is *false,* the half-plane containing $(1, 1)$ does *not* contain the solutions. The half-plane that does *not* contain $(1, 1)$ is the graph of the solution. We shade it to show that every point in that half-plane is a solution.

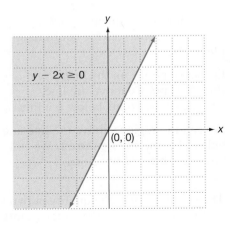

EXAMPLE 4   Graph $y < -2$ on a coordinate plane.

(a) We graph the boundary line $y = -2$, using a dashed line to show that the points on the line are not solutions of $y < -2$.

(b) We test a point that is not on the line, such as $(0, -3)$.

$$y < -2$$
$$-3 < -2 \quad \text{Substituting } -3 \text{ for } y$$

Since $-3 < -2$ is true, the half-plane containing $(0, -3)$ is the graph of the solution. We shade below the line to show that every point in that half-plane is a solution.

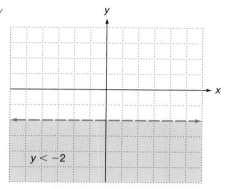

Try This   Graph on a coordinate plane.

c. $y > x - 1$ **d.** $2x + y \leq 4$
e. $y - 3x < 0$ **f.** $x \geq 2$

9-5 Exercises

A

1. Determine whether $(-3, -5)$ is a solution of $-x - 3y < 18$.

2. Determine whether $(5, -3)$ is a solution of $-2x + 4y \leq -2$.

3. Determine whether $\left(\frac{1}{2}, -\frac{1}{4}\right)$ is a solution of $7y - 9x > -3$.

Graph on a coordinate plane.

4. $x > 2y$	**5.** $x > 3y$	**6.** $y \leq x - 3$
7. $y \leq x - 5$	**8.** $y < x + 1$	**9.** $y < x + 4$
10. $y > 2$	**11.** $x \geq 3$	**12.** $x > 0$
13. $y \geq x - 2$	**14.** $y \geq x - 1$	**15.** $y \leq 2x - 1$
16. $y \leq 3x + 2$	**17.** $x + y \leq 3$	**18.** $x + y \leq 4$
19. $y \leq 0$	**20.** $y \geq -1$	**21.** $x \leq -2$
22. $x - y > 7$	**23.** $x - y > -2$	**24.** $x - 3y < 6$
25. $x - y < -10$	**26.** $2x + 3y \leq 12$	**27.** $5x + 4y \geq 20$
28. $y \geq 1 - 2x$	**29.** $y - 2x \leq -1$	**30.** $y + 4x > 0$
31. $y - x < 0$	**32.** $y > -3x$	**33.** $y < -5x$

34. **TEST PREP**   Which inequality has the same boundary line as

$y \geq 2x - 3$?

A. $2x + y \leq 3$ **B.** $y + 2x \geq 3$ **C.** $2x - y < -3$

D. $y - 2x > -3$ **E.** none of them

B
Write an inequality for each graph.

35.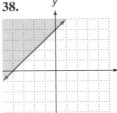

36.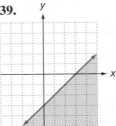

37.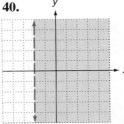

38.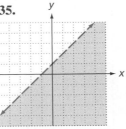

39.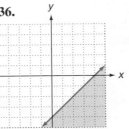

40.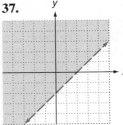

41. *Critical Thinking*   What compound inequality is shown in the graph? Can you find another inequality represented by the graph?

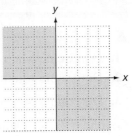

Challenge

Graph on a coordinate plane.

42. $|x| \leq y$ **43.** $|y| \geq x$

44. $|x| + |y| > 4$ **45.** $|x| - |y| \geq 6$

Graph on a number line.   **46.** $-5 \leq x$ and $x < 2$

47. $-4 < x$ and $x < -1$ **48.** $x \leq 0$ or $x > 3$ *4-1, 9-2*

Solve.   **49.** $5 < x + 8 \leq 13$ **50.** $2x + 1 \leq -7$ or $3x - 5 > 4$ *9-2*

Factor.   **51.** $m^2 - 15m + 50$ **52.** $2a^2 - 5a - 42$

53. $2x^2 + 3xa + a^2$ **54.** $6x^2 + 19x + 15$ *6-4, 6-5*

Graphing Systems of Linear Inequalities

Objective: Graph systems of linear inequalities in two variables.

Math in Action

The Sanderson Water Company must supply at least 8 million gallons of water per day (mgd) to the city of Sanderson. The water will come from either the local reservoir or from a pipeline to a water supply located in the mountains. The local reservoir has a daily yield of 4 mgd, which may not be exceeded. The pipeline can supply no more than 8 mgd. However, in order to use the pipeline, the company must agree to use a minimum of 6 mgd. What are possible amounts from each source that will satisfy these conditions?

In real-world situations there are often many conditions or constraints that must be considered. Constraints can often be translated into mathematical inequalities. Two or more linear inequalities for which a common solution is sought are called a **system of inequalities.**

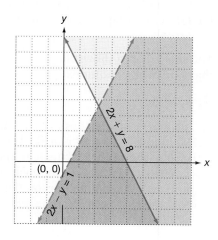

What You'll Learn

1 To graph systems of linear inequalities in two variables

...And Why

To find all the solutions of a system of inequalities by graphing

If the surface area of the reservoir is 1 mi^2, by how much will the water level drop if 4 million gallons are removed? (Hint: 1 mi$^2 \approx 27,900,000$ ft^2 1 ft$^3 \approx 7.5$ gal)

EXAMPLE 1 Solve this system by graphing.

$$2x + y \geq 8$$
$$2x - y > 1$$

(a) Graph the inequality $2x + y \geq 8$, graphing the boundary line $2x + y = 8$ (solid), and shading the half-plane above the boundary line in one color.

(b) Graph the inequality $2x - y > 1$, graphing the boundary line $2x - y = 1$ (dashed), and shading the half-plane below the line in another color.

The region where the shadings overlap is the graph of the solution to the system of inequalities.

Try This   Solve each system by graphing.

a. $y > 4x - 1$
$y < -2x + 3$

b. $y \geq x$
$y \leq -x + 1$

c. $x \leq 0$
$x - y > 1$

d. $x + y < -1$
$3x - y > 4$

EXAMPLE 2   Write an inequality for each of the conditions given in the Math in Action. Then graph these inequalities.

The Sanderson Water Company must supply at least 8 million gallons of water per day (mgd) to the city of Sanderson. The water will be provided from either the local reservoir or from a pipeline to a water supply located in the mountains. The local reservoir has a daily yield of 4 mgd, which may not be exceeded. The pipeline can supply no more than 8 mgd. However, in order to use the pipeline, the Sanderson Water Company must agree to use a minimum of 6 mgd. What are possible amounts from each source that will satisfy these conditions?

Let $x =$ the amount of water (mgd) supplied from the reservoir.
Let $y =$ the amount of water (mgd) supplied from the pipeline.

The water company must supply at least 8 mgd $\rightarrow$ $x + y \geq 8$

The reservoir can supply no more than 4 mgd $\rightarrow$ $x \leq 4$

The pipeline can supply no more than 8 mgd $\rightarrow$ $y \leq 8$

If used, the pipeline must supply at least 6 mgd $\rightarrow$ $y \geq 6$

Graph each of these inequalities on the same coordinate axes.

When graphing a system of three or more equations, we can use arrows to show which side of the boundary is included in the graph.

Finally, shade the region where all of the graphs overlap as indicated by the arrows.

The shaded area shows the values that satisfy all conditions.

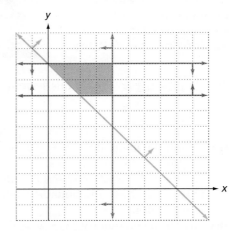

Try This

e. The math club decides to raise money by selling pencils. They order 300 blue and 400 red pencils. They must sell 100 pencils to break even. Each of the twenty students in the club agrees to sell at least 10 pencils.
  i. Write an inequality for each condition given in this situation.
  ii. Graph the inequalities on the same coordinate axes.
  iii. If the club sells 250 blue pencils and 300 red pencils, have they satisfied all of the conditions?

9-6 Exercises

Extra Help On the Web
Look for worked-out examples at the Prentice Hall Web site.
www.phschool.com

A

Solve each system by graphing.

1. $x > 2 + y$
   $y > 1$

2. $y < 3x$
   $x + y < 4$

3. $y < x$
   $y < -x + 1$

4. $y > x$
   $y > -x + 2$

5. $2y - y < 2$
   $x > 3$

6. $y > 4$
   $2y + x > 5$

7. $y > 4x - 1$
   $y \leq -2x + 3$

8. $y > 5x + 2$
   $y \leq -x + 1$

9. $x - 2y > 6$
   $x + 2y \leq 4$

10. $2y - x > 5$
   $x + y \leq 4$

11. $2x - 3y \geq 9$
   $2y + x > 6$

12. $3x - 2y \leq 8$
   $2x + y > 6$

13. $x + y < 3$
   $x - y \leq 4$

14. $x - y < 3$
   $x + y \geq 4$

15. $5x + 2y \geq 12$
   $2x + 3y \leq 10$

16. $x \leq 4$
   $x + y \leq 3$
   $y \leq x$

17. $y \leq x$
   $x \geq -2$
   $y \leq 1 - x$

18. $y > 0$
   $x > y$
   $x + y \geq 2$

19. $y > 2x$
   $y \leq x + 2$
   $x > -1$

20. $y \leq x$
   $y \geq -2$
   $y < 2x - 3$

21. $x - y > 3$
   $x > 0$
   $x + y \leq 5$

22. *Multi-Step Problem*   The school board is investigating ways to hire a faculty for the summer school program. They can hire teachers and aides. A minimum of 20 faculty members is needed to run the program, and there must be at least 12 teachers. For a proper teacher-to-aide ratio, the number of aides must be no more than twice the number of teachers. There can be no more than 50 faculty members altogether. (*Hint:* There cannot be a negative number of teachers or aides.)

   a. Write an inequality for each condition given in this situation.

   b. Graph the inequalities on the same coordinate axes.

   c. If the school board hires 12 teachers and 5 aides, will all of the conditions be satisfied?

23. *Multi-Step Problem*   The math club will sell rolls of wrapping paper and ribbon as a fundraiser. They can order up to 300 items, as long as they spend less than $600. They also must buy at least as many rolls of wrapping paper as rolls of ribbon. Each roll of wrapping paper costs the club $2. Each roll of ribbon costs the club $3.

   a. Write an inequality for each condition given in this situation.

   b. Graph the inequalities on the same coordinate axes.

   c. If the club buys 150 rolls of wrapping paper and 100 rolls of ribbon, will all of the conditions be satisfied?

B

Write a system of inequalities whose solution is shown by each graph.

24.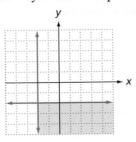

25.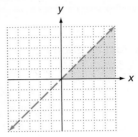

26.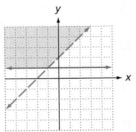

27.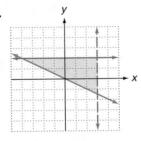

28. *Critical Thinking*   Write a system of inequalities such that the graph of its solution forms a square region with one corner at the origin and two adjacent sides on the *x*- and *y*-axis.

Challenge

The corner points of the graph of a system of inequalities are the points where the boundary lines intersect. Graph each system of inequalities and give the coordinates of each corner point.

29. $x - y \leq 1$
$x + 2y > 1$
$y < 1$

30. $x > 0$
$2y + x \leq 6$
$x + 2 \leq 2y$

31. Graph $(x - y - 3)(x + y + 2) > 0$. (*Hint*: Under what conditions is a product of two numbers positive?)

Mixed Review

Solve. **32.** $x + 5 \leq 16$ or $x - 3 > 5$ **33.** $-7 \leq -3x + 2 < -1$

34. $|4x| > 8$ **35.** $|4x| < 8$

36. $|2y + 1| > 9$ **37.** $|2y + 1| < 9$ *9-2, 9-4*

Factor.   **38.** $x^2 + 3yx + 2y^2$ **39.** $b^2 + 4b + 4$ **40.** $9x^4 - 25y^2$ *6-2, 6-4, 6-7*

41. A collection of dimes and quarters is worth $16.20. There are 81 coins in all. How many are dimes and how many are quarters?   *8-6*

Quantitative Comparisons

If you are asked to compare two expressions, you can often guess which expression is greater. However, you may want to check your answer by replacing the variables in the expressions with numbers. Select at least one positive integer, at least one negative integer, and zero as check points. If exponents are involved, you should also try a larger number like 10.

The choices for these kinds of test items are often
(A) if the quantity in column A is greater.
(B) if the quantity in column B is greater.
(C) if the two quantities are equal.
(D) if the relationship cannot be determined.

In the examples below, decide which of the choices above is correct.

EXAMPLE 1

Column A	Column B
$2x$	x

You may guess that $2x$ is greater than x. However, is $2x$ greater than x for all acceptable replacements?

$2(1)$	$>$	(1)	Substituting 1
$2(0)$	$=$	(0)	Substituting 0
$2(-1)$	$<$	(-1)	Substituting -1

Since the expressions are $>$, $=$, and $<$, depending on the value of the variable, the correct answer is (D), the relationship cannot be determined.

EXAMPLE 2

Column A	Column B
m^2	$1 + m^2$

1^2	$<$	$1 + 1^2$	Substituting 1
0^2	$<$	$1 + 0^2$	Substituting 0
$(-1)^2$	$<$	$1 + (-1)^2$	Substituting -1

Since Column B is always larger than Column A, the answer is (B), the quantity in Column B is greater.

EXAMPLE 3

	Column A		Column B
		a, b, c are all positive.	
	abc		$a + b + c$
First you let $a, b, c = 1$	$(1)(1)(1)$	$<$	$1 + 1 + 1$
Then you let $a, b, c = 2$	$(2)(2)(2)$	$>$	$2 + 2 + 2$

Since you get both $<$ and $>$, the answer must be (D), the relationship cannot be determined.

Problems

Compare the quantities in Column A with those in Column B, and choose statement (A), (B), (C), or (D).

	Column A		Column B
1.		$x < 0$	
	$(x + 1)(x + 4)$		$(x + 1)^2$
2.		$c < d < 0$	
	c		cd
3.		$a < b < c$	
	ab		bc
4.		$mn > 0$	
	$m + n$		$m - n$
5.	$5.0 \times 8{,}765$		$5.1 \times 8{,}765$
6.		$0 < c < d$	
	c		$-4d$
7.		$e > 1$	
		$f < 0$	
	$\dfrac{f}{e}$		ef
8.		$a > 0$	
	$(a - 2)(a + 5)$		$(a - 2)$
9.		$-3 < d < 3$	
		$d \neq 0$	
	$\dfrac{1}{d}$		d
10.		$(a + b) - c = a$	
	b		c

9-1

A **set** is a well-defined collection of objects called **members** or **elements.** To write a set using **roster notation,** list the elements of the set. To write a set using **set-builder notation,** specify a variable and a description of how to build the set.

Write using (a) roster notation and (b) set-builder notation.

1. the set A of whole numbers less than 9
2. the set B of odd whole numbers
3. the set C of positive multiples of 7 less than 30
4. the set D of negative integers greater than -5

The **intersection** of two sets A and B, $A \cap B$, is the set of all elements that are common to both sets. The **union** of the two sets A and B, $A \cup B$, is the set of all elements that are in A or B or both.

Let $A = \{2, 4, 8, 16, 32\}$, $B = \{4, 8, 12, 16, 20\}$, and $C = \{3, 6, 9, 12, 15, 18\}$. Find the following.

5. $A \cup B$
6. $A \cup C$
7. $A \cap B$
8. $B \cap C$
9. Let W be the set of whole numbers and P be the set of positive odd numbers. Find $W \cap P$.
10. Let Z be the set of integers and W be the set of whole numbers. Find $Z \cup W$.

Key Terms

boundary line (p. 417)
conjunction (p. 405)
disjunction (p. 407)
element (p. 400)
empty set (p. 401)
half-plane (p. 417)
intersection (p. 401)
member (p. 400)
roster notation (p. 400)
set (p. 400)
set-builder notation (p. 400)
system of inequalities (p. 421)
truth table (p. 410)
union (p. 402)

9-2

A **conjunction** of two statements is formed by the word "and" connecting the two statements and is true when both statements are true. The graph of a conjunction is the *intersection* of the two individual graphs. A **disjunction** of two statements is formed by the word "or" connecting the two statements and is true when one or both of the statements are true. The graph of the disjunction is the *union* of the two individual graphs.

11. Graph the conjunction $x \geq -2$ and $x \leq 1$.
12. Graph the conjunction $-1 < p < 12$.
13. Graph the disjunction $x < -2$ or $x > 4$.

Solve and graph.

14. $-2 \leq x + 3 < 7$
15. $-1 \leq x + 4 < 4$
16. $12 + 2x < 0$ or $-2 - x \leq 3$
17. $x + 3 < 4$ or $x - 2 > -5$

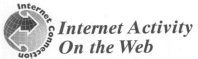
9-3

To solve an equation with absolute value, such as $|x + 1| = 5$, solve the
disjunction $x + 1 = 5$ or $x + 1 = -5$.

Solve.

18. $|x + 4| = 8$

19. $|3x - 6| = 18$

20. $|5x + 3| = 21$

21. $|3x - 5| = -7$

9-4

To graph an inequality such as $|x| < 5$, solve and graph the conjunction
$-5 < x < 5$. To solve an inequality such as $|x| > 5$, solve and graph the
disjunction $x > 5$ or $x < -5$.

Solve and graph.

22. $|5y| < 15$

23. $|y - 3| < 5$

24. $|2x - 9| \le 1$

25. $|3x| \ge 15$

26. $|5 + a| > 0$

27. $|-2y + 5| > 3$

9-5

To determine whether an ordered pair is a solution of an inequality, substitute
the numbers in the ordered pair for the variables to see whether the
inequality is true.

Determine whether the given point is a solution of the inequality $x - 2y > 1$.

28. $(0, 0)$

29. $(1, 3)$

30. $(4, -1)$

31. $(-2, -2)$

To graph an inequality in two variables, graph the equation of the boundary
line as a dashed or solid line. Then test a point that is not on the line to
determine which **half-plane** contains the solution.

Graph on a coordinate plane.

32. $y \le 9$

33. $2x + y \ge 6$

34. $x > 2 - 2y$

35. $x < -2$

9-6

To find the solutions of a **system of inequalities,** graph both inequalities on a
coordinate plane and find their intersection.

Solve each system by graphing.

36. $y \ge x$
   $y < x + 1$

37. $x > 1$
   $y < -2$

38. $x + y < 6$
   $2x - y < 7$

9 ▷ Chapter Assessment

Write using (a) roster notation and (b) set-builder notation.

1. the set A of whole numbers greater than 4

2. the set B of negative integers greater than -3

3. the set C of positive multiples of 3 less than -3

Let $A = (2, 4, 6, 8, 10, 12)$, $B = (5, 10, 15)$, and $C = (2, 3, 5, 7, 11)$. Find the following.

4. $A \cap C$

5. $A \cap B$

6. $B \cap C$

7. $A \cup B$

8. $B \cup C$

Solve and graph.

9. $0 < x - 4 < 3$

10. $-10 \leq x - 5 < -8$

11. $x + 2 < 1$ or $x + 3 \geq 5$

12. $2x < -2$ or $3x - 1 > 2$

Solve.

13. $|x - 2| = 4$

14. $|3x - 6| = 21$

Solve and graph.

15. $|3p| < 21$

16. $|x + 4| < 2$

17. $|9 - r| \leq 9$

18. $|4x| \geq 12$

19. $|2a - 1| > 5$

20. $|-3y + 6| > 12$

Solve each system by graphing.

21. $y \leq x$
$\quad y > x - 2$

22. $y > -3$
$\quad x < -2$

23. $y - x + 2 < 0$
$\quad 2y - 2 > x$

24. $x - y > 2$
$\quad x + y < 1$

CHAPTER 10

Skills & Concepts You Need for Chapter 10

2-6   Find the reciprocal.

1. $\frac{3}{5}$

2. $\frac{3x}{y}$

3-3 and 3-5   Solve.

3. $9 = 6(5x - 1)$

4. $11 - 2(y + 1) = 21$

5. $5(d + 4) = 7(d - 1)$

6. $5(t + 3) + 4 = 3(t - 2) + 1$

5-7, 5-8   Add or subtract.

7. $(2x^2 + 3x - 7) + (x^2 + x - 8)$

8. $(x^2 + 6x + 8) - (x^2 - 3x - 4)$

5-9 to 5-11   Multiply.

9. $2x(3x + 2)$

10. $(x + 1)(x^2 - 2x - 1)$

11. $(x - 2)(x + 2)$

12. $(x + 3)(x + 3)$

6-1 to 6-5   Factor.

13. $x^2 - 9$ **14.** $x^2 - 6x + 9$ **15.** $x^2 + 3x + 2$

16. $16x^6 - 32x^5$ **17.** $6a^2 + 5a - 6$

6-8   Solve.

18. $x^2 - 5x + 6 = 0$

19. $9x^2 - 4 = 0$

6-9

20. One more than a number times one less than a number is 24. Find the number.

Rational Expressions and Equations

The honeybee's storage system consists of an array of hexagonal cells. On page 432 you will learn about shapes other than hexagons that could be used for the cells.

10-1 ▷ Simplifying Rational Expressions

Objective: Simplify rational expressions.

Introducing the Concept: Rational Expressions

What You'll Learn

1 To simplify rational expressions

... And Why

To be able to simplify complex expressions and equations that are obtained when solving real-life problems

Bees tessellate the plane with regular hexagons. Find what other regular polygons tessellate the plane in the introduction to rational expressions at the right.

Geometric patterns that use repeated shapes to cover the plane without gaps or overlaps are called tessellations. Regular polygons have all sides congruent and all angles congruent. Tessellations made up of regular polygons are often used in architecture. Not all regular polygons tessellate the plane.

In the expression below, n represents the number of sides of a regular polygon. If the value of the expression is a whole number when you substitute for n, then the regular polygon with n sides will tessellate the plane.

$$\frac{2n}{n-2}$$

Find three values of n for which the expression gives a whole number. Sketch a tessellation using an n-sided regular polygon for each of the values of n you find. What relationship do you see between your sketches and the value of the above expression?

A **rational expression** is a quotient of two polynomials. A rational expression always indicates division. For example,

$$\frac{x^2 + 3x - 10}{3x + 2} \text{ means } (x^2 + 3x - 10) \div (3x + 2)$$

Rational expressions have the same properties as rational numbers. Since we cannot divide by 0, replacements for variables in the denominator that make the denominator 0 are not acceptable.

$\dfrac{5}{x}$ x cannot be 0.

$\dfrac{a}{b-2}$ b cannot be 2.

$\dfrac{5}{x-y}$ x cannot equal y.

A rational expression is in **simplest form** when the numerator and denominator have no common factors other than 1 or -1.

simplest form: $\dfrac{a + 2}{3a}$ Neither 3 nor a is a factor of $a + 2$.

not in simplest form: $\dfrac{5(x + 4)}{x(x + 4)}$ $x + 4$ is a factor of the numerator and the denominator.

To simplify rational expressions, factor the numerator and denominator. The common factors simplify to 1. We will restrict the values of the variables to values that will not make the denominator zero.

EXAMPLES Simplify.

1 $\dfrac{5x - 10}{5x} = \dfrac{5(x - 2)}{5x}$ Factoring the numerator

$= \dfrac{5(x - 2)}{5x}$ $\frac{5}{5} = 1$

$= \dfrac{x - 2}{x}$ Simplifying

2 $\dfrac{y^2 + 3y + 2}{y^2 - 1} = \dfrac{(y + 2)(y + 1)}{(y + 1)(y - 1)}$ Factoring the numerator and denominator

$= \dfrac{(y + 1)(y + 2)}{(y + 1)(y - 1)}$ $\frac{y + 1}{y + 1} = 1$

$= \dfrac{y + 2}{y - 1}$ Simplifying

Try This Simplify.

a. $\dfrac{12y + 24}{48y}$ **b.** $\dfrac{2x^2 + x}{3x^2 + 2x}$ **c.** $\dfrac{a^2 - 1}{2a^2 - a - 1}$

The numerator and denominator in the rational expression $\frac{x - 4}{4 - x}$ do not appear to have any common factors other than 1. Since $(x - 4)$ and $(4 - x)$ are additive inverses of each other, however, we can rewrite one of them as -1 times the other.

EXAMPLES Simplify.

3 $\dfrac{x - 4}{4 - x} = \dfrac{-1(-x + 4)}{(4 - x)}$

$= \dfrac{-1(4 - x)}{(4 - x)}$ $\frac{4 - x}{4 - x} = 1$

$= -1$

4 $\dfrac{3x - 6}{2 - x} = \dfrac{3(x - 2)}{2 - x}$ Factoring the numerator

$\quad\quad\quad = \dfrac{3(x - 2)}{-1(x - 2)}$ $2 - x = -1(-2 + x) = -1(x - 2)$

$\quad\quad\quad = -3$ Simplifying

5 $\dfrac{1 - y^2}{y^2 - 4y + 3} = \dfrac{(1 - y)(1 + y)}{(y - 1)(y - 3)}$ Factoring the numerator and denominator

$\quad\quad\quad\quad = \dfrac{-1(y - 1)(1 + y)}{(y - 1)(y - 3)}$

$\quad\quad\quad\quad = \dfrac{-1(1 + y)}{(y - 3)}$

$\quad\quad\quad\quad = \dfrac{-1 - y}{y - 3}$

Try This   Simplify.

d. $\dfrac{b - 7}{7 - b}$ **e.** $\dfrac{5 - 2a}{3(2a - 5)}$ **f.** $\dfrac{4x - 12}{6 - 2x}$

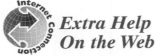

Extra Help On the Web

Look for worked-out examples at the Prentice Hall Web site.
www.phschool.com

10-1 Exercises

A
Simplify.

1. $\dfrac{4x^2y}{2xy^3}$

2. $\dfrac{a^3b^2}{-2a^5b}$

3. $\dfrac{4x - 12}{4x}$

4. $\dfrac{-2y + 6}{-4y}$

5. $\dfrac{3m^2 + 3m}{6m^2 + 9m}$

6. $\dfrac{4y^2 - 2y}{5y^2 - 5y}$

7. $\dfrac{6x^5 - x^4}{x^2 - x}$

8. $\dfrac{a^6 - a^5}{a^8 - a^7}$

9. $\dfrac{d + 7}{d^2 - 49}$

10. $\dfrac{a^2 - 9}{a^2 + 5a + 6}$

11. $\dfrac{t^2 - 25}{t^2 + t - 20}$

12. $\dfrac{2t^2 + 6t + 4}{4t^2 - 12t - 16}$

13. $\dfrac{a^2 - 1}{a - 1}$

14. $\dfrac{t^2 - 1}{t + 1}$

15. $\dfrac{x^2 + 1}{x + 1}$

16. $\dfrac{y^2 + 4}{y + 2}$

17. $\dfrac{6x^2 - 54}{4x^2 - 36}$

18. $\dfrac{8y^2 - 32}{4y^2 - 16}$

19. $\dfrac{6x + 12}{x^2 - x - 6}$

20. $\dfrac{5a + 5}{a^2 + 7a + 6}$

21. $\dfrac{b^2 - 10b + 21}{b^2 - 11b + 28}$

22. $\dfrac{2t - 8}{12 - 3t}$

23. $\dfrac{y^2 - 3y - 18}{y^2 - 2y - 15}$

24. $\dfrac{t^2 - 4}{(t + 2)^2}$

25. $\dfrac{(a - 3)^2}{a^2 - 9}$

26. $\dfrac{5x - 15}{3 - x}$

27. $\dfrac{6 - y}{y^2 - 2y - 24}$

28. $\dfrac{4 - 2y}{2y^2 + 10y - 28}$

29. $\dfrac{-12}{4x^2 - 1}$

30. $\dfrac{(a - b)^2}{b^2 - a^2}$

B

Simplify.

31. $\dfrac{a^4 - b^4}{b^2 - a^2}$

32. $\dfrac{x^4 - 16y^4}{(x^2 + 4y^2)(x - 2y)}$

33. $\dfrac{m^4 - n^4}{4m^2 + 4n^2}$

34. $\dfrac{2y^4 - 2z^4}{2y^2 - 2z^2}$

35. $\dfrac{(t - 3)^3(t^2 - 2t + 1)}{(t - 1)^3(t^2 - 4t + 4)}$

36. $\dfrac{(x^2 - y^2)(x^2 - 2xy + y^2)}{(x - y)^2(x^2 - 4xy - 5y^2)}$

Evaluate each expression before simplifying and after simplifying.

37. $\dfrac{(x + 3)^2}{x^2 - 9}$ for $x = 4$

38. $\dfrac{3a - 6}{2 - a}$ for $a = 2$

39. Critical Thinking   If a is a rational number, is it *sometimes*, *always*, or *never* true that $\dfrac{a^2 - 3a}{a - 3} = a$? Explain.

Error Analysis   Tell which of the rational expressions below were simplified correctly. For those that were not done correctly, tell what error was made.

40. $\dfrac{8x^4y^2}{2x^3y^2} = 4x$

41. $\dfrac{2y - 7}{2y} = -7$

42. $\dfrac{(m - 2)^2}{m^2 - 4} = m + 2$

43. $\dfrac{8y^2 - 32}{4y^2 - 16} = 2y^2 - 2$

Challenge

Determine which replacements of x are not acceptable.

44. $\dfrac{x + 1}{x^2 + 4x + 4}$

45. $\dfrac{x^2 - 16}{x^2 + 2x - 3}$

46. $\dfrac{x - 7}{x^3 - 9x^2 + 14x}$

Mixed Review

Solve.

47. $x^2 - 12x + 35 = 0$

48. $25x^2 - 9 = 0$

49. $6x^2 - x - 1 = 0$

50. $3x^2 + 2x - 8 = 0$

51. $3x - 4y = 6$
   $x + 4y = -14$

52. $x - y = -6$
   $3x + 4y = -4$

53. $2y + 7x = -4$
   $x = y - 7$ *6-8, 8-1, 8-2, 8-3*

10-2 ▷ Multiplying Rational Expressions

Objective: Multiply rational expressions.

To multiply rational numbers, we multiply the numerators and multiply the denominators.

$$\frac{3}{4} \cdot \frac{5}{6} = \frac{3 \cdot 5}{4 \cdot 6} = \frac{15}{24}$$

We multiply rational expressions in the same way.

EXAMPLES   Multiply. Simplify the product.

1 $\dfrac{5a^3}{4} \cdot \dfrac{2}{5a} = \dfrac{5a^3 \cdot 2}{4 \cdot 5a}$ Multiplying numerators and multiplying denominators

$\qquad = \dfrac{10a^3}{20a}$

$\qquad = \dfrac{a^2}{2}$ Simplifying: $\frac{10}{20} = \frac{1}{2}$ $\frac{a^3}{a} = a^{3-1} = a^2$

2 $\dfrac{4}{5x^2} \cdot \dfrac{x-2}{2x^3} = \dfrac{4(x-2)}{10x^5}$ Multiplying numerators and multiplying denominators

$\qquad = \dfrac{2(x-2)}{5x^5}$ Simplifying: $\frac{4}{10} = \frac{2}{5}$

3 $\dfrac{a-2}{3} \cdot \dfrac{a+2}{a+3} = \dfrac{(a-2)(a+2)}{3(a+3)}$ Multiplying numerators and multiplying denominators

There are no common factors other than 1. The answer is in simplest form. We could also write the product as $\frac{a^2-4}{3a+9}$. However, we usually write products of polynomials in factored form.

4   Multiply. Simplify the product.

$\qquad \dfrac{-2}{2y+6} \cdot \dfrac{3}{y-5} = \dfrac{-2 \cdot 3}{(2y+6)(y-5)}$ Multiplying numerators and multiplying denominators

$\qquad\qquad = \dfrac{-2 \cdot 3}{2(y+3)(y-5)}$ Factoring the denominator

$\qquad\qquad = \dfrac{-3}{(y+3)(y-5)}$ Simplifying: $\frac{-2}{2} = -1$

Try This   Multiply. Simplify the product.

a. $\dfrac{4a^4}{3} \cdot \dfrac{6}{5a^2}$ **b.** $\dfrac{x+3}{5} \cdot \dfrac{5(x+2)}{x+4}$ **c.** $\dfrac{-3}{4m+2} \cdot \dfrac{4}{2m-1}$

10-2 Exercises

Extra Help On the Web
Look for worked-out examples at the Prentice Hall Web site.
www.phschool.com

A
Multiply. Simplify the product.

1. $\dfrac{4x^3}{3x} \cdot \dfrac{14}{x}$

2. $\dfrac{32}{b^4} \cdot \dfrac{3b^2}{8}$

3. $\dfrac{3c}{d^2} \cdot \dfrac{4d}{6c^3}$

4. $\dfrac{8}{3x} \cdot \dfrac{x + 7}{6x^2}$

5. $\dfrac{y + 6}{2y} \cdot \dfrac{4y^2}{y + 6}$

6. $\dfrac{-5}{m} \cdot \dfrac{m^6}{m + 2}$

7. $\dfrac{-2n}{7(n + 2)} \cdot \dfrac{7n + 7}{n + 1}$

8. $\dfrac{-3y}{6(y - 1)} \cdot \dfrac{2y - 2}{y^2}$

9. $\dfrac{a - 6}{a^2} \cdot \dfrac{a + 2}{a + 1}$

10. $\dfrac{3x}{2} \cdot \dfrac{x + 4}{x - 1}$

11. $\dfrac{4y}{5} \cdot \dfrac{y - 3}{2y}$

12. $\dfrac{a - 1}{a + 2} \cdot \dfrac{a + 1}{a - 1}$

13. $\dfrac{m - 2}{m - 5} \cdot \dfrac{m + 5}{m - 2}$

14. $\dfrac{2x + 3}{4} \cdot \dfrac{4}{x - 5}$

15. $\dfrac{-5}{6y - 4} \cdot \dfrac{-6}{5y + 6}$

16. $\dfrac{a - 5}{a^2 + 1} \cdot \dfrac{a + 1}{a^2 - 1}$

17. $\dfrac{t + 3}{t^2 - 2} \cdot \dfrac{t + 3}{t^2 - 9}$

18. $\dfrac{x + 1}{2 + x} \cdot \dfrac{x - 1}{x + 1}$

19. $\dfrac{2x}{2x} \cdot \dfrac{x - 1}{x + 4}$

20. $\dfrac{3y - 1}{2y + 1} \cdot \dfrac{y}{y}$

21. $\dfrac{-1}{-1} \cdot \dfrac{3 - x}{4 - x}$

22. $\dfrac{-1}{-1} \cdot \dfrac{4 - a}{5 - a}$

23. $\dfrac{4(x + 2)}{5x} \cdot \dfrac{6x^2}{2x}$

24. $\dfrac{6(m - 3)}{5m} \cdot \dfrac{4m^2}{2(m - 3)}$

25. $\dfrac{(y - 4)^2}{3y} \cdot \dfrac{(y - 2)}{(y + 4)(y - 4)}$

26. $\dfrac{(x + 1)^2}{x + 3} \cdot \dfrac{(x + 3)^3}{x + 1}$

27. $\dfrac{5(m - 1)}{(m + 3)^2} \cdot \dfrac{m + 3}{(m - 1)^2}$

28. $\dfrac{6a + 12}{5} \cdot \dfrac{15a}{7a + 14}$

29. $\dfrac{25 - x^2}{12} \cdot \dfrac{6}{5 - x}$

30. $\dfrac{3}{x^2 - 1} \cdot \dfrac{x + 1}{3}$

31. $\dfrac{4 - 3a}{6} \cdot \dfrac{3}{3a - 4}$

32. $\dfrac{1 - x}{7} \cdot \dfrac{14}{x - 1}$

33. $\dfrac{7x}{4x + 3} \cdot (8x + 6)$

34. $\dfrac{4c}{2c - 1} \cdot (8c - 4)$

B

Multiply. Simplify the product.

35. $\dfrac{x^2 - 3x - 10}{(x - 2)^2} \cdot \dfrac{x - 2}{x - 5}$

36. $\dfrac{t^2}{t^2 - 4} \cdot \dfrac{t^2 - 5t + 6}{t^2 - 3t}$

37. $\dfrac{a^2 - 9}{a^2} \cdot \dfrac{a^2 - 3a}{a^2 + a - 12}$

38. $\dfrac{m^2 + 10m - 11}{m^2 - 1} \cdot \dfrac{m + 1}{m + 11}$

39. $\dfrac{4a^2}{3a^2 - 12a + 12} \cdot \dfrac{3a - 6}{2a}$

40. $\dfrac{5v + 5}{v - 2} \cdot \dfrac{v^2 - 4v + 4}{v^2 - 1}$

41. $\dfrac{x^4 - 16}{x^4 - 1} \cdot \dfrac{x^2 + 1}{x^2 + 4}$

42. $\dfrac{t^4 - 1}{t^4 - 81} \cdot \dfrac{t^2 + 9}{t^2 + 1}$

43. $\dfrac{(t - 2)^3}{(t - 1)^3} \cdot \dfrac{t^2 - 2t + 1}{t^2 - 4t + 4}$

44. $\dfrac{(y + 4)^3}{(y + 2)^3} \cdot \dfrac{y^2 + 4y + 4}{y^2 + 8y + 16}$

45. $\dfrac{m^2 - n^2}{2m + 1} \cdot \dfrac{2m^2 - 5m - 3}{m + n}$

46. $\dfrac{a^4 - b^4}{2ab} \cdot \dfrac{2a^2 - ab - 3b^2}{a^2 + b^2}$

47. $\dfrac{-4x^2 - 9xy - 2y^2}{x + 2y} \cdot \dfrac{-1}{4x^2 - 3xy - y^2}$

48. *Critical Thinking* Find two different pairs of rational expressions whose product is $\dfrac{8a^2 + 16a - 24}{a^2 + 13a + 40}$.

Challenge

Determine which replacements of x are not acceptable.

49. $\dfrac{x + 1}{x^2 + 4x + 4}$

50. $\dfrac{x^2 - 16}{x^2 + 2x - 3}$

51. $\dfrac{x - 7}{x^3 - 9x^2 + 14x}$

52. $\dfrac{x^2 - 4}{x^3 + x^2 - 6x}$

Let $A = \{-2, 0, 3, 5\}$, $B = \{0, 1, 2, 3, 4\}$, and $C = \{-3, -2, 0, 1\}$. Find the following. **53.** $A \cup B$ **54.** $A \cap C$ **55.** $B \cap C$ **56.** $A \cup \emptyset$ *9-1*

Solve. **57.** $x^2 - 4 = 3x$ **58.** $2y^2 - 6y = -4$ **59.** $3a^2 - 5 = 2a$ *6-8*

Solve each system. **60.** $x - \frac{2}{5}y = -2$ **61.** $2x - y = 4$

$\qquad\qquad\qquad\qquad\qquad 3x + 2y = 10 \qquad\quad \frac{3}{4}x + y = 7$ *8-2, 8-3*

Solve. **62.** $|y + 2| = 5$ **63.** $|2y - 6| = 16$ **64.** $|3x + 4| = 13$ *9-3*

65. Warne's Firewood Sales delivers and stacks seasoned firewood. A half cord costs $65. One cord costs $110. Assume a linear relationship fits these data using the ordered pairs (cords, price).

   a. Find the linear equation for the data points.

   b. Use this linear equation to find the cost of 5 cords of firewood. *7-7*

A cord of firewood is a stack that is 8 ft long, 4 ft high, and 4 ft wide. How many cords fill a woodbin that is 12 ft long, 4 ft high, and 2 ft deep? How much would it cost to fill the bin with Warne's firewood? (See Exercise 65.)

Dividing Rational Expressions

Objective: Divide rational expressions.

We can divide rational expressions using the same procedure as dividing two rational numbers. To divide rational expressions, multiply the first expression by the reciprocal of the divisor.

What You'll Learn

1 To divide rational expressions

. . . And Why

To be able to simplify algebraic expressions

EXAMPLES Divide and simplify.

1 $\dfrac{8n^5}{3} \div \dfrac{2n^2}{9} = \dfrac{8n^5}{3} \cdot \dfrac{9}{2n^2}$ Multiplying by the reciprocal of the divisor

$\qquad = \dfrac{72n^5}{6n^2}$ Multiplying numerators and multiplying denominators

$\qquad = 12n^3$ Simplifying

2 $\dfrac{2x + 8}{3} \div \dfrac{x + 4}{9} = \dfrac{2x + 8}{3} \cdot \dfrac{9}{x + 4}$ Multiplying by the reciprocal of the divisor

$\qquad = \dfrac{(2x + 8)(9)}{3(x + 4)}$ Multiplying

$\qquad = \dfrac{2(x + 4)(9)}{(x + 4)(3)}$ Factoring

$\qquad = 6$

3 $\dfrac{x + 1}{x + 2} \div \dfrac{x + 1}{x + 3} = \dfrac{x + 1}{x + 2} \cdot \dfrac{x + 3}{x + 1}$ Multiplying by the reciprocal of the divisor

$\qquad = \dfrac{(x + 1)(x + 3)}{(x + 2)(x + 1)}$ Factoring and identifying common factors

$\qquad = \dfrac{x + 3}{x + 2}$

4 $\dfrac{x + 1}{x^2 - 1} \div \dfrac{x + 1}{x^2 - 2x + 1} = \dfrac{x + 1}{x^2 - 1} \cdot \dfrac{x^2 - 2x + 1}{x + 1}$

$\qquad = \dfrac{(x + 1)(x^2 - 2x + 1)}{(x^2 - 1)(x + 1)}$

$\qquad = \dfrac{(x + 1)(x - 1)(x - 1)}{(x + 1)(x - 1)(x + 1)}$ Factoring and identifying common factors

$\qquad = \dfrac{x - 1}{x + 1}$

Try This   Divide and simplify.

a. $\dfrac{9a^4}{7} \div \dfrac{9a^2}{14}$ **b.** $\dfrac{4m - 8}{5} \div \dfrac{m - 2}{10}$ **c.** $\dfrac{3}{x^2 - 4} \div \dfrac{2}{x - 1}$

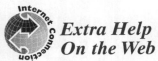

Extra Help On the Web

Look for worked-out examples at the Prentice Hall Web site.

www.phschool.com

10-3 Exercises

A

Divide and simplify.

1. $\dfrac{5x^4}{3} \div \dfrac{5x^2}{6}$

2. $\dfrac{-2x^6}{7} \div \dfrac{4x}{5}$

3. $\dfrac{3}{a^5} \div \dfrac{3}{a^2}$

4. $\dfrac{2}{t^5} \div \dfrac{8}{t^2}$

5. $\dfrac{6m^4}{5} \div 2m$

6. $\dfrac{4a^7}{3} \div 5a^2$

7. $\dfrac{5x - 5}{16} \div \dfrac{x - 1}{6}$

8. $\dfrac{-4 + 2x}{8} \div \dfrac{x - 2}{2}$

9. $\dfrac{-6 + 3x}{5} \div \dfrac{4x - 8}{25}$

10. $\dfrac{-12 + 4x}{4} \div \dfrac{-6 + 2x}{6}$

11. $\dfrac{a + 2}{a - 1} \div \dfrac{3a + 6}{a - 5}$

12. $\dfrac{t - 3}{t + 2} \div \dfrac{4t - 12}{t + 1}$

13. $\dfrac{x^2 - 4}{x} \div \dfrac{x - 2}{x + 2}$

14. $\dfrac{x^2 - 1}{x} \div \dfrac{x + 1}{x - 1}$

15. $\dfrac{x^2 - 9}{4x + 12} \div \dfrac{x - 3}{6}$

16. $\dfrac{4y - 8}{y + 2} \div \dfrac{y - 2}{y^2 - 4}$

17. $\dfrac{c^2 + 3c}{c^2 + 2c - 3} \div \dfrac{c}{c + 1}$

18. $\dfrac{x - 5}{2x} \div \dfrac{x^2 - 25}{4x^2}$

19. $\dfrac{8a - 32}{a + 1} \div \dfrac{16}{3a + 3}$

20. $\dfrac{17}{5x - 10} \div \dfrac{34x + 51}{3x - 6}$

21. $\dfrac{2y^2 - 7y + 3}{2y^2 + 3y - 2} \div \dfrac{6y^2 - 5y + 1}{3y^2 + 5y - 2}$

22. $\dfrac{x^2 - x - 20}{x^2 + 7x + 12} \div \dfrac{x^2 - 10x + 25}{x^2 + 6x + 9}$

23. $\dfrac{x^2 + 13x + 12}{x + 2} \div (x + 1)$

24. $\dfrac{a^2 - 5a + 6}{a - 3} \div (a - 2)$

25. $\dfrac{c^2 + 10c + 21}{c^2 - 2c - 15} \div (c^2 + 2c - 35)$

26. $\dfrac{1 - z}{1 + 2z - z^2} \div (1 - z)$

27. $(c + 3) \div \dfrac{c^2 + c - 6}{c + 2}$

28. $(2 - x) \div \dfrac{x^2 - 4}{x - 7}$

29. $\dfrac{(t + 5)^3}{(t - 5)^3} \div \dfrac{(t + 5)^2}{(t - 5)^2}$

30. $\dfrac{(y - 3)^3}{(y + 3)^3} \div \dfrac{(y - 3)^2}{(y + 3)^2}$

31. $\left(\dfrac{a + 7}{3}\right)^3 \div \left(\dfrac{a + 7}{2}\right)^2$

32. $\left(\dfrac{2x - 3}{2}\right)^4 \div \left(\dfrac{2x - 3}{2}\right)^3$

33. $\left(\dfrac{4}{b - 3}\right)^4 \div \left(\dfrac{3}{b - 3}\right)^5$

34. $\left(\dfrac{5}{y + 9}\right) \div \left(\dfrac{5}{y + 9}\right)^5$

B

Divide and simplify.

35. $\dfrac{2a^2 - 5ab}{c - 3d} \div (4a^2 - 25b^2)$

36. $\dfrac{3a^2 - 5ab - 12b^2}{3ab + 4b^2} \div (3b^2 - ab)$

37. $(x - 2a) \div \dfrac{a^2x^2 - 4a^4}{a^2x + 2a^3}$

38. $\dfrac{3x^2 - 2xy - y^2}{x^2 - y^2} \div (3x^2 + 4xy + y^2)$

39. $\dfrac{z^2 - 8z + 16}{z^2 + 8z + 16} \div \dfrac{(z - 4)^5}{(z + 4)^5}$

40. $xy \cdot \dfrac{y^2 - 4xy}{y - x} \div \dfrac{16x^2y^2 - y^4}{4x^2 - 3xy - y^2}$

41. *Critical Thinking* The volume of this figure is $a - 3$. What is its width?

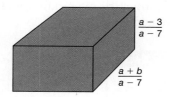

$\dfrac{a - 3}{a - 7}$

$\dfrac{a + b}{a - 7}$

Challenge

Divide and simplify.

42. $\dfrac{x^2 - x + xy - y}{x^2 + 6x - 7} \div \dfrac{x^2 + 2xy + y^2}{4x + 4y}$

43. $\dfrac{3x + 3y + 3}{9x} \div \dfrac{x^2 + 2xy + y^2 - 1}{x^4 + x^2}$

44. $\left(\dfrac{y^2 + 5y + 6}{y^2} \cdot \dfrac{3y^3 + 6y^2}{y^2 - y - 12}\right) \div \dfrac{y^2 - y}{y^2 - 2y - 8}$

45. $\dfrac{a^4 - 81b^4}{a^2c - 6abc + 9b^2c} \cdot \dfrac{a + 3b}{a^2 + 9b^2} \div \dfrac{a^2 + 6ab + 9b^2}{(a - 3b)^2}$

Mixed Review

Determine whether the graphs of the equations are parallel.

46. $2x - 3y = 9$
  $8x + 4 = -6y$

47. $4y + 9 = x$
  $5 + 2y = 8x$

48. $6y - 21x = 5$
  $8y - 5 = 28x$ *7-8*

Determine whether the graphs of the equations are perpendicular.

49. $5y = 2x - 10$
  $2y + 5x = 2$

50. $4y + 1 = 3x$
  $3y - 4x = 3$

51. $y = x + 3$
  $y + x = -3$ *7-8*

Solve for the indicated letter.   **52.** $Q = \dfrac{5mv}{s}$, for v **53.** $\dfrac{a}{b} = \dfrac{c}{d}$ for c *3-7*

Solve.   **54.** $2x + y = -1$
    $5 - y = 4x$

55. $2x + 3y = 8$
  $5y - x = 22$

56. $9y - 16 = 11x$
  $5x + 1 = 2y$ *8-2, 8-3*

Solve.   **57.** $9a^2 - 81 = 0$ **58.** $c^2 - 2c = 35$ **59.** $|2x + 3| > 5$ *6-8, 9-4*

60. Steve is half as old as Stacey. The sum of their ages five years ago was 8. How old are Steve and Stacey now?

Addition and Subtraction: Like Denominators

Objective: Add and subtract rational expressions with like denominators.

To add or subtract rational expressions with like denominators, add or subtract the numerators, and write the sum or difference over the common denominator.

EXAMPLES Add and simplify.

1 $\dfrac{4m}{3} + \dfrac{5m}{3} = \dfrac{4m + 5m}{3}$ Writing the sum over the common denominator

$= \dfrac{9m}{3}$ Adding the numerators

$= 3m$ Simplifying

2 $\dfrac{6a^2}{a + 2} + \dfrac{4a^2}{a + 2} = \dfrac{6a^2 + 4a^2}{a + 2}$

$= \dfrac{10a^2}{a + 2}$

3 $\dfrac{2x^2 + 3x - 7}{2x + 1} + \dfrac{x^2 + x - 8}{2x + 1} = \dfrac{2x^2 + 3x - 7 + x^2 + x - 8}{2x + 1}$

$= \dfrac{3x^2 + 4x - 15}{2x + 1}$

$= \dfrac{(x + 3)(3x - 5)}{2x + 1}$ Factoring to look for common factors

Try This   Add and simplify.

a. $\dfrac{3a}{4} + \dfrac{7a}{4}$ **b.** $\dfrac{8x^2}{x + 4} + \dfrac{2x^2}{x + 4}$ **c.** $\dfrac{x^2 - 4x - 10}{x - 7} + \dfrac{x - 18}{x - 7}$

EXAMPLE 4   Subtract and simplify.

$\dfrac{3a}{a + 2} - \dfrac{a - 4}{a + 2} = \dfrac{3a - (a - 4)}{a + 2}$ The parentheses are needed, since you must subtract the entire numerator.

$= \dfrac{3a - a + 4}{a + 2}$

$= \dfrac{2a + 4}{a + 2}$

$= \dfrac{2(a + 2)}{(a + 2)}$

$= 2$ Simplifying

Try This Subtract and simplify.

d. $\dfrac{4m + 5}{m - 1} - \dfrac{2m - 1}{m - 1}$ **e.** $\dfrac{2y^2 + 4y - 3}{y + 3} - \dfrac{y^2 - 2y - 12}{y + 3}$

Any number of expressions with common denominators can be added or subtracted by adding or subtracting the numerators and placing the result over the common denominator.

10-4 Exercises

Extra Help On the Web

Look for worked-out examples at the Prentice Hall Web site.
www.phschool.com

A

Add or subtract. Simplify.

1. $\dfrac{3a}{5} + \dfrac{2a}{5}$

2. $\dfrac{6m}{11} + \dfrac{8m}{11}$

3. $\dfrac{7s}{10} - \dfrac{2s}{10}$

4. $\dfrac{18xy}{7} - \dfrac{11xy}{7}$

5. $\dfrac{6b^2}{c} + \dfrac{7b^2}{c}$

6. $\dfrac{10x}{y} - \dfrac{7x}{y}$

7. $\dfrac{4x + 3}{x + 2} + \dfrac{3x + 4}{x + 2}$

8. $\dfrac{-6m}{m - 5} + \dfrac{m - 10}{m - 5}$

9. $\dfrac{a - 6}{a + 1} - \dfrac{3a - 4}{a + 1}$

10. $\dfrac{b + 4}{b + 2} - \dfrac{3b - 8}{b + 2}$

11. $\dfrac{y^2 + 5}{y + 2} - \dfrac{4y + 17}{y + 2}$

12. $\dfrac{x^2 + 3}{x - 2} - \dfrac{10x - 7}{x - 2}$

13. $\dfrac{3a + 5}{a - 1} + \dfrac{2a - 6}{a - 1}$

14. $\dfrac{4p - 3}{p + 2} + \dfrac{5 - 3p}{p + 2}$

15. $\dfrac{z - 6}{2z + 3} - \dfrac{5z}{2z + 3}$

16. $\dfrac{x - 9}{3x + 2} - \dfrac{7x - 5}{3x + 2}$

17. $\dfrac{y - 3}{y + 5} - \dfrac{2y - 7}{y + 5}$

18. $\dfrac{m + 9}{m + 3} - \dfrac{-4m - 6}{m + 3}$

19. $\dfrac{n^2 + 3n}{n + 4} + \dfrac{2n^2 - 13n - 8}{n + 4}$

20. $\dfrac{z + 6}{z + 5} + \dfrac{3z^2 + 19z + 19}{z + 5}$

21. $\dfrac{5x^2 - 3x + 2}{2x - 1} - \dfrac{3x^2 + 3x - 2}{2x - 1}$

22. $\dfrac{4y^2 + 2y - 3}{5y + 1} - \dfrac{3y^2 - 2y - 4}{5y + 1}$

23. $\dfrac{a - 1}{a^2 - 2a + 1} + \dfrac{5 - 3a}{a^2 - 2a + 1}$

24. $\dfrac{3m - 3}{m^2 + 3m - 4} + \dfrac{m - 7}{m^2 + 3m - 4}$

B

Add or subtract. Simplify.

25. $\dfrac{4a + 5}{a - 2} + \dfrac{6a - 4}{a - 2} + \dfrac{5}{a - 2}$

26. $\dfrac{5x - 3}{x + 1} + \dfrac{2x}{x + 1} + \dfrac{4}{x + 1}$

27. $\dfrac{3a + 3}{a + 2} + \dfrac{a^2 - 2a}{a + 2} + \dfrac{6}{a + 2}$

28. $\dfrac{2b}{b + 4} - \dfrac{4b}{b + 4} - \dfrac{-2b^2 - 3b + 5}{b + 4}$

29. $\dfrac{x^2 + 3x - 2}{x - 1} + \dfrac{2x + 4}{x - 1} + \dfrac{x^2 - x + 1}{x - 1}$

30. $\dfrac{4a^2 + 2a - 3}{3a + 4} + \dfrac{a^2 + 2a - 15}{3a + 4} + \dfrac{a^2 + 6a - 6}{3a + 4}$

31. $\dfrac{y^2 - 3y}{2y + 1} - \dfrac{3y^2 + 4y}{2y + 1} - \dfrac{y^2 + 3y}{2y + 1}$

32. $\dfrac{p^2 - 6}{3p + 8} + \dfrac{2p^2 + 5p - 3}{3p + 8} - \dfrac{3p^2 + p - 4}{3p + 8}$

33. $\dfrac{3x^2 + 4x - 12}{(3x + 4)(x - 1)} - \dfrac{5x^2 - 2x - 6}{(3x + 4)(x - 1)} - \dfrac{-14x^2 - 4x + 2}{(3x + 4)(x - 1)}$

34. $\dfrac{10b^2 + b - 2}{(5b + 2)(2b + 1)} + \dfrac{12b^2 - 5b}{(5b + 2)(2b + 1)} - \dfrac{-8b^2 - 7b + 4}{(5b + 2)(2b + 1)}$

35. *Critical Thinking*   The perimeter of the figure at the right is $2x + 5$. Find the length of the missing side.

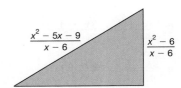
$\dfrac{x^2 - 5x - 9}{x - 6}$ $\dfrac{x^2 - 6}{x - 6}$

Challenge

Simplify.

36. $\dfrac{x^2}{3x^2 - 5x - 2} - \dfrac{2x}{3x + 1} \cdot \dfrac{1}{x - 2}$

37. $\dfrac{3}{x + 4} \cdot \dfrac{2x + 11}{x - 3} - \dfrac{-1}{4 + x} \cdot \dfrac{6x + 3}{3 - x}$

Mixed Review

Simplify.

38. $\dfrac{6x^2y}{3y^2}$

39. $\dfrac{m^2 - 36}{4m + 24}$

40. $\dfrac{4 - a}{a^2 - 16}$

41. $(-3t^2)^4$

42. $\left(\dfrac{y^4}{6}\right)^2$

43. $\left(\dfrac{m^4n^2}{2}\right)^6$

44. $(-3ab)^2$

45. $\left(\dfrac{-2x}{y}\right)^2$ *5-1, 5-2, 10-1*

Solve.   **46.** Find two numbers whose sum is -2 and whose product is -24.

47. The difference of two positive numbers is 2. The difference of the squares of the two numbers is 40. Find the numbers.   *8-6*

Addition and Subtraction: Unlike Denominators

PART 1 Addition with Unlike Denominators

Objective: Add rational expressions with unlike denominators.

If $\frac{p}{q}$ and $\frac{r}{s}$ represent rational numbers or rational expressions,

then $\frac{p}{q} + \frac{r}{s} = \frac{p}{q} \cdot \frac{s}{s} + \frac{r}{s} \cdot \frac{q}{q} = \frac{ps}{qs} + \frac{rq}{qs} = \frac{ps + rq}{qs}$.

The pattern $\frac{p}{q} + \frac{r}{s} = \frac{ps + rq}{qs}$ is useful for adding rational expressions with different denominators.

EXAMPLES   Add and simplify.

1 $\dfrac{3}{x^2} + \dfrac{6}{x} = \dfrac{3x + 6x^2}{x^2 \cdot x}$ Using the pattern for adding rational expressions

       $= \dfrac{3x(1 + 2x)}{x^2 \cdot x}$ Factoring to look for common factors

       $= \dfrac{3(1 + 2x)}{x^2}$ Simplifying

2 $\dfrac{3}{x + 1} + \dfrac{5}{x - 1} = \dfrac{3(x - 1) + 5(x + 1)}{(x + 1)(x - 1)}$ Using the pattern for adding rational expressions

       $= \dfrac{3x - 3 + 5x + 5}{(x + 1)(x - 1)}$

       $= \dfrac{8x + 2}{(x + 1)(x - 1)}$

       $= \dfrac{2(4x + 1)}{(x + 1)(x - 1)}$ Factoring to look for common factors

Try This   Add and simplify.

a. $\dfrac{2x}{3} + \dfrac{6}{x}$ **b.** $\dfrac{7x^2}{6} + \dfrac{3x}{16}$ **c.** $\dfrac{x}{x - 2} + \dfrac{4}{x + 2}$

PART 2 Subtraction with Unlike Denominators

Objective: Subtract rational expressions with unlike denominators.

To subtract expressions with unlike denominators, use the pattern

     $\dfrac{p}{q} - \dfrac{r}{s} = \dfrac{ps - rq}{qs}$

What You'll Learn

1 To add rational expressions with unlike denominators

2 To subtract rational expressions with unlike denominators

3 To add or subtract rational expressions using the least common multiple (LCM) of the denominators

...And Why

To be able to simplify algebraic expressions

EXAMPLES Subtract and simplify.

3 $\dfrac{x+2}{x-4} - \dfrac{x+1}{x+4} = \dfrac{(x+2)(x+4) - [(x+1)(x-4)]}{(x-4)(x+4)}$ Using the pattern for subtracting rational expressions

$$= \dfrac{x^2 + 6x + 8 - (x^2 - 3x - 4)}{(x-4)(x+4)}$$

$$= \dfrac{x^2 + 6x + 8 - x^2 + 3x + 4}{(x-4)(x+4)}$$

$$= \dfrac{x^2 - x^2 + 6x + 3x + 8 + 4}{(x-4)(x+4)}$$

$$= \dfrac{9x + 12}{(x-4)(x+4)}$$

$$= \dfrac{3(3x+4)}{(x-4)(x+4)}$$ Factoring to look for common factors

4 $3 - \dfrac{3}{x+4} = \dfrac{3}{1} - \dfrac{3}{x+4}$ Writing 3 as a fraction

$$= \dfrac{3(x+4) - 3(1)}{1(x+4)}$$

$$= \dfrac{3x + 12 - 3}{x+4}$$

$$= \dfrac{3x + 9}{x+4}$$

$$= \dfrac{3(x+3)}{x+4}$$

Try This   Subtract and simplify.

d. $\dfrac{4}{5x} - \dfrac{1}{x^2}$ **e.** $\dfrac{3}{2x+1} - \dfrac{2}{2x-1}$ **f.** $6 - \dfrac{1}{t-2}$

PART 3   **Using Least Common Multiples**

Objective: Add or subtract rational expressions using the least common multiple of the denominators.

Sometimes another method is useful in adding and subtracting rational expressions with unlike denominators. In this method we begin by finding the **least common multiple (LCM)** of the denominators.

Finding the Least Common Multiple

To find the LCM of two or more algebraic expressions,
1. factor each expression.
2. form the product using each factor the greatest number of times it occurs.

EXAMPLES

5 Find the LCM of $8x^2y^2$ and $-12xy^3$.

$$8x^2y^2 = 2 \cdot 2 \cdot 2 \cdot x \cdot x \cdot y \cdot y \quad -12xy^3 = -2 \cdot 2 \cdot 3 \cdot x \cdot y \cdot y \cdot y$$
$$\text{LCM} = 2 \cdot 2 \cdot 2 \cdot 3 \cdot x \cdot x \cdot y \cdot y \cdot y$$
$$= 24x^2y^3$$

6 Find the LCM of $x^2 + 5x - 6$ and $x^2 - 1$.

$$x^2 + 5x - 6 = (x + 6)(x - 1) \quad x^2 - 1 = (x + 1)(x - 1)$$
$$\text{LCM} = (x + 6)(x + 1)(x - 1)$$

7 Find the LCM of $x^2 + 4$ and $x + 1$.

These expressions are not factorable, so the LCM is their product, $(x^2 + 4)(x + 1)$.

8 Find the LCM of $y - 2$ and $2 - y$.

Since $y - 2 = -(2 - y)$ and $2 - y = -(y - 2)$, we can use either $2 - y$ or $y - 2$ as the LCM.

Try This   Find the LCM.

g. $12xy^2, 15x^3y$ **h.** $y^2 + 5y + 4, y^2 + 2y + 1$ **i.** $t^2 - 16, 4 - t$

To add or subtract rational expressions with unlike denominators, you can

1. find the LCM of the denominators. This is the least common denominator (LCD).
2. write each rational expression as an equivalent expression with the LCD as the denominator. To write an equivalent rational expression, multiply by an expression equivalent to 1.
3. add or subtract the numerators. Write the sum over the LCD.

EXAMPLES   Add or subtract and simplify.

9
$$\frac{x}{4x + 12} + \frac{2x}{5x + 15} = \frac{x}{4(x + 3)} + \frac{2x}{5(x + 3)} \qquad \text{Factoring to find that the LCD is } 4(5)(x + 3)$$

$$= \frac{x}{4(x + 3)} \cdot \frac{5}{5} + \frac{2x}{5(x + 3)} \cdot \frac{4}{4} \qquad \text{Multiplying each term by a form of 1 to get the LCD}$$

$$= \frac{5x}{20(x + 3)} + \frac{8x}{20(x + 3)}$$

$$= \frac{13x}{20(x + 3)}$$

10

$$\frac{k^2}{k-5} - \frac{2}{5-k} = \frac{k^2}{k-5} - \frac{2}{-1(k-5)}$$

Factoring out -1 because the denominators are additive inverses

$$= \frac{k^2}{k-5} - \frac{2}{-1(k-5)} \cdot \frac{-1}{-1}$$

Multiplying by a form of 1 to get the LCD $k-5$

$$= \frac{k^2}{k-5} - \frac{-2}{k-5}$$

$$= \frac{k^2 + 2}{k-5}$$

Try This   Add or subtract and simplify.

j. $\frac{3x}{25} + \frac{x^2}{10}$ **k.** $\frac{3}{xy^2} - \frac{x+y}{x^2y}$ **l.** $\frac{4}{3-b} + \frac{b}{2b-6}$

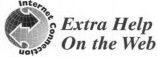

*Extra Help
On the Web*

Look for worked-out
examples at the Prentice
Hall Web site.
www.phschool.com

10-5 Exercises

A

Add and simplify.

1. $\frac{a^2}{2} + \frac{3a^2}{8}$ **2.** $\frac{8y}{10} + \frac{2y}{5}$ **3.** $\frac{4c}{15} + \frac{8c}{25}$

4. $\frac{2}{x} + \frac{5}{x^2}$ **5.** $\frac{4}{x} + \frac{8}{x^2}$ **6.** $\frac{5}{6r} + \frac{7}{8r}$

7. $\frac{3}{x-2} + \frac{3}{x+2}$ **8.** $\frac{2}{x-1} + \frac{2}{x+1}$ **9.** $\frac{3}{x+1} + \frac{2}{3x}$

Subtract and simplify.

10. $\frac{x-2}{6} - \frac{x+1}{3}$ **11.** $\frac{a+2}{2} - \frac{a-4}{4}$ **12.** $\frac{y-5}{y} - \frac{3y-1}{4y}$

13. $\frac{x-1}{4x} - \frac{2x+3}{x}$ **14.** $2 - \frac{2x+1}{5}$ **15.** $3x - \frac{x}{x-2}$

16. $\frac{2}{x+5} - \frac{3}{4x}$ **17.** $\frac{x+4}{x} - \frac{x}{x+4}$ **18.** $\frac{x}{x-5} - \frac{x-5}{x}$

Find the LCM.

19. c^2d, cd^2 **20.** $2x^2, 6xy$

21. $x-y, x+y$ **22.** $a-5, a+5$

23. $2(y-3), 6(3-y)$ **24.** $4(x-1), 8(1-x)$

25. $t+2, t-2$ **26.** $x+3, x-3$

27. x^2-4, x^2+5x+6 **28.** x^2+3x+2, x^2-4

29. t^3+4t^2+4t, t^2-4t **30.** y^3-y^2, y^4-y^2

31. $a+1, a^2-1$ **32.** $x^2-y^2, x^2+2xy+y^2$

33. m^2-5m+6, m^2-4m+4 **34.** $2x^2+5x+2, 2x^2-x-1$

Add or subtract and simplify.

35. $\frac{2}{9t} + \frac{11}{6t}$

36. $\frac{x + y}{xy^2} + \frac{3x + y}{x^2y}$

37. $\frac{2c - d}{c^2d} + \frac{c + d}{cd^2}$

38. $\frac{t}{t - 3} + \frac{5}{4t - 12}$

39. $\frac{3}{x - 1} + \frac{2}{(x - 1)^2}$

40. $\frac{2}{x + 3} + \frac{4}{(x + 3)^2}$

41. $\frac{4a}{5a - 10} + \frac{3a}{10a - 20}$

42. $\frac{3a}{4a - 20} + \frac{9a}{6a - 30}$

43. $\frac{x}{x^2 + 2x + 1} + \frac{1}{x^2 + 5x + 4}$

44. $\frac{7}{a^2 + a - 2} + \frac{5}{a^2 - 4a + 3}$

45. $\frac{3 - b}{b - 7} + \frac{2b - 5}{7 - b}$

46. $\frac{x}{x - 1} + \frac{1}{1 - x}$

47. $\frac{t^2}{t - 2} - \frac{4}{2 - t}$

48. $\frac{y^2}{y - 3} - \frac{9}{3 - y}$

49. $\frac{2z}{z - 1} - \frac{3z}{z + 1}$

50. $\frac{5x}{x^2 - 9} - \frac{4}{x + 3}$

51. $\frac{8x}{x^2 - 16} - \frac{5}{x + 4}$

52. $\frac{3}{2t^2 - 2t} - \frac{5}{2t - 2}$

53. $\frac{4}{5b^2 - 5b} - \frac{3}{5b - 5}$

54. $\frac{2s}{t^2 - s^2} - \frac{s}{t - s}$

55. $\frac{2x}{x^2 - 16} + \frac{x}{x - 4}$

56. $\frac{4x}{x^2 - 25} + \frac{x}{x + 5}$

B

Add or subtract and simplify.

57. $\frac{5}{z + 4} + \frac{3}{3z + 12}$

58. $\frac{5x + 3y}{2x^2y} - \frac{3x - 4y}{xy^2}$

59. $\frac{4x + 2t}{3xt^2} - \frac{5x - 3t}{x^2t}$

60. $\frac{5}{x + 5} - \frac{3}{x - 5}$

61. $\frac{y - 8}{y^2 - 16} + \frac{y - 8}{16 - y^2}$

62. $\frac{a + 3}{a - 5} - \frac{2a - 1}{5 - a}$

63. $\frac{3(x - 2)}{2x - 3} - \frac{3(x - 1)}{3 - 2x}$

64. $\frac{m - 2}{m^2 - 25} + \frac{m - 2}{25 - m^2}$

65. $\frac{x}{x^2 + 5x + 6} - \frac{2}{x^2 + 3x + 2}$

66. $\frac{x}{x^2 + 11x + 30} - \frac{5}{x^2 + 9x + 20}$

Find the LCM.

67. $8x^2 - 8, 6x^2 - 12x + 6$, and $10 - 10x$

68. $9x^3 - 9x^2 - 18x, 6x^5 - 24x^4 + 24x^3$

69. $x^5 + 2x^4 + x^3, 2x^3 - 2x, 5x - 5$

70. $x^5 + 4x^4 + 4x^3, 3x^2 - 12, 2x + 4$

Journal

When adding $\frac{2}{ab}$ and $\frac{3}{ac}$, discuss the advantages and disadvantages of using
• the pattern for adding rational expressions and
• the least common denominator method.

Add and simplify.

71. $\dfrac{5}{z + 2} + \dfrac{4z}{z^2 - 4} + 2$

72. $\dfrac{-2}{y^2 - 9} + \dfrac{4y}{(y - 3)^2} + \dfrac{6}{3 - y}$

73. $\dfrac{3z^2}{z^4 - 4} + \dfrac{5z^2 - 3}{2z^4 + z^2 - 6}$

74. Write $\dfrac{a + b}{a - b}$ as the sum of two rational expressions.

75. *Critical Thinking*   Write $\dfrac{5x^2 - 2xy}{x^2 + y^2}$ as the difference of two rational expressions, such that y occurs in the numerator of each expression.

Challenge

76. Two joggers leave the starting point of a circular course at the same time. One jogger completes one round in 6 minutes, and the second jogger finishes in 8 minutes. After how many minutes will they meet again at the starting place, assuming that they continue to run at the same pace?

The planets Earth, Jupiter, Saturn, and Uranus revolve around the sun about once each 1, 12, 30, and 84 years, respectively.

77. How often will Jupiter and Saturn appear in the same position in the night sky as seen from Earth?

78. How often will Jupiter, Saturn, and Uranus all appear in the same position in the night sky as seen from Earth?

Jupiter and Uranus revolve once around the sun about every 12 and 84 years, respectively. How often will Jupiter and Uranus appear in the same position in the night sky as seen from Earth?

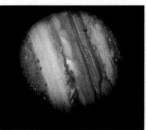
Jupiter

Saturn

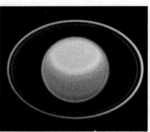
Uranus

Mixed Review

Determine whether the graphs of the equations are perpendicular.

79. $4y = 5x + 2$
  $8x = 3 - 10y$

80. $y + 3x = 4$
  $2x = 5 - 6y$

81. $6y + 4x = 11$
  $21 - 15y = 10x$ *7-8*

Solve and graph. **82.** $|11x| > 121$ **83.** $|3x - 5| \geq 4$

84. $|9x| \leq 108$ **85.** $|2x - x| > 0$ **86.** $|x - 1| \leq 5$ *9-4*

Simplify. **87.** $\dfrac{a^2 + 7a + 12}{a^2 - 9}$ **88.** $\dfrac{9x^2 - 25}{3x + 5}$ **89.** $\dfrac{3x - 6}{2 - x}$ *10-1*

Solving Rational Equations

Objective: Solve equations involving rational expressions.

A **rational equation** is an equation containing one or more rational expressions. Here are some examples.

$$\frac{1}{x} = \frac{1}{4-x} \qquad x + \frac{6}{x} = -5 \qquad \frac{x^2}{x-1} = \frac{1}{x-1}$$

To solve a rational equation multiply on both sides by the LCM of all the denominators.

EXAMPLE 1   Solve.

$$\frac{1}{x} = \frac{1}{4-x} \qquad \text{LCM is } x(4-x).$$

$$x(4-x) \cdot \frac{1}{x} = x(4-x) \cdot \frac{1}{4-x} \qquad \text{Multiplying on both sides by LCM}$$

$$4 - x = x$$
$$4 = 2x$$
$$2 = x$$

Check: $\dfrac{1}{x} = \dfrac{1}{4-x}$

$$\begin{array}{c|c} \dfrac{1}{2} & \dfrac{1}{4-2} \\[2mm] \dfrac{1}{2} & \dfrac{1}{2} ✔ \end{array}$$

The solution is 2.

Try This   Solve.

a. $\dfrac{3}{4} + \dfrac{5}{8} = \dfrac{x}{12}$ **b.** $\dfrac{1}{x} = \dfrac{1}{6-x}$

EXAMPLE 2   Solve.

$$x + \frac{6}{x} = -5$$

$$x\left(x + \frac{6}{x}\right) = -5x \qquad \text{LCM is } x.$$

$$x^2 + x \cdot \frac{6}{x} = -5x$$

$$x^2 + 6 = -5x$$

What You'll Learn

1 To solve equations involving rational expressions

...And Why

To be able to solve real-world problems using algebraic reasoning skills

Quick *Review*

You have used the LCM method to solve equations containing fractions or decimals in Lessons 3-6 and 3-9.

This is a second degree equation. Thus we set the equation equal to zero.

$$x^2 + 5x + 6 = 0$$
$$(x + 3)(x + 2) = 0 \qquad \text{Factoring}$$
$$x + 3 = 0 \quad \text{or} \quad x + 2 = 0$$
$$x = -3 \quad \text{or} \quad x = -2 \qquad \text{Using the principle of zero products}$$

Check:

$x + \dfrac{6}{x} = -5$		$x + \dfrac{6}{x} = -5$	
$-3 + \dfrac{6}{-3}$	-5	$-2 + \dfrac{6}{-2}$	-5
$-3 - 2$	-5	$-2 \quad -3$	-5
-5	-5 ✔	-5	-5 ✔

Both numbers check, so there are two solutions, -3 and -2.

EXAMPLE 3   Solve.

$$\frac{x^2}{x - 1} = \frac{1}{x - 1}$$
$$(x - 1) \cdot \frac{x^2}{x - 1} = (x - 1) \cdot \frac{1}{x - 1} \qquad \text{LCM is } x - 1.$$
$$x^2 = 1$$
$$x^2 - 1 = 0$$
$$(x - 1)(x + 1) = 0$$
$$x - 1 = 0 \quad \text{or} \quad x + 1 = 0$$
$$x = 1 \quad \text{or} \qquad x = -1$$

Check:

$\dfrac{x^2}{x - 1} = \dfrac{1}{x - 1}$		$\dfrac{x^2}{x - 1} = \dfrac{1}{x - 1}$	
$\dfrac{1^2}{1 - 1}$	$\dfrac{1}{1 - 1}$	$\dfrac{(-1)^2}{-1 - 1}$	$\dfrac{1}{-1 - 1}$
$\dfrac{1}{0}$	$\dfrac{1}{0}$	$-\dfrac{1}{2}$	$-\dfrac{1}{2}$ ✔

The solution is -1. The number 1 is not a solution, as it makes a denominator zero.

When both sides of an equation are multiplied by a variable, the equation is transformed into a new equation that may have extra or extraneous solutions. In Example 3 the number 1 is an **extraneous solution**. *When solving rational equations, it is necessary to check each solution of the new equation in the original rational equation.*

Try This   Solve.

c. $x + \dfrac{1}{x} = 2$ **d.** $\dfrac{x^2}{x + 2} = \dfrac{4}{x + 2}$ **e.** $\dfrac{1}{2x} + \dfrac{1}{x} = -12$

10-6 Exercises

Extra Help On the Web

Look for worked-out examples at the Prentice Hall Web site.
www.phschool.com

A

Solve.

1. $\frac{3}{8} + \frac{4}{5} = \frac{x}{20}$

2. $\frac{3}{5} + \frac{2}{3} = \frac{x}{9}$

3. $\frac{2}{3} - \frac{5}{6} = \frac{1}{x}$

4. $\frac{1}{8} - \frac{3}{5} = \frac{1}{x}$

5. $\frac{1}{6} + \frac{1}{8} = \frac{1}{t}$

6. $\frac{1}{8} + \frac{1}{10} = \frac{1}{t}$

7. $x + \frac{4}{x} = -5$

8. $x + \frac{3}{x} = -4$

9. $\frac{x}{4} - \frac{4}{x} = 0$

10. $\frac{x}{5} - \frac{5}{x} = 0$

11. $\frac{5}{x} = \frac{6}{x} - \frac{1}{3}$

12. $\frac{4}{x} = \frac{5}{x} - \frac{1}{2}$

13. $\frac{5}{3x} + \frac{3}{x} = 1$

14. $\frac{3}{4x} + \frac{5}{x} = 1$

15. $\frac{x - 7}{x + 2} = \frac{1}{4}$

16. $\frac{a - 2}{a + 3} = \frac{3}{8}$

17. $\frac{2}{x + 1} = \frac{1}{x - 2}$

18. $\frac{5}{x - 1} = \frac{3}{x + 2}$

19. $\frac{x}{6} - \frac{x}{10} = \frac{1}{6}$

20. $\frac{x}{8} - \frac{x}{12} = \frac{1}{8}$

21. $\frac{x + 1}{3} - \frac{x - 1}{2} = 1$

22. $\frac{x + 2}{5} - \frac{x - 2}{4} = 1$

23. $\frac{a - 3}{3a + 2} = \frac{1}{5}$

24. $\frac{x - 1}{2x + 5} = \frac{1}{4}$

25. $\frac{x - 1}{x - 5} = \frac{4}{x - 5}$

26. $\frac{x - 7}{x - 9} = \frac{2}{x - 9}$

27. $\frac{2}{x + 3} = \frac{5}{x}$

28. $\frac{3}{x + 4} = \frac{4}{x}$

29. $\frac{x - 2}{x - 3} = \frac{x - 1}{x + 1}$

30. $\frac{2b - 3}{3b + 2} = \frac{2b + 1}{3b - 2}$

31. $\frac{1}{x + 3} + \frac{1}{x - 3} = \frac{1}{x^2 - 9}$

32. $\frac{4}{x - 3} + \frac{2x}{x^2 - 9} = \frac{1}{x + 3}$

33. $\frac{x}{x + 4} - \frac{4}{x - 4} = \frac{x^2 + 16}{x^2 - 16}$

34. $\frac{5}{y - 3} - \frac{30}{y^2 - 9} = 1$

B

Solve.

35. $\dfrac{4}{y - 2} - \dfrac{2y - 3}{y^2 - 4} = \dfrac{5}{y + 2}$

36. $\dfrac{x}{x^2 + 3x - 4} + \dfrac{x + 1}{x^2 + 6x + 8} = \dfrac{2x}{x^2 + x - 2}$

37. $\dfrac{2a + 7}{8a^2 - 2a - 1} + \dfrac{a - 4}{2a^2 + 5a - 3} = \dfrac{4a - 1}{4a^2 + 13a + 3}$

38. $\dfrac{y}{y + 0.2} - 1.2 = \dfrac{y - 0.2}{y + 0.2}$

39. $\dfrac{x^2}{x^2 - 4} = \dfrac{x}{x + 2} - \dfrac{2x}{2 - x}$

40. $4a - 3 = \dfrac{a + 13}{a + 1}$

41. $\dfrac{14x - 2}{x - 3} = \dfrac{9x + 8}{-2}$

42. $\dfrac{y^2 - 4}{y + 3} = 2 - \dfrac{y - 2}{y + 3}$

43. *Critical Thinking*   Solve the equation $\dfrac{8}{x} - 4 = \dfrac{2}{x}$ using any problem-solving strategy.

Challenge

44. Solve. $\dfrac{n}{n - \frac{4}{9}} - \dfrac{n}{n + \frac{4}{9}} = \dfrac{1}{n}$

45. Suppose $t = \dfrac{x}{y}$ and $r = \dfrac{w}{z}$. Show that $\dfrac{xz + yw}{yz - xw} = \dfrac{t + r}{1 - tr}$.

46. Suppose $x = \dfrac{ab}{a + b}$ and $y = \dfrac{ab}{a - b}$. Show that $\dfrac{y^2 - x^2}{y^2 + x^2} = \dfrac{2ab}{a^2 + b^2}$.

Mixed Review

Multiply or divide and simplify.   **47.** $\dfrac{(x + 1)^2}{(x - 5)} \cdot \dfrac{(x - 3)}{(x + 1)}$

48. $\dfrac{3x + 3}{2} \div \dfrac{4}{9x + 9}$ **49.** $\dfrac{4a}{3a - 3} \cdot \dfrac{3(a - 1)}{16a}$ **50.** $\dfrac{x + 2}{x - 1} \div \dfrac{5x + 10}{x - 2}$ *10-2, 10-3*

Solve.   **51.** $|2x - 1| = 5$ **52.** $|x - 3| \leq 8$ *9-3, 9-4*

53. $x - 3 < -7$ or $x + 1 > 1$ **54.** $x - 2 < 3$ or $x + 4 > 11$

55. $11 - 8y < 6y + 39$ **56.** $3 - 7x < 9x + 67$ *4-4, 9-2*

57. The difference of two numbers is 4. Five times the larger number is fifteen times the smaller. Find the numbers.   *8-6*

454   Chapter 10   *Rational Expressions and Equations*

Using Rational Equations

Objective: Solve problems using rational equations.

PROBLEM-SOLVING GUIDELINES
■ UNDERSTAND the problem
Develop and carry out a PLAN
■ Find the ANSWER and CHECK

You can use the Problem-Solving Guidelines to help you solve problems involving rational equations.

What You'll Learn

1 To solve problems using rational equations

...And Why

To be able to solve real-world problems using algebraic reasoning skills

Suppose it takes a person 4 hours to do a certain job. Then, in 1 hour, $\frac{1}{4}$ of the job gets done. This diagram helps show this relationship.

Complete job

$\frac{1}{4}$ of the job can be done in 1 hour.

In general, if a job can be done in t hours, (or days, or some other unit of time), then $\frac{1}{t}$ of it can be done in 1 hour (or day, etc.).

EXAMPLE 1

Company A can install chairs in a theatre in 10 hours. Company B can install them in 15 hours. The owner of the theatre wants the chairs installed in less than one day (8 hours). If the companies work together, can they install the chairs in less than one day?

■ **UNDERSTAND the problem**

Question: Can the companies, working together, complete the job in less than 8 hours?

Data: Working alone, company A needs 10 hours and company B needs 15 hours.

■ **Develop and carry out a PLAN**

Company A can do $\frac{1}{10}$ of the job in 1 hour.

Company B can do $\frac{1}{15}$ of the job in 1 hour.

Let $t =$ the total number of hours needed to complete the job.

$\frac{1}{t} =$ the part of the job that can be completed in 1 hour.

Working together, they can do $\frac{1}{10} + \frac{1}{15}$ of the job in 1 hour, so

$$\frac{1}{t} = \frac{1}{10} + \frac{1}{15}$$

We can solve this equation for t.

$$\frac{1}{t} = \frac{3}{30} + \frac{2}{30}$$
$$\frac{1}{t} = \frac{1}{6}$$
$$t = 6$$

■ Find the ANSWER and CHECK

The job can be completed in 6 hours with both companies working together. Thus it can be completed in less than 1 day (8 hours). This is reasonable, since company A could do $\frac{5}{10}$ or half of the job in 5 hours, and company B could do about half of the job $\left(\frac{7}{15}\right)$ in 7 hours.

Try This   Solve.

a. A contractor finds that it takes crew A 6 hours to construct a wall of a certain size. Crew B takes 8 hours to construct a wall of the same size. How long will it take if they work together?

EXAMPLE 2

One car travels 20 km/h faster than another. While one of them travels 240 km, the other travels 180 km. Find their speeds.

■ UNDERSTAND the problem

Question: What are the speeds of the cars?
Data: One car travels 20 km/h faster than the other car. The faster car goes 240 km. The slower car goes 180 km. The time traveled is the same for both.

■ Develop and carry out a PLAN

Let r = the speed (rate) of the slower car.

$r + 20$ = speed of faster car

Let t = time each car traveled.

	Distance	Rate	Time
Slower car	180	r	t
Faster car	240	$r + 20$	t

Recording the data in a table helps show relationships.

If we solve the formula $d = rt$ for t, we get $t = \frac{d}{r}$. From the rows of the table, we can find two equations.

$$t = \frac{180}{r} \quad \text{and} \quad t = \frac{240}{r + 20}$$

Since the times are the same, we have the following equation.

$$\frac{180}{r} = \frac{240}{r+20}$$

$$\frac{180 \cdot r(r+20)}{r} = \frac{240 \cdot r(r+20)}{r+20} \qquad \text{Multiplying on both sides by the LCM, } r(r+20)$$

$$180(r+20) = 240r$$

$$180r + 3600 = 240r$$

$$\frac{3600}{60} = r$$

$$60 = r \qquad \text{Rate of the slower car}$$

$$80 = r + 20 \qquad \text{Rate of the faster car}$$

■ Find the ANSWER and CHECK

The speeds are 60 km/h for the slower car and 80 km/h for the faster car. In 3 hours the slow car would travel $60 \times 3 = 180$ km, and in 3 hours the faster car would travel $80 \times 3 = 240$ km. The answers check.

Try This   Solve.

b. One boat travels 10 km/h faster than another. While one boat travels 120 km, the other travels 155 km. Find their speeds.

EXAMPLE 3

The reciprocal of 2 less than a certain number is twice the reciprocal of the number itself. What is the number?

Let $x =$ the number.

$$\left(\begin{array}{c} \text{Reciprocal of 2 less} \\ \text{than the number} \end{array} \right) \text{ is } \left(\begin{array}{c} \text{twice the reciprocal} \\ \text{of the number.} \end{array} \right)$$

A ship's speed is sometimes measured in knots. A knot is one nautical mile per hour and a nautical mile is 6076.12 ft. If a ship is traveling at 10 mi/h, what is its speed in knots?

$$\frac{1}{x-2} = 2 \cdot \frac{1}{x} \qquad \text{Translating}$$

$$\frac{1}{x-2} = \frac{2}{x}$$

$$\frac{x(x-2)}{x-2} = \frac{2x(x-2)}{x} \qquad \text{Multiplying by LCM}$$

$$x = 2(x-2) \qquad \text{Simplifying}$$

$$x = 2x - 4$$

$$x = 4$$

The number is 4.

Try This   Solve.

c. The reciprocal of two more than a number is three times the reciprocal of the number. Find the number.

10-7 Exercises

A

Solve.

1. It takes painter A 3 hours to paint a certain area of a house. It takes painter B 5 hours to do the same job. How long would it take them, working together, to do the painting job?

2. By checking work records, a plumber finds that worker A can do a certain job in 12 hours. Worker B can do the same job in 9 hours. How long would it take if they worked together?

3. A tank can be filled in 18 hours by pipe A or in 24 hours by pipe B. How long would it take both pipes to fill the tank?

4. Team A can set up chairs in the gym in 15 minutes and team B can set up the chairs in 20 minutes. How long would it take them, working together, to set up the same chairs?

5. One car travels 40 km/h faster than another. While one travels 150 km, the other goes 350 km. Find their speeds.

6. A person traveled 120 miles in one direction. The return trip was accomplished at double the speed and took 3 hours less time. Find the speed going.

7. The speed of a freight train is 14 km/h slower than the speed of a passenger train. The freight train travels 330 km in the same time that it takes the passenger train to travel 400 km. Find the speed of each train.

8. The reciprocal of 4 plus the reciprocal of 5 is the reciprocal of what number?

9. The sum of half a number and its reciprocal is the same as 51 divided by the number. Find the number.

10. The additive inverse of a number divided by twelve is the same as one less than three times its reciprocal. Find the number.

B

11. Kirsten can type a 50-page paper in 8 hours. Last month Kirsten and Courtney, together, typed a 50-page paper in 6 hours. How long would it take Courtney to type a 50-page paper on her own?

12. Two road crews, working together, repaired 1 mile of a road in 4 hours. Working separately, one of the crews takes about 6 hours to repair a similar road. How long would it take the other crew, working alone, to repair a similar road?

13. One machine in a print shop can produce a certain number of pages twice as fast as another machine. Operating together, these machines can produce this number of pages in 8 minutes. How long would it take each machine, working alone, to produce this number of pages?

14. One watering system needs about 3 times as long to complete a job as another watering system. When both systems operate at the same time, the job can be completed in 9 minutes. How long does it take each system to do the job alone?

15. It takes 10 hours to fill a pool with water, and 20 hours to drain it. If the pool is empty and the drain is open, how long will it take to fill the pool?

16. It takes 8 hours to fill a tank with a particular chemical. Without treatment, all of the chemical in the tank would evaporate in 12 hours. If the tank is empty to start, and the chemical is not being treated as it enters the tank, how long will it take to have a full tank?

17. *Critical Thinking*   In Exercise 16, suppose it takes 9 hours to fill the tank. Without treatment, how long will it take to fill the tank?

Challenge

18. A carpenter can complete a certain job in 5 hours. After working on the job for 2 hours, an assistant helped finish the job. Together they completed the job in 1 hour. How long might it take the assistant, working alone, to complete a job similar to this one?

19. Dr. Wright allowed one hour to reach an appointment 50 miles away. After driving 30 miles she realized that her speed would have to be increased 15 mi/h for the remainder of the trip. What was her speed for the first 30 miles?

20. Together, Michelle, Bernie, and Kurt can do a job in 1 hour and 20 minutes. To do the job alone, Michelle needs twice the time that Bernie needs and two hours more than Kurt. How long would it take each to complete the job working alone?

Mixed Review

Add or subtract. Simplify.   **21.** $\dfrac{5x - 2}{x - 1} + \dfrac{3x - 1}{x - 1}$ **22.** $\dfrac{x^2 + 7}{x - 3} + \dfrac{7x + 3}{x - 3}$

23. $\dfrac{x^2 + 6x}{x + 4} - \dfrac{3x + 5}{x + 4} + \dfrac{1}{x + 4}$ **24.** $\dfrac{3}{x + 1} + \dfrac{3}{x - 1}$ *10-4, 10-5*

Solve.   **25.** $m^2 - 5m = 14$ **26.** $9n^2 = 16$

   27. $x^3 + 3x^2 + 2x = 0$ *6-7*

Solve.

28. On a test of 88 items, a student got 82 correct. What percent of the items were correct?

29. On a test of 88 items, a student got 87.5% of them correct. How many items were correct?

30. On a test, a student got 72 items correct, which was 80% of the total number of items. How many items were on the test?   *3-10*

10-8 ▷ Mixture Problems

Objective: Solve problems involving the mixture of substances.

What You'll Learn

1 To solve problems involving the mixture of substances

... And Why

To be able to solve real-world problems using algebraic reasoning skills

PROBLEM-SOLVING GUIDELINES
■ UNDERSTAND the problem
▨ Develop and carry out a PLAN
■ Find the ANSWER and CHECK

Some real-world situations require that two or more substances be combined to produce a mixture.

EXAMPLE 1

One solution is 80% acid and another one is 30% acid. How much of each solution is needed to make a 200 L solution that is 62% acid?

■ **UNDERSTAND the problem**

Question: How much of each solution is needed?
Data: first solution—80% acid
      second solution—30% acid
      final solution—200 L, 62% acid

▨ **Develop and carry out a PLAN**

Let x = amount of the first solution.
$200 - x$ = the amount of the second solution.
To solve this problem, it is helpful to record the data given and the unknowns in a table.

	Amount of solution	Percent acid	Amount of acid
1st solution	x	80%	$0.8x$
2nd solution	$200 - x$	30%	$0.3(200 - x)$
Final solution	200	62%	$0.62(200)$

We can now write an equation using the data in the table.

The sum of the amounts of acid in the two solutions gives the amount of acid in the final solution. Thus we have the equation

$$0.8x + 0.3(200 - x) = 0.62(200)$$
$$0.8x + 60 - 0.3x = 124$$
$$0.5x = 64$$
$$x = 128 \quad \text{The amount of the first solution needed}$$

Thus $200 - x = 200 - 128$.   Substituting to find the amount of the second solution

■ **Find the ANSWER and CHECK**

128 L of the 80% solution and 72 L of the 30% solution are needed.
80% of 128 is about 100, and 30% of 72 is about 20. The total,
100 + 20 = 120, is 60% of 200. The answer is reasonable.

EXAMPLE 2

From 1963 to 1984, the level of water in the Great Salt Lake
rose, expanding the surface area of the lake from 900 square
miles to 2300 square miles. During this period of time, the
salinity of the lake dropped from 20 percent to 6 percent.
How much water would you have to add to a liter of lake
water that is 20 percent salt to get a solution that is only
6 percent salt?

■ **UNDERSTAND the problem**

Question: What amount of water must be added?
Data: original solution of 1 liter of water is 20% salt;
final solution is to be 6% salt

■ **Develop and carry out a PLAN**

Let x = the amount of water added to the solution.
$1 + x$ = the amount in the new solution

Make a table to organize the data and the unknown
information.

	Amount of solution	Percent salt	Amount of salt
Original solution	1	20%	0.20(1)
Added water	x	0%	0
Final solution	$1 + x$	6%	0.06(1 + x)

Photosynthetic sulfur bacteria
color the waters of Great Salt Lake
a reddish-purple. Estimates of the
total biomass of sulfur bacteria
range from 180,000 tons to
2 million tons. How many times as
great is the greater estimate than
the lesser estimate?

The amount of salt in the original solution plus the amount added gives the
amount of salt in the new solution. Notice that since no salt is added, the total
amount of salt does not change.

$$0.20(1) + 0 = 0.06(1 + x)$$
$$20 = 6 + 6x$$
$$x \approx 2.33$$

■ **Find the ANSWER and CHECK**

The addition of approximately 2.33 liters of salt-free water for every
existing liter of lake water with 20 percent salinity will result in 6 percent
salinity in the lake.

Try This

a. A 280 mL solution is 20% salt. How much water should be added to make the solution 14% salt?

b. A grocer wishes to mix some nuts worth 90¢ per pound with some nuts worth $1.60 per pound to make 175 pounds of a mixture that is worth $1.30 per pound. How much of each should she use?

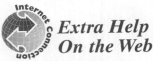

Extra Help On the Web

Look for worked-out examples at the Prentice Hall Web site.
www.phschool.com

10-8 Exercises

A

1. A lab technician has one solution that is 60% chlorinated and another that is 40% chlorinated. How much of each solution is needed to make a 100 L solution that is 50% chlorine?

	Amount of solution	Percent chlorine	Amount of chlorine
1st solution	x	60%	$0.60x$
2nd solution			
Final solution	100		

2. A 50-gallon barrel of milk is 6% butterfat. How much skim milk (no butterfat) should be mixed to make milk that is 3% butterfat?

	Amount (gallons)	Percent butterfat	Amount butterfat (gallons)
Original solution	50		
Skim milk	x		
Final solution			

3. *Multi-Step Problem*   Solution A is 50% acid and solution B is 80% acid. How much of each should be used to make 100 milliliters of a solution that is 68% acid?

a. Copy the table below. Write labels for the table.

b. Let x be the amount of the first solution. Complete the columns that show the amount of solution and the percent of acid.

c. To find the *amount* of acid in a solution, what two quantities must be multiplied?

d. Write expressions that show the amount of acid in each solution.

e. Write and solve an equation to answer the problem.

4. *Multi-Step Problem*   Seminole Dairy Farm has 100 gal of milk that is 4.6% butterfat. How much skim milk (no butterfat) should be mixed with it to make milk that is 3.2% fat?

a. Copy the table below. Write labels for the table.

b. Let x be the amount of skim milk. Complete the columns that show the amount and the percent of butterfat.

c. To find the *amount* of butterfat in a solution, what two quantities must be multiplied?

d. Write expressions that show the amount of butterfat in each solution.

e. Write and solve an equation to answer the problem.

5. A solution containing 30% insecticide is to be mixed with a solution containing 50% insecticide to make 200 L of a solution containing 42% insecticide. How much of each solution should be used?

6. A solution containing 28% fungicide is to be mixed with a solution containing 40% fungicide to make 300 L of a solution containing 36% fungicide. How much of each solution should be used?

7. The Nut Shoppe has 10 kg of mixed cashews and pecans, which sell for $8.40 per kilogram. Cashews alone sell for $8 per kilogram, and pecans sell for $9 per kilogram. How many kilograms of each are in the mix?

8. A coffee shop mixed Brazilian coffee worth $5 per kilogram with Turkish coffee worth $8 per kilogram. The mixture is to sell for $7 per kilogram. How much of each type of coffee should be used to make 300 kg of the mixture?

B

9. Northern Maywood voted 60% to 40% in favor of a water project. Southern Maywood voted 90% to 10% against the project. The project passed 55% to 45%. If 5900 people voted, how many were from Southern Maywood?

10. An employer has a daily payroll of $1950 when employing some workers at $120 per day and others at $150 per day. When the number of $120 workers is increased by 50% and the number of $150 workers is decreased $\frac{1}{5}$, the new daily payroll is $2400. Find how many workers were originally employed at each rate.

11. *Critical Thinking*   In Exercise 9, suppose that the project failed 45% to 55%. How many voters were from Southern Maywood?

Challenge

12. Bottle A, containing 12 L of 15% acid, is combined with bottle B, containing 3 L of 25% acid. Bottle C is 26% acid. How much of each solution is needed to have 24 L of a 20% acid solution?

Mixed Review

Solve.   **13.** $|x + 3| = 7$ **14.** $|2x - 4| = 16$ **15.** $|4x| - 5 = 19$

16. $8 - |x| > 4$ **17.** $|3x - 4| \leq 13$ **18.** $|5x - 4| + 3 < -19$ *9-3, 9-4*

19. A collection of dimes and quarters is worth $13.85. There are 83 coins in all. How many are dimes and how many are quarters?   *8-6*

◇◇ Connections: Reasoning

Problem: Aretha needs an antifreeze solution that is 50% alcohol. She has antifreeze that is 40% alcohol and antifreeze that is 60% alcohol. How much of each solution does she need to get 10 liters of the antifreeze that is 50% alcohol?

Solution A	Amount of solution	Percent alcohol	Amount of alcohol
1st antifreeze	x	0.60	
2nd antifreeze	$10 - x$	0.40	
Final solution	10	0.50	

Solution B	Amount of solution	Percent alcohol	Amount of alcohol
1st antifreeze	x	0.60	
2nd antifreeze	y	0.40	
Final solution	10	0.50	

Complete both tables and use the information in them to solve the problem. What mathematical concept is involved in Solution B?

Dividing Polynomials

PART 1   Dividing by a Monomial

Objective: Divide a polynomial by a monomial.

Rational expressions indicate division. To divide a polynomial by a monomial, divide each term by that monomial.

EXAMPLES   Divide.

1 $(6x^2 + 3x - 2) \div 3 = (6x^2 + 3x - 2) \times \frac{1}{3}$ Multiplying by the reciprocal

$\qquad\qquad\qquad = \frac{6x^2}{3} + \frac{3x}{3} - \frac{2}{3}$ Using a distributive property

$\qquad\qquad\qquad = 2x^2 + x - \frac{2}{3}$

2 $\dfrac{x^3 + 10x^2 + 8x}{2x} = \dfrac{x^3}{2x} + \dfrac{10x^2}{2x} + \dfrac{8x}{2x}$ Dividing each term by $2x$

$\qquad\qquad\qquad = \frac{1}{2}x^2 + 5x + 4$

Try This   Divide.

a. $\dfrac{4x^3 + 6x - 5}{2}$ **b.** $\dfrac{2x^3 + 6x^2 + 4x}{2x}$

PART 2   Dividing by a Polynomial

Objective: Divide a polynomial by a polynomial.

When the divisor is not a monomial, we can use long division.

EXAMPLE 3   Divide.

$(x^2 + 5x + 6) \div (x + 2)$

$$
\begin{array}{r}
x \\
x + 2 \overline{)x^2 + 5x + 6} \\
x^2 + 2x \\
\hline
3x
\end{array}
$$

Dividing first term by first term to get x

Multiplying x by divisor $x + 2$

Subtracting

What You'll Learn

1 To divide a polynomial by a monomial

2 To divide a polynomial by a polynomial

...And Why

To be able to simplify algebraic expressions

We now "bring down" the next term of the dividend, 6.

$$
\begin{array}{r}
x + 3 \hphantom{xxxxx} \longleftarrow \text{Dividing first term by first term to get 3} \\
x + 2\overline{)x^2 + 5x + 6} \hphantom{xxxxxxxxxxx} \\
\underline{x^2 + 2x} \hphantom{xxxxxxxxxxxxxxx} \\
3x + 6 \hphantom{xxxxxxxx} \\
\underline{3x + 6} \longleftarrow \text{Multiplying 3 by divisor } x + 2 \\
0 \longleftarrow \text{Subtracting} \hphantom{xxx}
\end{array}
$$

The quotient is $x + 3$. To check, multiply the quotient by the divisor and add the remainder, if any, to see if you get the dividend.

$$(x + 2)(x + 3) = x^2 + 5x + 6. \text{ The division checks.}$$

EXAMPLE 4   Divide.

$$(x^2 + 2x - 12) \div (x - 3)$$

$$
\begin{array}{r}
x + 5 \hphantom{xxxxx} \\
x - 3\overline{)x^2 + 2x - 12} \\
\underline{x^2 - 3x} \hphantom{xxxxxx} \\
5x - 12 \\
\underline{5x - 15} \\
3 \longleftarrow \text{Remainder}
\end{array}
$$

Check:
$$(x - 3)(x + 5) + 3 = x^2 + 2x - 15 + 3$$
$$= x^2 + 2x - 12$$

The answer can be written as quotient plus remainder over divisor.

$$\text{Quotient } \quad x + 5 + \dfrac{3}{x - 3} \quad \begin{array}{l}\longleftarrow \text{ Remainder} \\ \text{Divisor}\end{array}$$

When there are missing terms, we may represent them with 0's.

EXAMPLE 5   Divide.

$$(x^3 + 1) \div (x + 1)$$

$$
\begin{array}{r}
x^2 - x \hphantom{xxxxxx} + 1 \hphantom{x} \\
x + 1\overline{)x^3 + 0 \cdot x^2 + 0x + 1} \quad \text{Writing in the missing terms} \\
\underline{x^3 + \hphantom{xx} x^2} \hphantom{xxxxxxxxxx} \\
-x^2 + 0x \hphantom{xxxxx} \\
\underline{-x^2 - \hphantom{x} x} \hphantom{xxxxx} \\
x + 1 \\
\underline{x + 1}
\end{array}
$$

Try This   Divide.

c. $x - 2\overline{)x^2 + 2x - 9}$ 　　　 **d.** $(x^3 - 1) \div (x - 1)$

10-9 Exercises

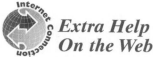

**Extra Help
On the Web**

Look for worked-out
examples at the Prentice
Hall Web site.
www.phschool.com

A

Divide.

1. $\dfrac{24x^4 - 4x^3 + x^2 - 16}{8}$

2. $\dfrac{12a^4 - 3a^2 + a - 6}{6}$

3. $\dfrac{u - 2u^2 - u^5}{u}$

4. $\dfrac{50x^5 - 7x^4 + x^2}{x}$

5. $\dfrac{15t^3 + 24t^2 - 6t}{3t}$

6. $\dfrac{25t^3 + 15t^2 - 30t}{5t}$

7. $\dfrac{20x^6 - 20x^4 - 5x^2}{-5x^2}$

8. $\dfrac{24x^6 + 32x^5 - 8x^2}{-8x^2}$

9. $\dfrac{9r^2s^2 + 3r^2s - 6rs^2}{-3rs}$

10. $\dfrac{4x^4y - 8x^6y^2 + 12x^8y^6}{4x^4y}$

Divide.

11. $(x^2 + 4x + 4) \div (x + 2)$

12. $(x^2 - 6x + 9) \div (x - 3)$

13. $(x^2 - 10x - 25) \div (x - 5)$

14. $(x^2 + 8x - 16) \div (x + 4)$

15. $(x^2 - 9) \div (x + 3)$

16. $(x^2 - 25) \div (x + 5)$

17. $(x^5 + 1) \div (x + 1)$

18. $(x^5 - 1) \div (x - 1)$

19. $\dfrac{a^3 + 6a^2 + 12a + 8}{a + 2}$

20. $\dfrac{x^3 - 4x^2 + x + 6}{x - 2}$

21. $\dfrac{8x^3 - 22x^2 - 5x + 12}{4x + 3}$

22. $\dfrac{2x^3 - 9x^2 + 11x - 3}{2x - 3}$

23. $(x^6 - 13x^3 + 42) \div (x^3 - 7)$

24. $(x^6 + 5x^3 - 24) \div (x^3 - 3)$

25. $(x^4 - 16) \div (x - 2)$

26. $(x^4 - 81) \div (x - 3)$

27. $(t^3 - t^2 + t - 1) \div (t - 1)$

28. $(t^3 - t^2 + t - 1) \div (t + 1)$

B

Divide.

29. $(x^4 + 9x^2 + 20) \div (x^2 + 4)$

30. $(y^4 + a^2) \div (y + a)$

31. $(5a^3 + 8a^2 - 23a - 1) \div (5a^2 - 7a - 2)$

32. $(15y^3 - 30y + 7 - 19y^2) \div (3y^2 - 2 - 5y)$

33. $(6x^5 - 13x^3 + 5x + 3 - 4x^2 + 3x^4) \div (3x^3 - 2x - 1)$

34. $(5x^7 - 3x^4 + 2x^2 - 10x + 2) \div (x^2 - x + 1)$

35. $(a^6 - b^6) \div (a - b)$

36. $(x^5 + y^5) \div (x + y)$

37. *Critical Thinking*   What polynomial has a quotient of $3a^2 + ab - b$
with a remainder of a when divided by $2a^2 - b$?

Challenge

38. Divide $6a^{3h} + 13a^{2h} - 4a^h - 15$ by $2a^h + 3$.

If the remainder is 0 when one polynomial is divided by another, then the divisor is a factor of the dividend. Find the value(s) of c for which $x - 1$ is a factor of each polynomial.

39. $x^2 + 4x + c$ **40.** $2x^2 + 3cx - 8$ **41.** $c^2x^2 - 2cx + 1$

42. One factor of $x^3 + 2x^2 - x - 2$ is $x + 2$. Find two other factors of this polynomial.

Mixed Review

Find the least common multiple (LCM).   **43.** $6(y - 1), 9 - 9y$ *10-5*

Add or subtract. Simplify.   **44.** $\dfrac{(x + y)}{x^2y} + \dfrac{(x + y)}{xy^2}$ **45.** $\dfrac{4}{7m} + \dfrac{1}{14m}$

46. $\dfrac{2}{x + 2} - \dfrac{3}{x - 2}$ **47.** $\dfrac{7}{x^2 - 9} - \dfrac{4}{2x - 6}$ **48.** $\dfrac{(x - 3)}{2x - 1} - \dfrac{4(x + 1)}{1 - 2x}$ *10-5*

Solve.   **49.** $x - \dfrac{3}{x} = 2$ **50.** $\dfrac{x - 3}{x + 2} = \dfrac{1}{2}$ **51.** $\dfrac{x + 2}{4} - \dfrac{x - 3}{3} = 1$ *10-6*

The Factor Theorem

If a polynomial such as $ax^2 + bx + c$ is divided by $x - d$ to get a quotient Q and a remainder R, then $ax^2 + bx + c = (x - d)Q + R$. When x has the value d, $(x - d)Q + R = (d - d)Q + R = (0)Q + R = R$. So when x has the value d, $ax^2 + bx + c = R$.

When x has the value d and the remainder is 0, $ax^2 + bx + c = 0$. This means that d is a root of the polynomial.

When x has the value d and the remainder is 0, $x - d$ divides $ax^2 + bx + c$ evenly. This means that $x - d$ is a factor of $ax^2 + bx + c$.

Therefore, $x - d$ is a factor of a polynomial whenever d is a root of the polynomial.

The statement we have just proved is known as the **factor theorem.**

Exercises

Factor the polynomial and use the factors to find its roots.

1. $x^2 - 9x + 8$ **2.** $x^2 + 11x + 28$ **3.** $x^2 - 2x - 15$

Evaluate the polynomial for each given value of x to find which values are roots. Use the roots to find the factors of the polynomial.

4. $2, -1, -2; x^2 - x - 2$ **5.** $\dfrac{7}{2}, \dfrac{5}{2}, \dfrac{3}{2}; 4x^2 - 20x + 21$

Objective: **Simplify complex rational expressions.**

A **complex rational expression** has a rational expression in its numerator or denominator or both. Here are some examples.

$$\frac{1 + \frac{2}{x}}{3} \qquad \frac{\frac{x + y}{2}}{\frac{2x}{x + 1}} \qquad \frac{\frac{1}{3} + \frac{1}{5}}{\frac{2}{x} - \frac{x}{y}}$$

To simplify a complex rational expression, multiply the numerator and denominator by an expression equivalent to 1. The expression selected should use the least common multiple of any denominators found in the numerator or denominator of the complex rational expression.

What You'll Learn

1 To simplify complex expressions

. . . And Why

To be able to simplify algebraic expressions

EXAMPLE 1   Simplify.

$$\frac{\frac{3}{4} + \frac{x}{2}}{\frac{x}{8}} = \frac{\frac{3}{4} + \frac{x}{2}}{\frac{x}{8}} \cdot \frac{8}{8} \qquad \text{The LCM of the denominators is 8.}$$

$$= \frac{\frac{3}{4} \cdot 8 + \frac{x}{2} \cdot 8}{\frac{x}{8} \cdot 8} \qquad \text{Using the distributive property}$$

$$= \frac{6 + 4x}{x} \qquad \text{Simplifying}$$

EXAMPLE 2   Simplify.

$$\frac{1 - \frac{1}{x}}{1 - \frac{1}{x^2}} = \frac{1 - \frac{1}{x}}{1 - \frac{1}{x^2}} \cdot \frac{x^2}{x^2} \qquad \text{The LCM of } x \text{ and } x^2 \text{ is } x^2.$$

$$= \frac{x^2(1) - x^2\left(\frac{1}{x}\right)}{x^2(1) - x^2\left(\frac{1}{x^2}\right)} \qquad \text{Using the distributive property}$$

$$= \frac{x^2 - x}{x^2 - 1}$$

$$= \frac{x(x - 1)}{(x + 1)(x - 1)} \qquad \text{Factoring}$$

$$= \frac{x}{x + 1} \qquad \text{Simplifying}$$

You can also simplify complex rational expressions by replacing a division by a product of the reciprocal. This method is particularly useful when the numerator and denominator are quotients.

EXAMPLE 3

$$\frac{\dfrac{4}{x^2 - y^2}}{\dfrac{2}{x - y}} = \frac{4}{x^2 - y^2} \div \frac{2}{x - y}$$

$$= \frac{4}{x^2 - y^2} \cdot \frac{x - y}{2}$$

$$= \frac{4(x - y)}{(x^2 - y^2)2}$$

$$= \frac{2 \cdot 2(x - y)}{(x + y)(x - y)2}$$

$$= \frac{2}{x + y}$$

Try This   Simplify.

a. $\dfrac{\dfrac{x}{2} + \dfrac{x}{3}}{\dfrac{1}{2}}$ **b.** $\dfrac{1 + \dfrac{1}{x}}{1 - \dfrac{1}{x^2}}$ **c.** $\dfrac{\dfrac{3}{(t + 2)(2t - 1)}}{\dfrac{t}{t + 2}}$

***Extra Help
On the Web***

Look for worked-out
examples at the Prentice
Hall Web site.
www.phschool.com

10-10 Exercises

A

Simplify.

1. $\dfrac{\dfrac{2}{7} + \dfrac{3}{7}}{\dfrac{3}{4}}$ **2.** $\dfrac{3 + \dfrac{5}{2}}{\dfrac{5}{4}}$ **3.** $\dfrac{1 + \dfrac{2}{x}}{\dfrac{3}{4}}$

4. $\dfrac{3 + \dfrac{x}{2}}{\dfrac{5}{4}}$ **5.** $\dfrac{1 + \dfrac{9}{16}}{1 - \dfrac{3}{4}}$ **6.** $\dfrac{\dfrac{5}{27} - 5}{\dfrac{1}{3} + 1}$

7. $\dfrac{\dfrac{1}{x} + 3}{\dfrac{1}{x} - 5}$ **8.** $\dfrac{\dfrac{3}{a}}{\dfrac{1}{a} - \dfrac{1}{3a}}$ **9.** $\dfrac{\dfrac{7}{y}}{\dfrac{1}{4} + \dfrac{2}{y}}$

10. $\dfrac{\dfrac{c}{d} + 3}{4 + \dfrac{c}{d}}$ **11.** $\dfrac{\dfrac{3}{s} + s}{\dfrac{s}{3} + s}$ **12.** $\dfrac{\dfrac{2}{y} + \dfrac{1}{2y}}{y + \dfrac{y}{2}}$

13. $\dfrac{4 - \dfrac{1}{x^2}}{2 - \dfrac{1}{x}}$

14. $\dfrac{\dfrac{1}{xy}}{\dfrac{1}{x} + \dfrac{1}{y}}$

15. $\dfrac{\dfrac{2}{a + b}}{\dfrac{4}{a^2 - b^2}}$

16. $\dfrac{\dfrac{p}{q} + \dfrac{q}{r}}{\dfrac{r}{s} + \dfrac{s}{t}}$

17. $\dfrac{\dfrac{x}{y} - \dfrac{y}{x}}{\dfrac{1}{y} + \dfrac{1}{x}}$

18. $\dfrac{\dfrac{1}{a} - \dfrac{1}{2}}{a - 2}$

19. $\dfrac{\dfrac{a}{(a + b)(2a + 1)}}{\dfrac{b}{(a + b)}}$

20. $\dfrac{\dfrac{m}{(m - n)(m + n)}}{\dfrac{n + 1}{(m + n)^2}}$

21. $\dfrac{\dfrac{x}{x - y}}{\dfrac{x^2}{x^2 - y^2}}$

22. $\dfrac{\dfrac{a}{b} + \dfrac{b}{c}}{\dfrac{c}{d} + \dfrac{d}{e}}$

23. $\dfrac{\dfrac{g}{2f} + \dfrac{g + 2}{f + 1}}{\dfrac{g^2}{f + 1} + \dfrac{2g + 3}{f}}$

24. $\dfrac{\dfrac{x + 1}{x + 2} + \dfrac{1}{x}}{\dfrac{x}{x + 2} + \dfrac{1}{x^2}}$

B

Simplify.

25. $\dfrac{1 + \dfrac{a}{b - a}}{\dfrac{a}{a + b} - 1}$

26. $\dfrac{\dfrac{a}{b} + \dfrac{c}{d}}{\dfrac{b}{a} + \dfrac{d}{c}}$

27. $\dfrac{\dfrac{a}{b} - \dfrac{c}{d}}{\dfrac{b}{a} - \dfrac{d}{c}}$

28. *Critical Thinking*   What values of a are unacceptable because they would make a denominator 0 in this fraction?

$$\dfrac{\dfrac{2a - 4}{a + 1}}{\dfrac{a + 2}{a - 2}}$$

Challenge

Solve.

29. $\dfrac{\dfrac{2a + 3}{a + 1}}{\dfrac{a - 2}{a + 1}} = 12$

30. $\dfrac{\dfrac{x + 1}{x - 1} + 1}{\dfrac{x + 1}{x - 1} - 1} = 10$

Mixed Review

Calculate and simplify.   **31.** $\dfrac{4x + 5}{x + 5} - \dfrac{x + 11}{x + 5}$ **32.** $\dfrac{5}{y + 2} + \dfrac{5}{y - 2}$

33. $\dfrac{m^2}{m - 5} + \dfrac{25}{5 - m}$ **34.** $\dfrac{2}{x + 1} + \dfrac{5}{2x}$ **35.** $\dfrac{x - 1}{x} - \dfrac{3x + 5}{2x}$ *10-4, 10-5*

Solve.   **36.** $\dfrac{5}{x + 1} = \dfrac{4}{x - 1}$ **37.** $\dfrac{x}{4} - \dfrac{x}{6} = \dfrac{1}{4}$ **38.** $\dfrac{x - 2}{3x} = \dfrac{1}{4}$ *10-6*

39. Find two numbers whose sum is -13 and whose difference is 21. *8-6*

10-11 ▷ Proofs

Objective: Prove theorems involving multiplication and division.

What You'll Learn

1 To prove theorems involving multiplication and division

... And Why

To become familiar with the properties of numbers and be able to use them to simplify algebraic equations

In our work with division of rational numbers and division of rational expressions, we used the division rule of multiplying by the reciprocal of the divisor. We can prove this rule.

Theorem

The Division Theorem

For any number a and any nonzero number b,
$$\frac{a}{b} = a \cdot \frac{1}{b}$$

EXAMPLE 1

To prove this theorem we will use the definition of division. That is, $\frac{a}{b} = c$ if $c \cdot b = a$. Thus to show that $a \cdot \frac{1}{b}$ is the quotient $\frac{a}{b}$, we will need to show that when b is multiplied by $a \cdot \frac{1}{b}$ the result is a.

Proof

1. $\left(a \cdot \frac{1}{b}\right) \cdot b = a \cdot \left(\frac{1}{b} \cdot b\right)$	1. Associative property of multiplication
2. $\qquad\qquad = a \cdot (1)$	2. Definition of reciprocal
3. $\qquad\qquad = a$	3. Multiplicative identity
4. $\left(a \cdot \frac{1}{b}\right) \cdot b = a$	4. Transitive property of equality

Thus, by the definition of division, $a \cdot \frac{1}{b} = \frac{a}{b}$.

Another theorem related to reciprocals concerns the reciprocal of a product.

Theorem

The Reciprocal Theorem

For any nonzero rational numbers a and b,
$$\frac{1}{ab} = \frac{1}{a} \cdot \frac{1}{b}$$
(The reciprocal of a product is the product of the reciprocals.)

EXAMPLE 2

To prove this theorem we will use the commutative and associative properties to show that $(ab) \cdot \left(\frac{1}{a} \cdot \frac{1}{b}\right)$ is 1.

Proof

1. $(ab)\left(\frac{1}{a} \cdot \frac{1}{b}\right) = \left(ab \cdot \frac{1}{a}\right) \cdot \frac{1}{b}$	1. Associative property of multiplication
2. $\qquad = \left(a \cdot \frac{1}{a} \cdot b\right) \cdot \frac{1}{b}$	2. Commutative property of multiplication
3. $\qquad = \left(a \cdot \frac{1}{a}\right)\left(b \cdot \frac{1}{b}\right)$	3. Associative property of multiplication
4. $\qquad = 1 \cdot 1$	4. Definition of reciprocal
5. $\qquad = 1$	5. Multiplicative identity
6. $ab\left(\frac{1}{a} \cdot \frac{1}{b}\right) = 1$	6. Transitive property of equality

Thus $\frac{1}{ab} = \frac{1}{a} \cdot \frac{1}{b}$.

This theorem gives us the procedure for multiplying two fractions or two rational expressions.

Theorem

For any rational numbers a, c, and any nonzero rational numbers b, d,
$$\frac{a}{b} \cdot \frac{c}{d} = \frac{ac}{bd}$$

Try This

a. Complete the following proof of the theorem presented above.

Proof

1. $\frac{a}{b} = a \cdot \frac{1}{b}$ and $\frac{c}{d} = c \cdot \frac{1}{d}$	1. Division theorem
2. $\frac{a}{b} \cdot \frac{c}{d} = \left(a \cdot \frac{1}{b}\right)\left(c \cdot \frac{1}{d}\right)$	2. Substituting $a \cdot \frac{1}{b}$ for $\frac{a}{b}$ and $c \cdot \frac{1}{d}$ for $\frac{c}{d}$
3. $\qquad = (a \cdot c)\left(\frac{1}{b} \cdot \frac{1}{d}\right)$	3.
4. $\qquad = ac\left(\frac{1}{bd}\right)$	4.
5. $\qquad = \frac{ac}{bd}$	5.
6. $\frac{a}{b} \cdot \frac{c}{d} = \frac{ac}{bd}$	6.

b. The subtraction theorem states that for any real numbers a and b, $a - b = a + (-b)$. Write a proof of the subtraction theorem.

10-11 Exercises

A

1. Complete the proof of the following theorem by supplying the reasons. For any numbers a, b, and any nonzero number c,

$$\frac{a}{c} + \frac{b}{c} = \frac{a + b}{c}.$$

(a) $\frac{a}{c} = a \cdot \frac{1}{c}$ and $\frac{b}{c} = b \cdot \frac{1}{c}$	(a) Division theorem
(b) $\frac{a}{c} + \frac{b}{c} = a \cdot \frac{1}{c} + b \cdot \frac{1}{c}$	(b) Substituting $a \cdot \frac{1}{c}$ for $\frac{a}{c}$ and $b \cdot \frac{1}{c}$ for $\frac{b}{c}$
(c) $\quad = (a + b)\frac{1}{c}$	(c)
(d) $\quad = \frac{a + b}{c}$	(d)
(e) $\frac{a}{c} + \frac{b}{c} = \frac{a + b}{c}$	(e)

2. Write a proof of the following theorem. For any numbers a, b, and any nonzero number c,

$$\frac{a}{c} - \frac{b}{c} = \frac{a - b}{c}$$

(Hint: Use Exercise 1 as a model for your proof.)

3. Prove that if $\frac{a}{b}$ is any nonzero rational number, then its reciprocal is $\frac{b}{a}$. (Hint: Show that $\frac{b}{a}$ satisfies the definition of reciprocal.)

4. Prove the property of proportion:

if $\frac{a}{b} = \frac{c}{d}$, then $ad = bc$.

Mixed Review

Simplify. **5.** $(2w)^5$ **6.** $\frac{a^2b^3}{ab^2c}$ **7.** $(y^9)^9$ **8.** $(-3m^5)^4$ *5-3*

Factor. **9.** $81c^2 - 16$ **10.** $5x^2 + 5x - 30$ **11.** $2x^2 + 3x - 5$ *6-2, 6-5*

12. $6x^2 + 25x + 4$ **13.** $6x^2 + 11x + 3$ **14.** $10x^2 + 23x + 12$

Solve. **15.** $\frac{x}{7} - \frac{7}{x} = 0$ **16.** $x - \frac{4}{x} = 0$ **17.** $\frac{a + 3}{2a + 2} = \frac{2}{3}$ *10-6*

18. $3x + y = 8$ **19.** $2x + 5y = 3$
$\ 5x - y = 8$ $\ 5x - 2y = -7$ *8-1, 8-2, 8-3*

Reasoning Strategies

Work Backward

Objective: Solve problems using the strategy *Work Backward* and other strategies.

PROBLEM-SOLVING GUIDELINES
■ UNDERSTAND the problem
▪ Develop and carry out a PLAN
■ Find the ANSWER and CHECK

Sometimes a problem describes a sequence of actions involving numbers, gives the result, and asks for the original number. A problem of this type can be solved using a strategy called *Work Backward*.

What You'll Learn

1 To solve problems using the strategy *Work Backward* and other strategies

. . . And Why

To be able to solve real-world problems more efficiently using reasoning skills

EXAMPLE

Ken had a package of graph paper for math class that he shared with 3 friends. He gave one quarter of the pack to Adele. Terry got one third of what was left. Then Phyllis took one sixth of the remainder. Ken had 30 sheets left for himself. How many sheets did he have to start?

To solve this problem, start with the number of sheets Ken had left for himself and *work backward* using the inverse operations.

Data in the Story

Ken started with some number of sheets of graph paper.

↓

Adele took $\frac{1}{4}$ of the paper.

↓

Terry took $\frac{1}{3}$ of what was left.

↓

Phyllis took $\frac{1}{6}$ of the remainder.

↓

Ken had 30 sheets left.   →

Work Backward

Ken started with 72 sheets.

↑

If Adele took $\frac{1}{4}$ of the pack, then the 54 sheets left must be $\frac{3}{4}$ of what was there z. If $\frac{3}{4}z = 54$, then $z = 72$.

↑

If Terry took $\frac{1}{3}$ of what was left, then the 36 sheets left must be $\frac{2}{3}$ of what was there y. If $\frac{2}{3}y = 36$, then $y = 54$.

↑

If $\frac{5}{6}x = 30$ then $x = 36$. There were 36 sheets before Phyllis took hers.

↑

If Phyllis took $\frac{1}{6}$ of the remaining sheets x, then 30 must be $\frac{5}{6}$ of x.

Ken had a total of 72 sheets of paper to start.

Writing Math

To solve this problem, you could write the following equations instead of the ones given.

$x - \frac{1}{6}x = 30$

$y - \frac{1}{3}y = 54$

$z - \frac{1}{4}z = 72$

Problem-Solving Strategies

Draw a Diagram	Try, Test, Revise	Write an Equation
Make an Organized List	Use Logical Reasoning	Make a Table
Look for a Pattern	Simplify the Problem	Work Backward

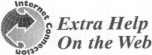

***Extra Help
On the Web***

Look for worked-out
examples at the Prentice
Hall Web site.
www.phschool.com

10-12 PROBLEMS

Solve using one or more of the strategies.

1. Four salespeople were sent into a particular region to find new stores to carry their product. If, together, they found 50 new stores to carry their product, they would each get a $500 bonus. Neil found twice as many stores as Gus. Gus found 4 fewer stores than Salvatore, and Salvatore found 4 more than Bonnie. Bonnie found 8 stores. Did each salesperson get the $500 bonus?

2. A rectangular swimming pool is 50 ft wide, 100 ft long, and 10 ft deep. The pool will be filled to a line 2 ft from the top. The water company charges $2.25/1000 foot^3. How much does it cost to fill this pool?

3. Ramon was going to visit his friend in a distant city. He had to travel on four different turnpikes to get there. He had to pay 50¢ to enter each turnpike and 50¢ to exit. On each turnpike, he stopped at one store for a snack and spent $\frac{1}{2}$ of the money he had after he entered that turnpike. After paying 50¢ to leave the last turnpike, Ramon was out of money. How much did he start with before entering the first turnpike?

4. You have two pails, one that will hold 4 qt and one that will hold 9 qt. There are no markings on either pail to indicate smaller quantities. How can you measure out 6 qt of water using these two pails? (Assume there is an unlimited supply of water.)

5. If a certain number, two thirds of it, half of it, and a seventh of it are added together, the result is 97. What is the number?*

6. ***Write a Convincing Argument***   Solve the problem below. Then write an argument that would convince a classmate that your solution is correct.

   An architect was hired to build a monument to a Civil War battle. The structure was a pyramid made out of cannonballs. The base was made of 100 cannonballs in the shape of a square, with 10 cannonballs on a side; the row on top of the base had 81 cannonballs with 9 on a side; and so on. How many cannonballs were used to build this monument?

El Morro in San Juan, Puerto Rico, begun in 1540, is a formidable six-level fortress rising 140 ft above the sea. This National Historic Site is a maze of tunnels, dungeons, barracks, outposts, and ramps. How many cannonballs are in this square pyramid?

*This problem appears in the Rhind Papyrus, which is probably the oldest mathematical book known, written around 1650 B.C. in Egypt.

10-1

A **rational expression** is in **simplest form** when the only common factor of the numerator and denominator is 1 or -1. To simplify a rational expression, factor the numerator and the denominator, and find common factors that simplify to 1.

Simplify.

1. $\dfrac{3x + 9}{3x}$ **2.** $\dfrac{6y^2 + 3y}{3y^2 + 6y}$ **3.** $\dfrac{3x - 3}{3x + 6}$ **4.** $\dfrac{3c + 5d}{25d^2 - 9c^2}$

10-2

To multiply two rational expressions, multiply the numerators and multiply the denominators.

Multiply. Simplify the product.

5. $\dfrac{9y^2}{5y^2} \cdot \dfrac{(y - 3)}{3}$ **6.** $\dfrac{2x}{x + 1} \cdot \dfrac{x + 1}{4x}$ **7.** $\dfrac{7(m - 2)}{5m} \cdot \dfrac{4m^2}{m - 2}$

10-3

To divide rational expressions, multiply the first expression by the reciprocal of the divisor.

Divide and simplify.

8. $\dfrac{3x + 3}{3} \div \dfrac{x + 1}{6}$ **9.** $\dfrac{y + 2}{y - 3} \div \dfrac{y + 2}{y + 1}$ **10.** $\dfrac{y + 3}{y^2 - 9} \div \dfrac{y - 3}{y^2 - 5y + 6}$

11. $\dfrac{b - 2}{b^2 + b} \div \dfrac{b^2 - 4}{b + 1}$ **12.** $\dfrac{4x - 6}{5} \div \dfrac{6x - 9}{25}$ **13.** $\dfrac{x^2 - y^2}{xy^2} \div \dfrac{xy + y^2}{x}$

10-4, 10-5

To add or subtract rational expressions, first determine the least common denominator and if necessary rewrite each expression as an equivalent expression with the LCD. Add or subtract the numerators, and write the sum or difference over the denominator.

Add or subtract. Simplify.

14. $\dfrac{3x^2 + 2x - 5}{5x + 1} + \dfrac{2x^2 - x + 6}{5x + 1}$ **15.** $\dfrac{5b}{2 + b} - \dfrac{b - 3}{2 + b}$

16. $\dfrac{3a}{3a} + \dfrac{-1}{a}$ **17.** $\dfrac{2a}{a + 1} + \dfrac{4a}{a^2 - 1}$ **18.** $\dfrac{3}{3x - 9} + \dfrac{x - 2}{3 - x}$

19. $\dfrac{3x - 1}{2x} - \dfrac{x - 1}{x}$ **20.** $\dfrac{15}{b^2 - 4} - \dfrac{7}{b - 2}$ **21.** $\dfrac{1}{x^2 - 25} - \dfrac{x - 5}{x^2 - 4x - 5}$

Key Terms

complex rational expression (p. 469)
Division Theorem (p. 472)
extraneous solution (p. 452)
Factor Theorem (p. 468)
least common multiple (LCM) (p. 446)
rational equation (p. 451)
rational expression (p. 432)
Reciprocal Theorem (p. 472)
simplest form of a rational expression (p. 433)

10-6

To solve an equation with rational expressions, first multiply both sides of the equation by the **LCM** of all the denominators.

Solve.

22. $\frac{3}{y} - \frac{1}{4} = \frac{1}{y}$

23. $\frac{15}{x} - \frac{15}{x+2} = 2$

24. $\frac{4x}{3} - \frac{2x-1}{5} = \frac{x+3}{2}$

25. $\frac{5}{x} + x = -6$

26. $\frac{x}{x-1} - \frac{2}{1-x^2} = \frac{8}{x+1}$

10-7

If a job requires n hours, then $\frac{1}{n}$ of the job can be done in 1 hour. You can use this principle to write an equation to solve work problems.

27. In checking records a contractor finds that crew A can pave a certain length of highway in 9 hours. Crew B can do the same job in 12 hours. How long would it take if both crews worked together?

The formula $d = r \cdot t$ or $t = \frac{d}{r}$ can be used to make a table and write an equation for solving motion problems.

28. A lab is testing two high-speed trains. One train travels 40 km/h faster than the other train. While one train travels 70 km, the other travels 60 km. Find their speeds.

10-8

29. Solution A is 30% alcohol and solution B is 60% alcohol. How much of each is needed to make 80 liters of a solution that is 45% alcohol?

10-9

To divide a polynomial by a monomial, divide each term by that monomial. To divide a polynomial by another polynomial, use the long division method.

Divide.

30. $\frac{12y^3 + 8y - 3}{3}$

31. $(2x^2 + 3x - 20) \div (x + 4)$

10-10

To simplify a complex rational expression, multiply both the numerator and the denominator by the LCM of all denominators in the complex expression.

Simplify.

32. $\dfrac{\frac{1}{x} + 1}{\frac{1}{x^2} - 1}$

33. $\dfrac{x + \frac{3}{y}}{x - \frac{2}{y^2}}$

10 ▷ Chapter Assessment

Simplify.

1. $\dfrac{5y + 15}{10}$

2. $\dfrac{14y^2 + 7y}{49y^2 + 14y}$

3. $\dfrac{4x^2 - 8xy + 4y^2}{3x - 3y}$

Multiply. Simplify the product.

4. $\dfrac{2x + 3y}{5} \cdot \dfrac{10}{4x + 6y}$

5. $\dfrac{25 - x^2}{12} \cdot \dfrac{6}{5 - x}$

6. $\dfrac{x^2 + x}{x^2} \cdot \dfrac{3x - 3}{x^2 - 1}$

Divide and simplify.

7. $\dfrac{4x - 6}{5} \div \dfrac{6x - 9}{25}$

8. $\dfrac{2x + x^2}{4x - 5} \div \dfrac{4x^2 + 2x^3}{16x - 20}$

Add or subtract. Simplify.

9. $\dfrac{16 + x}{x^3} + \dfrac{7 - 4x}{x^3}$

10. $\dfrac{5 - t}{t^2 + 1} - \dfrac{t - 3}{t^2 + 1}$

11. $\dfrac{x - 5}{x^2 - 1} + \dfrac{5}{x^2 - 1}$

Add or subtract. Simplify.

12. $\dfrac{x - 4}{x - 3} + \dfrac{x - 1}{3 - x}$

13. $\dfrac{5}{t - 1} + \dfrac{3}{t}$

14. $\dfrac{1}{x^2 - 16} - \dfrac{x + 4}{x^2 - 3x - 4}$

15. $\dfrac{6}{9 - a^2} - \dfrac{3}{12 + 4a}$

16. $\dfrac{4}{x^2 - 1} - \dfrac{2}{x^2 - 2x + 1}$

17. $\dfrac{3}{2a + 18} + \dfrac{27}{a^2 - 81}$

Solve.

18. $\dfrac{7}{y} - \dfrac{1}{3} = \dfrac{1}{4}$

19. $\dfrac{15}{x} - \dfrac{15}{x - 2} = -2$

20. Solution A is 25% acid and Solution B is 40% acid. How much of each is needed to make 60 liters of a solution that is 30% acid?

21. Mrs. Crowley has a stack of letters to be typed. If she can type all of the letters in 6 hours and Mr. Crowley can type all of the letters in 9 hours, how long will it take them if they work together?

Divide.

22. $(12x^4 + 9x^3 - 15x^2) \div 3x^2$

23. $\dfrac{6x^3 - 8x^2 - 14x + 13}{3x + 2}$

Simplify.

24. $\dfrac{\dfrac{1}{14y} - \dfrac{1}{2y^2}}{\dfrac{1}{7} - \dfrac{6}{7y} - \dfrac{1}{y^2}}$

25. $\dfrac{25 - \dfrac{9}{x^2}}{5 + \dfrac{3}{x}}$

CHAPTER 11

Skills & Concepts You Need for Chapter 11

1-2 Simplify.

1. $\frac{18}{50}$ **2.** $\frac{18}{66}$ **3.** $\frac{81}{27}$ **4.** $\frac{100}{50}$

1-3 What is the meaning of each?

5. 5^2 **6.** 4^3 **7.** x^5 **8.** 7^6

2-1 Simplify.

9. $|-8|$ **10.** $|-15|$ **11.** $|0|$

2-5 Multiply.

12. $\frac{5}{3} \cdot \frac{5}{3}$ **13.** $\left(-\frac{2}{9}\right) \cdot \frac{2}{9}$ **14.** $\left(-\frac{3}{16}\right) \cdot \left(-\frac{3}{16}\right)$

15. $\frac{11}{4} \cdot \left(-\frac{11}{4}\right)$ **16.** $(-5)(-5)$ **17.** $(-6)(-6)(-6)$

18. $\left(-\frac{3}{4}\right)\left(-\frac{3}{4}\right)$ **19.** $\left(-\frac{1}{5}\right)\left(-\frac{1}{5}\right)\left(-\frac{1}{5}\right)$

5-1 Multiply or divide. Simplify.

20. $x^3 \cdot x^3$ **21.** $(a^2b^3)(ab^2)$

22. $\frac{x^9}{x^4}$ **23.** $\frac{ab^3}{ab}$

6-1 to 6-5 Factor.

24. $x^3 - x^2$ **25.** $5x - 30x^2$

26. $x^2 + 2x + 1$ **27.** $x^2 - 14x + 49$

Radical Expressions and Equations

The period of a pendulum is the time it takes to swing from one side to the other and back. The pendulum on this clock is 1 ft long. Use the formula $T = 2\pi\sqrt{\frac{L}{32}}$, where L is the length of the pendulum in feet, to find the period T in seconds.

11-1 ▷ Real Numbers

What You'll Learn

1 To find the square roots of perfect squares

2 To tell whether a real number is rational or irrational

3 To use a table or a calculator to give an approximation for an irrational number

... And Why

To find and classify numerical radical expressions

PART 1 Square Roots

Objective: Find the square roots of perfect squares.

When we raise a number to the second power, we have squared the number. Sometimes we may need to find the number that was squared. We call this process finding a square root of a number.

Definition

The number c is a **square root** of a if $c^2 = a$.

Every positive number has two square roots, a positive square root and a negative square root. For example, the square roots of 25 are 5 and -5, because $5^2 = 25$ and $(-5)^2 = 25$.

The positive square root is also called the **principal square root.** The $\sqrt{}$ symbol is called a **radical sign.** The radical sign is used to denote the principal square root. To name the negative square root of a number, we use $-\sqrt{}$. Thus,

$$\sqrt{25} = 5 \text{ and } -\sqrt{25} = -5.$$

We can use the symbol $\pm\sqrt{}$ to name the positive and negative square roots.

The number 0 has only one square root, 0. Since any positive or negative number squared is positive, negative numbers do not have square roots in the set of real numbers.

EXAMPLE 1   Find the square roots of 81.

The numbers 9 and -9 are square roots. $9^2 = 81; (-9)^2 = 81$

EXAMPLES   Simplify.

2 $\sqrt{225} = 15$ Taking the principal square root

3 $-\sqrt{64} = -8$ Taking the negative square root

Try This

a. Find the square roots of 169.

Simplify. **b.** $-\sqrt{100}$ **c.** $\sqrt{256}$

PART 2 Real Numbers

Objective: Tell whether a real number is rational or irrational.

Each rational number can be matched to exactly one point on a number line. There are many points on the number line, however, for which there are no rational numbers. These points correspond to irrational numbers. Every point on a number line is associated with either a rational number or an irrational number. Combined, these numbers form the set of real numbers.

Definition

The **real numbers** consist of the rational numbers and the irrational numbers.

Quick Review

Like the rational numbers, the real numbers are a field, since they satisfy the field axioms found on p. 102.

Recall that any rational number can be written in the form $\frac{a}{b}$ where a and b are integers and $b \neq 0$.

We also know that decimal notation for a rational number either ends or continues to repeat the same group of digits.

$\frac{1}{4} = 0.25$ The decimal ends.

$\frac{1}{3} = 0.333\ldots$ The 3 repeats.

$\frac{5}{11} = 0.45\overline{45}$ The bar indicates that 45 repeats.

An irrational number cannot be expressed as a ratio of two integers. Decimal notation for an irrational number never ends and does not repeat any group of digits. The number π is an example.

$\pi = 3.1415926535\ldots$ and continues endlessly.

The numbers 3.1416, 3.14, or $\frac{22}{7}$ are only rational approximations for π.

Is $\sqrt{2}$ a rational number? If we look for a number $\frac{a}{b}$ for which $\left(\frac{a}{b}\right)^2 = 2$, we can find rational numbers whose squares are quite close to 2. But we cannot find one whose square is exactly 2. $\sqrt{2}$ is an irrational number.

Definition

An **irrational number** is a real number that cannot be written in the form $\frac{a}{b}$ where a and b are integers.

The square roots of most whole numbers are irrational. Only the perfect squares 0, 1, 4, 9, 16, 25, 36, and so on have rational square roots.

EXAMPLES Identify the rational numbers and the irrational numbers.

4 $\sqrt{3}$ $\sqrt{3}$ is irrational, since 3 is not a perfect square.

5 $\sqrt{25}$ $\sqrt{25}$ is rational, since 25 is a perfect square.

6 $\sqrt{35}$ $\sqrt{35}$ is irrational, since 35 is not a perfect square.

7 $-\sqrt{49}$ $-\sqrt{49}$ is rational, since 49 is a perfect square.

Try This Identify the rational numbers and the irrational numbers.

d. $\sqrt{5}$ **e.** $-\sqrt{36}$ **f.** $-\sqrt{32}$ **g.** $\sqrt{101}$

PART 3 Approximating Irrational Numbers

Objective: Use a table or a calculator to give an approximation for an irrational number.

We can use a rational number to approximate an irrational number. Table 1 in the Appendix contains rational approximations for square roots. We can also use a calculator to find rational approximations for square roots.

EXAMPLE 8 Approximate $\sqrt{10}$.

Using Table 1, find 10 in the first column headed N. Look in the third column headed $\sqrt{N}$ opposite 10. Thus $\sqrt{10} \approx 3.162$. The symbol $\approx$ means "is approximately equal to."

Calculators are very useful for finding square roots.

> ### Square Roots
>
> Most calculators have a square root key that is usually accessed using an
> INV   or   2nd   key with the x^2 key.
> $\sqrt{10} \rightarrow 10$ 2nd x^2 $\rightarrow$ 3.1622777
> Since $\sqrt{10}$ is an irrational number, the decimal shown on the calculator is a rational approximation.

Using either method, we find $\sqrt{10} \approx 3.162$ to the nearest thousandth.

Try This Approximate each square root to the nearest thousandth.

h. $\sqrt{7}$ **i.** $\sqrt{72}$ **j.** $\sqrt{18}$ **k.** $\sqrt{45}$

11-1 Exercises

Extra Help
On the Web

Look for worked-out examples at the Prentice Hall Web site.
www.phschool.com

A

Find the square roots of each number.

1. 1   **2.** 4   **3.** 16   **4.** 121   **5.** 169   **6.** 324

Simplify.

7. $\sqrt{4}$ **8.** $-\sqrt{9}$ **9.** $-\sqrt{25}$ **10.** $-\sqrt{64}$

11. $-\sqrt{81}$ **12.** $-\sqrt{225}$ **13.** $\sqrt{400}$ **14.** $\sqrt{361}$

15. $\sqrt{196}$ **16.** $\sqrt{289}$ **17.** $-\sqrt{36}$ **18.** $\sqrt{625}$

Identify each square root as rational or irrational.

19. $\sqrt{8}$ **20.** $\sqrt{49}$ **21.** $\sqrt{100}$ **22.** $\sqrt{75}$

23. $-\sqrt{4}$ **24.** $-\sqrt{12}$ **25.** $-\sqrt{125}$ **26.** $-\sqrt{196}$

Approximate these square roots to the nearest thousandth.

27. $\sqrt{5}$ **28.** $\sqrt{17}$ **29.** $\sqrt{93}$ **30.** $\sqrt{40}$ **31.** $\sqrt{54}$ **32.** $\sqrt{111}$

B

Identify each number as rational or irrational. If it is rational, is it best described as a whole number, an integer, or a rational number?

33. $\sqrt{120}$ **34.** $\sqrt{0.49}$ **35.** $\sqrt{196}$ **36.** $-\sqrt{215}$

Simplify.

37. $\sqrt{\sqrt{16}}$ **38.** $\sqrt{3^2 + 4^2}$ **39.** $\sqrt{(3 + 4)^2}$ **40.** $(\sqrt{5} + 13)^2$

41. **TEST PREP**   Which expression has the least value?

     A. $\sqrt{(5 + 6)^2}$ **B.** $\sqrt{5^2 + 6^2}$ **C.** $\left(\sqrt{5 + 6}\right)^2$

     D. $\sqrt{5^2} + \sqrt{6^2}$ **E.** The expressions have the same value.

42. Between what two consecutive integers is $-\sqrt{33}$?

43. Between what two consecutive integers is $-\sqrt{57}$?

Determine whether each statement is sometimes, always, or never true.

44. The expression $\sqrt{a^2 + b^2}$ is irrational.

45. The expression $\sqrt{(a + b)^2}$ is irrational.

46. If $\sqrt{a}$ is an integer, then $-\sqrt{a}$ is also an integer.

Challenge

47. 10.63 could be an approximation for the square root of what integer?

48. What number is halfway between x and y ?

49. *Critical Thinking*   Find a number that is the square of an integer and the cube of a different integer.

50. A formula for the energy of an object of mass (m) and velocity (v) is given by $E = \frac{1}{2}mv^2$. Find v in meters/second to the nearest tenth if $E = 20$ joules, and $m = 8$ kilograms.

51. Find y if $\sqrt{y+6}$ is

    a. 3   **b.** 7   **c.** 0   **d.** 10

Mixed Review

Simplify. **52.** $\dfrac{x^5 y^2}{-3xy}$ **53.** $\dfrac{5(x+1)}{8x} \cdot \dfrac{4x}{10}$ **54.** $\dfrac{3(x+1)}{5x^2} \cdot \dfrac{x^4}{9}$

55. $\dfrac{x^2+8x}{x+3} - \dfrac{3x+2}{x+3} + \dfrac{8}{x+3}$ **56.** $\dfrac{3x-10}{x^2-4} - \dfrac{5}{x+2}$ *10-1, 10-2, 10-4, 10-5*

Find the LCM. **57.** $25x - 10, 5x + 2$ **58.** $a + c, a - c$ *10-5*

Solve. **59.** $\dfrac{2}{3} + \dfrac{1}{4} = \dfrac{x}{6}$ **60.** $\dfrac{5}{8} + \dfrac{1}{2} = \dfrac{y}{24}$ **61.** $\dfrac{4}{9} - \dfrac{1}{3} = \dfrac{x}{36}$

62. $\dfrac{2}{3} - \dfrac{1}{5} = \dfrac{1}{a}$ **63.** $\dfrac{1}{6} + \dfrac{4}{9} = \dfrac{1}{a}$ **64.** $\dfrac{1}{4} - \dfrac{5}{6} = \dfrac{1}{b}$ *10-6*

Divide. **65.** $(x^2 - 9x + 20) \div (x - 4)$ **66.** $(y^4 - 81) \div (y - 3)$ *10-9*

Solve. **67.** $y - 6x = 1$ **68.** $4x + y = -4$

          $5x + y = 12$ $10x + 3y = -9$ *8-1, 8-2, 8-3*

Is $\sqrt{7}$ a Rational Number?

We can show that $\sqrt{7}$ is not a rational number by using an indirect proof, or *proof by contradiction*. We will use a fact proved in more advanced courses. If p is a prime factor of a^2, then p is a factor of a.

First, we assume that $\sqrt{7}$ is a rational number, which we write in simplest form as $\frac{a}{b}$ (where a and b are integers and $b \neq 0$). Since $\frac{a}{b}$ is in simplest form, we know that a and b have no common factors greater than 1.

$$\sqrt{7} = \frac{a}{b} \qquad \text{Assuming the opposite of what we wish to prove}$$

$$7 = \frac{a^2}{b^2} \qquad \text{Squaring both sides}$$

$$7b^2 = a^2 \qquad \text{Multiplying both sides by } b^2$$

The last equation shows that 7 is a factor of a^2. Since 7 is a prime number, 7 must also be a factor of a. So $a = 7k$ for some integer k.

$$7b^2 = (7k)^2 \qquad \text{Substituting } 7k \text{ for } a$$

$$7b^2 = 49k^2 \qquad \text{Raising a product to a power}$$

$$b^2 = 7k^2 \qquad \text{Multiplying both sides by } \tfrac{1}{7}$$

The last equation shows that 7 is a factor of b^2, and hence of b. Thus a and b have 7 as a common factor. But a and b have no common factor greater than 1. This contradiction shows our assumption that $\sqrt{7}$ is rational to be false. Therefore, $\sqrt{7}$ is an irrational number.

Exercise Show that $\sqrt{5}$ is irrational.

Writing Math

In an **indirect proof**, we assume that the opposite of what we wish to prove is true. Then we show that this assumption leads to a contradiction. Since it leads to a contradiction our assumption must be false, and what we wish to prove must be true.

Radical Expressions

Math History

Before symbols were used to describe mathematics, the words *root* or *side* were used to refer to the square root of a number. Because Arabic writers thought of a square number growing out of or being extracted from a root, works translated from Arabic used the word *radix* (root). Late medieval writers represented *radix* using the single symbol R_x, which was used for over a century. In 1484 the symbol R_x^2 appeared for square root. The symbol $\sqrt{}$ first appeared in print (in *Die Coss* by Christoff Rudolff) in 1525 and by the seventeenth century was widely accepted.

PART 1 — Nonnegative Radicands

Objective: Determine acceptable replacements for radicands.

When an expression is written under a radical, we have a **radical expression.** These are radical expressions.

$$\sqrt{14} \qquad \sqrt{x} \qquad \sqrt{x^2 + 4} \qquad \sqrt{\frac{x^2 - 5}{2}}$$

The expression written under the radical is called the **radicand.**

The square of any real number is always a positive number or zero. For example, $8^2 = 64$ and $(-11)^2 = 121$. Since there are no real numbers that can be squared to get negative numbers, radical expressions with negative radicands have no meaning in the real number system.

The following expressions do *not* represent real numbers.

$$\sqrt{-100} \qquad \sqrt{-49} \qquad -\sqrt{-3}$$

EXAMPLE 1

Evaluate the expression $\sqrt{1 - y}$ for $y = 6$. Is the result a real number?

If we replace y by 6, we get $\sqrt{1 - 6} = \sqrt{-5}$, which has a negative radicand and has no meaning in the real number system. This is not a real number.

EXAMPLES Determine the values of x that make each expression a real number.

2 $\sqrt{x}$ Any number greater than or equal to 0 can be used.

3 $\sqrt{x + 2}$ We solve the inequality $x + 2 \geq 0$. Any number greater than or equal to -2 can be used.

What You'll Learn

1 To determine acceptable replacements for radicands

2 To find the square root of perfect square radicands

. . . And Why

To simplify expressions with variables in the radicand

Reading Math

You read $\sqrt{x} - 1$ as *the difference of the square root of x and one.* You read $\sqrt{x - 1}$ as *the square root of the difference of x and one.*

EXAMPLE 4 Determine the values of x that make $\sqrt{x^2}$ a real number.

Squares of real numbers are never negative. All real number replacements are acceptable.

Try This

a. Evaluate the expression $\sqrt{15 - 2x}$ for $x = 8$. Is the result a real number?

Determine the values of x that make each expression a real number.

b. $\sqrt{x + 1}$ **c.** $\sqrt{x - 3}$ **d.** $\sqrt{2x - 5}$ **e.** $\sqrt{x^2 + 3}$

PART 2 Perfect Square Radicands

Objective: Simplify perfect square radicands.

Remember that $\sqrt{a}$ means the principal square root (positive or zero) of a. The symbol $\sqrt{x^2}$ means to square x and then find the principal square root. Is $\sqrt{x^2} = x$? Not necessarily.

Suppose $x = 3$. Then $\sqrt{x^2} = \sqrt{3^2}$, which is $\sqrt{9}$, or 3.
Suppose $x = -3$. Then $\sqrt{x^2} = \sqrt{(-3)^2}$, which is $\sqrt{9}$, or 3.

In either case, we have $\sqrt{x^2} = |x|$. In general, any radical expression $\sqrt{a^2}$ can be simplified to $|a|$.

EXAMPLES Simplify.

5 $\sqrt{(3x)^2} = |3x|$ or $3|x|$ **6** $\sqrt{a^2b^2} = \sqrt{(ab)^2} = |ab|$

7 $\sqrt{x^2 + 2x + 1} = \sqrt{(x + 1)^2} = |x + 1|$

Try This   Simplify.

f. $\sqrt{(xy)^2}$ **g.** $\sqrt{x^2y^2}$ **h.** $\sqrt{(x - 1)^2}$

i. $\sqrt{x^2 + 8x + 16}$ **j.** $\sqrt{25y^2}$ **k.** $\sqrt{\frac{1}{4}t^2}$

Evaluating Radical Expressions

You can use a calculator to evaluate radical expressions.
Evaluate $\sqrt{4x^2 - 5}$ for $x = 3$. Express the answer as a decimal to the nearest hundredth.

(	4	$\times$	3	x^2		$-$	5	)
2nd		x^2	5.5677644	$\approx$ 5.57				

11-2 Exercises

Extra Help On the Web

Look for worked-out examples at the Prentice Hall Web site.
www.phschool.com

A

1. Evaluate the expression $\sqrt{3x - 12}$ for $x = 4$. Is the result a real number?

2. Evaluate the expression $\sqrt{8 - 4y}$ for $y = 10$. Is the result a real number?

3. Evaluate $\sqrt{x + 12}$ for $x = -6$. Is the result a real number?

4. Evaluate $\sqrt{3y + 12}$ for $y = -5$. Is the result a real number?

Determine the values of the variable that make each expression a real number.

5. $\sqrt{5x}$ 6. $\sqrt{3y}$ 7. $\sqrt{t - 5}$ 8. $\sqrt{y - 8}$

9. $\sqrt{y + 8}$ 10. $\sqrt{x + 6}$ 11. $\sqrt{x + 20}$ 12. $\sqrt{m - 18}$

13. $\sqrt{2y - 7}$ 14. $\sqrt{3x + 8}$ 15. $\sqrt{t^2 + 5}$ 16. $\sqrt{y^2 + 1}$

Simplify.

17. $\sqrt{t^2}$ 18. $\sqrt{x^2}$ 19. $\sqrt{9x^2}$ 20. $\sqrt{4a^2}$

21. $\sqrt{(-7)^2}$ 22. $\sqrt{(-5)^2}$ 23. $\sqrt{(-4d)^2}$ 24. $\sqrt{(-3b)^2}$

25. $\sqrt{(x + 3)^2}$ 26. $\sqrt{(x - 7)^2}$ 27. $\sqrt{a^2 - 10a + 25}$

28. $\sqrt{x^2 + 2x + 1}$ 29. $\sqrt{4a^2 - 4a + 1}$ 30. $\sqrt{9a^2 - 12a + 4}$

B

Solve.

31. $\sqrt{x^2} = 6$ 32. $\sqrt{y^2} = -7$ 33. $-\sqrt{x^2} = -3$

34. $t^2 = 49$ 35. $\sqrt{(x - 3)^2} = 5$ 36. $\sqrt{4a^2 - 12a + 9} = 3$

Simplify.

37. $\sqrt{(3a)^2}$ 38. $\sqrt{(4a)^2(4a)^2}$ 39. $\sqrt{\dfrac{144x^8}{36y^6}}$

40. $\sqrt{\dfrac{y^{12}}{8100}}$ 41. $\sqrt{\dfrac{169}{m^{16}}}$ 42. $\sqrt{\dfrac{p^2}{3600}}$

43. Determine the values for the variable that will make each expression a real number.

    a. $\sqrt{m(m + 3)}$ b. $\sqrt{x^2(x - 3)}$

44. **Critical Thinking** Given a and c, what must be true of b to make $\sqrt{b^2 - 4ac}$ a real number?

    a. $a = -3, c = 2$ b. $a = 2, c = 8$

Determine whether each statement is sometimes, always, or never true.

45. $\sqrt{a^2 + b^2}$ is a real number. 46. $\sqrt{3 - t}$ is a real number for $t \geq 3$.

47. $\sqrt{a^2 - b^2}$ is a real number. 48. $\sqrt{a^2 + ab + b^2}$ is a real number.

Challenge

Determine the values for the variable that will make each expression a real number.

49. $\sqrt{(x + 3)(x - 2)}$

50. $\sqrt{x^2 + 7x + 12}$

51. $\sqrt{x^2 - 4}$

52. $\sqrt{4x^2 - 1}$

53. For a polynomial of the form $ax^2 + bx + c = 0$ to have real solutions, $\sqrt{b^2 - 4ac}$ must be a real number. Which of the following polynomials have real solutions?

a. $x^2 - 12x + 3 = 0$

b. $x^2 + 2x - 50 = 0$

c. $x^2 + 5x + 7 = 0$

d. $5x^2 + 2x + 1 = 0$

e. $-x^2 + x + 1 = 0$

f. $-x^2 + x - 1 = 0$

Mixed Review

Solve. **54.** $|x + 3| < 1$ **55.** $|x - 9| = -3$ **56.** $|y + 3| \geq 5$ *9-3, 9-4*

Simplify. **57.** $\frac{x - 3}{x + 2} - \frac{3x + 1}{x + 2}$ **58.** $\frac{6x + 7}{x - 3} - \frac{2x + 3}{x - 3}$

59. $\frac{5}{y + 5} + \frac{2}{(y + 5)^2}$ **60.** $\frac{5}{y + 4} - \frac{3}{y + 3}$ *10-4, 10-5*

Solve. **61.** $x - \frac{6}{x} = 5$ **62.** $\frac{6}{x} = \frac{5}{x} + \frac{1}{2}$ **63.** $\frac{y + 1}{y - 3} = 2$ *10-6*

The price of the larger can is $2.99. The price of the smaller can is $.89. Refer to the volumes in Exercise 3 to find the price per cubic centimeter. Which can is the better buy?

⟨⟩ Connections: Geometry

The formula for the volume of a cylinder is $V = \pi r^2 h$. The height of each cylinder and the volume are given. Find the radius of each figure. If you do not have a calculator with a $\boxed{\pi}$ key, use 3.14 for π. Round the radius to the nearest whole number.

1.

$h = 25$ in., $V = 2826$ in.^{3}

2.

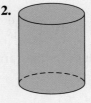

$h = 6.2$ cm, $V = 175$ cm^3

3. Use the photo at the left. The height of the larger can is 17 cm, and the volume is 3208 cm^3. The height of the smaller can is 11 cm, and the volume is 486 cm^3. Find the radius of each can.

Simplifying Radical Expressions

Objective: Simplify radical expressions.

Introducing the Concept: Square Roots

$\mathbf{F}$ind the following square roots.

$$\frac{\sqrt{225}}{\sqrt{400}} \qquad \frac{\sqrt{9}\cdot\sqrt{25}}{\sqrt{4}\cdot\sqrt{100}}$$

What do you notice about the results?

The above relationship suggests the following fact about square roots.

Product Property for Radicals

For any nonnegative real numbers a and b, $\sqrt{ab} = \sqrt{a}\cdot\sqrt{b}$.

To simplify radical expressions, we look for perfect square factors in the radicand. To simplify $\sqrt{50}$, we identify the perfect square 25.

$$\sqrt{50} = \sqrt{25\cdot 2}$$

Then we use the Product Property for Radicals to rewrite the expression.

$$= \sqrt{25}\cdot\sqrt{2}$$
$$= 5\sqrt{2}$$

A radical expression has been simplified when its radicand contains no perfect square factors. The radical expression $5\sqrt{2}$ is in its simplest form.

If you do not recognize perfect squares, try factoring the radicand into its prime factors.

$$\sqrt{50} = \sqrt{2\cdot 5\cdot 5} = 5\sqrt{2}$$

In many formulas and problems involving radical notation, variables do not represent negative numbers. Thus, absolute value is not necessary. *From now on we will assume that all radicands are nonnegative.*

EXAMPLE 1 Simplify.

$$\sqrt{18} = \sqrt{9\cdot 2} \qquad \text{Factoring the radicand with a perfect square factor}$$
$$= \sqrt{9}\cdot\sqrt{2} \qquad \text{Using the product property for radicals}$$
$$= 3\sqrt{2} \qquad \text{The radicand has no factors that are perfect squares.}$$

What You'll Learn

1 To simplify radical expressions

...And Why

To use the product property for radicals

EXAMPLES Simplify.

2 $\sqrt{48t} = \sqrt{16 \cdot 3t}$

Identifying perfect square factors

$= \sqrt{16} \cdot \sqrt{3t}$

Using the product property for radicals

$= 4\sqrt{3t}$

3 $\sqrt{72x^2} = \sqrt{36x^2 \cdot 2}$

Identifying perfect square factors

$= \sqrt{36x^2} \cdot \sqrt{2}$

Using the product property for radicals

$= 6x\sqrt{2}$

4 $\sqrt{3x^2 + 6x + 3} = \sqrt{3(x^2 + 2x + 1)}$

$= \sqrt{3} \cdot \sqrt{x^2 + 2x + 1}$ Using the product property for radicals

$= \sqrt{3} \cdot \sqrt{(x + 1)^2}$

$= \sqrt{3}(x + 1)$

Try This Factor and simplify.

a. $\sqrt{32}$ **b.** $\sqrt{25x^2}$ **c.** $\sqrt{60x}$

d. $\sqrt{45x^2}$ **e.** $\sqrt{7x^2 - 14x + 7}$

To take a square root of a power such as x^8, the exponent must be even. We then take half the exponent. Recall that $(x^4)^2 = x^8$.

EXAMPLES Simplify.

5 $\sqrt{x^6} = \sqrt{(x^3)^2}$

$= x^3$

6 $\sqrt{x^{22}} = x^{11}$

When odd powers occur, express the power as the product of the largest even power and x. Then simplify the even power.

EXAMPLE 7 Simplify.

$\sqrt{x^9} = \sqrt{x^8 \cdot x}$

$= \sqrt{x^8} \cdot \sqrt{x}$

$= x^4\sqrt{x}$

Try This Simplify.

f. $\sqrt{y^8}$ **g.** $\sqrt{(x + y)^{14}}$ **h.** $\sqrt{t^{15}}$ **i.** $\sqrt{a^{25}}$

11-3 Exercises

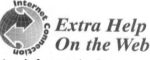

Extra Help On the Web

Look for worked-out examples at the Prentice Hall Web site.
www.phschool.com

A

Simplify. Assume that all variables are nonnegative.

1. $\sqrt{12}$
2. $\sqrt{8}$
3. $\sqrt{20}$
4. $\sqrt{45}$
5. $\sqrt{75}$
6. $\sqrt{50}$
7. $\sqrt{200}$
8. $\sqrt{300}$
9. $\sqrt{3x^2}$
10. $\sqrt{5y^2}$
11. $\sqrt{16a}$
12. $\sqrt{49b}$
13. $\sqrt{13x^2}$
14. $\sqrt{29t^2}$
15. $\sqrt{9x}$
16. $\sqrt{4y}$
17. $\sqrt{64y^2}$
18. $\sqrt{9x^2}$
19. $\sqrt{8t^2}$
20. $\sqrt{125a^2}$
21. $\sqrt{4x^2 + 8x + 4}$
22. $\sqrt{3x^2 + 12x + 12}$
23. $\sqrt{2x^2 + 12x + 18}$
24. $\sqrt{5x^2 + 30x + 45}$
25. $\sqrt{4x^2 + 12xy + 9y^2}$
26. $\sqrt{3x^2 + 30xy + 75y^2}$

Simplify.

27. $\sqrt{x^6}$
28. $\sqrt{x^{10}}$
29. $\sqrt{x^{12}}$
30. $\sqrt{x^{16}}$
31. $\sqrt{x^5}$
32. $\sqrt{x^3}$
33. $\sqrt{t^{19}}$
34. $\sqrt{p^{17}}$
35. $\sqrt{(y - 2)^8}$
36. $\sqrt{(x + 3)^6}$
37. $\sqrt{4(x + 5)^{10}}$
38. $\sqrt{16(a - 7)^4}$
39. $\sqrt{36m^3}$
40. $\sqrt{250y^3}$
41. $\sqrt{8a^5}$
42. $\sqrt{12b^7}$
43. $\sqrt{448x^6y^3}$
44. $\sqrt{243x^5y^4}$

45. **Error Analysis** What error did the student make in simplifying the radical expression?

$$\sqrt{9x^2y^3} = \sqrt{9x^2y^2}\sqrt{y} = 9xy\sqrt{y}$$

B

Simplify. Assume that all variables are nonnegative real numbers.

46. $3\sqrt{200}$
47. $2\sqrt{75}$
48. $4\sqrt{12}$
49. $-3\sqrt{72}$
50. $-2\sqrt{1000}$
51. $6\sqrt{36x}$
52. $4m\sqrt{20m^2}$
53. $2x\sqrt{50x^4}$
54. $5r^2\sqrt{32r^4s^3}$
55. $3a^3\sqrt{28a^3b^5}$

Evaluate and simplify for $r = 5$ and $s = \sqrt{5}$.

56. $\sqrt{3 + r^2}$
57. $\sqrt{r^2 - 1}$
58. $\sqrt{r + s^2}$
59. $\sqrt{50 - s^2}$

60. **Critical Thinking** Find $\sqrt{49}$, $\sqrt{490}$, $\sqrt{4900}$, $\sqrt{49,000}$, and $\sqrt{490,000}$. What pattern do you see?

Challenge

Use the proper symbol ($>$, $<$, or $=$) between each pair of values. Assume x is positive.

61. $15 \ \square \ \sqrt{14}$

62. $15\sqrt{2} \ \square \ \sqrt{450}$

63. $16 \ \square \ \sqrt{15}\sqrt{17}$

64. $3\sqrt{11} \ \square \ 7\sqrt{2}$

65. $5\sqrt{7} \ \square \ 4\sqrt{11}$

66. $8 \ \square \ \sqrt{15}\sqrt{17}$

67. $3\sqrt{x} \ \square \ 2\sqrt{2.5x}$

68. $4\sqrt{x} \ \square \ 5\sqrt{0.64x}$

69. $90\sqrt{100x} \ \square \ 100\sqrt{90x}$

70. $4\sqrt{5x} \ \square \ \sqrt{12x} + 4\sqrt{2x}$

Mixed Review

Solve. **71.** $5x + y = -9$
$2x - y = 2$

72. $2x + 3y = 11$
$5y - x = 1$

73. $5y + 3x = -1$
$2x - 2y = 10$ *8-2, 8-3*

Simplify. **74.** $\dfrac{6a^2 + 24}{12a^2 + 18a + 42}$

75. $\dfrac{(x + 3)}{x^2} \cdot \dfrac{(x + 2)}{(x + 3)}$ *10-1, 10-2*

Solve. **76.** The sum of two numbers is 51 and the difference of the two numbers is 19. Find the two numbers. *8-6*

Cube Roots

Objective: Find cube roots.

The number c is called the **cube root** of a if $c^3 = a$. We write this as $c = \sqrt[3]{a}$.

$\sqrt[3]{216} = 6$, since $6^3 = 216$ and $\sqrt[3]{-216} = -6$, since $(-6)^3 = -216$

The procedures you have learned for multiplying, factoring, and simplifying expressions involving square roots also apply to cube roots.

EXAMPLE Simplify.

$$\sqrt[3]{16a^4} = \sqrt[3]{8 \cdot 2 \cdot a^3 \cdot a} \qquad \text{Identifying factors that are perfect cubes}$$
$$= \sqrt[3]{2^3 \cdot 2 \cdot a^3 \cdot a}$$
$$= \sqrt[3]{2^3 \cdot a^3} \cdot \sqrt[3]{2a}$$
$$= 2a\sqrt[3]{2a}$$

Exercises

Simplify.

1. $\sqrt[3]{8}$

2. $\sqrt[3]{27}$

3. $\sqrt[3]{125}$

4. $\sqrt[3]{1000}$

5. $\sqrt[3]{-8}$

6. $\sqrt[3]{-64}$

7. $\sqrt[3]{-1}$

8. $\sqrt[3]{-8000}$

9. $\sqrt[3]{x^3}$

10. $\sqrt[3]{y^3}$

11. $\sqrt[3]{a^3b^3}$

12. $\sqrt[3]{mn^3}$

13. $\sqrt[3]{27x^6y^3}$

14. $\sqrt[3]{125m^9n^{12}}$

15. $\sqrt[3]{-8a^6b^9}$

16. $\sqrt[3]{-125p^{12}}$

Multiplying Radical Expressions

Objective: Multiply radical expressions.

We know that for nonnegative numbers,

$$\sqrt{ab} = \sqrt{a} \cdot \sqrt{b}.$$

We can use the product property for radicals to multiply radicals. It can also be used to simplify radicals.

What You'll Learn

1 To multiply radical expressions

. . . And Why

To perform operations with radicals

EXAMPLES Multiply.

1 $\sqrt{5} \cdot \sqrt{7} = \sqrt{5 \cdot 7} = \sqrt{35}$

2 $\sqrt{8} \cdot \sqrt{8} = \sqrt{8 \cdot 8} = \sqrt{64} = 8$

3 $\sqrt{\frac{2}{3}} \cdot \sqrt{\frac{4}{5}} = \sqrt{\frac{2}{3} \cdot \frac{4}{5}} = \sqrt{\frac{8}{15}}$

4 $\sqrt{2x} \cdot \sqrt{3x - 1} = \sqrt{2x(3x - 1)} = \sqrt{6x^2 - 2x}$

Try This Multiply.

a. $\sqrt{3} \cdot \sqrt{7}$ **b.** $\sqrt{5} \cdot \sqrt{5}$ **c.** $\sqrt{x} \cdot \sqrt{x + 1}$ **d.** $\sqrt{x + 1} \cdot \sqrt{x - 1}$

Sometimes we can simplify after multiplying. We can find perfect square factors and take their square roots.

EXAMPLES Multiply and simplify.

5 $\sqrt{2} \cdot \sqrt{14} = \sqrt{2 \cdot 14}$ Multiplying

$= \sqrt{2 \cdot 2 \cdot 7}$ Factoring to find perfect square factors

$= \sqrt{2 \cdot 2} \cdot \sqrt{7}$

$= 2\sqrt{7}$

6 $\sqrt{3x^2} \cdot \sqrt{9x^3} = \sqrt{3 \cdot 9x^5}$ Multiplying

$= \sqrt{3 \cdot 9 \cdot x^4 \cdot x}$ Factoring to find perfect square factors

$= \sqrt{9 \cdot x^4 \cdot 3 \cdot x}$ Identifying perfect squares

$= \sqrt{9} \cdot \sqrt{x^4} \cdot \sqrt{3x}$

$= 3x^2\sqrt{3x}$

Try This Multiply and simplify.

e. $\sqrt{3y} \cdot \sqrt{6}$ **f.** $\sqrt{2x} \cdot \sqrt{50x}$ **g.** $\sqrt{2x^3} \cdot \sqrt{8x^3y^4}$

h. $\sqrt{10xy^2} \cdot \sqrt{5x^2y^3}$ **i.** $\sqrt{12x^3y^2} \cdot \sqrt{3x^2y^6}$

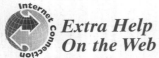

*Extra Help
On the Web*
Look for worked-out
examples at the Prentice
Hall Web site.
www.phschool.com

11-4 Exercises

A

Multiply.

1. $\sqrt{2} \cdot \sqrt{3}$ 2. $\sqrt{3} \cdot \sqrt{5}$ 3. $\sqrt{17} \cdot \sqrt{17}$

4. $\sqrt{25} \cdot \sqrt{3}$ 5. $\sqrt{2} \cdot \sqrt{x}$ 6. $\sqrt{x} \cdot \sqrt{x-3}$

7. $\sqrt{5} \cdot \sqrt{2x-1}$ 8. $\sqrt{x+2} \cdot \sqrt{x+1}$ 9. $\sqrt{x+4} \cdot \sqrt{x-4}$

10. $\sqrt{x-3} \cdot \sqrt{2x+4}$ 11. $\sqrt{2x+5} \cdot \sqrt{x-4}$ 12. $\sqrt{3a} \cdot \sqrt{3a+2b}$

13. $\sqrt{x} \cdot \sqrt{3x+4y}$ 14. $\sqrt{a-b} \cdot \sqrt{a+b}$ 15. $\sqrt{x-3} \cdot \sqrt{x+4}$

Multiply and simplify.

16. $\sqrt{3} \cdot \sqrt{18}$ 17. $\sqrt{15} \cdot \sqrt{6}$ 18. $\sqrt{3} \cdot \sqrt{27}$

19. $\sqrt{18} \cdot \sqrt{14x}$ 20. $\sqrt{7x} \cdot \sqrt{21y}$ 21. $\sqrt{11} \cdot \sqrt{11x}$

22. $\sqrt{5b} \cdot \sqrt{15b}$ 23. $\sqrt{6a} \cdot \sqrt{18a}$ 24. $\sqrt{2t} \cdot \sqrt{2t}$

25. $\sqrt{ab} \cdot \sqrt{ac}$ 26. $\sqrt{xy} \cdot \sqrt{xz}$ 27. $\sqrt{2x^2y} \cdot \sqrt{4xy^2}$

28. $\sqrt{15mn^2} \cdot \sqrt{5m^2n}$ 29. $\sqrt{18x^2y^3} \cdot \sqrt{6xy^4}$ 30. $\sqrt{12x^3y^2} \cdot \sqrt{8xy}$

31. $\sqrt{50ab} \cdot \sqrt{10a^2b^4}$ 32. $\sqrt{5a} \cdot \sqrt{20ab}$ 33. $\sqrt{7a^2b} \cdot \sqrt{42a^3b^2}$

34. $\sqrt{56x^2y^7} \cdot \sqrt{8xy}$ 35. $\sqrt{10x^6y^3} \cdot \sqrt{2x^5y}$ 36. $\sqrt{15xy^{12}} \cdot \sqrt{3x^3y^5}$

37. $\sqrt{8xyz^3} \cdot \sqrt{10x^3y^2z}$ 38. $\sqrt{12x^3y^5z} \cdot \sqrt{5xy^2z}$ 39. $\sqrt{12x^3} \cdot \sqrt{5x} \cdot \sqrt{45}$

40. $\sqrt{12x^6} \cdot \sqrt{7x^3} \cdot \sqrt{42x}$ 41. $\sqrt{6x^3} \cdot \sqrt{5x^5} \cdot \sqrt{10x^6}$

B

Multiply and simplify.

42. $(\sqrt{2y})(\sqrt{3})(\sqrt{8y})$ 43. $\sqrt{a}\left(\sqrt{a^3} - 5\right)$

44. $\sqrt{27(x+1)} \cdot \sqrt{12y(x+1)^2}$ 45. $\sqrt{18(x-2)} \cdot \sqrt{20(x-2)^3}$

46. $\sqrt{x} \cdot \sqrt{2x} \cdot \sqrt{10x^5}$ 47. $\sqrt{0.04x^{4n}}$

48. $\sqrt{2^{109}} \cdot \sqrt{x^{306}} \cdot \sqrt{x^{11}}$ 49. $\sqrt{147} \cdot \sqrt{y^{27}} \cdot \sqrt{x^{315}}$

50. $\sqrt{(x+9)^4} \cdot \sqrt{(x+9)^{99}}$ 51. $\sqrt{a^2 + 4ab + 4b^2} \cdot \sqrt{(a+2b)^{32}}$

52. $\sqrt{x^{2n}} \cdot \sqrt{y^{2n+1}}$ 53. $\sqrt{x^{2n}} \cdot \sqrt{x^3y^{3n}} \cdot \sqrt{y^{n+1}}$

54. *Critical Thinking*   We know that $\sqrt{a} \cdot \sqrt{b} = \sqrt{ab}$ for positive real numbers. Is it also true that $\sqrt{a} + \sqrt{b} = \sqrt{a+b}$? Explain.

Challenge

55. Simplify $\sqrt{y^n}$, given n is an even whole number ≥ 2.

56. Simplify $\sqrt{y^n}$, given n is an odd whole number ≥ 3.

57. Multiply $(x^2 + \sqrt{2}xy + y^2)$ by $(x^2 - \sqrt{2}xy + y^2)$. Use your result to factor $x^8 + y^8$.

Self-Test
On the Web
Check your progress. Look
for a self-test at the
Prentice Hall Web site.
www.phschool.com

Mixed Review

Simplify. **58.** $m^6 \cdot m^2$ **59.** $(3y^2)^3$ **60.** $(4x^3)(x^2)$ **61.** $(4c^2)(-2c^3)$
5-2

Factor. **62.** $a^2 - b^2$ **63.** $144y^2 - 1$ **64.** $4m^2 - 9n^2$ 6-2

Simplify. **65.** $\dfrac{-7x}{x+3} - \dfrac{2x+9}{x+3}$ **66.** $\dfrac{4}{x} + \dfrac{3}{x^2}$ **67.** $\dfrac{x+1}{2} - \dfrac{x-3}{4}$ 10-4, 10-5

Find the square roots of each number. **68.** 36 **69.** 121 **70.** 625 11-1

Simplify. **71.** $\sqrt{16}$ **72.** $-\sqrt{36}$ **73.** $-\sqrt{225}$ **74.** $\sqrt{81}$ 11-2

Rational Exponents

Objective: Simplify expressions with rational exponents.

Your work with exponents thus far has been with integer exponents.
Exponents can also be rational numbers.

If rational exponents are to follow the same rules as for integer exponents, it
must be true that $3^{\frac{1}{2}} \cdot 3^{\frac{1}{2}} = 3^{\frac{1}{2}+\frac{1}{2}} = 3^1 = 3$.
If we define $3^{\frac{1}{2}} = \sqrt{3}$, then our rules will work, since $\sqrt{3} \cdot \sqrt{3} = \sqrt{3^2} = 3$.

Definition

Rational Exponent: $a^{\frac{1}{k}} = \sqrt[k]{a}$ for any natural number k and any $a, a > 0$.

EXAMPLES Simplify.

1 $25^{\frac{1}{2}} = \sqrt{25} = 5$ **2** $8^{\frac{1}{3}} = \sqrt[3]{8} = 2$

Finding Roots

You can find a cube root or other roots of a number using the y^x key.

To find the cube root of 8, we first write $\sqrt[3]{8}$ using exponential notation.

$$\sqrt[3]{8} = 8^{\frac{1}{3}}$$

$8^{\frac{1}{3}} \rightarrow 8$ | y^x | | (| 1 | ÷ | 3 |) | | = | $\rightarrow 2$

Exercises

Simplify.

1. $16^{\frac{1}{2}}$ **2.** $81^{\frac{1}{2}}$ **3.** $27^{\frac{1}{3}}$ **4.** $125^{\frac{1}{3}}$ **5.** $343^{\frac{1}{3}}$

6. $\left(9^{\frac{1}{2}}\right)^3$ **7.** $\left(4^{\frac{1}{2}}\right)^3$ **8.** $\left(64^{\frac{1}{3}}\right)^2$ **9.** $\left(27^{\frac{1}{3}}\right)^2$ **10.** $\left(125^{\frac{1}{3}}\right)^2$

11-5 ▷ Dividing and Simplifying

What You'll Learn

1 To divide expressions involving radicals

2 To rationalize the denominator

...And Why

To rewrite radical expressions without radicals in the denominator

Introducing the Concept: Square Roots of Quotients

Compare the square roots $\dfrac{\sqrt{36}}{\sqrt{9}}$ and $\sqrt{\dfrac{36}{9}}$.

What do you notice about the results?

PART 1 Dividing with Radicals

Objective: Divide expressions involving radicals.

The above relationship suggests the following fact about square roots.

Division Property for Radicals

For any nonnegative real numbers a and b, where $b \neq 0$,

$$\sqrt{\frac{a}{b}} = \frac{\sqrt{a}}{\sqrt{b}} \quad \text{and} \quad \frac{\sqrt{a}}{\sqrt{b}} = \sqrt{\frac{a}{b}}$$

Fractional radicands with a perfect square numerator and a perfect square denominator can be simplified.

EXAMPLES Simplify.

1 $\sqrt{\dfrac{25}{9}} = \dfrac{5}{3}$, since $\dfrac{5}{3} \cdot \dfrac{5}{3} = \dfrac{25}{9}$

2 $\sqrt{\dfrac{1}{16}} = \dfrac{1}{4}$, since $\dfrac{1}{4} \cdot \dfrac{1}{4} = \dfrac{1}{16}$

Sometimes a fractional radicand can be simplified to a perfect square.

EXAMPLE 3 Simplify.

$$\sqrt{\frac{18}{50}} = \sqrt{\frac{9}{25} \cdot \frac{2}{2}} = \sqrt{\frac{9}{25}} = \frac{3}{5}$$

Try This Simplify.

a. $\sqrt{\dfrac{16}{9}}$ **b.** $\sqrt{\dfrac{1}{25}}$ **c.** $\sqrt{\dfrac{1}{9}}$ **d.** $\sqrt{\dfrac{18}{32}}$ **e.** $\sqrt{\dfrac{2250}{2560}}$

We can use the division property for radicals to simplify radicals with fractions and to divide radicals.

EXAMPLES Divide and simplify.

4 $\dfrac{\sqrt{27}}{\sqrt{3}} = \sqrt{\dfrac{27}{3}} = \sqrt{9} = 3$

5 $\dfrac{\sqrt{30a^3}}{\sqrt{6a^2}} = \sqrt{\dfrac{30a^3}{6a^2}} = \sqrt{5a}$

Try This Divide and simplify.

f. $\dfrac{\sqrt{50}}{\sqrt{2}}$ **g.** $\dfrac{\sqrt{42x^4}}{\sqrt{7x^2}}$

PART 2 Rationalizing the Denominator

Objective: Rationalize the denominator.

An expression containing radicals is simplified when the following conditions are met.

- The radicand contains no perfect square factors.
- A fraction in simplest form does not have a radical in the denominator.
- A simplified radical does not contain a fractional radicand.

The process of removing a fraction from the radicand or a radical from the denominator is called **rationalizing the denominator.**

EXAMPLES Simplify.

6 $\dfrac{\sqrt{2}}{\sqrt{3}} = \dfrac{\sqrt{2}}{\sqrt{3}} \cdot \dfrac{\sqrt{3}}{\sqrt{3}}$ Multiplying by 1; $\dfrac{\sqrt{3}}{\sqrt{3}} = 1$

$\quad = \dfrac{\sqrt{2} \cdot \sqrt{3}}{\sqrt{3} \cdot \sqrt{3}}$

$\quad = \dfrac{\sqrt{6}}{3}$ or $\dfrac{1}{3}\sqrt{6}$

7 $\dfrac{6}{\sqrt{2}} = \dfrac{6}{\sqrt{2}} \cdot \dfrac{\sqrt{2}}{\sqrt{2}}$ Multiplying by 1; $\dfrac{\sqrt{2}}{\sqrt{2}} = 1$

$\quad = \dfrac{6 \cdot \sqrt{2}}{\sqrt{2} \cdot \sqrt{2}}$

$\quad = \dfrac{6\sqrt{2}}{2}$

$\quad = 3\sqrt{2}$

8 $\frac{\sqrt{5}}{\sqrt{x}} = \frac{\sqrt{5}}{\sqrt{x}} \cdot \frac{\sqrt{x}}{\sqrt{x}}$ Multiplying by 1; $\frac{\sqrt{x}}{\sqrt{x}} = 1$

$\qquad = \frac{\sqrt{5} \cdot \sqrt{x}}{\sqrt{x} \cdot \sqrt{x}}$

$\qquad = \frac{\sqrt{5x}}{x}$

Try This   Simplify.

h. $\frac{\sqrt{5}}{\sqrt{7}}$ **i.** $\frac{8}{\sqrt{6}}$ **j.** $\frac{\sqrt{x}}{\sqrt{y}}$

If the radicand is a fraction, it can be simplified by writing it as a division of radicals and proceeding as above.

EXAMPLES   Simplify.

9 $\sqrt{\frac{3}{4}} = \frac{\sqrt{3}}{\sqrt{4}}$ Writing as a division of radicals

$\qquad = \frac{\sqrt{3}}{2}$

10 $\sqrt{\frac{5}{12}} = \frac{\sqrt{5}}{\sqrt{12}} \cdot \frac{\sqrt{3}}{\sqrt{3}}$ Multiplying by 1; $\frac{\sqrt{3}}{\sqrt{3}} = 1$

$\qquad = \frac{\sqrt{15}}{\sqrt{36}}$

$\qquad = \frac{\sqrt{15}}{6}$

11 $\sqrt{\frac{2y}{5x^3}} = \frac{\sqrt{2y}}{\sqrt{5x^3}}$

$\qquad = \frac{\sqrt{2y}}{\sqrt{5x^3}} \cdot \frac{\sqrt{5x}}{\sqrt{5x}}$ Multiplying by 1; $\frac{\sqrt{5x}}{\sqrt{5x}} = 1$

$\qquad = \frac{\sqrt{10yx}}{\sqrt{25x^4}}$

$\qquad = \frac{\sqrt{10yx}}{5x^2}$

Try This   Simplify.

k. $\sqrt{\frac{3}{7}}$ **l.** $\sqrt{\frac{5}{8}}$ **m.** $\sqrt{\frac{2}{27}}$ **n.** $\sqrt{\frac{5}{2a}}$

o. $\sqrt{\frac{7}{3b^5}}$ **p.** $\sqrt{\frac{x}{18y^3}}$

Extra Help On the Web

Look for worked-out examples at the Prentice Hall Web site.
www.phschool.com

A

Simplify.

1. $\sqrt{\dfrac{9}{49}}$　　**2.** $\sqrt{\dfrac{16}{25}}$　　**3.** $\sqrt{\dfrac{1}{36}}$　　**4.** $\sqrt{\dfrac{1}{4}}$

5. $-\sqrt{\dfrac{16}{81}}$　　**6.** $-\sqrt{\dfrac{25}{49}}$　　**7.** $\sqrt{\dfrac{64}{289}}$　　**8.** $\sqrt{\dfrac{81}{361}}$

9. $-\sqrt{\dfrac{9}{100}}$　　**10.** $-\sqrt{\dfrac{49}{100}}$　　**11.** $\sqrt{\dfrac{27}{75}}$　　**12.** $\sqrt{\dfrac{50}{18}}$

Divide and simplify.

13. $\dfrac{\sqrt{18}}{\sqrt{2}}$　　**14.** $\dfrac{\sqrt{20}}{\sqrt{5}}$　　**15.** $\dfrac{\sqrt{60}}{\sqrt{15}}$　　**16.** $\dfrac{\sqrt{108}}{\sqrt{3}}$

17. $\dfrac{\sqrt{75}}{\sqrt{15}}$　　**18.** $\dfrac{\sqrt{18}}{\sqrt{3}}$　　**19.** $\dfrac{\sqrt{3}}{\sqrt{75}}$　　**20.** $\dfrac{\sqrt{3}}{\sqrt{48}}$

21. $\dfrac{\sqrt{12}}{\sqrt{75}}$　　**22.** $\dfrac{\sqrt{18}}{\sqrt{32}}$　　**23.** $\dfrac{\sqrt{8x}}{\sqrt{2x}}$　　**24.** $\dfrac{\sqrt{18b}}{\sqrt{2b}}$

25. $\dfrac{\sqrt{63y^3}}{\sqrt{7y}}$　　**26.** $\dfrac{\sqrt{48x^3}}{\sqrt{3x}}$　　**27.** $\dfrac{\sqrt{15x^5}}{\sqrt{3x}}$　　**28.** $\dfrac{\sqrt{30a^5}}{\sqrt{5a}}$

29. $\dfrac{\sqrt{7}}{\sqrt{3}}$　　**30.** $\dfrac{\sqrt{2}}{\sqrt{5}}$　　**31.** $\dfrac{\sqrt{9}}{\sqrt{8}}$　　**32.** $\dfrac{\sqrt{4}}{\sqrt{27}}$

Simplify.

33. $\sqrt{\dfrac{2}{5}}$　　**34.** $\sqrt{\dfrac{2}{7}}$　　**35.** $\sqrt{\dfrac{3}{8}}$　　**36.** $\sqrt{\dfrac{7}{8}}$

37. $\sqrt{\dfrac{7}{12}}$　　**38.** $\sqrt{\dfrac{1}{12}}$　　**39.** $\sqrt{\dfrac{1}{18}}$　　**40.** $\sqrt{\dfrac{5}{18}}$

41. $\sqrt{\dfrac{1}{2}}$　　**42.** $\sqrt{\dfrac{1}{3}}$　　**43.** $\sqrt{\dfrac{8}{3}}$　　**44.** $\sqrt{\dfrac{12}{5}}$

45. $\sqrt{\dfrac{3}{x}}$　　**46.** $\sqrt{\dfrac{2}{x}}$　　**47.** $\sqrt{\dfrac{x}{y}}$　　**48.** $\sqrt{\dfrac{a}{b}}$

49. $\sqrt{\dfrac{x^2}{18}}$　　**50.** $\sqrt{\dfrac{x^2}{20}}$　　**51.** $\sqrt{\dfrac{6c}{2d^3}}$　　**52.** $\sqrt{\dfrac{x}{8y^7}}$

53. $\dfrac{\sqrt{2}}{\sqrt{5}}$　　**54.** $\dfrac{\sqrt{3}}{\sqrt{2}}$　　**55.** $\dfrac{2}{\sqrt{2}}$　　**56.** $\dfrac{3}{\sqrt{3}}$

57. $\dfrac{\sqrt{48}}{\sqrt{32}}$　　**58.** $\dfrac{\sqrt{56}}{\sqrt{40}}$　　**59.** $\dfrac{\sqrt{450}}{\sqrt{18}}$　　**60.** $\dfrac{\sqrt{224}}{\sqrt{14}}$

61. $\dfrac{\sqrt{3}}{\sqrt{x}}$　　**62.** $\dfrac{\sqrt{2}}{\sqrt{y}}$　　**63.** $\dfrac{4y}{\sqrt{3}}$　　**64.** $\dfrac{8x}{\sqrt{5}}$

65. $\dfrac{\sqrt{a^3}}{\sqrt{8}}$　　**66.** $\dfrac{\sqrt{x^3}}{\sqrt{27}}$　　**67.** $\dfrac{\sqrt{56}}{\sqrt{12x}}$　　**68.** $\dfrac{\sqrt{45}}{\sqrt{8a}}$

69. $\dfrac{\sqrt{27c}}{\sqrt{32c^3}}$　　**70.** $\dfrac{\sqrt{7x^3}}{\sqrt{12x}}$　　**71.** $\dfrac{\sqrt{y^5}}{\sqrt{xy^2}}$　　**72.** $\dfrac{\sqrt{x^3}}{\sqrt{xy}}$

B

Rationalize the denominator.

73. $\dfrac{\sqrt{2}}{3\sqrt{3}}$

74. $\dfrac{3\sqrt{6}}{6\sqrt{2}}$

75. $\dfrac{5\sqrt{2}}{3\sqrt{5}}$

76. $\dfrac{3\sqrt{15}}{5\sqrt{32}}$

77. $\dfrac{4\sqrt{\frac{6}{7}}}{\sqrt{\frac{12}{63}}}$

78. $\dfrac{\sqrt{\frac{2}{3}}}{\sqrt{\frac{3}{2}}}$

79. *Critical Thinking* Rationalize the denominator of $\dfrac{a\sqrt{b}}{b\sqrt{a}}$.

Challenge

Multiply.

80. $(\sqrt{5} + 7)(\sqrt{5} - 7)$

81. $(1 + \sqrt{5})(1 - \sqrt{5})$

82. $(\sqrt{6} - \sqrt{3})(\sqrt{6} + \sqrt{3})$

83. $(\sqrt{3} + \sqrt{2})(\sqrt{3} + \sqrt{2})$

84. The period T of a pendulum is the time it takes for a pendulum of length L to move from one side to the other and back.
A formula for the period is $T = 2\pi\sqrt{\dfrac{L}{32}}$ where T is in seconds and L is in feet. Use 3.14 for π.

  a. Find the periods of pendulums of lengths 2 ft, 8 ft, 64 ft, and 100 ft.

  b. Find the period of a pendulum of length $\frac{2}{3}$ in.

  c. The pendulum of a grandfather clock is $\dfrac{32}{\pi^2}$ feet long. How long does it take to swing from one side to the other?

This pendulum is 1 ft long. How long is its period? (See Exercise 84.)

Mixed Review

Identify the rational and irrational numbers.

85. $\sqrt{7}$ **86.** $\sqrt{9}$ **87.** $\sqrt{135}$ **88.** $\sqrt{16}$

89. $\sqrt{144}$ **90.** $\sqrt{220}$ **91.** $\sqrt{0}$ *11-1*

Factor. **92.** $16a^2 - 25c^4$ **93.** $x^2 - 2x - 15$

94. $5m^2 - 30m + 45$ **95.** $2am + bm - 6an - 3bn$ *6-2, 6-4, 6-5, 6-7*

Solve. **96.** $\dfrac{7}{2x} + \dfrac{2}{x} = 1$ **97.** $\dfrac{12}{x + 4} = \dfrac{3}{x - 2}$ **98.** $\dfrac{a + 1}{4a - 4} = \dfrac{1}{2}$ *10-6*

Determine the replacements for the variables that give real numbers.

99. $\sqrt{3x}$ **100.** $\sqrt{2x^2}$ **101.** $\sqrt{x - 2}$ **102.** $\sqrt{2x + 5}$ *11-2*

Operations with Rational Exponents

As you saw on page 497, exponents can be rational numbers. The rules for operations with rational exponents are the same as the rules for operations with integer exponents. Thus,

$$a^m \cdot a^n = a^{m+n} \qquad \frac{a^m}{a^n} = a^{m-n} \qquad a^{-m} = \frac{1}{a^m} \qquad (a^m)^n = a^{mn}$$

$$(ab)^n = a^n b^n \qquad \text{and } \left(\frac{a}{b}\right)^n = \left(\frac{a^n}{b^n}\right), \text{ when } b \text{ is not zero.}$$

Quick Review

To review operations with exponents, see Lessons 5-1 and 5-2.

EXAMPLES Simplify each expression if possible, then write the expression in radical form.

1 $12^{\frac{6}{8}} = 12^{\frac{3}{4}} = \sqrt[4]{12^3}$

2 $\left(5^{\frac{3}{2}}\right)\left(5^{\frac{1}{2}}\right) = 5^{\frac{3}{2}+\frac{1}{2}}$ Using $a^m(a^n) = a^{m+n}$

$\qquad\qquad\qquad = 5^2$ Adding exponents

$\qquad\qquad\qquad = 25$ Squaring

3 $\dfrac{y^{\frac{7}{9}}}{y^{\frac{1}{3}}} = y^{\frac{7}{9}-\frac{1}{3}}$ Using $\frac{a^m}{a^n} = a^{m-n}$

$\qquad\quad = y^{\frac{4}{9}}$ Subtracting exponents

$\qquad\quad = \sqrt[9]{y^4}$ Writing in radical form

4 $x^{\frac{3}{5}}\left(\frac{x^2}{2}\right)^{\frac{2}{5}} = x^{\frac{3}{5}}\left(\dfrac{x^{2\left(\frac{2}{5}\right)}}{2^{\frac{2}{5}}}\right)$ Using $\left(\frac{a}{b}\right)^n = \frac{a^n}{b^n}$

$\qquad\qquad = x^{\frac{3}{5}}\left(\dfrac{x^{\frac{4}{5}}}{2^{\frac{2}{5}}}\right)$ Multiplying exponents

$\qquad\qquad = \dfrac{x^{\frac{3}{5}+\frac{4}{5}}}{2^{\frac{2}{5}}}$ Using $a^m(a^n) = a^{m+n}$

$\qquad\qquad = \dfrac{x^{\frac{7}{5}}}{2^{\frac{2}{5}}}$ Adding exponents

$\qquad\qquad = \dfrac{x^{\frac{7}{5}}}{2^{\frac{2}{5}}}\left(\dfrac{2^{\frac{3}{5}}}{2^{\frac{3}{5}}}\right)$

$\qquad\qquad = \dfrac{2^{\frac{3}{5}}x^{\frac{7}{5}}}{2}$ Rationalizing the denominator

$\qquad\qquad = \frac{1}{2}\sqrt[5]{2^3 x^7}$ Writing in radical form

Exercises

Simplify each expression, then write in radical form.

1. $8^{\frac{4}{6}}$

2. $\left(7^{\frac{1}{3}}\right)^{\frac{2}{5}}$

3. $\left(10^{\frac{1}{4}}\right)\left(10^{\frac{5}{8}}\right)$

4. $\dfrac{2^{\frac{7}{4}}}{2^{\frac{3}{8}}}$

5. $t^{-\frac{2}{3}} \cdot t^{\frac{5}{9}}$

6. $\left(\dfrac{a^{\frac{1}{3}}}{a^{\frac{4}{6}}}\right)^{\frac{1}{2}}$

7. $\left(m^{\frac{5}{8}}n^{\frac{2}{3}}\right)^{\frac{3}{4}}$

8. $\left(\left(b^{\frac{2}{3}}\right)^{\frac{6}{10}}\right)^{\frac{1}{4}}$

9. $\left(x^{\frac{5}{3}}y^{\frac{1}{5}}\right)^{\frac{3}{6}} \cdot y^{\frac{3}{10}}$

10. $x^{\frac{2}{3}}y^{\frac{1}{3}} \cdot \sqrt[3]{xy^5}$

11. $\dfrac{\sqrt[3]{m^4 n^5}}{m^{\frac{2}{5}}n^{\frac{7}{3}}}$

12. $\sqrt[5]{6a^4 b^4} \cdot \left(5a^3 b^7\right)^{\frac{1}{5}}$

Operations with Rational Exponents **503**

11-6 ▷ Addition and Subtraction

Objective: Add and subtract radical expressions.

What You'll Learn

1 To add and subtract radical expressions

. . . And Why

To understand how the rules of addition and subtraction apply to radical expressions

When we have radical expressions with the same radicands we can simplify using the distributive property.

EXAMPLE 1   Add.

$$3\sqrt{5} + 4\sqrt{5} = (3 + 4)\sqrt{5} \qquad \text{Using the distributive property}$$
$$= 7\sqrt{5}$$

Sometimes we need to simplify the radicand before adding or subtracting.

EXAMPLES   Add or subtract.

2 $\sqrt{2} - \sqrt{8} = \sqrt{2} - \sqrt{4 \cdot 2}$
$\qquad\qquad = \sqrt{2} - 2\sqrt{2} \qquad$ Simplifying
$\qquad\qquad = (1 - 2)\sqrt{2} \qquad$ Using the distributive property
$\qquad\qquad = -\sqrt{2}$

3 $\sqrt{x} + \sqrt{4x} = \sqrt{x} + 2\sqrt{x} = 3\sqrt{x}$

4 $\sqrt{x^3 - x^2} + \sqrt{4x - 4} = \sqrt{x^2(x - 1)} + \sqrt{4(x - 1)} \qquad$ Factoring radicands
$\qquad\qquad\qquad\qquad\qquad = \sqrt{x^2}\sqrt{x - 1} + \sqrt{4}\sqrt{x - 1}$
$\qquad\qquad\qquad\qquad\qquad = x\sqrt{x - 1} + 2\sqrt{x - 1}$
$\qquad\qquad\qquad\qquad\qquad = (x + 2)\sqrt{x - 1} \qquad$ Using the distributive property

Try This   Add or subtract.

a. $3\sqrt{2} + 9\sqrt{2}$ **b.** $8\sqrt{5} - 3\sqrt{5}$ **c.** $2\sqrt{10} - 7\sqrt{40}$
d. $\sqrt{24y} + \sqrt{54y}$ **e.** $\sqrt{9x + 9} - \sqrt{4x + 4}$

Sometimes after rationalizing denominators, we can factor and combine expressions.

EXAMPLE 5

$$\sqrt{3} + \sqrt{\tfrac{1}{3}} = \sqrt{3} + \frac{\sqrt{1}}{\sqrt{3}}$$
$$= \sqrt{3} + \frac{\sqrt{1}}{\sqrt{3}} \cdot \frac{\sqrt{3}}{\sqrt{3}}$$
$$= \sqrt{3} + \frac{\sqrt{3}}{3}$$
$$= \tfrac{4}{3}\sqrt{3}$$

Try This   Add or subtract.

f. $\sqrt{2} + \sqrt{\dfrac{1}{2}}$ **g.** $\sqrt{\dfrac{5}{3}} - \sqrt{\dfrac{3}{5}}$ **h.** $\dfrac{x}{\sqrt{x}} + \sqrt{x}$

11-6 Exercises

**Extra Help
On the Web**

Look for worked-out
examples at the Prentice
Hall Web site.
www.phschool.com

A

Add or subtract.

1. $3\sqrt{2} + 4\sqrt{2}$ **2.** $8\sqrt{3} + 3\sqrt{3}$ **3.** $7\sqrt{5} - 3\sqrt{5}$

4. $8\sqrt{2} - 5\sqrt{2}$ **5.** $6\sqrt{x} + 7\sqrt{x}$ **6.** $9\sqrt{y} + 3\sqrt{y}$

7. $9\sqrt{x} - 11\sqrt{x}$ **8.** $6\sqrt{a} - 14\sqrt{a}$ **9.** $5\sqrt{8} + 15\sqrt{2}$

10. $3\sqrt{12} + 2\sqrt{3}$ **11.** $\sqrt{27} - 2\sqrt{3}$ **12.** $7\sqrt{50} - 3\sqrt{2}$

13. $\sqrt{45} - \sqrt{20}$ **14.** $\sqrt{27} - \sqrt{12}$

15. $\sqrt{72} + \sqrt{98}$ **16.** $\sqrt{45} + \sqrt{80}$

17. $2\sqrt{12} + \sqrt{27} - \sqrt{48}$ **18.** $9\sqrt{8} - \sqrt{72} + \sqrt{98}$

19. $3\sqrt{18} - 2\sqrt{32} - 5\sqrt{50}$ **20.** $\sqrt{18} - 3\sqrt{8} + \sqrt{50}$

21. $2\sqrt{27} - 3\sqrt{48} + 2\sqrt{18}$ **22.** $3\sqrt{48} - 2\sqrt{27} - 2\sqrt{18}$

23. $\sqrt{4x} + \sqrt{81x^3}$ **24.** $\sqrt{12x^2} + \sqrt{27}$

25. $\sqrt{27} - \sqrt{12x^2}$ **26.** $\sqrt{81x^3} - \sqrt{4x}$

27. $\sqrt{8x + 8} + \sqrt{2x + 2}$ **28.** $\sqrt{12x + 12} + \sqrt{3x + 3}$

29. $\sqrt{x^5 - x^2} + \sqrt{9x^3 - 9}$ **30.** $\sqrt{16x - 16} + \sqrt{25x^3 - 25x^2}$

31. $3x\sqrt{y^3x} - x\sqrt{yx^3} + y\sqrt{y^3x}$ **32.** $4a\sqrt{a^2b} + a\sqrt{a^2b^3} - 5\sqrt{b^3}$

33. $\sqrt{4(a + b)} - \sqrt{(a + b)^3}$ **34.** $\sqrt{x^2y} + \sqrt{4x^2y} + \sqrt{9y} - \sqrt{y^3}$

35. $\sqrt{3} - \sqrt{\dfrac{1}{3}}$ **36.** $\sqrt{2} - \sqrt{\dfrac{1}{2}}$

37. $5\sqrt{2} + 3\sqrt{\dfrac{1}{2}}$ **38.** $4\sqrt{3} + 2\sqrt{\dfrac{1}{3}}$

39. $\sqrt{\dfrac{2}{3}} - \sqrt{\dfrac{1}{6}}$ **40.** $\sqrt{\dfrac{1}{2}} - \sqrt{\dfrac{1}{8}}$

41. $\sqrt{\dfrac{1}{12}} - \sqrt{\dfrac{1}{27}}$ **42.** $\sqrt{\dfrac{5}{6}} - \sqrt{\dfrac{6}{5}}$

B

43. ***Error Analysis***   Three students were asked to simplify $\sqrt{10} + \sqrt{50}$.
Their answers were $\sqrt{10}(1 + \sqrt{5})$, $\sqrt{10} + 5\sqrt{2}$, and $\sqrt{2}(5 + \sqrt{5})$.

   a. Which, if any, is incorrect?

   b. Which is in simplest form?

Journal

Explain how rules for operations
with radicals are similar to the
rules for operations with
fractions.

Add or subtract.

44. $\sqrt{125} - \sqrt{45} + 2\sqrt{5}$

45. $3\sqrt{\frac{1}{2}} + \frac{5}{2}\sqrt{18} + \sqrt{98}$

46. $\frac{3}{5}\sqrt{24} + \frac{2}{5}\sqrt{150} - \sqrt{96}$

47. $\sqrt{ab^6} + b\sqrt{a^3} + a\sqrt{a}$

48. $\frac{1}{3}\sqrt{27} + \sqrt{8} + \sqrt{300} - \sqrt{18} - \sqrt{162}$

49. $x\sqrt{2y} - \sqrt{8x^2y} + \frac{x}{3}\sqrt{18y}$

50. $7x\sqrt{12xy^2} - 9y\sqrt{27x^3} + 5\sqrt{300x^3y^2}$

51. $\sqrt{x} + \sqrt{\frac{1}{x}}$

52. *Critical Thinking* You know that $\sqrt{x^2 + y^2} = \sqrt{x^2} + \sqrt{y^2}$ is not true for *all* real numbers. For what numbers is it true?

Challenge

Add or subtract. Simplify when possible.

53. $5\sqrt{\frac{3}{10}} + 2\sqrt{\frac{5}{6}} - 6\sqrt{\frac{15}{32}}$ **54.** $2\sqrt{\frac{2a}{b}} - 4\sqrt{\frac{b}{2a^3}} + 5\sqrt{\frac{1}{8}a^3b}$

55. Evaluate for $a = 1, b = 3, c = 2, d = 4$.

    a. $\sqrt{a^2 + c^2}, \sqrt{a^2} + \sqrt{c^2}$ **b.** $\sqrt{b^2 + c^2}, \sqrt{b^2} + \sqrt{c^2}$

    c. $\sqrt{a^2 + d^2}, \sqrt{a^2} + \sqrt{d^2}$ **d.** $\sqrt{b^2 + d^2}, \sqrt{b^2} + \sqrt{d^2}$

    e. $\sqrt{a^2 + b^2}, \sqrt{a^2} + \sqrt{b^2}$ **f.** $\sqrt{c^2 + d^2}, \sqrt{c^2} + \sqrt{d^2}$

Binomial pairs such as $1 + \sqrt{2}$ and $1 - \sqrt{2}$ are called **conjugates.** We can use conjugates to rationalize binomial denominators containing radicals. Rationalize each denominator.

56. $\dfrac{5}{1 - \sqrt{2}}$ **57.** $\dfrac{8 + \sqrt{3}}{3 - \sqrt{2}}$

Mixed Review

Simplify. **58.** $\sqrt{25y^2}$ **59.** $\sqrt{(-6)^2}$

          60. $\sqrt{(x + 2)^2}$ **61.** $\sqrt{y^2 + 10y + 25}$ *11-2*

Multiply. **62.** $\sqrt{5}\sqrt{15}$ **63.** $\sqrt{6}\sqrt{8}$

          64. $\sqrt{11}\sqrt{11}$ **65.** $\sqrt{a + c}\sqrt{a - c}$ *11-4*

Factor and simplify. **66.** $\sqrt{20}$ **67.** $\sqrt{16x^2y}$ **68.** $\sqrt{x^3 - 4x^2 + 4x}$ *11-3*

Solve by graphing. **69.** $x + 2 \leq y$ **70.** $x + y \leq 1$ **71.** $y - x \leq 1$

                           $y \geq -2$ $x + y \geq 1$ $2y + x \leq 2$ *9-6*

Injury Severity Score

Doctors in hospital emergency rooms must decide the order in which patients should be treated. Obviously, patients with the most serious injuries should be treated before those with less serious injuries. How do doctors determine the severity of an injury? Several scoring systems have been devised, the Injury Severity Score (ISS) among them. In the ISS system, each injury is assigned a severity code ranging from 1, for minor injuries, to 6, for injuries that are life-threatening. The ISS also assigns six body regions the letters A through F:

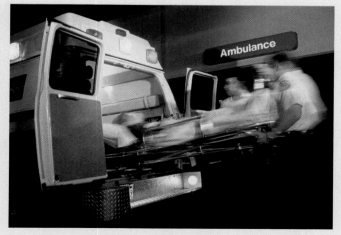

A Head and neck   D Abdomen
B Face   E Extremities
C Chest   F Skin

Emergency room doctors can use the Injury Severity Score (ISS) to determine which patients must be treated first. What is the highest ISS score a patient can have?

To compute the ISS, the doctor identifies the highest severity code for each region in which the patient has an injury. If the patient has any code 6 injury, the ISS is 75. Otherwise, the ISS is found by identifying the three highest codes from different body regions, squaring them, and finding their sum.

Suppose the three highest severity codes for a patient are as follows: Head and neck 2; Chest 1; Abdomen 4. Find the ISS.

> First, square each code: $2^2 = 4$, $1^2 = 1$, and $4^2 = 16$.
> Next, find the sum of the squares: $4 + 1 + 16 = 21$.
> The ISS for this patient is 21.

Suppose a patient has eight injuries as shown by the eight codes in the chart below. Find the ISS.

Region	Codes
A	5, 5, 4
C	3, 2
D	1
E	4, 4

Select the three highest codes from different body regions. They are 5 (from region A), 3 (from region C), and 4 (from region E). Thus the ISS is $5^2 + 3^2 + 4^2 = 25 + 9 + 16 = 50$.

Problems

Find the ISS for patients having these three highest codes.

1. Abdomen 3; Extremities 5; Skin 1
2. Head and neck 4; Face 5; Skin 3
3. Chest 5; Abdomen 6; Extremities 1
4. Head and neck 1; Abdomen 2; Skin 5

Find the ISS for the following cases.

5.	Region	Codes
	A	5, 2
	B	3
	C	2, 1
	D	2

6.	Region	Codes
	A	4, 3
	C	5, 2
	E	3, 1

7.	Region	Codes
	A	3, 2
	B	5, 3
	D	3, 1, 1
	E	2

8.	Region	Codes
	A	4, 4, 4, 4, 4, 4
	C	5, 4, 4, 4, 4
	E	4, 4, 3, 4, 4

9.	Region	Codes
	A	5, 5, 5, 5
	B	3, 3, 3, 3, 3
	C	2, 2, 2, 4
	D	3, 3, 3, 1, 1
	F	2, 2

10.	Region	Codes
	A	5, 4, 1
	B	2, 2
	C	1, 1
	D	1, 1, 1

11. Determine the order in which the patients in cases 5 through 10 should be treated.

12. If the probability of surviving injuries is found using the formula $P = 1 - \left(\frac{ISS}{80}\right)^2$, find the probability of survival for the patients in cases 5 through 10.

The Pythagorean Theorem

Objective: Solve triangles using the Pythagorean theorem.

In a right triangle, the longest side is called the **hypotenuse.** The hypotenuse is always the side opposite the right angle. The other two sides are called the **legs** of the triangle. We usually use the variables a and b to identify the legs and c for the hypotenuse. They are related as follows.

The Pythagorean Theorem

In any right triangle, if a and b are the lengths of the legs and c is the length of the hypotenuse, then

$$a^2 + b^2 = c^2$$

We will prove the Pythagorean theorem in geometry. The diagram below shows the relationship between the legs and the hypotenuse in a right triangle.

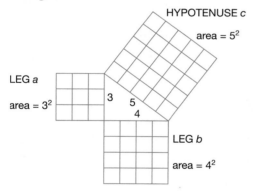

$$a^2 + b^2 = c^2$$
$$3^2 + 4^2 = 5^2$$
$$9 + 16 = 25$$

If we know the lengths of any two sides, we can find the length of the third side.

EXAMPLE 1

Find the length of the hypotenuse of this right triangle to the nearest thousandth.

$$4^2 + 5^2 = c^2$$
$$16 + 25 = c^2$$
$$41 = c^2$$
$$c = \sqrt{41}$$
$$c \approx 6.403$$

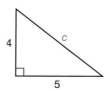

What You'll Learn

1 To solve triangles using the Pythagorean theorem

...And Why

To understand the relationship among the sides of a right triangle

EXAMPLE 2

Find the length of the leg of this right triangle to the nearest thousandth.

$$1^2 + b^2 = (\sqrt{7})^2$$
$$1 + b^2 = 7$$
$$b^2 = 7 - 1$$
$$b^2 = 6$$
$$b = \sqrt{6}$$
$$b \approx 2.449$$

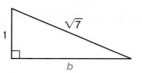

Try This   Find the missing length in each right triangle.

a.
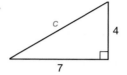

b.
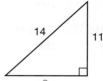

c.
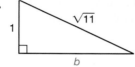

d.
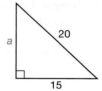

Extra Help On the Web

Look for worked-out examples at the Prentice Hall Web site.
www.phschool.com

11-7 Exercises

A

Find the length of the third side of each right triangle.

1.
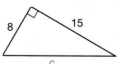

2.
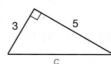

3.

4.
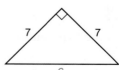

5.

6.
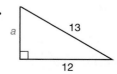

7.

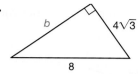

8.

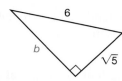

Find the length of the side not given for a right triangle with hypotenuse c and legs a and b.

9. $a = 10, b = 24$

10. $a = 5, b = 12$

11. $a = 9, c = 15$

12. $a = 18, c = 30$

13. $b = 1, c = \sqrt{5}$

14. $b = 1, c = \sqrt{2}$

15. $a = 1, c = \sqrt{3}$

16. $a = \sqrt{3}, b = \sqrt{5}$

17. $c = 10, b = 5\sqrt{3}$

18. $a = 3\sqrt{3}, c = 5\sqrt{3}$

19. *Error Analysis*   A student found the length of the hypotenuse. What error did the student make?

$$c^2 = a^2 + b^2$$
$$c^2 = 5^2 + 8^2$$
$$\sqrt{c^2} = \sqrt{5^2 + 8^2}$$
$$c = 5 + 8$$
$$c = 13$$

B

An equilateral triangle is shown to the right.

20. Find an expression for height h in terms of a.

21. Find an expression for area A in terms of a.

22. Find an expression for area A in terms of h.

23. **TEST PREP**   Which is longest?

    A. the diagonal of a square with 6 cm sides

    B. the diagonal of a rectangle with length 7 cm and width 5 cm

    C. the hypotenuse of a right triangle with legs 4 cm and 9 cm long

    D. the leg of a right triangle with the other leg 10 cm and the hypotenuse 15 cm long

24. Figure $ABCD$ is a square. Find AC.

25. *Critical Thinking*   A right triangle has sides whose lengths are consecutive integers. Find the lengths of the sides.

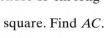

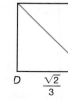

26. Suppose the length of a hypotenuse is $\sqrt{18}$. Find two pairs of values for the lengths of the legs.

Challenge

27. Find the length of the diagonal of a cube with side length 10 cm.

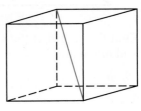

Find x.

28.
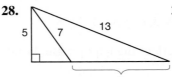

29.
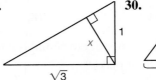

30.
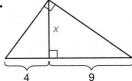

31. *Mathematical Reasoning*   The density property of rational numbers states that no matter how close two rational numbers are, there is a rational number between them.

  a. Find a real number between $\frac{3}{7}$ and $\frac{4}{7}$.
  b. Find a real number between –0.23 and –0.24.
  c. Find a real number between $\sqrt{2}$ and $\sqrt{3}$.
  d. Find a real number between $\sqrt{10}$ and $\sqrt{11}$.
  e. Do you think the density property holds for real numbers? Justify your reasoning.

Mixed Review

Simplify.   **32.** $-\sqrt{169}$ **33.** $\sqrt{(x+3)^2}$ **34.** $\sqrt{25y}$ **35.** $\sqrt{32a^2}$

36. $\sqrt{x^7}$ **37.** $\sqrt{a^{20}}$ **38.** $\sqrt{(x+5)^4}$ **39.** $\sqrt{(x-3)^3}$

40. $\sqrt{12a^5}$ **41.** $\sqrt{216x^4}$

42. $\sqrt{12x^3y}$ **43.** $\sqrt{18a^3b^4}$ *11-2, 11-3*

Solve.   **44.** $\frac{3}{2x} + \frac{1}{2} = \frac{10}{4x}$ **45.** $\frac{x}{4} - \frac{x}{12} = \frac{1}{2}$ **46.** $x + \frac{12}{x} = 7$ *10-6*

47. The product of two consecutive positive integers is 210. Find the numbers.

48. The sum of two numbers is 7. The difference of the two numbers is -17. Find the numbers.   *8-6*

The Distance Formula

Objective: Find the distance between two points on the coordinate plane.

The **distance formula** is based on the Pythagorean theorem and is used to find the distance between any two points in the plane if the coordinates of the points are known.

EXAMPLE 1 Find the distance between the points $(3, 2)$ and $(-3, -2)$.

We plot these points on a coordinate plane and construct a triangle as shown. The distance between the points $(3, 2)$ and $(-3, -2)$ is the hypotenuse of this triangle.

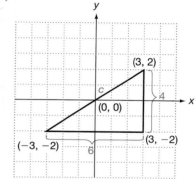

We can use the Pythagorean theorem to find this length.

$$c^2 = a^2 + b^2$$
$$= 6^2 + 4^2$$
$$= 36 + 16$$
$$= 52$$
$$c = \pm\sqrt{52}$$

Since distance cannot be negative, the distance is $\sqrt{52} \approx 7.2$.

The distance formula, which is derived from the Pythagorean theorem, can be used to compute the distance between two points.

Distance Formula

The distance between any two points (x_1, y_1) and (x_2, y_2) is given by

$$d = \sqrt{(x_1 - x_2)^2 + (y_1 - y_2)^2}$$

EXAMPLE 2 Find the distance between $(2, 2)$ and $(5, 6)$.

$$d = \sqrt{(2 - 5)^2 + (2 - 6)^2}$$
$$= \sqrt{(-3)^2 + (-4)^2}$$
$$= \sqrt{9 + 16}$$
$$= \sqrt{25}$$
$$d = 5$$

Exercises

Use the distance formula to find the distance between each pair of points.

1. $(8, -5)$ and $(3, 7)$ **2.** $(0, 4)$ and $(-4, 6)$ **3.** $(-3, -5)$ and $(-6, -8)$

4. $(5, 6)$ and $(-2, 6)$ **5.** $(-4, -4)$ and $(4, 4)$ **6.** $(7, 0)$ and $(-6, 4)$

11-8 ▷ Using the Pythagorean Theorem

Objective: Solve problems using the Pythagorean theorem.

What You'll Learn

1 To solve problems using the Pythagorean theorem

. . . And Why

To measure distances indirectly

PROBLEM-SOLVING GUIDELINES
■ UNDERSTAND the problem
▨ Develop and carry out a PLAN
■ Find the ANSWER and CHECK

Many real-world problems can be solved using the Pythagorean theorem. Use the Pythagorean theorem and the Problem-Solving Guidelines to help you solve these problems.

EXAMPLE 1

On a community baseball diamond, the distance between the bases is 60 ft. What is the distance from home plate to second base?

■ **UNDERSTAND the problem**

Question: What is the distance (d) from home plate to second base?
Data: Distance between home and first base = 60 ft;
distance between first and second base = 60 ft.

▨ **Develop and carry out a PLAN**

We can write and solve an equation using the Pythagorean theorem.

$$60^2 + 60^2 = d^2$$
$$3600 + 3600 = d^2$$
$$7200 = d^2$$
$$\sqrt{7200} = d$$
$$84.9 \approx d$$

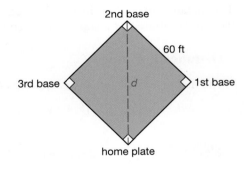

■ **Find the ANSWER and CHECK**

The distance from home plate to second base is about 84.9 ft. This answer is reasonable since the hypotenuse is greater than either leg.

Try This   Solve.

a. How long is a guy wire that reaches from the top of a 15-ft pole to a point on the ground 10 ft from the bottom of the pole?

b. A 12-ft ladder is leaning against a building. The bottom of the ladder is 7 ft from the building. How high is the top of the ladder?

Extra Help
On the Web
Look for worked-out examples at the Prentice Hall Web site.
www.phschool.com

A

Solve. Round answers to nearest tenth.

1. A 10-m ladder is leaning against a building. The bottom of the ladder is 5 m from the building. How high is the top of the ladder?

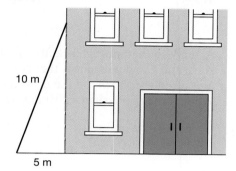

10 m

5 m

2. How long must a wire be to reach from the top of a 13-m telephone pole to a point on the ground 9 m from the foot of the pole?

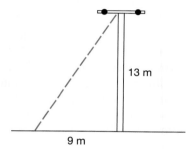

13 m

9 m

3. What amount of wire is needed to connect the top of the antenna to the hook 15 ft from the base of the antenna, as shown at right?

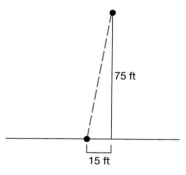

75 ft

15 ft

4. The distance between consecutive bases in professional baseball is 90 ft. Find the distance from home plate to second base.

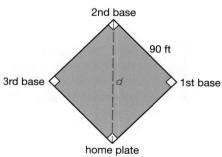

2nd base

90 ft

3rd base d 1st base

home plate

5. What is the distance across the garden shown at the right?

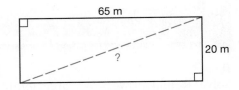

65 m

20 m

?

6. A surveyor had poles marked at points A, B, and C. The distances that could be measured are shown on the drawing. What is the approximate distance from A to C ?

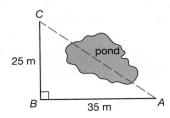

C

pond

25 m

B   35 m   A

7. Carla Chew lives 20 miles due north of her favorite radio station. While driving due east from her house, she was able to keep the radio signal for about 75 miles. What is the broadcasting range of her favorite radio station?

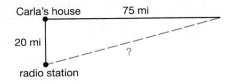

Carla's house   75 mi

20 mi

?

radio station

8. A cable television company needed to wire from its box at the corner of a lot to a corner of a house. The owner knew the house was 15 ft from the side of the lot and 60 ft from the back of the lot. How much wire was needed to go from the box to the house?

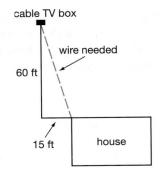

cable TV box

wire needed

60 ft

15 ft   house

9. An airplane is flying at an altitude of 4.1 km. The plane's slant distance from the runway is 15.1 km. How far must the plane travel to be directly above the runway?

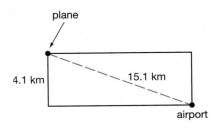

plane

4.1 km   15.1 km

airport

B

10. Suppose an outfielder catches the ball on the third base line about 40 feet behind third base. About how far would the outfielder have to throw the ball to first base?

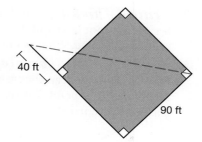

11. An A-frame tent is in the shape of an isosceles triangle. The base of the triangle is 7 ft and the two congruent sides are each 6 ft. What is the height of the tent?

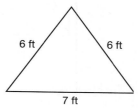

12. How far out is the ship? Using geometry, Kala found triangle *CDE* to be *congruent* (same size and shape) to triangle *CBA*.

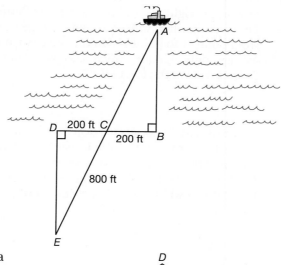

Suppose the tent in Exercise 11 is 9 ft long. Find the space inside (volume) of the tent.

13. A 48-ft-wide building has a roof that rises 4 ft for each 12-foot horizontal change. If the roof has a 2-foot overhang, what is the length of $\overline{CD}$?

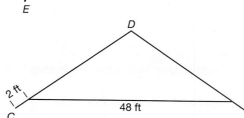

14. The diagonal of a square has length $8\sqrt{2}$ ft. Find the length of a side of the square.

15. Find the length of the diagonal of a rectangle whose length is 12 in. and whose width is 7 in.

16. One leg of a right triangle is 5 times the other leg. Find the longer leg if the hypotenuse is 60 ft.

17. *Critical Thinking*   In Exercise 13, suppose that the roof rises 3 feet for each 8-foot horizontal change, and that all other measurements remain the same. What is the length of $\overline{CD}$?

18. *Mathematical Reasoning*   Suppose one of your classmates claims that the Pythagorean theorem is $x^2 + y^2 = z^2$. Another classmate responds, "It depends." Write a paragraph explaining why the second classmate is correct.

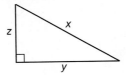

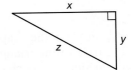

Challenge

19. Two major highways meet at a 90° angle. The known distances between cities are marked on the map at the right. An old road connects these cities. On the major highways, one can average 50 mi/h from point A to point C. On the old road, one can average only 30 mi/h. Which path would get you from A to C in the least time?

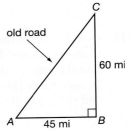

20. Two cars leave a service station at the same time. One car travels east at a speed of 50 mi/h, and the other travels south at a speed of 60 mi/h. After one-half hour, how far apart are they? When will they be 100 miles apart?

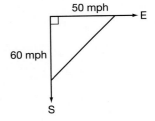

Mixed Review

Rationalize the denominator.   **21.** $\sqrt{\dfrac{3}{5}}$ **22.** $\dfrac{\sqrt{20}}{\sqrt{5y}}$ **23.** $\dfrac{\sqrt{y}}{\sqrt{xy}}$ *11-5*

Multiply and simplify.   **24.** $\sqrt{15}\sqrt{10}$ **25.** $\sqrt{xy}\sqrt{xyz}$ *11-4*

Add or subtract.   **26.** $\sqrt{2} + 4\sqrt{2}$ **27.** $4\sqrt{12} - 2\sqrt{3}$

28. $6\sqrt{12} - 4\sqrt{3}$ **29.** $\sqrt{45} + \sqrt{20}$ **30.** $2\sqrt{8} + 6\sqrt{18}$

31. $\sqrt{24} - \sqrt{6}$ **32.** $\sqrt{18} - 5\sqrt{8} + \sqrt{72}$ *11-6*

Equations with Radicals

Math in Action

Finding the speed of an automobile in an accident can help prevent future accidents. The formula $r = 2\sqrt{5L}$ can be used to approximate the speed (r), in miles per hour, of a car that has left a skid mark of length L, in feet.

PART 1 Solving Equations with Radicals

Objective: Solve equations involving radicals.

A **radical equation** contains a variable in a radicand. To solve radical equations, we first convert them to equations without radicals. We do this by squaring both sides of the equation.

The Principle of Squaring

If an equation $a = b$ is true, then the equation $a^2 = b^2$ is true.

EXAMPLE 1   Solve.

$$\sqrt{2x} - 4 = 7$$
$$\sqrt{2x} = 11 \qquad \text{Getting the radical alone on one side}$$
$$(\sqrt{2x})^2 = 11^2 \qquad \text{Squaring both sides}$$
$$2x = 121$$
$$x = \frac{121}{2}$$

Check:
$$\sqrt{2x} - 4 = 7$$

$$
\begin{array}{c|c}
\sqrt{2 \cdot \frac{121}{2}} - 4 & 7 \\
\sqrt{121} - 4 & 7 \\
11 - 4 & 7 \\
7 & 7 \ \checkmark
\end{array}
$$

The solution is $\frac{121}{2}$.

It is important to check. *When we square both sides of an equation, it is transformed into a new equation that may have extraneous solutions.* For example, the equation $x = 1$ has *one* solution, the number 1. When we square both sides we get $x^2 = 1$, which has *two* solutions, 1 and -1.

What You'll Learn

1 To solve equations involving radicals

2 To solve problems involving the solution of equations with radicals

. . . And Why

To solve more types of equations

EXAMPLE 2 Solve.

$$\sqrt{x + 1} = \sqrt{2x - 5}.$$
$$(\sqrt{x + 1})^2 = (\sqrt{2x - 5})^2 \qquad \text{Squaring}$$
$$x + 1 = 2x - 5 \qquad \text{both sides}$$
$$x = 6$$

Check:

$$\frac{\sqrt{x + 1}}{\sqrt{6 + 1}} \Big| \frac{\sqrt{2x - 5}}{\sqrt{2(6) - 5}}$$
$$\sqrt{7} \Big| \sqrt{12 - 5}$$
$$\sqrt{7} \Big| \sqrt{7} \; ✔$$

The solution is 6.

Try This Solve.

a. $\sqrt{3x} - 5 = 3$ **b.** $\sqrt{3x + 1} = \sqrt{2x + 3}$ **c.** $\sqrt{x - 2} - 5 = 3$

PART 2 Solving Problems

Objective: Solve problems involving the solution of equations with radicals.

This departing airplane is at an altitude of 250 m. Use the formula to find how far you could see.

The formula $V = 3.5\sqrt{h}$ tells how many kilometers (V) you can see from a height of h meters above Earth.

EXAMPLE 3

How far, to the nearest kilometer, can you see through an airplane window at a height, or altitude, of 12,321 meters?

$$V = 3.5\sqrt{12{,}321} \qquad \text{Substituting 12,321 for } h$$
$$V = 388.5 \text{ km}$$

Try This Approximate answers to the nearest kilometer.

d. How far can you see to the horizon through an airplane window at a height of 8000 m?

e. How far can a sailor see to the horizon from the top of a 20-m mast?

EXAMPLE 4

A person can see about 50 kilometers to the horizon from the top of a cliff. How high is the cliff to the nearest meter? Use $V = 3.5\sqrt{h}$.

$$50 = 3.5\sqrt{h} \qquad \text{Substituting 50 for } V$$
$$\frac{50}{3.5} = \sqrt{h}$$
$$14.3 \approx \sqrt{h} \qquad \text{Rounding to the nearest tenth}$$
$$(14.3)^2 \approx (\sqrt{h})^2$$
$$(14.3)^2 \approx h$$
$$204 \text{ m} \approx h$$

The cliff is about 204 meters high.

Try This Approximate to the nearest meter.

f. A person can see 61 km to the horizon from the roof of a building. How high is the rooftop?

11-9 Exercises

Internet Connection

***Extra Help
On the Web***

Look for worked-out examples at the Prentice Hall Web site.

www.phschool.com

A

Solve.

1. $\sqrt{x} = 5$

2. $\sqrt{x} = 7$

3. $\sqrt{x} = 6.2$

4. $\sqrt{x} = 4.3$

5. $\sqrt{x + 3} = 20$

6. $\sqrt{x + 4} = 11$

7. $\sqrt{2x + 4} = 25$

8. $\sqrt{2x + 1} = 13$

9. $3 + \sqrt{x - 1} = 5$

10. $4 + \sqrt{y - 3} = 11$

11. $6 - 2\sqrt{3n} = 0$

12. $8 - 4\sqrt{5n} = 0$

13. $\sqrt{5x - 7} = \sqrt{x + 10}$

14. $\sqrt{4x - 5} = \sqrt{x + 9}$

15. $\sqrt{x} = -7$

16. $-\sqrt{x} = 5$

17. $\sqrt{2y + 6} = \sqrt{2y - 5}$

18. $2\sqrt{x - 2} = \sqrt{7 - x}$

Solve. Use the formula $V = 3.5\sqrt{h}$ for Exercises 19–22.

19. How far can you see to the horizon from an airplane at 9800 m?

20. How far can a sailor see to the horizon from the top of a 24-m mast?

21. A person can see about 350 km to the horizon from an airplane window. How high is the airplane?

22. A person can see about 100 km to the horizon from the top of a hill. How high is the hill?

The formula $r = 2\sqrt{5L}$ can be used to approximate the speed (r), in mi/h, of a car that has left a skid mark of length L, in feet.

23. How far will a car skid at 50 mi/h? at 70 mi/h?

24. How far will a car skid at 60 mi/h? at 100 mi/h?

B

Solve.

25. $\sqrt{5x^2 + 5} = 5$

26. $\sqrt{x} = -x$

27. Find a number such that twice its square root is 14.

28. Find a number such that the opposite of three times its square root is -33.

The formula $T = 2\pi\sqrt{\dfrac{L}{32}}$ can be used to find the period (T), in seconds, of a pendulum of length L, in feet.

29. What is the length of a pendulum that has a period of 1.6 sec? Use 3.14 for π.

30. What is the length of a pendulum that has a period of 3 sec? Use 3.14 for π.

31. *Critical Thinking*   Find a number such that the square root of 4 more than 5 times the number is 8.

32. *Mathematical Reasoning*   Justify each step to prove the Principle of Squaring.

a. $a = b$ _____

b. $a \cdot a = a \cdot b$ _____

c. $a \cdot b = b \cdot b$ _____

d. $a \cdot a = b \cdot b$ _____

e. $a^2 = b^2$ _____

Challenge

Solve.

33. $x - 1 = \sqrt{x + 5}$ **34.** $\sqrt{y^2 + 6} + y - 3 = 0$

35. $\sqrt{x - 5} + \sqrt{x} = 5$ (Use the principle of squaring twice.)

36. $\sqrt{3x + 1} = 1 + \sqrt{x + 4}$

37. $4 + \sqrt{10 - x} = 6 + \sqrt{4 - x}$ **38.** $x = (x - 2)\sqrt{x}$

39. Solve $A = \sqrt{1 + \dfrac{a^2}{b^2}}$ for b.

The formula $t = \sqrt{\dfrac{2s}{g}}$ gives the time in seconds for an object, initially at rest, to fall s feet.

40. Solve the formula for s.

41. If $g = 32.2$, find the distance an object falls in the first 5 seconds.

42. Find the distance an object falls in the first 10 seconds.

Mixed Review

Determine the replacements for the variable that give real numbers.

43. $\sqrt{x + 1}$ **44.** $\sqrt{x - 1}$ **45.** $\sqrt{5x + 1}$ **46.** $\sqrt{x^2 + 4}$ *11-1*

Simplify.   **47.** $\sqrt{225}$ **48.** $\sqrt{m^2}$ **49.** $\sqrt{x^2 - 2x + 1}$

50. $\sqrt{(-9a)^2}$ **51.** $\sqrt{y^{13}}$ **52.** $\sqrt{9(y + 7)^4}$ **53.** $\sqrt{144m^5}$ *11-2*

Solve.   **54.** $y^2 - \dfrac{8}{15}y + \dfrac{15}{225} = 0$ **55.** $x^2 + \dfrac{1}{12}x - \dfrac{12}{144} = 0$ *6-5*

Odd and Even Problems

A common type of problem found on standardized tests is the "odd and even" problem. A variable is given to be an odd or an even number, and you must determine whether any of several expressions are odd or even. It is helpful to think about the following relationships involving the addition and multiplication of odd and even numbers.

odd + odd = even   odd × odd = odd
odd + even = odd   odd × even = even
even + even = even   even × even = even

EXAMPLE 1

If n is odd, which of the following can't be odd?
(A) $3n + 2$ **(B)** $3n + 4$ **(C)** $2n + 3$
(D) $6n + 3$ **(E)** $5n + 5$

We will look at the patterns above and determine whether the given expressions are even or odd.
(A) 3(odd) × n (odd) + 2(even) = odd + even = odd
(B) 3(odd) × n (odd) + 4(even) = odd + even = odd
(C) 2(even) × n (odd) + 3(odd) = even + odd = odd
(D) 6(even) × n (odd) + 3(odd) = even + odd = odd
(E) 5(odd) × n (odd) + 5(odd) = odd + odd = even

The correct answer is (E).

Another strategy is to substitute numbers according to the conditions given in the problem and evaluate the expressions.

EXAMPLE 2

If x is an integer, which of the following *must* be an even integer?
(A) $x^3 + 3$ **(B)** $5x + 1$ **(C)** $4x + 2$
(D) $x^2 + 1$ **(E)** $x^2 + x + 3$

Since x can be either odd or even, we will substitute an odd number and an even number and check each answer. If one odd number makes the answer even, any odd number will make the answer even.
(A) $x^3 + 3 = (1)^3 + 3 = 4$
    $x^3 + 3 = (0)^3 + 3 = 3$
(B) $5x + 1 = 5(0) + 1 = 1$ Since the answer is odd, you need not evaluate the second expression.

(C) $4x + 2 = 4(0) + 2 = 2$
    $4x + 2 = 4(1) + 2 = 6$

At this point, we know (C) is correct because both answers are even.

Problems

1. If a and b are odd integers, which of the following must be true?

   I. $\frac{a+b}{2}$ is odd.
   II. $a - b$ is even.
   III. $a + b$ is divisible by 2.

   (A) III only
   (B) I and II only
   (C) I and III only
   (D) II and III only
   (E) I, II, and III

2. For any integer n, which of the following represents three consecutive odd integers?
   (A) $n, n + 1, n + 2$
   (B) $n + 1, n + 3, n + 5$
   (C) $3n, 5n, 7n$
   (D) $2n + 1, 2n + 3, 2n + 5$
   (E) $2n, 2n + 2, 2n + 4$

3. For what whole number (W) is the sum of $W, W + 1$, and $W + 2$ odd?
   (A) For all W **(B)** For all even numbers W
   (C) For all odd numbers W **(D)** For no W
   (E) For some W, but for none of the sets above

4. If M is an odd integer and N is an even integer, which of the following *could* be an even integer?
   (A) $M + N$ **(B)** $M - N$ **(C)** $\frac{M}{2} + N$
   (D) $(M \times M) + M$ **(E)** $\frac{M}{2} + \frac{N}{2}$

5. If X, Y, and Z are integers such that $XY + Z$ is even, which of the following *might* be TRUE?
   (A) X and Y are even; Z is odd.
   (B) X and Y are odd; Z is even.
   (C) X and Z are even; Y is odd.
   (D) X and Z are odd; Y is even.
   (E) Y and Z are odd; X is even.

6. In the equations below, a is an odd integer and b is an even integer. Which of the following expressions must be odd?

   $$a^2 + ab^2 + 2b^3 = c$$
   $$b^2 + ba^2 + 2a^3 = d$$

   I. $c^2 + cd^2 + 2d^2$
   II. $3c^3 + 3d^2 + 2c^2$
   III. $c^2 + dc^2 + 2d^3$

   (A) I only   **(B)** II only   **(C)** III only   **(D)** I and II only
   (E) I, II, and III

11-1

The number c is a **square root** of a if $c^2 = a$. The square roots of 64 are 8 and -8. The **principal square root** of 64 is written $\sqrt{64} = 8$. The negative square root of 64 is written $-\sqrt{64} = -8$.

Simplify.

1. $\sqrt{36}$ **2.** $-\sqrt{81}$ **3.** $\sqrt{49}$ **4.** $-\sqrt{169}$

An **irrational number** cannot be named by fractional notation $\frac{a}{b}$. The rational numbers and irrational numbers make up the set of **real numbers.**

Identify each square root as rational or irrational.

5. $\sqrt{3}$ **6.** $\sqrt{36}$ **7.** $-\sqrt{12}$ **8.** $-\sqrt{4}$

11-2

In a radical expression, the expression written under the radical $\sqrt{x^2 + 5}$ is called the **radicand.** Radical expressions with negative radicands have no meaning in the real number system.

Determine the replacements for the variable so that the expression represents a real number.

9. $\sqrt{x + 7}$ **10.** $\sqrt{x - 10}$

Simplify.

11. $\sqrt{m^2}$ **12.** $\sqrt{49t^2}$ **13.** $\sqrt{p^2}$ **14.** $\sqrt{(x - 4)^2}$

11-3

For any nonnegative numbers, a and b, $\sqrt{ab} = \sqrt{a} \cdot \sqrt{b}$. You can use this property to simplify radical expressions. A simplified radical expression has no factors under the radical sign that are perfect squares.

To find the square root of an even power such as x^{10}, take half of the exponent. If the exponent is odd, write the power as a product of the largest even power and x. Then simplify the even power.

Factor and simplify. Assume that all variables are nonnegative.

15. $-\sqrt{48}$ **16.** $\sqrt{x^2 - 14x + 49}$ **17.** $\sqrt{64x^2}$

18. $\sqrt{36x}$ **19.** $\sqrt{x^{12}}$ **20.** $\sqrt{y^5}$

21. $\sqrt{(x - 2)^4}$ **22.** $\sqrt{75y^{15}}$

23. $\sqrt{25x^9}$ **24.** $\sqrt{(y + 7)^{10}}$

Key Terms

conjugate (p. 506)
cube root (p. 494)
distance formula (p. 513)
division property for radicals (p. 498)
hypotenuse (p. 509)
irrational number (p. 483)
leg (p. 509)
principal square root (p. 482)
principle of squaring (p. 519)
product property for radicals (p. 491)
Pythagorean theorem (p. 509)
radical equation (p. 519)
radical expression (p. 487)
radical sign (p. 482)
radicand (p. 487)
rationalizing the denominator (p. 499)
real number (p. 483)
square root (p. 482)

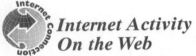
11-4

We can use the product property for radicals to multiply radicals. Sometimes we can simplify after multiplying. We can find perfect square factors and take their square roots.

Multiply.

25. $\sqrt{3} \cdot \sqrt{7}$

26. $\sqrt{a} \cdot \sqrt{t}$

27. $\sqrt{x-3} \cdot \sqrt{x+3}$

28. $\sqrt{2x} \cdot \sqrt{3y}$

29. $\sqrt{\frac{3}{4}} \cdot \sqrt{\frac{5}{7}}$

30. $\sqrt{3x} \cdot \sqrt{2x+1}$

Multiply and simplify.

31. $\sqrt{3} \cdot \sqrt{6}$

32. $\sqrt{2x^2} \cdot \sqrt{5x^5}$

33. $\sqrt{ab} \cdot \sqrt{bc}$

34. $\sqrt{5b} \cdot \sqrt{15b^3}$

11-5

For any nonnegative radicands A and B, $\dfrac{\sqrt{A}}{\sqrt{B}} = \sqrt{\dfrac{A}{B}}$.

A simplified expression may not have a radical in the denominator or a fractional radicand; you must remove the fraction from the radicand or the radical from the denominator by **rationalizing the denominator.**

Simplify.

35. $\sqrt{\dfrac{9}{16}}$

36. $\sqrt{\dfrac{1}{25}}$

37. $\sqrt{\dfrac{20}{45}}$

38. $\sqrt{\dfrac{9}{32}}$

Divide.

39. $\dfrac{\sqrt{48}}{\sqrt{3}}$

40. $\dfrac{\sqrt{45x^4}}{\sqrt{9}}$

41. $\dfrac{\sqrt{100x^3}}{\sqrt{25x^3}}$

42. $\dfrac{\sqrt{80y^4}}{\sqrt{5y^4}}$

Rationalize the denominator.

43. $\dfrac{\sqrt{3}}{\sqrt{5}}$

44. $\dfrac{5}{\sqrt{3}}$

45. $\dfrac{\sqrt{8}}{\sqrt{x}}$

46. $\dfrac{\sqrt{64a^3}}{\sqrt{6}}$

47. $\sqrt{\dfrac{1}{8}}$

48. $\sqrt{\dfrac{5}{y}}$

11-6

To add or subtract real numbers with the same radicand, use the distributive property. You may need to simplify the radicals first.

Add or subtract.

49. $10\sqrt{5} + 3\sqrt{5}$

50. $\sqrt{80} - \sqrt{45}$

51. $\sqrt{x} + \sqrt{9x}$

52. $3\sqrt{2} - 5\sqrt{\frac{1}{2}}$

53. $\sqrt{9x + 9} + \sqrt{x + 1}$

54. $\sqrt{12x^2} + \sqrt{3x^2}$

11-7

The **Pythagorean theorem,** $c^2 = a^2 + b^2$, can be used to find the hypotenuse (c) or the legs (a and b) of a right triangle.

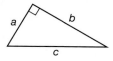

In a right triangle, find the length of the side not given.

55. $a = 15, b = 20$

56. $c = 5\sqrt{2}, b = 5$

57. $a = 6, c = 10$

58. $a = \sqrt{2}, b = \sqrt{5}$

59. $c = 18, b = 14$

60. $b = 6, a = 6\sqrt{3}$

11-8

Use the Pythagorean theorem and the Problem-Solving Guidelines to help you solve problems with right triangles.

Solve.

61. An 18-ft ladder leans against a house, reaching a point 14 ft above the ground. How far is the foot of the ladder from the bottom of the house?

62. How long must a wire be to reach from the top of a 12-ft pole to a point on the ground 8 ft from the pole?

11-9

To solve an equation with radicals, square both sides of the equation. You must always check for **extraneous solutions,** which are not solutions to the original equation.

Solve.

63. $\sqrt{x - 3} = 7$

64. $\sqrt{3x} - 8 = 13$

Solve. Use the formula $V = 3.5\sqrt{h}$.

65. A person can see 75.6 km to the horizon from the top of a mountain. How high is the mountain?

Simplify.

1. $\sqrt{64}$

2. $-\sqrt{25}$

Identify each number as rational or irrational.

3. $\sqrt{16}$

4. $-\sqrt{10}$

Simplify. The variables represent any real number.

5. $\sqrt{a^2}$

6. $\sqrt{36y^2}$

7. $\sqrt{(y+2)^2}$

Simplify. Assume that all variables are nonnegative.

8. $-\sqrt{40}$

9. $\sqrt{27}$

10. $\sqrt{25x-25}$

11. $\sqrt{x^6}$

12. $\sqrt{y^9}$

13. $\sqrt{(y+2)^4}$

Multiply.

14. $\sqrt{3} \cdot \sqrt{11}$

15. $\sqrt{3x} \cdot \sqrt{y}$

16. $\sqrt{\frac{2}{3}} \cdot \sqrt{\frac{5}{7}}$

Multiply and simplify. Assume that all variables are nonnegative.

17. $\sqrt{5} \cdot \sqrt{10}$

18. $\sqrt{3ab} \cdot \sqrt{6ab^3}$

19. $\sqrt{xy} \cdot \sqrt{y^2}$

Simplify. Assume that all variables are nonnegative.

20. $\sqrt{\frac{27}{12}}$

21. $\sqrt{\frac{144}{a^2}}$

22. $\sqrt{\frac{1}{36}}$

Divide. Assume that all radicands are nonnegative.

23. $\dfrac{\sqrt{36}}{\sqrt{12}}$

24. $\dfrac{\sqrt{75x^4}}{\sqrt{3}}$

25. $\dfrac{\sqrt{96y^3}}{\sqrt{16y}}$

Rationalize the denominator.

26. $\dfrac{\sqrt{2x}}{\sqrt{y}}$

27. $\dfrac{7}{\sqrt{2}}$

28. $\sqrt{\frac{2}{5}}$

Add or subtract.

29. $3\sqrt{18} - 5\sqrt{18}$

30. $\sqrt{5} + \sqrt{\frac{1}{5}}$

31. $\sqrt{20x^2} + \sqrt{45x^2}$

32. In a right triangle, the length of the hypotenuse is 91 and the length of one of the legs is 84. Find the length of the missing leg.

33. A slow pitch softball diamond is a square 65 ft on a side. How far is it from home to second base?

Solve.

34. $\sqrt{3x} + 2 = 14$

35. $\sqrt{y-2} + 3 = 9$

36. Use $r = 2\sqrt{5d}$. A car's rate (r) is 55 mi/h. How far (d) will it skid?

1-11 ▷ Cumulative Review

1-4 Evaluate.

1. $x - (x - 1) + (x^2 + 1)$ for $x = 10$
2. $xy + (xy)^2 + x + y$ for $x = 5$ and $y = 2$

1-5 Factor.

3. $121a + 88b$

4. $36x + 24y + 12z$

1-6 Write as an algebraic expression.

5. the product of x and 4 less than y divided by the difference of x and 8 times y
6. 19 more than the fifth power of a

2-3, 2-4 Simplify.

7. $-12.1 + 100.6 - 18.5$

8. $\frac{11}{9} - \frac{4}{18} + \frac{1}{6} - \frac{2}{3} + \frac{1}{2}$

2-5, 2-6 Multiply or divide.

9. $6(-12)$

10. $(-2.3)(-4.4)$

11. $\frac{-48}{-6}$

12. $\frac{18.6}{-6.2}$

2-7 Factor.

13. $-21x - 28w$

14. $144a^2 - 60b^2$

2-8 Simplify.

15. $-7(x - 1) + 2x$

16. $8[4 - (6x - 5)]$

3-4 Solve.

17. During the library marathon, Luis read twice as many books as Roger, but only half as many as Huong. If the three boys read 21 books, how many did Roger read?

3-5 Solve.

18. $5(a + 3) = 8a + 18$

19. $-3(m + 2) - 4 = -12 - (-2 + m)$

3-10 Translate to an equation and solve.

20. What percent of 1 is $\frac{1}{2}$?

21. 50 is 20% of what number?

22. 250% of what number is 6.25?

3-11 Translate to an equation and solve.

23. The ratio of apples to oranges sold in a local supermarket is 5 to 7. If 1320 pieces of fruit were sold in one week, how many were oranges?

4-4 Solve.

24. $8x - 2 \geq 7x + 5$ **25.** $-4x \geq 24$

26. $-3x < 30 + 2x$ **27.** $x + 3 > 6(x - 4) + 7$

4-5 Solve.

28. Amy received grades of 85, 87, 88, and 92 on her math tests. What must her grade be on her next test if her average is to be at least 90?

5-1, 5-2 Simplify.

29. $(a^2 b^4)(ab^5)$ **30.** $x^4 \cdot x^6 \cdot x$ **31.** $\frac{a^8 b^4}{a^5 b^3}$ **32.** a^0

33. 7^{-4} **34.** $(3^3)^2$ **35.** $(-3x^5 y^2)^3$ **36.** $\left(\frac{y^4}{2}\right)^3$

5-4 Write using scientific notation.

37. 346,000   **38.** 0.0000628

5-5 Collect like terms.

39. $10a^2 + 6a - 8a^2 + 3a - 2a^2 - 8a$

40. $(8m + 6n) - (12n + 7m) + 2(4m - 11n)$

5-9, 5-10 Multiply.

41. $(4 + 2b + c)(c - 1)$ **42.** $(2.5x - 0.3y)^2$

43. $(5x - 6y)(x + 2y)$ **44.** $(a + 2c + 1)(a + 2c - 1)$

45. $(h - 4k)^2$ **46.** $(2x + 7y)^2$

47. $(x^2 + 3)(x^2 - 3)$ **48.** $(4x + 2)(3x - 1)$

6-1 to 6-7 Factor.

49. $x^3y^3 + x^2y^2 - 4xy$ **50.** $a^8 + a^7 - a^6$ **51.** $4 - 9m^4$

52. $9x^2 - 9b^2$ **53.** $x^2 - 4x - 12$ **54.** $s^2 - 16s + 15$

55. $t^3 - 5t^2 + 6t$ **56.** $7x^2 - 6x - 1$

57. $20y^2 + 19y + 3$ **58.** $6y^2 + 9y - 15$

6-8 Solve.

59. $x^2 - 3x - 10 = 0$ **60.** $y(3y - 2) = 0$

7-5, 7-6 Write an equation for the line that satisfies each condition.

61. slope is 5, passes through the origin

62. passes through $(0, 3)$ and has x-intercept 6

63. slope is -1, y-intercept is -12

64. x-intercept is 7, y-intercept is -6

65. contains the points $(-1, 2)$ and $(2, 11)$

8-2, 8-3 Solve each system.

66. $6x + 3y = -6$ **67.** $2x + 3y = -3$
       $-2x + 5y = 14$ $y = 2x - 9$

8-4 to 8-6

68. Find two numbers such that their sum is 337 and their difference is 43.

69. The units digit of a certain number is one greater than twice the tens digit. If the digits are reversed, the new number is 36 more than the original number. Find the original number.

9-1

Let $A = \{0, 2, 4, 6, 8, 10, 12\}$ and $B = \{0, -2, -4, -6, -8, -10, -12\}$. Find the following.

70. $A \cup B$ **71.** $A \cap B$

9-3 Solve.

72. $|2x + 4| = 12$ **73.** $|2x - 5| = 7$

9-4 Solve and graph.

74. $|3y| < 12$ **75.** $|4x| \geq 20$

10-2 Multiply. Simplify the product.

76. $\dfrac{3y}{y+1} \cdot \dfrac{y+1}{2}$

77. $\dfrac{-4}{3y+3} \cdot \dfrac{y+1}{2}$

10-3 Divide. Simplify the quotient.

78. $\dfrac{2x-6}{5} \div \dfrac{x^2-9}{15}$

79. $\dfrac{x^2y+x^3y}{x} \div \dfrac{1+x}{x^2y}$

10-4, 10-5 Add or subtract. Simplify.

80. $\dfrac{4}{2x+8} + \dfrac{6}{x+4}$

81. $\dfrac{3y}{y+1} - \dfrac{2y+6}{y^2-1}$

82. $\dfrac{y^2}{x-2} + \dfrac{5}{x-2} - \dfrac{3x}{x-2}$

10-6 Solve.

83. $\dfrac{3}{x-3} - \dfrac{2}{x+3} = \dfrac{5}{x^2-9}$

84. $\dfrac{12}{y} - \dfrac{12}{y+1} = 1$

10-7

85. It takes two computers working together 10 hours to solve problems about a tail design for an airplane. One computer working alone can do the job in 16 hours. How long does it take the other computer to do the job alone?

10-9 Divide.

86. $x^2 + 5x - 28$ by $x + 8$

10-10 Simplify.

87. $\dfrac{\frac{1}{x}+3}{\frac{1}{x}-2}$

11-1, 11-2 Simplify.

88. $\sqrt{49}$ **89.** $-\sqrt{121}$ **90.** $\sqrt{64p^2}$

91. $\sqrt{(-7c)^2}$ **92.** $\sqrt{(x-2)^2}$ **93.** $\sqrt{x^2 - 6x + 9}$

11-3, 11-4 Simplify.

94. $-\sqrt{56}$ **95.** $\sqrt{x^8}$

96. $\sqrt{36b^5}$ **97.** $\sqrt{20x^4y^5}$

Multiply. Simplify where possible.

98. $\sqrt{6} \cdot \sqrt{8}$ **99.** $\sqrt{6a}\ \sqrt{3a^2b^2}$

100. $\sqrt{2b} \cdot \sqrt{5a + 3b}$ **101.** $\sqrt{x + 4y} \cdot \sqrt{2x - 5y}$

11-5 Divide. Simplify where possible.

102. $\sqrt{\dfrac{1}{81}}$ **103.** $\dfrac{\sqrt{200x^3}}{\sqrt{25x}}$

104. $\dfrac{6}{\sqrt{2}}$ **105.** $\sqrt{\dfrac{1}{9}}$

11-6 Add or subtract.

106. $6\sqrt{2} - 8\sqrt{2}$ **107.** $\sqrt{200} - \sqrt{8}$

108. $\sqrt{7} + \sqrt{\dfrac{1}{7}}$ **109.** $\sqrt{\dfrac{3}{4}} - \sqrt{\dfrac{4}{3}}$

11-7

In a right triangle, find the length of the side not given.

110. $c = 15, a = 9$ **111.** $a = 16, b = 30$

11-8

112. Larry wants to fit a circular piece of glass, 86 in. in diameter, through a doorway measuring 30 in. by 80 in. Will the glass fit through the doorway? What is the maximum diameter that could fit through the doorway?

11-9 Solve.

113. $\sqrt{x - 5} = 3$ **114.** $\sqrt{2y - 3} = \sqrt{y + 6}$

CHAPTER 12

What You'll Learn in Chapter 12

- How to recognize relations and functions and their graphs

- How to graph and use linear and quadratic functions

- How to use direct, inverse, joint, and combined variation

Skills & Concepts You Need for Chapter 12

1-1, 1-3 Evaluate for $x = 5$ and $y = -3$.

1. $-\frac{2x}{y}$ **2.** $x^2 + 1$ **3.** $y^3 - 4$

1-9 Evaluate.

4. $A = \frac{1}{2}bh$ for $b = 7$ and $h = 6$.

5. $I = Prt$ for $P = 1500$, $r = 0.12$, and $t = 2$.

3-7

6. Solve $A = \frac{1}{2}h(b_1 + b_2)$ for h.

7. Solve $C = 2\pi r$ for r.

3-9

8. The winner of an election won by a vote of 5 to 3, getting 1750 votes. How many votes did the loser get?

7-1

9. Plot these points on a coordinate plane.

     a. $(-2, 5)$ **b.** $(2, 3)$ **c.** $(4, 0)$

     d. $(-5, -6)$ **e.** $(0, -3)$ **f.** $(6, -1)$

7-3 Graph each equation.

10. $5y - 4 = 2x$ **11.** $3x + y = 8$

Relations and Functions

The thickness, tension, and length of a string all contribute to the wavelength of the tone that the string generates. In a harp, short strings produce shorter wavelengths and, therefore, higher pitches than long strings. The inverse variation function $p = \frac{k}{w}$ found on page 562 expresses this relationship.

12-1 ▷ Relations and Functions

What You'll Learn

1 To determine whether a given relation is a function

2 To find the value of a function

...And Why

To become familiar with function notation

Math in Action

The diagram below shows that the size of a motion picture on the screen is related to the distance of the movie projector from the screen.

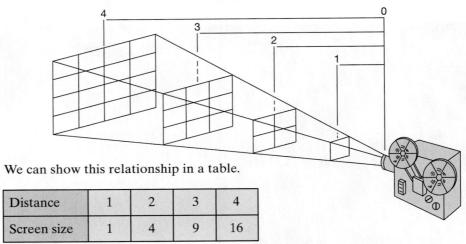

We can show this relationship in a table.

Distance	1	2	3	4
Screen size	1	4	9	16

We can also show this relationship using a formula. If d represents distance in units, and s represents screen size in squares, the formula $s = d^2$ shows the relationship between these quantities. We can see that for each value of d, we have one and only one value for s. In mathematics, this relationship is given a special name.

PART 1 Identifying Functions

Objective: Determine whether a given relation is a function.

The numbers in the table above could be written as **ordered pairs** (x, y) where x is the first member or coordinate and y is the second coordinate. We can express these numbers as a set of ordered pairs.

$$\{(1, 1), (2, 4), (3, 9), (4, 16)\}$$

Definition

A **relation** is a set of ordered pairs. The **domain** of a relation is the set of first coordinates. The **range** is the set of second coordinates.

The list and the set of ordered pairs below show the same relation. Each person is paired with a number representing his or her height.

Person	Height (cm)
Jorge	202
Carolyn	142
Elaine	138
Saul	142

{(Jorge, 202), (Carolyn, 142), (Elaine, 138), (Saul, 142)}

The domain is {Jorge, Carolyn, Elaine, Saul} and the range is {138, 142, 202}. Notice that for each person there is exactly one height. This is a special kind of relation called a **function.**

Definition

A **function** is a relation that assigns to each member of the domain exactly one member of the range.

The members of the domain can be called **inputs** and the members of the range can be called **outputs.** Arrows can be used to describe the function.

Domain	Range
(Set of inputs)	(Set of outputs)
Jorge	→202
Carolyn	→142
Elaine	→138
Saul	

EXAMPLE 1 Are the following relations functions?

f:

Domain	Range
a	→4
b	→0
c	

g:

Domain	Range
Cheese pizza	$9.75
Tomato pizza	$7.25
Meat pizza	$8.50

The relation f is a function, since each input is matched to only one output. The relation g is not a function, since the input Cheese pizza has more than one output.

EXAMPLE 2 Find the domain and range of each relation. Is the relation a function?

h: {(4, 0), (6, 0), (2, 0)} j: {(1, 5), (3, 7), (1, 7)}

For relation h, the domain is {2, 4, 6} and the range is {0}. The relation h is a function since each element of the domain is assigned to exactly one element of the range.

For relation j, the domain is $\{1, 3\}$ and the range is $\{5, 7\}$. The relation j is not a function since the domain value 1 is assigned to more than one range value.

Try This   Find the domain and range of each relation. Is the relation a function?

a. $\{(\text{Tom } 18), (\text{Sue}, 12), (\text{Sue}, 28)\}$ **b.**

PART **2** ## Function Notation

Objective: Find the value of a function.

The input-output process can also be thought of in terms of a function machine. Inputs from the domain are put into the machine. The machine then gives the proper output.

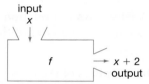

This function machine, for the relation f, assigns to each input x the output $x + 2$. It adds 2 to each input. The outputs for the inputs $8, -3, 0$, and 5 are as follows.

$$8 \to 10 \qquad -3 \to -1 \qquad 0 \to 2 \qquad 5 \to 7$$

The symbol $f(x)$ denotes the number assigned to x by the function f. If x is the input, $f(x)$ is the output. We can write the above results as follows where $f(x) = x + 2$.

$$f(8) = 8 + 2 = 10 \quad f(-3) = -3 + 2 = -1$$
$$f(0) = 0 + 2 = 2 \quad\; f(5) = 5 + 2 = 7$$

The outputs of a function are also called **function values.** For example, above we have $f(8) = 10$. We can say that "10 is the value of the function $f(x) = x + 2$ when $x = 8$."

Reading Math

The symbol *f(x)* is read "*f* of *x*." It is mathematical shorthand for "function of *x*."

EXAMPLE 3   Find the indicated outputs.

$f(t) = 2t^2 + 5$; find $f(-2)$, $f(0)$, and $f(3)$.

$$
\begin{aligned}
f(-2) &= 2(-2)^2 + 5 \\
&= 2 \cdot 4 + 5 \\
&= 13 \\
f(0) &= 2(0)^2 + 5 \\
&= 5 \\
f(3) &= 2(3)^2 + 5 \\
&= 2 \cdot 9 + 5 \\
&= 23
\end{aligned}
$$

Try This Find the indicated outputs.

c. $f(x) = x + 3$; find $f(5)$, $f(-8)$, and $f(-2)$.

d. $G(x) = 3x - x^2$; find $G(0)$, $G(-2)$, and $G(1)$.

e. $f(y) = 8y^2 + 3$; find $f(-1)$, $f(2)$ and $f\left(\frac{1}{2}\right)$.

f. $p(x) = 2x^2 + x - 1$; find $p(0)$, $p(-2)$, and $p(3)$.

12-1 Exercises

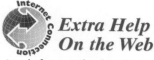
Extra Help On the Web

Look for worked-out examples at the Prentice Hall Web site.

www.phschool.com

A

Determine whether each relation is a function.

1.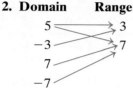

2.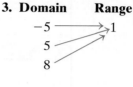

3.

Find the domain and range of each relation. Is the relation a function?

4. $\{(6, -6), (7, -7), (3, -3), (4, -4)\}$

5. $\{(a, b), (a, c), (d, e)\}$

6. $\{(4, 1), (7, 1), (-2, 4), (1, 1)\}$

Find the indicated output for each function machine.

7.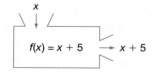

Find $f(3)$, $f(7)$, and $f(-9)$.

8.

$g(t) = t - 6 \longrightarrow t - 6$

Find $g(0)$, $g(6)$, and $g(18)$.

9.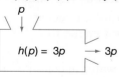

Find $h(-2)$, $h(5)$, and $h(24)$.

10.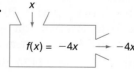

Find $f(6)$, $f\left(-\frac{1}{2}\right)$, and $f(20)$.

Find the indicated outputs for these functions.

11. $g(s) = 2s + 4$; find $g(1)$, $g(-7)$, and $g(6)$.

12. $h(x) = 19$; find $h(4)$, $h(-6)$, and $h(12)$.

13. $F(x) = 2x^2 - 3x + 2$; find $F(0)$, $F(-1)$, and $F(2)$.

14. $P(x) = 3x^2 - 2x + 5$; find $P(0)$, $P(-2)$, and $P(3)$.

Find the indicated outputs for these functions.

15. $h(x) = |x|$; find $h(-4)$, $h(4)$, and $h(-3)$.

16. $f(t) = |t| + 1$; find $f(-5)$, $f(0)$, and $f(-9)$.

17. $f(x) = |x| - 2$; find $f(3)$, $f(93)$, and $f(-100)$.

18. $g(t) = t^3 + 3$; find $g(1)$, $g(-5)$, and $g(0)$.

19. $h(x) = x^4 - 3$; find $h(0)$, $h(-1)$, and $h(3)$.

20. $f(m) = 3m^2 - 5$; find $f(4)$, $f(-3)$, and $f(6)$.

B

The cost of replacing a defective tire is a function of the tread depth. The chart below describes one such function. Refer to it for Exercises 21–24.

	Tread Depth in Millimeters								
	9	8	7	6	5	4	3	2	1
% charged	0%	20%	30%	40%	55%	70%	80%	90%	100%

21. Find the cost of replacing a tire whose regular price is \$64.50 and whose tread depth is 4 mm.

22. Find the cost of replacing a tire whose regular price is \$78.50 and whose tread depth is 7 mm.

23. Find the cost of replacing a tire whose regular price is \$67.80 and whose tread depth is 3 mm.

24. Find the cost of replacing a tire whose regular price is \$72.40 and whose tread depth is 5 mm.

25. The function $P(d) = 1 + \frac{d}{33}$ gives the pressure of salt water in atmospheres as a function of d, the depth in feet. Find the pressure at 20 feet, 30 feet, and 100 feet.

26. The function $R(t) = 33\frac{1}{3}t$ gives the number of revolutions of a $33\frac{1}{3}$ RPM record as a function of t, the time in minutes it is on the turntable. Find the number of revolutions at 5 minutes, 20 minutes, and 25 minutes.

27. The function $T(d) = 10d + 20$ gives the temperature in degrees Celsius inside the earth as a function of d, the depth in kilometers. Find the temperature at 5 km, 20 km, and 1000 km.

28. The function $W(d) = 0.112d$ gives the depth of water in centimeters as a function of d, the depth of snow in centimeters. Find the depth of water that results from these depths of snow: 16 cm, 25 cm, and 100 cm.

Find the range of each function for the given domain.

29. $f(x) = 3x + 5$ when the domain is the whole numbers less than 4.

30. $g(t) = t^2 - 5$ when the domain is the integers between -4 and 2.

31. $h(x) = |x| - x$ when the domain is the integers between -2 and 20.

32. *Critical Thinking* List all of the different relations between the elements in {a, b} and {1, 2}.

33. *Mathematical Reasoning* Suppose that a relation has exactly n elements in its domain. For each of the following conditions, is the relation *sometimes, always,* or *never* a function? Justify your answers.
a. The relation has exactly one element in its range.
b. The relation has exactly n elements in its range.
c. The relation has exactly $n + 1$ elements in its range.

Challenge

Use the functions $f(x) = 3x$ and $g(x) = -4x^2$ to find the following.

34. $f(8) - g(2)$ **35.** $f(0) - g(-5)$

36. $2f(1) + 3g(4)$ **37.** $g(-3) \cdot f(-8) + 16$

38. $f[g(-2)]$ **39.** $g[g(-1)]$

40. If $f(-1) = -7$ and $f(3) = 8$, find a linear equation for $f(x)$.

Mixed Review

Solve.   **41.** $x - y = -7$ **42.** $2x + 3y = 11$ **43.** $2y + 5x = 4$
              $x + y = 5$ $5y - x = 1$ $4x = 13 - 3y$

                                                                 8-1, 8-2, 8-3

Multiply.   **44.** $\sqrt{x}\sqrt{y}$ **45.** $\sqrt{y}\sqrt{y-2}$ **46.** $\sqrt{a}\sqrt{a+3}$

47. $\sqrt{m+n}\sqrt{m-n}$ **48.** $\sqrt{a+3}\sqrt{2a+1}$

49. $\sqrt{x-4} \cdot \sqrt{3x+2}$ *11-4*

Write an equation for the line that contains the given pair of points.

50. $(-2, 2)$ and $(3, 7)$ **51.** $(5, 1)$ and $(-7, 1)$

52. $(6, -1)$ and $(-2, -5)$ **53.** $(3, 3)$ and $(3, -1)$ *7-6*

Simplify.   **54.** $\sqrt{18}$ **55.** $\sqrt{144m^2}$ **56.** $\sqrt{20c^2}$ **57.** $\sqrt{32a^3}$ *11-2, 11-3*

Journal

Write a paragraph on the different meanings of the word *function.* Your paragraph should include real-world situations so that someone not studying algebra will understand the meaning of a mathematical function.

Operations with Functions

We can perform arithmetic operations on functions.

EXAMPLE Suppose $f(x) = 3x$ and $g(x) = 2x + 1$. Find $f(x) + g(x)$ and $f(x) \cdot g(x)$.

$f(x) + g(x) = 3x + (2x + 1) = 5x + 1$

$f(x) \cdot g(x) = 3x(2x + 1) = 6x^2 + 3x$

Suppose $f(x) = 5x$, $g(x) = \frac{1}{x}$, and $h(x) = \frac{2}{(x-3)}$. Find the following.

1. $f(x) - g(x)$ **2.** $f(x) \cdot g(x)$ **3.** $g(x) + h(x)$

4. $g(x) \cdot h(x)$ **5.** $g(x) \div h(x)$ **6.** $f(x) \cdot h(x)$

What You'll Learn

1 To recognize a function

2 To find the domain of a function

3 To graph a function

... And Why

To prepare for graphing linear and quadratic functions

Introducing the Concept: Graphs of Relations and Functions

Each equation below shows a relation between the variables x and y. Recall that a relation is a set of ordered pairs. Since we know how to graph ordered pairs, we know how to graph relations. Graph each of the following on separate coordinate axes.

- $y = x - 1$ for these replacements for x: $\{-2, -1, 0, 1, 2, 3\}$
- $y^2 = x + 1$ for these replacements for x: $\{-1, 0, 3, 8\}$
    (Hint: Be sure to find all values of y for each value of x.)

Recall that a function is a relation where there is a unique output value for each input value. In the relations above, the replacements for x are the input values, and the replacements for y are the output values.

Determine which of the relations above is a function and which is not. Can you determine from the graphs which is a function and which is not? How?

PART 1 Recognizing Functions

Objective: Recognize a function.

Writing Math

You should be able to recognize a function whether it is written as an equation, a set of ordered pairs, a graph, or with arrows.

We know that a function described by a set of ordered pairs in the form (x, y) has exactly one value for y for each value of x. Graphs A and B show the graphs of two relations. In Graph A, any vertical line that intersects the graph will intersect the graph in exactly one point. This means that there is only one y-value for each x-value. Therefore, Graph A is the graph of a function. The vertical dashed line in Graph B intersects the graph in two points. These points have the same x-coordinate but different y-coordinates. Graph B is *not* the graph of a function.

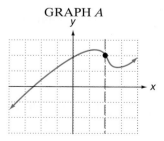
GRAPH A

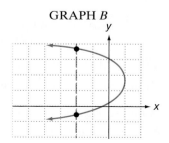
GRAPH B

EXAMPLE 1   Which of the following are graphs of functions?

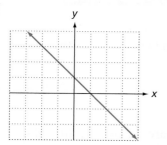

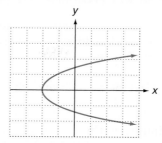

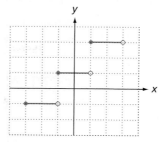

A function.
No vertical line crosses the graph more than once.

Not a function.
A vertical line crosses the graph more than once.

A function.
No vertical line crosses the graph more than once.

Try This   Which of the following are graphs of functions?

a.

b.

c.

We can use an equation to define a relation as the set of ordered pairs (x, y) that satisfy the equation. We can test the equation to see if the relation is a function, that is to see if it assigns exactly one y-value to each x-value.

EXAMPLE 2   Is the relation $x = |y|$ a function?

Begin by listing ordered pairs: $\{(1, -1), (1, 1), \ldots\}$

We can see immediately that the relation $x = |y|$ is *not* a function because it assigns two different y-values, -1 and 1, to the same x-value.

EXAMPLE 3   Is the relation $y = 3x$ a function?

For each real number x, the product $3x$ is a unique real number.

Thus, the relation $y = 3x$ is a function because it assigns exactly one y-value to each x-value.

Try This   Is the relation defined by each equation a function?

d. $y = x + 4$ **e.** $x = y^2$ **f.** $y = |x|$

When a function is defined by an equation and the domain of the function is not stated, we assume that the domain is all real numbers for which the value of the function is a real number.

EXAMPLES Find the domain of each function.

4 $f(x) = 2x - 5$

Since multiplication (by 2) and subtraction are defined for all real numbers, the domain of $f(x)$ is all real numbers.

5 $g(x) = \frac{1}{x - 2}$

$g(x)$ is not defined when $x - 2 = 0$. So, $x \neq 2$.
The domain is $\{x \mid x \neq 2\}$.

6 $h(x) = \sqrt{x + 6}$

$h(x)$ is not defined when $x + 6 < 0$. So $x + 6 \geq 0$, which occurs when $x \geq -6$.
The domain is $\{x \mid x \geq -6\}$.

Quick Review

To review set-builder notation, see Lesson 9-1.

Try This Find the domain of each function.

g. $f(x) = x^2 + 2$ **h.** $g(x) = \frac{1}{x + 5}$ **i.** $h(x) = \sqrt{x - 1}$

When the domain of a function has an infinite number of values, we graph the function by graphing some of the ordered pairs and connecting points.

EXAMPLE 7 Graph the function $g(x) = |x|$. Then find the range.

We cannot list all of the ordered pairs for this function, since there is an infinite number of real numbers. Thus we begin by listing some values of the function.

x	0	1	-1	2	-2	3	-3
$g(x)$	0	1	1	2	2	3	3

Now graph the ordered pairs. Connect the points to show all points whose coordinates are solutions of the equation $g(x) = |x|$.

Since the range consists of an infinite number of outputs, we use set-builder notation and the letter y. The range is $\{y \mid y \geq 0\}$.

$g(x) = |x|$

EXAMPLE 8 Graph the function $h(x) = 2x - 1$. Then find the range.

The domain of $h(x)$ is all real numbers. We recognize the form in which $h(x)$ is written as the equation of a line with slope 2 and y-intercept –1.

The range of $h(x)$ is all real numbers.

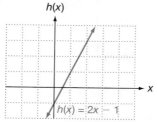

$h(x)$

$h(x) = 2x - 1$

Try This   Graph each function. Then find the range.

j. $f(x) = |x| - 1$ **k.** $g(x) = -x + 4$ **l.** $h(x) = -|x|$

12-2 Exercises

Internet Connection

Extra Help On the Web

Look for worked-out examples at the Prentice Hall Web site.

www.phschool.com

A

Graph each function.

1. $f(x) = x + 4$ where the domain is $\{-2, -1, 0, 1, 2, 3\}$.

2. $g(x) = x + 3$ where the domain is $\{-5, -4, -3, -2, -1, 0, 1\}$.

3. $h(x) = 2x - 3$ where the domain is $\{-3, -1, 1, 3\}$.

4. $f(x) = 3x - 1$ where the domain is $\{-1, 0, 2, 4, 6\}$.

Each relation below is a set of ordered pairs (x, y) that satisfy the given equation. Which of the relations are functions?

5. $y = -x$ **6.** $y = x^2$ **7.** $x = |y| - 1$

8. $x = y^2 + 2$ **9.** $y = |x + 3|$ **10.** $y = 6x + 9$

Which of the following are graphs of functions?

11.

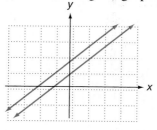

12.

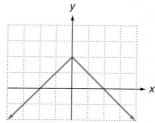

13.

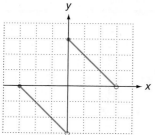

14.

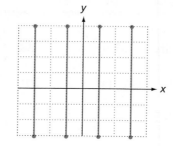

Find the domain of each function.

15. $f(x) = \frac{1}{3x}$ **16.** $g(x) = 10x$ **17.** $h(x) = \sqrt{x}$

18. $f(x) = \frac{5}{7-x}$ **19.** $g(x) = \sqrt{x+2}$ **20.** $h(x) = x^3$

21. $f(x) = \frac{1}{x+3}$ **22.** $g(x) = -2x - 9$ **23.** $h(x) = \sqrt{4-x}$

Graph each function. State the domain and the range.

24. $f(x) = x - 6$ **25.** $g(x) = 2|x|$ **26.** $h(x) = -2x + 1$

27. $f(x) = |x| - 3$ **28.** $g(x) = |x - 1|$ **29.** $h(x) = 4 - \frac{1}{2}x$

B

30. Here is the graph of a function. List the domain and the range of the function. Write an equation for this function.

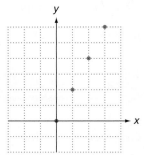

31. Draw the graph of $y = \frac{1}{x}$. Find the domain and range of the relation. Is this the graph of a function?

32. *Critical Thinking*   Sketch an absolute-value graph that is not a function.

33. [TEST PREP]   Which of the functions below has 0 in its domain?

A. $f(x) = \frac{1}{x+4}$ **B.** $f(x) = \frac{1}{x} - 4$

C. $f(x) = \sqrt{x-4}$ **D.** $f(x) = \frac{1}{\sqrt{x}}$

34. *Mathematical Reasoning*   When you graph a function by making a table and graphing ordered pairs, it is not always correct to connect the points you have graphed. Give an example of a function for which this is the case. (*Hint:* Consider a function for which the domain does not consist of all real numbers.)

Challenge

35. Describe the graph of any function of the form $g(x) = a|x| + b$.

36. For the function defined by $g(x) = a|x| + b$, what effect does changing the value of a have on the graph? What effect does changing the value of b have on the graph?

Mixed Review

Simplify.   **37.** $\frac{\sqrt{3}}{\sqrt{147}}$ **38.** $\frac{\sqrt{20}}{\sqrt{45}}$ **39.** $\frac{\sqrt{30}}{\sqrt{18}}$ **40.** $\frac{\sqrt{7}}{\sqrt{xy}}$ *11-5*

Divide.   **41.** $(x^2 - 9x + 20) \div (x - 4)$ **42.** $(y^4 - 9) \div (y - 3)$ *10-9*

Simplify.   **43.** $\frac{x^2 + 4x}{x+3} - \frac{3x+1}{x+3} - \frac{5}{x+3}$ **44.** $\frac{3y}{y^2 - 25} - \frac{2}{y+5}$ *10-4, 10-5*

Linear Functions

Objective: Solve problems involving linear functions.

The graph at the right is the graph of the equation $y = x + 3$. We can see that for each value of x on the graph there is only one value for y. Therefore, the equation $y = x + 3$ defines a function, which we call a linear function.

Since the equation $y = x + 3$ defines a function, we can write this equation using function notation as $f(x) = x + 3$.

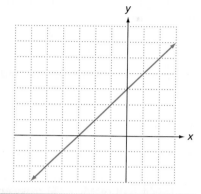

What You'll Learn

1 To solve problems involving linear functions

. . . And Why

To use linear functions as tools in a problem-solving plan

Definition

A function f defined by an equation of the form $y = mx + b$, where m and b are real numbers, is a **linear function** and can be written $f(x) = mx + b$.

We can see from the definition above that when the domain of a linear function is the set of real numbers, the graph is a line.

PROBLEM-SOLVING GUIDELINES
■ UNDERSTAND the problem
▢ Develop and carry out a PLAN
■ Find the ANSWER and CHECK

We can use the Problem-Solving Guidelines to help us solve problems involving linear functions.

The amount of antifreeze needed to protect a radiator against freezing to a temperature of −18°C is about half the capacity of the radiator. How much antifreeze is needed to protect a radiator with a capacity of 15 L?

■ **UNDERSTAND the problem**

Question: What amount of antifreeze is needed for a 15-L radiator?
Data: The amount needed is half the capacity.

▢ **Develop and carry out a PLAN**

Let x = the capacity of the radiator.
Let y = the amount of antifreeze needed.

We can now translate to an equation.

Amount needed is half of the capacity.

$$y = \frac{1}{2} \cdot x$$

This equation shows that for each value of x in the relation there is exactly one value for y. Therefore, the relation is a function. We can rewrite the equation to show this.

$$f(x) = \frac{1}{2}x$$

We can substitute 15 for x to find the amount of antifreeze needed.

$$f(15) = \frac{1}{2} \cdot 15$$
$$= 7.5$$

■ **Find the ANSWER and CHECK**

The amount of antifreeze needed is 7.5 L.
This is half of 15 L. The answer is reasonable.

Try This   Write a linear function. Then solve.

a. Frank's Baby-Sitting Service charges $3.50 plus $3.65 per hour. What is the cost of a nine-hour baby-sitting job?

12-3 Exercises

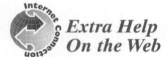

Extra Help On the Web

Look for worked-out examples at the Prentice Hall Web site.
www.phschool.com

A

Write a linear function describing each situation. Use the function to solve the problem.

1. The Triad Truck Rental Company charges $35 per day plus 21¢ per mile. Find the cost of renting a truck for a one-day trip of 340 miles.

2. A cable television provider charges $27 per month, plus $3.95 for any movies ordered. Find the total charge for a month in which 3 movies are ordered.

3. The cost of renting a chain saw is $5.90 per hour plus $6.50 for a can of gas. Find the cost of using the chain saw for 7.5 hours.

4. The airport parking garage charges $1.25 for the first hour and 70¢ for each additional hour. Find the cost of parking for 18 hours.

5. The cost of renting a floor waxer is $4.25 per hour plus $5.50 for the wax. Find the cost of waxing a floor if the time involved was 4.5 hours.

6. Sally rents a compact car for $29 per day plus 19¢ per mile. Compute the cost of a one-day trip of 280 miles.

7. A 40-cm spring will stretch (in cm) one third the weight (in kg) attached to it. How long will the spring be if a 15-kg weight is attached?

8. A 60-cm spring will stretch (in cm) one fifth the weight (in kg) attached to it. How long will the spring be if a 20-kg weight is attached?

B

9. A woman's phone bill is based on 15¢ per message unit charge plus a base charge. Her July bill was $18 and included 62 message units. Find the base charge. Her August bill included 76 message units. How much was her August bill?

10. The city's water department charges 23¢ per kiloliter (kL) plus a fixed charge. Mr. Ahmed's water bill for the use of 70 kL was $26.60. Find the fixed charge. The next month he used 85 kL. How much was his bill?

11. A parking garage in the city charges $2.00 for the first hour and $1.50 for each additional hour. Saturday and Sunday, the rates are decreased by 50%. How much does it cost to park a car from 5 p.m. on Friday until 2 a.m. on Saturday?

12. A truck rental company charges $41 per day plus 24¢ for each mile over 100 miles. Find the cost of renting a truck for three days during which it is driven 150 miles. How far can you drive in three days and keep the cost under $150?

13. A constant function is any function that can be described by an equation of the form $y = k$. Sketch the graph of a constant function.

14. *Critical Thinking* Make up a real-world example of a constant function.

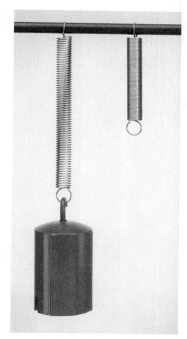

This 5-cm spring stretches (in cm) 0.02 times the weight (in grams) attached to it. How far does this spring stretch with a 200 g weight attached to it?

Challenge

15. Draw the graph of the function described by $f(t) = t^3$.

16. A restaurant has some fixed operating costs and some that vary with the number of people in attendance. If 4000 people visit the restaurant in one month, the operating costs are $1300. If 2800 people visit the restaurant in one month, the operating costs are $970. What would be the operating costs for this restaurant in a month where only 1500 people visit the restaurant?

Mixed Review

Add or subtract.   **17.** $3\sqrt{8} + 2\sqrt{2}$ **18.** $\sqrt{24} - \sqrt{6}$ *11-6*

Write using scientific notation.   **19.** 5, 470,000   **20.** 0.0034709   *5-4*

Simplify.   **21.** $\dfrac{6(x + 1)}{5x} \cdot \dfrac{35x}{21x + 21}$ **22.** $\dfrac{(y + 2)^3}{(y - 2)^2} \div \dfrac{(y + 2)^3}{(y - 2)^2}$ *11-4, 11-5*

Solve and graph.   **23.** $|3x| > 12$ **24.** $|2x| \geq 6$ **25.** $|x - 1| > 3$ *9-4*

⬦⬦   **Connections: Discrete Math**

Interval Graphs

In Chapter 7 you learned how to graph data using the Cartesian coordinate system. There are many other ways to represent data using graphs. One kind of graph, called an **interval graph,** can be used to solve problems involving the intersection of various time intervals. An interval graph is just a collection of points, called **vertices,** and line segments, called **edges,** connecting some of the vertices.

Interval graphs have been used to date artifacts from prehistoric sites in archeology, to identify genes, and to check the testimony of witnesses and suspects in crime investigations.

EXAMPLE

Several students spend Saturday morning at the library. It is a small library, and if two students are there at the same time, they are sure to see each other. Abdul arrives at 9 a.m. and stays for 2 hours. Becca arrives 45 minutes after 9. Carol arrives with Abdul and leaves with Becca, before Abdul is ready to leave. Doug arrives as Abdul is leaving and leaves at noon. Erik spends the shortest amount of time, but he sees Abdul, Becca, Carol, and Doug. Filipe sees Abdul but not Becca. How many students could Becca see at the library?

We represent each student with a vertex labeled by the first letter of his or her name. Whenever 2 students are at the library at the same time, we connect their vertices with an edge.

Since Abdul and Carol arrive at the same time, we connect their vertices. Becca arrives before Abdul leaves and leaves with Carol, so *B* should be connected with both *A* and *C*. Since Doug arrives as Abdul leaves, he misses Carol and Becca, so *D* is connected to *A* but not to *C* or *B*. Erik sees the first four students, so *E* is connected to *A*, *B*, *C*, and *D*. Filipe could arrive at 9 and leave before Becca arrives, in which case he would see Abdul and Carol.

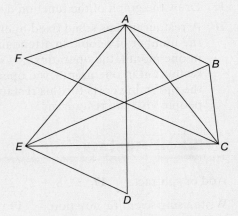

The graph indicates that Becca sees 3 other students: Abdul, Carol, and Erik.

We can also represent these data using a time line. The places where the intervals overlap represent the edges of the interval graph on the previous page. We know some of the endpoints (Becca's, Abdul's, and Carol's arrivals) but not some others (Becca's and Carol's departure). We can tell that Erik spends less than an hour and that his interval must overlap Becca's and Doug's. Check to see if this time line agrees with the interval graph on the previous page.

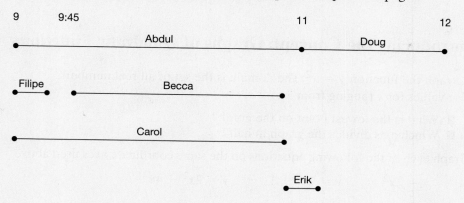

Problems

1. Check the information in the example and see if you can find another interval in which Filipe could visit the library. Draw a time line and an interval graph representing all the data if Filipe's interval is changed. Does your answer change the number of students Becca sees? Explain.

2. Six people are running the 1600-meter race in the Blackhawk conference. Below are the slow and fast times of each runner in minutes and seconds.

	Triggs	Carius	Nordvall	Oberle	Keller	Park
Slow	5:01	4:50	4:43	4:40	4:47	4:50
Fast	4:48	4:42	4:34	4:33	4:39	4:41

Assume that each runner's time is within his time interval.

a. Make an interval graph for the data. Remember that when the intervals of 2 runners intersect, you connect their vertices with an edge.

b. Make a time line representing the data.

c. Would it be possible for Triggs to beat Carius?

d. Would it be possible for Park to beat Oberle?

e. Would it be possible for Carius, Triggs, and Keller to finish first, second, and third?

f. Would it be possible for Nordvall to win?

12-4 ▷ Quadratic Functions

Objective: Graph quadratic functions.

What You'll Learn

1 To graph quadratic functions

. . . And Why

To find the vertex of a graph of a quadratic function

Introducing the Concept: Graphs of Quadratic Functions

Graph the function $y = x^2$. The domain is the set of all real numbers. Use values for x ranging from 3 to -3.

■ What is the lowest point on the graph?
■ Which axis divides the graph in half?

Graph each of the following equations on the same coordinate axes used above.

$$y = 2x^2 \qquad y = 2x^2 + 1 \qquad y = 2x^2 - 4x$$

■ How is the graph of $y = 2x^2$ related to the graph of $y = x^2$?

■ How is the graph of $y = 2x^2 + 1$ related to the graph of $y = 2x^2$?

■ How is the graph of $y = 2x^2 - 4x$ related to the graph of $y = 2x^2$?

■ How is the graph of $y = 2x^2 + 1$ related to the graph of $y = 2x^2 - 4x$?

The graph at the right is the graph of the equation $y = 2x^2 + 5x + 3$. We can see that for each value of x on the graph, there is exactly one value for y. Therefore, the equation $y = 2x^2 + 5x + 3$ defines a function. This equation is an example of a quadratic function. We can write $f(x) = 2x^2 + 5x + 3$.

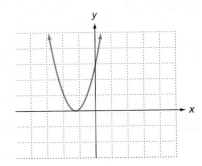

Definition

A function f defined by an equation of the form $y = ax^2 + bx + c$, where $a, b,$ and c are real numbers and $a \neq 0$, is a **quadratic function** and can be written $f(x) = ax^2 + bx + c$.

We can graph a quadratic function by making a table of values and graphing the ordered pairs. When the domain of the function is the set of real numbers, the graph is a **parabola.**

EXAMPLE 1   Graph the quadratic function $f(x) = 2x^2$. State the domain and the range.

Graph the ordered pairs (x, y) or $(x, f(x))$. The domain is all real numbers.

x	f(x)
−2	8
−1	2
0	0
1	2
2	8

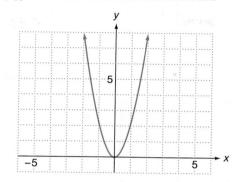

The range is $\{y \mid y \geq 0\}$.

Try This

a. Graph the quadratic function $f(x) = 3x^2 - 5$.

In Example 1, the point $(0, 0)$ on the graph is called the vertex of the parabola. The **vertex** is the maximum or the minimum point of a parabola. In Example 1, the vertex is the minimum point.

If you fold the graph so the two sides of the parabola coincide, then the fold line is the **axis of symmetry.** The y-axis is the axis of symmetry for the graph in Example 1. Notice in Example 1, the points, other than the vertex, occur in pairs that have the same y-coordinate.

Parabolas defined by equations of the form $y = ax^2$ will always have the vertex at the origin and the axis of symmetry will be the y-axis. We can use the following to find the vertex and the axis of symmetry for quadratic functions of the form $y = f(x) = ax^2 + bx + c$.

Vertex and Axis of Symmetry

For a parabola defined by the equation $y = ax^2 + bx + c$,

1. the x-coordinate of the vertex is $-\frac{b}{2a}$.

2. the axis of symmetry is the line $x = -\frac{b}{2a}$.

EXAMPLE 2   Graph the function $f(x) = -x^2 + 2x + 3$.

First find the vertex and the axis of symmetry.

x-coordinate of the vertex: $-\frac{b}{2a} = -\frac{2}{2(-1)} = 1$

Substitute the x-coordinate of the vertex into the original equation. Solve for y.

$$y = -x^2 + 2x + 3$$
$$= -(1)^2 + 2(1) + 3$$
$$y = 4$$

vertex: $(1, 4)$

The axis of symmetry is the line $x = 1$.
Now choose points on both sides of the vertex and graph the parabola.

x	y
-1	0
0	3
1	4
2	3
3	0

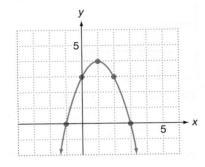

Try This   Graph each function.

b. $f(x) = -2x^2 + 4x + 1$ **c.** $g(x) = x^2 - 3x + 1$

In Example 2, the x-intercepts of the graph of $f(x) = -x^2 + 2x + 3$ are -1 and 3. We can also find find the x-intercepts by setting the function equal to zero and solving:

$$-x^2 + 2x + 3 = 0$$
$$(x + 1)(-x + 3) = 0 \qquad \text{Factoring}$$
$$x = -1, 3$$

Try This   Find the x-intercepts of each function.

d. $f(x) = x^2 - 5x + 6$ **e.** $g(x) = -x^2 + 3x + 4$

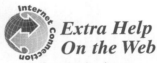

**Extra Help
On the Web**

Look for worked-out examples at the Prentice Hall Web site.
www.phschool.com

12-4 Exercises

A

Graph each function. State the domain and range.

1. $f(x) = -3x^2$ **2.** $f(x) = 3x^2$ **3.** $f(x) = 2x^2$

4. $f(x) = -2x^2$ **5.** $f(x) = \frac{1}{4}x^2$ **6.** $f(x) = 8x^2$

7. $f(x) = x^2 - 3$ **8.** $f(x) = -x^2 + 3$ **9.** $f(x) = 2x^2 - 1$

Graph each function.

10. $f(x) = x^2 + x - 6$

11. $f(x) = -x^2 + x - 1$

12. $f(x) = 8 - x - x^2$

13. $y = x^2 + 10x + 25$

14. $y = 2x^2 + 4x - 1$

15. $y = x^2 + 5$

Find the x-intercepts of the graph of each function.

16. $f(x) = x^2 - 3x - 10$

17. $y = x^2 + 2x$

18. $g(x) = -x^2 + 10x - 21$

19. $y = x^2 - 8x + 16$

20. $y = 2x^2 - 9x + 10$

21. $h(x) = -x^2 - 11x - 18$

B

22. Graph $f(x) = x^2 - 6x + 8$. What are the roots of $x^2 - 6x + 8$?

23. Graph $f(x) = -x^2 + x + 2$. What are the roots of $-x^2 + x + 2$?

24. For the graph of a linear function $f(x) = mx + b$, we know the y-intercept is b. Examine the graphs of the functions in Exercises 7–15. Describe the y-intercept of the graph of a quadratic function.

25. The graph of a quadratic function opens upward or opens downward. Examine the graphs in Exercises 7–15. What is true about functions whose graphs open upward? Downward?

Determine if the graph of each equation opens upward or downward.

   a. $y = 2x^2$ **b.** $y = -x^2 + 8$ **c.** $y = 5 + 3x - x^2$

26. The graph of each quadratic function has either a high point (maximum) or low point (minimum). Examine the graphs in Exercises 7–15. What types of graphs have a maximum or minimum?

27. Determine the minimum or maximum point for each equation. Indicate whether it is a minimum or maximum.

   a. $y = 3x^2 - 4$ **b.** $y = -x^2 + 7$ **c.** $y = 2 + 3x - 6x^2$

28. Find the axis of symmetry for each parabola graphed in Exercises 7–15.

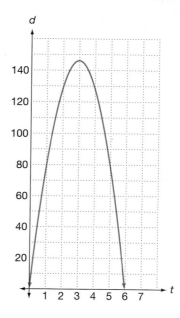

When a projectile is thrown into the air with an initial vertical velocity of r feet per second, its distance (d), in feet, above its starting point t seconds after it is thrown is approximately

$$d = rt - 16t^2$$

For a projectile launched from the ground with an initial upward velocity of 96 feet per second, the function is

$$d = 96t - 16t^2$$

Use the graph of this quadratic function to answer Exercises 29–31.

29. How many seconds after launch is the projectile 128 feet above the ground?

30. When does the projectile reach its maximum height? What is this height?

31. How many seconds after launch does the projectile return to the ground?

32. Multi-Step Problem To go over a tree, a golfer uses a 7-iron to hit the ball with an initial upward velocity of 80 feet per second.

    a. Write a quadratic function that gives the height of the ball t seconds after it is hit.

    b. Graph the function you found in part (a).

    c. How high will the ball be after 1 second? 2 seconds?

    d. After how many seconds will the ball be at its maximum height?

    e. What is the approximate maximum height the ball will reach?

33. Critical Thinking Use the same set of axes. Graph $y = x^2$, $y = 2x^2$, $y = 3x^2$, and $y = \frac{1}{2}x^2$. Describe the change in the graph of a quadratic function $y = ax^2$ as $|a|$ changes.

Challenge

34. Graph the equation $y = x^2 - x - 6$. Use your graph to approximate the solutions of $x^2 - x - 6 = 2$. (Hint: Graph $y = 2$ on the same set of axes as your graph of $y = x^2 - x - 6$.)

35. Graph $y = 2x^2 - 4x + 7$. Use the graph to approximate the solutions of $2x^2 - 4x + 7 = 0$. (Hint: Find the values of x when y is 0.)

36. What is the largest rectangular area that can be enclosed with 36 ft of fence?

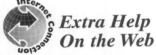

Extra Help On the Web

Look for worked-out examples at the Prentice Hall Web site.
www.phschool.com

Mixed Review

Write using decimal notation. **37.** 5.115×10^{-7} **38.** 4.7933×10^5 *5-4*

Solve. **39.** $\sqrt{x} = 17$ **40.** $\sqrt{2y - 1} = 9$ **41.** $11 - \sqrt{x + 1} = 2$

42. $2\sqrt{2x} = 20$ **43.** $\sqrt{3x + 4} = 5$ **44.** $5 + \sqrt{2x - 1} = 8$ *11-9*

Add or subtract. **45.** $\sqrt{\frac{5}{7}} - \sqrt{\frac{7}{5}}$ **46.** $x - \frac{x}{\sqrt{x}}$ **47.** $\sqrt{\frac{2}{5}} + \sqrt{\frac{1}{15}}$ *11-6*

Find the indicated outputs for these functions.

48. $f(m) = 2m - 1$; find $f(-1)$, $f(4)$, $f(2)$, and $f(-11)$

49. $g(x) = -3x + 5$; find $g(2)$, $g(-2)$, $g(0)$, and $g(5)$ *12-1*

Simplify. **50.** $\sqrt{36}$ **51.** $\sqrt{(x - 5)^2}$ **52.** $\sqrt{(-5y)^2}$ **53.** $\sqrt{243m^3}$ *11-2*

◇ Connections: Geometry

What is the largest rectangular area that can be enclosed with 16 ft of fence?

$$2w + 2l = 16$$
$$w + l = 8$$
$$w = 8 - l$$

Substitute for w in the formula for the area of a rectangle: $A = lw$. Graph the resulting quadratic function and find its maximum.

Direct Variation

Introducing the Concept: Direct Variation

The distance a bicycle travels varies as the rate of the bicycle and the time traveled. Suppose a bicycle travels at a constant rate of 10 km/h. Then the distance it travels will vary depending only on time. The table below shows the distance (d) a bicycle travels for several times (t) traveling at a rate of 10 km/h.

t (hours)	1	2	3	4
d (km)	10	20	30	40

We can see that the distance increases as the time increases. We can say that the distance "varies directly" as the time traveled. We can write

$$d = 10t$$

PART 1 Equations of Direct Variation

Objective: Give an equation of direct variation.

In an equation of the form $y = kx$, the variables are directly proportional or vary directly. If x is tripled, y is tripled. If x is halved, y is halved.

Definition

An equation of the form $y = kx$, where k is a nonzero constant, expresses **direct variation.** k is called the **constant of variation.**

When there is direct variation, $y = kx$, the constant of variation can be found if one pair of values of x and y is known.

EXAMPLE 1

Find an equation of direct variation where y varies directly as x. One pair of values is $y = 7$ when $x = 25$.

We substitute to find k.

$$y = kx$$
$$7 = k \cdot 25$$

What You'll Learn

 1 To give an equation of direct variation

2 To solve problems involving direct variation

. . . And Why

To become familiar with one of the types of variation

$\frac{7}{25} = k$, or $k = 0.28$

Then the equation of variation is $y = 0.28x$.

The relation given by $y = 0.28x$ is a function. Therefore, we can also write $f(x) = 0.28x$ as the equation of direct variation.

Try This   Find an equation of variation where y varies directly as x. One pair of values is given.

a. $y = 84$ when $x = 12$

b. $y = 50$ when $x = 80$

PART 2 Solving Problems

Objective: Solve problems involving direct variation.

EXAMPLE 2

The weight (J) of an object on Jupiter varies directly as its weight (E) on Earth. An object that weighs 225 lb on Earth has a weight of 594 lb on Jupiter. What is the weight on Jupiter of an object that has a weight of 115 lb on Earth?

First find an equation of direct variation. We substitute to find k. Then we can use our equation to find J for any value of E.

$$J = kE$$
$$594 = k \cdot 225$$
$$\frac{594}{225} = k$$
$$2.64 = k$$

The equation of variation is $J = 2.64E$.

Use the equation to find the weight on Jupiter of the 115 lb object.

$$J = 2.64E$$
$$J = 2.64(115)$$
$$J = 303.6$$

The object would have a weight of 303.6 lb on Jupiter.

Try This

c. The cost (c) of operating a TV varies directly as the number (n) of hours it is in operation. It costs $14.00 to operate a standard-size color TV continuously for 30 days. At this rate, about how much would it cost to operate the TV for 1 day? 1 hour?

d. The weight (V) of an object on Venus varies directly as its weight (E) on Earth. A person weighing 120 lb on Earth would weigh 106 lb on Venus. How much would a person weighing 150 lb on Earth weigh on Venus?

12-5 Exercises

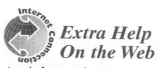

Extra Help On the Web
Look for worked-out examples at the Prentice Hall Web site.
www.phschool.com

A

Find an equation of variation where y varies directly as x, and the following are true.

1. $y = 28$ when $x = 7$

2. $y = 30$ when $x = 8$

3. $y = 0.7$ when $x = 0.4$

4. $y = 0.8$ when $x = 0.5$

5. $y = 400$ when $x = 125$

6. $y = 630$ when $x = 175$

7. $y = 200$ when $x = 300$

8. $y = 500$ when $x = 60$

Solve.

9. A person's paycheck (p) varies directly as the number (h) of hours worked. For working 15 hours, the pay is $236.25. Find the pay for 35 hours of work.

10. The number (b) of bolts a machine can make varies directly as the time it operates. It can make 6578 bolts in 2 hours. How many can it make in 5 hours?

11. The number (n) of servings of meat that can be obtained from a turkey varies directly as its weight (w). A turkey weighing 22 lb yields 40 servings of meat. How many servings can be obtained from a 14-lb turkey?

12. The number (n) of servings of meat that can be obtained from round steak varies directly as the weight (w). From 9 kg of round steak one can get 70 servings of meat. How many servings can one get from 12 kg of round steak?

13. The weight (M) of an object on the moon varies directly as its weight (E) on Earth. A person who weighs 115 lb on Earth weighs 19 lb on the moon. How much would a person who weighs 150 lb on Earth weigh on the moon?

14. The weight (M) of an object on Mars varies directly as its weight (E) on Earth. A person who weighs 115 lb on Earth weighs 44 lb on Mars. How much would a person who weighs 150 lb on Earth weigh on Mars?

15. The number of kg of water (W) in a human body varies directly as the total body weight (B). A person who weighs 75 kg contains 54 kg of water. How many kilograms of water are in a person weighing 95 kg?

16. The amount (A) that a family gives to charity varies directly as its income (I). Last year, the family earned $32,000 and gave $2560 to charity. How much will they give if they make $42,000 this year?

17. The distance between two cities is 1500 miles. They are shown to be 6 in. apart on a globe. What is the actual distance between two cities that are shown to be 10 inches apart on the globe?

18. The volume inside a balloon varies directly as the temperature. The volume of the balloon is 3 L at a temperature of 300° Kelvin. What is the volume if the temperature rises to 350° Kelvin?

B

Which of the following vary directly?

19. the amount of a gas in a tank in liters and the amount in gallons

20. the temperature in Fahrenheit degrees and in Celsius

21. the price per pound of carrots and the number of pounds

22. the total price of tomatoes and the number of pounds

23. a number and its reciprocal

Write an equation of direct variation for each situation.

24. The perimeter (P) of an equilateral polygon varies directly as the length of a side (S).

25. The circumference of a circle (C) varies directly as the radius (r).

26. The number of bags (B) of peanuts sold at a baseball game varies directly as the number (N) of people in attendance.

27. The cost (C) of building a new house varies directly as the area (A) of the floor space of the house.

28. *Critical Thinking*   Describe the graph of an equation of direct variation ($y = kx$). What is the relationship between k, the constant of variation and the graph of the equation?

Challenge

Write an equation of variation to describe these situations.

29. In a stream, the amount of salt (S) carried varies directly as the sixth power of the speed (V) of the stream.

30. The square of the pitch (P) of a vibrating string varies directly as the tension (t) on the string.

31. The surface area (A) of a sphere varies directly as the square of the radius (r).

Mixed Review

Determine the replacements for the variables that give real numbers.

32. $\sqrt{5t}$ **33.** $\sqrt{3x^2}$ **34.** $\sqrt{a - 7}$ **35.** $\sqrt{3m - 1}$

36. $\sqrt{y^2 + 3}$ **37.** $\sqrt{x^2 - 4x + 4}$ **38.** $\sqrt{a^2 + 6a + 9}$ *11-1*

Rationalize the denominator.   **39.** $\dfrac{\sqrt{y}}{\sqrt{xy}}$ **40.** $\dfrac{\sqrt{15x^3y^2}}{\sqrt{5x^2y}}$ **41.** $\dfrac{\sqrt{18m^2n}}{\sqrt{16n}}$ *11-5*

In a right triangle, find the length of the side not given.

42. $a = 7, c = 14$ **43.** $a = 10, b = 10$ **44.** $b = 12, c = 15$ *11-7*

Find the indicated outputs for these functions.

45. $f(t) = 2t^2 - 10$; find $f(1), f(-2), f(5), f(-4)$

46. $g(c) = |c| - 3$; find $g(1), g(5), g(-3), g(-7)$ *12-1*

Inverse Variation

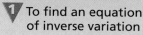
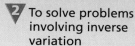
Introducing the Concept: Inverse Variation

he table below shows the time (t) needed for a trip of 10 km traveling at different rates (r).

r (km/h)	10	20	30	40
time (h)	1	$\frac{1}{2}$	$\frac{1}{3}$	$\frac{1}{4}$

We can see that the time decreases as the rate increases. We can say that the time "varies inversely" as the rate. We can write

$$t = \frac{10}{r}$$

PART 1 Equations of Inverse Variation

Objective: Find an equation of inverse variation.

In an equation of the form $y = \frac{k}{x}$, the variables are inversely proportional or vary inversely. If x is tripled, y is divided by 3. If x is halved, y is doubled.

Definition

An equation of the form $y = \frac{k}{x}$, where k is a constant, expresses **inverse variation.**

EXAMPLE 1 Find an equation of variation where y varies inversely as x. One pair of values is $y = 145$ when $x = 0.8$.

We substitute to find k.

$$y = \frac{k}{x}$$
$$145 = \frac{k}{0.8}$$
$$(0.8)145 = k$$
$$116 = k$$

The equation of variation is $y = \frac{116}{x}$.

The relation given by $y = \frac{116}{x}$ is a function. Therefore, we can also write $f(x) = \frac{116}{x}$ as the equation of inverse variation.

What You'll Learn

1 To find an equation of inverse variation

2 To solve problems involving inverse variation

... And Why

To become familiar with another type of variation

Try This   Find an equation of variation where *y* varies inversely as *x*.
One pair of values is given.

a. $y = 105$ when $x = 0.6$ **b.** $y = 45$ when $x = 20$

PART 2   Solving Problems

Objective: Solve problems involving inverse variation.

The thickness, tension, and length of a string all contribute to the wavelength of the tone that the string generates. In a harp, short strings produce shorter wavelengths and, therefore, higher pitches than long strings. A harpist adjusts the pitch of individual strings using foot pedals.

EXAMPLE 2

The pitch (P) of a musical tone varies inversely as its wavelength (W). One tone has a pitch of 660 vibrations per second and a wavelength of 1.6 feet. Find the wavelength of another tone which has a pitch of 440 vibrations per second.

Find an equation of variation.

$$P = \frac{k}{W}$$

$$660 = \frac{k}{1.6}$$

$$1.6(660) = k$$

$$1056 = k$$

The equation of variation is $P = \frac{1056}{W}$.

Use the equation to find the wavelength of the second tone.

$$P = \frac{1056}{W}$$

$$440 = \frac{1056}{W}$$

$$440W = 1056$$

$$W = 2.4$$

The wavelength is 2.4 feet.

Try This

c. The time (t) required to drive a fixed distance varies inversely as the speed (r). It takes 5 hours at 60 km/h to drive a fixed distance. How long would it take to drive the same distance at 40 km/h?

d. The time (t) required to do a certain job varies inversely as the number of people (n) working (assuming all work at the same rate). It takes 4 hours for 20 people working together to wash and wax the floors in a building. How long would it take 25 people working together to complete the same job?

12-6 Exercises

Extra Help On the Web

Look for worked-out examples at the Prentice Hall Web site.
www.phschool.com

A

Find an equation of variation where y varies inversely as x. One pair of values is given.

1. $y = 25$ when $x = 3$
2. $y = 45$ when $x = 2$
3. $y = 8$ when $x = 10$
4. $y = 7$ when $x = 10$
5. $y = 0.125$ when $x = 8$
6. $y = 6.25$ when $x = 0.16$
7. $y = 42$ when $x = 25$
8. $y = 42$ when $x = 50$
9. $y = 0.2$ when $x = 0.3$
10. $y = 0.4$ when $x = 0.6$
11. $y = 0.8$ when $x = 4$
12. $y = 80$ when $x = 0.7$
13. $y = \frac{2}{5}$ when $x = \frac{5}{2}$
14. $y = \frac{4}{3}$ when $x = \frac{3}{2}$

Solve.

15. It takes 16 hours for 2 people to resurface a gym floor. How long would it take 6 people to do the job?

16. It takes 4 hours for 9 cooks to prepare a school lunch. How long would it take 8 cooks to prepare the lunch?

17. The volume (V) of a gas varies inversely as the pressure (P) upon it. The volume of a gas is 200 cubic centimeters (cm^3) under a pressure of 32 kg/cm^2. What will be its volume under a pressure of 20 kg/cm^2?

18. The current (I) in an electrical conductor varies inversely as the resistance (r) of the conductor. The current is 2 amperes when the resistance is 960 ohms. What is the current when the resistance is 540 ohms?

19. The time (t) required to empty a tank varies inversely as the rate (r) of pumping. A pump can empty a tank in 90 minutes at the rate of 1200 L/min. How long will it take the pump to empty the tank at 2000 L/min?

20. The height (H) of triangles of fixed area varies inversely as the base (B). Suppose the height is 50 cm when the base is 40 cm. Find the height when the base is 8 cm. What is the fixed area?

B

Write an equation of inverse variation for each situation.

21. The cost per person (C) of chartering a fishing boat varies inversely as the number (N) of persons sharing the cost.

22. The number (N) of revolutions of a tire rolling over a given distance varies inversely as the circumference (C) of the tire.

23. The amount of current (I) flowing in an electric circuit varies inversely with the resistance (R) of the circuit.

24. The intensity of illumination (I) from a light source varies inversely as the square of the distance (d) from the source.

25. <u>**TEST PREP**</u>   Which one of the following varies inversely?

    A. the cost of sending a letter within the U.S. and the distance it travels
    B. a runner's speed in a race and the time it takes to run the race
    C. the area of a circle and the radius
    D. the weight of a turkey and the cooking time

26. *Critical Thinking*   Suppose y varies inversely as x. If the value of x is doubled, what happens to the value of y? If the value of y is doubled, what happens to the value of x?

Challenge

Write an equation of variation for each of the following.

27. The force (F) needed to keep a car from skidding on a curve varies directly as the square of the car's speed (S) and its mass (m) and inversely as the radius of the curve (r).

28. For a horizontal beam supported at both ends, the maximum safe load (L) varies directly as its width (w) and the square of its thickness (t) and inversely as the distance (d) between the supports.

Mixed Review

Simplify.   **29.** $\sqrt{2x^2 - 20x + 50}$ **30.** $\sqrt{ac^3}\ \sqrt{a^2c}$ *11-3, 11-4*

Solve.   **31.** $\sqrt{x - 2} = 4$ **32.** $7 - \sqrt{x + 3} = 1$ *11-9*

Determine whether the given point is a solution of $3x + 4y > 2$.

33. $(-3, 1)$ **34.** $(2, 0)$ **35.** $(0, 1)$ **36.** $(-1, 1)$ *9-5*

Graph the function.   **37.** $f(x) = x - 3$ where the domain is $\{-3, -1, 0, 1, 3\}$ **38.** $g(x) = 2x - 5$ **39.** $h(x) = |x + 1|$ *12-2*

◈ Connections: Reasoning

In each set of figures, the first two have a particular relationship. Which figure ($a, b, c,$ or d) has the same relationship to the third figure?

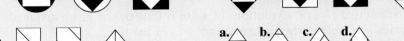

Joint and Combined Variation

Joint Variation

Objective: Find an equation of joint variation.

The formula for the area (A) of a triangle is $A = \frac{1}{2}bh$, where b is the base of the triangle and h is the height of the triangle. In this formula, the area varies directly as the base and the height of the triangle. We can say that the area of the triangle varies jointly as the base and the height.

Definition

An equation of the form $z = kxy$, where k is a nonzero constant, expresses **joint variation.**

EXAMPLE 1

Find an equation of joint variation where V varies jointly as B and h. One set of values for the relationship is $V = 35$, $B = 7$, and $h = 15$. Find V when $B = 18$ and $h = 6$.

We can write $V = kBh$ to show the joint variation.
Now we can substitute the given values to find the value of k.

$$V = k \cdot B \cdot h$$
$$35 = k \cdot 7 \cdot 15$$
$$35 = k \cdot 105$$
$$k = \frac{35}{105} = \frac{1}{3}$$

The equation for joint variation is $V = \frac{1}{3}Bh$.

We can now substitute the given values for B and h and solve for V.

$$V = \frac{1}{3}Bh$$
$$V = \frac{1}{3} \cdot 18 \cdot 6$$
$$V = 36$$

Try This

a. Find an equation of joint variation where w varies jointly as x, y, and z. One set of values is $w = 36$, $x = 3$, $y = 5$, and $z = 6$. Find the value of w when $x = 2$, $y = 8$, and $z = 5$.

What You'll Learn

1 To find an equation of joint variation

2 To solve problems involving combined variation

3 To solve problems involving joint variation

...And Why

To apply joint and combined variation to physical problems

Objective: Solve problems involving combined variation.

The formula $P = \frac{0.25W}{A}$ gives the recommended tire pressure for each tire for the total weight (W) of a car and the area (A) of the ground covered by each tire. The formula shows that the recommended tire pressure varies directly as the weight of the car and inversely as the area of the ground. The formula $P = \frac{0.25W}{A}$ expresses combined variation.

Definition

An equation of the form $z = \frac{kx}{y}$, where k is a nonzero constant, expresses **combined variation.**

EXAMPLE 2

Find an equation of combined variation where A varies directly as b and inversely as c. One set of values is $A = 4$, $b = 12$, and $c = 9$. Find A when $b = 7$ and $c = 3$.

We can write $A = \frac{kb}{c}$ to show the combined variation.

Now we can substitute to find the value of k.

$$A = \frac{kb}{c}$$

$$4 = k \cdot \frac{12}{9}$$

$$k = 3$$

The equation for combined variation is $A = \frac{3b}{c}$.

We can now substitute the given values for b and c and solve for A.

$$A = \frac{3b}{c}$$

$$A = 3 \cdot \frac{7}{3}$$

$$A = 7$$

Try This

b. Find an equation of combined variation where P varies directly as q and inversely as r. One set of values is $P = 0.064$, $q = 16$, and $r = 5$. Find P when $q = 12$ and $r = 10$.

Objective: Solve problems involving joint variation.

Joint variation has many real-world applications.

PROBLEM-SOLVING GUIDELINES
■ UNDERSTAND the problem
▢ Develop and carry out a PLAN
■ Find the ANSWER and CHECK

EXAMPLE 3

The volume of a pyramid varies jointly as the height of the pyramid and the area of its base. The volume of a pyramid with height 12 cm and base 5 cm^2 is 20 cm^3. Find the volume of the Great Pyramid whose height is 147 m and whose base has an area of 52,900 m^2.

We can write $V = kBh$ to show the joint variation. Now we can substitute the given values to find the value of k.

$$V = k \cdot B \cdot h$$
$$20 = k \cdot 5 \cdot 12$$
$$20 = k \cdot 60$$
$$k = \frac{20}{60} = \frac{1}{3}$$

The equation for the joint variation is $V = \frac{1}{3}Bh$.

We can now use this information to find the volume (in m^3) of the Great Pyramid. Substitute the values of B and h in the equation and solve for V.

$$V = \frac{1}{3}Bh$$

$$V = \frac{1}{3} \cdot 52,900 \cdot 147$$

$$V = 2,592,100$$

The volume of the Great Pyramid is 2,592,100 m^3.

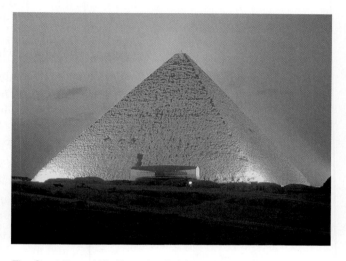

The Great Pyramid in Egypt has height 147 m and base area 52,900 m^2. The base of the Great Pyramid is a square. How long is each side of the base?

Try This

c. The temperature inside the chamber of a piston varies jointly as the pressure and the volume. The temperature is 300 Kelvin when the volume is 200 in.^{3} and the pressure is 100 pounds per square inch (lb/in.^{2}). Find the temperature when the pressure is 70 lb/in.^{2} and the volume is 400 in.^{3}

Extra Help
On the Web

Look for worked-out
examples at the Prentice
Hall Web site.
www.phschool.com

12-7 Exercises

A

Find an equation of joint variation. Then solve for the missing value.

1. r varies directly as s and t. One set of values is $r = 28$, $s = 7$, $t = 8$. Find r when $s = 12$ and $t = 9$.

2. m varies jointly as n and p. One set of values is $m = 86.4$, $n = 9$, and $p = 12$. Find m when $n = 20$ and $p = 6.5$.

3. q varies jointly as r and s. One set of values is $q = 2.4$, $r = 0.6$, and $s = 0.8$. Find q when $r = 1.6$ and $s = 0.1$.

4. a varies jointly as b and c. One set of values is $a = 1$, $b = 5$, and $c = 0.2$. Find a when $b = 2.4$ and $c = 0.01$.

5. x varies jointly as w, y, and z. One set of values is $x = 18$, $w = 2$, $y = 6$, and $z = 5$. Find x when $w = 5$, $y = 12$, and $z = 3$.

Find an equation of combined variation. Then solve for the missing value.

6. a varies directly as b and inversely as c. One set of values is $a = 14$, $b = 7$, and $c = 3$. Find a when $b = 4$ and $c = 8$.

7. m varies directly as n and inversely as p. One set of values is $m = 5$, $n = 2$, and $p = 4$. Find m when $n = 10$ and $p = 50$.

8. w varies directly as x and inversely as y. One set of values is $w = 3$, $x = 9$, and $y = 2$. Find w when $x = 15$ and $y = 5$.

9. p varies directly as q and inversely as r. One set of values is $p = 0.8$, $q = 8$, and $r = 7$. Find p when $q = 12$ and $r = 3$.

10. u varies directly as v and inversely as w. One set of values is $u = 5.75$, $v = 2.3$, and $w = 0.6$. Find u when $v = 0.5$ and $w = 0.8$.

B

11. A varies jointly as b and c and inversely as d. One set of values is $A = 0.525$, $b = 6$, $c = 7$, and $d = 8$. Find A when $b = 12$, $c = 7$, and $d = 3$.

12. W varies jointly as x and y and inversely as z. One set of values is $W = 112$, $x = 4$, $y = 8$, and $z = 0.2$. Find W when $x = 8$, $y = 10$ and $z = 4$.

13. The volume of a cone varies jointly as the height of the cone and the area of the base. The volume of a cone with height 15 cm and base 28 cm^2 is 140 cm^3. Find the volume of a cone with height 7 cm and base 12 cm^2.

14. A pitcher's earned run average (a) varies directly as the number of earned runs (r) allowed and inversely as the number of innings (i) pitched. Joe Price had an earned run average of 2.55. He gave up 85 earned runs in 300 innings. About how many earned runs would he have given up had he pitched 353 innings with the same average?

Use the following relationship: The lateral surface area of a cylinder varies jointly as the radius and height of the cylinder. A cylinder with radius 0.8 in. and height 6 in. has a lateral surface area of 30.2 in^2.

15. Find the height of a cylinder with radius 1.5 in. and lateral surface area 74.4 in^2.

16. Find the radius of a cylinder with height 6 cm and lateral surface area 111.6 cm^2.

17. *Critical Thinking*   The area of a circle varies directly as the square of the length of its diameter. What is the constant of variation?

18. *Error Analysis*   A student made the following incorrect statement. "If a pyramid has a square base and you double the length of the sides of the base and double the height, the volume of the new pyramid will be four times the volume of the original pyramid."
   a. Provide a counterexample to show that the statement is incorrect.
   b. Rewrite the statement with a corrected conclusion.

Challenge

19. Suppose y varies directly as x. What happens to the value of y if the value of x is doubled?

20. Suppose y varies directly as the square of x. What happens to the value of y if the value of x is doubled?

21. The stopping distance (d) of a car after the brakes are applied varies directly as the square of the speed (r). A car traveling 35 mi/h will travel about 106 ft after braking. What is the rate of a car that needs about 228 ft to stop?

22. The force of attraction of a body varies directly as its mass and inversely as the square of the distance from the body. A body of mass 10 kg has a force of attraction of 7.8 newtons at a distance of 20 m. How far away is the force of attraction of a 10 kg mass equal to 31.2 newtons?

Mixed Review

Rationalize the denominator.   **23.** $\dfrac{\sqrt{16}}{\sqrt{3}}$ **24.** $\dfrac{\sqrt{5}}{\sqrt{x}}$ **25.** $\dfrac{\sqrt{x}}{\sqrt{xy}}$

26. $\dfrac{\sqrt{18}}{\sqrt{2y}}$ **27.** $\dfrac{\sqrt{3x}}{\sqrt{12y}}$ **28.** $\dfrac{\sqrt{x^4y}}{\sqrt{xy^2}}$ **29.** $\dfrac{\sqrt{6c}}{\sqrt{8c^3}}$ **30.** $\dfrac{\sqrt{12cd}}{\sqrt{3c^4d^4}}$ *11-5*

In a right triangle, find the length of the hypotenuse.

31. $a = 10, b = 24$ **32.** $a = 6, b = 12$ **33.** $a = 24, b = 32$ *11-7*

Solve.   **34.** $\sqrt{2x + 3} = \sqrt{5x - 6}$ **35.** $-\sqrt{x} = 7$

36. $\sqrt{x + 7} = 2\sqrt{x - 5}$ **37.** $\sqrt{x + 30} = 3\sqrt{x - 2}$ *11-9*

Graph.   **38.** $h(x) = 3x - 2$ **39.** $f(x) = x^2 + 2$ *12-2, 12-4*

Application

Starting a Business

In the problems you have seen so far in this book, the data needed to find a solution have been given, and the question needed to be answered has been easily identified. Many real-world problems are not presented so conveniently.

In real-world situations you need to clarify, perhaps by asking many questions, exactly what you are being asked to do. You need to clarify the assumptions and collect the required data from a variety of sources. You may need to solve many subproblems before arriving at the final answer to the question. These problems are sometimes called situational problems.

PROBLEM-SOLVING GUIDELINES
■ UNDERSTAND the problem
▨ Develop and carry out a PLAN
■ Find the ANSWER and CHECK

The Problem-Solving Guidelines can be used to solve situational problems.

Situational Problem

You and three friends decide to start a summer business cleaning houses. You each want to save $500 for a trip at the end of the summer. You estimate that you will spend half a day cleaning each house, and you will clean each house once a week. You will need to purchase your own supplies and pay for transportation. You also may want spending money for other things during the summer.

Possible Assumptions

1. You do not have to pay for insurance for your business.
2. You will not hire others to work with you.
3. You each want $50 spending money.
4. You will each be able to work for two months.
5. You can sell your extra supplies at the end of the summer.

Possible Subproblems

1. How much will your expenses be for supplies that are reusable?
2. How much will your expenses be for consumable supplies?
3. How much will you charge per hour?
4. How much will you make for cleaning each house?
5. How much profit will you make for cleaning each house?

How many houses will you need to have for your business, and how much will you charge for cleaning a house?

12 ▷ Chapter Wrap Up

12-1

A **relation** is a set of ordered pairs; a **function** is a relation that assigns to each member of the **domain** (the set of first coordinates) exactly one member of the **range** (the set of second coordinates).

Are the following relations functions?

1. Domain   Range

-1 ⟶ 3
0 ⟶ 4
1 ⟶ 5

2. Domain   Range

-2 ⟶ 0
5 ⟶ 1
7 ⟶ 4

Find the indicated outputs for these functions.

3. $f(x) = 3x - 4$; find $f(2), f(0)$, and $f(-1)$

4. $g(t) = |t| - 3$; find $g(3), g(-5)$, and $g(0)$

5. $h(x) = x^3 + 1$; find $h(-2), h(0)$, and $h(-1)$

12-2

To graph a function, find some ordered pairs for the function, and plot the points. If the domain is the set of real numbers, then connect the points to show all the ordered pairs that belong to the function.

Graph each function with the given domain.

6. $f(x) = 2x + 3$ where the domain is $(-2, -1, 0, 1, 2)$

7. $g(x) = -3x$ where the domain is $(-4, -2, 0, 2, 4)$

Graph each function. State the domain and range.

8. $g(x) = x + 7$ **9.** $f(x) = x^2 - 3$ **10.** $h(x) = 3|x|$

Which of the following are graphs of functions?

11.

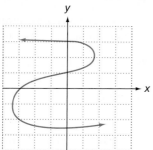

12.

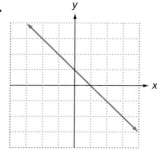

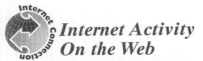
12-3

A function that can be described by $y = mx + b$ is a **linear function** and can be written $f(x) = mx + b$. You can use the Problem-Solving Guidelines to solve problems involving linear functions.

Solve.

13. A health club charges $30 for a one-month membership plus $1.50 for each aerobics class. Find the total cost for a month in which Adam attends 5 aerobics classes.

12-4

A function that can be described by $y = ax^2 + bx + c$ is a **quadratic function** and can be written $f(x) = ax^2 + bx + c$. If the domain of a quadratic function is the set of real numbers, then the graph of the function is a **parabola.** The x-coordinate of the **vertex,** the maximum or minimum point, is $-\frac{b}{2a}$.

Graph each function.

14. $f(x) = x^2 - 2$ **15.** $f(x) = \frac{1}{3}x^2$

12-5

An equation of the form $y = kx$, where k is constant, expresses **direct variation.** If one pair of values for x and y is known, substitute in the equation, $y = kx$, to find the value of k.

Find an equation of variation where y varies directly as x. One pair of values is given.

16. $y = 12$ when $x = 4$ **17.** $y = 4$ when $x = 8$

Solve.

18. A person's paycheck (P) varies directly as the number of hours (h) worked. The pay is $165 for working 20 hours. Find the pay for 30 hours of work.

12-6

An equation of the form $y = \frac{k}{x}$, where k is constant, expresses **inverse variation.** If one pair of values for x and y is known, substitute in the equation to find k.

Find an equation of variation where y varies inversely as x. One pair of values is given.

19. $y = 5$ when $x = 6$ **20.** $y = 0.5$ when $x = 2$

Solve.

21. It takes five hours for two washing machines to wash a fixed amount. How long would it take for ten washing machines to wash the same amount of clothes?

12-7

An equation of the form $z = kxy$, where k is a constant, expresses **joint variation.** An equation of the form $z = \frac{kx}{y}$, where k is a nonzero constant, expresses **combined variation.**

22. The area of a trapezoid varies jointly as its altitude and the sum of the bases. $A = ka(b_1 + b_2)$. If $A = 120$ when $a = 8$, $b_1 = 12$, and $b_2 = 18$,
   a. find the constant of variation.
   b. find A when $a = 6$, $b_1 = 8$, and $b_2 = 12$.

23. W varies jointly as x and y and inversely as the square of z. If $W = 189$, $x = 28$, $y = 16$, and $z = 8$,
   a. find the constant of variation.
   b. find W when $x = 24$, $y = 4$, and $z = 6$.

12 ▷ Chapter Assessment

1. $f(x) = \frac{1}{2}x + 1$; find $f(0)$, $f(1)$, and $f(2)$

2. $g(t) = -2|t| + 3$; find $g(-1)$, $g(0)$, and $g(3)$

Which of the following are graphs of functions?

3.

4.

5. Elena rents a car for $19 per day plus $0.20 per mile. Compute the cost of a 2-day trip of 310 miles.

Graph. State the domain and range.

6. $f(x) = x^2 + 4x + 4$ **7.** $f(x) = -x^2$

8. Find an equation of variation where y varies directly as x, and $y = 6$ when $x = 3$.

9. Find an equation of variation where y varies inversely with x and $y = 6$ when $x = 2$.

10. It takes 3 hours for 2 cement mixers to mix a certain amount. How long would it take 5 cement mixers to do the job?

11. y varies jointly with x and the square of z. One set of values is $y = 375$ when $x = 3$ and $z = 25$. Find y when $x = 8$ and $z = 6$.

12. x varies jointly with y and z and inversely with m. One set of values is $x = 2$ when $m = 3$, $y = 4$, and $z = 6$. Find x when $y = 7.5$, $m = 3$, and $z = 8$.

CHAPTER 13

Skills & Concepts You Need for Chapter 13

5-10 Multiply.

1. $(x - 5)^2$ **2.** $(3x + 1)^2$

6-8 Solve.

3. $x^2 - 6x = 0$ **4.** $x^2 - 5x + 6 = 0$

10-6 Solve.

5. $2x + \dfrac{8}{x} = 8$ **6.** $\dfrac{x - 2}{x + 2} = \dfrac{1}{4}$

11-3 Simplify.

7. $\sqrt{88}$ **8.** $\sqrt{20}$ **9.** $\sqrt{44}$ **10.** $\sqrt{32}$

11-5 Rationalize the denominator.

11. $\sqrt{\dfrac{7}{3}}$ **12.** $\sqrt{\dfrac{5}{2}}$ **13.** $\sqrt{\dfrac{1}{5}}$ **14.** $\sqrt{\dfrac{7}{8}}$

12-7 Graph the following quadratic functions.

15. $f(x) = x^2 - 1$ **16.** $y = -x^2 + 2$

Quadratic Equations

Water in the tallest stream reaches a height of $h = 20 + 84t - 16t^2$ feet at t seconds after leaving a nozzle on the fireboat. You can find the water's greatest height by finding the vertex of the parabola for $h = 20 + 84t - 16t^2$.

13-1 ▷ Introduction to Quadratic Equations

What You'll Learn

1 To write a quadratic equation in standard form

2 To solve an equation of the form $ax^2 + bx = 0$

3 To solve an equation of the form $ax^2 + bx + c = 0$

... And Why

To solve quadratic equations by factoring

Quick *Review*

Since −1 and 3 are values of x for which $x^2 - 2x - 3 = 0$, −1 and 3 are also roots of the quadratic polynomial $x^2 - 2x - 3$. See Lesson 6-8.

You learned in Chapter 12 that a quadratic function is a function that can be defined by an equation of the form $ax^2 + bx + c = y$, $a \neq 0$, and that the graph of a quadratic function is a parabola when the domain is the set of real numbers.

When $y = 0$ in the quadratic function $ax^2 + bx + c = y$, we have an equation of the form $ax^2 + bx + c = 0$. An equation that can be written in this form is called a quadratic equation.

Definition

An equation that can be written in the form $ax^2 + bx + c = 0$, where a, b, and c are real numbers and $a \neq 0$, is a **quadratic equation.**

We can graph the function $y = x^2 - 2x - 3$ as shown at the right. We can locate the points where $y = 0$.

The x-values at these points are −1 and 3 and are the solutions of the quadratic equation $0 = x^2 - 2x - 3$.

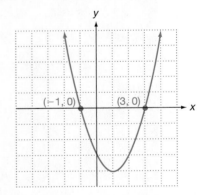

PART 1 Standard Form

Objective: Write a quadratic equation in standard form.

Quadratic equations may be written in various forms.

$$4x^2 + 7x = 5 \qquad 3x^2 = 7 \qquad 5x^2 = -4x$$

Work with quadratic equations is usually simplified when a quadratic equation is written in **standard form,** $ax^2 + bx + c = 0$.

EXAMPLES Write in standard form and determine a, b, and c.

1 $4x^2 + 7x = 5$
Standard form: $4x^2 + 7x - 5 = 0$; $a = 4$, $b = 7$, $c = -5$

2 $5x^2 = -4x$

Standard form: $5x^2 + 4x = 0$; $a = 5, b = 4, c = 0$

Try This   Write in standard form and determine a, b, and c.

a. $x^2 = 7x$ **b.** $3 - x^2 = 9x$ **c.** $5x^2 = -4$

PART
2   **Equations of the Form $ax^2 + bx = 0$**

Objective: Solve an equation of the form $ax^2 + bx = 0$.

When $c = 0$ in the standard form equation $ax^2 + bx + c = 0$, we have an equation of the form $ax^2 + bx = 0$. We can factor this equation and use the principle of zero products to find its solutions.

EXAMPLE 3   Solve.

$$20x^2 - 15x = 0$$
$$5x(4x - 3) = 0 \qquad \text{Factoring}$$
$$5x = 0 \quad \text{or} \quad 4x - 3 = 0 \qquad \text{Using the principle of zero products}$$
$$x = 0 \quad \text{or} \qquad x = \tfrac{3}{4}$$

Check: $\dfrac{20x^2 - 15x = 0}{}$

$$\begin{array}{c|c} 20(0)^2 - 15(0) & 0 \\ 0 - 0 & 0 \\ 0 & 0 \ \checkmark \end{array}$$

$$\dfrac{20x^2 - 15x = 0}{}$$

$$\begin{array}{c|c} 20\left(\tfrac{3}{4}\right)^2 - 15\left(\tfrac{3}{4}\right) & 0 \\ \tfrac{45}{4} - \tfrac{45}{4} & 0 \\ 0 & 0 \ \checkmark \end{array}$$

The solutions are 0 and $\tfrac{3}{4}$.

Any quadratic equation of the form $ax^2 + bx = 0$, or $x(ax + b) = 0$, always has 0 as one solution and $-\tfrac{b}{a}$ as the other solution.

Try This   Solve.

d. $3x^2 + 5x = 0$ **e.** $10x^2 - 6x = 0$

Quick *Review*

The principle of zero products says that if two factors have product zero, then at least one of the factors is 0. See Lesson 6-8.

Objective: Solve an equation of the form $ax^2 + bx + c = 0$.

We can also use the principle of zero products to solve equations of the form $ax^2 + bx + c = 0$, if $ax^2 + bx + c$ can be factored.

EXAMPLE 4 Solve.

$$y^2 - 5y + 6 = 6y - 18$$
$$y^2 - 11y + 24 = 0 \qquad \text{Standard form}$$
$$(y - 8)(y - 3) = 0 \qquad \text{Factoring}$$
$$y - 8 = 0 \quad \text{or} \quad y - 3 = 0$$
$$y = 8 \quad \text{or} \qquad y = 3$$

Substitution will show that 8 and 3 check. The solutions are 8 and 3.

Try This Solve.

f. $3x^2 + x - 2 = 0$ **g.** $x^2 + 4x + 8 = 8x + 29$

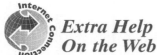

Extra Help On the Web

Look for worked-out examples at the Prentice Hall Web site.
www.phschool.com

13-1 Exercises

A

Write each equation in standard form and determine a, b, and c.

1. $x^2 - 3x + 2 = 0$ **2.** $x^2 - 8x - 5 = 0$ **3.** $2x^2 = 3$

4. $5x^2 = 9$ **5.** $7x^2 = 4x - 3$ **6.** $9x^2 = x + 5$

7. $5 = -2x^2 + 3x$ **8.** $2x = x^2 - 5$ **9.** $2x - 1 = 3x^2 + 7$

Solve.

10. $x^2 + 7x = 0$ **11.** $x^2 + 5x = 0$ **12.** $3x^2 + 6x = 0$

13. $4p^2 + 8p = 0$ **14.** $5x^2 - 2x = 0$ **15.** $3n^2 - 7n = 0$

16. $4x^2 + 4x = 0$ **17.** $2t^2 - 2t = 0$ **18.** $10x^2 - 30x = 0$

19. $10x^2 - 50x = 0$ **20.** $55x^2 - 11x = 0$ **21.** $33x^2 + 11x = 0$

22. $14x^2 - 3x = 0$ **23.** $17x^2 - 8x = 0$ **24.** $3x^2 - 81x = 0$

Solve.

25. $p^2 - 16p + 48 = 0$ **26.** $x^2 + 8x - 48 = 0$

27. $x^2 + 7x + 6 = 0$ **28.** $x^2 + 6x + 5 = 0$

29. $m^2 + 4m - 21 = 0$ **30.** $x^2 + 7x - 18 = 0$

31. $t^2 - 9t + 14 = 0$ **32.** $x^2 - 8x + 15 = 0$

33. $x^2 + 10x + 25 = 0$

34. $x^2 + 6x + 9 = 0$

35. $x^2 - 2x + 1 = 0$

36. $x^2 - 8x + 16 = 0$

37. $2x^2 - 13x + 15 = 0$

38. $6x^2 + x - 2 = 0$

39. $3a^2 - 10a - 8 = 0$

40. $9b^2 - 15b + 4 = 0$

41. $3x^2 - 7x = 20$

42. $6x^2 - 4x = 10$

43. $2x^2 + 12x = -10$

44. $12x^2 - 5x = 2$

45. $6x^2 + x - 1 = 0$

46. $6x^2 + 13x + 6 = 0$

47. $2x^2 + 3x = 35$

48. $12x^2 + 7x - 12 = 0$

B

Solve.

49. $t(t - 5) = 14$

50. $m(3m + 1) = 2$

51. $3y^2 + 8y = 12y + 15$

52. $18 + 2z = z^2 - 5z$

53. $t(9 + t) = 4(2t + 5)$

54. $16(p - 1) = p(p + 8)$

55. $(2x - 3)(x + 1) = 4(2x - 3)$

56. $(3x - 1)(2x + 1) = 3(2x + 1)$

57. $(2m - 1)(m + 3) = -2(m + 4)$

58. $(m + 2)(2m + 3) = (m + 2)^2$

59. $1 = \frac{1}{3}x^2$

60. $x^2 + \sqrt{3}x = 0$

61. $\sqrt{5}y^2 - y = 0$

62. $\sqrt{7}x^2 + \sqrt{3}x = 0$

63. $\sqrt{5}y^2 + y = 0$

64. $\sqrt{3}x^2 - \sqrt{8}x = 0$

65. *Critical Thinking*   Find a quadratic function, $f(x) = ax^2 + bx + c$, with $x = -\frac{3}{8}$ as its axis of symmetry and whose value for c is 7.

Challenge

Find an equation of the indicated form having the solutions shown.

Equation form	Solutions	Equation form	Solutions
66. $ax^2 + bx = 0$	$0, -6$	**67.** $ax^2 + bx + c = 0;$	$4, \frac{3}{4}$
68. $ax^2 + bx + c = 0$	$\frac{2}{5}, -5$	**69.** $ax^3 + bx^2 + cx = 0;$	$0, \frac{1}{2}, -3$

70. *Write a Convincing Argument*   How many equations have the form $ax^2 + bx + c = 0$ and solutions 2 and 5?

Determine the replacements for the variables that give real numbers.

71. $\sqrt{5x^2}$ **72.** $\sqrt{x - 3}$ **73.** $\sqrt{x + 5}$ **74.** $\sqrt{3x - 2}$ *11-1*

Factor.   **75.** $4m^2 - 10m - 6$ **76.** $c^2 - c - 90$ **77.** $y^2 - 121$

78. $9x^2 + 63x + 54$ **79.** $x^2y + 4xy + 4y$

80. $2ab + 2bc + 3ad + 3dc$ *6-2, 6-4, 6-5, 6-7*

Write roster notation for each set.   **81.** $G = \{x \mid x$ is a positive factor of 6$\}$

82. $H = \{y \mid y$ is a perfect square and $20 < y < 50\}$ *9-1*

13-2 ▷ More Solving Quadratic Equations

What You'll Learn

1. To solve an equation of the form $ax^2 = k$

2. To solve a quadratic equation by factoring one expression into a binomial square

3. To solve problems using quadratic equations

... And Why

To use models having the forms $ax^2 = k$ and $(x + a)^2 = k$

Quick Review

To rationalize a denominator, see Lesson 11-5.

PART 1 **Equations of the Form $ax^2 = k$**

Objective: Solve a quadratic equation of the form $ax^2 = k$.

When b, the coefficient of the x-term, is 0 in the quadratic equation $ax^2 + bx + c = 0$, we have a quadratic equation of the form $ax^2 = k$. We first solve for x^2 and then find the square roots.

EXAMPLES Solve.

1 $3x^2 = 18$

$x^2 = 6$ Dividing both sides by 3

$x = \pm\sqrt{6}$ Finding the square roots

$x = \sqrt{6}$ or $x = -\sqrt{6}$

Check:

$3x^2 = 18$		$3x^2 = 18$	
$3(\sqrt{6})^2$	18	$3(-\sqrt{6})^2$	18
$3(6)$	18	$3(6)$	18
18	18 ✔	18	18 ✔

The solutions are $\sqrt{6}$ and $-\sqrt{6}$.

2 $-3x^2 + 7 = 0$

$-3x^2 = -7$

$x^2 = \frac{7}{3}$

$x = \pm\sqrt{\frac{7}{3}}$ Finding the square roots

$x = \pm\sqrt{\frac{7}{3} \cdot \frac{3}{3}}$ Rationalizing the denominator

$x = \pm\frac{\sqrt{21}}{3}$

$x = \frac{\sqrt{21}}{3}$ or $x = -\frac{\sqrt{21}}{3}$

The solutions are $\frac{\sqrt{21}}{3}$ and $-\frac{\sqrt{21}}{3}$.

Try This Solve.

a. $2x^2 = 20$ **b.** $3y^2 = 5$ **c.** $4m^2 - 100 = 0$

d. $9h^2 + 4 = 4$

Squares of Binomials

Objective: Solve a quadratic equation by factoring one expression into a binomial square.

We can extend the square root method of the previous page to quadratic equations of the form $(x + a)^2 = k$.

EXAMPLES Solve.

3 $(x - 5)^2 = 9$

$x - 5 = \pm\sqrt{9}$

$x = 5 \pm \sqrt{9}$

$x = 5 \pm 3$

$x = 5 + 3$ or $x = 5 - 3$

$x = 8$ or $x = 2$

The solutions are 8 and 2.

4 $(x + 2)^2 = 7$

$x + 2 = \pm\sqrt{7}$

$x = -2 \pm \sqrt{7}$

The solutions are

$-2 + \sqrt{7}$ and $-2 - \sqrt{7}$.

5 $x^2 + 16x + 64 = 17$

$(x + 8)^2 = 17$

$x + 8 = \pm\sqrt{17}$

$x = -8 \pm \sqrt{17}$

The solutions are

$-8 + \sqrt{17}$ and $-8 - \sqrt{17}$.

Try This Solve.

e. $(x - 3)^2 = 16$ **f.** $(x + 3)^2 = 10$ **g.** $(m - 1)^2 = 5$

h. $x^2 - 14x + 49 = 3$ **i.** $z^2 + 22z + 121 = 169$

Solving Problems

Objective: Solve problems using quadratic equations.

An object that moves through the air and is solely under the influence of gravity is called a projectile. The approximate height (h) in meters of a projectile at t seconds after it begins its flight from the ground with initial upward velocity v_0 is given by the formula

$h = -5t^2 + v_0 t$

We can find when such a projectile is at ground level ($h = 0$) by solving

$0 = -5t^2 + v_0 t$

If a projectile begins its flight at height c, its approximate height at time t is $h = -5t^2 + v_0 t + c$. We can find when it hits the ground ($h = 0$) by solving

$0 = -5t^2 + v_0 t + c$

Journal

You may wish to note that

$h = -5t^2 + v_0 t + c$

is the formula when height is in meters and velocity is in meters per second.

$h = -16t^2 + v_0 t + c$

is the formula when height is in feet and velocity is in feet per second. Both formulas involve approximations.

EXAMPLE 6

A child tosses a ball upward with an initial velocity of 4 m/s from a height of 1 m. About how long will the ball be in the air?

Substitute $v_0 = 4$, $c = 1$, and $h = 0$ in

$$-5t^2 + v_0 t + c = h$$
$$-5t^2 + 4t + 1 = 0$$
$$-(5t^2 - 4t - 1) = 0$$
$$-(5t + 1)(t - 1) = 0$$
$$5t + 1 = 0 \quad \text{or} \quad t - 1 = 0$$
$$5t = -1 \quad \text{or} \quad t = 1$$
$$t = -\tfrac{1}{5} \quad \text{or} \quad t = 1$$

Since time cannot be negative, the ball will be in the air for about 1 second.

Try This

j. A marble is thrown upwards from a height of 3 m with an initial velocity of 14 m/s. In about how many seconds will it hit the ground?

Quick Review

Compound interest and the compound interest formula were introduced following Lesson 7-10.

Interest problems may be solved using quadratic equations. If you put money in some savings accounts, you receive interest at the end of the year. At the end of the second year you receive interest on both the original amount and the interest. This is called compounding interest annually. An amount of money P (the principal) is invested at an annual interest rate r. When compounded for t years it will grow to the amount A given by

$$A = P(1 + r)^t$$

EXAMPLE 7

Suppose $256 is invested at interest rate r compounded annually. In two years it grows to $289. What is the interest rate?

$$A = P(1 + r)^t$$
$$289 = 256(1 + r)^2 \quad \text{Substituting } A = 289, P = 256, t = 2$$
$$\tfrac{289}{256} = (1 + r)^2$$
$$\pm\sqrt{\tfrac{289}{256}} = 1 + r$$
$$-1 \pm \tfrac{17}{16} = r$$
$$\tfrac{1}{16} = r \quad \text{or} \quad -\tfrac{33}{16} = r$$

Since the interest rate cannot be negative, only $\tfrac{1}{16} = 0.0625 = 6.25\%$ is a solution. The interest rate must be 6.25% for $256 to grow to $289 in 2 years.

Try This

k. Suppose $400 is invested at interest rate r compounded annually and grows to $529 in two years. What is the interest rate?

13-2 Exercises

Extra Help On the Web

Look for worked-out examples at the Prentice Hall Web site.

www.phschool.com

A

Mental Math   Solve.

1. $x^2 = 121$ **2.** $x^2 = 10$ **3.** $5x^2 = 35$

4. $3x^2 = 30$ **5.** $5a^2 = 3$ **6.** $2x^2 = 5$

Solve.

7. $4t^2 - 25 = 0$ **8.** $9x^2 - 4 = 0$ **9.** $3x^2 - 49 = 0$

10. $5x^2 - 16 = 0$ **11.** $4y^2 - 3 = 9$ **12.** $49m^2 - 16 = 0$

13. $25n^2 - 36 = 0$ **14.** $5d^2 - 100 = 0$ **15.** $100x^2 - 5 = 0$

Solve.

16. $(x - 2)^2 = 49$ **17.** $(x + 1)^2 = 6$ **18.** $(d + 3)^2 = 21$

19. $(b - 3)^2 = 6$ **20.** $(x + 13)^2 = 8$ **21.** $(x - 13)^2 = 64$

22. $(x - 7)^2 = 12$ **23.** $(n + 1)^2 = 14$ **24.** $(x + 9)^2 = 34$

25. $(y + 4)^2 = 36$ **26.** $(m + 10)^2 = 15$ **27.** $(y - 5)^2 = 20$

Solve.

28. $x^2 + 2x + 1 = 81$ **29.** $x^2 - 2x + 1 = 16$

30. $y^2 + 10y + 25 = 121$ **31.** $y^2 - 12y + 36 = 49$

32. $m^2 + 4m + 4 = 29$ **33.** $c^2 + 16c + 64 = 15$

34. $x^2 - 6x + 9 = 91$ **35.** $x^2 - 14x + 49 = 19$

36. $n^2 - 8n + 16 = 15$ **37.** $d^2 + 24d + 144 = 8$

For Exercises 38–41, use the formula $-5t^2 + v_0 t + c = h$.

38. A ball is thrown upwards from a height of 20 m with an initial velocity of 15 m/s. In about how many seconds will it hit the ground?

39. Eddie threw a stone into the lake from the end of a pier that was 4 m above the lake surface. He released the stone with an upward velocity of 19 m/s. About how long did it take for the stone to hit the water?

40. A rock 80 m up the face of a cliff breaks loose. About how long does it take the rock to fall to the ground?

41. While cleaning a squirrel nest from a gutter on her house, Mrs. Daugherty threw an acorn downwards with a speed of 1 m/s ($v_0 = -1$). About how long did it take the acorn to fall 4 m to the ground?

The amount P is invested at interest rate r compounded annually and grows to the amount A in two years. Find the interest rate. Use $A = P(1 + r)^t$.

42. $P = \$100$, $A = \$121$

43. $P = \$2560$, $A = \$3610$

44. $P = \$6250$, $A = \$7290$

45. $P = \$400$, $A = \$453.69$

46. $P = \$1000$, $A = \$1267.88$

47. $P = \$4000$, $A = \$5267.03$

48. $P = \$1600$, $A = \$1772.41$

49. $P = \$1000$, $A = \$1232.10$

B

Solve for x.

50. $4x^2 - (x + 1)^2 = 0$

51. $(x - b)^2 = 4b^2$

52. $2(3x + 1)^2 = 8$

53. $5(5x - 2)^2 - 7 = 13$

54. $9x^2 - 24x + 16 = 2$

55. $64x^2 + 48x + 9 = 100$

56. $\dfrac{x - 1}{9} = \dfrac{1}{x - 1}$

57. $\dfrac{5}{x + 4} - \dfrac{3}{x - 2} = 4$

58. A diver springs upward from a 10-m diving board with a velocity of $\frac{7}{4}$ m/s. In about how many seconds will she enter the water?

When an object is dropped, or thrown downward with an initial downward velocity v_0, the approximate distance (d) in meters the object travels in t seconds is given by the formula $d = 5t^2 + v_0 t$.

59. A 134-m tall Detroit department store building was destroyed by controlled implosion in 1998. Use the formula above to estimate how long it took for a piece that broke away from the roof to reach the ground.

60. When a tall concrete chimney was imploded at a copper smelter in McGill, Nevada, in 1993, a piece of concrete from the top took 6.75 s to reach the ground. About how tall was the chimney?

61. a. *Multi-Step Problem*   Three of the most striking vertical geological features in the American West are Chimney Rock in Nebraska, Devils Tower in Wyoming, and El Capitan in California. They rise to heights of 136 m, 386 m, and 1095 m, respectively, above the surrounding land. For each of these natural landforms, how long (to the nearest tenth of a second) would it take a dropped object to fall a distance equal to the height?

b. An object is thrown downward from the top of El Capitan. What initial velocity must it have in order to fall 1095 m in the same time it takes a dropped object to fall 386 m? 136 m?

62. An object is dropped, in turn, from the tops of two of San Francisco's tallest buildings, one 260 m tall and the other 237 m tall.

a. What is the difference in the times it takes to reach the ground?

b. *Write a Convincing Argument*   The difference in the heights of the buildings is 23 m. Is the time difference in part a equal to the time it takes the object dropped from the taller building to travel the first 23 m, the last 23 m, or neither?

When a 100-m tall building is imploded, about how long does it take for a piece that breaks off from the roof to fall to the ground?

63. *Critical Thinking*   Solve the quadratic equation $x^2 + 4x + 4 = 9$.
Check each solution by substituting it for x in $x^2 + 4x + 4$ and
simplifying. Then solve the quadratic equation $x^2 + 4x + 4 = 8$.
Check its solutions by the same method.

The triangles shown are right triangles. Use the Pythagorean theorem to find
the value of a.

64.

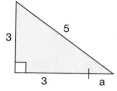

65.

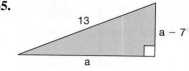

Challenge

In Exercises 66 and 67 the interest is compounded annually and the interest
rates are annual rates.

66. a. For an investment of $2000 to double in value in two years, what would
the interest rate have to be?

    b. *Mathematical Reasoning*   Will an interest rate of 30% double
the value of an investment P in 2 years for some, all, or no values of P?
Explain.

67. In two years you want to have $3000. How much do you need to invest
now if you can get an interest rate of 5.75%?

68. *Multi-Step Problem*   Solve $y^4 - 4y^2 + 4 = 0$. (Hint: Let $x = y^2$.
Solve for x, then solve for y after finding x.)

69. The amount of $1000 is invested at a quarterly interest rate of 2%
compounded quarterly. What is the total amount in the account at the end
of two years?

70. The amount of $2000 is invested at an annual interest rate of 12%
compounded quarterly. What is the total amount in the account at the end
of two years? (Hint: First calculate the quarterly interest rate.)

Mixed Review

Graph each function.   **71.** $f(x) = x^2 - 3$ **72.** $g(x) = 3 - x^2$ *12-4*

Divide and simplify.   **73.** $\dfrac{\sqrt{10}}{\sqrt{5}}$ **74.** $\dfrac{\sqrt{45y^3}}{\sqrt{5y}}$ **75.** $\dfrac{\sqrt{27a^2}}{\sqrt{9a^2}}$ **76.** $\dfrac{\sqrt{16}}{\sqrt{3}}$ *11-5*

Find the indicated outputs for these functions.
77. $f(t) = 2t^2 - 4t + 1$; find $f(-2)$, $f(1)$, and $f(3)$.
78. $g(x) = |x| - 5$; find $g(-7)$, $g(-2)$, and $g(1)$.
79. $h(s) = s^3 - 5$; find $h(-3)$, $h(1)$, and $h(3)$.
80. $f(x) = x^4 + 2$; find $f(-2)$, $f(0)$, and $f(3)$.   *12-1*

PART 1 **Completing the Square**

What You'll Learn

1 To complete a square for a quadratic equation

2 To solve a quadratic equation by completing the square

... And Why

To solve any quadratic equation that has one or two real solutions

Objective: Complete a square for a quadratic equation.

We have seen that a quadratic equation of the form $(x + h)^2 = d$ can be solved by finding the square roots of both sides. Thus if we can write a quadratic equation in this form, we can solve as before.

In the illustration below, look at the relationship between the constant in the binomial and the coefficients in the trinomial square.

$$(x + 3)^2 = x^2 + 2(3)x + 9$$
$$= x^2 + 6x + 9$$
$$\frac{6}{2} = 3 \rightarrow 3^2$$

This suggests a process for changing an expression like $x^2 + 10x$ to a trinomial square of the form $x^2 + 10x + c$. The process is called **completing the square.**

$$x^2 + 10x$$
$$\frac{10}{2} = 5 \qquad \text{Taking half the } x\text{-coefficient}$$
$$5^2 = 25 \qquad \text{Squaring}$$
$$x^2 + 10x + 25 \qquad \text{Adding 25 to complete the square}$$

The trinomial $x^2 + 10x + 25$ is the square of $x + 5$.

EXAMPLE 1 Complete the square.

$$x^2 - 5x$$
$$\left(\frac{-5}{2}\right)^2 = \frac{25}{4}$$
$$x^2 - 5x + \frac{25}{4}$$

The trinomial $x^2 - 5x + \frac{25}{4}$ is the square of $x - \frac{5}{2}$.

Try This Complete the square.

a. $x^2 - 8x$ **b.** $x^2 + 12x$ **c.** $y^2 + 7y$ **d.** $m^2 - 3m$

Objective: Solve a quadratic equation by completing the square.

We can use the technique of completing the square to solve quadratic equations. Recall that the addition property allows us to add a number to both sides of the equation.

EXAMPLE 2 Solve by completing the square.

$$x^2 - 4x - 7 = 0$$
$$x^2 - 4x = 7 \quad \text{Adding 7 to both sides}$$
$$x^2 - 4x + 4 = 7 + 4 \quad \text{Adding 4 to both sides to complete the square}$$
$$(x - 2)^2 = 11$$
$$x - 2 = \pm\sqrt{11}$$
$$x = 2 \pm \sqrt{11}$$

The solutions are $2 + \sqrt{11}$ and $2 - \sqrt{11}$.

To use the technique of completing the square to solve a quadratic equation, the coeffcient of the leading term (the second-degree term) must be 1. If the leading coefficient is not 1, we can use the multiplication property to make it 1.

EXAMPLE 3 Solve by completing the square.

$$2x^2 - 3x - 1 = 0$$
$$x^2 - \tfrac{3}{2}x - \tfrac{1}{2} = 0 \quad \text{Multiplying by } \tfrac{1}{2} \text{ to make the } x^2\text{-coefficient 1}$$
$$x^2 - \tfrac{3}{2}x = \tfrac{1}{2}$$
$$x^2 - \tfrac{3}{2}x + \tfrac{9}{16} = \tfrac{1}{2} + \tfrac{9}{16} \quad \text{Adding } \left(-\tfrac{3}{4}\right)^2 \text{ to both sides}$$
$$\left(x - \tfrac{3}{4}\right)^2 = \tfrac{8}{16} + \tfrac{9}{16}$$
$$\left(x - \tfrac{3}{4}\right)^2 = \tfrac{17}{16}$$
$$x - \tfrac{3}{4} = \pm\sqrt{\tfrac{17}{16}} = \pm\tfrac{\sqrt{17}}{4}$$
$$x = \tfrac{3}{4} \pm \tfrac{\sqrt{17}}{4} = \tfrac{3 \pm \sqrt{17}}{4}$$

The solutions are $\dfrac{3 + \sqrt{17}}{4}$ and $\dfrac{3 - \sqrt{17}}{4}$.

Journal

Show a calculator approximation for the two solutions of Example 3. Then explain how to use each approximation in a Check of these solutions.

Try This Solve by completing the square.

e. $x^2 + 8x + 12 = 0$ **f.** $2x^2 + 3x - 3 = 0$ **g.** $3x^2 - 2x - 3 = 0$

**Extra Help
On the Web**

Look for worked-out
examples at the Prentice
Hall Web site.
www.phschool.com

13-3 Exercises

A

Complete the square.

1. $x^2 - 6x$ **2.** $y^2 + 8y$ **3.** $m^2 + 7m$

4. $t^2 - 5t$ **5.** $x^2 + 4x$ **6.** $n^2 - 12n$

7. $z^2 - 20z$ **8.** $y^2 + 9y$ **9.** $x^2 + 15x$

Solve by completing the square.

10. $x^2 - 6x - 16 = 0$ **11.** $m^2 + 8m + 15 = 0$

12. $x^2 + 22x + 21 = 0$ **13.** $x^2 + 14x - 15 = 0$

14. $x^2 - 2x - 5 = 0$ **15.** $x^2 - 4x - 11 = 0$

16. $n^2 - 22n + 102 = 0$ **17.** $x^2 - 18x + 74 = 0$

18. $x^2 + 10x - 4 = 0$ **19.** $x^2 - 10x - 4 = 0$

20. $n^2 - 7n - 2 = 0$ **21.** $t^2 + 7t - 2 = 0$

22. $x^2 + 3x - 28 = 0$ **23.** $x^2 - 3x - 28 = 0$

24. $2x^2 + 3x - 17 = 0$ **25.** $2r^2 - 3r - 1 = 0$

26. $3x^2 + 4x - 1 = 0$ **27.** $3x^2 - 4x - 3 = 0$

28. $2x^2 - 9x - 5 = 0$ **29.** $2x^2 - 5x - 12 = 0$

B

Complete the square.

30. $x^2 + ? + 36$ **31.** $x^2 + ? + 55$ **32.** $4x^2 + 20x + ?$

33. $4x^2 + ? + 16$ **34.** $x^2 + ? + c$ **35.** $ax^2 + ? + c$

36. *Critical Thinking*   Solve $ax^2 + bx + c = 0$ by completing the square. Express your answer in terms of a, b, and c. If the equation has real-number solutions, what restrictions must there be on a, b, and c?

Challenge

Solve for x by completing the square.

37. $x^2 - ax - 6a^2 = 0$ **38.** $x^2 + 4bx + 2b = 0$

39. $x^2 - x - c^2 - c = 0$ **40.** $3x^2 - bx + 1 = 0$

41. $kx^2 + mx + n = 0$ **42.** $b^2x^2 - 2bx + c^2 = 0$

Mixed Review

Find an equation of variation where y varies directly as x, and the following are true.   **43.** $y = 11$ when $x = 4$ **44.** $y = 16$ when $x = 8$ *12-5*

Identify as rational or irrational.   **45.** $\sqrt{15}$ **46.** $\sqrt{225}$ **47.** $\sqrt{144}$ *11-1*

Solve.   **48.** $\sqrt{2x + 3} = 5$ **49.** $-\sqrt{4x} = 4$ *11-9*

The Quadratic Formula

13-4

Using the Quadratic Formula

Objective: Use the quadratic formula to solve quadratic equations.

Each time you solve quadratic equations by completing the square you follow the same steps. By looking at these steps we can find a formula for solving any quadratic equation.

Solve $ax^2 + bx + c = 0$, $a \neq 0$, for x.

We solve by completing the square.

$$x^2 + \frac{b}{a}x + \frac{c}{a} = 0 \qquad \text{Multiplying by } \tfrac{1}{a}$$

$$x^2 + \frac{b}{a}x = -\frac{c}{a} \qquad \text{Adding } -\tfrac{c}{a}$$

Half of $\frac{b}{a}$ is $\frac{b}{2a}$. The square is $\frac{b^2}{4a^2}$. We add $\frac{b^2}{4a^2}$ to both sides.

$$x^2 + \frac{b}{a}x + \frac{b^2}{4a^2} = -\frac{c}{a} + \frac{b^2}{4a^2}$$

$$\left(x + \frac{b}{2a}\right)^2 = \frac{b^2 - 4ac}{4a^2}$$

$$x + \frac{b}{2a} = \pm\sqrt{\frac{b^2 - 4ac}{4a^2}}$$

$$x = -\frac{b}{2a} \pm \frac{\sqrt{b^2 - 4ac}}{2a}$$

$$x = \frac{-b \pm \sqrt{b^2 - 4ac}}{2a}$$

$$x = \frac{-b + \sqrt{b^2 - 4ac}}{2a} \quad \text{or} \quad x = \frac{-b - \sqrt{b^2 - 4ac}}{2a}$$

The Quadratic Formula

If $ax^2 + bx + c = 0$, $a \neq 0$, then the **quadratic formula**

$$x = \frac{-b \pm \sqrt{b^2 - 4ac}}{2a}$$

gives the solutions of the quadratic equation.

What You'll Learn

1 To use the quadratic formula to solve quadratic equations

2 To use the discriminant to find the number of solutions for a quadratic equation

...And Why

To use a formulaic process to find information about a quadratic equation

---

EXAMPLE 1   Solve $5x^2 - 8x = -3$ using the quadratic formula.

First find the standard form and determine a, b, and c.

$$5x^2 - 8x + 3 = 0 \qquad \text{Standard form}$$
$$a = 5, b = -8, c = 3$$

Then use the quadratic formula.

$$x = \frac{-b \pm \sqrt{b^2 - 4ac}}{2a}$$

$$x = \frac{-(-8) \pm \sqrt{(-8)^2 - 4 \cdot 5 \cdot 3}}{2 \cdot 5} \qquad \text{Substituting for } a, b, \text{ and } c$$

$$x = \frac{8 \pm \sqrt{64 - 60}}{10} \qquad \text{Simplifying the radicand}$$

$$x = \frac{8 \pm \sqrt{4}}{10} = \frac{8 \pm 2}{10}$$

$$x = \frac{8 + 2}{10} \quad \text{or} \quad x = \frac{8 - 2}{10}$$

$$x = \frac{10}{10} = 1 \quad \text{or} \quad x = \frac{6}{10} = \frac{3}{5}$$

The solutions are 1 and $\frac{3}{5}$.

Try This   Solve using the quadratic formula.

a. $2x^2 = 4 - 7x$ **b.** $3m^2 - 8 = 10m$

EXAMPLE 2   Solve $3x^2 = 7 - 2x$ using the quadratic formula.

Approximate the solutions to the nearest tenth.

$$3x^2 + 2x - 7 = 0 \qquad \text{Standard form}$$
$$a = 3, b = 2, c = -7$$
$$x = \frac{-2 \pm \sqrt{88}}{6} \qquad \text{Substituting into the quadratic formula}$$

$$x = \frac{-2 \pm 2\sqrt{22}}{6}$$

$$x = \frac{-1 \pm \sqrt{22}}{3}$$

The solutions are $\dfrac{-1 + \sqrt{22}}{3}$ and $\dfrac{-1 - \sqrt{22}}{3}$.

Using a calculator, the solutions to the nearest tenth are 1.2 and -1.9. A check will show that these numbers are approximate roots of $3x^2 + 2x - 7$.

Try This   Solve using the quadratic formula. Approximate the solutions to the nearest tenth.

c. $2x^2 - 4x = 5$ **d.** $x^2 + 5x = -3$

We can use the quadratic formula to find the roots of a second-degree polynomial. First, write the polynomial in standard form to determine values of a, b, and c.

Try This   Use the quadratic formula to find the roots of each polynomial.

e. $6x^2 - 6 - 5x$ **f.** $6x^2 - 6x - 5$

PART 2 The Discriminant

Objective: Use the discriminant to find the number of solutions for a quadratic equation.

The quadratic equations you have solved so far have had two real-number solutions. Some quadratic equations have one or no real-number solutions. In the quadratic formula, the expression under the radical, $b^2 - 4ac$, is called the **discriminant.** We can use the discriminant to determine the number of real-number solutions of a quadratic equation.

This chart illustrates the three possible cases.

Solutions to $0 = ax^2 + bx + c$	Discriminant $b^2 - 4ac$	Graph of the Function
$0 = x^2 + 2x - 3$ $x = \dfrac{-2 \pm \sqrt{16}}{2}$ $x = 1$ or $x = -3$ 2 real-number solutions	$2^2 - 4(1)(-3) = 16$	$y = x^2 + 2x - 3$
$0 = x^2 + 4x + 4$ $x = \dfrac{-4 \pm \sqrt{0}}{2}$ $x = -2$ 1 real-number solution	$4^2 - 4(1)(4) = 0$	$y = x^2 + 4x + 4$
$0 = x^2 + x + 5$ $x = \dfrac{-1 \pm \sqrt{-19}}{2}$ 0 real-number solutions	$1^2 - 4(1)(5) = -19$	$y = x^2 + x + 5$

When the value of the discriminant is positive, there are two real-number solutions. When the discriminant is 0, there is one real-number solution. When the discriminant is negative, there are no real-number solutions.

Quick Review

For a polynomial containing one variable, any value of the variable that makes the value of the polynomial zero is a root of the polynomial.

Find the value of the discriminant to determine the number of real-number solutions.

3 $x^2 - x + 2 = 0$
$b^2 - 4ac = (-1)^2 - 4 \cdot 1 \cdot 2 = -7$
Since the discriminant is negative, there are no real-number solutions.

4 $3x^2 = 7 - 2x$
First rewrite the equation in standard form: $3x^2 + 2x - 7 = 0$
$b^2 - 4ac = 2^2 - 4(3)(-7) = 88$

Since the discriminant is positive, there are two real-number solutions.

Try This Find the value of the discriminant to determine the number of real-number solutions.

g. $2x^2 - 4x = 5$ **h.** $x^2 + 5x = -8$ **i.** $4x^2 = 8x - 4$

Summary of Related Quadratic Equations, Polynomials, and Functions

For real numbers $a, b,$ and c with $a \neq 0,$
$\quad 0 = ax^2 + bx + c$ is a quadratic equation,
$\quad\quad ax^2 + bx + c$ is the related quadratic polynomial, and
$\quad y = ax^2 + bx + c$ is the related quadratic function.

If the discriminant of the quadratic equation is positive, then
  • the quadratic equation has two real-number solutions (call them s_1 and s_2).
  • the related quadratic polynomial has roots s_1 and s_2.
  • the graph of the related quadratic function intersects the x-axis in two points, $(s_1, 0)$ and $(s_2, 0)$.

If the discriminant is 0, then
  • the quadratic equation has one real-number solution (call it s).
  • the related quadratic polynomial has one root s.
  • the graph of the related quadratic function intersects the x-axis in one point, the vertex $(s, 0)$.

If the discriminant is negative, then
  • the quadratic equation has no real-number solution.
  • the related quadratic polynomial has no real-number root.
  • the graph of the related quadratic function does not intersect the x-axis.

Try This Use the discriminant to determine whether the graph of each quadratic function intersects the x-axis in 0, 1, or 2 points.

j. $y = 3x^2 - 5x + 1$ **k.** $f(x) = x^2 - 3x + 7$ **l.** $y = x^2 - 12x + 36$

13-4 Exercises

**Extra Help
On the Web**

Look for worked-out
examples at the Prentice
Hall Web site.
www.phschool.com

A
Solve using the quadratic formula.

1. $x^2 - 4x = 21$ **2.** $x^2 + 7x = 18$ **3.** $x^2 = 6x - 9$

4. $x^2 = 8x - 16$ **5.** $3y^2 - 2y - 8 = 0$ **6.** $3y^2 - 7y + 4 = 0$

7. $4x^2 + 12x = 7$ **8.** $4x^2 + 4x = 15$ **9.** $x^2 - 9 = 0$

10. $x^2 - 4 = 0$ **11.** $x^2 - 2x + 1 = 0$ **12.** $x^2 - 4x - 7 = 0$

13. $y^2 - 10y + 22 = 0$ **14.** $y^2 + 6y - 9 = 0$ **15.** $x^2 + 4x + 4 = 7$

16. $x^2 - 2x + 1 = 5$ **17.** $3x^2 + 8x + 2 = 0$ **18.** $3x^2 - 4x - 2 = 0$

Use the quadratic formula to find the roots of each polynomial.

19. $4y^2 + 3y - 1$ **20.** $4y^2 + 4y + 1$ **21.** $3x^2 + 5x$

22. $5x^2 - 2x$ **23.** $4x^2 - 100$ **24.** $5t^2 - 80$

25. $2t^2 + 6t + 5$ **26.** $4y^2 + 3y + 2$ **27.** $3x^2 - 8x + 4$

28. The height of a drop of water at t seconds after being shot upward
from the fireboat is $h = 20 + 76t - 16t^2$ feet. Assuming no air
resistance, how long does it take for the drop to hit the river?
(Hint: Let $h = 0$.)

Solve using the quadratic formula. Give solutions to the
nearest tenth.

29. $x^2 - 4x - 7 = 0$ **30.** $x^2 + 2x - 2 = 0$ **31.** $y^2 - 6y - 1 = 0$

32. $4x^2 + 4x = 1$ **33.** $4x^2 = 4x + 1$ **34.** $3x^2 + 4x - 2 = 0$

35. $3x^2 - 8x + 2 = 0$ **36.** $2y^2 + 6y - 2 = 0$ **37.** $x^2 - 3x + 1 = 3$

38. $2x^2 - 10x + 9 = 0$ **39.** $5x^2 = 6 + 2x$ **40.** $7x^2 = 3$

Find the value of the discriminant to determine the number of real-number
solutions for each quadratic equation.

41. $x^2 - 5x + 7 = 0$ **42.** $x^2 - 8x + 3 = 0$

43. $a^2 + 12a + 36 = 0$ **44.** $2m^2 - m - 6 = 0$

Use the discriminant to determine whether the graph of each quadratic
function intersects the x-axis in zero, one, or two points.

45. $f(t) = 4t^2 - 3t + 3$ **46.** $y = 2x^2 - 4x - 6$

47. $f(x) = 3x^2 - 3x + 4$ **48.** $p = -3q^2 + 4q + 2$

Find the x-intercepts of the graph of each quadratic function.

49. $y = (x - 4)(x + 3)$ **50.** $y = (x - 5)^2$

51. $y = x^2 + 1$ **52.** $y = x(x + 10)$

A fireboat salutes by shooting
water into the air. How high does
the middle stream of water reach if
water height is described by the
function $h = 20 + 76t - 16t^2$?

B

Solve.

53. $5x + x(x - 7) = 0$ **54.** $x(3x + 7) - 3x = 0$

55. $3 - x(x - 3) = 4$ **56.** $x(5x - 7) = 1$

57. $(y + 4)(y + 3) = 15$ **58.** $(y + 5)(y - 1) = 27$

59. $(x + 2)^2 + (x + 1)^2 = 0$ **60.** $(x + 3)^2 + (x + 1)^2 = 0$

Use a graph to find the roots of each polynomial.

61. $x^2 + 2x - 8$ **62.** $x^2 - 8x + 16$ **63.** $x^2 + 1$

Use roots and the vertex to "quick sketch" a graph of each quadratic function. (Hint: The graph has an axis of symmetry.)

64. $y = (x + 4)(x - 2)$ **65.** $y = x(x + 6)$ **66.** $y = \frac{1}{5}(2x - 3)(2x + 7)$

67. *Critical Thinking*   For the given condition, will $ax^2 + bx + c = 0$ have two real-number solutions for some, all, or no values of b?

     a. when $b^2 > 4ac$ **b.** when $ac < 0$ **c.** when $a > 0$ and $c > 0$

Challenge

68. *Multi-Step Problem*   Use the two roots given by the quadratic formula.

     a. Find a formula for the sum of the roots.

     b. Find a formula for the product of the roots.

     c. Without solving, tell the sum and product of the solutions of $2x^2 + 5x - 3 = 0$.

     d. One solution of $2x^2 + bx - 3 = 0$ is –5. Find the other solution.

69. *Write a Convincing Argument*   By symmetry, the average of the roots of a quadratic function is the x-coordinate of the vertex of its graph. Use the roots given by the quadratic formula to show that the x-coordinate of the vertex is $-\frac{b}{2a}$.

70. If $f(x) = ax^2 + bx + c$, and r_1 and r_2 are two real roots given by the quadratic formula, show that $a(x - r_1)(x - r_2) = f(x)$.

Use factoring to determine whether the graph of each quadratic function has zero, one, or two x-intercepts. State the intercepts.

71. $f(x) = x^2 + x - 12$ **72.** $f(x) = 3x^2 - 6x + 3$

73. $f(x) = -6x^2 + 11x - 4$

Mixed Review

Write in standard form and determine a, b, and c.   **74.** $x^2 + 7x = 8$

75. $4x^2 + 16 = -5x$ **76.** $3x^2 - 12 = 8x + 10$ *13-1*

Find an equation of variation where y varies inversely as x. One pair of values is given.   **77.** $y = 16$ when $x = 4$ **78.** $y = 0.1$ when $x = 1$ *12-6*

Solve.   **79.** $11 - \sqrt{30 + x} = 5$ **80.** $\sqrt{2x + 2} = \sqrt{5x - 13}$ *11-9*

Factor.   **81.** $5m^2 - 30m + 45$ **82.** $c^3 - c^2 - c + 1$ *6-5, 6-7*

Solving Rational Equations

Objective: Solve rational equations involving quadratic equations.

Recall that we solve rational equations by multiplying both sides by the LCM of all the denominators. This can result in a quadratic equation, and also extraneous solutions. Therefore, you must check all possible solutions in the original equation.

EXAMPLES Solve.

1
$$\frac{a+1}{2} = \frac{1}{a}$$

$$\frac{a+1}{2}(2a) = \frac{1}{a}(2a)$$

$$(a+1)a = 2$$

$$a^2 + a = 2$$

$$a^2 + a - 2 = 0$$

$$(a+2)(a-1) = 0$$

$$a + 2 = 0 \quad \text{or} \quad a - 1 = 0$$
$$a = -2 \quad \text{or} \quad a = 1$$

Check $(a = -2)$: $(a = 1)$:

$$\frac{a+1}{2} = \frac{1}{a}$$

$\frac{-2+1}{2}$	$\frac{1}{-2}$
$-\frac{1}{2}$	$-\frac{1}{2}$ ✔

$$\frac{a+1}{2} = \frac{1}{a}$$

$\frac{1+1}{2}$	$\frac{1}{1}$
1	1 ✔

Quick Review

An extraneous solution is a solution of a transformed equation, but not a solution of the original equation. See Lesson 10-6.

2
$$\frac{3}{x-1} + \frac{5}{x+1} = 2 \quad \text{LCM is } (x-1)(x+1).$$

$$(x-1)(x+1)\left(\frac{3}{x-1} + \frac{5}{x+1}\right) = 2(x-1)(x+1)$$

$$(x-1)(x+1)\frac{3}{x-1} + (x-1)(x+1)\frac{5}{x+1} = 2(x-1)(x+1)$$

$$3(x+1) + 5(x-1) = 2(x-1)(x+1)$$

$$3x + 3 + 5x - 5 = 2(x^2 - 1)$$

$$8x - 2 = 2x^2 - 2$$

$$-2x^2 + 8x = 0$$

$$-2x(x-4) = 0 \quad \text{Factoring}$$

$$-2x = 0 \quad \text{or} \quad x - 4 = 0$$
$$x = 0 \quad \text{or} \quad x = 4$$

Substitution will show that both numbers check. The solutions are 0 and 4.

Try This   Solve. Use the quadratic formula, if necessary.

a. $x + 3 = \frac{10}{x}$ **b.** $1 = \frac{1}{a} + \frac{12}{a^2}$ **c.** $\frac{2}{x+2} + \frac{2}{x-2} = 1$

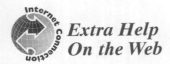
13-5 Exercises

A

Solve each rational equation. Use the quadratic formula as needed.

1. $\frac{7}{x+3} = x - 3$

2. $\frac{5}{y-2} = y + 2$

3. $\frac{x-2}{3} = \frac{1}{x}$

4. $\frac{a-1}{2} = \frac{3}{a}$

5. $\frac{5}{n^2} + \frac{4}{n} = 1$

6. $\frac{4}{a^2} - \frac{2}{a} = 2$

7. $x - 3 = \frac{5}{x-3}$

8. $x + 2 = \frac{3}{x+2}$

9. $\frac{x^2}{x-4} - \frac{7}{x-4} = 0$

10. $\frac{x^2}{x+3} - \frac{5}{x+3} = 0$

11. $\frac{y+2}{y} = \frac{1}{y+2}$

12. $\frac{8}{x-2} + \frac{8}{x+2} = 3$

13. $\frac{24}{x-2} + \frac{24}{x+2} = 5$

14. $1 + \frac{12}{x^2 - 4} = \frac{3}{x-2}$

15. $\frac{5}{t-3} - \frac{30}{t^2-9} = 1$

16. $\frac{4}{x+2} - \frac{5}{x-3} = 2$

17. $\frac{2}{y-1} + \frac{3}{y+1} = 1$

18. $\frac{1}{t+2} + \frac{5}{t} = 1$

19. $\frac{2}{a+1} - \frac{3}{a} = 2$

20. $\frac{x}{x+1} - \frac{x}{x-2} = 1$

21. $\frac{y}{y+3} - \frac{y}{y-1} = 1$

B

Solve each rational equation. Use the quadratic formula as needed.

22. $\frac{2x-1}{5} - \frac{2}{x} = \frac{x}{2}$

23. $\frac{n-1}{2} - \frac{1}{n} = \frac{n}{3}$

24. $\frac{6}{a+1} - \frac{1}{a} = \frac{1}{2}$

25. $\frac{2}{x-2} - \frac{1}{x} = \frac{1}{3}$

26. $\frac{x}{x+1} - \frac{x}{x-1} = \frac{1}{3}$

27. $\frac{y}{y-2} - \frac{y}{y+2} = \frac{1}{2}$

28. $\frac{1}{a-1} + \frac{2}{1-a} = 3a$

29. $\frac{1}{2x-1} + \frac{1}{1-2x} = x$

30. $\frac{1}{x-2} - \frac{2}{x^2-4} = 0$

31. $\frac{2}{x+3} + \frac{5}{x^2-9} = 0$

32. $\frac{1}{x+2} - \frac{2}{x^2-4} = \frac{2}{x}$

33. $\frac{2}{y+3} - \frac{1}{y^2-9} = \frac{1}{y}$

34. *Critical Thinking* The sum of an integer, $\frac{1}{2}$ its reciprocal, and one more than its reciprocal is $4\frac{1}{2}$. What is the number?

35. *Error Analysis* To solve $\frac{x}{x-2} - \frac{3}{x} = \frac{4}{x(x-2)}$, Leah multiplied both sides by the LCD, $x(x-2)$, and got $x^2 - 3x + 6 = 4$. For this equation, Leah claimed that the discriminant is negative, so there are no real number solutions. What error, if any, did Leah make?

36. **TEST PREP** Without solving the equation, give the only possible values of x that could be extraneous solutions of $\frac{5}{2x-2} = \frac{15}{x^2-1}$.

   A. 0 and 1   **B.** 1 and 2   **C.** −1 and 1   **D.** −1 and 0

37. *Mathematical Reasoning* Lon claimed that no equation can have 0 as an extraneous solution. Show by counterexample that this is not true.

Challenge

Solve.

38. $\frac{1}{x} - \frac{3}{1-x} = \frac{2}{x^2-x}$

39. $\frac{2}{y} + \frac{1}{1-y} = \frac{5}{y^2-y}$

40. $\frac{2}{x^2-x-6} + \frac{3}{x^2-7x+12} = \frac{1}{x-4}$

41. $\frac{-1}{x^2+4x-5} + \frac{2}{x^2+x-20} = \frac{2}{x-4}$

42. $\frac{1}{x^2+3x-4} + \frac{1}{x^2+2x-8} = \frac{1}{x^2-8x+12}$

43. $\frac{1}{x^2-2x-15} + \frac{1}{x^2+x-6} = \frac{1}{x^2+2x-8}$

Mixed Review

Solve.   **44.** $x^2 + 3x = 0$ **45.** $a^2 = 15$

46. $y^2 - 5y - 14 = 0$ **47.** $7x^2 + 4x = 0$

48. $9x^2 - 20 = 0$ **49.** $2x^2 - 7x - 15 = 0$ *13-1, 13-2, 13-3*

Graph.   **50.** $f(x) = 2x^2 - 5$ **51.** $g(x) = \frac{1}{2}x^2 + 1$

52. $h(x) = -2x^2 + 7$ **53.** $f(x) = -\frac{1}{2}x^2 - 4$ *12-4*

Find an equation of variation.   **54.** y varies directly as x, and $y = 0.6$ when $x = 0.4$.   **55.** y varies inversely as x, and $y = 2$ when $x = 3$.

56. y varies inversely as x, and $y = 5$ when $x = 2$.

57. y varies directly as x and inversely as z, and $y = 4$ when $x = 8$ and $z = 6$.   *12-5, 12-6, 12-7*

Write using scientific notation.   **58.** 3,485,117   **59.** 0.0070023   *5-4*

60. Find the slope of the line containing the points $(-5, -9)$, $(1, 1)$.   *7-5*

Internet Connection

Self-Test On the Web

Check your progress. Look for a self-test at the Prentice Hall Web site. www.phschool.com

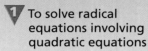

Solving Radical Equations

What You'll Learn

1 To solve radical equations involving quadratic equations

2 To solve formulas for given variables

... And Why

To solve equations in which the variable is under a radical symbol

PART 1 Radical Equations

Objective: Solve radical equations involving quadratic equations.

We can solve some radical equations by first using the principle of squaring to find a quadratic equation. When we do this we must be sure to check.

EXAMPLE 1   Solve.

$$x - 5 = \sqrt{x + 7}$$
$$(x - 5)^2 = (\sqrt{x + 7})^2 \quad \text{Using the principle of squaring}$$
$$x^2 - 10x + 25 = x + 7$$
$$x^2 - 11x + 18 = 0$$
$$(x - 9)(x - 2) = 0$$
$$x = 9 \quad \text{or} \quad x = 2$$

Check:

$x - 5 = \sqrt{x + 7}$		$x - 5 = \sqrt{x + 7}$	
$9 - 5$	$\sqrt{9 + 7}$	$2 - 5$	$\sqrt{2 + 7}$
4	4 ✔	-3	3

The number 9 checks, but 2 does not. Thus the only solution is 9.

EXAMPLE 2   Solve.

$$\sqrt{27 - 3x} + 3 = x$$
$$\sqrt{27 - 3x} = x - 3 \quad \text{Adding } -3 \text{ to get the radical alone}$$
$$(\sqrt{27 - 3x})^2 = (x - 3)^2 \quad \text{Using the principle of squaring}$$
$$27 - 3x = x^2 - 6x + 9$$
$$0 = x^2 - 3x - 18$$
$$0 = (x - 6)(x + 3)$$
$$x = 6 \quad \text{or} \quad x = -3$$

Check:

$\sqrt{27 - 3x} + 3 = x$		$\sqrt{27 - 3x} + 3 = x$	
$\sqrt{27 - 3 \cdot 6} + 3$	6	$\sqrt{27 - 3 \cdot (-3)} + 3$	-3
$\sqrt{9} + 3$	6	$\sqrt{27 + 9} + 3$	-3
6	6 ✔	$\sqrt{36} + 3$	-3
		9	-3

There is only one solution, 6.

Try This   Solve.

a. $\sqrt{x + 2} = 4 - x$ **b.** $\sqrt{30 - 3x} + 4 = x$

Objective: Solve formulas for given variables.

EXAMPLES Solve each formula for the given variable.

3 Solve $V = 3.5\sqrt{h}$ for h.

$V = 3.5\sqrt{h}$

$V^2 = (3.5)^2(\sqrt{h})^2$ Squaring both sides

$V^2 = 12.25h$

$\frac{V^2}{12.25} = h$ Multiplying by $\frac{1}{12.25}$ to get h alone

4 Solve $T = 2\pi\sqrt{\frac{L}{g}}$ for g. Justify each step.

$T = 2\pi\sqrt{\frac{L}{g}}$

$T^2 = \left(2\pi\sqrt{\frac{L}{g}}\right)^2$ *Square both sides.*

$T^2 = 2^2\pi^2\left(\sqrt{\frac{L}{g}}\right)^2$ *Raise a product to a power.*

$T^2 = \frac{4\pi^2 L}{g}$ *Definition of square root*

$gT^2 = 4\pi^2 L$ *Multiply by g.*

$g = \frac{4\pi^2 L}{T^2}$ *Multiply by $\frac{1}{T^2}$.*

5 Solve $A = P(1 + r)^2$ for r.

$A = P(1 + r)^2$

$\frac{A}{P} = (1 + r)^2$ Multiplying by $\frac{1}{P}$

$\sqrt{\frac{A}{P}} = 1 + r$ Taking the square root on both sides

$-1 + \sqrt{\frac{A}{P}} = r$

Since the interest rate (r) can only be positive, we do not need to find the negative square root, as it would lead to a negative solution.

Try This Solve for the indicated variable.

c. $r = 2\sqrt{5L}$; L **d.** $T = 2\pi\sqrt{\frac{L}{g}}$; L **e.** $c = \sqrt{\frac{E}{m}}$; m

f. $A = \pi r^2$; r **g.** $C = P(d - 1)^2$; d

Extra Help
On the Web

Look for worked-out examples at the Prentice Hall Web site.
www.phschool.com

13-6 Exercises

A

Mental Math   Solve each radical equation.

1. $\sqrt{a} = 6$

2. $\sqrt{x} = 9$

3. $\sqrt{x + 2} = 3$

4. $\sqrt{m - 4} = 5$

5. $\sqrt{\frac{x}{3}} = 2$

6. $\sqrt{\frac{m}{2}} = 5$

Solve each radical equation.

7. $\sqrt{2x + 3} = 7$

8. $\sqrt{5t - 2} = 1$

9. $\sqrt{2x + 3} = 3$

10. $\sqrt{4m - 1} = 5$

11. $\sqrt{\frac{x + 2}{3}} = 6$

12. $\sqrt{\frac{a - 3}{4}} = 2$

13. $x - 7 = \sqrt{x - 5}$

14. $\sqrt{x + 7} = x - 5$

15. $\sqrt{x + 18} = x - 2$

16. $x - 9 = \sqrt{x - 3}$

17. $\sqrt{5x + 21} = x + 3$

18. $\sqrt{2x + 3} = 6 - x$

19. $x = 1 + 6\sqrt{x - 9}$

20. $\sqrt{2x - 1} + 2 = x$

21. $x + 4 = 4\sqrt{x + 1}$

22. $x + 1 = 3\sqrt{x + 5}$

Solve each formula for the indicated variable.

23. $c^2 = a^2 + b^2; a$

24. $E = mc^2; c$

25. $c = \sqrt{a^2 + b^2}; b$

26. $N = 2.5\sqrt{A}; A$

27. $V = \pi r^2 h; r$

28. $s = \frac{gt^2}{2}; t$

29. $x^2 + y^2 + z^2 = r^2; x$

30. $P = \frac{V^2}{R}; V$

Solve for the indicated variable. Justify each step.

31. $F = \frac{GmM}{r^2}; r$

32. $\sqrt{\frac{2s}{a}} = t; s$

33. $\sqrt{\frac{P}{R}} = I; R$

34. $x = 2V + at^2; t$

35. $P = R(4 + I)^2; I$

36. $T = 2\pi\sqrt{\frac{l}{g}}; g$

B

Solve.

37. $\sqrt{x + 3} = \frac{8}{\sqrt{x - 9}}$

38. $\frac{12}{\sqrt{5x + 6}} = \sqrt{2x + 5}$

39. $\sqrt{4x^2 + 3} = 3x$

40. $\sqrt{2y^2 - 4} = y$

41. $6\sqrt{a} = 18\sqrt{7}$

42. $2\sqrt{x} = 5\sqrt{10}$

43. $\sqrt{t^2 + 1} = 1 - t$

44. $\sqrt{a^2 - 1} = 1 + a$

45. *Critical Thinking*   Find a formula for the area of a square in terms of the perimeter of the square. Then use the formula to express the perimeter of the square in terms of the area of the square.

46. *Critical Thinking* Find a formula for the circumference of a circle in terms of the area of a circle. Then use the formula to express the area of the circle in terms of the circumference of the circle.

Error Analysis Each exercise has an error commonly made by algebra students. Can you find and correct the error?

47. $\sqrt{3x + 7} = x + 3$
$$3x + 7 = x^2 + 9$$
$$0 = x^2 - 3x + 2$$
$$0 = (x - 2)(x - 1)$$
$$x - 2 = 0 \quad \text{or} \quad x - 1 = 0$$
$$x = 2 \quad \text{or} \quad x = 1$$

The solutions are 2 and 1.

48. $\sqrt{x + 1} = x - 5$
$$x + 1 = x^2 - 10x + 25$$
$$0 = x^2 - 11x + 24$$
$$0 = (x - 8)(x - 3)$$
$$x - 8 = 0 \quad \text{or} \quad x - 3 = 0$$
$$x = 8 \quad \text{or} \quad x = 3$$

The solutions are 8 and 3.

Mathematical Reasoning What, if any, extraneous solutions result when the principle of squaring is used to help solve each equation?

49. $\sqrt{x^2} = x$ **50.** $\sqrt{x^2} = -x$ **51.** $\sqrt{x^2} = |x|$ **52.** $\dfrac{1}{\sqrt{x}} = \sqrt{x}$

Challenge

53. Solve. $2\sqrt{x - 1} - \sqrt{3x - 5} = \sqrt{x - 9}$

54. Solve. $\sqrt{y + 1} - \sqrt{2y - 5} = \sqrt{y - 2}$

55. Solve $x + 1 + 3\sqrt{x + 1} - 28 = 0$ using two methods. First use the principle of squaring. Second, let $y = \sqrt{x + 1}$. (Then $y^2 = x + 1$.) Solve for y, then substitute to find x.

56. Solve $h = vt + 8t^2$ for t.

Solve the following systems of equations.

57. $2\sqrt{a} + 3\sqrt{b} = 21$
$\sqrt{a} - \sqrt{b} = -2$

58. $5\sqrt{m} + 2\sqrt{n} = 39$
$3\sqrt{m} - \sqrt{n} = 19$

59. $3r^2 + 2s^2 = 11$
$r^2 - 2s^2 = -7$

60. $5x^2 - 3y^2 = -7$
$-x^2 + 3y^2 = 23$

Mixed Review

Complete the square.   **61.** $x^2 + 4x$ **62.** $m^2 - 5m$ **63.** $a^2 - a$ *13-3*

Solve.   **64.** $9a^2 - 18a = 0$ **65.** $3x^2 - 13x + 4 = 0$

66. $2m^2 - 25 = 0$ **67.** $(x - 3)^2 = 36$ **68.** $(c - 5)^2 = 17$ *13-1, 13-2*

Simplify.   **69.** $\dfrac{\sqrt{1}}{\sqrt{81}}$ **70.** $-\dfrac{\sqrt{4}}{\sqrt{121}}$ **71.** $\dfrac{\sqrt{11}}{\sqrt{22}}$ **72.** $\dfrac{\sqrt{56}}{\sqrt{8}}$ **73.** $\dfrac{\sqrt{64}}{\sqrt{4}}$ *11-5*

Solve by graphing.   **74.** $y = x - 1$ **75.** $y = 2x$ **76.** $y = 1 - x$ *8-1*
$y = -x - 5$ $x + y = 0$ $x - y = 7$

77. The numerical value for the area of a square is 32 more than the perimeter. Find the length of a side.   *6-9*

13-7 ▷ Using Quadratic Equations

Objective: Solve problems involving quadratic equations.

What You'll Learn

1 To solve problems using quadratic equations

...And Why

To use models of the form $ax^2 + bx + c = 0$

PROBLEM-SOLVING GUIDELINES
■ UNDERSTAND the problem
Develop and carry out a PLAN
■ Find the ANSWER and CHECK

We can use Problem-Solving Guidelines to help solve problems involving quadratic equations.

EXAMPLE 1

A picture frame measures 20 cm by 14 cm. The picture, inside the frame, takes up 160 square centimeters. Find the width of the frame.

■ **UNDERSTAND the problem**

Question: What is the width of the frame?
Data: Picture frame is 20 cm × 14 cm; picture has area 160 cm².

■ **Develop and carry out a PLAN**

Let x = width of the picture frame.

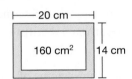

We can use the picture to help us express the other dimensions of the picture in terms of the width, x, of the picture frame. Also, recall that area can be found by multiplying the length by the width.

$$lw = A$$
$$lw = 160$$
$$(20 - 2x)(14 - 2x) = 160$$
$$280 - 68x + 4x^2 = 160$$
$$4x^2 - 68x + 120 = 0$$
$$x^2 - 17x + 30 = 0$$
$$(x - 15)(x - 2) = 0 \quad \text{Factoring}$$
$$x = 15 \text{ or } x = 2$$

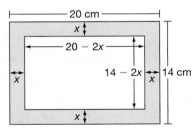

■ **Find the ANSWER and CHECK**

When $x = 15$, $20 - 2x = -10$, and $14 - 2x = -16$. Since the length and width of the picture cannot be negative, 15 is not an answer. When $x = 2$, $20 - 2x = 16$, and $14 - 2x = 10$. A 10 × 16 picture has an area of 160 cm². This answer is reasonable and checks. The width of the picture frame is 2 cm.

Try This   Solve.

a. A rectangular garden is 80 m by 60 m. Part of the garden is torn up to install a strip of lawn of equal width around the garden. The new area of the garden is 800 m². How wide is the strip of lawn?

EXAMPLE 2

The hypotenuse of a right triangle is 6 m long. One leg is 1 m longer than the other. Find the the lengths of the legs. Round to the nearest hundredth.

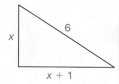

We first make a drawing. Let x = the length of one leg. Then $x + 1$ is the length of the other leg. Next we use the Pythagorean theorem.

$$x^2 + (x + 1)^2 = 6^2$$
$$x^2 + x^2 + 2x + 1 = 36$$
$$2x^2 + 2x - 35 = 0$$

Since we cannot factor, we use the quadratic formula.

$a = 2, b = 2, c = -35$, so $b^2 - 4ac = 284$

$$x = \frac{-b \pm \sqrt{b^2 - 4ac}}{2a}$$

$$= \frac{-2 \pm \sqrt{284}}{4}$$

$$= \frac{-2 \pm \sqrt{4 \cdot 71}}{4}$$

$$= \frac{-2 \pm 2 \cdot \sqrt{71}}{2 \cdot 2}$$

$$= \frac{-1 \pm \sqrt{71}}{2}$$

$$x = \frac{-1 + \sqrt{71}}{2} \approx 3.72 \quad \text{or} \quad x = \frac{-1 - \sqrt{71}}{2} \approx -4.72$$

Since the length of a leg cannot be negative, −4.72 can be discarded. Thus one leg is about 3.72 m and the other is about 3.72 + 1 = 4.72 m long. These lengths are reasonable, as the hypotenuse is greater than each leg. These lengths can also be checked, together with 6, in the Pythagorean theorem equation.

> **Reading Math**
>
> The numbers
> $\frac{-1 + \sqrt{71}}{2}$ and $\frac{-1 - \sqrt{71}}{2}$
> are exact solutions, while 3.72 and −4.72 are approximate solutions.

Try This   Solve.

b. The hypotenuse of a right triangle is 4 cm long. One leg is 1 cm longer than the other. Find the lengths of the legs. Round to the nearest tenth.

Had the wind speed been a little less than 3 mi/h, would the *Daedalus 88* have had to average more than or less than 15 mi/h to make the trip in 25 min?

EXAMPLE 3

In April, 1988, *Daedalus 88*, a man-powered aircraft weighing 70 pounds, made a historic 74-mile crossing from Crete to the Greek Isle of Santorini. In testing, the craft was able to fly a three-mile course *with* the wind and fly back *against* the wind in a total time of 25 minutes. If the speed of the wind was three miles per hour, what would be the speed of *Daedalus 88* in still air?

Let d represent the distance for both directions, as the distances were the same. Let r represent the speed of *Daedalus 88* in still air.

When traveling with the wind, the speed of the plane would be $r + 3$, and when traveling against the wind, the speed of the plane would be $r - 3$. Since $d = rt$, we know that $t = \frac{d}{r}$. Thus the time to travel against the wind would be $\frac{3}{r + 3}$. We summarize this in a chart.

	d	r (mi/h)	t (h)
With the wind	3	$r + 3$	$\frac{3}{r + 3}$
Against the wind	3	$r - 3$	$\frac{3}{r - 3}$

Since the total time is 25 minutes, or $\frac{5}{12}$ hour, we add the time *with* the wind and the time *against* the wind to get an equation for the total time.

$$\frac{3}{r + 3} + \frac{3}{r - 3} = \frac{5}{12} \qquad \text{LCM} = 12(r + 3)(r - 3)$$

$$12(r + 3)(r - 3)\left(\frac{3}{r + 3} + \frac{3}{r - 3}\right) = 12(r + 3)(r - 3)\frac{5}{12} \qquad \text{Multiplying by the LCM}$$

$$36(r - 3) + 36(r + 3) = 5r^2 - 45$$

$$5r^2 - 72r - 45 = 0$$

$$(5r + 3)(r - 15) = 0 \qquad \text{Factoring}$$

$$5r + 3 = 0 \quad \text{or} \quad r - 15 = 0 \qquad \text{Using the principle of zero products}$$

$$5r = -3 \quad \text{or} \quad r = 15$$

$$r = -\frac{3}{5} \quad \text{or} \quad r = 15$$

Since speed cannot be negative, $-\frac{3}{5}$ cannot be a solution. Thus the speed of the plane in still air would be 15 miles per hour, a speed that checks in the original situation.

Try This   Solve.

c. The speed of a boat in still water is 12 km/h. The boat travels 45 km upstream and 45 km downstream in a total time of 8 hours. What is the speed of the stream? (Hint: Let s = the speed of the stream. Then $12 - s$ is the speed upstream and $12 + s$ is the speed downstream).

13-7 Exercises

Extra Help On the Web

Look for worked-out examples at the Prentice Hall Web site.
www.phschool.com

A

Solve.

1. A picture frame is 20 cm by 12 cm. There are 84 cm² of a picture showing. Find the width of the frame.

2. A picture frame is 18 cm by 14 cm. There are 192 cm² of picture showing. Find the width of the frame.

3. The hypotenuse of a right triangle is 25 ft long. One leg is 17 ft longer than the other. Find the lengths of the legs.

4. The hypotenuse of a right triangle is 26 yd long. One leg is 14 yd longer than the other. Find the lengths of the legs.

5. The length of a rectangle is 2 cm greater than the width. The area is 80 cm². Find the length and width.

6. The width of a rectangle is 4 cm less than the length. The area is 320 cm². Find the length and width.

For Exercises 7 and 8, round your answers to the nearest tenth.

7. The hypotenuse of a right triangle is 8 m long. One leg is 2 m longer than the other. Find the lengths of the legs.

8. The hypotenuse of a right triangle is 5 cm long. One leg is 2 cm longer than the other. Find the lengths of the legs.

9. The current in a stream moves at a speed of 3 km/h. A boat travels 40 km upstream and 40 km downstream in a total time of 14 hours. What is the speed of the boat in still water?

10. The current in a stream moves at a speed of 4 mi/h. A boat travels 4 mi upstream and 12 mi downstream in a total time of 2 hours. What is the speed of the boat in still water?

11. The speed of a boat in still water is 10 km/h. The boat travels 12 km upstream and 28 km downstream in a total time of 4 hours. What is the speed of the stream?

12. An airplane flies 738 mi against the wind and 1062 mi with the wind in a total time of 9 hours. The speed of the airplane in still air is 200 mi/h. What is the speed of the wind?

B

13. Find the side of a square whose diagonal is 3 cm longer than a side.

14. Find r in this figure.
Round to the nearest hundredth.

1 cm

15. What should be the diameter (d) of a pizza so that it has the same area as two 10-in.-diameter pizzas? Do you get more to eat with a 15-in. pizza or two 10-in. pizzas?

16. In this figure, the area of the shaded region is 24 cm^2. Find r if $R = 6$ cm. Round to the nearest hundredth.

17. Trains A and B leave the same city at the same time. Train A heads north and train B heads east. Train B travels 5 mi/h faster than train A. After 2 hours they are 50 mi apart. Find the speed of each train.

18. *Write a Convincing Argument*   Solve the problem below. Then write an argument to convince a classmate that your solution is correct. A 10-ft long ladder leans against a wall. The bottom of the ladder is 6 ft from the wall. How much would the lower end have to be pulled away so that the top end would be pulled down the same amount?

Challenge

The formula $d = rt - 5t^2$ gives the approximate distance in meters of an object above its starting point t seconds after it is thrown with an initial upward velocity of r meters per second. Use this formula to solve the following problems.

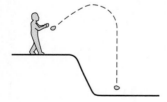

19. How high would a ball be in 5 seconds if it is thrown upward with an initial velocity of 45 meters per second?

20. How long would it take a ball batted upward at an initial velocity of 55 meters per second to be 50 meters above its starting point?

21. Where would a rock be (vertically) in 5 seconds if it is thrown as shown at the left with an initial upward velocity of 20 meters per second?

Mixed Review

Solve.   **22.** $\sqrt{m - 3} = 10$ **23.** $\sqrt{\frac{a}{3}} = 1$ **24.** $x + 7 = 2\sqrt{x + 7}$ *13-6*

Solve.   **25.** $x^2 + 2x - 15 = 0$ **26.** $x^2 - 10x + 25 = 0$

27. $x^2 + 5x + 2 = 0$ **28.** $x^2 - 7x + 12 = 0$ *13-3*

29. Find an equation of the line containing the points $(2, -4)$ and $(-3, -2)$.   *7-6*

Annual Percentage Rate

Banks often advertise interest rates by giving a compound percentage rate followed by a second rate labeled **APR.**

> 5.5% compounded daily,
> 5.65% APR

Which rate is correct?

The first is the actual rate used to compute the interest at any given time. Banks call this the **nominal rate.** The second, APR, is the **annual percentage rate,** and is sometimes called the **effective annual yield.** This rate is the equivalent simple interest for one year.

You can use the APR as simple interest to quickly determine the amount of interest you will pay or receive in one year. If you invested $1000 at the compound rate above, you would earn about $1000 × 0.0565 = $56.50. The APR gives an efficient way of comparing interest rates. If the APR is not given, you can use the following formula to find it.

CERTIFICATES OF DEPOSIT
WEEK OF 10 24
$ 1000 MIN. DEPOSIT

	RATE	ANNUAL YIELD
3 MONTHS	2.60%	2.63%
6 MONTHS	3.20%	3.25%
1 YEAR	3.94%	4.00%
18 MONTHS	4.67%	4.75%
2 YEARS	4.67%	4.75%
30 MONTH	4.67%	4.75%
3 YEARS	4.67%	4.75%
MONEY MARKET		2.50%

For the 3-year certificate of deposit above, is interest compounded yearly, quarterly, monthly, or daily? Use the formula on this page to find out.

Where E = effective annual yield or APR, r is the interest rate, and n is the number of compounding periods per year,

$$E = \left(1 + \frac{r}{n}\right)^n - 1.$$

Find the APR if the advertised interest rate is 7% compounded quarterly.

$$E = \left(1 + \frac{r}{n}\right)^n - 1$$
$$= \left(1 + \frac{0.07}{4}\right)^4 - 1 = (1.0175)^4 - 1 \approx 7.19\%$$

Find the APR if the advertised interest rate is $7\frac{1}{4}\%$ compounded yearly. Compare the results with the rate above.

Problems

1. How much interest will you receive on an investment of $2100 for 1 year in an account that has an APR of 6.2%?

2. Find the APR if the advertised interest rate is 6.2% compounded monthly.

3. Find the APR if the advertised interest rate is 4.1% compounded daily.

4. Which rate will yield more in one year, one that pays 8.1% compounded monthly or one that pays 8% compounded daily?

Designing a School Picnic

Some schools have end-of-the-year picnics for their students. These picnics usually involve games and, of course, food. It takes careful planning to assure that all the expenses can be paid (and that everyone gets enough to eat). You can use the Problem-Solving Guidelines to help organize a plan for a school picnic.

PROBLEM-SOLVING GUIDELINES
■ UNDERSTAND the problem
▨ Develop and carry out a PLAN
■ Find the ANSWER and CHECK

You can use the Problem-Solving Guidelines to help you solve the following situational problem about planning a picnic.

Use the Problem-Solving Guidelines to solve the following.

Situational Problem

Lincoln High School has 350 students in the sophomore class. The class has decided to plan an all-day class picnic. They plan to go to a state park that is 30 miles away. They have $200 in the class treasury to spend for the picnic. The students must share the additional expenses. Plan the expenses for this trip and the cost for each student to attend.

Possible Assumptions

1. You will have to provide 1 paper cup and 1 paper plate for each student.
2. There is no cost for supplies for games and activities that you select.
3. All the students in the class will attend the picnic.
4. The picnic will last the entire school day.

How will you design your picnic? What will be the cost per person?

Possible Subproblems

1. What type of food will you have at the picnic and how much of each type will you need?
2. How much will it cost for supplies for the picnic?
3. How much will it cost for transportation?
4. What state park fees are there?
5. What if the weather doesn't cooperate?
6. How much more than $200 will your class need for the picnic?

13 ▷ Chapter Wrap Up

13-1

To solve a **quadratic equation** in **standard form,** $ax^2 + bx + c = 0$, you may be able to factor the equation and use the principle of zero products to find the solutions.

Write in standard form.

1. $3x^2 + 6x = -4$

2. $5x^2 = 2x$

Solve.

3. $5x^2 - 7x = 0$

4. $3x^2 - 4x = 0$

5. $5x^2 - 8x + 3 = 0$

6. $3y^2 + 5y = 2$

Key Terms

complete the square (p. 586)
discriminant (p. 591)
quadratic equation (p. 576)
quadratic formula (p. 589)
standard form of a quadratic
   equation (p. 576)

13-2

To solve a quadratic equation of the form $ax^2 = k$ or $(x + a)^2 = k$, first solve for x^2 or $(x + a)^2$, and then find the square roots of each side.

Solve.

7. $5x^2 = 40$

8. $8x^2 = 24$

9. $(x + 8)^2 = 13$

10. $(x + 6)^2 = 49$

11. $4y^2 + 20y + 25 = 16$

12. Suppose we know a polygon has $d = 35$ diagonals. Use the formula $d = \frac{n^2 - 3n}{2}$ to find n the number of sides.

13. The sum of $1000 is invested at interest rate r. In 2 years the total grows to $1690. Use the formula $A = P(1 + r)^t$ to find the annual interest rate.

14. The sum of $4000, invested at 8% for 2 years, compounded annually, will grow to what amount?

13-3

To **complete the square** for an expression like $x^2 + 8x$, take half of the coefficient of x and square it. Add this new term to the binomial $x^2 + 8x$ to make a trinomial square, $x^2 + 8x + 16$. You can use the technique of completing the square to solve quadratic equations.

Complete the square.

15. $c^2 + 22c$

16. $w^2 - 7w$

Solve by completing the square.

17. $x^2 - 2x - 10 = 0$

18. $9x^2 - 6x - 9 = 0$

19. $3x^2 - 2x - 5 = 0$

20. $2x^2 + 7x - 1 = 0$

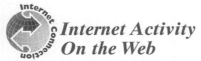

**Internet Activity
On the Web**

Look for extension problems
for this chapter at the
Prentice Hall Web site.
www.phschool.com

13-4

You can use the **quadratic formula** $x = \frac{-b \pm \sqrt{b^2 - 4ac}}{2a}$ to solve quadratic equations. The expression under the radical, $b^2 - 4ac$, is called the **discriminant.** When the discriminant is positive, there are two real-number solutions to the quadratic equation. When the discriminant is 0, there is only one real-number solution, and when the discriminant is negative, there are no real-number solutions.

Solve using the quadratic formula.

21. $x^2 - 6x - 9 = 0$ **22.** $3x^2 - x - 5 = 0$ **23.** $x^2 - 3x - 6 = 0$

24. $5x^2 + 3x - 4 = 0$ **25.** $x^2 + 6x + 7 = 0$ **26.** $x^2 - 14x + 49 = 0$

Compute the discriminant and determine how many real-number solutions there are.

27. $5x^2 - 8x + 2 = 0$ **28.** $x^2 - 18x + 83 = 0$

13-5

When you multiply both sides of a rational equation by the LCM of the denominators, you may get a quadratic equation. Be sure to check all possible solutions in the original equation.

Solve.

29. $\frac{15}{x} - \frac{15}{x + 2} = 2$ **30.** $x + \frac{1}{x} = 2$

13-6

To solve a radical equation, first square both sides. If a quadratic equation results, then solve by factoring or using the quadratic equation.

31. $\sqrt{x - 3} = 7$ **32.** $\sqrt{3x + 4} = \sqrt{2x + 14}$

33. Solve for F: $V = \sqrt{\frac{Fqr}{m}}$ **34.** Solve for r: $A = \frac{1}{3}\pi r^2$

13-7

You can use the Problem-Solving Guidelines to solve problems involving quadratic equations.

35. The length of a rectangle is 3 m greater than the width. The area is 70 m². Find the length and the width.

36. You can row upstream 5 miles and then row back downstream all in 3 hours and 20 minutes. If the river has an average current of 2 mi/h, at what rate are you able to row in still water?

37. One side of a right triangle is 1 ft, 4 in. shorter than the hypotenuse. The other side is 2 in. shorter than the hypotenuse. Find the lengths of the two legs.

Write in standard form.

1. $6x^2 = 3x + 4$

2. $3y = 2y^2$

Solve.

3. $4a^2 + 4a = 0$

4. $7x^2 + 8x = 0$

5. $x^2 + 2x - 48 = 0$

6. $3y^2 + 5y = 2$

7. $16b^2 - 25b = 0$

8. $7x^2 = 35$

9. $(x + 8)^2 = 13$

10. $(x - 1)^2 = 8$

Complete the square.

11. $x^2 + 8x$

12. $y^2 + 9y$

Solve.

13. $x^2 + 4x - 10 = 0$

14. $x^2 - 3x - 7 = 0$

15. $x^2 - x - 3 = 0$

16. $3x^2 - 7x + 1 = 0$

17. $x - \dfrac{2}{x} = 1$

18. $\dfrac{4}{x} - \dfrac{4}{x + 2} = 1$

Compute the value of the discriminant and use it to determine how many real-number solutions each quadratic equation has.

19. $3x^2 + 12x + 13 = 0$

20. $5x^2 + 17x + 14 = 0$

Solve.

21. $\sqrt{x + 1} = 6$

22. $\sqrt{6x + 1} = \sqrt{5x + 13}$

23. Solve $g = 2\sqrt{\dfrac{v}{kh}}$ for h.

24. The sum of $2000 is invested at the compound interest rate r. In 4 years it grows to $2621.59. Use the formula $A = P(1 + r)^t$ to find r.

25. The width of a rectangle is 4 m less than the length. The area is 16.25 m². Find the length and the width.

26. An airplane flies between two cities that are 700 miles apart, traveling with a wind of 25 mi/h when going, and traveling against it when returning. The trip out takes 15 minutes less time than the return flight. What is the speed of the plane in still air?

1–13 ▷ Cumulative Review

1-4 Evaluate.

1. $(x - 3)^2 + 5$ for $x = 10$
2. $(y - 1)^2 + (y + 6)^2$ for $y = 4$
3. $(x - y)^2 + 2(x + y)$ for $x = 10$ and $y = 2$

1-5 Use the associative property to write an equivalent expression.

4. $(7 + 6) + 4$
5. $a \cdot (b \cdot c)$

2-3, 2-4 Add.

6. $-12.8 + 2.6 + (-11.9) + 6.2 + 0.9$
7. $-\frac{1}{8} - 4 - \frac{3}{4} + 2\frac{1}{2} - 6\frac{1}{4}$
8. $2 + 6x - 14 - 5x$
9. $18a + 16b + 2a - 10b$

2-5 Multiply.

10. $(-8)(-5)$
11. $(-11.2)(3.1)$

2-6 Divide.

12. $-\frac{4}{7} \div \frac{1}{14}$
13. $-\frac{8}{9} \div -\frac{1}{3}$

3-3 to 3-5 Solve.

14. $3x - 12 = 2x$
15. $-\frac{7}{8}x + 7 = \frac{3}{8}x - 3$
16. $0.6x - 1.8 = 1.2x$
17. Three fifths of the automobiles entering the city each morning will be parked in city parking lots. These cars fill 3654 parking spaces. How many cars enter the city each morning?

3-7

18. Solve $A = \pi r^2$ for r.
19. Solve $A = 2\pi r^2 + 2\pi rh$ for h.

3-9

20. After election results of 378 votes were tallied, the new student-body president won by a margin of 5 to 4. How many votes did she get?

3-10 Solve.

21. What percent of 52 is 13?

22. What percent of 86 is 129?

23. 60 is what percent of 720?

24. 12 is what percent of 0.5?

25. 110% of what number is 11?

26. What is 25% of 16?

4-2 to 4-4 Solve.

27. $x - 9 < 12$

28. $3a + 8 \geq -5 + 2a$

29. $6y \leq 3$

30. $3c - 6 < 5c$

31. $7y + 2 > 5y - 8$

32. $23 - 7x - 3x \geq -11$

4-5

33. The width of a rectangle is 15 cm. What length will make the area at least 225 cm^2?

5-1, 5-2 Simplify.

34. $a^4 \cdot a^6$

35. $\frac{4m^5}{m^3}$

36. y^{-3}

37. $(2y^6)^3$

38. $\left(\frac{x}{y^3}\right)^2$

39. $(3x^5y^4)^3$

5-3, 5-4 Multiply.

40. $(-3y)(2y^2)$

41. $(-3ab^2c)(-4b^2c^4)$

Divide.

42. $\frac{-25x^4}{10x}$

43. $\frac{-18x^2y^3z}{-3xyz}$

5-7, 5-8 Add or subtract.

44. $(2m^3 - 9) + (5m^3 - 10m^2 + 10)$

45. $(-6a^2 - a + 3) - (a^3 - 10a^2 + a + 3)$

5-10 Multiply.

46. $(4b - 1)(4b + 3)$

47. $(2m + 3)(m - 6)$

48. $(7y + 6)(7y - 6)$

49. $(a + 2)^2$

50. $(a - 3)^2$

51. $(3m + 5)^2$

6-1 to 6-5 Factor.

52. $m^3 - m$

53. $49x^2 - 64$

54. $m^4 - 1$

55. $2x^2 + 13x - 99$

56. $7m^2 - 8m + 1$

57. $9x^2 - 24x + 16$

58. $9x^4 - 30x^2y + 25y^2$

59. $100x^3 + 60x^2 + 9x$

7-3 Graph each equation.

60. $x + y = 5$

61. $2x + 3y = -1$

62. $-y = 7$

7-5 Find the slope and y-intercept of each line.

63. $10x = 125 - 20y$

64. $2y - 3x + 1 = 0$

7-6 Write an equation for each line.

65. the line containing $(0, 10)$ and parallel to the x-axis

66. the line containing the origin and $(-3, 3)$

67. the line with slope of $-\frac{2}{3}$ that crosses the x-axis at -7

68. the line with x-intercept 6 and y-intercept -1

8-1

In Exercises 69–71, which of these pairs are solutions of the system of equations? $(0, 0), (-2, 1), (4, 3), (1, 1)$

69. $5x - 2y = -12$
$3x + 8y = 2$

70. $2y = 6$
$-3x = -12$

71. $x + 8y = 6$
$3x + 6y = 0$

8-2, 8-3 Solve each system of equations.

72. $y = x - 6$
$x + y = -2$

73. $\frac{1}{2}x + 2y = 9$
$4x + 3y = 7$

8-4 to 8-6

74. The difference of two numbers is 14. Three times the larger number is 45 less than four times the smaller. What are the two numbers?

75. In 15 years Dorothy will be three times as old as Stan. Five years ago the difference in their ages was 50. How old are Dorothy and Stan?

76. An airplane whose speed in still air is 530 mi/h carries enough fuel for 10 hours of flight. On a certain flight it flies against a wind of 30 mi/h. On the return flight it travels with a wind of 30 mi/h. How far can the plane fly without refueling?

77. For the school festival, 600 tickets were sold. Student tickets sold for $1.60, and adult tickets sold for $2.25. If the total amount received was $1122.50, how many tickets of each kind were sold?

9-1

Let $A = \{100, 105, 110, 115, 120\}$, $B = \{100, 102, 104, 106, 108, 110, 112\}$, and $C = \{99, 102, 105, 108, 111\}$.
Find the following.

78. $A \cup B$ **79.** $A \cup C$ **80.** $B \cup C$

81. $A \cap B$ **82.** $A \cap C$ **83.** $B \cap C$

9-4 Solve and graph.

84. $|x| < 4$ **85.** $|x| > 5$

86. $|x - 6| \leq 10$ **87.** $2|x| \geq 6$

10-2 Multiply. Simplify the product when possible.

88. $\dfrac{-5}{3x - 4} \cdot \dfrac{-6}{5x + 6}$

89. $\dfrac{x + 3}{x^2 - 2} \cdot \dfrac{x + 3}{x^2 - 2}$

90. $\dfrac{x^2 - 6x}{x - 6} \cdot \dfrac{x + 3}{x}$

91. $\dfrac{5a + 5}{a + 3} \cdot \dfrac{2a + 6}{a^2 + 2a + 1}$

10-3 Divide. Simplify the quotient.

92. $\dfrac{y + 4}{y^2 - 1} \div \dfrac{y^2 + y - 12}{y + 1}$

93. $\dfrac{8x - 12}{5} \div \dfrac{6x - 9}{35}$

10-4, 10-5 Add or subtract. Simplify.

94. $\dfrac{2x^2}{2x - 1} - \dfrac{1 - x}{2x - 1}$

95. $\dfrac{x^2}{x - 3} + \dfrac{9}{3 - x}$

96. $\dfrac{x - 5}{x} - \dfrac{x}{x - 5}$

97. $\dfrac{3}{12 + x - x^2} - \dfrac{2}{x^2 - 9}$

10-6, 10-7 Solve.

98. $\dfrac{6x - 2}{2x - 1} = \dfrac{9x}{3x + 1}$

99. $\dfrac{2}{x + 1} = \dfrac{5}{2x}$

100. In checking records a contractor finds that crew A can pave a certain length of highway in 8 hours. Crew B can do the same job in 10 hours. How long would it take if they worked together?

101. One boat travels 5 km/h slower than another. While one boat travels 85 km, the other travels 110 km. Find their speeds.

102. Two women were partners in a store, one investing $50,000 and the other $38,000. They agreed to share the profits in the ratio of the amount invested. The profits for the first year were $11,000. How much should each receive?

11-1 Simplify.

103. $\sqrt{49}$

104. $-\sqrt{81}$

11-2 Determine the replacements for the variable that will make each expression a real number.

105. $\sqrt{x + 4}$

106. $\sqrt{x - 6}$

Simplify.

107. $\sqrt{c^2 d^2}$

108. $\sqrt{(x + 1)^2}$

109. $\sqrt{64x^2}$

11-3 Simplify. Assume all variables are nonnegative.

110. $\sqrt{150}$

111. $\sqrt{9y}$

112. $\sqrt{16x - 16}$

113. $\sqrt{y^7}$

114. $\sqrt{8x^4 y^4}$

115. $\sqrt{9(a + 4)^2}$

11-4, 11-5 Multiply and simplify. Assume all variables are nonnegative.

116. $\sqrt{4xy^2} \cdot \sqrt{8x^2 y}$

117. $\sqrt{32ab} \cdot \sqrt{6a^4 b^2}$

Rationalize the denominator. Assume all variables are nonnegative.

118. $\sqrt{\frac{1}{6}}$

119. $\dfrac{\sqrt{5}}{\sqrt{18}}$

120. $\sqrt{\frac{x^2}{27}}$

11-6 Add or subtract.

121. $6\sqrt{a} + 7\sqrt{a}$

122. $\sqrt{81y^3} - \sqrt{4y}$

123. $3x\sqrt{x^2 y} - x\sqrt{x^2 y^3} - 2\sqrt{y^3}$

11-7

124. In a right triangle with hypotenuse c, $a = 9$ and $c = 41$. Find the length of side b.

12-1 Find the indicated output for the function $f(x) = 2x^2 + 7x - 4$.

125. $f(0)$

126. $f\left(\frac{1}{2}\right)$

127. $f(-2)$

12-4 Graph each function.

128. $g(x) = x^2 - 1$

129. $f(x) = \frac{1}{4}x^2$

12-5 to 12-7

130. When you swim underwater, the pressure in your ears varies directly as the depth at which you swim. At 50 ft the pressure is about 21.5 pounds per square inch (psi). Find the pressure at 20 ft.

131. The volume of a certain quantity of gas varies inversely as its pressure. If its pressure is 15 psi when its volume is 3 cubic feet, what will the pressure be when the gas is expanded to a volume of 5 cubic feet?

132. Assume that p varies directly as r and inversely as s, where p is 10 when r is 8 and s is 4. Find p when r is 10 and s is 2.

13-1 to 13-4 Solve.

133. $3x^2 = 30$

134. $3x^2 - 7x = 0$

135. $x^2 + 4 = 4x$

136. $6x^2 + x - 2 = 0$

137. $(x - 3)^2 = 6$

138. $x^2 - 10x - 4 = 0$

139. $9x^2 - 12x - 2 = 0$

140. $x^2 = 7x - 1$

13-5 Solve.

141. $\dfrac{x + 2}{x^2 - 2} = \dfrac{2}{2 - x}$

142. $1 + \dfrac{1}{x} = \dfrac{6}{x^2}$

13-6 Solve.

143. $p = \sqrt{4p - 3}$

144. $2\sqrt{x^2 - 1} = x - 1$

13-7

145. The speed of a boat in still water is 8 km/h. It travels 60 km upstream and 60 km downstream in a total time of 16 hours. What is the speed of the stream?

146. The width of a rectangle is half its length. The area is 32 m². Find the length and the width.

Additional Topics

A-1 ▷ Similar Right Triangles

Math in Action

Similar triangles have the same shape, but do not need to be the same size or positioned the same way. The distance across the river can be found using similar triangles.

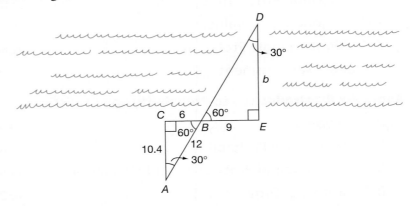

Similar Triangles

Objective: Write true proportions for similar right triangles.

In similar triangles, we identify corresponding angles and sides. Notice that angle B is the same in both triangles, angles C and E have the same measure, and angles A and D have the same measure.

Corresponding Angles	Corresponding Sides
$\angle B$ and $\angle B$	$\overline{AC}$ and $\overline{DE}$
$\angle C$ and $\angle E$	$\overline{AB}$ and $\overline{BD}$
$\angle A$ and $\angle D$	$\overline{BC}$ and $\overline{BE}$

When writing a statement such as $\triangle ACB \sim \triangle DEB$, we always list the vertices in corresponding order. For the triangles above, we could also write $\triangle BCA \sim \triangle BED$ or $\triangle CBA \sim \triangle EBD$.

Similar Triangles

Similar triangles have the following properties:
1. The lengths of the corresponding sides of a pair of similar triangles are proportional.
2. Corresponding angles are the same size.

EXAMPLE 1 $\triangle ABC \sim \triangle RST$. Write three true proportions.

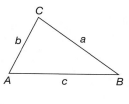

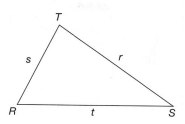

The small letters are the lengths of the sides.

These proportions are true.

$$\frac{a}{r} = \frac{b}{s}, \frac{c}{t} = \frac{a}{r}, \text{ and } \frac{b}{s} = \frac{c}{t}$$

There are others.

Try This

a. $\triangle PQR \sim \triangle XYZ$. Write three true proportions.

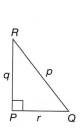 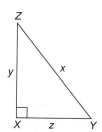

PART 2 Right Triangles

Objective: Find a missing side in a pair of similar right triangles.

A right triangle has one angle of 90°, often marked with a small square. The other two angles must each be less than 90°, since the sum of the interior angles of a triangle is 180°. Angles whose measures are less than 90° are called **acute angles.** If two angles of any triangle have the same measures as two angles of another triangle, then the third angles must also be equal. Therefore, two right triangles are similar if an acute angle of one triangle has the same measure as the acute angle of the other.

EXAMPLE 2 Which right triangles are similar?

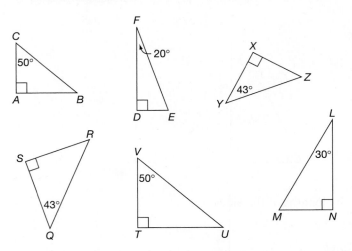

$\triangle ABC \sim \triangle TUV$ and $\triangle XYZ \sim \triangle SQR$.

When triangles are similar, the corresponding sides are proportional. We can use this relationship to find the length of a side whose length is not known.

EXAMPLE 3 $\triangle ACB \sim \triangle DEB$. Find length b.

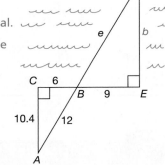

$$\frac{b}{10.4} = \frac{9}{6}$$ The corresponding sides are proportional.

$$10.4 \cdot \frac{b}{10.4} = \frac{9}{6} \cdot 10.4$$ Multiplying each side by 10.4

$$b = 15.6$$

The length b is 15.6.

Try This

b. $\triangle RST \sim \triangle WXY$. Find length x.

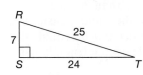

A

1. $\triangle ABC \sim \triangle DEF$. Name the corresponding sides and angles.

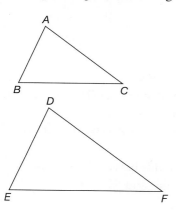

2. $\triangle PQR \sim \triangle WXY$. Name the corresponding sides and angles.

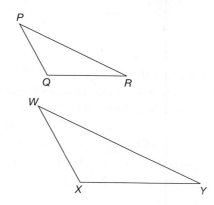

3. $\triangle STU \sim \triangle LMN$. Write three true proportions.

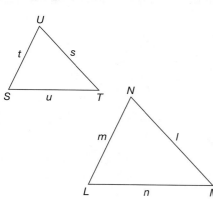

4. $\triangle FGH \sim \triangle JKL$. Write three true proportions.

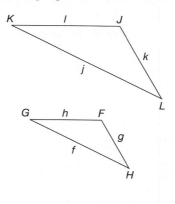

5. $\triangle ABC \sim \triangle DEF$. Find length f.

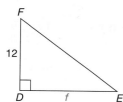

6. $\triangle LMN \sim \triangle HJK$. Find length h.

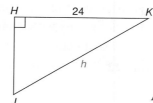

7. A rod 3 m tall casts a shadow 5 m long. At the same time, the shadow of a tower is 110 m long. How tall is the tower?

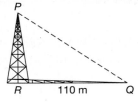

B

Assume that the three sides of $\triangle RST$ are 12, 16, and 20.

8. If $\triangle DEF$ is similar to $\triangle RST$ and the longest side of $\triangle DEF$ is 30, what are the lengths of the other two sides?

9. If $\triangle XYZ \sim \triangle RST$ and the shortest side of $\triangle XYZ$ is 6, what are the lengths of the other two sides?

10. *Critical Thinking* What relationship holds between the areas of $\triangle ABC$ and $\triangle DEF$ if the triangles are similar and $\frac{AB}{DE} = k$?

Challenge

11. There are three right triangles in the figure below. Name them, writing the right angle first.

12. Which of these proportions are true?

$$\frac{AB}{BC} = \frac{AC}{DB}$$

$$\frac{AC}{AB} = \frac{BC}{BD}$$

$$\frac{BD}{BC} = \frac{AB}{BC}$$

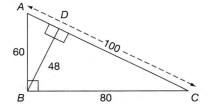

13. If $\frac{AD}{AB} = \frac{AB}{AC}$, find the length of $\overline{AD}$.

14. If $\frac{AD}{BD} = \frac{BD}{DC}$, find the length of $\overline{DC}$.

Mixed Review

Solve. **15.** $x^2 + 6x - 5 = 0$ **16.** $x^2 - 4x - 16 = 0$

Find the number of real-number solutions.

17. $x^2 - 10x + 25 = 0$ **18.** $y^2 - y + 1 = 0$

Write an equation of variation.

19. y varies inversely as x, and $y = 3$ when $x = 7$.

20. x varies jointly with y and z, and $x = 9$ when $y = 4$ and $z = 9$.

21. y varies directly as x, and $y = 1.2$ when $x = 4$.

Factor. **22.** $2m^3 - 8m^2 + 8m$ **23.** $a^4 - 72a^2 + 1296$ **24.** $x^2 - 25$

Trigonometric Ratios

A-2

For any right triangle six ratios of pairs of sides are possible. For the triangle at the right, we have these six ratios.

$$\frac{a}{c}, \frac{b}{c}, \frac{a}{b}, \frac{b}{a}, \frac{c}{a}, \frac{c}{b}$$

These six ratios are called *trigonometric ratios*.

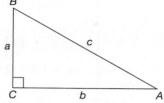

PART 1 Sine

Objective: Find the sine ratio of an angle.

Each of these six ratios has a name. First we discuss the **sine** ratio. We define the sine ratio as follows.

$$\text{sine of } A \text{ (or } \sin A) = \frac{\text{length of side opposite } \angle A}{\text{length of hypotenuse}} = \frac{a}{c}$$

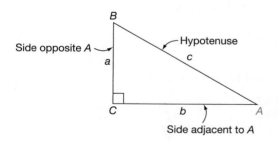

EXAMPLE 1

In $\triangle ABC$, find $\sin B$. Write this value to four decimal places.

$$\sin B = \frac{\text{length of side opposite } \angle B}{\text{length of hypotenuse}} = \frac{15}{17} \approx 0.8824$$

Try This

a. In $\triangle PQR$, find $\sin R$ to four decimal places.

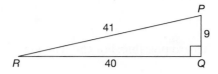

Objective: Find the cosine ratio of an angle.

For any acute angle A of a right triangle, we define the **cosine** ratio as follows.

$$\text{cosine of } A \text{ (or } \cos A) = \frac{\text{length of side adjacent to } \angle A}{\text{length of hypotenuse}} = \frac{b}{c}$$

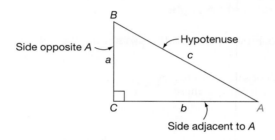

Side opposite A — a

Hypotenuse c

Side adjacent to A

EXAMPLE 2

In $\triangle CLF$, find $\cos F$. Write this value to four decimal places.

$$\cos F = \frac{\text{length of side adjacent to } \angle F}{\text{length of hypotenuse}} = \frac{32}{40}$$

$$= \frac{4}{5} = 0.8000$$

$$\cos F = 0.8000$$

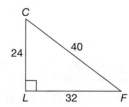

Try This

b. In $\triangle DEF$, find $\cos D$ to four decimal places.

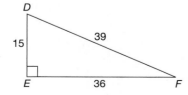

Objective: Find the tangent ratio of an angle.

For any acute angle A of a right triangle, we define the **tangent** ratio as follows.

The tangent of A:

$$\tan A = \frac{\text{length of opposite side}}{\text{length of adjacent side}} = \frac{a}{b}$$

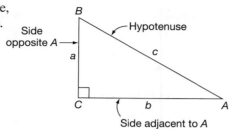

EXAMPLE 3

In $\triangle RST$, find $\tan S$. Write this value to four decimal places.

$$\tan S = \frac{\text{length of opposite side}}{\text{length of adjacent side}} = \frac{25}{60}$$

$$= \frac{5}{12} \approx 0.4167$$

$$\tan S \approx 0.4167$$

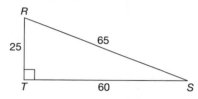

Try This

c. In $\triangle WXY$, find $\tan Y$.

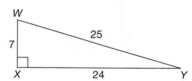

A-2 Exercises

A

Find the sine ratio for each triangle.

1. In $\triangle DEF$, find $\sin F$.

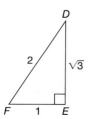

2. In $\triangle PQR$, find $\sin P$.

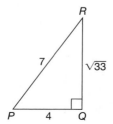

3. In $\triangle ABC$, find sin A.

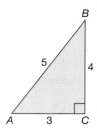

4. In $\triangle PQR$, find sin R.

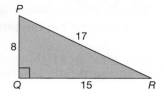

5. In $\triangle RST$, find sin T.

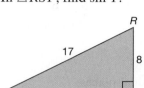

6. In $\triangle PQR$, find sin Q.

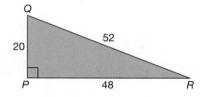

Find the cosine for each triangle.

7. Find cos S.

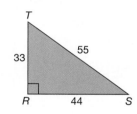

8. Find cos B.

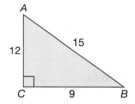

9. Find cos F.

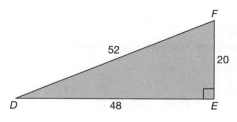

10. Find cos Z.

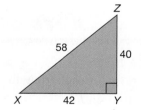

11. Find cos S.

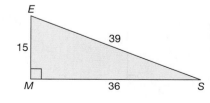

12. Find cos R.

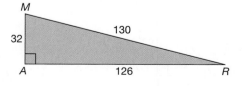

Find the tangent for each triangle.

13. Find tan R.

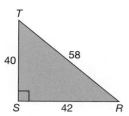

14. Find tan T.

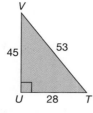

15. Find tan P.

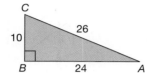

16. Find tan A.

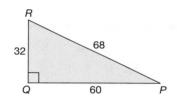

17. Find tan P.

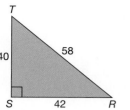

18. Find tan S.

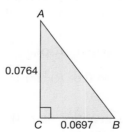

B

Use a calculator to solve.

19. In $\triangle PQR$, find cos R to four decimal places.

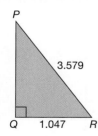

20. In $\triangle ABC$, find tan B to four decimal places.

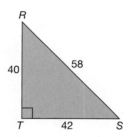

Use the Pythagorean theorem to find the length, to the nearest tenth, of the hypotenuse of a triangle with legs of the given lengths. Then find the sine ratio for each acute angle.

21. 9 and 12   **22.** 4 and 6   **23.** 5 and 13

24. 16 and 30   **25.** 24 and 32   **26.** 18 and 36

27. *Critical Thinking*   Show that the sine of an angle divided by the cosine of the same angle gives the tangent of the angle.

Challenge

28. Find sin T.

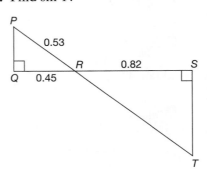

29. Find sin ($\angle BCD$).

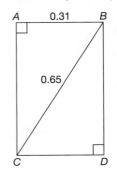

Solve.   **30.** $3x^2 + 12x = 0$ **31.** $y^2 - 2y = 8$ **32.** $4a^2 = 9$

33. $m^2 - 6m + 6 = 0$ **34.** $2x^2 - 7x + 15 = 0$ **35.** $3c^2 = 75$

Graph.   **36.** $f(x) = -x^2 + 4$ **37.** $g(x) = |x + 3| - 3$

Simplify.   **38.** $\dfrac{\sqrt{x^3 y}}{\sqrt{xy^3}}$ **39.** $\dfrac{\sqrt{12a^5}}{\sqrt{2a^2}}$ **40.** $\dfrac{\sqrt{(x-3)^3}}{\sqrt{(x-3)}}$ **41.** $\dfrac{1}{\sqrt{3}} - \dfrac{1}{\sqrt{27}}$

42. The cost of renting a paint sprayer is $12.50 plus $3.50 per hour. Find the cost of renting a paint sprayer for 5 hours.

43. A car leaves town and travels north at 36 mi/h. Two hours later a second car leaves town and travels north on the same road at 48 mi/h. When will the second car overtake the first?

Calculator Investigation

Find $(\sin R)^2$ and $(\cos R)^2$ for the triangle at the right.

1. What do you notice about the sum of these values?

2. Test other right triangles to see if this relationship seems to be true for any acute angle in a right triangle.

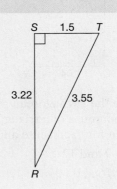

Trigonometric Values

A-3

Since corresponding sides of similar triangles are proportional, the sine ratio of 30° is the same in any right triangle. This is true for any trigonometric value of an angle in a right triangle. The values for angle measures can be found using a table, a calculator, or a computer.

PART 1 Finding Trigonometric Values

Objective: Find the value of a trigonometric ratio by reading a table or using a calculator.

The values of trigonometric ratios have been computed for angle measures between 0° and 90°. Table 4 (page 703) shows these values computed to four decimal places. Part of that table is shown below.

Degrees	Sin	Cos	Tan
56°	0.8290	0.5592	1.4826
57°	0.8387	0.5446	1.5399
58°	0.8480	0.5299	1.6003
59°	0.8572	0.5150	1.6643

EXAMPLE 1   Find tan 59°.

The entry in the Tan column opposite 59° is 1.6643. Thus, tan 59° ≈ 1.6643.

Try This   Use Table 4 to find the trigonometric values.

a. sin 57°   **b.** cos 77°   **c.** tan 46°

Many calculators are programmed to give the sine, cosine, or tangent of an angle.

Finding Trigonometric Values

Here is the key sequence to find the approximate angle for the sine, cosine, and tangent of a 56° angle.

56   [sin]   ⟶   0.8290376

56   [cos]   ⟶   0.5591929

56   [tan]   ⟶   1.4825609

Objective: Find an angle given the value of a trigonometric ratio.

The trigonometric table can also be used to approximate the measure of an angle if one of its trigonometric values is known.

EXAMPLE 2 Suppose cos A = 0.5592. Find A. Use Table 4 to find the angle.

In the Cos column find the entry 0.5592. Find the entry opposite 0.5592 in the Degree column. This is 56°, so A = 56°.

There are many trigonometric values that are not listed in the table. We can approximate the measure of the angle to the nearest degree by determining which value in the table is closest.

EXAMPLE 3 Suppose sin B = 0.8391. Find B to the nearest degree using Table 4.

In the Sin column the value 0.8391 is between two values.

$$0.8387 = \sin 57° \text{ and } 0.8480 = \sin 58°$$

Therefore, sin B is between 57° and 58°. Since 0.8391 is closer to 0.8387, sin B = 57° to the nearest degree.

Try This Use Table 4 to find the angle.

d. Suppose cos A = 0.6947. Find A.
e. Suppose sin B = 0.3584. Find B.
f. Suppose sin A = 0.8293. Find A to the nearest degree.
g. Suppose tan B = 3.0771. Find B to the nearest degree.

You can also find the angle value on a calculator if you know the trigonometric value by using the inverse key.

Finding Angles

Here is the key sequence to find the approximate angle for a given trigonometric value.

0.8290 | 2nd | sin → 55.99615 ≈ 56°

0.9613 | 2nd | cos → 15.99204 ≈ 16°

3.7321 | 2nd | tan → 75.00019 ≈ 75°

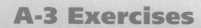

A-3 Exercises

A

Find these trigonometric values.

1. sin 38°   **2.** sin 47°   **3.** tan 56°   **4.** tan 84°   **5.** cos 9°

6. cos 31°   **7.** sin 60°   **8.** sin 30°   **9.** tan 45°   **10.** tan 55°

11. cos 1°   **12.** cos 89°   **13.** sin 71°   **14.** sin 45°   **15.** sin 15°

Find angle A.

16. sin $A = 0.2588$ **17.** sin $A = 0.9397$ **18.** cos $A = 0.8572$

19. cos $A = 0.1564$ **20.** tan $A = 0.4877$ **21.** tan $A = 2.2460$

22. cos $A = 0.7547$ **23.** cos $A = 0.9816$ **24.** tan $A = 9.5144$

25. tan $A = 1.1918$ **26.** sin $A = 0.7193$ **27.** sin $A = 0.0872$

Find angle A to the nearest degree.

28. sin $A = 0.1746$ **29.** sin $A = 0.8753$ **30.** tan $A = 2.9064$

31. tan $A = 0.7824$ **32.** cos $A = 0.8749$ **33.** cos $A = 0.4234$

34. tan $A = 9.5234$ **35.** tan $A = 2.8011$ **36.** sin $A = 0.9948$

B

37. One degree is 60 minutes (60′). The value of the trigonometric ratio of an angle measured in degrees and minutes can be approximated using the idea of proportion. For example, sin 37°10′ must lie between sin 37° and sin 38°. It is reasonable to assume that sin 37°10′ would be about $\frac{10}{60}$ of the difference between sin 37° and sin 38°. Find sin 37°10′, sin 37°20′, and sin 37°50′.

38. *Critical Thinking*   Find an angle that has the same sine and cosine.

39. Find an angle B such that sin $2B = $ cos B.

40. Find an angle B such that $B = \frac{A}{2}$ and 2 cos $A = $ sin A. (Hint: First show that tan $A = \frac{\sin A}{\cos A}$.)

Mixed Review

Solve.   **41.** $x - 7 = \dfrac{4}{x - 7}$ **42.** $\dfrac{y^2}{y + 1} - \dfrac{7}{y + 1} = 0$

43. $\dfrac{4}{a - 2} + \dfrac{6}{a + 2} = 1$ **44.** $5c^2 = 65$ **45.** $(m + 2)^2 = 16$

46. $x^2 + 4x - 16 = 0$ **47.** $x^2 + 20x + 91 = 0$

Determine whether the given point is a solution of the equation.

48. $(1, -2), 2y = x - 5$ **49.** $(3, -1), 2y = 3x - 7$

50. $(-2, 1), 5y - 2x = x + 11$ **51.** $(-2, 3), |x + y| - 3 = x$

A-4 ▷ Right Triangle Problems

Objective: Solve problems involving trigonometric functions.

PROBLEM-SOLVING GUIDELINES
■ UNDERSTAND the problem
Develop and carry out a PLAN
■ Find the ANSWER and CHECK

You can use the Problem-Solving Guidelines to help you solve problems where your plan involves the use of a trigonometric ratio.

EXAMPLE 1 In the right triangle ABC, $B = 61°$, $C = 90°$, and $c = 20$ cm. Find b.

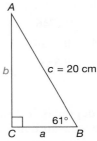

■ UNDERSTAND the problem

Question: What is the length of side b?
Data: $\angle B$ is 61°.
c is 20 cm and is the hypotenuse of a right triangle.

Drawing a diagram helps organize the data.

■ Develop and carry out a PLAN

We will use the sine ratio, since it relates the side opposite the given angle and the hypotenuse.

$$\sin B = \frac{b}{c}$$

$$\sin 61° = \frac{b}{20}$$

$$0.8746 \approx \frac{b}{20} \qquad \text{Finding } \sin 61°$$

$$20(0.8746) \approx b$$

$$17.492 \approx b$$

■ Find the ANSWER and CHECK

b is about 17.5 cm. If the drawing is accurate, we can see that 17.5 cm seems reasonable.

Try This

a. In right triangle ABC, B $= 42°$ and $c = 10$ cm. Find b.

EXAMPLE 2 In right triangle DEF, $D = 25°$ and $f = 18$ km. Find e.

$$\cos D = \frac{f}{e}$$

$$\cos 25° = \frac{18}{e}$$

$$0.9063 \approx \frac{18}{e} \qquad \text{Finding cos 25°}$$

$$0.9063e \approx 18$$

$$e \approx \frac{18}{0.9063}$$

$$e \approx 19.8609$$

e is about 19.9 km.

Try This

b. In right triangle DEF, $D = 36°$ and $f = 30$ m. Find e to the nearest tenth.

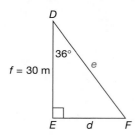

Trigonometric ratios can sometimes be used to help solve problems. We translate the information into a right triangle diagram.

EXAMPLE 3

The angle of elevation of an airplane is 12°. The distance to the plan is 16 km. How high is the plane?

Let the height of the plane be h.

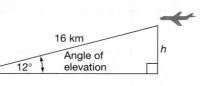

$$\sin 12° = \frac{h}{16}$$

$$0.2079 \approx \frac{h}{16} \qquad \text{Finding sin 12°}$$

$$16(0.2079) \approx h$$

$$3.3264 \approx h$$

The height of the airplane is about 3.3 km.

EXAMPLE 4

A fire warden's tower is 43 m tall. The angle of depression from the window of the tower to a fire in the woods is 5°. How far away from the base of the tower is the fire?

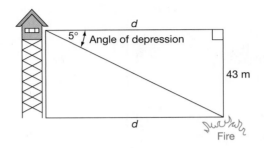

Let d be the distance from the fire to the base of the tower.

$$\tan 5° = \frac{43}{d}$$

$$0.0875 \approx \frac{43}{d} \qquad \text{Finding } \tan 5°$$

$$0.0875d \approx 43$$

$$d \approx 491.4$$

The distance to the fire is about 491 m.

Try This

c. A kite is flown with 180 m of string. The angle of elevation of the kite is 58°. How high is the kite? Round to the nearest tenth.

A-4 Exercises

A

Solve the following triangle problems. Round answers to the nearest tenth.

1. $B = 38°$ and $c = 37$ cm.
Find b.

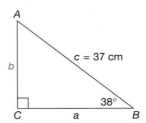

2. $B = 57°$ and $c = 24$ cm.
Find b.

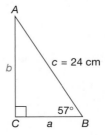

3. $D = 39°$ and $f = 42$ cm.
Find e.

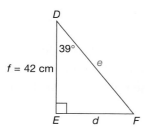

4. $D = 18°$ and $f = 16$ cm.
Find e.

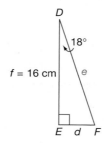

5. $k = 18$ cm and $g = 26$ cm.
Find K to the nearest degree.

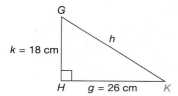

6. $k = 29$ cm and $g = 41$ cm.
Find K to the nearest degree.

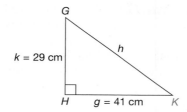

Solve. Draw a diagram first. Round answers to the nearest tenth.

7. The angle of elevation of an airplane is 9°. The distance to the plane is 21 km. How high is the plane?

8. A kite is flown with 210 m of string. The angle of elevation of the kite is 61°. How high is the kite?

9. The top of a lighthouse is 110 m above the level of the water. The angle of depression from the top of the lighthouse to a fishing boat is 18°. How far from the base of the lighthouse is the fishing boat?

10. An observation tower is 98 m tall. The angle of depression from the top of the tower to a historical marker is 23°. How far from the base of the tower is the marker?

11. A flagpole casts a shadow 4.6 m long. The angle of elevation of the sun is 49°. How high is the flagpole?

12. A water tower casts a shadow 23 m long. The angle of elevation of the sun is 52°. How tall is the water tower?

13. The firing angle of a missile is 28°. About how high is it after it has traveled 450 m?

14. A rocket is launched at an angle of 34°. About how high is it after it has traveled 670 m?

15. A pilot in a plane 3 km above the ground estimates that the angle of depression to a runway is 51°. What is the horizontal distance to the runway?

16. A balloonist 1.4 km above the ground estimates the angle of depression to a highway intersection to be 37°. How far is the balloonist horizontally from the intersection?

B

It can be shown that the area of a triangle equals one half the product of two adjacent sides times the sine of the angle between them. Use this formula, area of $\triangle ABC = \frac{1}{2}bc \sin \angle A$, to find the area of the following triangles to the nearest tenth.

17. $\triangle ABC$ where $A = 50°, b = 12$, and $c = 8$.

18. $\triangle MNP$ where $N = 67°, m = 40, p = 52$.

19. $\triangle XYZ$ where $Z = 12°, x = 18$, and $y = 18$.

20. $\triangle GHJ$ where $J = 24°, g = 6$, and $h = 6$.

21. *Critical Thinking* Lynnette is behind schedule. She is going to be late for an appointment in twenty minutes at the Texas Commerce Center. She knows that the building is 1002 ft tall, the angle to the building is 7°, and she is walking at a steady pace of 4 mi/h. How does she know that she will be late for her appointment? (5280 ft = 1 mi)

Challenge

22. Draw an acute triangle, ABC, with side a opposite $\angle A$, b opposite $\angle B$, and so on. Prove that $\frac{1}{2}bc \sin A$ is the area of the triangle. (Hint: Draw an altitude h.)

23. An equilateral isosceles triangle has two equal sides and two 45° angles. Use the Pythagorean theorem to find sin 45°.

Mixed Review

Write an equation for the line that contains the given pair of points.

24. $(-2, 2), (3, 7)$ **25.** $(3, 5), (3, -1)$ **26.** $(4, 1), (-2, -3)$

Solve.

27. $y = 3x - 10$ **28.** $5x + 2y = -11$ **29.** $x^2 + y = 7$
$\quad\quad x = 2y$ $3x - 2y = 3$ $y - 2x = 7$

Solve.   **30.** $8c^2 - 14c = 15$ **31.** $\sqrt{x - 7} = x - 13$

1. $\triangle PQR \sim \triangle SZW$. If $q = 25$, $r = 65$, $p = 60$, and $z = 75$, find w and s.
2. In $\triangle ABC$, find $\sin A$ to four decimal places.

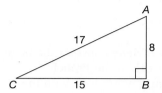

3. In $\triangle DEF$, find $\cos F$ to four decimal places.

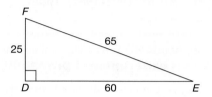

4. In $\triangle RST$, find $\tan R$ to four decimal places.

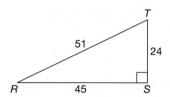

Use Table 4 for Exercises 5–8.

5. Find $\sin 13°$.
6. Find $\cos 52°$.
7. Suppose $\sin A = 0.9659$. Find A.
8. Suppose $\tan B = 0.6009$. Find B.
9. In right triangle GHK, K is the right angle, $H = 41°$, and $k = 60$ cm. Find h.
10. In right triangle MNQ, N is the right angle, $M = 18°$, and $n = 60$ m. Find q.
11. In right triangle PQR, R is the right angle, $q = 85$ km, and $p = 140$ km. Find Q to the nearest degree.
12. The angle of elevation of a hang glider is $15°$. The distance to the hang glider is 2 km. How high is the hang glider?
13. An observation tower is 95 m tall. The angle of depression from the top of the tower to a monument is $26°$. How far from the base of the tower is the monument?

B-1 ▷ Probability

Objective: Find the theoretical probability of a simple event.

Math History

The study of probability is less than 400 years old. Many consider the birth of this branch of mathematics to stem from the work of the French mathematician Blaise Pascal (1623–1662). His early work dealt with the calculation of probabilities for dice games. The development of sound foundations for the subject did not come until the early 1900s with the work of the Russian mathematician Andrei Kolmogoroff (1902–1987). Today, probability plays an important role in many careers.

If we toss a coin 1000 times and it comes up heads 503 times, we can say that the probability of getting a head is $\frac{503}{1000}$. This is **experimental probability.**

We could reason that there are only two ways a coin can fall, heads or tails. If the coin is fair, each outcome is equally likely, so we can say that the probability of getting a head is $\frac{1}{2}$. This is **theoretical probability.**

You can see that experimental probability and theoretical probability can differ. If an experiment is repeated many times, however, the two probabilities will become very close. In this chapter, we will consider theoretical probability.

The set of all possible outcomes of an experiment such as tossing a coin, rolling a number cube, or picking a card from a deck is called a **sample space.** An **event** is a set of outcomes that is a subset of the sample space.

Definition

If an event E can occur m ways out of n possible equally likely ways, the **probability** of that event is
$$P(E) = \frac{m}{n}$$

A cube with six faces, each containing a number of numerals from one to six, is called a **number cube.** We will consider the number cube to be fair. In other words, each face is equally likely to land up when tossed.

EXAMPLE 1   What is the probability of rolling a 4 on a number cube?

The sample space for rolling a number cube is $\{1, 2, 3, 4, 5, 6\}$. The event is $\{4\}$. Therefore, there is 1 way out of 6 possible ways that a 4 can be rolled. By the definition of probability, $P(4) = \frac{1}{6}$.

EXAMPLE 2   What is the probability of rolling an odd number on a number cube?

The event (odd) can occur in three ways $\{1, 3, 5\}$. The number of possible outcomes is 6. Thus, $P(\text{odd}) = \frac{3}{6} = \frac{1}{2}$.

Try This   A fair number cube is tossed.

a. What is the probability of rolling a factor of 6?
b. What is the probability of rolling a multiple of 2?

A standard deck of 52 cards consists of 13 black spades, 13 black clubs, 13 red hearts, and 13 red diamonds. Each suit has an ace, a king, a queen, a jack, and the numbers from 2 to 10.

EXAMPLES   A card is drawn from a well-shuffled deck of 52 cards.

3   What is the probability of drawing a queen?

The event (queen) can occur in 4 ways, namely, hearts, diamonds, spades, and clubs. There are 52 possible outcomes, so

$$P(\text{queen}) = \frac{4}{52} = \frac{1}{13}$$

4   What is the probability of drawing a card with a number printed on it that is less than 4?

The event $(n < 4)$ can occur in 8 ways, namely, 2 and 3 in each of the four suits, hearts, diamonds, clubs, and spades. There are 52 possible outcomes, so

$$P(n < 4) = \frac{8}{52} = \frac{2}{13}$$

5   What is the possibility of drawing a green card?

There are no green cards in a standard deck of cards. The event is the empty set, so

$$P(\text{green card}) = \frac{0}{52} = 0$$

These examples illustrate the following basic property of probability.

Basic Property of Probability

For any event E with a sample space S,
  $P(E)$ is a number between 0 and 1, or
  $P(E) = 0$ if the event cannot occur, or
  $P(E) = 1$ if the event is certain to occur.

Try This A card is drawn from a well-shuffled deck of 52 cards.

c. What is the probability of drawing a red card?

d. What is the probability of drawing a card with an even number?

e. What is the probability of drawing a blue card?

B-1 Exercises

A

A spinner numbered 1 to 8 is spun.

1. What is the probability of spinning an even number?
2. What is the probability of spinning a divisor of 12?
3. What is the probability of spinning a multiple of 3?
4. What is the probability of spinning a multiple of 4?
5. What is the probability of spinning a prime number?
6. What is the probability of spinning a factor of 10?
7. What is the probability of spinning a 9?

One card is drawn from a well-shuffled deck of 52 cards.

8. What is the probability of drawing an ace?
9. What is the probability of drawing a card with an odd number?
10. What is the probability of drawing a card with a number greater than 8?
11. What is the probability of drawing a face card?
12. What is the probability of drawing a card with the number 0?
13. What is the probability of drawing a card with a number that is divisible by 3?
14. What is the probability of drawing a card with a prime number?

B

15. Obtain a 3 × 5 index card and fold it in half widthwise. Toss the folded card 100 times and determine experimental probabilities for the card falling "flat," "on edge," or "as a tent."

Flat

On edge

Tent

16. Obtain a cap from a tube of toothpaste. Determine the various possibilities that can occur when the cap is tossed. Toss the cap 100 times, and determine experimental probabilities for the various events.

17. *Critical Thinking*   Suppose a fair coin has come up tails for the last 10 tosses. What is the probability of getting a head on the next toss? Why?

Challenge

Two number cubes are tossed.

18. What is the probability that the numbers on the number cubes will total 7?

19. What is the probability that the numbers on the number cubes will total 1?

20. What is the probability that the numbers on the number cubes will total 9?

21. What is the probability that the total will be greater than 10?

22. What total on the number cubes is most likely to be rolled? Why?

Mixed Review

Solve.   **23.** $m^2 - 8m = 0$ **24.** $y^2 - 5y = 6$ **25.** $12x^2 + 7x + 1 = 0$

26. $3a^2 - 5 = 16$ **27.** $(c + 7)^2 = 20$ **28.** $y^2 - 10y + 25 = 11$

Determine the nature of the solutions to these equations.

29. $x^2 - 121 = 0$ **30.** $y^2 - 3y + 9 = 0$ **31.** $a^2 - 4a + 4 = 0$

Use the figure to find the following:

32. the length of RT

33. $\tan R$ **34.** $\sin R$ **35.** $\sin T$

36. $\cos R$ **37.** $\cos T$ **38.** $\tan T$

B-2 ▷ More on Probability

Complementary Events

Objective: Find the theoretical probability of a complementary event.

Rolling a 1 on a number cube is an event, say E. *Not* rolling a 1 on a number cube is also an event, which we call the **complement of E,** or E'. E and E' are called complementary events.

Rolling an even number is the event $\{2, 4, 6\}$. The complement of this event, *not* rolling an even number (rolling an odd number), is $E' = \{1, 3, 5\}$. We can see that $P(E) = \frac{1}{2}$ and $P(E') = \frac{1}{2}$, and that

$$P(E) + P(E') = \frac{1}{2} + \frac{1}{2} = 1.$$

Complementary Events

For any event A, $P(A) + P(A') = 1$.

Since $P(A) + P(A') = 1$, we know that $P(A') = 1 - P(A)$.

EXAMPLE 1 Suppose that an event A has a probability of $\frac{2}{9}$.

What is $P(A')$?

$$P(A') = 1 - P(A)$$
$$= 1 - \frac{2}{9} = \frac{7}{9}$$

EXAMPLE 2 Suppose that the probability of rain today is 0.36.

What is the probability that it will not rain today?

Let the probability of rain be event R. Then the probability that it will *not* rain is R'.

$$P(R') = 1 - P(R)$$
$$= 1 - 0.36 = 0.64$$

Try This

a. Suppose that an event A has a probability of $\frac{4}{7}$. What is $P(A')$?

b. Suppose that the probability of sitting next to your best friend is 0.08. What is the probability that you will *not* sit next to your best friend?

Objective: Find the theoretical probability of two mutually exclusive events.

Two events that cannot both happen at the same time are called **mutually exclusive events.** An event and its complement are examples of mutually exclusive events.

Suppose there are 5 red marbles, 7 green marbles, and 11 blue marbles in a bag. Let us consider the mutually exclusive events *draw a green marble G* and *draw a red marble R*. We know that $P(R) = \frac{5}{23}$ and $P(G) = \frac{7}{23}$. We can easily see that $P(R \text{ or } G) = \frac{12}{23}$ since there are twelve marbles that are red or green. Note that $P(R \text{ or } G) = \frac{5}{23} + \frac{7}{23} = \frac{12}{23}$. The idea of adding probabilities when working with mutually exclusive events is true in general.

$P(A \text{ or } B)$ for Mutually Exclusive Events

If A and B are mutually exclusive events then
$$P(A \text{ or } B) = P(A) + P(B)$$

EXAMPLE 3   One number cube is tossed.

What is the probability that a 3 or a 5 will be rolled?

$P(3)$ and $P(5)$ are mutually exclusive events, so

$$P(3 \text{ or } 5) = P(3) + P(5)$$
$$= \frac{1}{6} + \frac{1}{6}$$
$$= \frac{2}{6} \text{ or } \frac{1}{3}$$

EXAMPLE 4   A block is chosen at random from a bag containing 6 white blocks, 4 black blocks, and 12 red blocks.

What is the probability that it will be a red block or a white block?

Choosing a red block and choosing a white block are mutually exclusive events, so

$$P(R \text{ or } W) = P(R) + P(W)$$
$$= \frac{12}{22} + \frac{6}{22}$$
$$= \frac{18}{22} \text{ or } \frac{9}{11}$$

Try This

c. What is the probability of rolling a 1 or a 6 on one toss of a number cube?

d. What is the probability that a block selected from the bag described in Example 4 will be black or white?

PART 3 **The Probability of *A* or *B***

Objective: Find the theoretical probability of two events.

Mutually exclusive events do not occur at the same time. There are, however, events that can occur at the same time. The sample space for one spin on the spinner shown is $S = \{1, 2, 3, 4, 5, 6, 7, 8\}$. What is the probability of spinning an even number *or* a number less than 5?

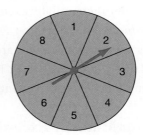

These two events can be represented by the sets $A = \{2, 4, 6, 8\}$ and $B = \{1, 2, 3, 4\}$. They are not mutually exclusive as shown in the diagram below.

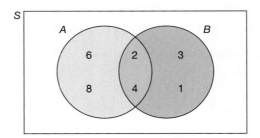

If we add the probabilities of event A and event B, we will count the probabilities of the intersection of these events twice. If we subtract $P(A \cap B)$ from $P(A) + P(B)$, however, we will eliminate this problem.

$$P(A \text{ or } B) = P(A) + P(B) - P(A \cap B) = \tfrac{4}{8} + \tfrac{4}{8} - \tfrac{2}{8} = \tfrac{6}{8} = \tfrac{3}{4}$$

The Probability of *A* or *B*

If A and B are events from a sample space S, then
$$P(A \text{ or } B) = P(A) + P(B) - P(A \cap B)$$

EXAMPLE 5 What is the probability of spinning a prime number or an odd number on a spinner numbered 1 to 8?

Let A be the event of spinning a prime number; $A = \{2, 3, 5, 7\}$, $P(A) = \frac{4}{8}$

Let B be the event of spinning an odd number; $B = \{1, 3, 5, 7\}$, $P(B) = \frac{4}{8}$

$$A \cap B = \{3, 5, 7\}, \text{ so } P(A \cap B) = \frac{3}{8}$$
$$P(A \text{ or } B) = P(A) + P(B) - P(A \cap B)$$
$$= \frac{4}{8} + \frac{4}{8} - \frac{3}{8}$$
$$= \frac{5}{8}$$

Try This

e. What is the probability of spinning an even number or a divisor of 8 on the spinner used for Example 5?

f. What is the probability of drawing a king or a black card from a well-shuffled deck of 52 cards?

B-2 Exercises

A

1. Suppose that an event A has a probability of $\frac{3}{8}$. What is $P(A')$?

2. Suppose that an event B has a probability of $\frac{7}{19}$. What is $P(B')$?

3. Suppose that the probability of snow is 0.58. What is the probability that it will *not* snow?

4. Suppose that the probability that you will win a contest is 0.001. What is the probability that you will *not* win the contest?

A card is chosen from a well-shuffled deck of 52 cards.

5. What is the probability that the card will be a king or a queen?

6. What is the probability that the card will be an ace or a card with a number less than 5?

7. What is the probability that the card will be a red jack or a black king?

8. What is the probability that the card will be a face card or a card with a prime number?

A spinner numbered 1 to 10 is spun. Each number is equally likely to be spun.

9. What is the probability of spinning an odd number or a power of 3?

10. What is the probability of spinning an even number or a multiple of 4?

11. What is the probability of spinning a number less than 8 or a divisor of 15?

A card is drawn from a well-shuffled deck of 52 cards.

12. What is the probability of drawing a diamond or a queen?

13. What is the probability of drawing a heart or a red jack?

14. What is the probability of drawing a black card or a card with a number less than 8?

15. What is the probability of drawing a spade or a black card?

B

16. If the set of whole numbers $\{0, 1, 2, 3, 4, 5, \ldots\}$ is the sample space, describe the complement of the set of even numbers.

17. A card is chosen from a well-shuffled deck of 52 cards. What is the probability that it will be a face card or an ace or a card with a number less than 4?

18. Two number cubes are tossed. What is the probability that a three will show face up?

19. *Critical Thinking*   Describe two easily understood events that can be confidently expected to have probabilities of 0 and 1, respectively.

Challenge

20. Two number cubes are tossed. What is the probability that the sum is three? What is the complement of this event?

21. Two number cubes are tossed. What is the probability that a four will show face up or that the sum of the two number cubes will be eight?

22. How can $P(A \text{ or } B \text{ or } C)$ be determined if events A, B, and C are *not* mutually exclusive?

23. Two events A and B are called independent if and only if $P(A \cap B) = P(A) \cdot P(B)$. A nickel and a number cube are tossed. What is the probability that the nickel shows tails and the number cube comes up even?

Mixed Review

Solve each formula for the given positive variable.   **24.** $A = \pi r^2; r$

25. $a^2 + b^2 = c^2; b$ **26.** $w^2 + x^2 + y^2 = z^2; y$ **27.** $A = \frac{1}{2}bh; b$

Solve.   **28.** $x + 5 = \dfrac{6}{x + 5}$ **29.** $\dfrac{y^2}{y - 2} - \dfrac{5}{y - 2} = 0$

30. $\dfrac{12}{a + 3} + \dfrac{2}{a - 3} = 2$ **31.** $x^2 + 6x + 4 = 0$

32. $3y^2 - 10y + 3 = 0$ **33.** $4m^2 - 1 = 7$

Find these trigonometric function values.   **34.** $\sin 16°$ **35.** $\cos 20°$

36. $\tan 80°$ **37.** $\sin 37°$ **38.** $\cos 40°$ **39.** $\tan 5°$

Experimental Probability and Simulation

Objective: Use simulation to find the experimental probability of an event.

Probabilities associated with events can be difficult to determine using theoretical probability. Because it is not always possible to actually perform an experiment, we can **simulate** the event in order to determine the desired probability. Simulations are also used to verify theoretical probabilities.

When developing and carrying out a plan for a simulation, you should *select an appropriate model* and *define a trial*. Then you are ready to *collect data* and *run a sufficient number of trials*.

EXAMPLE 1 A sock manufacturer makes an equal number of socks with red and blue stripes. Three pairs of socks are selected randomly to be packaged in each box. What is the probability that any box will have two pairs of socks with blue stripes and one pair of socks with red stripes?

■ **UNDERSTAND the problem**

The problem is to determine the probability that a given box contains two pairs of socks with blue stripes and one pair with red stripes.

■ **Develop and carry out a PLAN**

Since we are dealing with two color choices, we can simulate the color of a pair of stripes with a coin toss. A head stands for blue stripes and a tail for red stripes. Thus the *model* for our simulation is a coin toss.

Three successive tosses of a coin determine the colors of the socks in a given box. Hence, a *trial* for this simulation consists of three tosses of a coin, which provides data that we can *collect,* for instance HHT for two heads (blue) and one tail (red).

Finally, we need to run a fairly large number of trials to determine the frequency of the boxes with two pairs of socks with blue stripes and one pair with red stripes. Here are some sample results of 50 trials.

```
HHH  TTT  THH  TTH  HTH  HHT  THH  TTT  HTT  HHH
THT  TTT  HHT  HHT  THH  THT  TTH  THH  THH  HHH
HHH  THH  HHH  HTT  THT  TTH  TTH  THT  THH  TTT
HHT  HHT  HTT  TTT  HHT  HHH  THT  HHT  HHT  HTT
TTT  HHT  HTH  HHH  HHH  THT  TTH  THT  TTH  HTH
```

■ **Find the ANSWER and CHECK**

An examination of the trials shows that 19 of 50 result in exactly two heads (blue) and one tail (red). So we would estimate that the probability of getting a box with two pairs of socks with blue stripes and one pair of socks with red stripes is $\frac{19}{50}$. The probability of $\frac{19}{50}$ is an estimate derived from experimentation. The reliability of this estimate improves as the number of trials increases.

Try This

a. Use a simulation to find the probability that a box will have three pairs of socks with blue stripes.

How many trials should you run to find an accurate probability? This question does not have an easy answer. A famous theorem in probability called the **Law of Large Numbers** says that the more trials you run, the closer your simulation will come to the theoretical probability. So, the best answer to this question is to run as many trials as time will allow.

EXAMPLE 2 Two volleyball teams, the Hurricanes and the Tigers, are involved in a five-game playoff series. The outcome of any one game does not depend on what has happened in previous games. The Hurricanes and the Tigers are evenly matched.

a. Find the probability that the Hurricanes will win three or more games.

b. Find the probability that the Hurricanes will win exactly two games.

c. Find the probability that each team will win at least two games in a row.

These probabilities can be found if the simulation is carefully designed.

Since the Hurricanes and the Tigers are evenly matched, we can assume that the probability of either team's winning a given game is $\frac{1}{2}$. So the toss of a coin is a good model. A head represents a victory for the Hurricanes and a tail, a victory for the Tigers.

We need to conduct a large number of five-toss trials to simulate the five-game series. Each toss in the trial indicates the outcome of one game.

A trial like HTTHT indicates victories for the Hurricanes in the first and fourth games and victories for the Tigers in the other games.

To answer the questions, we run 50 trials. Sample results are as follows:

```
HHTTH    HTTHT    THTTH    HTHHT    HTTHH
HHTHH    HTTHT    HHTHH    THTTH    TTHHH
HTTTH    HTHTT    HTHTH    HTTTT    HHTTT
THTHH    HHHHT    HTTHH    HHTTT    TTHTT
TTTHT    THTTT    HHHTH    HTHHH    TTHTH
HTTTT    THTTH    HTTHT    HTTTT    HHTHT
TTHTT    THTTT    HHHHH    THHTH    THHTH
HTTHT    TTHHH    HTTHH    TTTHT    TTHHT
HHHTH    THTHT    TTTHH    TTHTT    HHHHT
THTTH    TTTHH    HTTTH    HHHTT    HTTHT
```

We can use these results to answer the questions.

a. An examination of the trials shows that we can expect the Hurricanes to win the series 21 out of 50 times. This is equivalent to the probability of $\frac{21}{50}$.

b. To find the probability that the Hurricanes will win exactly two games, we look for trials with two heads. There are 19 such trials, so we can expect a probability of $\frac{19}{50}$.

c. To find the number of series in which each team will win at least two games in a row, we look for series in which each team has at least two successive wins. There are 12 trials out of 50, so we can expect a probability of $\frac{12}{50}$ or $\frac{6}{25}$.

Try This

b. Find the probability that the winner of the five-game series will be decided in the fifth game of the series.

B-3 Exercises

A

1. What is the probability that a family with three children will have two boys and one girl?
   a. What are you being asked to find?
   b. What model can you use to simulate the event?
   c. Define the trial for this simulation.
   d. Run 20 trials and find the probability.

2. What is the probability that a family with three children will have at least two boys?
   a. What are you being asked to find?
   b. What model can you use to simulate the event?
   c. Define the trial for this simulation.
   d. Run 20 trials and find the probability.

For Exercises 3–6, use a number cube and 30 trials for your simulation. A tennis ball manufacturer packages four tennis balls to a tournament pack with white, orange, and yellow tennis balls equally likely. What is the probability that an individual pack has

  3. two white, one orange, and one yellow tennis ball?

  4. two white and two orange tennis balls?

  5. two white and two other tennis balls of the same color?

  6. no white tennis balls?

Suppose the freshman class sponsor told the class president that she would drive her van to the game if four of the seven officers wanted to go. If the probability that any one officer will want to go is $\frac{1}{2}$, answer the following questions.

  7. What is the probability that at least four officers will want to go to the game?

  8. What is the probability that only four officers will want to go to the game?

  9. What is the probability that less than four officers will want to go to the game?

  10. What is the probability that all seven officers will want to go to the game?

B

  11. Repeat the simulation in Example 2, this time collecting data from 100 trials. What probabilities did you get from the three questions? How did they change from the values obtained from only 50 trials? Which set of data do you think would give more reliable results?

  12. *Critical Thinking* In Example 1, a trial consisted of tossing a coin three times to simulate the color of the stripes on three pairs of socks. Instead, could we have tossed three coins for each trial? Explain.

Challenge

Six students travel to a speech contest. Suppose that the probability of each student getting laryngitis is $\frac{1}{3}$.

  13. What is the probability that at least four (4, 5, or 6) of the students will become ill?

  14. What is the probability that none of the six students will become ill?

Mixed Review

Write in standard form and determine a, b, and c.   **15.** $3x = 10 - 2x^2$

  16. $2x + 6 = x^2 - 9$ **17.** $8 - 3x = 47 - 5x^2$

  18. The length of a rectangle is 6 m greater than its width. The area of the rectangle is 187 m^2. Find the length and the width.

Statistics: Organizing Data

B-4

The branch of mathematics that deals with the collection, organization, display, and interpretation of data is called **statistics.** Statistics is used to solve many problems and to help in making decisions.

PART 1 Frequency Distributions

Objective: Construct a frequency distribution for a set of data.

When a set of data is collected it is often disorganized. We can organize data by using charts or tables. A **frequency distribution** is a type of table that is often used in statistics.

EXAMPLE 1 Here is a set of temperatures, in degrees Fahrenheit, recorded at noon each day during the month of April. Construct a frequency distribution.

49, 50, 49, 50, 50, 51, 49, 49, 51, 52, 51, 56, 53, 54, 50,
49, 53, 53, 55, 54, 50, 57, 49, 55, 56, 58, 54, 59, 55, 54

The temperatures range from a low of 49 to a high of 59. We make our frequency distribution as follows.

Temperatures	Tally	Frequency
49	ⅢⅠ Ⅰ	6
50	ⅢⅠ	5
51	Ⅲ	3
52	Ⅰ	1
53	Ⅲ	3
54	ⅢⅠ	4
55	Ⅲ	3
56	ⅠⅠ	2
57	Ⅰ	1
58	Ⅰ	1
59	Ⅰ	1

Try This

a. Here is a set of pulse rates on 25 patients. Construct a frequency distribution.

72, 70, 74, 72, 69, 68, 69, 72, 75, 74, 73, 70, 68,
69, 73, 75, 72, 76, 73, 73, 72, 68, 70, 71, 74

If the data are spread over a large range of numbers, we may group the data into intervals. We usually try to have from 10 to 15 intervals.

EXAMPLE 2 Construct a frequency distribution using intervals.

Here is a set of times, in hours, showing how long it took each of 24 light bulbs to burn out.

979, 986, 1134, 1213, 1097, 1089, 897, 1219, 1093, 992, 1228, 1298, 1226, 947, 1007, 1167, 1214, 895, 996, 1043, 1152, 982, 1231, 1099

Suppose that we want about 9 intervals. The smallest value is 895 and the largest value is 1298. We find the difference, $1298 - 895 = 403$, and divide 403 by 9. This is approximately 45, which suggests that a convenient interval length is 50. Thus the intervals can be 850–899, 900–949, 950–999, and so on.

Hours	Tally	Frequency
850–899	II	2
900–949	I	1
950–999	HH	5
1000–1049	II	2
1050–1099	IIII	4
1100–1149	I	1
1150–1199	II	2
1200–1249	HH I	6
1250–1299	I	1

Try This Construct a frequency distribution.

b. Here is a set of 33 monthly salaries. Use 8 intervals.

1120, 1200, 1150, 1400, 1550, 1475, 995, 1100, 1250, 1195, 1400, 1650, 1500, 1225, 1190, 980, 1650, 1425, 1320, 1119, 1235, 1545, 1399, 986, 1675, 1330, 1256, 1175, 1298, 1187, 1298, 1200, 1145

PART 2 Stem-and-Leaf Diagrams

Objective: Construct a stem-and-leaf diagram for a set of data.

Another useful way of organizing data is to construct a **stem-and-leaf diagram.**

EXAMPLE 3 Construct a stem-and-leaf diagram.

Here is a set of heights, in centimeters, of players on a high school basketball team.

172, 169, 183, 201, 203, 178, 183, 196, 198, 184, 195, 201, 199, 190, 186

As we look at these heights, we see that there are some that are in the 160s, some in the 170s, and so on. We use this idea to construct a stem-and-leaf diagram. We split each numeral into two parts, a stem and a leaf. The first value, 172, is split into 17 and 2. We write the stem, 17, in the first column and the leaf, 2, in the second column.

Stem	Leaf
16	9
17	2, 8
18	3, 3, 4, 6
19	6, 8, 5, 9, 0
20	1, 3, 1

We can see that the stem-and-leaf diagram has organized the data. It is easy to find the shortest height, 169, and the tallest height, 203. Also, it is obvious that many of the players have heights in the 190s.

Try This   Construct a stem-and-leaf diagram.

c. Here is a set of weights, in pounds, of people in a fitness class.

108, 112, 124, 106, 124, 148, 132, 129, 152, 132, 121, 118, 106, 109, 118, 114, 130, 126, 116, 113, 141, 137, 150, 127, 116, 134, 118, 129

B-4 Exercises

A

Construct a frequency distribution for each set of data.

1. The ages of the children in a nursery school class.

3, 4, 2, 2, 4, 3, 5, 4, 2, 2, 2, 4, 4, 3, 2, 3, 4, 4, 3, 3, 4, 4, 4, 3, 2, 2, 5

2. The numbers of "no-shows" on 30 regularly scheduled airline flights.

23, 25, 22, 17, 23, 22, 19, 21, 20, 19, 18, 25, 21, 22, 25,
24, 20, 21, 20, 18, 23, 20, 17, 19, 20, 20, 18, 24, 21, 19

Construct a frequency distribution using intervals.

3. The heights, in meters, of the 25 highest mountain peaks in the world. Use 10 intervals.

8750, 8156, 7885, 7937, 8126, 8068, 7902, 8033, 7897, 7925, 8598, 8470, 8048, 8047, 8172, 8078, 8013, 7893, 7852, 7821, 7952, 8501, 8153, 7852, 7829

4. The lengths, in feet, of 19 of the world's longest suspension bridges. Use 11 intervals.

2190, 2150, 2000, 3500, 2800, 2310, 3300, 4200, 2336, 3240, 2000, 2300, 2336, 3254, 4626, 3323, 4260, 2150, 3800

Construct a stem-and-leaf diagram for each set of data.

5. The distances, to the nearest centimeter, jumped by a class of middle-school girls.

   177, 180, 172, 168, 172, 165, 159, 165, 176, 181, 166, 174, 169, 170, 174, 165, 179, 180, 167, 178, 174, 167, 175, 164, 179, 176, 163, 158

6. The weight gains, in pounds, of a group of cattle eating a new brand of cattle feed.

   103, 107, 111, 108, 102, 103, 123, 143, 125, 132, 143, 135, 127, 119, 106, 154, 123, 165, 154, 138, 139, 146, 132, 128, 119, 129, 162, 152

7. The average verbal SAT scores for 28 high schools.

   402, 478, 417, 416, 467, 456, 463, 498, 476, 489, 476, 409, 429, 423, 471, 467, 438, 400, 439, 456, 448, 499, 439, 403, 427, 412, 487, 426

8. The weights, in pounds, of carry-on luggage as determined by a survey of 36 passengers at an airline check-in desk.

   27, 18, 28, 40, 36, 21, 13, 25, 45, 28, 16, 9, 11, 47, 32, 17, 32, 19, 51, 28, 46, 24, 18, 19, 33, 29, 40, 18, 10, 52, 34, 39, 50, 48, 19, 27

B

9. A *ranked* stem-and-leaf diagram has the values arranged in order from least to greatest. Choose any stem-and-leaf diagram that you have constructed for Exercises 5 to 8 and rank it.

10. *Critical Thinking*   Write a paragraph describing the advantages and disadvantages of frequency distributions compared with stem-and-leaf diagrams. Illustrate your response with an example.

Challenge

11. A number cube was rolled 120 times. A frequency distribution was made and shown at the right. Find the experimental probabilities $P(1)$, $P(3)$, and $P(6)$. Do you think that this number cube is fair? Why or why not?

Side	Frequency
1	12
2	21
3	15
4	18
5	24
6	30

Mixed Review

Solve.   **12.** $x^2 - 9x + 20 = 0$ **13.** $y^2 + 5y = 3$

In $\triangle ABC$, find the following.

14. $\sin B$ **15.** $\cos C$ **16.** $\tan B$

17. $\cos B$ **18.** $\tan C$ **19.** $\sin C$

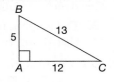

Find the equation of the line containing the given pair of points.

20. $(5, 2), (-1, 5)$ **21.** $(2, 6), (-7, 6)$ **22.** $(3, 1), (-3, 3)$

Write roster notation for each.   **23.** $A = \{x \mid x$ is a positive factor of 24$\}$
24. $B = \{y \mid y$ is a prime number and $6 < y < 50\}$

Graphs of Data

In statistics it is often helpful to give a pictorial representation of a set of data. Graphs are used for this purpose.

PART 1 Line Plots

Objective: Construct a line plot for a set of data.

One type of graph that can be constructed quickly is a **line plot.** To construct a line plot, we draw a portion of a number line and place a dot above the line for each occurrence of a value.

EXAMPLE 1 Construct a line plot.

Here is a set of morning temperatures, in degrees Celsius, for the month of March in a northeastern town.

5, 7, 4, 5, 3, 2, 0, 3, 2, 4, 5, 5, 4, 5, 6, 4, 7, 7, 9, 10, 9, 11, 12, 11, 13, 11, 10, 9, 10, 11, 13

The lowest temperature is 0° and the highest temperature is 13°. We draw a number line that includes these values and the values between. We place a dot above the line for each temperature.

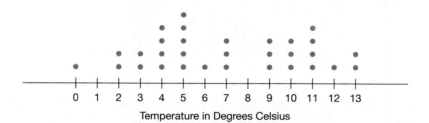

Temperature in Degrees Celsius

Try This Construct a line plot.

a. Here is a set of scores on an algebra test.

76, 80, 78, 68, 74, 69, 78, 80, 81, 80, 76, 65, 90, 88, 78, 81, 80, 76, 90, 73, 78

Objective: Construct a histogram for a set of data.

A bar graph, called a **histogram,** is useful for comparing data. A histogram always has a title and clearly labeled horizontal and vertical scales.

EXAMPLE 2   Construct a histogram.

Here is a stem-and-leaf diagram of the set of heights, in centimeters, of players on the high school basketball team from Example 3, page 654.

Stem	Leaf
16	9
17	2, 8
18	3, 3, 4, 6
19	6, 8, 5, 9, 0
20	1, 3, 1

For the histogram we let the horizontal scale represent the heights (160s, 170s, etc.) and the vertical scale represent the frequency (how many players have heights in the 160s, 170s, etc.).

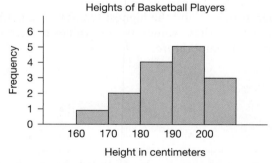

We can see from the histogram that there are two players whose heights are between 170 and 180, while four players have heights from 180 to 190.

Try This   Construct a histogram.

b. Here is a stem-and-leaf diagram of the number of games won by the great pitcher Cy Young each year from 1890 to 1911.

Stem	Leaf
0	9, 7, 7
1	8, 3, 9
2	7, 5, 9, 1, 5, 6, 0, 8, 6, 2, 1
3	6, 2, 5, 3, 2

Objective: Construct a frequency polygon for a set of data.

Another type of graph often used in statistics is the **frequency polygon.** An easy way to construct a frequency polygon is to connect the midpoints of the bars of a histogram with line segments. Here is a frequency polygon for the height data on the basketball players.

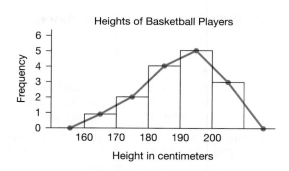

EXAMPLE 3 Construct a frequency polygon.

Here is the set of data from Try This **b.** concerning the number of games won by Cy Young.

Stem	Leaf
0	9, 7, 7
1	8, 3, 9
2	7, 5, 9, 1, 5, 6, 0, 8, 6, 2, 1
3	6, 2, 5, 3, 2

We first construct a histogram. We let the horizontal scale be the number of games won and the vertical scale be the frequency. We then connect the midpoints of the bars of the histogram.

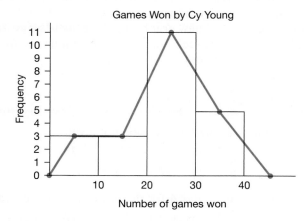

Try This Construct a frequency polygon.

c. Here are the heights, in feet, of some of the world's highest dams.
764, 761, 892, 777, 932, 770, 858, 778, 794, 932, 1017

A

Construct a line plot for each set of data.

1. The pulse rates of 30 patients.
   76, 78, 68, 73, 80, 78, 67, 76, 75, 78, 74, 75, 81, 75, 72,
   73, 81, 67, 68, 72, 70, 78, 76, 81, 69, 71, 68, 70, 74, 76

2. The golf scores of 25 high-school golfers.
   86, 79, 69, 74, 78, 87, 83, 81, 76, 80, 88, 79, 86, 90, 86,
   75, 78, 79, 80, 87, 78, 74, 87, 80, 79

3. The systolic blood pressure of 28 patients.
   120, 132, 127, 132, 137, 127, 123, 133, 133, 128, 133, 137, 129, 138,
   128, 120, 128, 139, 140, 132, 136, 126, 128, 133, 137, 121, 139, 141

4. The scores of 35 students on a ten-point biology quiz.
   7, 9, 4, 6, 5, 8, 8, 10, 5, 10, 4, 8, 7, 9, 10, 3, 9, 5,
   3, 0, 9, 10, 2, 5, 7, 8, 6, 9, 10, 7, 7, 5, 10, 9, 7

5–8. Construct a histogram for each set of data in Exercises 1–4.

9–12. Construct a frequency polygon for each set of data in Exercises 1–4.

B

13. Collect a set of data on a topic of interest to you. Construct a line plot, a histogram, and a frequency polygon for your set of data.

14. *Critical Thinking*   How can a histogram be quickly sketched if you have a stem-and-leaf diagram for a set of data?

15. Construct a frequency distribution for the biology quiz scores in Exercise 4. Add another column to the frequency distribution entitled **cumulative frequency.** In this column, opposite any score n, indicate the number of students that had a score of n or less. Use the frequency distribution to construct a new graph called a **cumulative frequency polygon.** Let the vertical scale represent the cumulative frequency and the horizontal scale represent scores.

Mixed Review

In a right triangle, find the length of the side not given.

16. $a = 5, c = 13$ **17.** $a = 11, b = 11$ **18.** $c = 25, b = 7$

Solve.   **19.** $2x^2 - 8x = 0$ **20.** $8a^2 - 6a + 1 = 0$

Use Table 4 or a calculator to find A for the following function values of A.

21. $\sin A = 0.956$ **22.** $\cos A = 0.799$ **23.** $\tan A = 2.605$

Find the probability of drawing each of the following from a well-shuffled deck of 52 cards.   **24.** a king   **25.** a black card   **26.** a heart

Measures of Central Tendency

B-6

Objective: Find the mean, median, and mode of a set of data.

A question often asked when analyzing a set of data is, "What single number best represents the set of data as a whole?" The *mean, median,* and *mode* are numbers that are used to answer this question. The mean, median, and mode are called **measures of central tendency** because they represent the center of a set of data.

The **mean** is the *average* of a set of values. To find the mean we find the sum of all the values and divide by the number of values.

EXAMPLE 1   Find the mean to the nearest tenth.

Here is a set of diameters, in miles, of the first ten asteroids discovered. Find the mean diameter.

485, 304, 118, 243, 50, 121, 121, 56, 78, 40

There are ten values. We find the sum and divide by 10.

The sum is 1616; $\frac{1616}{10} = 161.6$

The mean diameter is 161.6 miles.

Try This   Find the mean to the nearest tenth.

a. Here is a set of radar-recorded speeds, in miles per hour, of automobiles traveling on an interstate highway. Find the mean speed.

54, 58, 61, 65, 59, 60, 68, 55, 58, 49

The **median** of a set of data is the middle value when all the values are arranged in order.

EXAMPLE 2   Find the median.

Here is the number of children per family for the 25 families of the students in an algebra class. Find the median number of children per family.

2, 1, 5, 3, 4, 3, 3, 5, 2, 1, 3, 2, 1, 5, 3, 3, 6, 2, 6, 1, 2, 7, 3, 2, 4

We arrange the numbers in order from least to greatest.

1, 1, 1, 1, 2, 2, 2, 2, 2, 2, 3, 3, 3, 3, 3, 3, 3, 4, 4, 5, 5, 5, 6, 6, 7

There are 25 numbers. Thus the 13th number, 3, is the middle value. The median number of children per family is 3.

There is always a middle value when there is an odd number of values. If the number of values is even, then we use the average of the two middle values as the median.

EXAMPLE 3 Find the median.

This stem-and-leaf diagram shows the number of home runs hit by Babe Ruth each year from 1914 to 1935. Find the median number of home runs.

Stem	Leaf
0	0, 4, 3, 2, 6
1	1
2	9, 5, 2
3	5, 4
4	1, 6, 7, 6, 9, 6, 1
5	4, 9, 4
6	0

The stem-and-leaf diagram makes it easy for us to arrange the numbers in order from least to greatest.

$$0, 2, 3, 4, 6, 11, 22, 25, 29, 34, 35, 41, 41, 46, 46, 46, 47, 49, 54, 54, 59, 60$$

We find the average of the two middle values, 35 and 41. $\frac{35 + 41}{2} = 38$

The median number of home runs hit by Babe Ruth is 38.

Try This Find the median.

b. Here is a set of evacuation times, in minutes, for a series of fire drills in a school. Find the median evacuation time.

$$3.0, 2.7, 3.5, 2.7, 3.0, 2.6, 2.9, 3.2, 2.6, 2.7, 2.6, 2.8, 2.7, 2.9$$

The **mode** of a set is the value that occurs most often. Some sets of data have more than one mode, and some sets of data have no mode.

EXAMPLE 4 Find the mode.

Here is a set of shoe sizes of shoes sold one evening at a shoe store.

$$7A, 6B, 8AA, 7A, 8AA, 6D, 7\tfrac{1}{2}D, 6AA, 8AA, 7B, 6C, 8AA$$

The size 8AA occurs four times. It is the mode.

Try This Find the mode.

c. Here are the number of games won per year by the major-league pitcher Don Drysdale.

$$5, 17, 12, 17, 15, 13, 25, 19, 18, 23, 13, 13, 14, 5$$

A

Find the mean (to the nearest tenth), median, and mode for each set of data.

1. The number of home runs hit each year from 1954 to 1976 by Hank Aaron.

Stem	Leaf
1	3, 2, 0
2	7, 6, 4, 9, 0
3	0, 9, 4, 2, 9, 8, 4
4	4, 0, 4, 5, 4, 4, 7, 0

2. The scores of a high school gymnast on the floor exercise in 11 successive gymnastic meets.
6.7, 7.4, 8.1, 8.0, 7.9, 8.2, 7.9, 8.4, 9.0, 7.3, 8.8

3. The number of years served by the Chief Justice of the United States from John Jay in 1789 to Warren Burger in 1986.

Stem	Leaf
0	5, 0, 4, 8, 8, 4, 7
1	4, 0, 1, 5, 8
2	8, 1
3	4

4. The ages at the first inaugurations of the first 40 presidents of the United States.
57, 61, 57, 57, 58, 57, 61, 54, 68, 51, 49, 64, 50, 48, 65, 52, 56, 46, 54, 49, 50, 47, 55, 55, 54, 42, 51, 56, 55, 51, 54, 51, 60, 62, 43, 55, 56, 61, 52, 69

5. The lengths, in feet, of nine of the major U.S. 3-engine jet transport planes.
133.1, 133.1, 153.1, 153.1, 177.5, 164.2, 182.2, 181.6, 182.3

6. The depths, in meters, of certain points of the oceans and seas of the world.
10918, 9219, 7455, 5625, 4632, 5016, 4773, 3787, 3658, 2782, 3742, 3777, 660, 2211, 421, 6946, 183

B

7. Collect a set of data on some topic of interest to you. Find the mean, median, and mode of your set of data.

8. Extreme values can affect the mean. Recalculate the mean for Exercise 6 after deleting the highest and lowest value. Which mean is a better measure of central tendency?

9. If a set of data has two modes it is said to be **bimodal.** Are any of the six sets of data above bimodal?

10. *Critical Thinking* Which of the measures of central tendency in a set of 10 scores with 1 duplicate is most affected by the addition of another unique score? Which is least affected?

Challenge

11. A measure of how much a set of data varies from the mean of the data is called *variance*. The variance is the average of the squares of the differences of each data element from the mean of the data.

   a. Find the variance for the data in Exercise 2.

   b. Find the variance for the data in Exercise 4.

   c. Which set of data is clustered closer to its mean?

12. Compare the sets of home-run data for Babe Ruth (Example 3) and Hank Aaron (Exercise 1) with respect to the mean, median, and mode of each set. In your opinion, who was the greater home-run hitter? Defend your opinion with the data.

13. What are the advantages and disadvantages of the mean, median, and mode as measures of central tendency?

14. Roll three number cubes 10 times and record the sum for each toss. Find the mean, median, and mode for the set of data generated. Repeat the experiment with 50 rolls. Explain any differences between the two experiments. Which set of data most closely approximates the theoretical values (mean: 10.5, median: 10.5, mode: 10, 11)?

Mixed Review

Write an equation for the line that contains the given pair of points.

15. $(4, 1), (-1, 6)$ **16.** $(-3, 4), (-3, 0)$ **17.** $(2, 2), (-4, -13)$

Solve.   **18.** $\sqrt{x - 8} = x - 8$ **19.** $\sqrt{x + 6} = x$

20. $5y^2 - 15y = 0$ **21.** $m^2 + 8m + 15 = 0$ **22.** $a^2 - 2a = 15$

23. $3w^2 = -12w$ **24.** $25b^2 - 49 = 0$ **25.** $3x^2 + 13x - 10 = 0$

Graph these functions.

26. $y = |x - 2| + 3$

27. $y = (x - 2)^2 + 3$

Find the probability that each of the following will appear when a single number cube is tossed.

28. a factor of 4

29. an odd number

30. a prime number

31. The reciprocal of a number divided by eight is the same as two times the number. Find the number.

Scatter Plots and Data Relationships

Objective: Make scatter plots and determine data relationships.

Math in Action

The table below shows the number of hours a student studied and the grade received on eight separate exams.

Hours	0	0	1	2	2	4	5	5
Grade	30	40	60	60	70	80	90	95

Is there a relationship between hours studied and the grade received on each exam? An examination of the data shows that there is some relationship, but statisticians use a more objective method of analysis.

In Chapter 7 you learned how to find an equation for the line of best fit. In this lesson we will concentrate on using the line of best fit to determine whether a relationship exists between two variables. Statisticians spend a great deal of their time analyzing data from surveys and experiments, trying to find patterns of behavior or relationships between different pieces of information. They use a variety of techniques to do this, one of which is the **scatter plot.**

A scatter plot is a graph that shows the relationship between two variables. A scatter plot of the above data is shown at the right. If you draw a line of best fit, the line will have a positive slope. This is an indication that there is a **positive** relationship between *x* and *y*.

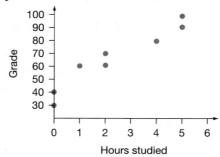

The following graphs show two other relationships that can occur.

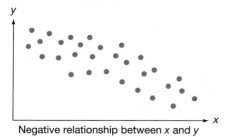

Negative relationship between *x* and *y*

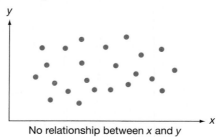

No relationship between *x* and *y*

EXAMPLE 1

The graph at the right represents data collected from a group of 30 adult males. Mentally draw the line of best fit and determine what type of relationship exists between a man's age and the amount he can lift.

The line of best fit has a negative slope, which indicates a negative relationship between the two variables.

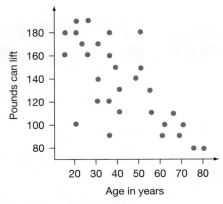

Pounds can lift (y-axis: 80, 100, 120, 140, 160, 180)
Age in years (x-axis: 20, 30, 40, 50, 60, 70, 80)

Try This What type of relationship exists between the variables in each graph?

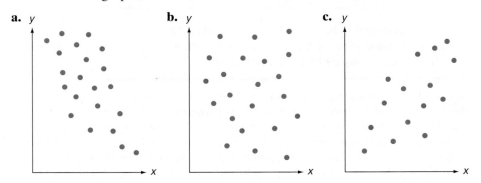

a. y   **b.** y   **c.** y

EXAMPLE 2

Use the data from the box score for a game from the 1988 National Basketball Association championship series to make a scatter plot representing the field goals attempted (fga) and the total points (total). What type of relationship exists?

Los Angeles	fga	fg	fta	ft	total
Green	2	2	8	6	10
Worthy	22	12	6	4	28
Abdul-Jabbar	14	3	8	8	14
E. Johnson	12	3	14	13	22
Scott	12	7	4	2	16
Thompson	6	3	2	1	7
Rambis	1	1	0	0	2
Cooper	3	1	2	2	4
Totals	72	32	43	35	103

Detroit	fga	fg	fta	ft	total
Dantley	10	3	8	8	14
Mahorn	3	2	0	0	4
Laimbeer	5	0	2	2	2
Dumars	12	7	2	2	16
Thomas	32	18	7	5	43
Salley	2	1	1	1	3
V. Johnson	7	2	2	1	5
Rodman	2	2	5	3	7
Edwards	6	4	0	0	8
Totals	79	39	27	22	102

We plot field goals attempted on the horizontal axis and total points on the vertical axis. We can plot each point using an L if it represents a player for Los Angeles and a D if it represents Detroit. The graph shows that players who attempt more field goals usually score more total points and players who attempt fewer field goals have fewer total points. Thus, there is a positive relationship between field goals attempted and total points scored.

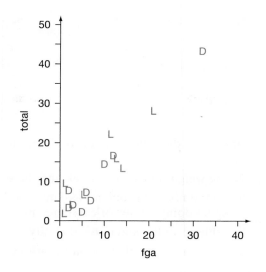

Try This

d. Use the box score to make a scatter plot representing the field goals attempted (fga) and the free throws attempted (fta). What type of relationship exists?

B-7 Problems

What type of relationship exists between the variables in each graph?

1.

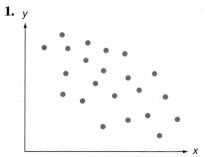

2.

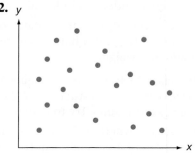

3.

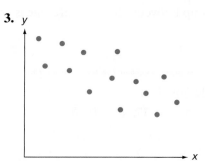

4.

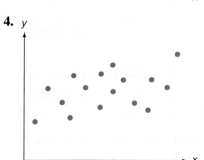

5.

6.

For each of the following sets of data, what type of relationship might you expect?

7. the weight of a sirloin steak and the selling price

8. the number of problems assigned for homework and the amount of time spent doing homework assignments

9. athletic ability and musical ability

10. math anxiety and score on a math exam

For Exercises 11 and 12, use the information shown in the following table.

Student	1	2	3	4	5	6	7	8	9	10	11	12
GPA	3.6	2.9	3.2	2.6	2.8	2.1	3.3	3.0	3.2	3.3	2.5	2.8
Shoe size	8.5	7.5	9	11	6	8	8.5	7	10	9.5	8	10.5
Height (in.)	65	69	70	71	62	66	68	65	69	70	63	71
Weight (lb)	141	145	163	170	109	150	156	138	166	168	118	188

11. Make a scatter plot for the data consisting of grade point average (GPA) and shoe size. Based on the scatter plot, what type of relationship exists between a student's grade point average and shoe size?

12. Make a scatter plot for the data consisting of height and weight. Based on the scatter plot, what type of relationship exists between a student's height and weight?

For Exercises 13 and 14, make a questionnaire and collect the needed data from approximately 20 students. Make a scatter plot and write a paragraph describing your results. Try to explain any trends or patterns.

13. Investigate whether there is a relationship between a person's height and the length of a person's arm from the elbow to the hand.

14. Investigate whether there is a relationship between the circumferences of a person's head and a person's neck.

Mixed Review

In a right triangle, find the length of the side not given.

15. $b = 18, c = 30$ **16.** $c = 5\sqrt{2}, a = 5$ **17.** $a = 10, b = 24$

Find these trigonometric function values.   **18.** $\tan 18°$ **19.** $\sin 34°$

20. $\cos 84°$ **21.** $\sin 67°$ **22.** $\cos 3°$ **23.** $\tan 77°$ **24.** $\cos 90°$

Appendix B Assessment

A spinner numbered 1 through 12 is spun.

1. What is the probability of spinning a multiple of 4?
2. What is the probability of spinning a factor of 12?
3. What is the probability of spinning a prime number?

A card is drawn at random from a well-shuffled deck of 52 cards. What is the probability that

4. the card is the seven of hearts? **5.** the card is an eight?

6. the card is a number less than six? **7.** the card is a five or a six?

8. the card is black or a six? **9.** the card is red or a multiple of three?

10. Suppose that event B has a probability of $\frac{7}{8}$. What is $P(B')$?

11. Suppose that the probability of rain today is 0.43. What is the probability that it will not rain today?

12. Define a trial for a simulation that could be used to find the probability that a family with four children has at least three girls.

The number of problems Laurel Nissan answered correctly on successive computer games was

| 148 | 172 | 144 | 167 | 149 | 150 | 149 | 148 |
| 152 | 161 | 149 | 152 | 154 | 177 | 159 | 163 |

13. Construct a stem-and-leaf diagram for this data.
14. Construct a line plot for this data.
15. Construct a histogram for this data.
16. Construct a frequency polygon for this data.

The temperature in San Francisco reached these highs over a one-week period in August: 85, 83, 79, 72, 68, 71, 72.

17. Find the mean to the nearest tenth for this data.
18. Find the median for this data.
19. Find the mode for this data.
20. What type of relationship would you expect between the number of dogs in 30 California cities and the number of cats in 30 Texas cities?

The table shows the number of absences and grades for 18 students.

Absences	3	6	0	9	4	2	5	8	3	9	0	2	4	6	1	1	4	7
Grade	85	64	90	41	83	88	78	60	82	50	98	90	85	71	93	87	79	63

21. Make a scatter plot for these data. What type of relationship seems to exist between absences and grades?

Mixed Practice 1

For use after Lesson 1-4

Write an equivalent expression.

1. $\frac{a}{3}$ Use $\frac{2}{2}$ for 1.
2. $\frac{3}{4}$ Use $\frac{m}{m}$ for 1.
3. $\frac{x}{7}$ Use $\frac{y}{y}$ for 1.

4. $5 \cdot (m \cdot n)$
5. $(s + 3) + t$
6. $a \cdot b \cdot 11$

7. $r(2 + s)t$
8. $1 + (2m^2 + n)$
9. $(xy)z + w$

Evaluate.

10. $9 + y + y$ for $y = 2$
11. $2a + 5b$ for $a = 3$ and $b = 7$

12. $\frac{3x}{5y}$ for $x = 10$ and $y = 2$
13. $\frac{2m + n}{3}$ for $m = 7$ and $n = 4$

14. $h + 3k$ for $h = 5$ and $k = 1$
15. $4(r + 6) - 3$ for $r = 7$

16. $(3a)^2$ for $a = 11$
17. $5y^2$ for $y = 1$
18. $6a^3$ for $a = 2$

19. $5r^2 + 1$ for $r = 2$
20. $m^3 + 4$ for $m = 0$
21. $x^3 - 7$ for $x = 2$

22. $(2c)^5$ for $c = 1$
23. $2c^2$ for $c = 1$
24. $5y^8$ for $y = 0$

25. $(3xy)^2$ for $x = 5$ and $y = 1$
26. $(ab)^3$ for $a = 2$ and $b = 3$

27. $(2mn)^4$ for $m = 0$ and $n = 2$
28. $(st)^5$ for $s = 1$ and $t = 1$

29. $(m - 4)(m + 1)$ for $m = 6$
30. $(9 - w)^2$ for $w = 5$

31. $y(11 - y)$ for $y = 5$
32. $5(a + 3)$ for $a = 9$

33. $\frac{a^2 + 4}{3a}$ for $a = 6$
34. $\frac{m^2 + 3m}{7m}$ for $m = 4$

Write using exponential notation.

35. $3 \cdot 3 \cdot 3 \cdot 3$
36. $7 \cdot n \cdot n \cdot n \cdot n$
37. w

Tell whether each pair of expressions is equivalent.

38. $3t + 5t$ and $8 + 2t$
39. $xy + yz$ and $xz + yy$
40. $mn + pq$ and $n \cdot p \cdot m \cdot q$

41. $a \cdot b + xyz$ and $xzy + ba$
42. $rs + tu$ and $r + s + t + u$
43. $hj + lm$ and $ml + jh$

Simplify.

44. $18 - 6 \times 8 - 2$
45. $19 - 2 \times 8 + 1$
46. $3 \times 8 - 6 \times 0$

47. $\frac{3w}{15w}$
48. $\frac{24mn}{6m}$
49. $\frac{11uvw}{2uw}$

50. $\frac{8ced}{2ec}$
51. $\frac{12st}{3rs}$
52. $\frac{5xtv}{7vxy}$

Calculate.

53. $(5 + 2)^2$
54. $5 + 2^2$
55. $5^2 + 2$

56. $(5 - 2)^2$
57. $5^2 - 2$
58. $5 - 2^2$

59. $5 \cdot 2^2$
60. $(5 \cdot 2)^2$
61. $5^2 \cdot 2^2$

For use after Lesson 1-9

Factor and check by multiplying.

1. $12a + 42b + 18$
2. $25x + 60y + 40z$
3. $14m + 10n + 6$

Simplify each expression. Factor and collect like terms as needed.

4. $xy + 3x + 6xy + 4x$
5. $6a^2 + 3ab + 2ab + 4a^2$

6. $8xy + 9xz + 4xy + 3xz$
7. $27c + 5 + 8c$

Write as an algebraic expression.

8. a number n divided among 5
9. a number y increased by 17

10. Let p be the number of problems Lonnie completed. Ray completed 8 more than Lonnie. Write an expression for the problems Ray completed.

11. Let b be the number of books Victor read. Donna read half as many books as Victor. Write an expression for the number of books Donna read.

12. Let w be Barbara's weight. Laurel weighs 6 pounds less than Barbara. Write an expression for Laurel's weight.

Evaluate.

13. $\frac{12m}{18n}$ for $m = 12$ and $n = 8$
14. $\frac{x \cdot y}{6} + \frac{x + 2}{2}$ for $x = 8$ and $y = 3$

Evaluate $\frac{2a + c}{5}$ when

15. a is 3 and c is 4.
16. c is 1 and a is twice c.

17. a is 15 and c is twice a.
18. c is 25 and a is half c.

Solve for the given replacement set.

19. $3m^2 - 1 = 47$ $\{2, 4, 6\}$
20. $y + 3 = 5y - 25$ $\{5, 6, 7\}$

Simplify, then solve mentally.

21. $6x + 3x = 36$
22. $n + 7n = 16$
23. $3t + 2t = 35$
24. $\frac{32m}{8} = 12$
25. $5a^2 = 5$
26. $\frac{15k}{3} = 20$

Determine whether each pair of equations is equivalent.

27. $3a + 6 = 12$
$3a + 6 - 6 = 12 + 6$

28. $10 + 3x = 12x - 4$
$10 + 3x - 3x = 12x - 4 + 4$

29. $2y - 5 = 19 - 4y$
$2y - 5 + 4y = 19 - 4y + 4y$

30. $17 - 5t = 2t - 4$
$17 - 5t + 5t = 2t - 4 - 5t$

31. Find the area (A) of a playing field with length (l) of 25 yd and width (w) of 50 ft using the formula $A = lw$.

32. Find the sales tax (T) paid on an item selling for a price (p) of \$12.50 using the formula $T = 0.06p$ (6% tax rate).

Mixed Practice 3

For use after Lesson 2-4

Name the integer that is suggested by each situation.

1. Letitia gained 3 pounds.   **2.** Lost Canyon is 1073 ft deep.

Find the absolute value.

3. $|22|$ **4.** $|-15|$ **5.** $|0.6|$ **6.** $|-1.295|$

Write a true sentence using < or >.

7. $-9 \ \square \ 7$ **8.** $3 \ \square \ 4$ **9.** $5 \ \square \ -8$ **10.** $-2 \ \square \ -3$

11. $-63 \ \square \ -51$ **12.** $0.01 \ \square \ 0.011$ **13.** $4.12 \ \square \ -4.13$ **14.** $7.52 \ \square \ 7.25$

15. $\frac{2}{3} \ \square \ \frac{1}{2}$ **16.** $-\frac{1}{8} \ \square \ -\frac{3}{16}$ **17.** $-\frac{2}{5} \ \square \ \frac{1}{3}$ **18.** $\frac{4}{5} \ \square \ \frac{7}{10}$

Add.

19. $-9 + (-2)$ **20.** $5 + (-18)$ **21.** $-6 + 8$

22. $-\frac{3}{8} + \frac{1}{2}$ **23.** $\frac{2}{5} + -\frac{4}{5}$ **24.** $-\frac{3}{4} + -\frac{1}{16}$

25. $17 + (-39) + 3.5$ **26.** $-21 + (-5) + 103$

27. $-\frac{2}{3} + \frac{5}{6} + -\frac{1}{4} + 1$ **28.** $3 + -\frac{1}{5} + -\frac{2}{3}$

Subtract.

29. $-7 - (-7)$ **30.** $19 - (-21)$ **31.** $-8 - 1.75$

32. $23 - (35.2)$ **33.** $-1.25 - (-3.4)$ **34.** $-9 - (-5.1)$

Evaluate.

35. $|2| + |-9|$ **36.** $|-4| \cdot |2| + |-7|$ **37.** $|3| + |-4| \cdot |0|$

38. $|a| - 17$ for $a = -23$ **39.** $|n| - |m|$ for $n = -5$ and $m = 6$

40. $2|x| \cdot |y|$ for $x = -3$ and $y = -4$ **41.** $16 - 3|t|$ for $t = -5$

Simplify.

42. $19 + (-27) - 5 - (-13)$ **43.** $-53 + (-19) - 41 - (-8)$

44. $-7 - (16) + (-9) - (-25)$ **45.** $11 - (3a) - 26a + 8 - (-17a)$

46. $21x - (17x) - (-32) + (-9x)$ **47.** $10 - (-5y) + (-9) + (-8y)$

Solve.

48. Bob entered the elevator on the eighth floor. The elevator went up 4 floors. Next it went down 10 floors. Then the elevator went up 3 floors and Bob got off. What floor was he on?

49. Cheryl's checking account was overdrawn by $102.75. After she made a deposit, she was overdrawn by $67.85. How much did she deposit?

50. At 4 a.m. the temperature at Anchorage was $-12°F$. By noon, the temperature was $39°F$. How many degrees did the temperature rise?

For use after Lesson 2-9

Simplify.

1. $2[5(6-4)+(-3)^2]$

2. $(-2)^3-(-1)^8+(-3)^2$

3. $3(-2)^3\cdot(-1)^{21}$

4. $5[-3(2^3)+(-2)^2(7)]$

5. $\dfrac{5(-11)+(-1)}{7}$

6. $3\frac{1}{8}\div5\frac{1}{2}$

7. $\dfrac{4^3}{(-2)^6}$

8. $2\frac{1}{3}\div5\frac{1}{4}$

9. $\dfrac{(-6)^3}{-(3^2)}$

10. $\dfrac{4+(-8)5}{-9}$

11. $\dfrac{(-8)^2}{(-2)^2}$

12. $\dfrac{10+2(-5)^2}{(2^2)(3)}$

13. $-4\frac{2}{5}\div2\frac{5}{8}$

14. $45-(-21)+(-7)-9+3-(-5)+(-12)-37$

15. $-11+(-36)+27-(-8)-15+(-2)+21-6$

16. $[3(x+5)-7]+[-5(x-2)+11]$

17. $[4(x-3)+18]-[3(x+1)+2]$

18. $[4(x+1)+11]-[7(x-3)-1]$

19. $[9(3-x)+7]+[4(5+x)-2]$

Evaluate for $x=-4$, $y=2$, $z=3$.

20. $(-2x)yz$

21. $5y^2+2xz$

22. $y(x^2)-5z$

23. $5(2y-x)+z$

24. $2[(x-y)+z]$

25. $z(9y+4x)$

26. $3|x|-yz$

27. $5x-2|y|$

28. $4|x|+7|z|-5y$

29. $|x|\cdot|y|+|z|$

30. $|x|\cdot|-y|\cdot|z|$

31. $|x|-|y|+|z|$

Multiply or divide.

32. $3(-5)(1.2)(1)(-2.5)(0.08)(-10)$

33. $-2(5)(1.4)(-0.25)(20)(0.5)$

34. $-\frac{1}{3}\left(\frac{2}{5}\right)\left(\frac{5}{7}\right)\left(-\frac{7}{8}\right)\left(-\frac{3}{8}\right)$

35. $\left(-\frac{2}{9}\right)\left(\frac{6}{5}\right)\left(-\frac{4}{7}\right)\left(-\frac{1}{8}\right)\left(\frac{3}{20}\right)$

36. $\frac{3}{8}\left(\frac{1}{5}x-\frac{2}{3}y+4\right)$

37. $-\frac{2}{5}\left(-\frac{3}{8}x+\frac{1}{2}y-\frac{2}{3}\right)$

38. $1.2(2x+4y-7)$

39. $-2.25(-5x+2.4y)$

40. $-\frac{2}{3}\div\frac{3}{8}$

41. $\frac{5}{6}\div\left(-\frac{3}{4}\right)$

42. $-\frac{3}{16}\div\left(-\frac{3}{4}\right)$

43. $107.25\div(-5.5)$

44. $-69.3\div(4.2)$

45. $-48.16\div(-8.6)$

Factor.

46. $256-80y$

47. $21x-56y+14$

48. $12x+12y-36z$

49. $-\frac{2}{3}x+y-\frac{1}{3}z$

50. $\frac{5}{24}x-\frac{5}{4}y$

51. $\frac{24}{5}x-\frac{4}{5}y+\frac{8}{15}$

Mixed Practice 5

For use after Lesson 3-5

Solve.

1. $-17.4t = 87$

2. $-9y = 193.5$

3. $-14x = -126$

4. $-\frac{2}{3}x = 4$

5. $\frac{5}{8}x = -\frac{3}{16}$

6. $-\frac{3}{4}y = \frac{1}{8}$

7. $m + \frac{2}{5} = -\frac{1}{2}$

8. $x + \frac{5}{8} = \frac{1}{4}$

9. $y - \frac{5}{6} = -\frac{3}{8}$

10. $x - 7.3 = -2.5$

11. $3.4 = r - 6.1$

12. $y + 9 = 5.4$

13. $10 - x - 7 = 3x - 1$

14. $18 + 3x - 5 = 7x - 14 - x$

15. $4a - (5a + 3) = -1$

16. $7y - 5 = 8(5 - y)$

17. $6(m + 3) = 2(m - 1)$

18. $7(a - 7) = -3(a + 3)$

19. $2(5t - 3) = 3(2t + 6)$

20. $4(2m + 1) = 2(3m - 1)$

21. $x + 5 = x + (9 - x)$

22. $20 - (4 - y) = 26$

23. $5x + 6 = 7x$

24. $4t + 5t = -27$

25. $3y - 9y = 102$

26. $4.3x - 7.9x = -18$

27. $4(5x - 7) - 8x = -16$

28. $2(9 - 6x) - 49 = 5$

29. $-2(4x + 5) - 11 = -5$

30. $6x - 5(3 + 2x) = 1$

Write as an algebraic expression.

31. 24 less than half a number

32. 3 times the sum of a number and its reciprocal

33. 4 times the difference of a number and 3

34. one-half of the product of a number and 5

Translate to an equation and solve.

35. Nine more than a number is -53. Find the number.

36. There are 64 members in the History Club. 11 less than half of the members are girls. How many members are boys?

37. The number of girls in Mrs. Busbee's class is 3 more than twice the number of boys. There are 19 girls. What is the total number of boys and girls in the class?

38. Mara reads an average of 0.75 pages a minute. At that rate, in how many minutes will she read 36 pages?

39. Rico spent $18.50 to rent a lawn mower. The fee for the first hour was $8.00. Each additional hour cost $3.50. For how many hours did he rent the mower?

40. Twelve times a number is 132. Find the number.

For use after Lesson 3-11

Write as a decimal.

1. 23%   **2.** 0.04%   **3.** 13.5%   **4.** 160%   **5.** 6.7%

Express as a percent. Round to the nearest tenth of a percent if necessary.

6. $\frac{3}{5}$ **7.** $\frac{1}{25}$ **8.** $\frac{5}{8}$ **9.** $\frac{2}{3}$ **10.** $\frac{37}{100}$

Solve.

11. $\frac{3}{2}x + \frac{3}{4}x + \frac{3}{8}x = 21$

12. $\frac{3}{4}n - \frac{1}{8}n = 6 + \frac{1}{8}n$

13. $\frac{1}{4} - x = \frac{1}{2}x + \frac{9}{4}$

14. $5|x| + 7 = 32$

15. $|y| + 7 = 3|y| - 9$

16. $|-x| = 14$

17. $A = \frac{1}{2}bh$, for h

18. $V = \frac{s}{t + r}$, for t

19. $B = 2(x + y)$, for x

20. What is 4% of 65?

21. 15 is 6% of what number?

22. 28 is what percent of 35?

Translate to an equation and solve.

23. The ratio of right-handed students to left-handed students in Mr. Duggan's class is 7 to 2. There are 27 students in the class. How many are right-handed?

24. The sum of three consecutive integers is 108. What are the integers?

25. At the end of the week, Lori had $440.28 in her account. She had written checks for $57.34, $19.09, and $30.77, and had made deposits of $42.00 and $15.85. How much was in her account at the beginning of the week?

26. Darrell bought a box of 36 ball point pens for $20.88. Find the cost of a single pen.

27. Raoul bought some $3 rolls of film and an $8 photo album. The total cost was $35. How many rolls of film did he buy?

28. Carl's age in years, 32, is 25 less than one-third his weight in pounds. How much does Carl weigh?

29. A movie theater had 46 more occupied seats than empty seats. It had a total of 320 seats. How many seats were occupied?

30. Alondra worked 55 hours and was paid $28.75. At that rate, how long will it take Alondra to earn $69?

For use after Lesson 4-3

Determine whether the given number is a solution of the inequality.

1. $x \le -1$ **a.** 2   **b.** -4 **c.** -1 **d.** 0

2. $y > -3$ **a.** 0   **b.** -2 **c.** -4 **d.** -3

3. $x < 4$ **a.** 3   **b.** 4   **c.** -1 **d.** 7

4. $x \le \frac{1}{3}$ **a.** $\frac{1}{8}$ **b.** $-\frac{1}{2}$ **c.** $\frac{1}{2}$ **d.** 0.5

5. $y \ge -\frac{3}{8}$ **a.** $\frac{3}{8}$ **b.** $-\frac{3}{5}$ **c.** -0.2 **d.** $-\frac{1}{8}$

Write the inequality shown by each graph.

6.

7.

8.

9.

10.

Solve.

11. $x + \frac{1}{2} < \frac{1}{8}$ **12.** $y - \frac{2}{3} > \frac{1}{4}$ **13.** $x - \frac{1}{5} \le \frac{2}{3}$

14. $x - \frac{1}{8} > 0$ **15.** $\frac{2}{5} + a < \frac{1}{2}$ **16.** $x + \frac{1}{8} \ge \frac{3}{4}$

17. $-6m < 102$ **18.** $9y \ge 31.5$ **19.** $-15x \ge 225$

20. $7y \le -98$ **21.** $9x - 7x \le 6$ **22.** $66 \ge 2y - 8y$

23. $5(x + 3) - 4x < 17$ **24.** $3y - 2(y + 4) > 2$ **25.** $-3(x + 5) + 4(x + 8) > 24$

26. $-5m + 4 + 6m < 2$ **27.** $5(x - 2) - 4x > 5$ **28.** $-2(x - 4) + 3x \le 1$

Classify each statement as true or false.

29. $-4 \le -5$ **30.** $7 \le -7$ **31.** $4.5 \ge 4.5$

32. $|-0.3| \ge 0$ **33.** $|-2| < |1|$ **34.** $3.01 < 3.10$

35. $|x| \ge x$ **36.** $|x| \ge 0$ **37.** $|x + 1| > x$

Solve and graph the solution.

38. $t + \frac{3}{5} \le \frac{9}{10}$ **39.** $m + \frac{1}{3} > -2$ **40.** $\frac{1}{3}x \le \frac{7}{6}$

41. $-6y > 9$ **42.** $8m > -4$ **43.** $5x + 4 - 7x \le 10$

For use after Lesson 4-6

Solve using the addition and multiplication properties.

1. $3(5 - x) \leq 2(x - 9)$
2. $4(x + 5) \leq 3(6 + x)$
3. $10 + 3y - 3 \geq 5y - 7$
4. $4x - 3 < 10x - 5$
5. $12 - 9c > 38 + 4c$
6. $2(x - 6) + 5 \geq 9$
7. $\frac{3}{8}y - 5 > \frac{7}{8}y$
8. $\frac{3}{4}x + 3 \leq x + \frac{1}{2}$
9. $1.6x - 0.5 \leq 1.2x + 1.5$
10. $2.2y + 3.2 < 3.4y - 1.6$
11. $6(1.5 - x) + 3x < 4(3 - x)$
12. $5(x + 2) - 4 > 3x$

Translate to an inequality.

13. 6 more than half a number is less than 7.
14. 9 less than twice a number is less than 2.
15. 15 is greater than or equal to half a number.
16. 7 more than 5 times a number is at most 31.
17. 6 less than 4 times a number is at least 40.
18. 3 more than half a number is at least 15.

Solve.

19. Find the greatest possible pair of integers such that one integer is 4 less than twice the other and their sum is at most 50.
20. Find all numbers such that the sum of the number and 24 is greater than 4 times the number.
21. The sum of four consecutive even integers is less than or equal to 116. Find the greatest possible values of the integers.
22. Roberta wants to buy a scarf and sweater and must not spend more than $56.00 for both. If the scarf costs $33.80, how much can she pay for the sweater?
23. Mitch scored 25 points in the first basketball game, 18 in the second, and 35 in the third. How many points must he score in the fourth game to maintain an average of at least 28 points scored for the four games?
24. The length of a rectangle is 22.5 cm. What width will make the area at least 405 cm^2?
25. Find the greatest possible pair of integers such that one integer is 2 less than three times the other and the sum is less than 42.

For use after Lesson 5-5

Simplify.

1. $(-8)^0$
2. $(x^3y)(x^2y)$
3. $(3^{-1})^4$
4. $(2w^9)^5$
5. $[2(-x^9)]^3$
6. $(-3m^4)^3$
7. $(2y^2)(y^5)^2$
8. $(x^2)^3(x^3)^2$

9. $\dfrac{2^5}{2^8}$
10. $\dfrac{(-2)^2}{(-2)^9}$
11. $\dfrac{x^3 \cdot y^4}{x^2y}$
12. $\dfrac{(4 \cdot 2^3)^2}{3}$

13. $\dfrac{(-y)^4}{2y}$
14. $\dfrac{(3y^4)^2}{27y^5}$
15. $\dfrac{-16m^5}{-4m^2n}$
16. $\dfrac{-3ab^2}{27a^2}$

Multiply or divide. Express the result using scientific and standard notation.

17. $(5.1 \times 10^3)(2.4 \times 10^{-5})$
18. $(1.1 \times 10^{-4})(3.0 \times 10^{-3})$
19. $\dfrac{1.8 \times 10^4}{2 \times 10^7}$

20. $\dfrac{3.5 \times 10^{-3}}{7 \times 10^{-5}}$
21. $\dfrac{(4.0 \times 10^3)(9.0 \times 10^5)}{(6.0 \times 10^5)}$
22. $\dfrac{(1.2 \times 10^4)(4.0 \times 10^{-3})}{(6.0 \times 10^7)}$

Evaluate each expression.

23. $x^2 \cdot x^1$ for $x = 10$
24. $2^a \cdot 2^b \cdot 2^c$ for $a = 1, b = 4, c = 0$
25. $7^a \cdot 5^a \cdot 3^a$ for $a = 0$
26. $10^x \cdot 10^y \cdot 10^z$ for $x = 3, y = 2, z = 1$

Write using standard notation.

27. 4.003×10^5
28. 9.6×10^{-4}
29. 1.392×10^3
30. 1.4×10^{-3}
31. 3.8×10^4
32. 3.752×10^{-5}

Identify the degree of each term and the degree of the polynomial.

33. $4x^3y - 19x^2y^2 + 21$
34. $-3x^5y^3 - 5x^4y^9 + 8xy^{21} + 15$
35. $4x^2 + 15 - 8x^3 + 11x$
36. $9x^2y^3 + 4x^5y - 2xy^2 - 1$

Write using scientific notation.

37. $9,475,001$
38. 0.00037
39. 65
40. 0.000001
41. 0.0939
42. $46,300$

Identify the terms. Give the coefficient of each term.

43. $-3a^3c + 11a^2c^2 + 5c^3$
44. $4x^2 - 6xy - 8y^2$
45. $-3x^3yz + 4x^2y^2z - 19xy^2z^3 + 15$

Collect like terms.

46. $9xy^3 - 3x^2y - 2xy^3$
47. $3m^2 - m^2 + 3m + m$
48. $\frac{3}{5}x^2 + 4 - 2x - x^2$

49. $\frac{1}{2}x + \frac{2}{3}x^2 - x + 3$
50. $2 - \frac{1}{2}x^3 - 2x + \frac{2}{3}x^3$
51. $\frac{1}{2}x^4 - 2x^2 - \frac{4}{5}x^4 + \frac{4}{5}x$

For use after Lesson 5-12

Collect like terms and then arrange in descending order for the variable x.

1. $5x^3 + 6x - 4x^2 - x + 4$

2. $xy - 7x^2 + 5xy + 21 - 3$

3. $3x - 3x^2 + 4x - x^2$

4. $5y^5 - x^2 + 4xy + 7x^2$

5. $-xy + 5x^2y^3 - 5 + 7xy - x^3 + 4xy + x^2y^3 - 2$

Add or subtract.

6. $(-3x^2 + 4x - 19) + (9x + 11 + 4x^2y - 5y)$

7. $(3m^2n + mn - 25) - (6m^2n - 5m + 9)$

8. $(4x^3 + 8x^2 - x + 4) - (3x^2 - 5x^3 + 1)$

9. $(2x^5y^2 - 4x^3 - 2x + 4) + (x^3 - 4x^5y^2 - 9x + 6)$

Simplify.

10. $(x^2 - x) + (x - 8) - (x + 5x^2) + (2x^2 - 9x + 1)$

11. $(5x^2 - 2x + 1) - (3x + 4) + (25 - 4x^2) - (9x + 7)$

12. $(4x^2y - 5x + 1) + (3y^2 - 4) - (7x + 4y^2 + 2x^2y)$

13. $(-4x^4 + 2xy) - (x^2 - 5xy + x^4) + (3x^4 + 2xy)$

Evaluate each polynomial for $x = -2$ and $y = 3$.

14. $4x^2 - 5xy$

15. $10 - 3x^2 - 5y$

16. $3x^2 + 10xy + 2y^2$

17. $x^3y^2 + 9x - 2y + 10$

18. $x^2y^3 + 15x - 20$

19. $2y^3 - 2y^2x + 4x^2 + 1$

Add or subtract using columns.

20. $(7y^5 + 4y^2 - 9) - (5y^3 - 7y^2 + 6y - 3)$

21. $(3x^5 - 9x^3y + 15 - 9x) + (14x^3y + 6x - y + 4 - 11x^5)$

22. $(4x^5y + 3x^3y^3 - 9xy + 4) - (2x^5y + 4x^4y^2 - 10xy - 3)$

23. $(-4mn^2 + 3m^4 + 6n - m^3) + (15n + 7m^3 - m^2 + 6mn^2 - 4)$

Multiply.

24. $(0.5x^3)(4x^5)$

25. $4x^2(x^3 - 5x + 16)$

26. $(5a^3 - 7)(-2a^2 + a)$

27. $(4x + 3)(3x - 4)$

28. $(4m + 0.5)(4m - 0.5)$

29. $(7 - 5x)^2$

30. $(3y + 2)^2$

31. $(2x^3 - 11)(2x^3 + 11)$

32. $(x^2 - 5)(x^3 - 2x^2 - 2)$

33. $(-2x^3 + 5x + 1)(x + 1)$

34. Find the area of a rectangle with length $= (a + 5)$ and width $= (a - 7)$.

35. Find the area of a square with each side $= (x + y)$.

36. Find three consecutive numbers, the sum of whose squares is 29 more than three times the square of the smallest.

For use after Lesson 6-5

Factor.

1. $m^4 - 25$ **2.** $81t^2 - 100s^4$ **3.** $-9 + 4y^2$ **4.** $49 - w^6$

5. $x^4 - 5x^3 + x^2$ **6.** $x^2 - 3x - 10$ **7.** $t^2 + 4t + 3$ **8.** $c^2 - 8c + 7$

State whether each expression is a difference of two squares.

9. $4y^2 - x$ **10.** $9x^2 - 25$ **11.** $m^2 + n^2$

12. $4a^3 - b^2$ **13.** $36 - 49t^2$ **14.** $12m^2 - 4n^2$

Factor.

15. $c^2 - 4$ **16.** $81m^2 - 25$

17. $y^{10} - z^{10}$ **18.** $49 - n^8$

19. $2a^4b + 2a^3b^2 - 2a^2b^2$ **20.** $5x^4y + 5x^2y - 10x$

21. $2x^2 - 8x - 10$ **22.** $2x^2 - 9x - 5$

23. $2x^2 + 3x - 5$ **24.** $2x^2 - 3x - 5$

State whether each expression is a trinomial square.

25. $x^2 - 2xy - y^2$ **26.** $4x^2 + 4xy + y^2$

27. $x^2 - 10xy + 25y^2$ **28.** $9x^2 - 18xy + 9y^2$

29. $2v^2 + 4vw + 4w^2$ **30.** $24x^2 + 20xy + 4y^2$

31. $x^2 + 2x + 1$ **32.** $y^2 - 6y - 9$

33. $c^4 + 4c + 4$ **34.** $7m^2 + 14m + 49$

Factor.

35. $m^4 - 9$ **36.** $4y^2 - 1$

37. $6x^2 + 3x - 9$ **38.** $10x^2 + x - 3$

39. $x^2 - 4x - 45$ **40.** $t^2 - 7t + 12$

41. $12 - x - x^2$ **42.** $2y^2 - 9y - 5$

Find three factorizations for each monomial.

43. $4x^2y$ **44.** $-9m^3n$ **45.** $15t^23$ **46.** $-12pq^2$

Factor.

47. $x^5 - 4x^3 + 3x$ **48.** $7x - 6 - 2x^2$ **49.** $4y^3 - 12y^2 + 4y$ **50.** $6a^2 - 2a + 10$

51. $x^2 + 5x - xy - 5y$ **52.** $6t^2 + 5t + 1$ **53.** $2x^2 - 9x + 4$ **54.** $3x^2 + 10x - 8$

For use after Lesson 6-9

Factor.

1. $2y^2 - 9y - 5$
2. $2t^2 + 25t + 12$
3. $4m^2 - 1$
4. $3y^2 + y - 10$
5. $x^2 + 4x - 21$
6. $y^2 - 12y + 36$
7. $10 + 3x - x^2$
8. $t^2 + 8t + 16$
9. $3x^3 + 3x^2 - 15x$
10. $x^3 + 3x^2 - x$

Solve.

11. $t^2 - 25 = 0$
12. $x^2 - x = 20$
13. $x^2 + 49 = 14x$
14. $3x^2 + x = 0$
15. $(2y - 1)(y - 5) = 0$
16. $t(t + 7) = 4(3 + 2t)$
17. $t^2 + 3t - 4 = 36$
18. $3y^2 + 17y + 10 = 0$
19. $t^2 - \frac{25}{4} = 0$
20. $\frac{3x^2}{4} = 27$

Factor by grouping.

21. $x^3 + 3x^2 - x - 3$
22. $2x^4 + 5x^3 + 2x + 5$
23. $6y^3 - 10y^2 + 9y - 15$
24. $x^3 + 2x^2 - 7x - 14$

Translate to an equation and solve.

25. Find two consecutive even integers whose product is 288.

26. Twelve more than the square of a number is seven times the number. Find the number.

27. The width of a rectangle is 7 ft less than the length. The area of the rectangle is 228 ft^2. Find the length and width.

28. If the sides of a square are lengthened by 4 in., the area becomes 256 in.^{2}. Find the length of a side of the original square.

29. Find two consecutive integers whose product is 182.

30. The sum of squares of two consecutive odd positive integers is 202. Find the integers.

31. The height of a triangle is 6 m more than the base. The area is 216 m^2. Find the base and height.

32. If a number is subtracted from its square, the result is 2. Find the number.

33. Four times the square of a number is 9. Find the number.

For use after Lesson 7-4

Find the coordinates of each point.

1. Q **2.** R **3.** S

4. T **5.** U **6.** V

Match each equation with its corresponding graph at the right.

7. $y = -2x + 2$ **8.** $y = \frac{1}{2}x - 1$

9. $y = -2x - 1$ **10.** $y = 2$

11. $y = \frac{1}{2}x + 2$

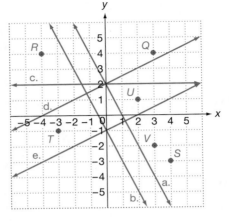

Find the slopes of the lines containing these points.

12. $(3, 7)$ $(6, 5)$

14. $(2, -2)$ $(10, 2)$

13. $(10, 9)$ $(2, 4)$

15. $(4, 13)$ $(7, 16)$

Determine whether the given point is a solution of the equation.

16. $(4, 1)$, $y = \frac{1}{2}x - 3$

17. $\left(-\frac{1}{2}, \frac{9}{8}\right)$, $y = -\frac{1}{4}x + 1$

18. $(0, 2)$, $5y = 2x + 10$

19. $(4, -4)$, $2y + 3x = 4$

Find three points that satisfy the following conditions.

20. The x-coordinate is half of the y-coordinate.

21. The x-coordinate is 3 less than the y-coordinate.

22. The x-coordinate is 5 less than twice the y-coordinate.

Solve.

23. A line contains $(-3, 10)$ and $(x, -5)$. It has slope -3. Find x.

24. A line contains $(-2, -17)$ and $(x, 8)$. It has slope 5. Find x.

25. A line contains $(2, 7)$ and $(x, -9)$. It has slope 2. Find x.

26. The vertices of a triangle are $A(3, 2)$, $B(4, -2)$, and $C(-1, -1)$. Find the slope of each side of the triangle.

27. Write an equation of a line that is parallel to the y-axis and 3 units to the left of it.

28. Write an equation of a line that is parallel to the x-axis and intersects the y-axis at $(0, -2.5)$.

In which quadrant is each point located?

29. $(27, -4)$ **30.** $(-6, -53)$ **31.** $(0, 4)$ **32.** $(2, 17)$

For use after Lesson 7-9

Write an equation for each line that contains the given pair of points.

1. $(1, 5)$ $(-4, -5)$

2. $(-3, 1)$ $(0, -1)$

3. $(2, 6)$ $(-4, -24)$

4. $(0, 5)$ $(3, -13)$

Graph each line using the slope and y-intercept.

5. $4y + 8x = -12$

6. $2y - 10 = 6x$

7. $5y + 20x = 5$

8. $x - y = 2$

Write an equation for each line.

9. the line containing $(-3, 1)$ and parallel to the line $y + 2x = 3$

10. the line containing $(2, 6)$ and perpendicular to the line $4y = x - 4$

11. the line containing $(3, 5)$ and parallel to the line $3y = 15x - 7$

12. the line containing $(2, -4)$ and perpendicular to the line $y = -3x + 5$

13. the line that has the same slope as the line described by $5y + 15 = 2x$ and contains the point $(-5, -1)$

14. the line that has the same slope as the line described by $2y + 4x = 6$ and contains the point $(-6, 5)$

15. the line that is perpendicular to the y-axis and intersects the y-axis at $(0, 3)$

Graph using intercepts.

16. $2x + 2y = 6$

17. $2y + 1 = x$

18. $3y + 6 = 15x$

19. $3y - 2x = 12$

Find the slope of each line by solving for y.

20. $8y + 3x = 16$

21. $-9x = -1 - y$

22. $2y + 4 = x - 2$

23. $2y + 8x = 14$

Write an equation for each line given the slope and y-intercept. Express the equation in slope-intercept form.

24. $m = -\frac{1}{3}, b = 2$

25. $m = \frac{4}{3}, b = \frac{1}{8}$

26. $m = 2, b = 0$

27. $m = 0, b = -1$

Solve. Assume a linear relationship fits the data.

28. A catering company advertised the following rates: "Complete Texas-style barbeque lunch just \$277.50 (d) for 50 people (p), or \$526.00 for 120 people." Use the ordered pairs (p, d).

   a. Find a linear equation for the data points.

   b. Use this linear equation to find the cost of lunch for 65 people.

Mixed Practice 15

For use after Lesson 8-3

Determine whether the given ordered pair is a solution of the system of equations.

1. $(4, 5)$; $\quad 2y - x = 6$
$\qquad\qquad y + x = 7$

2. $(-8, -8)$; $8y + 40 = 3x$
$\qquad\qquad\qquad y - x = 0$

3. $(4, 3)$; $\quad 4y + 8 = 5x$
$\qquad\qquad 2x - y = 5$

4. $(2, -7)$; $\quad 3x + y = -1$
$\qquad\qquad\qquad y + 5 = -x$

5. $(-2, 3)$; $2x - y = -7$
$\qquad\qquad\quad -y + x = -5$
$\qquad\qquad\qquad\quad y = 3$

6. $(7, -2)$; $\quad x + 2y = 3$
$\qquad\qquad\qquad -y + 9 = x$
$\qquad\qquad\qquad -x - y = -5$

Solve using the addition method.

7. $3x - 4y = 1$
$\quad -x + 2y = 3$

8. $3x - 5y = -2$
$\quad 5y - 2x = -2$

9. $3x + 2y = 1$
$\quad 5x + 3y = -1$

10. $4x + 9y = 6$
$\quad\; 5y + 3x = 1$

Solve using the substitution method.

11. $3y = x - 2$
$\quad\;\; y - x = -4$

12. $2y + 5x = 4$
$\quad\;\; x + y = 5$

13. $5y - x = -1$
$\quad\;\; 3y - 2x = 5$

14. $5x + 2y = 5$
$\quad\;\; 2x - y = 11$

Solve these systems graphically.

15. $2y = -x + 4$
$\quad\;\; x - y = 1$

16. $y - x = 5$
$\quad\;\; x + y = -1$

17. $x + y = -4$
$\quad\;\; 3y = x - 4$

18. $y + 1 = -x$
$\quad\;\; y = x - 7$

Translate to a system of equations and solve.

19. The perimeter of a rectangle is 61 m. The length of the rectangle is 7 less than twice the width. Find the length and width of the rectangle.

20. Find two numbers whose sum is 101 and whose difference is 45.

21. The difference between two numbers is 36. Five times the larger is 11 times the smaller. What are the numbers?

22. The sum of two numbers is 26. Two-fifths of the first number plus three-eighths of the second number is 10. Find the numbers.

For use after Lesson 8-6

Solve.

1. $2x - 5y = 7$
$2y - 3x = 6$

2. $2x - 3y = 4$
$5y - 3x = -5$

3. $6x + 12y = 5$
$6y - 10x = 9$

4. $x - 3y = 7$
$3x + 2y = 10$

5. $x + 2y = 15$
$5x - y = -2$

6. $4x + 7y = -3$
$2y - 3x = 24$

Solve by graphing.

7. $3y + 2x = 6$
$6y = 3x - 2$

8. $y = x + 5$
$2y + x = -2$

Translate to a system of equations and solve.

9. A collection of nickels and dimes totals $22.40. There are 304 coins in all. How many nickels are there?

10. The sum of the digits of a two-digit number is 11. When the number is reversed, the new sum is 27 less than the original number. Find the original number.

11. A fishing boat broke down after traveling 2 hours against a 4 km/h current. The boat was carried back to its starting point by the current. The whole trip took 5.5 hours. Find the speed of the boat in still water before the motor failed.

12. Admission to the gymnastics meet cost $2.40 for adults and $1.25 for students. If 540 tickets were sold for a total of $934.90, how many tickets of each kind were sold?

13. The sum of two numbers is 248. Their difference is 64. Find the numbers.

14. Two cars leave town at the same time traveling in opposite directions. One travels 51 mi/h and the other travels 45 mi/h. In how many hours will they be 432 miles apart?

15. A two-digit number is four times the sum of its digits. The ones digit is 4 more than the tens digit. Find the original number.

16. Two cars leave town at the same time going in the same direction on the same road. One travels 28 mi/h and the other travels 46 mi/h. In how many hours will they be 63 miles apart?

Mixed Practice 17

For use after Lesson 9-3

Solve.

1. $2x + 1 > 5$ or $x - 2 \le -1$
2. $2x + 1 < 5$ and $x - 2 \ge -1$
3. $|3x - 7| = 11$
4. $-|x - 3| = -5$
5. $-5 \le 2x + 3 < 21$
6. $-x + 1 > 3$ or $2x - 5 > 3$
7. $2|5x - 3| = 26$
8. $7 + |2x + 3| = 11$

Write the inequality shown by each group.

9.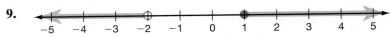

10.

11.

12.

Write using (a) roster notation and (b) set-builder notation.

13. the set W of positive multiples of 5 less than 38
14. the set P of prime numbers between 15 and 25
15. the set F of positive integers that are factors of 24
16. the set N of integers whose absolute values are less than 6

Write a compound sentence for each situation.

17. Water must be more than 0°C but less that 100°C to be in liquid form.
18. Special classes were created for students who scored less than 58 or more than 97 on the placement test.
19. Each crate of melons weighed at least 40 pounds and less than 45 pounds.

Let $A = \{2, 3, 5, 7\}$, $B = \{0, 3, 6, 9\}$, $C = \{1, 3, 5, 7, 9\}$, and $D = \{0, 1, 2, 3, 4, 5, 6\}$.

Find each of the following.

20. $A \cup B$
21. $C \cap D$
22. $A \cup C$
23. $B \cap C$
24. $A \cap D$
25. $B \cup C$
26. $A \cap C$
27. $B \cup D$

Solve and graph.

28. $-2 < x - 3 < 3$
29. $-2 > x + 3$ or $x + 6 \ge 7$
30. $-3x > 9$ or $2x - 5 > -3$
31. $-7 < 2x + 3 \le 7$

For use after Lesson 9-6

Graph on a number line.

1. $|y + 1| < 6$

2. $|3x| > 6$

3. $|x - 4| > 2$

Solve.

4. $|y + 4| = 6$

5. $|2x + 1| = -5$

6. $|2x + 1| > 3$

7. $4|3y| > 20$

8. $2|3x| < 20$

9. $|3y - 2| < 7$

10. $|3x + 2| < -3$

11. $2|-3x| = 24$

12. $|2x - 7| = 21$

13. $-2|x - 3| < -8$

14. $|2a + 5| < 1$

15. $|3x + 1.5| = 5.7$

Graph on a coordinate plane.

16. $-x < y$

17. $y < x - 1$

18. $2y < x + 4$

Determine whether the given point is a solution of the inequality.

19. $(1, 3); 2x - y > 5$

20. $(-2, 3); 2x + 3y \geq 5$

21. $(4, -1); 2x - 4y < 16$

22. $(-2, -7); y + 5x \leq 2$

Solve by graphing.

23. $y < 2x$
   $y < 4$

24. $y - x < 0$
   $3y + 2x > 1$

25. $x + y > 1$
   $x < 2$

Write an inequality for each graph.

26.

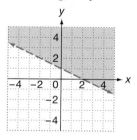

27.

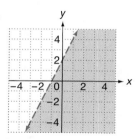

28.

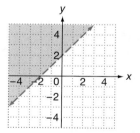

Write a system of inequalities whose solution is shown by each graph.

29.

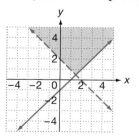

30.

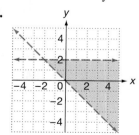

31.

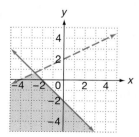

Mixed Practice 19

For use after Lesson 10-5

Simplify.

1. $\dfrac{x^2 - 2x - 3}{x^2 - 5x + 6}$

2. $\dfrac{25x^2 - 9}{5x + 3}$

3. $\dfrac{5x^2 - 5}{10x^2 - 10}$

4. $\dfrac{2y^2 + 5y - 7}{2y + 7}$

5. $\dfrac{16 - a}{a - 16}$

6. $\dfrac{2x^2 - 6x}{2x^2 + 2x}$

Add or subtract and simplify.

7. $\dfrac{2x + 9}{x + 7} + \dfrac{x + 12}{x + 7}$

8. $\dfrac{7x + 9}{3x + 2} - \dfrac{7x + 6}{3x + 2}$

9. $\dfrac{3y + 1}{y - 3} - \dfrac{2y - 4}{y - 3}$

10. $\dfrac{3}{y} - \dfrac{y + 4}{y^2}$

11. $\dfrac{3a}{a + 2} + \dfrac{12a}{a^2 - 4}$

12. $\dfrac{3m + 7}{4m} - \dfrac{4m + 11}{8m}$

13. $\dfrac{2 - x}{x^2 - 7x + 10} + \dfrac{x - 4}{x - 5}$

14. $\dfrac{x}{x + 1} - \dfrac{1}{x - 1}$

15. $\dfrac{1}{x} + \dfrac{x + 5}{x^2}$

16. $\dfrac{x^2}{x^2 - 1} - \dfrac{1}{x + 1}$

17. $\dfrac{x + 4}{2} + \dfrac{x + 4}{x}$

18. $\dfrac{a + 1}{a - 1} + \dfrac{a - 1}{a + 1}$

Multiply or divide and simplify.

19. $\dfrac{3}{2(x - 1)} \cdot \dfrac{4}{3(x - 1)}$

20. $\dfrac{x^2 - 1}{x^2 - 4} \cdot \dfrac{x + 2}{x + 1}$

21. $\dfrac{m}{m + 1} \cdot \dfrac{m^2 - m - 2}{m^2 + m}$

22. $\dfrac{6x^2}{6x^2 + 9x + 3} \cdot \dfrac{6x + 3}{2x}$

23. $\dfrac{mn + n^2}{m} \div \dfrac{m^2 - n^2}{mn^2}$

24. $\dfrac{x^2 - x - 12}{x + 2} \div \dfrac{(x - 4)^2}{x + 2}$

25. $\dfrac{x^2 - 3x - 10}{x^2 + 2x - 15} \cdot \dfrac{x^2 + 8x + 15}{x^2 - 7x + 10}$

26. $\dfrac{x^2 - 4x}{x + 1} \div \dfrac{x^2 - 16}{x^2 - 1}$

27. $\dfrac{x^2 - 9}{x + 5} \div \dfrac{x + 3}{x^2 + 2x - 15}$

28. $\dfrac{a^2 + 6a + 9}{a - 3} \div \dfrac{a^2 + 4a + 3}{a + 1}$

29. $\dfrac{x^2 - 4}{x + 1} \div \dfrac{x + 2}{x - 2}$

30. $\dfrac{m - 1}{5} \div \dfrac{m^2 - 2m + 1}{m^2 + 2m - 3}$

31. $\dfrac{2}{x^2 + 4x + 4} \cdot \dfrac{x + 2}{x - 2}$

Find the LCM.

32. $2x - 3, 4x^2 - 9$

33. $x^2 - 5x + 6, x^2 - 6x + 9$

34. $x^2 - 16, 2x + 8$

35. $10 - 2a, a^2 - 25$

36. $24a^3b, 18abc$

37. $x^2 - 1, x^2 - 3x + 2, \ x^2 + x - 6$

For use after Lesson 10-10

Solve.

1. $\dfrac{x + 2}{x - 2} = x - 1$

2. $\dfrac{x + 6}{x + 2} = \dfrac{x}{x - 1}$

3. $\dfrac{4x - 5}{2x + 1} + \dfrac{x + 1}{x - 1} = 3$

4. $2a - 1 = \dfrac{8a + 3}{a + 1}$

Write and solve an equation.

5. The Highway Department has purchased wildflower seed mixtures from two companies. Mixture A is 28% bluebonnets, and Mixture B is 48% bluebonnets. How much of each mix should be used to create 250 pounds of blended seed that is 35% bluebonnets?

6. The reciprocal of two more than a number is three-fourths of the reciprocal of the number itself. What is the number?

7. It takes Sylvia 8 hours to assemble a carton of widgets. Joe can do the same job in 12 hours. How long would it take them to assemble a carton of widgets if they worked together?

8. Marty drove his fully loaded moving van 270 miles to Memphis. With his van empty, Marty drove 15 mi/h faster and made the return trip in 1.5 hours less. Find the speed going to Memphis.

9. The reciprocal of 5 less than a number is 4 times the reciprocal of twice the number. Find the number.

Divide.

10. $\dfrac{3x^4 - 27x^3 + 3x^2}{3x^2}$

11. $\dfrac{16x^3 + 4x^2 - 4x - 1}{4x + 1}$

12. $x^2 + 4x - 24 \div x - 3$

13. $10a^2 + 7a - 12 \div (2a + 3)$

14. $2x^4 - x^2 - 15 \div x^2 - 3$

15. $y^4 - 4y^2 + 3 \div y - 1$

Simplify.

16. $\dfrac{\dfrac{x}{(3x - 1)(x - y)}}{\dfrac{y}{x - y}}$

17. $\dfrac{\dfrac{x(y - 3)}{y}}{\dfrac{y - 3}{x}}$

18. $\dfrac{\dfrac{1}{m} + \dfrac{1}{n}}{\dfrac{1}{m} - \dfrac{1}{n}}$

19. $\dfrac{1 - \dfrac{1}{a^2}}{1 - \dfrac{1}{a}}$

20. $\dfrac{\dfrac{x^2}{x^2 - y^2}}{\dfrac{x}{x + y}}$

21. $\dfrac{\dfrac{x}{2} + \dfrac{y}{3}}{\dfrac{2}{x} - \dfrac{3}{y}}$

For use after Lesson 11-5

Simplify. Assume that all radicands are nonnegative.

1. $\sqrt{169}$ **2.** $-\sqrt{49}$ **3.** $\sqrt{6^2 + 8^2}$ **4.** $\sqrt{(6 + 8)^2}$

5. $\sqrt{m^2 n^2}$ **6.** $\sqrt{25 y^4}$ **7.** $\sqrt{(-2x)^2}$ **8.** $\sqrt{x^2 - 6x + 9}$

9. $\sqrt{9 y^3}$ **10.** $\sqrt{(x - 2)^5}$ **11.** $2\sqrt{49 m^3}$ **12.** $\sqrt{75 x^5 y^2}$

13. $\sqrt{\dfrac{y^2}{100}}$ **14.** $\sqrt{\dfrac{9 m^4}{25 n^6}}$ **15.** $\sqrt{\dfrac{36 x^2}{49}}$ **16.** $\sqrt{\dfrac{x^2 - 8x + 16}{x^2 - 2x + 1}}$

Determine the values for the variable that will make each expression a real number.

17. $\sqrt{5y}$ **18.** $\sqrt{2x - 1}$ **19.** $\sqrt{2x - 10}$

20. $\sqrt{2x^2}$ **21.** $\sqrt{x^2 + 17}$ **22.** $\sqrt{x + 5}$

Multiply and simplify.

23. $\sqrt{25} \cdot \sqrt{32}$ **24.** $\sqrt{14} \cdot \sqrt{2}$ **25.** $\sqrt{5a} \cdot \sqrt{5ab}$ **26.** $\sqrt{3} \cdot \sqrt{3} \cdot \sqrt{3}$

27. $\sqrt{2x^2} \cdot \sqrt{2y}$ **28.** $\sqrt{8m} \cdot \sqrt{2m}$ **29.** $\sqrt{30b} \cdot \sqrt{2bc}$ **30.** $\sqrt{2}(\sqrt{2} - 2)$

31. $\sqrt{15} \cdot \sqrt{45a^3}$ **32.** $\sqrt{12xy} \cdot \sqrt{18xyz}$ **33.** $\sqrt{10^2} \cdot \sqrt{x^{31}}$ **34.** $\sqrt{8y^2} \cdot \sqrt{2y^3} \cdot \sqrt{12y^9}$

Simplify.

35. $\sqrt{512 x^{315}}$ **36.** $\sqrt{1500(x + 1)^3}$ **37.** $\sqrt{25(x^4 - 1)^2}$

38. $\sqrt{9 w^{32}}$ **39.** $\sqrt{18 m^4 n^5}$ **40.** $3a\sqrt{18 a^3}$

41. $\sqrt{4x^2 - 40x + 100}$ **42.** $\sqrt{8x^2 + 16x + 8}$ **43.** $\sqrt{25x^2 + 50xy + 25y^2}$

44. $\sqrt{\dfrac{100}{25}}$ **45.** $\sqrt{\dfrac{50}{6}}$ **46.** $\sqrt{\dfrac{y^7}{xy}}$ **47.** $\sqrt{\dfrac{x^2 y}{28}}$

48. $\sqrt{\dfrac{y^7}{x^3}}$ **49.** $\sqrt{\dfrac{48}{84}}$ **50.** $\sqrt{\dfrac{1}{256}}$ **51.** $\sqrt{\dfrac{75}{63}}$

Divide and simplify.

52. $\dfrac{\sqrt{36 x^3}}{\sqrt{6x}}$ **53.** $\dfrac{\sqrt{48 m^5}}{\sqrt{12 m^2}}$ **54.** $\dfrac{\sqrt{72}}{\sqrt{200}}$

55. $\dfrac{\sqrt{7}}{\sqrt{252}}$ **56.** $\dfrac{\sqrt{50 x^3}}{\sqrt{2x}}$ **57.** $\dfrac{\sqrt{7 y^5}}{\sqrt{21y}}$

58. $\dfrac{\sqrt{m^2 n}}{\sqrt{n^2 m}}$ **59.** $\dfrac{\sqrt{m^2 n^2}}{\sqrt{25}}$ **60.** $\dfrac{\sqrt{a - b}}{\sqrt{a + b}}$

For use after Lesson 11-9

Add or subtract.

1. $\sqrt{25x} - 3\sqrt{x}$

2. $\sqrt{54} - \sqrt{20}$

3. $\sqrt{18x + 9} + \sqrt{2x + 1}$

4. $3\sqrt{18} + 5\sqrt{12} - 3\sqrt{2}$

5. $2\sqrt{108} - 6\sqrt{3} + \sqrt{75}$

6. $2\sqrt{147} + \sqrt{12} - \sqrt{432}$

7. $\sqrt{18x^5y} + \sqrt{32xy^3} - \sqrt{128xy}$

8. $\sqrt{7x^4} - \sqrt{28x^2y^2} + \sqrt{7y^4}$

9. $\sqrt{\frac{3}{8}} + \sqrt{\frac{2}{3}} + \sqrt{\frac{8}{12}}$

10. $\sqrt{\frac{1}{12}} - \sqrt{\frac{1}{8}} + \sqrt{\frac{3}{4}}$

Rationalize the denominator.

11. $\dfrac{5\sqrt{7}}{7\sqrt{5}}$

12. $\dfrac{3\sqrt{8}}{2\sqrt{2}}$

13. $\dfrac{14}{\sqrt{7}}$

14. $\dfrac{24\sqrt{3}}{18\sqrt{2}}$

15. $\dfrac{10}{\sqrt{20}}$

16. $\dfrac{3\sqrt{21}}{5\sqrt{15}}$

17. $\dfrac{6\sqrt{27}}{4\sqrt{3}}$

18. $\dfrac{5\sqrt{338}}{8\sqrt{2}}$

19. $\dfrac{2\sqrt{\frac{3}{5}}}{3\sqrt{\frac{1}{20}}}$

20. $\dfrac{\sqrt{\frac{3}{5}}}{\sqrt{\frac{5}{8}}}$

21. $\dfrac{\sqrt{\frac{x}{y}}}{\sqrt{\frac{y}{x}}}$

22. $\dfrac{3\sqrt{\frac{15}{2}}}{2\sqrt{\frac{5}{3}}}$

Find the length of the side not given for a right triangle with hypotenuse c and legs a and b.

23. $a = 12, c = 20$

24. $a = 8, b = 15$

25. $c = 13, b = 12$

26. $b = 4, c = 5$

27. $a = 6, c = 10$

28. $a = 16, b = 30$

Simplify.

29. $7mn\sqrt{32m^3n^2}$

30. $-5\sqrt{24}$

31. $2x^2\sqrt{75xy}$

32. $\sqrt{27x} \cdot \sqrt{8x}$

33. $\sqrt{10}\sqrt{3a}\sqrt{5a^3}$

34. $\sqrt{x^{35}}\sqrt{10^{15}}\sqrt{10^4x^{21}}$

35. $\dfrac{\sqrt{18x^3}}{\sqrt{24x}}$

36. $\dfrac{\sqrt{27x^3y}}{\sqrt{48x}}$

37. $\dfrac{\sqrt{65xy}}{\sqrt{5xy}}$

Solve.

38. $3\sqrt{2x - 1} = 9$

39. $2\sqrt{3y - 2} = \sqrt{10y + 4}$

40. $\sqrt{2x + 20} = \sqrt{x + 8}$

41. $5\sqrt{3x + 7} = 2\sqrt{32x + 4}$

42. How long must a wire be to reach from the top of a 30-ft flag pole to a point on the ground 16 ft from the foot of the pole?

43. Find a number such that twice its square root is one fifth of the number itself.

44. Find a number such that nine times the inverse of its square root is -72.

For use after Lesson 12-4

Which of the following are graphs of functions?

1.
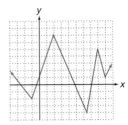

2.
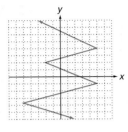

3.
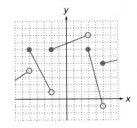

Find the indicated outputs for these functions.

4. $M(s) = |s| - 3s$; find $M(-4), M(-2), M(0), M(2), M(4)$.

5. $W(x) = 3x - 2$; find $W(-3), W(0), W(-1), W(2), W(3)$.

6. $h(x) = x^2 - 4$; find $h(-5), h(3), h(1), h(-1), h(0)$.

7. $f(t) = t^3$; find $f(-4), f(5), f(1), f(-1), f(2)$.

8. $g(a) = |a| - a$; find $g(-3), g(10), g(-2), g(0), g(4)$.

Graph each function.

9. $f(x) = -x + 4$ where the domain is $\{-3, -1, 0, 2, 5\}$

10. $h(x) = |x| - 1$ where the domain is all real numbers

11. $f(x) = 2x - 5$ where the domain is all real numbers

12. $g(x) = 2x - 1$ where the domain is $\{-3, -1, 0, 2, 3\}$

Write a linear function describing each situation. Use the function to solve the problem.

13. A fabric store sells flannel for $4.15 a yard. Find the total cost of 14 yards of flannel and a $3 spool of thread.

14. Each semester, Maria's college charges $180 per class unit plus a registration fee. Last semester Maria paid $2285 for 12 class units. Find the registration fee. Next semester, Maria will be taking 14 class units. How much will she have to pay?

15. Thi Tran makes advertising banners. He charges $40 per color plus $5.50 per letter. Find the cost of a three-color banner with 16 letters. How many letters can you have on a two-color banner and keep the cost under $125?

Graph each function. Find the vertex and axis of symmetry.

16. $y = x^2 + x$

17. $y = x^2 - 3x + 2$

18. $y = -x^2 + 4$

For use after Lesson 12-7

Find an equation of variation where y varies directly as x, and the following are true.

1. $y = 150$ when $x = 0.75$ **2.** $y = 128$ when $x = 16$

3. $y = 12$ when $x = 30$ **4.** $y = 0.36$ when $x = 45$

Find an equation of variation where y varies inversely as x. One pair of values is given.

5. $y = 26$ when $x = 18$ **6.** $y = 0.2$ when $x = 15$

7. $y = 1$ when $x = 100$ **8.** $y = 32$ when $x = 150$

Find an equation of joint or combined variation for each. Then solve for the missing value.

9. x varies jointly as y and z. One set of values is $x = 67.5$, $y = 6$, and $z = 9$. Find x when $y = 4$ and $z = 10$.

10. w varies directly as y and inversely as z. One set of values is $w = 12$, $y = 8$, and $z = 5$. Find x when $y = 9$ and $z = 15$.

11. a varies jointly as b, c, and d. One set of values is $a = 24$, $b = 3$, $c = 2$, and $d = 8$. Find a when $b = 10$, $c = 1$, and $d = 5$.

12. r varies directly as s and inversely as t. One set of values is $r = 2.7$, $s = 18$, and $t = 16$. Find r when $s = 10$ and $t = 4$.

Determine whether the following vary directly or inversely.

13. the amount of interest earned and the balance in a standard savings account

14. the amount of time required to do a job and the number of people working on the job

15. the size of a room and the amount of paint required to cover its walls

16. the distance a string is stretched by a hanging object and the weight of the object

17. the number of people that share a pizza and the size of each share

Solve.

18. The amount Tyler earns varies directly with the number of hours he works. He earns \$101.25 in 15 hours. How much does he earn in 40 hours?

19. The time required to set up the chairs for a school assembly varies inversely as the number of people working. It takes 5 hours for 3 people to do the job. How long will it take 20 people to set up the chairs?

For use after Lesson 13-4

Complete the square.

1. $a^2 + 18a$ 2. $x^2 - 7x$ 3. $x^2 - 20x$

4. $y^2 + 100y$ 5. $x^2 - 12x$ 6. $m^2 - 6m$

Write each equation in standard form and determine a, b, and c.

7. $3x^2 - 15 = 0$ 8. $x^2 + 4 = 6x$ 9. $5y^2 + 3y = 91$

10. $8t - 9 = t^2$ 11. $x^2 + 4 = 11x - 5$ 12. $35 + x^2 = 10x$

Find the value of the discriminant and determine the number of real-number solutions for each quadratic equation.

13. $x^2 + 12x + 32 = 0$ 14. $y^2 - 10y + 25 = 0$

15. $x^2 - 2x + 5 = 0$ 16. $x^2 = 11x$

Solve.

17. $3x^2 - 9x = 0$ 18. $2x^2 - 10x = 0$ 19. $4y^2 + 4y = 0$

20. $5x^2 = 20$ 21. $9y^2 - 64 = 0$ 22. $3x^2 - 243 = 0$

23. $(x - 5)^2 = 121$ 24. $(y + 3)^2 = 7$ 25. $(x + 4)^2 = 25$

26. $x(x - 2) = 15$ 27. $9y^2 - 14y = 10y - 16$ 28. $x^2 + 3x - 10 = 30$

29. $(y - 1)^2 - 81 = 0$ 30. $m^2 + 6m - 6 = 21$ 31. $x(2x + 1) = 28$

Solve by completing the square.

32. $x^2 - 6x - 16 = 0$ 33. $y^2 - 4y = 3$

34. $x^2 + 3x - 180 = 0$ 35. $x^2 - 6x + 8 = 0$

36. $a^2 - 7a + 12 = 0$ 37. $x^2 - 15x - 15 = 1$

Solve using the quadratic formula.

38. $x^2 - 5x + 4 = 0$ 39. $6t^2 - 5t - 6 = 0$

40. $8x^2 = 60$ 41. $2x^2 - x - 15 = 0$

42. $m^2 + 5m - 24 = 0$ 43. $x^2 - 4x - 77 = 0$

44. $2x(x - 2) = 3(4 - x)$ 45. $(3x + 4)(5x - 1) = 0$

Find all middle terms that complete the square.

46. $x^2 + ? + 81$ 47. $x^2 + ? + 30$ 48. $x^2 + ? + 24$

Solve.

49. $21x^2 = x$ 50. $4x^2 + 12x + 5 = 0$

51. $8x^2 = 14x + 15$ 52. $m^2 - 4m + 3 = 0$

53. $x^2 - 9 = 3x$ 54. $x^2 + 6x = 27$

For use after Lesson 13-7

Solve each rational equation.

1. $\dfrac{9}{x-3} - \dfrac{x-4}{x-3} = \dfrac{1}{4}$

2. $\dfrac{1}{x-1} + \dfrac{2}{x} = 0$

3. $\dfrac{y^2}{6} = \dfrac{y}{3} + \dfrac{1}{2}$

4. $\dfrac{m}{m-3} + \dfrac{6}{m+3} = 1$

5. $x - 3 = \dfrac{1}{x-3}$

6. $x - 6 = \dfrac{x}{x-6}$

7. $x + \dfrac{x}{x+1} = \dfrac{4x+3}{x+1}$

8. $\dfrac{1}{x+5} + \dfrac{5}{x^2-25} = 0$

Solve each radical equation.

9. $\sqrt{3x-5} = 4$

10. $\sqrt{x+5} = \sqrt{2x-3}$

11. $\sqrt{x-3} = 6 - x$

12. $\sqrt{y-5} = y - 7$

13. $\sqrt{x} + \sqrt{7} = \sqrt{x+7}$

14. $m + \sqrt{2m-6} = 3$

Solve.

15. $2x^2 - 5x + 3 = 0$

16. $(x+2)(x-1) = 10$

17. $6x^2 - x = 1$

18. $3t^2 + 5t = 28$

19. $(3y-10)^2 = 0$

20. $10x - 19 = x^2$

Solve.

21. Quentin deposited $500 in his savings account. In two years it grew to $561.80. What is the interest rate? (Use $A = P(1+r)^t$.)

22. A picture frame is 30 cm by 24 cm. There are 520 cm^2 of picture showing. Find the width of the frame.

23. The hypotenuse of a right triangle is 13 m long. One leg is 7 m shorter than the other. Find the lengths of the legs.

24. The length of a rectangle is 15 ft greater than the width. The area is 1000 ft^2. Find the length and width.

25. The current in a stream moves at a speed of 5 km/h. A boat travels 20 km upstream and 20 km downstream in a total of 3 hrs. Find the speed of the boat in still water.

26. Marla can type a 24-page report in 3 hours. If Marla and Gene work together, they can type the same report in 2 hours. How long would it take Gene alone to type the report?

27. Find the side of a square whose diagonal is 5 cm longer than a side.

Carl Friedrich Gauss called mathematics the queen of the sciences. Clearly then, mathematicians are her courtiers. To fully enjoy mathematics, you need a sense of its development and of the people who have devoted their lives to its exploration. **Milestones in Mathematics** is a partial list of important events in mathematical history. You may want to find additional information in the library or on the Internet to learn more about these and other mathematicians and their contributions to the field of mathematics.

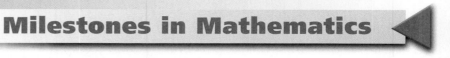

c. 30,000 + BC		The knucklebones of animals were used as dice in games of chance.
c. 20,000 + BC		A wolfbone with 55 notches in two rows divided into groups of five was used for counting (discovered at Vestonice in the Czech Republic).
c. 8000	BC	First evidence of recorded counting.
c. 2000	BC	The Egyptians had arrived at a value for pi of $\pi = 4\left(\frac{8}{9}\right)^2$.
c. 1900	BC	Babylonian scholars used cuneiform numerals for the base 60 in the oldest known written numeration for place value.
c. 1700	BC	Sumerian notation was used to solve quadratic equations by the equivalent of the formula we use today.
c. 800	BC	Queen Dido founded the great city of Carthage by solving the geometric "Problem of Dido." A rigorous proof of this problem—what closed curve of specified length will enclose a maximum area—did not come until the 19th century.
c. 700	BC	Zero appeared in the Seleucid mathematical tables.
c. 550	BC	Pythagoras developed a logical, deductive proof of the Pythagorean theorem.
c. 300	BC	Euclid wrote the first geometry text, *Elements*.
c. 250	BC	Archimedes wrote *On Mechanical Theorems, Method* for his friend Eratosthenes.
c. 250	AD	An initial-letter shorthand for algebraic equations was developed.
c. 300	AD	Pappus of Alexandria discussed the areas of figures with the same perimeter in the *Mathematical Collection*.
c. 375	AD	Earliest known Mayan Initial Series inscriptions for expressing dates and periods of time.
c. 400	AD	Hypatia, the foremost mathematician in Alexandria, lectured on Diophantine algebra.
595		Date of an Indian deed on copper plate showing the oldest known use of the nine numerals according to the place value principle: the first written decimal numeration with the structure used today.
825		A treatise on linear and quadratic equations was published by Mohammed Al-Khwarizmi.

Milestones in Mathematics

850	Mahavira contributed to the development of algebra in India.
1202	Leonardo of Pisa, also called Fibonacci, wrote *Liber abaci,* introducing Arabic numerals to Europe. This book contains his "rabbit problem" involving the numbers we now call Fibonacci.
1261	Yang Hui of China wrote on the properties of the binomial coefficients.
1557	The equal sign ($=$) came into general use during the 16th century. (The twin lines as an equal sign were used by the English physician and mathematician Robert Recorde with the explanation that "noe .2. thynges, can be moare equalle.")
1614	John Napier invented logarithms.
1639	René Descartes published his treatise on the application of algebra to geometry (analytic geometry).
1654	Blaise Pascal described the properties of the triangle we now call Pascal's triangle.
1657	Major contributions to number theory were made by Pierre de Fermat, including his formulation of the "Pell" equation.
1670	G. Mouton devised a decimal-based measuring system.
1687	The calculus was published by Isaac Newton in his *Principia.*
1735	Graph theory was originated by Leonard Euler in his paper on the problem "The Seven Bridges of Konigsberg."
1784	Maria Agnesi developed new ways to deal with problems involving infinite quantities in her book *Analytical Institutions.*
1799	The fundamental theorem of algebra was delineated by Carl Friedrich Gauss, who also developed rigorous proof as the requirement of mathematics.
1816	Sophie Germain published equations that stated the law for vibrating elastic surfaces.
1832	Evariste Galois wrote the theorem stating the conditions under which an equation can be solved.
1854	George Boole developed the postulates of "Boolean Algebra" in *Laws of Thought.*
1854	Mary Fairfax Somerville wrote books to popularize mathematics and extend the influence of the work of mathematicians.
1859	George F. B. Riemann published his work on the distribution of primes; "Riemann's Hypothesis" became one of the famous unsolved problems of mathematics.
1886	Modern combinatorial topology was created by Henri Poincaré.

1888	Sonya Kovalevskaya was awarded the Prix Bordin for her paper "On the Rotation of a Solid Body About a Fixed Point."
1897	David Hilbert published his monumental work on the theory of number fields and later clarified the foundations of geometry.
1906	Grace Chisholm Young and William Young published the first text on set theory.
1914	Srinivasa Ramanujan went to England to collaborate with G. H. Hardy on analytic number theory.
1925	Hermann Weyl published fundamental papers on group theory.
1931	Gödel showed that there must be undecidable propositions in any formal system, and that one of those undecidable propositions is consistency.
1932	A completely general theory of ideal numbers was built up, on an axiomatic basis, by Emmy Noether.
1936	The minimax principle in probability and statistics was developed by Abraham Wald.
1937	Goldbach's conjecture that every even number is the sum of two primes ($12 = 5 + 7, 100 = 3 + 97$) was established by I. M. Vinogradov for every sufficiently large even number that is the sum of, at most, four primes.
1938	Claude E. Shannon discovered the analogy between the truth values of propositions and the states of switches and relays in an electric circuit.
1942	Jacqueline Ferrand created the concept of preholomorphic functions, using these to produce a new methodology for mathematical proofs.
1951	Elizabeth Scott, Jerzy Newyman, and C. D. Shane applied statistical theories to deduce the existence of clusters of galaxies.
1953	Maria Pastori extended the usefulness of the tensor calculus in the pure mathematical investigation of generalized spaces.
1960	Advances in the application of probability and statistics were made by Florence Nightingale David.
1976	The four-color problem was proved using electronic computing in concert with human deduction.
1985	A new algorithm for factoring large numbers by using elliptic curves was developed by Hendrik W. Lenstra, Jr.
1985	David Hoffman discovered a fourth minimal surface, the first new minimal surface discovered since the 1700s.
1994	Andrew Wiles proved "Fermat's Last Theorem" on the impossibility of separating any power above the second into two powers of the same degree.

Table 1: Squares and Square Roots

N	N^2	$\sqrt{N}$	N	N^2	$\sqrt{N}$
1	1	1	51	2,601	7.141
2	4	1.414	52	2,704	7.211
3	9	1.732	53	2,809	7.280
4	16	2	54	2,916	7.348
5	25	2.236	55	3,025	7.416
6	36	2.449	56	3,136	7.483
7	49	2.646	57	3,249	7.550
8	64	2.828	58	3,364	7.616
9	81	3	59	3,481	7.681
10	100	3.162	60	3,600	7.746
11	121	3.317	61	3,721	7.810
12	144	3.464	62	3,844	7.874
13	169	3.606	63	3,969	7.937
14	196	3.742	64	4,096	8
15	225	3.873	65	4,225	8.062
16	256	4	66	4,356	8.124
17	289	4.123	67	4,489	8.185
18	324	4.243	68	4,624	8.246
19	361	4.359	69	4,761	8.307
20	400	4.472	70	4,900	8.367
21	441	4.583	71	5,041	8.426
22	484	4.690	72	5,184	8.485
23	529	4.796	73	5,329	8.544
24	576	4.899	74	5,476	8.602
25	625	5	75	5,625	8.660
26	676	5.099	76	5,776	8.718
27	729	5.196	77	5,929	8.775
28	784	5.292	78	6,084	8.832
29	841	5.385	79	6,241	8.888
30	900	5.477	80	6,400	8.944
31	961	5.568	81	6,561	9
32	1,024	5.657	82	6,724	9.055
33	1,089	5.745	83	6,889	9.110
34	1,156	5.831	84	7,056	9.165
35	1,225	5.916	85	7,225	9.220
36	1,296	6	86	7,396	9.274
37	1,369	6.083	87	7,569	9.327
38	1,444	6.164	88	7,744	9.381
39	1,521	6.245	89	7,921	9.434
40	1,600	6.325	90	8,100	9.487
41	1,681	6.403	91	8,281	9.539
42	1,764	6.481	92	8,464	9.592
43	1,849	6.557	93	8,649	9.644
44	1,936	6.633	94	8,836	9.695
45	2,025	6.708	95	9,025	9.747
46	2,116	6.782	96	9,216	9.798
47	2,209	6.856	97	9,409	9.849
48	2,304	6.928	98	9,604	9.899
49	2,401	7	99	9,801	9.950
50	2,500	7.071	100	10,000	10

Rectangle
Area: $A = \ell w$
Perimeter: $P = 2\ell + 2w$

Parallelogram
Area: $A = bh$

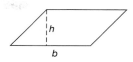

Square
Area: $A = s^2$
Perimeter: $P = 4s$

Trapezoid
Area: $A = \frac{1}{2}h(a + b)$

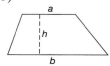

Triangle
Area: $A = \frac{1}{2}bh$
Sum of Angle Measures:
$A + B + C = 180°$

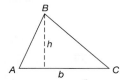

Circle
Area: $A = \pi r^2$
Circumference:
$C = \pi d = 2\pi r$

Right Triangle
Pythagorean Theorem:
$a^2 + b^2 = c^2$

Rectangular Solid
Volume: $V = \ell wh$

Polygon
Sum of Angle Measures:
$S = 180(n - 2)$

Number of Diagonals:
$N = \dfrac{n(n - 3)}{2}$

$n = 5$

Cylinder
Volume: $V = \pi r^2 h$

Prism
Volume: $V = Bh$
B = base area

Cone
Volume: $V = \frac{1}{3}\pi r^2 h$

$+$	positive		[ ]	set brackets
$-$	negative		$\in$	is a member of
$\cdot$	times ($\times$)		$\cap$	the intersection of
$\pm$	positive or negative		$\cup$	the union of
$=$	is equal to		$\subset$	is a subset of
$\neq$	is not equal to		$\emptyset$	the empty set
$\approx$	is approximately equal to		(x, y)	ordered pair
$<$	is less than		$f(x)$	f of x, the value of f at x
$>$	is greater than		$\{x \mid x > 1\}$	the set of all numbers x such that $x > 1$
$\leq$	is less than or equal to			
$\geq$	is greater than or equal to		$\triangle$	triangle
$-n$	additive inverse of n		$\angle$	angle
$\lvert n \rvert$	absolute value of n		$\sim$	is similar to
b^n	n^{th} power of b		$\overline{AB}$	segment AB
$a : b$	ratio of a to b		AB	the length of $\overline{AB}$
$\%$	percent		$\sin A$	the sine of A
$^\circ$	degree		$\cos A$	the cosine of A
$\sqrt{}$	principal square root		$\tan A$	the tangent of A
π	pi, approximately 3.14		$P(A)$	the probability of event A
$\{\ \}$	set braces		A'	the complement of event A
$(\ )$	set parentheses		$P(A \text{ or } B)$	the probability of two events

Table 4: Trigonometric Function Values

Degrees	Sin	Cos	Tan	Degrees	Sin	Cos	Tan
0°	0.0000	1.0000	0.0000				
1°	0.0175	0.9998	0.0175	46°	0.7193	0.6947	1.0355
2°	0.0349	0.9994	0.0349	47°	0.7314	0.6820	1.0724
3°	0.0523	0.9986	0.0524	48°	0.7431	0.6691	1.1106
4°	0.0698	0.9976	0.0699	49°	0.7547	0.6561	1.1504
5°	0.0872	0.9962	0.0875	50°	0.7660	0.6428	1.1918
6°	0.1045	0.9945	0.1051	51°	0.7771	0.6293	1.2349
7°	0.1219	0.9925	0.1228	52°	0.7880	0.6157	1.2799
8°	0.1392	0.9903	0.1405	53°	0.7986	0.6018	1.3270
9°	0.1564	0.9877	0.1584	54°	0.8090	0.5878	1.3764
10°	0.1736	0.9848	0.1763	55°	0.8192	0.5736	1.4281
11°	0.1908	0.9816	0.1944	56°	0.8290	0.5592	1.4826
12°	0.2079	0.9781	0.2126	57°	0.8387	0.5446	1.5399
13°	0.2250	0.9744	0.2309	58°	0.8480	0.5299	1.6003
14°	0.2419	0.9703	0.2493	59°	0.8572	0.5150	1.6643
15°	0.2588	0.9659	0.2679	60°	0.8660	0.5000	1.7321
16°	0.2756	0.9613	0.2867	61°	0.8746	0.4848	1.8040
17°	0.2924	0.9563	0.3057	62°	0.8829	0.4695	1.8807
18°	0.3090	0.9511	0.3249	63°	0.8910	0.4540	1.9626
19°	0.3256	0.9455	0.3443	64°	0.8988	0.4384	2.0503
20°	0.3420	0.9397	0.3640	65°	0.9063	0.4226	2.1445
21°	0.3584	0.9336	0.3839	66°	0.9135	0.4067	2.2460
22°	0.3746	0.9272	0.4040	67°	0.9205	0.3907	2.3559
23°	0.3907	0.9205	0.4245	68°	0.9272	0.3746	2.4751
24°	0.4067	0.9135	0.4452	69°	0.9336	0.3584	2.6051
25°	0.4226	0.9063	0.4663	70°	0.9397	0.3420	2.7475
26°	0.4384	0.8988	0.4877	71°	0.9455	0.3256	2.9042
27°	0.4540	0.8910	0.5095	72°	0.9511	0.3090	3.0777
28°	0.4695	0.8829	0.5317	73°	0.9563	0.2924	3.2709
29°	0.4848	0.8746	0.5543	74°	0.9613	0.2756	3.4874
30°	0.5000	0.8660	0.5774	75°	0.9659	0.2588	3.7321
31°	0.5150	0.8572	0.6009	76°	0.9703	0.2419	4.0108
32°	0.5299	0.8480	0.6249	77°	0.9744	0.2250	4.3315
33°	0.5446	0.8387	0.6494	78°	0.9781	0.2079	4.7046
34°	0.5592	0.8290	0.6745	79°	0.9816	0.1908	5.1446
35°	0.5736	0.8192	0.7002	80°	0.9848	0.1736	5.6713
36°	0.5878	0.8090	0.7265	81°	0.9877	0.1564	6.3138
37°	0.6018	0.7986	0.7536	82°	0.9903	0.1392	7.1154
38°	0.6157	0.7880	0.7813	83°	0.9925	0.1219	8.1443
39°	0.6293	0.7771	0.8098	84°	0.9945	0.1045	9.5144
40°	0.6428	0.7660	0.8391	85°	0.9962	0.0872	11.4301
41°	0.6561	0.7547	0.8693	86°	0.9976	0.0698	14.3007
42°	0.6691	0.7431	0.9004	87°	0.9986	0.0523	19.0811
43°	0.6820	0.7314	0.9325	88°	0.9994	0.0349	28.6363
44°	0.6947	0.7193	0.9657	89°	0.9998	0.0175	57.2900
45°	0.7071	0.7071	1.0000	90°	1.0000	0.0000	

Abscissa (p. 304) See *x-coordinate*.
Abscisa Ver *Coordenada x.*

Absolute value (p. 56) The absolute value of a number *n*, represented as |*n*|, is its distance from 0 on the number line. For any number *n*, |*n*| = *n* if *n* is a positive number or zero, and |*n*| = −*n* if *n* is a negative number.
Valor absoluto El valor absoluto de un número *n*, representado con |*n*|, es su distancia a 0 sobre la recta numérica. Para cualquier número *n*, |*n*| = *n* si *n* es un número positivo o cero, y |*n*| = −*n* si *n* es un número negativo.

Addend Any one of a set of numbers to be added. In the sum 1 + 2 + 3, 1, 2, and 3 are the addends.
Sumando Cualquiera de los miembros de un conjunto de números que se van a sumar. En la suma 1 + 2 + 3, 1, 2 y 3 son sumandos.

Addition method (p. 367) A method for solving systems of equations in which the equations are added together to obtain an equation with fewer variables. One or both equations may first be multiplied by a constant. The result is a *linear combination* of the original equations.
Método de suma Método para resolver ecuaciones en donde las ecuaciones se suman para obtener otra con menos variables. Una o las dos ecuaciones se pueden multiplicar por una constante. El resultado es una *combinación lineal* de las ecuaciones originales.

Addition property of equality (p. 114) For all real numbers *a*, *b*, and *c*, if *a* = *b* then *a* + *c* = *b* + *c*.
Propiedad aditiva de la igualdad Para cualquier terna de números reales *a*, *b*, y *c*, si *a* = *b*, entonces *a* + *c* = *b* + *c*.

Addition property of inequalities (p. 175) For all real numbers *a*, *b*, and *c*, if *a* < *b*, then *a* + *c* < *b* + *c*; if *a* > *b*, then *a* + *c* > *b* + *c*. Similar statements hold for ≤ and ≥.
Propiedad aditiva de la desigualdad Para cualquier terna de números reales *a*, *b* y *c*, si *a* < *b*, entonces *a* + *c* < *b* + *c*; si *a* > *b*, entonces *a* + *c* > *b* + *c*. Afirmaciones similares son válidas para ≤ y ≥.

Additive identity (p. 10) The number 0 is the additive identity. For any real number *a*, *a* + 0 = *a* and 0 + *a* = *a*.
Identidad aditiva El número 0 es la identidad aditiva. Para cualquier número *a*, *a* + 0 = *a* y 0 + *a* = *a*.

Additive inverse (p. 66) If the sum of two numbers or expressions is 0, they are additive inverses of each other.
Inverso aditivo Si la suma de dos números o expresiones es 0, son inversos aditivos uno del otro.

Adjacent sides Two sides of a polygon are adjacent if their endpoints form a vertex.
Lados adyacentes Dos lados de un polígono son adyacentes si sus puntos extremos forman un vértice.

Algebraic expression (p. 4) An expression that contains at least one variable.
Expresión algebraica Expresión que contiene al menos una variable.

Angle Two rays with a common endpoint called the vertex.
Ángulo Dos rayos con un punto extremo en común llamado vértice.

Antecedent (p. 192) See *If-then statement*.
Antecedente Ver *Afirmaciones de la forma si-entonces*.

Area The size of a surface expressed in square units.
Área Tamaño de una región del plano expresado en unidades cuadradas.

Ascending order (p. 226) A polynomial is in ascending order for a variable if the term with the smallest exponent for that variable (often a constant term) is first, the term with the next smallest exponent for that variable is second, and so on.
Orden ascendente Un polinomio está en orden ascendente respecto a una variable si el término con el exponente más chico para tal variable (con frecuencia un término constante) aparece primero, el término con el siguiente exponente más grande es el segundo, etcétera.

Associative properties (pp. 20–21) For all real numbers *a*, *b*, and *c*,
Addition: $a + (b + c) = (a + b) + c$.
Multiplication: $a \cdot (b \cdot c) = (a \cdot b) \cdot c$.
Propiedades asociativas Para cualquier terna de números reales *a*, *b* y *c*:
Suma: $a + (b + c) = (a + b) + c$.
Multiplicación: $a \cdot (b \cdot c) = (a \cdot b) \cdot c$.

Axes (p. 304) See *Coordinate axes*.
Ejes Ver *Ejes coordenados*.

Axiom (p. 102) A property that is accepted to be true without proof.
Axioma Una propiedad que se supone verdadera sin demostración.

Axis of symmetry of a parabola (p. 553) If the graph of the parabola is folded so that its two sides coincide, the line on which the fold occurs is the axis of symmetry. For a parabola defined by the equation $y = ax^2 + bx + c$, the axis of symmetry is the line $x = -\frac{b}{2a}$.
Eje de simetría de una parábola Si la gráfica de una parábola se dobla de tal manera que sus dos lados coincidan, la recta sobre la que se produce el dobles es el eje de simetría. Para la parábola definida por la ecuación $y = ax^2 + bx + c$, el eje de simetría es la recta $x = -\frac{b}{2a}$.

English/Spanish Glossary

Base (p. 15) In exponential notation n^x, n is the base.
  Base En la notación exponencial n^x, n es la base.

Binomial (p. 222) A polynomial with exactly two terms.
  Binomio Polinomio con dos términos exactamente.

Binomial expansion (p. 285) The expansion of a binomial power. For example, the binomial expansion of $(a + b)^3$ is $a^3 + 3a^2b + 3ab^2 + b^3$.
  Expansión binomial La expansión de una potencia binomial.

Boundary line (p. 417) A line that separates a plane into two half-planes.
  Recta frontera Recta que divide el plano en dos semiplanos.

Circumference The distance around a circle.
  Circunferencia La distancia alrededor de un circulo.

Closure properties (p. 102) For any real numbers a and b, Addition: $a + b$ is a real number. Multiplication: $a \cdot b$ is a real number.
  Propiedades de cerradura Para cualquier par de números reales a y b: Suma: $a + b$ es un número real. Multiplicación: $a \cdot b$ es un número real.

Coefficient (p. 222) In any term, the coefficient is the numeric factor of the term or the number that is multiplied by the variable. In $-3x$, the coefficient is -3; in x^4, the coefficient is 1.
  Coeficiente En cualquier término, el coeficiente es el factor numérico del término o el número que multiplica a la variable. En $-3x$, el coeficiente es -3; en x^2 el coeficiente es 1.

Collect like terms (p. 26) The process of using the distributive property to simplify expressions containing like terms.
  Reducción de términos semejantes Procedimiento en el que se utiliza la propiedad asociativa para simplificar expresiones que contienen términos semejantes.

Combined variation (p. 566) An equation of the form $z = \frac{kx}{y}$, where k is a nonzero constant, expresses combined variation.
  Variación combinada Una ecuación de la forma $z = \frac{kx}{y}$, donde k es una constante diferente de cero, expreso una variación combinada.

Commutative properties (p. 9) For any real numbers a and b, Addition: $a + b = b + a$. Multiplication: $a \cdot b = b \cdot a$.
  Propiedades conmutativas Para cualquier par de números reales a y b: Suma: $a + b = b + a$. Multiplicación: $a \cdot b = b \cdot a$.

Complementary angles (p. 371) Two angles are complementary if their sum is $90°$.
  Ángulos complementarios Dos ángulos son complementarios si sus medidas suman $90°$.

Completing the square (p. 586) Adding a constant to an expression of the form $ax^2 + bx$ to form a trinomial square.
  Compleción de cuadrados La suma de una constante a una ecuación de la forma $ax^2 + bx + c$ para formar un trinomio cuadrado perfecto.

Complex rational expression (p. 469) An expression with a rational expression in its numerator or denominator or both.
  Expresiones racionales complejas Expresión racional con una expresión racional en su numerador o en su denominador, o en ambos.

Compound interest (p. 346) A percentage of both the amount of borrowed money and of previously computed interest.
  Interés compuesto Un porcentaje del principal y del interés previamente computado.

Compound sentence (p. 405) Two simple sentences joined by a connective such as "and" or "or."
  Afirmación compuesta Dos afirmaciones simples unidas por un conectivo como "y" u "o."

Conclusion (p. 192) See *If-then statement*.
  Conclusión Ver *Afirmaciones de la forma si-entonces*.

Conditional statement (p. 192) A statement of the form *If a, then b.*
  Afirmación condicional Una afirmación de la forma *si a, entonces b.*

Congruent Two geometric figures are congruent if they have the same size and shape.
  Congruencia Dos figuras geométricas son congruentes si tienen el mismo tamaño y forma.

Conjugate (p. 506) Binomial pairs such as $1 + \sqrt{2}$ and $1 - \sqrt{2}$ are called conjugates.
  Conjugado Los pares binomiales con la forma $1 + \sqrt{2}$ y $1 - \sqrt{2}$ son conjugados.

Conjunction (p. 405) A conjunction of two statements is formed by connecting them with "and" and is true when *both* statements are true.
  Conjunción La conjunción de dos afirmaciones se forma conectándolas con "y" y es verdadera cuando *ambos* afirmaciones son verdaderas.

Consecutive even integers (p. 158) Integers that follow each other when counting by twos, beginning with an even integer.
Enteros pares consecutivos Números que se siguen uno al otro al contar en pares, comenzando con un número par.

Consecutive integers (p. 158) Integers such as 22, 23, and 24 that follow each other when counting by ones.
Enteros consecutivos Números que, como 22, 23 y 24, se siguen uno al otro al contar en unidades.

Consecutive odd integers (p. 158) Integers that follow each other when counting by twos, beginning with an odd integer.
Enteros impares consecutivos Números que se siguen uno al otro al contarlos terciados, comenzando con un número impar.

Consequent (p. 192) See *If-then statement.*
Consecuente Ver *Afirmaciones de la forma si-entonces.*

Consistent system of equations (p. 360) A system of equations that has one or more solutions.
Sistema consistente de ecuaciones Un sistema de ecuaciones que tiene una o más soluciones es consistente.

Constant (p. 214) A term with no variables.
Constante Un término sin variables.

Constant of variation (p. 557) In an equation of variation $y = kx$ or $y = \frac{k}{x}$, k is the constant of variation.
Constante de variación En una ecuación de variación $y = kx$ o $y = \frac{k}{x}$, k es la constante de variación.

Converse (p. 192) The converse of a conditional statement is found by interchanging the hypothesis and the conclusion.
Converso El converso de una afirmación condicional se encuentra intercambiando la hipótesis y la conclusión.

Coordinate axes (p. 304) The *x*- and *y*-axes in the coordinate plane.
Ejes coordenados Los ejes *x* y *y* en el plano coordenado.

Coordinate of a point on the number line (p. 59) The number that corresponds to the point.
Coordenada de un punto en una recta numérica El número que corresponde al punto.

Coordinate plane (p. 304) A plane in which a coordinate system has been set up.
Plano coordenado Plano en donde se ha colocado un sistema coordenado.

Coordinates (p. 304) The numbers in an ordered pair, used to locate a point on a plane.
Coordenadas Los números de una pareja ordenada se usan para localizar un punto en el plano coordenado.

Coordinate system (Cartesian) (p. 304) A system for graphing ordered pairs of numbers as points in a plane using two perpendicular number lines, called the *coordinate axes,* which intersect at the zero point of each.
Sistema coordenado (cartesiano) Sistema para graficar pares ordenados de números como puntos en un plano, utilizando dos rectas numéricas perpendiculares llamadas *ejes coordenados,* que se intersecan en el punto cero de cada una.

Corner points (p. 424) The corner points of the graph of a system of inequalities are the points where the boundary lines intersect.
Punto esquina Los puntos esquina de la gráfica de un sistema de desigualdades son puntos donde las rectas frontera se intersecan.

Counterexample (p. 14) An example that shows that a statement is false.
Contraejemplo Un ejemplo que muestra que una afirmación es falsa.

Cube root (p. 494) A number c is a cube root of a if $c^3 = a$.
Raíz cúbica Un número c es la raíz cúbica de a si $c^3 = a$.

Degree of an angle A unit used to measure angles. There are 90 degrees (90°) in a right angle.
Grado de un ángulo Unidad utilizada para medir ángulos. Hay 90 grados (90°) en un ángulo recto.

Degree of a polynomial (p. 223) The greatest degree of any of its terms after it has been simplified.
Grado de un polinomio El grado mayor de cualquiera de los términos después de la simplificación.

Degree of a term (p. 223) The degree of a term is the sum of the exponents of the variables in the term.
Grado de un término El grado de un término es la suma de los exponentes de las variables que hay en el término.

Denominator In $\frac{a}{b}$, b is the denominator.
Denominador En $\frac{a}{b}$, b es el denominador.

Density property (p. 62) The density property for rational (real) numbers states that between any two rational (real) numbers there is another rational (real) number.
Propiedad de densidad La propiedad de densidad de los números reales establece que entre cualquier par de números reales diferentes existe otro número real.

Dependent system of equations (p. 360) A system of equations that has an infinite number of solutions.
Dependiente Un sistema de ecuaciones que tiene un número infinito de soluciones es dependiente.

Descending order (p. 226) A polynomial is in descending order for a variable if the term with the greatest exponent for that variable is first, the term with the next greatest exponent for that variable is second, and so on.
Orden descendente Un polinomio está en orden descendente respecto a una variable si el término con el exponente más grande para tal variable (con frecuencia un término constante) aparece primero, el término con el siguiente exponente más chico es el negundo, etcétera.

Diagonal of a polygon A line segment that connects two nonadjacent vertices of the polygon.
Diagonal de un polígono Segmento de recta que une dos vértices no adyacentes de un polígono.

Diameter The diameter of a circle is the length of a line segment that passes through the center of the circle and has endpoints on the circle.
Diámetro El diámetro de un círculo es la longitud de un segmento que pasa por su centro y que tiene sus puntos extremos sobre el círculo.

Difference (p. 71) For all real numbers a and b, the difference $a - b$ is the number c, such that $c + b = a$.
Diferencia Para todo par de números a y b, la diferencia $a - b$ es el número c tal que $c + b = a$.

Difference of two squares (p. 266) A binomial whose two terms are squares and have a minus sign between them.
Diferencia de cuadrados Un binomio cuyos términos son cuadrados y tienen un signo de menos entre ellos.

Direct variation (p. 557) An equation of the form $y = kx$, where k is a nonzero constant, expresses direct variation.
Variación directa Función que se puede describir mediante una ecuación $y = kx$, donde k es una constante diferente de cero.

Discriminant (p. 591) For a quadratic equation $ax^2 + bx + c = 0$, the expression $b^2 - 4ac$ is the discriminant.
Discriminante Para cualquier ecuación cuadrática $ax^2 + bx + c = 0$, la expresión $b^2 - 4ac$ es el discriminante.

Disjunction (p. 407) A disjunction of two statements is formed by connecting them with "or" and is true when *one or both* statements are true.
Disyunción Una disyunción de dos afirmaciones se forma uniéndolas con un "o" y es verdadera cuando una o ambas afirmaciones son verdaderas.

Distance formula (p. 513) The distance between any two points (x_1, y_1) and (x_2, y_2) is given by
$$d = \sqrt{(x_1 - x_2)^2 + (y_1 - y_2)^2}.$$
Fórmula de la distancia La distancia entre dos puntos (x_1, y_1) y (x_2, y_2) está dada por
$$\sqrt{(x_1 - x_2)^2 + (y_1 - y_2)^2}.$$

Distributive property of multiplication over addition (p. 24) For any real numbers a, b, and c, $a(b + c) = ab + ac$, and $(b + c)a = ba + ca$.
Propiedad distributiva de la multiplicación sobre la suma Para cualquier terna de números reales a, b y c, $a(b + c) = ab + ac$ y $(b + c)a = ba + ca$.

Distributive property of multiplication over subtraction (p. 89) For any real numbers a, b, and c, $a(b - c) = ab - ac$, and $(b - c)a = ba - ca$.
Propiedad distributiva de la multiplicación sobre la resta Para cualquier terna de números reales a, b y c, $a(b - c) = ab - ac$ y $(b - c)a = ba - ca$.

Division Property for Radicals (p. 498) For any nonnegative real numbers a and b, where $b \neq 0$,
$$\sqrt{\frac{a}{b}} = \frac{\sqrt{a}}{\sqrt{b}} \text{ and } \frac{\sqrt{a}}{\sqrt{b}} = \sqrt{\frac{a}{b}}.$$
Propiedad de división de los radicandos Para cualquier par de números reales no negativos a y b,
donde $b \neq 0$, $\sqrt{\frac{a}{b}} = \frac{\sqrt{a}}{\sqrt{b}}$ y $\frac{\sqrt{a}}{\sqrt{b}} = \sqrt{\frac{a}{b}}$.

Division Theorem (p. 472) For any number a and any nonzero number b, $\frac{a}{b} = a \cdot \frac{1}{b}$.
Teorema de la división Para cualquier número a y cualquier número b diferente de cero, $\frac{a}{b} = a \cdot \frac{1}{b}$.

Domain (p. 536) The domain of a relation is the set of first coordinates.
Dominio El dominio de una relación es el conjunto de las primeras coordenadas.

Element of a set (p. 400) Any object in the set; also called *member of a set.*
Elemento de un conjunto Cualquier objeto de un conjunto. También se llama *miembro de un conjunto.*

Empty set (p. 80) The set with no elements, symbolized $\emptyset$; also called the *null set.*
Conjunto vacio El conjunto sin elementos, simbolisado con $\emptyset$.

Equality (p. 103) A mathematical sentence $a = b$ states that a and b are expressions for the same number.
Igualdad Una afirmación matemática $a = b$ establece que a y b son expresiones para el mismo número.

Equation (p. 33) A mathematical sentence that uses an equal sign to state that two expressions represent the same number or are equivalent. An equation may be true, false, or, if it contains a variable, open.
Ecuación Afirmación matemática que utiliza el signo igual para establecer que dos expresiones representan el mismo número o son equivalentes. Una ecuación puede ser verdadera, falsa o, si contiene una variable, abierta.

Equilateral triangle A triangle with all three sides of equal length.
Triángulo equilátero Triángulo con sus tres lados de igual longitud.

Equivalent equations (p. 35) Equations with the same solution set.
Ecuaciones equivalentes Ecuaciones con el mismo conjunto solución.

Equivalent expressions (p. 9) Expressions that have equal values for the same replacement values of their variables.
Expresiones equivalentes Expresiones que siempre don como resultado el mismo número para cualquier sustitución de la variable.

Evaluate an expression (p. 4) To evaluate an expression, replace each variable in the expression by a given value and simplify the result.
Evaluación de una expresión Para evaluar una expresión se sustituye cada variable en la expresión con un valor dado y se simplifica el resultado.

Even integer Any integer that has 2 as a factor.
Entero par Un entero que tiene 2 como factor.

Exponent (p. 15) In exponential notation n^x, x is the exponent. The exponent tells how many times the base is used as a factor.
Exponente En notación exponencial n^x, x es el exponente. El exponente indica cuántas veces la base se utiliza como factor.

Exponential notation (p. 15) The expression x^n is exponential form for the nth power of x.
Notación exponencial La expresión x^n está en forma exponencial para la potencia enésima de x.

Expression (p. 4) A number, or two or more numbers together with operation signs.
Expresión Un número, o dos o más números junto con sus signos de operación.

Extraneous solution (p. 452) When an equation is transformed, for example by squaring both sides, the transformed equation may have solutions that are not solutions to the original equation. These solutions are called extraneous.
Solución imprevista Cuando una expresión se transforma, por ejemplo al elevar al cuadrado ambos lados, la ecuación resultante puede tener soluciones que no satisfacen la ecuación original. Estas soluciones se llaman soluciones imprevistas.

Factor (p. 12) When two or more numbers (or expressions) are multiplied, each is a factor of the product.
Factor Cuando se multiplican dos o más números (o expresiones), cada uno es factor del producto.

Factor by grouping (p. 281) A method for factoring a polynomial in which different terms are first factored from different parts of the polynomial.
Factorización por agrupación Método para factorizar polinomios en donde los términos se factorizan primero en las diferentes partes del polinomio.

Factor completely (p. 268) A polynomial is factored completely if the factors have no common factors other than 1.
Factorización completa Un polinomio está factorizado completamente si los factores no tienen factores comunes diferentes de 1.

Factoring (p. 25) To factor a number or expression is to write an equivalent expression that is the product of two or more numbers or expressions.
Factorizar Factorizar un número o una expresión es escribir una expresión equivalento que es producto de dos o más números o expresiones.

Factorization (p. 262) A representation of an expression as a product of two or more expressions.
Factorización Una representación de una expresión como el producto de dos o más expresiones.

Factor Theorem (p. 468) $x - d$ is a factor of a polynomial whenever d is a root of the polynomial.
Teorema del factor Si $x - d$ es un factor de un polinomio, entonces d es una raíz del mismo polinomio.

Field (p. 102) Any number system with two operations for which the field axioms hold.
Campo Cualquier sistema numérico donde están definidas dos operaciones que satisfacen los axiomas de campo.

Field axioms (p. 103) The closure, commutative, associative, identity, inverse, and distributive properties.
Axiomas de campo Las propiedades de cerradura, conmutativa, asociativa, de la identidad, del inverso y distributiva.

FOIL method (p. 241) A method for finding the product of two binomials. The product is written as the product of the first term of each binomial, plus the product of the outside terms, plus the product of the inside terms, plus the product of the last terms.
Método PEIF Método para encontrar el producto de dos binomios. El producto se expresa como el producto de los primeros términos de cada binomio, más el producto de los términos exteriores, más el producto de los términos interiores, más el producto de los términos finales.

Formula (p. 40) An equation that shows the relationship between two or more quantities.
Fórmula Ecuación que muestra la relación entre dos o más cantidades.

Fraction See *Rational number.*
Fracción Ver *Número racional.*

Fractional equation See *Rational equation.*
Ecuación fraccionaria Ver *Ecuación racional.*

Fractional expression See *Rational expression.*
Expresión fraccionaria Ver *Expresión racional.*

Function (p. 537) A relation that assigns to each member of its *domain* exactly one member of its *range.*
Función Una relación que asigna a cada miembro de su *dominio* exactamente un miembro de su *contradominio.*

Function values (p. 538) The outputs of a function.
Valores funcionales Las salidas de una función.

Graph of a function (p. 542) A graph of all the ordered pairs that make up the function.
Gráfica de una función Gráfica de todas las parejas ordenadas que forman una función.

Graph of an equation (p. 310) The graph of an equation consists of all the points whose coordinates satisfy the equation.
Gráfica de una ecuación La gráfica de una ecuación consta de todos los puntos cuyas coordenadas satisfacen la ecuación.

Graph of an inequality (p. 172) The graph of an inequality consists of all the points whose coordinates satisfy the inequality.
Gráfica de una desigualdad La gráfica de una ecuación consta de todos los puntos cuyas coordenadas satisfacen la desigualdad.

Graph of an ordered pair (p. 304) The point on the coordinate plane that corresponds to the ordered pair.
Gráfica de una pareja ordenada El punto sobre el plano coordenado que corresponde a la pareja ordenada.

Graph of a number (p. 59) The point on the number line that corresponds to the number.
Gráfica de un número Sobre la recta numéricas, el punto que corresponde al número.

Grouping symbols (p. 5) Symbols, such as parentheses or brackets, that indicate that the operations within them should be done first. When an expression contains more than one pair of grouping symbols, the computations in the innermost grouping should be done first.
Signos de agrupamiento Signos que, como los paréntesis y los corchetes, indican que las operaciones dentro de ellos se deben hacer primero.

Half-plane (p. 417) One of the two regions into which a line separates a plane. The line itself is called a *boundary line* and may or may not be included in the half-plane.
Semiplano Una de las dos regiones en que una linea divide el plano. La recta en el se llama *recta frontera* y puede estar incluida o no en el semiplano.

Horizontal line (p. 315) A line that is parallel to the x-axis (or the x-axis itself).
Recta horizontal Recta que es paralela al eje x.

Hypotenuse (p. 509) The side of a right triangle opposite the right angle.
Hipotenusa El lado de un triángulo rectángulo que queda opuesto al ángulo recto.

Hypothesis (p. 192) See *If-then statement.*
Hipótesis Ver *Afirmaciones del tipo si-entonces.*

Identity (p. 138) An equation that is true for all acceptable replacements of the variables.
Identidad Una ecuación que es verdadera para todos los valores aceptables de las variables.

Identity properties (p. 10) For any real number a,
Addition: $a + 0 = a$ and $0 + a = a$.
Multiplication: $1 \cdot a = a$ and $a \cdot 1 = a$.
Propiedad de las identidades Para cualquier número a:
Suma: $a + 0 = a$ y $0 + a = a$.
Multiplicación: $1 \cdot a = a$ y $a \cdot 1 = a$.

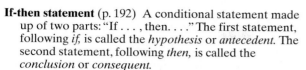

If-then statement (p. 192) A conditional statement made up of two parts: "If . . . , then. . . ." The first statement, following *if,* is called the *hypothesis* or *antecedent.* The second statement, following *then,* is called the *conclusion* or *consequent.*
    Afirmación de la forma si-entonces Una afirmación condicional está formada de dos partes: "Si . . . , entonces. . . ." La primera afirmación, que sigue al *si,* se llama *hipótesis* o *antecedente.* La segunda afirmación, que sigue al *entonces,* se llama *conclusión* o *consecuente.*

Inconsistent system of equations (p. 360) A system of equations that has no solution.
    Inconsistente Un sistema de ecuaciones que no tiene soluciones es inconsistente.

Inequality (p. 172) A mathematical sentence containing an inequality symbol between two expressions.
    Desigualdad Afirmación matemática que contiene un signo de desigualdad entre dos expresiones.

Inequality symbols (p. 172) The symbols $<$, $>$, $\le$, and $\ge$.
    Signos de desigualdad Los signos $<$, $>$, $\le$ y $\ge$.

Inputs (p. 537) The members of the domain of a function.
    Entradas Los miembros del dominio de una función.

Integers (p. 54) The numbers in the set $\{\ldots, -3, -2, -1, 0, 1, 2, 3, \ldots\}$.
    Enteros Los números del conjunto $\{\ldots, -3, -2, -1, 0, 1, 2, 3, \ldots\}$.

Interest (p. 346) A charge for the use of money, paid by the borrower to the lender.
    Interés Cargo por la utilización del dinero que el prestatario paga al prestamista.

Interior angles The interior angles of a polygon are those inside the figure.
    Ángulos interiores Los ángulos interiores de un poligono son aquellos que están en el interior de la figura.

Intersection (p. 401) The intersection of two sets is the set of all members that are common to both sets, symbolized $A \cap B$.
    Intersección La intersección de dos conjuntos es el conjunto de todos los miembros que son comunes a los dos conjuntos, y su símbolos es $A \cap B$.

Interval graph (p. 550) A graph used to solve problems involving the intersections of various time intervals.
    Gráfica de subintervalos Gráfica utilizada para resolver problemas sobre la intersección de varios subintervalos de tiempo.

Inverse of a sum property (p. 94) For any real numbers a and b, $-(a + b) = -a + (-b)$. (The additive inverse of a sum is the sum of the additive inverses.)
    Propiedad de los inversos de la suma Para cualquier par de números reales a y b, $-(a + b) = -a + (-b)$.

Inverse properties (p. 102) Addition: For each real number a, there is an additive inverse $-a$ such that $a + (-a) = 0$. Multiplication: For each real number a not equal to 0, there is a multiplicative inverse $\frac{1}{a}$ such that $a \cdot \frac{1}{a} = 1$.
    Propiedad de los inversos Suma: Para cada número real a, existe un inverso aditivo, $-a$, tal que $a + (-a) = 0$. Multiplicación: para cada número real a diferente de cero, existe un inverso multiplicativo $\frac{1}{a}$ tal que $a \cdot \frac{1}{a} = 1$.

Inverse variation (p. 561) An equation of the form $y = \frac{k}{x}$, where k is a nonzero constant, expresses inverse variation.
    Variación inversa Función que se puede describir mediante una ecuación $y = \frac{k}{x}$, donde k es una constante diferente de cero.

Irrational number (p. 483) A real number that *cannot* be written in the form $\frac{a}{b}$ where a and b are integers.
    Número irracional Un número real que *no* se puede expresar en la forma $\frac{a}{b}$ donde a y b son enteros.

Isosceles triangle A triangle with two sides of equal length.
    Triángulo isósceles Triángulo con dos lados de la misma longitud.

Joint variation (p. 565) An equation of the form $z = kxy$, where k is a nonzero constant, expresses joint variation.
    Variación conjunta Una ecuación de la forma $z = kxy$, donde k es una constante diferente de cero, expresa una variación conjunta.

Leading coefficient (p. 223) The coefficient of the leading term.
    Coeficiente principal El coeficiente del término principal.

Leading term (p. 223) The term of a polynomial with the highest degree.
    Término principal El término de un polinomio con mayor grado.

Least common denominator (LCD) of two rational expressions (p. 447) The least common multiple of their denominators.
    Mínimo común denominador (MCD) de unas expresións racionales La expresión de grado mínimo que es múltiplo de los denominadores de unas expresiónes dadas.

Least common denominator (LCD) of two rational numbers (p. 139) The least common multiple of their denominators (expressed as positive integers).
    Mínimo común denominador (MCD) de números racionales El mínimo común múltiplo de los denominadores (expresado como enteros positivos).

Least common multiple (LCM) of two algebraic expressions (p. 446) The expression of smallest degree that is a multiple of both expressions.
Mínimo común múltiplo (MCM) de expresiones racionales La expresión de grado mínimo que es múltiplo de dos o más expresiones.

Least common multiple (LCM) of two positive integers The smallest positive integer that is a multiple of both integers.
Mínimo común múltiplo de los enteros positivos El mínimo entero positivo que es multiplo de dos o más números dados.

Legs of a right triangle (p. 509) The two sides of the triangle that form the right angle.
Cateto de un triángulo Los dos lados de un triángulo rectángulo que forman un ángulo recto.

Like terms (p. 26) Terms whose variable factors are exactly the same.
Términos semejantes Términos cuyos factores variables son exactamente los mismos.

Line of best fit (p. 334) The line that best approximates a linear relationship for a set of data points.
Recta de mayor aproximación La recta que más se acerca a los puntos que representan la relación linear de los datos.

Linear combination (p. 368) A constant multiple of one equation added to a constant multiple of a second equation results in a linear combination of the two equations.
Combinación lineal Un múltiplo constante de una ecuación sumado a un múltiplo constante de una segunda ecuación da como resultado una combinación lineal de dos ecuaciones.

Linear equation (p. 313) An equation whose graph is a line. An equation is linear if the variables occur to the first power only, there are no products of variables, and no variable is in a denominator.
Ecuación lineal Una ecuación cuya gráfica es una línea recto. Una ecuación es lineal si las variables aparecen sólo a la primera potencia, no hay producto de variables y ninguna variable aparece en un denominador.

Linear function (p. 547) A function in the form $f(x) = mx + b$, where m and b are real numbers.
Función lineal Una función de la forma $f(x) = mx + b$, donde m y b son números reales y $m \neq 0$.

Line segment A set of points containing two points and all the points between them in a line.
Segmento de recta Un conjunto que contiene a dos puntos y a todos los puntos que están entre ellos en una recta.

Measures of central tendency (p. 661) A value that tells what number is at the middle, or center, of a set of data. Measures of central tendency include *mean* (p. 661), *median* (p. 661), and *mode* (p. 662).
Medidas de tendencia central Valores que indican cuál número está a la mitad, o al centro. Las medidas de tendencia central son *media, mediana* y *moda*.

Member of a set (p. 400) Any object in the set; also called *element of a set*.
Miembro de un conjunto Cualquier objeto de un conjunto. También llamado *elemento del conjunto*.

Moment (p. 87) The product of the force exerted on a lever and the distance of the force from the fulcrum. Also known as *torque*.
Momento El producto de la fuerza que ejerce cada carga en una palanca y su distancia al fulcro. También conocido como *torca*.

Monomial (p. 214) An expression that is the product of numerals and variables.
Monomio Expresión que es el producto de numerales y variables.

Multiplication property of equality (p. 119) For all real numbers a, b, and c, if $a = b$, then $ac = bc$.
Propiedad multiplicativa de la igualdad Para cualquier terna de números reales a, b y c, si $a = b$, entonces $ac = bc$.

Multiplication property of inequalities (p. 180) For all real numbers a, b, and c, if $a > b$ and $c > 0$, then $ac > bc$. If $a > b$ and $c < 0$, then $ac < bc$.
Propiedad multiplicativa de la desigualdad Para cualquier terna de números reales a, b y c, si $a > b$ y $c > 0$, entonces $ac > bc$. Si $a > b$ y $c < 0$, entonces $ac < bc$.

Multiplicative identity (p. 10) The number 1 is the multiplicative identity. For any real number a, $1 \cdot a = a$ and $a \cdot 1 = a$.
Identidad multiplicativa El número 1 es la identidad multiplicativa. Para cualquier número real a, $a \cdot 1 = a$ y $1 \cdot a = a$.

Multiplicative inverse (p. 82) See *Reciprocal*.
Inverso multiplicativo Ver *Reciproco*.

Multiplicative property of zero (p. 78) The product of any real number and 0 is 0.
Propiedad multiplicativa del cero El producto de cualquier número real y 0 es 0.

Natural numbers (p. 5) The numbers we use for counting. They are 1, 2, 3, 4, and so on.
Números naturales Los números utilizados para contar. Son 1, 2, 3, 4, etcétera.

Negative number (p. 54) Any number that is less than 0.
 Números negativos Cualquier número menor que 0.

Null set (p. 80) See *Empty set.*
 Conjunto nulo Ver *Conjunto vacío.*

Numeral A symbol that names a number.
 Numeral Signo que nombra a un número.

Numerator In $\frac{a}{b}$, a is the numerator.
 Numerador En $\frac{a}{b}$, a es el numerador.

Odd integer An integer that does not have 2 as a factor.
 Entero impar Un entera que no tiene a 2 como factor.

Open sentence (p. 33) An equation or inequality that contains at least one variable.
 Afirmación abierta Una ecuación o desigualdad que tiene al menos una variable.

Opposites (p. 54) Numbers, such as 3 and -3, that are the same distance from 0 but on opposite sides of 0 on the number line.
 Opuestos Números, como 3 y -3, que están a la misma distancia del 0, pero en lados opuestos del cero en la recta numérica.

Order of operations (p. 16) A rule for the order in which operations should be done. The order of operations is (1) compute within grouping symbols; (2) compute powers; (3) multiply and divide in order from left to right; and (4) add and subtract in order from left to right.
 Jerarquia de las operaciones Regla para el orden en que se deben efectuar las operaciones. El orden de las operaciones es (1) calcular dentro de los signos de agrupamiento; (2) calcular potencias; (3) multiplicar y dividir en orden de izquierda a derecha; y (4) sumar y restar en orden de izequierda a derecha.

Ordinate (p. 304) See *y-coordinate.*
 Ordenada Ver *Coordenada y.*

Origin (p. 304) The point at which the axes of a plane or graph cross; the point $(0, 0)$ in the Cartesian coordinate system.
 Origen Punto en donde se cruzan los ejes de un plano o gráfica; en el sistema coordenado cartesiano es el punto $(0, 0)$.

Outputs (p. 537) The members of the range of a function.
 Salidas Los miembros de contradominio de una función.

Parabola (p. 552) The graph of a quadratic function $f(x) = ax^2 + bx + c, a \neq 0$, is a parabola.
 Parábola La gráfica de una función cuadrática $f(x) = ax^2 + bx + c, a \neq 0$, es una parábola.

Parallel lines (p. 338) Lines in the same plane that never intersect.
 Rectas peralelas Rectas en el mismo plano que no se intersecan.

Parallelogram A four-sided polygon in which the opposite sides are parallel and of equal length.
 Paralelogramo Poligono de cuatro lados en donde los lados opuestos son paralelos y de igual longitud.

Percent (p. 152) Literally, "per one hundred"; represented by the symbol %.
 Porcentaje Literalmente, "por cada cien"; se representa con el signo %.

Percent of decrease (p. 157) The ratio of an amount of decrease compared with the original amount, expressed as a percent.
 Porcentaje de disminución La razón de la cántidad de disminución y la cantidad original, expresado como un porcentaje.

Percent of increase (p. 157) The ratio of an amount of increase compared with the original amount, expressed as a percent.
 Porcentaje de aumento La razón de la cantidad de aumento y la cantidad original, expresado como un porcentaje.

Perfect square An expression whose square root can be written without radicals.
 Cuadrado perfecto Una expresión cuya raíz cuadrada se puede escribir sin radicales.

Perimeter The sum of the lengths of the sides of a polygon.
 Perímetro Suma de las longitudes de los lados de un poligono.

Perpendicular lines (p. 339) Two lines that intersect to form right angles.
 Rectas perpendiculares Dos rectas que se intersecan en un ángulo recto.

Point-slope equation (p. 329) A nonvertical line that contains a point (x_1, y_1) and has slope m has a point-slope equation $y - y_1 = m(x - x_1)$.
 Ecuación pendiente punto Una recta no vertical que contiene un punto (x_1, y_1) y cuya pendiente es m tiene una ecuación $y - y_1 = m(x - x_1)$.

English/Spanish Glossary

Polygon A closed plane figure formed by three or more segments that intersect only at their endpoints so that exactly two segments meet at each endpoint. In a *regular polygon*, all angles are congruent and all line segments are congruent.
Polígono Figura plana cerrada formada por tres o más segmentos que se intersecan sólo en sus puntos extremos de manera que sólo dos segmentos se tocan en un punto extremo. En un *poligono regular*, todos los ángulos son congruentes y todos los segmentos de recta son congruentes.

Polynomial (p. 221) A monomial or a sum of monomials.
Polinomio Monomio o suma de monomios.

Positive number (p. 54) Any number greater than zero.
Número positivo Cualquier número que es mayor que cero.

Power (p. 15) A number that can be named with exponential notation as x^n. The nth power of x is
$$\underbrace{x \cdot x \cdot x \cdot \ldots \cdot x}_{n \text{ factors}}.$$
Potencia Número que se puede nombrar en notación exponencial como x^n. La potencia *enésima* de x es
$$\underbrace{x \cdot x \cdot x \cdot \ldots \cdot x}_{n \text{ factores}}.$$

Prime number Any integer greater than 1 that has no integral factors other than 1 and itself.
Número primo Cualquier entero mayor que 1 que no tiene factores enteros diferentes de 1 y él mismo.

Principal (p. 346) An amount of money that is invested or loaned.
Capital Cantidad de dinero que se invierte o que se presta.

Principle of moments (p. 88) When several parallel forces act on an object, it will be in balance if the sum of the moments is 0.
Principio del momento Cuando varias fuerzas paralelas actúan sobre un objeto, éste estará en equilibrio si la suma de los momentos es 0.

Principle of squaring (p. 519) If an equation $a = b$ is true, then the equation $a^2 = b^2$ is true.
Principio del cuadrado Si $a = b$ es cierto, entonces $a^2 = b^2$ es cierto.

Principle of zero products (p. 286) For any real numbers a and b, if $ab = 0$, then $a = 0$ or $b = 0$; if $a = 0$ or $b = 0$, then $ab = 0$.
Principio de los productos nulos Para cualquier par de números reales a y b, si $ab = 0$ entonces $a = 0$ o $b = 0$; si $a = 0$ o $b = 0$, entonces $ab = 0$.

Principal square root (p. 482) The positive square root of a positive number.
Raíz cuadrada principal La raíz cuadrada no negativa de un número positivo.

Probability (p. 640) If an event E can occur m ways out of n possible equally-likely ways, the theoretical probability of that event is $P(E) = \frac{m}{n}$. The experimental probability is the estimated likelihood of an event, found by performing a number of trials and dividing the number of successful trials by the total number of trials.
Probabilidad Si un evento E puede ocurrir de m maneras de n maneras posibles igualmente probables, la probabilidad teórica de tal evento es $P(E) = \frac{m}{n}$. La probabilidad experimental es la ocurrencia estimada de un evento, calculada realizando varios ensayos y dividiendo el número de éxitos entre el número total de ensayos.

Product Property for Radicals (p. 491) For any nonnegative real numbers a and b, $\sqrt{ab} = \sqrt{a} \cdot \sqrt{b}$.
Propiedad del producto para radicales Para cualquier par de números reales no negativos a y b, $\sqrt{ab} = \sqrt{a} \cdot \sqrt{b}$.

Proof (p. 342) A convincing argument that a statement is true, using definitions, axioms, and other known facts.
Demostración Un argumento convincente de que una afirmación es cierta utilizando definiciones, axiomas y otros hechos conocidos.

Property of additive inverses (p. 66) For each real number a, there is one and only one real number $-a$ such that $a + (-a) = 0$.
Propiedad del inverso aditivo Para cada número real a, existe un solo número real $-a$, tal que $a + (-a) = 0$.

Property of multiplicative inverses (p. 82) For each nonzero real number a, there is one and only one real number $\frac{1}{a}$ such that $a \cdot \frac{1}{a} = 1$.
Propiedad del inverso multiplicativo Para cada número real a diferente de cero, existe un inverso multiplicativo $\frac{1}{a}$ tal que $a \cdot \frac{1}{a} = 1$.

Property of -1 (p. 93) For any real number a, $-1 \cdot a = -a$.
Propiedad de -1 Para cualquier número a, $-1 \cdot a = -a$.

Proportion (p. 148) An equation that states that two ratios are equal.
Proporción Ecuación que establece que dos razones son iguales.

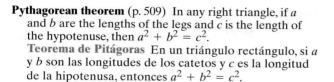

Pythagorean theorem (p. 509) In any right triangle, if a and b are the lengths of the legs and c is the length of the hypotenuse, then $a^2 + b^2 = c^2$.
Teorema de Pitágoras En un triángulo rectángulo, si a y b son las longitudes de los catetos y c es la longitud de la hipotenusa, entonces $a^2 + b^2 = c^2$.

Quadrant (p. 306) One of the four regions into which coordinate axes divide a plane.
Cuadrante Una de las cuatro regiones en que los ejes coordenados dividen al plano.

Quadratic equation (p. 576) An equation that can be written in the form $ax^2 + bx + c = 0$, where a, b, and c are real numbers and $a \neq 0$.
Ecuación cuadrática Una ecuación que se puede escribir en la forma $ax^2 + bx + c = 0$, donde a, b, y c son números reales y $a \neq 0$.

Quadratic formula (p. 589) A formula for finding the solutions of a quadratic equation $ax^2 + bx + c = 0$. The formula is $x = \frac{-b \pm \sqrt{b^2 - 4ac}}{2a}$.
Fórmula cuadrática Fórmula para encontrar soluciones de una ecuación cuadrática $ax^2 + bx + c = 0$. La fórmula es $x = \frac{-b \pm \sqrt{b^2 - 4ac}}{2a}$.

Quadratic function (p. 552) A function in the form $f(x) = ax^2 + bx + c$, where a, b, and c are real numbers and $a \neq 0$.
Función cuadrática Una función de la forma $f(x) = ax^2 + bx + c = 0$, donde a, b y c son números reales y $a \neq 0$.

Quotient (p. 81) For all real numbers a and b, $b \neq 0$, the quotient $\frac{a}{b}$ (or $a \div b$) is the number c such that $cb = a$.
Cociente Para todo par de números reales a y b, el cociente $\frac{a}{b}$ (o $a \div b$), si existe, es el número c tal que $cb = a$.

Radical equation (p. 519) An equation that contains a variable in a radicand.
Ecuación radical Una ecuación que contiene una variable en el radicando.

Radical expression (p. 487) When an expression is written under a radical, the result is a radical expression.
Expresión radical Cuando una expresión se escribe bajo el signo radical, el resultado es una expresión radical.

Radical sign (p. 482) The symbol $\sqrt{}$.
Signo de radical El signo $\sqrt{}$. Cualquier expresión quo contiene un signo radical se llama *expresión radical*.

Radicand (p. 487) The expression under a radical sign.
Radicando Expresión que está bajo un signo radical.

Radius The radius of a circle is the distance from any point on the circle to its center.
Radio El radio de un círculo es la distancia de cualquier punto sobre el círculo a su centro.

Range (p. 536) The range of a relation is the set of second coordinates.
Contradominio El contradominio es el conjunto de las segundas coordenadas.

Rate A ratio that compares quantities involving two different units.
Tasa Razón que compara dos unidades diferentes.

Ratio (p. 148) A comparison of two quantities, often expressed as a fraction.
Razón Comparación de un número con otro, expresado en forma de cociente.

Rational equation (p. 451) An equation containing one or more rational expressions.
Ecuación racional Una ecuación que contiene una o más expresiones racionales.

Rational expression (p. 432) The quotient of two polynomials.
Expresión racional El cociento de dos polinomios.

Rationalizing the denominator (p. 499) Simplifying a radical expression so that there are no radicals in the denominator and no fractions in the radicand.
Racionalización del denominador Simplificar una expresión radical de tal manera que no haya radicales en el denominador y sólo queden números completos y variables en el radicando.

Rational number (p. 59) Any number that can be expressed as the ratio of two integers in the form $\frac{a}{b}$ where $b \neq 0$.
Número racional Cualquier número que se puede expresar como cociente de dos enteros en la forma $\frac{a}{b}$, donde $b \neq 0$.

Real number (p. 61) The real numbers consist of the rational numbers and the irrational numbers. There is a real number for each point of the number line.
Números reales Los números reales constan de los números racionales o irracionales. Existe un número real para cada punto en la recta numérica.

Reciprocal (p. 82) Two expressions are reciprocals if their product is 1. A reciprocal is also called a *multiplicative inverse*.
Recíprocos Dos expresiones son recíprocas si su producto es 1. Un recíproco también se llama *inverso multiplicativo*.

English/Spanish Glossary

Reciprocal Theorem (p. 472) For any nonzero rational numbers a and b, $\frac{1}{ab} = \frac{1}{a} \cdot \frac{1}{b}$.
Teorema del recíproco Para cualquier par de números racionales a y b, $\frac{1}{ab} = \frac{1}{a} \cdot \frac{1}{b}$.

Reflexive property of equality (p. 103) For any real number a, $a = a$ is always true.
Propiedad reflexiva de la igualdad Para cualquier número real a, $a = a$ siempre es cierto.

Regular polygon (p. 432) See *Polygon*.
Polígono regular Ver *Polígono*.

Relation (p. 536) Any set of ordered pairs.
Relación Cualquier conjunto de parejas ordenadas.

Relatively prime (p. 264) Two polynomials are relatively prime if they have no common factors other than constants.
Primos relativos Dos polinomios son primos relativos si no tienen factores en común diferentes de las constantes.

Repeating decimal (p. 86) A decimal in which the same number or group of numbers repeats endlessly.
Decimal periódico Un decimal donde el mismo número o grupo de números se repite sin fin.

Replacement set (p. 34) The set of all values that may replace a variable in a sentence.
Conjunto de sustituciones El conjunto de todos los valores que pueden sustituir a las variables en una afirmación.

Right angle An angle that measures 90°.
Ángulo recto Ángulo que mide 90°.

Right triangle A right triangle has one angle of 90°.
Triángulo rectángulo Triángulo con un ángulo de 90°.

Rise (p. 318) The difference between the y-coordinates of two points; used to determine the slope of a line.
Aumento La diferencia entre las coordenadas y de dos puntos, utilizada para calcular la pendiente de una recta.

Root (p. 288) For a polynomial in one variable, a root is any value of the variable that makes the value of the polynomial equal 0; also called a *zero* of the polynomial.
Raíz Una raíz de un polinomio es un número tal que hace que el polinomio valga cero. También se llama un *cero* del polinomio.

Roster notation (p. 400) A listing of all the members in a set.
Notación de la lista Lista de todos los miembros de un conjunto.

Run (p. 318) The difference between the x-coordinates of two points; used to determine the slope of a line.
Curso La diferencia entre las coordenadas x de dos puntos, utilizada para calcular la pendiente de una recta.

Scientific notation (p. 217) A number expressed as the product of a power of 10 and a numeral greater than or equal to 1 but less than 10. The numbers 4.25×10^3 and 2.3×10^{-2} are expressed in scientific notation.
Notación científica Un número expresado como producto de una potencia de 10 y un numeral mayor o igual que 1, pero menor que 10. Los números 4.25×10^3 y 2.3×10^{-2} están expresados en notación científica.

Set (p. 400) A well-defined collection of objects.
Conjunto Una colección bien definida de objetos.

Set-builder notation (p. 400) A notation used to express the members of a set of numbers. For example, the set of negative integers can be written in set-builder notation as $\{x \mid x$ is an integer and $x < 0\}$.
Notación constructiva Una notación utilizada para expresar los miembros de un conjunto de números. Por ejemplo, el conjunto de los enteros negativos se puede escriber $\{x \mid x$ es un entero y $x < 0\}$.

Similar triangles (p. 620) Two triangles that have three pairs of angles of the same size. For similar triangles $\triangle ABC$ and $\triangle XYZ$, $\angle A$ and $\angle X$ have equal measure, $\angle B$ and $\angle Y$ have equal measure, and $\angle C$ and $\angle Z$ have equal measure. The corresponding sides are $\overline{AB}$ and $\overline{XY}$, $\overline{BC}$ and $\overline{YZ}$, and $\overline{AC}$ and $\overline{XZ}$. Corresponding sides are proportional.
Triángulos semejantes Dos triángulos que tienen tres pares de ángulos del mismo tamaño. En los triángulos semejantes $\triangle ABC$ y $\triangle XYZ$, $\angle A$ y $\angle X$ tienen la misma medida; igualmente, $\angle B$ y $\angle Y$, y $\angle C$ y $\angle Z$ tienen la misma medida. Los lados correspondientes son $\overline{AB}$ y $\overline{XY}$, $\overline{BC}$ y $\overline{YZ}$, y $\overline{AC}$ y $\overline{XZ}$.

Simple interest (p. 346) A percentage of an amount of borrowed money paid by the borrower to the lender.
Interés simple Porcentaje de la suma de dinero prestado que el prestatario paga al prestamista. El monto del préstamo se llama *capital*.

Simplest form of a radical expression (p. 499) A radical expression is in simplest form when its radicand contains no perfect square factors and is not fractional, and any fraction does not contain a radical in the denominator.
Forma más simple de una expresión radical Un radical está en su forma más simple cuando el radicando no contiene factores cuadrados perfectos y no es fraccional, y cualquier fracción no contiene radicales en el denominador.

Simplest form of a rational expression (p. 433) A rational expression is in simplest form when the numerator and denominator have no common positive factors other than 1.

Forma más simple de una expresión racional Una expresión racional está en su forma más simple cuando el numerador y el denominador no contienen factores en común diferentes de 1 y -1.

Simplifying an expression (p. 12) The process of finding the simplest form of an expression.

Simplificación de una expresión Proceso de encontrar la forma más simple de una expresión.

Simultaneous equations (p. 358) See *System of equations.*

Ecuaciones simultáneas Ver *Sistemas de ecuaciones.*

Slope (p. 318) A number that tells how steeply a line slants; the ratio of rise to run.

Pendiente Número que indica cuán inclinada está una recta; la razón del aumento entre el curso.

Slope-intercept equation (p. 324) A line with slope m and y-intercept b has a slope-intercept equation $y = mx + b$.

Ecuación pendiente ordenada Una recta con pendiente m y ordenada al origen b tiene una ecuación $y = mx + b$.

Solution of an equation (p. 34) A replacement for the variable that makes the equation true.

Solución de una ecuación Sustitución de la variable que hace verdadera la ecuación.

Solution of an equation in two variables (p. 309) An ordered pair that makes the equation true.

Solución de una ecuación en dos variables Pareja ordenada que hace de la ecuación una afirmación verdadera.

Solution of an inequality (p. 172) A replacement for the variable that makes the inequality true.

Solución de una desigualdad Sustitución de la variable que hace verdadera la desigualdad.

Solution of an inequality in two variables (p. 417) An ordered pair that makes the inequality true.

Solución de una desigualdad en dos variables Pareja ordenada que hace verdadera la desigualdad.

Solution of a system of two equations in two variables (p. 358) An ordered pair that makes both equations true.

Solución de un sistema de ecuaciones en dos variables Pareja ordenada que hace verdaderas ambas ecuaciones.

Solution set of an equation (p. 34) The set of all replacements for the variable that make the equation true.

Conjunto solución de una ecuación El conjunto de todas las sustituciones que hacen la ecuación verdadera.

Solve an equation (p. 34) To find the solution set of the equation.

Resolución de una ecuación Encontrar el conjunto solución de una ecuación.

Speed (p. 40) A ratio that compares change in distance to change in time. *Velocity* describes the ratio if change in distance can be positive or negative.

Velocidad La tasa del cambio de la distancia con respecto al tiempo.

Square of a number (p. 482) The second power of the number.

Cuadrado de un número Un número que se ha elevado a la segunda potencia.

Square root (p. 482) A number c is a square root of a if $c^2 = a$.

Raíz cuadrada Un número c es la raíz cuadrada de a si $c^2 = a$.

Standard form of a linear equation (p. 315) The standard form of a linear equation is $Ax + By = C$ where A, B, and C are constants and A and B are not both 0.

Forma general de una ecuación lineal La forma general de una ecuación lineal es $Ax + By = C$ donde A, B y C son constantes y A y B no son ambos 0.

Standard form of a quadratic equation (p. 576) The standard form of a quadratic equation is $ax^2 + bx + c = 0$.

Forma general de una ecuación cuadrática La forma general de una ecuación cuadrática es $ax^2 + bx + c = 0$.

Standard notation (p. 217) A number in its decimal form, such as 100 or 3.21, is written in standard notation.

Notación normal Un número como 100 o 3.21 escrito en forma decimal están en notación normal.

Subset (p. 80) Set A is a subset of set B if every element of set A is an element of set B.

Subconjunto El conjunto A es subconjunto de B si todo elemento de A es un elemento de B.

Substituting for a variable (p. 4) To replace a variable with a number or expression.

Sustitución Reemplazar una variable con un número o expresión.

Substitution method (p. 362) A method for solving systems of equations in which one equation is solved for one of the variables and the result is substituted for that variable in the other equation.

Método de sustitución Método para resolver sistemas de ecuaciones en donde una variable se despeja de una ecuación y el resultado se sustituye en la otra ecuación.

English/Spanish Glossary

Symmetric property of equality (p. 103) For any real numbers a and b, if $a = b$, then $b = a$.
Propiedad simétrica de la igualdad Para cualquier par de números reales a y b, si $a = b$, entonces $b = a$.

System of equations (p. 358) Two or more equations for which a common solution is sought; also called *simultaneous equations*.
Sistema de ecuaciones Dos o más ecuaciones para las cuales se busca una solución común (también llamadas *ecuaciones simultáneas*).

System of inequalities (p. 421) Two or more linear inequalities for which a common solution is sought.
Sistema de desigualdades Dos o más desigualdades para las cuales se busca una solución común.

Term (p. 26) An expression that is a single numeral or variable, or the product of numerals and variables.
Término Una expresión que es el producto de numerales y variables.

Terminating decimal (p. 86) A number that can be written in decimal form with a finite number of digits.
Decimal finito Un número que se puede escribir en forma decimal con un número finito de dígitos.

Term of a polynomial (p. 222) In a polynomial, each monomial is a term.
Término de un polinomio En un polinomio cada monomio es un término.

Tessellation (p. 432) A pattern formed by covering a surface with congruent shapes.
Teselación Patrón que se forma al cubrir una superfice con formas congruentes.

Theorem (p. 102) A property that can be proved using axioms, definitions, and other theorems.
Teorema Propiedad que se puede demostrar con axiomas, definiciones y otros teoremas.

Transitive property of equality (p. 103) For any real numbers a, b, and c, if $a = b$ and $b = c$, then $a = c$.
Propiedad transitiva de la igualdad Para cualquier terna de números reales a, b y c, si $a = b$ y $b = c$, entonces $a = c$.

Trapezoid A four-sided polygon with exactly two parallel sides.
Trapecio Polígono de cuatro lados con exactamente dos lados paralelos.

Trigonometric ratios (p. 625) Ratios of the lengths of the sides of right triangles. They are sine (p. 625), cosine (p. 626), and tangent (p. 627).
Razones trigonométricas Los razones de los lados de un triángulo rectángulo. Son seno (pág. 625), coseno (pág. 626), y tangente (pág. 627).

Trinomial (p. 222) A polynomial with exactly three terms.
Trinomio Polinomio con exactamente tres términos.

Trinomial square (p. 270) A trinomial that is the square of a binomial.
Trinomio cuadrado perfecto Trinomio que es el cuadrado de un binomio.

Union (p. 402) The union of two sets is the set of all members that are in either set (or in both), symbolized $A \cup B$.
Unión La unión de dos conjuntos es el conjunto de todos los miembros que están en cualquiera de los dos conjuntos; se simboliza como $A \cup B$.

Variable (p. 4) A letter (or some other symbol) used to represent one or several numbers.
Variable Letra (u otro signo) utilizada para representar uno o varios números.

Velocity See *Speed*.
Velocidad Ver *Velocidad*.

Vertex of an angle The point at which two rays meet (pl. *vertices*).
Vértice de un ángulo El punto donde dos rayos se tocan.

Vertex of a parabola (p. 553) The maximum or minimum point of the graph of $y = ax^2 + bx + c$ ($a \neq 0$). The x-coordinate of the vertex is $-\frac{b}{2a}$.
Vértice de una parábola El máximo o mínimo punto de la gráfica de $y = ax^2 + bx + c$ ($a \neq 0$). La abacisa del vértice es $-\frac{b}{2a}$.

Vertical line (p. 315) A line that is parallel to the y-axis (or the y-axis itself).
Recta vertical Recta que es paralela al eje y.

Volume The size of a solid expressed in cubic units.
Volumen El tamaño de un sólido expresado en unidades cúbicas.

Whole number (p. 5) Any natural number or 0.
Número completo Cualquier número natural o 0.

x-axis (p. 304) The horizontal axis or number line in a coordinate plane.
Eje x El eje o recta numérica horizontal en el plano coordenado.

x-coordinate (p. 304) The first number in an ordered pair used to locate a point on a plane; also called the *abscissa*.
Coordenada x El primer número en una pareja ordenada se usa para localizar un punto en el plano coordenado. También se llama *abscisa*.

x-intercept (p. 314) The *x*-coordinate of the point where a graph intersects the *x*-axis.
Abscisa al origen La coordenada *x* del punto donde un gráfico cruza el eje *x*.

y-axis (p. 304) The vertical axis or number line in a coordinate plane.
Eje *y* El eje o recta numérica vertical del plano coordenado.

y-coordinate (p. 304) The second number in an ordered pair used to locate a point on a plane; also called the *ordinate*.
Coordenada *y* El segundo número en una pareja ordenada se usa para localizar un punto en el plano coordenado. También se llama *ordenada*.

y-intercept (p. 314) The *y*-coordinate of the point where a graph intersects the *y*-axis.
Ordenada al origen La coordenada *y* del punto donde un gráfico cruza el eje *y*.

Selected Answers

Chapter 1

Skills & Concepts You Need for Chapter 1   **1.** $\frac{5}{7}$
2. $\frac{13}{24}$ **3.** $16\frac{3}{8}$ **4.** $15\frac{5}{12}$ **5.** $\frac{1}{3}$ **6.** $\frac{13}{30}$ **7.** $1\frac{1}{8}$ **8.** $6\frac{3}{8}$ **9.** $\frac{9}{16}$
10. $\frac{45}{4}$ or $11\frac{1}{4}$ **11.** $15\frac{3}{5}$ **12.** $7\frac{2}{3}$ **13.** 1   **14.** $\frac{3}{8}$ **15.** $2\frac{2}{3}$ **16.** 9
17. 2.35   **18.** 26.35   **19.** 1.22   **20.** 2.62   **21.** 5.11   **22.** 8.14
23. 52.5   **24.** 0.00225   **25.** 61.778   **26.** 0.0228   **27.** 1.16
28. 4958.75   **29.** 0.4   **30.** 9.7   **31.** 5123.08   **32.** 0.11

LESSON 1-1

Try This   **a.** 17   **b.** 8   **c.** 11   **d.** 3   **e.** 18   **f.** 9   **g.** 10   **h.** 12
i. 6   **j.** 2   **k.** 15   **l.** 16   **m.** 4   **n.** 21   **o.** 15   **p.** 11   **q.** 2

Exercises   **1.** 13   **3.** 10   **5.** 35   **7.** 7   **9.** 2   **11.** 48   **13.** 27
15. 6   **17.** 9   **19.** 9   **21.** 16   **23.** 19   **25.** 9   **27.** 26   **29.** 16
31. 14   **33.** 30   **35.** 2   **37.** 1   **39.** 3   **41.** 5   **43.** 6   **45.** 9
47. Rob did not use the order of operations. He added before dividing.   **49.** 12 and 5

Mixed Review   **51.** 72   **53.** 57   **55.** 14.1   **57.** $1\frac{1}{28}$ **59.** $2\frac{1}{6}$
61. $\frac{15}{28}$

LESSON 1-2

Try This   **a.** $9 + x$ **b.** qp **c.** $yx + t$, $t + xy$, or $t + yx$ **d.** $\frac{28}{20}$
e. $\frac{15}{40}$ **f.** $\frac{yz}{2xz}$ **g.** $\frac{2mp}{np}$ **h.** $\frac{2}{3}$ **i.** $\frac{8}{3}$ **j.** $\frac{8}{7}$ **k.** $\frac{1}{2}$ **l.** 4   **m.** $\frac{5y}{3}$
n. $\frac{1}{8n}$ **o.** $2a$

Exercises   **1.** $8 + y$ **3.** nm **5.** $9 + yx$ or $yx + 9$ or $xy + 9$
7. $c + ab$ or $c + ba$ or $ba + c$ **9.** $\frac{40}{48}$ **11.** $\frac{600}{700}$ **13.** $\frac{st}{20t}$ **15.** $\frac{1}{8}$
17. 12   **19.** $\frac{a}{9}$ **21.** $\frac{1}{8p}$ **23.** $\frac{9}{17q}$ **25.** $\frac{3}{s}$ **27.** $\frac{13r}{3h}$ **29.** 8
31. No   **33.** No   **35.** Yes   **37.** $\frac{r}{g}$
39. Answers may vary. $\frac{8ab}{2c}$, $\frac{4abd}{cd}$ No, $12 \div 4 \neq 4 \div 12$

Mixed Review   **41.** 16   **43.** 42   **45.** $\frac{15}{16}$ **47.** 0.48

LESSON 1-3

Try This   **a.** $5 \cdot 5 \cdot 5 \cdot 5$ **b.** $b \cdot b \cdot b$ **c.** $2 \cdot x \cdot x \cdot x$
d. $12 \cdot y \cdot y \cdot y \cdot y$ **e.** 9^3 **f.** y^5 **g.** $4n^5$ **h.** $15x^4$ **i.** $10b^3$
j. 100   **k.** 32   **l.** 0   **m.** 29   **n.** 40   **o.** 64   **p.** 1000   **q.** 27

Exercises   **1.** $2 \cdot 2 \cdot 2 \cdot 2$ **3.** 3   **5.** $a \cdot a \cdot a$ **7.** 10^6 **9.** x^5
11. $5m^4$ **13.** 27   **15.** 19   **17.** 248   **19.** 66   **21.** 3   **23.** 32
25. 1296   **27.** 20,736   **29.** 0   **31.** 10^5 **33.** 8^4 **35.** No; for
example, $2^3 = 8$ and $3^2 = 9$.   **37.** Answers may vary.
Example: 1; $1^2 = 1$.   **39.** 9   **41.** 81

Mixed Review   **43.** $\frac{7}{8}$ **45.** $12\frac{1}{2}$ **47.** 10   **49.** 8   **51.** $\frac{9}{y}$

LESSON 1-4

Try This   **a.** 225   **b.** 75   **c.** 32   **d.** 512   **e.** 8   **f.** 36   **g.** 16
h. 4   **i.** 139   **j.** 120   **k.** $2\frac{3}{10}$ **l.** 8   **m.** 63   **n.** $(a + b) + 2$
o. $(3 \cdot v) \cdot w$ **p.** Ex. $4 \cdot (u \cdot t)$ or $u \cdot (4 \cdot t)$ or $t \cdot (4 \cdot u)$
q. Ex. $r + (s + 2)$ or $(2 + s) + r$ or $(r + s) + 2$

Exercises   **1.** 400   **3.** 80   **5.** 11   **7.** 81   **9.** 9   **11.** 1   **13.** 4
15. 125   **17.** 76   **19.** 925   **21.** 66   **23.** 343   **25.** 60   **27.** $\frac{4}{5}$
29. 1   **31.** $a + (b + 3)$ **33.** $(3 \cdot a) \cdot b$ **35.** $(2 + b) + a$,
$(2 + a) + b$, $b + (a + 2)$ **37.** $v + (w + 5)$, $(5 + w) + v$,
$w + (5 + v)$ **39.** $(y \cdot 3) \cdot x$, $x \cdot (3 \cdot y)$, $y \cdot (x \cdot 3)$
41. $a \cdot (b \cdot 7)$, $(a \cdot 7) \cdot b$, $b \cdot (7 \cdot a)$
43. $c \cdot (2 \cdot d)$, $d \cdot (c \cdot 2)$, $2 \cdot (d \cdot c)$
45. $7 \cdot (n \cdot m) + 3$, $3 + m \cdot (7 \cdot n)$ **47.** $6(mp)n$, $m(6n)p$
49. $(3 + 5) + 7y + 4$; $5 + 3 + (4 + 7y)$, Answers may vary.
51. Any number except 0 or -2 **53.** Any number except 1.
0 is not acceptable.   **55.** 9; 1; No, $9 \neq 1$ **57. a.** No; 2 @ 3 = 7
and 3 @ 2 = 8   **b.** No; (1 @ 2) @ 3 = (4 @ 3) = 11 and
1 @ (2 @ 3) = 1 @ 7 = 9

Mixed Review   **59.** $9\frac{1}{10}$ **61.** $1\frac{5}{12}$ **63.** $\frac{8}{5}$ or $1\frac{3}{5}$ **65.** $\frac{6}{7y}$
67. $\frac{6n}{11t}$ **69.** 3375   **71.** 7   **73.** 30   **75.** 2   **77.** 4

LESSON 1-5

Try This   **a.** $4x + 4y + 4z$ **b.** $5y + 15$ **c.** $16a + 6$
d. $6x + 12y + 30$ **e.** $5(x + 2)$ **f.** $3(4 + x)$
g. $3(2x + 4 + 3y)$ **h.** $5(x + 2y + 1)$ **i.** $3(3x + y)$
j. $5(1 + 2x + 3y)$ **k.** $8y$ **l.** $11x + 8y$ **m.** $14p + 13q$ **n.** $8x^2$

Exercises   **1.** $2b + 10$ **3.** $7 + 7t$ **5.** $3x + 3$ **7.** $4 + 4y$
9. $30x + 12$ **11.** $7x + 28 + 42y$ **13.** $2(x + 2)$ **15.** $5(6 + y)$
17. $7(2x + 3y)$ **19.** $5(x + 2 + 3y)$ **21.** $7(2c + 9d + 1)$
23. $9(r + 3s + 2)$ **25.** $9(x + 3)$ **27.** $3(3x + y)$
29. $8(a + 2b + 8)$ **31.** $11(x + 4y + 11)$ **33.** $5(x + 2y + 9z)$
35. $19a$ **37.** $11a$ **39.** $8x + 9z$ **41.** $7x + 15y^2$
43. $101a + 92$ **45.** $11a + 11b$ **47.** $14u^2 + 13t + 2$
49. $50 + 6t + 8y$ **51.** $1b$ or b **53.** $\frac{13}{4}y$ or $3\frac{1}{4}y$ **55.** $10x + 5y$
57. $12p^2 + 6p$ **59.** $9xy + 6x + 3y$ **61.** $9x + 27$
63. $12a + 16b$ **65. a.** $P(1 + rt)$ **b.** \$412   **67.** No; when
either x or y is 0.   **69.** Both answers are correct.
$ax + ay + bx + by = a(x + y) + b(x + y)$ and
$ax + ay + bx + by = ax + bx + ay + by =$
$xa + xb + ya + yb = x(a + b) + y(a + b)$.   **71.** $\frac{4}{3}$
73. $q(1 + r + rs + rst)$ **75.** $a + ab + abc + abcd$

Mixed Review   **77.** 48   **79.** 0   **81.** $\frac{1}{3a}$ **83.** $8x$ **85.** 24   **87.** 15

LESSON 1-6

Try This   **a.** $n + 7$ **b.** $4n$ **c.** $y - 4$ **d.** $x - 6$ **e.** $m - n$
f. $2y$ **g.** $b - a$ **h.** $7n$ **i.** $\frac{a}{7}$ **j.** $c - 24$

Exercises **1.** $b + 6$ **3.** $c - 9$ **5.** $q + 6$ **7.** $a + b$ **9.** $y - x$
11. $w + x$ **13.** $n - m$ **15.** $r + s$ **17.** $2x$ **19.** $5t$ **21.** $3b$
23. $2h$ **25.** $x - y$ **27.** $m - 5$ **29.** $a + 5$ **31.** $m - \$4.50$
33. $a + \$45$ **35.** $w - 2$ **37.** $3K$ **39.** $\frac{1}{4}t$ or $\frac{t}{4}$ **41.** $R - 3$
43. $y + 2x$ **45.** $2x - 3$ **47.** lw **49.** 2 **51.** $\frac{31}{4}$ **53.** 9 **55.** 24
57. a. $x - 6$ **b.** $\frac{x - 6}{3}$ **c.** $\frac{x - 6}{3} + 4$ **d.** $\frac{x - 6}{3} + 4 - \frac{x}{9}$
e. 8 students **59.** $w + 4$ **61.** $t + 3, t - 3$ **63.** 4

Mixed Review **65.** 48 **67.** $3(x + 2)$ **69.** $8(1 + 2x + 5y)$
71. $12a + 7b$ **73.** $11y$ **75.** $9 + 7c$

LESSON 1-7

Try This **a.** False **b.** True **c.** Open **d.** {3} **e.** {2} **f.** $x = 6$
g. $y = 24$ **h.** $y = 5$ **i.** $x = 17$ **j.** 4 was added to both sides
of the equation. **k.** 5 was subtracted from both sides of the
equation. **l.** Both sides of the equation were divided by 2.

Exercises **1.** False **3.** True **5.** {8} **7.** {0} **9.** {12}
11. $m = 23$ **13.** $y = 27$ **15.** $y = 9$ **17.** $c = 48$ **19.** 5 was
added to both sides. **21.** 10 was subtracted from both sides.
23. Both sides were multiplied by 4. **25.** Both sides were
multiplied by 8. **27.** Both sides were multiplied by 4.
29. $y = 2$ **31.** $y = 31$ **33.** $x = \frac{1}{2}$ **35.** $k = 2$ **37.** Add 12 to
both sides. **39.** Divide both sides by 3. **41.** Multiply both
sides by 8. **43.** 5 was added to the left side, but subtracted
from the right side. **45.** D **47.** Ex. $3x = 2$ **49.** Ex. $12x = 0$

Mixed Review **51.** $5n^5$ **53.** 64 **55.** 27 **57.** $13(t + 4)$
59. $8(2 + y)$ **61.** $3(3x + 1)$

LESSON 1-8

Problems **1.** The underwater mountain is 5550 ft high.
3. The booster is 90 ft long, the fuel tank is 75 ft long, and the
cargo and navigation section is 15 ft long.

LESSON 1-9

Try This **a.** 1695 km/h **b.** 1370 mi/h **c.** $P = 39$ cm
d. $A = 49$ in.^{2} **e.** $r = 9$ ft/sec **f.** $V = 20$ ft^3

Exercises **1.** 440 mi **3.** $6.80 **5.** 1435 ft/s **7.** 364 m^2
9. 198 yd or 594 ft **11.** $900 **13.** 0.7 mL **15.** 0.6 mL
17. 56.25 ft **19.** 206.25 ft **21.** 17 ft^2 **23.** $2\frac{1}{2}$ m^2
25. a. Andrew did not convert 0.5 km to meters. Marie did not
convert 150 m to kilometers. **b.** 75,000 m^2 or 0.075 km^2
27. Answers may vary. Ex: $a^2 - b^2$.

Mixed Review **29.** $t + 5$ **31.** $3k$ **33.** $16c$ **35.** 9

LESSON 1-10

Problems **1.** 7 **3.** 7 **5.** 8 **7.** 9 **9.** 5 **11.** The numbers are
12 and 48. **13.** 24 in., 12 in. **15.** 45°, 45°, 90° **17.** 22 and 11
19. 59 **21.** Eunpyo worked 11 hours of overtime. **23.** Peter
earned $15.25 the first week.

CHAPTER 1 WRAP UP

1. 11 **2.** 9 **3.** 5 **4.** 32 **5.** 72 **6.** 8 **7.** 2 **8.** 33 **9.** 53
10. 10 **11.** 4 **12.** 54 **13.** $8 + x$ **14.** $ab + 11, ba + 11$, or
$11 + ba$ **15.** $\frac{36}{45}$ **16.** $\frac{2xz}{yz}$ **17.** $\frac{1}{3}$ **18.** $\frac{7}{2}$ **19.** $\frac{a}{3c}$ **20.** $\frac{4}{xy}$ **21.** $\frac{n}{6}$
22. $\frac{q}{8}$ **23.** 6^5 **24.** $3y^4$ **25.** 64 **26.** 72 **27.** 62 **28.** 19
29. 216 **30.** 100,000 **31.** 400 **32.** 55 **33.** 70 **34.** 28
35. $a + (b + 6)$ **36.** $7 \cdot (y \cdot x)$ **37–38.** Answers may vary.
37. $1 + (n + m), n + (m + 1), m + (1 + n)$ **38.** $4 \cdot (y \cdot x),$
$y \cdot (x \cdot 4), x(y \cdot 4)$ **39.** $7y + 35$ **40.** $18m + 12n + 15$
41. $6(3x + y)$ **42.** $4(1 + 3b + 9a)$ **43.** $8a + 9b$
44. $19m^2 + 12m$ **45.** $5n$ **46.** $n - 7$ **47.** $n + 4$ **48.** $2n$
49. $x + 2x$ or $3x$ **50.** $a + 12$ **51.** {3} **52.** {0, 1} **53.** $a = 7$
54. $c = 24$ **55.** 5 was subtracted from both sides. **56.** Both
sides were multiplied by 10. **57.** 93.75 cm^2 **58.** 28.26 ft^2

Chapter 2

Skills & Concepts You Need for Chapter 2 **1.** $\frac{4}{9}$
2. $\frac{1}{4b}$ **3.** 13 **4.** $\frac{6c}{5}$ **5.** 64 **6.** 24 **7.** 24 **8.** $5a + 5b + 5d$
9. $11w + 44$ **10.** $21z + 7y + 14$ **11.** $9(5 + y)$
12. $3(a + 4b)$ **13.** $2(2x + 5 + 4y)$ **14.** $7x + 3y$
15. $5b^2 + 3a$ **16.** $8t + 9$ **17.** {7} **18.** {0.5}

LESSON 2-1

Try This **a.** -12 **b.** 8 **c.** -5 **d.** -3 **e.** > **f.** > **g.** <
h. 17 **i.** 8 **j.** 14 **k.** 21 **l.** 0 **m.** 21

Exercises **1.** -12 **3.** 18 **5.** 2500 **7.** -125 **9.** 3,000,000
11. > **13.** > **15.** > **17.** < **19.** > **21.** > **23.** 7
25. 11 **27.** 4 **29.** 325 **31.** 5.5 **33.** 120.2 **35.** 340 **37.** 0.3
39. 0.07 **41.** 3.75 **43.** 34 **45.** 0 **47.** 11 **49.** $-23, -17, 0, 4$
51. $-24, -16, -14, -13, -5, 12, 15$ **53.** 21 **55.** 31
57. a. $-3, -7, -11$ **b.** $-4, -9, -15$ **c.** $-17, -23, -30$
d. $-11, -18, -29$ **59.** B **61.** A **63.** D **65.** <
67. = **69.** < **71.** =

Mixed Review **73.** $21m$ **75.** $11x^2 + 7x$ **77.** $4(m + 6c)$
79. $7(2x + 4y + 1)$ **81.** {361} **83.** {2.7} **85.** $x = 22$
87. $y = 90$ **89.** $x = 24$

Selected Answers

LESSON 2-2

Try This a. $\frac{45}{10}$ or $\frac{9}{2}$ b. $-\frac{10}{1}$ c. $-\frac{143}{10}$ d. $-\frac{1}{100}$

e. (number line from -1 to 3, point at $2\frac{12}{5}$)

f. (number line from -5 to 0, point at -4.8)

g. (number line from -5 to -3, point at $-\frac{18}{4}$)

h. (number line from -2 to 1, point at 0.5)

i. $>$ j. $>$ k. $<$ l. $>$

Exercises 1. $\frac{14}{1}$ 3. $\frac{42}{10}$ or $\frac{21}{5}$ 5. $-\frac{5}{10}$ or $-\frac{1}{2}$ 7. $\frac{3444}{1000}$ or $\frac{861}{250}$

9. $-\frac{68}{100}$ or $-\frac{17}{25}$ 11. $\frac{15}{2}$

13. (number line from -1 to 4, point at $3\frac{10}{3}$)

15. (number line with point at -4.3) 17. C 19. $<$ 21. $<$

23. $>$ 25. $>$ 27. $>$ 29. $<$ 31. Ex: $\frac{3}{8}$ 33. Ex: 0.455

35. $-\frac{8}{8}, -\frac{4}{8}, \frac{1}{8}, \frac{3}{8}, \frac{5}{8}, \frac{7}{8}$ 37. $\frac{4}{9}, \frac{4}{8}, \frac{4}{6}, \frac{4}{5}, \frac{4}{3}, \frac{4}{2}$

39. Answers may vary. $\frac{2}{3} > \frac{4}{7}, \frac{3}{2} > \frac{5}{3}, \frac{3}{2} > \frac{4}{5}, \frac{4}{5} > \frac{2}{7}, \frac{7}{2} > \frac{5}{4}$

41. Sometimes; true when $a = b$.

Mixed Review 43. $\frac{y}{x}$ 45. $4w$ 47. 2.3 49. $\frac{1}{5}$ 51. $\frac{1}{6}$ 53. 72
55. 22 57. 51

LESSON 2-3

Try This a. 7 b. -3 c. -2 d. -6 e. $\frac{4}{4}$ or 1 f. 0 g. -20

h. -25 i. 0.53 j. 13 k. -7 l. $-\frac{2}{4}$ or $-\frac{1}{2}$ m. $-\frac{7}{8}$ n. $-\frac{3}{35}$

o. -58 p. -56 q. 19 r. -54 s. 0 t. 7.4 u. $\frac{8}{3}$

v. $-14, 14$ w. $-1, 1$ x. $19, -19$ y. 12 yd gained

Exercises 1. -7 3. -4 5. 0 7. -8 9. -7 11. -27

13. 0 15. -42 17. -43 19. $-\frac{1}{6}$ 21. $-\frac{23}{24}$ 23. $-\frac{11}{18}$

25. $\frac{3}{4}$ 27. -5 29. -1093 31. $14 + (-35)$ 33. $-\frac{3}{5} + \frac{3}{5}$

35. -24 37. 9 39. 26.9 41. -9 43. $\frac{14}{3}$ 45. -0.101

47. -65 49. $\frac{5}{3}$ 51. never 53. sometimes 55. sometimes

57. 999 mb 59. 542 above last year's 61. $1715 63. $6.41
65. When x is negative 67. Negative; $-n$ is negative and m is negative, so their sum is negative. 69. Zero; $-m$ is the additive inverse of n, so their sum is zero. 71. Answers may vary, but should include the idea that since $-n + n = 0$, the additive inverse of $-n$ is n. 73. No value 75. 21

Mixed Review 77. 2.4 79. 12 81. $>$ 83. $>$ 85. 2
87. 2.03 89. 13

LESSON 2-4

Try This a. -8 b. -6 c. -5 d. -5 e. 10 f. -21 g. 9
h. $\frac{5}{8}$ i. -9 j. 21.6 k. $5x + 5$ l. $90

Exercises 1. -4 3. -7 5. 7 7. 0 9. 0 11. 14 13. 11
15. -14 17. 5 19. -5 21. -49 23. -193 25. 500

27. -2.8 29. -3.53 31. $-\frac{1}{2}$ 33. 0 35. $-\frac{41}{30}$ 37. $-\frac{1}{156}$

39. 37 41. -62 43. -139 45. 4 47. $-3x + 46$
49. $15x + 39$ 51. $330.54 53. $7°$ 55. 116 males 57. 116 m
59. A 61. A 63. A 65. a. 10.7 b. 5.7 c. 6.6 d. 19.4
e. -15.3 f. -14.8 67. False; $3 - 0 \neq 0 - 3$ 69. True
71. True 73. No 75. All; $a - 1$ is to the left of a on the number line.

Mixed Review 77. 49 79. 81 81. 243 83. 18 85. $y = 1$
87. $y = \frac{1}{4}$ 89. $2a + 8b + 4c$ 91. $6(x + 4y - 3z)$

LESSON 2-5

Try This a. -18 b. -100 c. -90 d. $-\frac{3}{2}$ e. 20 f. 0
g. 12.6 h. $\frac{3}{56}$ i. -90 j. 120 k. -6

Exercises 1. -16 3. -42 5. -24 7. -72 9. 16 11. 42
13. -120 15. -238 17. 1200 19. 98 21. $\frac{-2}{45}$ 23. 1911

25. 50.4 27. $\frac{10}{189}$ 29. -960 31. 17.64 33. $-\frac{5}{784}$ 35. 0

37. -0.104 39. 72 41. -6 43. 1944 45. -32 47. 13
49. -79 51. -69 53. $12, -7$ 55. Either m or n is negative and the other is positive. 57. Always; for all values of a and b, $|ab| \geq 0$, $|-a| \geq 0$, and $|-b| \geq 0$. Both sides of the given equation equal $|a| \cdot |b|$. 59. $z < 0$

Mixed Review 61. 4 63. 0 65. 15 67. $<$ 69. $<$
71. $2(2x + 5 + 4y)$ 73. 24

LESSON 2-6

Try This a. -5 b. 3 c. 4 d. -7 e. 2 f. -5 g. 3
h. -21 i. $\frac{6}{3}$ or 2 j. $-\frac{1}{4}$ k. -2 l. $\frac{3}{4}$ m. $\frac{y}{x}$ n. $-6(5)$

o. $-5\left(\frac{1}{7}\right)$ p. $(x^2 - 2)\frac{1}{3}$ q. $x\left(\frac{1}{y}\right)$ r. $-15x$ s. $-\frac{4}{7}\left(-\frac{5}{3}\right)$

t. $13\left(-\frac{3}{2}\right)$ u. ab v. $\frac{11}{20}$ w. $-\frac{12}{5}$ x. -16.2 y. -26.2

Exercises 1. -6 3. -2 5. 4 7. -2 9. -25 11. 9

13. None 15. 0 17. $\frac{8}{3}$ 19. $-\frac{12}{31}$ 21. $-\frac{1}{10}$ 23. $-\frac{5}{2}$ 25. $\frac{3}{8}$

27. $\frac{t}{s}$ 29. $-8a$ 31. $-\frac{3x}{4y}$ 33. $4\left(\frac{-1}{9}\right)$ 35. $-12\left(\frac{1}{41}\right)$ 37. $x \cdot y$

39. $(5a - b)\left(\frac{1}{5a + b}\right)$ 41. $-\frac{7}{4}$ 43. $\frac{2}{3}$ 45. $\frac{24}{25}$ 47. None

49. -1 51. $-\frac{10}{9}$ 53. A 55. B 57. D 59. $-\frac{17}{2}$ 61. -9

63. $\frac{40}{49}$ 65. $\frac{1}{8}$ 67. 0.238095238 69. Yes, this is true for 1 and also for -1. 71. No, $(12 \div 6) \div 2 = 2 \div 2 = 1$ but
$12 \div (6 \div 2) = 12 \div 3 = 4$. 73. Yes; $\frac{1}{\left(\frac{a}{b}\right)} \cdot \frac{\left(\frac{b}{a}\right)}{\left(\frac{b}{a}\right)} = \frac{\left(\frac{b}{a}\right)}{1} = \frac{b}{a}$

Mixed Review **75.** 7 **77.** 7 **79.** $2m$ **81.** $25 - x$ **83.** $\frac{1}{2}$
85. $\frac{1}{3}$

Terminating and Repeating Decimals **1.** $0.\overline{36}$
3. $2.\overline{5}$ **5.** $0.\overline{4}$ **7.** There are 6 numbers in the repeating pattern of remainders: 1, 3, 2, 6, 4, 5, . . . **9.** For the divisor 17, the 16 possible remainders are 1, 2, . . . , 16. As soon as any remainder repeats, the digits in the quotient repeat. So there can be no more than 16 digits in the quotient that repeat.

Application **1.** Some examples are 15 ft, 1000 lb; and 30 ft, 500 lb. **3.** 600 lb **5.** The fulcrum would have to be 60 cm from the 10-kg weight and 40 cm from the 15-kg weight.

LESSON 2-7

Try This **a.** $8y - 56$ **b.** $\frac{5}{6}x - \frac{5}{6}y + \frac{35}{6}z$ **c.** $-5x + 15y - 40z$
d. $4(x - 2)$ **e.** $3(x - 2y - 5)$ **f.** $b(x - y + z)$
g. $-2(y - 4z + 1)$ or $2(-y + 4z - 1)$ **h.** $4(3z - 4x - 1)$
i. $5a, -4b, 3$ **j.** $-5y, -3x, 5z$ **k.** $3x$ **l.** $6y$ **m.** $0.56m$
n. $3x + 3y$ **o.** $-4x - 5y - 15$

Exercises **1.** $7x - 14$ **3.** $-7y + 14$ **5.** $45x + 54y - 72$
7. $-4x + 12y + 8z$ **9.** $-3.72x + 9.92y - 3.41$
11. $2a - 4b + 6$ **13.** $\frac{2}{5}x - \frac{8}{15}y + \frac{4}{5}$ **15.** $8(x - 3)$
17. $4(8 - y)$ **19.** $2(4x + 5y - 11)$ **21.** $a(x - 7)$
23. $a(x - y - z)$ **25.** $\frac{1}{4}(3x - y - 1)$
27. $4x, 3z$ **29.** $7x, 8y, -9z$ **31.** $12x, -13.2y, \frac{5}{8}z, -4.5$
33. $-2x$ **35.** $5n$ **37.** $4x + 2y$ **39.** $7x + y$ **41.** $0.8x + 0.5y$
43. $-2y - 3x$ **45.** $-9t + 5p$ **47.** $32a - 17b - 17c$
49. $8.5d + 3a$ **51.** $\frac{3}{5}x + \frac{3}{5}y$ **53.** $8(x - y)$ **55.** $3(a + b) - 7a$
or $3b - 4a$ **57.** No; $1 \cdot (3 - 2) = 1, 1 - (3 \cdot 2) = -5$
59. $5420(41\frac{1}{8} - 37\frac{3}{4})$ or $5420(41\frac{1}{8}) - 5420(37\frac{3}{4})$; $18,292.50

Mixed Review **61.** $-\frac{11}{6}$ **63.** $3c$ **65.** $12x$ **67.** $-\frac{3}{16}$ **69.** 2

LESSON 2-8

Try This **a.** $-x - 2$ **b.** $-5x - 2y - 8$ **c.** $-a + 7$
d. $-3c + 4d - 1$ **e.** $-6 + t$ **f.** $4a - 3t + 10$
g. $-18 + m + 2n - 4t$ **h.** $2x - 9$ **i.** $8x - 4y + 4$
j. $-9x - 8y$ **k.** $-16a + 18$ **l.** -1 **m.** 4 **n.** $2x - y + 4$

Exercises **1.** $-2x - 7$ **3.** $-5x + 8$ **5.** $-4a + 3b - 7c$
7. $-6x + 8y - 5$ **9.** $-3x + 5y + 6$ **11.** $8x + 6y + 43$
13. $5x - 3$ **15.** $-3a + 9$ **17.** $5x - 6$ **19.** $-19x + 2y$
21. $9y - 25z$ **23.** $-2x + 6y$ **25.** $3m - 6n$ **27.** 0
29. $a + 4b$ **31.** 7 **33.** -40 **35.** 19 **37.** $12x + 30$
39. $3x + 30$ **41.** $x - (y + a + b)$
43. $6m - (-3n + 5m - 4b)$ **45.** $2a + 4$
47. 0; $a + b + (-a) + (-b) = a + (-a) + b + (-b) = 0$
49. $-2x - f$ **51.** $5y - 4$

Mixed Review **53.** $2(a - 3b + 6)$ **55.** 54 **57.** 50 **59.** -8
61. $-\frac{7}{45}$ **63.** $2x^2 + x$ **65.** $3x - 5$

LESSON 2-9

Problems **1.** (B) or (C) **3.** (A) or (B) **5.** (B) or (C)
7-23: Answers may vary. Examples are given. **7.** Let $h = $ the height of the Statue of Liberty. $h + 203 = 295$ **9.** Let $a = $ the amount of money Alberto has. $a = 115 - 48$
11. Let $p = $ the price of a ticket. $117p = 438.75$ **13.** Let $a = $ the area of Lake Ontario. $4a = 78,114$ **15.** Let $a = $ the area of Rhode Island. $483a = 1,519,202$ **17.** Let $d = $ the distance from Earth to the moon. $391d = 150,000,000$
19. Let $t = $ time. $325 = 50t$ **21.** Let $q = $ the number of quarters required. $7q = 45$ **23.** Let $t = $ the time it takes the sound to reach you. $1087t = 10,000$

LESSON 2-10

Try This **a.** Associative prop. of addition **b.** Inverse prop. of multiplication **c.** Inverse prop. of addition **d.** No; yes
e. Reflexive **f.** Transitive **g.** Symmetric **h.** 2. Distributive property 3. Distributive property **i.** 4. Distributive property 6. Multiplicative identity 7. Additive inverses

Exercises **1.** Commutative property of addition
3. Distributive property of multiplication over addition
5. Additive inverses **7.** Additive inverses **9.** Associative property of multiplication **11.** Distributive property of multiplication over addition **13.** Multiplicative inverse
15. Reflexive property of equality **17.** Reflexive property of equality **19.** Yes; no, $4 - 2$ is not a whole number; yes; no, $1 \div 2$ is not a whole number. **21.** Yes; yes; yes; no, $1 \div -2$ is not an integer. **23.** Yes. The sum of two even numbers $2a$ and $2b$ where a and b are whole numbers equals $2(a + b)$ by the distributive property. $2(a + b)$ is even because $a + b$ is a whole number. **25.** Yes. The product of $3a$ and $3b$ where a and b are whole numbers is $(3a)(3b)$ which equals $3(3(ab))$ by the associative and commutative properties of multiplication. ab is a whole number, so $3(ab)$ is a whole number.

27.

Statement	Reason
1. $-(a + b)$ $= -1(a + b)$	1. Property of -1
2. $= -1(a) + -1(b)$	2. Distributive property
3. $= -a + (-b)$	3. Property of -1
4. $-(a + b)$ $= -a + (-b)$	4. Transitive property of equality

Mixed Review **29.** $16(a - 3)$ **31.** $15(3 - n)$ **33.** $9 - 17c$

CHAPTER 2 WRAP UP

1. -25 2. $+50$ 3. 38 4. 91 5. 0.02
8. 6.   7.

9. $>$ 10. $<$ 11. $<$

12. $-\frac{42}{10}$ 13. $\frac{8}{5}$ 14. $-\frac{8}{1}$ 15. -19 16. $-\frac{6}{4}$ or $-\frac{3}{2}$ 17. 3.5
18. -4 19. -6.4 20. -27 21. 7.45 22. $\frac{7}{3}$ 23. 34 24. 5
25. 8 yd gain 26. -2 27. -4 28. $-\frac{14}{10}$ or $-\frac{7}{5}$ 29. 19
30. $11y - 16$ 31. 4000 ft 32. $16.95 33. -24 34. $-\frac{2}{7}$
35. 210 36. -3 37. 5 38. $-\frac{7}{10}$ 39. $12x - 2$
40. $-7 - 28x$ 41. $-6a + 9b - 3c$ 42. $9(a - 1)$
43. $8(x - 4y - 1)$ 44. $7(6z - 3x + 1)$ 45. $7x$ 46. $2a$
47. $2m + 6$ 48. $-x - 7$ 49. $-7a - 12b - c$ 50. $-6 + z$
51. $-5a - 3$ 52. $-3x - 1$ 53. $-4a - 5b$ 54. $-29p + 12$
55. 1 56. 21 57. (A) or (C) 58. $162a = 1{,}289{,}170$

Chapter 3

Skills & Concepts You Need for Chapter 3 1. -11
2. -6 3. 3.7 4. 22 5. 2.9 6. $-\frac{7}{30}$ 7. -36 8. $-\frac{6}{7}$ 9. $\frac{-5}{12}$
10. -48 11. 33 12. 35 13. -6 14. $\frac{7}{6}$ 15. 93.7
16. $9(y - 5)$ 17. $b(w + x - y)$ 18. $3(y + 5 - 7x)$
19. $2(3w - 6x + 5)$ 20. $3x - 15$ 21. $32 + 8w$ 22. $2x - 6$
23. $3w + 5$ 24. 22 25. $15x + 26$

LESSON 3-1

Try This a. -5 b. 5 c. 9 d. $x + 82 = 675$; $593

Exercises 1. 4 3. 11 5. -14 7. -18 9. 15 11. -14
13. 2 15. 20 17. -6 19. 43 21. -20 23. 4.6 25. -6.5
27. 6.9 29. $\frac{1}{4}$ 31. $\frac{-3}{2}$ 33. $\frac{19}{12}$ 35. $-\frac{7}{10}$ 37. $x + 6 = 57$; 51
39. $x - 4 = 11$; 15 41. A 43. a. $t - 55$ b. $-35°$ c. The average daily low temperature in Key West in January
d. $t - 55 = -35$ e. $t = 20°$ 45. a. $c + 15{,}918{,}215$
b. 18,870,730 c. The newspaper's circulation
d. $c + 15{,}918{,}215 = 18{,}870{,}730$ e. Less f. $c = 2{,}952{,}515$
47. -10 49. $a - b$ 51. $1 - c - a$ 53. $118.40
55. Sometimes; when $k = 0$ and $a = b$. Always; If $k + a = b$, then $a - b = -k$. Using $-k$ for x, $x - a = -k - a = a - b - a = -b$ and $-k$ is a solution of $x - a = -b$.
57. 11,074 59. a. All values of x are solutions. Adding $-x$ to both sides gives $3 = 3$, which is true for all values of x.
b. No solution. Adding $-x$ to both sides gives $-3 = 3$, which is not true for any value of x.

Mixed Review 61. $7y - 4$ 63. $-7w + 24$ 65. $51 - 12y$
67. 100 69. 32 71. $\frac{1}{5}$ 73. -2 75. $-\frac{98}{75}$

LESSON 3-2

Try This a. 5 b. $-\frac{7}{4}$ c. 14 d. -12 e. $-\frac{5}{4}$ f. -6 g. 50
h. 36 i. -24 j. $12x = 6.72$; $0.56

Exercises 1. 6 3. 9 5. 12 7. -40 9. 1 11. -7 13. -6
15. 6 17. -63 19. 36 21. -21 23. $\frac{-3}{5}$ 25. $\frac{3}{2}$ 27. $\frac{9}{2}$
29. 7 31. -7 33. 8 35. $-8x = 744$; -93 37. a. $8p$
b. $170 c. The price of one ticket d. $8p = 170$ e. Less; if each ticket costs $30, 8 tickets would cost $240.
f. $p = 21.25$ 39. a. $42w$ b. 258,295 c. the population of Winnemucca d. $42w = 258{,}295$ e. about 6000
f. $w = 6150$ (approximately) 41. $1131 = \frac{1}{3}f$; 3393
43. 2,730,000 45. 12 47. 60 49. 5 51. $\frac{a^2 + 1}{c}$
53. Answers may vary. 55. a. Yes; If $a = b$, then $a^2 = ab$. Also, $ab = b^2$. Therefore, $a^2 = b^2$. b. No; for example, $3^2 = (-3)^2$, but $3 \neq -3$.

Mixed Review 57. $-4a - 4$ 59. 0 61. 0 63. -42
65. 18.6 67. 216 69. 3 71. $4(x + 2y - 3z)$

LESSON 3-3

Try This a. 5 b. -4 c. 13 d. -1 e. 3 f. 4 g. -3 h. 7
i. 2

Exercises 1. 5 3. 8 5. 10 7. 14 9. -8 11. -7 13. 15
15. 6 17. 6 19. 5 21. -3 23. 1 25. -20
27.

$$4x - 8 = 32 \qquad 4x - 8 = 32 \qquad \text{Yes.}$$
$$\tfrac{1}{4}(4x - 8) = \tfrac{1}{4}(32) \qquad 4x = 40$$
$$x - 2 = 8 \qquad x = 10$$
$$x = 10$$

29. 6 31. $-\frac{1}{3}$ 33. 9 35. -9 37. -24 39. -3 41. $\frac{8}{3}$
43. a. Using the distributive property b. Using the addition property c. Simplifying d. Using the multiplication property
e. Simplifying 45. a. Using the commutative property
b. Using the associative property c. Collecting like terms
d. Using the addition property e. Simplifying f. Using the multiplication property g. Simplifying 47. 0.18 49. -3
51. 1 53. $0.074/mi or 7.4¢ per mile 55. $x = -\frac{1}{3}$, $y = -5$

Mixed Review 57. $<$ 59. $>$ 61. $<$ 63. $\frac{12}{25}$
65. $x = 15$ 67. $y = 6$ 69. $3(a - c - d)$ 71. $12x - 16y$

Connections: Geometry 1. 16 ft

LESSON 3-4

Try This a. $2n - 3$ b. $\frac{1}{2}(n - 1)$ c. $4(n + 3)$ d. $10n - 2$
e. $2n - 5$ f. $\frac{1}{2}t + 2$ g. 7 h. 1.5

Exercises 1. $5n - 3$ 3. $\frac{1}{2}n - 18$ 5. $\frac{n}{5} - 3$ 7. $4(n - 1)$
9. $\frac{1}{2}(n + 6)$ 11. $\frac{1}{3}n - 4$ 13. $2y + 2$ 15. $\frac{1}{2}a + 2$
17. a. $s + 15$ b. $L - 15$

19. a.

```
|<--------------- 55 mi --------------->|
|<--- 20 mi --->|<------- 10h ------->|
```

b. $10h + 20$ **c.** the number of additional hours that Elena must ride   **d.** $10h + 20 = 55$ **e.** $h = 3\frac{1}{2}$ Elena must ride $3\frac{1}{2}$ hours more.   **21.** B   **23.** 75   **25.** \$0.75   **27.** 2 days   **29.** \$120

Mixed Review   **31.** 4   **33.** $12n^3m^2$ **35.** $30t^3$ **37.** 20   **39.** $\frac{15}{14}$

LESSON 3-5

Try This   **a.** 1   **b.** 2   **c.** 2   **d.** 9   **e.** −2   **f.** $-\frac{1}{2}$

Exercises   **1.** 7   **3.** 2   **5.** 5   **7.** 2   **9.** 10   **11.** 4   **13.** 5   **15.** 8   **17.** 4   **19.** 17   **21.** −3   **23.** −3   **25.** 2   **27.** 5   **29.** 3 ft   **31.** 2   **33.** −1   **35. a.** Yes; true for all values of x.   **b.** No; true only for $x = 0$.   **37.** $\frac{d - e + ac}{ab + 1}$

Mixed Review   **39.** $-\frac{1}{5}x + \frac{3}{7}y$ **41.** $\frac{1}{3}a + \frac{1}{3}$ **43.** $5(n - 2)$

LESSON 3-6

Try This   **a.** 2   **b.** 21   **c.** 6   **d.** −4.3

Exercises   **1.** 4   **3.** 8   **5.** 6   **7.** −1   **9.** −2   **11.** 4   **13.** $\frac{1}{2}$ **15.** $-\frac{2}{3}$ **17.** 28   **19.** −4   **21.** 0.8   **23.** 1   **25.** 12   **27.** 5   **29.** $\frac{5}{4}$ **31.** 84 yr   **33.** 72

Mixed Review   **35.** <   **37.** <   **39.** $2n - 5$ **41.** −3   **43.** 6   **45.** $\frac{8}{3}$ **47.** 28

LESSON 3-7

Try This   **a.** $r = \frac{C}{2\pi}$ **b.** $l = \frac{P - 35}{2}$ **c.** $c = 4A - a - b - d$ **d.** $n = \frac{y}{r}$

Exercises   **1.** $\frac{A}{h}$ **3.** $\frac{d}{t}$ **5.** $\frac{l}{rt}$ **7.** $\frac{F}{m}$ **9.** $\frac{P - 2l}{2}$ **11.** $\frac{A}{\pi}$ **13.** $\frac{2A}{h}$ **15.** $\frac{E}{c^2}$ **17.** $3A - a - c$ **19.** $\frac{3k}{v}$ **21.** $\frac{360A}{\pi r^2}$ **23.** $\frac{2.5H}{N}$ **25.** $\frac{1}{A}$ **27.** $8h - 4r$ **29.** $\frac{a^2 - b^2}{2c}$ **31.** $\frac{b}{d}$ **33.** $\frac{d - a + l}{d}$ **35.** $t = \frac{R - 3.85}{-0.00625}$ or $-160R + 616$ **37.** $\frac{y}{1 - b}$ **39.** $\frac{x - b}{1 - 2b}$ **41.** $4r + 2q$

Mixed Review   **43.** $4(x + 3)$ **45.** $3y - 2x$ **47.** 3   **49.** 5   **51.** 3

LESSON 3-8

Try This   **a.** 17, −17   **b.** 6, −6   **c.** 7, −7

Exercises   **1.** 19, −19   **3.** 4, −4   **5.** 0   **7.** 12, −12   **9.** 2, −2   **11.** 7, −7   **13.** 28, −28   **15.** 2, −2   **17.** 6, −6   **19.** 0   **21.** 7, −7   **23.** 3, −3   **25.** 20, −20   **27.** $\frac{5}{4}$, $-\frac{5}{4}$ **29.** 4, −4   **31.** 175, −175   **33.** The absolute value of a number cannot be negative.   **35.** true for $x = -2$; false for $x = 2$ **37.** true for $x = -2$; false for $x = 2$ **39.** true for $x = -2$, $y = 3$; false for $x = 2$, $y = 3$ **41.** 12, −12   **43.** 4, −4   **45.** 3, −3   **47.** 1, −1   **49.** 2, −2   **51.** $a = 4, -4$ **53.** $x = 7, -7$ **55.** $-x$ **57.** 5, −9   **59.** 2, −3   **61.** Always; a number and its opposite are the same distance from 0.   **63.** Sometimes; false only for $x = y = 0$.   **65.** Sometimes; true for $x = 3$, $y = 2$; false for $x = 3$, $y = -2$.   **67.** The correct solution is $x = -\frac{1}{3}$.   **69.** The correct solution is $c = 1$ or $c = -1$.

Mixed Review   **71.** −3   **73.** 12   **75.** 14   **77.** $\frac{5}{2}a - \frac{32}{5}b$ **79.** 46, 48   **81.** 30°, 60°, 90°

LESSON 3-9

Try This   **a.** 20   **b.** $\frac{5}{2}$ **c.** $\frac{14}{3}$ **d.** 250 km   **e.** $133\frac{1}{3}$ miles

Exercises   **1.** 1   **3.** $\frac{27}{2}$ **5.** $\frac{18}{5}$ **7.** 25   **9.** $\frac{5}{2}$ **11.** $\frac{55}{9}$ **13.** 24   **15.** 63   **17.** 12   **19.** 25   **21.** $\frac{63}{4}$ **23.** 35   **25.** 40   **27.** $\frac{4}{15}$ minute   **29.** 80   **31.** 24   **33.** 5075   **35.** 35,936   **37.** 12   **39.** 5:9   **41.** 5888 marbles   **43.** 12 meters

Mixed Review   **45.** $-\frac{7}{2}$ or $-3\frac{1}{2}$ **47.** 3   **49.** 12   **51.** ±3   **53.** 0   **55.** $x = \frac{55}{2}$ **57.** $m = \frac{y - b}{x} = \frac{y}{x} - \frac{b}{x}$ **59.** $r = \frac{I}{Pt}$ **61.** $-6x - 16$

LESSON 3-10

Try This   **a.** 0.48   **b.** 0.03   **c.** 1.45   **d.** 0.005   **e.** 75%   **f.** 37.5%   **g.** 490%   **h.** 49.6%   **i.** 0.004%   **j.** 7.5%   **k.** 37.5%   **l.** 18.75   **m.** 6   **n.** 5   **o.** 30%   **p.** 30%

Exercises   **1.** 0.41   **3.** 0.07   **5.** 1.25   **7.** 0.008   **9.** 0.015   **11.** 75%   **13.** 96%   **15.** 33.3%   **17.** 62.5%   **19.** 18.8%   **21.** 25%   **23.** 24%   **25.** 150   **27.** 2.5   **29.** 125%   **31.** 0.8   **33.** 5%   **35.** 5   **37.** 86.4%   **39.** \$1569.23   **41.** 36 cm³; 436 cm³   **43.** 133.3%   **45.** \$20   **47.** 4%   **49.** 20 cm by 33.3 cm   **51.** 62.5%   **53.** Equal. Both earn \$15.50 interest on \$100 over two years.

Mixed Review   **55.** −4.1   **57.** −16   **59.** $10c + 8$ **61.** $5t - 6$ **63.** 0   **65.** −33   **67.** −3

LESSON 3-11

Try This   **a.** $\frac{1}{2}g + g$ or $b + 2b$ **b.** $x + x + 2 + x + 4 = 3x + 6$ **c.** Width is 30 cm; length is 45 cm   **d.** 9, 10   **e.** \$9250

Selected Answers

Exercises **3–5.** Answers may vary. Examples are given.
1. Let c = cost of one CD. $c + (c - 3.50)$ or $2c - 3.50$
Let t = cost of one tape. $t + (t + 3.50)$ or $2t + 3.50$
3. Let e = number of English books. $e + (e - 9)$ or $2e - 9$
Let m = number of math books. $m + (m + 9)$ or $2m + 9$
5. Let p = cost of paperback book. $p + 3(p + 7)$ or $4p + 21$
Let h = cost of hardback book. $3h + (h - 7)$ or $4h - 7$
7. $x + (x + 2) = 2x + 2$ **9.** $x + 2(x + 2) = 3x + 4$
11. $x + (x + 2) + (x + 4) = 3x + 6$
13. $x + \frac{1}{2}(x + 2) + \frac{1}{4}(x + 4) = \frac{7}{4}x + 2$ **15.** 40   **17.** 37, 39
19. 41, 42, 43   **21.** 41, 42, 43; 61, 63, 65   **23.** 18°
25. Amazon 6437 km, Nile 6671 km   **27.** 3 ft, 9 ft, 36 ft
29. $5916.98   **31.** 151 million   **33.** 4, 16   **35.** 19   **37.** $32.03
39. a. The driver owed only $9.10 + (0.09)(9.10) \approx \$9.92$.
b. If the pump registered $10, the driver owed
$10 + (0.09)10 = \$10.90$, less the 9% discount, or
$10.90 - (0.09)(10.90) = \$9.92$.   **41.** $1056

Mixed Review   **43.** $\frac{10}{7}$ **45.** 9   **47.** 4   **49.** 36

LESSON 3-12

Problems   **1.** There will be 72 games played when each team
has played each other team twice.

3. a. 1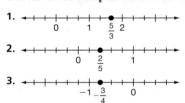

b. 3

c. 5

d. 12

5. The garden's measurements were 10 m by 12 m.
7. Charles and Eva will both be off on a Monday five weeks
later.

CHAPTER 3 WRAP UP

1. -20 **2.** 4   **3.** 25   **4.** $-\frac{8}{7}$
5. $591   **6.** 85°   **7.** 4   **8.** -192 **9.** $-\frac{3}{2}$ **10.** -11 **11.** 27
12. 4   **13.** -3 **14.** 9   **15.** 3   **16.** 3   **17.** 3   **18.** $2n + 6$
19. $5n - 18$ **20.** $\frac{1}{3}n - 6$ **21.** $\frac{1}{2}(n + 10)$ **22.** $2n - 3$
23. $2x + 10$ **24.** 40   **25.** 4 h 10 min or 250 min   **26.** 38
27. 2   **28.** -12 **29.** 6   **30.** 12   **31.** true for all values of x;
an identity   **32.** true for all values of x; an identity   **33.** -1
34. -2.8 **35.** 7   **36.** -3 **37.** $h = \frac{V}{B}$ **38.** $A = \frac{br}{3}$
39. $x = \frac{P - 2w}{2}$ **40.** $A = \frac{3V}{r}$ **41.** 5, -5 **42.** 10, -10
43. 11, -11 **44.** 36   **45.** 10   **46.** 216   **47.** 702 km   **48.** 0.48
49. 0.07   **50.** 1.5   **51.** 33.3%   **52.** 87.5%   **53.** 1.2%
54. 40%   **55.** 250   **56.** $55.25   **57.** 40%   **58.** $2x + x = 3x$
59. $x + x + 2 = 2x + 2$ **60.** 57, 59   **61.** 11 cm, 17 cm

Chapter 4

Skills & Concepts You Need for Chapter 4

1.

2.

3.

4. $<$ **5.** $<$ **6.** $>$ **7.** 3   **8.** -4 **9.** 7   **10.** 8   **11.** 5
12. 1   **13.** $n + n + 2 + n + 4$ **14.** $\frac{1}{2}n + 12$ **15.** $2n - 32$
16. $3n + 2$ **17.** 3   **18.** $\frac{24}{5}$ **19.** $\frac{3}{2}$ **20.** 7   **21.** 24   **22.** $\frac{1}{2}$
23. 15   **24.** 1600

LESSON 4-1

Try This   **a.** (1) Yes   (2) Yes   (3) Yes   (4) No   (5) No
b. (1) Yes   (2) No   (3) No   (4) Yes   (5) No
c.

d.

Exercises   **1. a.** No   **b.** No   **c.** No   **d.** Yes   **3. a.** No   **b.** No
c. Yes   **d.** Yes   **5. a.** No   **b.** No   **c.** Yes   **d.** No   **7. a.** Yes
b. Yes   **c.** Yes   **d.** No
9.

11.

13.

15.  (number line with point at −4, scale showing −4 and 0)

17. (number line with point at 5, scale showing 0 and 5)

19. (number line with point at −3, scale showing −3 and 0)

21. T **23.** F **25.** $s \leq 25$ **27.** $x \leq -2$ **29.** $x < 0$ **31.** $x \leq 7$

33. (number line, open circles at −1 and 3, shaded between; scale −1 0 3)

35. (number line, open circles at 2 and 5, shaded between; scale 0 2 5)

Mixed Review **37.** $-\frac{1}{6}$ **39.** 12 **41.** ±15 **43.** No solution **45.** 6

LESSON 4-2

Try This

a. $x > 2$ (number line, open circle at 2, shaded right; scale 0 2)

b. $x \leq 13$ (number line, closed circle at 13, shaded left; scale 0 13)

c. $x \geq 9$ (number line, closed circle at 9, shaded right; scale 0 9)

d. $x < 2$ (number line, open circle at 2, shaded left; scale 0 2)

e. $y < -\frac{1}{2}$ (number line, open circle at $-\frac{1}{2}$, shaded left; scale −1 $-\frac{1}{2}$ 0)

f. $y \geq \frac{1}{2}$ (number line, closed circle at $\frac{1}{2}$, shaded right; scale 0 $\frac{1}{2}$ 1)

g. $y \leq -3$ (number line, closed circle at −3, shaded left; scale −3 0)

h. $x < -3$ (number line, open circle at −3, shaded left; scale −3 0)

Exercises

1. $x > -5$ (number line, open circle at −5, shaded right; scale −5 0)

3. $y > 3$ (number line, open circle at 3, shaded right; scale 0 3)

5. $x \leq -18$ (number line, closed circle at −18, shaded left; scale −19 −18)

7. $a < -6$ (number line, open circle at −6, shaded left; scale −6 0)

9. $x \leq 16$ (number line, closed circle at 16, shaded left; scale 15 16)

11. $x > 8$ (number line, open circle at 8, shaded right; scale 0 8)

13. $y > -5$ (number line, open circle at −5, shaded right; scale −5 0)

15. $m < 2$ (number line, open circle at 2, shaded left; scale 0 2)

17. $x \leq -3$ **19.** $n < 4$ **21.** $y \leq -11$ **23.** $m \leq \frac{1}{4}$ **25.** $x > \frac{7}{12}$
27. $c \leq -\frac{1}{2}$ **29.** D **31.** $r \geq -13$ **33.** $m \geq 5$ **35.** $y < 6$
37. $a < -8$ **39.** −6 **41.** $-2 - q$ **43.** $7 + 2y$ **45.** Answers may vary. Ex: $x + 7 \leq 2$, $2x - 6 \leq -16$ **47.** False
49. $y \leq 4$ **51. a.** $x \leq 5$ **b.** $x \geq -3$ **c.** $x < \frac{-3}{2}$ or $x > \frac{-3}{2}$
d. $x \geq y$ **e.** $x \leq -y$ **f.** $-x > y$ or $-x < y$

Mixed Review **53.** 9 **55.** $-\frac{1}{21}$ **57.** ±25 **59.** 5 **61.** $2x + 3$
63. 42 oz of peanuts

LESSON 4-3

Try This

a. $x < 8$ (number line, open circle at 8, shaded left; scale 0 8)

b. $y \geq 32$ (number line, closed circle at 32, shaded right; scale 0 32)

c. $t < 28$ (number line, open circle at 28, shaded left; scale 0 28)

d. $s > 9$ (number line, open circle at 9, shaded right; scale 0 9)

e. $x \leq -6$ (number line, closed circle at −6, shaded left; scale −6 0)

f. $y > -\frac{13}{5}$ (number line, open circle at $-\frac{13}{5}$, shaded right; scale $-\frac{13}{5}$ −2 0)

g. $t > 5$ (number line, open circle at 5, shaded right; scale 0 5)

h. $n < -2$ (number line, open circle at −2, shaded left; scale −2 0)

i. $y \leq -\frac{1}{2}$ (number line, closed circle at $-\frac{1}{2}$, shaded left; scale −1 $-\frac{1}{2}$ 0)

j. $x > -\frac{1}{18}$ (number line, open circle at $-\frac{1}{18}$, shaded right; scale −1 $-\frac{1}{18}$ 0)

k. $x \geq -\frac{5}{16}$ (number line, closed circle at $-\frac{5}{16}$, shaded right; scale −1 $-\frac{5}{16}$ 0)

l. $y \leq \frac{3}{28}$ (number line, closed circle at $\frac{3}{28}$, shaded left; scale 0 $\frac{3}{28}$ 1)

Exercises

1. $x < 7$ (number line, open circle at 7, shaded left; scale 0 7)

3. $y \leq 9$ (number line, closed circle at 9, shaded left; scale 0 9)

5. $y > 12$ (number line, open circle at 12, shaded right; scale 0 12)

7. $x < \frac{13}{17}$ (number line, open circle at $\frac{13}{7}$, shaded left; scale 0 1 $\frac{13}{7}$)

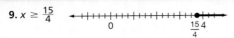

9. $x \geq \frac{15}{4}$

11. $y \leq \frac{1}{2}$

13. $y \geq -3$

15. $x < -3$

17. $y \geq -\frac{2}{5}$ **19.** $x \geq -6$ **21.** $y \geq -4$ **23.** $y < -60$
25. $x > 2$ **27.** $y \leq 2$ **29.** $x > \frac{17}{2}$ **31.** $y \leq \frac{31}{8}$ **33.** $y > -\frac{1}{21}$
35. $x \leq 0.9$ **37.** $x > -5.0625$ **39.** $x < -3$ **41.** $t < 0$
43. $m \leq 4$ **45.** False; $-2 > -3$ but $4 < 9$.

Mixed Review **47. a.** No **b.** No **c.** Yes **d.** No **e.** Yes
49. $11x + 5$ **51.** $8x$ **53.** -20

LESSON 4-4

Try This **a.** $x > 2$ **b.** $a \geq -1$ **c.** $m > 6$

Exercises **1.** $x < 8$ **3.** $x \leq 6$ **5.** $x < -3$ **7.** $x \geq -2$
9. $y < -3$ **11.** $x > -3$ **13.** $y < -\frac{10}{3}$ **15.** $x \leq 7$
17. $x > -10$ **19.** $y < 2$ **21.** $y \geq 3$ **23.** $y > -2$
25. $y > -2$ **27.** $y \leq \frac{33}{7}$ **29.** $x < \frac{9}{5}$ **31.** C **33.** $z < \frac{65}{16}$
35. $y > 1.8$ **37.** $x > 2$ **39.** $x \geq -25$ **41.** $x < \frac{30}{7}$
43. $b \geq -4$ **45.** $y \leq 10$ **47.** $t \leq -\frac{19}{3}$ **49.** $d < \frac{3}{22}$
51. $w > 1.5$ **53. a.** Using the addition property
b. Simplifying **c.** Using the addition property
d. Simplifying **e.** Using the multiplication property
f. Simplifying **55. a.** Using the multiplication property
b. Using the distributive property **c.** Simplifying
d. Using the addition property **e.** Simplifying **f.** Using the
multiplication property **g.** Simplifying **57.** Sometimes
59. In the second step the student added 1 to the right side,
but subtracted 1 from the left side. **61.** $x \leq -4a$ **63.** $x \geq \frac{3y}{2}$
65. $x < c + 3$ **67.** $x \geq y$ and $x \leq y$, so $x = y$ **69.** $x^2 < |x|$

Mixed Review **71.** 3 **73.** 18 **75.** $z < -3$ **77.** 4
79. $\frac{9}{5}$, 180% **81.** $\frac{3}{5}$, 60% **83.** $M - 2$ **85.** $3L$

LESSON 4-5

Try This **a.** $x \geq 8$ **b.** $t < 12$ **c.** $x \leq 4\frac{1}{2}$ **d.** $n \geq 0$
e. $n - 3 > 4$ **f.** $p \geq 10$; at least 10 **g.** $s \geq 94$; at least 94
h. 16, 17

Exercises **1.** $y > 3$ **3.** $h \geq 4\frac{5}{6}$ **5.** $x \geq 0$ **7.** $x + 2 > 9$
9. $\frac{x}{2} \leq 6$ **11.** $2x - 4 \leq 18$ **13.** $3x + 2 \leq 11$ **15.** 97
17. 9, 18 **19.** 0, 2, 4, 6; 2, 4, 6, 8; 4, 6, 8, 10 **21.** $A > 12$,

$D > 15$; Armando worked more than 12 hours, and Drew
worked more than 15 hours. **23.** $w > 14$ cm **25.** $b > 4$ cm
27. $x < 57$ **29.** Cut all three links of one section (30¢). Use
each link to join the remaining 4 sections, requiring 3 welds
(60¢). The total cost will be 90¢.

Mixed Review **31.** $-\frac{5}{6}$ **33.** $-\frac{1}{15}$ **35.** -1 **37.** $a \geq -4$
39. D **41.** B

Connections: Deductive Reasoning
1. If we can't play
soccer, then it's raining. False. Counterexample: It is a sunny
day but we can't play soccer because no one can find the ball.
3. If a number is even, then it is divisible by 4. False.
Counterexample: 10 is even and is not divisible by 4. **5.** If
$x < 10$, then $x < 5$. False. Counterexample: 7 is less than 10
and is not less than 5.

Connections: Inductive Reasoning
1. 625
3. Counterexamples may vary. Ex: $\frac{1}{2} \cdot \frac{1}{3} = \frac{1}{6}$, and $\frac{1}{6} < \frac{1}{2}, \frac{1}{6} < \frac{1}{3}$

LESSON 4-6

Problems **1.** William coaches racquetball. Carrie coaches
tennis. Lester coaches volleyball. Rosa coaches basketball.
3. The student earned $283.50 for painting the house
numbers. **5.** Here are two ways the five tiles could be
arranged.

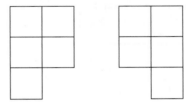

7. Nellie lives in Jackson; Meg lives in Springstown; Scott lives
in Mowetown; and Jeff lives in Newton.

CHAPTER 4 WRAP UP

1. a. Yes **b.** Yes **c.** Yes **d.** No
2. a. Yes **b.** No **c.** Yes **d.** Yes
3.

4.

5.

6. $y > -2$

7. $b \geq \frac{9}{4}$

8. $a < 6$

9. $x > -4$ **10.** $a \le \frac{1}{6}$ **11.** $y \le 20$

12. $x < 5$

13. $b \le -7$

14. $y < -\frac{3}{2}$

15. $y < 7$ **16.** $a \le -\frac{13}{2}$ **17.** $y < 3$ **18.** $y < 3$ **19.** $x > -\frac{11}{7}$
20. $a \le \frac{11}{3}$ **21.** 120 lbs **22.** $T \ge 87$ **23.** 12, 14, 16
24. 1, 3, 5, 7; 3, 5, 7, 9; 5, 7, 9, 11

CHAPTERS 1–4 CUMULATIVE REVIEW

1. $\frac{3}{2}$ **3.** 8 **5.** $y + 12$ **7.** $\frac{3x}{4z}$ **9.** 16 **11.** 10,000 **13.** 1000
15. $3 \cdot (y \cdot z)$ **17.** $15x + 25y + 10z$ **19.** $6(9y + 1)$
21. $15b + 22y$ **23.** $2w - 4$ **25.** $\{9\}$ **27.** $\{6\}$ **29.** Both sides
were multiplied by 7. **31.** $p = 40.8$ m **33.** $>$ **35.** 14 **37.** $>$

39.

41. 3 **43.** 1 **45.** $3 - 10x$ **47.** 420 **49.** -105 **51.** $-\frac{32}{125}$
53. $-12x - 8$ **55.** $5x + 5$ **57.** $-2(x + 4)$
59. $-9d - 3a + 1$ **61.** $-2x - y$ **63.** $8x$
65. Transitive property **67.** $3\frac{5}{6}$ **69.** 12 **71.** $-\frac{12}{5}$ **73.** 7
75. $-3\frac{1}{3}$ or $-3.3\overline{3}$ **77.** $r = \frac{L}{2h}$ **79.** 9, -9 **81.** $\frac{32}{3}$ **83.** 56.9 L
85. 50 **87.** $1500 **89.** No **91.** Yes
93. $x \ge \frac{5}{6}$

95. $x > -6$

97. $l > 20$ ft, $w > 16$ ft

Chapter 5

Skills & Concepts You Need for Chapter 5 **1.** 8^4
2. $12b^3$ **3.** 11 **4.** 48 **5.** $3s + 3t + 3w$ **6.** $-7x - 28$
7. $9x + 13y$ **8.** $9b^2 + 9b + 8$ **9.** 30 **10.** $-\frac{5}{16}$ **11.** 8
12. $-\frac{3}{2}$ **13.** $-4x + 7y - 2$ **14.** $-12r - 7p + 9s$
15. $-4y - 2$ **16.** $-19b + 8$

LESSON 5-1

Try This **a.** 5^6 **b.** a^8 **c.** y^{10} **d.** m^5n^8 **e.** 7^4 **f.** a^5 **g.** m^2
h. x^2y **i.** $\frac{1}{2^2}$ **j.** $\frac{1}{y^4}$ **k.** $\frac{3}{c^2}$ **l.** $\frac{1}{16}$ **m.** 1 **n.** 1

Exercises **1.** 2^7 **3.** 8^{14} **5.** x^7 **7.** n^4 **9.** x^4 **11.** m^7 **13.** x^7
15. a^9 **17.** a^8b^7 **19.** $p^3q^4r^5$ **21.** $5^2s^4t^4$ **23.** 7^3 **25.** 8^6
27. 1 **29.** y^4 **31.** 1 **33.** 1 **35.** a^2b^3 **37.** $4x^2$ **39.** $\frac{1}{3^2}$
41. $\frac{1}{x^4}$ **43.** $\frac{3}{a}$ **45.** $\frac{1}{2y}$ **47.** $\frac{5}{c^4}$ **49.** $\frac{1}{3a}$ **51.** $\frac{1}{16}$ **53.** $\frac{1}{125}$ **55.** 1
57. 1 **59.** 64 **61.** 9 **63.** $\frac{1}{16}$ **65.** $-\frac{1}{8}$ **67. (a)** x^{-4} **(b)** $\frac{1}{x^4}$
69. (a) a^{-4} **(b)** $\frac{1}{a^4}$ **71.** 256 **73.** 64 **75. a.** $\frac{1}{2}, \frac{1}{4}, \frac{1}{8}, \frac{1}{16}$
b. $2^{-1}, 2^{-2}, 2^{-3}, 2^{-4}$ **c.** 2 raised to the opposite of the
figure number **d.** 2^{-10} **77.** $x^5 \cdot x \cdot x^2 = x^{5+1+2} = x^8$
79. 256 **81.** b^{-2} or $\frac{1}{b^2}$ **83.** 256 **85.** x^2 **87.** No; let
$a = 1, b = 2, m = 3, 27 \ne 9$ **89.** 2^6 **91.** 2^{13} **93.** 3^{10} **95.** $\frac{b^3}{a^3}$

Mixed Review **97.** $-(m + 3n)$ **99.** $12a^2 + 14a$
101. $ac - 8$ **103.** 369 **105.** 5 **107.** $27 or less

LESSON 5-2

Try This **a.** 5^{12} **b.** 2^{10} **c.** a^{18} **d.** n^{16} **e.** $9y^2$ **f.** $1296m^4$
g. $8a^9$ **h.** $16x^6$ **i.** $256y^{12}$ **j.** $243x^{20}y^{35}z^{30}$ **k.** $49x^{18}y^{12}$
l. $-y^{45}$ **m.** $\frac{y^6}{4}$ **n.** $\frac{a^{15}}{27}$ **o.** $\frac{x^4}{y^6}$

Exercises **1.** 2^{10} **3.** 5^6 **5.** y^{45} **7.** m^{32} **9.** a^{30} **11.** p^{100}
13. $81y^4$ **15.** $343y^3$ **17.** $25m^2$ **19.** $2401x^4$ **21.** $4m^4$
23. $125y^{12}$ **25.** $-216t^6$ **27.** $512k^{12}$ **29.** $4x^{16}y^6$
31. $-8x^6y^{12}$ **33.** $256x^8y^{12}z^4$ **35.** $\frac{27}{a^6}$ **37.** $\frac{x^8}{256}$ **39.** $\frac{m^{12}}{n^6}$
41. $\frac{1728}{125}$ **43.** $\frac{x^3y^6}{z^3}$ **45.** $\frac{4x^4y^{12}}{25}$ **47.** $-\frac{64m^6n^{15}}{27}$ **49.** x^{30}
51. $-\frac{x^3}{27y^3}$ **53.** $\frac{x^6y^3}{z^3}$ **55.** $\frac{9a^4b^8}{16c^6}$ **57.** $54n^7$ **59.** $19a^2$
61. $8z^8$ **63.** $6z^7 - 25z^6$ **65.** $18c^9$ **67.** $-432a^{12}b^{14}$ **69.** B
71. x^{3a+2b} **73.** x^{2a+1} **75.** $x^{3a}y^{3a-9}$ **77.** $x^{a+4}y^3$
79. $a = 11$ **81.** $a = \frac{10}{3}$

Mixed Review **83.** $12 - x$ **85.** $\frac{8}{5c}$ **87.** $\frac{2}{m}$ **89.** $m = -1$

Connections: Geometry **1.** $(2x)^3$ or $8x^3$ **3.** $(8x)^3$ or $512x^3$

LESSON 5-3

Try This **a.** $-15x$ **b.** $-m^2$ **c.** y^2 **d.** x^5 **e.** $12p^7q^5$
f. $-8x^{11}y^9$ **g.** $14y^8$ **h.** $-21a^{13}$ **i.** x^3 **j.** $\frac{3}{2m^3}$ **k.** xy^3 **l.** $-4xy$

Exercises **1.** $42x^2$ **3.** x^4 **5.** $-x^8$ **7.** $6a^6$ **9.** $28t^8$
11. $-18g^7$ **13.** $-6x^{11}$ **15.** $25n^8$ **17.** x^7y^6 **19.** $8a^8b^{10}$
21. $6y^8$ **23.** $40m^9$ **25.** x^4 **27.** $2x^3$ **29.** 3 **31.** $\frac{5}{a^4}$ **33.** $-\frac{1}{2}h$
35. $\frac{1}{4}x^5$ **37.** -4 **39.** $3x$ **41.** $5x^2y^3$ **43.** $-4b^6$ **45.** $\frac{-3p^2}{r}$
47. $\frac{-5a^6}{7b^2}$ **49.** x^{11} **51.** a^{18} **53.** $18x^8$ **55.** $36x^{18}$ **57.** $6x^6y^6$
59. a^9b^{14} **61.** $4x$ **63.** y^2 **65.** $\frac{a^2}{3b}$ **67.** $\frac{1}{2mn^6}$ **69.** It must be
equal to one. **71.** $\frac{-32}{m^3}$ **73.** $-\frac{3}{m^{15}}$ **75.** 15 **77.** $\frac{5r^6}{qs}$

Selected Answers

Mixed Review **79.** $4y^2 + 7x$ **81.** $-2m$ **83.** $9a - 2b$
85. 0.0004 **87.** $x < -7$ **89.** $x > -1$

LESSON 5-4

Try This **a.** 1250 **b.** 700,000 **c.** 0.0048 **d.** 0.00018
e. 3.2×10^3 **f.** 1.39×10^5 **g.** 3.07×10^{-2}
h. 2.004×10^{-1} **i.** 5.5×10^{-15} **j.** 2.0×10^3

Exercises **1.** 5543 **3.** 0.00235 **5.** 57,000 **7.** 0.000034
9. 0.0006 **11.** 0.003007 **13.** 4.25×10^2 **15.** 1.24×10^4
17. 4.5×10^{-2} **19.** 1.25×10^5 **21.** 5.2×10^6
23. 5.6×10^{-6} **25.** 1.4×10^7 **27.** 3.2×10^{11}
29. 1.0×10^{-10} **31.** 2.0×10^5 **33.** 4.2×10^{-2}
35. 5.0×10^1 **37.** $4.08 \times 10^4 = 40,800$
39. $8.32 \times 10^{-8} = 0.0000000832$ **41–47.** Precision of answers
may vary. **41.** 1.5×10^8 km $= 150,000,000$ km
43. Answers may vary. **45.** C **47.** $1.5 \times 10^4 = 15,000$ s
49. 8×10^2 **51.** 2.5×10^{-1}

Mixed Review **53.** $3(3a + 2)$ **55.** $4(3m - n)$ **57.** $7x - 6$
59. $a - 15$

LESSON 5-5

Try This **a.** No **b.** Yes; binomial **c.** Terms: $5y^3$, $6y$, -3.
Coefficients: 5, 6, -3 **d.** Terms: m^4, $-3m$, -6.
Coefficients: 1, -3, -6 **e.** Terms: $-3m^4n^2$, $-m^2n$, $2n$.
Coefficients: -3, -1, 2 **f.** $2x - 10x^3 - 24$ **g.** $6m^2 - m - 7$
h. $4x^2y^2 - y^2 + y^3 - 1$ **i.** $b^5 + 5ab^3$ **j.** 4, 2, 1, 0; 4
k. 11, 7, 7, 1; 11

Exercises **1.** No **3.** Yes; binomial **5.** No **7.** Yes; binomial
9. Yes; monomial **11.** Yes; trinomial **13.** Yes; monomial
15. Terms: $-4m^9$, $6m$, -1. Coefficients: -4, 6, -1
17. Terms: $2x^2y$, $5xy^2$, $-6y^4$. Coefficients: 2, 5, -6
19. Terms: $8p^3$, $2pq$, -4. Coefficients: 8, 2, -4
21. Terms: $-3n^6$, $3n$, -3. Coefficients: -3, 3, -3
23. Terms: x^8y^6, $-2x^6y^6$, $8x^4y^7$, $-4xy^8$.
Coefficients: 1, -2, 8, -4 **25.** $-3x$ **27.** $10x^2$ **29.** $-x^3 - 5x$
31. $3x^4 + 7$ **33.** $3x^3 - 3$ **35.** $4a^4$ **37.** $3xy^2 + 5x^2y$
39. $6ab^2 + 3ab - 5a^2b$ **41.** The student should have
subtracted the coefficients of the like terms.
$7x^3 - x^3 = 7x^3 - 1x^3 = (7 - 1)x^3 = 6x^3$ **43.** 2, 1, 0; 2

45. 2, 1, 6, 4; 6 **47.** 9, 9, 4; 9 **49.** $\frac{3}{4}x^5 - 2x - 5$

51. $\frac{7}{6}a^4 - 4a^2 - 3$ **53.** $14y + 17$ $11\frac{1}{2}a + 10$

55. $n(n + 2) - 3 = n^2 + 2n - 3$

Mixed Review **57.** c^{10} **59.** x^7y^{11} **61.** $9c^{-4}$ or $\frac{9}{c^4}$ **63.** $-\frac{1}{12}$
65. $\frac{11}{8}$ **67.** $a \geq 3$

LESSON 5-6

Try This **a.** $6x^7 + 3x^5 - 2x^4 + 4x^3 + 5x^2 + x$
b. $7x^5 - 5x^4 + 2x^3 + 4x^2 - 3$
c. $-14x^7 - 10x^3y^2 + 7x^2y^3 - 14y$ **d.** $-2m^2 - 3m + 2$
e. $3m^3y - 6m^2y$ **f.** -19 **g.** -14 **h.** 56 **i.** 196 ft
j. $\approx 23.9¢$ per mile **k.** 3.83 L

Exercises **1.** $x^5 + 6x^3 + 2x^2 + x + 1$
3. $15x^9 + 7x^8 + 5x^3 - x^2 + x$
5. $-5y^8 - y^7 + 9y^6 + 8y^3 - 7y^2$
7. $m^6 + m^4$ **9.** $13m^3 - 9m + 8$ **11.** $-5m^2 + 9mp$

13. $12m^4 - 2m + \frac{1}{4}$ **15.** 98 **17.** 78 **19.** 9 **21.** -448

23. -18 **25.** 19 **27.** -12 **29.** -13 **31.** 5 **33.** 2 **35.** 448.6
37. $x^2 - 16$ **39.** $a = 5$ **41.** 24 **43.** $a = 0.4$, $b = -40$,
$2ax = -b$, $2(0.4)x = -(-40)$, $0.8x = 40$, $x = 50$. The age with
the lowest daily accidents is age 50.

Mixed Review **45.** $\frac{x^9}{8}$ **47.** $\frac{3c^3}{a^3}$ **49.** 0.007662

LESSON 5-7

Try This **a.** $2x^2 - 4$; $6x + 3$; $2x^2 + 6x - 1$
b. $(2x + 1) + (x^2 - x + 4) + (3x^2 - 5)$; $4x^2 + x$
c. $x^2 + 7x + 3$ **d.** $24m^4 + 5m^3 + m^2 + 1$ **e.** $2a^2b - 7a - 1$
f. $8n^3 - m^3n^2 - 7n - 3m - 5$
g. $m^4 - 2m^3 - 11m^2 + 5m - 14$ **h.** $-2x^4y^3 + x^2 - 3xy + 7$

Exercises **1.** $2x^2 + 8x - 2$ **3.** $3x^2 + 5x + 10$ **5.** $-x + 5$
7. $-4x^4 + 6x^3 + 6x^2 + 2x + 4$ **9.** $12x^2 + 6$
11. $5x^4 - 2x^3 - 7x^2 - 5x$
13. $9x^8 + 8x^7 - 3x^4 + 2x^2 - 2x + 5$
15. $-3cd^4 + 3d^2 + 4cd$ **17.** $5a^4 + 3a^3 - a^2 + 5a + 2$
19. $7y^5 - y^3 + 6y^2 + 4$ **21.** $-2h^3 - 2h^2k + 3hk + 4$
23. $12x^2y + 7xy^2 - 2xy + 5$ **25. a.** $3x^2 + x^2 + x^2 + 4x =$
$5x^2 + 4x$ **b.** 57 **c.** 352 **27. a.** $n + 5$, $n + 10$
b. $n - 2$, $n + 3$, $n + 8$ **c.** $3n + 9$ **d.** 20 **e.** 20, 25, 30
f. $\frac{20}{5} = 4$, $\frac{25}{5} = 5$, $\frac{30}{5} = 6$; 18, 23, 28; $18 + 23 + 28 = 69$
29. Answers may vary. Some differences are that coefficients
of polynomials cannot be carried and that adding polynomials
can involve adding negative coefficients.
31. $(ax + b) + (cx + d) = (a + c)x + (b + d)$;
$(cx + d) + (ax + b) = (c + a)x + (d + b) =$
$(a + c)x + (b + d)$
Addition of binomials is commutative. **33.** See 31 above.

Mixed Review **35.** Additive inverse **37.** Commutative
property of multiplication **39.** Commutative property of
addition **41.** $18a^7$ **43.** $12m^2n^2$ **45.** $y(xz + 5 - 9z)$

LESSON 5-8

Try This **a.** $-12x^4 + 3x^2 - 4x$
b. $13x^6y^4 - 2x^4y + 3x^2 - xy + \frac{5}{13}$ **c.** $5x^4 - 2x^2 + 5$
d. $-5m^3 + 2m + 8$ **e.** $4a^3 - 14a^2b^4 + 5ab + 2a + 2$
f. $2x^3 + 5x^2 - 2x - 5$ **g.** $-ab^2 + 4ab - 4a - 4$

Exercises 1. $5x$ **3.** $x^2 - 10x + 2$ **5.** $-12x^4y + 3x^3 - 3$
7. $2x^2 + 14$ **9.** $-2x^5 - 6x^4 + x + 2$ **11.** $9b^2 + 9b - 8$
13. $7m^3 - 3m - 11$ **15.** $3y^4 + 8y^3 - 5y - 3$
17. $6v^4u + 9v^2 - 7$
19. $9mn^5 + n^4 + mn^4 - 3mn^3 + 3n^2 + 1$ **21.** $3x + 6$
23. $4c^3 - 3c^2 + c + 1$ **25.** $11x^4 + 12x^3 - 9x^2 - 8x$
27. $-4m^5 + 9m^4 + 6m^2 + 16m + 6$ **29.** $x^4y^2 + x^2y$
31. $y - 9$ **33.** $11a^2 - 18a - 4$ **35.** $-10y^2 - 2y - 10$
37. $-3xy^4 - y^3 + 5y - 2$ **39.** $2x + 1$ **41.** $2x^2 - 2x + 8$
43. No, $-3(-x)^2 = -3x^2$

Mixed Review 45. 1.594×10^3 **47.** 9.361×10^4
49. Terms: $5n^4m$, $7n^2m^2$, $-2m$, 3 Coefficients: 5, 7, -2, 3;
Factors: 5, n^4 and m; 7, n^2 and m^2; -2 and m; 3 **51.** 3

LESSON 5-9

Try This a. $8x^2 + 16x$ **b.** $-15a^5 + 6a^3 - 21a^2$
c. $40st^4 - 20s^3 - 45st - 55s$ **d.** $x^2 + 7x + 12$
e. $x^2 - 2x - 15$ **f.** $2x^2 + 9x + 4$ **g.** $2x^3 - 4x^2 - 3x + 6$
h. $12x^5 + 10x^3 + 6x^2 + 5$ **i.** $y^6 - 49$
j. $-2x^8 + 2x^6 - x^5 + x^3$ **k.** $-6a^2 - 14ab - 4b^2$
l. $2xy^3 - 8xy$ **m.** $3r^3s + 2r^3 + 6r^2s^3 + 4r^2s^2$
n. $5x^2 - 17x - 12$ **o.** $6y^3 - 10y^2 - 9y + 15$
p. $6a^2 - ab - b^2$ **q.** $18m^3 - 6m^2n^2 + 3mn - n^3$
r. $4p^2q^2 + 3p^3q - p^4$ **s.** $\frac{1}{4}r^4s^2 - s^2$

Exercises 1. $-3x^2 + 15x$ **3.** $12x^3 + 24x^2$ **5.** $-6m^4 - 6m^2x$
7. $3x^6 + 15x^3$ **9.** $18y^6 + 24y^5$ **11.** $6x^3 + 8x^2 - 6x$
13. $15a^4 + 30a^3 - 35a^2$ **15.** $-8y^9 - 8y^8 + 4y^7 - 20y^6$
17. $-7h^4k^6 + 7h^4k^4 + 7h^4k^3 - 7h^4k$
19. $-10a^9b + 2a^3 - 24a^2b$ **21.** $x^3 + x^2 + 3x + 3$
23. $x^4 + x^3 + 2x + 2$ **25.** $a^2 - a - 6$ **27.** $9x^2 + 15x + 6$
29. $5x^2 + 4x - 12$ **31.** $9x^2 - 1$ **33.** $4x^2 - 6xy + 2y^2$
35. $x^2 - \frac{1}{16}$ **37.** $x^2 - 0.01$ **39.** $2x^3 + 2x^2 + 6x + 6$
41. $-2x^2 + 13x - 6$ **43.** $x^2 + 14xy + 49y^2$
45. $6x^7 + 18x^5 + 4x^2 + 12$ **47.** $8x^6 + 65x^3 + 8$
49. $4x^3 - 12x^2 + 3x - 9$ **51.** $4x^6 + 4x^5 + x^4 + x^3$
53. $a^2b^2 - 9b^4$ **55.** $a^2 + 2ab + b^2$ **57.** $4x^2 + 12x + 9$
59. $84y^2 - 30y$ **61.** $m^2 - 28$ **63.** $2x + 1$
65. The answer is correct. **67.** The first term should be $-2x^5$.
The third term should be $6x^3$. The correct answer is
$-2x^5 - 6x^4 + 6x^3 - 4x^2$ **69.** $V = 4x^3 - 48x^2 + 144x$;
$S = -4x^2 + 144$ **71. a.** $2x^2 - 18x + 28$ **b.** 0
73. a. $2x^2 - 112$ **b.** $-6x$ **75.** 2

Mixed Review 77. $\frac{n+3}{2}$ **79.** $3(7-n)$ **81.** 7 **83.** -2

LESSON 5-10

Try This a. $x^2 - 4$ **b.** $x^4 - 49$ **c.** $9t^2 - 25$ **d.** $4x^6 - y^2$
e. $x^2 + 4x + 4$ **f.** $y^2 - 18y + 81$ **g.** $16x^2 - 40x + 25$
h. $a^2 - 8a + 16$ **i.** $25x^4 + 40x^2 + 16$ **j.** $16x^4 - 24x^3 + 9x^2$

Exercises 1. $x^2 - 16$ **3.** $d^2 - 36$ **5.** $36 - m^2$ **7.** $4x^2 - 1$
9. $16a^2 - 49$ **11.** $16x^4 - 9$ **13.** $9x^8 - 4$ **15.** $x^{12} - x^4$
17. $49c^2 - 4d^2$ **19.** $36t^2 - s^2$ **21.** $x^2 + 4x + 4$
23. $t^2 - 6t + 9$ **25.** $4x^2 - 4x + 1$ **27.** $16a^2 - 24ab + 9b^2$
29. $16s^2 + 40st + 25t^2$ **31.** $x^2 - \frac{1}{2}x + \frac{1}{16}$
33. $4x^2 + 28x + 49$ **35.** $9x^2 - 4y^2$ **37.** $25x^4 - 10x^2 + 1$
39. $4x^2 - \frac{4}{5}x + \frac{1}{25}$ **41.** $4x^6 - 0.09$ **43. a.** ac, ad, bc, bd
b. $ac + ad + bc + bd$ **c.** $ac + ad + bc + bd$, equal
45. 10, 11, 12 **47.** D **49. a.** Additive inverses
b. Both $= x^2 - 2xy + y^2$ **c.** $a^2 = (-a)^2$ for any a
51. $(5a + 7)(5a - 7)$

Mixed Review 53. $20x - 13$ **55.** $27m^{15}$ **57.** $30y^7$ **59.** 6
61. 11 **63.** 68

LESSON 5-11

Try This a. $b^4 + 3b^3 + b^2 + 15b - 20$
b. $6x^2 - xy - 12y^2 + 15x + 20y$
c. $3a^4 + 13a^3 - 3a^2 + 18a + 4$
d. $-20x^4 - 11x^3 - 44x^2 - 30x - 16$
e. $8n^5 + 4n^4 - 20n^3 - 16n^2 + 7n + 10$
f. $3x^7y^2 + 3x^6y^3 - 4x^5 - 4x^4y - 5x^3 - 5x^2y$
g. $x^2 + 11x + 30$ **h.** $x^2 - 16$ **i.** $-8x^5 + 20x^4 + 40x^2$
j. $81x^4 + 18x^2 + 1$ **k.** $4x^2 + 6x - 40$ **l.** $3x^3 - 14x^2 - x + 6$

Exercises 1. $x^3 - 1$ **3.** $4x^3 + 14x^2 + 8x + 1$
5. $3y^4 - 6y^3 - 7y^2 + 18y - 6$ **7.** $x^6 + 2x^5 - x^3$ **9.** $a^4 - b^4$
11. $x^4 - x^2 - 2x - 1$ **13.** $4x^4 + 8x^3 - 9x^2 - 10x + 8$
15. $6t^4 + t^3 - 16t^2 - 7t + 4$
17. $-4x^4 + 6x^3 - 2x^2 - 13x + 10$ **19.** $x^9 - x^5 + 2x^3 - x$
21. $b^4 - 1$ **23.** $x^4y - 2x^3y - 4x^2y + 9y$ **25.** $x^2 - 16x + 64$
27. $x^2 - 64$ **29.** $x^2 - 3x - 40$ **31.** $4x^3 + 24x^2 - 12x$
33. $4x^4 - 2x^2 + \frac{1}{4}$ **35.** $36a^6 - 1$ **37.** $-9x^2 + 4$
39. $36x^8 + 48x^4 + 16$ **41.** $-6x^5 - 48x^3 + 54x^2$
43. $12q^5 + 6q^3 - 2q^2 - 1$ **45.** $\frac{9}{16}x^2 + \frac{9}{4}x + 2$
47. $4x^3 + 13x^2 + 22x + 15$ **49.** $3x^5 - 14x^4 + 13x^3 - 20x^2$
51. $x^3 + 3x^2y + 3xy^2 + y^3$
53. $x^5 + 5x^4y + 10x^3y^2 + 10x^2y^3 + 5xy^4 + y^5$
55. $x^4 + x^3 + x^2 + x + 1$ **57.** $x^5 + x^4 + x^3 + x^2 + x + 1$
59. Answers may vary. Ex: $(x^2 - x + 2)(x + 1)$

Mixed Review 61. $x^2 + 6x + 9$ **63.** $-7a$
65. $-3y^2 + 9y - 1$ **67.** 21,000,000 **69.** 7, 3, 0; 7 **71.** 9 ft

Application 1. $14.938\% \approx 15\%$
3. 2.4747 Liters ≈ 2.5 Liters

LESSON 5-12

Problems 1. Job B will pay more money for the 10-year
period. **3.** Seven people bought the stamp, each paying $29.
5. The company would have 204,775 salespeople after 12 weeks.

Selected Answers

CHAPTER 5 WRAP UP

1. 7^6 **2.** y^8 **3.** x^{11} **4.** a^5b^5 **5.** x^8y^{10} **6.** $l^3m^{13}n^6$ **7.** 7^2
8. a^5 **9.** x^7y^4 **10.** $\frac{1}{7^3}$ **11.** $\frac{1}{y^2}$ **12.** 1 **13.** 5^6 **14.** 3^{16}

15. x^{12} **16.** a^9 **17.** $9a^2$ **18.** $8b^3$ **19.** $8x^9$ **20.** $64p^6$

21. $9x^4y^2z^8$ **22.** $-8x^{18}y^6$ **23.** n^{30} **24.** $\frac{y^{12}}{81}$ **25.** $6a^2$

26. $-6x^3$ **27.** $-20b^3c^6$ **28.** $10y^8$ **29.** $15w^3z^7$ **30.** $32x^3y^4$
31. a^3 **32.** $-n^4$ **33.** $-3x^2y^3$ **34.** $4m^7n$ **35.** $-6b^7c^4$
36. $4x^2y^2$ **37.** 3250 **38.** 0.0057 **39.** 2.426×10^6
40. 4.5×10^{-5} **41.** $4x^3 + 4$ **42.** $-3x^5 + 25$ **43.** 5, 3, 0; 5
44. 2, 1, 0; 2 **45.** $7x^5 - 2x^4 + 3x^2 - 2x + 5$
46. $-4x^5 - 2x^3y^2 + 7x^2y^3 + 3y$ **47.** $-x^5 + 10x^4 - 7x - 1$
48. $8x^4y^3 + 3x^3 - 7xy^2 + 6y$ **49.** 25 **50.** 16
51. $7x^3 + 4x^2 + 4x$ **52.** $6x^4 - 6x^3 + 3x^2 + x - 9$
53. $3x^5 - x^4 - 4x^3 + 3x^2 - 3$ **54.** $3a^3 + 7a^2b - 4ab^2$
55. $4y^3 + 14$ **56.** $2x^2 - 4x - 6$
57. $x^5 + 8x^4 - 3x^3 - 2x^2 + 8$ **58.** $-2y^2 - 2y + 11$
59. $-x^5 + x^4 - 5x^3 - 2x^2 + 2x$ **60.** $15x^2 + 18x$
61. $15x^6 - 40x^5 + 50x^4 + 10x^3$ **62.** $x^2 - 3x - 28$
63. $a^2 - 9$ **64.** $b^4 + 5b^2 + 6$ **65.** $6x^4 + 15x^3y - 6x^2 - 15xy$
66. $x^2 - 9$ **67.** $a^2 - 64$ **68.** $4y^2 - 9$ **69.** $9x^4 - 16$
70. $4y^2 - 49x^2$ **71.** $4 - 9y^2$ **72.** $a^2 + 8a + 16$
73. $9x^2 + 36x + 36$ **74.** $12x^3 - 23x^2 + 13x - 2$
75. $2a^4 + 3a^3 - 10a^2 - 12a + 8$
76. $4b^4 + 6b^3 - 14b^2 + 11b - 3$
77. $x^7 + x^5 - 3x^4 + 3x^3 - 2x^2 + 5x - 3$

Chapter 6

Skills & Concepts You Need for Chapter 6

1. $6(x + y)$ **2.** $24(w + z)$ **3.** $4(y + 7 + 3z)$ **4.** $2n + 10$
5. $2(n + 6)$ **6.** 1 **7.** $\frac{4}{3}$ **8.** 80 cm, 60 cm **9.** $-12x^{13}$

10. $-24x^3y^6$ **11.** $36x^2 + 63x$ **12.** $18st^4 - 6s^3 - 9st - 18s$
13. $3x^2 - 13x - 56$ **14.** $5x^2 + 8x - 21$
15. $16x^3 - 48x^2 + 8x$ **16.** $x^2 + 2x - 24$ **17.** $y^2 - 5y - 24$
18. $28w^2 + 17w - 6$ **19.** $x^2 - 18x + 81$
20. $25x^2 + 30x + 9$ **21.** $a^2 - 49$ **22.** $4 - 25y^2$

LESSON 6-1

Try This **a–c.** Answers may vary.
a. $(4x^2)(2x^2)$, $(4x)(2x^3)$, $(8x)(x^3)$
b. $(2m)(3m^4)$, $(m^2)(6m^3)$, $(2m^3)(3m^2)$
c. $(6ab)(2ab)$, $(6a^2)(2b^2)$, $(12)(a^2b^2)$ **d.** $x(x + 3)$
e. $ab(a + 2)$ **f.** $x^2(3x^4 - 5x + 2)$ **g.** $3x^2(3x^2 - 5x + 1)$
h. $pq(2p^2q + p + 1)$ **i.** $3m^2n^2(4m^2n^2 + m + 2)$

Exercises **1–9.** Answers may vary. **11.** $y(y + 8)$
13. $3p(p - 1)$ **15.** $5(x^2 + 2x + 6)$ **17.** $7y^2(4 + 3y^2)$
19. $x^3(9 + 25x^4)$ **21.** $18y^4$ **23.** $3(2x^2 + x - 5)$
25. $a^2b(4a^2b + 1)$ **27.** $5m^3(m^2n + 2)$
29. $2xy^2(x^2 + 3y + 4)$ **31.** $16x(x^5 - 2x^4 - 3)$
33. $x(5x^4 + 10x - 8)$ **35.** $x^3(x^6 - x^4 + x + 1)$
37. $5(2x^3 + 5x^2 + 3x - 4)$ **39.** $5pq^2(p^2 + 2p - 4)$
41. $m^2n^2(6mn + 3m + 1)$ **43.** No **45.** No **47.** No **49.** Yes
51. Yes **53.** Yes **55.** Yes **57.** $3t$ **59.** $24t^2$

Mixed Review **61.** x^{13} **63.** $-18t^7$ **65.** 3.075×10^2
67. $-5m^3 - 2m^2 + 12$

Connections: Geometry **1.** $3x + y$, $3x + y$

LESSON 6-2

Try This **a.** Yes **b.** No **c.** No **d.** No **e.** Yes **f.** Yes
g. $(x + 3)(x - 3)$ **h.** $(y + 8)(y - 8)$ **i.** $(2y + 7)(2y - 7)$
j. $(4x - 5y)(4x + 5y)$ **k.** $(a^4b^2 - 2)(a^4b^2 + 2)$
l. $(5a^5 - 6b^4)(5a^5 + 6b^4)$ **m.** $8y^2(2 + y^2)(2 - y^2)$
n. $5(1 + 2y^3)(1 - 2y^3)$ **o.** $ab(a + 2b)(a - 2b)$
p. $x^4y^4(8 - 5xy^2)(8 + 5xy^2)$ **q.** $(3x + 1)(3x - 1)(9x^2 + 1)$
r. $(4m^2 + n^4)(2m - n^2)$

Exercises **1.** Yes **3.** No **5.** No **7.** Yes **9.** $(x + 2)(x - 2)$
11. $(x + 3y)(x - 3y)$ **13.** $(4a + 3)(4a - 3)$
15. $(2x + 5)(2x - 5)$ **17.** $(5m + 7)(5m - 7)$
19. $(x^2 + 3)(x^2 - 3)$ **21.** $(m^8 + 5)(m^8 - 5)$
23. $(2x^2 + 4)(2x^2 - 4)$ **25.** $(8y^2 + 9)(8y^2 - 9)$
27. $(6x^6 + 7)(6x^6 - 7)$ **29.** $x(6 + 7x)(6 - 7x)$
31. $y^2(9y^2 + 5)(9y^2 - 5)$ **33.** $2(2x + 7y)(2x - 7y)$
35. $2(4x + 5y)(4x - 5y)$ **37.** $3(5m^3n + 7)(5m^3n - 7)$
39. $(x^2 + 1)(x + 1)(x - 1)$ **41.** $4(x^2 + 4)(x + 2)(x - 2)$
43. $(4 + y^2)(2 + y)(2 - y)$ **45.** $(25 + m^2)(5 + m)(5 - m)$
47. $x(4 + 9x)(4 - 9x)$ **49.** $(b^4 + a^2)(b^2 + a)(b^2 - a)$
51. $x^2(x^7 + 3)(x^7 - 3)$ **53.** $(7a^2 + 9)(7a^2 - 9)$
55. $(x^6 + 4)(x^3 + 2)(x^3 - 2)$ **57.** $a^2(a^5 + 2)(a^5 - 2)$
59. $(5a^2 + 3)(5a^2 - 3)$ **61.** $(3c^4 + 7)(3c^4 - 7)$

63. $3x^3(x + 2)(x - 2)$ **65.** $2x\left(3x + \frac{2}{5}\right)\left(3x - \frac{2}{5}\right)$

67. $x\left(x + \frac{1}{4}\right)\left(x - \frac{1}{4}\right)$ **69.** $(0.8x + 1.1)(0.8x - 1.1)$

71. $x(x + 6)$ **73.** $3(a - 1)(3a + 11)$
75. $(y^4 + 16)(y^2 + 4)(y + 2)(y - 2)$
77. No; any product of the form $(x + a)(x + c)$ has 3 terms:
$x^2 + (a + c)x + ac$. For the product to have 2 terms, a and c
must be opposites; but if a and c are opposites, then ac must
be negative, and ac cannot equal b^2 for any value of b.
79–81. Answers may vary. Examples are given.
79. $(x^2 - 2)(x^2 + 2) = x^4 - 4$
81. $(a + 2b)(a + b)(a - b) = a^3 - ab^2 + 2a^2b - 2b^3$

Mixed Review **83.** $x^2 + 14x + 49$ **85.** 1, 0; 1 **87.** 5, 2, 0; 5
89. 0.08 **91.** 0.065 **93.** 5 **95.** The base is 18 cm.

LESSON 6-3

Try This **a.** Yes **b.** Yes **c.** No **d.** Yes **e.** No **f.** Yes
g. $(x + 1)^2$ **h.** $(x - 1)^2$ **i.** $(5x - 7)^2$ **j.** $3(4m + 5n)^2$

Exercises **1.** Yes **3.** No **5.** Yes **7.** No **9.** No **11.** $(x - 7)^2$
13. $(x + 8)^2$ **15.** $(x - 1)^2$ **17.** $(x + 2y)^2$ **19.** $(y - 3x)^2$
21. $2(x - 1)^2$ **23.** $x(x - 9)^2$ **25.** $5(2x + 5)^2$ **27.** $(7y - 3x)^2$
29. $5(y^2 + 1)^2$ **31.** $(y^3 + 13)^2$ **33.** $(4x^5 - 1)^2$
35. $(2x^2 + 1)^2$ **37.** $(9x^3 + 4y)^2$ **39.** Not possible
41. $(x + 11)^2$ **43.** Not possible **45.** $7(9x - 4)$
47. $y^4(x^2 - 3)(x^2 + 3)$ **49.** $(x^4 + 16)(x^2 + 4)(x + 2)(x - 2)$
51. $(y + 4)^2$ **53.** $(2a + 15)^2$ **55.** $(x + 5)^2$ **57.** $a = 2$
59. $(x^n + 5)^2$ **61.** $(y + 3)^2 - (x + 4)^2$
$= (y + x + 7)(y - x - 1)$ **63.** 16

Mixed Review **65.** $-2x^3 - x^2 + 18x + 9$ **67.** $3x(2x - 3)$
69. $3y(3y^2 + 1)$ **71.** 359,400

LESSON 6-4

Try This **a.** $(x + 4)(x + 3)$ **b.** $(x + 9)(x + 4)$
c. $(x - 5)(x - 3)$ **d.** $(x - 4)(x - 5)$ **e.** $(x - 3)(x - 4)$
f. $(m + 3n)(m + 5n)$ **g.** $(a + 3b)(a + 2b)$
h. $(p + 4q)(p + 2q)$ **i.** $(x + 6)(x - 2)$ **j.** $(x - 6)(x + 2)$
k. $(a + 7b)(a - 2b)$ **l.** $(x - 6y)(x + 5y)$

Exercises **1.** $(x + 5)(x + 3)$ **3.** $(x + 4)(x + 3)$ **5.** $(x + 3)^2$
7. $(x + 7)(x + 2)$ **9.** $(b + 4)(b + 1)$ **11.** $(a - 8)(a - 6)$
13. $(m + 7)(m + 3)$ **15.** $(z - 4)(z - 6)$ **17.** $(a - 5b)(a - 4b)$
19. $(c - 5d)(c - 2d)$ **21.** $(y - 10z)(y - z)$
23. $(x + 7)(x - 6)$ **25.** $(x - 9)(x + 2)$ **27.** $(x - 8)(x + 2)$
29. $(y - 9)(y + 5)$ **31.** $(x - 11y)(x + 9y)$
33. $(c + 8d)(c - 7d)$ **35.** $(a + 7b)(a - 5b)$ **37.** $(x + 10)^2$
39. $(x - 25)(x + 4)$ **41.** $(x - 24)(x + 3)$ **43.** $(x - 16)(x - 9)$
45. $(a + 12)(a - 11)$ **47.** $(15y - x)(8y - x)$
49. $(12y + x)(9y - x)$ **51.** $(n - 3)$ hours **53. a.** The signs of a
and b must be opposite. **b.** Since the middle term is positive,
the number with the larger absolute value must be positive.
Therefore, b is a negative integer.
55. $-49, -23, -5, 5, 23, 49$ **57.** $-x(x - 23)(x + 1)$

Mixed Review **59.** Answers may vary.
Ex: $8y(y^2)$, $(4y^2)(2y)$, $(2y^2)(4y)$ **61.** a^4b **63.** $5y^2 + 8$ **65.** c
67. $2, -2$

LESSON 6-5

Try This **a.** $(3x + 2)(2x + 1)$ **b.** $(4x - 1)(2x + 3)$
c. $(6x + 1)(x - 7)$ **d.** $3(x - 3)(x - 4)$ **e.** $2(2x + 1)(2x - 1)$
f. $3(3a + 1)(a - 2)$ **g.** $2(x + 3)(x - 1)$ **h.** $2(2a + 3)(a - 1)$
i. $3(2m - n)(m + 3n)$

Exercises **1.** $(2x + 1)(x - 4)$ **3.** $(5x - 9)(x + 2)$
5. $(2x + 7)(3x + 1)$ **7.** $(3x + 1)(x + 1)$ **9.** $(2x + 5)(2x - 3)$
11. $(2x + 1)(x - 1)$ **13.** $(3x + 8)(3x - 2)$

15. $(3x + 1)(x - 2)$ **17.** $(3x + 4)(4x + 5)$
19. $(7x - 1)(2x + 3)$ **21.** $(3p + 4)(3p + 2)$ **23.** $(7 - 3b)^2$
25. $(x + 2)(24x - 1)$ **27.** $(7x + 4)(5x - 11)$
29. $2(5 - x)(2 + x)$ **31.** $4(3x - 2)(x + 3)$
33. $6(5x - 9)(x + 1)$ **35.** $2(3x + 5)(x - 1)$
37. $(3a - 1)(a - 1)$ **39.** $4(3x + 2)(x - 3)$
41. $(2x - 1)(x + 1)$ **43.** $(3b - 8)(3b + 2)$
45. $5(3x + 1)(x - 2)$ **47.** $(6x + 5y)(3x - 2y)$
49. $(5m + 2n)(3m - 5n)$ **51.** $(5x - 2y)(7x - 4y)$
53. $(3x^2 + 2)(3x^2 + 4)$ **55.** $(3x - 7)^2$ **57.** $2a(3a + 5)(a - 1)$
59. Not factorable **61.** $x(x^2 + 3)(x^2 - 2)$ **63.** $a = 4, c = 9$
65. $(10x^n + 3)(2x^n + 1)$ **67.** $(x^{3a} - 3)(x^{3a} + 2)$
69. $-2(a + 1)^n(a + 3)^2(a + 6)$

Mixed Review **71.** $\frac{a + b}{2}$ **73.** $\frac{r}{s + t}$ **75.** $t < -3$

LESSON 6-6

Try This **a.** $(4x + 1)(2x^2 + 3)$ **b.** $(2x + 3)(2x^2 - 3)$
c. $(x + 1)(x + 1)(x - 1)$ **d.** $(a - 2b)(3 + 5a)$

Exercises **1.** $(x + 3)(x^2 + 2)$ **3.** $(y + 3)(2y^2 + 1)$
5. $(2a - 3)(4a^2 + 3)$ **7.** $(3x - 4)(4x^2 + 1)$
9. $(b + 8)(b^2 - 3)$ **11.** Not factorable **13.** $(x - 4)(2x^2 - 9)$
15. $(a - b)(x + y)$ **17.** $(n + p)(n + 2)$ **19.** $(a + y)(a - 3)$
21. $(2x^2 + 3)(2x^3 + 3)$
23. $(c^2 + 1)(c + 1)(c + 1)(c - 1)(c - 1)$
25. $(x - y + z)(x - y - z)$ **27.** $(a + b + 1)(a + b - 1)$
29. $D = abc$ **31.** $28x^3 + 20x^2 + 7x + 5$, $(7x + 5)(4x^2 + 1)$

Mixed Review **33.** $m^2 + 2mn + n^2$ **35.** $m^2 - n^2$
37. $(y + 3)(y + 3)$ or $(y + 3)^2$ **39.** $(c + 9)(c - 10)$
41. $(5 - x)(4 - y)$ **43.** $(3a^2 + b)(3a^2 - b)$

LESSON 6-7

Try This **a.** $3(m^2 + 1)(m + 1)(m - 1)$ **b.** $(x^3 + 4)^2$
c. $2x^2(x + 3)(x + 1)$ **d.** $(x + 4)(3x^2 - 2)$
e. $8x(x + 5)(x - 5)$ **f.** $y^3(y - 7)(y + 5)$

Exercises **1.** $2(x + 8)(x - 8)$ **3.** $(a - 5)^2$
5. $(2x - 3)(x - 4)$ **7.** $x(x + 12)^2$ **9.** $6(2x + 3)(2x - 3)$
11. $4x(x - 2)(5x + 9)$ **13.** Not factorable **15.** $x^3(x - 7)^2$
17. Not factorable **19.** $4(x^2 + 4)(x + 2)(x - 2)$
21. $(y^4 + 1)(y^2 + 1)(y + 1)(1 - y)$ **23.** $x^3(x - 3)(x - 1)$
25. $(x - 2)(x + 2)(x + 3)$ **27.** $x(x - 3)(x^2 + 7)$
29. $(a + 1)(a + 1)(a - 1)(a - 1)$ **31.** $-2(x - 2)(x + 5)$ or
$2(2 - x)(5 + x)$ **33.** $(y - 2)(y + 3)(y - 3)$
35. $(a + 4)(a^2 + 1)$ **37.** $2ab(2ab - 1)(3a + 1)$
39. $x^2y(x + 1)(3x - 2y)$ **41.** $x + 2$
43. $(x^4 + 16)(x^2 + 4)(x + 2)(x - 2)$

Mixed Review **45.** $\frac{1}{x}$ **47.** $6a^5 - 3a^3$

Selected Answers

Connections: Discrete Math

1. $m^5 + 5m^4n + 10m^3n^2 + 10m^2n^3 + 5mn^4 + n^5$

3. $a^4 + 16a^3 + 96a^2 + 256a + 256$

5. $a^6 + 6a^5b + 15a^4b^2 + 20a^3b^3 + 15a^2b^4 + 6ab^5 + b^6$

LESSON 6-8

Try This   a. $3, -4$ b. $7, 3$ c. $0, \frac{17}{3}$ d. $-\frac{1}{4}, \frac{2}{3}$ e. $3, -2$

f. $8, -7$ g. $7, -4$ h. -3 i. $0, -4$ j. $\frac{4}{5}, -\frac{4}{5}$

Exercises   1. $-8, -6$ 3. $3, -5$ 5. $-12, 11$ 7. $0, -5$

9. $0, 13$ 11. $0, -10$ 13. $4, \frac{1}{4}$ 15. $0, \frac{2}{3}$ 17. $0, 18$ 19. $\frac{1}{9}, \frac{1}{10}$

21. $2, 6$ 23. $\frac{1}{3}, 20$ 25. $0, \frac{2}{3}, \frac{1}{2}$ 27. $-5, -1$ 29. $-7, 3$

31. $0, 8$ 33. $0, -19$ 35. $\frac{2}{3}, -\frac{2}{3}$ 37. -3 39. $\frac{2}{3}, -\frac{1}{4}$

41. $7, -2$ 43. $\frac{9}{8}, -\frac{9}{8}$ 45. $-\frac{9}{4}, \frac{1}{2}$ 47. $0, \frac{6}{5}$ 49. 1 51. $\frac{5}{3}, -1$

53. $-\frac{9}{2}, -8$ 55. $4, -4$ 57. $7, 2$ 59. $4, -\frac{5}{3}$ 61. $4, -5$

63. $9, -3$ 65. $\frac{1}{8}, \frac{-1}{8}$ 67. $4, -4$ 69. $x^2 - 16, x^2 - 15x - 16,$
$x^2 + 15x - 16, x^2 - 6x - 16, x^2 + 6x - 16$

71. a. $x^2 + 2x - 3 = 0$ b. $x^2 - 2x - 3 = 0$

c. $x^2 - 4x + 4 = 0$ d. $x^2 - 7x + 12 = 0$

e. $x^2 + x - 12 = 0$ f. $x^2 - x - 12 = 0$

g. $x^2 + 7x + 12 = 0$ h. $x^2 - x + \frac{1}{4}$ or $4x^2 - 4x + 1 = 0$

i. $x^2 - 25 = 0$ j. $x^3 - \frac{14}{40}x^2 + \frac{1}{40}x$ or $40x^3 - 14x^2 + x = 0$

Mixed Review   73. $3n + 8$ 75. $\frac{n-15}{2}$ 77. $a^2 + b^2$

79. $2(2y - 1)(y + 3)$ 81. $(2y - 3)(3y + 2)$

LESSON 6-9

Try This   a. $7, 8$ b. $0, 1$ c. $5, -5$ d. $5, -4$ e. $6, -6$
f. 5 cm, 3 cm   g. $21, 22; -21, -22$

Exercises   1. $\frac{-3}{4}$ or 1 3. 2 or 4 5. 13 and 14, -13 and -14
7. 12 and 14, -12 and -14 9. 15 and 17, -15 and -17
11. 12 m, 8 m   13. 5 ft   15. 4 cm, 14 cm   17. 6 m
19. 5 and 7   21. D   23. $6x + 1 = (x - 1)^2, x = 8$ 25. The
student subtracted two from the number before squaring
instead of squaring the number then subtracting two.
27. a. 1 second   b. 2 seconds   29. 7 in.   31. 8, 9
33. 30 cm by 15 cm

Mixed Review   35. 1.17203×10^5 37. $10,000m^8$
39. $-15a^4b^5$ 41. 680   43. $3(2c + 1)(c - 3)$
45. $(2m^2 - 1)(m - 2)$ 47. $5(x + 7)^2$

Preparing for Standardized Tests   1. (C)   3. (B)
5. (C)   7. (B)   9. (D)

CHAPTER 6 WRAP UP

1–2. Answers many vary.   3. $x(x - 3)$ 4. $3y(2y^2 + 4y + 1)$
5. $4x^4(2x^2 - 8x + 1)$ 6. $2a^2(3a^2b^4 - ab + 4)$ 7. No
8. Yes   9. $(3x - 2)(3x + 2)$ 10. $(2x - 5)(2x + 5)$
11. $2(x - 5)(x + 5)$ 12. $3(x - 3)(x + 3)$
13. $(x^2 + 9)(x - 3)(x + 3)$ 14. $(4x^2 + 1)(2x - 1)(2x + 1)$
15. No   16. No   17. Yes   18. No   19. $(x - 3)^2$ 20. $(x + 7)^2$
21. $(3x - 5)^2$ 22. $(5x - 2)^2$ 23. $2(3x - 1)^2$ 24. $3(2x + 5)^2$
25. $(x - 5)(x - 3)$ 26. $(x + 6)(x - 2)$ 27. $(y + 4)(y + 5)$
28. $(b - 6)(b + 3)$ 29. $(m + 7)(m + 8)$ 30. $(p - 8)(p + 1)$
31. $(2x + 1)(x - 4)$ 32. $(2y - 1)(3y - 1)$
33. $2(a - 6)(3a + 4)$ 34. $(x^2 + 3)(x + 1)$
35. $(x^3 - 2)(x + 4)$ 36. $(x - 1)(x + 1)(x + 3)$
37. $(3x + 2)(2x^2 + 1)$ 38. $7(x - 1)(x + 1)$
39. $-3x(5x - 2)^2$ 40. $(a - 7)(a + 3)$ 41. $(x + 15)(x - 13)$
42. $(x + 4)(x^2 - 3)$ 43. $(1 + a^4)(1 + a^2)(1 + a)(1 - a)$

44. $1, -3$ 45. $0, \frac{3}{2}$ 46. $-7, 5$ 47. $-4, 3$ 48. $-\frac{1}{3}, 2$
49. $\frac{4}{3}, -\frac{4}{3}$ 50. 3 or -2 51. $-18, -16$ or 16, 18
52. $-19, -17$ or 17, 19   53. $\frac{5}{2}$ or -2 54. 12 cm

Chapter 7

Skills & Concepts You Need for Chapter 7   1. 15

2. 4   3. 38   4. 56   5. $<$ 6. $>$ 7. $>$ 8. $>$ 9. $\frac{13}{6}$ 10. -11

11. 12   12. -2 13. $-\frac{16}{21}$ 14. $\frac{3}{16}$ 15. 7   16. 10   17. -5

18. -2 19. 8   20. $k = \frac{ds}{5}$ 21. $v = \frac{Mp^2}{mS}$

LESSON 7-1

Try This   a–i.

j. I   k. III   l. IV   m. II
n. $(4, 3), (-4, -3), (2, -4), (1, 5), (-2, 0), (0, 3)$

Exercises   1–15 Odd

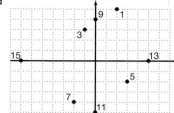

17. II   **19.** IV   **21.** III   **23.** I   **25. a.** *y, x*   **b.** Positive, negative
27. A (3, 3), B (0, −4), C (−5, 0), D (−1, −1), E (2, 0)
29–35. Answers may vary. Examples are given.
29. (−3, 3), (−4, 4), (5, 5)   **31.** (4, −2), (9, 3), (1, −1)
33. (q, r), and (r, q) are
symmetrical about
the line y = x.

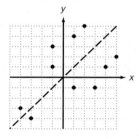

35. (2, 3), (4, 1), (0, 5)   **37.** 32.5

Mixed Review   **39.** $(x^2 + 2)(x − 5)$ **41.** $4ab − 3bc$
43. $−4mn − 3pq$

LESSON 7-2

Try This   **a.** No   **b.** Yes   **c.** Answers may vary. Ex: (0, 3),
(1, 5), (−1, 1), (−2, −1)

d.

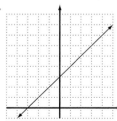

e.

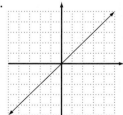

Exercises   **1.** Yes   **3.** No   **5.** Yes   **7–15.** Answers may vary.

17.

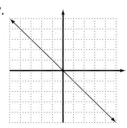

19.

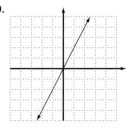

21.

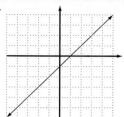

23.

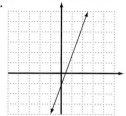

25.

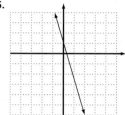

27.

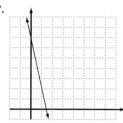

29.

x	−4	−3	−2	−1	0	1	2	3	4
y	5	4	3	2	1	2	3	4	5

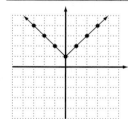

31. Yes   No   No   No   **33.** 68x + 76y = 864 , let x = y, each
machine runs for 6 h

Mixed Review   **35.** 1   **37.** $x(7x^3 + 1)$ **39.** 0   **41.** −6, 3
43. −1, −3   **45.** $(mn^2)(mn + 2)$ **47.** $(x + 3y)^2$
49. $(3x − 2)(2x − 1)$ **51.** $r = \frac{A − P}{Pt}$

LESSON 7-3

Try This

a.

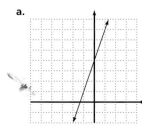

b.

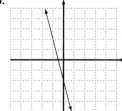

Selected Answers

c.
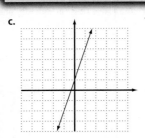

d.
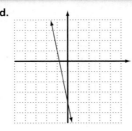

Exercises

1.
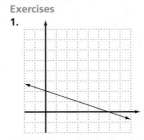

3.
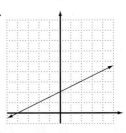

e.
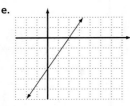

f.
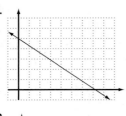

5.
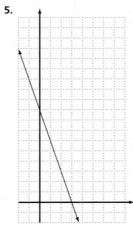

7.
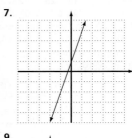

g.
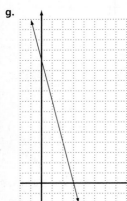

h.
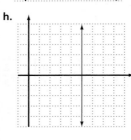

9.
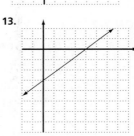

i.
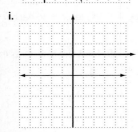

j.
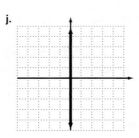

11.
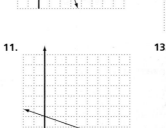

13.
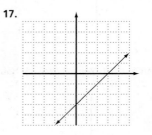

15.
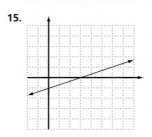

17.

k.
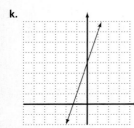

19.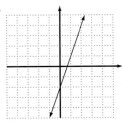

21.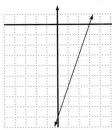

23.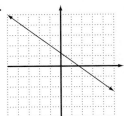

25.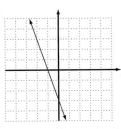

27.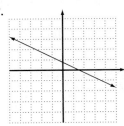

29.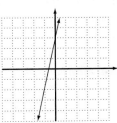

31.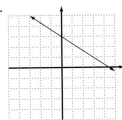

33.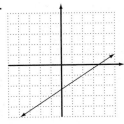

35.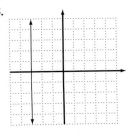

37.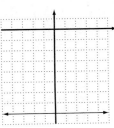

39.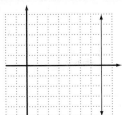

41.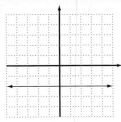

43. $(-3, 6)$ **45.** c   **47.** d   **49.** e   **51.** Changing the constant raises or lowers the graph.   **53.** $x = 13$ **55.** $x = -3\frac{1}{2}$ **57.** e; b and g, a and f, d and h

Mixed Review   **59.** Yes   **61.** Yes   **63.** $(xy + 2)(xy - 4)$ **65.** $r = \frac{v^2}{a}$ **67.** About 38.5 minutes

Connections: Reasoning   **1.** D   **3.** F

LESSON 7-4

Try This

a.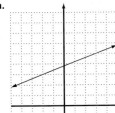

b.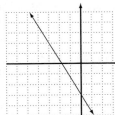

Slope $= \frac{2}{5}$ Slope $= -\frac{5}{3}$

c. $\frac{7}{6}$ **d.** $\frac{4}{7}$ **e.** $-\frac{1}{2}$ **f.** $\frac{-15}{14}$ **g.** 0   **h.** No slope   **i.** $-\frac{1}{3}$

Exercises   **1.** $m = 3$ **3.** $m = -\frac{9}{7}$ **5.** $m = -\frac{5}{6}$ **7.** $m = -\frac{4}{5}$ **9.** $m = 2$ **11.** 7   **13.** $-\frac{2}{3}$ **15.** -2 **17.** 3   **19.** 2   **21.** No slope   **23.** Zero slope   **25.** No slope   **27.** Zero slope   **29.** 6   **31.** 12   **33.** 39%   **35. a.** $\frac{12}{5}, \frac{18}{5}, \frac{24}{5}$ **b.** All values from 4 to 0   **37.** -1 **39.** In using the slope formula, Garth subtracted the y-coordinates (numerator) and the x-coordinates (denominator) in opposite orders.

Mixed Review   **41.** $(ab + 2)(ab - 1)$ **43.** Yes   **45.** 0.002575   **47.** $-2, 9$ **49.** -2

LESSON 7-5

Try This   **a.** $-\frac{4}{5}$ **b.** $-\frac{3}{8}$ **c.** $-\frac{1}{5}$ **d.** $\frac{5}{4}$ **e.** 5, 0   **f.** $-\frac{3}{2}, -6$ **g.** $-\frac{3}{4}, 4$ **h.** $-\frac{7}{5}, -5$

Selected Answers

i.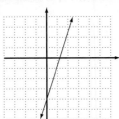

j.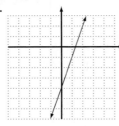

41.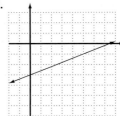

43.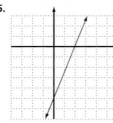

k.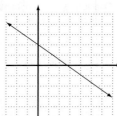

45.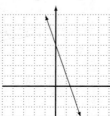

47. -2 **49.** $y = 8x$
51. $y = -7x + 4$
53. $y = -6x + \frac{3}{4}$
55. $m = 11, b = 9$
57. Slopes: $-3, 3$; vertex $(0, 5)$

Exercises   1. $-\frac{3}{2}$ **3.** $-\frac{1}{4}$ **5.** 2   **7.** $\frac{4}{3}$ **9.** $\frac{1}{2}$ **11.** $\frac{1}{2}$ **13.** $\frac{7}{5}$
15. $-\frac{2}{3}$ **17.** $-\frac{8}{9}$ **19.** $m = -4, b = -9$ **21.** $m = -\frac{2}{3}, b = 3$
23. $m = -\frac{8}{7}, b = -3$ **25.** $m = 3, b = -\frac{5}{3}$
27. $m = -\frac{3}{2}, b = -\frac{1}{2}$

29.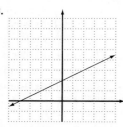

31.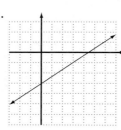

33.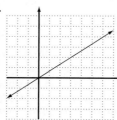

35.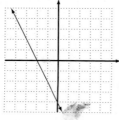

37.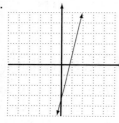

39.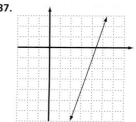

Mixed Review   59. IV   **61.** I   **63.** IV   **65–67.** Answers may vary. Examples are given.   **65.** $(-1, 3)$, $(1, 2)$, $(2, \frac{3}{2})$
67. $(0, 2), (1, -1), (-1, 5)$ **69.** $(5b + 4a)(5b - 4a)$
71. $(m + 3)(n + 5)$ **73.** $-3, 3$ **75.** $-5, 5$

Connections: Reasoning   a. Same slope, but $b = 6$
c. Same line   **e.** Same y-intercept, but $m = -\frac{1}{3}$

LESSON 7-6

Try This   a. $y = 5x - 18$ **b.** $y = -3x - 5$ **c.** $y = -\frac{2}{3}x + \frac{22}{3}$
d. $y = \frac{9}{2}x + \frac{17}{2}$ **e.** $y = 6x - 13$ **f.** $y = -\frac{2}{3}x + \frac{14}{3}$
g. $y = x + 2$ **h.** $y = -\frac{7}{6}x - \frac{2}{3}$

Exercises   1. $y = 5x - 5$ **3.** $y = \frac{3}{4}x + \frac{5}{2}$ **5.** $y = x - 8$
7. $y = -3x + 3$ **9.** $y = \frac{1}{2}x + 2$ **11.** $y = \frac{5}{2}x + 13$
13. $y = \frac{1}{4}x + \frac{5}{2}$ **15.** $y = -\frac{1}{2}x + 4$ **17.** $y = -\frac{3}{2}x + \frac{13}{2}$
19. $y = \frac{2}{5}x - 2$ **21.** $y = \frac{3}{4}x - \frac{5}{2}$ **23.** $y = \frac{4}{5}x - 3$
25. $y = \frac{3}{2}x + 6$ **29.** $y = \frac{1}{5}x - 2$ **31.** $y = \frac{2}{3}x - \frac{31}{3}$
33. a. $(1, -3)$ **b.** $(0, 0)$ **c.** $(1, 2)$ **d.** $(0, 0)$ **35.** $(0, \frac{19}{3})$

Mixed Review
39. 163.2   **41.** $-7, 7$ **43.** $-9, 4$
45. $9, -\frac{5}{3}$ **47.** $4(m - 4)(m - 5)$
49. $(3c^2 - 1)(3c - 1)$
51. $(xy - z)(xy + z)$ **53.** p^2
55. 249 million

37.

LESSON 7-7

Try This   **a.** (1) $r = -0.01t + 30$ (2) 10.1 s
b. Answers may vary. Ex: $c = \frac{5}{6}d$

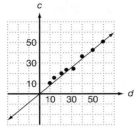

Exercises   **1. a.** $p = 0.05m + \$0.60$ **b.** $\$1.60$
3. a. $t = -\frac{1}{100}h + 15$ **b.** 0°C
5. a. $r = -0.0075t + 18.5$ **b.** 3.575
7. Answers may vary.
Ex: Using (10, 5) and
(40, 20), $y = \frac{1}{2}d$.

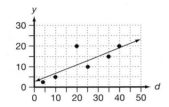

9. Answers may vary. Ex: Using (3, 60) and (6, 35),
$c = -\frac{25}{3}d + 85$.

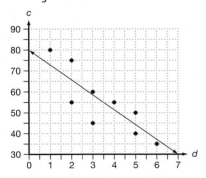

11. $\$250$ **13.** 55 ft   **15.** (0, 0), $(1, \frac{21}{20})$, $(2, \frac{11}{5})$, $(3, \frac{69}{20})$,
$(4, \frac{24}{5})$, $(5, \frac{25}{4})$; No

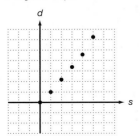

Mixed Review
17. $m = -4$ **19.** $3y^5 - 6y^4$
21. $2y^2(5y + 6)(5y - 6)$ **23.** $(a - 6)(b + 3)$
25. $n(n + 1) = 110;$ 10, 11 or $-11, -10$

LESSON 7-8

Try This   **a.** Yes   **b.** No   **c.** Yes   **d.** No   **e.** $y = -\frac{1}{2}x$
f. $y = 2x - 1$

Exercises   **1.** Yes   **3.** No   **5.** No   **7.** Yes   **9.** Yes   **11.** Yes
13. No   **15.** Yes   **17.** Yes   **19.** No   **21.** No   **23.** No   **25.** No
27. $y = -\frac{1}{3}x + 6$ **29.** $y = -3x + 2$ **31.** $y = 3x + 6$
33. $y = \frac{1}{3}x + 2$ **35. a.** $y = -2x + 7$ **b.** No; the line
$x - 2y = 6$ contains $(4, -1)$.   **37.** Answers may vary.
39. 16   **41.** $4y + 3x = -1, 3y - 4x = -7$

Mixed Review
43. $m = -\frac{1}{2}, b = \frac{5}{4}$ **45.** $m = 2, b = \frac{2}{3}$
47. $m = \frac{2}{3}, b = -\frac{4}{3}$ **49.** $y = -2x + 5$
51. $(3a - 7b)(3a + 7b)$ **53.** $(2m + 3)(m + 3)(m - 3)$
55. $9t^6$ **57.** $6x^5y^2z^3$ **59.** $6x^2 + 9xy + 3y^2$

LESSON 7-9

Try This   **a.** The y-intercept of a line is the point where the
line crosses the y-axis. Thus, the x-coordinate of the point is
zero. Let $x = 0$ in the equation $y = mx + b$. $y = m \cdot 0 + b$,
$y = 0 + b$, $y = b$. Thus, b is the y-intercept.   **b.** Suppose that
(x_1, y_1) and (x_2, y_2) are any two points on a vertical line. The
slope of the line is $\frac{y_2 - y_1}{x_2 - x_1}$. Since the line is vertical, the
x-coordinates are the same, so the slope is $\frac{y_2 - y_1}{0}$. Division by
0 is not allowed, so the line has no slope.

Exercises   **1.** First, show that a point (x_2, y_2) on a nonvertical
line with slope m and containing (x_1, y_1) must satisfy the
equation $y - y_1 = m(x - x_1)$. By the slope formula,
$m = \frac{y_2 - y_1}{x_2 - x_1}$. Multiplying each side of the equation
by $x_2 - x_1$ (Multiplication principle), we have
$m(x_2 - x_1) = y_2 - y_1$, or $y_2 - y_1 = m(x_2 - x_1)$. Thus, the
point (x_2, y_2) satisfies the equation $y - y_1 = m(x - x_1)$.
Next, show that a point that satisfies the equation
$y - y_1 = m(x - x_1)$ lies on a nonvertical line with slope m
and containing (x_1, y_1). Suppose (x_2, y_2) is such a point.
Then, $y_2 - y_1 = m(x_2 - x_1)$. If $x_2 = x_1$, then $y_2 - y_1 =$
$m(x_2 - x_1) = 0$, so $y_2 = y_1$. This means that (x_1, y_1) and
(x_2, y_2) are one and the same point, a point that does
indeed lie on the desired line. Now suppose $x_2 \neq x_1$. Then
$x_2 - x_1 \neq 0$, so multiply both sides of the equation by $\frac{1}{x_2 - x_1}$
to get $\frac{y_2 - y_1}{x_2 - x_1} = m$. Thus, the line through (x_1, y_1) and (x_2, y_2) is
nonvertical with slope m. (x_2, y_2) lies on this line and the
proof is complete.

Mixed Review 3. 2, 0; 2 **5.** 6, 3; 6 **7.** $-35 + 8c$
9. $3(a^3)$, $(3a)(a^2)$, $(3a^2)(a)$ **11.** Answers may vary.
Ex: $(-4, -\frac{3}{4})$, $(3, 1)$, $(4, \frac{5}{4})$ **13.** $(2y + 3)(2y - 3)$

LESSON 7-10

Problems 1. The perimeter would be 72. **3.** 18 different
matches could be played. **5.** Five baseball fans are neither
soccer fans nor football fans. **7.** There are 140 different
squares.

Application a. $10{,}000\left(1 + \frac{0.11}{1}\right)^{2 \cdot 1} = \$12{,}321$

c. $10{,}000\left(1 + \frac{0.11}{4}\right)^{2 \cdot 4} = \$12{,}423.81$

e. $10{,}000\left(1 + \frac{0.11}{365}\right)^{2 \cdot 365} = \$12{,}460.35$

CHAPTER 7 WRAP UP

1–6.

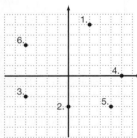

7. IV **8.** III **9.** I **10.** II **11.** (4, 3)
12. $(-3, 5)$ **13.** $(-4, -3)$
14. Yes **15.** No

16.

x	y
0	-1
1	1
2	3

17.

x	y
0	5
1	7
2	9

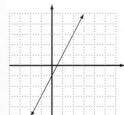

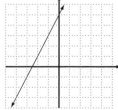

18.

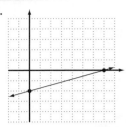

19.

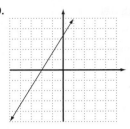

20.

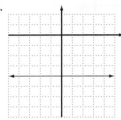

21.

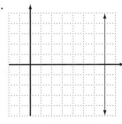

22. $\frac{3}{2}$ **23.** 0 **24.** No slope **25.** -6 **26.** $\frac{3}{2}$ **27.** $-\frac{5}{3}$
28. $\frac{3}{5}$, $-\frac{4}{5}$ **29.** $\frac{1}{3}$, -2

30.

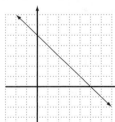

31.

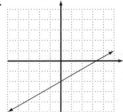

32.

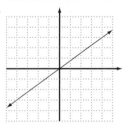

33. $y = 3x - 4$ **34.** $y = 5x$ **35.** $y = 3x - 1$
36. $y = -2x + 4$ **37.** $y = -\frac{1}{2}x + 3$ **38.** $y = x + 2$
39. $y = \frac{1}{2}x - 1$ **40.** $y = \frac{3}{2}x - 3$ **41.** $y = -\frac{2}{3}x + 2$
42. $C = \frac{5}{9}F - \frac{160}{9} = \frac{5}{9}(F - 32)$ **43.** 25°C **44.** Yes **45.** No
46. Yes **47.** No **48.** Parallel **49.** Perpendicular
50. Parallel **51.** Neither

CHAPTERS 1–7 CUMULATIVE REVIEW

1. 22 **3.** Answers may vary. Ex: $4x + y \cdot 3$, $x \cdot 4 + 3y$, $3y + 4x$
5. $\frac{1}{12p}$ **7.** 4 **9.** 25 **11.** $12x + 16y + 4z$ **13.** $9x^2 + 2y + 2z$

15. $x - 3y$ **17. a.** Open **b.** False **c.** Open **19.** No solution **21.** 59°F **23.** > **25.** 18 **27.** > **29.** < **31.** −15
33. $-\frac{2}{3}$ **35.** 1 **37.** 6 **39.** 1 **41.** $-2(3 + x + 6y)$ or $2(-3 - x - 6y)$ **43.** $-5y - 6$ **45.** Distributive property
47. 2.6 **49.** $\frac{9}{2}$ **51.** $-\frac{1}{2}$ **53.** 10 **55.** $12d = 9$; $0.75
57. $\frac{-33}{4}$ **59.** $-\frac{2}{7}$ **61.** $r = \frac{C}{2\pi}$ **63.** 61, −61 **65.** 28 **67.** 60%
69. $y \le 4$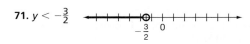

71. $y < -\frac{3}{2}$

73. 31, 33, 35 **75.** $\frac{1}{z^3}$ **77.** $27x^6 y^3$ **79.** $24b^5 c^7$ **81.** $-6m^2$
83. $\frac{1}{3p^3 r^5}$ **85.** 3.75×10^{-5} **87.** $-4x^3 - x^2 - 2$
89. $x^4 + 2x^3 - 9x^2 - 7$ **91.** $-y^3 - 2y^2 - 2y + 7$
93. $8x^5 - 4x^4 + 28x^3$ **95.** $x^2 y^2 - 49y^4$
97. $4a^2 - 20ab + 25b^2$ **99.** $2 - 10x^2 + 12x^4$ **101.** $4x^6 - 1$
103. $36x^2 - 60x + 25$ **105.** $x(x - 4)$ **107.** $4x(3 - x - 12x^3)$
109. $2(x - 2)(x + 2)$ **111.** $(x - 7)^2$ **113.** $(x - 4y)^2$
115. $2(3x - 4)^2$ **117.** $(x - 7)(x + 5)$
119. $(2x + 1)(4x + 3)$ **121.** $2(3x - 2)(x - 4)$
123. $(x^3 - 3)(x + 2)$ **125.** $(x + 5)(x + y)$
127. 2, −6 **129.** 14, 16 or −16, −14 **131.** II
133.

x	y
0	−2
−1	−5
−2	−8

135.

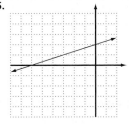

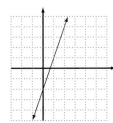

137. $\frac{3}{4}$ **139.** $m = -2, b = 4$
141. $y = -x + 3$
143. $y = \frac{2}{3}x + \frac{11}{3}$ **145.** Parallel

Chapter 8

Skills & Concepts You Need for Chapter 8 **1.** −5
2. $\frac{2}{9}$ **3.** 4 **4.** 5 **5.** $\frac{45}{8}$ **6.** 2 **7.** $2n + 8$ **8.** $10x + 5y$ **9.** 2
10. −10 **11.** −5 **12.** 6 **13.** 11 **14.** Yes **15.** No
16–18. Answers may vary.

19.

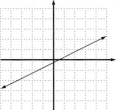

20.

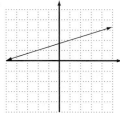

21.

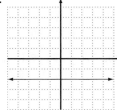

22.

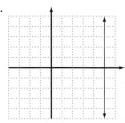

LESSON 8-1

Try This **a.** Yes **b.** No **c.** $(-2, -1)$ **d.** (0, 5) **e.** No solution **f.** Infinitely many solutions

Exercises **1.** Yes **3.** No **5.** Yes **7.** Yes **9.** (2, 1)
11. $(-12, 11)$ **13.** (2, 2) **15.** (5, 3) **17.** $\left(\frac{1}{3}, 1\right)$ **19.** No solution **21.** All except 19 and 20 **23.** Exercises 19 and 20
25. (0, 1), (2, 1) **27.** Noninteger solutions are difficult to approximate from graphs. Other methods are needed. $\left(\frac{2}{3}, \frac{3}{7}\right)$
29. Answers may vary.

Mixed Review **31.** $m = 2, b = -1$ **33.** $y = 3x - 2$
35. $y(y^2 + 2y + 5)$ **37.** 2, −7 **39.** 9 and 11

LESSON 8-2

Try This **a.** (3, 2) **b.** $(1, -3)$ **c.** (3, 5) **d.** $\left(\frac{24}{5}, \frac{-8}{5}\right)$ **e.** $\left(\frac{5}{2}, 5\right)$ **f.** (1, 6) **g.** $(2, -1)$ **h.** 63, 21

Exercises **1.** (1, 3) **3.** (1, 2) **5.** (4, 3) **7.** $(-2, 1)$ **9.** (5, 3)
11. $(2, -4)$ **13.** $\left(\frac{17}{3}, \frac{2}{3}\right)$ **15.** $(-12, 11)$ **17.** $(4, -2)$ **19.** (1, 2)
21. $\left(\frac{3}{4}, 0\right)$ **23.** 19, 17 **25.** 37, 29 **27.** 22, 4

29. Substitution yields $15 = 15$. Since this equation is true for all values of x, there are infinitely many solutions. Graphically the lines coincide:

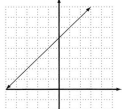

Selected Answers

31. $A = 6$, $B = 4$ **33.** $(2, -1, 3)$ **35.** Answers may vary.
Ex: $x = 10 - z$ and $y = 10 - z$, so $(10 - z) +$
$(10 - z) + z = 10$ or $z = 10$. $x = 10 - z$, so $x = 0$, and
$y = 10 - z$, so $y = 0$. Then $x + y = 0$, but we know
$x + y = 10$, so there is no solution.

Mixed Review **37.** Yes **39.** $(3a - b)^2$ **41.** $(x - 2yz^2)^2$
43. -5 **45.** $5, -5$ **47.** 95 cm, 80 cm

LESSON 8-3

Try This **a.** $(3, 2)$ **b.** $(1, -1)$ **c.** $(1, 4)$ **d.** $\left(3, \frac{13}{11}\right)$ **e.** $(1, 1)$
f. $(13, 3)$ **g.** $(-1, 2)$ **h.** $(1, -1)$ **i.** $(2, -4)$ **j.** 126, 90

Exercises **1.** $(9, 1)$ **3.** $(3, 5)$ **5.** $(3, 0)$ **7.** $\left(\frac{-1}{2}, 3\right)$ **9.** $\left(-1, \frac{1}{5}\right)$
11. No solution **13.** $(-3, -5)$ **15.** $(4, 5)$ **17.** $(4, 1)$ **19.** $(4, 3)$
21. $(1, -1)$ **23.** $(-3, -1)$ **25.** $(2, -2)$ **27.** $\left(5, \frac{1}{2}\right)$ **29.** $(4, 8)$
31. 68, 47 **33.** $\frac{37}{3}$ in., $\frac{20}{3}$ in. **35.** $62°$, $28°$ **37.** C **39.** $(2, 0)$
41. $(0, -1)$ **43.** $x = \frac{ce - bf}{ae - bd}$, $y = \frac{af - cd}{ae - bd}$ **45.** $\left(\frac{-b - c}{a}, 1\right)$
47. $(4, 3)$

Mixed Review **49.** No **51.** Yes **53.** $(-4, 2)$
55. $3(y + 2)(y - 2)$ **57.** $-2a^2b + ab^2$

LESSON 8-4

Try This **a.** 70 trucks, 110 vans **b.** 16 km **c.** 4 **d.** 14, 21
e. $0.08, $0.21

Exercises **1. a.** $n + d = 150$ **b.** $n + 12 = d$
c. $n + d = 150$, $n + 12 = d$ **d.** 69 nickels, 81 dimes
3. 44¢, 36¢ **5.** 48, 24 **7.** $71\frac{1}{9}$ ft, $8\frac{8}{9}$ ft **9.** 150 mi
11. $0.32, $0.48 **13.** 18 $21 tickets, 11 $27 tickets
15. 4 12-oz, 6 16-oz **17.** 120, 121 **19.** No solution
21. $1100x + 1800(x + 0.015) = 288$; 9%, 10.5%

Mixed Review **23.** -1 **25.** -5 **27.** $y = 6x + 7$ **29.** t
31. y **33.** $(9x - 7y)^2$

LESSON 8-5

Try This **a.** 168 km **b.** 275 km/h
c. $35t + 40t = 200$, $t = 2\frac{2}{3}$ h
d. $d = 35t$, $d + 15 = 40t$, $t = 3$ h

Exercises

1. a.
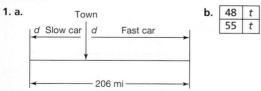
Town
d Slow car | d Fast car
206 mi

b.

48	t
55	t

c. $48t + 55t = 206$ **d.** $t = 2$; in 2 hours they will be 206 miles
apart. **3. a.**

Station
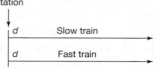

| d | Slow train |
| d | Fast train |

b.

d		$t + 3$
	120	

c. $d = 72(t + 3)$, $d = 120t$ **d.** $t = 4.5$; 4.5 hours after the
second train leaves, the second train will overtake the first
train. **5.** 4.6 h **7.** 14 km/h **9.** 384 km **11.** 330 km/h
13. 15 mi **15.** ≈ 317.03 km/h **17.** 90 mi, 48 mi
19. After 40 min **21.** 6:34 A.M.

Mixed Review **23.** Yes **25.** 9, -2 **27.** a^5b^6 **29.** $x^9y^2z^2$

Error Analysis **1.** The next to the last equation should
be $-y = 4 - 12$. The solution is $(4, 8)$.

LESSON 8-6

Try This **a.** 14 **b.** 43 **c.** 7 quarters, 13 dimes **d.** 8 dimes,
11 nickels **e.** 135, 31

Exercises **1.** 18 **3.** 75 **5.** 70 dimes, 33 quarters **7.** 8
nickels, 40 dimes **9.** 226 children, 203 adults **11.** 130 adults,
70 students **13.** 130 5-g bolts, 170 10-g bolts **15.** 86 **17.** 54
19. 336 **21.** 100 dimes, 40 quarters

Mixed Review **23.** $4(2a^4 + 3)(2a^4 - 3)$ **25.** $c(c - 5)$
27. $(5m - 9)(9m - 5)$ **29.** $0, -4$ **31.** $2, -5$ **33.** $x^3y^3z^3$
35. $x^2 + 2x + 1$ **37.** $a^2 + 14a + 49$ **39.** $2a^2 - 6a - 20$
41. $x = 2$, $y = -1$

PREPARING FOR STANDARDIZED TESTS **1.** (C),
variation **3.** (C), variation **5.** (B), substitution
7. (D), variation **9.** (C), variation **11.** (D), variation

Application **1.** No **3.** Yes **5.** $1.42 **7.** $2.84 **9.** $0.71

CHAPTER 8 WRAP UP

1. No **2.** Yes **3.** Yes **4.** No **5.** $(6, -2)$ **6.** $(6, 2)$ **7.** $(2, -3)$
8. No solution; lines are parallel **9.** $(0, 5)$ **10.** $(-2, 4)$
11. $(1, -2)$ **12.** $(-3, 9)$ **13.** $(1, 4)$ **14.** $(3, -1)$ **15.** $(35, -5)$
16. $(3, 1)$ **17.** $(1, 4)$ **18.** $(5, -3)$ **19.** $(-4, 1)$ **20.** $(-2, 4)$
21. $(-2, -6)$ **22.** $(3, 2)$ **23.** $(2, -4)$ **24.** $(12, 15)$
25. Roberta 46, Cindy 21 **26.** length = 27.5, width = 10.5
27. 135 mi/h **28.** 15 **29.** 60 quarters, 100 dimes

Chapter 9

Skills & Concepts You Need for Chapter 9 **1.** <
2. > **3. (a)** Yes **(b)** Yes **(c)** Yes

4. [number line with open circle at −3, marked −3, 0]

5. [number line with closed circle between 0 and 1, marked 0 1]

6. $x < -6$ [number line with open circle at −6, marked −6, 0]

7. $x > -13$ [number line with open circle at −13, marked −13 −12]

8. $x > 6$ [number line with open circle at 6, marked 0, 6]

9. $x \le 0$ [number line with closed circle at 0, marked 0]

10. (a) No **(b)** Yes **(c)** Yes **11.** Yes **12.** No **13.** (3, 2)
14. (−2, 0)

LESSON 9-1

Try This **a. (a)** $G = \{6, 7, 8, \ldots\}$ **(b)** $G = \{x \mid x$ is a whole
number and $x > 5\}$ **b. (a)** $T = \{20, 15, 10, 5, 0, -5, \ldots\}$
(b) $T = \{x \mid x$ is a multiple of 5 and $x < 24\}$
c. (a) $P = \{2, 3, 5, 7, 11, 13, 17, 19\}$ **(b)** $P = \{x \mid x$ is a prime
number and $x < 20\}$ **d.** $\{0, 1\}$ **e.** $\{1, 6\}$ **f.** $\{-3, 1\}$ **g.** $\emptyset$
h. E **i.** $\{0, 2\}$ or T **j.** $\emptyset$ **k.** S **l.** T **m.** $\{-4, -3, -2, 0, 4, 5, 6\}$
n. $\{-3, -2, 0, 1, 3, 4, 5\}$ **o.** D **p.** $\{x \mid x$ is a whole number\}
q. M

Exercises **1. (a)** $A = \{0, 1, 2, 3\}$ **(b)** $A = \{x \mid x$ is a whole
number and $x < 4\}$ **3. (a)** $N = \{-1, -2, -3, -4\}$
(b) $N = \{x \mid x$ is an integer and $-5 < x < 0\}$
5. (a) $H = \{3, 6, 9, 12, 15, 18, 21\}$ **(b)** $H = \{x \mid x$ is a multiple
of 3 and $0 < x \le 21\}$ **7. (a)** $E = \{2, 4, 6, 8, \ldots\}$
(b) $E = \{x \mid x$ is an even integer and $x > 0\}$ **9. (a)** $m = \{2\}$
(b) $m = \{x \mid x$ is an even prime number\} **11.** $\{1, 2\}$ **13.** $\{4, 5\}$
15. $\emptyset$ **17.** $\emptyset$ **19.** $\{0, 2, 4, 6, 8, \ldots\}$ or E
21. $\{-5, -4, -3, -2, -1, 0\}$ or P
23. $\{-5, -4, -3, -2, -1, 0, 5, 6, 7, 8\}$
25. $\{-1, 0, 1, 2, 3, 4, 5, 6, 7, 8\}$
27. $\{-5, -4, -3, -2, -1, 0\}$ or P **29.** $\{0, 1, 2, 3, \ldots\}$ or W
31. T **33.** T **35.** T **37.** T **39.** F **41.** T **43.** A **45.** A
47. $\{2, 4, 6, 8, \ldots\}$ **49.** Answers may vary. Ex: $\{5, 1, 0\}$
and $\{1, 9\}$
51.   **53.** $B = \{3, 7, 10, 15\}$

Mixed Review **55.** $(7 - 2c)(7 + 2c)$ **57.** $(2a - 3)^2$
59. $2(x + 3y)(4x - 3y)$ **61.** (5, 3) **63.** $y = 3x$
65. $y = \frac{1}{3}x - 4$ **67.** 9, 4

LESSON 9-2

Try This
a. [number line, open circles at −3 and 4, marked −3, 0, 4]
b. [number line, closed circle at −2, open circle at 7, marked −2, 0, 7]
c. [number line, open circle at −2, closed circle at 4, marked −2, 0, 4]
d. [number line, open circle at −7, closed circle at −3, marked −7, −3, 0]
e. $\{x \mid -4 < x \le 1\}$ [number line, open circle at −4, closed circle at 1, marked −4, 0 1]
f. $\emptyset$ **g.** [number line, closed circle at −1, open circle at 4, marked −1 0, 4]
h. $\{x \mid x < -5$ or $x > 3\}$ [number line, open circles at −5 and 3, marked −5, 0, 3]
i. $\{x \mid x < -5$ or $x > 5\}$ [number line, open circles at −5 and 5, marked −5, 0, 5]

Exercises
1. [number line, open circles at 4 and 9, marked 0, 4, 9]
3. [number line, open circle at 0, closed circle at 5, marked 0, 5]
5. [number line, closed circle at −7, marked −7, 0]
7. $\{x \mid 1 < x < 3\}$ [number line, open circles at 1 and 3, marked 0 1, 3]
9. $\{x \mid 6 < x < 10\}$ [number line, open circles at 6 and 10, marked 0, 6, 10]
11. $\{x \mid -4 \le x \le 3\}$ [number line, closed circles at −4 and 3, marked −4, 0, 3]
13. $\{x \mid 3 \le x \le 4\}$ [number line, closed circles at 3 and 4, marked 0, 3 4]
15. $\{x \mid 2 \le x \le 6\}$ [number line, closed circles at 2 and 6, marked 0, 2, 6]
17. [number line, open circles at −1 and 2, marked −1 0, 2]
19. [number line, closed circles at −4 and 4, marked −4, 0, 4]
21. [number line, closed circle at −6, open circle at 2, marked −6, 0, 2]
23. $\{x \mid x < 2$ or $x > 7\}$ [number line, open circles at 2 and 7, marked 0, 2, 7]
25. $\{x \mid x \le -1$ or $x > 9\}$ [number line, closed circle at −1, open circle at 9, marked −1 0, 9]
27. $\{x \mid x < 4$ or $x > 5\}$ [number line, open circles at 4 and 5, marked 0, 4 5]
29. $\{x \mid x \le -5$ or $x > 3\}$ [number line, closed circle at −5, open circle at 3, marked −5, 0, 3]

31. A **33.** all numbers on the number line **35.** $\{x \mid x < -2\}$
37. $\{x \mid x < 7\}$ **39.** $x \le -5$ or $x > 5$ **41.** $4 \le x$ and $x \le 9$ or $4 \le x \le 9$ **43.** $x < 1$ or $x > 1$ **45.** $-230{,}000{,}000 \le M$ and $M \le -60{,}000{,}000$ or $-230{,}000{,}000 \le M \le -60{,}000{,}000$
47. $L < -39$ or $L > 357$ **49.** $x \le 2$ and $x \ne -3$ OR $x < -3$ or $(-3 < x$ and $x \le 2)$
51. $x \le -5$ or $x \ge 3$
53. $x < -2$ or $x > 1$

Mixed Review **55.** 2, 0; 2 **57.** 9, 6; 9 **59.** $y = 2x + 5$
61. $(1, -7)$ **63.** 14 nickels, 27 dimes

Connections: Reasoning **1.** False **3.** True **5.** True

LESSON 9-3

Try This **a.** $\{-2, -14\}$ **b.** $\{16, -4\}$ **c.** $\emptyset$

Exercises **1.** $\{9, -27\}$ **3.** $\{-17, -5\}$ **5.** $\emptyset$ **7.** $\{5, -1\}$
9. $\left\{1, -\frac{3}{7}\right\}$ **11.** $\left\{2, \frac{8}{5}\right\}$ **13.** $\emptyset$ **15.** $\left\{-\frac{1}{6}, -\frac{1}{2}\right\}$ **17.** $\left\{\frac{3}{8}, \frac{5}{8}\right\}$
19. $\{-1, -9\}$ **21.** $\{0.2, -0.28\}$ **23.** $\left\{\frac{19}{3}, -5\right\}$ **25.** $\{0, 2\}$
27. $\{1, -7\}$ **29.** $\{3, 1\}$ **31.** $\emptyset$ **33.** $\{1, -3\}$ **35.** $\{x \mid x \ge 4\}$
37. $\left\{-\frac{3}{5}, -1\right\}$

Mixed Review **39.** $m = -4$, $b = -7$ **41.** $m = \frac{2}{5}$, $b = -1$
43. $2x(x - 3)(x + 1)$ **45.** $(3a + 2)(3a - 2)$ **47.** $(1, -4)$
49. 1, -2 **51.** 25 yr

LESSON 9-4

Try This

a. $\{x \mid -7 < x < 7\}$

b. $\{x \mid -6 < x < 6\}$

c. $\{x \mid -14 \le x \le 4\}$

d. $\left\{x \mid \frac{2}{3} \le x \le 2\right\}$

e. $\{x \mid x < -1$ or $x > 1\}$

f. $\{x \mid x \le -3$ or $x \ge 3\}$

g. $\{x \mid x < -5$ or $x > 5\}$

h. $\{x \mid x < -5$ or $x > 5\}$

i. $\{x \mid x \le -1$ or $x \ge 9\}$

j. $\{x \mid x \le -10$ or $x \ge 6\}$

Exercises
1. $\{x \mid -1 < x < 1\}$

3. $\{x \mid -4 \le x \le 4\}$

5. $\left\{x \mid -\frac{11}{2} < x < \frac{11}{2}\right\}$

7. $\{t \mid -7 < t < 7\}$

9. $\{x \mid -5 \le x \le 5\}$

11. $\{x \mid -7 \le x \le 3\}$

13. $\{x \mid -8 < x < -4\}$

15. $\left\{y \mid -\frac{5}{4} < y < \frac{9}{4}\right\}$

17. $\{x \mid -3 \le x \le 2\}$

19. $\{d \mid 0.989 < d < 1.011\}$

21. $\{d \mid 1.999 \le d \le 2.001\}$

23.

25.

27. $\{x \mid x < -4$ or $x > 4\}$

29. $\{t \mid t \le -3$ or $t \ge 3\}$

31. $\{x \mid x \le -5$ or $x \ge 7\}$

33. $\{x \mid x \le -2$ or $x \ge 20\}$

35. $\left\{y \mid y < -\frac{5}{3}$ or $y > 1\right\}$

37. $\left\{x \mid x \le -2$ or $x > \frac{5}{3}\right\}$

39. The second line is not correct. If $|x - 3| > 5$, then $x - 3 > 5$ or $x - 3 < -5$. **41.** $\{x \mid -6 \le x \le 3\}$ **43.** $\{y \mid y \le -8$ or $y \ge 7\}$
45. $\left\{-\frac{3}{2}, -\frac{7}{4}\right\}$ **47.** $\emptyset$ **49. a.** $|x + 1| \le 3$ **b.** $\left|x - \frac{1}{2}\right| > \frac{5}{2}$

Mixed Review **51.** $\{11, 13, 17, 19, 23, 29\}$ **53.** $\{0, 2\}$
55. $\{-2, -1, 0, 1, 2, 4, 6\}$ **57.** $\{-6, -4, -2, -1, 0, 1, 2\}$

LESSON 9-5

Try This   a. Yes   **b.** No

c.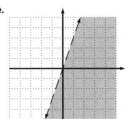

d.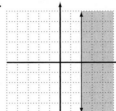

e.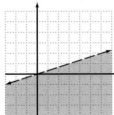

f.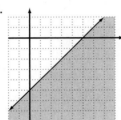

Exercises   1. No   **3.** No

5.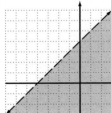

7.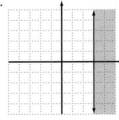

9.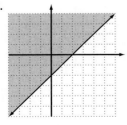

11.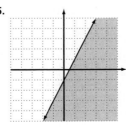

13.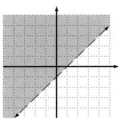

15.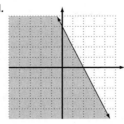

17.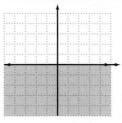

19.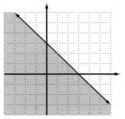

21.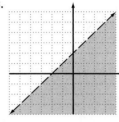

23.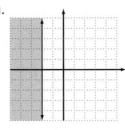

25.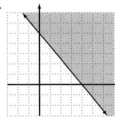

27.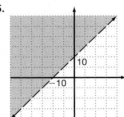

29.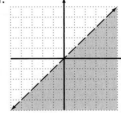

31.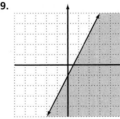

35. $y < x + 1$ **37.** $y > x - 2$ **39.** $y \le x - 3$
41. ($x \ge 0$ and $y \le 0$) or ($x \le 0$ and $y \ge 0$); $xy \le 0$

43.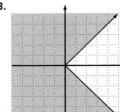

45.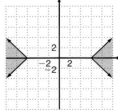

Mixed Review   47.

49. $-3 < x \le 5$ **51.** $(m - 5)(m - 10)$ **53.** $(2x + a)(x + a)$

Selected Answers

LESSON 9-6

Try This

a.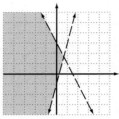

b.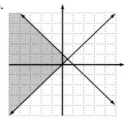

c.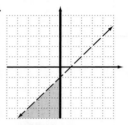

d.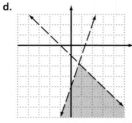

e. i. $0 \le b \le 300$
$0 \le r \le 400$
$b + r \ge 100$
$b + r \ge 200$

iii. Yes

ii.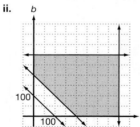

Exercises

1.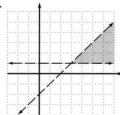

3.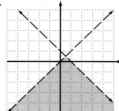

5.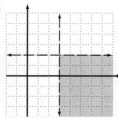

7.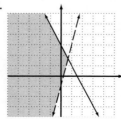

9.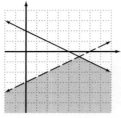

11.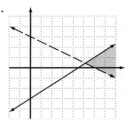

13.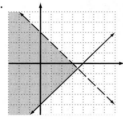

15.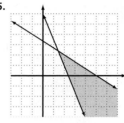

17.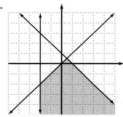

19.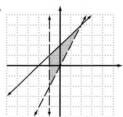

21.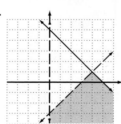

23. a. $2p + 3r < 600$
$p + r \le 300$
$p \ge r$

b.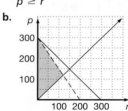

c. No, the total amount spent is not less than $600.

25. $y \ge 0, x > y$ **27.** $x < 3, y \le 2, y \ge \frac{1}{2}x$

29. $(-1, 1), (1, 0), (2, 1)$

31.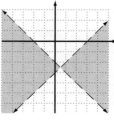

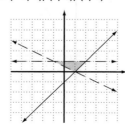

Mixed Review **33.** $1 < x \le 3$ **35.** $-2 < x < 2$
37. $-5 < y < 4$ **39.** $(b + 2)^2$ **41.** 27 dimes, 54 quarters

Preparing for Standardized Tests **1.** (D) **3.** (D)
5. (B) **7.** (A) **9.** (D)

CHAPTER 9 WRAP UP

1. a) $A = \{0, 1, 2, 3, 4, 5, 6, 7, 8\}$ **b)** $A = \{x | x$ is a whole number and $x < 9\}$ **2. a)** $B = \{1, 3, 5, \dots\}$ **b)** $B = \{x | x$ is a whole number and x is an odd number$\}$
3. a) $C = \{7, 14, 21, 28\}$ **b)** $C = \{x | x$ is a positive multiple of 7 and $x < 30\}$ **4. a)** $D = \{-4, -3, -2, -1\}$ **b)** $D = \{x | x$ is a negative integer and $x > -5\}$ **5.** $\{2, 4, 8, 12, 16, 20, 32\}$
6. $\{2, 3, 4, 6, 8, 9, 12, 15, 16, 18, 32\}$ **7.** $\{4, 8, 16\}$ **8.** $\{12\}$
9. $W \cap P = P$ **10.** $Z \cap W = Z$

11.
   $\quad\quad -2\ \ 0\ 1$

12. ⊶┼┼┼┼┼┼┼┼┼┼┼⊷┼┼⊷
   $\quad -1\ 0 \quad\quad\quad\quad\quad 12$

13. ┼┼┼⊷┼┼┼┼┼⊷┼┼┼┼
   $\quad\quad -2\quad 0\quad\quad 4$

14. $-5 \le x < 4$ ┼┼┼●┼┼┼┼┼┼┼┼⊷┼┼┼┼
   $\quad\quad\quad\quad -5\quad\quad 0\quad\quad 4$

15. $-5 \le x < 0$ ┼┼┼●┼┼┼┼┼⊷┼┼┼┼┼┼┼
   $\quad\quad\quad\quad -5\quad\quad\quad 0$

16. $-x < -6$ or $x \ge -5$ ⊷●┼┼┼┼┼┼┼┼┼┼┼
   $\quad\quad\quad\quad\quad\quad -6\ -5\quad\quad 0$

17. All numbers on the number line
   ┼┼┼┼┼┼┼┼┼┼┼┼┼┼┼
   $\quad\quad\quad\quad 0$

18. $\{4, -12\}$ **19.** $\{-4, 8\}$ **20.** $\left\{\frac{18}{5}, -\frac{24}{5}\right\}$ **21.** $\emptyset$

22. $-3 < y < 3$ ┼┼┼┼⊷┼┼┼┼⊷┼┼┼┼
   $\quad\quad\quad\quad -3\quad 0\quad 3$

23. $-2 < y < 8$ ┼┼⊷┼┼┼┼┼┼┼┼┼⊷┼┼
   $\quad\quad\quad -2\quad 0\quad\quad\quad\quad\quad 8$

24. $4 \le x \le 5$ ┼┼┼┼┼┼┼┼┼┼●●┼┼
   $\quad\quad\quad\quad 0\quad\quad\quad\quad 4\ 5$

25. $x \le -5$ or $x \ge 5$ ┼●┼┼┼┼┼┼┼┼●┼┼
   $\quad\quad\quad\quad -5\quad\quad 0\quad\quad\quad 5$

26. $a < -5$ or $a > -5$
All numbers except -5 ┼┼⊷┼┼┼┼┼┼┼┼┼┼
   $\quad\quad\quad\quad\quad\quad -5\quad\quad 0$

27. $y < 1$ or $y > 4$ ┼┼┼┼┼┼┼┼⊷┼┼⊷┼┼
   $\quad\quad\quad\quad\quad\quad 0\ 1\quad\quad 4$

28. No **29.** No **30.** Yes **31.** Yes

32.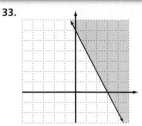

33.

34.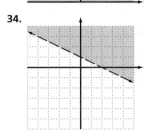

35.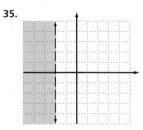

36.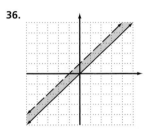

37.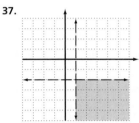

38.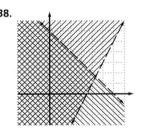

Chapter 10

Skills & Concepts You Need for Chapter 10 **1.** $\frac{5}{3}$
2. $\frac{y}{3x}$ **3.** $\frac{1}{2}$ **4.** -6 **5.** $\frac{27}{2}$ **6.** -12 **7.** $3x^2 + 4x - 15$
8. $9x + 12$ **9.** $6x^2 + 4x$ **10.** $x^3 - x^2 - 3x - 1$ **11.** $x^2 - 4$
12. $x^2 + 6x + 9$ **13.** $(x - 3)(x + 3)$
14. $(x - 3)(x - 3)$ or $(x - 3)^2$ **15.** $(x + 2)(x + 1)$
16. $16x^5(x - 2)$ **17.** $(3a - 2)(2a + 3)$ **18.** 2, 3 **19.** $\frac{2}{3}, -\frac{2}{3}$
20. 5, -5

Selected Answers

LESSON 10-1

Try This a. $\dfrac{y+2}{4y}$ b. $\dfrac{2x+1}{3x+2}$ c. $\dfrac{a+1}{2a+1}$ d. -1 e. $-\dfrac{1}{3}$
f. -2

Exercises 1. $\dfrac{2x}{y^2}$ 3. $\dfrac{x-3}{x}$ 5. $\dfrac{m+1}{2m+3}$ 7. $\dfrac{x^3(6x-1)}{x-1}$
9. $\dfrac{1}{d-7}$ 11. $\dfrac{t-5}{t-4}$ 13. $a+1$ 15. Already simplified 17. $\dfrac{3}{2}$
19. $\dfrac{6}{x-3}$ 21. $\dfrac{b-3}{b-4}$ 23. $\dfrac{y-6}{y-5}$ 25. $\dfrac{a-3}{a+3}$ 27. $\dfrac{-1}{y+4}$
29. Already simplified 31. $-a^2-b^2$ 33. $\dfrac{m^2-n^2}{4}$
35. $\dfrac{(t-3)^2}{(t-1)(t-2)^2}$ 37. 7; 7 39. Sometimes; It is true for all
values of a except $a=3$. 41. Incorrect; only factors can be
simplified, not individual terms. 43. Incorrect; the expression
was factored incorrectly. The correct answer is 2. 45. $-3, 1$

Mixed Review 47. 5, 7 49. $\dfrac{1}{2}, -\dfrac{1}{3}$ 51. $(-2, -3)$
53. $(-2, 5)$

LESSON 10-2

Try This a. $\dfrac{8a^2}{5}$ b. $\dfrac{(x+3)(x+2)}{x+4}$ c. $\dfrac{-6}{(2m+1)(2m-1)}$

Exercises 1. $\dfrac{56x}{3}$ 3. $\dfrac{2}{c^2d}$ 5. $2y$ 7. $\dfrac{-2n}{n+2}$ 9. $\dfrac{(a-6)(a+2)}{a^2(a+1)}$
11. $\dfrac{2(y-3)}{5}$ 13. $\dfrac{m+5}{m-5}$ 15. $\dfrac{15}{(3y-2)(5y+6)}$
17. $\dfrac{t+3}{(t^2-2)(t-3)}$ 19. $\dfrac{x-1}{x+4}$ 21. $\dfrac{x-3}{x-4}$ 23. $\dfrac{12(x+2)}{5}$
25. $\dfrac{(y-4)(y-2)}{3y(y+4)}$ 27. $\dfrac{5}{(m+3)(m-1)}$ 29. $\dfrac{5+x}{2}$ 31. $-\dfrac{1}{2}$
33. $14x$ 35. $\dfrac{x+2}{x-2}$ 37. $\dfrac{(a-3)(a+3)}{a(a+4)}$ 39. $\dfrac{2a}{a-2}$
41. $\dfrac{(x-2)(x+2)}{(x-1)(x+1)}$ 43. $\dfrac{(t-2)}{(t-1)}$ 45. $(m-n)(m-3)$
47. $\dfrac{1}{x-y}$ 49. -2 51. 0, 2, 7

Mixed Review 53. $\{-2, 0, 1, 2, 3, 4, 5\}$ 55. $\{0, 1\}$
57. 4, -1 59. $\dfrac{5}{3}, -1$ 61. $(4, 4)$ 63. 11, -5
65. a. $y=90x+20$ b. $470

LESSON 10-3

Try This a. $2a^2$ b. 8 c. $\dfrac{3(x-1)}{2(x+2)(x-2)}$

Exercises 1. $2x^2$ 3. $\dfrac{1}{a^3}$ 5. $\dfrac{3m^3}{5}$ 7. $\dfrac{15}{8}$
9. $\dfrac{15}{4}$ 11. $\dfrac{a-5}{3(a-1)}$ 13. $\dfrac{(x+2)^2}{x}$ 15. $\dfrac{3}{2}$ 17. $\dfrac{c+1}{c-1}$

19. $\dfrac{3(a-4)}{2}$ 21. $\dfrac{y-3}{2y-1}$ 23. $\dfrac{x+12}{x+2}$ 25. $\dfrac{1}{(c-5)^2}$ 27. $\dfrac{c+2}{c-2}$
29. $\dfrac{t+5}{t-5}$ 31. $\dfrac{4(a+7)}{27}$ 33. $\dfrac{4^4(b-3)}{3^5}$ 35. $\dfrac{a}{(c-3d)(2a+5b)}$
37. 1 39. $\dfrac{(z+4)^3}{(z-4)^3}$ 41. $\dfrac{(a-7)^2}{a+b}$ 43. $\dfrac{x(x^2+1)}{3(x+y-1)}$
45. $\dfrac{a-3b}{c}$

Mixed Review 47. No 49. Yes 51. Yes 53. $c=\dfrac{ad}{b}$
55. $(-2, 4)$ 57. ± 3 59. $x>1, x<-4$

LESSON 10-4

Try This a. $\dfrac{5a}{2}$ b. $\dfrac{10x^2}{x+4}$ c. $x+4$ d. $\dfrac{2(m+3)}{m-1}$ e. $y+3$

Exercises 1. a 3. $\dfrac{s}{2}$ 5. $\dfrac{13b^2}{c}$ 7. $\dfrac{7(x+1)}{x+2}$ 9. -2 11. $y-6$
13. $\dfrac{5a-1}{a-1}$ 15. -2 17. $\dfrac{-y+4}{y+5}$ 19. $\dfrac{(3n+2)(n-4)}{n+4}$
21. $\dfrac{2(x-2)(x-1)}{2x-1}$ 23. $\dfrac{-2(a-2)}{(a-1)(a-1)}$ 25. $\dfrac{2(5a+3)}{a-2}$
27. $\dfrac{a^2+a+9}{a+2}$ 29. $\dfrac{2x^2+4x+3}{x-1}$ 31. $\dfrac{-y(3y+10)}{2y+1}$
33. $\dfrac{2(2x-1)}{x-1}$ 35. $\dfrac{-2x-15}{x-6}$ 37. $\dfrac{30}{(x+4)(x-3)}$

Mixed Review 39. $\dfrac{m-6}{4}$ 41. $81t^8$ 43. $\dfrac{m^{24}n^{12}}{64}$ 45. $\dfrac{4x^2}{y^2}$
47. 11, 9

LESSON 10-5

Try This a. $\dfrac{2x^2+18}{3x}$ b. $\dfrac{56x^2+9x}{48}$ c. $\dfrac{x^2+6x-8}{(x-2)(x+2)}$
d. $\dfrac{4x-5}{5x^2}$ e. $\dfrac{2x-5}{(2x+1)(2x-1)}$ f. $\dfrac{6t-13}{t-2}$ g. $60x^3y^2$
h. $(y+1)^2(y+4)$ i. t^2-16 or $(t+4)(4-t)$ j. $\dfrac{5x^2+6x}{50}$
k. $\dfrac{3x-xy-y^2}{x^2y^2}$ l. $\dfrac{b-8}{2(b-3)}$ or $\dfrac{8-b}{2(3-b)}$

Exercises 1. $\dfrac{7a^2}{8}$ 3. $\dfrac{44c}{75}$ 5. $\dfrac{4(x+2)}{x^2}$ 7. $\dfrac{6x}{(x-2)(x+2)}$
9. $\dfrac{11x+2}{3x(x+1)}$ 11. $\dfrac{a+8}{4}$ 13. $\dfrac{-7x-13}{4x}$ 15. $\dfrac{x(3x-7)}{x-2}$
17. $\dfrac{8(x+2)}{x(x+4)}$ 19. c^2d^2 21. $(x-y)(x+y)$ 23. $6(y-3)$ or
$6(3-y)$ 25. $(t+2)(t-2)$ 27. $(x+2)(x-2)(x+3)$
29. $t(t+2)^2(t-4)$ 31. $(a-1)(a+1)$
33. $(m-2)^2(m-3)$ 35. $\dfrac{37}{18t}$ 37. $\dfrac{c^2+3cd-d^2}{c^2d^2}$
39. $\dfrac{3x-1}{(x-1)^2}$ 41. $\dfrac{11a}{10(a-2)}$ 43. $\dfrac{x^2+5x+1}{(x+1)^2(x+4)}$
45. $\dfrac{8-3b}{b-7}$ or $\dfrac{3b-8}{7-b}$ 47. $\dfrac{t^2+4}{t-2}$ 49. $\dfrac{z(5-z)}{(z-1)(z+1)}$

51. $\dfrac{3x + 20}{(x - 4)(x + 4)}$ **53.** $\dfrac{4 - 3b}{5b(b - 1)}$ **55.** $\dfrac{x(x + 6)}{(x - 4)(x + 4)}$

57. $\dfrac{6}{z + 4}$ **59.** $\dfrac{4x^2 - 13xt + 9t^2}{3x^2 t^2}$ **61.** 0   **63.** 3

65. $\dfrac{x - 3}{(x + 1)(x + 3)}$ **67.** $120(x + 1)(x - 1)^2$

69. $10x^3(x + 1)^2(x - 1)$ **71.** $\dfrac{(z + 6)(2z - 3)}{z^2 - 4}$

73. $\dfrac{11z^4 - 22z^2 + 6}{(2z^2 - 3)(z^2 + 2)(z^2 - 2)}$ **75.** Answers may vary.

Ex: $\dfrac{5x^2 + y}{x^2 + y^2} - \dfrac{2xy + y}{x^2 + y^2}$ **77.** Every 60 years

Mixed Review   **79.** Yes   **81.** No

83. $\left\{x \mid x \geq 3 \text{ or } x \leq \frac{1}{3}\right\}$

85. $\{x \mid x \neq 0\}$ **87.** $\dfrac{a + 4}{a - 3}$
89. -3

LESSON 10-6

Try This   **a.** $\frac{33}{2}$ **b.** 3   **c.** 1   **d.** 2   **e.** $-\frac{1}{8}$

Exercises   **1.** $\frac{47}{2}$ **3.** -6 **5.** $\frac{24}{7}$ **7.** $-4; -1$ **9.** $4; -4$ **11.** 3
13. $\frac{14}{3}$ **15.** 10   **17.** 5   **19.** $\frac{5}{2}$ **21.** -1 **23.** $\frac{17}{2}$ **25.** No
solution   **27.** -5 **29.** $\frac{5}{3}$ **31.** $\frac{1}{2}$ **33.** No solution   **35.** 7
37. $4, -2$ **39.** $0, -1$ **41.** $\frac{4}{3}, -\frac{7}{3}$ **43.** $\frac{3}{2}$

45. $\dfrac{\frac{x}{y} + \frac{w}{z}}{1 - \frac{x}{y} \cdot \frac{w}{z}} = \dfrac{\frac{xz + yw}{yz}}{\frac{yz - xw}{yz}} \cdot \dfrac{yz}{yz} = \dfrac{xz + yw}{yz - xw}$

Mixed Review   **47.** $\dfrac{(x + 1)(x - 3)}{x - 5}$ **49.** $\frac{1}{4}$ **51.** $-2, 3$
53. $x < -4$ or $x > 0$ **55.** $y > -2$ **57.** 2, 6

LESSON 10-7

Try This   **a.** $3\frac{3}{7}$ h   **b.** $34\frac{2}{7}$ km/h, $44\frac{2}{7}$ km/h   **c.** -3

Exercises   **1.** $1\frac{7}{8}$ h   **3.** $10\frac{2}{7}$ h   **5.** 30 km/h, 70 km/h
7. p: 80 km/h, f: 66 km/h   **9.** $\frac{1}{2}x + \frac{1}{x} = \frac{51}{x}$, $x = 10$ or -10
11. 24 h   **13.** 12 min, 24 min   **15.** 20 h   **17.** 36 h
19. $\frac{30}{r} + \frac{20}{r + 15} = 1$; 45 mi/h

Mixed Review   **21.** $\dfrac{(8x - 3)}{(x - 1)}$ **23.** $x - 1$ **25.** 7, -2
27. $0, -1, -2$ **29.** 77

LESSON 10-8

Try This   **a.** 120 mL   **b.** 75 lb, 100 lb

Exercises

1.

100 − x	40%	0.40(100 − x)
	50%	0.50(100)

50 L of 60%, 50 L of 40%

3. a, b, d.

	Amt. of solution	% Acid	Amount of acid
Soln. A	x	50%	0.50x
Soln. B	100 − x	80%	0.80(100 − x)
Final soln.	100	68%	0.68(100)

c. (Percent acid)(Amount solution)
e. $0.50x + 0.80(100 - x) = 0.68(100)$; 40 mL of A, 60 mL of B
5. 80 L of 30%, 120 L of 50%   **7.** 6 kg of cashews, 4 kg of
pecans   **9.** 590 from Southern Maywood   **11.** 1770

Mixed Review   **13.** 4, -10 **15.** 6, -6 **17.** $-3 \leq x \leq \frac{17}{13}$
19. 46 dimes, 37 quarters

Connections: Reasoning

Solution A:

0.60x
0.40(10 − x)
0.50(10)

Solution B:

0.60x
0.40y
0.50(10)

5 L of each   Systems of equations

LESSON 10-9

Try This   **a.** $2x^4 + 3x - \frac{5}{2}$ **b.** $x^2 + 3x + 2$ **c.** $x + 4 + \dfrac{-1}{x - 2}$
d. $x^2 + x + 1$

Exercises   **1.** $3x^4 - \frac{x^3}{2} + \frac{x^2}{8} - 2$ **3.** $1 - 2u - u^4$
5. $5t^2 + 8t - 2$ **7.** $-4x^4 + 4x^2 + 1$ **9.** $-3rs - r + 2s$
11. $x + 2$ **13.** $x - 5 + \dfrac{-50}{x - 5}$ **15.** $x - 3$
17. $x^4 - x^3 + x^2 - x + 1$ **19.** $a^2 + 4a + 4$
21. $2x^2 - 7x + 4$ **23.** $x^3 - 6$ **25.** $x^3 + 2x^2 + 4x + 8$
27. $t^2 + 1$ **29.** $x^2 + 5$ **31.** $a + 3 + \dfrac{5}{5a^2 - 7a - 2}$
33. $2x^2 + x - 3$ **35.** $a^5 + a^4b + a^3b^2 + a^2b^3 + ab^4 + b^5$
37. $6a^4 + 2a^3b - 5a^2b - ab^2 + b^2 + a$ **39.** -5 **41.** 1

Mixed Review   **43.** $-18(y - 1)$ or $18(y - 1)$ **45.** $\frac{9}{14m}$
47. $\dfrac{-1(2x - 1)}{(x + 3)(x - 3)}$ **49.** $-1, 3$ **51.** 6

The Factor Theorem   **1.** $(x - 8)(x - 1)$; 8, 1
3. $(x - 5)(x + 3)$; 5, -3 **5.** 0, -4, 0; roots: $\frac{7}{2}, \frac{3}{2}$

LESSON 10-10

Try This **a.** $\frac{5x}{3}$ **b.** $\frac{x}{x-1}$ **c.** $\frac{3}{t(2t-1)}$

Exercises **1.** $\frac{20}{21}$ **3.** $\frac{4(x+2)}{3x}$ **5.** $\frac{25}{4}$ **7.** $\frac{1+3x}{1-5x}$ **9.** $\frac{28}{y+8}$

11. $\frac{9+3s^2}{4s^2}$ **13.** $\frac{2x+1}{x}$ **15.** $\frac{a-b}{2}$ **17.** $x-y$

19. $\frac{a}{b(2a+1)}$ **21.** $\frac{x+y}{x}$ **23.** $\frac{4f+3fg+g}{2(fg^2+2fg+3f+2g+3)}$

25. $\frac{a+b}{a-b}$ **27.** $\frac{-ac}{bd}$ **29.** $\frac{27}{10}$

Mixed Review **31.** $\frac{3(x-2)}{(x+5)}$ **33.** $(m+5)$ **35.** $\frac{-1(x+7)}{2x}$

37. 3 **39.** $-17, 4$

LESSON 10-11

Try This **a.** 3. Associative and commutative properties
4. Reciprocal theorem **5.** Division theorem **6.** Transitive property of equality
b.

1. $[a+(-b)]+b$ $= a + [(-b) + b]$	1. Associative property
2. $= a + 0$	2. Property of additive inverse
3. $= a$	3. Identity property
4. $[a+(-b)] + b = a$	4. Transitive property

Thus, by the definition of subtraction, $a + (-b) = a - b$.

Exercises **1.** (c) Distributive property (d) Division theorem
(e) Transitive property of equality

3. Show $\frac{1}{\frac{a}{b}} = \frac{b}{a}$.

1. $\frac{1}{\frac{a}{b}} = \frac{1 \cdot b}{\frac{a}{b} \cdot b}$	1. Mult. identity; $\frac{b}{b} = 1$
2. $= \frac{b}{\frac{a}{b} \cdot b}$	2. Mult. identity
3. $= \frac{b}{\left(a \cdot \frac{1}{b}\right) \cdot b}$	3. Division theorem
4. $= \frac{b}{a\left(\frac{1}{b} \cdot b\right)}$	4. Associative property
5. $= \frac{b}{a(1)}$	5. Definition of reciprocal
6. $= \frac{b}{a}$	6. Mult. identity
7. $\frac{1}{\frac{a}{b}} = \frac{b}{a}$	7. Transitive property of equality

Mixed Review **5.** $32w^5$ **7.** y^{81} **9.** $(9c+4)(9c-4)$
11. $(2x+5)(x-1)$ **13.** $(3x+1)(2x+3)$ **15.** $7, -7$ **17.** 5
19. $(-1, 1)$

LESSON 10-12

Problems **1.** Together they found 44 new stores. They did not get the bonus. **3.** Before entering the first turnpike, Ramon had $22.50. **5.** The number is 42.

CHAPTER 10 WRAP UP

1. $\frac{x+3}{x}$ **2.** $\frac{2y+1}{y+2}$ **3.** $\frac{x-1}{x+2}$ **4.** $\frac{1}{5d-3c}$ **5.** $\frac{3(y-3)}{5}$ **6.** $\frac{1}{2}$

7. $\frac{28m}{5}$ **8.** 6 **9.** $\frac{y+1}{y-3}$ **10.** $\frac{y-2}{y-3}$ **11.** $\frac{1}{b(b+2)}$ **12.** $\frac{10}{3}$

13. $\frac{x-y}{y^3}$ **14.** $\frac{5x^2+x+1}{5x+1}$ **15.** $\frac{4b+3}{2+b}$ **16.** $\frac{a-1}{a}$ **17.** $\frac{2a}{a-1}$

18. -1 **19.** $\frac{x+1}{2x}$ **20.** $\frac{-7b+1}{(b+2)(b-2)}$

21. $\frac{-x^2+x+26}{(x-5)(x+5)(x+1)}$ **22.** 8 **23.** $(-5, 3)$ **24.** 3

25. $(-1, -5)$ **26.** $(5, 2)$ **27.** $5\frac{1}{7}$ hours **28.** 240 km/h, 280 km/h **29.** 40 liters of each **30.** $4y^3 + \frac{8}{3}y - 1$

31. $2x - 5$ **32.** $\frac{x}{1-x}$ **33.** $\frac{y(xy+3)}{xy^2-2}$

Chapter 11

Skills & Concepts You Need for Chapter 11 **1.** $\frac{9}{25}$

2. $\frac{3}{11}$ **3.** 3 **4.** 2 **5.** 5×5 **6.** $4 \times 4 \times 4$

7. $x \times x \times x \times x \times x \times x$ **8.** $7 \times 7 \times 7 \times 7 \times 7 \times 7$ **9.** 8

10. 15 **11.** 0 **12.** $\frac{25}{9}$ **13.** $-\frac{4}{81}$ **14.** $\frac{9}{256}$ **15.** $-\frac{121}{16}$ **16.** 25

17. -216 **18.** $\frac{9}{16}$ **19.** $-\frac{1}{125}$ **20.** x^6 **22.** a^3b^5 **22.** x^5

23. b^2 **24.** $x^2(x-1)$ **25.** $5x(1-6x)$ **26.** $(x+1)^2$

27. $(x-7)^2$

LESSON 11-1

Try This **a.** $13, -13$ **b.** -10 **c.** 16 **d.** Irrational
e. Rational **f.** Irrational **g.** Irrational **h.** 2.646 **i.** 8.485
j. 4.243 **k.** 6.708

Exercises **1.** $1, -1$ **3.** $4, -4$ **5.** $13, -13$ **7.** 2 **9.** -5
11. -9 **13.** 20 **15.** 14 **17.** -6 **19.** Irrational **21.** Rational
23. Rational **25.** Irrational **27.** 2.236 **29.** 9.644 **31.** 7.348
33. Irrational **35.** Rational, whole number **37.** 2 **39.** 7
41. B **43.** $-8, -7$ **45.** Sometimes **47.** $\sqrt{113}$
49. Ex: 1 is $(-1)^2$ and 1^3, 64 is 8^2 and 4^3 **51. a.** 3 **b.** 43
c. -6 **d.** 94

Mixed Review **53.** $\frac{x+1}{4}$ **55.** $x+2$ **57.** $5(5x+2)(5x-2)$
59. $\frac{11}{2}$ **61.** 4 **63.** $\frac{18}{11}$ **65.** $x-5$ **67.** $(1, 7)$

LESSON 11-2

Try This **a.** $\sqrt{-1}$; No **b.** $x \geq -1$ **c.** $x \geq 3$ **d.** $x \geq \frac{5}{2}$ **e.** All replacements **f.** $|xy|$ **g.** $|xy|$ **h.** $|x-1|$ **i.** $|x+4|$
j. $5|y|$ **k.** $\frac{1}{2}|t|$

Exercises **1.** 0; Yes **3.** $\sqrt{6}$; Yes **5.** $x \geq 0$ **7.** $t \geq 5$
9. $y \geq -8$ **11.** $x \geq -20$ **13.** $y \geq \frac{7}{2}$ **15.** Any value **17.** $|t|$
19. $3|x|$ **21.** 7 **23.** $4|d|$ **25.** $|x + 3|$ **27.** $|a - 5|$
29. $|2a - 1|$ **31.** 6, -6 **33.** 3, -3 **35.** $-2, 8$ **37.** $3|a|$
39. $\frac{2x^4}{|y^3|}$ **41.** $\frac{13}{m^8}$ **43. a.** $m \geq 0$ or $m \leq -3$ **b.** $x \geq 3$ or $x = 0$
45. Always **47.** Sometimes **49.** $x \geq 2$ or $x \leq -3$
51. $x \geq 2$ or $x \leq -2$ **53. a.** Real **b.** Real **c.** Not real
d. Not real **e.** Real **f.** Not real

Mixed Review **55.** No solution **57.** -2 **59.** $\frac{5y + 27}{(y + 5)^2}$
61. 6, -1 **63.** 7

Connections: Geometry **1.** 6 in.
3. larger can, 7.75 cm; smaller can, 3.75 cm

LESSON 11-3
Try This **a.** $4\sqrt{2}$ **b.** $5x$ **c.** $2\sqrt{15x}$ **d.** $3x\sqrt{5}$ **e.** $\sqrt{7}(x - 1)$
f. y^4 **g.** $(x + y)^7$ **h.** $t^7\sqrt{t}$ **i.** $a^{12}\sqrt{a}$

Exercises **1.** $2\sqrt{3}$ **3.** $2\sqrt{5}$ **5.** $5\sqrt{3}$ **7.** $10\sqrt{2}$ **9.** $x\sqrt{3}$
11. $4\sqrt{a}$ **13.** $x\sqrt{13}$ **15.** $3\sqrt{x}$ **17.** $8y$ **19.** $2t\sqrt{2}$
21. $2(x + 1)$ **23.** $(x + 3)\sqrt{2}$ **25.** $2x + 3y$ **27.** x^3 **29.** x^6
31. $x^2\sqrt{x}$ **33.** $t^9\sqrt{t}$ **35.** $(y - 2)^4$ **37.** $2(x + 5)^5$
39. $6m\sqrt{m}$ **41.** $2a^2\sqrt{2a}$ **43.** $8x^3y\sqrt{7y}$
45. $\sqrt{9x^2y^2} = 3xy$, not $9xy$ **47.** $10\sqrt{3}$ **49.** $-18\sqrt{2}$
51. $36\sqrt{x}$ **53.** $10x^3\sqrt{2}$ **55.** $6a^4b^2\sqrt{7ab}$ **57.** $2\sqrt{6}$ **59.** $3\sqrt{5}$
61. $>$ **63.** $>$ **65.** $<$ **67.** $<$ **69.** $<$

Mixed Review **71.** $(-1, -4)$ **73.** $(3, -2)$ **75.** $\frac{x + 2}{x^2}$

Cube Roots **1.** 2 **3.** 5 **5.** -2 **7.** -1 **9.** x **11.** ab
13. $3x^2y$ **15.** $-2a^2b^3$ **17.** xy^2 **19.** $a^2b^3\sqrt[3]{30ab^2}$

LESSON 11-4
Try This **a.** $\sqrt{21}$ **b.** $\sqrt{25}$, or 5 **c.** $\sqrt{x^2 + x}$ **d.** $\sqrt{x^2 - 1}$
e. $3\sqrt{2y}$ **f.** $10x$ **g.** $4x^3y^2$ **h.** $5xy^2\sqrt{2xy}$ **i.** $6x^2y^4\sqrt{x}$

Exercises **1.** $\sqrt{6}$ **3.** 17 **5.** $\sqrt{2x}$ **7.** $\sqrt{10x - 5}$
9. $\sqrt{x^2 - 16}$ **11.** $\sqrt{2x^2 - 3x - 20}$ **13.** $\sqrt{3x^2 + 4xy}$
15. $\sqrt{x^2 + x - 12}$ **17.** $3\sqrt{10}$ **19.** $6\sqrt{7x}$ **21.** $11\sqrt{x}$
23. $6a\sqrt{3}$ **25.** $a\sqrt{bc}$ **27.** $2xy\sqrt{2xy}$ **29.** $6xy^3\sqrt{3xy}$
31. $10ab^2\sqrt{5ab}$ **33.** $7a^2b\sqrt{6ab}$ **35.** $2x^5y^2\sqrt{5x}$
37. $4x^2yz^2\sqrt{5y}$ **39.** $30x^2\sqrt{3}$ **41.** $10x^7\sqrt{3}$ **43.** $a^2 - 5\sqrt{a}$
45. $6(x - 2)^2\sqrt{10}$ **47.** $0.2x^{2n}$ **49.** $7y^{13}x^{157}\sqrt{3xy}$
51. $(a + 2b)^{17}$ **53.** $x^{n+1}y^{2n}\sqrt{xy}$ **55.** $y^{\frac{n}{2}}$
57. $x^4 + y^4$; $(x^4 + \sqrt{2}x^2y^2 + y^4)(x^4 - \sqrt{2}x^2y^2 + y^4)$

Mixed Review **59.** $27y^6$ **61.** $-8c^5$ **63.** $(12y - 1)(12y + 1)$
65. $\frac{-9(x + 1)}{x + 3}$ **67.** $\frac{x + 5}{4}$ **69.** ± 11 **71.** 4 **73.** -15

Rational Exponents **1.** 4 **3.** 3 **5.** 7 **7.** 8 **9.** 9

LESSON 11-5
Try This **a.** $\frac{4}{3}$ **b.** $\frac{1}{5}$ **c.** $\frac{1}{3}$ **d.** $\frac{3}{4}$ **e.** $\frac{15}{16}$ **f.** 5 **g.** $x\sqrt{6}$ **h.** $\frac{\sqrt{35}}{7}$
i. $\frac{4\sqrt{6}}{3}$ **j.** $\frac{\sqrt{xy}}{y}$ **k.** $\frac{\sqrt{21}}{7}$ **l.** $\frac{\sqrt{10}}{4}$ **m.** $\frac{\sqrt{6}}{9}$ **n.** $\frac{\sqrt{10a}}{2a}$ **o.** $\frac{\sqrt{21b}}{3b^3}$
p. $\frac{\sqrt{2xy}}{6y^2}$

Exercises **1.** $\frac{3}{7}$ **3.** $\frac{1}{6}$ **5.** $-\frac{4}{9}$ **7.** $\frac{8}{17}$ **9.** $-\frac{3}{10}$ **11.** $\frac{3}{5}$ **13.** 3
15. 2 **17.** $\sqrt{5}$ **19.** $\frac{1}{5}$ **21.** $\frac{2}{5}$ **23.** 2 **25.** $3y$ **27.** $x^2\sqrt{5}$
29. $\frac{1}{3}\sqrt{21}$ **31.** $\frac{3}{4}\sqrt{2}$ **33.** $\frac{1}{5}\sqrt{10}$ **35.** $\frac{1}{4}\sqrt{6}$ **37.** $\frac{1}{6}\sqrt{21}$
39. $\frac{1}{6}\sqrt{2}$ **41.** $\frac{1}{2}\sqrt{2}$ **43.** $\frac{2}{3}\sqrt{6}$ **45.** $\frac{1}{x}\sqrt{3x}$ **47.** $\frac{1}{y}\sqrt{xy}$
49. $\frac{x\sqrt{2}}{6}$ **51.** $\frac{\sqrt{3cd}}{d^2}$ **53.** $\frac{\sqrt{10}}{5}$ **55.** $\sqrt{2}$ **57.** $\frac{\sqrt{6}}{2}$ **59.** 5
61. $\frac{\sqrt{3x}}{x}$ **63.** $\frac{4y\sqrt{3}}{3}$ **65.** $\frac{a\sqrt{2a}}{4}$ **67.** $\frac{\sqrt{42x}}{3x}$ **69.** $\frac{3\sqrt{6}}{8c}$
71. $\frac{y\sqrt{xy}}{x}$ **73.** $\frac{\sqrt{6}}{9}$ **75.** $\frac{\sqrt{10}}{3}$ **77.** $6\sqrt{2}$ **79.** $\frac{\sqrt{ab}}{b}$ **81.** -4
83. $5 + 2\sqrt{6}$

Mixed Review **85.** Irrational **87.** Irrational **89.** Rational
91. Rational **93.** $(x + 3)(x - 5)$ **95.** $(m - 3n)(2a + b)$
97. 4 **99.** $x \geq 0$ **101.** $x \geq 2$

Operations with Rational Exponents **1.** 4
3. $\sqrt[8]{10^7}$ or $\sqrt[8]{10,000,000}$ **5.** $\frac{\sqrt[9]{t^8}}{t}$ **7.** $\sqrt[32]{m^{15}n^{16}}$
or $\sqrt[32]{m^{15}}\sqrt{n}$ **9.** $\sqrt[6]{x^5}\sqrt[5]{y^2}$ or $\sqrt[30]{x^{25}y^{12}}$ **11.** $\sqrt[3]{\frac{m^2}{n^2}}$

LESSON 11-6
Try This **a.** $12\sqrt{2}$ **b.** $5\sqrt{5}$ **c.** $-12\sqrt{10}$ **d.** $5\sqrt{6y}$
e. $\sqrt{x + 1}$ **f.** $\frac{3}{2}\sqrt{2}$ **g.** $\frac{2\sqrt{15}}{15}$ **h.** $2\sqrt{x}$

Exercises **1.** $7\sqrt{2}$ **3.** $4\sqrt{5}$ **5.** $13\sqrt{x}$ **7.** $-2\sqrt{x}$ **9.** $25\sqrt{2}$
11. $\sqrt{3}$ **13.** $\sqrt{5}$ **15.** $13\sqrt{2}$ **17.** $3\sqrt{3}$ **19.** $-24\sqrt{2}$
21. $6\sqrt{2} - 6\sqrt{3}$ **23.** $(2 + 9x)\sqrt{x}$ **25.** $(3 - 2x)\sqrt{3}$
27. $3\sqrt{2x + 2}$ **29.** $(x + 3)\sqrt{x^3 - 1}$
31. $(-x^2 + 3xy + y^2)\sqrt{xy}$ **33.** $(2 - a - b)\sqrt{a + b}$ **35.** $\frac{2\sqrt{3}}{3}$
37. $\frac{13\sqrt{2}}{2}$ **39.** $\frac{\sqrt{6}}{6}$ **41.** $\frac{\sqrt{3}}{18}$ **43. a.** None **b.** $\sqrt{10} + 5\sqrt{2}$
45. $16\sqrt{2}$ **47.** $(b^3 + ab + a)\sqrt{a}$ **49.** 0 **51.** $\frac{x + 1}{x}\sqrt{x}$

Selected Answers

53. $\frac{\sqrt{30}}{12}$ **55. a.** $\sqrt{5}, 3$ **b.** $\sqrt{13}, 5$ **c.** $\sqrt{17}, 5$ **d.** 5, 7
e. $\sqrt{10}, 4$ **f.** $2\sqrt{5}, 6$ **57.** $\frac{24 + 3\sqrt{3} + 8\sqrt{2} + \sqrt{6}}{7}$

Mixed Review   **59.** 6   **61.** $|y + 5|$ **63.** $4\sqrt{3}$ **65.** $\sqrt{a^2 - c^2}$
67. $4x\sqrt{y}$

69.   **71.**

Application   **1.** 35   **3.** 62   **5.** 38   **7.** 43   **9.** 50   **11.** From highest score to lowest: 8, 6, 9, 7, 5, 10 or 8, 9, 6, 7, 5, 10

LESSON 11-7

Try This   **a.** $\sqrt{65} \approx 8.062$ **b.** $\sqrt{75} \approx 8.660$ **c.** $\sqrt{10} \approx 3.162$
d. $\sqrt{175} = 5\sqrt{7} \approx 13.229$

Exercises   **1.** 17   **3.** $4\sqrt{2}$ or 5.657   **5.** 12   **7.** 4   **9.** 26
11. 12   **13.** 2   **15.** $\sqrt{2}$ **17.** 5   **19.** $\sqrt{5^2 + 8^2} = \sqrt{25 + 64}$
$= \sqrt{89}$, not $5 + 8 = 13$.   **21.** $\frac{a^2}{4}\sqrt{3}$ **23.** D   **25.** 3, 4, 5
27. $10\sqrt{3}$ **29.** $\frac{\sqrt{3}}{2} \approx 0.87$ **31.** Answers may vary. Examples are given.   **a.** $\frac{1}{2}$ **b.** -0.237 **c.** $\sqrt{2.4}$ **d.** $\sqrt{10.79}$ **e.** Yes. The average of two numbers will always be another real number between the two.

Mixed Review   **33.** $|x + 3|$ **35.** $4|a|\sqrt{2}$ **37.** a^{10}
39. $(x - 3)\sqrt{x - 3}$ **41.** $6x^2\sqrt{6}$ **43.** $3ab^2\sqrt{2a}$ **45.** 3
47. 14, 15

The Distance Formula   **1.** 13   **3.** $3\sqrt{2}$ **5.** $8\sqrt{2}$

LESSON 11-8

Try This   **a.** ≈ 18.0 ft   **b.** ≈ 9.7 ft

Exercises   **1.** ≈ 8.7 m   **3.** ≈ 76.5 ft   **5.** ≈ 68.0 m
7. ≈ 77.6 mi   **9.** ≈ 14.5 km   **11.** $\sqrt{27.75} \approx 4.9$ ft
13. $8\sqrt{10} + 2 \approx 27.3$ ft   **15.** $\sqrt{193} \approx 13.9$ in.
17. $3\sqrt{73} + 2 \approx 27.6$ ft   **19.** Old road 2.5 h, major highways 2.1 h; major highways

Mixed Review   **21.** $\frac{\sqrt{15}}{5}$ **23.** $\frac{\sqrt{x}}{x}$ **25.** $xy\sqrt{z}$ **27.** $6\sqrt{3}$
29. $5\sqrt{5}$ **31.** $\sqrt{6}$

LESSON 11-9

Try This   **a.** $\frac{64}{3}$ **b.** 2   **c.** 66   **d.** ≈ 313 km   **e.** ≈ 16 km
f. About 300 m

Exercises   **1.** 25   **3.** 38.44   **5.** 397   **7.** 310.5   **9.** 5   **11.** 3
13. $\frac{17}{4}$ **15.** No value   **17.** No value   **19.** ≈ 346 km
21. $\approx 10,000$ m   **23.** 125 ft, 245 ft   **25.** 2 or -2 **27.** 49
29. 2.1 ft   **31.** 12   **33.** 4   **35.** 9   **37.** $\frac{15}{4}$ **39.** $\pm\sqrt{\frac{a^2}{A^2 - 1}}$
41. 402.5 ft

Mixed Review   **43.** $x \geq -1$ **45.** $x \geq -\frac{1}{5}$ **47.** 15   **49.** $|(x - 1)|$
51. $y^6\sqrt{y}$ **53.** $12m^2\sqrt{m}$ **55.** $-\frac{1}{3}, \frac{1}{4}$

Preparing for Standardized Tests   **1.** (D)   **3.** (B)
5. (C)

CHAPTER 11 WRAP UP

1. 6   **2.** -9 **3.** 7   **4.** -13 **5.** Irrational   **6.** Rational
7. Irrational   **8.** Rational   **9.** $x \geq -7$ **10.** $x \geq 10$ **11.** $|m|$
12. $7|t|$ **13.** $|p|$ **14.** $|x - 4|$ **15.** $-4\sqrt{3}$ **16.** $x - 7$
17. $8x$ **18.** $6\sqrt{x}$ **19.** x^6 **20.** $y^2\sqrt{y}$ **21.** $(x - 2)^2$
22. $5y^7\sqrt{3y}$ **23.** $5x^4\sqrt{x}$ **24.** $(y + 7)^5$ **25.** $\sqrt{21}$ **26.** $\sqrt{at}$
27. $\sqrt{x^2 - 9}$ **28.** $\sqrt{6xy}$ **29.** $\sqrt{\frac{15}{28}}$ **30.** $\sqrt{6x^2 + 3x}$ **31.** $3\sqrt{2}$
32. $x^3\sqrt{10x}$ **33.** $b\sqrt{ac}$ **34.** $5b^2\sqrt{3}$ **35.** $\frac{3}{4}$ **36.** $\frac{1}{5}$ **37.** $\frac{2}{3}$
38. $\frac{3\sqrt{2}}{8}$ **39.** 4   **40.** $x^2\sqrt{5}$ **41.** 2   **42.** 4   **43.** $\frac{\sqrt{15}}{5}$ **44.** $\frac{5\sqrt{3}}{3}$
45. $\frac{2\sqrt{2x}}{x}$ **46.** $\frac{4a\sqrt{6a}}{3}$ **47.** $\frac{\sqrt{2}}{4}$ **48.** $\frac{\sqrt{5y}}{y}$ **49.** $13\sqrt{5}$ **50.** $\sqrt{5}$
51. $4\sqrt{x}$ **52.** $\frac{\sqrt{2}}{2}$ **53.** $4\sqrt{x + 1}$ **54.** $3x\sqrt{3}$ **55.** $c = 25$
56. $a = 5$ **57.** $b = 8$ **58.** $c = \sqrt{7}$ **59.** $a = 8\sqrt{2}$ **60.** $c = 12$
61. ≈ 11.3 ft   **62.** ≈ 14.4 ft   **63.** 52   **64.** 147   **65.** 466.56 m

CHAPTERS 1–11 CUMULATIVE REVIEW

1. 102   **3.** $11(11a + 8b)$ **5.** $\frac{x(y - 4)}{x - 8y}$ **7.** 70   **9.** -72 **11.** 8
13. $-7(3x + 4w)$ **15.** $-5x + 7$ **17.** 3 books   **19.** 0   **21.** 250
23. 770 oranges   **25.** $x \leq -6$ **27.** $x < 4$ **29.** a^3b^9 **31.** a^3b
33. $\frac{1}{7^4}$ **35.** $-27x^{15}y^6$ **37.** 3.46×10^5 **39.** a
41. $3c + 2bc + c^2 - 4 - 2b$ **43.** $5x^2 + 4xy - 12y^2$
45. $h^2 - 8hk + 16k^2$ **47.** $x^4 - 9$ **49.** $xy(x^2y^2 + xy - 4)$
51. $(2 - 3m^2)(2 + 3m^2)$ **53.** $(x - 6)(x + 2)$
55. $t(t - 2)(t - 3)$ **57.** $(4y + 3)(5y + 1)$ **59.** $-2, 5$
61. $y = 5x$ **63.** $y = -x - 12$ **65.** $y = 3x + 5$ **67.** $(3, -3)$
69. 37   **71.** {0}   **73.** 6, -1

75. $x \leq -5$ or $x \geq 5$

77. $-\frac{2}{3}$ **79.** x^3y^2 **81.** $\frac{3y^2 - 5y - 6}{(y + 1)(y - 1)}$ **83.** -10

85. $26\frac{2}{3}$ h or 26 h 40 min   **87.** $\frac{1 + 3x}{1 - 2x}$ **89.** -11 **91.** $7|c|$

93. $|x - 3|$ **95.** x^4 **97.** $2x^2y^2\sqrt{5y}$ **99.** $3|ab|\sqrt{2a}$

101. $\sqrt{2x^2 + 3xy - 20y^2}$ **103.** $2|x|\sqrt{2}$ **105.** $\frac{1}{3}$ **107.** $8\sqrt{2}$

109. $\frac{-\sqrt{3}}{6}$ **111.** $c = 34$ **113.** 14

Chapter 12

Skills & Concepts You Need for Chapter 12   **1.** $\frac{10}{3}$
2. 26   **3.** -31 **4.** 21   **5.** 360   **6.** $\frac{2A}{b_1 + b_2}$ **7.** $\frac{C}{2\pi}$ **8.** 1050

9.

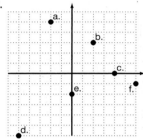

10.

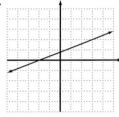

11.

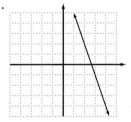

LESSON 12-1

Try This   **a.** Domain: {Tom, Sue}, Range: {12, 18, 28}; no
b. Domain: {3, 6, 7}, Range: {35, 36}; yes   **c.** 8, -5, 1
d. 0, -10, 2   **e.** 11, 35, 5   **f.** -1, 5, 20

Exercises   **1.** Yes   **3.** Yes   **5.** Domain: {a, d}, Range: {b, c, e};
no   **7.** 8, 12, -4 **9.** -6, 15, 72   **11.** 6, -10, 16   **13.** 2, 7, 4
15. 4, 4, 3   **17.** 1, 91, 98   **19.** -3, -2, 78   **21.** \$45.15
23. \$54.24   **25.** $1\frac{20}{33}$, $1\frac{30}{33}$, $4\frac{1}{33}$ **27.** 70°, 220°, 10,020°
29. {5, 8, 11, 14}   **31.** {0, 2}   **33. a.** Always; every domain
element is assigned to exactly one range element.
b. Sometimes; a domain element could be assigned to more
than one range element.   **c.** Never; at least one domain
element must be assigned to two range elements.   **35.** 100
37. 880   **39.** -64

Mixed Review   **41.** $(-1, 6)$ **43.** $(-2, 7)$ **45.** $\sqrt{y^2 - 2y}$
47. $\sqrt{m^2 - n^2}$ **49.** $\sqrt{3x^2 - 10x - 8}$ **51.** $y = 1$ **53.** $x = 3$
55. $12|m|$ **57.** $4|a|\sqrt{2a}$

Operations with Functions   **1.** $\frac{5x^2 - 1}{x}$ **3.** $\frac{3x - 3}{x(x - 3)}$
5. $\frac{x - 3}{2x}$

LESSON 12-2

Try This   **a.** Yes   **b.** No   **c.** No   **d.** Yes   **e.** No   **f.** Yes
g. All real numbers   **h.** $\{x \mid x \neq -5\}$ **i.** $\{x \mid x \geq 1\}$

j.

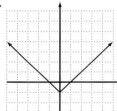

$\{y \mid y \geq -1\}$

k.

All real numbers

l.

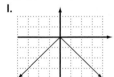

$\{y \mid y \leq 0\}$

Exercises

1.

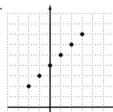

5. Yes   **7.** No   **9.** Yes   **11.** No
13. Yes   **15.** $\{x \mid x \neq 0\}$
17. $\{x \mid x \geq 0\}$ **19.** $\{x \mid x \geq -2\}$
21. $\{x \mid x \neq -3\}$
23. $\{x \mid x \leq 4\}$

25.

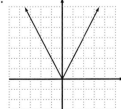

Domain: all real numbers
Range: $\{y \mid y \geq 0\}$

27.

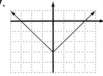

Domain: all real numbers
Range: $\{y \mid y \geq -3\}$

29.

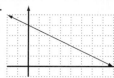

31.

Domain: all real numbers
Range: all real numbers

Domain: $\{x \mid x \neq 0\}$
Range: $\{y \mid y \neq 0\}$; yes

33. A **35.** $\vee$ shaped, or $\wedge$ if a is negative, with "point" on the y-axis b units up or down from the origin

Mixed Review **37.** $\frac{1}{7}$ **39.** $\frac{\sqrt{15}}{3}$ **41.** $(x - 5)$ **43.** $(x - 2)$

LESSON 12-3

Try This **a.** $c(h) = 3.50 + 3.65h$; $c(9) = \$36.35$

Exercises **1.** $c(k) = 35 + 0.21k$; $c(340) = \$106.40$
3. $c(h) = 6.50 + 5.90h$; $c(7.5) = \$50.75$
5. $c(h) = 5.50 + 4.25h$; $c(4.5) = \$24.63$
7. $L(w) = \frac{1}{3}w + 40$; $L(15) = 45$ cm **9.** \$8.70; \$20.10
11. \$12.50 **13.** A horizontal line

Mixed Review **17.** $8\sqrt{2}$ **19.** 5.47×10^6 **21.** 2
23. $x > 4$ or $x < -4$

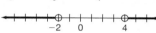

25. $x > 4$ or $x < -2$

Connections: Discrete Math **1.** Filipe could also visit the library just after Becca leaves, while Abdul is still at the library. This would not change the number of students that Becca sees because she does not see Filipe in either case.

LESSON 12-4

Try This

a.

b.

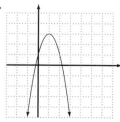

c.

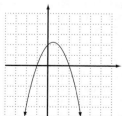

d. 2, 3 **e.** −1, 4

Exercises

1.

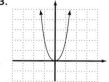

Domain: all real numbers
Range: $\{y \mid y \leq 0\}$

3.

Domain: all real numbers
Range: $\{y \mid y \geq 0\}$

5.

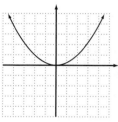

Domain: all real numbers
Range: $\{y \mid y \geq 0\}$

7.

Domain: all real numbers
Range: $\{y \mid y \geq -3\}$

9.

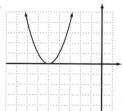

Domain: all real numbers
Range: $\{y \mid y \geq -1\}$

11.

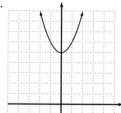

13.

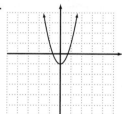

15.

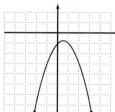

17. −2, 0 **19.** 4 **21.** −9, −2
23.

The x-intercepts of the graph are −1 and 2. The roots of the polynomial are −1 and 2.

25. $a > 0$; $a < 0$ **a.** upward **b.** downward **c.** downward

27. a. $(0, -4)$ min. pt. **b.** $(0, 7)$ max. pt. **c.** $\left(\frac{1}{4}, \frac{19}{8}\right)$ max. pt.
29. 2 s, 4 s **31.** 6 s **33.** As $|a|$ increases, the graph narrows.
35. If the graph of the function does not cross the x-axis, then the equation has no real-number solution.

Mixed Review **37.** 0.0000005115 **39.** 289 **41.** 80 **43.** 7

45. $\frac{-2\sqrt{35}}{35}$ **47.** $\frac{3\sqrt{10} + \sqrt{15}}{15}$ **49.** $-1, 11, 5, -10$ **51.** $|x - 5|$

53. $9|m|\sqrt{3m}$

LESSON 12-5

Try This **a.** $y = 7x$ **b.** $y = 0.625x$ **c.** $46\frac{2}{3}¢, 1\frac{17}{18}¢$ **d.** 132.5 lb

Exercises **1.** $y = 4x$ **3.** $y = 1.75x$ **5.** $y = 3.2x$ **7.** $y = \frac{2}{3}x$
9. $551.25 **11.** Approx. 25 servings **13.** Approx. 25 lb
15. 68.4 kg **17.** 2500 miles **19.** Yes **21.** No **23.** No
25. $C = kr(k = 2\pi)$ **27.** $C = kA$ **29.** $S = kV^6$ **31.** $A = kr^2$

Mixed Review **33.** Any real no. **35.** $m \geq \frac{1}{3}$ **37.** Any real no.

39. $\frac{\sqrt{x}}{x}$ **41.** $\frac{3|m|\sqrt{2}}{4}$ **43.** $10\sqrt{2}$ **45.** $-8, -2, 40, 22$

LESSON 12-6

Try This **a.** $y = \frac{63}{x}$ **b.** $y = \frac{900}{x}$ **c.** $7\frac{1}{2}$ hr **d.** 3.2 h or $3\frac{1}{5}$ h

Exercises **1.** $y = \frac{75}{x}$ **3.** $y = \frac{80}{x}$ **5.** $y = \frac{1}{x}$ **7.** $y = \frac{1050}{x}$
9. $y = \frac{0.06}{x}$ **11.** $y = \frac{3.2}{x}$ **13.** $y = \frac{1}{x}$ **15.** $5\frac{1}{3}$ hr **17.** 320 cm³
19. 54 min **21.** $C = \frac{k}{N}$ **23.** $I = \frac{k}{R}$ **25.** B **27.** $F = \frac{kS^2m}{r}$

Mixed Review **29.** $|x - 5|\sqrt{2}$ **31.** 18 **33.** No **35.** Yes

37. 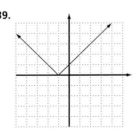 **39.**

Connections: Reasoning **1.** d **3.** a

LESSON 12-7

Try This **a.** $w = 0.4xyz; 32$ **b.** $P = \frac{0.02q}{r}; 0.024$ **c.** $420 k$

Exercises **1.** $r = \frac{1}{2}st; 54$ **3.** $q = 5rs; 0.8$ **5.** $x = \frac{3}{10}wyz; 54$
7. $m = \frac{10n}{p}; 2$ **9.** $p = \frac{0.7q}{r}; 2.8$ **11.** 2.8 **13.** 28 cm³
15. 8 in. **17.** $\frac{\pi}{4}$ **19.** y is doubled **21.** Approx. 51 mi/h

Mixed Review **23.** $\frac{4\sqrt{3}}{3}$ **25.** $\frac{\sqrt{y}}{y}$ **27.** $\frac{\sqrt{xy}}{2y}$ **29.** $\frac{\sqrt{3}}{2c}$ **31.** 26

33. 40 **35.** No real-number solution **37.** 6

CHAPTER 12 WRAP UP

1. No **2.** Yes **3.** 2; -4; -7 **4.** 0; 2; -3 **5.** -7; 1; 0
6. 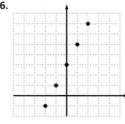 **7.**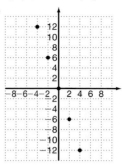

8. 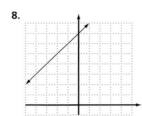 **9.**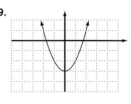

10. 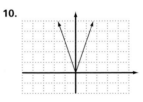 **11.** No **12.** Yes
13. $c(m) =$
$0.35 + 0.25(m - 1)$;
$1.35

14. 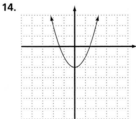 **15.**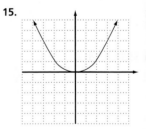

16. $y = 3x$ **17.** $y = \frac{1}{2}x$ **18.** $247.50 **19.** $y = \frac{30}{x}$ **20.** $y = \frac{1}{x}$
21. 1 h **22. a.** $k = \frac{1}{2}$ **b.** $A = 60$ **23. a.** $k = 27$ **b.** $W = 72$

Chapter 13

Skills & Concepts You Need for Chapter 13

1. $x^2 - 10x + 25$ **2.** $9x^2 + 6x + 1$ **3.** 0, 6 **4.** 2, 3 **5.** 2
6. $\frac{10}{3}$ **7.** $2\sqrt{22}$ **8.** $2\sqrt{5}$ **9.** $2\sqrt{11}$ **10.** $4\sqrt{2}$ **11.** $\frac{\sqrt{21}}{3}$
12. $\frac{\sqrt{10}}{2}$ **13.** $\frac{\sqrt{5}}{5}$ **14.** $\frac{\sqrt{14}}{4}$

15. 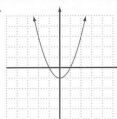 **16.**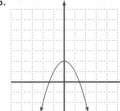

LESSON 13-1

Try This   a. $x^2 - 7x = 0; a = 1, b = -7, c = 0$
b. $x^2 + 9x - 3 = 0; a = 1, b = 9, c = -3$
c. $5x^2 + 0x + 4 = 0; a = 5, b = 0, c = 4$ **d.** $\frac{-5}{3}, 0$ **e.** $\frac{3}{5}, 0$
f. $-1, \frac{2}{3}$ **g.** $7, -3$

Exercises   1. $x^2 - 3x + 2 = 0; a = 1, b = -3, c = 2$
3. $2x^2 - 3 = 0; a = 2, b = 0, c = -3$ **5.** $7x^2 - 4x + 3 = 0;$
$a = 7, b = -4, c = 3$ **7.** $2x^2 - 3x + 5 = 0; a = 2, b = -3,$
$c = 5$ **9.** $3x^2 - 2x + 8 = 0; a = 3, b = -2, c = 8$ **11.** $0, -5$
13. $0, -2$ **15.** $0, \frac{7}{3}$ **17.** $0, 1$ **19.** $0, 5$ **21.** $0, -\frac{1}{3}$ **23.** $0, \frac{8}{17}$
25. $4, 12$ **27.** $-1, -6$ **29.** $3, -7$ **31.** $2, 7$ **33.** -5 **35.** 1
37. $\frac{3}{2}, 5$ **39.** $4, -\frac{2}{3}$ **41.** $4, -\frac{5}{3}$ **43.** $-1, -5$ **45.** $\frac{1}{3}, -\frac{1}{2}$
47. $-5, \frac{7}{2}$ **49.** $-2, 7$ **51.** $3, -\frac{5}{3}$ **53.** $4, -5$ **55.** $\frac{3}{2}, 3$
57. $-1, -\frac{5}{2}$ **59.** $\pm\sqrt{3}$ **61.** $\frac{\sqrt{5}}{5}, 0$ **63.** $-\frac{\sqrt{5}}{5}, 0$
65. Ex: $f(x) = 4x^2 + 3x + 7$ **67.** Ex: $4x^2 - 19x + 12 = 0$
69. $2x^3 + 5x^2 - 3x = 0$

Mixed Review   71. Any value   **73.** $x \geq -5$
75. $2(2m + 1)(m - 3)$ **77.** $(y - 11)(y + 11)$ **79.** $y(x + 2)^2$
81. $\{1, 2, 3, 6\}$

LESSON 13-2

Try This   a. $\pm\sqrt{10}$ **b.** $\pm\frac{\sqrt{15}}{3}$ **c.** ± 5 **d.** 0 **e.** $7, -1$
f. $-3 \pm \sqrt{10}$ **g.** $1 \pm \sqrt{5}$ **h.** $7 \pm \sqrt{3}$ **i.** $2, -24$ **j.** 3 **k.** 15%

Exercises   1. ± 11 **3.** $\pm\sqrt{7}$ **5.** $\pm\frac{\sqrt{15}}{5}$ **7.** $\pm\frac{5}{2}$ **9.** $\pm\frac{7\sqrt{3}}{3}$
11. $\pm\sqrt{3}$ **13.** $\pm\frac{6}{5}$ **15.** $\pm\frac{\sqrt{5}}{10}$ **17.** $-1 \pm \sqrt{6}$ **19.** $3 \pm \sqrt{6}$
21. $21, 5$ **23.** $-1 \pm \sqrt{14}$ **25.** $2, -10$ **27.** $5 \pm 2\sqrt{5}$
29. $-3, 5$ **31.** $13, -1$ **33.** $-8 \pm \sqrt{15}$ **35.** $7 \pm \sqrt{19}$
37. $-12 \pm 2\sqrt{2}$ **39.** 4 s   **41.** $\frac{4}{5}$ s   **43.** 18.75% **45.** 6.5%
47. 14.75% **49.** 11% **51.** $3b, -b$ **53.** $\frac{4}{5}, 0$ **55.** $-\frac{13}{8}, \frac{7}{8}$
57. $1, -\frac{5}{2}$ **59.** About 5 s   **61. a.** 5.2 s, 8.8 s, 14.8 s   **b.** About
81 m/s; about 184 m/s   **63.** $x = 1, x = -5; x = -2 \pm \sqrt{2}$
65. $a = 12$ **67.** \$2682.63   **69.** \$1171.66

Mixed Review
71. Parabola, opens up, vertex $(0, -3)$ **73.** $\sqrt{2}$ **75.** $\sqrt{3}$
77. $17, -1, 7$ **79.** $18, 2, 83$

LESSON 13-3

Try This   a. $x^2 - 8x + 16 = (x - 4)^2$
b. $x^2 + 12x + 36 = (x + 6)^2$ **c.** $y^2 + 7y + \frac{49}{4} = \left(y + \frac{7}{2}\right)^2$
d. $m^2 - 3m + \frac{9}{4} = \left(m - \frac{3}{2}\right)^2$ **e.** $-2, -6$ **f.** $\frac{-3 \pm \sqrt{33}}{4}$
g. $\frac{1 \pm \sqrt{10}}{3}$

Exercises   1. $x^2 - 6x + 9$ **3.** $m^2 + 7m + \frac{49}{4}$ **5.** $x^2 + 4x + 4$
7. $z^2 - 20z + 100$ **9.** $x^2 + 15x + \frac{225}{4}$ **11.** $-5, -3$
13. $-15, 1$ **15.** $2 \pm \sqrt{15}$ **17.** $9 \pm \sqrt{7}$ **19.** $5 \pm \sqrt{29}$
21. $\frac{-7 \pm \sqrt{57}}{2}$ **23.** $-4, 7$ **25.** $\frac{3 \pm \sqrt{17}}{4}$ **27.** $\frac{2 \pm \sqrt{13}}{3}$
29. $-\frac{3}{2}, 4$ **31.** $\pm 2x\sqrt{55}$ **33.** $\pm 16x$ **35.** $\pm 2x\sqrt{ac}$
37. $3a, -2a$ **39.** $c + 1, -c$ **41.** $\frac{-m \pm \sqrt{m^2 - 4nk}}{2k}$

Mixed Review   43. $y = \frac{11}{4}x$ **45.** Irrational   **47.** Rational
49. No real-number solution

LESSON 13-4

Try This   a. $\frac{1}{2}, -4$ **b.** $4, -\frac{2}{3}$ **c.** $2.9, -0.9$ **d.** $-0.7, -4.3$
e. $\frac{3}{2}, -\frac{2}{3}$ **f.** $\frac{3 \pm \sqrt{39}}{6}$ **g.** 56, two real-number solutions
h. -7, no real-number solutions   **i.** 0, one real-number
solution   **j.** 13, two points   **k.** -19, no points   **l.** 0, one point

Exercises   1. $-3, 7$ **3.** 3 **5.** $-\frac{4}{3}, 2$ **7.** $-\frac{7}{2}, \frac{1}{2}$ **9.** $-3, 3$
11. 1 **13.** $5 \pm \sqrt{3}$ **15.** $-2 \pm \sqrt{7}$ **17.** $\frac{-4 \pm \sqrt{10}}{3}$ **19.** $-1, \frac{1}{4}$
21. $-\frac{5}{3}, 0$ **23.** $-5, 5$ **25.** No real-number roots   **27.** $\frac{2}{3}, 2$
29. $-1.3, 5.3$ **31.** $-0.2, 6.2$ **33.** $-0.2, 1.2$ **35.** $0.3, 2.4$
37. $-0.6, 3.6$ **39.** $-0.9, 1.3$ **41.** -3, no real-number solutions
43. 0, one real-number solution   **45.** zero points
47. zero points   **49.** $-3, 4$ **51.** None   **53.** $0, 2$ **55.** $\frac{3 \pm \sqrt{5}}{2}$
57. $\frac{-7 \pm \sqrt{61}}{2}$ **59.** No real-number solutions   **61.** $-4, 2$
63. no real roots   **65.** Parabola, x-intercepts $-6, 0,$
vertex $(-3, -9)$ **67. a.** all   **b.** all   **c.** some
69. The two roots are $\frac{-b - \sqrt{b^2 - 4ac}}{2a}$ and $\frac{-b + \sqrt{b^2 - 4ac}}{2a}$.
Their average is $\frac{1}{2}\left(\frac{-b - \sqrt{b^2 - 4ac}}{2a} + \frac{-b + \sqrt{b^2 - 4ac}}{2a}\right) =$
$\frac{1}{2}\left(\frac{-2b}{2a}\right) = -\frac{b}{2a}$ **71.** two; $-4, 3$ **73.** two; $\frac{1}{2}, \frac{4}{3}$

Mixed Review   75. $4x^2 + 5x + 16 = 0; a = 4, b = 5, c = 16$
77. $y = \frac{64}{x}$ **79.** 6 **81.** $5(m - 3)^2$

LESSON 13-5

Try This   a. $-5, 2$ **b.** $-3, 4$ **c.** $2 \pm 2\sqrt{2}$

Exercises   1. $4, -4$ **3.** $3, -1$ **5.** $5, -1$ **7.** $3 \pm \sqrt{5}$ **9.** $\pm\sqrt{7}$
11. No real-number solution   **13.** $10, -\frac{2}{5}$ **15.** 2 **17.** $0, 5$
19. No real-number solution   **21.** $-3 \pm 2\sqrt{3}$ **23.** $\frac{3 \pm \sqrt{33}}{2}$

25. $-1, 6$ **27.** $4 \pm 2\sqrt{5}$ **29.** 0 **31.** $\frac{1}{2}$ **33.** $\frac{7 \pm \sqrt{13}}{2}$

35. Leah computed the discriminant (-15) of $x^2 - 3x + 6$ instead of the discriminant (1) of $x^2 - 3x + 2$.

37. Answers may vary. Ex: $\frac{x+2}{x} = \frac{2}{x}$ **39.** 7 **41.** $\frac{-7 \pm \sqrt{145}}{4}$

43. $\frac{-3 \pm \sqrt{61}}{2}$

Mixed Review **45.** $\pm\sqrt{15}$ **47.** $0, -\frac{4}{7}$ **49.** $5, -\frac{3}{2}$

55. $y = \frac{6}{x}$ **57.** $y = \frac{3x}{z}$ **59.** 7.0023×10^{-3}

LESSON 13-6

Try This **a.** 2 **b.** 7 **c.** $\frac{r^2}{20}$ **d.** $\frac{T^2 g}{4\pi^2}$ **e.** $\frac{E}{c^2}$ **f.** $\sqrt{\frac{A}{\pi}}$

g. $1 \pm \sqrt{\frac{C}{P}}$

Exercises **1.** 36 **3.** 7 **5.** 12 **7.** 8 **9.** 3 **11.** 106 **13.** 9

15. 7 **17.** 3 **19.** 13, 25 **21.** 0, 8 **23.** $a = \sqrt{c^2 - b^2}$

25. $b = \sqrt{c^2 - a^2}$ **27.** $r = \sqrt{\frac{V}{\pi h}}$ or $\frac{\sqrt{V\pi h}}{\pi h}$

29. $\sqrt{r^2 - y^2 - z^2}$ **31.** $\sqrt{\frac{GmM}{F}}$ **33.** $\frac{P}{I^2}$ **35.** $\sqrt{\frac{P}{R}} - 4$

37. 13 **39.** $\sqrt{\frac{3}{5}}$ or $\frac{\sqrt{15}}{5}$ **41.** 63 **43.** 0

45. $A = \frac{p^2}{16}, p = 4\sqrt{A}$ **47.** The student squared $x + 3$ incorrectly. $(x + 3)^2 = x^2 + 6x + 9$. The correct solutions are -2 and -1. **49.** all numbers $x < 0$ **51.** none **53.** 10

55. 15 **57.** $a = 9, b = 25$ **59.** $(-1, -2), (1, -2), (-1, 2), (1, 2)$

Mixed Review **61.** $x^2 + 4x + 4$ **63.** $a^2 - a + \frac{1}{4}$ **65.** $\frac{1}{3}, 4$

67. $9, -3$ **69.** $\frac{1}{9}$ **71.** $\frac{\sqrt{2}}{2}$ **73.** 4 **75.** $(0, 0)$ **77.** 8 units

LESSON 13-7

Try This **a.** 20 m **b.** 2.3 cm, 3.3 cm **c.** 3 km/h

Exercises **1.** 3 cm **3.** 7 ft, 24 ft **5.** 8 cm, 10 cm **7.** 4.6 m, 6.6 m **9.** 7 km/h **11.** 4 km/h **13.** $3 + 3\sqrt{2}$ or 7.243 cm **15.** 14.14 in.; a 15-in. pizza **17.** 15 mi/h, 20 mi/h **19.** 100 m **21.** -25 or 25 m below the starting point

Mixed Review **23.** 3 **25.** $3, -5$ **27.** $\frac{-5 \pm \sqrt{17}}{2}$

29. $y = -\frac{2}{5}x - \frac{16}{5}$

Application **1.** \$130.20 **3.** 4.18%

CHAPTER 13 WRAP UP

1. $3x^2 + 6x + 4 = 0$ **2.** $5x^2 - 2x = 0$ **3.** $0, \frac{7}{5}$ **4.** $0, \frac{4}{3}$

5. $\frac{3}{5}, 1$ **6.** $\frac{1}{3}, -2$ **7.** $2\sqrt{2}, -2\sqrt{2}$ **8.** $\sqrt{3}, -\sqrt{3}$

9. $-8 \pm \sqrt{13}$ **10.** $1, -13$ **11.** $-\frac{1}{2}, -\frac{9}{2}$ **12.** $n = 10$

13. 30% **14.** \$4665.60 **15.** $c^2 + 22c + 121$

16. $w^2 - 7w + \frac{49}{4}$ **17.** $1 \pm \sqrt{11}$ **18.** $\frac{1 \pm \sqrt{10}}{3}$ **19.** $\frac{5}{3}, -1$

20. $\frac{-7 \pm \sqrt{57}}{4}$ **21.** $3 \pm 3\sqrt{2}$ **22.** $\frac{1 \pm \sqrt{61}}{6}$ **23.** $\frac{3 \pm \sqrt{33}}{2}$

24. $\frac{-3 \pm \sqrt{89}}{10}$ **25.** $-3 \pm \sqrt{2}$ **26.** 7 **27.** 24, two real-number solutions **28.** -8, no real-number solutions **29.** $3, -5$ **30.** 1

31. 52 **32.** 10 **33.** $F = \frac{mV^2}{qr}$ **34.** $\sqrt{\frac{3A}{\pi}}$ **35.** 10 m, 7 m

36. 4 mi/h **37.** 10 in., 24 in. or 2 ft

CHAPTERS 1–13 CUMULATIVE REVIEW

1. 54 **3.** 88 **5.** $(a \cdot b) \cdot c$ **7.** $-8\frac{5}{8}$ **9.** $20a + 6b$

11. -34.72 **13.** $\frac{8}{3}$ **15.** 8 **17.** 6090 cars **19.** $h = \frac{A}{2\pi r} - r$ or

$\frac{A - 2\pi r^2}{2\pi r}$ **21.** 25% **23.** $8\frac{1}{3}$% **25.** 10 **27.** $x < 21$ **29.** $y \leq \frac{1}{2}$

31. $y > -5$ **33.** $I \geq 15$ **35.** $4m^2$ **37.** $8y^{18}$ **39.** $27x^{15}y^{12}$

41. $12ab^4c^5$ **43.** $6xy^2$ **45.** $-a^3 + 4a^2 - 2a$

47. $2m^2 - 9m - 18$ **49.** $a^2 + 4a + 4$ **51.** $9m^2 + 30m + 25$

53. $(7x + 8)(7x - 8)$ **55.** $(2x - 9)(x + 11)$ **57.** $(3x - 4)^2$

59. $x(10x + 3)^2$

61.

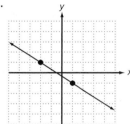

63. $m = -\frac{1}{2}, b = \frac{25}{4}$

65. $y = 10$

67. $y = -\frac{2}{3}x - \frac{14}{3}$

69. $(-2, 1)$ **71.** $(-2, 1)$

73. $(-2, 5)$ **75.** Dorothy is 60 years old; Stan is 10 years old. **77.** 350 student tickets, 250 adult tickets

79. $\{99, 100, 102, 105, 108, 110, 111, 115, 120\}$ **81.** $\{100, 110\}$

83. $\{102, 108\}$

85. $x < -5$ or $x > 5$

87. $x \leq -3$ or $x \geq 3$

89. $\frac{x^2 + 6x + 9}{x^4 - 4x^2 + 4}$ **91.** $\frac{10}{a + 1}$ **93.** $\frac{28}{3}$ **95.** $x + 3$

97. $\frac{-5x + 17}{(x - 4)(x + 3)(x - 3)}$ **99.** -5 **101.** 17 km/h, 22 km/h

103. 7 **105.** $x \geq -4$ **107.** $|cd|$ **109.** $8|x|$ **111.** $3\sqrt{y}$

113. $y^3\sqrt{y}$ **115.** $3(a + 4)$ **117.** $8a^2b\sqrt{3ab}$ **119.** $\frac{\sqrt{10}}{6}$

121. $13\sqrt{a}$ **123.** $(3x^2 - x^2y - 2y)\sqrt{y}$ **125.** -4 **127.** -10

129.

131. 9 psi **133.** $\sqrt{10}, -\sqrt{10}$

135. 2 **137.** $3 \pm \sqrt{6}$

139. $\frac{2 \pm \sqrt{6}}{3}$ **141.** $\frac{\pm 2\sqrt{6}}{3}$

143. 1, 3 **145.** 2 km/h

Index

Index

Index

Index

STAFF CREDITS

The people who helped produce Prentice Hall *Algebra 1*—representing design services, editorial, editorial services, marketing, marketing services, market research, on-line services & multimedia development, production services, project office, publishing processes—are listed below.

Barbara Bertell, Todd Christy, Sheila DeFazio, Jo DiGiustini, Deborah Faust, Frederick Fellows, Catherine Maglio, Tim McDonald, Perrin Moriarty, Paul W. Murphy, Cindy Noftle, Suzanne Schineller, Debby Sommer, Stuart Wallace, Joe Will, Stewart Wood, Carol Zacny

ADDITIONAL CREDITS

Leora Adler, Charles Carpenter, Paula C. Foye, Al Jacobson, Ann McSweeney, PoYee Oster, Sydney Schuster, Nancy Smith

Cover Design: Studio Montage

Cover Image: Conrad Zobel/Corbis
Pete Saloutos/The Stock Market

Book Design: Thompson Steele

Front Matter: Sue Gerould

Photo Research: PoYee Oster

Photography:
Chapter 1: Page 3, Dominique Sarraute/ The Image Bank; **4,** Yellow Dog Productions/ The Image Bank; **15,** Dominique Sarraute/ The Image Bank; **24,** Georg Gerster/Photo Researchers; **31,** Jim Corwin/Stock Boston; **40,** Steve Krongard/The Image Bank.

Chapter 2: Page 53, Jeff Foott/Tom Stack & Associates; **55,** Charles Krebs/The Stock Market; **69,** M. Antman/The Image Works; **71,** Jeff Foott/Tom Stack & Associates; **87,** Adam Jones/Photo Researchers; **100,** Rafael Macia/Photo Researchers.

Chapter 3: Pages 113, 117, Joseph Sohm; ChromoSohm Inc./CORBIS; **119,** Kenneth W. Fink/Photo Researchers; **123,** Reuters Newmedia Inc./CORBIS; **130,** Billy E. Barnes/Stock Boston; **143,** Ron J. Berard/Duomo Photography; **151,** Mark Burnett/Stock Boston; **161,** Stone.

Chapter 4: Page 171, Stone/Chris Everard; **174,** Photo Edit; **179,** Stone/Chris Everard; **188,** PhotoDisc.

Chapter 5: Pages 203, 217, Michael Dalton/Fundamental Photographs; **221,** ©Corbis; **227,** Jeff Hunter/The Image Bank; **253,** Eric Herzog/Custom Medical Stock Photo; **254,** A. Ramey/PhotoEdit.

Chapter 6: Page 261, Richard Megna/Fundamental Photographs; **269,** Pearson Education/PH College; **277,** J. Cochin/Photo Researchers; **292,** Patrick Ward/Stock Boston; **295,** Richard Megna/Fundamental Photographs.

Acknowledgments

Chapter 7: Page 303, Stone/Pat O'Hara;
307, Vincent DeWitt/Stock Boston;
313, Donald G. Oke; **322,** PhotoDisc;
334, W. Spunbarg/PhotoEdit;
337, Stone/Pat O'Hara.

Chapter 8: Page 357, Brian Parker/Tom Stack &
Associates; **376,** Robert Brenner/PhotoEdit;
386, Brian Parker/Tom Stack & Associates; **390
(FDR),** Franklin D. Roosevelt Library; **390
(dime),** PhotoDisc, Inc.

Chapter 9: Pages 399, 409, Stone/Bob Thomason;
414, Juneberg Clark/Photo Researchers;
421, PhotoDisc.

Chapter 10: Pages 431, 432, Mark A.
Chappell/Animals Animals; **438,** Stone/Pal
Hermansen; **450(left, middle, right),** NASA;
457, Daniel MacDonald/Stock Boston; **461,** Scott T.
Smith/Corbis; **476,** Jeremy Horner/Corbis.

Chapter 11: 481, Robert Mathena/Fundamental
Photographs; **490,** Tony Freeman/PhotoEdit;
502, Robert Mathena/Fundamental Photographs;
507, ATC Productions/The Stock Market;
517, Gary Milburn/Tom Stack & Associates;
520, Richard Pasley/Stock Boston.

Chapter 12: Page 535, Richard Gross/The Stock
Market; **549,** Richard Megna/Fundamental
Photographs; **562,** Richard Gross/The Stock
Market; **567,** Stone/Stephen Studd.

Chapter 13: Page 575, Philip James
Corwin/Corbis; **584,** Stone/David Hoffman;
593, Philip James Corwin/Corbis; **604,** Charles
O'Rear/Corbis; **607,** Jeff Greenberg/PhotoEdit.